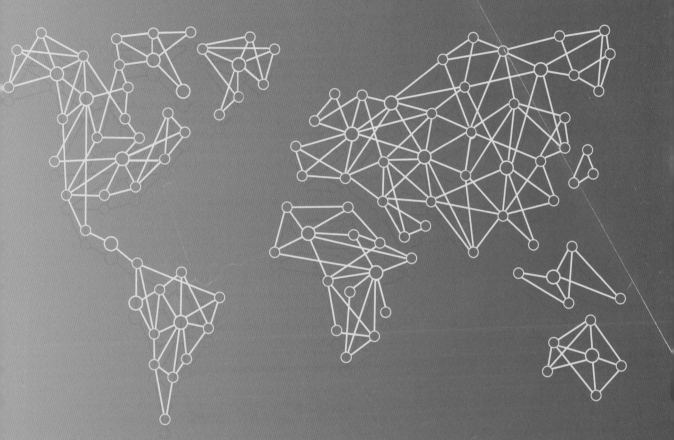

INTERNATIONAL BUSINESS

Mike Peng and Klaus Meyer

Second Edition

CENGAGE
Learning®

Australia • Brazil • Mexico • Singapore • United Kingdom • United States

International Business, 2nd Edition
Mike Peng and Klaus Meyer

Publisher: Annabel Ainscow

Commissioning Editor: Abigail Jones

Content Project Manager: Sue Povey

Manufacturing Manager: Eyvett Davis

Marketing Manager: Vicky Pavlicic

Typesetter: MPS Limited

Cover design: Adam Renvoize Creative

Text design: Design Deluxe Ltd

For product information and technology assistance, contact **emea.info@cengage.com**.

For permission to use material from this text or product, and for permission queries, email **emea.permissions@cengage.com**.

British Library Cataloguing-in-Publication Data
A catalogue record for this book is available from the British Library.

ISBN: 978-1-4737-2264-4

Cengage Learning EMEA
Cheriton House, North Way, Andover, Hampshire, SP10 5BE
United Kingdom

Cengage Learning products are represented in Canada by Nelson Education Ltd.

For your lifelong learning solutions, visit **www.cengage.co.uk**

Purchase your next print book or e-book at
www.cengagebrain.com

Printed in China by RR Donnelley
Print Number: 03   Print Year: 2017

To our students:
past, present and future

BRIEF CONTENTS

PART ONE FOUNDATIONS 1

1 Globalizing Business 3
2 Formal Institutions: Political, Economic and Legal Systems 29
3 Informal Institutions: Culture, Religion and Languages 57
4 Firm Resources: Competitiveness and Growth 88

PART TWO BUSINESS ACROSS BORDERS 117

5 Trading Internationally 119
6 Investing Abroad Directly 151
7 Exchange Rates 184

PART THREE GLOBALIZATION 211

8 European Integration 213
9 Global Integration and Multilateral Organizations 246
10 Socially Responsible Business 278

PART FOUR THE FIRM ON THE GLOBAL STAGE 307

11 Starting International Business 309
12 Foreign Entry Strategies 337
13 Competitive Dynamics 363
14 Global Strategies and Acquisitions 390

PART FIVE OPERATIONS IN THE GLOBAL MNE 419

15 Organizing and Innovating in the MNE 421
16 People in the MNE 451
17 Customers and Suppliers of the MNE 477

PART SIX INTEGRATIVE CASES 505

Integrative Cases 1-14

Glossary 581
Credits 593
Name Index 594
Subject Index 596
Organizations Index 602

CONTENTS

List of Boxes   ix
Preface to the 1st Edition   xiii
Preface to the 2nd Edition   xviii
Acknowledgements for the 2nd Edition   xix
Scholarly Journals xx
About the authors   xxii

PART ONE
FOUNDATIONS 1

1 GLOBALIZING BUSINESS   3

European and Global Business   5
Why Study International Business?   7
A Unified Framework   9
Understanding Globalization   12
A Glance at the Global Economy   18
Implications for Practice   22

2 FORMAL INSTITUTIONS: POLITICAL, ECONOMIC AND LEGAL SYSTEMS   29

An Institution-Based View
   of International Business   32
Political Systems   35
Economic Systems   40
Legal Systems   44
Debates and Extensions   46
Implications for Practice   51

3 INFORMAL INSTITUTIONS: CULTURE, RELIGION AND LANGUAGES   57

Cultures   60
Languages   69
Religions   72
Ethics   74
Debates and Extensions   77
Implications for Practice   80

4 FIRM RESOURCES: COMPETITIVENESS AND GROWTH   88

Identifying Resources   90
Appraising Resources: The Vrio Framework   97
Applying Resource Analysis: Benchmarking   101
Debates and Extensions   106
Implications for Practice   108

PART TWO
BUSINESS ACROSS BORDERS 117

5 TRADING INTERNATIONALLY   119

Why Do Nations Trade?   123
Theories of International Trade   126
National Institutions and International Trade   136
Debates and Extensions   142
Implications for Practice   145

6 INVESTING ABROAD DIRECTLY   151

The FDI Vocabulary   154
Ownership Advantages   158
Location Advantages   160
Internalization Advantages   165
Benefits and Costs of FDI   168
National Institutions and FDI   170
Debates and Extensions   174
Implications for Practice   178

7 EXCHANGE RATES   184

Markets for Currencies   188
Institutions of the International Monetary
   System   194
Managing Exchange Risks   198
Debates and Extensions   202
Implications for Practice   204

8 EUROPEAN INTEGRATION 213

Overcoming Divisions   216
The EU as Institutional Framework for
   Business   222
The Euro as a Common Currency   228
Debates and Extensions   236
Implications for Practice   239

9 GLOBAL INTEGRATION AND MULTILATERAL ORGANIZATIONS 246

The Multilateral Trade System   249
The Multilateral Monetary System   256
Regional and Bilateral Economic Integration   259
Debates and Extensions   265
Implications for Practice   271

10 SOCIALLY RESPONSIBLE BUSINESS 278

Stakeholders of the Firm   282
CSR in the Global Economy   288
Institutions, Stakeholders and CSR   292
Debates and Extensions   295
Implications for Practice   299

11 STARTING INTERNATIONAL BUSINESS 309

Going International   312
Resources and Internationalization   323
Institutions and Internationalization   326

Debates and Extensions   327
Implications for Practice   328

12 FOREIGN ENTRY STRATEGIES 337

Strategic Objectives of Establishing
   Foreign Subsidiaries   340
Where to Enter?   342
When to Enter?   344
How to Enter?   346
How to Organize Your Operations   353
Institutions and Foreign Entry Strategies   353
Debates and Extensions   355
Implications for Practice   357

13 COMPETITIVE DYNAMICS 363

Dynamics of Competition   366
Competition and Collusion   368
Institutions Governing Competition   372
Resources Influencing Competition   377
Debates and Extensions   380
Implications for Practice   384

14 GLOBAL STRATEGIES AND ACQUISITIONS 390

Strategizing Globally   392
Growth by Acquisitions   397
Institutions Governing Acquisitions   403
Resource-Based Perspectives on
   Acquisitions   407
Debates and Extensions   408
Implications for Practice   411

15 ORGANIZING AND INNOVATING IN THE MNE 421

Organizational Structures in MNEs   423
Managing Knowledge in Global MNEs   429
Institutions and the Choice of Organizational
   Structure   438

Resource-Based Considerations   439
Debates and Extensions   440
Implications for Practice   442

16 PEOPLE IN THE MNE   451

Approaches to Managing People   453
Expatriates   455
Managing People Abroad   464
Institutions and Human Resource
   Management   466
People as Resources   468
Debates and Extensions   469
Implications for Practice   471

17 CUSTOMERS AND SUPPLIERS OF THE MNE   477

Understanding Consumers around the
   World   479
The Marketing Mix   482
Price   484
Supply Chain Management   487
Institutions, Marketing and Supply Chain
   Management   493
Resources, Marketing and Supply Chain
   Management   494
Debates and Extensions   495
Implications for Practice   498

PART SIX

INTEGRATIVE CASES   505

1 Xiaomi Challenges Global Smartphone
   Leaders   506
2 Rolls Royce: From Insolvency to World
   Leadership   511
3 Agrana: From Local Supplier to Global Player   520
4 Bharti Airtel Acquires Resources and
   Companies   525
5 Enhancing UK Export Competitiveness   528
6 Canada and the EU Negotiate CETA   534
7 German Chamber of Commerce Develops Social
   Responsibility in China   540
8 Tackling Corrupt Practices: GSK China   544
9 Fan Milk in West Africa   550
10 ESET: From Living Room to Global Player in
   Antivirus Software   556
11 The LG-Nortel Joint Venture   561
12 Beko Washes Clothes Across Europe   566
13 SG Group: Managing European Acquisitions   570
14 Just Another Move to China?   576

Glossary   581
Credits   593
Name Index   594
Subject Index   596
Organizations Index   602

LIST OF BOXES

	Case	Locations	Industry
Chapter 1			
Opening Case	adidas: sales, suppliers and stakeholders around the world	Germany	Fashion (sportswear)
In Focus 1.1	Setting the Terms Straight	—	—
In Focus 1.2	Globalization in the year 1900	—	—
In Focus 1.3	GE Innovates from the Base of the Pyramid	India, USA	Medical instruments
Closing Case	Coca-Cola Dives into Africa	USA, Africa	Soft drinks
Chapter 2			
Opening Case	Managing business risks in Turkey	Turkey	—
In Focus 2.1	Elections around the globe	France, Germany, India, USA	—
In Focus 2.2	Father of the market economy	Germany	—
In Focus 2.3	Protecting intellectual property internationally	China	—
In Focus 2.4	Who is breaking whose copyright?	Denmark, UK	Furniture
Closing Case	Carlsberg faces political risk in Russia	Russia	Brewing
Chapter 3			
Opening Case	Party invitations in Saudi Arabia and in China	Saudi Arabia, China, Switzerland	Civil engineering
In Focus 3.1	Limitations of Hofstede's framework	—	—
In Focus 3.2	Multilinguists in multinational enterprises	Finland	Elevators
In Focus 3.3	The OECD anti-corruption convention	—	—
Closing Case	What's in a (Maasai) name?	Kenya, Tanzania	Clothing, etc.
Chapter 4			
Opening Case	SAP drives industry 4.0	Germany	IT software and services
In Focus 4.1	Capabilities in distribution: *Wal-Mart*	USA	Retail
In Focus 4.2	Burberry makes Britishness its core capability	UK	Fashion retail
In Focus 4.3	Poland competes with India for BPO	Poland, India	Business services
In Focus 4.4	Ostnor offshores and reshores	Sweden, China	Bathroom engineering
Closing Case	Lego's secrets	Denmark	Toys

	Case	Locations	Industry
Chapter 5			
Opening Case	EU exports: emerging economy opportunities	EU	—
In Focus 5.1	Port of Rotterdam: gateway to the world	Netherlands	Trading and shipping
In Focus 5.2	Comparative advantage and YOU	—	—
Closing Case	US anti-dumping against Chinese apple juice concentrate producers	USA, China	Processed foods
Chapter 6			
Opening Case	Spanish MNEs enter the global stage	Spain	—
In Focus 6.1	Grupo Antolin pursues OLI advantages	Spain	Automotive supplier
In Focus 6.2	Wind energy agglomerates in Jutland	Denmark	Engineering
In Focus 6.3	State enterprises meet market economy	Dubai, China	—
In Focus 6.4	Corporate taxation drives US FDI in Europe	USA, Europe	—
Closing Case	Politics and FDI in Argentina	Argentina, Spain	—
Chapter 7			
Opening Case	The economic crisis upsets exchange rates	Poland, Hungary, Latvia, Slovakia	—
In Focus 7.1	Hong Kong and Argentina: a tale of two currency boards	Hong Kong, Argentina	—
In Focus 7.2	Local councils mess with taxpayers' funds	Germany	—
Closing Case	Jobek do Brasil's foreign exchange challenges	Brazil	Furniture
Chapter 8			
Opening Case	A day in European business	Poland	IT (software)
In Focus 8.1	Rebuilding institutions in Central and Eastern Europe	Europe	—
In Focus 8.2	Mobile students: the Bologna Process	EU	Education
In Focus 8.3	Boom and bust in the eurozone	Spain	—
In Focus 8.4	Half in, half out: the British	UK	—
Closing Case	The Eco-design Directive: Nokia goes to Brussels	Finland, EU	Mobile phones
Chapter 9			
Opening Case	WTO mediates between Airbus and Boeing	EU, USA	Aircraft manufacturing
In Focus 9.1	Russia in the WTO	Russia, EU	—
In Focus 9.2	Beef and shrimp: is the WTO over-reaching?	USA, EU	Processed Foods
In Focus 9.3	Food versus trade?	India	—

	Case	Locations	Industry
In Focus 9.4	ASEAN integrates regional economies	ASEAN	—
In Focus 9.5	Disputes over ISDS tribunals	Canada, Germany, Australia	—
In Focus 9.6	Why are the rating agencies so powerful?	USA	Rating agencies
Closing Case	The future of globalization: Wärtsilä scenarios	Finland	Energy
Chapter 10			
Opening Case	Starbucks: standards in the spotlight	USA	Restaurants
In Focus 10.1	IKEA adapts in Saudi Arabia	Norway	Aquaculture
In Focus 10.2	Farming salmon	Sweden, Saudi Arabia	Retail
In Focus 10.3	Working poor	Central America	Garments
Closing Case	M&S: . . . because there is no 'Plan B'	UK	Retail
Chapter 11			
Opening Case	Kaspersky Lab is scaling the globe	Russia	IT software
In Focus 11.1	Tourism: exporting experiences	—	Tourism
In Focus 11.2	Building bridges	Bahrain, Qatar	Construction
In Focus 11.3	Scandinavia A/S: a small publisher for small people worldwide	Denmark	Publishing
Closing Case	Better generation: the global generation of business	UK, China, Hong Kong	Green energy
Chapter 12			
Opening Case	Pearl River Piano enters foreign markets	China	Musical instruments
In Focus 12.1	Tata and Geely acquire capabilities	India, China	Car manufacturing
In Focus 12.2	Thai Union acquires market access	Thailand	Processed foods
In Focus 12.3	Joint venture ZF Kama in Russia	Russia, Germany	Automotive supplier
Closing Case	Danone and Wahaha: 'failed' joint ventures	France, China	Processed foods
Chapter 13			
Opening Case	Gulf Airlines challenge a global industry	UAE	Airlines
In Focus 13.1	Haier pursues niche in the USA	USA, China	White goods
In Focus 13.2	Caught colluding in Germany	Germany	—
In Focus 13.3	Is anti-dumping discriminatory?	USA, EU	—
In Focus 13.4	Patent lawsuits: competing in the courts	South Korea, USA	Mobile phones
Closing Case	Brussels vs Microsoft and Google	EU, USA	IT (software and services)

	Case	Locations	Industry
Chapter 14			
Opening Case	Danisco: the rise and sale of a global leader	Denmark	Food ingredients
In Focus 14.1	Nomura	Japan, Europe	Investment banking
In Focus 14.2	Focusing and refocusing Nokia	Finland	Network infrastructure
Closing Case	Daimler merges and demerges	Germany	Car manufacturing
Chapter 15			
Opening Case	The global organizational design of the 'Big Four'	—	Consultants
In Focus 15.1	Reverse innovation at McDonalds	USA	Restaurants
In Focus 15.2	Siemens' ShareNet: a knowledge management system	Germany	Engineering
Closing Case	Subsidiary initiative at Schenck Shanghai Machinery	China	Automotive supplier
Chapter 16			
Opening Case	EADS: managing human resources in a European context	France, Germany, Spain	Aircraft manufacturing
In Focus 16.1	Expatriate spouses	China	—
In Focus 16.2	Practical tips for getting started in Asia	Hong Kong, Taiwan	—
In Focus 16.3	Competing for talent in China	China	—
Closing Case	Dallas vs Delhi	India, USA	—
Chapter 17			
Opening Case	Zara rewrites the rules on marketing and supply chain management	Spain	Fashion retail
In Focus 17.1	Honest Films	UK, China	Marketing services
In Focus 17.2	C&A: failed European standardization	Germany, Netherlands, Spain	Fashion retail
In Focus 17.3	Online shop #1	China	E-business
In Focus 17.4	A volcano focuses minds on supply chain agility	Iceland	Airlines
In Focus 17.5	B2B marketing: BMS plastics for laptops	Germany	Plastics
Closing Case	Li & Fung: from trading company to supply chain manager	Hong Kong	Logistics services

PREFACE TO THE 1st EDITION

A EUROPEAN VIEW ON INTERNATIONAL BUSINESS

This book offers a European perspective on international business. In the age of globalization, isn't that a contradiction? Why did we set out to write a textbook specifically for you as students in Europe? There are five considerations why we have been writing this book:

- Students learn best from cases and examples that they can relate to. Thus we have developed a number of cases and examples specifically for this book that tell the experiences of European businesses. At the same time, we wish to broaden your horizon and equip you with an understanding of businesses in different parts of the world. As an international manager you will need to understand both, the regional and the global dimensions of business. Thus we also include a large number of cases and examples from all over the world.

- In Europe, international business (IB) is relevant for (almost) every business. Most textbooks in this field have been written primarily for American students, and thus treat global business primarily as a phenomenon that big companies have to deal with, with internationally operating entrepreneurs being an exception. That is understandable given the vast size of the domestic market of the USA. However, in Europe, where national markets are much smaller, even small- and medium-sized firms soon hit the limits of their domestic markets, and IB becomes a natural part of everything they do. Thus we relate much more to the needs and challenges faced by smaller firms, especially in a European context.

- Textbooks written by American authors typically draw primarily on scholarly work by US-based authors. However, there is important work by European scholars that is, in our view, not sufficiently appreciated in these textbooks. Thus we pay special attention to work by European scholars, for example the work by Hall and Soskice on varieties of capitalism, and by Zweigert and Kotz on legal systems (Chapter 2), by Hofstede and other Dutch authors on culture and by Marschan-Piekkari on languages (Chapter 3), by Dunning, Buckley and Casson on foreign direct investment (Chapter 6), by Matten, Moon and others on corporate social responsibility (Chapter 10), by Nordic scholars in the tradition of Johansen and Vahlne on internationalization processes (Chapter 11), and by scholars across Europe on knowledge management and governance (Chapter 15) and on expatriate management (Chapter 16).

- European businesses deal with a variety of subtle differences when engaging in neighbouring countries as well as with big differences when going to, for example, China. This contrasts with US businesses for whom IB is a big strategic change from domestic operations (unless they go to Canada), and thus involves substantial differences. Thus we treat IB as a natural and integrated part of business activity, but subject to a range of subtle differences when dealing with nearby yet still foreign institutions and businesses.

- European businesses do most of their IB elsewhere in the Europe, where they operate within the institutional framework of the European Union (EU). Understanding this framework is thus essential. Therefore, we devote one entire chapter specifically to the institutional framework of the EU (Chapter 8), and we relate to the EU regulatory framework in later chapters of the book, for example EU competition policy in Chapters 13 and 14.

Of course, as an alternative to using an English-language 'European' textbook such as ours, instructors may consider adapting a textbook in local languages, for example in German or French. This approach has advantages – students may be more at ease with their own language, and examples are even more local. However, we would encourage instructors to adopt our textbook as a core or recommended reading because:

- Engaging in global business in most parts of the world requires competences in English, and the classroom is an ideal place to acquire and polish English language skills.

- An important aspect of building competences for IB is to put oneself in the position of a business partner or competitor in order to understand how they would handle a certain situation. Successful international managers are also able to critically reflect on the merits and demerits of their own country, its institutions and its businesses. The development of these capabilities requires looking 'beyond the horizon' of your national economy, and engaging with individuals and businesses in other countries. Our European view encourages students to broaden their horizon beyond national boundaries.

- Both authors, being non-native speakers of English, remember how hard it is to start using English in a classroom setting. Thus we have written the text avoiding unnecessarily complex or colloquial expressions that may be inaccessible to students whose first language is not English.

OUR PERSPECTIVE AS AUTHORS

We, your authors, have studied, worked and taught global business throughout our careers. This personal experience and expertise gives us our foundation for writing this book, and enables us to offer you diverse yet complementary perspectives on international business:

- We have conducted research ourselves on many of the issues discussed in this text. Mike Peng has investigated, for example, the institution-based view of business (Chapters 2 and 3), the resource-based view (Chapter 4) and strategies of global firms (Chapters 13 and 14). Klaus Meyer has also contributed to the institution-based view (Chapter 2), and investigated in particular foreign direct investment (Chapter 6) and foreign entry strategies (Chapters 11 and 12). This work has been published in leading scholarly journals in the field, such as the *Journal of International Business Studies*, *Strategic Management Journal* and *Journal of Management Studies*.

- In our research, we have investigated a wide range of different contexts, including in particular emerging economies. Mike Peng's research has focused on contemporary management research in China and other transition economies, while Klaus Meyer has studied businesses in the countries of Central and Eastern Europe as well as Asian economies such as Vietnam and Taiwan, and multinational firms from Germany, Denmark and the UK.

- We have taught at universities quite literally around the globe, and thus learned from discussions with students offering a wide variety of perspectives and experiences. Mike Peng has taught at the University of Hawaii at Manoa, Ohio State University and University of Texas at Dallas (all USA), as well as at the Chinese University of Hong Kong and a number of universities in mainland China. Klaus Meyer has taught at Copenhagen Business School (Denmark), Hong Kong University of Science and Technology (Hong Kong), National Cheng-Chi University (Taiwan), as well as the University of Reading and the University of Bath (both UK). In addition, both of us have given numerous guest lectures at other universities throughout Europe, Asia and North America.

- Last but not least, we have lived in different countries, and thus complement each other's personal experiences. Mike Peng grew up in China and has spent most of his professional life in the USA, while Klaus Meyer grew up in Germany and has spent most of his professional life in Denmark and the UK. These personal experiences help us in linking theory to practice, notably on cross-cultural matters.

PEDAGOGICAL FEATURES OF THIS BOOK

In designing this book, we have been guided by three main pedagogical ideas:

1 We want to provide a comprehensive yet solidly research-grounded overview of the field.

2 We want to facilitate learning of the essential concepts and analytical framework.

3 We want to stimulate students' own critical reflection and discussions that go beyond rote learning of the material presented in the text.

COMPREHENSIVE, RESEARCH-GROUNDED

International business is a very broad topic that integrates many scholarly disciplines. In selecting and presenting the material, we have been guided by two objectives: to integrate complex materials in an accessible style and to build on contemporary research. First, to provide a consistent structure that helps to analyze this complex subject, we organize the book around a unified framework that integrates all chapters. Given the wide range of topics in IB, many textbooks present the discipline item by item: 'This is how MNEs manage X.' Rarely do authors address: 'Why do MNEs manage X in this way?' More importantly, What are the big questions that the field is trying to address? Our framework suggests that the discipline can be united by one big question and two core perspectives. The big question is: what determines the success and failure of firms around the globe? To address this question, we introduce two core perspectives: (1) an institution-based view, and (2) a resource-based view. The unified framework presents an extension of our own research that investigates international business topics using these two perspectives. This focus on one big question and two core perspectives enables this book to analyze a variety of IB topics in a coherent fashion.

Second, this book engages leaders through an evidence-based approach. We have endeavoured to draw on the latest research, as opposed to the latest fads. The comprehensive yet research-grounded coverage is made possible by drawing on the most comprehensive range of the literature. Specifically, we have read and considered every article over the past ten years in the *Journal of International Business Studies*, and other leading IB and general management journals. In addition, we have consulted numerous specialty journals for specific chapters. As research for the book progressed, our respect and admiration for the diversity of insights of our field and the relevance of neighbouring disciplines grew substantially. The result is a comprehensive set of evidence-based insights on IB. While citing every article is not possible, we cover work from a wide range of relevant scholars. Feel free to check the authors found in the Name Index to verify this claim.

Furthermore, we provide evidence through contemporary examples that illustrate theoretical concepts in practice. These up-to-date examples are found all over the world, with an emphasis on European business. They not only encourage students to build bridges between theoretical frameworks and the contemporary world of business, but also encourage them to find further examples in newspapers and magazines, such as *Financial Times* and *The Economist*. Many of the cases have been contributed by scholars from around the world, who have first-hand knowledge of the companies and contexts concerned, including Finland, Italy, France, Germany, the UK and the USA.

SUPPORTING LEARNING

The comprehensive nature of IB means that students of the subject have to engage with a wide range of concepts and frameworks based on current research. To facilitate the accessibility of this material, we use a clear, engaging, conversational style to tell the 'story'. Relative to other books, our chapters are generally more lively. Moreover, we have introduced a number of features aimed to facilitate the learning of key concepts, facts and frameworks:

- We explicitly state **learning objectives** at the outset and in the margin throughout each chapter. These learning objectives are the basis for a brief **chapter summary** at the end of each chapter.
- An **Opening case** about a firm or country provides a taster of the issues from a real world perspective, and a basis to reflect over issues introduced in the Chapter.
- Engaging in international business requires knowledge of many concepts. We therefore state the definitions of key concepts as **margin notes** when they are first introduced, and we include a **Glossary** at the end of the book containing all key concepts in alphabetical order.
- **In Focus** boxes illustrate key concepts on the basis of shorter, real world examples.
- So what? We conclude every chapter with **Implications for practice**, which clearly summarizes the key learning points from a *practical* standpoint in one or more tables.

CRITICAL REFLECTION AND DISCUSSION

The field of IB is subject to many debates, and many broader debates on globalization affect internationally operating MNEs. While it is important to 'learn' concepts and frameworks, we strongly believe that, it is also important to critically engage with the 'how' and 'why' questions surrounding the field. It is debates that drive the field of practice and research forward. We therefore aim to encourage students to critically reflect over the material presented (we expect most students to find at least one argument where they disagree with us) and to engage in cutting-edge debates. Several features aim to provoke discussion and critical reflections in each chapter:

- **Debates and extensions** section for *every* chapter (except Chapter 1, which is a big debate in itself).
- **Photo questions** challenge you to think about the consequences of the material presented. We use photos not only to illustrate the text, but as a stimulus for developing your own ideas and arguments.
- **Recommended readings** provide a basis for further study, for example when you want to prepare a class assignment of a dissertation on a topic.
- **Critical discussion questions** at the end of each chapter provide a basis for group discussions or individual work on the issues in the chapter, and their broader implications for society. Many of these questions concern ethical issues that have increasingly come to the forefront of public debates on international business.
- **Closing cases** to each chapter provide the story of a specific company engaged in international business. Analysis of this case along the questions provided will help gain deeper insights on the topic of the chapter, and help relating concepts to the real world of business.
- A set of **Integrative cases** provide further opportunities to deepen the study material, and to discuss how firms may handle specific challenges they encounter in international business.

Our ambitions in writing this book have been quite high, aiming to provide a teaching and learning foundation for students in Europe and beyond that is comprehensive and specific, theoretically grounded and hands-on, and explaining concepts while stimulating critical thought. The writing process has been challenging, but with the support of numerous colleagues we believe we have produced a solid and innovative book. We hope you enjoy studying and working with this book and, in the process, become as enthusiastic about international business as we are. Happy reading!

Mike W Peng and Klaus E Meyer
Dallas, Texas and Bath, Somerset
June 2010

PREFACE TO THE 2nd EDITION

In the five years since the publication of the first edition of this textbook, the international economy has evolved in many ways. Some trends highlighted in our book, like the rise of emerging economies and heightened volatility, have accelerated. New phenomena, such as emerging economy MNEs and international arbitrage tribunals, gained prominence and thus deserve consideration in a broad based textbook. Therefore, time has come to prepare a second edition.

The main focus of the revision has been on introducing new debate and extension sections on contemporary issues as well as new business cases, often researched by ourselves. For example, the eurozone and its crisis are now extensively discussed in Chapter 8, supported by extensive empirical data. Along with numerous updates on the global business environment, we also have used the opportunity to sharpen some of the conceptual frameworks, and to incorporate recent research. For example, the discussion of mergers and acquisition in Chapter 14 has been substantially extended.

Since the publication of the first edition, I (Klaus Meyer) have relocated to Shanghai, where I have been teaching at China Europe International Business School. I thus have able to gather first-hand experiences on international business challenges that inform several of the case studies in this 2nd edition, especially the Integrative cases on *Xiaomi*, *GSK China*, German Chamber of Commerce and *SG Group*. Similarly, the discussion of expatriates in Chapter 17 has benefitted from numerous interactions with expats living in Shanghai and elsewhere in Asia. These and other updated real world cases strengthen the bridge between theory and practice, making this textbook not only scholarly grounded, but – we hope – a foundation and stimulation for many international business careers.

Klaus Meyer
Shanghai, May 2015

ACKNOWLEDGEMENTS FOR THE 2nd EDITION

The revision of the textbook has benefited from comments and feedback from our students and colleagues to whom we are grateful. Among them, I would like to especially thank Grazia Santangelo (University of Catania), Christian Schwens (Heinrich-Heine-University Düsseldorf), and Lydia Price and Juan Fernandez (CEIBS) who provided detailed comments on selected chapters. I moreover thank Alexandra Han, Melody Zhang, Jenny Zhu, Coco Zhao and Vicky Nee for their research assistance and administrative support.

The CEIBS research centre for emerging market studies, which in turn is funded by *Ernst & Young*, has provided financial support for my research, which I greatly appreciate. These resources have in particular enabled the preparation of new original case studies for this book.

Abigail Jones and her colleagues at Cengage EMEA have, as usual, been very helpful in guiding us through the publishing process, and conveying us the market feedback.

The publisher would like to thank the following academics for their valuable suggestions for both the first and second editions:

- Ursula Ott, Loughborough University, UK
- Robert Read, Lancaster University, UK
- Sangeeta Khorana, University of Wales, Aberystwyth, UK
- Saleema Kauser, Manchester Metropolitan University, UK
- Gabriel R.G. Benito, BI Norwegian School of Management, Norway
- Erik de Bruijn, University of Twente, Netherlands
- Camilla Jensen, University of Southern Denmark, Denmark
- Christine Mortimer, York St John University, UK

The publisher would also like to thank Jason Evans, Marketing and Strategy Group, Aston University, UK and Mirko H. Benischke, Rotterdam School of Management, Erasmus University, the Netherlands for their work on the digital resources that accompany this book.

SCHOLARLY JOURNALS

Throughout this book, we make extensive reference to publications in scholarly journals. To report these references in an efficient way, we use abbreviations for management and economics journals such as *JIBS, AMJ, JMS,* or *IBR*, as reported below. You will normally find these sources through your university library's databases, though a search through *Google* Scholar may also get you to the right place. When citing journals in other fields as well as newspapers and magazine, we report the full name (*Business Week, The Economist*). To trace newspaper articles, it is often easiest to go to these publications' own homepage and type the full title of the article in the search engine.

JOURNAL ACRONYMS

The most frequently cited journals are set in **bold.**

AE – *Applied Economics;* AER – *American Economic Review;* AIM – *Advances in International Marketing;* AJS – *American Journal of Sociology;* AMA – *Academy of Management Annals* – AME – *Academy of Management Executive;* AMJ – ***Academy of Management Journal;*** AMLE – *Academy of Management Learning & Education;* AMR – ***Academy of Management Review;*** APJM – ***Asia Pacific Journal of Management;*** ASR – *American Sociological Review;* ASQ – *Administrative Science Quarterly;* ARS – *Annual Review of Sociology;* BEQ – *Business Ethics Quarterly;* BH – *Business History;* B&S – *Business and Society* – BSR – *Business Strategy Review;* CBR – *China Business Review;* CCM – *Cross Cultural Management: An International Review;* CES – *Comparative Economic Studies;* CJAS – *Canadian Journal of Administrative Studies;* CJE – *Canadian Journal of Economics;* CJWB – *Columbia Journal of World Business;* CMR – *California Management Review;* CPIB – *Critical Perspectives in International Business;* ECLR – *European Competition Law Review;* EER – *European Economic Review;* EJ – *Economic Journal;* EJE – *European Journal of Education;* EJM – *European Journal of Marketing;* EJPE – *European Journal of Political Economy;* ELJ – *European Law Journal;* EMJ – *European Management Journal;* EMR – *European Management Review;* EoT – *Economics of Transition;* ETP – *Entrepreneurship Theory and Practice;* FA – *Foreign Affairs;* HBR – ***Harvard Business Review;*** HR – *Human Relations;* HRM – *Human Resource Management;* HRMR – *Human Resource Management Review;* IBR – ***International Business Review;*** ICC – *Industrial and Corporate Change;* IE – *International Economy;* IJCCR – *International Journal of Cross-Cultural Management;* IJHRM – ***International Journal of Human Resource Management;*** IJKM – *International Journal of Knowledge Management;* IJMR – *International Journal of Management Reviews;* IJPE – *International Journal of Production Economics;* IMR – *International Marketing Review;* JAMS – *Journal of the Academy of Marketing Science;* JAP – *Journal of Applied Psychology;* JB – *Journal of Business;* JBE – ***Journal of Business Ethics;*** JBF – *Journal of Banking and Finance;* JBR – *Journal of Business Research;* JBV – *Journal of Business Venturing;* JCMS – *Journal of Common Market Studies;* JCR – *Journal of Consumer Research;* JEBO – *Journal of Economic Behavior and Organization;* JEI – *Journal of Economic Issues;* JEL – ***Journal of Economic Literature;*** JEP – ***Journal of***

Economic Perspectives; JEPP – *Journal of European Public Policy;* JES – *Journal of Economic Surveys;* JFE – *Journal of Financial Economics;* JHE – *Journal of Health Economics;* JIA – *Journal of International Affairs;* JIBS – ***Journal of International Business Studies;*** JID – *Journal of International Development;* JIE – *Journal of International Economics;* JIM – ***Journal of International Management;*** JKM – *Journal of Knowledge Management;* JLAS – *Journal of Latin American Studies;* JM – *Journal of Management;* JMM – *Journal of Marketing Management;* JMS – ***Journal of Management Studies;*** JMR – *Journal of Marketing Research;* JOB – *Journal of Organizational Behavior;* JOM – *Journal of Operations Management;* JPA – *Journal of Public Affairs;* JPE – *Journal of Political Economy;* JSM – *Journal of Strategic Management;* JWB – ***Journal of World Business;*** JWT – *Journal of World Trade;* LODJ – *Leadership and Organizational Development Journal;* LRP – *Long Range Planning;* MBR – *Multinational Business Review;* MIR – ***Management International Review;*** MQ – *McKinsey Quarterly;* MS – *Management Science;* OBES – *Oxford Bulletin of Economics and Statistics;* OD – *Organizational Dynamics;* ODS – *Oxford Development Studies;* OEP – *Oxford Economic Papers;* OSc – ***Organization Science;*** OSt – *Organization Studies;* POM – *Production and Operations Management;* PoP – *Perspectives on Politics;* PSJ – *Policy Studies Journal;* QJE – *Quarterly Journal of Economics;* RDM – *R&D Management;* RES – *Review of Economics and Statistics;* RIE – *Review of International Economics;* RP – *Research Policy;* SC – *Strategic Change;* SJM – *Scandinavian Journal of Management;* SMJ – ***Strategic Management Journal;*** SMR – *MIT Sloan Management Review;* S&P – *Society and Politics;* TIBR – *Thunderbird International Business Review;* TNC – *Transnational Corporations (United Nations);* WD – *World Development;* WE – *World Economy.*

ABOUT THE AUTHORS

MIKE W. PENG

Mike W. Peng (PhD, University of Washington) is the Jindal Chair of Global Business Strategy at the Jindal School of Management, University of Texas at Dallas, a National Science Foundation CAREER Award winner, and a Fellow of the Academy of International Business. He is also Executive Director of the Center for Global Business, which he founded.

Professor Peng's research focuses on firm strategies in countries such as China, Hong Kong, Japan, Russia, South Korea, Thailand and the United States. He has published over 100 articles in leading academic journals, such as the *Academy of Management Review*, *Strategic Management Journal* and *Journal of International Business Studies*. He published two textbooks with Cengage Learning, *Global Strategy* (3rd edition 2014) and *Global Business* (3rd edition 2014), which have become best sellers around the world, and have been translated into other languages such as Chinese, Portuguese and Spanish.

Professor Peng is active in scholarly associations such as the Academy of International Business and the Strategic Management Society. He co-edited a special issue of the *Journal of International Business Studies* published in 2010, and from 2007 to 2009, he served as the Editor-in-Chief of the *Asia Pacific Journal of Management*. Professor Peng's personal website is available at: www.utdallas.edu/~mikepeng/.

KLAUS E. MEYER

Klaus E. Meyer (PhD, London Business School) is Professor of Strategy and International Business at China Europe International Business School (CEIBS). Previously, he was Professor of Strategy and International Business at the University of Bath, UK, and held faculty position at University of Reading (UK) and Copenhagen Business School (Denmark) as well as visiting positions and Hong Kong University of Science and Technology, as well as National Chang-chi University in Taipei. Professor Meyer is a Fellow of the Academy of International Business.

Professor Meyer's research focuses on strategies of multinational enterprises in emerging economies. He is particularly interested in how firms adapt their business strategies to the specific conditions prevailing in each emerging economy. His work also extends to the impact of foreign investors on the economic transition and development of the host economies. Recent research has focused in particular on the strategies and operations of multinational enterprises originating from emerging economies. This work has led to four books and more than 70 articles in leading scholarly journals such as the *Journal of International Business Studies*, *Journal of Management Studies* and *Strategic Management Journal*. In 2015, Professors Meyer and Peng together won the 2005 Decade Award of the Journal of International Business Studies for their co-authored article published in 2005.

Professor Meyer holds responsibilities in scholarly journals, including the role of Deputy Editor-in-Chief of *Management and Organization Review*, and Consulting Editor of the *Journal of International Business Studies*. He also served in numerous roles in the Academy of International Business, in particular as Vice President (2012–2015) with responsibility for the 2014 Vancouver annual conference program. His personal website is www.klausmeyer.co.uk.

Turn the light on with MindTap

MindTap represents a new approach to online learning. A fully online learning solution, MindTap combines all of your learning tools, readings, multimedia, activities and assessments, into a singular Learning Path that guides you through your course.

Lecturers can easily personalize the experience by customizing the presentation of these learning tools and content to their students so that they have access to course content exactly when they need it.

MindTap can be fully integrated into most Learning Management Systems giving you a seamless experience. You will also have a dedicated team of Digital Course Support professionals to make your use of MindTap a success.

To find out more students can go to **login.cengagebrain.com** and instructors can go to **login.cengage.com** or speak to their local Cengage Learning EMEA representative.

MindTap is available with some of our bestselling titles across multiple disciplines including Accounting, Economics, Management, Psychology, Engineering and Chemistry

PART ONE

FOUNDATIONS

1   Globalizing Business
2   Formal Institutions: Political, Economic and Legal Systems
3   Informal Institutions: Culture, Religion and Languages
4   Firm Resources: Competitiveness and Growth

CHAPTER ONE

GLOBALIZING BUSINESS

LEARNING OBJECTIVES

After studying this chapter, you should be able to

1 Explain the concept of international business (IB)

2 Articulate what you hope to learn by reading this book and taking this course

3 Identify one fundamental question and two core perspectives that provide a framework for studying this field

4 Participate in the debate on globalization with a reasonably balanced and realistic view

5 Summarize some basic trends in the global economy

6 Draw implications for action by integrating global and local knowledge

 **OPENING CASE**

adidas: *sales, suppliers and stakeholders around the world*

On Shanghai's fashionable Huaihai Road, not far from the outlets of *Apple, Nike* and *Gucci*, a multi-story fashion store invites shoppers to try a brand hailing from a small town in Germany. In Herzogenaurach, the intense rivalry between *adidas* and *Puma* has propelled both sports shoe manufacturers onto the international stage. *adidas* pulled ahead with innovative approaches to sport sponsorship, placing its three stripes on the dresses of international competitors in many sports. After taking over *Reebok* in 2005, *adidas* became the world's second largest provider of sports shoes and clothing (after *Nike*), a segment that evolved into a much broader market of leisure clothing.

By 2014, *adidas* sales had a truly global footprint, with an equally strong presence on all continents. Western Europe was still the most important region accounting for 28.3% of sales, followed by North America with 20.4%. Yet about half of *adidas*' sales already came from emerging economies, including European emerging economies (13.3%), Greater China (12.5%), other Asia (14.3%), and Latin America (11.2%). The success in China is the result of over two decades of brand building, and a major marketing push ahead of the 2008 Olympics, featuring adverts associating *adidas* with the Chinese national team and its successes. In a highly competitive premium segment in China, global premium brands *Nike* and *adidas* have been challenged by local brands like *Li Ning*, but by focusing on innovation and brand quality they sustained their popularity among increasingly affluent young urban people.

However, not only sales have become global; the value chain of the company also extends across the globe. In particular, the labour-intensive parts of shoes and clothing manufacturing have, since the 1980s, been moved to locations with low labour costs, often to independent suppliers. By 2015 *adidas* had 891 primary suppliers around the world, many of which are based in emerging countries like China (227), Vietnam (63), India (30), Indonesia (45), and Korea (51). They were complemented by suppliers in advanced economies like the USA (83), Japan (52), Italy (12), UK (24), Spain (8), and Germany (19).

With global supply chains labour relations have also become global, and consumers in Europe and North America take an active interest in where and how their shoes are made. Thus *adidas* is continuously developing its codes of conduct for the company and its suppliers, which cover a wide range of issues including forced labour, child labour, discrimination, wage and benefits, hours of work, collective bargaining, disciplinary practices, environmental requirements and community involvement.

These codes are supplemented by comprehensive inspection programmes. An initial audit in 2000 found many incidences of standards not being kept, such as maximum work hours ignored, poor age documentation, wages below minimum wage, and working rules not publicly displayed in the work place. Unusually, *adidas* made this report public. The violations identified varied considerably across countries due to different emphasis of laws, law enforcement and informal norms. Informed by this report, *adidas* launched several initiatives to spread its standards of engagement, including identification of suppliers further down the supply chain, development of auditing tools and

procedures, and hiring staff to support these activities. Audit teams visited factories not only to monitor compliance, but also to train the management in the use of the standards of engagement and to explain the likely benefits of higher standards for the business itself. The teams rate each factory on a scale from 1 to 5 on several criteria. At the same time, they aim to engage in a constructive dialogue to provide solutions to problems that occur. On its website, *adidas* publishes a list of its suppliers as well as annual 'performance data' containing details such as (aggregate) supplier ratings from audit reports, number of warning letters sent to suppliers and suppliers terminated.

The standards of engagement led to improvement in business practices in supplier firms, especially in those firms that chose a proactive approach. An independent study found rising product quality, fewer accidents, lower staff turnover and rising productivity in a proactive supplier firm, while reluctant adoption of the code in another supplier firm led to inferior economic performance. *adidas* is cooperating with the *Fair Labor Association* (FLA), which provides external, independent monitoring, complaints procedures and public reporting. Other recognition for *adidas*' efforts in the area of social responsibility comes from industry organizations. Most notably, *Dow Jones Sustainability Index* (DJSI) recognized *adidas* as industry leader since 2003, and named it 'Global Supersector Leader' 2009/2010 for the sector 'Personal & Household Goods' for the second consecutive time. In 2013, *adidas* was named both the global sustainability 'Sector Leader' and 'Gold' for the second consecutive time.

Sources: (1) adidas-Salomon, 2000, *Our World: Social and environmental report 2000*, Herzongenaurach: adidas-Salomon; (2) S. Frenkel & D. Scott, 2002, *Compliance, collaboration, and codes of labor practice: The adidas connection*, CMR, 45, 29–49 (3) L. Hartman, R. Wokutch & J. French, 2003, adidas-Salomon, in: L. Hartman, D. Arnold & R. Wokutch, eds, *Rising Above Sweatshops*, Westport: Praeger, 191–248; (4) www.adidas-group.com; (accessed March 2015).

Were you surprised to learn how many people in different countries are involved with *adidas* – not just wearing their shoes and sports clothings, but as labourers, NGOs, or brand managers? Did you expect *adidas* to be so concerned what people think about its labour practices around the world? Did you realize that its marketing practices are locally adapted, even when refering to the same global brand? International business (IB) has become an integral part of many businesses – and products. Yet, managing IB activities – for example coordinating multiple suppliers of components – is challenging even for experienced managers. This book is about these sorts of challenges faced by managers of firms operating around the globe. In particular, we will be exploring what determines the success and failure of firms engaged in international business.

EUROPEAN AND GLOBAL BUSINESS

International business (IB) is about (1) businesses (firms) engaging in international (cross-border) economic activities and/or (2) the activity of doing business abroad. The IB course thus adds an explicitly international dimension to the curriculum of your business education. The most important actors in international business are known as multinational enterprise (MNE), defined as a firm that engages in foreign direct investment (FDI) by directly investing in, controlling and managing value-added activities in other countries.[1] For example, *adidas*, an MNE, has undertaken many FDI projects, such as manufacturing plants in the UK or retail shops in China. In addition, it has a variety of relationships with other businesses (from suppliers to distributors), sports teams it sponsors, and last but not least, consumers. These others may not be MNEs themselves, but they engage in IB too. For example domestic firms actively compete and/or collaborate with foreign entrants. They are the other side of the coin of international competition.[2]

There are two key words in IB: international (I) and business (B). The I indicates that we will spend substantial time on analysing the international environment of business, especially in Chapters 2, 3, 8 and 9. The B indicates why we study the international environment: we want to know how and why it is important for business. It also indicates that we are not focused on one function, such as management, marketing, or finance, but on the overall picture of business. Does it matter? Of course! It means that your IB course is an integrative course that has the potential to provide you with an overall business perspective (as opposed to a functional view) grounded in a global environment. Therefore, we aim to provide you with both the I and B parts in this textbook.

The realities of international and domestic business are increasingly blurred because many previously national (domestic) markets have opened to international competition. For example, suppliers of computer parts need to be able and willing to cooperate with the computer maker, for example *Dell*, *Acer* or *Lenovo*, at multiple sites around the world if they want to sell to the brand. Moreover, with creation of the single market in the European Union (EU), the definition of a home market is increasingly ambiguous. Especially in business-to-business markets, such as computer parts, customers are often operating internationally as well, such that competition in a single country would hardly be sustainable. Thus, it becomes difficult to tell what is international and what is domestic.

This book goes beyond traditional IB textbooks in two important ways. First, we focus on issues relevant to European businesses and managers. In Europe, domestic markets are smaller than, for example, in the USA and China. Hence, IB is an important element of business for almost all firms – large and small. Most of its business is

LEARNING OBJECTIVE

1 Explain the concept of international business (IB)

international business (IB)
(1) A business (firm) that engages in international (cross-border) economic activities and/or (2) the action of doing business abroad.

multinational enterprise (MNE)
A firm that engages in foreign direct investments and operates in multiple countries.

foreign direct investment (FDI)
Investments in, controlling and managing value-added activities in other countries.

Figure 1.1 International trade in Europe

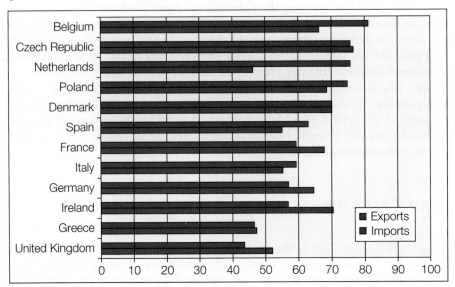

Note: Share of intra-EU exports and imports in the countries' total exports and imports, in %.

Source: Authors' creation using data from Eurostat database, accessed January 2015.

conducted with neighbouring countries. For example, France and Germany are each other's main trading partners. For most European businesses, the EU member countries account for more than half of their international activities. Only British (44%) and Greek (47%) exporters sell less than half their overseas sales within the EU, while their Czech counterparts sell 81% within the EU (see Figure 1.1). That is like working Monday to Thursday on EU markets and Friday on the rest of the world. Even the biggest MNEs do most of their business in their home region,[3] truly global companies like *adidas* remain the exeption rather than the rule. Within their own region, however, businesses face different kinds of challenges than when expanding beyond their home region. Notably, they operate under the auspices of the EU and the rules that the EU has established for business (see Chapter 8). Moreover, in neighbouring countries differences in institutions are relatively small, yet big enough to derail unsuspecting business people (Chapters 2 and 3). On the other hand, the rest of the world presents some of the most attractive (profitable) business opportunities and recently much larger growth potential. For example, *adidas* has been able to tap into both traditional West European markets and fast growing Asian markets. Hence, as an IB executive you need competence for both Europe and beyond.

This book aims to give you *both*, which distinguishes it from most English-language textbooks, which are often written by leading scholars based in the USA, and thus focus on issues of interest to Americans going international. Typically these are large companies dealing in distant markets because the home market in the USA is so big. Thus our European focus implies that we are paying more attention than other textbooks to (1) business in nearby countries, (2) institutions of the EU, (3) small and medium-sized enterprises (SMEs), and (4) research by European scholars on these issues.

Second, this book is going beyond developed economies by devoting extensive space to emerging economies (also known as emerging markets). These are economies that only recently established institutional frameworks that facilitate international trade and investment, typically with low- or middle-level income and above average economic growth. How important are emerging economies? Figure 1.2 provides some indications. The largest four emerging economies are indicated in

emerging economies (emerging markets) Economies that only recently established institutional frameworks that facilitate international trade and investment, typically with low- or middle-level income and above average economic growth.

Figure 1.2 The contributions of emerging economies

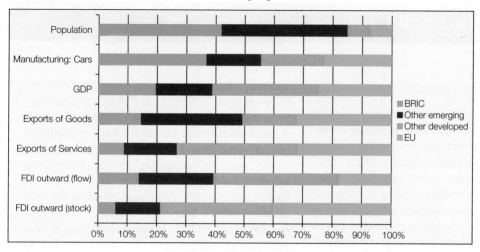

Sources: Authors' creation using data extracted from (1) United Nations, 2014, *World Investment Report 2014*, New York and Geneva: UN; (3) World Bank, 2014, *World Development Indicators* database. (4) World Trade Organization, 2014, *WTO Statistics* database, (4) *The Economist*, 2014, Pocket World in Figures, London: The Economist. All data refer to 2013.

blue: Brazil, Russia, India and China (also known as BRIC). About 85% of the people of the world live in an emerging market but they collectively contribute only about 30% of global gross domestic product (GDP), the most common measure of the economic power of an economy (In Focus 1.1). However, their participation in the global economy is rapidly increasing. For example, 55% of all cars are built in an emerging economy (25% in China alone). Together, emerging economies account for almost half of all goods exports and a quarter of all service exports. Their position in FDI is still small, but rapidly increasing; note the much larger share in new FDI (FDI flow) in the year 2013 compared to the existing FDI operations (FDI stock). The rapid growth of some emerging economies is evident. Today's students – and tomorrow's business leaders – will find rich opportunities in emerging economies. This book will help you to recognize them.

gross domestic product (GDP)
The sum of value added by resident firms, households and governments operating in an economy.

WHY STUDY INTERNATIONAL BUSINESS?

International business is one of the most exciting, challenging and relevant subjects offered by business schools. In addition to the requirements at your university or business school that usually classify this course as a core or recommended course, there are at least two compelling reasons you should study it.

First, for ambitious students who aspire to lead a business unit or an entire firm, expertise in IB is normally a prerequisite. It is increasingly difficult, if not impossible, to find top managers without significant international competences, even in small and medium-size enterprises. Of course, eventually, hands-on global experience, not merely knowledge acquired from this course, will be required. However, mastery of the knowledge of and demonstration of interest in IB during your education will set you apart as a candidate for fast-track career development that involves expatriate assignments – job assignments located abroad (see Chapter 16).

Thanks to globalization, low-skilled jobs not only command lower salaries, but are also more vulnerable to international competition. However, top management capabilities, especially those that create connections across the world, are in demand in companies that operate across national boundaries. For example, if a factory in

LEARNING OBJECTIVE

2 Articulate what you hope to learn by reading this book and taking this course

expatriate assignment
A temporary job abroad with a multinational company.

IN FOCUS 1.1

Setting the Terms Straight

GDP, GNP, GNI, PPP – there is a bewildering variety of acronyms that are used to measure economic development. It is useful to set these terms straight before proceeding. Gross domestic product (GDP) is measured as the sum of value added by *resident* firms, households and government operating in an economy. For example, the value added by foreign-owned firms operating in Mexico would be counted as part of Mexico's GDP. However, the earnings of *non-resident* sources that are sent back to Mexico (such as earnings of Mexicans who do not live and work in Mexico and dividends received by Mexicans who own non-Mexican stocks) are not included in Mexico's GDP. One measure that captures this is **gross national product (GNP)**. More recently, the World Bank and other international organizations have used a new term, **gross national income (GNI)**, to supersede GNP. Conceptually, there is no difference between GNI and GNP. What exactly is GNI/GNP? It comprises GDP plus income from non-resident sources abroad.

While GDP, GNP, and now GNI are often used as yardsticks of economic development, differences in cost of living make such a direct comparison less meaningful. In particular, the costs of living in emerging economies, especially services such as housing and haircuts, tend to be much lower than in developed economies. For example, €1 spent in Nairobi, Kenya can buy a lot more than in €1 spent in Oslo, Norway. The **purchasing power parity (PPP)** exchange rate considers such differences. The PPP between two countries is the rate at which the currency of one country needs to be converted into that of a second country to ensure that a given amount of the first country's currency will purchase the same volume of goods and services in the second country.

For example, according to the International Monetary Fund (IMF, see Chapter 9), the Swiss per capita GDP is US$81 276 based on official (nominal) exchange rates – a lot *higher* than the US per capita GDP of US$53 001. However, everything is more expensive in Switzerland. A Big Mac costs US$6.83 in Switzerland versus US$4.80 in the USA. Thus, Switzerland's per capita GDP based on PPP is only US$53 977 – only slightly higher than the US per capita GDP based on PPP, US$53 001 (the IMF uses the USA as benchmark in PPP calculation). Overall, when we read statistics about GDP, GNP and GNI, always pay attention to whether these numbers are based on official exchange rates or PPP, which can make a huge difference. However, PPP values have been created to compare standards of living, they only weakly proxy the 'real' size of an economy. Also, be aware of intra-country variations in PPP. If you live as an expatriate in Manila or Shanghai, you will find many actual expenses to be quite similar to Europe: the cheap food or local transport does not meet the same quality and safety standards that most Europeans expect.

Sources: (1) *The Economist*, 2014, Calculating European GDP, August 23; (2) *The Economist*, 2014, The Big Mac index, July 26; (3) International Monetary Fund, 2014, *Report for selected countries and subjects (PPP valuation of country GDP)*, Washington: IMF.

gross national product (GNP)
Gross domestic product plus income from non-resident sources abroad.

gross national income (GNI)
GDP plus income from non-resident sources abroad. GNI is the term used by the World Bank and other international organizations to supersede the term GNP.

Europe is shut down and the MNE sets up a similar factory in China, only a few dozen people may keep their jobs. Yes, you guessed it: these jobs are top-level positions such as the chief executive, chief financial officer, factory director and chief engineer. They may be sent by the MNE as expats to China to lead operations there. To motivate their best people to take such challenging assignments, MNEs typically offer them a higher salary and extra perks during their stay. Knowledge of IB and the ability to contribute to discussion on global business issues are a foundation for becoming a sought after, globetrotting manager.

Second, even if you do not have the aspiration to move around the world in your professional life, you may find yourself dealing with foreign-owned suppliers and buyers, competing with foreign-invested firms in your home market, and perhaps even managing investments abroad. Very few companies in Europe are able to pursue their business without regular interaction across international borders. Moreover, you may also find yourself working for a foreign-owned firm, as your domestic employer is acquired by a foreign player. Understanding how global business decisions are made may facilitate your own career in such MNEs.[4] If there is a strategic rationale to downsize your unit, you would want to be able to figure this out and be the first one to talk to alternative employers. In other words, it is your career that is at stake. Don't be the last in the know! In short, in this age of global competition, how do you prevent your job from being offshored to India or China? A good place to start is to study hard and do well in your IB course.

purchasing power parity (PPP)
A conversion that determines the equivalent amount of goods and services different currencies can purchase. This conversion is usually used to capture the differences in cost of living in different countries.

A UNIFIED FRAMEWORK

International business is a vast subject area. It is one of the few courses that will make you appreciate why your university requires you to take a number of (seemingly unrelated) general education courses. Here we draw on major social sciences, such as economics, geography, history, political science, psychology and sociology, as well as a number of business disciplines, such as finance and marketing. It is very easy to lose sight of the 'forest' while scrutinizing various 'trees' or even 'branches'. The subject is not difficult, and most students find it to be fun. The number one student complaint (based on previous student feedback) is an overwhelming amount of information, which is also our number one complaint as your authors.

LEARNING OBJECTIVE

3 Identify one fundamental question and two core perspectives that provide a framework for studying this field

To address your possible complaint and make your learning more manageable (and ideally, more fun), we develop a unified framework as a consistent theme throughout this book (Figure 1.3). This will provide continuity to facilitate your learning. Specifically, we will focus on one fundamental question. This question acts to define a field and to orient the attention of students, practitioners and scholars in a certain direction. Our 'big question' is: *What determines the success and failure of firms around the globe?*[5] To answer this question, we focus on two core perspectives throughout this book: (1) an institution-based view, and (2) a resource-based view. The remainder of this section outlines why this is the case.

One Fundamental Question

What is it that we do in IB? Why is it so important that practically every student in a business school around the world is either required or recommended to take such a course? Although there are certainly a lot of questions, 'what determines the success

Figure 1.3 A Unified framework for global business

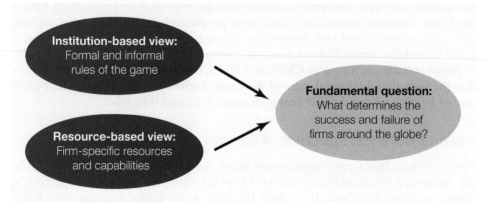

and failure of firms around the globe?' serves to focus our studies. IB, fundamentally, is about not limiting yourself to your home country and about treating the entire global economy as your potential playground (or battlefield). Some firms may be successful domestically. However, when they venture abroad they fail miserably. Other firms successfully translate their strengths from their home market to other countries. If you were to lead your firm's efforts to enter a particular foreign market, wouldn't you want to find out what is behind the success and failure of other firms in that market?

Overall, firm performance in all their operations around the globe is, more than anything else, of concern to managers in internationally operating firms. Numerous other questions all relate in one way or another to this most fundamental question. For example, how do firms affect those they cooperate or compete with, their employees and suppliers, and society as a whole? This broader perspective is part of what constitutes the 'success' of firms looking beyond profits. In this spirit, the primary focus of the field of IB – and of this book – is: *what determines the success and failure of firms around the globe?*

First Core Perspective: An Institution-Based View

Like sports or board games, businesses have to play by certain rules. These 'rules of the game' are commonly known as 'institutions', and they come in many forms. However, they also vary considerably across countries, or even within countries. To succeed in IB, you need intimate knowledge about the formal and informal rules of doing business in each country in which you are operating. In a nutshell, an institution-based view suggests that success and failure of firms are enabled and constrained by the different rules of the game.[6]

Some *formal* rules of the game, such as the requirements to treat domestic and foreign firms as equals, would enhance the potential odds for foreign firms' success. Hong Kong is well known to treat all comers, ranging from neighbouring mainland China (whose firms are still technically regarded as 'non-domestic') to far-away Chile, the same as it treats indigenous Hong Kong firms. It is thus not surprising that Hong Kong attracts a lot of outside firms. Other rules of the game, which may discriminate against foreign firms, would undermine the chances for foreign entrants. For example, Central and Eastern Europe started attracting foreign investors only after 1990, when the region shed the legacies of socialism, removed barriers to foreign investment, and aligned its formal institutions to those of the EU.

In addition to formal rules, *informal* rules such as culture, norms and values play an important part in shaping the success and failure of firms around the globe. For example, because founding new firms tends to deviate from the social norm of working for other bosses, individualistic societies, such as Australia, Britain and the USA, tend to have a relatively higher level of entrepreneurship as reflected in the number of business start-ups. Conversely, collectivistic societies such as Japan often have a hard time fostering entrepreneurship; most people feel discouraged from sticking their neck out to found new businesses. Yet such collectivist societies may find it easier to mobilize teams to work towards common goals over long periods of time.

As we will discuss further in Chapters 2 and 3, the institution-based view suggests that the formal and informal rules of the game, known as institutions, shed a great deal of light on what is behind firm performance around the globe.

Second Core Perspective: A Resource-Based View

The institution-based view suggests that firms' success and failure around the globe are influenced by their environments. However, insightful as this perspective is, there is a major drawback. If we push this view to its logical extreme, then firms' performance around the globe would be entirely determined by their environments. The validity of this extreme version is certainly questionable.

This is where the resource-based view comes in.[7] While the institution-based view primarily deals with the external environment, the resource-based view focuses on a firm's internal resources and capabilities. It starts with a simple observation: in harsh, unattractive environments, most firms either suffer or exit. However, against all odds, a few superstars thrive in these environments. For instance, the worldwide automotive industry has been under pressure from overcapacity. Yet, some European manufacturers like *Audi* and *BMW* have been increasing their market share, while US manufacturers *General Motors* (*GM*) and *Ford* needed a government bail-out in 2009. On the other hand, *Toyota* suffered a major drop in sales due to quality control problems and a US government investigation. Likewise, in the global airline industry, where most of the major airlines around the world have been losing money in recent years, a small number of players, such as *Southwest* in the USA and *Ryanair* in Ireland, have been profitable year after year. How can these firms succeed in very challenging environments? A short answer is that *BMW*, *Audi*, *Southwest* and *Ryanair* must have certain valuable and unique firm-specific resources and capabilities that are not shared by competitors in the same environments.

Doing business outside one's home country is challenging. Foreign firms have to overcome a liability of outsidership, which is the inherent disadvantage that outsiders experience in a new environment because of their lack of familiarity with local contexts and networks (See Figure 1.4).[8] Just think of all the differences in regulations, languages, cultures and norms. Your ability to operate depends on your familiarity with the local context. Thus the liability of outsidership increases the more a firm's origins differ from the host environment,[9] the less the firm has experience in the host country,[10] and the further away its nearest prior affiliate.[11]

Against such significant odds, the primary weapon of foreign firms is overwhelming resources and capabilities that after offsetting the liability of outsidership, still result in some significant competitive advantage. Many of us take it for granted that year in and year out, *Coca-Cola* (see Closing Case) is the best-selling soft drink in many countries, and *Microsoft Word* is the market-leading word processing software virtually everywhere around the world. We really shouldn't take it for granted because it is *not* natural for these foreign firms to dominate non-native markets. Behind such remarkable success stories, these firms must possess some powerful firm-specific resources that enabled them to attain these leadership positions around the globe. Chapter 4 will explore how the resource-based view can be used to analyze businesses and business opportunities.

liability of outsidership
the inherent disadvantage that outsiders experience in a new environment because of their lack of familiarity.

Figure 1.4 Liability of outsidership

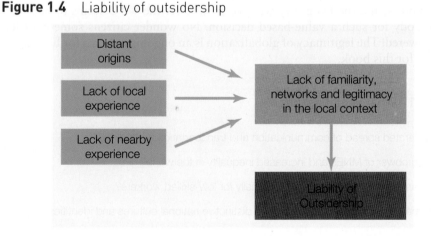

UNDERSTANDING GLOBALIZATION

LEARNING OBJECTIVE

4 Participate in the
debate on globaliza-
tion with a reason-
ably balanced and
realistic view

The rather abstract word 'globalization' is hotly debated across the world. Those who approve of globalization praise its contributions to economic growth and standards of living, sharing of technologies, and more extensive cultural exchange. Critics argue that globalization undermines wages in rich countries, exploits workers in poor countries, and gives MNEs too much power. So, what exactly is globalization? This section (1) provides a first glance of what globalization is all about, (2) sets it in a historical perspective, and (3) outlines the current wave of globalization. We will further explore the forces driving globalization in Chapter 9.

Views on Globalization

Many people talk about globalization, yet they do not necessarily mean the same thing (Table 1.1). For young people, globalization is often first and foremost the internet and the information and communication technology that comes with it. It is now as easy to chat with your friends at the other end of the world as if you were sitting in the same room. Imagine the days when letters took days or even weeks to be delivered. You may be studying anywhere in the world, but you can easily update yourself about activities of the authors of your textbook over the internet – what a difference to your fellow students only a decade ago. *Facebook*, *Twitter*, *YouTube* and *Flickr* are certainly expressions of globalization affecting your daily life. The accelerated pace at which technologies spread around the globe is an important aspect of globalization.

A second view associates globalization primarily with rising power of MNEs and growing inequality around the world.[12] Many people feel that they are losing control over their lives as a result of forces unleashed by globalization, and beyond the control of even their elected representatives. MNEs have grown big (see next section), and have attained considerable bargaining power when negotiating with national governments. Nations appear to have less control over what happens within their borders, and politicians have lost some of their power to shape events.[13] For example, in 2009 the EU banned the import of seal-based products, notably sealskin, following a long period of lobbying by environmental groups and a vote by the European Parliament. Yet it is doubtful whether the strong popular desire to protect seals will translate into action: Canada immediately announced that it would challenge the EU's import ban at the World Trade Organization because it is 'a trade decision … which is not based on science'.[14] It took another five years until the WTO ruled that the prevention of animal cruelty was a legitimate reason to block imports, and the EU policy was acceptable. Yet the WTO seems to be a very remote body for such a value-based decision. No wonder citizens sometimes feel disempowered! The legitimacy of globalization is an ongoing concern for businesses, and thus for this book.

Table 1.1 What is globalization?

- Accelerated spread of communication and transportation technology?
- Rising power of MNEs and increased inequality in the world?
- Increased competition for jobs, especially for low-skilled workers?
- A force eliminating differences among distinctive national cultures and identities?

Third, unskilled workers appear to lose out, at least in relative terms. The relative income of the highest skilled people is rising, while the share of income from capital is rising relative to income from labour. According to French economist Thomas Piketty and American Nobel Prize winner Robert Solow, these trends are likely to continue.[15] Moreover, in Western Europe, international competition creates pressures on the welfare state,[16] while low-skilled workers fear that their job will be offshored to India, China, Poland or Romania. Other economists point to the fundamentally positive effects. In particular, increased global trade allows greater specialization and greater synergies of pooling resources, which increases productivity and thus creating potentially more wealth that should eventually benefit all (Chapter 5). Advocates of this view thus argue that fine-tuning of regulations – rather than wholesale rejection of globalization – would be the appropriate way to ensure benefits of globalizations are shared more broadly.[17]

Fourth, some interpret globalization as a force that makes us all more similar, and that eliminates the distinctiveness of our national cultures and identities. Some scholars, especially in marketing, argue that the world is on a path of convergence where consumers become more alike, and companies thus sell the same products everywhere on the globe.[18] This expectation has created substantial anxieties, especially in more traditional communities.[19] For some consumer electronics, it may hold true, as demonstrated by the success of Asian consumer electronics manufacturers of computers and smartphones. Yet such strategies have their limits, and in fact almost all products are in one way or another adapted to local contexts, even the infamous Coca-Cola (see Closing Case). People around the world may be watching Hollywood movies, yet they live their daily lives in distinctly different ways. Thus we may see some convergence – especially amongst the middle classes – but there is little evidence to suggest that globalization would create a homogenous 'global culture' any time soon.

The following definition by sociologist Mauro Guillén nicely sums up this discussion: globalization is '*a process leading to greater interdependence and mutual awareness (reflexivity) among economic, political and social units in the world, and among actors in general.*'[20] In other words, globalization has created unprecedented contacts between cultures, but it has only marginally reduced clashes between them. Hence, in business you have to work more frequently with others who operate under quite different conditions than yourself. This book aims to help you deal with the challenges and opportunities that this creates.

globalization
A process leading to greater interdependence and mutual awareness among economic, political and social units in the world, and among actors in general.

Trends of Globalization

Globalization is not new; it has long been part and parcel of human history. People have been trading over long distances for more than five millennia, with early traces of internationally operating businesses going as far back as the Assyrian and Phoenician Empires.[21] From 50 BCE to 500 CE, the Roman Empire ruled the Mediterranean region and created road and shipping infrastructure as well as political and legal structure, notably a common currency that facilitated trade, while the Silk Road connected Europe to Asia. In the Middle Ages, the Hanseatic League created a trading network of cities in Northern Europe that stretched from Novgorod in Russia to London in England. The League established common rules (or 'institutions'), that applied to merchants in member cities, and thus overcame the fragmented political structures at the time. Technological progress, notably in shipping and navigation techniques, has been advancing the speed and scope of international trade throughout the Middle Ages and into modern times.

Globalization accelerated in the 19th century following major innovations in manufacturing, communication and transport, as well as legal changes.[22] Industrialization took off with the invention of the steam engine, which powered the new railway networks and steam ships as well as mechanized mass production. Communication accelerated first by faster transport, and then by the invention of the telegraph in 1838. However, these technological changes alone would probably not have brought about the rapid economic growth of the 19th century; they were accompanied by major liberalization, the removal of regulatory restrictions on business, such as the abolishment of guild systems for trades and crafts. The introduction of the limited liability company permitted new forms of ownership and thus larger companies, while new patent laws encouraged entrepreneurs to innovate – and reap the benefits of their innovations. Many countries adopted the gold standard, which provided stable exchange rates, and allowed unrestricted transfers of capital. Migration was uninhibited by passport controls, visas or work permits. MNEs played a major role in this global economy, the level of world FDI relative to GDP reached an estimated 9% in 1913, a level that was reached again only in the 1990s.

The wave of globalization of the 19th century peaked with the outbreak of World War I (see In Focus 1.2). While technological advances continued, politics interfered with a lot of the benefits that our grandparents might have enjoyed. Tariffs started to be introduced from the 1850s; by 1914 only Britain, the Netherlands and Denmark were committed to free trade. During the 1920s, many countries raised tariffs to record levels, and new quotas and trade barriers were created as countries aimed to protect their domestic industries. During World War I, many MNE subsidiaries were expropriated, and all foreign investors lost their assets in Russia after the revolution of 1917.

Many developing countries nationalized natural resource investments between the 1930s and 1960s. New FDI was made less attractive by restrictions on foreign ownership and by exchange controls that inhibited the repatriation of profits. Migration has become more restricted since World War I. The USA started requiring passports and visas, and soon added work restrictions: its annual immigration rate fell from 1.16% of the population in 1913 to 0.04% after the war. The stable exchange rate system broke down when Britain abandoned the gold standard in 1931, and others followed with competitive devaluations, thus raising the costs and uncertainty of trading across currency areas. As a consequence, international trade declined during World War I, recovered moderately during the 1920s, and then collapsed in the depression of the 1930s. In a nutshell, globalization is nothing new and it is marching on, but there have been quite substantial and costly setbacks. Hence, following business historian Geoff Jones, we suggest that waves of globalization may appropriately describe the world economy.[23]

What is Globalization?

The current wave of globalization gradually evolved after World War II. A new fixed exchange rate system was created and provided stability until the late 1960s (see Chapter 7). However, in the 1950s and 1960s barriers to trade and capital movements were pervasive, even among the countries that had embraced the principles of a market economy. Many developing countries, such as Argentina, Brazil, India and Mexico, focused on fostering and protecting domestic industries, while socialist countries, such as China and the (then) Soviet Union, sought to develop self-sufficiency. Even in Western Europe, trade barriers were substantial – not only shielding European businesses from outside competition, but also inhibiting companies operating across borders within Europe.[24] However, barriers to global trade and investment ended up breeding uncompetitive industries focused on domestic markets only.

Gradually, international integration gathered pace. At a regional level, initiatives such as the European Communities, predecessor of the EU, created an institutional framework for intra-regional trade (see Chapter 8), while global agreements such as the GATT aimed to liberalize trade globally (see Chapter 9). However, in the 1970s

liberalization
The removal of regulatory restrictions on business.

waves of globalization
The pattern of globalization arising from a combination of long-term trends and pendulum swings.

IN FOCUS 1.2

Globalization in the Year 1900

The world economy was highly globalized at the start of the 20th century. By some measures, the same levels of global integration were only reached again in the 1990s. For instance the ratio of FDI-stock to GDP reached 9% in 1913, dropped to 4.4% by the 1960s, before rising to 8.8% in 1990 and 28.4% in 2007 (before falling back to 24.5% in 2008). However, the nature of global business was quite different. European powers ruled large colonial empires, and a lot of international trade was bringing raw materials to Europe, and manufactured goods from Europe were sold worldwide.

The mining industry led international investment. Many natural resources required by the rapidly industrializing nations of Europe and North America were found in colonies: petroleum, copper, tin and other metals. MNEs led the exploitation of these resources employing imported technologies and capital. Concessions, once obtained, were relatively generous, giving these early MNEs a free hand to manage their affairs, and few taxes or charges were levied by the host countries. The notion that natural resources underground belong to the nation was only developed early in the 20th century. A leading player in the global exploitation of natural resources was *Standard Oil*, one of the largest companies of the world until it was broken up by US anti-trust legislation in 1911.

Many renewable resources in demand by the early industrial societies were also found in the colonies. In some industries, MNEs controlled the entire value chain from the plantation to the retailer: for instance, *United Fruit* controlled the banana trade between Central America and North America, while British trading houses not only imported tea but invested in tea plantations in South Asia. Elsewhere, British entrepreneurs took seeds from Brazil to build rubber plantations in Malaya (modern day Malaysia) that came to dominate world markets. In other industries, such as cotton, tobacco and coffee, multinational trading houses sourced from local farmers and sold on the big exchanges in Europe and North America.

Resource exploiting companies were often organized as free-standing MNEs. They would be headquartered in the leading financial markets of London or New York, but operate solely in distant locations or colonies. Often these firms started out designing and implementing major projects, such as railways and mines. Entrepreneurs would bring together engineering skills and capital from the home country with knowledge of local geology, geography, economics and politics. This business model enabled raised risk capital from European or American investors, and used it where high returns could be earned. After the initial construction phase, the operation of the railway or mine was often transferred to a local management company – similar to modern build-own-operate contracts.

The earliest manufacturing MNEs were established in the 1850s, including *Singer Sewing Machines* (USA) and *Siemens* (Germany). Yet integrated global operations as we know them in the 21st century were rare in the year 1900 because distance – in particular the time it took to communicate over long geographic distances – inhibited the establishment of effective control mechanisms. Many businesses thus entrusted subsidiaries to a family member or clan member, and gave him (rarely her) a free hand to manage it locally. Hierarchical organizational forms to manage MNEs only evolved later with advances in technology and marketing practices.

In many industries, businesses organized international cartels to reduce the uncertainty created by free competition, and to protect their profits. Especially in small countries, many industries were thus highly concentrated, with tacit or even formal agreements between international competitors not to enter each other's home markets. Liberal policies at the time also meant absence of effective merger control or constraints on private monopolies. Moreover, protection of industrial workers was still in its infancy. Unprecedented wealth was created in the late 19th century, but it took several decades longer for this wealth to spread to all strata of society.

Sources: (1) J.F. Hennart, 1994, International financial capital transfers, *BH*, 36, 51–70; M.C. Casson, 1994, Institutional diversity in overseas enterprise, *BH*, 36, 95–108; (2) G. Jones, 2005, *Multinationals and Global Capitalism*, Oxford: Oxford University Press; (3) S. Fellman, M.J. Iversen, H. Sjögren & L. Thue, eds., 2008, *Creating Nordic Capitalism*, Basingstoke: Palgrave-Macmillan; (4) M. Bucheli, 2008, Multinational corporations, totalitarian regimes and economic nationalism: United Fruit Company in Central America 1899–1975, *BH*, 50, 433–454.

IN FOCUS 1.3

GE Innovates from the Base of the Pyramid

MNEs such as *General Electric (GE)* historically innovate new products in developed economies, and then localize these products by tweaking them for customers in emerging economies. However, such expensive products developed with customers in developed economies in mind often flop in emerging economies not only because of their price tag, but also because of their lack of consideration for the specific needs and wants of local customers. In recent years, some firms have turned this pattern around.

For example, *GE Healthcare*, a unit of *GE*, traditionally build ultrasound machines that sell in the US and Japanese markets for €100 000 and up. In emerging economies, these devices sold poorly because not every hospital imaging centre could afford them. More than 80% of China's population relies on rural hospitals or clinics that are poorly funded. Conventional ultrasound machines were simply out of reach for these facilities. Since most Chinese patients could not come to the ultrasound

machines, the machines, thus, have to go to the patients. Scaling down its existing complex ultrasound machines was not going to serve that demand. *GE Healthcare* realized that it needed a revolutionary product – a compact, portable ultrasound machine. It thus developed a compact ultrasound machine that was operated with a regular laptop computer, and sold for €12 000. These portable ultrasounds not only became a hit in smaller cities in China, but generated dramatic growth throughout the world for *GE*, including developed economies. These machines combine a new dimension previously unavailable to ultrasound machines – portability – with a low price, in developed economies where containing health care cost is increasingly paramount.

Portable ultrasound machines in China are not the only such innovation. In Africa, healthcare service providers like *GE*, *Philips*, *Siemens* and *Elektra* offering slimmed down and adapted products experience double digit growth. However, they adjust not only their products, but also their business models. Governments are concerned that hospital equipment is often used by poorly-trained doctors, and maintained

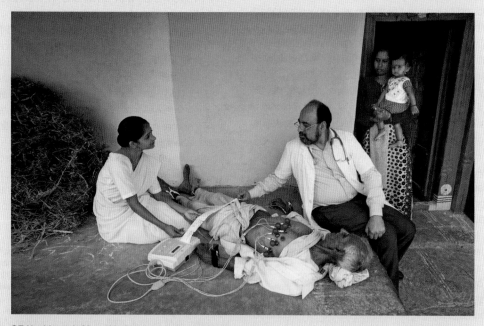

GE Healthcare's Mac 400 electrocardiogram (ECG) machines, seen here being used in rural India, was developed for India and China. In 2009, *GE Healthcare* brought a newer model, the Mac 800 (pictured) into the USA, where it is finding new applications, such as at accident sites.

under challenging climatic conditions. In Kenya, *GE Healthcare* develops with innovative service contracts rather than traditional product sales.

These experiences in emerging economies change the mental map of first world healthcare equipment providers. Their strategic attention moves to emerging economies and they transfer innovative ideas between emerging economies – and eventually back to their home regions. Such strategy also prepares them to face new competitors from the developing world such as Chinese *Mindray*.

Sources: (1) *The Economist*, 2009, GE: Losing its magic touch, March 21; (2) GE Report, 2009, www.gereports.com; (3) J. Immelt, V. Govindarajan, & C. Trimble, 2009, How GE is disrupting itself, *HBR*, October: 56–65; (4) K. Manson, 2015, GE and Philips scan African market as disease burden grows, *Financial Times*, March 6.

and 1980s, globalization remained largely a matter for the developed economies in the Triad, three regions that consist of North America, Western Europe and Japan.

Globalization accelerated dramatically in the 1990s. While world output grew by 23% over the decade, global trade expanded by 80% and the total flow of FDI increased fivefold.[25] A major contributor to the acceleration were emerging economies that joined the global stage, bringing billions of people with much lower incomes into the fold. More and more countries, such as China and Latin America in the 1980s, and Central and Eastern Europe and India in the 1990s, realized that joining the world economy was a must. As these countries started to emerge as new players in the world economy, they become collectively known as 'emerging markets'[26] or 'emerging economies'. Over the past three decades, many often them have risen from 'cheap workbenches', to major markets for consumer goods, and some even become sources of innovation (In Focus 1.3). The largest emerging economies – Brazil, Russia, India and China (collectively known as BRIC) – have not only achieved remarkable economic development, but have also become major political players.[27]

The active participation of emerging economies in the global economy has created new awareness of the pyramid structure of the global economy (Figure 1.5). The top consists of about one billion people with per capita annual income of €15 000 or higher. However, the vast majority of humanity – about four billion people – live at the base of this pyramid, making less than €1500 a year. These people at the base of

Triad
Three regions of developed economies (North America, Western Europe and Japan).

BRIC
Brazil, Russia, India and China.

base of the pyramid
The vast majority of humanity, about four billion people, who make less than €1500 a year.

Figure 1.5 The global economic pyramid

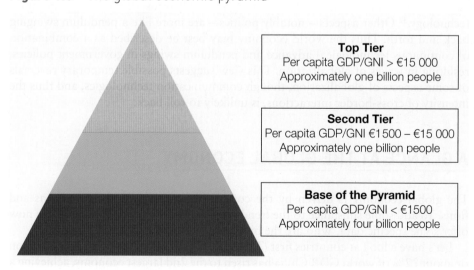

Top Tier
Per capita GDP/GNI > €15 000
Approximately one billion people

Second Tier
Per capita GDP/GNI €1 500 – €15 000
Approximately one billion people

Base of the Pyramid
Per capita GDP/GNI < €1500
Approximately four billion people

Sources: (1) C. K. Prahalad & S. Hart, 2002, The fortune at the bottom of the pyramid, Strategy + Business, 26: 54–67, and (2) S. Hart, 2005, Captialism at the Crossroads (p. 111), Philadelphia: Wharton School Publishing.

the pyramid provide new resources, and new demand (see Closing Case, and Integrated Case Fan Milk).[28]

Like a pendulum, globalization is unable to keep going in one direction. Opposing pressures arise from at least two sources. First, it created fear among many people in developed economies because emerging economies not only seem to compete away many low-end manufacturing jobs, but also appear to threaten some high-end jobs. Second, some factions in emerging economies complained against the onslaught of MNEs, which allegedly not only destroy local companies but also local cultures and values, as well as the environment.

The inter-connectedness of the global economy, and hence the power of competitive pressures, became evident to everyone in the 2008/9 global financial crisis. Deteriorating housing markets in the USA, fuelled by unsustainable subprime lending practices, led to massive government bailouts of financial services firms starting in September 2008. The crisis quickly spread around the world, forcing numerous governments to bail out their own troubled banks. Global output, trade and investment plummeted, while unemployment started rising.[29]

During the crisis, many citizens in countries in Eastern and Southern Europe, such as Hungary, Latvia, Romania and Greece, were bitter.[30] Prior to 2008, these countries were first enthusiastic about their integration with the EU, and many consumers felt they could afford to enjoy rich Europe's living standards by borrowing from the banks. However, when the financial crisis upset exchange rates and triggered a recession, the region was hard hit. The International Monetary Fund (IMF) came to the rescue, but not without harsh medicines of belt tightening, credit squeezing and spending cuts. Not surprisingly, this intervention triggered lots of debates over the role of the IMF (see Chapter 9).

After unprecedented intervention throughout developed economies, the global economy turned the corner. However, economic recovery was slow in some developed economies, especially Southern Europe, whereas some emerging economies rebounded faster, especially China. The recession reminded all firms and managers of the importance of risk management – the identification and assessment of risks and the actions taken to minimize the impact of rare, unfortunate events.[31] Considerations of risk are thus central for how firms develop their strategies on the global stage (Chapter 14), and specifically for the management of global supply chains (Chapter 17).

risk management
The identification and assessment of risks and the actions taken to minimize their impact.

Overall, globalization is seen by everyone and rarely comprehended. Some aspects of globalization are continuously advancing – notably transport and communication technology.[32] Other aspects – notably politics – are more like a pendulum swinging back and forth. Thus the world economy may best be described as a combination of continuous technological advance and pendulum swings in government policies, resulting in waves of globalization. This view suggests possible temporary reversals of some aspects of globalization, though communication technologies, and thus the intensity of cross-border interactions, is unlikely to roll back.

A GLANCE AT THE GLOBAL ECONOMY

LEARNING OBJECTIVE

5 Summarize some basic trends in the global economy

The global economy is driven by the competitive interplay between nations and firms. To add some substance to the trends explored in the previous section, we now offer some specific data. Who are the biggest players in the global economy?

Let's have a look at countries first (Table 1.2). The USA accounts for €13.5 trillion or about 22% of world GDP. China has risen to the 2nd largest economy, achieving a GDP of €7.2 trillion, and with regularly higher growth rates its weight in the global economy is continuously growing. The EU as a whole is however bigger than either

Table 1.2 Top 25 economies in 2013

	Country	GDP (€ billion)	Population (million)	Exports (€ billion)	Stock of Outward FDI (€ billion)
1	USA	13 479	319.3	1 264	5 166
2	China (PR)	7 413	1 367.2	1 773	492
3	Japan	3 932	127.1	559	797
4	Germany	2 916	80.8	1 198	1 372
5	France	2 198	66.1	464	1 313
6	UK	2 023	64.1	652	1 512
7	Brazil	1 802	203.6	196	235
8	Russia	1 682	146.3	413	402
9	Italy	1 662	60.8	380	480
10	India	1 506	1 264.1	251	96
11	Canada	1 466	35.5	368	588
12	Australia	1 259	23.7	202	191
13	Spain	1 090	46.5	367	516
14	South Korea	1 047	50.4	447	176
15	Mexico	1 012	119.7	298	115
16	Indonesia	697	252.2	144	13
17	Turkey	658	76.7	134	26
18	Netherlands	642	16.9	463	860
19	Saudi Arabia	598	30.8	302	32
20	Switzerland	522	8.2	184	1 010
21	Argentina	491	42.7	68	27
22	Sweden	448	9.7	146	350
23	Nigeria	419	178.5	75	7
24	Poland	415	38.5	162	44
25	Norway	411	5.2	124	185

Sources: (1) IMF (2014): *International Financial Statistics*, Washington: IMF; (2) UNCTAD (2014): *World Investment Report*, Geneva: United Nations.

of these countries; its combined GDP adds to €13 trillion. Looking at other indicators of economic power, however, quite different rankings emerge. Four of the five most populous countries are emerging economies: China (1.37 billion people), India (1.26 billion), Indonesia (252 million) and Brazil (204 million). The biggest exporters in 2013 were China (€1.8 trillion), USA (€1.3 trillion) and Germany (€1.2 trillion). The countries of the EU together export over €5.0 trillion, most of which is traded

Table 1.3 Top 25 companies by revenues in the global economy

	Company	Headquarters	Industry	Sales € bn	Assets € bn	Employment	TNI*
1	Royal Dutch Shell	UK	Petroleum	362	287	92 000	72.8
2	Exxon Mobil	USA	Petroleum	313	278	75 000	62.6
3	BP	UK	Petroleum	304	245	83 900	69.7
4	Volkswagen	Germany	Motor vehicles	210	358	572 800	58.6
5	Toyota Motor	Japan	Motor vehicles	206	323	333 498	58.6
6	Glencore Xstrata	Switzerland	Mining & quarrying	187	124	190 000	82.8
7	Total	France	Petroleum	183	192	98 799	79.5
8	Chevron	USA	Petroleum	170	204	64 600	59.3
9	Apple	USA	Electrical & electronic	137	166	84 400	59.6
10	EON	Germany	Utilities	130	144	62 239	73.3
11	Eni	Italy	Petroleum	122	153	83 887	71.2
12	General Electric	USA	Electrical & electronic	115	527	307 000	48.8
13	GDF Suez	France	Utilities	95	176	147 199	55.2
14	Honda Motor	Japan	Motor vehicles	95	122	190 338	74.3
15	Fiat	Italy	Motor vehicles	92	96	225 587	80.2
16	Enel	Italy	Electricity, gas and water	86	181	71 394	57.3
17	Nissan	Japan	Motor vehicles	84	115	160 530	67.4
18	BMW	Germany	Motor vehicles	81	153	110 351	68.0
19	EDF	France	Utilities	81	284	158 467	34.0
20	Nestlé	Switzerland	Food, beverages and tobacco	80	104	333 000	97.1
21	Siemens	Germany	Electrical & electronic	80	111	362 000	77.8
22	Deutsche Telekom	Germany	Telecommunications	64	131	228 596	61.9
23	ArcelorMittal	Luxembourg	Metal and metal products	64	90	232 000	89.0
24	Mitsubishi	Japan	Wholesale trade	61	119	65 975	43.0
25	Johnson & Johnson	USA	Pharmaceuticals	57	106	128 100	62.3

Notes: Data refer to the world's top 100 non-financial TNCs, ranked by foreign assets, 2013; * TNI (transnationality index) = average of three ratios: foreign/total assets, foreign/total employment and foreign/total sales.

Source: UNCTAD, 2014, *World Investment Report 2014*, Geneva: United Nations.

within the EU. Yet exports to the rest of the world still account for €1.7 trillion, second only to China. The country with the largest investments by its MNEs abroad is the USA, with €5.2 trillion of assets overseas, followed by the UK, Germany and France.[33] However, look further in the table and you will note that some smaller countries also are major homes to MNEs, notably the Netherlands and Switzerland.

Do study the numbers in Table 1.2 in more detail, or better even download and analyze the latest data from databases on the internet or held in your university library. You will note that these numbers are highly volatile because growth trends and exchange rates fluctuate. Exchange rate realignments affect the relative position of countries, for instance, the Swiss franc appreciated by 35% relative to the euro from 2005 to 2015, 15% of which was over just one week in January 2015 (See Chapter 7).

A frequent observation in the globalization debate is the enormous size of MNEs. The size of these leading MNEs is indeed striking: the largest MNE – oil and gas major *Shell* – generated more turnover in 2013 (Table 1.3) than the GDPs of Venezuela and Austria (€352 and €333 billion respectively), ranked 27th and 28th. Of course, you can't quite compare sales revenues and GDP figures, but this comparison indicates the economic power that some of these MNEs may attain, especially when operating in smaller countries. The largest private employer of the world is US retailer *Wal-Mart*, with 2.2 million employees; that's more people than the populations of Slovenia or Latvia, or the inhabitants of Paris. Second comes *Hon Hai* of Taiwan (better known under its trade name *Foxconn*), which employs 1.3 million people, which is more than those living in Estonia, or in the cities of Milan or Munich.

Many of these big companies do most of their business overseas, as indicated by the transnationality index (TNI), which measures the share of activities outside the home country. Most of the largest firms do more than half of their business abroad, especially those originating from a small country. An unusual case is *Arcelor Mittal* (TNI = 89.0%), which is registered in Luxembourg, though it is controlled by the Indian Mittal family and has operations spread across Europe and Asia. Why activities in different countries are organized within a single firm – a MNE – is the focal question of Chapter 6.

Total annual sales of the largest 500 firms listed by *Fortune* magazine in 2013 exceeded €24 trillion. Table 1.4 documents the change in the makeup of the 500 largest firms. In general, over 80% of the 500 largest firms used to come from the Triad (North America, Europe and Japan). Since 1990, the USA has contributed about one-third of these firms, the EU has maintained a reasonably steady increase, and Japan has experienced a dramatic variation corresponding to its economic boom and bust, with several years of delay.

Among MNEs from emerging economies, those from South Korea and Brazil have largely maintained a continuing presence in the *Fortune* Global 500. However, MNEs from China have come on strong – from zero in 1990 to 100 in 2014. Beijing is now headquarters of 52 Fortune Global 500 firms, followed by Tokyo (41) and New York (20). The rise of emerging economy MNEs will be a theme running throughout this book (e.g. Integrative cases *Xiaomi* and *SG Group*).

A group of particularly powerful players in the global economy are banks and other financial intermediaries. They do not appear in rankings by sales turnover; their influence is usually proxied by the asset they have under their management. In 2013, for the first time, a Chinese bank, *ICBC*, was the largest bank worldwide, and in 2014 *ICBC* again came first with total assets of €2.3 billion. It was followed by *HSBC* (UK) with €2.0 billion, and *China Construction Bank* (China) and *BNP Paribas* (France) both with €1.9 billion. Other major European banks are ranked 9 to 11: *Credit Agricole* (France), *Barclays* (UK) and *Deutsche Bank* (Germany) all with about €1.7 billion of assets.[34] These rankings however change frequently with economic cycles and currency swings.

Table 1.4 Changes in the Fortune Global 500, 1990–2014

Country	1990	1995	2000	2005	2010	2014
USA	164	153	185	170	133	128
EU	129	148	136	165	149	121
Japan	111	141	95	70	68	57
Canada	12	6	13	14	11	10
Korea (South)	11	12	8	12	10	17
Switzerland	11	16	10	12	15	13
Australia	9	4	7	8	8	8
China	0	2	10	20	61	100
Brazil	3	4	3	4	7	7
Russia	0	0	2	3	7	8
India	0	1	1	5	8	8
Others	50	13	30	17	23	23
Total	500	500	500	500	500	500

Sources: Based on data from various issues of *Fortune Global 500*. Finland and Sweden are included as 'others' prior to 1996 and as European Union after 1996.

IMPLICATIONS FOR PRACTICE

LEARNING OBJECTIVE

6 Draw implications for action by integrating global and local knowledge

The field of IB is full of debates. First, policy debates concern how societies should influence the path of globalization (see Chapters 8 and 9). Second, debates concern the responsibility of business toward the consequences of globalization, often discussed under the topic of corporate social responsibility (Chapter 10). Third, businesses debate how they can develop their strategies to take advantage of the opportunities of globalization (Chapters 11 to 14). Fourth, managers debate how to manage people and organizations exposed to the trends of globalization (Chapters 15 to 17). Be prepared for a lot of debates as you go through the course of IB!

It is important to approach these debates with an open mindset to recognize international connections and analyze their interactions. We believe that two types of people are bound to fail in IB. The first are those who believe that the 'best practices' their organization has developed in one place should consistently be rolled out worldwide. They tend to have an ethnocentric perspective, which is when one views the world through the lens of one's own culture and believes in the superiority of that culture. Their confidence in their 'superior practices' may be grounded in success in their own country, prior to growing their business internationally. The others are those who reject advice from outside because of the advisors' presumed lack of local knowledge. Let's call them 'exceptionalists'. Their not-invented-here syndrome,[35] which is a tendency to distrust new ideas coming from outside of one's own organization or community, is particularly prevalent in countries with distinct social histories and limited international exchange; China and Russia at the onset of economic transition were prime examples.

Neither of the two is likely to enjoy long-term success in IB. Those approaching IB with an ethnocentric perspective will hit a wall when their 'best practices'

ethnocentric perspective
A view of the world through the lens of one's own culture.

not-invented-here syndrome
The tendency to distrust new ideas coming from outside of one's own organization or community.

Table 1.5 Implications for practice

- Think global!

- Think local!

- Integrate your global and local knowledge!

- Communicate effectively with those who are not in the global jet set!

fail to deliver; complaints about the incompetence of local employees or customers are symptoms of that phenomenon. The exceptionalist is likely to fail even in their home country because international competition is a reality virtually everywhere (at least in Europe). Complaining about foreigners enjoying unfair advantages makes for good media coverage, but not for a viable business. There is a lot you can learn from other countries, no matter how good you already are.

Successful managers operate within the spectrum between universalists and exceptionalists. They know that some practices are effective in a wide range of different countries, but that they may need fine-tuning to accommodate local idiosyncrasies. They also know that each country has unique institutions, but adapted practices informed by experiences elsewhere may outperform traditional local practices. In other words, successful managers not only *know* about global best practices and local idiosyncrasies, they are able to *integrate* such knowledge to develop practices that outperform competitors in a given context.[36]

Hence, as an international manager, you have to iterate across levels: think global, think local, and integrate those two lines of thinking! (Table 1.5). Consider two examples of global linkages relevant to virtually every business. First, supply chains crossing countries and continents face risks of disruptions through events in a one part of the world that impact business at the other end of the world. Such disruptions may be caused by natural disasters such as epidemics (like Ebola or avian flu), earthquakes, typhoons, tsunamis or volcanic eruptions. For example, when volcano Eyjafjallajökull erupted unexpectedly in 2010, aircraft across Europe were grounded and many firms had to stop production because components could not be delivered on time. Other disruptions are man-made: wars and acts of terrorism in particular.[37] Businesses operating around the globe thus have to continuously ask questions about their business environment, and be able to respond flexibly.

Second, the financial crisis of 2008/9 has highlighted global interdependencies. The credit crunch spread rapidly from the USA through the financial sector to banks in numerous countries, and caused an unprecedented credit squeeze as inter-bank lending came to a virtual hold. This in turn hit the real economy as businesses faced liquidity squeezes and consumers cut back their expenses.[38] The crisis caused subtle shifts in politics as protectionism was politically advocated by more and more pressure groups. Economic events in one part of the world thus can have political and social consequences in other parts of the world.

At the same time, you have to think local. Every country has its own peculiarities. In this book we are emphasizing the institutional view as a conceptual lens to identify and analyze such idiosyncrasies. Consider two example of local knowledge. First, Europe shares common rules that are created by the EU, and which are implemented by national governments (Chapter 8). Yet not all is harmonized in the EU. For example, the rules by which we elect political leaders are very different. Similarly, what is or is not acceptable business practice still varies across countries.

As another example, consider China. In only four years, *Xiaomi* became the largest mobile phone manufacturer in China, and number four in the world (see Integrative case). *Xiaomi* certainly learned from the best in the world, yet fundamentally its business model was grounded in deep understanding of Chinese consumers, the evolution of online business models in China, and access to the best manufacturing sites in China. Deeply grounded in China, they need to develop a deep understanding of, say, India in their drive to expand overseas.

In the complex interaction of global and local forces many business leaders are well at ease with globalization and its opportunities. As cosmopolitans, they embrace the cultural diversity and the personal and professional opportunities that globalization brings. Most elites in both developed and emerging economies – executives, policy makers and scholars – tend to adopt cosmopolitan views.[39] In fact, many business school students already share the beliefs and biases in favour of globalization.[40]

Yet the fact that these elites share certain perspectives on globalization does *not* mean that other members of the society share the same views. Those other people are important to you, even if you one day find yourself as a leader of a major MNE and join the global jet set. Those people work for your company, they buy your products – and they vote in the elections for the governments that eventually set the rules under which your business operates. It is not enough to mix with the global jet set, you also need to empathize with people who spend most of their lives in their home town, and rarely engage with people outside their country. They may be very concerned about how globalization affects them. They want to be taken seriously too. Thus the message we wish you to remember in future when you have made it is: show respect and listen to people in local communities.

cosmopolitans
The people embracing cultural diversity and the opportunities of globalization.

CHAPTER SUMMARY

1 Explain the concepts of international business (IB)

- IB is defined as (1) a business (firm) that engages in international (cross-border) economic activities, and (2) the action of doing business abroad.

- This book places special emphasis on the challenges faced by European businesses, and the challenges of emerging economies.

2 Articulate what you hope to learn by reading this book and taking this course

- To better compete in the corporate world that will require global expertise.

- To enhance your understanding of what is going on in the global economy.

3 Identify one fundamental question and two core perspectives that provide a framework for studying this field

- Our most fundamental question is: What determines the success and failure of firms around the globe?

- The two core perspectives are (1) the institution-based view, and (2) the resource-based view.

4 Participate in the debate on globalization with a reasonably balanced and realistic view

- Globalization has created unprecedented contacts between nations and cultures, with both positive and negative consequences for individuals.

- Globalization has been evolving in waves, with a major peak in the late 19th/early 20th century.

- The recent wave of globalization has accelerated with the rising powers of emerging economies, yet it remains highly volatile.

5 Summarize some basic trends in the global economy

- MNEs, especially large ones from developed economies, are sizeable economic entities.

6 Draw implications for action by integrating global and local knowledge

- International managers need to think global, think local, and integrate the two perspectives.

- People with cosmopolitan worldviews and experience need to remember that not everyone shares their broad perspectives and experiences.

KEY TERMS

Base of the pyramid
BRIC
Cosmopolitans
Emerging economies (emerging markets)
Ethnocentric perspective
Expatriate assignments

Foreign direct investment (FDI)
Globalization
Gross domestic product (GDP)
Gross national income (GNI)
Gross national product (GNP)
International business (IB)
Liability of outsidership

Liberalization
Multinational enterprise (MNE)
Not-invented-here syndrome
Purchasing power parity (PPP)
Risk management
Triad
Waves of globalization

CRITICAL DISCUSSION QUESTIONS

1 A classmate says: 'Global business is relevant for top executives such as CEOs in large companies. I am just a lowly student who will struggle to gain an entry-level job, probably in a small domestic company. Why should I care about it?' How do you convince her that she should care about it?

2 A classmate says: 'The world economy has changed so much; all those textbooks and historical cases don't really help me in the 21st century.' How do you convince him that he should care about lessons from the past?

3 What are some of the darker sides (in other words, costs) associated with globalization? How can business leaders make sure that the benefits of their various actions outweigh their drawbacks (such as job losses in developed economies)?

4 Some argue that aggressively investing in emerging economies is not only economically beneficial but also highly ethical because it may potentially lift many people out of poverty (see Closing Case). However, others caution that in the absence of reasonable hopes of decent profits, rushing to emerging economies is reckless. How would you participate in this debate?

RECOMMENDED READINGS

J.N. Bhagwati, 2004, *In Defence of Globalization,* Oxford: Oxford University Press – an esteemed economist outlines the benefits of globalization, and how they can be made even better.

P. Dicken, 2015, *Global Shift: Mapping the Changing Contours of the World Economy,* 7th ed., London: Sage – a thorough analysis of the economic trends of globalization in a variety of industries.

K.E. Meyer, 2004, Perspectives on multinational enterprises in emerging economies, *JIBS* 34: 259–277 – outlines an agenda for IB scholars looking beyond the firm to its wider impact on society.

K.E. Meyer, 2011, What is and to what purpose do we study international business? *AIB Insights* 13(1): 10–13 – an essay reflecting why IB is an important field for study and research.

M.W. Peng, 2004, Identifying the big question in international business research, *JIBS,* 35: 99–108 – outlines an agenda for IB scholars focused on the performance of firms in the global economy.

T. Piketty, 2014, *Capital in the Twenty-First Century,* Cambridge, MA: Harvard University Press – a much-discussed book offering a lot of data to support the argument that globalization causes increased inequality within countries.

 # CLOSING CASE

Coca-Cola *Dives into Africa*

Founded in 1892, *Coca-Cola* first entered Africa in 1929. While many businesses have long viewed Africa as an economic 'backwater', it has recently emerged as a major growth market. Of the $27 billion that *Coca-Cola* will invest in emerging economies between 2010 and 2020, $12 billion is to be used to upgrade plants and distribution facilities in Africa. Why does *Coca-Cola* show such a strong interest in a 'deep dive' in Africa? Both the push and pull effects are at work.

The push comes from the quest for new sources of growth for this mature firm, which has promised investors of 7%–9% earnings growth. In July 1998, its stock reached a high-water mark at $87 but it dropped to $38 in May 2003. From 2009 to 2014, the share price rallied again, rising from $43 to a new peak of $89.66 in November 2014 (adjusted for a 2 : 1 share split in 2012). Can Coca-Cola reach higher?

Its home markets are unlikely to help. Between 2006 and 2011, US sales declined for five consecutive years. Further, health advocates accused Coca-Cola of contributing to an epidemic of obesity in the US and proposed to tax soft drinks to pay for health care. While Coca-Cola defeated the tax initiative, it is fair to say the room for growth at home is limited. In Europe and Japan, sales are similarly flat. Elsewhere, in China, strong local rivals have made it tough for Coca-Cola to break out. Its acquisition of a leading local fruit juice firm was blocked by the government. In India, Pepsi is so popular that 'Pepsi' has become the Hindi shorthand for all bottled soft drinks (including Coke!). In Latin America, sales are encouraging but growth may be limited. Mexicans on average are already guzzling 665 servings of Coca-Cola products every year, the highest in the world.

In contrast, Coca-Cola is pulled by Africa, where it leads with 29% market share versus Pepsi's 15%. With 65 000 employees and 160 plants, Coca-Cola is Africa's largest private sector employer. Yet annual per capita consumption of Coca-Cola products is only 39 servings in Kenya. For the continent as a whole, disposable income is growing. In 2010, 60 million Africans earned at least $5000 per person, and the number is likely to reach 100 million by 2014. While Africa has some of the poorest countries in the world, 12 African countries (with a combined population of 100 million) have a GDP per capita that is greater than China's. Coca-Cola is hoping to capitalize on Africa's improved political stability and physical infrastructure.

Coca-Cola is present in all African countries. The challenge, according to chairman and CEO Muhtar Kent, is to deep dive into 'every town, every village, every township'. This will not be easy. War, poverty and poor infrastructure inhibit distribution and marketing in hard-to-access regions. Undaunted, Coca-Cola is in a street-by-street campaign to increase awareness and consumption of its products. The crowds and the poor roads dictate that some of the deliveries have to be done manually on pushcarts or trolleys. Throughout the continent, Coca-Cola has set up 3000 Manual Distribution Centres. Learning from its experience in Latin America, especially Mexico, Coca-Cola has aggressively courted small corner stores. Coca-Cola and its bottlers offer small corner store owners delivery, credit and direct coaching – ranging from the tip not to ice down the Cokes until the midday rush to save electricity, to helping with how to buy a house after vendors make enough money.

However, Africa is not Coca-Cola's marketing paradise free from criticisms. It has to defend itself from critics that accuse it of depleting fresh water, encouraging expensive and environmentally harmful refrigeration,

and hurting local competitors who hawk beverages. In response, *Coca-Cola* often points out the benefits it has brought. In addition to the 65 000 jobs it has directly created, one million local jobs are indirectly created by its vast system of distribution, which moves beverages from bottling plants deep into the slums and the bush, a few crates at a time.

CASE DISCUSSION QUESTIONS

1 Do you believe African countries are attractive markets for Western consumer goods such as *Coca-Cola*?

2 What are the challenges that *Coca-Cola* is likely to face to grow its business in Africa?

3 What ethical questions is *Coca-Cola* likely to face when pushing into Africa?

Sources: (1) M. Blanding, 2010, *The Coke Machine*, New York: Avery; (2) *Bloomberg Businessweek*, 2010, Coke's last round, November 1: 54–61; (3) *Bloomberg Businessweek*, 2010, For India's consumers, Pepsi is the real thing, September 20: 26–27; (4) *Bloomberg Businessweek*, 2011, Can Coke surpass its record high of $88 a share? June 6: 49–50; (5) D. Zoogah, M.W. Peng, & H. Woldu, 2015, Institutions, resources, and organizational effectiveness in Africa, *Academy of Management Perspectives* (in press).

NOTES

'For journal abbreviations please see page xx–xxi.'

1 This definition of the MNE can be found in R. Caves, 1996, *Multinational Enterprise and Economic Analysis*, 2nd ed. (p. 1), Cambridge: Cambridge University Press; J. Dunning & S. Lundan, 2008, *Multinational Enterprises and the Global Economy*, Cheltenham: Elgar. Other terms are multinational corporation (MNC) and transnational corporation (TNC), which are often used interchangeably with MNE. To avoid confusion, in this book, we use MNE.

2 O. Shenkar, 2004, One more time: International business in a global economy (p. 165), *JIBS*, 35: 161–171. See also J.-F. Hennart, 2009, Down with MNE-centric models! *JIBS*, 40: 1454.

3 A. Rugman & A. Verbeke, 2004, A perspective on the regional and global strategies of multinational enterprise, *JIBS* 35: 3–18; A. Rugman, 2005, *The Regional Multinational*, Cambridge: Cambridge University Press.

4 W. Newburry, 2001, MNC interdependence and local embeddedness influences on perceptions of career benefits from global integration, *JIBS*, 32: 497–508.

5 M.W. Peng, 2004, Identifying the big question in international business research, *JIBS*, 35: 99–108.

6 C. Oliver, 1997, Sustainable competitive advantage: combining institutional and resource based views, *SMJ*, 18: 697–713; Peng, M.W. 2003. Institutional transitions and strategic choices, *AMJ*, 28: 275–296. W. Henisz & B. Zelner, 2005, Legitimacy, interest group pressures, and change in emergent institutions, *AMR*, 30: 361–382; M. Gelbuda, K.E. Meyer & A. Delios, 2007, International business and institutional development in Central and Eastern Europe, *JIM*, 14: 1–11; M.W. Peng, D. Wang & Y. Jiang, 2008, An institution-based view of international business strategy, *JIBS*, 39: 920–936.

7 J. Barney, 1991, Firm resources and sustained competitive advantage, *JM*, 17: 99–120, R. Grant, 1996, Towards a knowledge-based theory of the firm, *SMJ*, 17 (winter special issue): 109–122; M.W. Peng, 2001, The resource-based view and international business, *JM*, 27: 803–829; M. Peteraf, 2003, The foundations of competitive advantage: a resource-based view, *SMJ*, 14: 179–191.

8 J. Johansen & J. Vahlne, 2009, the Uppsala internationalization process model revised: From liability of foreignness to liability of outsidership, *JIBS*, 40, 1411–1432. Originally this concept was known as liability of foreignness, see J. Johanson & J. Vahlne, 1977, The internationalization process of the firm, *JIBS*, 8: 23–32; S. Zaheer, 1995, Overcoming the liability of foreignness, *AMJ*, 38: 341–363; J. Mezias, 2002, Identifying liabilities of foreignness and strategies to minimize their effects, *SMJ*, 23: 229–244.

9 B. Kogut & H. Singh, 1988, The effect of national culture on the choice of entry mode, *JIBS*, 19: 411–432; D. Xu & O. Shenkar, 2002, Institutional distance and the multinational enterprise, *AMR*, 27: 608–618; S. Estrin, D. Baghdasaryan & K.E. Meyer, 2009, Institutional and human resource resource distance on international entry strategies, *JMS*, 46: 1171–1196.

10 P. Li & K.E. Meyer, 2009, Contextualizing experience effects in international business, *JWB*, 44: 370–382; J. Clarke, R. Tamaschke & P. Liesch, 2012, International experience in international business research, *IJMR*, 15(3): 265–279.

11 T. Hutzschenreuther & J. Voll, 2008, Performance effects of added cultural distance in the path of international expansion, *JIBS*, 39: 53–70.

12 A. Giddens, 1999, *Runaway World*, London: Profile;
   J. Stiglitz, 2013, *The Price of Inequality*, New York:
   Penguin; D. Rodrik, 2011, *The Globalization Paradox*,
   Oxford: Oxford University Press.

13 R. Vernon, 1971, *Sovereignty at Bay: The Multinational
   spread of US Enterprises*, New York: Basic Books.
   J.M. Stopford & S. Strange, *Rival State, Rival Firms*,
   Cambridge: Cambridge University Press; S. Kobrin,
   2001, Sovereignty @ Bay: Globalization, multinational
   enterprise and the international political system, in:
   A.M. Rugman & T. Brewer, eds, *Oxford Handbook of
   International* Business, Oxford: Oxford University Press.

14 *BBC News*, 2009, EU seal ban challenged by Canada,
   July 27; *BBC News*, 2011, Canada launches challenge
   against EU seal product ban, February 14.

15 T. Piketty, 2014, *Capital in the Twenty-First Century*,
   Cambridge, MA: Harvard University Press; R. Solow,
   2014, Thomas Piketty is right, *New Republic*, April 22;
   C. Jones, 2015, Pareto and Piketty, *JEL*, 29: 29–46;
   T. Piketty, 2015, putting distribution back at the center
   of economics, *JEL*, 29: 67–88.

16 D. Snower, A. Brown & C. Merkl, 2009, Globalization
   and the welfare state, *JEL*, 47: 136–158.

17 R. Rajan & L. Zingales, 2003, *Saving Capitalism from
   the Capitalists*, New York: Crown; J. Bhagwati, 2004, *In
   Defence of Globalization*, New York: Oxford University
   Press; D. Acemoglu & J. Robinson, 2015, The rise and
   decline of general laws of capitalism, *JEL*, 29: 3–28.

18 T. Levitt 1983. The globalization of markets, *HBR*,
   May/June; K. Ohmae 1989. Managing in a borderless
   world, *Harvard Business Review*, May/June 1989; F.
   Fukuyama, 1992, *The End of History and the Last Man,*
   New York: The Free Press.

19 J. Johansson, 2004, *In Your Face: How American
   Marketing Excess Fuels Anti-Americanism*. Upper
   Saddle River, NJ: Prentice Hall.

20 M. Guillén, 2001, Is globalization civilizing, destructive
   or feeble? A critique of five key debates in the social
   science literature, *ARS*, 27: 235–60. Similar definitions
   are used by J. Stiglitz, 2002, *Globalization and Its
   Discontents* (p. 9), New York: Norton; R. Narula, 2003,
   Globalization and Technology, London: Polity Press.

21 K. Moore & D. Lewis, 2000, Multinational enterprise in
   ancient Phoenicia, *BH*, 42(2): 17–42; *The Economist*,
   2013, When did globalization start? September 23.

22 Data in this paragraph and the next are based on G.
   Jones, 2005, *Multinationals and Global Capitalism: from
   the Nineteenth Century to the Twenty-first Century*,
   Oxford: Oxford University Press; also see A. Kenwood
   & A. Longhead, 1999, *The Growth of the International
   Economy*, Abington: Routledge; D. Hummels, 2007,
   Transportation cost and international trade in the
   second era of globalization, *JEP*, 21 (3): 131–154;
   Fellman, Iversen, Sjögren & Thue, 2008, *as above*.

23 G. Jones, 2004, *Multinationals and Global Capitalism
   from the Nineteenth Century to the Twenty-first Century*,
   Oxford: Oxford University Press.

24 G. Jones, 2005, *as above*.

25 United Nations, 2000, *World Investment Report 2000*,
   New York and Geneva: United Nations.

26 The term *emerging markets* was probably coined in the
   1980s by Antonie van Agtmael, a Dutch officer at the
   World Bank's International Finance Corporation (IFC).
   See A. van Agtmael, 2007, *The Emerging Markets
   Century*, New York: Simon and Schuster.

27 *The Economist*, 2009, BRICs, emerging markets and
   the world economy: Not just straw men, June 20.

28 T. London & S. Hart, 2004, Reinventing strategies for
   emerging markets, *JIBS*, 35: 350–370; S. Hart, 2005,
   Capitalism at the Crossroads, Philadelphia: Wharton
   School Publishing; C.K. Prahalad, 2005, *The Fortune
   at the Bottom of the Pyramid*, Philadelphia: Wharton
   School Publishing; T. London, 2009, Making better
   investments at the base of the pyramid, *HBR,* May:
   106–113.

29 J. Stiglitz, 2010, *Freefall*, New York: Allen Lane; S.
   Johnson & J. Kwak, 2010, *13 Bankers*, New York:
   Pantheon; A. Mian & A. Sufi, 2014, *House of Debt*,
   Chicago: Chicago University Press.

30 S. Leong et al., 2008, Understanding consumer
   animosity in an international crisis, *JIBS*, 39: 996–1009.

31 N. Taleb, D. Goldstein & M. Spitznagel, 2009, The six
   mistakes executives make in risk management, *HBR*,
   October: 78–81.

32 Narula, 2003, *as above*.

33 On the limitations of using FDI assets overseas as
   measure of the scope of MNEs see S. Beugelsdijk,
   J.F. Hennart, A. Slangen & R. Smets, 2011, Measures
   of multinational activity, *JIBS*, 41: 826–843.

34 *The Banker*, 2014, Top 1000 World Banks, *The Banker*
   (magazine).

35 R. Katz & T. Allen, 1982, Investigating the Not Invented
   Here (NIH) syndrome, *R&D Management*, 12: 7–20.

36 K.E. Meyer, 2011, What is and to what purpose do we
   study international business? *AIB Insights* 13(1): 10–13.

37 G. Suder, ed., 2004, *Terrorism and the International
   Business Environment*, Cheltenham, Elgar; R. Spich &
   R. Grosse, 2005, How does homeland security affect
   U.S. firms' international competitiveness? *JIM*, 11:
   457–478; M. Czinkota, G. Knight, P. Liesch & J. Steen,
   2010, Terrorism and international business, *JIBS*, 41,
   826-843.

38 P. Krugman, 2008, *The Return of Depression
   Economics and the Crisis of 2008*, London: Penguin;
   A. Krishnamurthy, 2010, How debt markets have
   malfunctioned in the crisis, *JEP*, 24(1): 3–28; F. Mishkin,
   2011, Over the cliff: From the subprime to the global
   financial crisis, *JEP*, 25(1): 49–70.

39 A. Bird & M. Stevens, 2003, Toward an emergent global
   culture and the effects of globalization on obsolescing
   national cultures, *JIM*, 9: 395–407; L. Brimm, 2010,
   Global Cosmopolitans, Basingstoke: Palgrave
   Macmillan.

40 M.W. Peng & H. Shin, How do future leaders view
   globalization, *TIBR*, 50: 175–182.

CHAPTER TWO

FORMAL INSTITUTIONS: POLITICAL, ECONOMIC AND LEGAL SYSTEMS

LEARNING OBJECTIVES

After studying this chapter, you should be able to

1 Explain the concept of institutions and their key role in reducing uncertainty

2 Explain the basic differences between political systems

3 Explain the systemic differences between economic systems

4 Explain the basic differences between legal systems

5 Participate in three leading debates on institutions in international business

6 Draw implications for action

OPENING CASE

Managing business risks in Turkey

Throughout the 20th century, Turkey has been iterating between military and democratically-elected governments that varyingly pursued protection of national industries and economic liberalization. Since the 1980s, the trend has been towards more stable democracy, liberalization of foreign trade and formalization of a legal framework facilitating the operations of local and foreign businesses. A major milestone was an agreement in 1988 with the European Union (EU) to reduce and then phase out import tariffs, which resulted in a customs union in 1996. With protective barriers removed and industry exposed to dramatically more intensive competition, Turkish exports and imports took off. Some Turkish businesses, such as Beko (see Integrative Case), were able to use the customs-free access to the EU to develop major market positions in EU countries.

However, for the next decade, the Turkish economy remained very volatile, with high inflation (peaking at 106% in 1994) and periodic currency devaluation. In 2001, Turkey needed another IMF-led support program in which the government committed to economic liberalization and tight fiscal policy.

In 2003, the Justice and Development Party won parliamentary elections and Recep Tayyip Erdoğan became prime minister. Under his leadership, Turkey advanced economic reforms, not only stabilizing and liberalizing the economy, but also aligning the regulatory framework with the EU. Moreover, Turkey pursued solid macroeconomic policies, including monetary policy led by an independent Central Bank focused on controlling inflation and government budget deficits that were stable. Banks appeared properly supervised, and had strong balance sheets.

Thus West European companies considered Turkey an attractive location for business. Since the labour force was younger than in Western Europe, and wages were substantially lower too, especially labour-intensive manufacturing plants were built. For example, *Fiat* and *Renault* invested with Turkish joint venture partners in new car assembly plants, while *Ford* expanded its existing operations. The qualifications of the workforce (outside the elite) were still substantially lower and on many aspects of the business environment, Turkey was less sophisticated than, for example, Spain and Italy. However, compared to other emerging economies, Turkey showed promising development on several dimensions (Table 2.1).

Despite the praise for a predictable environment for business, and annual economic growth of almost 4% in real terms, many potential investors were concerned about the country. The policies of the AKP government gradually shifted towards value-conservative policies, such as promoting traditional family values and large-size families, restricting entertainment businesses and tightening regulation of alcohol consumption. Added to this were restrictions on the access to the internet, including temporary bans *Twitter* and *YouTube*, and a general perception that Erdoğan was acting increasingly like an autocratic leader.

Table 2.1 Institutional environment: Turkey and benchmark countries

	Turkey	Spain	Italy	Hungary	Romania	Russia	India	China
		EU	EU	EU	EU	EE	EE	EE
Quality of education and research institutions[1]	33.3	48.3	42.1	37.9	29.1	44.5	22.7	43.3
Quality of technology infrastructure[1]	35.6	56.7	49.8	45.6	41.7	41.1	32.1	45.0
Openness and effectiveness of markets[1]	49.1	64.7	51.0	42.1	42.9	42.5	51.2	50.5
Cost and time of procedure to start a business[2]	83.6	88.1	91.2	90.0	91.9	92.2	68.4	77.4
Cost and time of procedure to enforce a contract[2]	61.0	62.7	45.6	73.4	65.0	75.9	25.8	68.2
Strength of the legal protection of minority shareholders[2]	55.0	64.2	66.7	47.5	61.7	50.8	72.5	45.0
Transparency (absence of corruption)[3]	50	56	43	54	43	28	36	40
Constraints on political power[4]	37.3	83.6	75.7	73.3	73.5	73.1	70.2	n/a

Note: All indices have been scaled such that a high index reflects a more market-oriented economy. EU = member of the European Union, EE = emerging economy.

Sources: (1) Global Innovation Index, INSEAD, (www.globalinnovationindex.org) Scale 1 to 100 (100 = innovation friendly); (2) Doing Business Index, World Bank (www.doingbusinessin.org); (3) Corruption Perception Index 2013, Transparency International, http://www.transparency.org; (4) PolCon Index 2012, (scale 0 to 100; original multiplied by 100) Henisz, W. 2000, The Institutional Environment for Economic Growth, *Economics and Politics* 12(1): 1–31, https://mgmt.wharton.upenn.edu/profile/1327.

Moreover, power battles within the country took place throughout Erdoğan's time in government. In the early years, the government tried to neutralize old elites and the military, notably by putting dozens of generals on trial for an alleged coup (some observers claim the evidence presented in court was fabricated). Journalists were not safe either: in 2013 Turkey reportedly put more journalists in jail than China (a *much* larger country). In December 2013, prosecutors and police went public with investigations into corruption of high-ranking government officials, to which the government reacted by dismissing numerous officials, claiming this to be a plot by a powerful network known as Gülenists, early supporters of Erdoğan who later turned against him.

The unhappiness of the secular urban youth with such policies led to extensive demonstrations around Istanbul's central Gezi Park in the spring of 2013. Protesters were initially objecting to a commercial development (a shopping mall) in a popular park. However, following incidents of police suppression, their aims broadened to the abuse of power by Erdoğan's government, and the protections of the right to peaceful protest without harassment by the police. The protests gained attention in the international media, which in turn concerned potential investors in Turkey. Similarly, business leaders within Turkey expressed concerns. For example Muharrem Yılmaz, the head of Turkey's industry lobby Tusiad, described Turkey as:

"a country where the rule of law is ignored, where the independence of regulatory institutions is tainted, where companies are pressured through tax penalties and other punishments, where rules on tenders are changed regularly, [it] is not a fit country for foreign capital."

The prime minister returned in kind, accusing Yılmaz of treason.

Changes in the law also created practical challenges – or even economic losses – for some foreign investors. For example, in 2011, *Diageo*, the world's largest distiller, acquired *Mey Icki*, a maker of raki liquor, traditionally Turkey's national drink. In addition to growing the raki business, *Diageo* intended to grow the sales of its global brands in Turkey using *Mey Icki*'s distribution channels. However, in 2013 the Turkish government introduced a new law that forbade alcohol advertising and severely restricted when and where alcoholic beverages can be sold. *Mey Icki*'s business prospects nosedived, and consequently *Diageo*'s share price fell by as much as 8%.

These changes to the political and legal system of Turkey also dampened the prospect of the country joining the EU. The formal start of EU membership negotiations in 2005 initially enhanced business confidence. On the one hand, some politicians in Western Europe interpreted political events and changes in legal practice as Turkey moving away from the shared norms and values of the EU. On the other hand, cultural and religious differences have long created major barriers to mutual understanding.

Despite these concerns, the governing AKP party enjoyed continuous strong support in the population, especially in the economically less prosperous parts of the country. The AKP again won local elections in 2013, and Erdoğan won the presidential elections of 2014. In part, this reflected the weakness of opposition parties, but the policy agenda that many outside observers (and potential investors) found objectionable, is supported by large parts of Turkish society. Thus, while many businesses may worry about the rules of the game in Turkey, the government continues to receive democratic legitimacy.

Sources: (1) F. Nowak-Lehman, D. Herzer, I. Martinez-Zarzoso & S. Vollmer, 2007, The impact of a customs union between the Turkey and the EU on Turkey's exports to the EU, *JCMS* 45: 719–743. (2) E. Largo & K. Jørgensen, eds, 2007, *Turkey and the European Union*, Basingstoke: Palgrave-Macmillan; (3) B. Yinanç, 2013, Turkey a 'success story for the troubled IMF, *Hürriyet Daily News*, May 20; (4) K. Stock, 2013, Diageo's $2.1 billion Turkish hangover, *BloombergBusinessweek*, June 24; (5) *Financial Times*, 2013, Supplement 'Investing in Turkey', November 28; (6) D. Acemoglu, 2014, The failed autocrat, *Foreign Affairs*, May 24; (7) D. Rodrik, 2014, The Plot Against the Generals, mimeo (32 pages), June; (8) J. Parkinson & E. Peker, 2014, Turkey election: Erdoğan wins landmark victory, *Wall Street Journal*, August 1; (9) A. Evans-Pritchard, 2014, Turkey spoils emerging market story as politics go haywire, *The Telegraph*, February 19.

Although Turkey offers attractive business opportunities, developments in the country's political, economic and legal sphere create numerous uncertainties. The rules for business are different from elsewhere in Europe, and recent changes are not necessarily making the rules more similar to the rest of Europe. How can businesses play by the rules when the rules of the game are uncertain and keep changing? This chapter explores the variations in the rules of the game that firms face when entering a foreign country.

As the Opening Case illustrates, different countries have different institutions, popularly known as 'the rules of the game'. More formally, economic historian Douglass North, a Nobel laureate, defines institutions as 'the humanly devised constraints that structure human interaction'.[1] Firms doing business abroad encounter such rules in their home country, in host countries, and in international and regional organizations such as the World Trade Organization (WTO) and the European Union (EU). The institutional framework governing a particular context is made up of formal and informal institutions governing individual and firm behaviour.

The success and failure of firms are to a large extent determined by firms' ability to understand and take advantage of the different rules of the game. This calls for firms to constantly monitor, decode and adapt to the changing rules of the game. As a result, such an institution-based view has emerged as a leading perspective on international business.[2] This chapter first introduces the institution-based view, and then reviews *formal* institutions in political, economic and legal systems. *Informal* institutions, such as culture, ethics and norms, are discussed in Chapter 3.

AN INSTITUTION-BASED VIEW OF INTERNATIONAL BUSINESS

The idea that context influences economic behaviour has a long tradition. The historical school in Germany and Austria, developed since the mid-18th century, taught that economic processes in different countries could only be explained as a consequence of their national histories.[3] In the early 20th century, sociologist Max Weber studied how contextual phenomena such as religion influence economic growth. More recently, economists of the 'ordo-liberal' tradition such as Walter Eucken have been promoting the idea that the role of the state is to set the rules or legal framework, which would then ensure that the market economy functions without major distortion.[4]

A second intellectual source of the institutional perspective is transaction costs economics, as developed by Ronald Coase in the 1930s and Oliver Williamson in the 1970s (both winners of the Nobel Prize). Essentially, this work argues that it is costly to organize transactions using the market mechanism, and as a consequence economic actors organize themselves in less costly ways, notably by establishing firms. These costs of organizing transactions are known as transaction costs. Oliver Williamson compares them with frictions in mechanical systems: 'Do the gears mesh, are the parts lubricated, is there needless slippage or other loss of energy?' He goes on to suggest that transaction costs can be regarded as 'the economic counterpart of frictions: Do the parties to exchange operate harmoniously, or are there frequent misunderstandings and conflicts?'[5] These transaction costs, however, are to a large extent influenced by the institutions governing the market.

The institutional perspective applied in this book draws in particular on the work of Douglass North, who integrated different lines of thought and emphasized the complementary, and often interdependent, role of formal and informal institutions.

---

institutions
Formal and informal rules of the game.

institutional framework
Formal and informal institutions governing individual and firm behaviour.

institution-based view
A theoretical perspective suggesting that firm performance is, at least in part, determined by the institutional frameworks governing firms.

LEARNING OBJECTIVE

1 Explain the concept of institutions and their key role in reducing uncertainty

transaction costs
The costs of organizing economic transactions.

Table 2.2 Dimensions of institutions

Degree of formality	Examples	Supportive pillars
Formal institutions	● Laws ● Regulations ● Rules	● Regulatory (coercive)
Informal institutions	● Norms ● Cultures ● Ethics	● Normative ● Cognitive

Shown in Table 2.2, formal institutions include laws, regulations and rules that are set by the authorized bodies. On the national level, this is normally the government, although the authority to set rules may have been delegated to specific bodies within a country (say, a ministry, the competition authority, or local councils), or to supra-national bodies such as the EU (see Chapter 8). In Turkey, it was the democratically elected government that changed rules on advertising; domestic and foreign firms failing to adapt how and where they advertise alcohol will face legal prosecution (see Opening Case).

On the other hand, informal institutions are rules that are not formalized but exist in, for example, norms and values. They concern what behaviours are morally right and wrong, and what is important and what is not within a society. They create pressures on individuals that shape behaviours without being 'cast in iron'. For example, formal rules may create minimum standards on how much environmental pollution is acceptable, and how much to pay its workers. Yet norms in a society may create pressures on companies to do more than what is legally required, or else face protests or boycotts.

Institutions can also be classified according to three 'pillars' identified by W. Richard Scott, a leading sociologist (Table 2.2).[6] The first regulatory pillar reflects the coercive power of governments and largely corresponds to formal institutions. The normative pillar refers to how the norms, values, beliefs and actions of other relevant players influence the behaviour of focal individuals and firms. The cognitive pillar refers to the internalized, taken-for-granted assumptions of how the world works that (usually unconsciously) guide individual and firm behaviour. The financial crisis of 2008 revealed that banks made major mistakes in their risk management practices.[7] Probing deeper, it emerged that a combination of cognitive and normative pressures may have been at fault.[8] Risk managers widely believed AAA-rated assets to be safe, as events that eventually happened were not conceived to be possible – a cognitive limitation. Moreover, the norms of many financial organizations favoured the aggressive attitudes of the traders, who want their money-making transactions approved, rather than the cautious, risk-averse attitude of the risk department. The norms of the organization, however, often favoured the traders, a bias that eventually proved fatal for banks such as *Bear Stearns* and *Lehman Brothers*.

formal institutions
Institutions represented by laws, regulations and rules.

informal institutions
Rules that are not formalized but exist in for example norms, values and ethics.

regulatory pillar
The coercive power of governments.

normative pillar
The mechanism through which norms influence individual and firm behaviour.

cognitive pillar
The internalized, taken-for-granted values and beliefs that guide individual and firm behaviour

What do institutions do?

Although institutions do many things, their key role, in two words, is to *reduce uncertainty*.[9] Specifically, institutions influence individuals' and firms' decision-making by signalling what conduct is legitimate and acceptable and what is not.

Basically, institutions constrain the range of acceptable actions, and thereby reduce uncertainty. Why is it so important to reduce uncertainty? Political uncertainty, such as the possibility of expropriation, may render long-term planning obsolete. Economic uncertainty, such as volatile exchange rates or high inflation, makes it difficult to predict returns on investments. Behavioural uncertainty, such as fear that a partner may fail to carry out obligations set out in a contract, may result in economic losses. Hence uncertainty reduces people's willingness to make long-term commitments, or any commitments at all. This had a devastating effect during the financial crisis in 2008: after the failure of *Lehman Brothers*, banks were so worried that another major bank might go bust that they virtually stopped lending to each other, even for short-term loans. The institutions of the financial markets stopped working efficiently, and interbank lending dropped dramatically.[10]

opportunistic behaviour
Seeking self-interest with guile.

Moreover, businesses take extra pecautions when they believe that others may behave opportunistically, defined as self-interest seeking with guile. Examples include misleading, cheating and confusing other parties in a transaction. Institutional frameworks can reduce the potential for opportunistic behaviour by explicitly establishing the rules of the game, so that violations (such as failure to fulfil a contract) can be mitigated with relative ease (such as through formal arbitration and courts). Other institutional contexts may reduce potential opportunistic behaviour by creating trust between members of a group, or by creating punishments on those who cheat.

Without stable institutional frameworks, costs of doing business may become prohibitively high, to the extent that certain transactions simply are not undertaken at all. For example, in the absence of a credible institutional framework that protects investors, foreign investors are unlikely to invest in a country,[11] and domestic investors may choose to put their money abroad. Wealthy Russians, for example, may thus purchase foreign assets such as a football club in London or a seaside villa in Cyprus instead of investing in Russia.

institutional transition
Fundamental and comprehensive changes introduced to the formal and informal rules of the game that affect organizations as players.

Institutions are not static; they evolve over time under the influence of economic and political actors.[12] Institutional transition, defined as 'fundamental and comprehensive change introduced to the formal and informal rules of the game that affect organizations as players,'[13] is common, especially in emerging economies. Such transition can happen gradually, or through a radical change of formal institutions. China and Russia in the 1990s represent examples of these contrasting approaches. China followed an incremental, 'gradualist' approach, whereas Russia pursued a radical, 'big bang' reform. Both approaches have their merits. On the one hand, radical reforms in Russia may have been necessary to create private ownership in order to prevent falling back on a central plan regime. On the other hand, China's economic accomplishments suggest that it is possible to achieve major change by initiating substantive but localized economic reforms, which – if successful – may create a political dynamic that leads to more comprehensive reforms. By most economic measures, China has outperformed Russia over the past two decades.

Two core propositions

Firm behaviours are often a reflection of the formal and informal constraints of a particular institutional framework.[14] Why? The institution-based view suggests two core propositions (Table 2.3). First, managers and firms *rationally* pursue their interests and make choices within institutional constraints. For example, in some countries, labour laws – a formal institution – protect workers from the threat of unemployment by requiring long notice periods and substantial redundancy payment. Then, employees are much safer in their job in an economic downturn (unless

Table 2.3 Two core propositions of the institution-based view

Proposition 1	Managers and firms *rationally* pursue their interests and make choices within the formal and informal constraints in a given institutional framework.
Proposition 2	Although formal and informal institutions combine to govern firm behaviour, in situations where formal constraints are unclear or fail, informal constraints will play a *larger* role in reducing uncertainty and providing constancy to managers and firms.

the firm goes bankrupt). However, employers would also be more reluctant to hire new people because hiring implies a long-term commitment to employ the person largely irrespective of market fluctuations. This explains why unemployment tends to rise early in a recession in the UK (UK firms find it easy to fire), but is more persistent in France and Italy when the recession ends (French and Italian firms are more reluctant to hire).

The second proposition is that formal and informal institutions combine to govern firm behaviour, but in situations where formal constraints are unclear or fail, informal constraints play a *larger* role in reducing uncertainty and providing constancy to managers and firms.[15] For example, when the formal regime collapsed with the breakup of the former Soviet Union, entrepreneurial firms pursued their ambitions largely relying on informal rules based on personal relationships and connections (called *blat* in Russian) among managers and officials.[16]

Also in developed economies, formal rules only make up a small (although important) part of institutional constraints, and informal constraints are pervasive. Just as firms compete in product markets, they also compete in the political marketplace characterized by informal relationships.[17] In particular, they may lobby political decision makers and regulators to change or interpret rules in their favour.[18] For example, in September 2008, a rapidly falling *Merrill Lynch* was able to sell itself to *Bank of America* for a hefty $50 billion. Supported by US government officials, this 'mega deal' was arranged over 48 hours (shorter than the time most people take to decide on which cars to buy) and the negotiations took place *inside* the Federal Reserve building in New York. In contrast, *Lehman Brothers* failed to secure government support and had to file for bankruptcy. Overall, the skilful use of a country's institutional frameworks to acquire advantage is at the heart of the institution-based view.

In this chapter we focus on *formal* institutions; informal institutions will be covered in Chapter 3. In particular, we discuss three spheres of countries' national institutional framework: (1) political systems, (2) economic systems and (3) legal systems.

POLITICAL SYSTEMS

A **political system** refers to the rules of the game on how a country is governed politically. Businesses interact with political systems only indirectly, yet businesspeople need to understand the political system because it shapes the commercial rules and regulations for business, and it is a major source of risk. At a broad level, there are two primary political systems: (1) totalitarianism and (2) democracy. At a more detailed level, democratic countries vary considerably in how they make and implement rules.

LEARNING OBJECTIVE

2 Explain the basic differences between political systems

political system
A system of the rules of the game on how a country is governed politically.

Totalitarianism

Totalitarianism (or dictatorship) is defined as a political system in which one person or party exercises absolute political control over the population. Although the number of totalitarian regimes has declined in recent decades, business may still encounter them. In Europe, probably only Belarus would qualify as totalitarian at present. Why do totalitarian regimes persist when democracy has been sweeping around the world? The answer is usually a combination of ideology and control over military and police forces.

An important ideology supporting totalitarian regimes is communism, which was embraced throughout Central and Eastern Europe and the then Soviet Union until the late 1980s. It is still the official ideology in China, Cuba, Laos, North Korea and Vietnam. Other totalitarian regimes are motivated by a combination of nationalism, religious motives and a fear of communism. In this nationalist totalitarianism, one political party, typically backed by the military, restricts political freedom, arguing that such freedom would lead to communism or chaos. In the 20th century, Spain, Portugal and most countries in Latin America and South-East Asia experienced periods of nationalist totalitarianism before becoming democracies.

Democracy

Democracy is a political system in which governments derive their legitimacy from election by their citizens. For example, the citizens of Turkey in three elections (2002, 2007 and 2011) gave the Justice and Development Party (AKP) the majority in parliament, which in turn elected Recep Tayyip Erdoğan as prime minister (Opening Case). After stepping down as prime minister, voters in 2014 elected Erdoğan as president of the country.[19] National elections such as these give a parliament and the government the legitimacy to issue new rules for business that are considered binding (provided they are consistent with the constitution).

However, democracies vary considerably in the way they translate the votes of the public into legislation, taxation and other government actions. Like the economy, institutions govern the political system. The rules are usually laid down in a constitution, and they determine how elections are organized, how the public vote is translated into seats in parliament, and how much power the elected officials or members of parliament attain. These democratic processes influence the relative influence of different interest groups, and the ability of ruling elites to retain their power. Crucial variations among democracies include:[20]

- **Proportional representation versus first-past-the-post:** Most European countries have some form of proportional representation which implies that, essentially, all votes are added up and seats are allocated to political parties proportionately to the number of their votes. This system comes closest to the ideal that all voters are equally important in choosing a country's leaders. Usually, such a system is combined with a minimum threshold share of votes that parties have to attain, such as 2% in Denmark, 4% in Sweden and 5% in Germany. In the absence of such a hurdle, the parliament may become fragmented and unable to support a stable government, as experienced for example in Italy and Israel. In contrast, many Anglo-Saxon countries, including the UK, USA and India, have a first-past-the-post system, in which each constituency elects *one* representative only. This system tends to favour the relative strongest political parties and gives less influence to smaller parties (apart from regional parties).

- **Direct versus indirect elections of governments:** Most European countries have an indirect democracy in which voters elect their representatives in parliament, who on their behalf elect and monitor the government and the most powerful official in the country, normally the prime minister. However, some countries directly elect a president with executive power who then appoints government ministers, notably in France and the USA (see In Focus 2.1).

IN FOCUS 2.1

Elections around the globe

It can be quite exciting to watch the news from elections around the world and compare how the will of the people translates into the creation of governments. When the people of **France** went to vote in May 2012, they chose their president in a two-stage direct election. At the first stage, François Hollande of the Socialist party gained 28.6% of the votes ahead of incumbent president Nicolas Sarkozy of the centre-right UMP party (27.2%), the Front National's Marine Le Pen (17.9%) and the Front Gauche's Jean-Luc Mélenchon (11.1%). Only the two leading candidates of the first round proceeded through to the run-off held two weeks later, which Hollande won with 51.6% against Sarkozy's 48.4%. This system of a run-off election ensures that the president actually is backed by a majority of the electorate, thus avoiding situations where the vote is split among multiple candidates, leaving the winner with with 40% or less of the vote, as can easily happen in single-round presidential elections.

When the people of the **USA** went to vote for a president in November 2012, they had already endured over a year of political campaigning. Initially, the race had been on for the presidential candidates of the two main parties, Republicans and Democrats. Over several weeks from January to May 2012, both parties held primary elections. The Democrats quickly gathered behind incumbent president Barak Obama. The Republicans' primary was fought until May, when Mitt Romney clinched enough delegates to make his last serious competitor, Newt Gingrich, concede. The November election looked like a direct election, but actually voters are voting for electoral college representatives of their states who then vote for the president, with the (relative) winner in each state receiving all the state's votes. Obama was first across the finishing line with 332 electoral college votes, compared to Romney's 206. Obama also received a majority of the actual votes with 51%, which is not always the case; in fact rarely does a president receive over 50% of the popular vote. In 2000, Al Gore actually lost even though he received more popular votes (48.4%) than George Bush (47.9%), because Gore had fewer electoral college votes (266 to 271, after the Florida recount controversy).

When the people of **Germany** went to vote in September 2013, they were choosing between party lists in a system of proportional representation similar to those used in most continental European countries (except France). The parties' share of seats in the parliament represents their share in the direct vote, provided that they attain at least 5% of the popular vote. Four parties passed this threshold: the Christian Democrats (41.5%), Social Democrats (25.7%), The Left (8.6%) and The Greens (8.4%). The allocation of seats then follows a complex system that takes into account both the constituency seats that parties obtained directly, and the votes they received in each state. Proportional representation typically leads to coalition governments in which the contributing parties have to negotiate and compromise on their policies. Thus Chancellor Angela Merkel formed a new coalition government with the Social Democrats, as her previous coalition partner, the Free Democrats, missed the 5% threshold.

When the people of **India** went to vote in April and May 2014, 814 million voters were eligible to vote – the largest exercise in democracy in the world. The election took place on nine dates over five weeks.

How are votes translated into political power?

Voters elected one Member of Parliament in each constituency, a system modelled on the British first-past-the-post system. The Bharatiya Janata Party (BJP) led by Narendra Modi received 31.0% of the votes and obtained a majority of seats in the parliament, 282 of 543 seats. The long-governing Congress Party – once led by Jawaharlal Nehru and Indira Ghandi – dropped to 19.3% of the votes and 44 seats. The parliament with the majority of BJP members then elected Narendra Modi as prime minister. A similar first-past-the-post system is used in the **UK**, where in 2015 the Conservatives received 36.8% of the vote but obtained an absolute majority in parliament with 331 of 650 seats. Second by votes came Labour with 30.4% (231 seats) and UKIP with 12.6% but only 1 seat.

Sources: Website of the national election offices: (1) France: www.conseil-constitutionnel.fr; (2) USA: www.fec.gov/pubrec/fe2012/federalelections2012.pdf; (3) Germany: http://www.bundeswahlleiter.de; (4) India: http://www.pib.gov.in/elections2014/; (5) UK: http://news.bbc.co.uk/1/hi/uk_politics/election_2010/default.stm, all accessed February 2015.

- **Representative versus direct democracy:** In most countries, voters elect representatives (members of parliament) who then act on their behalf. Thus the parliament, by majority vote of the peoples' representatives, decides on new laws, taxation, or government spending, for example. However, in some territories, voters can vote directly for certain laws, notably in Switzerland and in several US states. This system gives voters more power, but may lead to inconsistencies and rigidities in the overall legal framework, as experienced recently in California.[21]

- **Centralization of power:** Normally the national government is the centre of power, but people also elect local representations and in some countries regional assemblies. The power vested in these sub-national parliaments varies considerably. Especially in federal systems such as Australia, Germany and the USA, state-level governments actually wield considerable power, and may even have to approve certain legislative changes at the federal level.

Why are political elections – even in other countries – important for businesses?

Beyond politics, these rules also determine what selection processes are considered fair and legitimate in other organizations. For instance, students in continental Europe elect representatives in a student parliament by voting for different groups, and each group will receive seats in proportion to their votes. The student union is then elected by this parliament, usually from the largest group. In contrast, students at UK or US universities typically directly elect individuals to specific posts within the student union.

Why does all this matter for international business? First, political systems determine who sets the rules, and whose interest may be reflected in the rules. For example, in first-past-the-post systems, regionally concentrated interest groups, such as farmers or industries clustered in certain cities or region, tend to have a lot of influence on 'their' representatives in parliament. With an indirect election, a poorly performing prime minister is likely to be ousted by his or her own party, a concern that US President Obama and French President Hollande do not need to worry about. In a direct democracy, interest groups and lobbyists may appeal directly to the electorate, which opens opportunities for those with major financial resources. In a centralized country, such as France or the UK, the regulations and taxation rates tend to be uniform across the country, while decentralized countries such as the USA may have considerable variations that require adaptation even within the country.

Second, political systems also determine where and how businesses may be able to influence legislative processes through lobbying (mostly legal) or corruption (usually illegal). Third, they influence how frequently the rules of the game for business are changed, a major source of political risk – risk associated with political changes that may negatively impact domestic and foreign firms.[22] The more stable a political system, and the more entities needed to approve changes of regulations, the lower is the political risk (see Closing Case).

political risk
Risk associated with political changes that may negatively impact domestic and foreign firms.

ECONOMIC SYSTEMS

LEARNING OBJECTIVE

3   Explain the systemic differences between economic systems

economic system
Rules of the game on how a country is governed economically.
market economy
An economy that is characterized by the 'invisible hand' of market forces.
command economy
An economy in which all factors of production are government- or state-owned and controlled, and all supply, demand and pricing are planned by the government.

An economic system refers to the rules of the game on how a country is governed economically. The theoretical prototypes are a pure market economy and a command economy, yet between them exists a wide variety of capitalism.

A pure market economy is characterized by the 'invisible hand' of market forces first noted by Adam Smith in *The Wealth of Nations* in 1776. The government takes a hands-off approach known as *laissez-faire*. All factors of production are privately owned, and individuals are free to engage in all sorts of contracts. The government only performs functions the private sector cannot perform (such as providing roads and defence). Historically, many countries had a system that came close to the model of a pure market economy in the 19th century, notably the UK and the USA (see Chapter 1).

A pure command economy is defined by a government, in the words of Lenin, taking the 'commanding heights' in the economy. All factors of production are government- or state-owned and controlled, and all supply, demand and pricing are planned by the government. During the heyday of communism, the former Soviet Union approached such an ideal. Yet even the Soviet Union was never a complete command economy; black markets for small products from agricultural produce to cigarettes existed practically everywhere.

Pure market economy and pure command economy are theoretical ideas at opposite ends of a scale. In practice, economic systems vary in the relative distribution of market forces versus other forms of coordination. In the early 21st century, almost all countries have become market economies. Thus when we say a country has a market economy, it is really a shorthand version for a country that organizes its economy *mostly* (but not completely) by market forces, and that still has certain elements of non-market coordination. But even the effective functioning of a market economy may need some institutions backed by a strong government (In Focus 2.2). Variations among market economies thus concern not only the rules that companies have to respect, but also the degree to which governments intervene discretionarily on a case-by-case basis, say to protect employment in a loss-making enterprise.

IN FOCUS 2.2

Father of the market economy

In Germany, many scholars honour Walter Eucken as 'father of the market economy', while the general public often gives that title to Ludwig Erhard, minister of the economy in the 1950s. Eucken was the intellectual inspiration for many of the policies that in the 1950s enabled the German economic miracle. His ideas in many ways anticipated the institutional perspective developed in this chapter.

The core of Eucken's argument is that competition based on prices is the best mechanism to ensure economic prosperity. Yet a market economy needs some

sort of regulatory institutions because 'laissez-faire liberalism' like in the 19th century, if left unchecked, may deliver economic growth but not yield socially desirable outcomes. In an anniversary speech, German President Joachim Gauck captured the essence of Eucken's advice:

'Competition . . . is an opening force. It breaks up inhertited priviledges and cemented power structures, and thereby offers space for more participation. It offers – even in case of failure – ideally second and further chances. If it is designed well, it is also fair'.

How did Walter Eucken enable the German economic miracle?

However, Eucken believed that these outcomes will only be achieved if a strong state secures the rules, or what we today call 'formal institutions'. At the same time, the state should not directly interfere in economic activities. Eucken identified six primary and four supporting sets of institutions that need to be in place for competition to deliver the desired outcomes

(see Figure 2.1). Three of the primary institutions are grounded in the legal system: (1) the right to private property; (2) the freedom to make contracts with others to exchange private property; and (3) the economic liability of economic agents. This third item specifies that individuals are liable for negative effects of their (economic) actions on others – for instance when the delivery of faulty products causes harm to consumers.

A further three primary institutions concern the way the government is running the economy: (4) markets should be open to international trade to enable both effective integration in the world economy and international competition to pre-empt domestic collusion or monopolies; (5) the currency should be stable and not manipulated by government in pursuit of short term objectives; and (6) economic policy should be consistent and predictable to allow economic agents to make long term commitments.

The supporting institutions aim to secure the sustainability of the system, and the generation of socially acceptable outcomes. Eucken identified four types:

1 Competition rules and regulations should (a) prevent the creation of monopolies, cartels and other concentration of market power in the hands of a

Figure 2.1 Principles of a competition-based economic system (based on Walter Eucken, 1952)

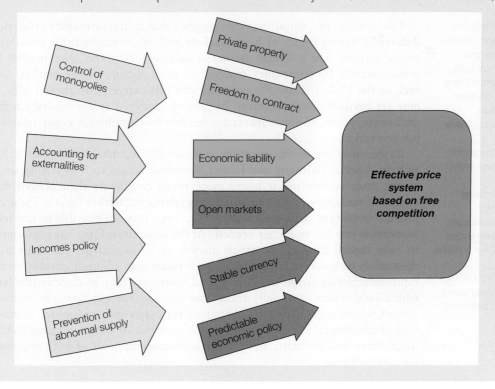

few, and (b) force those with market power to act as *if* they are exposed to competitive markets. For Eucken and his collaborators, this was a major concern (also see Chapter 13).

2 Accounting systems should account for externalities. In other words, businesses creating costs for others have to pay for them. This idea has been developed later especially in environmental economics – if you pollute a river you have to pay the fishermen who lose their catch.

3 Incomes policy should create socially acceptable distribution of wealth. Eucken favoured progressive taxation as a simple and not too intrusive means in influence distribution. Of course, in his day income taxes were nowhere near as high as they are today.

4 Policy interventions should also prevent abnormal supply behaviour such as increasing supply when prices go down, a behaviour that can happen in labour markets in combination with poverty: labourers work as long as necessary to feed their family.

Such institutions to support the economic system that underpins European prosperity did not arise spontaneously. They are shaped by deliberate policy decisions, and they are continuously evolving. Politicians and powerful businesses are often tempted to cement structures, yet giving in to such pressures would undermine the market mechanism. In the words of Joachim Gauck:

'Only the restriction of power through fair and free competition enables many people to participate. Therefore it is so important to ensure that competition is not benefitting a few powerful people, but creates opportunities for as many people as possible.'

The question is, do politicians in today's Germany (and Europe more generally) appreciate the importance of constraining power, including their own, once they have attained it?

Sources: (1) W. Eucken, 1952, *Grundsätze der Wirtschaftspolitik*, (7th ed. 2004), Tübingen: Mohr Siebeck; (2) N. Goldschmidt & M. Wohlgemuth, eds., 2008, *Grundtexe zur Freiburger Tradition der Ordnungsökonomik*, Tübingen: Mohr Siebeck; (3) J. Gauck, 2014, Speech at Walter Eucken Institute, University of Freiburg (translation KM).

varieties of capitalism
A scholarly view suggesting that economies have different inherent logics on how markets and other mechanisms coordinate economic activity.
liberal market economy (LME)
A system of coordination primarily through market signals.
coordinated market economy (CME)
A system of coordinating through a variety of other means in addition to market signals.
apprenticeship system
Vocational training system for crafts and professions.

The varieties of capitalism view suggests that different market economies have different inherent logics of how markets and other mechanisms coordinate economic activity.[23] In a liberal market economy (LME), the coordination happens predominantly by companies reacting to price signals of the market. Countries such as the USA, UK and Canada fall into this category. In these LMEs, companies are predominantly financed by issuing shares that are traded on the stock exchanges, while labour markets are flexible and employees enjoy relatively little job protection.

At the other end of the spectrum, in a coordinated market economy (CME) such as Italy, Austria, Germany and France, economic actors such as businesses, governments, trade unions and industry associations coordinate their actions through a variety of mechanisms; they are not purely relying on market signals. These countries provide employees with more legal protection – it is not possible to just tell people 'tomorrow you are no longer needed'. At the same time, firms have less opportunity to raise capital through the stock market, or to incentivize managers by linking their salary or bonus to stock market performance. In addition, employees may have representatives on corporate boards, and businesses may be directly involved in the educational system, especially vocational training. For example, the apprenticeship system, which is the backbone of training for crafts and professions in many countries of continental Europe, relies on close cooperation between businesses, industry associations and the state, and on long-term commitments of both apprentices and their employers.

Figure 2.2 Varieties of capitalism

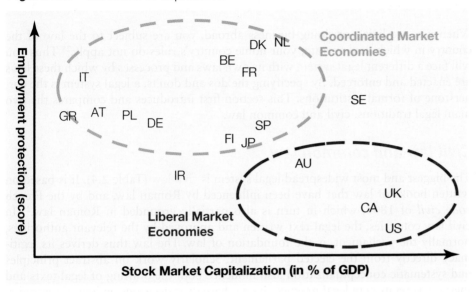

Abbreviations: AT = Austria, AU = Australia, BE = Belgium, CA = Canada, DE = German, DK = Denmark, FI = Finland, FR = France, IT = Italy, IR = Ireland, JP = Japan, NL = Netherlands, PL = Poland, SE = Sweden, SP = Spain, UK = United Kingdom, US = USA.

Source: Authors' creation using data from *OECD* and *World Bank*. All data refer to 2013.

The elements of LME and CME are combined in different ways in different countries (Figure 2.2). The Nordic countries combine an extensive welfare state (typical for a CME) with flexible labour markets, strong capital markets and an open trade regime (typical for an LME). For example, the Danish agricultural industry is organized in cooperatives owned by the farmers, yet they are fiercely competitive internationally, including the largest exporters of meat (*Danish Crown*) and dairy products (*Arla*), and they have a long record of advocating free trade, which is rather unusual for farmers.[24]

Moreover, these economic systems are in constant flux. For example, Sweden had an LME during its early industrialization in the 19th century, and a financial capital-driven economy until a major banking crash in 1932. Only thereafter Sweden developed its well-known welfare economy with a high degree of coordination. However, since the 1970s, the pendulum has been swinging back towards an intermediate position, with the Swedish stock markets gaining in importance for finance and corporate governance.[25]

In South-East Asia, many countries have embraced the principles of an LME by the end of the 20th century, yet with a strong state providing directions and vision regarding the envisaged path of economic development.[26] Singapore, often seen as a role model of a market economy, in fact sees very active guidance of the economy by the government, along with the ownership of some large corporations. Likewise in China, the state continues to maintain a major role both as owner and investor of enterprises, as well as a regulator of industries. There is considerable debate on the future direction of Chinese capitalism; many experts suggest the active role of government involvement within a market economy in France most closely resembles the system that China is evolving towards.[27]

LEGAL SYSTEMS

LEARNING OBJECTIVE

4   Explain the basic
     differences between
     legal systems

legal system
The rules of the game on
how a country's laws are
enacted and enforced.

civil law
A legal tradition that uses
comprehensive statutes and
codes as a primary means
to form legal judgments.

common law
A legal tradition that is
shaped by precedents and
traditions from previous
judicial decisions.

case law
Rules of law that have been
created by precedents of
cases in court.

When you are living or doing business abroad, you are subject to the law of the country in which you operate; your home country's rules do not apply.[28] Thus you will face a different legal system with its own laws and processes by which these laws are enacted and enforced. By specifying the dos and don'ts, a legal system is the cornerstone of formal institutions. This section first introduces and compares the two main legal traditions: civil and common law.

Civil law and common law

The biggest and most widespread legal system is civil law (Table 2.4). It is based on written books of law that have been influenced by Roman law, and by the French *code civil* of 1804, which in turn is also partially grounded in Roman law.[29] In civil law countries, the legal text written and approved by the relevant authorities, normally the parliament, is the foundation of law. The law thus derives its legitimacy directly from the elected parliament. Scholarly work on abstract principles and systematic conceptualization also influence both the drafting of legal texts and their interpretation in legal practice. Judges base their decisions on logical reasoning grounded primarily in the text and the purpose of the law, and on decisions by higher courts. Judicial practice has over time filled gaps in the legal texts, but (contrary to common law) this is a supplementary source.[30]

Common law which is English in origin, is shaped by statutes as well as precedents and traditions from previous judicial decisions. It gives more weight to customary law, and the courts play a more central role in defining the law, the so-called case law. Statutes passed by legislators cover only specific areas, and tend to be interpreted narrowly.[31] Hence common law is continuously evolving as judges resolve specific disputes with primary reference to precedents set in previous cases of similar nature. Such extensions of the law then may give new meaning to the law, which will shape future cases.

Table 2.4   Civil and common law

	Civil law	Common law
Historical origins	Roman law and French *code civil* of 1804	English customary law
Primary sources of laws	Codified in books of law, scholarly conceptualization	Statutes, customs, court decisions
Court proceedings	Judges lead the proceedings, including asking questions and taking decisions.	Judges as arbiters, lawyers dominate proceedings, and juries as decision makers
Business practice	Contracts and codes of practice comparatively brief, traditionally more protection of employees and consumers.	Greater freedom to design contracts and codes of practice; detailed contracts filling gaps in the legal framework; extensive use of lawyers.

Note: These characteristics are stylized, practices vary considerably across countries.

Sources: K. Zweigert & K. Kötz, 1999, *An Introduction to Comparative Law*, 3rd ed., Oxford: Oxford University Press.

Common law may provide businesses with greater freedom to set their own rules, for instance when writing contracts. However, courts will only consider the exact wording of the written contract. This means that contracts tend to be rather long and detailed, partially substituting for the absence of detailed legal regulations. Corporate lawyers are therefore likely to be essential in business negotiations from the outset to define the terms of the relationship. The contract freedom tends to benefit those with more bargaining power, i.e. big business. As an unsuspecting consumer, you are more likely to find surprising clauses that you do not like in your mobile phone or credit card service provider's contracts in a common law country. On the other hand, businesses may appreciate civil law because of the greater clarity of rules and the reduced need to negotiate detailed contracts. Many issues are already covered in legal codes, and courts will consider the spirit and intentions of the contracting partners when interpreting a contract. Contracts thus normally cover only the specifics of the transaction and the deviations from the rules in the relevant legal statutes. Moreover, there tends to be less need for industry or corporate 'codes of conduct' to make up for voids in the legal framework in civil law systems (Chapter 10).[32]

Legal processes

Not only does the content of the law differ, but also the processes by which it is enacted. Probably you have seen US law in action in Hollywood movies: lawyers arguing with each other, and juries having to make tricky decisions of fact. American common law is highly confrontational (and thus an attractive setting for movies) because plaintiffs and defendants, through their lawyers, must argue their case in front of judge and jury. Juries of twelve laypeople often have to decide whether a person is guilty, or whether and how much compensation is to be paid. In contrast, you probably have rarely seen a civil law court in action in a movie. That's because it lacks the drama and excitement. Civil law is less confrontational because comprehensive statutes and codes serve to guide judges. Another key difference is that in the USA each party has to pay its own legal costs. This implies that even if you win a case, you may end up paying a lot of money. Unsurprisingly, more lawyers are needed in the common law systems – and they tend to be very expensive.

If you are used to common law, you may find civil law countries very bureaucratic because there seems to be fairly detailed rules for almost everything, and not knowing all the rules can easily get you in trouble. On the other hand, if you are used to civil law, you may find common law countries very bureaucratic: each organization has its own rules, and a lot of activities have to be documented in great detail both for independent evaluators (whose criteria are vaguely defined), and as a protection against possible legal action. You may not find as much legal certainty, that is, clarity over the relevant rules that apply in a given situation. The codification of civil law makes it more accessible to everyone. In fact Napoleon himself challenged legislators to produce a 'readable' code back in the early 1800s when the French were drafting their *code civil*.[33] This codification established the unity of the law in its territory, reduced uncertainty, and secured equality before the law, as proclaimed by the French Revolution.

Most countries of the world have adapted legal codes based on civil or common law. In British colonies, the law usually developed along the principles of common law but incorporated local legal traditions, and this mix was retained after gained independence. Countries that at some stage in their history wished to introduce an entirely new and coherent set of rules often adapted civil law to local conditions.[34] For example, many Latin American countries opted for the French *code civil*, while Turkey imported the Swiss civil code (Table 2.5). German civil law is also the

legal certainty
Clarity over the relevant rules applying to a particular situation.

Table 2.5 Legal traditions

Family of law	Sub-group	Examples
Civil Law	French *code civil*	France, Spain, Italy, Belgium, Netherlands, Poland, Romania, Latin America, French-speaking Africa
	Germanic civil law	Germany, Austria, Switzerland, Hungary, Greece, Turkey, Japan, Korea, Taiwan
	Nordic civil law	Denmark, Finland, Iceland, Norway, Sweden
Common law	English law	England & Wales, Australia, Canada, Ireland, New Zealand
	English law with local customary law	Former British colonies in Africa and Asia
	American common law	USA
	Mixed common & civil law	South Africa, Scotland, Quebec (Canada), Louisiana (USA)
Other	Islamic law	Iran, Libya, Morocco, Saudi Arabia

Note: Most countries have been influenced by multiple legal traditions; the table indicates the main influence on current legal practice.

Sources: (1) K. Zweigert & K. Kötz, 1999, *An Introduction to Comparative Law*, 3rd ed., Oxford: Oxford University Press; (2) R. LaPorta, F. Lopez-de-Silvanes, A. Shleifer & R.W. Vishny, 1998, Law and Finance, *JPE* 106: 1113–1155.

foundation of legal codes in East Asia, notably Japan, Korea and Taiwan. Yet application of the law is quite different in these Asian countries, as preference is given to peaceful conciliation and arbitrage rather than public proceedings in court.

DEBATES AND EXTENSIONS

The formal institutions of the political, economic and legal systems represent some of the broadest and most comprehensive forces affecting international business. They provoke some significant debates. In this section, we focus on three: (1) property rights, (2) corporate governance and (3) political risk.

Property rights

property rights
The legal rights to use an economic property (resource) and to derive income and benefits from it.

A fundamental economic function of institutions is to protect property rights – the rights to use an economic property (resource) and to derive income and benefits from it.[35] Examples of property include homes, offices and factories as well as intellectual property. Property rights provide the basic economic incentive system that shapes resource allocation. In principle, property rights can be defined by formal arrangements or informal conventions and customs regarding the allocations and uses of property. However, informal conventions are rarely effective beyond clearly defined communities.

What difference do property rights supported by an effective legal system make? A great deal. Clearly defined property rights enable people and businesses to make contracts over such property, and thus to engage in business – most business transactions concern the transfer of some sort of property, or rights to property. For example, owners of land, buildings or trademarks who hold legal titles documenting their rights can derive income and benefits from it and enabling prosecution of violators through legal means. With legal titles, tangible property can lead an invisible, parallel life alongside its material existence. It can be used as collateral for credit. For example, the single most important source of funds for new start-ups in the USA is the mortgage of entrepreneurs' houses.

However, if you live in a house but cannot produce a title document specifying that you are the legal owner (which is a very common situation throughout the developing world, especially in 'shanty towns'); no bank will accept your house as collateral for credit. To start a new firm, you may have to resort to borrowing funds from family members, friends and other acquaintances through *informal* means. Such insecure property rights also result in using technologies that employ little fixed capital and do not entail long-term investment. Thus, lack of formal protection of property rights is a major barrier to economic growth in many developing countries.[36]

Although the term *property* traditionally refers to *tangible* pieces of property (such as land), intellectual property specifically refers to *intangible* property that results from intellectual activity (such as writing, creating and inventing). Intellectual property rights (IPRs) are rights associated with the ownership of intellectual property (In Focus 2.3). IPRs primarily include rights associated with (1) patents, (2) copyrights and (3) trademarks.

intellectual property rights
Rights associated with the ownership of intellectual property.

IN FOCUS 2.3

Protecting intellectual property internationally

Intellectual property rights (IPRs) are usually asserted and protected on a country-by-country basis, which raises a pressing issue internationally: how are IPRs protected when countries have uneven levels of IPR enforcement? IPRs need to be asserted and enforced through a *formal* system, which is designed to provide an incentive for people and firms to innovate and to punish violators. However, the intangible nature of IPRs makes their protection difficult. Around the world,

the unauthorized use of IPRs is widespread, ranging from unauthorized sharing of music files to deliberate counterfeiting of branded products.

A prerequisite for this to happen is ineffective formal IPR protection. China has significantly strengthened its IPR laws in line with the WTO TRIPS Agreement. However, what is lacking is enforcement. In America, convicted counterfeiters face fines of up to €1.5 million and ten years in prison for a *first* offence. In China, counterfeiters will not be prosecuted if their profits do not exceed approximately €7000. If they are caught and are found to make less than €7000, they can usually get away with a €700 fine, which is a small cost of doing business. In many cases, local governments and police have little incentive to enforce IPR laws.

To stem counterfeits, four 'Es' are necessary. The first E, *enforcement*, even if successful, is likely to be short-lived as long as demand remains high. *Education* not only refers to educating IPR law enforcement officials but also the general public about the perils of counterfeits. Educational efforts ideally encourage young entrepreneurs to favour ethical and legitimate businesses. *External pressures* have to be applied skilfully. Confronting host governments is not likely to be effective. For example, *Microsoft*, when encountering extensive software piracy in China, chose to collaborate with the Ministry of Electronics to develop new software instead of challenging it head on. *Microsoft* figured that once the government has a stake in the sales of legitimate *Microsoft* products, it may have a stronger interest in cracking down on pirated software.

Finally, *economic growth* and home-grown brands are the most effective remedies in the long run. In the 1960s, Japan was the global leader in counterfeits. In the 1970s, this dubious distinction passed on to Hong Kong, and later to South Korea and Taiwan. Now it is China's turn. As these countries developed their own industries, local inventors developed an interest in

protecting their IPR and lobbied for stronger IPR laws. This experience suggests that China and other leading counterfeiting nations may gradually extend their IPR protection laws and enforcement. In fact, consumers eager to show off their 'real' wealth appreciate the prestige of the 'real' brand and advocate their protection.

Sources: Based on (1) M.W. Peng, 2001, How entrepreneurs create wealth in transition economies, *AME*, 15: 95–108; (2) C. Hill, 2007, Digital piracy: Causes, consequences, and strategic responses, *APJM*, 24: 9–24; (3) *The Economist*, 2007, Counterfeit Goods in China: Mind games, November 10; (4) *The Economist*, 2012, Brands in China: Pro Logo, January 14.

patents
Legal rights awarded by government authorities to inventors of new technological ideas, who are given exclusive (monopoly) rights to derive income from such inventions.

copyrights
Exclusive legal rights of authors and publishers to publish and disseminate their work.

trademarks
Exclusive legal rights of firms to use specific names, brands and designs to differentiate their products from others.

- Patents are legal rights awarded by government authorities to inventors of new technological ideas, who are given exclusive (monopoly) rights to derive income from such inventions through activities such as manufacturing, licensing or selling.

- Copyrights are the exclusive legal rights of authors and publishers to publish and disseminate their work (such as this book, a photo, a piece of software or a design).

- Trademarks are the exclusive legal rights of firms to use specific names, brands and designs to differentiate their products from others.

The definition of property rights is one issue; their enforcement is an entirely different one. The rise of the internet has created new challenges to the definition and enforcement of IPR, including images, music, texts and movies. The enforcement of IPR on the internet is technologically difficult, and raises important civil liberties issues.[37] Some countries are also slow in enforcing conventional IPR. In fact, counterfeiting – the production of copied products – is a thriving international business. Thus the creation and enforcement of IPR has created some hotly debated issues, such as the IPR of traditional practices, farmers' rights to their seeds and living organisms. Even variations in the length of the protection of IPR in different countries can result in major conflicts for the businesses concerned (see In Focus 2.4). More challenging recent empirical evidence suggests that actual IPR systems are used for rent seeking and do not enhance innovation or productivity at a national level.[38]

IN FOCUS 2.4

Who is breaking whose copyright?

A fascinating aspect about newspapers in most countries is that they like to report stories where foreigners break 'our' people's copyright, with scant attention to copying done in their own country. Chinese businesses have, for good reason, been in the firing line

for copying product designs for both domestic use and export. However, in Denmark, a newspaper took aim at British manufacturers: '*Uphill Danish struggle against British Furniture Copies*'. Danes are very proud of a number of their architects and designers of the 1950s and 1960s, such as Arne Jacobsen. Their designer chairs, lamps and other furnishings continue to attain premium prices, and they also export products sought by fashionable Asian consumers. However, a British manufacturer has been copying those products and selling them in shops in London and on the internet (and hence also to Denmark) for a fraction of the price. 'Breach of copyright!', shout the Danes. 'Perfectly legal!', reply the British.

The underlying legal issue is that protection for design lasts for 70 years after the death of the designer in Denmark and most other European countries, but only 25 years in the UK. So, it is legal to produce 1960s Danish designs in the UK. But is it also legal to export them? In a long-running conflict, Danish courts have ruled that the Britons may not sell such furniture to Denmark because they breach copyright. But how can such a ruling be enforced on internet sales? While Danish businesses seek ways to enforce the copyrights, the British happily sell their copies.

In the European common market, it is a cause of political tension if products are legal in one country, but illegal in another. Products flow freely across borders, and copyright holders can't stop them from entering their country. Whether 70 years or 25 years is appropriate is a different question, but a common definition of copyright is necessary to prevent the British (in this case) from undercutting businesses having to pay for copyright in their own country.

Sources: (1) *Berlinske Tidende*, 2008, Engelske kopimøbler rykker ind i Danmark, February 8; (2) *Berlingske Tidende*, 2012, Forgaeves dansk kamp mod britiske kopimøbler, May 31, page B12.

Corporate governance

Another aspect of formal institutions that is essential for business is corporate governance, that is the rules by which shareholders and other interested parties control corporate decision makers (typically managers). The rules of corporate governance specify the distribution of rights and responsibilities among different participants in the corporation, such as the board, managers, shareholders and other stakeholders, and spells out the rules and procedures for making decisions on corporate affairs.[39] Corporate governance is important to ensure that managers act in the best interest of the firm, rather than their personal interest. Without effective corporate governance no one would put their money into someone else's firm – and thus firms would remain small.

corporate governance Rules by which shareholders and other interested parties control corporate decision makers.

Variations in corporate governance around the world are closely associated with variations in economic and legal systems. Common law systems have evolved in ways that provide strong protection to financial investors. Thus shareholders are at the centre of corporate governance. Managers have to serve shareholders' interests, who monitor them through the stock market, while employees and other stakeholders normally have rather little influence. In particular, stock options provide powerful incentives for managers to act in shareholders' interest. Moreover, takeovers provide a mechanism by which widespread equity ownership may rapidly become concentrated.[40] Managers act in anticipation of potential hostile takeover and thus aim to keep the share price high, which is in the interest of shareholders. This focus of the legal framework on shareholders explains why common law countries generally qualify as LME.

In contrast, legislators in civil law countries (especially in French *code civil*) tend to offer less protection to outside shareholders, and hence we see more family and state ownership in these countries. Germanic civil law is strong in protecting creditors, and thus provides a stronger basis for bank financing. Moreover, many Germanic and Nordic civil law countries give stakeholders such as banks and non-managerial employees a formal role in governance. For example, German banks play an important role in the monitoring of firms, as most individual shareholders delegate their voting rights to a bank, which then votes in shareholder meetings on behalf of its clients. Moreover, firms often entertain close relationships with their bank. As lenders, banks have access to inside information and take a central role in monitoring management. These rules reinforce the coordination aspect of a CME. In addition, employee representatives sit on corporate supervisory boards of large firms, and thus directly participate in corporate governance.[41] However, a global trend over the past two decades has led to more legal protection of shareholders, and reduced role of bank governance. For instance, banks in Germany have been divesting their equity stakes in non-bank businesses. Thus corporate governance rules are converging across legal systems.

Institutions and political risk

political risk
Risk associated with political changes that may negatively impact on domestic and foreign firms.

Businesses like stable institutional environments, which make it easier to plan for the long term. However, changes in the law, such as new taxation or regulation, are common around the world, and represent a mild form of political risk; even small changes can shift the playing field between foreign and local players. More serious political risks arise from military embargoes or trade sanctions, as Danish investors experienced in Russia during the Crimean crisis (see Closing Case). Other sources of political risk include civil wars, riots, protests and breakdowns of public order. Such disruptions can cause major losses to businesses. The most extreme political risk is the nationalization (expropriation) of foreign assets. The last time this happened on a large scale was in the 1979 Iranian revolution,[42] yet singular incidents happen occasionally, as when Spanish *Repsol* was expropriated by the Argentinean government who took control of its subsidiary *YPF* (see Chapter 6, Closing Case).

Totalitarian political systems, or formally democratic countries dominated by an autocratic acting leader are a particular challenge for businesses. For example, ahead of the Arab spring of 2011, it was often necessary to develop close ties to political leaders to do business in Arab countries like Tunisia, Egypt and Libya. Yet with the revolutions, such carefully cultivated ties could turn into liabilities.[43] Likewise, the overthrow of President Suharto in Indonesia in 1998 led to substantial losses for foreign investors who had closely aligned themselves with the extensive business network of the Suharto family. Another form of political risk arises by posting expatriates to a crisis area. For example, whose responsibility is it to bring out British expatriates who are trapped on oil fields in the Libyan dessert? The British media (and relatives of expats) argued that the Foreign Office had a responsibility, while others suggested that it was the employer's responsibility. Moreover, should companies pay ransom if their employees get kidnapped, and if so who should pay it?

In democracies, political risk tends to be more moderate than in totalitarian states. For example, each election entails the possibility that the opposition wins, and then changes the legal framework to their liking. For example, many supporters of presidential candidate Barak Obama in the USA in 2008 advocated restrictions on free trade or inward investment. From the perspective of foreign businesses doing business in the USA, this represents a political risk – the possibility that such measures are implemented and have negative effect on their business. In another example, the UK and Irish governments have considered restricting packaging design for cigarettes. From the perspective of branded cigarette manufacturers like *Japan Tobacco* and *Imperial Tobacco* (who have together almost 90% market share), this represents a risk to their revenue streams, and they threatened to sue the governments.[44] However, democracies are subject to division of powers: in the USA, not only the president but both Houses of Congress have to approve new laws; in case of high-level disputes even the Supreme Court may be involved. Hence changes in the law are unlikely to be very radical unless they have broad support of the political decision makers in the country.

How can companies assess political risk? First, they could ask a panel of country experts about their personal views, and combine these perceptions into an aggregate country risk index. A number of agencies, such as the *Economist Intelligence Unit*, *Euromoney* and the *World Bank* (see Chapter 9), produce such ratings of political risk. However, great caution must be exercised when using such indices. For example, they failed to provide warning of sudden political changes in Indonesia, Malaysia, South Korea and Thailand triggered by the 1997 East Asian financial crisis. In fact, these had often been rated as the least risky countries, as East Asia was widely regarded as an 'economic miracle' region. The velocity of the crisis shocked the vast majority of investors and politicians, as well as international executives and political risk experts. When the perception-based risk indicators were eventually adjusted, it was too late for many. Hence, perception-based measures may miss important aspects of political risk![45]

Two complementary approaches thus have been developed. Some commercial providers compile indices based on *symptoms* of political instability such as crime rates, poverty and labour strikes. Additionally, scholars have proposed to look at a country's underlying political system.[46] For example, the political constraint index (POLCON) focuses on the identifiable and measurable number of veto points in a political system, such as multiple branches of the government and judicial independence.[47] The assumption is that a political system with no checks and balances would have no constraints on the leading politicians because nobody possesses the power to veto key decisions. In such a system, political change may become highly unpredictable, thus presenting a lot of risk.

IMPLICATIONS FOR PRACTICE

Focusing on *formal* institutions, this chapter has sketched the contours of an institution-based view of international business, which is one of the two core perspectives we present throughout this book (Chapter 3 will reinforce this view with a focus on *informal* institutions). How does the institution-based view help us answer the fundamental question of this book: What determines the success and failure of firms around the globe? In a nutshell, this chapter suggests that firm performance is, at least in part, determined by the institutional frameworks governing firm behaviour. It is the growth of the firm that, in the aggregate, leads to the growth of the economy. Not surprisingly, persistent economic growth is typically supported by clearly defined and effectively implemented market-supporting formal institutions, while long periods of slow growth are often associated with vague, ineffective or market-depressing formal institutions. In other words, when markets work smoothly, behind the scenes the formal institutions are reducing the uncertainty facing business.

For managers, this chapter suggests two broad implications for action (Table 2.6). First, managerial choices are made rationally within the constraints of a given institutional framework. Therefore, when entering a new country, managers need to do

LEARNING OBJECTIVE

6 Draw implications for action

Table 2.6 Implications for action

- When entering a new country, do your homework by developing a thorough understanding of the formal institutions governing firm behaviour.

- Beware of small institutional differences among superficially similar countries, not recognizing such differences can costs your business a lot of money.

- Changes in formal institutions can be anticipated, or even influenced, by engaging in processes in the economic, political and legal systems.

their homework to attain a thorough understanding of the formal institutions in the host locations. This will help to understand not only *why* local businesses do things in a certain way, but also what strategies are different yet feasible in that context. A superficial understanding may not get you very far and may even be misleading or dangerous. For example, understanding the legal system and codes applying to your industry may help you understand why local firms act the way they do – and how a foreign entrant might gain competitive advantage by doing business differently yet within the scope of what is permitted.

Second, there are huge variations in political, economic and legal systems, even among 'Western' societies. Many people think of issues such as political risks, incomprehensible legal practices, or opaque economic structures when they consider investment distant countries, notably places they have never visited. The differences between Western societies may be small, but when it comes to running a business with a healthy margin or at a loss, even small differences in the institutional environment can make a big difference. Therefore, don't underestimate the challenge of doing business in a neighbouring country. Not a few businesses faltered because they thought it was easy just across the border.[48]

Third, formal institutions are not fixed for all times, they do change. Such change is usually gradual and based on clearly defined processes in the economic, political and legal systems. Thus, businesses operating in other countries ought to closely follow what is happening in their host country to anticipate possible changes. Understanding these processes reduces political risk, and firms may even be able to influence change through lobbying at the appropriate places.

CHAPTER SUMMARY

1 Explain the concept of institutions and their key role in reducing uncertainty

- Institutions are commonly defined as 'the rules of the game'.

- Institutions have formal and informal components, each with different supportive pillars.

- Their key functions are to reduce uncertainty, curtail transaction costs and constrain opportunism.

- Managers and firms *rationally* pursue their interests and make choices within formal and informal institutional constraints in a given institutional framework.

- When formal constraints are unclear or fail, informal constraints will play a *larger* role.

2 Explain the basic differences between political systems

- Totalitarianism is a political system in which one person or political party exercises overwhelming political control.

- In democracies, citizens elect representatives to govern the country, yet the institutions governing this selection vary widely.

3 Explain the systemic differences between economic systems

- A pure market economy is characterized by *laissez-faire* and total control by market forces.

- In liberal market economies (LMEs), companies are predominantly financed through the stock market, while labour markets are highly flexible.

- In coordinated market economies (CMEs), businesses, governments, trade unions, industry association and other economic actors coordinate their actions not only through markets.

4 Explain the basic differences between legal systems

- Civil law uses comprehensive statutes and codes as a primary means to form legal judgments.

- Common law is shaped by precedents and traditions from previous judicial decisions.

5 Participate in three leading debates on institutions in international business

- Property rights are legal rights to use an economic resource and to derive income and benefits from it.

- Corporate governance systems specify how managers are controlled by other interested parties of the firm.

- Political risk takes many forms, and is hard to capture using formal indices.

6 Draw implications for action

- Managers considering working abroad should have a thorough understanding of the formal institutions before entering a country.

KEY TERMS

Apprenticeship system
Case law
Civil law
Cognitive pillar
Command economy
Common law
Coordinated market economy (CME)
Corporate governance
Copyrights
Democracy
Economic system

Formal institutions
Informal institutions
Institutional framework
Institutional transitions
Institution-based view
Institutions
Intellectual property rights
Legal certainty
Legal system
Liberal market economy
Market economy

Normative pillar
Opportunistic behaviour
Patents
Political risk
Political system
Property rights
Regulatory pillar
Totalitarianism (dictatorship)
Trademarks
Transaction costs
Variety of capitalism

CRITICAL DISCUSSION QUESTIONS

1 What are the relative merits of a coordinated market economy (CME) and a liberal market economy (LME)? Would you rather work/study/retire in a CME or an LME?

2 What is in your view the most legitimate way to select student union representatives at your university?

3 As a manager, you discover that your firm's products are counterfeited by small family firms employing child labour in rural Bangladesh. You are aware of the corporate plan to phase out these products soon. You also realize that once you report this to the authorities, these firms will be shut down, employees will be out of work, and families and children will be starving. How would you proceed?

4 Your multinational is the largest foreign investor and enjoys good profits in (1) Sudan, where government forces are reportedly cracking down on rebels and killing civilians and (2) Belarus, where elections fail to meet normal European standards. As a country manager, you understand that your firm is pressured by activists to exit these countries. The alleged government actions, which you personally find distasteful, are not directly related to your operations. How would you proceed?

RECOMMENED READINGS

P.A. Hall & D. Soskice, eds, 2001, *Varieties of Capitalism,* Oxford: Oxford University Press – an introduction and discussion of the varieties of capitalisms view.

D.C. North, 1991, Institutions, *Journal of Economic Perspectives* 5(1): 97–112 – the foundation of contemporary institutional economics.

M. W. Peng, D. Wang & Y. Jiang, 2008, An institution-based view of international business strategy, *Journal of International Business Studies* 39: 920–936 – an introduction to institutional perspectives on international business topics.

M.A. Witt & G. Redding, eds., 2013, *The Oxford Handbook of Asian Business Systems,* Oxford: Oxford University Press – in depth descriptions and analysis of how Asian economies work, and how they differ from each other.

K. Zweigert & H. Kötz, 1999, *An Introduction to Comparative Law,* 3rd ed., Translated by T. Weir, Oxford: Oxford University Press – a systematic overview of the main legal systems around the world.

CLOSING CASE

Carlsberg faces political risk in Russia

In the early 1900s, Danish businessmen were rushing to invest in Russia, building cement plants, slaughterhouses and engine factories. Their advanced technologies gave them competitive advantages in the vast Russian market that gradually opened up to foreign investment. Then came the revolution of 1917, and all was lost as factories were expropriated. For the next seven decades, Russia was under Soviet rule and, with very few exceptions, closed to foreign investors.

When Soviet rule came to an end in 1990, Danish businesses – led by shipping company *Maersk*, pump maker *Grundfos* and building materials giant *Rockwool* – began setting up operations in Russia. *Carlsberg* was particularly successful, building a market share of 38% in the Russian beer market; their *Baltica* brands achieved market shares of 49% in the mainstream segment, and 37% in the premium segment. As part of its commitment to Russia, *Carlsberg* sponsored the national hockey league and the *Sochi Olympic Games*. Thus *Carlsberg* earned about 35% of its global revenues in Russia in 2013.

The success in Russia, however, exposed *Carlsberg* to the economic and political volatilities of Russia. In the 1990s, while Russia was experimenting with democracy, the economy had collapsed; by official estimates GDP fell approximately 40%. In the early 2000s, the economy was recovering at 7% annually, but remained highly volatile. Russia was highly dependent on exports of oil and gas, and thus on the world market prices of these commodities. Moreover, as Russia became richer and stronger (thanks to high oil prices), the government became more assertive *vis-à-vis* foreign businesses, for example putting pressure on foreign oil companies such as *BP* to reduce control over their operations in Russia.

While brewing is not a particularly sensitive activity, institutional changes still had a profound impact on *Carlsberg*. Russian leaders, from the czars to Boris Yeltsin, periodically tried to convince Russians to drink less alcohol, especially vodka. Vladimir Putin made a fresh attempt by increasing alcohol taxation, and in consequence the beer market shrank. Moreover, new laws banned TV, radio and outdoor advertising, and prohibited the sale of alcohol at non-stationary kiosks, which traditionally accounted for 26% of the off-trade (i.e. not in restaurants, clubs, or hotels) sales of beer in Russia.

These institutional changes had profound impact on brewers like *Carlsberg*. First, the demand surged ahead of the deadline of the new taxation as people stocked up their supplies, only to sharply drop in the next quarter as people destocked their supplies, creating challenges for logistics. Second, marketing resources had to be reallocated to, for example, in-store displays and channel marketing. Third, constraints on sales channels and advertising shifted the pattern of demand, leading to drop of sales especially in the economy segment. The economic crisis further reduced the demand for beer, especially in the premium and super-premium segment. By early 2014, capacity utilization in *Carlsberg*'s Russian breweries dropped to below 60%, creating speculation about possible brewery closures.

In 2014, Carlsberg was hit by the deteriorating Russian economy, worsening political relationships between Russia and the EU, and the collapse of the rouble. The trade sanctions introduced by the EU did not hit *Carlsberg* directly, because most of the beer it sold in Russia was brewed in Russia. Yet the economic crisis did: beer consumption dropped (especially of the more expensive brands) and the value of its Russian investments depreciated when the rouble dropped in value. Thus every time there was bad news from Russia, *Carlsberg*'s share price took a hit; in the second half of 2014, *Carlsberg* shares lost 20% of their value. Even so, *Carlsberg* remained committed to the Russian market, hoping for economic recovery, even though it reduced overcapacity by closing two breweries in early 2015. But not everyone did; some foreign investors, such as *Rockwool*, were concerned that Russia might introduce capital controls and divested some Russian assets. When the rouble collapsed, importing companies especially faced major losses if they had already contracted sales in the local currency. Some, like *Renault Nissan*, stopped taking orders as they could not price their cars appropriately.

CASE DISCUSSION QUESTIONS

1 Why is investment in Russia considered risky?

2 Why do West European MNEs invest in Russia, despite the political risks?

3 If you were a board member of Carlsberg, would you vote 'yes' or 'no' for a new project to acquire a local company in Russia?

Sources: (1) *Carlsberg Shareholder News*, 2012–2014, various issues, (2) *Carlsberg Annual Reports*, 2011–2014, various issues; (3) *The Economist*, 2011, BP in Russia: Dancing with bears, February 5; (4) M. Jes-Iversen, 2014, Kun en tåbe frygter ikke Rusland, *Børsen*, August 21; (5) J. Nymark & M. Butler, 2014, Russiske nedskæringer i vente, *Børsen*, August 21; (6) *BBC News*, 2014, Manufacturers face 'bloodbath' in Russia, says Renault Nissan boss, December 19; (7) P. Day, 2014, A tale of two sanctions, *BBC podcast*, http://downloads.bbc.co.uk/podcasts/radio/worldbiz/worldbiz_20141127-2100a.mp3.

NOTES

'For journal abbreviations please see page xx–xxi.'

1 D. North, 1990, *Institutions, Institutional Change, and Economic Performance* (p. 3), New York: Norton; O. Williamson, 2000, The new institutional economics, *JEL*, 38, 595–613; D. North, 2005, *Understanding the Process of Economic Change*, Princeton: Princeton University Press.

2 M.W. Peng, D. Wang & Y. Jiang, 2008, An institution-based view of international business strategy, *JIBS*, 39: 920–936; K.E. Meyer & M.W. Peng, 2005, 'Probing theoretically into Central and Eastern Europe: transactions, resources, and institutions', *JIBS*, 36: 600–621.

3 H. Nau & P. Steiner, 2002, Schmoller, Durkheim and the old European institutionalist economics, *JIE*, 36: 1005-1024; B. Sandelin, H. Trautwein & R. Wundrack, 2008, *A Short History of Economic Thought*, 2nd ed., London: Routledge.

4 W. Eucken, 1940, *Grundlagen der Nationalökonomie*, Jena: Fischer; P. Koslowski, ed., 2000, *The Theory of Capitalism the German Economic Tradition*, Berlin: Springer; N. Goldschmidt & M. Wohlgemut, eds, 2008, *Grundtexte zur Freiburger Tradition der Ordnungsokonomik*, Tubingen: Mohr Siebeck.

5 O. Williamson, 1985, *The Economic Institutions of Capitalism* (pp. 1–2), New York: Free Press.

6 W.R. Scott, 1995, *Institutions and Organizations*, Thousand Oaks, CA: Sage; M. Gelbuda, K.E. Meyer & A. Delios, 2008, International business and institutional development in Central and Eastern Europe, *JIM*, 14: 1–12.

7 A. Haldane, 2009, Why Banks failed the stress test, Mimeo, Bank of England, February 13. H. Shin, 2009, Reflections on Northern Rock, *JEP*, 23(1): 101–119.

8 *The Economist*, 2009, A personal view of the crisis: Confessions of a risk manager, August 9.

9 D.C. North, 1990, *as above*; J. Hooker, 2003, *Working Across Cultures*, Stanford: Stanford University Press.

10 *The Economist*, 2008, Derivatives: A nuclear winter? September 18; *The Economist*, 2008, Rethinking Lehman Brothers: The price of failure, October 2.

11 S. Globerman & D. Shapiro, 2003, Governance infrastructure and US foreign direct investment, *JIBS*, 34: 19–34; A. Bevan, S. Estrin & K.E. Meyer, 2004, Institution building and the integration of Eastern Europe in international production, *IBR*, 13: 43–64.

12 North, 1990, *as above*; A. Greif, 2006, *Institutions and the Path to the Modern Economy*, Cambridge: Cambridge University Press.

13 M.W. Peng, 2003, Institutional transitions and strategic choices (p. 275), *AMR*, 28: 275–296; see also E. George, P. Chattopadhyay, S. Sitkin & J. Barden, 2006, Cognitive underpinning of institutional persistence and change, *AMR*, 31: 347–365.

14 P. Moran & S. Ghoshal, 1999, Markets, firms, and the process of economic development, *AMR*, 24: 390–412; M. Kotabe & R. Mudambi, 2003, Institutions and international business, *JIM*, 9: 215–217; K.E. Meyer, S. Estrin, S. Bhaumik & M.W. Peng, 2009, Institutions, Resources, and Entry Strategies in Emerging Economies, *SMJ*, 31: 61–80; A. Chacar, W. Newburry & B. Vissa, 2010, Bringing institutional factors into performance persistence research, *JIBS*, 41: 1 119–1 140.

15 M.W. Peng, 2003, *as above*; G. Helmke & S. Levitsky, 2004, Informal institutions and comparative politics: A research agenda, Perspective on Politics, 2; 725–740; S. Estrin & M. Prevezer, 2011, The role of informal institutions in corporate governance: Brazil, Russia, India, and China compared, APJM 28: 41–67.

16 R. Aidis, S. Estrin & T. Mickiewicz, 2008, Institutions and entrepreneurship development in Russia, *JBV*, 23: 656–672; S. Puffer, D. McCarthy & M. Boisot, 2010, Entrepreneurship in Russia and China, *ETP*, 34: 441–467.

17 A. McWilliams, D. van Fleet & K. Cory, 2002, Raising rivals' costs through political strategy, *JMS*, 39: 707–723; M. Lord, 2003, Constituency building as the foundation for corporate political strategy, *AME*, 17: 112–124; A. Hillman & W. Wan, 2005, The determinants of MNE subsidiaries' political strategies, *JIBS*, 36: 322–340;

P. Sun, K. Mellahi & M. Wright, 2012, The contingent value of corporate political ties, *AMP*, 26: 68–82.

18 J. Crystal, 2003, *Unwanted Company: Foreign Investment in American Industries*, Ithaca: Cornell University Press; J. Bonardi, G. Holburn & R. Bergh, 2006, Nonmarket strategy performance, *AMJ*, 49: 1 209–1 228; J.P. Lindeque, 2007, A firm perspective of anti-dumping and countervailing duty cases in the United States, *JWT* 41: 559–579.

19 J. Parkinson & E. Peker, 2014, Turkey election: Erdoğan wins landmark victory, *Wall Street Journal*, August 11.

20 A. Lijphart, 1995, *Electoral Systems and Party Systems: A Study of Twenty-Seven Democracies*, Oxford: Oxford University Press; D.M. Farrell, 2001, *Electoral Systems: A Comparative Introduction*, Basingstoke: Palgrave.

21 B.S. Frey, 1994, Direct democracy, *AER*, 84: 338–348; J.G. Matsuoka, 2005, Direct democracy works, *JEP*, 19, 185–206; *The Economist*, 2009, Charlemagne: The Swiss in the middle, December 5; B.S. Frey, 2009, Letter: Popular politics, *The Economist*, December19; *The Economist*, 2009, Direct democracy: The tyranny of the majority, December 19.

22 S. Kobrin, 1979, Political risk, *JIBS*, 10: 67-80.T.L. Brewer, 1993, Government policies, market imperfections, and foreign direct investment, *JIBS*, 24: 101–120.

23 P. Hall & D. Soskice, eds, 2001, *Varieties of Capitalism*, Oxford: Oxford University Press; G. Morgan, R. Whitley & E. Moen, 2005, *Changing Capitalism?* Oxford: Oxford University Press; M. Carney, E. Gedajlovic & X. Yang, 2009, Varieties of Asian capitalism, *APJM*, 26: 361–380; W. Judge, S. Fainshmidt & L. Brown, 2014, Which model of capitalism best delivers both wealth and equality? *JIBS*, 45: 363–386.

24 M. Mordhorst, 2008, Arla from a decentralized co-operation to an MNE, in: S. Fellman, M.J. Iversen, H. Sjögren & L. Thue, eds, *Creating Nordic Capitalism*, Basingstoke: Palgrave-MacMillan.

25 H. Sjögren, 2008, Welfare capitalism: the Swedish economy 1850–2005, in: Fellman et al., eds, 2008, *as above*.

26 F. Tipton, 2009, Southeast Asian capitalism, *APJM*, 26: 401–434; M. Witt & G. Redding, 2013, Asian business systems, *Socio-Economic Review*, 11: 265-300; M. Witt & G. Redding, eds., 2013, *The Oxford Handbook of Asian Business Systems*, Oxford: Oxford University Press.

27 N. Fligstein & J. Zhang, 2011, A New Agenda for research on the trajectory of Chinese capitalism, *MOR*, 7: 39–62; N. Lin, 2011, Capitalism in China, *MOR*, 7: 63–96.

28 M. Dixon, 2007, *A Textbook on International Law*, 7th ed., Oxford: Oxford University Press; M.N. Shaw, 2009, *International Law*, 6th ed., Cambridge, Cambridge University Press.

29 O.F. Robinson, T.D. Fergus & W.M. Gordon, 1994, *European Legal History*, London: Butterworth; F.

Wieacker, 1996, *A History of Private Law in Europe*, Translated by T. Weir, Oxford: Oxford University Press.

30 K. Zweigert & H. Kötz, 1999, *An Introduction to Comparative Law*, 3rd ed., Translated by T. Weir, Oxford: Oxford University Press (Chapters 9 & 18).

31 Zweigert & Kötz, 1999, *as above* (Chapters 15 & 18); V. Bogdanor, 2009, *The new British constitution*, Oxford: Hart.

32 G. Jackson & A. Apostolakou, 2010, Corporate social responsibility in Western Europe? *JBE*, 94: 371–394.

33 Zweigert & Kötz, 1999, *as above*.

34 Zweigert & Kötz, 1999, *as above*. (Chapters 8, 11, 13 & 21).

35 Y. Barzel, 1997, *Economic Analysis of Property Rights*, 2nd ed., Cambridge: Cambridge University Press; R. Posner, 2003, *Economic Analysis of Law*, 6th ed., New York: Aspen.

36 H. de Soto, 2000, *The Mystery of Capital*, New York: Basic Books.

37 A. Johns, 2010, *Piracy: The Intellectual Property Wars from Gutenberg to Gates*, Chicago: University of Chicago Press; L. Menand, 2014, Crooner in rights spat, *New Yorker*, October 20.

38 M. Boldrin & D. Levine, 2013, The case against patents, *JEP*, 27(1): 3–22.

39 R. Monks & N. Minow, 1995, *Corporate Governance*, Oxford: Blackwell; OECD, 2004, *OECD Principles of Corporate Governance*, Paris: OECD.

40 LaPorta et al., 1997, *as above*.

41 J.C. Coffee, 2001, The rise of dispersed ownership: the roles of law and the state in the separation of ownership and control, *Yale Law Journal*, 111, 1–82; Hall & Soskice, 2001, *as above*.

42 R. Click, 2005, Financial and political risks in US direct foreign investment, *JIBS*, 36: 559–575.

43 *The Economist*, 2011, Schumpeter: Beyond Economics – Businesspeople need to think harder about political risk, February 12.

44 K. Shubber, 2015, Tobacco groups poised to sue over plain packaging, *Financial Times*, January 23; S. McCabe, 2015, No smoke without ire: Big Tobacco gets angry, *Independent.ie*, February 22.

45 G. Holburn & B. Zelner, 2010, Political capabilities, policy risk, and international investment strategy, *SMJ*, 31: 1 290–1 315.

46 P. Vaaler, B. Schrage & S. Block, 2005, Counting the investor vote, *JIBS*, 36: 62–88.

47 The data are available at: http://www-management. wharton.upenn.edu/henisz/; see also W. Henisz & A. Delios, 2001, Uncertainty, imitation, and plant location, *ASQ*, 46: 443–475; W. Henisz & J. Macher, 2004, Firm and country-level tradeoffs and contingencies in the evaluation of foreign investment, *OSc*, 15: 537–554.

48 K. Brouthers, 2001, Explaining the national cultural distance paradox, *JIBS*, 32:177–189.

CHAPTER THREE

INFORMAL INSTITUTIONS: CULTURE, RELIGION AND LANGUAGES

LEARNING OBJECTIVES

After studying this chapter, you should be able to

1 Discuss how cultures systematically differ from each other

2 Explain how language competences shape intercultural interactions

3 Explain how religions shape cultures

4 Explain why 'acting ethically' is sometimes very challenging in international business

5 Participate in leading debates on variations in cultures

6 Draw implications for action

OPENING CASE

Party invitations in Saudi Arabia and in China

The French engineering giant ALSTOM is building infrastructure projects all over the world. As is typical for engineering and construction firms, ALSTOM sends its engineers out, often on short-term expatriate assignments for a few months. Their construction projects are typically in remote locations far away from the major urban hubs, where the engineers have to work with a local workforce and live in a local community. They thus have to learn to adapt – quickly. For example, they may be invited to a party, and be expected to actively participate. A Swiss ALSTOM engineer recalls his experiences from Saudi Arabia:

'Once, there was a farewell for someone from the building site. On this occasion, there was a little celebration. We were told, at midday, after work, there would be a party. We waited and were wondering what would happen, where they would do it, and if they would bring something. There were neither chairs nor tables. Around 2 pm, they came with huge aluminium tablets, the size of a wagon wheel, filled up with rice, and in the middle a huge piece of mutton, grilled mutton. Finally, three or four of these tablets were standing on the floor of the workshop. They just put them on the floor! Of course we had cleaned up before. They came dressed in their celebratory dresses, and we expected some sort of ceremony. But they just sat down on the floor in their white gowns, around the tablets, and started eating.

The [Swiss] colleague who was with me was vegetarian. He said, 'Listen, I won't squat on the floor like that, and I won't eat anything either'. Everyone had a piece of mutton in his hand – it was incredible. One would hold the mutton, and another pulled out a chunk and passed it to me: 'here, mutton, that's good, you must eat'. We had no plates or anything. Everyone grabbed into the bowl, and scooped out a handful of rice. And now, my mate said 'I won't squat on the floor like that', and I say, 'come on, let's just sit down, you don't have to eat mutton, but you can at least do as if you are'.

They were very happy that we were there, and that they could invite us for this meal. It was important to them that we would participate. We had known these people from work, but still, initially the atmosphere was a bit uncomfortable. We didn't know how to behave. But then, after we sat down, and meat was passed around, it got really interesting. We got talking, and relaxed. My mate also sat down and afterwards he said he enjoyed it very much. The English vocabulary of those people was quite limited, so we had to talk 'with hands and feet'. Even so, we have been chatting about work, and what kind of rice this was, and what was in this rice. It was typical Saudi rice with raisins and the taste was quite fantastic. We couldn't talk much, the language barrier was just there, but then we picked up a few bits of Arabic, and the next morning we could say 'Good morning' in Arabic. Every day a word more, they had immense joy hearing us speak Arabic.'

No alcohol was served at this party, as you would expect in a Muslim society. Yet this was quite different from the experiences of an Italian engineer who was posted by ALSTOM to China. He was an experienced serial expatriate when he arrived in Foshan, a smaller city in China (1.1 million inhabitants), where he and his team settled down in a local hotel for a couple of weeks. But work is not separate from the rest of life in China:

'In China, we knew to party – the staff of the Chinese [JV partner] company, we the ALSTOM people and all of us together. Parties didn't happen in a regular pattern, but when a party was announced, everyone dressed up, queued at the buffet, and toasted with their glasses.

After dinner came the inevitable: karaoke, or as they call it KTV. We Europeans politely said 'no thanks', with one very talented exception. Among the Chinese, however, a group dynamic developed, there was no avoiding: everyone had to accept the microphone at least once. Not even the bosses at the top of the hierarchy could have an exception. I remember how we often had to endure with tightly closed ears three or four horrible performances in a row before a more talented singer took the mic.

.... At the banquets, a lot of alcohol came on the table. One morning, I knew that this must have been the case the previous evening. How my colleagues got me back to the hotel, I do not recall. When I met the same Chinese people who also were at the party on the construction site, I was showered with congratulations. 'You are our hero.' Apparently, I must have gone to the highest boss, and had challenged him to 'ganbei'. Ganbei is a popular game where people challenge each other to drink a glass empty, and those who didn't join were considered ill-mannered. I stood there and didn't know what to think of these compliments. Was it the fact that I had the courage to do that, or did they have an especially good time with their boss that evening?'

Food is a central part of both Italian and Chinese culture. In fact, both love noodles, which reportedly were brought by Marco Polo from China to Italy in the 13th century. Yet there are also differences that can be quite challenging, which the expatriate describes with typical Italian flair:

'The menus of the Chinese cuisine would certainly allow eating a different dish every day for months. That's because there is an incredible diversity in preparation methods and sauces in Chinese cooking. Moreover, it seems that Chinese people eat everything that moves, or has once moved: cockroaches, dogs, cats, monkeys, rats, snakes.

I have my own experience with snakes. That was probably the biggest surprise event for me. It started with a bet that I had with the deputy director, a young Chinese man. Our deal was that both of us would invite the other to a local meal, and the other had to eat at least one bite. The snakes were still alive when I had to tell the cook my preference, and we could watch the chosen animal being prepared. I did manage to swallow a bit of the fried dish, but the sight of the cooked dish already deterred me from trying. The next week we had our revenge. In an international restaurant I ordered a rare steak, well seasoned but without sauce – just the way I like it. After one bite, my Chinese colleague asked me to relieve him of the plate. I can still see his desperate eyes, and hear him saying 'I am sorry, but I cannot eat this'.

Sources: (1) N. Felix, 2007, *Dann hat man es gewusst, und dann war gut*, p. 29–37 (p. 30); (2) L. Etter, 2007, *Geröstet nicht geröstet*, p. 98–104 (p. 99–100 & 103–104), both in; (3) M. Spisak & H. Stalder, eds: *In der Fremde*, Bern: Haupt. Translated by Klaus Meyer.

Sharing food with new friends from afar can be one of the most enjoyable aspects of international business, or in fact of studying with international classmates. Yet even in a simple setting like a party invitation, lots of cross-cultural misunderstandings can happen. At a party, such communication problems can usually be quickly sorted out. Businesses, however, face far more complex cross-cultural settings, for example in negotiations, in managing cross-cultural teams, or in hiring foreign employees. How can companies know what the rules are if they are not even written down? More fundamentally, what informal institutions govern individual and firm behaviour in different countries?

Following Chapter 2, this chapter continues our coverage on the institution-based view by exploring informal institutions, rules that are not formalized but exist in for example norms, values and ethics. Of the two propositions in the institution-based view, the first proposition – managers and firms rationally pursue their interests within a given institutional framework – deals with both formal and informal institutions. The second proposition – in situations where formal institutions are unclear or fail, informal institutions play a larger role in reducing uncertainty – is more important and relevant in this chapter. When formal institutions are not securing effective functioning of the economy, then informal institutions may substitute them,

informal institutions
Rules that are not formalized but exist in for example norms, values and ethics.

or set up competing systems of economic order.[1] As shown in the Opening Case, this chapter is more than about how to present business cards correctly and wine and dine differently. Informal institutions influence individuals' behaviour in ways that they themselves may not even be aware of. Understanding the often unwritten rules that guide your business partners can make or break your business activities abroad.

Recall from Chapter 2 that formal institutions clearly specify the dos and don'ts. Informal institutions, by definition, are more elusive. Since they are not written down in law, their enforcement is also informal. Yet they are no less important, especially to businesspeople operating abroad (Chapter 16), and when marketing to consumers in different cultures (Chapter 17).[2] Here we are going to first discuss culture and how to compare it across countries, and then we focus on language as a feature of culture, and religion as a source of culture. We then discuss how cultural differences can lead to ethical conflicts. The debates section explores the impact of cultural variations not just among nations, but also between groups in the same country.

CULTURES

LEARNING OBJECTIVE

1 Discuss how cultures systematically differ from each other

Where do informal institutions come from? They are socially transmitted within societies, and are part of the heritage that we call culture. They tell individuals in a society what behaviours are considered right and proper, and what would be unacceptable. For instance, a person considered rude by his or her peers may not be invited to the next party, or to the next business deal.

Culture is probably the most frequently discussed aspect of informal institutions. What is culture? Culture is everywhere, though we notice it especially when we are in unfamiliar territory: people create different arts and architecture, admire different sorts of heroes, eat different foods and follow different sports (see photo). All of this is culture. Yet it is only the visible surface of culture, also known as artefacts of culture. For example, postcards in tourist destinations depict some of these artefacts; in fact picture postcards themselves are artefacts of culture. Beneath these artefacts, however, are differences in the shared values, norms and assumptions in a society, which are much less visible. In other words, culture is embedded in daily routines, and some aspects are encoded in language. These invisible differences make up the essence of culture, and create major challenges for international business.

artefacts of culture
Physical objects that represent the visible surface of culture.

The concept of culture is complex, and scholars use a variety of definitions to describe the phenomenon. For example, anthropologist Victor Barnouw defined culture as:

'a way of life of a group of people, the configuration of all the more or less stereotyped patterns of learned behaviour, which are handed down from one generation to the next through means of language and imitation'.[3]

culture
The collective programming of the mind that distinguishes the members of one group or category of people from another.

Many management scholars prefer more specific definitions, such as the one proposed by Geert Hofstede, a Dutch management professor:

'Culture is a collective phenomenon that is shared with people who live or lived within the same social environment, which is where it was learned. It is the collective programming of the mind which distinguishes the members of one group or category of people from another.'[4]

Culture thus is shared in a group, connecting members of the group with each other, and with their history. Note that although it is customary to talk about the American culture or Brazilian culture, there is no strict one-to-one correspondence between cultures and nation-states. Many subcultures exist within countries, even in Europe, notably in Belgium, Russia, Switzerland and the UK. In this chapter, we

What do tourist postcards tell us about culture?

focus on nation states as the relevant group; other groups are discussed in Debates and Extensions.

Each one of us is a walking encyclopedia of our own culture; most travellers have some anecdotes to tell about cross-cultural experiences or misunderstandings. Sometimes it can be frustrating to feel bombarded with a seemingly random collection of the numerous informal 'rules of the game': do this in Muslim countries, don't do that in Catholic countries, and so on. These are all interesting stories and features, but let us not forget that we are more interested in the overall picture. The point about seeing the overall picture is to understand how cultures are *systematically* different. This section outlines two approaches to systematically understand cultural differences: (1) cultural clusters and (2) dimensions of culture.

Cultural clusters

A basic approach to illustrating culture is to group countries that share similar cultures together as one cluster. There are three influential sets of clusters; Table 3.1 illustrates them side-by-side. Viewing them together can allow us to see their similarities and differences.

cluster
Countries that share similar cultures together.

Table 3.1 Cultural clusters

Ronen and Shenkar clusters[1]	GLOBE clusters[2]	Huntington civilizations
Anglo	Anglo	Western
Nordic	Nordic Europe	Western
Germanic	Germanic Europe	Western
Latin Europe	Latin Europe	Western
East Europe	Eastern Europe	Slavic-Orthodox
Arab	Middle East	Islamic
Near East[3]	–	–
Africa	Sub-Sahara Africa	African
Latin America	Latin America	Latin American
Far East[4]	Southern Asia	Hindu
Confucian	Confucian Asia	Confucian (Sinic)
Confucian	Confucian Asia	Japanese

Notes: [1] Ronen and Shenkar 2013 classified 11 clusters covering 70 countries; [2] GLOBE includes ten clusters, covering 62 countries; [3] Near Eastern includes Turkey and Greece; [4] Far East includes countries of Southeast Asia along with India, Iran, Jamaica, Pakistan and Zimbabwe.

Sources: (1) R. House, P. Hanges, M. Javidan, P. Dorfman & V. Gupta eds, 2004, *Culture, Leadership, and Organizations: The GLOBE Study of 62 Societies*, Thousand Oaks, CA: Sage; (2) S. Huntington, 1996, *The Clash of Civilizations and the Remaking of World Order*, New York: Simon & Schuster; (3) S. Ronen & O. Shenkar, 2013, Mapping world cultures: Cluster formation, sources and implications, *JIBS*, 44(9): 867–897.

The first set is provided by management professors Simcha Ronen and Oded Shenkar.[5] Using empirical techniques that integrate many characteristics, they obtained 11 clusters: (1) Anglo, (2) Nordic, (3) Germanic, (4) Latin Europe, (5) East Europe, (6) Latin America, (7) Near East, (8) Arab, (9) Far East, (10) Confucian and (11) Africa. The second set of clusters is called the GLOBE clusters, named after the Global Leadership and Organizational Behavior Effectiveness project led by management professor Robert House.[6] The GLOBE project identifies ten clusters using data from their own very large survey of business leaders; the results closely resemble those of the Ronen and Shenkar clusters, though their labels and country coverage vary slightly.

The third set of clusters is the Huntington civilizations, popularized by political scientist Samuel Huntington. A civilization is 'the highest cultural grouping of people and the broadest level of cultural identity people have'.[7] Huntington divides the world into eight civilizations: (1) African, (2) Confucian (Sinic), (3) Hindu, (4) Islamic, (5) Japanese, (6) Latin American, (7) Slavic-Orthodox and (8) Western. Although this classification shares a number of similarities with the Ronen and Shenkar and GLOBE clusters, Huntington's Western civilization is a very broad cluster that aggregates the Anglo, Germanic, Latin Europe and Nordic clusters. This usage of the term Western culture (or 'civilization'), which aggregates Europe with North America, Australia and New Zealand, reflects a common way of thinking in the USA. However, it is problematic, and explains why Americans are often surprised to discover that Europeans (or even Canadians) are not just like them.

civilization
The highest cultural grouping of people and the broadest level of cultural identity people have.

Western culture
An aggregate term for European, North American, Australian and New Zealand cultures.

Culture dimensions

Although clustering of countries can be very helpful, it is a very crude tool. The cluster approach has relatively little to offer regarding differences between countries *within* one cluster. For example, what are the differences between Italy and Spain, both of which belong to the same Latin Europe cluster? By focusing on multiple dimensions of cultural differences both within and across clusters, the dimension approaches provide a more fine-grained picture. While there are several competing frameworks,[8] the work of Geert Hofstede is most widely used[9] and thus is our main focus. He identified five dimensions by which cultural norms vary across countries (Table 3.2). We add to this the high low context dimension introduced later.

First, power distance is the extent to which less powerful members within a society expect and accept that power is distributed unequally. The appreciation of hierarchy is often reflected in the use of titles. For instance, in the USA, subordinates often address their bosses on a first-name basis, which indicates a relatively low power distance. While this boss, Mary or Joe, still has the power to fire you, the distance appears to be shorter than if you have to address this person more formally as Doctor X, Professor Y or Manager Z. Another indication of power distance is the practice of addressing people with the formal pronoun 'sie' in German, 'vous' in French and 'usted' in Spanish, which do not have an exact equivalent in modern English. High power distance tends to be associated with high income inequality: in Brazil, the richest 10% of the population earn approximately 50% of the national income, and most people accept this as 'the way it is'. In low power distance Sweden, the richest 10% only get 22% of the national income.[10]

These cultural differences are reflected in business practice. For instance, managers in high power distance countries such as France and Italy have a greater penchant for centralized authority.[11] Solicitation of subordinate feedback and participation is a daily routine in low power distance Nordic countries, but it is often regarded as a sign of weak leadership in high power distance countries such as China, Egypt, Russia and Turkey.[12]

Second, individualism refers to the perspective that the identity of an individual is fundamentally his or her own, whereas collectivism refers to the idea that the identity of an individual is primarily based on the identity of his or her collective group (such as family, village or company). In individualist societies (led by the USA), ties between individuals are relatively loose, and individual achievement and freedom are highly valued. In contrast, in collectivist societies (such as many countries in Africa, Asia and Latin America), ties between individuals are relatively close, and collective accomplishments are often sought after. We will return to this important dimension in the Debates and Extensions section.

Third, the masculinity versus femininity dimension refers to the relative importance of values traditionally held by men and women. Masculine societies favour leaders that are assertive, decisive and 'aggressive' (only in masculine societies does this word carry a positive connotation), along with focus on career progression and material rewards. Such values are commonly associated with traditionally male professions such as politicians, soldiers and investment bankers. Feminine values include compassion, relationships, care for others and job satisfaction – or more generally *quality of life*.[13] The stylized manager in feminine societies thus is 'less visible, intuitive rather than decisive, and accustomed to building consensus'.[14] These values are found in professions traditionally more associated with women, such as teaching and nursing, and they also more likely to support social and environmental responsibility. Highly masculine societies (led by Japan) typically maintain a sharp role differentiation along gender lines, with most leadership positions taken by men.

power distance
The extent to which less powerful members within a country expect and accept that power is distributed unequally.

individualism
The perspective that the identity of an individual is fundamentally his or her own.

collectivism
The idea that the identity of an individual is primarily based on the identity of his or her collective group.

masculinity
Values traditionally associated with male role, such as assertive, decisive and aggressive.

femininity
Values traditionally associated with female role, such as compassion, care and quality of life.

Table 3.2   Hofstede's dimensions of culture[1]

	1. Power distance	2. Individualism	3. Masculinity	4. Uncertainty avoidance	5. Long-term orientation
1	Malaysia (104)	USA (91)	Japan (95)	Greece (112)	China (118)
2	Guatemala (95)	Australia (90)	Austria (79)	Portugal (104)	Hong Kong (96)
3	Panama (95)	UK (89)	Venezuela (73)	Guatemala (101)	Taiwan (87)
4	Philippines (94)	Canada (80)	Italy (70)	Uruguay (100)	Japan (80)
5	Mexico (81)	Netherlands (80)	Switzerland (70)	Belgium (94)	South Korea (75)
6	Venezuela (81)	New Zealand (79)	Mexico (69)	El Salvador (94)	Brazil (65)
7	Arab countries (80)	Italy (76)	Ireland (68)	Japan (92)	India (61)
8	Ecuador (78)	Belgium (75)	Jamaica (68)	Yugoslavia (88)	Thailand (56)
9	Indonesia (78)	Denmark (74)	UK (66)	Peru (87)	Singapore (48)
10	India (77)	Sweden (71)	Germany (66)	France (86)	Netherlands (44)
11	West Africa (77)	France (71)	Philippines (64)	Chile (86)	Bangladesh (40)
12	Yugoslavia (76)	Ireland (70)	Colombia (64)	Spain (86)	Sweden (33)
13	Singapore (74)	Norway (69)	South Africa (63)	Costa Rica (86)	Poland (32)
14	Brazil (69)	Switzerland (68)	Ecuador (63)	Panama (86)	Germany (31)
15	France (68)	Germany (67)	USA (62)	Argentina (86)	Australia (31)
16	Hong Kong (68)	South Africa (65)	Australia (61)	Turkey (85)	New Zealand (30)
17	Colombia (67)	Finland (63)	New Zealand (58)	South Korea (85)	USA (29)
18	El Salvador (66)	Austria (55)	Greece (57)	Mexico (82)	UK (25)
19	Turkey (66)	Israel (54)	Hong Kong (57)	Israel (81)	Zimbabwe (25)
20	Belgium (65)	Spain (51)	Argentina (56)	Colombia (80)	Canada (23)
21	East Africa (64)	India (48)	India (56)	Venezuela (76)	Philippines (19)
22	Peru (64)	Japan (46)	Belgium (54)	Brazil (76)	Nigeria (16)
23	Thailand (64)	Argentina (46)	Arab countries (53)	Italy (75)	Pakistan (0)
24	Chile (63)	Iran (41)	Canada (52)	Pakistan (70)	
25	Portugal (63)	Jamaica (39)	Malaysia (50)	Austria (70)	
26	Uruguay (61)	Brazil (38)	Pakistan (50)	Taiwan (69)	
27	Greece (60)	Arab countries (38)	Brazil (49)	Arab countries (68)	
28	South Korea (60)	Turkey (37)	Singapore (48)	Ecuador (67)	
29	Iran (58)	Uruguay (36)	Israel (47)	Germany (65)	
30	Taiwan (58)	Greece (35)	Indonesia (46)	Thailand (64)	
31	Spain (57)	Philippines (32)	West Africa (46)	Iran (59)	

	1. Power distance	2. Individualism	3. Masculinity	4. Uncertainty avoidance	5. Long-term orientation
32	Pakistan (55)	Mexico (30)	Turkey (45)	Finland (59)	
33	Japan (54)	East Africa (27)	Taiwan (45)	Switzerland (58)	
34	Italy (50)	Yugoslavia (27)	Panama (44)	West Africa (54)	
35	Argentina (49)	Puerto Rico (27)	Iran (43)	Netherlands (53)	
36	South Africa (49)	Malaysia (26)	France (43)	East Africa (52)	
37	Jamaica (45)	Hong Kong (25)	Spain (42)	Australia (51)	
38	USA (40)	Chile (23)	Peru (42)	Norway (50)	
39	Canada (39)	West Africa (20)	East Africa (41)	South Africa (49)	
40	Netherlands (38)	Singapore (20)	El Salvador (40)	New Zealand (49)	
41	Australia (36)	Thailand (20)	South Korea (39)	Indonesia (48)	
42	Cost Rica (35)	El Salvador (19)	Uruguay (38)	Canada (48)	
43	Germany (35)	South Korea (18)	Guatemala (37)	USA (46)	
44	UK (35)	Taiwan (17)	Thailand (34)	Philippines (44)	
45	Switzerland (34)	Peru (16)	Portugal (31)	India (40)	
46	Finland (33)	Costa Rica (15)	Chile (28)	Malaysia (36)	
47	Norway (31)	Pakistan (14)	Finland (26)	UK (35)	
48	Sweden (31)	Indonesia (14)	Yugoslavia (21)	Ireland (35)	
49	Ireland (28)	Colombia (13)	Costa Rica (21)	Hong Kong (29)	
50	New Zealand (22)	Venezuela (12)	Denmark (16)	Sweden (29)	
51	Denmark (18)	Panama (11)	Netherlands (14)	Denmark (23)	
52	Israel (13)	Ecuador (8)	Norway (8)	Jamaica (13)	
53	Austria (11)	Guatemala (6)	Sweden (8)	Singapore (8)	

Note: [1] When scores are the same, countries are tied according to their alphabetical order. Arab, East Africa, and West Africa are clusters of multiple countries. Germany and Yugoslavia refer to the former West Germany and the former Yugoslavia, respectively.

Source: G. Hofstede, 1997, *Cultures and Organizations: Software of the Mind* (pp. 25, 26, 53, 84, 113, 166), New York: McGraw-Hill. © Geert Hofstede B.V. Quoted with permission.

In contrast, in highly feminine societies (led by Sweden), women increasingly become politicians and soldiers, and men are entitled to, and actually take, paternity leave.[15]

In some masculine societies, it is considered good manners to show appreciation to women in ways that may be misunderstood in more feminine societies: for example, when a French manager was transferred to a US subsidiary and met his American secretary (a woman) for the first time, he greeted her with a kiss on the cheek – a practice appreciated as courteous in France. However, the secretary later filed a complaint for sexual harassment.[16] More seriously, *Mitsubishi Motors*, from world leader in masculinity Japan, encountered major problems when operating in the USA, where women not only account for a higher share of the labour force but

Why do women in Nordic countries find it easier to reconcile career and family?

expect to be promoted like their male colleagues. In 1998, its North American division paid $34 million to settle sexual harassment charges.

uncertainty avoidance
The extent to which members in different cultures accept ambiguous situations and tolerate uncertainty.

Fourth, uncertainty avoidance refers to the extent to which members in different cultures accept ambiguous situations and tolerate uncertainty. Members of high uncertainty avoidance cultures (led by Greece) place a premium on job security and retirement benefits. They also tend to resist change, which, by definition, is uncertain. Low uncertainty avoidance cultures (led by Singapore) are characterized by a greater willingness to take risks and less resistance to change. For example, when the swine-flu arrived in Europe, a Danish manufacturer of safety clothing and equipment quickly reported to be sold out because of surging demand from Germany, while sales in Denmark were slow. A customer, a German insurance company, explained that Germans like to be prepared for all eventualities[17] – a symptom of higher uncertainty avoidance.

long-term orientation
A perspective that emphasizes perseverance and savings for future betterment.

Finally, long-term orientation emphasizes perseverance and focus on long-term objectives. China, which has the world's longest continuous written history of nearly 4000 years, and the highest contemporary savings rate, leads the pack in Hofstede's study. On the other hand, members of short-term orientation societies (led by Pakistan) prefer quick results and instant gratification. Unsurprisingly, saving rates are higher in long-term oriented East Asian countries than in short-term oriented USA.

In cultures with a long-term orientation, firms are more likely to nurture long-term ambitions. For instance, Japan's *Matsushita* has a 250-year plan, which was put together in the 1930s. While this is certainly an extreme case, Japanese and Korean firms tend to focus more on the long term.[18] In comparison, Anglo-American firms often focus on relatively short-term profits (often on a *quarterly* basis). Yet this varies within societies too. Young Chinese exhibit some very short-term oriented behaviours, while their government takes much longer perspectives in its foreign policy than their American counterpart.[19]

low-context culture
A culture in which communication is usually taken at face value without much reliance on unspoken context.

Of numerous other dimensions introduced by scholars, Edward Hall's high low context dimension is probably most useful (Figure 3.1).[20] Whereas Hofstede's dimensions are concerned with cultural norms, this sixth dimension concerns directness of communication. In low-context cultures (such as in North American and Western

Figure 3.1 High-context versus low-context cultures

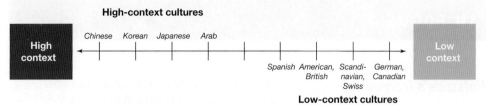

European countries), communication is usually taken at face value without much reliance on unspoken context. In other words, yes means yes. In contrast, in high-context cultures (such as Arab and Asian countries), communication relies a lot on the underlying unspoken context, which is as important as the words used. For example, 'yes' does not necessarily mean 'yes, I agree', it might mean 'yes, I hear you'.

Why are such communication differences important? This is because failure to understand the differences in interaction styles may lead to misunderstandings. For instance, in Japan, a high-context culture, negotiators prefer not to flatly say 'no' to a business request. They may say something like 'We will study it' and 'We will get back to you later'. Their negotiation partners are supposed to understand the context of these responses that lack enthusiasm and figure out that these responses essentially mean no (although the word 'no' is never mentioned). In high-context countries, initial rounds of negotiations are supposed to create the 'context' for mutual trust and friendship. Business activities thus involve frequent social activities, for example in Saudi Arabia and in China (see Opening Case). For individuals brought up in high-context cultures, decoding the context and acting accordingly are second nature. Straightforward communication and confrontation, typical in low-context cultures, often baffle them. In contrast, people from low-context cultures like to 'get down to business' quickly, focus on the facts, and spell out what is agreed explicitly in letters of intent, standards of engagements or contracts. This approach, however, may miss (or miscommunicate) the more subtle ways of communicating in high context cultures.

high-context culture A culture in which communication relies a lot on the underlying unspoken context, which is as important as the words used.

Working with culture clusters and dimensions

The clusters and dimensions that we have introduced here provide an interesting starting point for interpreting cultural differences.[21] They provide insights into how interactions between members within different groups or nations vary. This helps businesspeople to interpret their counterparts when negotiating with a team from another culture, or to create a shared working culture when working with people from different cultures in a team (Chapter 16). However, it is important to note that Hofstede's dimensions in particular have attracted their share of criticisms (In Focus 3.1). They are a greatly simplified analytical tool for complex and evolving phenomena in the real world.[22] Variations of norms and values are often hard to observe, and thus require great sensitivity when dealing with people from other countries.

The first point to remember is that culture is about shared values within a society, and hence helps to explain how people from that culture interact with each other. Thus indices like Hofstede's may help you when you travel abroad and are surrounded by people from that – for you – foreign society. They may also help you when you receive a large group of visitors – a tourist group or a business delegation – and observe how they interact with each other. The Hofstede dimensions are much less helpful when it comes to dealing with individual visitors from another culture.

IN FOCUS 3.1

Limitations of Hofstede's framework

Despite the influence of Hofstede's framework, it has attracted a number of criticisms.

- Cultural boundaries are not the same as national boundaries.

- Although Hofstede tried to remove some of his own cultural biases, the 'Dutch software' of his mind, as he acknowledged, 'will remain evident to the careful reader'. Being more familiar with European cultures, Hofstede might inevitably be more familiar with dimensions relevant to distinguishing European cultures. Thus crucial dimensions relevant to Asian or African cultures could be missed.

- Hofstede's research was based on surveys of more than 116 000 IBM employees working at 72 national subsidiaries during 1967–1973. This had both pros and cons. On the positive side, it not only took place in the same industry but also in the same company. Otherwise, it would have been difficult to attribute whether findings were due to differences in national cultures or industrial/organizational cultures. However, because of such a single firm/single industry design, it was possible that Hofstede's findings captured what was unique to that industry or to IBM. In other words, Hofstede's empirical data would reflect the interaction of the IBM organizational culture with local culture, rather than local culture as such. Thus, it was difficult to ascertain whether employees working for IBM were true representatives of their respective national cultures.

- Because the original data are now over 40 years old, critics contend that Hofstede's framework

fails to reflect aspects of cultural change, which have been quite substantive in those countries that have experienced major social or political upheaval, like transition economies. Moreover, the data for some countries are based on small samples or subsequent studies in other organizations, which makes them imprecise estimates at best.

Hofstede has responded to all four criticisms. First, he acknowledged that his focus on national culture was a matter of expediency, with all its trappings. Second, since the 1980s, Hofstede and colleagues relied on a questionnaire derived from cultural dimensions most relevant to the Chinese and then translated it from Chinese to multiple languages. That was how he uncovered the fifth dimension: long-term orientation (originally labelled 'Confucian dynamism'). In response to the third and fourth criticisms, Hofstede pointed out a large number of studies by other scholars using a variety of countries, industries and firms. Many results were supportive of his original findings, while others suggest that cultures indeed change over time. Overall, Hofstede's work is imperfect, but on balance, its values seem to outweigh its drawbacks.

Sources: (1) B. McSweeney, 2002, Hofstede's model of national cultural differences and their consequences, *HR*, 55: 89–118; (2) T. Fang, 2003, A critique of Hofstede's fifth national culture dimension, *IJCCR*, 3: 347–368; (3) M. Javidan, R. House, P. Dorfman, P. Hanges & M. Luque, 2006, Conceptualizing and measuring cultures and their consequences, *JIBS*, 37: 897–914; (4) P. Smith, 2006, When elephants fight, the grass gets trampled, *JIBS*, 37: 915–921; (5) G. Hofstede, 2007, Asian management in the 21st century, *Asia Pacific Journal of Management*, 24: 411–420; (6) R. Maseland & A. van Hoorn, 2009, Explaining the negative correlation between values and practices: A note on the Hofstede-GLOBE debate, *JIBS*, 40: 527–532; (7) T. Fang, 2010, Asian management research needs more self-confidence: Reflection on Hofstede 2007 and beyond, *APJM*, 27: 155–170

stereotype
A sets of simplistic often inaccurate generalizations about a group that allows others to categorize them.

When people talk about other groups of people they often use stereotypes, which refers to sets of simplistic often inaccurate generalizations about a group that allows others to categorize them. The Hofstede dimensions can be seen as a scientifically-refined stereotype. They offer an initial idea of what to expect of a group of strangers. Yet you have to be very careful how you use stereotypes. Bad managers simply treat people 'as if' their stereotypes hold true – and usually quickly make enemies. Successful businesspeople look beyond stereotypes to develop deeper understanding of each individual.[23] Remember that indices are based on averages obtained in large survey studies. Individual respondents will have answered questions regarding their values in different ways, and then the scholars calculated average scores that are the basis for the index. In other words, what the index tells is that, for example, British are *on average* more individualistic than Spaniards. Yet your British classmate might hold values below the British mean, and thus be less individualistic than your Spanish friend.

LANGUAGES

Among approximately 6000 languages in the world, Chinese is the world's largest in terms of the number of native speakers.[24] English is a distant second, followed closely by Hindi and Spanish. What is language and why does it matter? In the first instance, language is a system of shared meanings that enables people to effectively communicate. These meanings however are often complex and contextually embedded, and thus not easy to transfer from one language to another.[25] Therefore, two people who speak different mother tongues and lack a shared language in which both are fluent may face considerable language barriers. These barriers not only inhibit the exchange of information and knowledge, but they inhibit social interactions and thereby for example cohesion in work teams and the development of mutual trust.[26]

Translators can be very helpful. Yet communicating through a translator can lead to many misunderstandings. For example, many terms do not have an exact expression in other languages: you may find 'noodle soup' and 'dumplings' on restaurant menus in both Vienna, Austria and Hong Kong, China. And yet those dishes have next to nothing in common! This lack of direct translation is even more challenging for abstract terms such as 'fair' or 'considerate'.[27] For example, what does it mean if your boss describes your work as 'not bad'? In America, you probably just survived and better improve next time round. However if your boss is a traditional Chinese, an English gentlemen or a Dane from the rural area of Jutland, this is probably the highest praise you are ever going to get. A good translator will thus not transfer statements word-by-word but reinterpret the meaning of the statement.[28] However, even a good translator will only provide you with an approximation of the original meaning.

How can individuals and organizations handle language differences? Table 3.3 provides some suggestions. As individual, if you face a difficult situation, you might informally ask a colleague or friend for translation or summary. However, if you disrupt a meeting too often for that purpose you will not be appreciated. An organization committed to equal opportunities might consider translating all relevant documents, and hiring interpreters to offer simultaneous or sequential translation of everything that is said in a meeting. But this quickly proves highly impractical, as demonstrated by the experience of the European Union (see Chapter 8). It has all major documents translated into 24 official languages for 28 member countries, an exercise costing the EU €1.1 billion a year.[29] International managers often have to deal with two, or even three, languages on a daily basis.

Individuals adapt their habits to facilitate communication across language barriers, especially when communicating with others who are less fluent or less confident.[30] They may for example use email instead of the telephone because this gives them time to compose a message, and gives the reader more time to make sense of it. Also, they may adapt their language use. For example, in writing this book, we assume that many of the readers are non-native speakers of English. Therefore, we try to avoid colloquialisms and complex sentence structures.

LEARNING OBJECTIVE

2 Explain how language competences shape intercultural interactions

language
A system of shared meanings that enables people to effectively communicate.

language barriers
Communication barriers between people who speak different mother tongues and lack a shared language in which all are fluent.

Table 3.3 Handling language differences

	Individuals	Companies
Translation and interpretation	• Consult with a colleague or friend	• Translate all official documents • Hire interpreters for important meetings
Ad hoc remedies	• Build redundancy into communications • Adjust mode of communication	• Adopt a corporate language • Encourage non-native speakers to engage • Provide summaries of discussions, instructions and achievements
Support people	–	• Place multilingual people in key positions • Facilitate informal networks
Build capabilities	• Learn foreign languages	• Provide language training to employees and business partners

Sources: (1) A. Harzing, K. Köster & U. Magner, 2011, Babel in business, *JWB*, 46: 179–287; (2) H. Tenzer, M. Pudelko & A. Harzing, 2014, The impact of language barriers on trust formation in multinational teams, *JIBS*, 45:508–535; (3) S. Yamao & T. Sekiguchi, 2015, Employee commitment to corporate globalization, *JWB*, 50: 168–179.

corporate language
The language used for communications between entities of the same MNE in different countries.

lingua franca
The dominance of one language as a global business language.

In MNEs, such informal means are often insufficient because knowledge sharing is essential for modern MNEs (see Chapter 15). Therefore many MNE have adopted an (official or unofficial) corporate language (In Focus 3.2).[31] In European businesses, this is typically English. Even without formal adoption, English often emerges as the default language of international communication, thus becoming a global business language, known as the lingua franca as many people speak it as a second language. A corporate language clearly facilitates formal communication, but not everyone is fluent in English. People with modest knowledge of English may be OK with talking English informally, but get stressed if they have to speak English to their boss, or in a large group meeting.[32] How to handle that? Team leaders can help a lot, for example by creating awareness of language barriers, encouraging less confident people to speak, and by highlighting or summarizing key points of a discussion. For example, *ABB*'s former CEO Göran Lindahl famously claimed that his company's official language was 'poor English' to make the point that 'no one should be embarrassed to forward an idea because of a lack of perfection in English'.[33]

However, people who face lower language barriers can communicate more effectively both internally and externally and will hence be more effective in their work. Non-native speakers of English who can master English, such as the Taiwanese-born Hollywood director Ang Lee, Icelandic-born singer Björk and Colombian-born pop star Shakira (or in fact both authors of this book) have better job and career prospects. MNEs often pay close attention to language skills in recruitment, promotion and overseas postings. For example, some foreign investors in places such as China like to hire graduates from language programmes as they consider good communication more important than subject-specific skills to start a career. At the same time, they would prefer to send a Chinese speaker as expat to head their local operation. Even when there is no formal language policy, multilinguals can play an important

IN FOCUS 3.2

Multilinguists in multinational enterprises

In MNEs, not only top management but technical experts and middle managers have to regularly interact across language barriers when talking to people in other units abroad, or with foreign customers and suppliers. Although companies may have an official corporate language, staff in subsidiaries may speak a local language, and staff in headquarters may be more comfortable with yet another language, especially if the MNE is from a small country, such as Finland. Language competence in the corporate language is thus often a precondition for career advancement. Less obvious, however, is that knowledge of other languages can place individuals in critical bridging positions, to help communicate with each other.

For example, in *Kone Elevators*, a study found that multilinguals often become critical communication intermediaries, which enhances their personal network and their access to knowledge. For example, fluent English speakers in subsidiaries were more likely to be sent to corporate training courses, while headquarter staff with Spanish language competence were sought out by staff in subsidiaries in Spanish-speaking countries as their primary contact. Shared language thus became a powerful glue in informal networks that facilitated knowledge flows within the MNE.

The multilingual individuals who connected different people in different locations and networks acquired knowledge, reputation and influence well beyond their formal role, which substantially helped their career progression. More generally, language skills open new opportunities not only by handling specific situations more effectively, but by providing new insights and broader awareness about the company and its business partners.

Sources: (1) R. Marschan-Piekkari, D. Welch & L. Welch, 1999, In the shadow: the impact of language on structure, power and communication in the multinational, *IBR* 8: 421–440; (2) V. Peltokorpi & E. Vaara, 2012, Language policies and practices in wholly owned foreign subsidiaries, *JIBS*, 43(9): 808–833; (3) W. Barner-Rasmussen, M. Ehrnrooth, A. Koveshnikov & K. Mäkelä, 2014, Cultural and language skills as resources for boundary spanning within the MNC, *JIBS*, 45: 886–905.

role in informal networks that facilitate internal communication (In Focus 3.2). Thus, language capabilities can greatly enhance individuals' career prospects.[34]

In meetings, people tend to use the language they expect most members of the group to understand at least minimally, which in practice is often English. The dominance of English might give native speakers of English an initial advantage in international business. However, speaking only English has disadvantages. Learning a language helps to develop sensitivity for subtleties of other cultures – and for the mistakes non-natives make when speaking English, such as Chinese confusing 'he' and 'she', Russians dropping articles and Germans and Japanese moving verbs to the end of complex sentences. Thus some non-native speakers of English find it easier to understand and relate to other non-native speakers. Some may even resent Britons or Americans for speaking too fast and for using obscure idioms and slang.[35] Linguistic fluency can be a competitive advantage, but it needs to be handled carefully. Even basic skills in another foreign language can help to show respect to your host and to build trust.

In conclusion, try not to remain monolingual if you have international career ambitions. English is the norm in many places, and an additional language (in addition to your native tongue) can give you a critical edge. Thus you will be better off if you can pick up at least one language – in addition to English – during your university studies! Last but not least, languages will make your social life much more fun, as you can participate in more local events (see Opening Case).

RELIGIONS

LEARNING OBJECTIVE

3   Explain how religions shape cultures

Religion is a major manifestation of culture, and it is the source of some of the differences in norms and values that we discussed before. The leading religions are (1) Christianity (approximately 1.7 billion adherents), (2) Islam (1 billion), (3) Hinduism (750 million) and (4) Buddhism (350 million), see Figure 3.2. Of course, not everybody claiming to be an adherent actively practises a religion. For instance, some Christians may go to church only once a year – on Christmas. Because religious differences have led to numerous challenges, knowledge about religions is crucial even for non-religious managers. Religious beliefs and activities affect business through (1) religious festivals, (2) daily and weekly routines and (3) people's perceptions about their environment.

First, religious festivals are focal events of social life, and thus create direct and indirect opportunities for business – as well as periods when businesses and government offices are shut down. For example, in Christian countries, the Christmas season represents the peak season in shopping and consumption. In the USA, half of toys sold are done so in the month before Christmas. Since children in the USA consume half of the world's toys, this means 25% of world toy output is sold in one country in one month, thus creating severe production, distribution and coordination challenges. Thus for toy makers and stores, getting the timing of their product launches, marketing and logistics right is key to their success. But remember that Christmas is on December 25 in Western Europe, but on January 7 in the Eastern Orthodox churches, e.g. in Greece. Similar seasonal patterns of demand exist in conjunction with, for example, Diwali in India, Chinese New Year in East Asia, and Ramadan in Muslim countries.

Second, daily and weekly routines vary. The monotheistic religions (Christianity, Islam and Judaism) have a lot in common, yet they differ on which day of the week the faithful worship: Christians go to church on Sundays, while Muslims and Jews worship respectively on Fridays and Saturdays. Also, daily routines vary. For instance, faithful Muslims interrupt their activities five times a day at specific times for prayer. As an expatriate in Indonesia, you may experience that your driver stops the car in the middle of the traffic, takes out his prayer carpet and performs his prayer routine. Knowing this practice, a small adjustment of daily work schedules can minimize such disruptions.[36]

Third, religious beliefs also influence how people perceive themselves and what happens around them. For example, if people believe in a god that is watching over them and whom they will face on a 'judgement day', this may encourage them not to cheat other people.[37] Moreover, some beliefs attach symbolic value to certain objects or activities, which leads to rules on what the faithful are allowed to do, or not to do. Objects or activities considered holy deserve particular respect. For example, cows are holy in Hindu religion, and thus may not be disturbed (let alone be eaten). Other objects are considered taboo or dirty, and thus may not be touched or eaten. For example, Muslims are not supposed to eat pork. Managers and firms ignorant of religious taboos may end up with embarrassments. A US firm blundered in Saudi Arabia by sending a project proposal bound with an expensive pigskin leather cover hoping to impress the clients. The proposal was never read because Muslims avoid pig products.[38] Religiously sensitive managers and firms should be able to avoid such blunders.

In secular societies, societies where religion does not dominate public life, such concerns are not paramount. Yet religions have shaped cultures even where people are no longer aware of it, like businesses closing on Sundays in secular European societies. Moreover, some groups are very faithful, and your customer or your business partner may just be one of them. Thus it pays to be prepared and able to accommodate religious sensitivities. Many conflicts actually arise from

holy
An item or activity that is treated with particular respect by a religion.
taboo
An item of activity considered unclean by a religion.

secular societies
Societies where religions do not dominate public life.

Religions of the World: A Part of Culture

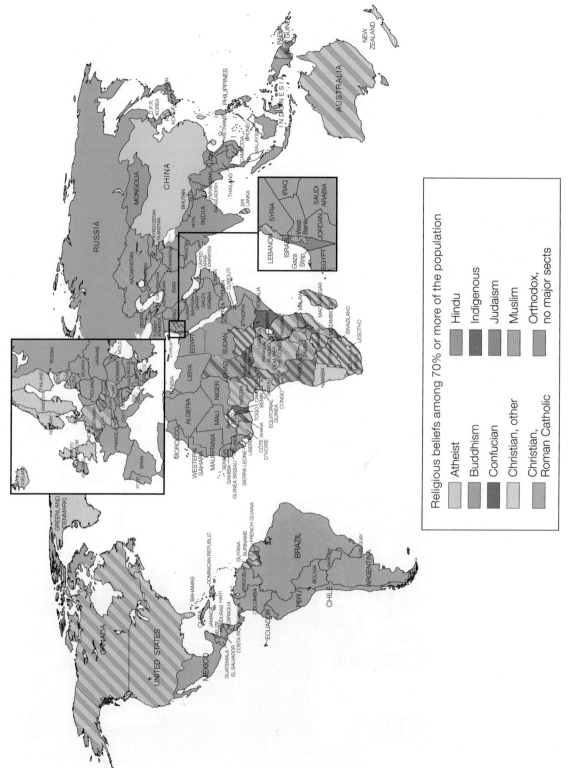

Religious beliefs among 70% or more of the population

- Atheist
- Buddhism
- Confucian
- Christian, other
- Christian, Roman Catholic
- Hindu
- Indigenous
- Judaism
- Muslim
- Orthodox, no major sects

Sources: *CIA – The World Factbook 2000.* Note that Confucianism, strictly speaking, is not a religion but a set of moral codes guiding interpersonal relationships.

discrepancies between the values held by secular societies and religious groups. Consider for example, the relationships between men and women: in secular societies non-discrimination is considered a basic human right (even enshrined in national constitutions). Yet former Irish president and human rights activist Mary Robinson argues that elsewhere religious traditions have been used by those in power to justify and entrench inequalities, including teachings and practices that give men power over female members of their families and societies.[39] Such tensions between religiously motivated differences in values can create a minefield for multinational enterprises.

Religious differences, more than any other differences, tend to raise emotions – and thus are challenging to handle for businesses. If you are used to a secular society, you may find it difficult to appreciate the intensity of feeling that some people attach to their religion. Yet showing respect for other religions and associated values will help you avoiding conflict and creating a basis for doing business.

ETHICS

LEARNING OBJECTIVE

4 Explain why 'acting ethically' is sometimes very challenging in international business

ethics
The principles, standards and norms of conduct governing individual and firm behaviour.

code of conduct
Written policies and standards for corporate conduct and ethics.

Ethics refers to the principles, standards and norms of conduct governing individual and firm behaviour.[40] Ethics are not only an important part of informal institutions but are also reflected in formal laws and regulations. To the extent that laws reflect a society's minimum standard of conduct, there is a substantial overlap between what is ethical and legal and between what is unethical and illegal. However, there is a grey area, because what is legal may be considered unethical by different groups. For example, US online retailer *Amazon* was accused in Europe of sub-standard labour practices, of paying sub-standard wages, of unfair bargaining tactics *vis-à-vis* book publishers and of using tax loopholes to pay virtually no corporation tax in Europe.[41] All these practices seemed consistent with formal institutions, yet were considered unethical by some groups of people, and received considerable media attention.

Challenged by exposure in the media, numerous firms have introduced codes of conduct – a set of guidelines for making ethical decisions (Chapter 10).[42] These guidelines often apply not only to employees, but to suppliers, franchisees and others using the brand name of the company, as we will discuss further in Chapter 10.

What do you think a company's code of conduct should say about workers in supplier firms overseas?

However, managing ethics overseas is challenging because what is ethical in one country may be unethical elsewhere.[43] For example, firing staff on short notice to secure profitability is a normal practice in countries such as the USA, yet it is unethical or even illegal in, for example, France and Germany. In some cases, firms face clear guidelines, or even regulatory restrictions, established in their home countries. On other issues, they have to make decisions 'on the ground' and communicate them to the relevant parties.

How should companies navigate this minefield? There are two schools of thought.[44] First, ethical relativism follows the cliché, 'When in Rome, do as the Romans do'. If women in Muslim countries are discriminated against, so what? Likewise, if industry rivals in China can fix prices, who cares? Adapting those practices might be the quickest way to a local contract. Second, ethical imperialism refers to the absolute belief that 'There is only one set of ethics, and we have it'. Europeans and Americans have a reputation for expecting that their ethical values should be applied universally.[45] For example, since sexual discrimination and price fixing are wrong in Europe, they must be wrong everywhere else.

In practice, however, neither of these schools of thought is realistic. At the extreme, ethical relativism would get you in trouble with headquarters, whereas ethical imperialism may cause resentment and backlash among locals. As we will discuss in Chapter 10, many companies choose a blended approach, with three elements. First, respect for human dignity and basic rights (such as those concerning health, safety and the need for education instead of working at a young age) should determine the absolute minimal ethical thresholds for *all* operations around the world.

Second, respect for local traditions suggests cultural sensitivity. If gifts are banned, foreign firms can forget about doing business in China and Japan, where gift giving is part of the business norm. Although hiring employees' children and relatives instead of more qualified applicants is illegal according to European equal opportunity laws, Indian companies routinely practise such nepotism, which would strengthen employee loyalty. What should European companies setting up subsidiaries in India do?

Let us consider corruption, defined as the abuse of public power for private benefits, usually in the form of bribery (in cash or in kind).[46] It varies greatly across countries (see Table 3.4). In some places, it appears deeply embedded in the culture, while elsewhere it is considered the worst sin a business person might commit. Corruption distorts the basis for competition, thus causing misallocation of resources, slowing

ethical relativism
A perspective that suggests that all ethical standards are relative.

ethical imperialism
The absolute belief that 'there is only one set of Ethics (with the capital E), and we have it'.

corruption
The abuse of public power for private benefits, usually in the form of bribery.

Table 3.4 The least and the most corrupt

	TI Index	Countries
Most transparent	8.9. to 9.1	Denmark, New Zealand, Finland, Sweden
	8.5 to 8.6	Norway, Singapore, Switzerland
	8.1 to 8.3	Netherlands, Australia, Canada
	7.8 to 8.0	Luxemburg, Iceland, Germany
	7.5 to 7.6	Barbados, Belgium, Hong Kong, UK
Most corrupt	2.0	Eritrea, Venezuela
	1.9	Chad, Equatorial Guinea, Guinea-Bissau, Haiti
	1.6 to 1.8	Yemen, Syria, Turkmenistan, Uzbekistan, Iraq
	1.4 to 1.5	Libya, South Sudan
	1.1 to 0.8	Afghanistan, North Korea, Somalia, Sudan

Note: Index: 10 = highly transparent to 0 = highly corrupt, index values refer to 2013.

Source: Transparency International, *Global Corruption Report 2014*.

IN FOCUS 3.3

The OECD anti-corruption convention

How does corruption affect foreign investors? Bribery is a criminal offence in most countries, yet prosecution is inconsistent in many countries, as it is often difficult to prove, or the relevant authorities do not really care. Foreign investors need to be particularly vigilant because catching a foreign briber can be a particular big scoop for an ambitious local police commissioner – be careful, your conversations may be taped. On the other hand, experienced foreign investors may find ways around this risk by letting local partners do the 'dirty work', and by moving staff out of the country quickly when it gets too hot. The latter approach however no longer works.

In 1997, the OECD agreed a Convention on Combating Bribery of Foreign Public Officials, which subsequently has been implemented into law in all 30 OECD countries (essentially all developed economies). Under this convention, states not only criminalize bribery, but prosecute MNEs and their employees at home for bribery committed abroad. The convention departs from the basic principle of international law that prosecution is the responsibility of the country where the crime has been committed. It supports a fairly new precept in international law known as nationality principle, which states that countries have some jurisdiction (but not unconditional) over their own citizens wherever they may be. In practice this can be difficult, because few countries are willing to extradite their own nationals to other countries (especially those perceived to be corrupt). OECD countries thus established laws with extra-territorial effect that should prevent their firms from acting corruptly abroad.

The convention has started biting: in the UK, the first penalty of £6.6 million under the Bribery Act was handed to construction firm *Mabey & Johnson* for paying bribes in Jamaica and Ghana, and for having broken the UN sanctions of Iraq. In contrast, Britain's (and Europe's) largest defence contractor *BAE* was investigated for alleged bribes to Saudi princes, but the investigation was stopped in 2006 by intervention of Prime Minister Tony Blair because of the need to safeguard national and international security. Few companies have as powerful connections to get away with that, and the net is tightening – both on companies, and on politicians. Even *BAE* later had to pay a $400 million fine in the USA.

Sources: (1) S. Wei, 2000, How taxing is corruption on international investors? *RES*, 82: 1–11; (2) M. Habib & L. Zurawicki, 2002, Corruption and foreign direct investment (p. 295), *JIBS*, 33: 291–307; (3) *The Economist*, 2009, BAE Systems: See you in court, October 3; (4) *The Guardian*, 2010, BAE admits guilt over corrupt arms deals, February 5.

economic development and deterring foreign investors.[47] According to *Transparency International*, an anti-corruption non-governmental organization (NGO), the correlation between a high level of corruption and a low level of economic development is strong. In other words, corruption and poverty go together. On this issue, a broad consensus thus has evolved that MNEs should *not* 'when in Rome do as the Romans do'. Home countries thus try to prevent MNEs from being drawn into corrupt practices (In Focus 3.3), yet not always do business people face clear guidelines (see Closing Case).

Finally, respect for institutional context calls for a careful understanding of local institutions. Codes of conduct banning bribery are not very useful unless accompanied by guidelines for the scale and scope of appropriate gift giving and receiving. *The Economist* allows its journalists to accept any gift that can be consumed in a single day – a bottle of wine is acceptable, but a case of wine is not.[48] US multinational, *Texas Instruments* includes in its guidelines to employees in China the following two quick tests:[49]

- Reciprocity Test. Ask this question: based on your knowledge of TI's policy and culture, would TI under similar circumstances allow you to provide a

TI business partner a gift of an equivalent nature? If the answer is no, then politely refuse the offer.

- Raise Eyebrow Test. Ask those questions: Would you 'raise eyebrows' or feel uncomfortable in giving or receiving the gift in the presence of others in a work area? Would you feel comfortable in openly displaying the gift you are offering or receiving? Would you feel embarrassed if it were seen by other TI business partners or by your colleagues/supervisor?

DEBATES AND EXTENSIONS

Informal institutions such as culture, ethics and norms provoke debates that often get emotional. In this section, we introduce three: (1) social groups that share a culture, (2) limits to generalizations on human behaviours, and (3) in-groups versus out-groups in collectivist societies.

Units of culture: social groups

In this chapter, we have focused on national culture, which is the most apparent variation that businesses experience in the global economy. As indicated earlier, this is a simplification for two reasons. First, in most countries, many subcultures co-exist.[50] For example, many Scots, Catalans and Bavarians identify themselves with their regional culture rather than with British, Spanish or German culture. In reverse, non-Bavarian Germans can get quite annoyed when 'German festivals' abroad portray Germany with Bavarian stereotypes such as people wearing *lederhosen* and eating pork knuckle and *sauerkraut*. Moreover, groups such as ethnic minorities, religious groups or social strata may develop their own cultures. Likewise, culture in urban centres often varies from rural areas, with rural people holding more conservative and religious values, as evident for example in Turkey (Chapter 2, Opening Case). Thus, when we talk about national cultures, we are really talking about averages, and about informal rules that apply when members of different subgroups interact with each other.

Second, cultures evolve and change. Although such change may be slow, few would dispute that cultures change at least moderately from one generation to the next. Hence, the cultural values held by people of different generations may be quite different – think of your own grandparents. Some people predict this cultural change to converge towards 'modern' Western values such as individualism and consumerism.[51] Worldwide spread of Western products and brands such as *McDonalds*, *Coca-Cola* and Hollywood movies, seems to support this view. Likewise, the rise of the internet, and the ascendance of English as a commercial language suggest some cultural convergence – at least among the urban youth. For example, relative to the average citizens, younger Chinese, Georgian, Japanese and Russian managers are becoming more individualist and less collectivist than the older generation.[52]

However, the popularity of Western brands around the world does not imply a 'Westernization of values'. For example, the increasing popularity of Asian foods and games in Europe does not necessarily mean that Europeans are converging towards 'Asian values'. In fact, a major study found more evidence of divergence than of convergence of cultures.[53] Thus, we will continue to see inter-generational differences in culture, as well as cross-national ones.

Third, within a firm, one may find a specific organizational culture that is shared by people working in the organization, and perhaps by customers and suppliers as well.[54] Such shared values and beliefs are often inspired by the founders of a firm,

LEARNING OBJECTIVE

5 Participate in leading debates on variations in cultures

organizational culture
Culture shared by people working in the organization.

Does the popularity of Asian food in Europe suggest a convergence of cultures?

and they help create a common sense of purpose as well as rules for interacting within the firm. For example, the founder of the Indian *Tata* group, Jamseti Tata, established in the late 1800s his 'creed' as the foundation of a socially responsible business; and his creed to this day shapes how employees think about *Tata*, which in the 2000s encompasses European businesses like *Tetley Tea*, *Corus Steel* and *Jaguar Land Rover*.[55] An organizational culture can be shared within a company that transcends national boundaries, and facilitates interaction of individuals originating from different national cultures. Empirical studies suggest that in large MNEs, organizational culture is more important than national culture in explaining business unit performance.[56]

Limits to generalization

Cultural differences, such as those discussed in this chapter, also have profound implications for the social sciences and the transferability of management practices. A major debate has erupted about the general validity of many key insights and theories in psychology and other social sciences. The reason? Most empirical studies underlying key ideas in psychology have been conducted with people that are Western, educated, industrialized, rich and democratic (WEIRD). In fact, most studies in experimental psychology and economics have been conducted with American undergraduate students.

The question thus is, how much do we really know about human behaviours if the bulk of evidence is from one particular kind of people? It might not matter much if these WEIRD people were representative of the people of the world. Yet an influential article by psychologists of the University of British Columbia recently argued that WEIRD people are highly non-representative.[57] On many key motivations and behaviours Westerners are outliers in the world, and even among Westerners, Americans are outliers. Sociologist Seymour Lipset argued that among industrialized societies, Americans are most patriotic, litigious, philanthropic, church-going, optimistic and least class conscious. Such cultural idiosyncrasies explain at least in part why the USA score among the highest in the Western world in terms of crime rate, working hours, divorce rate, poverty and inequality, yet are least supportive of government interventions.[58] Certainly on some aspects of human behaviours we are similar across the globe, such as perceptions of colour and emotional expressions.[59] However, the questions of what knowledge does or does not hold generally true for all human beings hangs over a lots our social science theories.

This debate has profound implications for management practice. Geert Hofstede once argued that *'there are no such things as universal management theories . . . not only practices but also the validity of theories may stop at national borders'*.[60] In fact, he pointed out, the term 'management' has different meanings in different languages, thus how can there be a universal theory if even the core concept of that theory cannot be generalized? Some management practices may be effective in a wide range of context, yet each cultural context has unique features that call for locally adapted practices. Successful international managers not only appreciate these global practices and local idiosyncrasies, but they are able to integrate such knowledge to develop practices that outperform competitors in a given context.[61]

Limits of collectivism[62]

A common stereotype is that players from collectivist societies (such as China) are more collaborative and trustworthy, and those from individualist societies (such as the USA) are more competitive and opportunistic.[63] However, this is not necessarily the case. Collectivists are more collaborative *only* when dealing with their own in-group members: individuals and firms regarded as part of their own collective. The flip side is that collectivists discriminate more harshly against out-group members – individuals and firms not regarded as part of 'us'.[64] It is quite easy for those not part of an in-group to wonder what happened to the collective nature of the so-called collective society. On the other hand, individualists, who believe that every person (firm) is on his or her (its) own, make less distinction between in-group and out-group. Therefore, while individualists may indeed act more opportunistically than collectivists when dealing with in-group members (this fits the stereotype), collectivists may be *more* opportunistic when dealing with out-group members. This can be seen at the street level. In China, drivers do not yield to pedestrians and even press the horn when pedestrians cross the street in front of their cars. In Europe, drivers normally yield to pedestrians to let them cross the street first. To drivers, pedestrians by definition are out-group members. The same Chinese drivers who are rude to pedestrians likely show impeccable courtesy when dealing with their in-group members. Thus, on balance, the average Chinese is not inherently more trustworthy than the average American. The Chinese motto regarding out-group members (including other Chinese) is: 'Watch out for strangers. They will screw you!'[65]

This helps explain why the USA, the leading individualist country, is among societies with a higher level of spontaneous trust, whereas there is greater interpersonal and inter-firm *distrust* in the large society in China.[66] This also explains why it is so important to establish *guanxi* (relationship) for individuals and firms in China, otherwise life can be very challenging in a sea of strangers.

These cultural traits also impact on the growth of e-commerce. One study reported that although Britain and Hong Kong have comparable levels of per capita income, 24% of the internet users shopped online in Britain, whereas only 7% did so in Hong Kong.[67] Shopping online means having some trust in the out-group – the website to which credit card details are provided, and the anonymous 'system' that processes payment. Internet users in Hong Kong are more reluctant to do so. A professor in Hong Kong confirmed this when asking his MBA students about their use of the internet.[68] Only a couple of students had ever purchased anything online, though many had made travel reservations. They simply would not pre-pay, even when told about the online guarantee of the travel website, the travel providers (e.g. hotel) and even their credit card company. Such is the power of culture. In consequence, e-commerce took off in mainland China only after intermediaries such

in-group
Individuals and firms regarded as part of 'us'.
out-group
Individuals and firms not regarded as part of 'us'.

as *Alipay* had established themselves as trustworthy intermediaries for the handling of online payments.

This insight can help managers and firms to better deal with one another. Only through repeated social interactions can collectivists assess whether to accept new-comers as in-group members.[69] For example, Russians are said to do business only with people with whom they have become drunk together at least once.[70] If foreigners, who by definition are from an out-group, refuse to show any interest in joining the in-group, then it is fair to take advantage of them. For example, don't refuse a friendly cup of coffee from a Saudi businessman, it might be considered an affront. Most of us do not realize that 'Feel free to say no when offered food or drink' reflects the cultural underpinning of individualism, and people in collectivist societies do not necessarily view this as an option (also see Opening Case). Watch out for statements like 'it isn't really necessary' or 'do not be influenced by what our company did before'. These are often signals 'it is necessary' or 'you should recall what we did before, and reciprocate accordingly'. Such misunderstanding, in part, explains why many cross-culturally naïve Western managers and firms complain that they have been taken advantage of in collectivist societies. In reality, they are simply being treated as 'deserving' out-group members.

IMPLICATIONS FOR PRACTICE

LEARNING OBJECTIVE

6 Draw implications
   for action

cultural intelligence
An individual's ability to
understand and adjust to
new cultures.

A contribution of the institution-based view is to emphasize the importance of informal institutions for businesses around the world. How does this perspective answer our fundamental question: what determines the success and failure of firms around the globe? The institution-based view argues that firm performance is, at least in part, determined by the informal rules of the game.

For managers around the globe, this emphasis on informal institutions suggests three broad implications (Table 3.5). First, they need to develop cultural intelligence, defined as an individual's ability to understand and adjust to new cultures.[71] Nobody can become an expert (the chameleon in Table 3.6) in all cultures. However, a genuine interest in foreign cultures will open your eyes. Acquisition of cultural intelligence passes through three phases: (1) awareness, (2) knowledge and (3) skills.[72] *Awareness* refers to the recognition of both the pros and cons of your 'mental software' and the appreciation of people from other cultures. *Knowledge* refers to ability to identify the symbols, rituals and taboos in other cultures – also known as cross-cultural literacy. Although you may not share (or even may disagree with) their values, you will at least obtain a road map of the informal institutions governing their behaviour. Finally, *skills* are based on awareness and knowledge, plus good practice.

While skills can be taught, the most effective way to develop cultural intelligence is total immersion within a foreign culture. Even for gifted individuals, learning a new language and culture to function well at a managerial level will take several

Table 3.5   Implications for action: preparing for cultural differences

- Develop cultural intelligence in terms of awareness, knowledge and skills, and invest in learning foreign languages.

- Beware of subtle shifts in informal rules over time, and of inconsistencies between formal and informal rules.

- 'Respect cultural differences' is likely the most important rule.

Table 3.6 Five profiles of cultural intelligence

Profiles	Characteristics
The Local	A person who works well with people from similar backgrounds but does not work effectively with people from different cultural backgrounds.
The Analyst	A person who observes and learns from others and plans a strategy for interacting with people from different cultural backgrounds.
The Natural	A person who relies on intuition rather than on a systematic learning style when interacting with people from different cultural backgrounds.
The Mimic	A person who creates a comfort zone for people from different cultural backgrounds by adopting their general posture and communication style. This is not pure imitation, which may be regarded as mocking.
The Chameleon	A person who may be mistaken for a native of the foreign country. He/she may achieve results that natives cannot, due to his/her insider's skills and outsider's perspective. This is very rare.

Sources: (1) P.C. Earley & S. Ang, 2003, *Cultural Intelligence: Individual Interactions across Cultures*, Palo Alto, CA: Stanford University Press; (2) P.C. Earley & E. Mosakowski, 2004, Cultural intelligence, *HBR*, October: 139–146; (3) P.C. Earley & E. Mosakowski, 2004, Toward culture intelligence: Turning cultural differences into a workplace advantage, *AME*, 18 (3): 151–157.

months of study. Many employers do not give their managers that much time to learn before sending them abroad. Thus, many expat managers are inadequately prepared, and the costs for firms, individuals and families can be very high (see Chapter 16). This means that you, a student studying this book, are advised to further invest in your own career by picking up at least one foreign language (beyond English), joining an international student group such as *AIESEC*, spending a semester (or year) abroad, and reaching out to make some international friends. Such an investment during university studies will make you stand out among the crowd and propel your career to new heights.

Second, managers need to be aware of the prevailing norms and their changes. The norms guiding international business in the 2010s call for more cultural and ethnic sensitivity than, say, in the 1970s. This is not to suggest that every local norm needs to be followed. However, failing to understand and adapt to local ways may lead to unsatisfactory or disastrous results. At the same time, local norms are shifting. For example, as societies such as China become more affluent, they expect foreign businesses to pay them more respect, not only by aligning to their cultural norms, but by paying attention to their social and environmental concerns. A few years ago, certain practices may have been informal norms that certain laws are not rigorously enforced. Those same practices may now no longer be acceptable.[73] For example, some degree of corruption may have been tolerated in China, but a new government since 2013 decided to enforce the existing rules more stringently, thus changing what is or is not acceptable practice (also see Integrated Case *GSK*). The best managers expect norms to shift over time by constantly deciphering the changes in the informal rules of the game and by taking advantage of new opportunities.

Finally, in dealing with unfamiliar values, norms and practices, the single most important advice is the need to show respect. Most people are attached to the culture in which they grew up and they do not take kindly to being told, implicitly or explicitly, that they are wrong. Showing respect for your host's culture, particularly the local cuisine (which locals tend to be very proud of) and an openness to learn, will often go a long way towards establishing trust with those from other cultures and countries.

CHAPTER SUMMARY

1 Discuss how cultures systematically differ from each other

- The cluster approach groups similar cultures together.

- Hofstede and colleagues have identified five dimensions of cultural norms: (1) power distance, (2) individualism/collectivism, (3) masculinity/femininity, (4) uncertainty avoidance and (5) long-term orientation.

- The context dimension differentiates cultures based on the high- versus low-context dimension.

2 Explain how language competences shape intercultural interactions

- Language barriers inhibit effective communication and thereby business processes such as trust building and knowledge sharing.

- Individuals and team leaders can reduce language barriers by adapting how they communicate.

- Language skills are important for individuals engaged in international operations.

3 Explain how religions shape cultures

- Religions are an important source of variations in routines, norms and values.

- Religious symbols can create strong emotional reactions and sensitivities.

4 Explain why 'acting ethically' is sometimes very challenging in international business

- When managing ethics overseas, two schools of thought are ethical relativism and ethical imperialism.

- Three 'middle-of-the-road' principles help guide managers to make ethical decisions.

5 Participate in leading debates on variations in cultures

- These are (1) units of culture, (2) limits to generalization and (3) limits to collectivism.

6 Draw implications for action

- It is important to enhance cultural intelligence, leading to cross-cultural literacy.

- It is crucial to understand and adapt to changing norms.

- Respect for your hosts' culture will often get you a long way.

KEY TERMS

Artefacts of culture	Ethics	Low-context culture
Civilization	Femininity	Masculinity
Cluster	High-context culture	Organizational culture
Code of conduct	Holy	Out-group
Collectivism	Individualism	Power distance
Corporate language	Informal institutions	Secular societies
Corruption	In-group	Stereotype
Cultural intelligence	Language	Taboo
Culture	Language barriers	Uncertainty avoidance
Ethical imperialism	Lingua franca	Western culture
Ethical relativism	Long-term orientation	

CRITICAL DISCUSSION QUESTIONS

1 When you take an airline flight, the passenger sitting next to you tries to have a conversation with you. He or she asks, 'What do you do?' You would like to be nice, but don't want to give too much information about yourself (such as your name). How would you answer this question? A typical US manager may say: 'I am a marketing manager' – without mentioning the employer. A typical Japanese manager may say: 'I work for Honda.' Why are there such differences?

2 You meet a classmate who has just arrived from a distant country. What are the most important things you want to tell him or her about *your own* country's culture? Would that be big issues related to cultural values, or something simple like 'be careful of staring at people on the bus'.

3 Have a look at the postcards of Valencia (page 61). Do they represent the culture of Valencia as experienced by foreign tourists? Do you think local people of Valencia like to be associated with these images? How can local people and tourist communicate their understanding of Spanish culture?

4 Your new male colleague informs you that he cannot shake hands with female colleagues or clients because his religion forbids shaking hands (or any physical contact) with women. How do you react?

5 Based on Table 3.6, which best describes your cultural intelligence profile: a Local, Analyst, Natural, Mimic or Chameleon? Why?

6 Assume you work for a Norwegian company exporting a container of salmon to Azerbaijan or Haiti. The customs official informs you that there is a delay in clearing your container through customs, and it may last a month. However, if you are willing to pay an 'expediting fee' of €200, he will try to make it happen in one day. What are you going to do?

RECOMMENDED READINGS

N.A. Boyacigiller, R.A. Goodman & M.E. Philips, eds, 2003, *Crossing Cultures: Insights from the Master Teachers*, London: Routledge – a collection of teaching materials for practical learning about the challenges of cross-cultural management.

G. Hofstede, 1997, *Cultures and Organizations*, New York: McGraw-Hill – a classic book explaining Hofstede's five dimensions of culture and their implications for business.

J. Hooker, 2003, *Working Across Cultures*, Stanford: Stanford University Press – explores and explains the multifaceted phenomenon of culture and its implications for businesspersons.

J. Henrich, S.J. Heine, & A. Norenzayan, 2010, Most people are not WEIRD, *Science*,

466: 29 – a short article by psychologists explaining why generalizations on human behaviour are problematic; the intellectually curious may read the same authors' article in *Behavioral and Brain Sciences* (2010).

R. House, P. Hanges, M. Javidan, P. Dorfman & V. Gupta, eds, 2004, *Culture, Leadership, and Organizations: The GLOBE Study of 62 Societies*, Thousand Oaks, CA: Sage – a very comprehensive study developing new constructs to measure cultural variations with focus on leadership styles.

T. Khanna, 2014, Contextual Intelligence. *HBR*, 95 (September): 58–66 – a concise statement as to what is needed be a successful manager in a culturally diverse world.

CLOSING CASE

What's in a (Maasai) name?

Living in Kenya and Tanzania, the Maasai represent one of the most iconic tribes in Africa. As semi-nomadic pastoralists, the Maasai have been raising cattle and hunting with some small-scale agriculture near Africa's finest game parks such as the Serengeti for ages. Known as fierce warriors, the Maasai have won the respect of rival tribes, colonial authorities and modern governments of Kenya and Tanzania. Together with wildlife safaris, a Maasai village is among the 'must-see' places for a typical African safari trip.

Those of you who cannot travel so far to visit Africa, you can still get a piece of the colourful Maasai culture. *Land Rover* marketed a limited-edition version of its Freelander 4x4 named Maasai. *Louis Vuitton* developed

a line of menswear and womenswear fashion inspired by the Maasai dress. *Diane von Fürstenberg* offered a red pillow and cushion line simply called the Maasai. The Switzerland-based *Maasai Barefoot Technology* (MBT) developed a line of round bottom shoes to simulate the challenge of Maasai walking barefoot on soft earth. Italian pen maker *Delta* named its high-end fountain pen with a striking red cap the Maasai. A single pen retails at $600, 'which is like three or four good cows', according to a Maasai tribesman. These are just high-profile examples. Experts estimate that perhaps 10 000 firms around the world use the Maasai name, selling everything from hats to legal services.

All of this sounds fascinating, except there is a catch. While these firms made millions, neither a single Maasai individual nor the tribe has ever received a single

What rights do these Maasai have to the name Maasai?

penny. This is where a huge ethical and legal debate has erupted. Legally, the Maasai case is weak. The tribe has never made any formal effort to enforce any intellectual property rights (IPR) of its culture and identity. With approximately two million members spread between Kenya and Tanzania, who can officially represent the Maasai? An expert laughed at this idea, by saying, 'Look, if it could work, the French budget deficit would be gone by demanding royalties on French fries.'

However, from an ethical standpoint, all the firms named above claim to be interested in corporate social responsibility (CSR). If they indeed are interested in the high road to business ethics, expropriating – or, if you may, 'ripping off' or 'stealing' – the Maasai name without compensation has obviously become a huge embarrassment.

Although steeped in tradition, the Maasai are also in touch with the modern world. Their frequent interactions with tourists have made them aware how much value there is in the Maasai name. But they are frustrated by their lack of knowledge about the rules of the game concerning IPR. Ron Layton, a retired New Zealand diplomat runs a non-profit organization advising groups in the developing world, such as the Maasai. Layton previously helped the Ethiopian government wage a legal battle with *Starbucks*, which marketed *Harrar, Sidamo* and *Yirgacheffe* coffee lines from different regions of Ethiopia without compensation. Although *Starbucks* projects an image of being very serious about CSR, it initially fought these efforts but eventually agreed to recognize Ethiopia's claims.

Emboldened by the success in fighting *Starbucks*, Layton worked with Maasai elders to establish a non-profit organization registered in Tanzania called Maasai Intellectual Property Initiative (MIPI). They crafted MIPI bylaws that would reflect traditional Maasai cultural values and that would satisfy the requirements of Western courts – in preparation for an eventual legal showdown. A $1.25 million grant from the US Patent and Trademark Office (USPTO) did help defray some of the expenses. The challenge now is to have more tribal leaders and elders to sign up with MIPI so that MIPI would be viewed both externally and internally as the legitimate representative of the Maasai tribe. How the tribe can monetize its name remains to be seen in the future.

CASE DISCUSSION QUESTIONS

1 Assuming you can afford (and are interested in) some of the 'Maasai' products, would you like to pay more for these products if royalties are paid to the Maasai?

2 As CEO of one of the firms mentioned, how are you going to respond?

3 If you were a judge in the home country of any of these firms named, how would you proceed with the legal dispute (assuming MIPI can represent the tribe and press legal charges)?

Sources: (1) *Bloomberg Businessweek*, 2013, Maasai™, October 24: 84–88; (2) ca.mbt.com; (3) V. Kaster, 2014, Maasai tribe wants control over commercial uses of its name, March 6, iplegalfreebies. wordpress.com; (4) www.dvf.com; (5) www.louisvuitton.com; (6) www.jaguarlandrover.com.

NOTES

'For journal abbreviation, please see page xx-xxi.'

1 G. Helmke & S. Levitsky, 2004, Informal institutions and comparative politics, *PoP*, 2: 725–740; S. Estrin & M. Prevezer, 2011, The role of institutions in corporate governance, *APJM*, 28: 41–67.

2 T. Kostova & S. Zaheer, 1999, Organizational legitimacy under conditions of complexity, *AMR*, 24: 64–81; L. Busenitz, C. Gomez & J. Spencer, 2000, Country institutional profiles, *AMJ*, 43: 994–1003; M. Lounsbury, 2007.

3 V. Barnouw, 1985, *Culture and Personality*, 4th. ed., Homewood, IL: Dorsey Press.

4 Hofstede, 1997, *Cultures and Organizations*.

5 S. Ronen & O. Shenkar, 1985, Clustering countries on attitudinal dimension, *AMR*, 10: 435–454; S. Ronen & O. Shenkar, 2013. Mapping world culture: Cluster formation, sources and implications, *JIBS*, 44(9): 867–897. Data reported in this chapter relate to the 2013 paper.

6 R. House, P. Hanges, M. Javidan, P. Dorfman & V. Gupta eds, 2004, *Culture, Leadership, and Organizations: The GLOBE Study of 62 Societies*, Thousand Oaks, CA: Sage.

7 S. Huntington, 1996, *The Clash of Civilizations and the Remaking of World Order* (p. 43), New York: Simon & Schuster.

8 S. Schwartz, 1994, Cultural dimensions of values, in U. Kim et al. eds, *Individualism and Collectivism* (pp. 85–119), Thousand Oaks, CA: Sage; F. Trompenaars, 1993, *Riding the Waves of Culture*, Chicago: Irwin; R. Drogendijk & A. Slangen, 2006, Hofstede, Schwartz, or managerial perceptions, *IBR*, 15, 361–380.

9 K. Sivakumar & C. Nakata, 2001, The stampede toward Hofstede's framework, *JIBS*, 32: 555–574.

10 World Bank, 2004, *World Development Indicators*, www.worldbank.org.

11 M. Erramilli, 1996, Nationality and subsidiary ownership patterns in multinational corporations, *JIBS*, 27: 225–248.

12 J. Parnell & T. Hatem, 1999, Behavioral differences between American and Egyptian managers, *JMS*, 36: 399–418; C. Fey & I. Björkman, 2001, The effect of HRM practices on MNC subsidiary performance in Russia, *JIBS*, 32: 59–75; E. Pellegrini & T. Scandura, 2006, Leader-member exchange (LMX), paternalism, and delegation in the Turkish business context, *JIBS*, 37: 264–279.

13 N. Adler & A. Gundersen, 2008, *International Dimensions of Organizational Behaviour*, 5th ed., Cengage Learning.

14 Hofstede, 1997, *Cultures and Organizations* (p. 94).

15 *The Economist*, 2010, Women in the workforce: Female power, January 2.

16 P.C. Earley & E. Mosakowski, 2004, Toward culture intelligence (p. 155), *AME*, 18 (3): 151–157.

17 *Copenhagen Post*, 2009, Company reaps benefits from German flu fears, July 24; also see Hooker, 2003, *Working Across Cultures*, Stanford: Stanford University Press (Chapter 6).

18 K. Laverty, 1996, Economic 'short-termism,' *AMR*, 21: 825–860; L. Thomas & G. Waring, 1999, Competing capitalism, *SMJ*, 20: 729–748; R. Peterson, C. Dibrell & T. Pett, 2002, Long- vs. short-term performance perspectives of Western European, Japanese, and U.S. companies, *JWB*, 37: 245–255.

19 H. Kissinger, 2011, *On China*, New York: Penguin.

20 E.T. Hall & M. Hall, 1987, *Hidden Differences*, Garden City, NY: Doubleday; J. Hooker, 2003, *as ave*, (Chapter 2).

21 House et al., 2004, *as above*; B. Kirkman, K. Lowe & C. Gibson, 2006, A quarter century of culture's consequences, *JIBS*, 37: 285–320; K. Leung, R. Bhagat, N. Buchan, M. Erez & C. Gibson, 2005, Culture and international business, *JIBS*, 36: 357–378.

22 P. Earley, 2007, Leading cultural research in the future, *JIBS,* 37: 922–931; C. Ooi, 2007, Unpacking packaged cultures, *East Asia: An International Quarterly,* 24: 111–128.

23 Adler & Gundersen, 2008, *as above*.

24 D. Graddol, 2004, The future of language, *Science*, 303: 1329–1331.

25 R. Piekkari, D. Welch & L. Welch, 2014, *Language in International Business*, Cheltenham: Elgar.

26 H. Tenzer, M. Pudelko & A. Harzing, 2014, The impact of language barriers on trust formation in multinational teams, *JIBS*, 45:508–535; P. Hinds, T. Neeley & C. Cramton, 2014, Language as lighting rod, *JIBS*, 45: 536–561.

27 K.E. Meyer, 2006, Asian management research needs more self-confidence, *APJM*, 23: 119–137.

28 A. Chidlow, E. Plakoyiannaki & C. Welch, 2014, Translation in cross-language international business research, *JIBS*, 45: 562–582; N. Holden & S. Michailova, 2014, A more expansive perspective on translation in IB research, *JIBS*, 45: 906–918.

29 *The Economist*, 2006, Brussels v the English language: Babelling on, December 16: 50.

30 A. Harzing, K. Köster & U. Magner, 2011, Babel in business, *JWB*, 46

31 R. Marschan-Piekkari, D. Welch & L. Welch, 1999, Adopting a common language, *IJHRM* 10: 377–390.

32 J. Lauring & A. Klitmøller, 2015, Corporate language-based communication avoidance in MNCs, *JWB*, advance online.

33 V. Govindarajan & A. Gupta, 2001, Building an effective global business team, *SMR*, Summer: 63–71; Harzing et al., 2001, *as above*.

34 S. Itani, M. Järlström & R. Piekkari, 2015, The meaning of language skills for career mobility in the new career landscape, *JWB*, advance online.

35 *The Economist*, 2009, Charlemagne: English is coming, February 14.

36 N. Felix, 2007, Dann hat man es gewusst, und dann war gut, in: M. Spisak & H. Stalder, eds, *In der Fremde*, Bern: Haupt, p. 29–37.

37 A. Norenzayan, 2013, *Big Gods: How Religions Transformed Cooperation and Conflict*, Princeton: Princeton University Press.

38 D. Ricks, 1999, *Blunders in International Business*, 3rd ed., Oxford: Blackwell. (p. 31).

39 M. Robinson, 2009, Realising rights: the role of religion in human rights and the future, Speech upon receiving honorary degree of doctor of law from the University of Bath (webcast: www.bath.ac.uk/play/video/1253532480, last accessed October 2009).

40 A. Crane & D. Matten, 2007, *Business Ethics*, 2nd ed., Oxford: Oxford University Press; L. Treviño & K. Nelson, 2007, *Managing Business Ethics*, 4th ed., New York: Wiley.

41 *Handelsblatt*, 2013, Amazon will Vorwürfe wegen Leiharbeitern prüfen, February 14; *Handelsblatt*, 2013, Riesiger Markt, winzige Steuerrechnung, July 12; *Handelsblatt*, 2014; Wie Amazon Autoren bedrängt, August 14; *Handelsblatt*, 2014, Die eiserne Lady des Versandhandels, December 18.

42 I. Maignan & D. Ralston, 2002, Corporate social responsibility in Europe and the US, *JIBS*, 33: 497–514; A. Kolk & R. van Tulder, 2004, Ethics in international business, *JWB*, 39: 49–60; J. Stevens, H. K. Steensma, D. Harrison & P. Cochran, 2005, Symbolic or substantive document? *SMJ*, 26: 181–195; R. Durand, H. Rao & P. Monin, 2007, Code of conduct in French cuisine, *SMJ*, 28: 455–472.

43 S. Puffer & D. McCarthy, 1995, Finding common ground in Russian and American business ethics, *CMR*, 37: 29–46; A. Spicer, T. Dunfee & W. Bailey, 2004, Does national context matter in ethical decision making? *AMJ*, 47: 610–620; K. Parboteeah, J. Cullen, B. Victor & T. Sakano, 2005, National culture and ethical climates, *MIR*, 45: 459–519; J.A. Al-Khatib, A. Malshe & N.A. Kader, 2008, Perception of unethical negotiation tactics: A comparative study of US and Saudi managers, *IBR*, 17: 78–102.

44 T. Donaldson, 1996, Values in tension, *HBR*, September–October: 4–11.

45 D. Vogel, 1992, The globalization of business ethics, *CMR*, Fall: 30–49.

46 P. Rodriguez, K. Uhlenbruck & L. Eden, 2004, Government corruption and the entry strategies of multinationals, *AMR*, 30: 383–396; A. Cuervo-Cazurra, 2006, Who cares about corruption? *JIBS*, 37: 807–822; N. Khatri, E. Tsang & T. Begley, 2006, Cronyism, *JIBS*, 37: 61–75.

47 J. Doh, P. Rodriguez, K. Uhlenbruck, J. Collins & L. Eden, 2003, Coping with corruption in foreign markets, *AME*, 17: 114–127; J.G. Lambsdorff, 2003, How corruption affects productivity, *Kyklos*, 56: 457–474; C. Dirienzo, J. Das, K. Cort & J. Burbridge, 2006, Corruption and the role of information, *JIBS*, 38: 320–332; P. Meschi, 2008, Impact de la corruption d'Etat sur l'évolution des participations européennes dans les coentreprises internationals, *M@n@gement*, 11: 1–26.

48 *The Economist*, 2006, The etiquette of bribery: How to grease a palm, December 23.

49 Texas Instruments, 2014, *Comprehensive Guidelines on Gifts, Entertainment, and Travel in China*.

50 K. Au, 1999, Intra-cultural variation, *JIBS*, 30: 799–813; G. Cheung & I. Chow, 1999, Subcultures in Greater China, *APJM*, 16: 369–387.

51 T. Levitt, 1983, The globalization of markets, *HBR*, May–June: 92–102; M. Heuer, J. Cummings & W. Hutabarat, 1999, Cultural change among managers in Indonesia? *JIBS*, 30: 599–610.

52 C. Chen, 1995, New trends in allocation preferences, *AMJ*, 38: 408–428; D.A. Ralston, C.P. Egri, S. Stewart, R.H. Terpstra & K. Yu, 1999, Doing business in the 21st century with the new generation of Chinese managers, *JIBS*, 30: 415–428; A. Ardichvili & A. Gasparishvili, 2003, Russian and Georgian entrepreneurs and non-entrepreneurs, *OSt*, 24: 29–46.

53 S. Ronen & O. Shenkar, 2013, Mapping world cultures: Cluster formation, sources and implications, *JIBS*, 44: 867–897.

54 E. Schein, 2010, *Organizational Culture and Leadership*, 4th ed., San Francisco: Jossey-Bass.

55 V. Venema, 2015, The men of steel with a softer side, *BBC World Service*, February 3.

56 B. Gerhart, 2009, How Much Does National Culture Constrain Organizational Culture? *MOR*, 5: 241–259; M. Naor, K. Linderman & R. Schroeder, 2010, The globalization of operations in Eastern and Western countries, *JOM*, 28: 194–205; E. Vaara, R. Sarala, G. Stahl, I. Björkman, 2012, The Impact of Organizational and National Cultural Differences, *JMS*, 49: 1–27.

57 J. Henrich, S.J. Heine & A. Norenzayan, 2010. The Weirdest people of the world? *Behavioral and Brain Sciences*, 33: 61–83; see also J. Henrich, R. Boyd, S.

Bowles, C. Camerer, E. Fehr, H. Gintis & R. McElreath, 2001. In search of homo economicus, *AER*, 91 (papers & proceedings): 73–78.

58 S. Lipset, 1996, *American exceptionalism*, New York: W.W. Norton.

59 Henrich, et al., 2010, *as above*.

60 Hofstede, G. 1993, Cultural constraints in management theories, *AME*, 7: 81–82.

61 T. Khanna, 2014, Contextual Intelligence. *HBR*, 95 (September): 58–66.

62 This section draws heavily on C. Chen, M.W. Peng & P. Saparito, 2002, Individualism, collectivism, and opportunism, *JM*, 28: 567–583.

63 J. Cullen, K.P. Parboteeah & M. Hoegl, 2004, Cross-national differences in managers' willingness to justify ethically suspect behaviors, *AMJ*, 47: 411–421.

64 M. Muethel & M. Bond, 2013, National context and individual employees' trust of the out-group, *JIBS*, 44: 312–333.

65 M.J. Chen, 2001, *Inside Chinese Business*, Boston: Harvard Business School Press.

66 F. Fukuyama, 1995, *Trust*, New York: Free Press; G. Redding, 1993, *The Spirit of Chinese Capitalism*, 2nd ed., Berlin, De Gruyter.

67 K. Lim, K. Leung, C. Sia & M. Lee, 2004, Is e-commerce boundaryless? *JIBS*, 35: 545–559.

68 This example is based on personal communication with Prof David Ahlstrom, Chinese University of Hong Kong.

69 J. Graham & N. Lam, 2003, The Chinese negotiation, *HBR*, 81: 82–91.

70 N. Holden, C. Cooper & J. Carr, 1998, *Dealing with the New Russia*, New York: Wiley.

71 P. Earley & E. Mosakowski, 2004, Cultural intelligence, *HBR*, October: 139–146; J. Johnson, T. Lenartowicz & S. Apud, 2006, Cross-cultural competence in international business, *JIBS*, 37: 525–543; A. Bartel-Radic, 2009, La competence interculturelle, *MI/IM/GI*, 13 (4): 11–26.

72 Hofstede, 1997, *as above* (p. 230).

73 M. Zhao, S. Park & N. Zhou, 2014, MNC strategy and social adaptation in emerging markets, *JIBS*, 45: 842–861.´

CHAPTER FOUR

FIRM RESOURCES: COMPETITIVENESS AND GROWTH

LEARNING OBJECTIVES

After studying this chapter, you should be able to

1 Explain what firms' resources are

2 Assess the resources of a firm using the VRIO framework

3 Use benchmarking to consider outsourcing and offshoring decisions

4 Participate in two leading debates on resources in an international context

5 Draw implications for action

OPENING CASE

SAP *drives industry 4.0*

In manufacturing, the buzzword of the decade is 'industry 4.0', which stands for new forms of organizing and coordinating economic processes. 'Smart factories' are envisaged, with components identified individually by RFID tags communicating directly with robots assembling mass-customized products, thus changing not only factories, but entire systems of coordination of human activity. A leader in this technological transformation is *SAP*, a business software company. Founded in 1972, *SAP*

is world leader for enterprise resource planning (ERP) software – programmes that help other businesses to make best use of their resources. What are the foundations for *SAP*'s success, how is it developing its capabilities for the next industrial revolution?

SAP was founded by five entrepreneurs in 1972. They had new ideas about how to use computers more efficiently to analyze accounting data, yet their employer – *IBM* – didn't think much of their proposals. So they established their own company. Within just one year they generated turnover of €300 000,

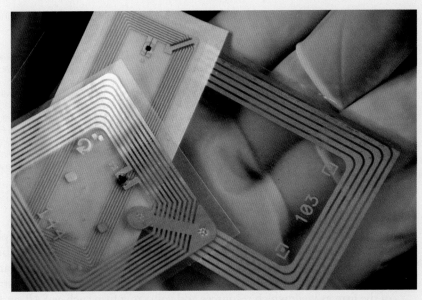

How do advances in information technology change the ways firms manage their resources?

and the growth became unstoppable. By 1980, the majority of Germany's top 100 companies were running *SAP* software on *IBM* mainframe computers. By 1993, turnover exceeded €1 billion, and in 2007 it went above €10 billion. After set-backs during the financial crisis, it reached €17.6 billion in 2014 with a profit margin of 25%. The small town of Walldorf (near Heidelberg in south-western Germany) remains the hub of *SAP*'s global operations.

SAP invented and developed the market for ERP software. Essentially, it provides electronic information systems that integrate data from different parts of an organization, such as manufacturing efficiency, inventories, sales and customer feedback. ERP software is like the central nervous system of a company, gathering information, and conveying it in real time to decision makers in an accessible form – including fancy tables and graphs.

The business model combines products with service; customers would buy not only software, but a maintenance contract that includes regular software upgrades, thus generating two income streams for *SAP* – one at the time of the sale, and one spread over several years. As a business-to-business (B2B) supplier, *SAP* is working closely with many of the world's largest MNEs. Independent IT service partners help clients to implement *SAP* systems in their organization.

SAP built on German strengths in quality and reliability of engineering, yet soon that was not enough. From the 1990s onwards, research and software development have been internationalized,

with eight centres around the globe. An operation in Palo Alto, California served as an ideas factory and to stay in touch with the latest trends in Silicon Valley. This internationalization allowed *SAP* to tap into human capital around the world. To stay ahead of the competition, *SAP* pushed further than most firms by aiming to hire the best software engineers – wherever in the world they were found. Thus gradually the hub of the development and the top management was shifting away from Walldorf. This internationalization was appreciated by clients and investors outside Germany, but received a mixed response in Walldorf. Disgruntled employees talked in the local media about the 'Americanization' and the loss of traditional values, such as commitment to quality and the entrepreneurial spirit of the early years. Having to speak English in internal meetings did not please many of the older engineers.

However, in this fast-growing industry, new generations of technology often required new ways of organizing software. *Oracle* and *Mi*... became major pl............ market, and .... flexibly redes.............. new start-up........... model. In par............ developed 'so............ paid by mon............ model of insta............ and then regul............ investing in inf............

based on cloud computing to stay ahead of its competitors.

At the same time, *SAP* took the lead in developing new IT systems that would enable higher levels of integration of manufacturing processes, known as 'industry 4.0'. Next-generation systems integrate data across multiple platforms from multiple players in the value chain, including consumers, and thus enable new forms of complex coordination. *SAP* thus invests in new capabilities not only in software and cloud computing but also in helping firms manage those complex systems,

and to engage stakeholders in discussing the wider social impact of industry 4.0.

Sources: (1) P. Dvorak & L. Abboud, 2007, Internal revolution, *Wall Street Journal Europe*, May 11; (2) A. Kaiser, 2010, Abschied vom nationalen Champion, *Manager Magazin*, February 8; (3) M. Palmer, 2010, SAP vows to return to double-digit sales growth, *Financial Times*, March 2; (4) *Frankfurter Allgemeine Zeitung*, 2011, Wir wollen ein 20-Milliarden-Euro-Unternehmen werden', February 27; (5) D. Schafer & M. Watkins, 2011, The 'bosses' with two, *Financial Times*, April 18; (6) T. Weber, 2011, Can software giant SAP survive the IT revolution? *BBC News*, April 28; (7) SAP (2014): *Annual Report* 2013; (8) www.plattform-i40.de; (9) www.sap.com (accessed February 2015).

resource-based view
A leading perspective in global business that posits that firm performance is fundamentally driven by firm-specific resources.

The resource-based view focuses on the inside of the firm, thus complementing the institutional view, which focuses on firms' external environment. In business, many key decisions concern the alignment of the firm – and its resources in particular – with its environment. Thus to make the best decisions, you need to understand the inside of the firm as well: which resources add value to a firm such as *SAP*, and how can you systematically assess them? How can firms manage their resources to create value, while protecting them from their competitors? How can you develop new resources?

This chapter introduces tools to address these sorts of questions. We first define resources and then introduce several complementary classification schemes for resources. Then we focus on value (V), rarity (R), imitability (I), and organization (O) through a VRIO framework. We apply these concepts in a value chain analysis on the decision to keep an activity in-house or outsource it. Finally, debates and extensions follow.

LEARNING OBJECTIVE

1 Explain what firms' resources are

IDENTIFYING RESOURCES

competitive advantage
The ability of a firm to outperform its rivals.
primary resources
The tangible and intangible assets as well as human resources that a firm uses to choose and implement its strategies.
capability
firm-specific abilities to ~~re~~sources to achieve ~~organiza~~tional objectives.

A basic proposition of the resource-based view is that a firm consists of a bundle of productive resources. These provide the basis for firms to attain competitive advantage in their markets; that is the ability to outperform their rivals. Moreover, resources enable firms to grow into new activities and markets.[1]

Resources come in many different forms. For analytical purposes it is often helpful to distinguish between primary resources as the productive assets of a firm, and capabilities as firms' ability to use them. More precisely we define primary resources as the tangible and intangible assets as well as the human resources that a firm uses to implement its strategies.[2] Such resources can principally be purchased on open markets and customized for use. Individually, they are however insufficient to provide an advantage over competitors, firms have to know how to use them. This knowledge and associated routines and practices are known as capabilities, defined as firm-specific abilities to use resources to achieve organizational objectives. Capabilities are normally developed internally and depend to some degree on tacit knowledge; they are specific to the firm and do not take the form of assets that can be traded or knowledge picked up from a textbook. For example, *SAP* is able to offer better services than its competitors in terms of helping clients to implement *SAP* software. This capability is grounded in specific resources such as the skills of its software engineers and the practical knowledge of its network of specialized business partners. However, the capability 'comes alive' in the processes by which *SAP*'s employees and partners interact and use these resources to create a unique service.[3]

In practice, primary resources and capabilities are often hard to distinguish; we thus use the simpler term 'resources' to refer to all of them.

Managers and consultants often have to analyze the resources of a firm as a foundation for developing strategic advice. If you want to advise a business what to do next, you first need to know the firms' resources. Equally, you need to know the resources of the competitors. So, how do analyze the resources of a firm, be it your own or those of a competitor? Start by studying the company's annual report and other documents to identify its primary resources.

Primary resources

On firms' balance sheets, you can find two types of resources: tangible assets and intangible assets. Tangible assets are those items that are observable and quantifiable. They are normally reported in two categories (Table 4.1):

tangible assets
Assets that are observable and easily quantified.

- **Financial assets** reflect the depth of a firm's financial pockets. They include internal funds, such as shareholders' capital and retained profits, as well as external capital, like loans provided by banks.
- **Physical assets** include plants, offices, infrastructure and equipment, as well as inventories of raw materials, components and finished goods. For example, although many people attribute the success of *Amazon* to its online portal (which makes sense), a crucial reason why *Amazon* has emerged as the largest bookseller is because it has built some of the largest physical warehouses in key locations around the globe.

Table 4.1 Examples of primary resources

Tangible Resources	Examples
Financial	Cash, securities, borrowing capacity
Physical	Plants, equipment, sales outlets, land, natural resources
Intangible Resources	**Examples**
Technological	Patents, trademarks, copyrights, trade secrets
Reputational	Brands, relationships, corporate goodwill (e.g. reputation as a quality manufacturer or as a socially responsible corporate citizen)
Human Resources	**Examples**
Skills and know-how	Job-specific skills and know-how held by individual employees
Communication and collaboration abilities	Interpersonal skills and learning capacity for team work and collaboration, emotional intelligence
Organizational culture	Values, traditions, organizational norms

Sources: (1) J. Barney, 1991, Firm resources and sustained competitive advantage, *Journal of Management*, 17: 101; (2) R. Hall, 1992, The strategic analysis of intangible resources, *Strategic Management Journal*, 13: 135–144; (3) R. Grant, 2012, *Contemporary Strategy Analysis*, 8th ed., Oxford: Wiley-Blackwell.

While the information on tangible assets on the balance sheet is precise, it may still be insufficient to assess their true value for the company's strategy. Many assets are reported at historical costs (the original costs that the company paid for it), and depreciated over a number of years. The actual value, however, depends on their contribution to the products and services that the company can sell in the marketplace: *Amazon*'s warehouses are valuable beyond their resale value because of their role in *Amazon*'s business model.

intangible assets
Assets that are hard to observe and difficult (or sometimes impossible) to quantify.

- Intangible assets are also found on companies' balance sheets, but they are much harder to value, and they are not always reported. They include technological and reputational resources:

- **Technological resources** include patents, licences and copyrights that entitle the firm to intellectual property rights in technologies or products and enable it to generate valuable products.[4] For example, the value of pharmaceutical companies such as *Roche, Novartis* or *Sanofi* is grounded in their patented medicines. In a broader sense, they also include less clearly defined resources such as trade secrets and databases that support the firm's business activity.

goodwill
The value of a firm's abilities to develop and leverage its reputation.

- **Reputational resources** reflect the value of the reputation of a firm as a provider of quality goods and services, responsive an attractive employer, and/or a socially responsible corporate citizen. On the balance sheet, the entry for goodwill captures the value of a firm's abilities to develop and leverage its reputation. The reputation of a firm is closely associated with the values associated with its brands. For example, carmakers *BMW* and *Daimler* focus on quality and reliability as the key attributes of their brand. Others build their reputation around socially responsible business practices (Chapter 10). For example, British cosmetics retailer *Body Shop* built a reputation as an 'ethical' brand that appealed to many especially young consumers. This made it an attractive acquisition target for French cosmetics giant *L'Oreal*, who aimed to strengthen its position with this important consumer group.[5]

human resources
Resources embedded in individuals working in an organization.

Some resources are embedded in the individuals working in an organization, and thus known as human resources (or human capital). They are not owned by the firm (and are thus not on the balance sheet) but the firm can use them based on individual contracts. Human resources include:

- Individual employees' skills, talent and knowledge, including both knowledge acquired in formal education and through experiential learning on the job.

- Individual employees' capacity for collaboration and their abilities for interpersonal interaction that are not captured by the firm's formal systems and structures.[6] For instance, internet start-ups such as *Facebook* are known for their (relative) youth, technological wizardry and competitive orientation, which enable them to continuously develop new software products.

organizational culture
Employees' shared values, traditions and social norms within an organization.

- Employees' shared values, traditions and social norms within an organization. This organizational culture has been identified as a key factor in explaining superior financial performance in many firms, yet it is notoriously hard to define and value.[7] For example, British chocolate maker *Cadbury* attributed its success to its unique organizational culture grounded in the founders' Quaker philosophy,[8] which became hard to sustain after *Cadbury* was acquired by the American food conglomerate *Kraft*.

Human resources are a key foundation for most capabilities on which MNEs compete, which is evident in the efforts firms put into the management of their human resources (Chapter 16).

Capabilities

Capabilities are, by definition, harder to observe and more difficult (or sometimes impossible) to quantify. Yet it is widely acknowledged that they must be 'there' because no firm is likely to generate competitive advantage by relying on primary resources.[9] How can we make an inventory of capabilities?

The first approach is to look at the value chain, which illustrates how the different activities of a firm come together to add value. In principle, a firm may have capabilities in any of its activities. Shown in Figure 4.1, most goods and services are produced through a chain of vertical activities (from upstream to downstream) that add value – in short, a value chain.[10] For example, a manufacturing process may flow from raw materials, to primary components, to intermediate components, to

value chain
A chain of activities vertically related in the production of goods and services.

Figure 4.1   The value chain

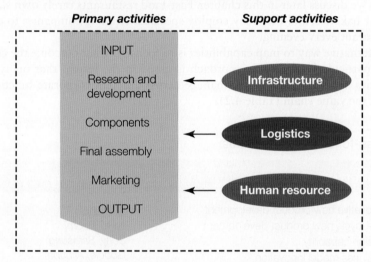

Panel A. An example of value chain with firm boundaries

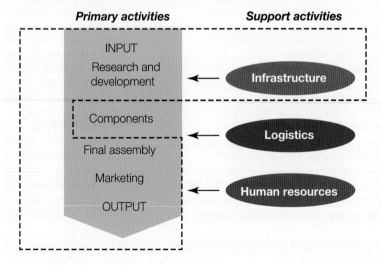

Panel B. An example of value chain with some outsourcing

Note: Dotted lines represent firm boundaries.

assembly, to sales and to after-sales service. These primary activities are backed up by support activities, such as finance and human resources. As an example, a fast-food hamburger may be manufactured in a fairly simple value chain: farmers grow cows, wheat, tomatoes and other raw materials. These are slaughtered or harvested, processed and aggregated in transportable primary components. Further processes such as baking bread and frying the hamburger create intermediate components that are delivered to the restaurant. The assembly kicks in when you order, and the sale involves you exchanging money for a meal. The after-sales service includes listening to any complaints you may have, and cleaning up after you left.

Each activity along the value chain requires a number of resources. Value chain analysis forces managers to think about firm resources at an activity-based level.[11] Given that no firm is likely to have enough resources to be good at all primary and support activities, the key is to examine whether the firm has resources to perform a particular activity in a manner superior to competitors. Some companies may have particular capabilities in product development and sales, others are relatively stronger in production. Hence, firms may concentrate on selected stages of the value chain, as we discuss later in this chapter. Fast-food restaurants rarely own slaughter-houses or bakeries, and they may employ specialist cleaning companies to clean up the restaurant every evening.

An alternative way to map capabilities is to focus on what outcome the company delivers particularly well. This approach is based in the insight that many critical capabilities arise from abilities to manage across different corporate functions and stages of the value chain (Table 4.2).

Table 4.2 Examples of cross-functional capabilities

Processes	Examples of capabilities	Exemplar companies
Innovation	● Innovative new product development ● Fast-cycle new product development ● Design capability ● Business model innovation	*3M, Apple* *Zara, Xiaomi* *Sony, Samsung* *Google, Alibaba*
Operations	● Continuous product quality improvement ● Efficiency in volume manufacturing ● Low-cost delivery of customer service	*Rolls Royce, SAP, Toyota* *Flextronics, Foxconn* *Hainan Airlines, EasyJet*
Marketing	● Management of consumer brands ● Reputation for quality ● Reputation for exclusivity and luxury ● Responsiveness to market trends	*LVMH, Nestlé, P&G, Unilever* *BMW, Mercedes, Siemens* *Bentley, Gucci, Burberry* *MTV, L'Oreal, Zara*
Logistics and service	● Efficiency of order processing and distribution ● Effective distribution management ● Quality and effectiveness of customer service ● Control of unique service platforms	*Dell, Amazon, Yihaodian* *Wal-Mart, Li & Fung* *Singapore Airlines, Virgin Atlantic* *Google, Apple, Alibaba, Uber*
Corporate operations	● Ability to attract and manage financial resources ● Strategic management of multiple businesses ● Ability to manage government relations ● Attraction and development of global talent ● Managing financial risks	*Exxon Mobil, PepsiCo* *General Electric, P&G* *Halliburton, Royal Bank of Scotland* *McKinsey, BCG* *HSBC, Santander*

- **Capabilities in innovation** are a firm's assets and skills to (1) research and develop new products and services and (2) innovate and change ways of organizing.[12] Some firms are renowned for innovations. For instance, *Apple* often pioneers new classes of products, such as the Mac, the iPod, the smartphone and the iPad.

- **Capabilities in operations** are a firm's ability to effectively implement its regular activities, notably the manufacturing process. For example, many German engineering firms such as *BMW* and *Mercedes* are known for producing reliable, high-quality machines, engines or software. Some firms, such as *Dell* computers and *Zara* fashion, are better than anyone else in their industry in adjusting operations to changing markets; others, such as *Ryanair* and *EasyJet*, excel at delivering service at low costs.

- **Capabilities in marketing** enable firms to develop and sustain brands and to induce consumers to buy these brands. Such capabilities often integrate a firm's ability to recognize (potential) consumer demands, develop products to fit this demand, and communicate the benefits of the product to consumers. For example, many popular food brands are owned and managed by MNEs specialized in brand management, such as *Unilever, Procter & Gamble* and *Nestlé*.

- **Capabilities in logistics and service** enable firms to manage interactions with (potential) customers and in bringing products to the right customer at the right time. Such capabilities are often grounded in efficiency-oriented management processes as well as IT systems and supporting technologies. *Wal-Mart* is known for its capability to manage complex distribution networks (In Focus 4.1), though internet retailers from *Amazon* to *Zelando* are beating them by innovating logistics.

- **Capabilities in corporate coordination** include a firm's planning, command and control systems. In general, younger firms tend to rely more on the visions of

IN FOCUS 4.1

Capabilities in distribution: Wal-Mart

A 120 000 m² distribution centre in Bentonville, Arkansas, USA, is the hub of *Wal-Mart's* North American logistics operation. *New York Times* journalist Thomas Friedman describes how he discovered the capabilities underlying its success:

'We climbed up to a viewing perch and watched the show. On one side of the building, scores of white Wal-Mart trailer trucks were dropping off boxes of merchandise from thousands of different suppliers. Boxes large and small were fed up a conveyor belt, like streams feeding into a powerful river. Twenty-four hours a day, seven days

a week, the suppliers' trucks feed the twelve miles [19 km] of conveyor streams, and the conveyor streams feed into a huge Wal-Mart river of boxed products. But that is just half the show. As the Wal-Mart river flows along, an electric eye reads the bar codes on each box on its way to the other side of the building. There, the river parts again into a hundred streams. Electric arms from each stream reach out and guide the boxes – ordered by particular Wal-Mart stores – off the main river and down its stream, where another conveyor belt sweeps them into a waiting Wal-Mart truck, which will rush these particular products onto the shelves of a particular Wal-Mart store somewhere in the country.'

What capabilities enable *Wal-Mart* to run the world's largest retail operation?

The whole process was semi-automatic, initiated by signals that were triggered when a consumer picked a product from the shelves.

'That signal will go out across the Wal-Mart *network to the supplier of that product – whether that supplier's factory is in coastal China or in coastal Maine [USA]. That signal will pop up on the supplier's computer screen and prompt him to make another of that item and ship it via the* Wal-Mart *supply chain, and the whole cycle will start anew. So no sooner does your arm lift a product off the local* Wal-Mart's *shelf and onto the checkout counter than another mechanical arm starts making another one somewhere in the world.'*

The resources and capabilities that enable *Wal-Mart* to provide US consumers with the lowest price consumer goods are only partly visible to those consumers. They include a relentless focus on costs in everything from store lay-out to supplier bargaining and (controversially) employee pay. But behind that stand unique capabilities of supply chain management that make every product flow smoothly through warehouses and lorries to the shelf, where it is picked up by the consumer.

Sources: Quotes from T.L. Friedman, 2007, *The World is Flat*, 3rd ed., New York: Picador (pp. 151–152).

managers (often founders), whereas more established firms usually have more formalized systems and structures. In emerging economies, corporate functions often include navigating complex institutional frameworks, and the management of relationships with authorities.[13] A related capability, which has proven to be pivotal during the financial meltdown of 2008, is corporate risk management, as those who lack financial foresight were most likely to go under.[14]

Note that firms rarely excel at all these resources; they tend to have strength in some areas and weaknesses in others. For example, *Wal-Mart*'s operational efficiency (In Focus 4.1) comes at the expense of a particularly weak reputation for social responsibility.

A resource audit is often the first step for many types of analysis that you may be doing during your studies, and in your managerial career. For example, when analyzing the potential for synergies in mergers and acquisitions (Chapter 14), a thorough assessment of the resources of both firms is a crucial first step. The classification schemes for resources provided here provide a starting point for a resource audit. The next step then is to assess them.

APPRAISING RESOURCES: THE VRIO FRAMEWORK

How can you know how useful your (firm's) resources are? An important line of work on the resource-based view focuses on the value creation (V), rarity (R), imitability (I), and organization (O) aspects of resources, leading to a VRIO framework.[15] These four important questions have a number of ramifications for competitive advantage.

LEARNING OBJECTIVE

2 Assess the resources of a firm using the VRIO framework

VRIO framework
The resource-based framework that focuses on the value creation (V), rarity (R), imitability (I), and organizational (O) aspects of resources.

The question of value creation

The most fundamental question is, do the resources add value?[16] In other words, do they enable a firm to exploit an external opportunity, and/or neutralize an external threat? Machines that convert trees into furniture obviously add value as long as the furniture is more valuable than the trees (that is, the market price of the output is higher than the price of the inputs). If the value of the trees increases (say because of their carbon capture capacity) or if the value of wooden furniture falls (say, because it is out of fashion), then the machines no longer add value – even if they are technologically still fully operational.

Only value-creating resources can possibly lead to competitive advantage, whereas non-value-creating capabilities may lead to competitive *dis*advantage. With changes in the competitive landscape, previously value-creating resources may become obsolete. The evolution of *IBM* is a case in point. *IBM* historically excelled in making hardware, including tabulating machines in the 1930s, mainframes in the 1960s and 1970s, and personal computers (PCs) in the 1980s. However, as competition for hardware was heating up, *IBM*'s core capabilities in hardware not only added little value, but also increasingly became core rigidities that stood in the way of the firm moving into new areas.[17] Since the 1990s, *IBM* has been transformed to focus on software and services, where it has developed new value-creating capabilities, becoming an information technology-related service provider for corporations. As part of this new strategy, *IBM* sold its PC division to China's *Lenovo* in 2004.

The relationship between value-creating resources and firm performance is straightforward. However, non-value-creating resources, such as *IBM*'s historical expertise in hardware, may become weaknesses. If firms are unable to get rid of non-value-creating resources, they are likely to suffer below-average performance.[18] In the worst case, they may become extinct, a fate *IBM* narrowly skirted during the early 1990s. 'Continuous strategic renewal,' in the words of Gary Hamel, a strategy guru, 'is the only insurance against irrelevance.'[19]

The ability to create value, however, is often context-specific. Firms may be highly successful at home, but struggle when they try to transfer their capabilities abroad. For example, *Wal-Mart* (In Focus 4.1) failed to transfer its business model to Germany, partly because it couldn't achieve the necessary scale, and partly because its work practices were not acceptable to German work forces.

The question of rarity

Simply possessing value-creating resources may not be enough. The next question is: how rare are these resources? Value-creating but common resources will at best lead to competitive parity but not to an advantage over competitors. Consider *SAP* software used by businesses worldwide. It certainly creates value by enabling firms to organize their processes more efficiently. Yet it is difficult to derive competitive advantage from the software alone; implementation is key. For example, using *SAP* 'industry 4.0' software, *Harley-Davidson* reorganized its production processes, which reduced the time to produce a customized motorcycle from 21 days to six hours.[20] As an early mover of new technology, and integrating it with its operational processes, *Harley-Davidson* could dramatically enhance its operational flexibility, which gave it a temporary competitive advantage.

temporary competitive advantage
The ability to outperform rivals for a limited time.

Only value-creating and rare resources have the potential to provide temporary competitive advantage; they enable outperformance of competitors for a limited time.[21] In the *Harley-Davidson* example, it is the application of the software that was rare, rather than the software itself. Many IT firms exploit their intellectual property (IP) by licensing their patents to others. However, this potentially reduces their rarity. There is always a danger that their licensees (or their licensees' employees) use the technology for purposes other than those originally intended. Although patent infringement is illegal, smart reverse engineering, by inventing 'around' a given patent, is legal. Thus Indian IT company *Wipro* prefers to hold on to their innovations rather than patenting and licensing them. It calls these inventions 'IP blocks', which are bits of software or processes taken from work for one client that it can draw on to serve multiple clients better. Around 10 000 *Wipro* engineers are involved with such high-end design and development work for numerous clients, but *Wipro* has fewer than ten patents.[22] By developing and keeping the technology (mostly) in-house, *Wipro* protects the rarity of such expertise, and uses it as a competitive advantage when competing for contracts. Overall, the question of rarity is a reminder of the cliché: if everyone has it, you cannot make money from it.

The question of imitability

Value-creating and rare resources can be a source of temporary competitive advantage, but this will disappear quickly if competitors can imitate the resources. The third question thus is, how difficult is it for competitors to imitate the resources? It is relatively easy to imitate many tangible resources (such as plants), but it is a lot more challenging and often impossible to imitate intangible resources (such as tacit knowledge, superior motivation and managerial talents).[23] In an effort to maintain a high-quality manufacturing edge, many Japanese firms employ 'supertechnicians' – an honour designated by the Japanese government – to handle mission-critical work, such as mounting tiny chips onto circuit boards for laptops at *Sharp*.[24] Although robots can be purchased by rivals, no robots, and few humans elsewhere, can imitate the skills and dedication of the supertechnicians in Japan. In an effort to create an inimitable brand, *Burberry* focused on its British heritage as the core of its brand identity (In Focus 4.2).

causal ambiguity
The difficulty of identifying the causal determinants of successful firm performance.

Imitation is difficult. Why? In two words: causal ambiguity, which refers to the difficulty of identifying the causal determinants of successful firm performance.[25] In an abstract economic model, you can easily establish which variable influences which other variable. However, in the real world, organizations have complex internal patterns and processes that escape systematic modelling. For example, why do Italian fashion houses like *Versace* and *Gucci* stay ahead in the world of fashion for decades? Is it the training that designers and tailors received in their apprenticeship? Is it the close-knit networks of small firms in northern Italy? Is it the experience of designers growing up in a fashion-oriented culture? Or, is it simply that people elsewhere associate Italian names with 'fashionable'? Outsiders usually have a hard time understanding what a firm – or a network of firms – does inside its

IN FOCUS 4.2

Burberry *makes Britishness its core capability*

Asked to name an iconic British fashion brand, many people would probably nominate *Burberry*. Founded in 1856, *Burberry* grew to become a leading global fashion house with €3 billion of revenue in 2014. Most famous for its trench coats, *Burberry* became such a part of British culture that it earned a royal warrant as an official supplier to the royal family.

However, by the mid 2000s, *Burberry* had lost its focus. It had 23 licensees in a variety of products and locations around the world, each doing something different, ranging from dog cover-ups and leashes to kilts. In luxury, ubiquity, by definition, is the killer of exclusivity. Among numerous *Burberry* products, outerwear exemplified by the 'boring old trench coat' only represented 20% of its global revenue. While luxury sales were growing globally, Burberry seemed to be losing out, with a lacklustre growth rate of only 2% per year by 2006. Global luxury goods rivals *LVMH* and *Gucci* achieved ten times Burberry's revenue and grew much faster. How could *Burberry*, as a 'David', grow against such 'Goliaths'?

In 2006, the new CEO Angela Ahrendts led a significant soul search at *Burberry*. Deploying the classic resource-based logic, the firm realized that its greatest assets lay in its Britishness, more specifically its trench coat roots – hence the highest value it could deliver. Further, such a focus on Britain's exquisite country-of-origin image would be rare in a world largely populated by French and Italian luxury brands. It would also be difficult (or sometimes impossible) to imitate if this heritage were emphasized and strengthened.

With this powerful insight, *Burberry* adopted a new strategy centred on the iconic trench coat – its first social media platform was named www.artofthetrench.com. Before the transformation, *Burberry* sold just a few styles of trench coats and almost all were beige with the signature check lining. Now with consistent design (a significant intangible capability), it sells more than 300 types and sizes of trench coats in a wide variety of styles and colours. Of its revenues, 60% came from apparel, and outerwear made up more than half of that. Many of its stylish trench coats are priced over €1000. Furthermore, instead of outsourcing, *Burberry* has concentrated its trench coat production at Castleford in the north of England, adding more than 1000 jobs in the UK in two years (of a global labour force of 9000). The *Burberry* trench coat designed and manufactured in the UK thus became valuable, rare and impossible to imitate by rivals.

Burberry has been rewarded handsomely by the market. In five years (2007–2012), its revenue and operating income doubled. In 2011, *Interbrand* named it the fourth fastest-growing global brand (behind *Apple, Google* and *Amazon*) and the fastest-growing luxury brand. So impressed was *Apple* that in 2013 it poached Ahrendts, who quit *Burberry* and became *Apple*'s senior vice-president in charge of retail and online operations.

Sources: (1) A. Ahrendts, *2013,* Burberry's CEO on turning an aging British icon into a global luxury brand, *HBR*, January, 39–42; (2) *Daily Mail*, 2013, Burberry share price plummets after CEO Angela Ahrents quits fashion house to take key role at Apple, October 13; (3) www.artofthetrench.com; (4) www.burberry.com.

boundaries. We can try, as many rival luxury goods manufacturers have, to identify the Italian recipe for success by drawing up a long list of possible reasons labelled as 'capabilities' in our classroom discussion. But in the final analysis, as outsiders, we are not sure.[26]

What is even more fascinating is that often managers of a successful firms do not know either exactly what contributes to their success. In fact, different managers of the same firm may have different lists. When probed as to which capability is 'it', they usually suggest that it is all of the above in *combination*. This is probably one of the most interesting and paradoxical aspects of the resource-based view: if insiders have a hard time figuring out what explains their firm's performance, it is not surprising that outsiders' efforts in understanding and imitating these capabilities usually fail.[27]

social complexity
The socially complex ways of organizing typical of many firms.

The difficulties of imitation are related to a phenomenon known as social complexity, which refers to the socially complex ways of organizing, typical of many firms. Many MNEs consist of thousands of people scattered in many different countries. How they overcome cultural differences and are organized as one corporate entity and achieve organizational goals is profoundly complex.[28] Often it is their invisible relationships that add value.[29] Such organizationally embedded capabilities are thus very difficult for rivals to imitate. This emphasis on social complexity refutes what is half-jokingly called the 'Lego toy' view of the firm, in which a firm can be assembled (and disassembled) from modules of technology and people (à la Lego toy blocks). By treating employees as identical and replaceable blocks, this view fails to realize that the social capital associated with complex relationships and knowledge permeating many firms can be a source of competitive advantage.[30]

The social complexity underlying many capabilities, especially in knowledge-intensive industries, also has implications for crisis management: laying people off in difficult times may imply losing capabilities for good that cannot be recreated by hiring new people when the economy picks up again. Such capabilities based on social complexity are thus valuable, rare and hard to imitate and can provide the basis for a sustainable competitive advantage.

The question of organization

sustainable competitive advantage
The ability to deliver persistently above-average performance.

Even value-creating, rare, and hard-to-imitate resources may not give a sustainable competitive advantage, the ability to deliver persistently above-average performance, if the firm is not properly organized. For example, companies developing new mobile phone apps are often very popular, and thus seem to have value-creating, rare, and hard-to-imitate resources. Yet many of them fail to deliver profits for the firms that created the service. More generally, the question of organization asks: are other policies and procedures of the firm organized to enable and support the exploitation of its value-creating, rare and costly-to-imitate resources? If customers enjoy the value created by an internet company, but nobody pays for it, then the business in unsustainable. In economics, this issue is known as appropriability, the ability of the firm to appropriate the values for itself. This depends on (1) revenues received from customers, and (2) expenses paid to suppliers.

appropriability
The ability of the firm to appropriate the values for itself.

First, how do you ensure that customers pay for the goods or services they benefit from? This question is particularly challenging for online service providers that are used by many people who don't pay. How do social networking websites such as *LinkedIn, Xing* or *Facebook* survive financially? The (main) answer is advertising revenues; a secondary answer is premium services, such as special database search functions (*LinkedIn, Xing*) or online games (*Facebook*). Second, firms have to ensure that they keep a large share of the revenues, and don't overpay their suppliers. This is challenging for firms where 'star performers' are a crucial element in their resource mix, for example, football clubs, movie studios or TV stations. These star performers tend to have large bargaining power that they can use to attain a share of the revenues generated by the firm.

Overall, only valuable, rare and hard-to-imitate resources that are organizationally embedded and exploited can lead to sustainable competitive advantage.[31] Because resources cannot be evaluated in isolation, the VRIO framework presents four interconnected and increasingly difficult hurdles for them to become a source of sustainable competitive advantage (Table 4.3).

Table 4.3 The VRIO framework

Criterion	Question	Resource 1	Resource 2	Resource 3	Resource 4
Value-creating	*Does the resource add value?*	No	Yes	Yes	Yes
Rare	*How rare is the resource?*	—	No	Yes	Yes
Imitability	*How difficult is it for others to imitate the resource?*	—	No	No	Yes
Organization	*Are other policies and procedures organized to support the exploitation of this resource?*	No	Yes	Yes	Yes
		↓	↓	↓	↓
Competitive implications		Disadvantage	Parity	Temporary advantage	Sustained advantage

Sources: (1) J. Barney, 2002, *Gaining and Sustaining Competitive Advantage*, 2nd ed. (p. 173), Upper Saddle River, NJ: Prentice Hall; (2) R. Hoskisson, M. Hitt, & R.D. Ireland, 2004, *Competing for Advantage* (p. 118), Cincinnati, OH: Thomson South-Western.

APPLYING RESOURCE ANALYSIS: BENCHMARKING

Benchmarking as an analytical tool

A key tool for analyzing resources is benchmarking.[32] The essence of benchmarking is to compare your resources against those of your competitors on the basis of two questions: (1) Which resources are most important in conferring sustainable competitive advantage in **your industry?** (2) How strong are your strengths and weaknesses as compared to your competitors? Benchmarking then involves four steps:

1 **Choose a benchmark organization** to compare yourself with. To assess your own competitiveness you have to benchmark against your competitors, in particular the 'best in class'. If you are facing a single most important competitor, you may learn most from benchmarking directly against that competitor, rather than an industry average. Alternatively, you can benchmark against the industry leader in another country to explore your potential for further improvement.

2 **Identify the relevant resources.** This step is essentially the resources audit that we have discussed earlier. You can classify resources using the categories of primary resources (Table 4.1), the value chain (Figure 4.1) and the list of cross-functional capabilities (Table 4.2).

3 **Assess the importance of your resources.** As decision maker, you need to focus on those resources that are most relevant to compete *in your industry*. The VRIO framework can help you in this assessment: resources meeting the VRIO criteria (Table 4.3) are more likely to be important. However, keep

LEARNING OBJECTIVE

3 Use benchmarking to consider outsourcing and offshoring decisions

benchmarking
An examination of resources to perform a particular activity compared against competitors.

Figure 4.2 Benchmarking SAP

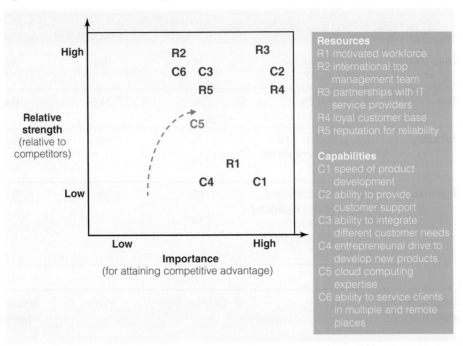

Note: These are indicative examples based on publicly available information only.

in mind that the importance of resources shifts; in this analysis you need to assess the importance in the future. For example, as cloud computing capabilities are becoming important, firms like *SAP* or *Oracle* would want to be ahead of their competitors in developing such capabilities!

4 **Assess the relative strengths** of the resources you have identified, compared to your benchmark organization(s). The challenge here is to be objective: it is easy to be swayed by past glories and successes. For example, *Toyota*'s business model has been widely admired inside and outside the company, which may have inhibited top management from recognizing early warning signs of an impending crisis and major quality control issues in 2009/10.[33] An outside advisor can be very helpful in providing an unbiased assessment.

Plotting capabilities in the style of Figure 4.2 will help you identify what your firm is good at, and what you need to improve. We illustrate the use of this framework with *SAP*, the chapter's Opening Case. Capabilities in the top right quadrant of Figure 4.2 indicate growth potential; you may consider exploiting them further by expanding into new businesses. For example, capabilities in reliable customer support enable *SAP* to retain the trust of a loyal customer base. Capabilities in the bottom right quadrant are potential weaknesses that you need to overcome to keep up with your competitors. For example, *SAP*'s leadership had to address issues of speed of innovation and internal cohesion in a multinational workforce. In this analysis, however, keep in mind that the importance and relative strengths are constantly changing, especially in fast moving industries such as information technology.

Benchmarking is a useful analytical tool – but no more than that. The generation, display and discussion of data in a benchmarking analysis provides managers with insight and understanding of their own organization. An inferior score suggests that an issue may need to be addressed, but it does not imply that the competitor's structure and processes should be imitated – that may not be feasible because many key capabilities are organizationally embedded. Moreover, benchmarking only tells you where you have catch-up potential; it doesn't tell you how to overtake your competitor. To overtake, you need to be better than they are – which may require entirely different processes and capabilities. Hence the insights from the benchmarking exercise provide critical input for making strategic decisions, such as outsourcing and offshoring; they do not automatically suggest a conclusion.

Application: outsourcing

One way to overcome a strategic weakness is to outsource the activity (Figure 4.1). Outsourcing is defined as turning over an activity to an outside supplier that will perform it on behalf of the focal firm.[34] For example, many consumer products companies (such as *adidas* and *Nike*), which possess strong capabilities in upstream activities (such as design) and downstream activities (such as marketing), have outsourced manufacturing to independent suppliers at home and abroad.

In addition to manufacturing processes, a number of service activities, such as information technology (IT), human resources (HR) and logistics, are frequently outsourced to service providers in a process known as business process outsourcing (BPO). A driving force is that many specialist service providers have developed capabilities in activities that are needed in multiple industries. For example, *IBM*, *TCS* and *Infosys* provide IT services; *Hewitt Associates* and *Manpower* administer HR; *Flextronics* and *Videoton* offer contract manufacturing; while *DHL* and *Li & Fung* manage other firms' logistics. These specialist firms enable such activities to be broken off from their client firms and leveraged to serve multiple clients with greater economies of scale.[35] For client firms, such outsourcing results in 'leaner and meaner' organizations that utilize their core capabilities.

Outsourcing can take place at home or internationally. In fact, when you head for lunch you may be served by a company contracted by your university or employer to run their cafeterias. That is outsourcing too. Often outsourcing is a domestic transaction with a local business partner. Yet that partner can be an MNE operating around the world. For example, *Sodexho* from France specializes in hotel and catering services, including the management of company cafeterias; UK-based *G4S* provides security services from guards to money transports; and *ISS* from Denmark cleans offices and public spaces – you may have seen cleaners wearing their logo at airports around the world.

Benchmarking can help to assess outsourcing opportunities. For this purpose, the resources and the performance of the internal organization need to be benchmarked against those of a potential outsourcing service provider. If that partner is better at a particular activity, say analyzing financial data or managing the company cafeteria, then outsourcing should be considered. However, the second question then is whether the interface with the external partner can be managed as smoothly and efficiently as the interface between units of the same firm. We return to this question in Chapter 6.

Application: offshoring

The decision to outsource is often closely related to the geographic dimension – domestic versus foreign locations.[36] When activities are moved from a firm's main country of operations to another country, we talk of offshoring. Decisions over offshoring are largely driven by differences in production costs, taking into consideration

outsourcing
Turning over an activity to an outside supplier that will perform it on behalf of the firm.

business process outsourcing (BPO)
The outsourcing of business services such as IT, HR or logistics.

offshoring
Moving an activity to a location abroad.

IN FOCUS 4.3

Poland competes with India for BPO

Poland is emerging as a favourite location for back-office operations in Europe. Rather than sending their work to India, financial service firms, IT providers and logistics firms opt for nearshoring. Central and Eastern Europe has become an attractive location for offshoring from Western Europe, especially for complex back-office operations. For example, Warsaw hosts *Citigroup*'s global anti-money laundering operation and *Procter & Gamble*'s logistics and supply coordination unit. Similarly, strategy consultants like *Cap Gemini* and *Accenture* and IT service providers like *IBM* and *Infosys* (from India!) have established offices in Poland.

Poland and its neighbouring countries offer several attractions. A wide range of technical skills and competencies in European languages are readily available. The cultural differences that often undermine the effectiveness of interactions with partners in India or China are much lower. Moreover, Poland operates under EU rules and regulations, which makes some administrative processes easier. Also, the practicalities of managing an operation are easier than in East Asia: transportation costs are lower, smaller time zone differences facilitate communication, and bosses from Western Europe can visit their staff in single-day trips.

Even warehousing and logistics are nearshored: *Amazon* operates three fulfilment centres in Poland, even though it is not present in the Polish retail market. These centres serve customers in Western Europe, especially Germany. *Amazon* can save a lot of money in this way. In Germany, *Amazon* pays its logistics workers on average £7.40 per hour, and faces hostile unions that went on strike during the busy Christmas season on 2014. In contrast, Amazon pays its Polish workers £2.35, according to *Financial Times* estimates.

Source: (1) T. Mayer, 2006, Nearshoring to Central and Eastern Europe, *Deutsche Bank Research*, August 14; (2) H. Foy, 2015, Cost-focused businesses beat a path to Poland, *Financial Times*, January 23; (3) D. Rzasa & M. Ahmed, 2015, Lower wages lure Amazon, *Financial Times*, January 23.

---

also transportation costs for both raw materials and finished products, and the need to coordinate between units based in different locations. For example, in the textile and footwear industry, labour costs are so substantially cheaper in China or Vietnam compared to France or Germany that cost savings of offshoring are substantial.

Yet transportation costs and time may reduce total cost savings. Thus some Western European business prefer to offshore their activities to Eastern Europe, including Italian fashion businesses in Slovenia and BPO in Poland (In Focus 4.3). Known as **nearshoring**, offshoring within Europe keeps travel and transport costs low, while reducing institutional differences.[37]

nearshoring
Offshoring to a nearby location, i.e. within Europe.
reshoring
Bringing activities back to a firm's home country.

A decision to offshore involves a lot of sunk cost, but it is not permanent. Some companies have been **reshoring** activities, i.e. bringing them back to their home country. There are three main reasons for this trend.[37] First, labour costs are rising fast in China and other emerging economies, which diminishes the labour cost advantage, while higher fuel costs increase transportation costs. Second, companies have become more aware of the risks of offshoring (and offshore outsourcing in particular), especially the negative effects on innovation and the risk of disruptions in complex supply chains. For example, *Steiff*, a German maker of teddy bears and other children's toys, moved its production back to Europe in 2008 because the two months of shipping toys from Asia to Europe reduced the company's ability to react to changes in market trends in Europe.[38] Similarly, bathroom armature maker *Ostnor* moved manufacturing back to Sweden after experiencing quality and supply chain problems in China (In Focus 4.4).

IN FOCUS 4.4

Ostnor *offshores and reshores*

In a small town in Sweden, four hours north of Stockholm, a company named *Ostnor* has made bathroom armatures and mixers since 1965. Faced with German and Swiss competitors invading its Swedish home market, *Ostnor* decided in 2003 to follow the trend and offshore outsource its production to China. However, business did not develop well: lead times for new product introduction became longer, capital employed increased because of the need to hold more stock in the warehouses, and quality control consumed substantial resources. The relocation of production to China turned into a nightmare.

In 2010, a new CEO, Claes Seldeby decided to turn back time. The new vision was reshoring, bringing back the business to its hometown of Mora. Swedish craftsmen from the local community were again to make the armatures using high technology and local inputs. Yet reshoring wasn't easy either. Young people in the local area were looking for job opportunities, but they needed to be trained – and manufacturing jobs were not so popular in the internet generation. So, *Ostnor* invited school classes to visit their factories to see the high tech nature of the work, aiming to attract future apprentices. Another challenge was finding suppliers for manufactured components in Europe; Chinese suppliers were either not interested or not able to deliver the relatively small volumes to Sweden.

'Made in Sweden' thus became central to the identity of the firm. Consumers valued the Swedish identity because they had become sceptical of the reliability of products imported from the Far East. Moreover, bringing all key activities together was also critical for other capabilities that *Ostnor* needed to build to compete in the top end of the market. For example, innovation processes were modernized to stay in close touch with consumer preferences. When Claes Seldeby arrived in 2010, the R&D unit was almost all male. Yet 82% of purchasing decisions for bathroom and kitchen equipment were made by women in Sweden! So, he brought new people into the innovation team that would understand not only the technologies but also the consumers. Moreover, *Ostnor* enhanced its capabilities in workflow organization, supply chain management and collaborations with customers, suppliers and designers – all of which were strengthened by proximity between partners in Sweden.

After developing its capabilities to support a top-end brand, *Ostnor* set its eyes on international markets. In 2013, 76% of its sales were still in Sweden. In 2014, *Ostnor* acquired a Danish competitor, *Damixa,* and together they became number one or number two in all five Nordic countries. Elsewhere, *Ostnor* was pursuing market niches with own-sales subsidiaries in Germany, the Netherlands, Belgium, Singapore and China, and distributors to the UK, France, Russia, Australia and the Baltic countries. Yet many of its competitors enjoyed much larger scale economies. Thus the critical question remained, how much of a premium are customers willing to pay for quality 'made in Sweden'?

Source: (1) Presentation by Claes Seldeby to scholarly workshop in Mora, 2014; (2) Ostnor Annual Report 2013; (3) *Fyens Stiftstidende*, 2013, Damixa solgt til svensk konkurrent, May 6; (4) T. Nilsson, 2013, Det krävs stordåd för ny svensk production, *Dagens Industri*, December 2.

Because the two terms outsourcing and offshoring have emerged rather recently, there is a great deal of confusion, especially among some journalists, who often casually equate them. So, to minimize confusion, we go from two terms to four in Figure 4.3, based on locations and modes (in-house versus outsource): (1) offshore outsourcing, (2) domestic outsourcing, (3) captive offshoring (setting up subsidiaries abroad – the work done is in-house, but the location is foreign) and (4) domestic in-house activity.[39] For example, a firm contracting a supplier in India to manage its IT services is actually engaged in offshore outsourcing. Since Indian companies such as *TCS, Wipro* and *Infosys* have developed special competences for such services – and global players like *IBM* and *Accenture* also use India as a base – offshore

offshore outsourcing
Outsourcing to another firm doing the activity abroad.

domestic outsourcing
Outsourcing to a firm in the same country.

captive offshoring
setting up subsidiaries abroad – the work done is in-house but the location is foreign.

Figure 4.3   Offshoring and outsourcing

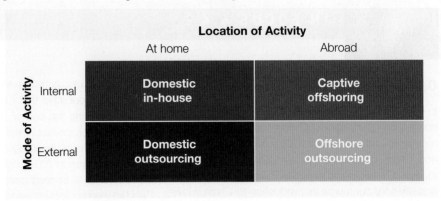

outsourcing of IT to India not only enables firms to cut costs, but to tap into the best capability pools around the world.[40]

DEBATES AND EXTENSIONS

LEARNING OBJECTIVE

4 Participate in two
   leading debates
   on resources in an
   international context

Challenges in the application of the resource-based view relate in particular to its long-term implications. In the short-run, firms may do well by exploiting their existing resources. Yet taking a longer view, their attention needs to turn to the protection, renewal and enhancement of their resources.[41] We here discuss to challenges arising from this challenge: (1) long-term consequences of offshoring and (2) dynamic capabilities.

Long-term consequences of outsourcing

As noted earlier, outsourcing – or more specifically, offshore outsourcing – has emerged as a major corporate strategy in the 21st century. What has become very controversial recently is the outsourcing of increasingly high-end services, especially BPO, to countries such as India. Because digitization of service work was enabled only recently by the rise of the internet and the reduction of international communication costs, whether such outsourcing will bring long-term benefit or hindrance to Western firms and economies is a hot debate.[42]

Proponents argue that outsourcing creates enormous value for firms. Western firms are able to tap into low-cost and high-quality labour, translating into significant cost savings. They can also focus on their core capabilities, which may add more value than dealing with non-core (and often uncompetitive) activities. For example, *Apple*'s products are essentially all assembled by companies such as *Foxconn* or *Pegatron*, mostly in China. Yet the value added is mostly captured by *Apple* itself, and hence by shareholders and employees of the company. Of the costs of an iPad, only 2% go to Chinese labour, 5% to labour elsewhere, 31% to costs of materials and 15% to distribution and retail.[43] A whopping 47% of the price of an iPad goes to profits (30% to *Apple*, 17% to others). The 31% for materials of course also include raw materials or components that are made in China, or elsewhere in Asia.

However, if European firms follow the advice of outsourcing gurus, 'even core functions like engineering, R&D, manufacturing and marketing can – and often

Figure 4.4 From original *equipment* manufacturer (OEM) to original *design* manufacturer (ODM)

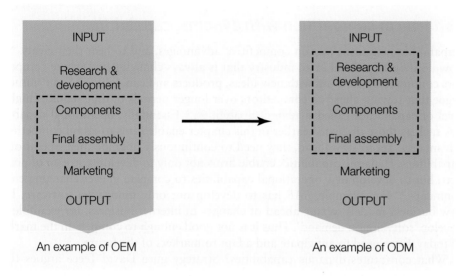

An example of OEM   An example of ODM

Note: Dotted lines represent organizational boundaries. A further extension is to become an original *brand* manufacturer (OBM), which would incorporate brand ownership and management in the marketing area. For graphic simplicity, it is not shown here.

should – be moved outside',[44] what does this imply for the firms' long-term development of capabilities? Does offshore outsourcing nurture rivals?[45] Indian IT service providers like *Infosys* and *TCS* are emerging as strong rivals of *Accenture* and *IBM*. They are able to do so in part because they built up their capabilities doing work for European and American clients in the 1990s.

Offshoring service providers are gradually moving up the value chain. In manufacturing, many Asian firms, which used to be original equipment manufacturers (OEMs) executing design blueprints provided by Western firms, now want to have a piece of action in design by becoming original design manufacturers (ODMs) (see Figure 4.4). Having mastered low-cost and high-quality manufacturing, Asian firms such as *Foxconn*, *Pegatron* and *Huawei* are indeed capable of capturing some design function from Western firms such as *Dell*, *HP* and *Apple*.[46] They tend to start with small design changes that facilitate the production process, and gradually upgrade to adding new features and creating entirely new products.

As they upgrade, however, suppliers can become a competitive threat to their former masters. Several Asian firms have openly announced that their real ambition is to become original brand manufacturers (OBMs). For example, *HTC* from Taiwan has for many years built mobile phones as an ODM for Western operators such as *Verizon* and *Orange*. Based on this experience, it set out to develop its own brand to challenge *Apple* and *Nokia*.[47] While *HTC*'s success was shortlived, several others follow their trail into the smartphone industry, including *Huawei*, *ZTE* and *Lenovo*. In fact, *Xiaomi* has been able to build its own smartphone by tapping into the supplier network created by the market leaders (Integrative Case *Xiaomi*). For the time being, it seems that the main value added by new products is still in the development and marketing offices located in, for example, California. Similarly, with the increasing emphasis in electronics on digital (as opposed to analogue) products, countries such as Germany, the UK and the USA with strong software development expertise have

original equipment manufacturer (OEM) A firm that executes the design blueprints provided by other firms and manufactures such products.

original design manufacturer (ODM) A firm that both designs and manufactures products.

original brand manufacturer (OBM) A firm that designs, manufactures and markets branded products.

been able to reassert themselves in industries, such as consumer electronics. But for how much longer?

Long-term competition with dynamic capabilities

Capabilities help firms to gain competitive advantages, and to beat their rivals. Yet how do they stay ahead in an industry that is always changing and where competitors continuously come up with new ideas, products and capabilities? Some authors argue that staying ahead of competitors over longer periods of time requires higher level of capabilities called dynamic capabilities.[48] Essentially, operational capabilities such as those discussed earlier in this chapter enable firms to attain competitive advantages. Yet to stay ahead, they need to continuously upgrade their operational capabilities. Dynamic capabilities enable firms not only to develop a stream of products, but to develop new operational capabilities to compete in ever-changing environments.[49] For example, *SAP* has to develop not only innovative software, but new business models to stay ahead of changes in internet business, for example to develop 'software on demand'. Thus it is not good enough to compete in the market of today, firms need to anticipate and adapt to markets of the future.

dynamic capabilities
Higher level capabilities that enable an organization to continuously adapt to new technologies and changes in the external environment.

What constitutes dynamic capabilities? Strategy guru David Teece argues that three types of managerial activities can make a capability dynamic.[50] First is sensing, which means identifying and assessing opportunities outside your company. For example, based in Silicon Valley, *Apple* engineers were in touch with latest trends and idea. *Nokia* also had a lab in Silicon Valley, but their key development people were in Finland, and not close enough to the 'vibe' of Silicon Valley. Second is seizing, which means mobilizing your resources to capture value from those opportunities. Steve Jobs built *Apple*'s capabilities step-by-step; including digital rights management, how best to cut deals with studios and recording companies, and design capabilities that enabled presenting technology in a user-friendly device. Third is transforming or continuous renewal of the enterprise. *Apple* has reinvented itself several times, reorganizing the company's capabilities to lead in new generations of technologies – from PCs to iPods and to iPhones. *Apple*'s ability to reinvent itself is closely associated with its his management team.

Sceptics of the dynamic capabilities approach argue that dynamic capabilities are impossible to identify because they are so diverse and abstract. Looking back, it may be possible to say what made a firm successful over long periods of time (such as Steve Jobs' leadership style), but no one knows what dynamic capabilities will allow firms to thrive in the future. In theory it makes sense to distinguish operational and dynamic capabilities, but it is hard to derive specific managerial tools from this insight.

IMPLICATIONS FOR PRACTICE

LEARNING OBJECTIVE

5 Draw implications for action

How does the resource-based view answer the big question: what determines the success and failure of firms around the globe? The answer is straightforward: winners exploit some value-creating, rare, hard-to-imitate and organizationally embedded resources that competitors do not have.[51] In international business, the challenge thus is to use resources to compete in foreign markets through exports (Chapter 5) or direct investment (Chapter 6), to use imports and foreign operations to strengthen a company's core resources. In translating the resource-based view into strategies, two fundamental questions arise for managers: (1) how can we best exploit our current resources and (2) how should we build resources that we can exploit tomorrow?

Table 4.4 Implications for action

- Managers need to understand their resources, based on the VRIO framework, to optimize their resource exploitation.

- Managers need to continuously create new resources, in part by benchmarking against the best, and in part by developing entirely new capabilities that go beyond the state-of-the-art competitors.

- Students are advised to make themselves 'untouchables' whose jobs cannot be offshored.

The questions apply not only to firms but to you as students preparing your career (Table 4.4).

First, managers need to focus on the identification, development, and leveraging of their capabilities. The subtlety comes when managers attempt, via the VRIO framework, to distinguish resources that are value-creating, rare, hard-to-imitate and organizationally embedded from those that do not share these attributes. Managers, who cannot pay attention to every resource, must have some sense of what really matters, and what is likely to matter in the future. Benchmarking and the VRIO framework help managers to evaluate their firms' capabilities relative to rivals, and thus to provide a basis for strategic decisions. What really matters are not primary resources that are relatively easy to imitate, but knowledge-based capabilities that are harder for rivals to get hold of. This is why many people call the new global economy a 'knowledge economy'.[52]

Second, managers need to continuously upgrade their capability to remain competitive in rapidly-changing environments. Benchmarking plays an important part in this, as firms aim to catch up in functions and activities where they are lagging, while preventing others catching up where they are leading. However, imitation of best practice may not be enough. Follower firms that meticulously replicate every resource possessed by winning firms can hope to attain competitive parity, though by the time they catch up to the leader, the leader may already have moved on.[53] To achieve competitive advantage, firms need to develop their own unique capabilities. The best performing firms often create new ways of adding value.

Leaders, on the other hand, need to be aware that no competitive advantage lasts forever. Over time, all advantages may erode. Each of *IBM*'s product-related advantages associated with tabulating machines, mainframes, and PCs was sustained for a period of time. But eventually these advantages disappeared. Therefore, the lesson for all firms, including current market leaders, is to develop strategic *foresight* – 'over-the-horizon radar' is a good metaphor – that enables them to anticipate future needs and move early to identify and develop resources for future competition.

Finally, here is a very personal and relevant implication for action. As a student who is probably studying this book in a developed (read: high-wage and thus high-cost!) country in Western Europe, you may be wondering: What do I get out of this? How do I cope with the future of global competition? There are two lessons you can learn. First, the debate on offshoring, a part of the larger debate on globalization (Chapters 1 and 9), is very relevant and directly affects your future as a manager, a consumer and a citizen. So do not be a couch potato. Be active, become informed, get involved and be prepared, because it is not only *their* debate; it is *yours* as well. Second, be very serious about the advice of the resource-based view. Although this view has been developed to advise firms, there is no reason you cannot develop that into a resource-based view of the *individual*. That is, you should develop your personal capabilities to prepare your career.

CHAPTER SUMMARY

1 Explain what firms' resources are

- Resources include primary resources and capabilities that provide the basis for firms to attain competitive advantages, and to grow.

- Primary resources include tangible and intangible assets, as well as human resources.

- Capabilities can be classified by stages of the value chain, or by processes integrating functions within an organization.

2 Assess the resources of a firm using the VRIO framework

- A VRIO framework suggests that only resources that are value-creating, rare, hard to imitate and organizationally embedded will generate sustainable competitive advantage.

3 Use benchmarking to consider outsourcing and offshoring decisions

- Benchmarking is a technique of comparing a firm's capabilities to its rivals.

- Outsourcing is defined as turning over all or part of an activity to an outside supplier.

- Offshoring is defined as relocating an activity to another country, either in-house or with outsourcing, to take advantage of locational advantages in that country.

4 Participate in two leading debates on resources in an international context

- In the long run, is offshoring beneficial or detrimental for Western firms and economies?

- In the long run, how can dynamic capabilities help firms to stay ahead in ever-changing industries?

5 Draw implications for action

- Managers need to understand their resources based on the VRIO framework to optimize their resource exploitation.

- Managers need to continuously create new resources, in part by benchmarking against the best, and in part by developing entirely new capabilities that go beyond the competitors' state-of-the-art.

- Students are advised to make themselves 'untouchables' whose jobs cannot be offshored.

KEY TERMS

Appropriability
Benchmarking
Business process outsourcing (BPO)
Capability
Captive (in-house) offshoring
Competitive advantage
Causal ambiguity
Domestic outsourcing
Dynamic capabilities
Goodwill
Human resources
Intangible resources
Intangible resources

Internationally transferable resources
Location-bound resources
Nearshoring
Offshore outsourcing
Offshoring
Organizational culture
Original brand manufacturer (OBM)
Original design manufacturer (ODM)
Original equipment manufacturer (OEM)
Outsourcing

Primary resources
Reshoring
Resource-based view
Resources
Social complexity
Sustainable competitive advantage
Tangible assets
Tangible resources
Temporary competitive advantage
Value chain
VRIO framework

CRITICAL DISCUSSION QUESTIONS

1 Pick any pair of rivals (such as *Samsung/Apple*, *Lego/Mattel* and *Boeing/Airbus*) and explain why one outperforms another. Apply both a benchmark analysis (Figure 4.2) and a VRIO framework (Table 4.3) to the resources of the chosen pair.

2 Conduct a VRIO analysis of your business school or university in terms of (1) perceived reputation (such as rankings), (2) faculty strength, (3) student quality, (4) administrative efficiency, (5) IT and (6) building maintenance, relative to the top-three rival schools/universities. If you were the dean with a limited budget, where would you invest scarce financial resources to make your school number one over its rivals? Why?

3 One reason why outsourcing service providers have lower costs is that their labour force may not be unionized. Would it be appropriate for an established industry leader to outsource to such a company?

4 Since firms read information posted on competitors' websites, is it ethical to provide misleading information on resources on corporate websites? Do the benefits outweigh the costs?

RECOMMENDED READINGS

-J. Barney, 1991, Firm resources and sustained competitive advantage, *JM*, 17: 99–120 – the original paper that explained and popularized the resource-based view.

R. Grant, 2012, Contemporary strategy analysis, 8th ed., Oxford: Blackwell – a strategy textbook that is grounded in the resource-based view, see especially chapters 5 and 6.

G. Hamel & C.K. Prahalad, 1994, *Competing for the Future*, Boston: Harvard Business School Press – a management guru book using resource-based thinking.

C. Helfat, S. Finkelstein, W. Mitchell, M. Peteraf, H. Singh, T. Teece & S.G. Winter, 2007, *Dynamic Capabilities: Understanding Strategic Change in Organizations*, Oxford: Blackwell – leading scholars discuss the state-of-the-art of the resource-based view and of dynamic capabilities research.

M.W. Peng, 2001, The resource-based view and international business, *JM*, 27: 803–829 – a paper applying resource-based reasoning to the international sphere.

CLOSING CASE

Lego's secrets

Lego is everywhere – toys, games, books, magazines, competitions, retail stores, theme parks and now movies. If all the approximately 400 billion colourful interlocking bricks ever produced by *Lego* were to be divided equally among the world's population, each person would have 86 bricks! *Fortune* magazine half-joked that 'at least ten billion are under sofa cushions and three billion are inside vacuum cleaners'. By itself, a single plastic brick is lifeless. But snap two of these inorganic blocks together, and suddenly they take on a life of their own and a world of nearly infinite possibilities opens up. Igniting the imagination of millions of children and adults around the world, the little *Lego* brick has become a universal building block for fostering creativity. Around the world *Lego* fan clubs abound, often with their own conferences and

competitions. 'With the possible exception of *Apple*, arguably no brand sparks as much cult-like devotion as *Lego*,' noted an expert. What are *Lego*'s secrets?

Innovation and experimentation are among the foremost characteristics of *Lego*. Derived from the Danish *leg godt* ('play well'), *Lego* was founded in 1932 by Ole Kirk Christiansen, a carpenter from Billund, a rural town in the West of Denmark (*Lego* Group is still head-quartered in Billund.) As a firm self-styled 'to stimulate children's imagination and creativity' and 'to nurture the child in each of us,' *Lego* is known for being willing to entertain numerous experiments in order to capture the hearts and minds of its fickle primary customers – boys aged seven to 16 – as well as the wallets of their parents. *Lego* started with wooden toys. In 1947, it became the first Danish toymaker to experiment with plastics, even though trade magazines at that time predicted that plastics would never replace wooden toys.

Lego tinkered with the brick, and initial efforts were not successful. The bricks snapped together, but could not be separated easily. *Lego* continued to experiment, eventually hitting a stud-and-tube coupling design that was patented in 1958. When a child snaps two bricks together, they would stick with a click and stay together until the child separated them with an easy tug. Because such bricks would not come apart, kids could build from the ground up, leveraging what *Lego* continues to call 'clutch power'. While the brick proved to be one of the toy industry's greatest innovations, *Lego*'s experiment marched on, with numerous hits and also numerous misses in the last five decades.

Another *Lego* hallmark is insisting on excellence. Coming from the founder, 'only the best is good enough' is a company motto engraved on a plaque that graces the entrance to *Lego* Group headquarters' cafeteria even today. The seemingly simple tight fit of two bricks – and their easy separation – calls for extremely precise manufacturing. Since the size of each brick is so tiny, misalignment in the range of a few millimeters can easily create a misfit when bricks are stacked together. Competitors can produce *Lego* look-alikes that tolerate higher levels of variations, but kids often quickly figure out *Lego* is the best after playing with competing products for a short while. This is not to say *Lego*'s quality is perfect. It is not, as on average 18 out of one million bricks produced fail to meet *Lego*'s quality standards and have to be tossed. In addition to tight fit and easy separation, *Lego* is also known for its strength. It is legendarily indestructible:

more than half a million people have 'liked' the *Facebook* page 'For those who have experienced the pain caused by stepping on *Lego*'!

Lego is also world-famous for generating a system, not merely a product. Long before the days when computer programmes were supposed to be backward compatible (a new version of Windows needs to allow users to open old files), *Lego* made its bricks backward compatible – new bricks would click with old bricks of the 1950s vintage. As a result, kids (and adults) can mix and match old and new sets and the *Lego* universe can grow exponentially.

Of course it has not always been plain sailing for *Lego*. In the 1990s, Lego entered numerous related lines of business, ranging from book publishing to business consulting inspired by playing children. For example, Lego diversified into themeparks known as *Legoland* – first in Billund, and later also in Germany and the UK. While these parks were popular among children and their parents, the finances never quite worked out and *Lego* kept losing money. In 2005, *Lego* eventually sold its themeparks to *Merlin Entertainment*. In the early 2000s, Lego also produced products like Harry Potter-branded toys under licence of Hollywood film studio *Warner Brothers*. While this venture was profitable in the short term, it distracted the focus of the company.

After many years of poor performance, Jørgen Vig Knudstorp was brought in as new CEO in 2004. The first question he had to address was, what does the *Lego* name stand for? A toy brand, or specific type of

toy, or an experience? His team developed the new vision 'to inspire and develop the builders of tomorrow'. Under Knudstorp's leadership, *Lego* radically refocused on its core business, the bricks, as an inspiration for creative children – and adults. New product lines, such as '*Lego* Friends' targeted at girls, built on the age-old idea of using the brick to create new playing and learning experiences.

A more specific problem was the high costs in the primary production sites in Denmark and Switzerland. *Lego* in 2006 thus offshore outsourced production to *Flextronics* plants in Hungary and the Czech Republic. Yet *Flextronics* was unable to deliver the expected quantity and quality of bricks; both *Lego* and *Flextronics* had underestimated how difficult it is to manufacture those simple yet very precise bricks. Thus in 2008 *Lego* bought those *Flextronics* plants and invested in automation and quality control to ensure that every

brick ever sold under the *Lego* name would easily click with any other *Lego* brick.

CASE DISCUSSION QUESTIONS

1 Applying the VRIO framework, what are the sources of *Lego*'s success?

2 How sustainable is *Lego*'s success in the long run?

3 How did *Lego* recover from a decade of poor performance in the late 1990s/early 2000s?

Sources: (1) N. Lunde, 2012, Miraclet i Lego, Copenhagen: Jyllands-Postens Forlag; (2) *Economist*, 2013, Lego in Asia, November 16: 72; (3) *Economist*, 2014, Unpacking Lego, March 8: 71; (4) D.C. Robertson, 2013, *Brick by Brick: How LEGO Rewrote the Rules of Innovation and Conquered the Global Toy Industry*, New York: Crown Business; (5) *Bloomberg*, 2014, Brick by brick: inside Lego, online video, www.bloomberg.com/news/videos/b/4a56e664-4427-49fc-82fb-2d5e4a6f4502; (6) www.lego.com.

NOTES

'For journal abbreviations please see page xx–xxi.'

1 E. Penrose, 1959, *The Theory of the Growth of the Firm*, London: Blackwell; M. Pettus, 2001, The resource-based view as a developmental growth process, *AMJ*, 44: 878–896; K.E. Meyer, 2006, Globalfocusing: From Domestic Conglomerate to Global Specialist, *JMS*, 43, 1109–1144; C. Pitelis & A. Verbeke, 2007, Edith Penrose and the future of the multinational enterprise, *MIR*, 47: 139–149.

2 J. Barney, 2001, Is the resource-based view a useful perspective for strategic management research? (p. 54), *AMR* 26: 41–56.

3 R. Grant, 1991, The resource-based theory of competitive advantage, *CMR*, 33, 114–135; J. McGee, H. Thomas & D. Wilson, 2005, *Strategy Analysis & Practice*, Maidenhead: McGraw Hill.

4 A. Phene, K. Fladmoe-Lindquist & L. Marsh, 2006, Breakthrough innovations in the US biotechnology industry, *SMJ*, 27: 369–388; E. Danneels, 2007, The process of technological competence leveraging, *SMJ*, 28: 511–533; M. Reitzig & P. Puranam, 2009, Value appropriation as an organizational capability, *SMJ*, 30: 765–789.

5 *The Economist*, 2006, Ethical Business: The body beautiful, March 25.

6 N. Hatch & J. Dyer, 2004, Human capital and learning as a source of competitive advantage, *SMJ*, 25: 1155–1178.

7 C.F. Fey & D.R. Denison, 2003, Organizational culture and effectiveness, *OSc*, 14: 686–706; D.R. Denison, S. Haaland & P. Goelzer, 2004, Corporate culture and organizational effectiveness, *OD*, 33, 98–109;

8 N. O'Regan & A. Ghobadian, 2009, Successful strategic re-orientation: Lessons from Cadbury's experience, *JSM*, 2, 405–412.

9 H. Itami & T. Roehl, 1987, *Mobilizing Invisible Assets*, Cambridge, MA: Harvard University Press; S. Dutta, O. Narasimhan & S. Rajiv, 2005, Conceptualizing and measuring capabilities, *SMJ*, 26: 277–285;

10 M. Porter, 1985, *Competitive Advantage*, New York: Free Press; C. Stabell & O. Fjeldstad, 1998, Configuring value for competitive advantage, *SMJ*, 19: 413–437.

11 G. Johnson, L. Melin & R. Whittington, 2003, Micro strategy and strategizing, *JMS*, 40: 3–22; A. Parmigiani, 2007, Why do firms both make and buy? *SMJ*, 28: 285–311.

12 J. Birkinshaw, R. Nobel & J. Ridderstråle, 2002, Knowledge as a contingency variable, *OSc*, 13: 274–289; M. Subramaniam & M. Youndt, 2005, The influence of intellectual capital on the types of innovative capabilities, *AMJ*, 48: 450–463.

13 W. Henisz, 2003, The power of the Buckley and Casson thesis, *JIBS*, 34: 173–184; M.W. Peng, 2003, Institutional transitions and strategic choices, *AMR*, 28: 275–296.

14 T. Holcomb, M. Holmes & B. Connelly, 2009, Making the most of what you have, SMJ, 30: 457–485; N. Taleb, D. Goldstein & M. Spitznagel, 2009, The six mistakes executives make in risk management, HBR, October: 78–81.

15 J. Barney, 2001, Is the resource-based view a useful perspective for strategic management research? AMR 26: 41–56; J.B. Barney & W.S. Hesterly, 2008, Strategic Management and Competitive Advantage: 2nd ed., Upper Saddle River: Pearson Prentice-Hall.

16 S. Lippman & R. Rumelt, 2003, A bargaining perspective on resource advantage, SMJ, 24: 1069–1086; R. Adner & P. Zemsky, 2006, A demand-based perspective on sustainable competitive advantage, SMJ, 27: 215–239; J. Anderson, J. Narus & W. Van Rossum, 2006, Customer value propositions in business markets, HBR, March: 91–99.

17 D. Leonard-Barton, 1992, Core capabilities and core rigidities, SMJ, 13: 111–125; B. Vissa & A. Chacar, 2009, Leveraging ties, SMJ, 30: 1179–1191.

18 N. Siggelkow, 2001, Change in the presence of fit, AMJ, 44: 838–857; G.P. West & J. DeCastro, 2001, The Achilles heel of firm strategy, JMS, 38: 417–442; D. Lavie, 2006, Capability reconfiguration, AMR, 31: 153–174.

19 G. Hamel, 2006, Management innovation (p. 78), HBR, February: 72–84.

20 German Chamber Ticker (China), 2015, In Person Clas Neumann, February, p. 42.

21 N. Carr, 2003, Does IT Matter? Boston: Harvard Business School Press.

22 The Economist, 2005, Patents and Technology: Thinking for themselves, October 22; S. Ethiraj, P. Kale, M. Krishnana & J. Singh, 2005, Where do capabilities come from and how do they matter? SMJ, 26: 25–45.

23 A. Knott, D. Bryce & H. Posen, 2003, On the strategic accumulation of intangible assets, OSc, 14: 192–208; D. Miller, 2003, An asymmetry-based view of advantage, SMJ, 24: 961–976; G. Ray, J. Barney & W. Muhanna, 2004, Capabilities, business processes, and competitive advantage, SMJ, 25: 23–37.

24 Business Week, 2005, Better than robots, December 26.

25 A. King, 2007, Disentangling interfirm and intrafirm causal ambiguity, AMR, 32: 156–178; T. Powell, D. Lovallo & C. Caringal, 2006, Causal ambiguity, management perception, and firm performance, AMR, 31: 175–196; S. Jonsson & P. Renger, 2009, Normative barriers to imitation, SMJ, 30: 517–536.

26 M. Lieberman & S. Asaba, 2006, Why do firms imitate each other? AMR, 31: 366–385.

27 A. Lado, N. Boyd, P. Wright & M Kroll, 2006, Paradox and theorizing within the resource-based view, AMR, 31: 115–131.

28 S. Tallman, 1991, Strategic management models and resource-based strategies among MNEs in a host market, SMJ, 12: 69–82; J. Birkinshaw & N. Hood, 1998, Multinational subsidiary evolution, AMR, 23: 773–795.

29 T. Kostova & K. Roth, 2003, Social capital in multinational corporations and a micro-macro model of its formation, AMR, 28: 297–317; P. Moran, 2005, Structural vs. relational embeddedness, SMJ, 26: 1129–1151.

30 K.E. Meyer & M.W. Peng, 2005, Probing Theoretically into Central and Eastern Europe, JIBS, 36, 600–621

31 S. McEvily & B. Chakravarthy, 2002, The persistence of knowledge-based advantage, SMJ, 23: 285–305; S. Zahra & A. Nielsen, 2002, Sources of capabilities, integration, and technology commercialization, SMJ, 23: 377–398.

32 R. Grant, 2010, Contemporary Strategy Analysis, 7th ed., Oxford: Blackwell (140–144).

33 The Economist, 2009, Briefing: Toyota: Losing its shine, December 12; D. Pilling, 2010, How Toyota engineered its own downfall, Financial Times, February 11.

34 J. Barthelemy, 2003, The seven deadly sins of outsourcing, AME, 17 (2): 87–98; F. Rothaermel, M. Hitt & L. Jobe, 2006, Balancing vertical integration and strategic outsourcing, SMJ, 27: 1033–1056.

35 M. Jacobides & S. Winter, 2005, The co-evolution of capabilities and transaction costs (p. 404), SMJ, 26: 395–413; M. Kang, J. Mahoney & D. Tan, 2009, Why do firms make unilateral investments specific to other firms? SMJ, 30: 117–135.

36 S. Beugelsdijk, T. Pedersen & B. Petersen, 2009, Is there a trend towards global value chain specialization? JIM, 15: 126–141; J. Doh, K. Bunyaratavej & E. Hahn, 2009, Separable but not equal, JIBS, 40: 926–943; M. Kotabe & R. Mudambi, 2009, Global sourcing and value creation, JIM, 15: 121–125.

37 J. Lamont & J. Leahy, 2010, US matches Indian outsourcing costs, Financial Times, August 17; The Economist, 2013; Special report outsourcing and offshoring: Here, there and everywhere, January, 19.

38 S. Bottler, 2010, Wenn Unternehmen nach Deutschland zurückkehren, Handelsblatt, February 4.

39 M. Kenney, S. Massini & T. Murtha, 2009, Offshoring administrative and technical work, JIBS, 40: 887–900; B. Kedia & D. Mukherjee, 2009, Understanding offshoring, JWB, 44: 250–261; K. Kumar, P. van Fenema & M. von Glinow, 2009, Offshoring and the global distribution of work, JIBS, 40: 642–667; F. Contractor, V. Kumar, S. Kundu & T. Pedersen, eds, 2010, Outsourcing and Offshoring of Business Activities, Cambridge: Cambridge University Press.

40 M. Joseph, 2012, How India became an outsourcing magnet, New York Times, March 28.

41 J. Uotila, M. Maula, T. Keil & A. Zahra, 2009, Exploration, exploitation, and financial performance, SMJ, 30: 221–231; S. Raisch, J. Birkinshaw, G. Probst & M. Tushman, 2009, Organizational ambidexterity, OSc, 20: 685–695.

42 J. Doh, 2005, Offshore outsourcing, *JMS*, 42: 695–704.

43 *The Economist*, 2012, Trade Statistics: iPadded, January 21.

44 M. Gottfredson, R. Puryear & S. Phillips, 2005, Strategic sourcing (p. 132), *HBR*, February: 132–139.

45 C. Rossetti & T. Choi, 2005, On the dark side of strategic sourcing, *AME*, 19 (1): 46–60.

46 A. van Agtmael, 2007, *The Emerging Market Century*, New York: Simon & Schuster.

47 *The Economist*, 2009, Face value: Upwardly mobile, July 11.

48 C.E. Helfat & M. Peteraf, 2003, The dynamic resource-based view, *SMJ*, 24: 997–1010; D. Teece, G. Pisano & A. Shuen, 1997, Dynamic capabilities and strategic management, *SMJ*, 18: 509–533; K.M. Eisenhart & J.A. Martin, Dynamic Capabilities: What are they? *SMJ*, 21: 1105–1121; S.E. Dixon, K.E. Meyer & M. Day, 2010, Stages of organizational transformation in transition economies: A dynamic capabilities approach, *JMS*, 47: 416–436.

49 C.E. Helfat & M. Lieberman, 2002, The birth of capabilities, *ICC*, 12, 725–760.

50 D. Teece, 2007, Explicating dynamic capabilities, *SMJ*, 28: 1319–1350; D. Teece, 2014, A dynamic capabilities-based entrepreneurial theory of the multinational enterprise, *JIBS* 45: 8–37.

51 W. DeSarbo, C. Nenedetto, M. Song & I. Sinha, 2005, Revisiting the Miles and Snow strategic framework, *SMJ*, 26; 47–74; G.T. Hult, D. Ketchen & S. Slater, 2005, Market orientation and performance, *SMJ*, 26: 1173–1181.

52 N. Foss, 2005, *Strategy, Economic Organization, and the Knowledge Economy*, Oxford: Oxford University Press.

53 G. Hamel & C.K. Prahalad, 1994, *Competing for the Future*, Boston: Harvard Business School Press.

PART TWO

BUSINESS ACROSS BORDERS

5   Trading Internationally
6   Investing Abroad Directly
7   Exchange Rates

CHAPTER FIVE

TRADING INTERNATIONALLY

LEARNING OBJECTIVES

After studying this chapter, you should be able to

1 Use the resource-based and institution-based views to explain why nations trade

2 Understand classic and modern theories of international trade

3 Appreciate how economic and political institutions influence international trade

4 Participate in two leading debates on international trade

5 Draw implications for action

OPENING CASE

EU exports: emerging economy opportunities

The growth of emerging economies, such as China, is creating tremendous opportunities for European businesses. Traditionally seen primarily as a source for cheap imports of manufacturing goods and raw materials, emerging economies have become major markets for European exports. Large countries like Russia, India and Brazil, offer large markets, while especially the four 'Asian tigers' (Korea, Taiwan, Hong Kong and Singapore) demand sophisticated industrial inputs and consumer brands. Countries in geographic proximity, like Turkey, Ukraine, Algeria and Morocco, offer opportunities to trade without the hassles of long-distance travel and shipments.

However, the pattern varies across countries (Figure 5.1). British companies are strong in India,

Figure 5.1   EU exports to emerging economies (in per cent of total exports)

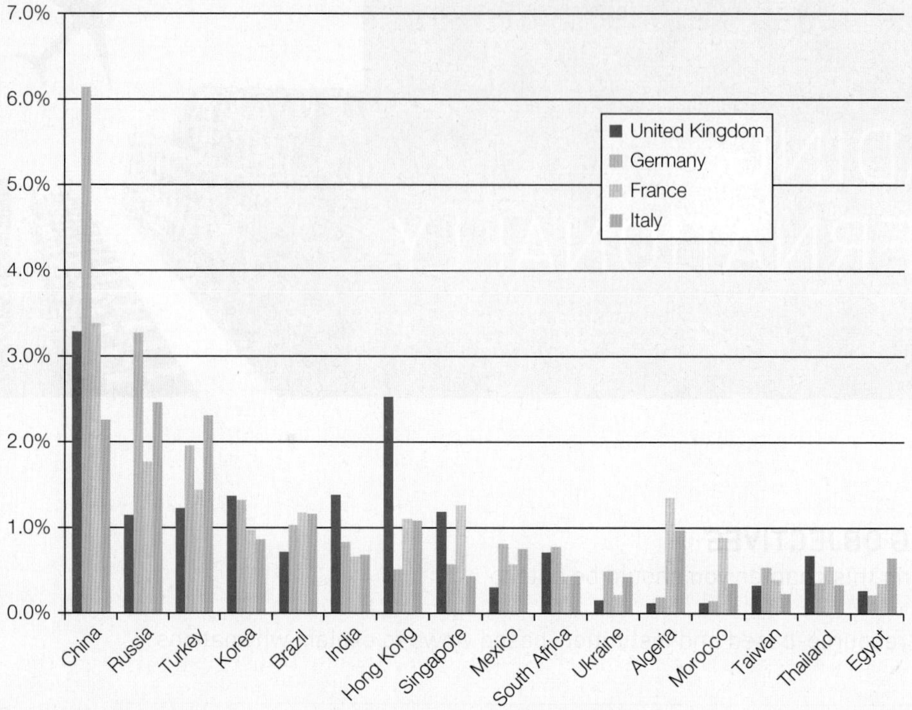

Note: Destination countries are in order of their share in EU exports. Data refer to 2013.

Source: Authors' creation using Eurostat data.

Hong Kong and South Africa, where they can build on shared language and historical ties that date back to colonial times. French exports are particularly strong in the western part of the Mediterranean (Algeria and Morocco), whereas Italian businesses focus more on the eastern Mediterranean (Turkey and Egypt). East European EU members, like Poland and Lithuania, have strong trade ties with Russia, Ukraine and Belarus. Clearly geography and history still matter a lot in international trade!

In contrast, China is a distant country, which did not enjoy a long continuous trade relationship with Europe. Yet its recent economic growth offers large trade opportunities. In only ten years, from 2005 to 2014, EU exports to China tripled(!) in volume, from €52 billion to €165 billion. Who has been taking advantage of the growth opportunities in China? The Chinese in fact hold strong views – or country-of-origin images – for some European countries. German products are believed to be of high quality and reliable, which explains why German products account

for a remarkable 46% of EU imports to China. French and Italian products are regarded as fashionable and luxurious; think of *L'Oreal* or *Gucci*. France and Italy thus account for 10% and 6% respectively. The second-largest volume of EU imports are from Britain, which has both high-tech brands like *Rolls Royce* and fashionable brands like *Burberry*. The real European number 2, however, is not in the EU: Switzerland exports more than the UK or France, and its exports received another boost from a free-trade agreement with China in 2014.

Of course, in part there are lots of German exports because Germany is big. To assert who is most savvy in the pursuit of the China market, we should look for how much China accounts relative to all of a country's exports (Figure 5.2). In fact, German businesses are most China oriented; 6.6% of German exports go to China, which is almost twice the weighted average across all EU countries of 3.5%. UK firms sharply increased their China orientation in 2014 when the China share increased from 3.3% to 5.1%.

Figure 5.2   EU exports to China (in per cent of total exports)

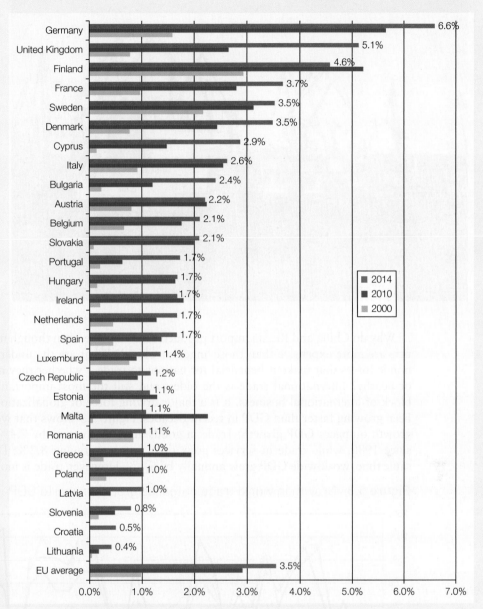

Note: Data for Croatia 2000 and 2010 are not available.

Source: Authors' creation using Eurostat data.

The Nordic countries have also been very active in the China market. In Finland, the rise and decline of *Nokia* is evidence of Finland's China trade, while Sweden and Denmark are fast catching up (Figure 5.2). On the other hand, Eastern and Southern European countries are relatively less directly active in China. Yet the data disguise an important indirect effect. Many cars and car components may be exported from Germany, but their value chain extends across the continent. Hence engines made in Hungary and assembled into cars in Germany count as Hungarian exports to Germany, and as German exports to the country of the final consumer. Some automotive suppliers in, for example, Slovakia may also directly export to factories of *VW* or *BMW* in China.

Why do China and Russia import products from Europe, even though most products are more expensive than those 'made in China'? What are the underlying economic forces that make it beneficial for nations to trade – whether they are distant or nearby? International trade is the oldest and still the most important building block of international business. It is a major driving force of globalization and has been growing faster than GDP in recent decades. Figure 5.3 shows that world trade growth outpaces GDP growth. Trade in goods grew on average by 7.4% per year since 1980, while trade in services grew even faster, averaging 8.2%. During the same time, worldwide GDP grew annually by 6.1%. However, trade is more volatile

Figure 5.3   Growth in world trade outpaces growth in world GDP

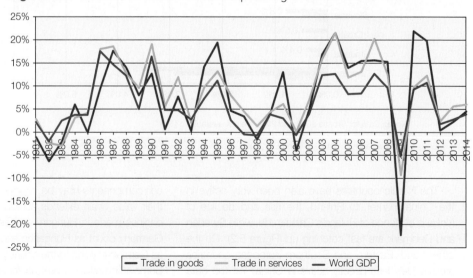

Note: Annual percentage growth; world trade estimated from sum of national export data.

Source: Authors' creation using data from WTO (WTO database, 2014 version); IMF (World Economic Outlook database, October 2014 version).

than GDP: in the recessions of 1982, 1998 and 2001 trade in goods shrank; during the recession of 2008 it fell by as much as 22.3%.

Unsurprisingly, international trade is also a hot topic in politics, as the benefits of trade are often unevenly distributed. Debates on international trade tend to be very ferocious, because so much is at stake. This chapter will help you to participate in such debates. We start by outlining the theoretical foundations of international trade. These theories provide a structured way of thinking and analyzing issues that are central to both businesses and government policy. We begin by outlining how the two core perspectives introduced in earlier chapters – namely, resource-based and institution-based views – can help us understand the crucial issue of why nations trade. The remainder of the chapter deals with (1) theories and (2) institutions shaping international trade. As before, debates and implications for action follow.

WHY DO NATIONS TRADE?

Most nations actively participate in international trade, which consists of exporting (selling abroad) and importing (buying from abroad). Table 5.1 provides a snapshot of the top ten exporting and importing nations in the two main sectors: goods and services. In goods exports, Germany has for many years been the world champion, though China has taken the lead in recent years. In services, the US leads with the UK leapfrogging into second place, mainly due to its financial services. As importers, the USA, China and Germany lead both the goods and the services tables.

Relative to domestic trade, international trade entails much greater complexities. So why do nations go through these troubles to trade internationally? They involve not just the exporter and importer, but specialist intermediaries such as logistics firms and ports through which goods are shipped (In Focus 5.1); and despite the money these intermediaries make, the trade is profitable. Without getting into details, we can safely say that there must be economic gains from trade. More important, such gains must be shared by *both* sides; otherwise, there would be no willing exporters and importers. In other words, international trade is a *win-win* deal. Empirical evidence suggests that openness to international trade is, on average, associated with lower unemployment and higher economic growth.[1] How are these gains from trade created? This chapter sheds some light on these questions.

Before proceeding, it is important to clarify that 'nations trade' is a misleading statement. A more accurate expression would be 'firms from different nations trade'.[2] Unless different governments directly buy and sell from each other (such as arms sales), the majority of trade is conducted by firms, which pay little attention to country-level ramifications. For example, oil majors such as *Shell* and *BP* import oil to Europe (often via Rotterdam) and do not export much. They thus directly contribute to the trade deficit (a surplus of imports over exports) of countries like France and Spain, which is something their government may not like. However, in most countries, governments cannot tell firms, such as *Shell* or *BP*, what to do (and not to do) unless firms engage in illegal activities. Therefore, we need to be aware that when we ask 'Why do nations trade?' we are really asking 'Why do firms from different nations trade?' When discussing imbalance of trade where Germany and China run a trade surplus (a surplus of exports over imports), we are really referring to thousands of firms buying from and selling to Germany and China, which also have thousands of firms buying from and selling to other countries. The aggregation of such buying (importing) and selling (exporting) by both sides leads to the country-level balance of trade – namely, whether a country has a trade surplus or deficit.

Having acknowledged the limitations of statements such as 'nations trade,' we will still use them. This is not only because these expressions have been commonly

LEARNING OBJECTIVE

1 Use the resource-based and institution-based views to explain why nations trade

exporting
Selling abroad.

importing
Buying from abroad.

trade deficit
An economic condition in which a nation imports more than it exports.

trade surplus
An economic condition in which a nation exports more than it imports.

balance of trade
The aggregation of importing and exporting that leads to the country-level trade surplus or deficit.

Table 5.1   Leading trading nations

	Top 10 exporters of goods	Value (€ billion)	World share (%)		Top 10 importers of goods	Value (€ billion)	World share (%)
1	China	1 772	11.70	1	USA	1 869	12.30
2	USA	1 268	8.40	2	China	1 564	10.30
3	Germany	9 189	7.70	3	Germany	954	6.30
4	Japan	574	3.80	4	Japan	668	4.40
5	Netherlands	539	3.60	5	France	546	3.60
6	France	465	3.10	6	United Kingdom	526	3.50
7	Korea	449	3.00	7	Hong Kong	499	3.30
8	United Kingdom	435	2.90	8	Netherlands	473	3.10
9	Hong Kong	430	2.80	9	Korea	414	2.70
10	Russia	420	2.80	10	Italy	383	2.50
	World total	**15 096**	**100**		**World total**	**15 155**	**100**
	Top 10 exporters of services	Value (€ billion)	World share (%)		Top 10 importers of services	Value (€ billion)	World share (%)
1	USA	426	14.30	1	USA	347	9.80
2	United Kingdom	189	6.30	2	China	264	7.50
3	Germany	184	6.20	3	Germany	254	7.20
4	France	152	5.10	4	France	152	4.30
5	China	132	4.40	5	United Kingdom	140	4.00
6	India	97	3.20	6	Japan	130	3.70
7	Netherlands	95	3.20	7	Singapore	103	2.90
8	Japan	93	3.10	8	Netherlands	102	2.90
9	Spain	93	3.10	9	India	100	2.80
10	Hong Kong	86	2.90	10	Russia	99	2.80
	World total	**2 989**	**100**		**World total**	**3 515**	**100**

Source: Authors' creation using data from World Trade Organization, 2014, *World Trade Report 2014*. All data are for 2013.

used but also because they serve as a shorthand version of the more accurate but more cumbersome ones such as 'firms from different nations trade'. This clarification does enable us to use the two *firm-level* perspectives introduced earlier – resource- and institution-based views – to shed light on why nations trade.

Recall from Chapter 4 that resources and capabilities determine the competitive advantage of a firm. Applied to international trade, this insight suggests that firms use their resources and capabilities to produce goods and services that have a competitive advantage in markets abroad, and hence they export. Firms in different countries have different resources and capabilities, and thus export different

IN FOCUS 5.1

Port of Rotterdam: gateway to the world

The Netherlands has a long tradition as a trading nation dating back to the *Dutch East India Company* in the 17th century. The hub of modern trade is the Port of Rotterdam, Europe's largest. It stretches over 40 kilometres and covers 12 000 hectares of land. Every day, over one million tons of goods are loaded, unloaded and distributed in Rotterdam – more than twice the turnover of the next largest European ports, Antwerp and Hamburg. Worldwide, Rotterdam is the largest port outside of East Asia. Every year, 30 000 ocean-going ships call at the port, 7.0 million containers are transferred and 130 million cubic metres of crude oil and mineral oil products arrive to be refined and distributed throughout Europe. The transportation businesses in the port add €6.3 billion to Dutch GDP, while other industries, especially petroleum and chemical industries located in the vicinity, add another €6.6 billion. Over 90 000 people work in the port area, including 27 000 in road transport.

Seaports are key nodes of international trade, as 90% of world trade (by volume) is transported by ship. The Port of Rotterdam is the main hub for sea-bound transportation in and out of Europe. Containers arrive from Asia on mega-ships that are too large even for medium-sized ports such as Hamburg or Le Havre. Thus containers are transferred in Rotterdam to smaller ships sailing to ports along the Atlantic coast into the North and Baltic Seas, up the river Rhine and across to the UK. More than 500 liner services connect Rotterdam with over 1000 ports worldwide.

Huge investments have expanded the port, and more are planned for the future. The infrastructure is built around the Nieuwe Waterweg (New Channel), which opened in 1870 and connects the city of Rotterdam directly to the North Sea. It has been continuously widened and deepened, while far out in the North Sea a man-made channel allows easy access even for the largest ships of the world. Maasvlakte 1, which contains the largest container terminals, was reclaimed from the estuary 30 years ago. A new expansion of the port, called Maasvlakte 2, is to extend the port further into the North Sea, creating 1000 hectares of industrial land directly on deep water by the year 2030.

The fastest growing businesses of the Port of Rotterdam, and of maritime transport worldwide, is container shipping. Containers are standardized and allow a much faster transfer over different modes of transport. In Rotterdam, over 100 mega-cranes work day and night to unload containers arriving from overseas, and reload them to regional container ships, inland boats, trains and trucks.

The Dutch government has invested heavily in transportation infrastructure to connect Rotterdam with its hinterland, including regional shipping lines, inland waterways (especially the Rhine connecting to Germany, France and Switzerland), oil pipelines, roads and railways – with strategically located transshipment points between different transport modes. Many goods from the German industrial heartlands of the Ruhr region are loaded on riverboats or direct trains in Duisburg, and then shipped downstream to Rotterdam, and from there out into the world. Yet traffic jams hold up trucks, and the regional and national authorities are under pressure to invest in upgrading the infrastructure connecting Rotterdam with Duisburg and other secondary hubs.

Sources: (1) R. Wrights, 2007, Rotterdam struggles to contain its enthusiasm as demand surges ahead, *Financial Times*, December 5; (2) Port of Rotterdam, 2014, *Port Statistics*, mimeo, (3) www.portofrotterdam.com (accessed March 2015).

products. Therefore, the exchange of goods though exports and imports is mutually beneficial. Theories of international trade explore in more detail why this is so.

Further, recall from Chapters 2 and 3 that numerous politically and culturally derived rules of the game, known as institutions, constrain individual and firm behaviour. In international trade, various regulations in the form of both tariffs and non-tariff barriers (NTBs) hamper trade around the world. On the other hand, we also see the rise of rules that facilitate trade, such as those promoted by the World Trade Organization (WTO) (see Chapter 9). Explanations of the actual flows of trade thus need to consider these institutions. The remainder of this chapter expands on these two perspectives.

THEORIES OF INTERNATIONAL TRADE

Theories of international trade provide one of the oldest, richest and most influential bodies of economics. In this section, we briefly review major theories of international trade in the order in which they evolved: (1) mercantilism, (2) absolute advantage, (3) comparative advantage, (4) product life cycle, (5) strategic trade and (6) national competitive advantage. The first three are often regarded as classic trade theories, and the last three are viewed as modern trade theories.

Mercantilism

classic trade theories
The major theories of international trade that were advanced before the 20th century, which consist of mercantilism, absolute advantage and comparative advantage.

modern trade theories
The major theories of international trade that were advanced in the 20th century, which consist of product life cycle, strategic trade and national competitive advantage.

theory of mercantilism
A theory that holds the wealth of the world (measured in gold and silver) is fixed and that a nation that exports more and imports less would enjoy the net inflows of gold and silver and thus become richer.

protectionism
The idea that governments should actively protect domestic industries from imports and vigorously promote exports.

free trade
Trade uninhibited by trade barriers.

theory of absolute advantage
A theory that suggests that under free trade, each nation gains by specializing in economic activities in which it has absolute advantage.

absolute advantage
The economic advantage one nation enjoys that is absolutely superior to other nations.

In the 1600s and 1700s, international trade was widely regarded as a zero-sum game. Politicians like French statesman Jean-Baptiste Colbert believed in the theory of mercantilism, which suggests that the wealth of the world (measured in gold and silver at that time) was fixed and that a nation that exported more and imported less would enjoy the net inflows of gold and silver and thus become richer. On the other hand, a nation experiencing a trade deficit would see its gold and silver flowing out and, consequently, would become poorer. The implication? Exports are good; imports are bad.

Although mercantilism is largely discredited by scholars, it is not an extinct dinosaur. Very much alive, mercantilism is the direct intellectual ancestor of modern-day protectionism, which is the idea that governments should actively protect domestic industries from imports and vigorously promote exports. During the recession of 2009, many politicians advocated mercantilist policies to (in the short run) protect jobs in their own country.

Absolute advantage

The theory of absolute advantage, advocated by Adam Smith in *The Wealth of Nations* in 1776, opened the floodgates of the free trade movement that is still going on today. Smith argued that in the aggregate, it is the 'invisible hand' of markets, rather than governments, that should determine the scale and scope of economic activities. Thus the principles of a market economy (Chapter 2) should apply for international trade as they apply for domestic trade. By trying to be self-sufficient and to (inefficiently) produce a wide range of goods, mercantilist policies *reduce* the wealth of a nation in the long run. Smith thus argued for free trade, which is the idea that free market forces should determine how much to trade with little (or no) government intervention.

Specifically, Smith proposed a theory of absolute advantage: under free trade, each nation gains by specializing in economic activities in which a nation has absolute advantage. What is absolute advantage? It is the economic advantage one nation enjoys that is absolutely superior to other nations. For example, Smith argued that because of better soil, water and weather, Portugal enjoyed an absolute advantage over England in the production of grapes and wines. Likewise, England had an absolute advantage over Portugal in the production of sheep and wool. England could grow grapes at a greater cost and with much lower quality. Smith suggested that England should specialize in sheep and wool, Portugal should specialize in grapes and wines, and they should trade with each other. Smith's greatest insights were in the argument (1) that by specializing in the production of goods for which each has an absolute advantage, both can produce more and (2) that by trading, both can benefit more. In other words, international trade is not a zero-sum game as suggested by mercantilism. It is a *win-win* game.

Figure 5.4 Absolute advantage

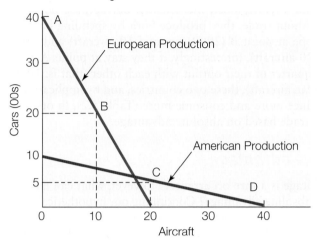

How can this be? Let us use an example with hypothetical numbers (Figure 5.4 and Table 5.2). For the sake of simplicity, assume there are only two nations in the world: Europe and America. They produce only two products: cars and aircraft. Production of cars or aircraft, naturally, requires resources such as labour, land and technology. Assume that both are equally endowed with 800 units of resources. Between the two activities, America has an absolute advantage in the production of aircraft – it takes 20 resources to produce an aircraft (for which Europe needs 40 resources) and the total American capacity is 40 aircraft if it does not produce cars (point D in Figure 5.4). Europe has an absolute advantage in the production of cars – it takes 20 resources to produce 100 cars (for which America needs 80 resources) and the total European capacity is 4000 cars if it does not

Table 5.2 Absolute advantage

Each country has 800 resources		Europe	America	Total
	Resources for 100 cars	20	80	
	Resources for 1 aircraft	40	20	
1. Production and consumption with no specialization and without trade (each country devotes half of its resources to each activity)	cars	2000	500	2500
	aircraft	10	20	30
2. Production with complete specialization at point A and D respectively	cars	4000	0	4000
	aircraft	0	40	40
3. Consumption after each country trades one-fourth of its output	cars	3000	1000	4000
	aircraft	10	30	40
4. Gains from trade	cars	+1000	+500	+1500
	aircraft	0	+10	+10

make aircraft (point A). It is important to note that America can build cars and Europe can build aircraft, albeit inefficiently. But because both nations need cars and aircraft, without trade, they produce both by spending half of their resources on each – Europe at point B (2000 cars and 10 aircraft) and America at point C (500 cars and 20 aircraft). Interestingly, if they stay at points A and D, respectively, and trade one-quarter of their output with each other (that is, 1000 European cars with 10 American aircraft), these two countries, and by implication the global economy, both produce more and consume more (Table 5.2). In other words, there are *net* gains from trade based on absolute advantage.

Comparative advantage

Absolute advantage is a rare occurrence. However, what can nations do when they do *not* possess absolute advantage? Continuing our hypothetical two-country example of Europe and America, what if Europe was absolutely inferior to America in the production of both cars and aircraft? What should Europe do? What should America do? Obviously, the theory of absolute advantage runs into a dead end.

In response, British economist David Ricardo developed a theory of comparative advantage in 1817. This theory suggests that even if America has an absolute advantage over Europe in both cars and aircraft, as long as Europe is not equally less efficient in the production of both goods, Europe can still choose to specialize in the production of one good (such as cars) in which it has comparative advantage – defined as the relative (not absolute) advantage in one economic activity that one country enjoys in comparison with another country.[3] Figure 5.5 and Table 5.3 show that Europe's comparative advantage lies in its *relatively less inefficient* production of cars: if Europe devotes all resources to cars it can produce 1000 units, which is four-fifths of the 1250 cars America can produce. However, at a maximum, Europe can produce only 20 aircraft, which is merely one-half of the 40 aircraft America can make. By letting Europe specialize in the production of cars and importing some cars from Europe, America is able to leverage its strengths by devoting its resources to aircraft. For example, if (1) America devotes four-fifths of its resources to aircraft and one-fifth to cars (point C of Figure 5.5), (2) Europe concentrates 100% of its resources on cars (point E) and (3) trading with each other, both countries produce and consume more than they would if they devote half of their resources to each activity (see Table 5.3).

theory of comparative advantage
A theory that focuses on the relative (not absolute) advantage in one economic activity that one nation enjoys in comparison with other nations.

comparative advantage
Relative (not absolute) advantage in one economic activity that one nation enjoys in comparison with other nations.

Figure 5.5 Comparative advantage

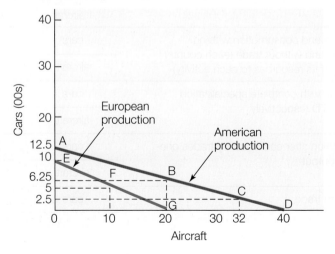

Table 5.3 Comparative advantage

Each country has 800 resources		Europe	USA	Total
	Resources for 100 cars	80	64	
	Resources for 1 aircraft	40	20	
1. Production and consumption with no specialization and without trade (each country devotes half of its resources to each activity), at point F and B respectively	cars	500	625	1125
	aircraft	10	20	30
2. Production with specialization (Europe devotes all resources to cars, and America devotes one-fifth of its resources to cars and four-fifths to aircraft), at point E and C respectively	cars	1000	250	1250
	aircraft	0	32	32
3. Consumption after Europe trades 400 cars for 11 US aircraft	cars	600	650	1250
	aircraft	11	21	32
4. *Gains* from trade	cars	+100	+25	125
	aircraft	+1	+1	2

Again, there are net gains from trade, this time from comparative advantage. One crucial concept here is opportunity cost – given the alternatives (opportunities), the cost of pursuing one activity at the expense of another activity. For America, the opportunity cost of concentrating on cars at point A in Figure 5.5 is tremendous relative to producing aircraft at point D, because it is only 25% more productive in cars than Europe, but is 100% more productive in aircraft.

The theory of comparative advantage may seem counterintuitive, compared to absolute advantages. However, this theory is far more realistic and useful to explain the patterns of trade in the real world. It may be easy to identify an absolute advantage in a highly simplified, two-country world, as in Figure 5.4, but how can each nation decide what to specialize in when there are more than 200 nations in the world? It is simply too complex to ascertain that one nation is absolutely better than all others in one activity. The theory of comparative advantage suggests that even without an absolute advantage, America can still profitably specialize in aircraft as long as it is *relatively* more efficient than others. The message of comparative advantage is that it may pay to import products from countries that are absolutely inferior in the production of these products, just as it may pay for you to delegate some of your work (see In Focus 5.2). Hence comparative rather than absolute advantage explains the pattern of international trade.

Where do absolute and comparative advantages come from? In one word, productivity. Smith looked at *absolute* productivity differences, and Ricardo emphasized *relative* productivity differences. In this sense, absolute advantage is really a special case of comparative advantage. But what leads to such productivity differences? In the early 20th century, Swedish economists Eli Heckscher and Bertil Ohlin argued that absolute and comparative advantages stem from different resource endowments – namely, the

opportunity cost
Given the alternatives (opportunities), the cost of pursuing one activity at the expense of another activity.

resource (factor) endowments
The extent to which different countries possess various resources (factors), such as labour, land and technology.

IN FOCUS 5.2

Comparative advantage and YOU

Despite the seemingly abstract reasoning, the theory of comparative advantage is very practical. Although you may not be aware of it, you have been a practitioner of this theory almost *every day*. How many of you grow your own food, knit your own jumpers and write your own software? Hardly any! You probably buy most of what you consume. By doing this, you are actually practising this theory. This is because buying your food, jumpers and software from producers frees up the time it would have taken you to grow your own food, knit jumpers and write software – even assuming you are multi-talented and capable of doing all of the above. As students, you are probably using this time wisely to study a subject (ranging from accounting to zoology) in which you may have some comparative advantage. After graduation, you will trade your skills (via your employer) with others who need these skills from you. By specializing and trading, rather than producing everything yourself, you help channel the production of food, jumpers and software to more efficient producers. Some of them may be foreign firms. You and these producers mutually benefit because they can produce more for everyone to consume, and you can concentrate on your studies and build your tradeable skills.

Let's assume that at your university, you are the best student. At the same time, you also drive a taxi

at night to earn enough money to put you through university. In fact, you become the best taxi driver in town, knowing all the side streets, never getting lost, and making more money than other taxi drivers. Needless to say, by studying during the day and driving a taxi at night, you don't have a life. However, your efforts are handsomely rewarded when the best company in town hires you after graduation, and very soon, as a fast-tracker, you become the best manager in town. Of course, you quit driving a taxi after joining the firm. The best taxi driver can earn about €50 000 a year, whereas the best manager can make €500 000, so your choice would be obvious. One day, you leave your office and jump into a taxi to rush to the airport. The taxi driver misunderstands your instruction, gets lost, and is unnecessarily stuck in a bad traffic jam. As soon as you become irritated because you may miss your flight, you start to smile because you remember today's lecture. 'Yes, I have an absolute advantage both in driving a taxi and being a good manager compared with this poor taxi driver. But by focusing on my comparative advantage in being a good manager,' you remember what your professor said, 'this taxi driver, whose abilities are nowhere near my taxi driving skills, can tap into his comparative advantage (funny, he has one!), trade his skills with me, and can still support his family.' With this pleasant thought, you end up giving the driver a big tip when arriving at the airport.

---

factor endowment theory (or Heckscher-Ohlin theory)
A theory that suggests that nations will develop comparative advantage based on their locally abundant factors.

extent to which different countries possess various resources, such as labour, land and technology. These resources are in economics known as 'factors of production'. The factor endowment theory (or Heckscher-Ohlin theory) thus suggests that nations tend to export goods whose production requires a lot of those resources that the country has a lot of. In other words, nations develop comparative advantage based on their *locally abundant* factors.[4] Numerous examples support the theories of comparative advantage and resource (factor) endowments. For instance, when Indian firms set up call centres to service Western clients, they use human labour, a resource that is very abundant in India, to replace some automation functions when answering the phone. In Europe and North America, labour shortage has driven the development of telephone automation technology. However, many people still prefer talking with a live person rather than buttons on a machine (press 1 for this, press 2 for that). This creates opportunities for trade in call centre services.

In summary, *classic* theories, (1) mercantilism, (2) absolute advantage and (3) comparative advantage (which includes resource endowments) have evolved from approximately 300 years ago to the beginning of the 20th century. More recently, three *modern* theories, outlined next, have emerged.

Product life cycle

Up to this point, classic theories all paint a *static* picture: if England has an absolute or comparative advantage in textiles (mostly because of its resource endowments such as favourable weather and soil), it should keep producing them. However, this assumption of no change in resource endowments and trade patterns does not always hold in the real world. In Adam Smith's time, over 200 years ago, England was a major exporter of textiles; today England's textile industry is insignificant. So what happened? One may argue that in England, weather has changed and soil has become less fertile, but it is difficult to believe that weather and soil have changed so much in 200 years, which is a relatively short period for climatic changes. For another example, since the 1990s, Japan turned from a net exporter to a net importer of personal computers (PCs), while Malaysia transformed itself from a net importer to a net exporter – and this example has nothing to do with weather or soil change. Why do patterns of trade in PCs change over time? Classic theories would have a hard time answering this intriguing question.

In the 1960s, Raymond Vernon of Harvard and Seev Hirsch of Tel Aviv developed the product life cycle theory, which was the first *dynamic* theory to account for changes in the patterns of trade over time.[5] Vernon divided the world into three categories: (1) lead innovation nation (which, according to him, is typically the USA), (2) other developed nations and (3) developing nations. Further, every product has three life cycle stages: new, maturing and standardized. In the first stage, production of a new product that commands a price premium will concentrate in the USA, which exports to other developed nations. In the second, maturing stage, demand and ability to produce grow in other developed nations (such as Australia and Italy) so it is now worthwhile to produce there. In the third stage, the previously new product is standardized (or commoditized). Therefore, much production will now move to low-cost developing nations, which export to developed nations. In other words, comparative advantage may change over the life time of a product.

> **product life cycle theory**
> A theory that accounts for changes in the patterns of trade over time by focusing on product life cycles.

This theory was first proposed in the 1960s, and some later events (such as the migration of PC production) have supported its prediction. However, the theory has been criticized on two accounts. First, it assumes that the USA will always be the lead innovation nation for new products. This was probably true in the immediate post-WWII period, but that was an exceptional period. For example, the fanciest mobile phones are now routinely pioneered in Asia and Europe. Second, this theory assumes a stage-by-stage migration of production that takes at least several years (if not decades). The reality of the 21st century, however, is an increasing number of firms now *simultaneously* launch new products (such as iPods or game consoles) around the globe.

Strategic trade theory

Except for mercantilism, all the theories discussed so far have nothing to say about the role of governments. Since the days of Adam Smith, government intervention is usually regarded by economists as destroying value, because it allegedly distorts free trade. However, government intervention is extensive and is not going away. Can government intervention actually add value? Since the 1970s, a new theory, strategic trade theory, has been developed to explain why.[6]

Strategic trade theory suggests that strategic intervention by governments in certain industries can enhance their odds for international success. What are these

> **strategic trade theory**
> A theory that suggests that strategic intervention by governments in certain industries can enhance their odds for international success.

industries? They have high up-front costs of entry, notably investments in research and in capability development, and they tend to be highly capital-intensive, which creates high entry barriers. In consequence, these industries feature substantial first-mover advantages – namely, advantages that first entrants enjoy and do not share with late entrants. Typical examples are the jet engine industry and the aircraft industry. Founded in 1915, and strengthened by large military orders during World War II, *Boeing* has long dominated the commercial aircraft industry. In the jumbo jet segment, *Boeing*'s first-mover advantages associated with its 400-seat 747, first launched in the late 1960s, are still significant today. Alarmed by such US dominance, in the late 1960s, European governments realized that if they did not intervene in this industry, individual European aerospace firms on their own would be driven out of business by US rivals. Therefore, British, French, German and Spanish governments joined together to launch and subsidize *Airbus*. In four decades, *Airbus* has risen from nowhere to a position where it now has a 50-50 split of the global market with *Boeing*. A similar pattern of competition exists between *GE* and *Rolls Royce* (see Integrative case *Rolls Royce*).

How do governments help *Airbus*? Let us use a recent example: the very large, superjumbo aircraft, which is larger than the Boeing 747. Both *Airbus* and *Boeing* are interested in entering this market. However, the demand in the next 20 years is only about 400 to 500 aircraft, and a firm needs to sell at least 300 just to break even, which means that only one firm can be profitably supported. Shown in Figure 5.6 (panel A), if both enter, the outcome will be disastrous because each will lose €5 billion (cell 1). If one enters and the other does not, the entrant will make €20 billion (cells 2 and 3). It is possible that both will enter and clash

first-mover advantage
Advantage that first entrants enjoy and do not share with late entrants.

Figure 5.6 Entering the superjumbo aircraft market?

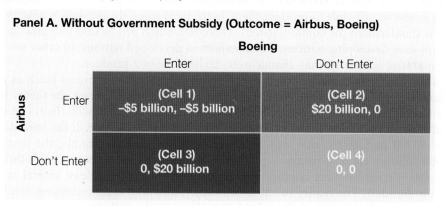

Panel A. Without Government Subsidy (Outcome = Airbus, Boeing)

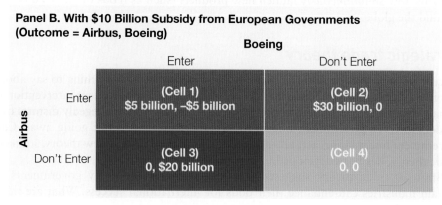

Panel B. With $10 Billion Subsidy from European Governments (Outcome = Airbus, Boeing)

(see Chapter 11). *Airbus* is promised a subsidy of, say, €10 billion if it enters, then the picture changes to panel B. Regardless of what *Boeing* does, *Airbus* finds it lucrative to enter. In cell 1, if *Boeing* enters, it will lose €5 billion as before, whereas *Airbus* will make €5 billion (€10 billion subsidy minus €5 billion loss). So *Boeing* has no incentive to enter. Therefore, the more likely outcome is cell 2, where *Airbus* enters and enjoys a profit of €30 billion. Thus the subsidy has given *Airbus* a *strategic* advantage, and the policy to assist *Airbus* is known as a strategic trade policy.[7] This has indeed been the case, as the 550-seat A380 will enter service when this book is published.

strategic trade policy
Government subsidies inspired by strategic trade theory.

Strategic trade theorists do not advocate a mercantilist policy to promote all industries. They only propose to help a few strategically important industries. However, this theory has been criticized as impractical on two accounts. First, the argument assumes that governments have very detailed information about cost structures in an industry, and can make rational decisions. What if governments are not sophisticated and objective enough to do this job? Second, a lot of industries claim that they are strategically important. For instance, farmers in many countries successfully argued that agriculture would be a strategic industry (guarding food supply against foreign dependence or terrorists) to justify more subsidies. Overall, where to draw the line between strategic and nonstrategic industries is tricky.

National competitive advantage of industries

The most recent theory is known as the theory of national competitive advantage of industries (Table 5.4). This is popularly known as the 'diamond' model because its principal architect, Harvard professor Michael Porter, presents it in a diamond-shaped diagram.[8] This theory focuses on why certain *industries* (but not others) within a nation are competitive internationally. For example, although Japanese electronics and automobile industries are global winners, Japanese service industries are notoriously inefficient.

theory of national competitive advantage of industries (or 'diamond' model)
A theory that suggests that the competitive advantage of certain industries in different nations depends on four aspects that form a 'diamond'.

Porter argues that the competitive advantage of certain industries is driven by capabilities that firms develop in response to opportunities and pressures in their home environment. Four aspects are particularly critical. First, resource endowments in terms of natural and human resource repertoires have also been emphasized by the Heckscher-Ohlin theory. For example, the coal and steel industry historically developed where coals and iron ore were found, for example in England and Wales, as well as in northern France and western Germany. The paper industry is flourishing in Scandinavia, where forests are plentiful and thus timber is readily available. High-tech clusters are developing around university cities such as Munich or Cambridge because scientists and graduates – both scarce human resources – are readily available in these areas. The resource endowment element of the diamond thus builds on insights from previous theories. But different from traditional trade theories, Porter argues that resource endowments are not enough.

Table 5.4   A theory of national competitive advantage

National competitive advantage is created through opportunities and pressures created by
● resource endowment in terms of natural and human resources
● sophistication and scale of domestic demand
● strategies, structure and rivalry of domestic competitors
● availability-related and supporting industries.

Second, domestic demand propels firms to scale new heights. Why are Japanese consumer electronics firms so competitive worldwide? One reason is that Japanese consumers demand the most novel technology and the highest standards of quality for items such as mobile phones, iPods and games consoles. Endeavouring to satisfy such domestic demand, manufacturers are driven to satisfy these most demanding customers, which then provides them with a quality product they can also sell in other markets. In other words, abilities to satisfy a tough domestic crowd may make it possible to successfully deal with less demanding overseas customers.

Third, domestic firm strategy, structure and rivalry in one industry play a huge role in its international success or failure. Historically, world leaders in many industries have emerged from close geographic proximity, driven by the intense rivalry between two firms. The most famous example is probably *Puma* and *adidas*, which both hail from Herzogenaurach, a small town in Germany. Another example is the Japanese electronics industry, which is driven by a domestic rivalry that is probably the most intense in the world. When shopping for digital cameras or camcorders, if you are tired with some 20 models in an average European electronics store, you will be more exhausted when shopping in Japan: the average store there carries about 200 models! Most firms producing such a bewildering range of models do not make money. However, the few top firms (such as *Canon*) that win the tough competition domestically, may have a relatively easier time when venturing abroad, because overseas competition is less demanding.

Finally, related and supporting industries provide the foundation upon which key industries can excel. In the absence of strong related and supporting industries such as engines, avionics and materials, a key industry such as aerospace cannot become globally competitive. Each of these related and supporting industries requires years (or even decades) of hard work. For instance, emboldened by the *Airbus* experience, Chinese, Korean and Japanese governments poured money into their own aerospace industry. However, they realized that Europe's long history of excellence in a series of crucial related industries made it possible for *Airbus* to succeed. A lack of supporting industries has (so far) prevented the Chinese, Korean and Japanese aerospace industry from taking off.

Overall, Porter argues that the dynamic interaction of these four aspects explains what is behind the competitive advantage of leading industries in different nations. This is the first *multilevel* theory to realistically connect firms, industries and nations, whereas previous theories only work on one or two levels. However, critics argue that the 'diamond model' places too much emphasis on domestic conditions.[9] The recent rise of India's IT industry suggests that its international success is not entirely driven by domestic demand, which is tiny compared with overseas demand. It is overseas demand that matters a lot more in this case.

Evaluating theories of international trade

In case you are tired after studying the six theories, you have to appreciate that we have just gone through over 300 years of research, debates and policy changes around the world in about ten pages! As a student, that is not a small accomplishment. Table 5.5 enables you to see the 'big picture'.

Today, the classic pro-free trade theories seem like common sense. However, we need to appreciate that they were revolutionary in the late 1700s and early 1800s in a world of mercantilism. These theories attracted numerous attacks. But eventually they defeated mercantilism, at least intellectually. Influenced by these classic theories, England in the 1830s dismantled its protectionist Corn Laws, which contributed

Table 5.5 Theories of international trade: a summary

Classic theories	Main points	Strengths and influences	Weaknesses and debates
Mercantilism (Colbert, 1600s–1700s)	• International trade is a zero-sum game – trade deficit is dangerous • Governments should protect domestic industries and promote exports	• Forerunner of modern-day protectionism	• Inefficient allocation of resources • Reduces the wealth of the nation in the long run
Absolute advantage (Smith, 1776)	• Nations should specialize in economic activities in which they have an absolute advantage and trade with others • By specializing and trading, each nation produces more and consumes more, wealth increases	• Birth of modern economics • Forerunner of the free trade movement • Defeats mercantilism, at least intellectually	• When one nation is absolutely inferior to another, the theory is unable to provide any advice • When there are many nations, it may be difficult to find an absolute advantage
Comparative advantage (Ricardo, 1817; Heckscher, 1919; Ohlin, 1933)	• Nations should specialize in economic activities in which they have a comparative advantage and trade with others • Even if one nation is absolutely inferior to another, the two nations can still gainfully trade • Factor endowments underpin comparative advantage	• More realistic guidance to nations (and their firms) interested in trade but having no absolute advantage • Explains patterns of trade based on factor endowments	• Relatively static, assuming that comparative advantage and factor endowments do not change over time
Modern theories			
Product life cycle (Vernon, 1966; Hirsch, 1975)	• Comparative advantage first resides in the lead innovation nation, which exports to other nations • Production migrates to other advanced nations and then developing nations in different product life cycle stages	• First theory to incorporate dynamic changes in patterns of trade • More realistic with trade in industrial products in the 20th century	• Many innovations originate outside the USA. • Many new products are now launched simultaneously around the world

Modern theories			
Strategic trade (Brander, Spencer, Krugman, 1980s)	● Strategic intervention by governments may help domestic firms reap first-mover advantages in industries with high barriers to entry ● First-mover firms may have better odds at winning internationally	● More realistic and positively incorporates the role of governments in trade ● Provides direct policy advice	● Ideological resistance from many 'free trade' scholars and policymakers ● Invites many industries to claim they are strategic
National competitive advantage of industries (Porter, 1990)	● Competitive advantage of different industries in different nations depends on the four interacting aspects ● The four aspects are (1) factor endowments, (2) domestic demand, (3) firm strategy, structure and rivalry and (4) related and supporting industries	● Most recent, most complex, and most realistic among various theories ● As a multilevel theory, it directly connects firms, industries and nations	● Has not been comprehensively tested ● Overseas (not only domestic) demand may stimulate the competitiveness of certain industries

to the surge of international trade during the first wave of globalization in the late 1800s (see Chapter 1).

All theories simplify to make their point. Classic theories rely on highly simplistic assumptions of a model consisting of only two nations and two goods. They also assume perfect resource mobility – that is, one resource removed from cars production can be moved to make aircraft. In reality, both industries require highly specialized skills. Further, classic theories assume no foreign exchange complications and zero transportation costs. So, in the real world of many countries, numerous goods, imperfect resource mobility, fluctuating exchange rates, high transportation costs and product life cycle changes, is free trade still beneficial as Smith and Ricardo suggested? Most economists would still answer 'yes', and they can show lots of data to support the basic arguments.[10] But not everyone agrees. We return to this question in Debates and Extensions.

resource mobility
The ability to move resources from one part of a business to another.

NATIONAL INSTITUTIONS AND INTERNATIONAL TRADE

LEARNING OBJECTIVE

3   Appreciate how economic and political institutions influence international trade

Theories of international trade generally assume that the rules of the game are the same in every country. Yet international trade takes place in a web of national and international institutions, created by complex political processes that do not always favour the overall best arrangements. Many institutions, or 'rules of the game' are created by nation states, and act as barriers to international trade. Some are grounded in historical differences across countries, while others are deliberately created to protect a domestic industry. Let us examine how they affect international trade, and why they are created.

Tariff barriers

There are two broad types of trade barriers: (1) tariff barriers and (2) non-tariff barriers (NTBs). As a major tariff barrier, an import tariff is a tax imposed on imports. A simple analysis shows how import tariffs distort international trade – and why consumers lose out.[11] Figure 5.7 uses rice tariffs in Japan as a hypothetical example to show that there are *unambiguously* net losses – known as deadweight loss.

tariff barrier
Trade barriers that rely on tariffs to discourage imports.
non-tariff barrier (NTB)
Trade barriers that rely on non-tariff means to discourage imports.
import tariff
A tax imposed on imports.
deadweight loss
Net losses that occur in an economy as the result of tariffs.

- Panel A: In the absence of international trade, the domestic price is P_1 and domestic wheat farmers produce Q_1, determined by the intersection of domestic supply and demand curves.

- Panel B: Because the domestic rice price P_1 is higher than world price P_2, foreign farmers export to Japan. In the absence of tariffs, Japanese farmers reduce output to Q_2. Japanese consumers enjoy more rice at Q_3 at a much lower price P_2.

- Panel C: The government imposes an import tariff, effectively raising the price from P_2 to P_3. Japanese farmers increase production from Q_2 to Q_4, and consumers pay more at P_3 and consume less by reducing consumption from Q_3 to Q_5. Imports fall from Q_2Q_3 in panel B to Q_4Q_5 in panel C.

Who is better or worse off with tariffs? The gains are represented by areas in Panel C. Farmers sell more rice at a higher price, they gain area A. The government pockets tariffs on the imports, area C. However, consumers are worse off having to pay higher prices, and some of them not buying rice at all, represented by the area consisting of A, B, C and D. Hence we can calculate the deadweight loss:

$$\text{Deadweight loss} = \text{Loss to consumer} - \text{Gains to farmers}$$
$$- \text{Tariff revenues to government}$$
$$= \text{Area } (A + B + C + D) - \text{Area } (A) - \text{Area } (C)$$
$$= \text{Area } (B + D)$$

The deadweight loss (areas B and D) represents unambiguous economic inefficiency to the nation as a whole. Tariffs such as these are common around the world, not only for agricultural produce: an *Apple* iPad mini that retails for about €250

Figure 5.7 Tariff on rice imports

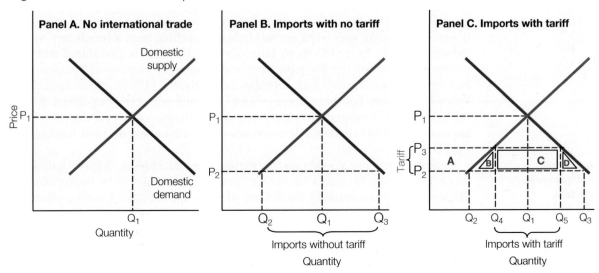

in the USA costs about €560 in Brazil because Brazil charges high import tariffs on technology products. In 2009, the USA slapped a 35% import tariff on tyres made in China. Brazilian iPad users and American tyre buyers have to pay more, and some may be unable to afford the products. While not being able to buy an iPad will have no tangible damage, some financially struggling US drivers who should have replaced their worn-out tyres may delay replacing them, which increases the possibility of accidents.[12]

Given the well-known net losses, why are tariffs imposed? The answer boils down to politics. Although almost every consumer in a country is hurt because of higher import prices, it is very costly, if not impossible, to politically organize geographically scattered individuals and firms to advance the case for free trade.[13] On the other hand, certain special interest groups tend to be geographically concentrated and well organized to advance their interest. Farmers tend to be particularly powerful around the world. In Europe, they represent 2% of the population, but they had a strong impact on the original design of EU rules in the 1950s, and these rules are slow to change (see Chapter 8). In Japan, although farmers represent less than 5% of the population, they have a disproportionate vote in the Diet (Japanese parliament). Why? Diet districts were drawn up in the aftermath of World War II, when most Japanese lived in rural areas. Such districts were never rezoned, although the majority of the population now lives in urban areas. Likewise, in the USA, each state has two representatives in the Senate, which gives a large political weight to thinly-populated rural states such as Kansas or Wisconsin. Thus when the powerful farm lobby speaks, governments listen.

Non-tariff barriers (NTBs)

Tariff barriers have been reduced in recent decades, mainly on the basis of international agreements. Yet NTBs persist. In fact, since the financial crisis in 2008, an increase of such NTBs has been observed in several countries.[14] NTBs include (1) subsidies, (2) import quotas, (3) export restraints, (4) local content requirements, (5) administrative practices and (6) anti-dumping duties.

subsidy
Government payments to (domestic) firms.

Subsidies are government payments to domestic firms. They lower firms' costs of production, provide an additional revenue stream, and allow firms to stay in business even when they lack competitive advantages. Subsidies are often paid indirectly, as open subsidies would attract too much attention from taxpayers. For example, the US government supports businesses by providing manufacturers of military hardware – tanks, airplanes or ships – with R&D support and long-term contracts. This gives these firms a competitive edge when exporting, or when using the same technologies for civilian uses – the aircraft industry has long been a beneficiary of such indirect subsidies. In the EU, many farm subsidies are paid via guaranteed minimum prices, which means the EU pays for the difference between world market price and its 'intervention price'. Such subsidies are costly: the EU's Common Agricultural Policy (CAP) costs European taxpayers €47 billion a year, eating up about 40% of the EU budget.[15] European taxpayers may complain about CAP, yet the main losers are probably farmers in developing countries, who cannot export their foodstuffs to the EU.

import quota
Restrictions on the quantity of imports.

Import quotas are restrictions on the quantity of imports. Import quotas are worse than tariffs because with tariffs, foreign goods can still be imported if tariffs are paid. By constraining the volume of trade, quotas have a similar effect as a monopoly: supply is constrained and prices go up, producers earn higher rents, and consumers pay more. The main difference from tariffs is that governments do not earn tariff revenues.[16] Quotas are thus the most straightforward denial of absolute or comparative advantage. For example, the textile industry in developed economies

Was the EU right to slam quotas on imports of clothing from China?

had been 'temporarily' protected by quotas for about 40 years – until 2005.[17] As soon as the protectionist Multi-fibre Arrangement (MFA) was phased out and textile quotas were lifted on January 1 2005, China's comparative (and probably absolute) advantage in textiles immediately shone. In the first quarter of 2005, the number of Chinese trousers exported to the USA rose 1573%, T-shirts 1277% and underwear 318%.[18] In the second quarter of 2005, both the USA and European Union said 'Enough!' and slapped quotas on Chinese textiles again.

Because import quotas are protectionist pure and simple, there are political costs that countries have to shoulder in today's largely pro-free trade environment. In response, voluntary export restraints (VERs) have been developed to show that, on the surface, exporting countries *voluntarily* agree to restrict their exports. VERs in essence are export quotas. One of the most (in)famous examples are the VERs that the Japanese government agreed upon in the early 1980s to restrict US-bound automobile exports. This, of course, was a euphemism, because the Japanese did not volunteer to restrict their exports. Only when faced with concrete threats did the Japanese agree. Later, empirical studies of these VERs suggested that they raised prices in *both* Japan and the US: some Japanese firms benefited from higher profits, US authorities lost tariffs revenues, and US consumers were the biggest losers.[19] In part, this is because Japanese companies established production facilities in the USA and thus 'jumped over' the trade barriers (yet they still were subject to regulation, so-called local content requirements – see Chapter 6).

Administrative practices refer to bureaucratic rules that make it harder to import foreign goods. For example, public procurement offices in various countries have introduced preferences for locally-produced products, while other countries have introduced new requirements for the tax inspection procedures for imports.[20] The nature of such barriers can be quite subtle. For example, the US implemented the Mandatory Country of Origin Labelling (mCOOL) legislation, requiring US firms to track and notify consumers of the country of origin of meat. Many young Canadian pigs were exported to the US, and were mixed with indigenous US pigs for fattening. After several months,

voluntary export restraint (VER)
An international agreement in which exporting countries voluntarily agree to restrict their exports.

administrative practices
Bureaucratic rules that make it harder to import foreign goods.

separating the (immigrant) Canadian pigs from the (native-born) US pigs was next to impossible. As a result, major US pork producers simply stopped buying pigs from Canada. Such a seemingly innocent move in the name of protecting consumers provoked fierce protests from the Canadian government, which eventually sued the US government at the WTO.[21]

Finally, the arsenal of trade warriors also includes anti-dumping duties levied on imports that have been sold at less than a 'fair' price – or 'dumped' – and thus harm domestic firms. The argument is that foreign competitors may sell at low price until domestic firms go out of business, and then ratchet up their prices to recover losses from their aggressive market entry strategy. Although there is little economic basis for the use of anti-dumping duties, they are a frequent and powerful instrument in international trade. Once allegations of dumping have been filed, potential importers have to prove their innocence, which creates a huge administrative burden for them – and deters all but the most savvy importers (Closing Case).[22]

Taken together, trade barriers reduce or eliminate international trade. Although certain domestic industries and firms benefit, the entire country – or at least a majority of its consumers – tends to suffer. Given these well-known negative aspects, why do people make arguments against free trade? The next two sections outline economic and political arguments against free trade.

Economic arguments against free trade

Prominent among economic arguments against free trade include (1) the need to protect domestic industries, (2) the necessity to shield infant industries and (3) distribution effects. The oldest and most frequently used argument against free trade is the urge to protect domestic industries, firms and jobs from 'unfair' foreign competition – in short, protectionism. The following excerpt is from an 1845 petition of the French candle makers to the French government:

> 'We are subject to the intolerable competition of a foreign rival, who enjoys such superior capabilities for the production of light, that he is flooding the domestic market at an incredibly low price. From the moment he appears, our sales cease, all consumers turn to him, and a branch of French industry whose ramifications are innumerable is at once reduced to complete stagnation. This rival is nothing other than the sun. We ask you to be so kind as to pass a law requiring the closing of all windows, skylights, shutters, curtains, and blinds – in short, all openings, holes, chinks, and fissures through which sunlight penetrates . . .'[23]

Although this was a hypothetical satire written by a French free trade advocate Fredric Bastiat over 150 years ago, similar points are often heard today. Such calls for protection are not limited to commodity producers like candle makers in the 19th century, but they are frequently made by traditional industries and farmers around the world. For example, Canadian cheese and wine producers made such argument when calling for an exemption in the free trade negotiations between Canada and the EU (see Integrative Case EU Canada CETA).

A second argument is the infant industry argument. If domestic firms are as young as 'infants', in the absence of government intervention, they stand no chance of surviving and will be crushed by mature foreign rivals. Thus governments are asked to level the playing field by assisting infant industries. This argument has been advanced in the 19th century by John Stuart Mills in Britain and Friedrich List in Germany, and it periodically reappears in public debates. From a theoretical perspective, it is feasible that with the *temporary* protection by trade barriers, a young industry can develop its capabilities to a level where it can compete with more established competitors elsewhere.[24]

anti-dumping duty
Costs levied on imports that have been 'dumped' (selling below costs to 'unfairly' drive domestic firms out of business).

infant industry argument
The argument that temporary protection of young industries may help them to attain international competitiveness in the long run.

There is plenty of evidence of temporary tariffs helping an industry, from the US tin industry in the 19th century to machinery and electronics in Korea and Taiwan in the 1960s. Unfortunately, governments have a tendency of prolonging such tariffs when companies fail to achieve international competitiveness. For example, Latin America replied heavily on protectionism in the 1960s and 1970s, invoking the infant industry argument. Yet the tariffs remained in place for decades, seriously hampering economic development. The infant industry argument only works when firms are exposed to competition – and tariffs indeed are temporary. In reality, they are rarely quickly abandoned, but become persistent trade barriers.

A third argument concerns the distribution of the gains of free trade. If a trade barrier is removed, some industries and their workers will often lose out. The theories discussed before show that society as a whole is better off as a result of free trade – but that does not mean every worker is better. For example, after the removal of trade barriers for the textile industry in Europe, French and Italian textile workers found themselves competing with Chinese and Bangladeshi workers. Since they were often specialized and low-skilled, they had few alternative employment opportunities. In fact, as far back as 1941, economists Wolfgang Stolper and Paul Samuelson have shown that, under some realistic assumption, some people will always lose out, even in the long run.[25] In theory, a payment from those who gain from trade liberalization (i.e. buyers of cheap textiles) to these workers should resolve the problem. Yet in practice that is difficult to implement. Therefore, some economists like Dani Rodrik challenge their colleagues to carefully consider the distribution consequences before advocating 'free trade for all'.[26]

Political arguments against free trade

Political discussions of free trade incorporate nations' political, social and environmental agenda, independent of possible economic gains from trade. These arguments include (1) national security, (2) consumer protection, (3) foreign policy and (4) environmental and social responsibility.

First, national security concerns are often invoked to protect defence-related industries. Many nations fear that if they rely on arms imports, their national security may be compromised if there are political or diplomatic disagreements between them and the arms-producing nation. The largest buyer of military hardware, the US military, is subject to strict regulations requiring that a major part of the manufacturing is done in the US, even when buying from non-US suppliers. Even so, it is rare that a non-US supplier actually receives a major order. For example, in February 2008 the US Air Force selected a consortium of *Northrop Grumman* and *EADS* to supply 179 tanker aircraft. *Boeing* complained and politicians in Washington went into overdrive; reasons to cancel the contract were found, and a new tender was announced in September 2009. *Northrop Grumman* did not participate in the new tender, *EADS* submitted its own bid, but in 2011 the contract worth $35 billion was awarded to *Boeing*.[27] Similarly, France has a long-standing commitment to maintain an independent defence industry, even though arguably it would be cheaper to procure from large US and British suppliers.

Second, consumer protection has frequently been used as an argument for nations to erect trade barriers. In the 1990s, many countries – even within the EU – banned British beef for fears that mad cow disease might spread to humans. Likewise, any incidence of disease in cattle tends to trigger swift reaction from trading partners to protect their famers' livestock, and their consumers. For example, an outbreak of African swine fever in the Baltic States and Poland in 2014 induced countries like China to stop imports of pork products from the affected countries, while Russia blocked imports of pork from anywhere in the EU.[28]

Should Western governments use trade sanctions against hostile governments?

trade embargo
Politically motivated trade sanctions against foreign countries to signal displeasure.

Third, foreign policy objectives are often sought through trade intervention. Trade embargoes are politically motivated trade sanctions against foreign countries to signal displeasure. Many Arab countries maintain embargoes against Israel, and until 2012 many countries embargoed all trade with Myanmar.[29] After the annexation of the Crimea by Russia, many countries and the EU introduced a trade embargo on Russia; Russia retaliated by banning food imports from the EU, purportedly due to health concerns. Sanctions are popular, even though there is little evidence that a trade embargo is effective.[30] The only successful case was probably the anti-apartheid sanctions against South Africa before 1994.

Finally, environmental and social responsibility can be used as a political argument to initiate trade intervention against certain countries. Developed countries tend to have sophisticated standards that apply to all aspect of manufacturing, such as labour standards and limits on environmental emissions. Some interest groups argue that imported goods ought to be manufactured by the same standards, even where the local regulations and standards are fundamentally different. The producing countries may see such interference in their internal matters as an illegitimate trade barrier. For example, the EU introduced a ban on fish imports from Sri Lanka because the country's fishing practices were not sustainable. Illegal, unreported and unregulated fishing threatened to destroy the fish population in Sri Lankan waters. Fish exports to the EU are important for Sri Lanka, amounting to €74 million (or 1% of Sri Lankan exports), and the foreign minister went to Brussels to negotiate support for Sri Lanka to improve its fish stock management practices.[31]

DEBATES AND EXTENSIONS

LEARNING OBJECTIVE

4 Participate in two leading debates on international trade

As has been shown, international trade has a substantial mismatch between theory and reality, resulting in numerous debates. This section highlights two leading debates: (1) trade deficit versus surplus and (2) impact of trade on job markets.

Trade deficit versus trade surplus

Smith and Ricardo would probably turn in their graves if they heard that one of today's hottest trade debates still echoes the old debate between mercantilists and free traders 200 years ago. Nowhere is the debate more ferocious than in the USA, which runs the world's largest trade deficit. In 2006, it reached a record US$817 billion (6% of GDP). During the recession, it dropped to US$503 billion in 2009, before growing again, reaching US$689 billion in 2013. Should this level of trade deficit be of concern? Free traders argue that this is not a grave concern. They suggest that the USA and its trading partners mutually benefit by developing a deeper division of labour based on comparative advantage. The 2008 Nobel laureate in economics Paul Krugman argued in 1993:

> 'International trade is not about competition, it is about mutually beneficial exchange . . . Imports, not exports, are the purpose of trade. That is, what a country gains from trade is the ability to import things it wants. Exports are not an objective in and of themselves: the need to export is a burden that a country must bear because its import suppliers are crass enough to demand payment.'[32]

Critics disagree. They argue that international trade *is* about competition between nations – about markets, jobs and incomes. The debate in the USA tends to focus on a particular country with which the country runs the largest deficit: Japan in the 1980s and 1990s and China in the 2000s and 2010s. The US runs trade deficits with all of its major trading partners – Canada, the EU, Japan and Mexico – and is in trade disputes with them most of the time (see Closing Case). Nevertheless, the China trade debate is emotionally charged and politically explosive, perhaps fuelled by the political and cultural barriers between the two countries. Table 5.6 summarizes major arguments and counterarguments in this debate.[33] Two things seem certain: (1) given Americans' appetite for imports, the US trade deficit is difficult to eliminate and (2) drastic measures proposed by some protectionist members of US Congress (such as slapping Chinese imports with 20% to 30% tariffs if the yuan does not appreciate 'satisfactorily') are unrealistic and would violate US commitments to the WTO. As China's export drive continues, according to *The Economist*, China will be the 'scapegoat of choice' for the economic problems of the USA for a long time.[34] (We will discuss the currency issue in Chapter 7.) Similar tensions have arisen within the Eurozone, as Germany persistently generates a large export surplus, while other countries have structural trade deficits and wish the Germans would buy more of their produce.

What about jobs?

What happens in the real world when comparative advantages shift over time? In recent years, China and India have upgraded their resources – both capital and skilled labour – in areas where Europe and the US traditionally enjoyed comparative advantages, such as car components and information technology. For example, a study of the value chain of cars 'made in Germany' found that from 1995 to 2008 the value added in Germany declined, especially the contribution by low-skilled workers (from 7% to 4%) and medium-skilled workers (34% to 25%). Who are the winners? They are in emerging economies, the owners of capital (8% to 15%), and high-skilled workers (3% to 6%).[35] Paul Samuelsen, who won a Nobel Prize for his research on the gains from international trade,[36] thus argued that a loss of comparative advantage can in fact make the US economy *worse* off as a whole, because those losing their jobs cannot be adequately compensated.[37]

Table 5.6   Debate on the US trade deficit with China

US trade deficit with China is a huge problem	US trade deficit with China is not a huge problem
Naive trader versus unfair protectionist • The US is a 'naive' trader with open markets. China has 'unfairly' protected its markets.	*Market reformer versus unfair protectionist* • China's markets are already unusually open. Its trade volume (merchandise and services) is 53% of GDP, whereas the US volume is only 30%.
Greedy exporters • Unscrupulous Chinese exporters threaten US manufacturing jobs and drive US rivals out of business.	*Eager foreign investors* • Two-thirds of Chinese exports are generated by foreign-invested firms in China, and numerous US firms have invested in and benefited from such operations in China.
The demon that has caused deflation • Cheap imports sold at 'the China price' push down prices and cause deflation.	*Thank China for low prices* • Every consumer benefits from cheap prices brought from China by US firms such as *Wal-Mart*.
Intellectual property (IP) violator • Chinese violate IP rights, valued by US firms as billions of dollars per year a year.	*Inevitable step in development* • True, but (1) the US did that in the 19th century (to the British) and (2) IP protection is improving in China.
Currency manipulator • The yuan is severely under-valued (maybe up to 40%), giving Chinese exports an 'unfair' advantage in being priced at an artificially low level.	*Currency issue is not relevant* • The yuan may be somewhat under-valued, but (1) US and other foreign firms producing in China benefit and (2) the US also manipulates its own currency via quantitative easing.
Trade deficit will make the USA poorer • Since imports have to be paid, the USA borrows against its future with disastrous outcomes.	*Trade deficit does not cause a fall in the US standard of living* • As long as the Chinese are willing to invest in the US economy (such as Treasury bills), what's the worry?
Something has to be done • If the Chinese don't do it 'our way', the US should introduce drastic measures (such as slapping 20% to 30% tariffs on all Chinese imports).	*Remember the gains from trade argued by classic theories?* • Tariffs will not bring back US jobs, which will simply go to Mexico or Malaysia, and will lead to retaliation from China, a major *importer* of US goods and services.

Note: This table is a representative sample – not an exhaustive list – of major arguments and counter-arguments in this debate. Other issues include (1) statistical reporting differences, (2) environmental damage, (3) human rights and (4) national security, which are not discussed to make this table manageable.

Sources: (1) *BusinessWeek,* 2009, Free trade in the slow lane, September 21: 50; (2) *The Economist,* 2005, From T-shirts to T-bonds, July 30: 61–63; (3) *The Economist,* 2014, A number of great import, February 15: 40; (4) *The Economist,* 2014, Picking the world champion of trade, January 18: 72–73; (5) *The Economist,* 2014, Trading places, April 5: 49; (6) M. W. Peng, D. Ahlstrom, S. Carraher, & W. Shi, 2014, How history can inform the debate over intellectual property, Working paper, Jindal School of Management, University of Texas at Dallas; (7) O. Shenkar, 2005, *The Chinese Century,* Philadelphia: Wharton School Publishing.

The reaction has been swift. Jagdish Bhagwati, an Indian-born Columbia University trade expert, and his colleagues countered Samuelson by arguing that classic pro-free trade theories still hold.[38] Bhagwati and colleagues wrote:

'Imagine that you are exporting aircraft, and new producers of aircraft emerge abroad. That will lower the price of your aircraft, and your gains from trade will diminish. You have to be naïve to believe that this can never happen. But you have to be even more naïve to think that the policy response to the reduced gains from trade is to give up the remaining gains as well. The critical policy question we must address is: when external developments, such as the growth of skills in China and India, for instance, do diminish the gains from trade to the US, is the harm to the US going to be reduced or increased if the US turns into Fortress America? The answer is: the US will only increase its anguish if it closes its markets.'[39]

In any case, according to Bhagwati and colleagues, the 'threat' posed by Indian innovation is vastly exaggerated, and relative to the entire US economy offshoring is too small to matter much. Moreover, higher-level jobs will replace those lost to offshoring, thus creating greater earnings potential. However, here is a catch: Where are such newer and higher-level jobs? Will there be enough of such jobs in Western Europe and the USA? Creating higher-level jobs requires foresighted investment in education, training and skill development. Ultimately, countries with persistently high trade deficits face the question, how can we develop new capabilities that make our businesses internationally competitive – and enable us to sustain our standard of living?

IMPLICATIONS FOR PRACTICE

How does this chapter answer the big question in global business adapted for the context of international trade: what determines the success and failure of firms' exports around the globe? The two core perspectives lead to two answers. Fundamentally, the various economic theories underpin the resource-based view, suggesting that successful exports are generated by firms endowed with resources and capabilities that give them a competitive edge over their foreign rivals. However, the political realities stress the explanatory power of the institution-based view: as rules of the game, institutions such as laws and regulations promoted by various special interest groups can protect certain domestic industries, firms and individuals, erect trade barriers and make the nation as a whole worse off.

As a result, three implications for action emerge (Table 5.7). First, location, location, location! In international trade, managers' primary role is to leverage comparative advantage of world-class locations. For instance, as managers aggressively tapped into Argentina's comparative advantage in wine production, its wine exports grew from $6 million in 1987 to $500 million in 2008.

> **LEARNING OBJECTIVE**
>
> 5   Draw implications for action

Table 5.7   Implications for action

- Discover and leverage comparative advantage of world-class locations.
- Monitor and nurture the current comparative advantage of certain locations and take advantage of new locations.
- Be politically aware to demonstrate, safeguard and advance the gains from international trade.

Second, comparative advantage is not fixed. Managers need to constantly monitor and nurture the current comparative advantage of a location and take advantage of new promising locations. Managers who fail to realize the departure of comparative advantage from certain locations are likely to fall behind. For instance, numerous German managers have moved production elsewhere, citing Germany's reduced comparative advantage in basic manufacturing. However, they still concentrate on top-notch, high-end manufacturing in Germany, leveraging its excellence in engineering.

Third, managers need to be politically active if they are to gain from trade. Although managers at many uncompetitive firms have long mastered the game of twisting politicians' arms for more protection, managers at competitive firms, who tend to be pro-free trade, have a tendency to shy away from 'politics'. They often fail to realize that free trade is *not* free – it requires constant efforts and sacrifices to demonstrate, safeguard and advance the gains from such trade.

CHAPTER SUMMARY

1 Use the resource-based and institution-based views to explain why nations trade

- The resource-based view suggests that nations trade because some firms use their unique resources and capabilities to produce goods in demand in other nations.

- The institution-based view suggests that national and international 'rules of the game' influence the actual flows of international trade.

2 Understand classic and modern theories of international trade

- Classic theories include (1) mercantilism, (2) absolute advantage and (3) comparative advantage.

- Modern theories include (1) product life cycles, (2) strategic trade and (3) the 'diamond model'.

3 Appreciate how economic and political institutions influence international trade

- The net impact of various tariffs and NTBs is that the whole nation is worse off while certain special interest groups (such as certain industries, firms and regions) benefit.

- Economic arguments against free trade centre on (1) protection from 'unfair' competition, (2) infant industries and (3) unequal distribution of cost and benefits.

- Political arguments against free trade focus on (1) national security, (2) consumer protection, (3) foreign policy and (4) environmental and social responsibility.

4 Participate in two leading debates on international trade

- The first debate deals with whether persistent trade deficit is of grave concern or not.

- The second deals with rich countries' response to shifts in comparative advantage.

5 Draw implications for action

- Discover and leverage comparative advantage of world-class locations.

- Monitor and nurture current comparative advantage of certain locations and take advantage of new locations.

- Be politically engaged to demonstrate, safeguard and advance the gains from international trade.

KEY TERMS

Absolute advantage
Administrative practices
Anti-dumping duty
Balance of trade

Classic trade theories
Comparative advantage
Deadweight loss
Exporting

Factor endowment theory
   (Heckscher-Ohlin theory)
First-mover advantage
Free trade

Import quota
Import tariff
Importing
Infant industry argument
Modern trade theories
Non-tariff barrier (NTB)
Opportunity cost
Product life cycle theory
Protectionism

Resource (factor) endowments
Resource mobility
Strategic trade policy
Strategic trade theory
Subsidy
Tariff barrier
Theory of absolute advantage
Theory of comparative advantage
Theory of mercantilism

Theory of national competitive
   advantage of industries
   ('diamond' model)
Trade deficit
Trade embargo
Trade surplus
Voluntary export restraint (VER)

CRITICAL DISCUSSION QUESTIONS

1 After the 2008–09 crisis, is the trade policy of your country's government turning into more protectionist? Why?

2 What is the ratio of total volume of international trade (exports + imports) to GDP in your country? How about the ratio for the following: the US, the European Union, Japan, Russia, China and Singapore? Do these ratios help you answer question 1?

3 As a foreign policy tool, trade embargoes, such as US embargoes against Cuba, Myanmar (until 2012)

and North Korea, are meant to discourage foreign governments. But they also cause a great deal of misery among the population (such as shortage of medicine and food). Are embargoes ethical?

4 Although the nation as a whole may gain from free trade, there is no doubt that certain regions, industries, firms and individuals may lose their jobs and livelihood due to foreign competition. How can the rest of the nation help the unfortunate ones cope with the impact of international trade?

RECOMMENDED READINGS

J. Bhagwati, A. Panagariya & T. Sribivasan, 2004, The muddles over outsourcing, *Journal of Economic Perspectives*, 18, 93–114 – a recent statement of the benefits of free trade, applied to the question of outsourcing.

R.C. Feenstra, 2004, Advanced International Trade: Theory and Evidence, Princeton: Princeton University Press – a specialized textbook that explains the theories and institutions of international trade.

P.R. Krugman & M. Obstfeld, 2011, International Economics: Theory and Practice, 9th ed., Boston: Pearson – a textbook that covers international trade extensively.

P. Rivoli, 2005, *The Travels of a T-shirt in the Global Economy*, Hoboken: Wiley – an economist is tracing and explaining the interdependencies of international trade using the case of a T-shirt.

P. Samuelson, 2004, Where Ricardo and Mill rebut and confirm arguments of mainstream economists supporting globalization, *Journal of Economic Perspectives*, 18, 135–146 – an esteemed international trade economist outlining some concerns regarding free trade.

CLOSING CASE

US anti-dumping against Chinese apple juice concentrate producers

The US Commerce Department (in short, 'Commerce') frequently initiates anti-dumping investigations of Chinese imports. In most cases, Chinese producers are found to be guilty of dumping in the USA and suffer high punitive tariffs. However, the tide turned when Chinese apple juice concentrate (AJC) producers took Commerce to court.

Commerce's probe into AJC production in China started in response to a petition filed by American apple juice producers. They requested a 92% anti-dumping rate and then dropped to 52% after they heard that Chinese AJC producers started to fight by responding. If the Chinese did not respond to the investigation, they would obviously lose.

China was the world's largest producer of AJC, exporting about 90% of its AJC production. The proposed anti-dumping rate of 52%, if imposed, would have devastated Chinese AJC producers and apple growers. Among about 30 Chinese AJC producers involved in the US anti-dumping investigation, 15 companies agreed to respond and then 11 companies collectively hired experienced American lawyers, with one firm dropping out later. The case took four and a half years (1999–2004) and cost about US$3.6 million in legal fees for the Chinese respondents.

A key point of contention was how much it would cost to produce AJC in a market economy. Since China was not considered a 'market economy,' Commerce chose India and other surrogate factors of production for valuation purposes. Commerce concluded that Chinese AJC exports were sold at less than 'fair market value' and the US International Trade Commission determined that the Chinese dumping materially injured US industry. As a result, an anti-dumping rate of 15% was imposed on the Chinese exporters, with one firm receiving zero tariffs, while the 52% rate remained the same for Chinese firms that had not responded.

Nine Chinese respondents appealed the case to the US Court of International Trade, challenging the selection of India as a surrogate country and Indian prices for juice apple and calculation of expenses. Unusually, the Court did not support Commerce's decision, and the Chinese AJC producers won. When choosing India

as a surrogate country, Commerce relied on the data in a private market study prepared for US petitioners by a paid consultant because there were no official countrywide data about AJC production in India. According to the Court, this information was insufficiently reliable. Thus Commerce failed to adequately explain how the data in the market study could serve as substantial evidence of the Indian AJC industry as a whole and thus led to its conclusion that India was a significant producer of comparable merchandise (AJC) to be a proper surrogate country.

Accordingly, Commerce observed the Court's decisions and used Turkey as the surrogate country. It then amended the weighted average dumping margins to

1.5% (3.83% for four Chinese respondent firms and 0% for six firms), while the same rate (52%) was maintained to other Chinese AJC exporters that did not respond. To the ten Chinese respondents, reducing the punitive tariff first from 92% to 52%, then to 15%, and finally to 1.5% on average was as a major victory in the US anti-dumping game whose rules were typically stacked against them. Since these ten AJC producers represented 80% of Chinese AJC exports, this effectively opened the US market. AJC exports from China to the USA grew from 227 tons in 2005 to 388 tons in 2010. More recently, rising demand in China and lower costs in other producer countries has stopped the rise of the Chinese export.

This case taught Chinese businesses an important lesson: as long as they operate within the framework of WTO, they don't need to be afraid of unreasonable anti-dumping charges. Challenging a decision by a US government department in court may be expensive, but can be successful.

DISCUSSION QUESTIONS

1 Considering absolute and comparative advantages, how would you explain the growth AJC exports from China to the United States?

2 From an institutional perspective, what explains the imposition and the reduction of tariffs for AJC?

3 Is this form of international trade beneficial to home and host societies?

Sources: This case was prepared by Professor Lianlian Lin (California State Polytechnic University Pomona) and updated by Klaus Meyer. Based on (1) A-570-855, Department of Commerce, International Trade Administration, 2004, Certain non-frozen apple juice concentrate from the People's Republic of China, *Federal Register,* 69(30), February 13; (2) X. Wang, 2004, Taking 4.5 years, Chinese agricultural product firms won US Commerce Department for the first time, *Economic Information Newspaper,* February 12, news.xinhuanet.com; (3) Juice Camber of CFNA, en.cccfna.org.cn/ (accessed march 2015); (4) S. Zhou & X. Cai, 2010, US lifts tariffs on apple juice concentrates *China Daily,* November 18.

NOTES

'For journal abbreviations please see page xx–xxi.'

1 G. Felbermayr, J. Prat & H.-J. Schmerer, 2011, Trade and unemployment: What do the data say?, *EER,* 55: 741–758.

2 J. Baggs & J. Brander, 2006, Trade liberalization, profitability, and financial leverage, *JIBS,* 37: 196–211; also see A.B. Bernard, J.B. Jensen, S.J. Redding & P.K. Schott, Firms in international trade, *JEP,* 31(3); 105–130.

3 J. Eaton & S. Kortum, 2012, Putting Ricardo to work, *JEP,* 26(2): 65–90.

4 B. Ohlin, 1933, *Interregional and International Trade,* Cambridge, MA: Harvard University Press. In this work, Ohlin summarized and extended E. Heckscher's research first published in 1919. Another implication of this theory is that trade does not benefit everyone in an economy, but only those who own the relatively abundant resources.

5 R. Vernon, 1966, International investments and international trade in product life cycle, *QJE,* May: 190–207; S. Hirsch, 1975, The product cycle model of international trade, *OBES,* 37, 305–317.

6 J.A. Brander & B. Spencer, 1985, Export subsidies and international market share rivalry, *JIE,* 18: 83–100; P. Krugman ed., 1986, *Strategic Trade Policy and the New International Economics,* Cambridge, MA: MIT Press; J.A. Brander, 1995, Strategic trade policy, NBER Working Paper #W5020.

7 P. Krugman, 1994, *Peddling Prosperity,* New York: Norton.

8 M. Porter, 1990, *Competitive Advantage of Nations,* New York: Free Press.

9 J. Dunning, 1993, *The Globalization of Business,* London: Routledge; H. Moon, A. Rugman & A. Verbeke, 1998, A generalized double diamond approach to the global competitiveness of Korea and Singapore, *IBR,* 7: 135–151; H. Davies & P. Ellis, 2001, Porter's *Competitive Advantage of Nations:* Time for the final judgment? *JMS,* 37: 1189–1215.

10 R. Baldwin, 1992, Measureable dynamic gains from trade, *JPE,* 100, 162–174; D. Bernhofen & J. Brown, 2005, An empirical assessment of the comparative advantage gains from trade, *AER,* 95: 208–225.

11 R.C. Feenstra, 1992, How costly is protectionism, *JEP,* 6, 159–178.

12 Tire Industry Association (TIA), 2009, Tire Industry Association expresses disappointment with President's decision concerning Chinese tire tariff, September 14, Bowie, MD: TIA, www.tireindustry.org.

13 J. Bhagwati, 2004, *In Defense of Globalization,* New York: Oxford University Press.

14 *The Economist,* 2009, Globalization and trade: The nuts and bolts come apart, March 28; *The Economist,* 2009, World trade: unpredictable tides, July 15; A. Lowrey, 2012, An Increase in Barriers to Trade Is Reported, *New York Times,* June 22.

15 *The Economist,* 2005, Special Report: The EU's agricultural policy, December 10; *BBC News,* 2013, Euro MPs reject radical CAP farm subsidy reforms, March 13.

16 R.C. Feenstra, 1992, *as above.*

17 H. Nordas, 2004, The global textile and clothing industry beyond the Agreement on Textiles and Clothing (p. 34), Discussion paper no. 5, Geneva: WTO Secretariat.

18 *The Economist,* 2005, The textile industry: The great stitch-up, May 28.

19 S. Berry, J. Levinsohn & A. Pakes, 1999, Voluntary export restrains on automobiles, *AER,* 8, 400–430.

20 WTO, 2012, *Report on G-20 Trade Measures,* Geneva: WTO; European Commission, 2012, *Ninth report on potentially restrictive measures,* Brussels: EC.

21 *Globe and Mail,* 2009, Canada turns to WTO over US label law, October 8: B7; 'United States – certain country of origin labeling (COOL) requirements – request for the establishment of a panel by Canada', WTO document #WT/DS38418, www.wto.org.

22 T. Klitgaard & K. Schiele, 1998, Free trade vs fair trade, *Current Isssues in Economics and Finance,* 4, 1–6; J.P. Lindeque, 2007, A firm perspective of anti-dumping and countervailing duty cases in the United States of America, *JWT,* 41, 559–579.

23 F. Bastiat, 1964, *Economic Sophisms,* A. Goddard (ed. and trans.), New York: Van Nostrand.

24 P. Dasgupta & J. Stiglitz, 1988, Learning-by-doing, market structure and industrial and trade policies, *OEP,* 40, 246–268.

25 W. Stolper & P. Samuelson, 1942, Protection and real wages, *Review of Economic Studies,* 9: 58–73.

26 D. Rodrik, 2011, *The Globalization Paradox,* Oxford: Oxford University Press; R. Driskill, 2012, Deconstructing the argument for free trade, *Economics and Philosophy,* 28: 1–30.

27 *The Economist,* 2009, Airbus and Boeing resume the feud: Hard pounding, June 18; C. Drew, 2011, Boeing wins contract to build air force tankers, *New York Times,* February 24.

28 *Moscow Times,* 2014, EU says Moscow overreacting on swine fever, February 2; *Reuters,* 2014, China suspends Polish pork imports over swine fever, February 27.

29 K.E. Meyer & H. Thein, 2014, Business under adverse home country institutions: The case of international sanctions against Myanmar, *JWB,* 49: 156–171.

30 G. Hufbauer, J. Schott & K. Elliott, 2007, *Economic Sanctions Reconsidered,* 3rd ed., Washington, DC: Peterson Institute for International Economics.

31 J. Fioretti, 2014, EU to ban fish from Sri Lanka, *Reuters,* October 14; *Colomo Gazette,* 2015, EU begins Sri Lanka import ban, January 15; Government of Sri Lanka, 2015, Sri Lankan Foreign Minister's statement in parliament on EU visit, Fishing & GSP, February 20.

32 P. Krugman, 1993, What do undergrads need to know about trade? (p. 24), *AER,* 83: 23–26.

33 O. Shenkar, 2005, *The Chinese Century,* Philadelphia: Wharton School Publishing; M. Feldstein, 2008, Resolving global imbalance, *JEP,* 22(3), 113–125.

34 *The Economist,* 2003, Tilting at dragons, October 25; *The Economist,* 2007, America's fear of China, May 17.

35 M. Timmer, A. Eruban, B Los, R. Stehrer & G. De Vries, 2014, Slicing up global value chains, *JEP,* 99–118.

36 P. Samuelson, 1962, The gains from international trade once again, *EJ,* 72: 820–829.

37 P. Samuelson, 2004, Where Ricardo and Mill rebut and confirm arguments of mainstream economists supporting globalization, *JEP,* 18(3): 135–146.

38 J. Bhagwati, A. Panagariya, & T. Srinivasan, 2004, The muddles over outsourcing, *JEP,* 18(4): 93–114.

39 J. Bhagwati & A. Panagariya, 2004, Trading opinions about free trade (p. 20), *Business Week,* December 27.

CHAPTER SIX

INVESTING ABROAD DIRECTLY

LEARNING OBJECTIVES

After studying this chapter, you should be able to

1   Understand the vocabulary associated with foreign direct investment (FDI)

2   Explain why ownership advantages are necessary for firms to engage in FDI

3   Explain what location advantages attract foreign investors

4   Explain and apply the concept on internalization advantages

5   Appreciate the benefits and costs of FDI to host and home countries

6   Explain how home and host country institutions affect FDI

7   Participate in three leading debates on FDI

8   Draw implications for action

OPENING CASE

Spanish MNEs enter the global stage

Spanish multinational enterprises (MNEs) have been relative latecomers to international business. Yet by 2010, Spain was among the top ten source and recipient countries for foreign direct investment (FDI). Foreign firms' stock of FDI in Spain grew from €201 billion in 2001 to €605 billion in June 2014, while Spanish firms owned €541 billion of FDI stock abroad, up from €264 billion in 2001.

Since the early 1980s, liberalization and privatization not only increased competition from foreigners entering

Spain, but also propelled Spanish enterprises to compete abroad. EU membership in 1986, the EU common market in 1993 and the adoption of the euro in 1999 further levelled barriers to trade and investment.

In the 1990s, Spanish MNEs expanded abroad. Initially many focused on Latin America, exploiting the similarities of language, culture and development process. Moreover, Latin America was undergoing privatization and liberalization processes not unlike Spain's experience a decade earlier. Hence business leaders saw opportunities to enter new markets that were not too different from Spain and to contribute their experience and competence to the industrial development of their hosts. This drive into Latin America was led by six of the largest companies in Spain that accounted for over 90% of all Spanish FDI in that region: *Banco Santander* and *BBVA* in banking, *Endesa* and *Iberdola* in public utilities, *Repsol* in oil and gas, as well as *Telefónica*, Spain's main telephone operator. In the years 1999 and 2000, Spanish firms invested more than US firms in Latin America, while Spain accounted for more than half of the EU's investment in Latin America.

In the early 2000s, Spanish MNEs refocused their attention on Western Europe, exploiting the opportunities of market integration and expansion in the EU. In particular consumer goods and tourism businesses expanded from Spain to other parts of Europe. For example, the entrepreneurial start-ups in the fashion industry, like *Inditex* (owner of *Mango* and *Zara*), successfully entered the international stage by pioneering new concepts of fast fashion, expanding first across Europe, and then to other parts of the world. Thus the pattern of FDI from Spain became more geographically diversified by reducing the focus on Latin America (Figure 6.1).

The leading Spanish MNEs are concentrated in several industries. In banking, *BBVA* and *Santander* have become market leaders in many countries of Latin America. Starting in the 1990s, they became the largest foreign banks in Latin America through some 20 acquisitions. In 2004, *Santander* also entered retail banking in the UK by acquiring *Abbey National* for €12.5 billion. Meanwhile, *Santander* acquired *Sovereign Bankcorp* to build a bridgehead in the USA, the world's largest financial market. *Santander* escaped relatively unscathed from the financial crisis due to its geographic diversification and its prudent risk management. *Santander* even used the crisis to acquire assets from banks in financial difficulties,

Figure 6.1 Spanish outward FDI flows

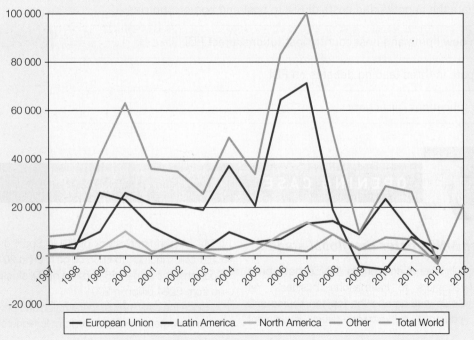

Source: Authors' creation based on data from OECD and Banco de España.

including *Banco Real* in Brazil from *ABN AMRO* and *Bank America*'s stake in *Serfin* in Mexico. In Poland, *Santander* acquired *Bank Zachodni*, the third-largest bank, from *Allied Irish Bank*. In the UK, *Santander* acquired two mortgage banks that faltered during the financial crisis, and bought 318 branches of the then state-controlled *Royal Bank of Scotland*. *Santander* thus grew into the second-largest retail bank in the UK, with 11% market share serving 26 million customers through its 1400 branches.

In the utilities industry, privatized companies led the international expansion. Opportunities for acquisition in these sectors are often created by privatization. For example, *Endesa*, an electric utilities operator, started its international acquisition spree with a major investment in 1997 in Chile, which was the first Latin American country to create a legal framework for FDI that reduced the business risk to acceptable levels. *Endesa* subsequently became market leader in Chile, Argentina and Peru.

Similarly, telephone operator *Telefónica* began its internationalization by acquiring equity stakes in companies in Latin America. In 2010, it took full control of Brazilian phone operator *Brasilcel* by buying out minority shareholders for €8.5 billion, thus becoming the market leader. In Europe, *Telefónica* acquired *O2*, the mobile phone operator in the UK, Germany and Ireland for €26 billion. London later also became *Telefónica*'s hub for its digital economy operations. In China, *Telefónica* holds almost 10% in *China Netcom*, which in turn owns 1.7% of *Telefónica*.

In the construction sector, companies like *Ferrovial*, *ACS* and *Sacyr Vallehermoso* have grown on the back of the construction boom, while expanding into the operation of infrastructure, such as motorways and airports, moving away from construction and into services. In the 2000s, *Ferrovial* embarked on a major acquisition drive with two objectives: (1) to reduce its dependence on the Spanish market and (2) to reduce the volatility of its revenues, which previously were derived mainly from the very cyclical construction industry. Across Europe, *Ferrovial* acquired construction businesses such as *Amey* in the UK and *Budimex* in Poland, as well as airport operators such as *Swissport* in Switzerland and *BAA* in the UK. Many UK airports, such as *Heathrow* and *Gatwick*, were thus owned by this Spanish MNE. Meanwhile, *ACS* acquired Germany's largest construction company, *Hochtief*, in 2011.

At the same time, Latin American businesses, such as Mexican cement maker *CEMEX*, use Spain as a springboard to European markets. *CEMEX* originally established its Spanish operations as a means to access European capital markets and thus to lower

How did Spanish bank Santander become a common sight on British high streets?

its capital costs. Since then, *CEMEX* has used Spain as a basis to expand across Europe, and it still uses Spain as a base for its regional headquarters. A foreign investor in Spain itself, *CEMEX* is thus also a major outward foreign investor from Spain.

The financial crisis, however, also hit Spanish multinationals. Some divested projects overseas. For example, *Ferrovial* sold 10.6% of its *equity* in BAA to *Qatar Investment Authority*, a sovereign wealth fund. Others used their overseas affiliate to raise funds to channel money back to Spain. Hence in some years, and for some countries, Spanish outward FDI was negative. For example, in 2012 Spanish MNEs withdrew more than €2 billion from *each* of Mexico,

Switzerland, the USA and the UK. By 2013 however, the situation normalized, and Spanish MNEs continued their international growth.

Sources: (1) J. Galan, J. Gonzáles-Benito & J. Zuñiga, 2007, Factors determining the location decisions of Spanish MNEs, *JIBS*, 38: 975–997; (2) P. Ghemawat, 2007, *Redefining Global Strategy*, Cambridge, MA, Harvard Business School Press; (3) *The Economist*, 2007, Conquistadores on the beach, May 5; (4) P. Toral, 2008, The foreign direct investments of Spanish multinational enterprises in Latin America, *JLAS*, 40: 513–544; (5): N. Puig & P. Pérez, 2009, A silent revolution: The internationalization of large Spanish family firms, *BH*, 51: 462–483; (6) *The Economist*, 2009, Spanish companies in Latin America: A good bet? May 2; (7) W. Chislet, 2011, Spain's multinationals, Real Instituto Elcano, working paper 17/2011; (8) A. Parker, M. Johnson & C. Hall, 2012, Qatar move illustrates attraction of BAA, *Financial Times,* August 21; (9) Bank of Spain website (www.bde.es, accessed February 2014).

Why are Spanish firms increasingly interested in investing in FDI in Latin America and Europe? Is it because of the the pull of low labour costs? Or is it lucrative markets abroad? Or both? Why do they choose direct investment rather than trade (Chapter 5) or financial investment (Chapter 7)? Why are these particular firms investing abroad, while other domestically successful firms are not? Recall from Chapter 1 that foreign direct investment (FDI) is defined as directly investing in activities that control and manage value creation in other countries.[1] Also recall from Chapter 1 that firms that engage in FDI are known as multinational enterprises (MNEs). Focusing on FDI, this chapter builds on our coverage of international trade in Chapter 5. International trade and FDI are closely related. MNEs are not only trading with other firms, they transfer goods and services internally, which creates intra-MNE international trade.

We start by clarifying the terms. Then we address a crucial question: why do firms engage in FDI? We present a famous analytical framework, the OLI paradigm, which integrates aspects of the resource-based and institution-based views. On this basis, we explore how national institutions affect the flow of FDI and how FDI impacts on host countries. Debates and implications for action follow.

foreign direct investment (FDI)
Investment in, controlling and managing value-added activities in other countries.
multinational enterprise (MNE)
A firm that engages in foreign direct investment and operates in multiple countries.

THE FDI VOCABULARY

LEARNING OBJECTIVE

1   Understand the vocabulary associated with foreign direct investment (FDI)

Foreign investment comes in many forms and shapes. As a basis for systematic analysis, we need to reduce this complexity by setting the terms straight. Specifically, we will discuss (1) the key word in FDI, (2) horizontal versus vertical FDI, (3) FDI flow and stock and (4) MNE versus non-MNE.

The key word is 'direct'

foreign portfolio investment (FPI)
Investment in a portfolio of foreign securities such as stocks and bonds.

There are two primary kinds of international investment: FDI and foreign portfolio investment (FPI). FPI refers to investment in a portfolio of foreign financial assets, such as stocks and bonds, that do not entail the active management of foreign business operations. In contrast, the key word in FDI is 'direct' – namely, the direct management of foreign assets. Undertaking FPI is normally not a full-time job. If you own foreign stocks and bonds, you don't need to do anything else – just collect your dividends or interest. In contrast, engaging in FDI requires substantial resource commitments – including managerial time to oversee the operations – you have to 'get your feet wet' by actively managing foreign operations. In other words, foreign direct investors participate in the strategic decision-making of the local firm.

For statistical purposes, FDI is defined by the United Nations as involving an equity stake of 10% or more in a foreign-based enterprise.[2] Hence FDI includes joint ventures, which are operations with shared ownership by several domestic or foreign companies. Larger equity stakes, ideally 100%, give foreign investors more control over the operation. However, investors like to share control under certain circumstances, for example when both partners contribute intangible resources to the business, as we shall discuss in Chapter 12.

joint venture
An operation with shared ownership by several domestic or foreign companies.

Horizontal and vertical FDI

FDI establishes a new operation that can stand in various relationships with the existing company. Recall the value chain introduced in Chapter 4, through which firms perform value-adding activities stage by stage in a vertical fashion (from upstream to downstream). Horizontal FDI creates operations abroad at the same position in the value chain as the operation in the home country (see Figure 6.2). For example, *Endesa* generates and distributes electricity in Spain. Through horizontal FDI, it does the same type of activity in host countries in Latin America.

If a firm through FDI moves upstream or downstream in different value chain stages in a host country, we label this vertical FDI (Figure 6.3). For instance, if *VW* (hypothetically) only assembles cars and does not manufacture components in Germany, but does so in Spain, it enters into components manufacturing through FDI (an upstream activity), this would be upstream vertical FDI. Likewise, if *VW* does not engage in car distribution in Germany, but invests in car dealerships in France or Italy (a downstream activity), it would be downstream vertical FDI. In practice, many FDI projects have horizontal and vertical elements, yet the horizontal–vertical terminology helps to describe how different operations stand in relation to each other.

horizontal FDI
FDI that creates operations abroad at the same position in the value chain as the operation in the home country.

vertical FDI
A type of FDI in which a firm moves upstream or downstream in different value chain stages in a host country.

upstream vertical FDI
A type of vertical FDI in which a firm engages in an upstream stage of the value.

downstream vertical FDI
A type of vertical FDI in which a firm engages in a downstream stage of the value chain in two different countries.

Measuring FDI

How much FDI is there? There are two ways to look at this question: by flow and by stock. FDI flow is the amount of FDI capital transferred by MNEs in a given period (usually a year) in a certain direction. FDI inflow refers to inbound FDI moving into a country, and FDI outflow refers to outbound FDI moving out of a country. Figure 6.4 illustrates the pattern of FDI outflows over time. The most striking observation is the highly cyclical nature of FDI: in a recession much less is invested in form of FDI. This is in part because mergers and acquisitions account for a major part of FDI flows, and their valuations go down during a recession. Also note that these capital flow data do not include capital raised by MNEs in host countries; actual investments by MNEs in a given country may thus be considerably larger. On the other hand, if MNEs use overseas capital markets to raise funds and channel them back home, this counts as negative outflow of FDI. For example, when financial markets were tight in Spain in 2010, the French subsidiary

FDI flow
The amount of FDI moving in a given period (usually a year) in a certain direction.

Figure 6.2 Horizontal FDI

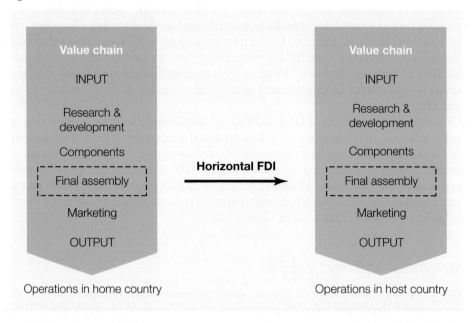

Figure 6.3 Vertical FDI

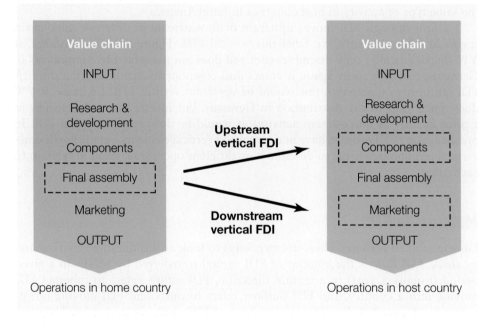

of Spanish infrastructure operator *Abertis* issued €750 million in bonds. The deal allowed *Abertis* to benefit from the stronger credit rating of its French unit.[3] Deals such as this explain the negative value in Spanish FDI in the EU in 2009 and 2010 (Figure 6.1).

Emerging economies as a group attracted over 60% of the FDI inflows in 2013, with China, Russia and Hong Kong the most important destinations. Firms from

Figure 6.4 FDI outflows

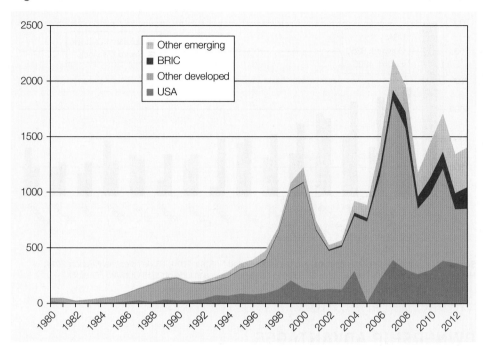

Source: Authors' creation using data extracted from: UNCTAD, various years, *World Investment Report 2014*, Geneva: UNCTAD.

some emerging economies, such as those from India and China, have also become major players on the global stage, generating 33% of FDI outflows worldwide.[4]

FDI stock is the book value of foreign-owned firms operating in a country, or controlled by a country's firms abroad. Hypothetically, between two countries A and B, if firms from A undertake €10 billion of FDI in B in year 1 and another €10 billion in year 2, then we can say that in each of these two years, B receives annual FDI inflows of €10 billion and, correspondingly, A generates annual FDI outflows of €10 billion. If we assume that there was no revaluation (for instance due to currency fluctuations), then this investment added €20 billion to the stock of FDI in B by the end of year 2.

Figure 6.5 shows the inward FDI and outward FDI stock from countries that are the largest players in the global economy. The USA is by far the largest source of FDI; in 2013 assets worth US$6.3 trillion were under control of American MNEs around the world. The largest four European source countries – UK, Germany, France and the Netherlands – together(!) achieve a similar magnitude. The US is also the largest host to foreign MNEs who own US$4.9 trillion of assets with in the USA. If you inspect Figure 6.5 further, you will note that some smaller countries also make a strong appearance, for example, Switzerland and Belgium. This is in part due to their ability to foster the growth of indigenous MNEs, and in part due to them hosting European headquarters of MNEs who thus both invest in the country, and use the country as a base to invest in third countries. Hong Kong may also strike you as odd; it isn't even a country, right? (It has been part of China since 1997.) Yet in official statistics it is still reported as separate entity, and it plays an important role as intermediary for investment both from and to mainland China.

FDI stock
The total accumulation of inbound FDI in a country or outbound FDI from a country across a given period of time (usually several years).

Figure 6.5 Top 15 source countries of FDI stock

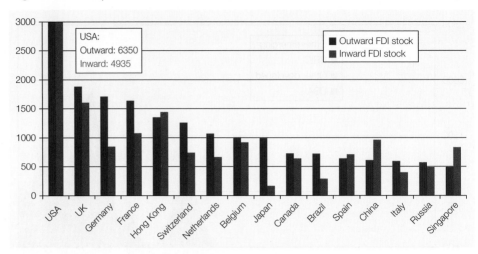

Source: Authors' creation based on data extracted from United Nations, 2014, *World Investment Report 2014*, New York and Geneva: UN (Annex Table 2). Ranking based on the magnitude of 2013 Outward FDI stock.

OWNERSHIP ADVANTAGES

LEARNING OBJECTIVE

2 Explain why ownership advantages are necessary for firms to engage in FDI

OLI paradigm
A theoretical framework positing that ownership (O), location (L) and internalization (I) advantages combine to induce firms to engage in FDI.

ownership advantages
Resources of the firm that are transferable across borders, and enable the firm to attain competitive advantages abroad.

locational advantages
Advantages enjoyed by firms operating in certain locations.

internalization advantages
Advantages of organizing activities within a multinational firm rather than using a market transaction.

Why do so many firms become MNEs by engaging in FDI? There must be economic gains for these firms from using FDI rather than other forms of international business. What are the sources of such gains? British economist John Dunning developed a framework known as OLI paradigm, which proposes that FDI is the most appropriate form of international business if three conditions are met (Table 6.1):[5]

1 The firm possesses ownership advantages (O-advantages), defined as resources of the firm that are transferable across borders, and that enable the firm to attain competitive advantages abroad. Firms are at a natural disadvantage when competing in a foreign country, what we call the liability of outsidership (Chapter 1). O-advantages enable MNEs to overcome this liability when competing abroad.

2 The local context provides some sort of locational advantage (L-advantage), that is an operation at that location allows the MNEs to create value that it would not be able to create at home. L-advantages include in particular access to local markets and to resources, such as human capital and raw materials.

3 The activities in both locations are better organized within a multinational firm rather than using a market transaction, a condition known as internalization advantages (I-advantages). They arise for example from the transaction costs of using international markets. Firms may be able to organize certain activities more effectively internally. Such internalization replaces cross-border markets (such as exporting and importing) with one firm (the MNE) locating in two or more countries.

Thus firms become MNEs because FDI provides ownership, location and internalization advantages that they otherwise would not obtain. Let us have a closer look at the three conditions.

Table 6.1 OLI paradigm

Types of O-advantages	Examples
● Resources created in one country that can be exploited in other countries.	● Proprietary technology and managerial know-how (e.g. *VW*).
● Capabilities arising from combining business units in multiple countries.	● Logistics based on superior coordination between business units in different locations (e.g. *Wal-Mart*).
● Capabilities arising from organizational structures and culture.	● Operation manuals, codes of conduct, organizational norms and practices (e.g. *IKEA, Carrefour*).

Types of L-advantages	Examples
● Markets	● Size and growth consumer demand (e.g. China), presence of key clients (e.g. *Antolin*), high income consumers (e.g. *Haier* in the USA).
● Location-bound human resources	● Human capital, such a skilled labour force (e.g. pharmaceuticals labs near Oxford and Cambridge).
● Natural resources	● Oil, gas and mining deposits (e.g. *Shell, BP, Sinopec*) and agriculture.
● Agglomeration	● Geographic cluster of potential customers and suppliers (e.g. cars in Slovakia).
● Institutions	● Incentive schemes to attract FDI (e.g. Hungary).

I-advantages: types of market failure	Examples
● Asset specificity	● FDI versus exports (e.g. aluminium industry) or outsourcing (e.g. *Flextronics, Wipro*).
● Information asymmetry	● FDI versus outsourcing where monitoring of the actual process is important (e.g. *Nike, adidas*).
● Dissemination risk	● FDI versus licensing of technology (e.g. automotive components).
● Tacit knowledge transfers	● FDI versus licensing/franchising of complex knowledge (e.g. *Marks & Spencer*).

Do firms that are successful domestically have what it takes to win internationally? Not necessarily. In fact, domestic focus is common in a business that you probably encounter almost daily: retailing. In France, you may shop at *E.Leclerc* or *Géant*; in Germany, you may go to *Tengelmann* or *Edeka*; while in Spain your first choice might be *El Corte Inglés*. Few outside the country will have heard of these names. Why is that? knowledge of local customers and suppliers along with distribution networks are key capabilities in the business of retailing. Yet these capabilities are difficult to transfer across borders. They are location-bound resources tied to the location. Firms with such location-bound resources are likely to grow domestically, for instance by branching out in related industries.

location-bound resources
Resources that cannot be transferred abroad.

The essence of O-advantages is that they are *not* location bound, but they enable a firm to compete abroad, where they face the natural disadvantage of being an outsider. In other words, O-advantages are internationally transferable, and enable the firm to achieve competitive advantages abroad. Successful retailers must have some other capabilities that indeed are transferable. These are usually managerial capabilities related to managing large stores and in coordinating complex supply chains (see In Focus 4.1). For example, Swedish furniture retailer *IKEA* has found that its Scandinavian style of furniture combined with do-it-yourself flat packaging is very popular around the globe. *IKEA* thus has become a cult brand in many countries.

O-advantages can take many forms, including capabilities that the MNE has created at home and transferred abroad, capabilities arising from the multinational operations as such, and capabilities embedded in the organizational structures and culture of an MNE. For example, proprietary technological and management know-how initially enabled *VW* to compete abroad; nowadays these capabilities are reinforced by a global network of operations that enable *VW* to enter further markets. Mature MNEs usually combine these types of O-advantages, which gives them additional competitive advantages over single-country firms that only have access to resources of a single country.

LOCATION ADVANTAGES

LEARNING OBJECTIVE

3   Explain what
    location advantages
    attract foreign
    investors

Foreign direct investors are by definition outsiders in the location where they invest. Given the liability of outsidership, foreign locations must offer compelling advantages to doing business.[6] We may regard the continuous expansion of international business, such as FDI, as an unending saga in search of location-specific advantages. They come in many forms, including (1) markets, (2) resource endowments, (3) agglomeration and (4) institutions. This section outlines these types of locational advantages; in Chapter 12 we discuss more specifically how firms interact with them when choosing where and how to enter.

Markets as L-advantages

Many foreign investors are primarily pursuing access to foreign markets. Hence they invest where they expect future demand for their products, looking for both large markets and fast-growing markets. Thus many businesses have been investing in sales operations in China, attracted by the prospect of potentially over a billion consumers, and high growth rates in recent years. But why do they need to establish FDI close to their markets – can't they just export? Five different reasons encourage firms to set up operations close to their markets.

- **Protectionism**, in the form of tariffs or non-tariff barriers, may inhibit exports (Chapter 5). However, MNEs can quite literally jump over such protectionist barriers by setting up local production.

- **Transportation costs** continue to be a major barrier to trade in some industries, despite their drastic decline over the past century. However, products are still costly to transport over long distances if they are perishable (e.g. fresh fruit), breakable (e.g. sheet glass for windows), heavy (e.g. cement) or bulky (e.g. certain construction materials). In these industries, local production often allows serving a market at lower costs. For example Mexican *CEMEX* has built or acquired cement factories geographically distributed across the countries in which it competes to be close to all major construction sites.

- **Direct interaction with the customer** is essential in industries where associated services such as just-in-time delivery or after sales services are an essential part of the product offering. For example, suppliers to the automotive industry need to produce near the brand manufacturers to integrate in their supply chain, which has motivated FDI by automotive suppliers such as *Grupo Antolin* (In Focus 6.1).

IN FOCUS 6.1

Grupo Antolin *pursues OLI advantages*

Grupo Antolin is a Spanish family-owned manufacturer of automotive components, which emerged in Burgos, a small city in Northern Castille in the 1950s. By 2013 it had sales of €2.7 billion and over 14 800 employees and operations in 25 countries, and was the world's largest maker of internal lining for cars. The industry has gone through major changes in recent years, as suppliers are not only delivering parts, but also designing, developing and manufacturing entire 'modules'. *Grupo Antolin* developed into a full service supplier for interior modules, including overhead systems, door functions and seat functions. It developed unique ownership advantages in the development and manufacturing of such modules, integrating multiple technologies and materials, including in particular electronics, and associated services. Normally, modules are delivered just-in-time and just-in-sequence to the clients assembly line.

The shift in the industry has triggered major changes in the international activities of *Antolin*. Traditionally, *Antolin* has mainly supplied *VW*'s Spanish affiliate *SEAT*, and then production sites of the *VW* group worldwide, such as Wolfsburg (Germany) and Mlada Boleslav (Czech Republic). However, dependence on one key client is risky. *Antolin* thus diversified its clients to include all major car manufacturers, while developing its specialization in the area of interior components. This strategy allowed strengthening of its ownership advantages in the delivery of complex modules, and exploiting these in a wider arrange of markets. Hence *Antolin* invested in production facilities, logistics centres and technical-commercial offices at the locations of clients' production sites (to integrate in their supply chain) and development centres (to collaborate on product development). The location advantages

sought thus were both attractive markets (i.e. presence of key customers) and availability of technical competences.

Antolin diversified its customer portfolio, with *VW* (28% of sales) as biggest client, followed by *Ford* (15%), *Peugeot-Citroën* (15%) and *Renault* (13%). In emerging economies, *Antolin* has been supplying foreign investors' assembly plants, as well as emergent local firms such as *Tata* and *Mahindra* in India. At the same time, *Antolin* could tap into new skilled workforces, for example with its Design Centre in Pune, India. The FDI took many different forms, dependent on the local conditions, including greenfield plants, acquisitions of local companies, joint ventures, and, though rarely, licensing of specific technologies to local firms. Internalization advantages in many cases suggested taking full ownership of the foreign operation to maintain control over the technology transferred.

Recent FDI projects include, for example, the acquisition of a headliner plant in Leamington Spa (UK), a greenfield plant manufacturing seat systems in Jarney (France) aimed at supplying *Renault*, and a new plant in Ostrava (Czech Republic) to supply *Hyundai*. In 2012, *Grupo Antolin* took over the Italian specialist for vehicle lighting systems *CML Innovative Technologies* to become one of the leading European companies in vehicle interior lighting. As a consequence of this aggressive expansion strategy, by 2015 *Antolin* had become the 56th largest automotive supplier worldwide. One in four cars produced worldwide contains interiors provided by *Antolin*, including *VW* Golf, *Ford* Fiesta, *Toyota* Corolla and *Renault* Clio.

Sources: (1) M.H. Antolin-Raybaud, 2009, Antolin company presentation, EIBA conference, Valencia, December; (2) *Business Week*, 2008, Grupo Antolín Irausa enters into joint venture with Ningbo Huaxing Electronic Co, June 7; (3) www.grupoantolin.com.

- **The production and sale of some services** cannot be physically separated, for example, in hotels, banking or consultancy. The delivery of such services thus normally requires a local presence. For example, Spanish banks use local branches to serve clients in Latin America, as well as Spanish MNEs operating in the region (see Opening Case).
- **Marketing assets** may be important for a fast-entry strategy. FDI enables MNEs to acquire local firms that control sought-after assets, such as distribution networks and brand names. For example, *Wal-Mart* entered the UK by acquiring local supermarket chain *Asda*, which provided an established brand name and a network of sales outlets.

Markets are important even in low-income/low-cost locations. *Grupo Antolin* is building factories in China not because it is cheap to make car seats in China (In Focus 6.1): the country's inefficiencies in advanced engineering and transportation costs of bringing seats back to Europe would more than offset the savings achieved due to cheap labour. *Antolin* has one clear goal: seeking greater access to car manufacturers in China, including both local and foreign brands.

Resources as L-advantages

For most of this book, we talk about resources controlled by the firm. Yet location-bound resources are tied to a specific country, and form part of a country's L-advantages. These include natural resources like raw materials, agricultural land and geography, but also created assets, such as human capital and infrastructure.[7] Foreign investors try to tap into these resources and use them for their objectives. For example, oil majors like *Shell* and *BP* invest in oil exploration at many inhospitable places around the world. More recently, Chinese MNEs have joined the quest for natural resources, not only oil, gas and minerals, but also in agriculture.

Some of these resources are controlled by local firms, others are available on local markets, and a few may even be free (such as the sunshine that a solar energy plant might exploit). If resources are controlled by local firms, such as research teams or brand names, then FDI is likely to be undertaken as JV or acquisition. For example, MNEs like *Tata* from India and *Geely* from China are investing abroad to access resources that they need to compete on the global stage, in particular technology and brand names. They can enhance their competitiveness both in Europe and in their home country by combining their own with such resources acquired by taking over firms in Europe or North America (see Chapter 12 for details).

Agglomeration as L-advantages

agglomeration
The location advantages that arise from the clustering of economic activities in certain locations.

L-advantages also arise from the clustering of economic activities in certain locations – referred to as agglomeration.[8] Many investors, especially those seeking innovations, like to locate in clusters of related businesses. The basic idea dates back at least to Alfred Marshall, a British economist who first published it in 1890. Advantages of locating in a cluster stem from (1) knowledge spillovers among closely-located firms that attempt to hire individuals from competitors, (2) industry demand that creates a skilled labour force whose members may work for different firms without having to move out of the region and (3) industry demand that facilitates a pool of specialized suppliers and buyers to also locate in the region.[9] Agglomeration explains why certain cities and regions, in the absence of obvious geographic advantages, can attract businesses. In particular, suppliers follow downstream manufacturers, and industry newcomers locate near industry leaders.[10] For instance, Slovakia produces more cars per capita than any other country in the world, thanks to the quest for agglomeration benefits by global automakers. Denmark has become a global hub for the design and manufacturing of windmills, and attracts leading companies from around the world (In Focus 6.2). Overall, agglomeration advantages stem from:

- knowledge spillovers (knowledge diffused from one firm to others) among closely located firms that attempt to hire individuals from competitors
- industry demand that creates a skilled labour force whose members may work for different firms without having to move out of the region
- industry demand that facilitates a pool of specialized suppliers and buyers also located in the region.[11]

knowledge spillover
Knowledge diffused from one firm to others among closely located firms.

Institutions as L-advantages

The institutional environment can also be an L-advantage, or a locational *dis*advantage. Countries that offer free access and equal opportunities for foreign investors are obviously more attractive to invest in than those that create barriers to foreign investors. Hence clear and simple rules, low levels of corruption and an efficient bureaucracy make a country more attractive to invest in.[12] We discuss these issues further when considering the institutional view in the next section.

Location-specific advantages are not constant; they grow, evolve and/or decline. If policymakers fail to maintain the institutional attractiveness (for example, by raising taxes) or if companies overcrowd and bid up factor costs such as land and talents, some firms may move out of certain locations previously considered advantageous.[13] For example, policy shifts of the Turkish government over the past decades gradually changed the rules of the game for foreign investors. In the early 2000s, Turkey became more attractive as a foreign investment location, yet in the 2010s this trend

IN FOCUS 6.2

Wind energy agglomerates in Jutland

On a clear day, passengers on planes taking off and landing at Copenhagen airport can see dozens of huge offshore wind turbine parks. Chances are that these wind turbines are also developed and made in Denmark. Thanks to visionary government policies, Denmark became a first mover and now a world leader in the wind turbine industry. Twenty-eight per cent of the Danish electricity grid is already powered by wind, and the target is to become the first country in the world to meet 50% of its energy needs with wind power by 2020. Underpinning these ambitions is a cluster of wind turbine manufacturers and suppliers in Jutland, a peninsula in west Denmark (Figure 6.6).

The origins of the cluster are Danish industrial policies in the 1980s that encouraged the development of wind energy technology by guaranteeing relatively high feed-in tariffs that made it attractive for farmers and other landowners to invest in a windmill, and sell surplus energy to the grid. With this support, Danish companies like *Vestas* and *Bonus Energy* (both founded 1979) became worldwide technology leaders. Meanwhile, the nearby port of Esbjerg on the North Sea coast established itself as the preferred port for exports of wind turbines made in Denmark, and for construction and servicing of offshore wind farms, not only in Danish coastal waters but also throughout the North Sea.

Based in Aarhus (Denmark's second city), *Vestas* is the world leader in terms of installed turbines (60 GW), accounting for nearly one-fifth of the total capacity of all the installed turbines in the world. *Vestas* employs 15 000 people, including 4000 in Denmark. *Siemens Wind Power* has been headquartered about 80 kilometres west of Aarhus since *Siemens* acquired *Bonus*

Figure 6.6   Denmark wind energy cluster

Energy in 2004. *Siemens Wind Power* has 23 GW of installed turbines and 11 000 employees worldwide (of which 5500 are in Denmark). In addition, major Danish-owned suppliers *LM Wind Power* and *AH Industries* are also nearby.

Several other international players in the wind energy industry, such as India's *Suzlon* and China's *Envision Energy*, were attracted to the know-how of the cluster. Japan's *Mitsubishi Heavy Industries (MHI)* invested $400 million in a 50-50 joint venture with *Vestas* – named *MHI Vestas Offshore Wind* – which focuses on huge 8.0 MW turbines. Suppliers to the industry also joined the cluster. For example, Chinese *Titan Wind* bought a wind tower factory from *Vestas*, primarily as a means to develop a long-term supplier relationship with *Vestas* and others in the cluster. Likewise, *PricewaterhouseCoopers (PwC)* established a specialized unit of its tax and advisory services that caters to the industry, and knows how energy businesses can best navigate tax laws when operating across national boundaries within the North Sea.

Anders Rebsdorf, director of *Envision Energy (Denmark)*, echoes many in articulating his firm's location choice:

'Our choice of Denmark is directly related to the country's strong cluster of know-how in the area of turbine design. It is also important that there are manufacturers of turbine components and experts in turbine service. The entire value chain is represented to a degree that is not found anywhere else .... If we are to earn the right to join the battle for international orders, then we must be visible where the competition is fierce.'

Sources: Based on (1) J. Hansen, C. Jensen & E. Madsen, 2003, The establishment of the Danish windmill industry – Was it worthwhile? *Review of World Economics*, 139: 324–347; (2) J. Lipp, 2007, Lessons for effective renewable electricity policy from Denmark, Germany and the United Kingdom, *Energy Policy*, 35: 5481–5495; (3) *Wall Street Journal*, 2013, Vestas, Mitsubishi form offshore joint venture, September 27; (4) *Focus Denmark*, 2014, Titans of wind energy arm for battle, summer-autumn: 18–23; (5) Vestas, 2014, MHI Vestas Offshore Wind now operational, press release, April 1; (6) D. Chng, 2014, Titan Wind, mimeo, June.

has been reversed (see Chapter 2, Opening Case). Similarly, changing practices of law enforcement in China have at times made China more attractive, and at other times raised concerns among foreign investors (see Integrative Case *GSK*).

INTERNALIZATION ADVANTAGES

A key advantage of FDI over other modes is the ability to replace ('internalize') external market relationships, with one firm (the MNE) owning, controlling and managing activities in two or more countries. When firms interact in a market, they incur transaction costs, defined as the costs of organizing a transaction. Transaction costs arise firstly from transaction-related activities such as searching for partners, monitoring product quality and enforcing contracts. Secondly, transaction costs may also arise from sub-optimal allocation of resources due to unrealized transactions (also known as opportunity costs).

Transaction costs are important in international business because they tend to be higher for cross-border transactions compared with domestic transactions. For example, obtaining information and verifying a business partner's reputation is both more costly and more time-consuming. Likewise, costs of monitoring performance are higher where language and other communication barriers arise. Enforcing a contract when a partner behaves opportunistically is more complex because laws and regulations are typically enforced on a nation-state basis. Suing the other party in a foreign country is not only costly, but also uncertain (Chapter 2). In the worst case, such imperfections are so grave that markets fail to function.

High transaction costs can result in market failure – imperfections of the market mechanisms that make some transactions prohibitively costly and sometimes prevent transactions from taking place. In response, MNEs emerge as an alternative organizational form that does not rely on these imperfect (external) markets.[14] This section outlines how internalization enables MNEs to overcome market failure by discussing three types of decisions: (1) FDI versus exporting, (2) FDI versus licensing and (3) FDI versus outsourcing.

FDI versus exporting

Let us consider a simple example of trade:[15] an aluminium smelting firm in Europe and a bauxite mine in Latin America. The bauxite is transformed by aluminium smelters into aluminium, a critical component in many products, such as cars. Thus the two companies may engage in international trade: the bauxite mine exports and the aluminium smelter imports the bauxite. However, the markets for bauxite are subject to market failure because the aluminium smelting plant needs to be adapted to the specific properties of the bauxite. Thus aluminium smelters need to make an investment in their plants that is specific to the mine supplying the bauxite, a problem known as asset specificity. The specificity of the relationship between the bauxite mine and the aluminium smelter creates a dependence that could be exploited opportunistically by the bauxite mine. For example, after the deal is signed, the bauxite mine may demand higher than agreed-upon prices, citing a variety of reasons such as inflation, natural disasters or simply rising prices. The aluminium smelter thus has to either (1) pay more than the agreed-upon price or (2) refuse to pay and suffer from the huge costs of keeping expensive facilities idle. In other words, the bauxite mine's opportunistic behaviour can cause the aluminium smelter to lose a lot of money.

FDI overcomes such market failure through internalization. By replacing an external market relationship with a single organizational spanning both countries,

LEARNING OBJECTIVE

4 Explain and apply the concept on internalization advantages

transaction costs
The costs of organizing a transaction.

market failure
Imperfections of the market mechanism that make some transactions prohibitively costly.

asset specificity
An investment that is specific to a business relationship.

the MNE thus reduces cross-border transaction costs and increases efficiencies.[16] In theory, there are two possibilities: (1) the aluminium smelter undertakes upstream vertical FDI by owning bauxite mines in Latin America or (2) the bauxite mine undertakes downstream vertical FDI buying aluminium smelting assets in Europe (Figure 6.7, Panel A). FDI essentially transforms the international trade between two independent firms in two countries intra-firm trade between two subsidiaries in two countries controlled by the same MNE. The MNE is thus able to coordinate cross-border activities better, an I-advantage. However, in other industries, such as tin, where no such specific investments are required, firms are less likely to integrate vertically (Figure 6.7, Panel B).

intra-firm trade
International trade between two subsidiaries in two countries controlled by the same MNE.

Figure 6.7   Overcoming market failure through FDI

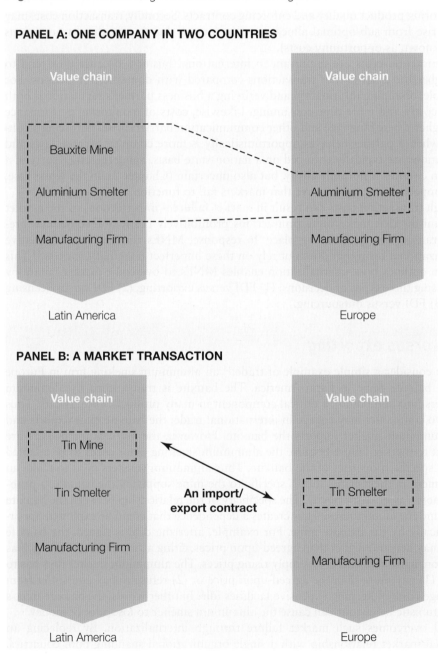

PANEL A: ONE COMPANY IN TWO COUNTRIES

PANEL B: A MARKET TRANSACTION

FDI versus licensing

In some cases, a company may face the choice between licensing the technology to a local firm and FDI establishing its own production facilities. How to choose between these two options? Three reasons may compel firms to prefer FDI to licensing.

First, FDI affords a high degree of direct management control that reduces the risk of firm-specific resources and capabilities being opportunistically taken advantage of. A key risk abroad is dissemination risk, defined as the risk associated with unauthorized diffusion of firm-specific know-how. If a foreign company grants a licence to a local firm to manufacture or market a product, 'it runs the risk of the licensee, or an employee of the licensee, disseminating the know-how or using it for purposes other than those originally intended'.[17] Owning and managing proprietary assets through FDI does not completely shield firms from dissemination risks (after all, their employees can quit and join competitors), but FDI is better than licensing that provides no such management control. Consequently, FDI is extensively used in knowledge-intensive, high-tech industries, such as automobiles, electronics, chemicals and IT.[18]

Second, even if there is no opportunism on the part of licensees and if they are willing to follow the wishes of the foreign firm, certain types of knowledge may be too difficult to transfer to licensees without FDI.[19] Knowledge has two basic categories: (1) explicit and (2) tacit (implicit). Explicit knowledge is codifiable (that is, it can be written down and transferred without losing much of its richness). Tacit knowledge, on the other hand, is non-codifiable, and its acquisition and transfer require hands-on practice. For instance, a driving manual represents a body of explicit knowledge. However, mastering this manual without any road practice does not make you a good driver. Tacit knowledge is evidently more important and harder to transfer and learn; it can only be acquired through learning by doing (in this case, driving practice supervised by an experienced driver). Likewise, operating a department store chain like French *Carrefour*'s stores entails a great deal of knowledge, some explicit (often captured in an operational manual) and some tacit. However, simply giving foreign licensees a copy of the *Carrefour* operational manual will not be enough. Foreign employees will need to learn from *Carrefour* personnel side-by-side (learning by doing). From a resource-based standpoint, it is *Carrefour*'s tacit knowledge that gives it competitive advantage (see Chapter 4). *Carrefour* owns such crucial tacit knowledge, and it wants to ensure that its competences are properly deployed to protect its reputation and to maximize its return on investment. Therefore, properly transferring and controlling tacit knowledge calls for FDI.[20]

Finally, FDI provides more direct and tighter control over foreign operations. Even when licensees (and their employees) have no opportunistic intention to take away 'secrets', they may not follow the wishes of the foreign firm that provides the know-how. Without FDI, the foreign firm cannot order or control its licensee to move ahead. For example, *Starbucks* entered South Korea by licensing its format to *ESCO*. Although *ESCO* soon opened ten stores, *Starbucks* felt that *ESCO* was not aggressive enough in growing the chain. But there was very little Starbucks could do. Eventually, *Starbucks* switched from licensing to FDI, which allowed *Starbucks* to directly 'call the shots' and promote the aggressive growth of the chain in South Korea.

FDI versus offshore outsourcing

Internalization advantages also arise for offshoring, though that is a very different sort of transaction. Rather than transferring a technology, it involves the transfer of activities to be delivered back to the parent firm. Recall from Chapter 4 that outsourcing to a foreign location becomes 'offshore outsourcing', whereas FDI – that

licensing
Firm A's agreement to give Firm B the rights to use A's proprietary technology (such as a patent) or trademark (such as a corporate logo) for a royalty fee paid to A by B.

dissemination risks
The risks associated with unauthorized diffusion of firm-specific know-how.

tacit knowledge
Knowledge that is non-codifiable, and whose acquisition and transfer require hands-on practice.

is, performing an activity in-house at an overseas location – is in-house offshoring (see Figure 4.3). Like licensing, this involves a complex relationship between the two operations, and the question arises: can this transaction be handled using the market, or should it be internalized? Three types of problems can arise in offshore outsourcing: (1) hold-up problems due to asset specificity, (2) unauthorized dissemination of technology and (3) costs of monitoring quality and standards.

First, if the activity would require substantial specific investment by the service provider, the problem of asset specificity arises. This may lead to one-sided dependence of one partner on the other, and market failure is likely. Hence you rarely see outsourcing of activities that are unique to a firm. Typically, firms outsource activities that are common across several industries, where there is scope for other firms to develop complementary specialist capabilities for that activity. For example, *Flextronics* is a specialist for assembly of electronics products, while *Wipro* specializes in IT services. They know how to manage these operations, and enable their customers to focus on product development and marketing.

Second, the outsourcing service provider may use knowledge of the firm's technology for other purposes, for instance helping competitors or entering the industry itself. Thus offshore outsourcing requires safeguards on the use of technology. For instance, it is standard practice that service providers may not simultaneously provide similar services to a competitor. But even such safeguards may not suffice when latest and non-patented knowledge is involved. In such a situation, a firm may prefer to operate its offshore manufacturing plant itself (i.e. in-house offshoring).

Third, for some activities companies may find it necessary to monitor the actual manufacturing process, rather than simply buying the finished products. For example, considerable concern has been raised that suppliers of textile and footwear in developing countries are using child labour or other work practices deemed unethical by consumers in Europe. In consequence, companies such as *Nike* and *adidas* have developed detailed codes of conduct as well as training for their suppliers.[21] However, ownership of the relevant production facilities as in-house offshoring would provide even better mechanisms to ensure compliance with the firm's code of conduct (see Chapter 10).

BENEFITS AND COSTS OF FDI

LEARNING OBJECTIVE

5 Appreciate the benefits and costs of FDI to host and home countries

Why do countries restrict or regulate FDI? Many economists and managers argue that MNEs generally are good for society, yet there are also widespread concerns. Even leading economists acknowledge that at least some forms of MNE activity may be harmful to host economies.[22] These perceptions of potential negative effects shape political views of FDI and thus the institutional environment in different countries. Therefore, to understand why institutions offer a mix of incentives and obstacles, we need to analyze the benefits and costs associated with FDI. Foreign direct investors interact in many ways with firms and individuals in their host country, which makes the assessment of their costs and benefits very complex.[23] Table 6.2 provides a simplified overview of some potential benefits and costs from the perspective of local people, firms, government and the environment.

- **Consumers** generally appreciate foreign investors that bring new consumer goods of better quality and/or lower prices. Some may however mourn the disappearance of traditional local producers that are no longer able to compete.
- **Suppliers** to the foreign investors may benefit from new orders and from training in modern production and supply chain management practice.[24]

Table 6.2 Potential benefits and costs of FDI for host countries

	Potential benefits of FDI	Potential negative effects of FDI
Consumers	● access to international quality products and brands ● lower prices due to scale economies and competition	● reduces variety of traditional local brands (if local firms are crowded out)
Suppliers	● technology transfer enhancing productivity ● opportunity to become an international supplier	● crowding out by international sourcing
Competitors	● technology spillovers enable learning ● competition may trigger upgrading and innovation	● crowding out by overwhelming competition
Workers	● employment opportunities ● typically higher labour standards than local firms ● training and knowledge transfer	● often less labour-intensive production (thus fewer work places) than local firms
Government	● tax revenues ● economic growth	● costs of subsidies and other incentives
Natural environment	● MNEs often have higher environmental standards than local firms	● MNEs may locate highly polluting activities in places with less stringent regulation

Note: The effects vary substantially across countries, industries and FDI projects.

Sources: (1) M. Blomström & A. Kokko, 1998. Multinational corporations and spillovers, *JES,* 12, 247–77; (2) K.E. Meyer, 2004, Perspectives on Multinational Enterprises in Emerging Economies, *JIBS,* 34, 259–277; (3) K.E. Meyer, ed., 2008, Editors' Introduction, in: *Multinational Enterprises and Host Economies*, Cheltenham: Elgar; (4) K.E. Meyer & E. Sinani, 2009, When and where does foreign direct investment generate positive spillovers? *JIBS,* 40, 1 075–1 094.

These benefits however occur only if the foreign investors actually source locally; some foreign investors prefer to import their components from their established suppliers, and thus offer few opportunities for local firms.

● **Competitors** have a very ambiguous relationship with foreign entrants. On the one hand, they may learn by observing the advanced technologies and management practices. These knowledge spillovers may enable some local firms to upgrade their own practices, and thus increase sales and even increase their exports.[25] However, knowledge spillovers are difficult to realize if the gap between locals and foreign investors is too big. Weaker local firms may be overwhelmed by the foreign competition and thus forced to close down.

● **Workers** benefit from new jobs created directly or indirectly by the FDI. Direct benefits arise when MNEs employ individuals locally, and train them in latest technologies and management practices. For example, in Ireland, more than 50% of manufacturing employees work for MNEs.[26] In the UK, one of the largest private sector employers is India's *Tata* group with over 50 000 employees working for a variety of businesses such as *Jaguar Land Rover*, *Tata Steel* (formerly *Corus*), *Tetley Tea* and *Tata Consultancy Services*

(*TCS*).[27] Indirect benefits include jobs created when local suppliers increase hiring and when MNE employees spend money locally resulting in more jobs. On the other hand, foreign-owned production facilities in emerging economies are often more capital-intensive and thus create fewer jobs than local firms using more traditional production processes.

- **Host governments** benefit from increased tax revenues, provided they have not agreed to generous tax holidays or other financial incentives for the investors. Moreover, if foreign investors stimulate growth in the local economy, this has indirect positive effects for the society and government revenues.

- **The natural environment** may be negatively affected if foreign investors establish polluting industrial plants, or destroy a natural habitat. However, arguably, this is more a side-effect of industrialization than of FDI as such. Foreign investors typically use more environmentally-friendly technologies than comparable local firms, because they allow them to standardize their operations and to satisfy interest groups back home.[28]

The actual benefits and costs of FDI thus vary greatly across FDI projects, and across various aspects of the relationship between foreign investors and the local society. Political proponents can easily find positive or negative examples supporting their particular view: some FDI projects are undoubtedly beneficial for the hosts, while some are harmful. Empirical research suggests that suppliers and employees typically are better off because of the presence of foreign investors, but the actual benefits and costs depend on the specific characteristics of the FDI projects.

NATIONAL INSTITUTIONS AND FDI

Host country institutions

LEARNING OBJECTIVE

6   Explain how home and host country institutions affect FDI

In view of the complex benefits and costs of receiving FDI, many countries have developed institutions designed to influence the FDI they receive. Most countries nowadays expect that, at least in principle, FDI leads to a win-win situation for both home and host countries, and have thus adopted FDI-friendly policies. However, most countries have retained some institutions that either (1) restrict the presence of FDI or (2) regulate the operations of FDI. Restrictive institutions come in three forms.

- **Outright bans on FDI** that rule out FDI completely have become rare. Some governments in developing countries hostile to FDI have in the past nationalized MNE assets, and banned new investment[29] – spectacularly, for example, the Iranian government in 1979. In the 2010s, bands of FDI tend to be limited to specific sectors of industry, such as mining or oil and gas industries in countries ranging from China to Venezuela and Argentina (see Closing Case).

- **Case-by-case approvals of FDI** substitute for outright bans of FDI, and make every FDI subject to a registration and approval process. In practice, this often means that governments can impose a wide range of conditions that are subject to negotiation with the foreign investors. Such approval procedures are common in emerging economies. For instance, at early stages of their economic opening, China and Vietnam would vet every investor, only gradually did they move to automatic approval for most industries. More recently, countries like the US have introduced

IN FOCUS 6.3

State enterprises meet market economy

In 2006, a controversy erupted when *Dubai Ports World*, a Dubai government-owned company, purchased US ports from another *foreign* firm, Britain's *P&O*. This entry gave *Dubai Ports World* control over terminal operations at the ports of New York/New Jersey, Philadelphia, Baltimore, Miami and New Orleans. Although Dubai has been a US ally for three decades, then Senator Hillary Clinton argued, 'Our port security is too important to place in the hands of foreign governments.' She was not alone; many politicians, journalists and activists opposed such FDI. In this 'largest political storm over US ports since the Boston Tea Party,' *Dubai Ports World* eventually withdrew.

The conflict apparently started when *Eller & Co*, a US ports operator in a commercial conflict with *P&O*, lobbied the US government. In pursuit of its economic interests, they exploited an anti-Arab mood in the US at the time, and triggered a very emotional national security debate that overlooked the fact that Dubai was in fact a key US ally in the Middle East. A few years later, Dubai companies (including SWFs) engaged again in acquisitions in the US, including a defence contractor *Standard Aero Group*, without triggering such a storm of resistance.

Similar political storms have been unleashed by some Chinese investments in the USA. Notably, in 2005, the US Congress challenged the bid of *CNOOC*, a Chinese state-owned enterprise, to buy *Unocal* – an American oil and gas company – for $18.5 billion, because of national security concerns. Economic analysts, such as those of the conservative Cato institute,

argued that such concerns were unfounded: '*A reasonable understanding of how international oil markets actually work in practice is sufficient to dismiss the worries of those who fear Chinese control of oil-producing assets or long-term contracts with producer states.*'

However, political opposition gained its own dynamics, and *CNOOC* eventually withdrew its offer. Similarly, telecom networks company *Huawei* regularly faces accusations of being too close to the Chinese government, and consequently excluded from public procurement contracts in the USA; many US journalists describe it as state-owned enterprise, even though in fact it is owned by its employees. Yet when political commentators get involved, economic arguments do not always prevail. Chinese state enterprises also stirred up controversy when acquiring local companies in the energy or mining sectors in Canada and Australia (both countries with strong mining sectors). Both countries introduced rules that require extra governmental review for investment projects by foreign state entitities above certain thresholds.

Sources: (1) J. Tayler, 2005, CNOOC Bid for Unocal No Threat to Energy Security, Free Trade Bulletin no.19, Cato Institute; (2) *The Economist*, 2006, America's ports and Dubai: Trouble on the waterfront, February 2; (3) B. Simpfendorfer, 2009, *The New Silk Road: How A Rising Arab World is Turning away from the West and Rediscovering China*, Basingstoke: Palgrave-Macmillan (pages 55–60); (4) K. Sauvant, 2010, Is the United States ready for foreign direct investment from emerging markets? in: K. Sauvant, W. Maschek & G. McAllister, eds, *Foreign Direct Investments From Emerging Markets*. New York: Palgrave Macmillan; (5) F. WU, L. Hoon & Y. Zhang, 2011, Dos and don'ts for Chinese companies investing in the United States: Lessons from Huawei and Haier, *TIBR*, (6) K.E. Meyer, Y. Ding, J. Li & Z. Hua, 2014, Overcoming distrust, *JIBS*, 45: 1 005–1 028.

case-by-case special procedures if the investor was a foreign state-owned enterprise (In Focus 6.3).

- **Ownership requirements** are a specific form of restriction that disallow full foreign ownership, but allow foreign investors to operate in a county if they establish a joint venture with a local firm. For example, Vietnam did not allow the acquisition of local firms until about 2001, thus forcing foreign investors who wanted to access a local firm to establish a joint venture. Even in developed economies, foreign investors face such restrictions in selected industries. For example, the USA does not allow foreign majority ownership in domestic air transportation and other sectors deemed sensitive because of national security.

Even when foreign investors are free to set up their own operations, they are not necessarily free to do as they like; they are subject to the institutional setting of the host economy. The regulation of FDI comes in three parts:

- **General regulatory institutions of business.** From the perspective of a host country, an FDI establishes a new firm that – like any firm – is subject to the laws and regulations of the country. Thus the operations of a foreign investor are subject to the host country's institutional framework, which may be quite different from what the investor is used to at home. For example, foreign investors have to comply with specific regulations, such as restrictions on advertising, the pricing of utilities or the need for building permits. Theoretically, these rules should be applied without discriminating between domestic and foreign investors. However, allegation of unequal application of the law are common, even in Europe. For example, the Polish authorities are reported to favour local state-owned firms over foreign investors in the energy and mining sector,[30] while the Hungarian authorities introduced a retroactive bank tax that hit foreign banks in particular,[31] and the Greek authorities, after the election of a new government, revoked permissions that Canadian *Eldorado Gold* had received to operate a major mining project in the Halkidiki region.[32]

local content requirements
Requirement that a certain proportion of the value of the goods made in a country originates from that country.

- **FDI specific regulation.** Some countries make the operation of FDI subject to specific regulations. For example, local content requirements require a certain proportion of the value of the goods made in the country to originate from that country.[33] The Japanese automobile VERs discussed in Chapter 5 are a case in point here. Starting in the mid 1980s, because of VERs, Japanese automakers switched to producing cars in the USA through FDI. However, initially, such factories were 'screwdriver plants', because the majority of components were imported from Japan and only the proverbial screwdrivers were needed to tighten the screws. To deal with this issue, many countries impose local content requirements, mandating that a 'domestically-produced' product will still be treated as an 'import' subject to tariffs and NTBs unless a certain fraction of its value is produced locally.

- **Corporate taxation.** Companies have to pay corporate tax in each country where they operate, but some countries deliberately design their tax codes to attract foreign investors.[34] Some countries keep their overall corporate tax rates low to attract global or region headquarters. Others offer temporary tax relief for companies creating jobs in the country. For example, prior to joining the EU, the Czech Republic ran a scheme that offered new foreign investors tax relief for up to ten years, and duty-free importing. In addition, in areas with high unemployment, job creation subsidies and training grants for up to 25% of training costs were available.[35] Companies thus have opportunities to reduce their tax payments through tax avoidance strategies that enable them to legally(!) move profits to jurisdictions where tax rates are lower (In Focus 6.4).[36]

tax avoidance
Reducing tax liability by legally moving profits to jurisdictions where tax rates are lower.

Home country institutions

Home countries generally do not have specific policies to encourage or discourage outward FDI. However, some see MNEs as vital to achieving national economic objectives, such as the transformation of an economy or a means to access scarce resources. For example, in the 1960s and 1970s the Japanese government encouraged companies to move labour-intensive operations overseas to enable the technological

IN FOCUS 6.4

Corporate taxation drives US FDI in Europe

What are the preferred foreign locations for US MNEs to invest abroad? Countries with cultural ties rank highly as hosts for US inward FDI stock, including the UK (second) and Canada (fourth). However, some other top destinations may be more surprising. The largest share of outward FDI stock from the USA goes to the Netherlands (14.5%), with Luxembourg in third place (8.6%) and Ireland fifth (4.6%). These countries are also important sources for FDI stock in the USA, the Netherlands is third and Luxembourg seventh. While the Netherlands is an important trading nation, and home to some large MNEs (such as *Unilever, Shell* and *Philips*), there must be something else going on here.

An important motivation for these investments is corporate taxation. For example, the corporate tax rate in Ireland is 12.5%, much lower than in the UK (21%), Germany (29.6%), Italy (31.4%) and France (33.3%). Other countries, such as Luxembourg and the Netherlands, grant generous exemptions for some types of operations, notably corporate headquarters. Ireland even allows legal constructions, known a 'double Irish', which enable firms to collect profits in their Irish subsidiary and then route those profits out of Ireland through a second Irish subsidiary with tax residency in a tax havens such as the Bermuda or Isle of Man. In consequence Ireland, the Netherlands and Luxembourg have become preferred locations for incorporating global companies and for European headquarters.

A business strategy that has become very controversial in the USA is 'tax inversion' acquisitions. US companies merging with a foreign company can move their place of registration (and hence where they have to pay corporate tax) out of the USA. For example, when two of the largest suppliers of chip-making equipment, *Applied Materials* (United States) and *Tokyo Electron* (Japan), merged in 2013, they set up a holding company in the Netherlands. The existing companies became US and Japanese affiliates of the Dutch holding company through share swaps.

Tax avoidance strategies also became very controversial in Europe. Some companies channel their profits from countries of their operation to their European headquarters, thereby avoiding taxes in the those countries. For example, affiliates in the UK may pay a licence fee to the European headquarters in Ireland and thereby minimize their tax payments in the UK. According to one study, *McDonalds* channelled its Europe-wide profits to *McD Europe Franchising Sàrl* in Luxembourg, a company with 13 employees that in 2009 to 2013 reported turnover of €3.7 billion and paid just €16 million in tax. Totally legal! Another loophole in international tax treaties is that warehouses often do not trigger a tax residency, which has been used by online retailer *Amazon* to channel €15 billion of sales through Luxembourg, where it pays no tax. An investigation by news agency *Reuters* found that three quarters of the 50 largest US technology companies used tax avoidance strategies to channel their profits into locations with lower corporate tax, including *Google, Apple, Adobe* and *eBay*, with the 'double Irish' subsidiary structure particularly popular among firms delivering services through the internet. Since the EU does not harmonize corporate tax rules to allow for tax competition, and lacks rules preventing transfer of profits through transfer pricing or excessive license fees, this creates quite substantive distortions.

Why have American companies in particular been in the firing line of the critics? In the USA, companies only have to pay tax on their profits when the profits are repatriated to the USA. Hence they can lower their tax burden by exploiting international differences. In contrast, many European countries tax global profits (while allowing for double taxation), which means that European MNEs have fewer incentives to channel profits between subsidiaries, but they may still choose to register their corporate headquarters in a low-tax country.

Governments promise to tighten regulation, but that turns out to be difficult in practice. The OECD issued new guidelines, while the Obama government in the USA initiated new laws to tax non-repatriated profits and to prevent 'tax inversion'. British politicians have also been vocal in the debate, yet they are reluctant to take firm action. On the one hand, action would require coordination on taxation in the EU, which the British government dislikes. On the other hand, rich individuals find British taxation regimes very favourable; action against companies evading taxes in the

UK by locating outside would certainly trigger others to respond in kind and demand the UK to be less welcoming to tycoons around the world moving their money into London. The bottom line is that many of the tax loopholes that politicians complain about in fact have been deliberately created by politicians trying to attract foreign investors!

Corporate tax avoidance strategies also have implications for the interpretation of FDI data: a large volume of investment does not necessary imply a large operation in the country. Keep this in mind when you review Figures 6.4 and 6.5 or other FDI data provided by UNCTAD.

Sources: (1) J. Smith, 2013, Adobe gets creative with Ireland's tax rules, *Financial Times*, September 13; (2) UNCTAD, 2014, *World Investment Report 2014*, Geneva: UNCTAD (pp. 79–80); (3) *Reuters*, 2014, OECD unveils proposals to curb corporate tax avoidance, September 16; (4) J. Drucker, 2014, Double Irish's slow death leaves Google executives calm, *Bloomberg*, October 15; (5) P. Lewis, 2015, Obama will propose mandatory tax on US companies' earning held overseas, *The Guardian*, February 1; (6) D. Robinson, 2015, McDonald's avoided €1 billion in taxes, says report, *Financial Times*, February 26; (7) KPMG, no date, Corporate tax rates table, www.kpmg.com (accessed February 2015).

upgrading of the Japanese economy.[37] The Chinese government in the early 2000s actively supported companies investing overseas in natural resources, as China is scarce in resources like minerals or agricultural produce (see In Focus 6.3).[38] Such support is especially crucial at early stages of countries' outward FDI.

Others are concerned that the transfer of capital or jobs may be detrimental to the home economy, and thus oppose some forms of FDI. On the one hand, efficiency considerations suggest that in many cases relocation of labour-intensive parts of the value chain may actually enhance competitiveness and thus benefit the company and the home country in the long run. On the other hand, a relocation of production may often be opposed by trade unions fearing the loss of jobs, but it is rare that governments publicly intervene to dissuade MNEs not to establish production overseas. A rare exception happened in 2010 when *Renault* announced its intention to relocate production of the Clio to Turkey. French government ministers issued strong statements condemning the action, and – with reference to the state's 15% equity stake in *Renault* – put pressure on *Renault* to cancel its plans.[39] Yet later Renault invested in a new engine and engine part facility with its Turkey JV partner.

Paradoxically, the main argument for restricting FDI to a particular destination country is that it might help the economy of the other country. For example, the USA have tight bans on FDI and many other forms of business with several countries considered hostile, such as Iran, Sudan and Cuba. From the late 1990s until 2012, many countries banned investment in Myanmar, which induced firms to pursue low-profile, non-equity strategies of engagement in the country.[40] The merits of such boycotts are controversial. With one exception, there is little evidence that an investment ban actually induces political change in another country. That exception is the apartheid regime in South Africa, whose downfall was widely attributed to persistent pressure and boycotts from most of its potential trading partners.

DEBATES AND EXTENSIONS

LEARNING OBJECTIVE

7 Participate in three leading debates on FDI

MNEs are widely regarded as the embodiment of globalization. Not surprisingly, they have stimulated a lot of debates. At the heart of these debates is the age-old question: can we trust foreigners and foreign firms in making decisions important to our economy? This section discusses (1) the interaction between MNEs and host governments, (2) emerging economy multinationals and (3) sovereign wealth funds.

How MNEs and host governments bargain

For small firms, institutions and government policies are largely 'given', and the firms have to adjust. However, larger firms – and small firms acting together – may have some power to influence institutions and political processes, or at least the application of particular rules in a particular case. Governments tend to be interested in some of the benefits of FDI, for example the creation of jobs or the upgrading of technology. Hence the actual FDI and the regulations applying to it are to some degree the outcome of a bilateral negotiation process. The relationship between MNEs and host governments is thus shaped by their relative bargaining power – their ability to extract a favourable outcome from negotiations due to one party's strengths.[41] MNEs typically prefer to minimize the interventions from host governments and maximize the incentives provided by host governments. Host governments usually want to ensure a certain degree of control and minimize the subsidies paid to MNEs. Sometimes, host governments try to induce MNEs to undertake activities that they would otherwise not do, such as investing in advanced R&D or locating in less prosperous regions. They may use financial incentives, such as tax holidays, because MNEs have options to invest elsewhere.

The bargaining between MNEs and FDI does not end with the initial investment decision, it often continues over the entire lifetime of an FDI operation. A well-known phenomenon is the obsolescing bargain, a renegotiation of a deal *after* the initial FDI entry, when the relative bargaining positions have changed.[42] This is a concern in particular for projects that require large, non-recoverable up-front investment (called sunk costs) and long pay-back periods, as in natural resource exploration and infrastructure operations.[43] Likewise, investors in power plants, telecommunication networks, bridges or airports, are very concerned about the regulatory regime *after* the initial construction has been completed. In such situations, a government may opportunistically take advantage of the shifting bargaining power by renegotiating in three stages.

- In stage one, the MNE and the government negotiate a deal that involves assurances of property rights and incentives.

- In stage two, the MNE makes its investment by building the bridge or power plant, in the expectation of recovering the investment from future revenue streams.

- In stage three, the MNE sells its services, and thus recovers its investment and, after a while, may earn handsome profits. Observing such profits along with perceived high prices for electricity or bridge tolls (and perhaps less than perfect service), domestic political groups may pressurize the government to renegotiate the deal that seems to yield 'excessive' profits to the foreign firm (which, of course, regards these as 'fair' return on their risky investment). The previous deal, therefore, becomes obsolete. The government's tactics may include changing rules applying to pricing of electricity or bridge tolls, demanding a higher share of profits and taxes, or even confiscating foreign assets – in other words, expropriation.

At stage three, the MNE has already invested substantial resources that it cannot recover and often has to accommodate some new demands. Otherwise, it may face expropriation or exit at a huge loss. Not surprisingly, MNEs do not appreciate the risk associated with such obsolescing bargains, and they seek long-term guarantees from host governments to reduce their exposure. Unfortunately, recent actions in Venezuela and Argentina suggest that obsolescing bargains are not necessarily becoming obsolete (see Closing Case).[44] The political stability of a country thus is a

---

bargaining power
The ability to extract a favourable outcome from negotiations due to one party's strengths.

obsolescing bargain
Refers to the deal struck by MNEs and host governments, which change their requirements after the initial FDI entry.

sunk cost
Up-front investments that are non-recoverable if the project is abandoned.

expropriation
Government's confiscation of private (foreign-owned) assets.

major concern for MNEs in mining, oil exploration, infrastructure and other capital intensive industries.

Emerging economy multinationals

Since about 2005, Chinese, Indian and other companies from emerging economies have become major players on the global stage. Traditionally, FDI originated from advanced economies that were both capital rich and technologically advanced. These conditions provided a foundation for firms to develop O-advantages that they could then exploit overseas. From this perspective, it may be surprising that MNEs emerge from less-advanced economies to invest in advanced economies. Does this mean there is a gap in the theory? Probably not. Two considerations help explaining the emergence of emerging economy MNEs.[45]

First, emerging economy MNEs may have different types of O-advantages from firms in advanced economies.[46] For example, companies like *Foxconn* may have capabilities in managing large-scale labour-intensive operations, while IT companies like *Infosys* or *TCS* serve clients in Europe via delivery centres in Poland or Hungary. Others can use their experience in managing in highly volatile and imperfect institutional environments to invest in other countries facing similar challenges (see Integrative Case *Xiaomi*). Also, access to the vast market in the home country can be a valuable asset when connected to foreign products or brands potentially in demand (see Integrative Case *SG Group*). Yet others benefit from finance via a development bank or other forms of government support, as is common in China.[47] State enterprises especially may have access to resources at lower costs (In Focus 6.3). The concept of O-advantage is very broad. While most famous MNEs have O-advantages grounded in technology and brands, this is not a requirement.

Second, emerging economy MNEs are only beginning to develop global operations. Hence their investment should be seen in a catch-up perspective. They are in the early stages of a learning process: their outward FDI serves both to build capabilities, and to exploit them. This learning process involves many small projects that enable firms to develop capabilities to compete overseas (see Chapter 11); though some emerging economy MNEs with rich financial resources make large investments aimed at building the capabilities of their operations both at home and globally (see Chapter 12).[48]

Sovereign wealth fund investments

A sovereign wealth fund (SWF) is 'a state-owned investment fund composed of financial assets such as stocks, bonds, real estate or other financial instruments funded by foreign exchange assets'.[49] Investment funds that we now call SWFs were first created in 1953 by Kuwait. Most SWFs are based in countries in the Middle East and Asia that generate current account surpluses, for instance from oil and gas revenues (Table 6.3). The only major European SWF is Norway's *Government Pension Fund*, which is investing the nation's saving from oil revenues for future generations. These SWFs undertake FDI, yet they operate differently from conventional MNEs: (1) they are state-owned or controlled and (2) they typically acquire equity stakes sufficient to influence target forms, yet they do not get involved in day-to-day management or integrate operations.[50]

While most SWFs make relatively passive FPI, some have become more active, direct investors as they hold larger stakes in recipients. For example, during the financial crisis in 2007/08, the *Abu Dhabi Investment Authority* injected $7.5 billion (4.9% of equity) into *Citigroup*, while *China Investment Corporation* (*CIC*) invested $5 billion for a 10% equity stake in *Morgan Stanley*.[51] The investment drive

emerging economy MNEs
MNEs that originate from an emerging economy, and are headquartered there.

sovereign wealth fund (SWF)
A state-owned investment fund composed of financial assets such as stocks, bonds, real estate or other financial instruments.

Table 6.3 The 15 largest sovereign wealth funds

Sovereign wealth fund	Owner	Assets (US$ billion)	Origins	Foundation	Transparency Index*
Government Pension Fund of Norway	Norway	893.0	oil/gas	1990	10
Abu Dhabi Investment Authority	United Arab Emirates	773.0	oil/gas	1976	6
SAMA Foreign Holdings	Saudi Arabia	757.2	oil/gas	1952	4
China Investment Corporation	China	652.7	other	2007	8
SAFE Investment Company	China	567.9	other	1997	4
Kuwait Investment Authority	Kuwait	548.0	oil/gas	1953	6
Hong Kong Monetary Authority Investment Portfolio	Hong Kong	400.2	other	1998	8
GIC Private Limited	Singapore	320.0	other	1981	6
Qatar Investment Authority	Qatar	256.0	oil/gas	2005	5
National Social Security Fund	China	240.0	other	2000	5
Temasek Holdings	Singapore	177.0	other	1974	10
Australian Future Fund	Australia	95.0	other	2006	10
Abu Dhabi Investment Council	United Arab Emirates	90.0	oil/gas	2007	n/a
Reserve Fund	Russia	88.9	oil/gas	2008	5
Korea Investment Corporation	South Korea	84.7	other	2005	9

Notes: *Scale from 1 (fund provides contact information) to 10 (fund provides details of investment strategy, origins of wealth, ownership structure etc.); n/a = data not available.

Source: Data extracted from various items posted at Sovereign Wealth Fund Institute, 2015, Current news, www.swfinstitute.org (accessed February 2015).

continued after the recovery. For example, the *Qatar Investment Authority* acquired 20% of *Heathrow Airport* in 2012 and took over the London landmark Canary Wharf in 2015.[52]

Such large-scale investments have ignited considerable debate. On the one hand, SWFs have brought much needed cash to desperate Western firms. On the other hand, concerns are raised by host countries. A primary concern is national security in that SWFs may be politically (as opposed to commercially) motivated. Other concerns are agency conflicts in the governance structure of SWFs, and their inadequate transparency.[53] For example, the *Libyan Investment Authority*, an SWF, was closely associated with Colonel Gaddafi, which became a major liability after the fall of the Libyan government.[54]

Governments in developed economies like the USA, in fear of the influence of foreign governments, have created measures to defend their companies from SWF takeovers. SWFs in turn created a voluntary code of conduct, known as the 'Santiago Principles', which are designed to alleviate some of the concerns and to enhance the transparency and the commercial (non-political) viability of such investment.

IMPLICATIONS FOR PRACTICE

The big question in global business, adapted to the context of FDI, is: what determines the success and failure of FDI around the globe? The answer boils down to two components. First, from a resource-based view, some firms are very good at FDI because they leverage ownership, location and internalization advantages in a way that is value-creating, rare, hard to imitate by rival firms and organizationally embedded. Second, from an institution-based view, institutions in home and host countries either enable or constrain FDI from reaching its full economic potential. Therefore, the success and failure of FDI also significantly depend on institutions governing FDI as 'rules of the game'.

As a result, three preliminary implications for action emerge (Table 6.4) that we will explore further in Chapter 12. First, carefully assess whether FDI is justified in light of other opportunities, such as exporting, outsourcing and licensing. This exercise needs to be conducted on an activity-by-activity basis as part of the value chain analysis (see Chapter 4). If internalization advantages are deemed not crucial, organizational forms other then FDI are recommended.

Second, once a decision to undertake FDI is made, pay attention to the old adage: 'location, location, location!' The quest for location advantages has to create a fit with the firm's strategic goals. For example, if a firm is searching for the best 'hot spots' for innovations, this location shortlist is likely to be limited to a few hubs of that particular industry, such as Denmark for windmills (In Focus 6.2).

Finally, given the political realities around the world, be aware of the institutional constraints. Recent events suggest that MNE managers should not take FDI-friendly policies for granted. Setbacks are likely. In the long run, MNEs' interests in home and host countries can be best safeguarded if they accommodate society. In practical terms, contributions to local employment, job training, education, pollution control and financial support for local infrastructure, schools, research and sports will demonstrate MNEs' commitment to the countries in which they operate.[55] For example, German firms in China engage with the local community in various ways, including extensive vocational training, sharing of environmental protection related know-how, and donations to charitable causes to demonstrate that they are in China not just for a 'quick buck' but with a long-term commitment to the society (see Integrative Case *German Chamber of Commerce*).[56] Such engagement reduces liabilities of outsidership and enhances MNEs' legitimacy in the eyes of governments and the public.

Table 6.4   Implications for action

- Carefully assess whether FDI is justified in light of other foreign entry modes, such as outsourcing and licensing.

- Pay careful attention to the location advantages in combination with the firm's strategic goals.

- Be aware of the institutional constraints and enablers governing FDI and enhance legitimacy in host countries.

CHAPTER SUMMARY

1 Understand the vocabulary associated with foreign direct investment (FDI)

- FDI refers to directly investing in activities that control and manage value creation in other countries.
- MNEs are firms that engage in FDI.
- FDI can be classified as horizontal FDI and vertical FDI.
- FDI flow is the amount of FDI moving in a given period in a certain direction (inflow or outflow).
- FDI stock refers to the assets under control of foreign MNEs.

2 Explain why ownership advantages are necessary for firms to engage in FDI

- Ownership refers to MNEs' resources that are internationally transferable and enable firms to attain competitive advantages abroad.

3 Explain what location advantages attract foreign investors

- Location refers to certain locational advantages that can help MNEs attain their strategic goals.

4 Explain and apply the concept on internalization advantages

- Internalization refers to the replacement of cross-border market relationship with one firm (the MNE) locating in two or more countries. Internalization helps to overcome market imperfections.
- Exporting, licensing and outsources provide alternatives to FDI when market failures are unlikely to affect the operation.

5 Appreciate the benefits and costs of FDI to host and home countries

- Foreign direct investors interact with a variety of stakeholders in the host economy, each of which may benefit directly or indirectly, while some may be worse off.

6 Explain how home and host country institutions affect FDI

- Host countries may restrict FDI by outright bans, case-by-case approval, or limits on foreign ownership, but such restrictions have become less common in recent years.
- Foreign investors are subject to the same regulatory institutions as local firms, plus in some countries special regulations for foreign investors.
- Variations in corporate taxation rules also influence the pattern of FDI.

7 Participate in three leading debates on FDI

- The relationship between MNEs and host governments is subject to 'obsolescing bargain'.
- Emerging economy MNEs and sovereign wealth funds (SMEs) are important new players in the global economy.
- Sovereign wealth funds from resource-rich countries are becoming important international investors.

8 Draw implications for action

- Carefully assess whether FDI is justified, in light of other options such as outsourcing and licensing.
- Pay careful attention to locational advantages in combination with the firm's strategic goals.
- Be aware of the institutional constraints governing FDI and enhance legitimacy in host countries.

KEY TERMS

Agglomeration
Asset specificity
Bargaining power
Dissemination risks
Downstream vertical FDI
Emerging economy MNEs
Expropriation
FDI flow
FDI stock
Foreign direct investment (FDI)
Foreign portfolio investment (FPI)

Horizontal FDI
Internalization
Internalization advantages
Intra-firm trade
Joint venture
Knowledge spillovers
Licensing
Local content requirements
Location-bound resources
Locational advantages
Market failure

Multinational enterprise (MNE)
Obsolescing bargain
OLI paradigm
Ownership advantages
Sovereign wealth fund
Sunk cost
Tacit knowledge
Tax avoidance
Transaction costs
Upstream vertical FDI
Vertical FDI

CRITICAL DISCUSSION QUESTIONS

1 Identify the top five (or ten) source countries of FDI into your country. Then identify the top ten (or 20) foreign MNEs that have undertaken inbound FDI in your country. Why do these countries and companies provide the bulk of FDI into your country?

2 Identify the top five (or ten) recipient countries of FDI from your country. Then identify the top ten (or 20) MNEs headquartered in your country that have made outbound FDI elsewhere. Why do these countries attract FDI from the top MNEs in your country?

3 Worldwide, which countries were the largest recipient and source countries of FDI last year? Why? Will this situation change in five years? Ten years? How about 20 years down the road? Why?

4 MNEs are bargaining with host governments that – in many countries – are elected by the population. Is it legitimate to pressure governments to make concessions that the voting public would not agree with? Should agreements between MNEs and governments always be made public?

RECOMMENDED READINGS

J.H. Dunning, 2000, The eclectic paradigm as an envelope for economic and business theories of MNE activities, *IBR,* **12, 141–171** – a summary of the OLI paradigm.

J.H. Dunning & S. Lundan, 2008, *Multinational Enterprises and the Global Economy,* **2nd ed., Cheltenham: Elgar** – the most comprehensive book on the multinational enterprise, including theoretical foundations, empirical evidence and policy issues.

M. Forsgren, 2013, *Theories of the multinational firm,* **2nd ed., Cheltenham: Elgar** – a monograph critically reviewing five alternative theoretical perspectives on MNEs.

R. Grosse, ed., 2005, *International Business and Government Relations in the 21st Century,* **Cambridge: Cambridge University Press** – a collection of articles examining institutions and politics surrounding multinational enterprises.

K.E. Meyer, ed., 2008, *Multinational Enterprises and Host Economies* **(2 vols), Cheltenham: Elgar** – a collection of articles on the theme of benefits and costs of FDI.

UNCTAD, annual, *World investment Report,* **Geneva: United Nations** – a rich source for FDI data and analysis of current trends.

CLOSING CASE

Politics and FDI in Argentina

Argentina's relationship with foreign investors in its energy industry has historically been rocky. Yet since the 1990s, pro-market reform policies centred on trade liberalization, deregulation and privatization brought more stability. More foreign investors showed up. In 1993, *YPF*, the state-owned oil giant, was privatized. In 1999, Spain's *Repsol* bought 57% of the shares of *YPF* and became its controlling shareholder. Although Argentina suffered from the government's default on its $155 billion public debt (a world record at that time) in 2002, and the country struggled to recover, *Repsol*'s operations had been relatively smooth – until 2012.

Argentina was again engulfed in a major crisis. Facing a severe trade deficit, the government, under President Cristina Fernández de Kirchner, introduced radical measures to curb imports. Importers of foreign cars were required to find export buyers of Argentine wines, otherwise port authorities would not release their cars. Foreign print publications, including magazines and newspapers, were held at Buenos Aires airport unless subscribers went there to pay a highly unpopular fee – an import tax of sorts.

In addition to making the life of Argentine firms and citizens harder, Fernández also targeted big businesses. Specifically, *Repsol* was singled out as a high-profile target. Its alleged wrongdoing was that it failed

to boost oil and natural gas production needed to keep up with rising local demand. In 2003, when Néstor Kirchner, Fernández's ex-husband and predecessor, took office, Argentina was a net energy exporter. Ten years later, Argentina imported 15% more than its energy production, resulting in more than $10 billion of cash outflows. The government argued that the largest producer, YPF, which contributed 45% of the country's energy production, was responsible, because it failed to invest in the infrastructure needed by the sector.

Fernández's measures were popular with ordinary Argentines. Many of them blamed the free-market reforms and privatization of the 1990s for the economic devastation of the 2000s. A popular view was that the privatization of 1993 sold YPF under value, thus enabling associates of the then president Carlos Menem to enrich themselves. The YPF renationalization bill passed Congress by a landslide, and in May 2012, Fernández signed the measure into law and formally (re)nationalized – initially without compensation – Repsol's assets, which according to Repsol were worth more than €7.4 billion. Fernández also nationalized the country's private pension funds and (re)nationalized the flagship airline, Aerolineas Argentinas. So she did not just target foreign investors such as Repsol.

Outraged, both Repsol and the Spanish government protested, but there was little they could do. In retaliation, Spain limited imports of biofuels from Argentina, which annually exported over €1 billion to Spain. Spain also threatened to initiate complaints to the World Trade Organization, called for EU-wide boycotts of Argentine products, and took the case to the World Bank's International Centre for Settlement of Investment Disputes (ICSID).

While renationalizing YPF brought more revenues and helped the president's popularity, according to The Economist, 'it is a disaster for Argentina'. In the short run, Argentina and Repsol fought over compensation and the valuation of YPF, and Repsol sued the Argentine government in Spanish courts. In the long run, the expropriation had ramifications far beyond the oil industry and beyond foreign investors from Spain, as foreign investors became more cautious about sinking their funds into Argentina. This was not helped by news such as the suspension of Procter & Gamble's business in Argentina over a dispute over taxes in November 2014.

DISCUSSION QUESTIONS

1 From a resource-based perspective, what has motivated Repsol's direct investment in Argentina?

2 From an institution-based view, how can companies protect their interest in countries with instable institutions, such as Argentina?

3 Why did the Argentinian government act the way it did?

Sources: Based on (1) *Bloomberg Businessweek*, 2012, Argentina goes rogue again, April 23: 16–17; (2) *The Economist*, 2012, Cristina scrapes the barrel, April 21; (3) *The Economist,* 2012, Fill 'er up, April 21; (4) M. Guillén, 2001, *The Limits of Convergence* (p. 135), Princeton, MJ: Princeton University Press; (5) Hernandez, V. 2012, YPF nationalization: Is Argentina playing with fire? *BBC News Online*, April 17; (6) *El Pais*, 2012, Repsol acusa a Argentina de expropiar YPF para tapar la crisis económica y social, April 17; (7) *Reuters*, 2012, Argentina nationalizes oil company YPF, May 4 (8) *BBC News*, 2014, Argentina suspends P&G over tax claims, November 3.

NOTES

'For journal abbreviations please see page xx–xxi.'

1 R. Caves, 1996, *Multinational Enterprise and Economic Analysis*, 2nd ed., Cambridge: Cambridge University Press.

2 United Nations, 2014, *World Investment Report 2014*, New York and Geneva: United Nations.

3 R. Minder, 2011, Spanish Companies Look Abroad for Growth, *New York Times*, October 14.

4 United Nations, 2014, *as above.*

5 J.H. Dunning, 1993, *Multinational Enterprises and the Global Economy*, Reading, MA: Addison-Wesley; J.H. Dunning & S. Lundan, 2009, *Multinational Enterprises and the Global Economy*, 2nd ed., Cheltenham: Elgar.

6 P. Buckley & N. Hashai, 2004, A global system view of firm boundaries, *JIBS*, 35: 33–45; J. Dunning, 1998, Location and the multinational enterprise, *JIBS*, 29: 45–66; R. Grosse & L. Treviño, 2005, New institutional economics and FDI location in Central and Eastern Europe, *MIR*, 45: 123–145.

7 R. Narula & J.H. Dunning, 2000, Industrial development, globalization and multinational enterprises, *ODS*, 28: 141–167.

8 W. Chung & A. Kalnins, 2001, Agglomeration effects and performance, *SMJ*, 22: 969–988; E. Maitland, S. Nicholas, W. Purcell & T. Smith, 2004, Regional learning networks, *MIR*, 44: 87–100; J. M. Shaver & F. Flyer, 2000, Agglomeration economies, firm heterogeneity, and foreign direct investment in the United States, *SMJ*, 21: 1175–1193.

9 S. Tallman, M. Jenkins, N. Henry & S. Pinch, 2004, Knowledge, clusters, and competitive advantage, *AMR*, 29: 258–271; L. Canina, C. Enz & J. Harrison, 2005, Agglomeration effects and strategic orientations, *AMJ*, 48: 565–581; E. Maitland, E. Rose & S. Nicholas, 2005, How firms grow, *JIBS*, 36: 435–451; L. Nachum & C. Wymbs, 2005, Product differentiation, external economies, and MNE location choices, *JIBS*, 36: 415–434.

10 Shaver & Flyer, 2000, as above.

11 A. Kalnins & W. Chung, 2004, Resource-seeking agglomeration, *SMJ*, 25: 689–699; L. Nachum, 2000, Economic geography and the location of TNCs, *JIBS*, 31: 367–385; M. Porter, 1998, *On Competition*, Boston: Harvard Business School Press.

12 S. Globerman & D. Shapiro, 2003, Governance infrastructure and US foreign investment, *JIBS*, 34: 19–39; A. Bevan, S. Estrin & K.E. Meyer, 2004, Institution building and the integration of Eastern Europe in international production, *IBR,* 13, 43–64; K.E. Meyer & H. Nguyen, 2005, Foreign investment strategies and sub-national institutions in emerging markets, *JMS*, 42, 63–93.

13 N. Driffield & M. Munday, 2000, Industrial performance, agglomeration, and foreign manufacturing investment in the UK, *JIBS*, 31: 21–37; Kalnins & Chung, 2004, as above.

14 P. Buckley & M. Casson, 1976, *The Future of the Multinational Enterprise*, London: Macmillan; J.F. Hennart, 1982, *A Theory of Multinational Enterprise*, Ann Arbor: University of Michigan Press.

15 This example is inspired by J.F. Hennart, 1988, Upstream vertical integration in the aluminum and tin industries, *JEBO*, 281–299.

16 J. Campa & M. Guillén, 1999, The internalization of exports, *MS*, 45: 1463–1478; P. Buckley & M. Casson, 2009, The internalization theory of the multinational enterprise, *JIBS*, 40, 1563–1580.

17 C. Hill, P. Hwang & C. Kim, 1990, An eclectic theory of the choice of international entry mode (p. 124), *SMJ* 11: 117–128.

18 J. Denekamp, 1995, Intangible assets, internalization, and foreign direct investment in manufacturing, *JIBS*, 26: 493–504; M. Cannice, R. Chen & J. Daniels, 2004, Managing international technology transfer risk, *MIR*, 44: 129–139; K.E. Meyer & Y. Wang, 2015, Transaction cost perspectives on alliances and joint ventures, in: J. Larimo, N. Nummela & T. Mainela, eds *Elgar Handbook of International Alliances and Network Research*, Cheltenham: Elgar.

19 B. Kogut & U. Zander, 1993, Knowledge of the firm and the evolutionary theory of the multinational corporation, *JIBS*, 24: 625–646.

20 X. Martin & R. Salomon, 2003, Tacitness, learning, and international expansion, *OSc*, 14: 297–311.

21 S. Frenkel & D. Scott, 2002, Compliance, collaboration, and codes of labor practice, *CMR,* 45, 29–49; L. Hartman, D.G. Arnold & R.E. Wokutch, eds, 2003, *Rising above Sweatshop*, New York: Praeger.

22 R.E. Caves, 1996, *Multinational Enterprise and Economic Analysis*, 2nd ed., Cambridge: Cambridge University Press; L.T. Wells, 1998, Multinational enterprise and the developing countries, *JIBS*, 29, 101–114; D. Rodrik, 1999. The new global economy and developing countries, Policy Essay #24, John Hopkins University Press, Washington, DC.

23 M. Blomström & A. Kokko, 1998, Multinational corporations and spillovers, *JES,* 12, 247–277; K.E. Meyer, 2004, Perspectives on multinational enterprises in emerging economies, *JIBS*, 35: 259–276.

24 S. Lall, 1980, Vertical inter-firm linkages in LDCs: An empirical study, *OBES* 42, 203–226. R. Belderbos, G. Capannelli & K. Fukao, 2001, Backward vertical linkages of foreign manufacturing affiliates, *WD*, 29, 189–208.

25 B. Aitken & A. Harrison, 1999, Do domestic firms benefit from direct foreign investment? *AER*, 89: 605–618;

H. Görg & E. Strobl, 2001, Multinational companies and productivity spillovers, *EJ*, 111: 723–739; P. Buckley, J. Clegg & C. Wang, 2002, The impact of inward FDI on the performance of Chinese manufacturing firms, *JIBS*, 33: 637–655; B. Javorcik, 2004, Does foreign direct investment increase the productivity of domestic firms? *AER*, 94: 605–627; K.E. Meyer & E. Sinani, 2009, When and where does foreign direct investment generate positive spillovers? *JIBS*, 40, 1075–1094.

26 F. Barry & C. Kearney, 2006, Multinational enterprises and industrial structure in host countries, *JIBS*, 37: 392–406.

27 *The Economist*, 2011, Tata for now, September 10: 61–62.

28 L. Zarsky, 1999, Havens, halos and spaghetti: Untangling the evidence about FDI and the environment, conference paper, Paris: OECD, January, (www.olis. oecd.org/olis/1998doc.nsf/LinkTo/CCNM-EMEF-EPOC-CIME(98)5); P. Christmann, 2004, Multinational companies and the natural environment: Determinants of global environmental policy standardization, *AMJ,* 47, 747–760.

29 T. Poynter, 1982, Government intervention in less developed countries, *JIBS*, 13: 9–25; R. Vernon, 1977, *Storm over the Multinationals*, Cambridge, MA: Harvard University Press.

30 H. Foy, FT Big Read Poland: Barriers to business, *Financial Times*, April 6.

31 A. Byrne, 2015, Hungary also accused of homegrown bias, *Financial Times*, April 6.

32 K. Hope, 2015, Athen digs in over golden opportunity, *Financial Times*, April 4.

33 S. Lall & R. Narula, 2004, Foreign direct investment and its role in economic development, *EJDR* 16, 447–464.

34 C. Oman, 2000, *Competition Policy for Foreign Direct Investment*, Paris: OECD; R. Grosse, ed., 2003, *International Business and Government Relations*, Cambridge: Cambridge University Press.

35. T. Mallya, A. Kukulka & C. Jensen, 2004, Are incentives a good investment for the host country? *TNC*, 13, 109–148.

36. G. Zucman, 2014, Taxing across Borders, *JEL*, 28(4): 121–148.

37 K. Kojima, 1985, Japanese and American direct investment in Asia, *Hitotsubashi Journal of Economics* 26, 1–36; T. Ozawa, 1979, International investment and industrial structure, *OEP*, 31, 72–92.

38 X. Yang, Y. Jiang, R. Kang & Y. Ke, 2007, A comparative analysis of the internationalization of Chinese and Japanese firms, *APJM*, 26, 141–162; S. Globerman & D. Shapiro, 2009, Economic and strategic considerations surrounding Chinese FDI in the United States, *APJM*, 26: 163–183.

39 E. Bembaron, 2010, L'État contre la délocalisation de la Clio en Turquie, *Le Figaro*, January 11; *Le Monde*, 2010, Le gouvernement s'insurge contre la délocalisation de la Clio en Turquie, January 11.

40 K.E. Meyer & H. Thein, 2014, Business under adverse home country institutions: The case of international sanctions against Myanmar, *JWB*, 49(1): 156–171

41 D. Lecraw, 1984, Bargaining power, ownership, and profitability of transnational corporations in developing countries, *JIBS*, 15: 27–43; T. Murtha & S. Lenway, 1994, Country capabilities and the strategic state, *SMJ*, 15: 113–129; J. Nebus & C. Rufin, 2010, Extending the bargaining power model, *JIBS*, 41: 996–1015.

42 T.L. Brewer, 1992, An issue-area approach to the analysis of MNE-government relations, *JIBS*, 23: 295–309; R. Ramamurti, 2001, The obsolescing 'bargain model', *JIBS*, 32, 23–39; L. Eden, S. Lenway & D.A. Schuler, 2005, From obsolescing bargain to the political bargaining model, in: R. Grosse, ed., *International Business and Government Relations in the 21st Century*, Cambridge: Cambridge University Press.

43 J. Doh & R. Ramamurti, 2003, Reassessing risk in developing country infrastructure, *LRP*, 36: 337–353.

44 *Business Week*, 2006, Venezuela: You are working for Chavez now, May 15; *The Economist*, 2006, Bolivia: Now it's the people's gas, May 6.

45 J. Hennart, 2012, Emerging market multinationals and the theory of the multinational enterprise, *GSJ*, 2: 168–187; R. Narula, 2012, Do we need different frameworks to explain infant MNEs from developing countries?, *GSJ*, 2: 188–204.

46 M. Zeng & P. Williamson, 2007, *Dragons at Your Door*, Boston: Harvard Business School Press; R. Ramamurti 2012, What is really different about emerging market multinationals? *GSJ*, 2: 41–47.

47 Y. Luo, Q. Xue & B. Han, 2010, How emerging market governments promote outward FDI, *JWB* 45: 68–79.

48 K.E. Meyer & O. Thaijongrak, 2013, The dynamics of emerging economy MNEs, *APJM*, 30(4): 1125–1153.

49 SWF Institute, 2009, About sovereign wealth fund, www.swfinstitute.org.

50 K. Sauvant, L. Sachs & W. Jongbloed, eds, 2012, *Sovereign Investment: Concerns and Policy Reactions*, Oxford: Oxford University Press.

51 T. Hemphill, 2009, Sovereign wealth funds, *TIBR,* 51: 551–566.

52 P. Day, 2014, In Business: Sovereign Wealth Funds, *BBC podcast*, Dec 7 (Audio); *The Telegraph*, 2015, Canary Wharf to be bought by Qatar for £2.6bn, January 28.

53 S. Bernstein, J. Lerner & A. Schoar, 2013, The investment strategies of sovereign wealth funds, *JEP*, 27(2): 219–38.

54 M. Peel & L. Saignol, 2011, Wealth fund hides hard truths, *Financial Times*, August 24.

54 E. Iankova & J. Katz, 2003, Strategies for political risk mediation by international firms in transition economies, *JWB*, 38: 182–203.

56 B. Bartsch, K. Hellkoetter & M. Menant, 2015, *More than a Market*, report, Bertelsmann Foundation, March.

CHAPTER SEVEN

EXCHANGE RATES

LEARNING OBJECTIVES

After studying this chapter, you should be able to

1 Understand the determinants of exchange rates

2 Track the evolution of the international monetary system

3 Identify firms' strategic responses to deal with exchange movements

4 Participate in two leading debates on exchange movements

5 Draw implications for action

OPENING CASE

The economic crisis upsets exchange rates

The year 2009 was a difficult year for many businesses and citizens in Central and Eastern Europe. Countries across the region embarked on capitalism from fairly similar starting points in the early 1990s, but they have evolved quite differently in recent years. A key difference has been their exchange rate regime: the rules that determine the price of their currency. This had major implications on their ability to cope with the global economic crisis in 2008/09 – and how individual

citizens were affected. Let's have a brief look at four countries that joined the EU in 2004: Poland, Hungary, Latvia and Slovakia (Table 7.1).

Poland and Hungary adopted flexible exchange rates. **Poland** had been most radical in its economic stabilization and market-oriented reforms in the early 1990s, and became the fastest-growing country in the region in the late 1990s. This healthy growth continued in the 2000s, with a GDP growth of 6.8% in 2007. When the crisis reached Europe in 2008, Poland suffered only a mild, slow downturn of growth at 4.9%, and in the crisis year of 2009 achieved a positive

Table 7.1 Economic crisis in selected CEE countries

Country	Exchange rate regime	GDP per capita 2008 (billion €)	GDP Growth 2009	Foreign currency mortgages (% of total)
Poland	Floating	12 432	1.6%	40%
Hungary	Floating	10 198	– 6.5%	70%
Latvia	Fixed	9 459	–17.1%	83%
Slovakia	Euro	10 501	– 4.8%	1%

growth of 1.4%, a rare achievement at that time. The banking system remained relatively stable, and with a large domestic economy, Poland was less affected by the downturn of world trade.

However, all was not well in Poland. The Polish zloty lost 28% of its value from mid 2008 to February 2009. Thus Poles found it more difficult to pay for their travels abroad, and prices of imported goods went up. Moreover, home owners with a mortgage faced stiff challenges. Before the crisis, interest rates on mortgages in euro or Swiss francs were considerably lower than those in Polish zloty. Thus 40% of mortgages were in foreign currencies, equivalent to about 12% of Polish GDP, according to IMF estimates. Most of these borrowers had their assets (notably their house) and their income (salary) in zloty. With the depreciation of the zloty – unexpected by most borrowers – they needed more zlotys to pay their euro or Swiss francs debt. Unable to afford the higher mortgage payments, many people lost their homes. In a way, these home buyers were acting like a hedge fund – but often without understanding the risks they were taking when signing their mortgage.

Hungary, too, had a flexible exchange rate, but it faced considerably more challenges. The economy had been growing steadily at around 4% or higher until 2006, but slowed down in 2007. In addition, Hungary had for a long time been burdened with a relatively high debt, which made it more vulnerable. When the crisis hit, Hungary had to negotiate a special financing programme with the IMF and the EU for €18 billion in October 2008. The programme committed Hungary to stabilize its macroeconomy, which required cuts in budget spending and higher interest rates. The Hungarian forint depreciated by 22% from summer 2008 to February 2009. As in Poland, businesses and individuals faced steep increases in their debt payments for loans taken out in foreign currencies. In addition, they faced the consequences of a recession at home, which reduced their ability to earn the money to service their debt.

Other countries had fixed exchange rates, and they faced different sorts of challenges. The Baltic States Estonia, Latvia and Lithuania had adopted a fixed exchange rate based on a 'currency board' as a centrepiece of their economic policy since the early 1990s. For many years it served them well. They emerged from the Soviet Union to implement radical market-oriented reforms, achieved economic growth far above European average, and joined the EU in the first wave of new members from the transition economies in 2004.

However, the economic crisis tested their resolve. Without the flexibility of floating exchange rates, defence of the exchange rate became first policy priority during the crisis – and that almost failed. **Latvia** was particularly hard hit. Extensive bank lending, particularly for construction and consumer loans, had fuelled an economic boom, with over 10% annual GDP growth from 2005 to 2007. However, the crisis came suddenly and severely. First, the housing bubble burst. Then, the main locally-owned bank, *Parex*, went bust and had to be nationalized. In December 2008, Latvia had to ask the IMF for a €7.5 billion bailout. To get that money, the Latvian government had to commit to tight fiscal policy: government budgets were cut and interest rates were raised. The economy shrank by a staggering 17.1% in 2009 before achieving a steady growth rate of 4% to 5% from 2011 onwards.

With the expectation of joining the euro soon, even more Latvian borrowers – over 80% of all mortgages – had taken out their mortgages in foreign currencies: the interest rates were lower, and with pegged exchange rates, what is the risk? If the government maintains the peg, indeed, home owners save a lot of money that way. However, with the economy in a deep recession and local construction firms going bust, many borrowers struggled to keep their earnings up. The Latvian government faced a dilemma. Devaluation of the Latvian currency would help exports and thus help boost the economy, yet it risked bankrupting a large number of its own people. Hence the government opted for a very tough adjustment economic programme. Eventually, Latvia joined the euro in 2014.

Two countries had entered the eurozone before the crisis hit, courtesy of their strong economic record in the early 2000s: Slovakia and Slovenia. Thus they enjoyed the full protection of the currency union, which helped them to get through the recession relatively well. **Slovakia** attracted billions of FDI, especially in the car industry, and these direct investors are more resilient than financial investors: they can't easily shut down when economic prospects become more uncertain. However, due to the strong euro, Slovakia – like Greece or Spain – faced challenges to its competitiveness because it could not devalue its currency when some key competitors had done so. On the other hand, Slovak home buyers had no reason to consider a currency other than the euro, and compared to their neighbours they were relatively safe.

Sources: (1) *The Economist*, 2009, Ex-communist economies: the whiff of contagion, February 28; (2) *The Economist*, 2009, Foreign-currency mortgages: The bills are alive, October 10; (3) D.M. Nuti, 2009, Eastern Europe: from slowdown to nosedive, Blog, dmarionuti.blogspot.com, May 10; (4) EBRD, 2009, *Transition Report 2009*, London: European Bank of Reconstruction and Development.

Why is the exchange rate regime so important? What determines exchange rates? How do exchange rates affect trade and investment? How do firms manage their exposure to volatile exchange rates? Continuing from our two previous chapters on trade (Chapter 5) and foreign direct investment (FDI) (Chapter 6), this chapter addresses these crucial questions regarding financial flows in international business.

exchange rate
The price of one currency in another currency.
appreciation
(of a currency)
An increase in the value of a currency.
depreciation (of a currency)
A decrease in the value of a currency.

An exchange rate is the price of one currency in another currency. The exchange rates between the world's major currencies are constantly on the move. Some of them are highly volatile, as illustrated in the Opening Case. Figure 7.1 and 7.2 show the volatility of two of Europe's most important currencies, the Swiss franc and the euro. We use the terms appreciation and depreciation to describe shifts in the values of currencies. An appreciation describes an increase in the value of the currency, that is foreigners have to pay more for one unit, while a depreciation is a loss of value of the currency. The price of the euro (€) in Swiss francs (SF) increased from SF0.70 = €1 in 2010 to SF0.93 = €1 in August 2011, before falling back SF0.81 by October. After a period of stability, it again increased in January 2015 with a peak of SF1 = €1. Hence the SF appreciated *vis-à-vis* the euro from 2009 to August 2011, and depreciated sharply in autumn 2011 (Figure 7.1). Seen from the perspective of the euro, it first depreciated over two years (from 1.46 in 2009 to 1.08 in August 2011), before appreciating over the next two months to 1.20 €/SF. Figure 7.2 shows the volatility of the British pound (£) during the same time period. The pound depreciated by 30% at the onset of the financial crisis in 2007/2008, but regained that loss over the next six years.

Figure 7.1 Exchange rate: SF/€ from 2006 to 2015

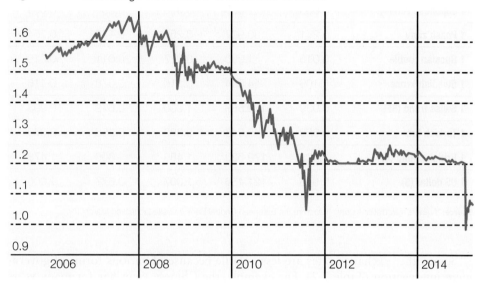

Note: The graphs show the price of €1 in Swiss francs (SF). A high value thus indicates a strong euro and a weak franc.

Source: Author's creation using website of the European Central Bank (accessed March 2015).

Figure 7.2 Exchange rate: £/€ from 2006 to 2015

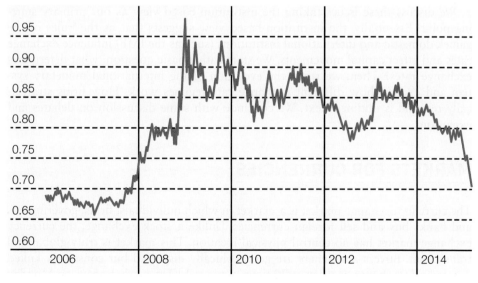

Note: The graphs show the price of €1 in British pounds (£). A high value thus indicates a strong euro and a weak pound.

Source: Author's creation using website of the European Central Bank (accessed March 2015).

Table 7.2 Examples of key currency exchange rates

	€	¥	SF	£	$
1 euro (€)	1.000	128.403	1.065	0.715	1.057
1 Chinese yuan	0.151	19.402	0.161	0.108	0.160
1 Indian rupee	0.015	1.927	0.016	0.011	0.016
1 Japanese yen (¥)	0.008	1.000	0.008	0.006	0.008
1 Polish zloty	0.241	30.907	0.256	0.172	0.254
1 Russian rouble	0.016	1.990	0.017	0.011	0.016
1 Swedish krone	0.109	14.034	0.116	0.078	0.116
1 Swiss franc (SF)	0.939	120.583	1.000	0.672	0.993
1 Turkish lira	0.359	46.045	0.382	0.256	0.379
1 British pound (£)	1.398	179.520	1.489	1.000	1.478
1 US dollar ($)	0.946	121.456	1.007	0.677	1.000

Source: Authors' calculations using data from the European Central Bank website (accessed March 15).

Some other exchange rates are less volatile because of various forms of government intervention (Table 7.2). For example, the Chinese yuan has for many years been pegged to the dollar, and then moved within narrow bands, due to government intervention. Also the Swiss National Bank aimed to stabilize the Swiss franc by pegging it to the euro (more on that later). Yet in January of 2015 the peg proved to be unsustainable, leading to major upsets in currency markets. There is already an important lesson from simply looking at these figures: exchanges rates are more volatile than even many experts believe.

We discuss these issues taking the institution-based view as our primary starting point. Essentially, the institution-based view suggests that as the 'rules of the game', domestic and international institutions (such as the IMF) influence exchange rates and affect capital movements. We start with a basic question: what determines exchange rates? Then, we track the evolution of the international monetary system and explain how different exchange rate regimes work. How firms strategically respond is outlined next. We conclude with some discussion on debates and extensions.

LEARNING OBJECTIVE

1 Understand the determinants of exchange rates

currency exchange market
A market where individuals, firms, governments and banks buy and sell foreign currencies.

MARKETS FOR CURRENCIES

The **currency exchange market** is a market in which individuals, firms, governments and banks buy and sell foreign currencies. Unlike a stock exchange, the currency exchange market has no central physical location. This market is truly global and transparent. Buyers and sellers are geographically dispersed but constantly linked (quoted prices change as often as 20 times a minute).[1] The market opens on Monday morning first in Tokyo and then Hong Kong followed by Singapore. Gradually, Frankfurt, Zurich, Paris, London, New York, Chicago and San Francisco 'wake up' and come online.

Operating on a 24/7 basis, the currency market is the largest and most active market in the world. On average, the worldwide volume averages $5.3 trillion a *day*.[2] To put this mind-boggling number in perspective, the amount of one single *day* of currency exchange transactions is roughly double the amount of entire worldwide FDI outflows in one *year* and roughly equals close to one-quarter of worldwide merchandise exports in one *year*. What drives the prices in these currency markets?

The concept of an exchange rate as the price of a commodity – one country's currency – helps us understand its determinants. Basic economic theory suggests that the price of a commodity is most fundamentally determined by its supply and demand. Strong demand will lead to price hikes, and oversupply will result in price drops. Of course, we are dealing with a most unusual commodity here, money, because currency transactions are often an indirect outcome of other transactions. Yet the basic underlying principles still apply.

First, when French exporters sell products to the UK, they often demand that they be paid in euro, because that is more convenient for them. Likewise, British tourists need to buy euros to pay for their hotels, restaurants and other expenses in France (which are technically speaking French service exports). British importers of French products will somehow have to generate euros to pay for their imports. The easiest way to generate euros is to *export* to France (or other countries using the euro), and be paid in euros. In this example, the euro is the common transaction currency involving both French imports and French exports. Hence the British importer of French goods would buy euros from their bank that in turn buys them on international currency markets. On the other hand, British exporters receive euros as payments for their goods; they would thus sell their euros. This first source of supply and demand on currency markets is international trade in goods or services (Chapter 5).

Second, FDI (Chapter 6) triggers demand and supply for currencies. When a company builds a factory or buys another company abroad, it needs to buy foreign currency to pay for the expense. This creates a demand for the host country's currency. On the other hand, when overseas affiliates repatriate profits, that creates a demand for the home country's currency. The third source of supply and demand is financial investors who buy a portfolio of assets in another country, such as shares or bonds, purely for financial reasons. These financial investors account by far for most transactions in financial markets.

Because currencies are such unique commodities, their markets are influenced not only by economic factors but also by a lot of political and psychological factors. We next explore five underlying forces that contribute to the supply and demand for currencies: (1) relative price differences, (2) inflation and monetary supply, (3) interest rates, (4) productivity and balance of payments, (5) exchange rate policies, and (6) investor psychology.

Relative price differences and purchasing power parity

Recall from international trade theory (Chapter 5) that countries export products for which they have a comparative advantage. The price importers are willing to pay reflects their domestic price. Hence there will be an upward pressure in the price in the exporting country until the goods have the same price in both countries. The purchasing power parity (PPP) hypothesis suggests that the exchange rates between two countries will equate prices in the two markets, which is essentially the 'law of one price'. In the absence of trade barriers (such as tariffs or transport costs), the price for identical products sold in different countries must be the same. Otherwise, arbitragers may 'buy low' and 'sell high'. The PPP hypothesis suggests that in the

purchasing power parity (PPP) hypothesis
Hypothesis suggesting that, in the long run, baskets of goods would cost the same in all currencies ('law of one price').

long run, exchange rates should move toward levels that would equalize the prices of an identical basket of goods in any two countries.[3]

You can test the PPP hypothesis yourself by buying the same product in several countries as you travel. If it is a tradeable product, and there are no differences in taxation and no tariff barriers, it should – in theory – cost the same in every country. *The Economist* magazine does this exercise regularly using a *McDonald*'s Big Mac hamburger. In January 2015, a Big Mac cost $4.79 in the USA and – at market exchange rates – $4.26 in the eurozone.[4] According to this calculation, the euro was 11% 'undervalued' against the dollar. The Ukrainian hryvnia and the Russian rouble were the most undervalued currencies, whereas the Swiss franc is most overvalued. In other words, the Big Mac in Ukraine and Russia had the best 'value' in the world, based on official exchange rates. They only cost $1.20 and $1.36, respectively. Hence the data suggest that the PPP hypothesis does not hold in the strict version. However, the Big Mac is not really a tradeable good – it is largely made from local ingredients and with local labour. Hence it is domestic demand and supply that determine the price of a Big Mac.[5] To truly test the PPP hypothesis, you have to use a tradeable good such as a T-shirt, an iPod or a car (and you have to deduct value-added tax). Thus the answer to the question 'Why is Zürich much more expensive than Kiev?' is that goods are not perfectly free to trade across countries.

Inflation and money supply

relative PPP hypothesis
Hypothesis suggesting that changes in exchange rates will be proportional to differences in inflation rates.

inflation
The (average) change of prices over time.

The PPP in its strict interpretation may at best apply in the long term – the Big Mac index has for many years suggested that the Swiss franc is overvalued and various emerging economy currencies are undervalued. However, a weaker version of PPP, known as relative PPP hypothesis, suggests that *changes* in prices should be the same in both countries, after considering the exchange rate. Thus when prices rise more slowly (the inflation is higher) in Switzerland than in the eurozone, then the Swiss franc should depreciate relative to the euro proportional to the difference in the inflation rate.

Inflation is closely associated with the amount of money in circulation. A high level of inflation is essentially too much money chasing too few goods in an economy – technically, an expansion of a country's money supply. The more money people have in their purse, the higher the prices they are able to pay. A government, when facing budgetary shortfalls, may choose to print more currency to increase the money supply, which tends to stimulate inflation. In turn, this would cause its currency to depreciate. This makes sense because as the supply of a given currency (such as the Swiss franc) increases while the demand stays the same, the per unit value of that currency goes down. Therefore, the exchange rate is very sensitive to changes in monetary policy. It responds swiftly to changes in money supply. To avoid losses, investors anticipating a change in monetary policy sell assets denominated in the depreciating currency for assets denominated in other currencies. Such massive sell-offs may often worsen the depreciation. The appreciation of the Swiss franc relative to the euro in January 2015 may thus have been caused by the *Swiss National Bank*'s tighter monetary policy, compared to the *European Central Bank*.

Interest rates and interest rate parity

Financial investors are not so much interested in the prices of Big Macs, or other goods they might buy in either country; they focus on their return on investment. In the short run, variations in interest rates have a powerful effect. A basic consideration is this: should I invest my money at home, or should I invest abroad? If markets are efficient, then these two investment alternatives should yield the same outcome.

This is known as interest rate parity. It suggests that the return should be the same for the following two transactions:

1 Invest in a one-year government bond in your own country.

2 (a) Buy foreign currency at today's rate (the spot market rate), (b) invest in a one year foreign currency government bond, and (c) sell foreign currency for delivery in one year's time.

You can actually sell currency for delivery at specified days in the future, typically 30, 60, 90 or 180 days, a forward transaction. This means you commit yourself to deliver the currency at that time at that price (the forward exchange rate) – independent of where the current exchange rate is in the future. The forward exchange rate reflects market participants' expectations of the future exchange rate. This expectation may be driven by, for example, the differences in inflation rates, and thus the relative PPP hypothesis discussed above. Before proceeding, do a little experiment. Pick up the latest issue of a financial newspaper, such as the *Financial Times*, and find current rates for the following: (1) today's exchange rate, (2) forward exchange rates one year from today, and (3 & 4) interest rates for money market investment in the two currencies. Can you demonstrate that interest rate parity holds? (If you look at a shorter time period, you will need to adjust the interest rate earned, for example 90/360 for three months).

Since investors have these two investment alternatives, logically, exchange rates and interest rates are very closely related. If one country increases its interest rate while the other does not, then either the current exchange rate or the forward exchange rate has to adjust. If the inflation rates are the same (and expected to stay the same), then the forward exchange rate is likely to stay stable, and the current exchange rate is likely to appreciate. If increases in interest rates also affect inflation expectations, then the main adjustment may be in the forward exchange rate.

Productivity and balance of payments

In international trade, the rise of a country's productivity, relative to other countries, will improve its competitive position – this is a basic proposition of the theories of absolute and comparative advantage discussed in Chapter 5. Productivity fuels exports, which in turn increases demand for a country's currency. One recent example is China. All the China-bound FDI inflows in dollars, euros and pounds have to be converted to local currency, boosting the demand for the yuan. Hence the yuan would appreciate unless the government was neutralizing the effect by buying massive amounts of US government bonds. Other examples are not hard to find. The rise in relative Japanese productivity over the past three decades led to a long-run appreciation of the yen, which rose from about ¥310 = $1 in 1975 to ¥80 = $1 in 2011 before declining to ¥120 in 2015.

Recall from Chapter 5 that changes in productivity will change a country's balance of trade. A country that is highly productive in manufacturing may generate a surplus in trade in goods, whereas a country that is less productive in manufacturing may end up with a deficit on its trade account. These have ramifications for the balance of payments (BoP) – officially known as a country's international transaction statement. Table 7.3 illustrates the components of the BoP for the UK in the year 2013. In that year, the UK imported more goods than it exported, leading to a deficit of £110.2 billion on the trade balance. In services, the UK generated an export surplus of £78.1 billion, the biggest contributor being financial services. The UK also had a deficit on income, most of which arises from FDI undertaken in the UK in the past. The UK paid more in transfer overseas than it received; this category included payments to and from the EU as well as, for example, development aid. The sum of

interest rate parity
Hypothesis suggesting that the interest rate in two currencies should be the same after accounting for spot and forward in exchange rates.
spot market rate
The exchange rate for immediate payment.
forward transaction
A currency exchange transaction in which participants buy and sell currencies now for future delivery, typically in 30, 90 or 180 days, after the date of the transaction.
forward exchange rate
The exchange rate for forward transactions.

balance of payments (BoP)
A country's international transaction statement, including merchandise trade, service trade and capital movement.

Table 7.3 The UK balance of payments, 2013 (billion pounds)

	Current account	Export (income)	Import (payments)	Balance
1	Trade in goods	306.81	417.006	−110.196
2	Trade in services	204.465	126.369	78.096
3	Income	161.756	174.890	−13.134
4	Transfers	17.621	44.783	−27.162
5	Current account balance (line 1 + 2 + 3 + 4)			−71.396

	Capital and financial account	Foreign investment in the UK	UK investment abroad	Balance
6	Capital account	1.795	1.265	0.530
7	Direct investment (FDI)	27.378	−12.700	40.078
8	Financial investment	−167.819	−195.294	27.500
9	Reserve assets		4.961	4.961
10	Capital and financial account balance (line 6 + 7 + 8 + 9)			73.044
11	Net errors and omissions (line 10 + 5)			1.648

Source: Authors' creation using data extracted from: Office for National Statistics, 2014, *Statistical Bulletin*, Balance of Payments: 2013.

current account (of the BoP)
Exports and imports of goods and services.
capital and financial account (of the BoP)
Sales and purchases of financial assets.

all these transactions, known as the current account, adds to a deficit of £71.4 billion in the UK for 2013.

This deficit was financed by a variety of financial flows recorded in the capital and financial account. There were net inflows of FDI of £40.1 billion, meaning more foreign investors were investing in the UK than British MNEs investing overseas. Note that capital flows arising from UK outward FDI were negative, which indicated that UK firms withdrew capital from overseas subsidiaries: they either made loans from the subsidiary to headquarters, or they divested (sold) business units abroad. Financial investments also show large negative entries for inflows and outflows, which are related to the reduction of currencies holdings, presumably due to tighter banking regulation (see Chapter 9). Other countries with a substantial current account deficit, such as the USA, have to finance it by selling government bonds to foreign investors, which also would show up in this BoP line. In 2013, the Bank of England (the central bank of the UK) increased its position of foreign reserve assets by £5.0 billion, which also shows up as investment abroad in the BoP. These numbers add up to the capital and financial account of £73.0 billion. In theory, the capital and current account should balance – in practice, however, they don't. There is quite a substantial measurement error in these data because the central bank does not know details of all transactions and needs to make estimates for some of these numbers.

To make a long story short, a country experiencing a current account surplus will see its currency appreciate; conversely, a country experiencing a current account deficit will see its currency depreciate. This may not happen overnight, but it will happen in a span of years and decades. Going back to the 1950s and 1960s, the rise of the dollar was accompanied by a sizeable US surplus on merchandise trade. By the 1970s and 1980s, the surplus gradually turned into a deficit. By the 1990s and 2000s, the US current account deficit became ever increasing, forcing the dollar to depreciate relative to other currencies, such as the euro, the Japanese yen and the Chinese yuan. Broadly speaking, the value of a country's currency is an embodiment of its economic productivity and balance of payments positions.

Investor psychology

Although theories on price equality, interest rates, inflation and money supply, and balance of payments policies predict long-run movements of exchange rates, they often fall short of predicting short-run movements. It is investor psychology, some of which is fickle and thus very hard to predict, that largely determines short-run movements. Professor Richard Lyons at the University of California, Berkeley, is an expert on exchange rate theories. However, he was baffled when he was invited by a friend to observe currency trading first hand:

> *'As I sat there, my friend traded furiously all day long, racking up over $1 billion in trades each day. This was a world where the standard trade was $10 million, and a $1 million trade was a 'skinny one.' Despite my belief that exchange rates depend on macroeconomics, only rarely was news of this type his primary concern. Most of the time he was reading tea leaves that were, at least to me, not so clear . . . It was clear my understanding was incomplete when he looked over, in the midst of his fury, and asked me: 'What should I do?' I laughed. Nervously.'*[6]

Investors – currency traders (such as the one Lyons observed), foreign portfolio investors and average citizens – may move as a 'herd' at the same time in the same direction, resulting in a bandwagon effect. The bandwagon effect seemed to be at

bandwagon effect
The result of investors moving as a herd in the same direction at the same time.

What drives the day-to-day activities of currency traders?

play in August 2014, when the Argentinean peso plunged against key currencies, such as the US dollar and the euro. Essentially, a large number of individuals and firms exchanged the pesos for the key foreign currencies in order to minimize their exposure to Argentina's sovereign default (its second since 2001) – a phenomenon known as capital flight. This would push down the demand for, and thus the value of, domestic currencies. Then, more individuals and companies joined the herd, further depressing the exchange rate and setting off a major economic crisis.

Overall both economics and psychology are involved in determining exchange rates. However, so far we have discussed currency markets *as if* they are freely driven by supply and demand. Of course, that is not entirely true. The markets for some currencies are heavily influenced by governments (more precisely, by central bank interventions). To understand how and why, we first need to make a historical excursion.

capital flight
A phenomenon in which a large number of individuals and companies exchange domestic currencies for a foreign currency.

INSTITUTIONS OF THE INTERNATIONAL MONETARY SYSTEM

LEARNING OBJECTIVE

2 Track the evolution of the international monetary system

Three eras are commonly distinguished in the evolution of the institutions governing currency exchange markets, known as the international monetary system, over the past 150 years. They are (1) the gold standard, (2) the Bretton Woods system, and (3) the post-Bretton Woods system.

The gold standard (1870–1914)

gold standard
A system in which the value of most major currencies was maintained by fixing their prices in terms of gold, which served as the common denominator.

The gold standard was a system in place between the 1870s and 1914, when the value of most major currencies was maintained by fixing their prices in terms of gold. Gold was used as the common denominator for all currencies. This was essentially a global fixed-rate system, with little volatility and every bit of predictability and stability. To be able to redeem its currency in gold at a fixed price, every central bank needed to maintain gold reserves. The system provided powerful incentives for countries to avoid current account deficits, as that would quickly deplete their reserves of gold.

The gold standard was severely undermined in 1914 when World War I broke out and several combatant countries printed excessive amounts of currency to finance their war efforts. After World War I, many countries rejoined the gold standard. However, during the Great Depression (1929–1933), countries engaged in competitive devaluations in an effort to boost exports at the expense of trading partners. But no country could win such a 'race to the bottom', and the gold standard eventually had to be abandoned.

The Bretton Woods system (1944–1973)

Bretton Woods system
A system in which all currencies were pegged at a fixed rate to the US dollar.

Towards the end of World War II, at an allied conference in Bretton Woods, New Hampshire, USA, a new system – known as the Bretton Woods system – was agreed upon by 44 countries. The Bretton Woods system was centred on the US dollar as the new common denominator. All currencies were pegged at a fixed rate to the dollar, and changes in exchange rates were rare. The USA became the anchor of the system by promising that other countries could at any time convert their dollars to gold at $35 per ounce.

At the Bretton Woods conference, two institutions were created that were to secure the stability of this new monetary system, and the world economy more generally. Both continue to play an important role in the globally-integrated economy of the 21st century (see Chapter 9). The International Monetary Fund (IMF) provides financial assistance to countries experiencing temporary imbalances in their balance of payment, and helps countries to secure macroeconomic stability. The World Bank provides loans for specific projects in developing countries to support their economic development, for example, construction of airports, reforms of the education system or administration of privatization programmes.

In the Bretton Woods system, the dollar was given a pivotal role in the global economy, making it the most used reserve currency of countries around the world. This was appropriate in the late 1940s because the US economy had the highest levels of productivity and contributed approximately 70% of the global GDP. The system was sustained by the large US trade surplus with the rest of the world; the USA was the export engine of the world when the rest of the world was recovering from World War II. Overall, the system served the world well for about 25 years.

By the late 1960s and early 1970s, a combination of rising productivity elsewhere and US inflationary policies put pressures on Bretton Woods. First, West Germany and other countries caught up with productivity and exported more, and the USA ran its first post-1945 trade deficit in 1971. This pushed the German mark to appreciate and the dollar to depreciate – a situation very similar to the yen-dollar relationship in the 1980s and the yuan-dollar relationship in the 2000s. Second, in the 1960s, to finance the Vietnam War, the USA increased government spending not by additional taxation but by increasing the money supply. These actions led to rising inflation levels and strong pressures for the dollar to depreciate.

Per Bretton Woods agreements, the US Treasury was obligated to dispense one ounce of gold for every $35 brought by a foreign central bank such as the Bundesbank. For several years, an informal agreement between central banks maintained the presumption of $35 per ounce of gold, despite the growing imbalance between gold reserves and dollars in circulation. However, currency traders gradually realized that the $35 rate was no longer realistic, and they started selling dollars. In April 1971, the Bundesbank gave up its attempts to buy dollars to keep the exchange rate fixed, and allowed the mark to appreciate. In August 1971, to stop this loss of its gold reserves, the US government unilaterally revoked its commitment to convert dollars into gold. After tense negotiations, major countries collectively agreed to relinquish the Bretton Woods system by allowing their currencies to float in 1973. In retrospect, the Bretton Woods system had been built on two conditions: (1) the US inflation rate had to be low, and (2) the US could not run a substantial trade deficit. When both these conditions were violated, the demise of the system was inevitable.

The post-Bretton Woods System (1973–present)

As a result, today we live in the post-Bretton Woods system. This system is essentially built around floating exchange rates between the world's major currencies (dollar, euro, yen), with a diversity of exchange rate regimes, ranging from various floating systems to various fixed rates. Its main drawback is turbulence and uncertainty. Since the early 1970s the US dollar has no longer been the official common denominator. However, it has retained a significant amount of 'soft power' as a key currency, accounting for about 65% of the reserve currencies held by central banks. The leading role is unlikely to change in the near future, as dollar-denominated financial markets are most liquid.[7]

Since 1973, countries have been able to choose between three major exchange rate policies: (1) a floating rate, (2) a pegged rate, or (3) adoption of another (or common) currency. Governments adopting the floating (or flexible) exchange rate policy tend to be free market believers, willing to let the demand and supply conditions determine exchange rates – usually on a daily basis, via the currency exchange

International Monetary Fund (IMF) International organization that provides financial assistance to countries experiencing temporary imbalances in their balance of payment, and helps securing macroeconomic stability.
World Bank International organization that provides loans for specific projects in developing countries.

post-Bretton Woods system A system of flexible exchange rate regimes with no official common denominator.

floating (or flexible) exchange rate policy The willingness of a government to let the demand and supply conditions determine exchange rates.

free float
A pure market solution to determine exchange rates.
managed float
The common practice of influencing exchange rates through selective government intervention.

market. However, few countries adopt a free float, which would be a pure market solution. Most countries practice a managed float, with selective government intervention. Of the major currencies, the US, Canadian and Australian dollars, the yen and the pound have been under managed float since the 1970s. Since the late 1990s, several developing countries, such as Brazil, Mexico and South Korea, have also joined the managed float regime, as did Hungary and Poland (see Opening Case). The severity of intervention is a matter of degree. Heavier intervention moves the country closer to a fixed exchange rate policy, and less intervention enables a country to approach the free float ideal. A main objective of intervention is to prevent the emergence of erratic fluctuations that may trigger macroeconomic turbulence.

pegged exchange rate
An exchange rate of a currency attached to that of another currency.
crawling band
A limited policy of keeping the exchange rate within a specified range, which may be changing over time.

An alternative exchange rate regime is the pegged exchange rate policy – countries 'peg' the exchange rate of their currency relative to another currency, typically the dollar or the euro. This means that the currency is allowed to fluctuate only within a more or less narrow band relative to that other currency. For example, the Danish krone (DKK) is pegged to the euro. Thus between 2010 and 2014, the DKK/€ rate only fluctuated between 7.430 and 7.462. Others choose a continuously adjusting exchange rate – known as crawling band – which may be suitable for a country that wishes to allow for a slightly higher inflation than the currency it is pegged to. China has at times adopted a crawling band to gradually adjust its exchange rate.

There are two benefits to a peg policy. First, a peg stabilizes the import and export prices for smaller economies that otherwise may experience high volatility in their exchange rate. Second, many developing countries with high inflation have pegged their currencies to the dollar or the euro (currencies with relatively low inflation) to restrain domestic inflation. However, there are two drawbacks of pegging an exchange rate. First, interest rates have to be set to support the pegged exchange rate (remember interest rate parity) and cannot be used for other economic policy objectives. Second, the peg has to be credible. Currency exchange traders are likely to attack a currency if they believe that a pegged rate is not sustainable, for example, because the inflation rate is too high or the central bank does not have enough reserves. The expectation that the currency will be devalued creates a big profit opportunity for those selling the currency just before the devaluation. This expectation can be so powerful that it overwhelms even the most esteemed central banks. The UK experienced such a devaluation in 1992, which severely disrupted business and ultimately led to the downfall of the Thatcher government.

fixed exchange rate
An exchange rate of a currency relative to other currencies.
currency board
A monetary authority that issues notes and coins convertible into a key foreign currency at a fixed exchange rate.

An extreme case of a pegged exchange rate is a fixed exchange rate, which allows no movements of the currency at all. Such fixed rates have become rare since the 1970s. The most extreme fixed rate policy is a currency board, which is a monetary authority that issues notes and coins convertible into a key foreign currency at a fixed exchange rate. Usually the fixed exchange rate is set by law, making changes to the exchange rate politically very costly for governments. To honour its commitment, a currency board must back the domestic currency with 100% of equivalent foreign currencies. In the case of Hong Kong's currency board, every HK$7.8 in circulation is backed by US$1. By design, a currency board is passive. When more US dollars flow in, the board issues more Hong Kong dollars and interest rates fall. When more US dollars flow out, the board reduces money supply and interest rates rise. The Hong Kong currency board has been jokingly described as an Asian outpost of the US Federal Reserve. This is technically accurate because interest rates in Hong Kong are essentially determined by the US Federal Reserve. While the Hong Kong currency board was a successful bulwark against speculative attacks on the Hong Kong dollar in 1997 and 1998, a currency board is not necessarily a panacea, as evidenced by Argentina's experience (In Focus 7.1).

The third option is to give up your own monetary policy entirely, and thus rely on another country, or a common central bank, to manage inflation and exchange

IN FOCUS 7.1

Hong Kong and Argentina: a tale of two currency boards

Hong Kong is usually cited as an example that has benefited from a currency board. In the early 1980s, Hong Kong had a floating exchange rate. As Britain and China intensified their negotiations over the colony's future, the fear that the 'Hong Kong way of life' might be abandoned after 1997 shook business confidence, pushed down real estate values, and caused panic buying of vegetable oil and rice. The result was 16% depreciation in the Hong Kong dollar against the US dollar. In 1983, the Hong Kong government ended the crisis by adopting a currency board that pegged the exchange rate at HK$7.8 = US$1. The currency board almost immediately restored confidence. The second major test of the currency board came in 1997, in the first autumn after Hong Kong was returned to Chinese sovereignty. During the Asian financial crisis of 1997–1998, Hong Kong's currency board stood like a rock, successfully repelled speculative attacks, and maintained its peg to the US dollar.

In Argentina, hyperinflation was rampant in the 1980s. Prices increased by more than 1000% in both 1989 and 1990. In 1991, to tame its tendency to

finance public spending by printing pesos, Argentina adopted a currency board and pegged the peso at parity with the US dollar (1 peso = US$1). At first the system worked, as inflation was reduced to 2% by 1995. However, by the late 1990s, Argentina was hit by multiple problems. First, appreciation of the dollar made its exports less competitive. Second, rising US interest rates spilled over to Argentina. Third, depreciation of Brazil's real resulted in more imports from Brazil and fewer exports from Argentina to Brazil. To finance budget deficits, Argentina borrowed dollars on the international market, as printing more pesos was not possible under the currency board. When further borrowing became impossible in 2001, the government defaulted on its $155 billion public debt (a world record), ended the peso's convertibility, and froze most dollar-denominated deposits in banks. In 2002, Argentina was forced to give up its currency board. After the de-link, the peso plunged, hitting a low of 3.5 to the dollar. Riots broke out as people voiced their displeasure with politicians.

Sources: (1) F. Gunter, 2004, Why did Argentina's currency board collapse? *The World Economy*, May: 697–704; (2) R. Carbaugh, 2007, *International Economics*, 11th ed. (p. 492–495), Cincinnati, OH: Thomson South-Western.

rate. Such a common currency is used for example in West Africa, where 14 countries use the 'CFA franc', which in turn is fixed to the euro. Thus monetary policy for these countries in Africa is effectively determined by the European Central Bank in Frankfurt. Of course, the euro itself is a common currency shared by 19 countries in 2015, as we will discuss in greater detail in the next chapter. Some small countries have one-sidedly adopted another currency, for example, the dollar is used in Panama and the euro is used in Montenegro.

common currency
A currency shared across several countries, such as the euro and the CFA franc.

Pegged versus floating exchange rates

With the blending of pegged and floating exchange rate regimes, the debate has never ended on which would be better. Proponents of pegged and floating exchange rates argue that these rates impose monetary discipline by preventing governments from engaging in inflationary monetary policies (essentially, printing more money). Proponents also suggest that pegged exchange rates reduce uncertainty and thus encourage trade and FDI, not only benefiting the particular economy but also helping the global economy.[8]

Proponents of floating exchange rates believe that market forces should take care of supply, demand and thus the price of any currency.[9] Under a pegged (or fixed) exchange rate, central banks have to continuously intervene to guarantee the exchange rate. A trade deficit would result in diminishing of currency reserves, which is not sustainable over longer periods of time. Floating exchange rates create an automatic adjustment mechanism where trade surpluses lead to currency appreciation that then increases the prices of exports, and thus reduces the trade surplus. In other words, flexible exchange rates may help avoid the sudden crises that occur under fixed exchange rates when expectations of an impending devaluation arise. For example, Thailand probably would not have been devastated so suddenly in July 1997 (generally regarded as the triggering event for the 1997 Asian financial crisis) had it operated a floating exchange rate system. In addition, floating exchange rates allow each country to make its own monetary policy. A major problem of the Bretton Woods system was that in the late 1960s other countries were not happy about fixing their currencies to the currency of a country, the USA, which conducted inflationary monetary policies.

MANAGING EXCHANGE RISKS

LEARNING OBJECTIVE

3   Identify firms' stra-
    tegic responses to
    deal with exchange
    movements

**exchange rate risk
(or currency risk)**
The risk of financial losses
because of unexpected
changes in exchange rates.

Firms engaging in international business are almost always exposed to exchange rate movements. Even if you are not exporting or importing, you may be exposed to currency risks in other ways (In Focus 7.2). Thus they face exchange rate risk (or currency risk), which is the possibility of financial losses because of unexpected changes in exchange rates. Whenever a foreign currency transaction involves a payment to be made at a later time – such as payment for goods upon delivery – firms are exposed to exchange risks. In volatile markets, this exchange risk can potentially undermine the profitability of a business transaction; in extreme cases it has driven companies into bankruptcy. For example, when the Swiss franc appreciated in January 2015, brokers with high-risk business models, such as *Alpari* in the UK and *Global Broker* in New Zealand, paid the ultimate price and went bankrupt.[10]

The fundamental principle for minimizing exchange risk is to ensure that future revenue streams and future expenses are in the same currency. Whenever expected financial flows are in different currencies, companies are exposed to currency risk.[11] In a flexible exchange rate regime, the exchange rate risk is evident from the volatility of the exchange rates in the past (see Figures 7.1 and 7.2). In a fixed exchange rate regime, the risk is more difficult to assess. There is a large probability that the exchange rate stays the same. However, there is also a small probability that the fixed exchange rate breaks down – and then a very substantial adjustment may occur. Companies can address this risk in two ways: (1) by strategically structuring their business in such a way that revenues are in the same currencies as expenses, or (2) by using financial market instruments to manage risk exposure (Table 7.4).

Table 7.4 Managing exchange rate risk

Strategic	Financial
• Invoicing in your own currency	• Spot market transaction plus investing or borrowing in foreign currency
• Strategic hedging by balancing currencies of cost and revenue streams	• Forward market transactions
• Diversification by trading in multiple currencies	• Swap market transactions

IN FOCUS 7.2

Local councils mess with taxpayers' funds

Local governments are managing some taxpayers' funds, depositing temporary surpluses in a bank, and taking out loans when they need more money. Since they are handling taxpayers' money, you would expect them to act conservatively – read 'risk adverse' – in their financial management. Yet some do not!

In the early 2000s, city treasurers in German cities like Essen, Bochum and Gelsenkirchen found a smart way to save money, or so they thought. Interest rates in Swiss francs were almost two percentage points lower than for euros. So they decided to issue bonds in francs. For a while they smiled while paying lower interest rates than neighbouring towns. Then the financial crisis hit, and the euro weakened relative to the franc, the exchange rate dropped from 1.60 SF/€ in 2005 until the Swiss National Bank stabilized the rate in 2011 to 1.20 SF/€.

Analyzing the situation in September 2014, city treasurers acknowledged their loss – which so far was only on the books. The big bill would come when the bonds were due – a one million franc bond raised about €625 000 (= 1/1.60) in 2005, yet on the due day the repayment would be €833 000 if the exchange rate remained at 1.20 SF/€. If you add that up for outstanding bonds of 450 million francs, as in the case of Essen, that comes to a lot of money. The one or two percentage points saved every year in interest covered only a small part of those losses. So, they were playing for time, and hoping for the best. Bochum's treasurer said 'all we can do is wait until the exchange rate one day moves in our favour'.

However, things turned a lot worse. After months of speculation and increasing capital inflows to Switzerland, in January 2015 the Swiss National Bank stopped its currency market interventions. The Swiss franc again became free floating, and jumped to a new price of 1.02 SF/€. The city of Essen alone lost about €70 million that day; together the municipalities in North Rhine Westphalia may have lost as much as €900 million. Meanwhile, the Austrian capital city of Vienna saw its debt soar by about €300 million.

Why did the promising financing opportunity turn so badly wrong? The city treasurers appear to have ignored some basic rules of international finance:

- Rule number 1: if it looks too good to be true, it probably is! More precisely, there are likely to be hidden risks that are not obvious to a lay person.

- Rule number 2: match the currencies of your revenues and costs! More precisely, if your expected revenues are mostly in euro (as is the case for local councils), you should also raise funds in euro!

Sources: (1) M. Kohlstadt, 2014, Revier-Städte verzocken Millionen mit Schweiser Krediten, *Westdeutsche Allgemeine Zeitung,* September 15; (2) M. Schymiczek, 2015, Kursbeben in der Schweiz verschärft Finanzkrise in Essen, *Westdeutsche Allgemeine Zeitung,* January 16; (3) T. Döring, 2015, Deutsche Kommunen in der Franken-Falle, *Handelsblatt,* January 16; (4) *Wirtschaftsblatt,* 2015, Franken-Kredite in Österreich, January 16.

Strategic responses

Companies can reduce their exposure to exchange rate risk in three ways: (1) by invoicing in their own currency, (2) by strategic hedging, or (3) by risk diversification. The most basic way to reduce exchange rate risk is to invoice customers in your own currency, and to only accept payment in your own currency. This may sound very simple, but it is actually the most powerful way to protect yourself. In practice, the currency of invoicing is subject to negotiation, and you may have to agree to a slightly less favourable price. Invoicing in your own currency is a low risk option, but it is not completely risk free: you still face the (normally small) possibility that your business partner goes bankrupt in a financial market upheaval, and thus is unable to pay.

Second, a more sophisticated strategy is strategic hedging, which involves organizing activities in such a way that currencies of expenditures and revenues match. For example, a British firm receiving a major export order from France may in return order some components in France. It then can use the euro received for its export order to pay for its own imports. Or, companies may establish a local production facility. If part of the production occurs locally, then some of the costs are in local currency, which reduces the exchange rate exposure.[12] Strategic hedging was one of the key motivations behind *Toyota*'s 1998 decision to set up a new factory in France instead of expanding its existing British operations (which would cost less in the short run). France is in the eurozone, which the British refused to join. Strategic hedging refers to arranging your operations such as to reduce your exposure to exchange rate risk, through sourcing or FDI. This is more strategic because it establishes long-term structures that reduce the need for complex financial management, and it involves managers from many functional areas (such as production, marketing and sourcing) in addition to those from finance.

Third, companies may diversify their exchange rate risk by engaging with a number of countries using different currency zones to offset the currency losses in certain regions through gains in other regions.[13] Such currency risk diversification reduces exposure to unfavourable exchange movements from any one currency. For example, a European firm selling to a wide range of countries (and invoicing in local currency) in 2008 may have experienced substantial losses on its orders from Iceland, but made gains on orders to the USA. This strategy, however, does not work if your own country experiences a major crisis. Imagine a (hypothetical) British company in early 2007 ordering construction of a building to be completed and paid in a mix of euros and dollars at the end of 2008. Since the pound sharply depreciated in 2008, this company would have struggled to pay the agreed amount of euro and dollars. A different strategy is required, and that's where financial markets can help.

Financial management responses

How can companies use financial markets to manage their exchange rate risks? There are three primary types of exchange transactions: (1) spot transactions, (2) forward transactions, and (3) swaps. Spot transactions are the classic single-shot exchange of one currency for another. For example, through spot transactions, Russian tourists may buy several thousand euros with their roubles and will get their euros from a bank right away. A Russian business expecting an invoice in euro in a year's time could in principle also buy the euros on the spot market, and then invest them in German government bonds until the invoice arrives. In practice, however, the company may not have the money available already at this earlier time.

The second option is to use forward markets. Recall that forward transactions allow participants to buy and sell currencies now for future delivery, typically in 30, 90 or 180 days, after the date of the transaction. The primary benefit of such transactions is to protect investors from exposure to the fluctuations of the spot rate, an act known as currency hedging. Currency hedging is essentially a way to minimize the exchange rate risk inherent in all non-spot transactions. Traders and investors expecting to make or receive payments in a foreign currency in the future are concerned whether they will have to make a greater payment or receive less in terms of the domestic currency should the spot rate change. For example, if the forward rate of the euro (€/$) is exactly the same as the spot rate, the euro is 'flat'. If the forward rate of the euro per dollar is *higher* than the spot rate, the euro has a forward discount. If the forward rate of the euro per dollar is *lower* than the spot rate, the euro then has a forward premium.

Hypothetically, assume that (1) today's €/$ exchange rate is 1, (2) a US firm expects to be paid €1 million six months from now, and (3) the euro is at a 180-day forward discount of 1.1. The US firm may take out a forward contract now, and convert euro earnings into a dollar revenue of $909 091 (€1 million/1.1) after six months. Does such a move make sense? There can be two answers. Yes, if the firm knew in advance that the future spot rate would be 1.25. With the forward contract, the US firm would make $909 091 instead of $800 000 (€1 million/1.25) – the difference is $109 091 (14% of $800 000). However, the answer would be no if the spot rate after six months was below 1.1. If the spot rate remained at 1, the firm could have earned $1 million, *without* the forward contract, instead of only $909 091. This simple example suggests a powerful observation: currency hedging may lead to a win or loss compared to a strategy of 'wait and buy on the spot market' (see Closing Case). However, the waiting strategy exposes the firm to a currency risk – exchange rates can go up as well as down. Remember, that the best bet available for the future exchange rate is the rate in the forward market. Only if you believe that you are smarter than the market would it make sense to bet against the market (and there are a lot of smart people active in that market). Of course, *afterwards* a lot of people will say 'you should have. . .' – but with hindsight advice is always cheap!

A third major type of currency exchange transaction is a swap. A currency swap is the conversion of one currency into another at Time 1, with an agreement to revert it back to the original currency at a specific Time 2 in the future. *Deutsche Bank* may have an excess balance of pounds but needs dollars. At the same time, *Union Bank of Switzerland (UBS)* may have more dollars than it needs at the moment but is looking for more pounds. They can negotiate a swap agreement in which *Deutsche Bank* agrees to exchange with *UBS* pounds for dollars today and dollars for pounds at a specific point in the future.

The primary participants of the currency exchange market are large international banks, such as *Deutsche Bank*, *HSBC*, and *Santander*, that trade among themselves. How do these banks make money by trading money? They make money by capturing the difference between their offer rate (the price to sell) and bid rate (the price to buy) – the bid rate is *always* lower than the offer rate. The difference of this 'buy low, sell high' strategy is technically called the spread. For example, *Deutsche Bank* may quote offer and bid rates for the British pound at US$0.6630 and $0.6625, respectively, and the spread is $0.0005. That is, *Deutsche Bank* is willing to sell one million pounds for $663 000 and buy one million pounds for $662 500. If *Deutsche Bank* can simultaneously buy and sell one million pounds, it can make $500 (the spread of $0.0005 × £1000 000).

Given the instantaneous and transparent nature of the electronically-linked currency exchange market around the globe, the opportunities for trading, or arbitrage, can come and go very quickly. The globally integrated nature of this market leads to three outcomes:

- Razor-thin spread
- Quick (literally split-second) decisions on buying and selling (remember Professor Lyons' observation earlier)
- Ever-increasing volume to make more profits (recall the daily volume of $5.3 trillion). In the earlier example, $500 is obviously just 'peanuts' for *Deutsche Bank*. Do a little maths: how much trading does *Deutsche Bank* have to do to make $1 million in profits for itself?

Overall, the importance of currency management cannot be overstressed for firms of all kinds interested in doing business abroad. Firms whose performance is otherwise stellar can be devastated by unfavourable currency movements.

currency swap
A currency exchange transaction between two firms in which one currency is converted into another in Time 1, with an agreement to revert it back to the original currency at a specific Time 2 in the future.

offer rate
The price offered to sell a currency.
bid rate
The price offered to buy a currency.
spread
The difference between the offered price and the bid price.

From a resource-based view, it seems imperative that firms develop resources and capabilities that can combat currency risks in addition to striving for excellence in, for example, operations and marketing.[14] MNE subsidiary managers in certain countries may believe that there are lucrative opportunities to expand production. However, if these countries suffer from high currency risks, it may be better – for the multinational as a whole – to curtail such expansion and channel resources to other countries whose currency risks are more manageable. Developing such expertise is no small accomplishment because, as noted earlier, prediction of currency movements remains an art or a highly imprecise science. Because of such challenges, financial market capabilities are essential for firms to profit from (or at least avoid being crushed by) unfavourable currency movements.

DEBATES AND EXTENSIONS

LEARNING OBJECTIVE

4 Participate in two
   leading debates
   on exchange
   movements

In the highly uncertain world of exchange rate movements, stakes are high, and debates are numerous. We review two major debates here: (1) a strong versus a weak dollar, and (2) hedging versus not hedging.

A strong dollar versus a weak dollar

With the leading roles of the US dollar as the world's foremost trading and reserve currency, the value of the dollar is essential not just for the US, but for economies around the world. Yet this value is often very volatile as a consequence of American domestic policies, notably fiscal and monetary policy, as well as the trade deficit. During the financial crisis, the value of the dollar fell to $1.60 per euro in July 2008. In the next years, the dollar fluctuated around $1.30 to $1.50 per euro. Only in late 2014, when the European Central Bank introduced looser monetary policy, the dollar strengthened again, one euro cost only $1.05 in March 2015.[15] At the same time, the dollar is still strong compared to the Chinese yuan, which is pegged to the dollar despite the two countries experiencing very different economic conditions.[16]

What are the implications of a weak dollar for the rest of the world? Although a weak dollar hurts exporters in Asia and Europe, it helps remedy the US balance of payments and results in more global balancing. As the US economy slows down and thus is unable to absorb more imports (the USA already has by far the world's largest current account deficit), a weak dollar forces Asian and European economies to boost their domestic demand. Thus the world economy may become less unbalanced with a gradual slide of the dollar.

However, the rest of the world has two reasons to support a strong dollar. First, the rest of the world holds so many dollars as currency reserves that most countries fear the capital loss they would suffer if the dollar falls too deep. China leads the world by holding over €2.6 trillion(!) of foreign reserves, 70% of which are in US dollars.[17] A devaluation of the dollar would result in a huge loss for those holding dollar-denominated assets. Since the US Federal Reserve has been issuing new money to fund stimulus packages (with the euphemism 'quantitative easing'), China is deeply worried that a cheapening dollar will be a nasty hit to Chinese holdings of US Treasury bonds. There is some fundamental soul-searching among Beijing's economic mandarins.[18] Second, many countries prefer to keep the value of their currencies down to promote exports. A weak dollar benefits American exporters facing Chinese competitors, not only in their home market, but also when they compete in third countries such as Europe.

Currency hedging versus not hedging

Given the unpredictable nature of exchange rates (at least in the short term), it seems natural that firms that deal with transactions in foreign currencies would engage in currency hedging (see Closing Case). Firms that fail to hedge are at the mercy of the spot market. In 1997, *Siam Cement*, a major chemicals firm in Thailand, had $4.2 billion debt denominated in foreign currencies and hedged none of it. When the Thai baht sharply depreciated against the US dollar in July 1997, *Siam Cement* had to absorb a $517 million loss, which wiped out all the profits it made during 1994–1996.[19] This was a common occurence during the Asian crisis, and in several of the financial crises that followed, from Russia in 1998 to Iceland in 2008, as well as in Hungary and Poland (see Opening Case).

Hedging your currency in financial markets has a similar effect as an insurance. If everything went well, you wonder whether it was worth the effort. However, there are costs and risks that are easily overlooked: (1) bank fees, (2) counter party risk, and (3) uncertainty in the underlying business transaction.

First, hedging is not free; after all, banks do charge for their services and for the risk that they may assume in the transaction. This cost can be quite substantial if you want to hedge over long time periods, unusual contract length, or in less-traded currencies.

Second, counter party risk is the risk that the bank with which you have a hedging contract goes bankrupt. Usually this possibility is seen as remote, and many finance texts may not bother to mention it in the context of currency exchange markets. However, when *Lehman Brothers* went down in autumn of 2008, some businesses suddenly found themselves with claims that they could not realize.

Third, what happens if the underlying transaction does not take place as expected, and thus future revenues or expenses do not materialize? For example, when the oil price soared in 2007, many airlines anticipated having to pay a much higher price (in dollars) for petrol in the future – petrol always being a major cost factor in this industry. Thus they expected to need a lot of dollars in the future, and bought them using forward contracts. However, in 2008 the oil price collapsed, while demand for air travel grew slower than expected – hence, airlines needed fewer dollars than expected. However, having entered forward contracts at a time when the dollar was relatively expensive, they had to sell those dollars at a lower price in the spot market. In consequence *Cathay Pacific Airways* had to write off close to $1 billion, while *Ryanair*, *Air France-KLM* and *Southwest* also made substantive losses.[20]

Given the theoretical arguments in favour of hedging, it may be surprising that in 2008 only about 55% of large firms engaged in financial hedging, up from 45% in the previous year.[21] Among America's largest firms, about two thirds do not use financial hedging, including many large firms, such as *3M*, *Deere*, *Eastman Kodak*, *ExxonMobil* and *IBM*. Managers argue that currency hedging eats into profits. A simple forward contract may cost up to half a percentage point per year of the revenue being hedged. More complicated transactions and longer time horizons may cost more. As a result, many firms believe that the ups and downs of various currencies balance out in the long run. Some, such as *IBM*, focus on strategic hedging and risk diversification, but refrain from currency hedging. Such a strategy may be viable for larger firms that have only a small part of their costs and revenues in foreign currencies, and that have diversified their risk exposure (typical for big US firms). However, for small firms with a large share of international business, for firms exposed to a small number of currencies, and for firms originating from a small country that is subject to substantial exchange rate uncertainty, such a strategy can be fatal – as the *Siam Cement* example illustrates.

counter party risk
The risk of a business partner not being able to fulfil a contract.

IMPLICATIONS FOR PRACTICE

LEARNING OBJECTIVE

5   Draw implications
    for action

The big question in global business, adapted to the context of exchange rate movements, is: what determines the success and failure of currency management around the globe? The answer boils down to two components. First, from an institution-based standpoint, the changing rules of the game – economic, political and psychological – enable or constrain firms. *Wal-Mart*'s low-cost advantage from made-in-China products stems at least in part from the Chinese government's policy to peg its yuan at a favourable level against the dollar. Consequently, *Wal-Mart*'s low-cost advantage may be eroded as the yuan appreciates. Second, from a resource-based perspective, firms' capabilities in currency management may make or break them.

As a result, three implications for action emerge (Table 7.5). First, managers must be aware of their currency risk exposure, which arises from differences in the currencies of their expected revenues and expenditures. This requires constant monitoring of the firm's financial data, and of contractual commitments and claims that are expected to result in payments at a later time.

Second, risk analysis of any country must include its currency risks. Previous chapters have advised managers to pay attention to the political, regulatory and cultural features of various countries. Here, a crucial currency risk dimension is added. To assess currency risks, they need not only pay attention to the broad long-run movements informed by PPP, productivity changes and balance of payments, but also to the fickle short-run fluctuations triggered by interest rate changes and investor mood swings. An otherwise attractive country may suffer from high inflation, resulting in devaluation of its currency on the horizon. Countries in Southeast Asia prior to 1997, and in Central and Eastern Europe prior to 2008, are examples of such scenarios. Numerous firms ignoring such currency risk were burned badly in these financial crises.

Finally, a country's high currency risks do not necessarily suggest that this country needs to be totally avoided. Instead, it calls for a prudent currency risk management strategy via strategic or financial hedging. Not every firm has the stomach or capabilities to do both. Smaller, internationally inexperienced firms (such as *Jobek do Brazil*, see Closing Case) may outsource currency hedging to specialists in their bank. Strategic hedging may be unrealistic for such smaller firms without operations abroad. On the other hand, many larger, internationally experienced firms choose not to touch currency hedging, but focus on strategic hedging and risk diversification. Although there is no fixed formula, firms not having a well-thought-out currency management strategy may be caught off guard when currency movements take a wrong turn.

Table 7.5   Implications for action

- Managers must at all times be aware of their currency risk exposure.
- Risk analysis of any country must include an analysis of its currency risks.
- A currency risk management strategy is necessary via currency hedging, strategic hedging or both.

CHAPTER SUMMARY

1 Understand the determinants of exchange rates

- An exchange rate is the price of one currency expressed in another.

- Basic determinants of exchange rates include (1) relative price differences and PPP, (2) inflation, (3) interest rates, (4) productivity and balance of payments, (5) exchange rate policies and (6) investor psychology.

2 Track the evolution of the international monetary system

- The international monetary system evolved from the gold standard (1870–1914), to the Bretton Woods system (1944–1973) and eventually to the current post-Bretton Woods system (1973–present).

- The current system is characterized by a mix of managed floats between major currencies and pegged exchange rates for many other currencies.

3 Identify firms' strategic responses to deal with exchange movements

- Firms' strategic responses include (1) invoicing in their own currency, (2) strategic hedging and (3) risk diversification.

- Financial markets can be used to manage exchange rate risk by using (1) spot transactions, (2) forward transactions and (3) currency swaps.

4 Participate in two leading debates on exchange movements

- These are: (1) a strong versus a weak dollar and (2) currency hedging versus not hedging.

5 Draw implications for action

- Managers must at all times be aware of their currency risk exposure.

- Risk analysis of any country must include an analysis of its currency risks.

- A currency risk management strategy is necessary via currency hedging, strategic hedging or both.

KEY TERMS

Appreciation (of a currency)
Balance of payments (BoP)
Bandwagon effect
Bid rate
Bretton Woods system
Capital flight
Common currency
Counter party risk
Crawling band
Current account (BoP)
Currency board
Currency exchange market
Currency hedging
Currency risk diversification
Currency swap

Depreciation (of a currency)
Exchange rate
Exchange rate risk
   (currency risk)
Financial account (BoP)
Fixed exchange rate
Floating (flexible) exchange
   rate policy
Forward discount
Forward premium
Forward transaction
Free float
Gold standard
Inflation
Interest rate parity

International Monetary
   Fund (IMF)
Managed float
Offer rate
Pegged exchange rate
Post–Bretton Woods system
Purchasing power parity (PPP)
   hypothesis
Relative PPP hypothesis
Spot market rate
Spread
Strategic hedging
World Bank

CRITICAL DISCUSSION QUESTIONS

1 Identify the currencies of the top three trading partners of your country in the last ten years. Find the exchange rates of these currencies, relative to your country's currency, ten years ago and now. Explain the changes then predict the movement of these exchange rates ten years from now.

2 Should China revalue the yuan against the dollar? If so, what impact may this have on (1) US balance of payments, (2) Chinese balance of payments, (3) relative competitiveness of Mexico and Thailand, (4) European firms importing from China and (5) European retail consumers?

3 As a finance manager in a European company (accounting in euro), one of your sales managers proudly tells you that he has just signed a contract for a sale to Russia due in two years' time, to be paid in Russian roubles. How do you react?

4 The English Premier League earns £250 million annually from broadcasting contracts abroad, of which 16% arise from Southeast Asia. Contracts are usually signed for three year periods after a competitive tender.[22] As manager of a television company in Southeast Asia, you want a share of the cake and prepare a bid for a contract for broadcast rights in your country. Tender conditions specify payment in British pounds spread over the three year period. How do you manage the associated exchange rate risk?

RECOMMENDED READINGS

S.Y. Cross, 1998, *The Foreign Exchange Market in the United States,* New York: Federal Reserve Bank of New York – a clear exposition of the institutions and practice in currency markets.

J. Fox. 2009, *The Myth of the Rational Market: The History of Risk, Reward, and Delusion on Wall Street,* New York: Harper – explains how financial markets really work, how their interpretation has evolved over the past 100 years and what theory does or does not explain.

C. Henderson, 2006, *Currency Strategy,* 2nd ed., New York: Wiley – a comprehensive, though somewhat theoretical, treatment of a variety aspects of currency exchange markets.

M. Taylor, 1995, The economics of exchange rates, *JEL* 33, 13–47 – a comprehensive review of the economics underlying the formation of exchange rates.

J. Williamson, 1998, *Crawling Bands or Monitoring Bands: How to Manage Exchange Rates in a World of Capital Mobility,* Washington, DC, Institute of International Economics (www.iie.com/publications/papers/paper.cfm?ResearchID=319) – a review of the alternative ways for countries to manage their currencies.

CLOSING CASE

Jobek do Brasil's *foreign exchange challenges*

by Dirk Michael Boehe

Jobek do Brasil is an outdoor furniture and hammock manufacturer and exporter, based in Brazil. Focusing on European markets, it had to constantly deal with foreign exchange challenges. In 2008, sales went down by more than 60%, thanks to the global financial crisis. The existing business model – based on in-house manufacturing in Brazil's northeast and an administrative, purchasing, quality assurance and sales unit in Germany – was no longer viable. Fixed costs were substantial, and manufacturing inputs had already been purchased. Sitting in debt and running short of working capital, Barny, the owner, shut down

Jobek's plant in 2010; outsourced production to *Reed Isaac*, a former local partner; closed down the German unit; and signed a long-term supply contract with *Stern GmbH* in Germany. The measures were necessary to refocus the business and drive down costs.

After more than a decade of high inflation, low growth, debt default and failed stabilization policies, the Brazilian government introduced a new currency, the real (BRL), in 1994. The new currency, initially valued at BRL1 per US$, was pegged to the US dollar, and could oscillate within an adjustable band until 1999. Then, subject to central bank interventions, the real depreciated rapidly and reached BRL2.25 per dollar in January 2002. During the presidential campaign of 2002, investors got increasingly concerned about the likely policies of the likely winner and drove down the value of the real to BRL3.83 per dollar by October 2002. The BRL/euro exchange rate evolved similarly (see Figure 7.3). However, Lula's government soon gained the confidence of international financial markets by pursuing conservative fiscal and monetary policy. After paying back its last IMF loan in 2005, the country obtained investment grade rating in 2008. The international financial markets honoured that and billions of US dollars poured into the country over the next years. This macroeconomic stabilization, however, came at a cost: the BRL continuously appreciated from 2004 and about 2700 (12%) exporters quit international markets between 2004 and 2011.

However, *Jobek* did not want to give up on exports. It had built up a strong premium brand, especially in Germany, associating *Jobek* with Latin American lifestyle, as well as social responsibility and high quality. Selling the rights to the brand in Europe to *Stern* was a hard decision. Now, *Stern* owned the rights of the *Jobek* brand for Europe, while Barny maintained the rights for the rest of the world. In exchange, *Stern* committed to buying all products it sold under the *Jobek* brand from Barny for the next ten years.

Barny approached *Jobek*'s account managers at *Banco do Brasil*, Brazil's largest and partly state-owned bank, and asked them to make an offer for a swap contract over BRL1 million. After six months, Barny still had not received the contract, and grumbled that 'here in the northeast of Brazil, they are 20 years back in some areas'. Indeed, hedging the exposure to the euro is sometimes a problem in a country where, according to a financial risk consultant, 'the US dollar is still a synonym for foreign exchange'.

More black clouds moved across the horizon and tapped the usually strong sunshine in Brazil's northeast. With the euro in its deepest crisis since its introduction in 2002, many feared that quantitative easing might be used to get rid of the eurozone's mounting debt. Barny read an article in *Valor Econômico*: 'Dilma Roussef [the new Brazilian president] sent a message to Mrs Merkel [the German chancellor] complaining about 'the monetary *tsunami*' that is threatening to flood Brazil and other emerging economies with

Figure 7.3 Exchange rate: BRL/€ from 2008 to 2015

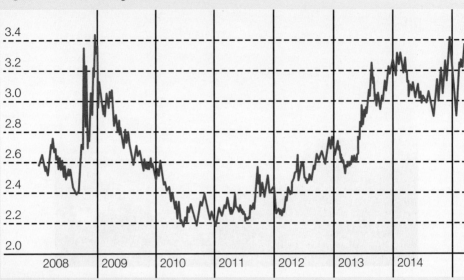

Source: Author's creation using website of the European Central Bank (accessed March 2015).

cheap money made available by the European Central Bank.' In fact, Brazil was attracting foreign money as never before, and received a record amount of FDI of US$66 billion in 2011.

Barny complained that 'with the resulting real appreciation, our clients are not very happy'. He noted: 'On November 29, 2011, *Stern* placed an order based on an exchange rate of BRL2.49 per euro. Today, March 2, 2012, the euro dropped to BRL2.28, that's an appreciation of about 10% in a very short period. The only way we can sell our products is because we have a strong brand name.'

The telephone ringing interrupted Barny's thoughts. It was João Gonçalves, the boss at *Reed Isaac*, shouting through the handset: 'You know, I am very concerned with the high minimum wage increases that Mrs Dilma Roussef has pushed through congress, not to mention the ever rising tax charges. We can hardly survive at such costs and I am sorry but I need to talk to you about a price adjustment.' Although disappointed, Barny politely asked João if he would like to have lunch together. Then Barny scratched his head on how he would respond to João's request over lunch.

CASE DISCUSSION QUESTIONS

1 How do you evaluate *Jobek*'s situation from the resource-based and institution-based views? Why have resources and institutions hindered Barny from coping with the foreign exchange situation, but simultaneously helped him to turn his company around?

2 How do you evaluate *Jobek*'s strategic response to foreign exchange risks?

3 What would you do if you were Barny? Why?

Sources: This case was written by **Dirk Michael Boehe** (University of Adelaide). It is based on (1) the author's interviews; (2) internal information provided by *Jobek do Brasil*, www.jobek.com.br; (3) Brazilian Central Bank, www.bacen.gov.br; (4) Brazilian Ministry of Economic Development, www.mdic.gov.br; (5) Exchange rate converter, www.oanda.com; (6) *Forbes*, 2011. BRIC worker: A look at labor costs in the big EMs, March 11, www.forbes.com/sites/kenrapoza/2011/03/11/bric-worker-a-look-at-labor-costs-in-the-big-ems/; (6) Doing Business 2012 – Paying taxes, World Bank, www.doingbusiness.org/ data/exploretopics/paying-taxes; (7) *Valor Econômico*, 2012, Dilma: países ricos estão inundando o mundo com um 'tsunami monetário', March 1; (8) *Economist*, 2011, Latin America's economies: Waging the currency war, January 13, www.economist.com/node/17906027.

NOTES ·

'For journal abbreviation, please see page xx–xxi.'

1 R. Carbaugh, 2007, *International Economics*, 11th ed. (p. 360), Cincinnati, OH: Thomson South-Western.

2 In this chapter, we follow financial markets in using the $ sign to denote the US$, unless otherwise specified. This is a simplification, as Australia, Canada, Hong Kong, Singapore and Taiwan also call their currency 'dollar'.

3 A. Taylor & M. Taylor, 2004, The purchasing power parity debate, *JEP*, 18: 135–158.

4 *The Economist*, 2010, The Big Mac index, www.economist.com/content/big-mac-index/ (accessed March 2015).

5 D.M. Nuti, 2009, The Economist's burgernomics, Blog, dmarionuti.blogspot.com, August 14; *The Economist*, 2011, Beefed-up burgernomics, July 30

6 R. Lyons, 2001, *The Microstructure Approach to Exchange Rates* (p. 1), Cambridge, MA: MIT Press.

7 R. Copper, 2009, *The Future of the dollar*, Washington, DC: Peterson Institute of International Economics.

8 e.g. R.I. McKinnon, 1988, Monetary and exchange rate policies for international financial stability, *JEP*, 2(1), 82–103.

9 e.g. J. Williamson, 2006, *Choosing monetary arrangements for the 21st Century*, Washington, DC: Peterson Institute of International Economics.

10 *Handelsblatt*, 2015, Finanzinstitute mit Einbußen in Millionenhöhe, January 19.

11 F. Carrieri & B. Majerbi, 2006, The pricing of exchange risk in emerging stock markets, *JIBS*, 37: 372–391; L. Jacque & P. Vaaler, 2001, The international control conundrum with exchange risk, *JIBS*, 32: 813–832.

12 K.D. Miller & J.J. Reuer, 1998, Firm strategy and economic exposure to foreign exchange rate movements, *JIBS*, 29, 493–514.

13 B. Kogut & N. Kulatilaka, 1994, Operating flexibility, global manufacturing, and the option value of a multinational network, *MS*, 40: 123–139; C. Pantzalis, B. Simkins & P. Laux, 2001, Operational hedges and the foreign exchange exposure of US multinational corporations, *JIBS*, 32: 793–812.

14 R. Faff & A. Marshall, 2005, International evidence on the determinants of foreign exchange rate exposure of multinational corporations, *JIBS*, 36: 539–558; R. Weiner, 2005, Speculation in international crises, *JIBS*, 36: 576–587.

15 Exchange rates taken from European Central Bank website: www.ecb.europa.eu/stats/exchange/eurofxref/html/index.en.html (accessed March 2015)

16 *The Economist*, 2009, Banyan: Currency contortions, December 19.

17 *The Economist*, 2011, Who wants to be a triple trillionaire? April 16.

18 *The Economist*, 2011, China's currency: Stranger than fiction, January 22

19 Carbaugh, 2007, *as above* (p. 380).

20 *The Economist*, 2009, Corporate hedging gets harder: The perils of prudence, June 18.

21 *The Economist*, 2009, Corporate hedging . . . , *as above*.

22 H. Richards, 2010, Dealmaking skill adds to the score, *Financial Times*, April 21.

PART THREE

GLOBALIZATION

8   European Integration

9   Global Integration and Multilateral Organizations

10 Socially Responsible Business

CHAPTER EIGHT

EUROPEAN INTEGRATION

LEARNING OBJECTIVES

After studying this chapter, you should be able to

1 Explain the origins and the evolution of the EU

2 Explain how and why the institutional framework created by the EU is pivotal for business

3 Discuss the merits and drawbacks of the euro as a common currency

4 Participate in debates over the political institutions of the EU

5 Draw implications for action

OPENING CASE

A day in European business

It is Tuesday morning 5 a.m., and a nearly empty motorway lies ahead of Marcus as he drives his company Audi on a familiar route: he is heading for the Munich airport. As a manager with European responsibilities, travelling and engaging with other cultures is his daily job.

Marcus is Vice President (VP) Northern Europe of an entrepreneurial software company providing computer-aided design software for use in businesses, such as large architectural firms, municipalities, automotive suppliers, aviation manufacturers, media and entertainment and designers. His responsibilities include the definition of strategies for the region, budgeting for several European countries, negotiations with new potential business partners, and business reviews with his own local teams, suppliers and partners.

After leaving the car on deck 12 of the spacious car park and writing down the exact location (important!), he heads for the security check and his gate at International Departures. With the boarding pass on his mobile phone, he can jump the queue at the gate. Early in the morning, *Lufthansa* departure times are quite reliable and the flight departs on time: two hours to read the morning news, to get an update on worldwide financials, to enjoy a cup of tea or two and to have an unspectacular sandwich.

Arriving in Warsaw airport, there is less border security than in the past. Since Poland joined the Schengen Agreement in 2003 there are no longer any passport controls. Business travellers try to avoid check-in luggage to save time, and 10 minutes later he is greeted by his local Country Manager. Unfortunately, he cannot take advantage of the EU's monetary union, and still has to use five different wallets. In addition to the 'euro wallet', he needs one for Swedish kroner, one for Romanian leu, one for British pounds, and finally one for Polish zloty, which is what he is carrying today. It's quite a challenge to grab the right one when leaving home at 4:30 in the morning . . .

While an experienced driver takes Marcus and his Country Manager through Warsaw's rush hour traffic, they discuss the latest development at the Polish office. Since joining the EU, the level of professionalism has significantly increased at all levels of management in Poland, and English has become the norm for conversations with local staff. This was not the case when Marcus started doing business in Poland

in 2001. Initially, he could communicate only with the Country Manager directly in English. For the first year, all employees were enrolled in English language training every Friday afternoon. Now this training has paid off, and Marcus can easily communicate directly with everyone in the office.

This time, his first appointment is with a major supplier in the centre of Warsaw to review the business development for the next months: three hours of PowerPoint presentations, financial reports and marketing reviews. A quick business lunch at a Chinese restaurant and two hours in the car to his company's Polish office in Łodz are followed by an internal staff meeting with updates by all business unit managers. It is the VP's job to make sure the right mindset is present everywhere in the sales channel, service levels are met and staff's compensation schemes keep them hungry to do more and develop the business to the next level.

Marcus' visits to a country office typically take three days, packed with meetings to justify the expense of the journey. Modern technology allows video conferencing at high quality, yet it cannot replace the extremely important 'human' factor in business negotiations. Marcus prefers face-to-face discussions, because recognizing subtle expressions on someone's face often can make a difference between closing a deal and coming home empty handed.

Doing business in different European countries, Marcus faces differences in bureaucracy at almost every step. In Poland, for example, it seems that everything needs to be filed in several copies, stamped and signed. Notaries hold 'a licence to print money' because more or less everything related to the administration of a limited company (called 'sp. z o.o.') needs to be signed in the presence of a notary. The easiest way to discover this is by having a dinner. Why? If you want to use the restaurant receipt as proof of expenses related to a business, you have to ask the waiter. After ten minutes he might come back to you with a huge document (three pages) that needs to be filled in with the company's long tax ID number, signed several times and finally stamped by the restaurant before it is accepted. In Germany, Marcus would just take his credit card receipt – that's all.

After a long day, it is time to check in at one of the business hotels. Besides the construction of highways and roads, this is an area where the progress of economic transition and development of Poland is most visible. In 2001, business travellers in Łodz had the choice of one hotel. Today, international hotel chains like *Ibis* and *Radisson* provide facilities of very high standard. With travelling as part of a business life, Marcus' views on hotels are different from those of a tourist. How close to the airport? 100% non-smoking environment? What internet bandwidth is available? Wireless LAN? Any sports facilities for a quick workout? International newspapers available? Member of a frequent flyer programme? These are questions he considers prior to booking the 'right' spot. It will be past 10 p.m. when he returns from his business dinner to the hotel, and he will have to prepare for another busy day in European business.

Source: Based on personal communications with a business executive who prefers to remain anonymous.

A business trip across Europe has become an everyday event for many managers in Europe. How have the rules of the game in Europe changed to make business in neighbouring countries so much easier in recent years? What are the political developments behind these changes that have led to the European Union (EU) as we know it today? A few years ago crossing borders required a lot of effort and costs. Only since 1993 have people been able to freely chose their workplace anywhere in the EU; only since 2002 have people used the euro (some Europeans still don't); and only in 2004, transition economies such as Poland have joined the union.

This chapter introduces the key institutions that businesses have to be aware of when doing business in the EU, along with their historical origins and contemporary controversies. The EU has been a driving force of regional integration in Europe, and it has gone through several stages of integration. It started in the 1950s as a free trade area by abolishing tariffs on trade between member countries, and soon moved to a customs union by introducing common external tariffs. Such forms of regional integration also exist elsewhere in the world (see Chapter 9). Yet the EU has gone much further. In 1993 it adopted a common market based on the principle of free movement of goods, services, capital and labour. Since then, it has moved towards an economic union that also coordinates aspects of its fiscal and monetary policy, harmonizes regulatory institutions, and conducts, for example, EU-wide competition policy. Some members have adopted a monetary union by sharing a common currency – the euro. However, the EU continues to be an association of sovereign nations, and thus is not considered a political union (Figure 8.1).

This chapter first outlines the historical evolution that led to the current structure of the EU. On that basis, we then explore the institutional framework of the EU, which is pivotal for many aspects of business in Europe. In particular, we look at the rules governing the free movement of goods, services, capital and people, along with competition policies. In a separate section, we discuss the monetary union known as the eurozone. In the debates and extensions section, we review the political processes in the EU that drive the evolution of the economic institutions.

European Union (EU)
The political and economic organization of 27 countries in Europe.

euro
The currency of the European Monetary Union.

free trade area
A group of countries that remove trade barriers among themselves.

customs union
One step beyond a free trade area, a customs union imposes common external policies on non-participating countries.

common market
Combining everything that a customs union has, a common market permits free movement of goods and people.

economic union
In addition to all features of a common market, members of an economic union coordinate and harmonize economic policies.

monetary union
Countries sharing a common currency and monetary policy.

political union
The integration of political and economic affairs of a region.

Figure 8.1 Types of regional integration

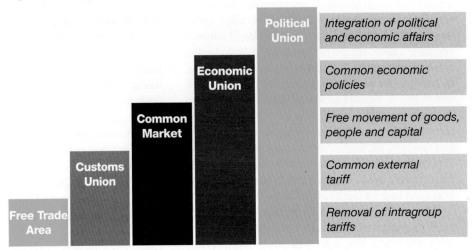

OVERCOMING DIVISIONS

Origins[1]

LEARNING OBJECTIVE

1 Explain the origins
   and the evolution of
   the EU

The idea of political and economic integration across Europe has a long tradition. In the inter-war period, politicians like Aristide Briand in France and Gustav Stresemann in Germany promoted ideas for a Europe without borders, but they were ahead of their time. The rise of nationalism in the wake of the economic depression of 1929 set a premature end to their visions. They failed to convince the people across the continent, and their failure proved costly. The rise of nationalism, especially the Nazi party in Germany, deepened divisions and eventually led to the disaster of World War II.

After World War II, several initiatives promoted the idea of European integration. Civil movements across Europe promoted ideas of working together, and overcoming the historical divisions. Political initiatives led to the creation of the Council of Europe (not to be confused with the Council of the EU!) by initially ten Western European nations in 1949 (Table 8.1), which aimed to promote greater unity amongst its member states. Nation states maintained their sovereignty, but entered commitments to improve citizens lives and prevent future wars through conventions and policy declarations. The Council of Europe's most famous achievement is the European Convention on Human Rights, which was adopted in 1950, and created the European Court of Human Rights in Strasbourg – an institution that to this day protects the rights of European people and operates independently of the EU.

Council of Europe
A loose association in which essentially all European countries are members.
European Convention on Human Rights
A charter defining human rights in Europe.
European Court of Human Rights
An international court assessing human rights cases in Europe.

The formation of the EU was set in motion in May 1950 by the 'Schuman Plan' in which French Foreign Minister Robert Schuman proposed the creation of a common market for coal, steel and related products. These industries were the backbones of European economies during the time of industrialization and post-war reconstruction because they provided critical inputs to leading industries such as railways, automotive, shipbuilding and machine engineering. At the same time, coal and steel were of significant military importance, thus supra-national coordination was expected not only to advance economic recovery but also to constrain re-militarization of these industries. The Schuman Plan led to the Treaty of Paris in 1951 and creation of the European Coal and Steel Community (ECSC).

Table 8.1 European integration processes

Event	Date[a]	Main objectives	Comments
Treaty of London	September 1949	Creation of the Council of Europe	Independent of the EU
European Convention on Human Rights	November 1950	Codifying individual human rights; creation of European Court of Human Rights	Ratified and in force 1953
Treaty of Paris	April 1951	European Coal and Steel Community (ECSC)	In force 1952, now defunct
Treaties of Rome	March 1957	Creation of the European Economic Community (EEC) and Euroatom	In effect from January 1958, with a completion target date set to December 1969
First direct election to the European Parliament	June 1979	Monitoring of EU bureaucracy and its budget; co-decisions regarding European legislation	Elected every fifth year directly by the citizens of the Union
Schengen Treaty	June 1985	Abolition of border controls.	Implemented 1995, see also Figure 8.1
Single European Act	February 1986	Creation of the European single market	Single market effective January 1, 1993
Maastricht Treaty	February 1992	Creation of the monetary union, extension of political cooperation, EEC becomes European Union (EU)	In force 1993; see also Figure 8.2
Copenhagen Criteria	June 1993	Conditions that new members have to fulfil to join the union	
Amsterdam Treaty	October 1997	Further streamlining of decision-making processes; tidying up gaps in Maastricht treaty	In force 1999
Bologna Declaration	June 1999	Creation of a single European higher educational area	An agreement outside the EU initiating the Bologna Process (see In Focus 8.3)
Nice Treaty	February 2001	Further streamlining of decision-making processes; realignment of voting power	In force 2003
Constitution	October 2004	Integrating the treaties; creating new structures and policy areas	Never ratified
Lisbon Treaty	December 2007	Integration of agreements; simplification of institutions	In force December 2009
European Stability Mechanism	December 2011	Organization providing support for countries in financial difficulties	September 2012

Note: [a]Date when the agreement was signed.

Sources: Based on (1) D. Dinan 2014, *Europe Recast: A History of European Union, 2nd ed.* Palgrave-Macmillan; (2) European Commission, no date, eur-lex.europa.eu/collection/eu-law/treaties-overview.html (accessed December 2014); (3) G. Suder 2008, *Business in Europe*, Los Angeles: Sage.

Coal and steel, however, were not enough. Initiatives for more comprehensive political and economic integration led to the Treaties of Rome in 1957 creating the European Economic Community (EEC) and the European Atomic Energy Community (Euratom). These institutions later developed into the EU, such that the signing of the Treaties of Rome on March 25, 1957 is generally considered as the founding date of the EU. With the memory of the two world wars still fresh, there has been a strong desire to create institutions that would prevent future wars between the nations of Europe. These political objectives became an important motivation for the economic integration. Economic objectives thus became the focus of the EEC Treaty, as stated in its Article 2:

'It shall be the aim of the Community, by establishing a Common Market and progressively approximating the economic policies of Member States, to promote throughout the Community a harmonious development of economic activities, a continuous and balanced expansion, an increased stability, an accelerated raising of the standard of living and closer relations between its Member States.'[2]

The Treaties of Rome established an action programme that guided European governments over the next decades. Initially, the focus was on establishing a customs union with a common external tariff, and common policies for agriculture, transport, trade and the support of developing countries. Early achievements included a common price level for agricultural products, and reduction of external tariffs. By 1968, all internal tariffs were abolished, though it took much longer to remove non-tariff barriers.

A growing union

Over the next half century, the union grew and deepened integration. With increasing membership, more people joined the union, the internal market grew in size, and the union gained political weight in world politics. As early as 1960, the UK, Ireland, Norway and Denmark applied for membership. Yet their entries were delayed by French objections until 1973 (Table 8.2). Norwegian voters, however, rejected membership in a referendum in 1972 (and again in 1994), mainly because they wished to retain control over their national fishing grounds. In the 1980s, Spain, Portugal and Greece joined after replacing their totalitarian governments with democracies. In 1990, former East Germany joined the EU by joining the Federal Republic of Germany (West Germany). Finland, Sweden and Austria joined in 1995.

The process of accepting new members was formalized in 1993 with the establishment of the Copenhagen Criteria. These criteria require that new members have a stable democracy and a fully-functioning market economy. Moreover, they must demonstrate a good human rights record on, the ability to cope with the competitive pressures of the common markets, and the ability to take on obligations of membership, also known as *acquis communautaire*.[3] These rules have been the basis for admitting new members in Central and Eastern Europe (CEE).

During the Cold War, CEE developed a system of central planning under the guidance (and military pressure) of the Soviet Union. International trade within CEE took place in the context of the Comecon, an economic integration scheme that, like the national economies, was grounded on the principles of central planning. Transactions between East and West normally took the form of counter-trade negotiated with state-trade monopolies. After the fall of the Berlin wall, the countries of CEE faced the dual challenge of economic transition. They not only had to build entirely different economic system (In Focus 8.1), but also had to re-integrate themselves into the European and global economy.

Treaties of Rome
The first treaties establishing European integration, which eventually led to the EU.

Copenhagen Criteria
Criteria the new members have to fulfil to be admitted as members of the EU.
Central and Eastern Europe (CEE)
The common name used for the countries east of the former Iron Curtain.
Comecon
The pre-1990 trading bloc of the socialist countries.
economic transition
The process of changing from central plan to a market economy.

Table 8.2 Countries of the Union

Country	Member of EEC/EU since	Member of Schengen area since	Member of Eurozone since[b]
Belgium	1958	1995	2002
France	1958	1995	2002
Germany	1958	1995	2002
Luxembourg	1958	1995	2002
Netherlands	1958	1995	2002
Italy	1958	1997	2002
Denmark	1973	2001	Opt out
Ireland	1973	Partial 2002[a]	2002
United Kingdom	1973	Partial 2000[a]	Opt out
Greece	1981	2000	2002
Portugal	1986	1995	2002
Spain	1986	1995	2002
Austria	1995	1997	2002
Finland	1995	2001	2002
Sweden	1995	2001	Not implemented
Cyprus	2004	Not yet implemented	2008
Czech Republic	2004	2007	Not implemented
Estonia	2004	2007	2011
Hungary	2004	2007	Not implemented
Latvia	2004	2007	2014
Lithuania	2004	2007	2015
Malta	2004	2007	2008
Poland	2004	2007	Not implemented
Slovakia	2004	2007	2009
Slovenia	2004	2007	2007
Bulgaria	2007	Not yet implemented	Not implemented
Romania	2007	Not yet implemented	Not implemented
Croatia	2013	2015	Not implemented
Iceland	EEA only[c]	2001	Not member
Norway	EEA only	2001	Not member
Switzerland	Not member	2008	Not member
Lichtenstein	EEA only	2009	Not member

Country	Member of EEC/EU since	Member of Schengen area since	Member of Eurozone since[b]
FYR Macedonia	Candidate	Not member	Not member
Serbia	Candidate	Not member	Not member
Turkey	Candidate	Not member	Not member

Notes: [a]Ireland and the UK implemented police and judicial cooperation rules only, and are not committed to removing border controls.
[b]Year from when euro notes officially became sole currency; the euro has also been adopted in Montenegro, Kosovo, Andorra, Monaco, San Marino and the Vatican.
[c]EEA = European Economic Area, an extension of the single market to non-members.

Sources: (1) D. Dinan, 2014, *Europe Recast: A History of European Union, 2nd ed.* Palgrave-Macmillan; (2) *European Commission*, various years, Eur-lex, (eur-lex.europa.eu/, accessed December 2014).

IN FOCUS 8.1

Rebuilding institutions in Central and Eastern Europe

From the 1950s to the 1980s, countries of CEE were governed by Communist governments grounded in an ideology focused on collective values and the working class. The economies were coordinated by central plans that left little scope for individual initiative. This central plan determined which factory would produce what, with which inputs, and deliver to whom. The plan focused on quantitative output targets, with few incentives for quality and customer service. Thus firms were not responsive to consumer demand, nor would they be free to choose their suppliers. This created huge inefficiencies and no incentives to innovate. Technologically, business in CEE fell far behind the West. The lack of adequate hotels in places like Łodz (see Opening Case) is typical of CEE during that time.

In 1990, the economic system of central planning collapsed. The nations of CEE thus entered a painful process of economic transition to replace their defunct economic systems with a market economy. Initial reform programmes followed three primary aims: liberalization, stabilization and privatization. Liberalization should enable individuals and businesses to take their own decisions and initiatives, and thus set free entrepreneurial spirits. Stabilization had to combat macroeconomic imbalances, notably external debt and hidden inflation that emerged when price controls were removed. Privatization was to transfer ownership from the state to private shareholders, and thus give private owners appropriate incentives to make the best of the firms.

However, these reforms did not kick-start an economic miracle. Several economies quite literally collapsed, with GDP dropping at an unprecedented rate. In Russia, the output dropped for seven years, by which time the level of GDP had fallen by 47% from its 1990 level. Central European economies turned their economies around more quickly. Even so, Hungary, Poland and the Czech Republic experienced two to three years of recession and lost 15% to 18% of their GDP. How could this happen?

The reforms were slow to implement a fourth aspect of transition, the creation of institutions that secure the effective functioning of a market economy. You may find this surprising because you have read Chapters 2 and 3, and know about the importance of formal and informal institutions. Yet new institutions cannot be created overnight. The formal structures of the old system disintegrated before new institutions supporting a market economy were in place. Hence businesses in CEE started life in a market economy where market failure was pervasive. They lacked, for example, legal institutions to enforce contracts and information systems to provide market data. Moreover, rules that did exist were often unstable, and at times inconsistent, and hence could not support long-term decisions.

Businesses thus had to act on markets that did not yet exist; and they lacked the (often tacit) knowledge on how to use the market mechanism. At the same time, the informal institutions of the old system, such as norms and values formed during the socialist period, were still in peoples' minds, and businesses often fell back on informal networks that had helped in overcoming shortages in the old regime.

However, during the period of radical change in the early 1990s, new institutions were created, often under the influence of the EU accession process. They provided new foundations for business and continue to shape the institutional framework in each transition economy.

Sources: (1) World Bank 1996, *World Development Report 1996: From Plan To Market*, New York: Oxford University Press; (2) Lavigne, 1999, *The Economics of Transition*, London: Macmillan (Chapters 7 & 8); (3) K.E. Meyer 2001, Transition Economies, in: T. Brewer & A. Rugman, eds: *Oxford Handbook of International Business*, Oxford: Oxford University Press, pp. 715–759; (4) S. Estrin, 2002, Competition and corporate governance in transition, *JPE*, 36: 1947–1982; (5) D. Gros & A. Steinherr, 2004, *Economic Transition in Central and Eastern Europe*, Cambridge: Cambridge University Press; (6) K.E. Meyer & M.W. Peng, 2005, Probing theoretically into Central and Eastern Europe, *JIBS*, 36: 600–621.

The transition economies opened up to international trade and FDI early in the transition process. Within a few years, trade pattern realigned, FDI surged and the structure of industry adapted to new pan-European patterns of international business.[4] Western businesses started flooding in well ahead of EU membership; for example, Marcus' software firm established its Polish office in Łodz in 2001 (Opening Case).

The external opening was in part motivated by the aspiration to join the EU. Each country went through several stages of agreements with the EU, political reforms, and changes in the legal framework. The EU provided a mix of financial support and pressures for regulatory reform, notably a push to adopt aspects of the EU regulatory frame as spelled out in the Copenhagen Criteria. However, in 2004, the first wave of CEE countries joined the EU (see Table 8.2), followed by Bulgaria and Romania in 2007, and Croatia in 2013. Five countries soon also joined the common currency: Slovenia (2007), Slovakia (2009), Estonia (2011), Latvia (2014), and Lithuania (2015).

Continuous deepening

After a trip to Europe in 1986, the American humourist PJ O'Rourke told his compatriots about his experiences 'among the Euro-Weenies'. He joked about 'dopey little countries', 'pokey borders', 'itty-bitty' languages and 'Lilliputian' drink measures. Most poignantly, he claimed 'you can't swing a cat without sending it through customs'.[5] How arrogant! Yes, but there was a grain of truth in this. However, by the time of his visit, Europeans were well on their way to overcoming their historical divisions and fragmented markets.

How was this integration achieved? The key stepping-stones were a succession of treaties and agreements between the member states, often known by the cities where crucial meetings took place, notably Maastricht, Amsterdam and Lisbon (Table 8.1). In the 1970s and early 1980s, European economies were struggling with their competitiveness, being held back by rigid institutional frameworks and small, fragmented markets. Policy initiatives, notably the Single European Act (SEA) adopted in 1986, aimed to reinvigorate the European integration process along with economic liberalization. This act reformed the institutions and prepared for the single market to come into effect on January 1, 1993. Crucially, it introduced weighted majority decision-making in selected policy areas to facilitate reaching agreements; before 1986 national vetoes had frequently inhibited change. In preparation for the single market, the EU adopted nearly 280 separate items of legislation in the period 1986 to 1992.[6] This legislation opened hitherto closed national markets, and reduced the complexity and costs for businesses selling their goods and services in other countries of the union.

Single European Act (SEA)
The agreement that established the basis for the single European market.
single market
The EU's term of its common market.

Maastricht Treaty
A major treaty deepening
integration in Europe.

The next big step was the Maastricht Treaty of 1993, which both deepened and broadened the scope of the union. In particular, it set the foundations for common foreign and security policy, and for cooperation in police and judicial matters. In the economic sphere, it established the timeline and the criteria of the establishment of the monetary union, and thus the introduction of the euro as a common currency. Since the Maastricht Treaty, the organization has been known as the European Union (EU).

The treaties of Amsterdam (1999) and Nice (2003) revised the procedures of decision-making to reduce the power of national vetoes and increasing the power of parliament. Moreover, they created further areas of policy coordination, such as on asylum seekers and law enforcement. However, the legal basis of the EU continued to be based on an amalgam of treaties rather than a coherent set of rules. This abnormality was supposed to be addressed by the European Constitution, which had been prepared in 2002/3 by the European Convention, which was comprised of representatives of national parliaments, national governments, the European Parliament and the European Commission. It aimed to facilitate decision-making in the union, create new and simpler institutional structures, and to integrate fundamental human rights in the EU's legal foundations.[7] However, voters in both France and the Netherlands voted against this, partly because they were concerned about further losses of national sovereignty, and partly because they wished to penalize their national politicians promoting the constitution. After the European Constitution went nowhere, the Lisbon Treaty signed in 2007 was designed to substitute it, but with somewhat less ambitious reforms.[8] This series of treaties thus advanced European integration and the shared institutions of the EU, while opening for new members.

European Constitution
An ambitious project to create a new legal foundation for the EU, which failed.

THE EU AS INSTITUTIONAL FRAMEWORK FOR BUSINESS

The institutional framework of the EU sets many of the rules by which businesses compete. New members and associated countries have adopted parts of this framework, often ahead of membership. These institutions have succeeded in removing most internal trade barriers. For example, it used to take Spanish lorry drivers 24 hours to cross the border into France due to numerous paperwork requirements and checks. Since 1992, customs controls have been disbanded, and since 1996 even passport controls have been abolished. Border checkpoints between the two countries are no longer manned, as people no longer need to show their passport. Now Spanish lorry drivers can move from Barcelona to Paris – and on as far as the Arctic Circle – just like they would travel from Barcelona to Granada.

LEARNING OBJECTIVE
2 Explain how and why the institutional framework created by the EU is pivotal for business

The rules set by the EU thus have direct relevance to businesses. They continue to evolve in inter-governmental agreements and decisions by bodies such as the Council and the Parliament. We here explore five aspects of this institutional framework that are particularly relevant to international businesses in Europe: the free movement of goods, services, capital and people, as well as European competition policy. The 'four freedoms', namely the freedom of movement goods, services, capital and people, are the cornerstones of the single market that came into effect in 1993.[9] Everyone in the union can benefit from these four freedoms: as an individual citizen you have the right to live, work, study or retire in another EU country. As a consumer, you benefit from lower prices and a wider choice of things to buy, which are the results of increased competition and scale economies. As a business, you can obtain easier and cheaper access to markets and suppliers in other countries of the union.

four freedoms of the EU single market
Freedom of movement of people, goods, services and capital.

Such a single market can however not be created by a simple stroke of a pen. Every country used to have its own formal and informal institutions, often grounded in centuries of national history. Aligning these national rules and eliminating frictions between them has been a complex process.

Free movement of goods

The first principle of the single market is that the free movement of goods may only be restricted in special cases, for instance when there are risks related to public health, environment or consumer protection. On the other hand, sectors that are not subject to such concerns are generally not subject to EU legislation. They are regulated by the principle of 'mutual recognition', introduced by the SEA in 1986. This implies that products that meet the necessary laws and technical standards in any one country may also be sold throughout the EU. About half of intra-EU trade falls under these rules.[10]

mutual recognition
The principle that products recognized as legal in one country may be sold throughout the EU.

When is a common regulation better, and when should national laws plus 'mutual recognition' prevail? The Maastricht Treaty introduced the subsidiarity principle, which establishes a priority for decentralization. Thus the EU is supposed to take action only if it is more effective than actions taken at national, regional or local level (in addition to areas which are defined as the EU exclusive competence). This principle was to prioritize the rights of national and local governments, though it does give the EU more power in areas where national differences may inhibit free trade.

subsidiarity
The EU takes action only if it is more effective than actions taken at lower levels.

In sectors where the EU sees higher risks for customers, national regulations in each country have been replaced by common European rules, such as the 'directive on the eco-design of energy-using products' (Closing Case). In this harmonized sector, the EU aims to harmonize technical regulations to increase transparency, minimize risks and ensure legal certainty. Thus the regulation of pharmaceuticals, for example, is based on a two-tier structure: (1) a centralized procedure across all member states for drug authorization for specified groups of medications governed by the European Agency for the Evaluation of Medicinal Products (EMEA) (see also Integrative Case *Novo Nordisk*); (2) a decentralized procedure applying for the majority of conventional medicinal products governed by national authorities, but providing EU-wide marketing authorization. The harmonization often implies higher costs, for example in the food industry, where harmonization raised safety standards, and thus increased compliance costs for companies. Smaller firms complain that these costs often affect them more because the initial investment in procedures and documentation are similar for all firms.[11]

harmonized sector
Sectors of industry for which the EU has created common rules.

Creating such harmonized rules is often challenging. For example, in 2008, the EU discussed a new directive to regulate the use of pesticides in agriculture, which affected consumers of foods anywhere in the single market. The harmonization has however been controversial. Some national politicians felt it would infringe their sovereignty and would unduly restrict the industry and raise costs. Others accused the EU of failing to protect consumers from the dangers of chemical pollution.[12] Thus scientists, farmers, the food industry and consumer organizations joined the debate. Many commentators came with a long wish list, often ignoring the fact that political decisions such as these require sensitive trade-offs. It is a tough job to be a European lawmaker – be it in the Commission or in the Parliament (see Closing Case).

Free movement of services

The single market for services has been even more difficult to implement, for two reasons.[13] First, many service sectors have very complex regulatory regimes, for example banking or telecommunications. Second, most services need some form of local delivery, because you cannot pack them up and send them by mail or freight like a chocolate bar, a pair of shoes or even a car. Self-employed people may in principle move between member states to provide services on a temporary or permanent basis. Yet to offer your services, you need to be sure that your professional qualifications will be recognized. Service providers thus are subject to both home country and host country regulations. The horizontal services directive of 2006 aimed to eliminate obstacles to trade in services, yet its implementation was complex due to the interdependence with domestic regulatory reform. It had profound implications even for businesses operating only nationally because it triggered major legal changes in national law. In Germany, for example, EU service sector liberalization forced radical liberalization of traditional regulation in several sectors, from the opening of electricity and telecommunications industry to fundamental reform of the crafts sector.[14]

Even with this harmonization, the single market for services is not really a single market, *yet*. Residual barriers increase costs and lower quality of services provided in other countries. Smaller businesses especially complain about administrative and legal requirements. Several studies suggest that despite some progress, the overly restrictive national regulation still not only inhibits free trade in services, it makes many national service sectors less effective than they could be.[15]

Free movement of capital

Another sensitive area is the free movement of capital. In principle, EU citizens should be able to conduct their financial transactions in any EU country, including opening bank accounts, buying shares in companies and purchasing real estate. However, this principle requires mutual liberalization of capital markets, and – especially in the wake of financial market crash of 2008 – coordination of financial market regulation and supervision.[16] Some of the rules affecting these types of transactions, however, remain governed by national regulators, and may thus vary between countries. For example, Icelandic bank *Landisbanken* operated in the UK through an internet bank, attracting savers by promising higher interest rates. Yet when it went bankrupt in 2008, a major row broke out between the British and Icelandic governments over who should pay for reimbursing those who had deposited large funds with the bank.[17]

If EU-wide harmonization is making life so much easier for businesses and consumers, why don't we see enthusiastic support for it across Europe? First, European laws are usually a compromise between national legislators who each prefer principles in use in their own country. Political compromises between such positions often add to the complexity of the legislation. Second, any new legislation affects different countries and interest groups differently, and thus triggers political action from those facing major adjustments. Thus with benefits widely shared and costs falling of specific groups, building and retaining political support for such reforms is challenging.

Free moving people

The Single European Act of 1986 established the right of individuals to move freely in the EU to live, work, study or retire. Initially focused on opening European labour markets, this right has over the years been extended to cover all citizens, thus fulfilling a dream of the founders in the 1950s.[18] However, many obstacles and uncertainties still prevent people from relocating across Europe.

Are you thinking of moving to another country? Then a major concern may be the recognition of your professional qualification – for example your university degree. Traditionally, many countries would only recognize qualifications obtained under their own jurisdiction. The EU has thus introduced rules to guarantee mutual recognition of qualifications. These rules include:[19]

- the harmonization of training requirements which allow for automatic recognition of selected professional qualifications, in particular in the health sector and for architects
- the mutual recognition of all the other professions that require a qualification
- the automatic recognition of professional experience for professions of craft, commerce and industry sectors.

The EU has also instigated a number of programmes that actively encourage mobility of people across borders, now collectively known as Erasmus+ Programme. Since 1987, Erasmus has helped over 2 million students spend part of their studies in another European country by providing scholarships, regulating credit transfer and supporting networking between universities. Similarly, the Grundvig programme supports individuals in adult education, while vocational training is supported by the Leonardo da Vinci scheme. Marie Curie scholarships help with conducting research in other countries, while Jean Monnet scholars receive support for teaching and researching Europe-related themes.[20] In parallel, EU countries participate in the Bologna Process, which aims to advance higher education across Europe (see In Focus 8.2).

Erasmus+ Programme
An EU programme encouraging student mobility in Europe.

Bologna Process
A political process aimed at harmonizing European higher education.

IN FOCUS 8.2

Mobile students: the Bologna Process

For students, an important aspect of the free movement of people is the so-called Bologna Process. It was initiated in 1999 with the Bologna Declaration, by Ministers of Education from 29 European countries at the University of Bologna, Italy. By 2015, 47 countries in Europe and Central Asia had joined the process, involving 5600 higher education institutions and 31 million students. It has profound implications for how university education is organized in Europe and beyond. The main aim is to facilitate the mobility of students and professionals within Europe by making the standards of academic degrees more comparable and compatible throughout Europe. The enhanced mobility was expected to strengthen Europe's knowledge base, and to ensure the further development of cutting-edge research in Europe. Moreover, the Bologna process is hoped to attract more students from outside Europe and to facilitate the convergence of university systems in Europe and the USA.

The Bologna Process is not an EU initiative and does not have the status of EU legislation, though EU institutions help with its implementation. The Bologna agreement is a separate arrangement involving both EU members and non-members. Moreover, it is not a treaty or convention, and thus it does not create legal obligations for the signatory states; the extent of participation is entirely voluntary. However, it has created a dynamic political process that led to monitored coordination among participating nations.

A cornerstone of the Bologna Process is a common course structure based on ECTS credits and a degree structure with Bachelor, Masters and PhD degrees. This common structure helps exchange students to fit a semester or year abroad into their degree programme, and it makes it easier to move to a university in another country. The basic structure is an academic year of 60 ECTS credits that are equivalent to 1500–1800 hours of study. A Bachelor degree typically requires 180–240 ECTS credits (three to four years of study). A Masters degree builds on a completed Bachelor degree and encompasses typically 90–120 ECTS credits (18 to 24 months). A doctoral degree builds on a Masters degree, and is expect to take another three years. Beyond the basic guidelines,

226   PART THREE GLOBALIZATION

How and why does the Bologna process help students study abroad?

however, individual countries have considerable freedom to design their educational programs.

Some countries, like Denmark, had already adopted the 3 + 2 + 3 structure in the 1970s, and thus faced few adjustments. In Germany and some Eastern European countries, the 3 + 2 + 3 structure and the focus on examinations for each course, rather than comprehensively at the end of the studies, represented a radical break, and many professors struggled to adjust their teaching to the new system. Yet the implementation was largely voluntary and thus

often partial. Notably, the UK has adopted only a few aspects of this framework, and most British universities continue to offer three-year Bachelor degrees and one-year Master degrees.

Sources: (1) B. Wächter, 2004, The Bologna Process: Developments and prospects, *EJE*, 39: 265–273; (2) C. Tauch, 2004, Almost half-time in the Bologna Process: Where do we stand? *EJE* 39: 275–288; (3) I. Bache, 2006, The Europeanization of higher education: Markets, politics or learning? *JCMS*, 44: 231– 248; (4) C. Sin, 2012, Academic understandings and responses to Bologna, *EJE*, 47: 392–404.

Schengen Agreement
The agreement that laid the basis for passport-free travel.

Schengen area
The area covered by the Schengen agreement.

The most visible aspect of the freedom of movement of people has been the abolition of border controls. Until 1995, travellers still had to show their passports each time they crossed a border within the EU (except between the Benelux countries). The basis for the removal of border controls has been the Schengen Agreement, originally a separate agreement signed by five countries in the town of Schengen in Luxembourg in 1985.

The abolition of passport controls, desirable as it is for travellers, does however require a closer coordination in a number of other areas. For example, how to make sure criminals don't just disappear across the border. Hence the police and judicial systems had to cooperate more closely, and the external borders of the so-called Schengen area needed to be managed more tightly. Consequently, the Schengen Agreement coordinates procedures and policies regarding a number of judicial matters, such as entry into and short stays by non-EU citizens, police cooperation, political asylum seekers, and combatting cross-border drugs-related crime.[21]

The implementation of these rules took ten years from the signing of the agreement to the actual removal of border controls on March 26, 1995. All members of the EU have since joined the agreement, though some have yet to implement it (see Figure 8.2.).

Figure 8.2 The Schengen Area

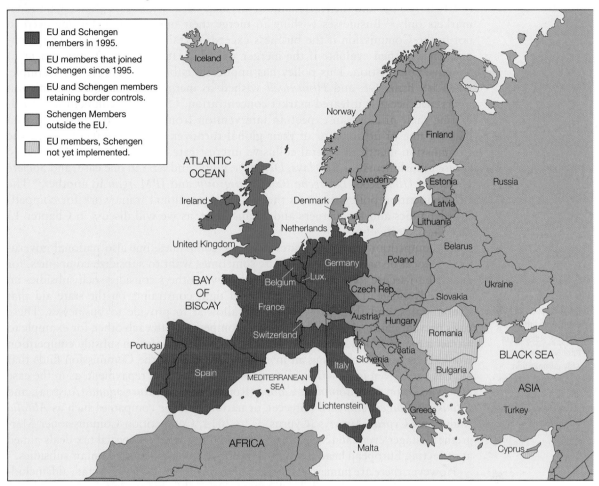

It was absorbed into the legal framework of the EU with the Amsterdam Treaty in 1999. However, the UK and Ireland only adopted the police and judicial cooperation; they continue passport controls at their intra-EU borders. The Schengen Area of free travel also extends beyond the EU to Iceland, Lichtenstein, Norway and Switzerland.

The Schengen arrangement also benefits visitors from other parts of the world. Holders of many passports can obtain a 'Schengen visa', which permits stay in the Schengen area and travel between Schengen states as long as the conditions for entry are still fulfilled.[22] The visa can be obtained at the embassies of any Schengen country. Yet this simplification comes at the expense of a more complex application process.

Schengen visa
Visa giving non-citizens access to the Schengen area.

EU competition policy

Markets are probably the best way to ensure the efficient allocation of goods and services, and to create incentives for businesses to constantly improve their offerings. However, these functions of the market only work well if everyone plays by the rules, and no one attains so much power as to control the market. An important aspect of the institutional framework thus is competition policy (Chapter 2). Competition regulators aim to ensure that competition is not distorted by dominant players, or by illegal collusion.

The European Commission acts as a regulatory authority to secure fair competition within the union. Cases affecting multiple EU countries are handled by the

Commission itself, while national authorities such as the Office for Fair Trading (OFT) in the UK and the Kartellamt in Germany deal with cases affecting national markets only.[23] Businesses wishing to merge their operations in Europe need to notify the Commission if the business exceeds certain size thresholds. The Commission will then evaluate if the merger would create substantial impediment to effective competition. This policy has implications beyond Europe. For example, when US firms *GE* and *Honeywell* wished to merge in 2001, the Commission intervened because it feared market concentration.[24] Similarly, competitors coordinating their pricing can expect an intervention from the EU that may lead to a massive fine of up to 10% of their global turnover.[25] For example, in 2013 the Commission identified several collusive interest rate manipulations, which led to severe punishments for *Barclays, Deutsche Bank*, and *RBS* in one case, and *Société Générale, UBS, RBS, Deutsche Bank, Citigroup* and *JPMorgan* in another.[26] The EU competition policy thus sets the formal institutional framework for competitive dynamics and for mergers and acquisitions, as we will discuss in Chapter 13 and 14, respectively.

EU competition policy regulates not only companies, but also national governments. Local or national governments sometimes want to subsidize companies, for example to secure jobs in a local area. However, others consider such subsidies an unfair advantage. Thus the EU has placed tight constraints on the state aid that nation states, and their sub-entities, are allowed to provide to businesses. These rules prevent national or local authorities competing with each other, for example to attract a major production plant. The main beneficiary of such subsidy competition would be the MNE choosing an investment location. If the Commission finds that aid has been given in violation of its rules, it may demand repayment, as in the case of privatization of *Automobile Caiova* (Romania), *Bank Burgenland* (Austria), and *Ellinika Nafpigeia* shipyard (Greece), or national airline companies such as *Alitalia* (Italy) and *Cyprus Airways* (Cyprus).[27] In 2014, Competition Commissioner Margrethe Vestager even launched an investigation into whether special tax deals aimed at attracting European headquarters of multinationals constituted unfair subsidies.[28]

However, there are numerous exemptions from the prohibition of state aid, including support for research and development, renewable energy and energy efficiency, broadband networks, and the development of designated disadvantaged regions. The financial crisis of 2008/9 tested the EU's anti-subsidy commitment, as many national governments bailed out firms experiencing a liquidity crisis, especially in the banking sector. The EU approved aid and broader schemes to support the financial sector, but it is expected that such support would not be approved under normal circumstances.

THE EURO AS A COMMON CURRENCY

Introduction of the euro[29]

One of the EU's proudest accomplishments has been the introduction of a common currency, the euro (€). The economies using the euro, known as the eurozone, account for about one fifth of world GDP. The euro was introduced in two phases. In 1999, the euro became 'virtual money' in 11 countries, used only for financial transactions, but not in circulation (Figure 8.3). Exchange rates with national currencies were fixed at that point. In 2002, the euro was introduced as banknotes and coins. To meet the cash needs of over 300 million people, the EU printed 14.25 billion banknotes and minted 56 billion coins – with a total value of €660 billion. The new banknotes would cover the distance between the earth and the moon five times![30] Overall, the introduction of the euro was an amazing logistical achievement.

state aid
Financial support from government to firms through e.g. subsidies or tax rebates.

subsidy competition
The competition between governments trying to attract investors by offering subsidies.

LEARNING OBJECTIVE

3   Discuss the merits and drawbacks of the euro as a common currency

eurozone
The countries that have adopted the euro as their currency.

Figure 8.3 The eurozone

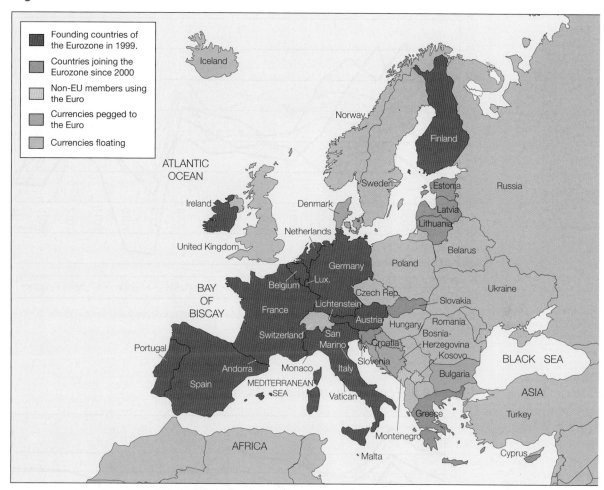

In the Maastricht Treaty of 1992, member states had legally committed themselves to introduce a monetary union no later than January 1, 1999. The treaty established criteria, known as Maastricht Criteria, that countries had to fulfil to be accepted into the monetary union: countries were required to have annual budget deficits not exceeding 3% of GDP, public debt under 60% of the GDP, inflation rates within 1.5% of the three lowest rates in the EU, long-term interest rates within 2% of the three EU countries with the lowest rate, and exchange rate stability. The euro went ahead on time, with 11 member countries in 1999, even though several countries failed the convergence criteria: inflation rates had not converged as much as expected (Figure 8.4); some budget deficits were below the limit only in the benchmark year (Figure 8.5); and Belgium, Greece and Italy exceeded the debt criterion (Figure 8.6, Maastricht criterion indicated by a red arrow). With the introduction of the new currency, the European Central Bank (ECB), based in Frankfurt, took over responsibility for monetary policy from the national central banks.

Euro notes and coins were introduced on January 1, 2002 and replaced the national currencies in initially 12 countries (11 founders, plus Greece, who was admitted in 2010). Since then, the eurozone has grown to 18 members. Outside the EU, the euro is used in a handful of countries and territories without formal agreement with the ECB, for instance in Montenegro.

Maastricht Criteria
Criteria that countries have to fulfil to join the eurozone.

European Central Bank (ECB)
The central bank for the eurozone.

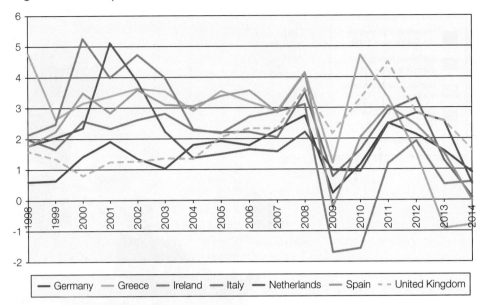

Figure 8.4 European inflation rates in %

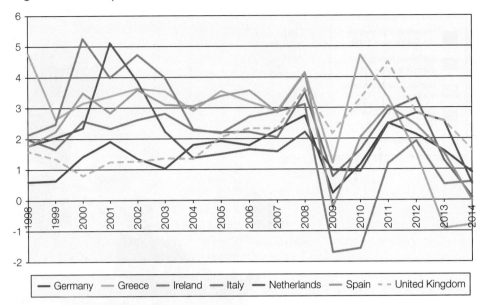

Source: Authors' creation using data extracted from IMF: World Economic Outlook database, version October 2014.

Figure 8.5 European budget deficits, as % of GDP

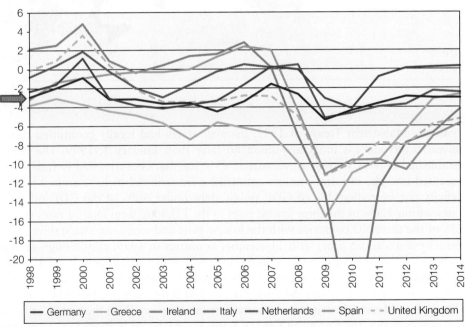

Note: Ireland's budget deficit was 29.3% in 2010.

Source: Authors' creation using data extracted from IMF: World Economic Outlook database, version October 2014.

Figure 8.6 European government debt, as % of GDP

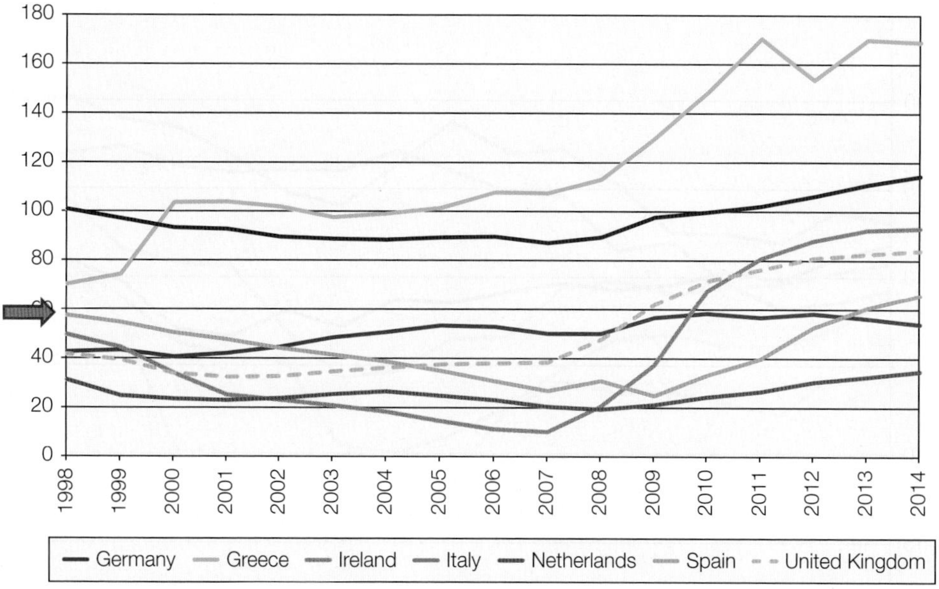

Source: Authors' creation using data extracted from IMF: World Economic Outlook database, version October 2014.

Costs and benefits of the euro

Adopting the euro has four major benefits. First, it reduces currency conversion costs. Travellers no longer need to pay processing fees to convert currencies for tourist activities or hedging purposes (see Chapter 7). Second, direct and transparent price comparisons are now possible, thus channelling more resources towards more competitive firms. Third, the elimination of exchange rate risk means that businesses face less risk when contracting or investing in other countries; likewise tourists can better plan the costs of their holiday.

Fourth, adopting the euro was supposed to impose macroeconomic discipline on participating governments. Prior to adopting the euro, different governments independently determined exchange rates. Italy, for example, sharply devalued its lira in 1992 and in 1995. Although Italian exports became cheaper and more competitive overseas, other EU members, especially France, were furious.[31] Also, when confronting recession, governments often printed more currency and increased spending. Such actions cause inflation, which may spill over into neighbouring countries. By adopting the euro, member countries agreed to abolish national monetary policy as a tool to solve macroeconomic problems. The economic stability thus boosted intra-EU trade by approximately 10% over the next decade, and supported economic growth, notably in Spain, Ireland and Greece (Figure 8.7 and 8.8). Moreover, the euro has become a global reserve currency as the only competitor to the US dollar, commanding 27% of global currency reserves (compared to 19% in 1999).[32]

However, there are also significant costs involved, some of which were underestimated in the 1990s. First, while giving up independent monetary policy reduces politicians' ability to create spurious inflation-fuelled short-term growth, it can be a severe disadvantage when business cycles or production costs develop differently within the eurozone. For example, over the 2000s, inflation and labour costs have been rising faster in Spain, Italy and Greece compared with Germany (Figure 8.4), which contributed to rising trade deficits in these countries, while Germany accumulated trade surpluses (Figure 8.7). The need to agree on a common monetary policy under such circumstances is challenging.[33]

Figure 8.7 European trade balances, as % of GDP

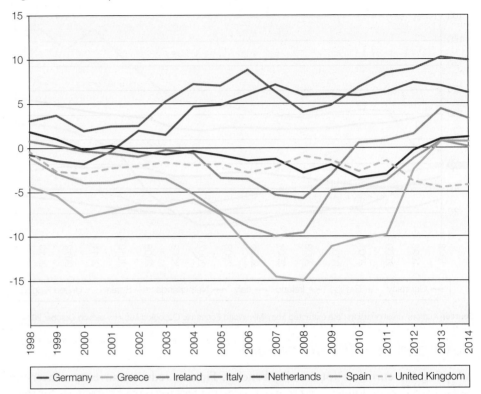

Source: Authors' creation using data extracted from IMF: World Economic Outlook database, version October 2014.

Figure 8.8 European real GDP (index 1998 = 100)

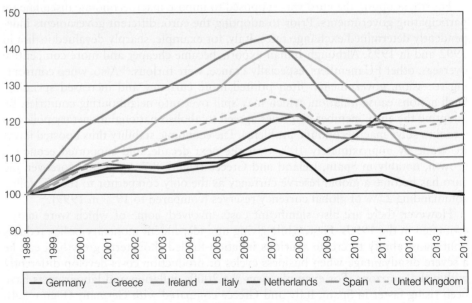

Source: Authors' creation using data extracted from IMF: World Economic Outlook database, version October 2014.

Second, the agreed limits on budget deficit reduce the flexibility in fiscal policy, in particular government spending financed through debt. When a country runs into fiscal difficulties it may be faced with inflation, high interest rates, and a loss of confidence in its currency. When countries share a common currency, the risks of high public debt are spread. If a country becomes a 'free rider' by not fixing their domestic fiscal problems, other more responsible countries may end up sharing the burden. To prevent such free riding, the eurozone countries entered a Stability and Growth Pact that committed them to stick to the Maastricht Criteria, notably for their budget deficit not to exceed 3% of GDP. However, the enforcement of this rule has been difficult, as fining a country already in fiscal difficulties is politically problematic. Hence the Commission has been warning countries exceeding this limit, including France and Germany, but has not been effective in enforcing the rule (Figure 8.5).

The challenge became even more daunting in 2008, as many people argued that the best policy to combat the global recession would be increased government spending.[34] In 2009, most eurozone countries exceeded the 3% limit, with most serious fiscal difficulties in Greece (15.6%). In 2010, Ireland even hit 29.3% due to the costs associated with the bank bailout (Figure 8.6). Subsequent to this crisis, it was difficult to re-enforce the 3% rule, as penalty threats lost credibility, which led to drawn-out political tensions between eurozone countries. In fact, the huge deficits in some countries endangered the stability of the euro itself, which led to the creation of the European Stability Mechanism (ESM) in December 2011, a fund that can support member countries who find it difficult to raise money on the capital markets.

> **European Stability Mechanism (ESM)**
> A fund to support member countries with difficulties raising money on the capital markets.

Third, at the outset, joining the euro was seen as a credible commitment to structural reforms that would make economies more competitive. For example, the then governor of the Bank of Greece (and late Prime Minister) Lucas Papademos stated, in 2001:

> 'After entry into the euro area, . . . it will certainly be impossible to improve the economy's international competitiveness by changing the exchange rate of our new currency, the euro. The objectives of higher employment and output growth will therefore have to be pursued through structural reforms and fiscal measures aimed at enhancing international competitiveness by increasing productivity, improving the quality of Greek goods and services and securing price stability.'[35]

However, in the early 2000s structural reforms were introduced in Germany and North European countries, substantially reforming labour markets.[36] Yet few structural reforms were implemented in Southern Europe, in part because the inflow of capital during early years of the euro created the illusion of strong competitiveness.[37] Later, the rules agreed to secure the stability of the euro have become a scapegoat for national politicians failing in their national economic policies. In other words, countries wanted stable and predictable monetary policies modelled on the German Bundesbank because of the benefits of lower inflation rates. Yet informal norms of wage bargaining and price setting were not adjusted, which led to higher inflation eroding competitiveness, notably in Greece and Spain. Likewise, failure to enforce tax collection or to implement market liberalization created unsustainable budget deficits (Figure 8.5) and led to the bailout packages that had to be underwritten by eurozone partners.

The eurozone as an optimum currency area

So, who should join the eurozone, and who should stay out? In this debate (Table 8.3), a key idea is the 'optimum currency area'.[38] Economies with closely-related business cycles are less likely to have different needs in monetary policy, and thus should

> **optimum currency area**
> A theory establishing criteria for the optimal size of an area sharing a common currency.

Table 8.3   Advantages and disadvantages of joining the euro

Advantages	Disadvantages
• Reduce currency conversion costs	• Unable to implement independent monetary policy
• Facilitate direct price comparisons	• Limits on fiscal policy, notably deficit spending
• Reduction of exchange rate risk	• *De facto* shared responsibility to support weaker member countries
• Impose monetary discipline	• National politicians blame eurozone instead of addressing their own failings

join a currency union. On the other hand, countries may be better off with separate currencies if they are affected by asymmetric shocks, such as oil price fluctuation or a financial sector crisis, or if they have very divergent economic policies that affect national competitiveness, for instance with respect to labour market flexibility or welfare spending. In fact, the eurozone was hit by an asymmetric shock that nobody expected: a financial crisis that induced national governments to bail out banks, and thus to assume extraordinary financial obligations. The national debt created from these bailouts caused severe strains on national economies, such as Ireland (Figure 8.6).

Even if the business cycles are not perfectly aligned, labour mobility may help easing tensions. For example, when California was particularly hard hit by the economic crisis in 2008/9, while Texas was doing comparatively well, people packed up their cars and moved east in search of new jobs.[39] Yet in Europe labour is less mobile, and labour markets are less flexible (see In Focus 8.3), and difference in unemployment therefore quite persistent (Figure 8.9). Thus some argue that the eurozone has reached its optimal size, or is already too large.

Figure 8.9   European unemployment rates in % of the workforce

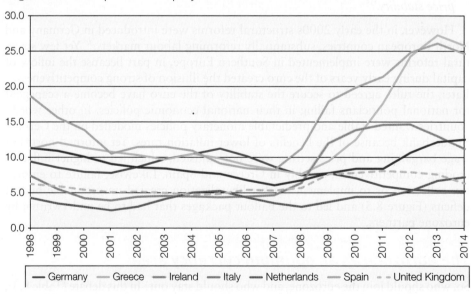

Source: Authors' creation using data extracted from IMF: World Economic Outlook database, version October 2014.

IN FOCUS 8.3

Boom and bust in the eurozone

The joys and pains of the eurozone become visible in the economic data of the member countries. You can go to the website of the IMF yourself (www.imf .org/external/pubs/ft/weo/2014/02/weodata/index .aspx) and download data from their World Economic Outlook Database. This database contains economic data for all major economies of the world; you can download them into Excel to create your own graphs for whichever country you are interested in. Newspapers often focus on changes in recent data, but you will gain a much better picture if you look at longer trends. Therefore, in this chapter we have chosen to present data from 1998 onwards, the year before the eurozone came into effect. Let us examine the experience of Spain on the basis of Figures 8.4 to 8.9; you can then analyze other countries yourself.

Spain joined the euro from the outset, and enjoyed a decade of very successful economic growth. GDP grew by an annual average of 3.7% over the decade to 2006, compared to 2.1% in the remainder of the eurozone (Figure 8.8), thus creating over five million new jobs. The euro contributed to this success story: it lowered Spain's costs of servicing the government debt, and confidence in the stability of the currency attracted foreign investment. This prosperity was strengthened by prudent fiscal policy, running budget surpluses when times were good (Figure 8.5), and a comparatively robust banking sector.

However, the prosperity had side effects. Private consumers and businesses took advantage of the combination of a solid currency and low interest rates to go on a spending spree. This led to a current account deficit of 10% in 2007 (Figure 8.7), and rapidly rising property prices. A major part of the economic growth happened in the housing market: the construction industry increased its share to 7.5% of GDP. When the economic crisis hit, credit flows dried up and the housing bubble burst. Construction projects were stopped, and unemployment surged. The tourism sector, which contributes 11% of employment in Spain, was particularly hit as foreign visitors spent less money, or remained home.

What options did the Spanish government have to tackle the crisis? Monetary policy had been transferred to the ECB, and devaluation of the currency was not an option. Thus the Spanish economy needed other sources of flexibility to get back on its feet. Prudent fiscal policy gave the government some leverage to increase government spending, which softened the impact somewhat. One might also expect pressure on wages to keep costs down and thus maintain international competitiveness of Spanish exports, yet this did not happen. The Spanish labour market had developed a two-tier structure. Two thirds of workers enjoyed safe long-term employment, while the rest were on short-term contracts. The recession hit the two parts of the labour markets unequally. Those in long-term contracts were even able to negotiate pay rises of 3% in real terms, while those in short-term employment bore the brunt of rising unemployment. While the drop of Spanish GDP was only a notch below the EU average (Figure 8.8), unemployment increased from 11% in 2007 to a record 26% in 2013 (Figure 8.9).

While the euro has undoubtedly helped Spain in its long run of above-average economic growth (Figure 8.8), it is hard to say whether staying out of the eurozone would have eased the impact of the global crisis. Hypothetically, what would have happened? First, the Spanish peseta might have devalued in 2008, similar to the British pound, which might have stimulated exports, thus allowing the Spanish economy to recover quicker, albeit from a lower level of real income. Second, wild speculation and high volatility of the exchange rates within Europe might have further accelerated the disruptive effects of economy, possibly even leading to an Iceland-style collapse.

Sources: (1) C. Giles & V. Mallet, 2009, Britain and Spain: A tale of two housing bubbles, *Financial Times*, January 11; (2) V. Mallet, 2009, Spain's recession: After the fiesta: *Financial Times*, February 17; (3) *The Economist* (2009): Unemployment in Spain: Two-tier flexibility, July 11; (4) S. Bentolila, P. Cahuc, J. Dolado & T. LeBarbanchon, 2012, Two-tier labour markets in the great recession: France versus Spain, *EJ*, 122: F155–187; J. Fernández-Villaverde, L. Garicano, & T. Santos, 2013, Political credit cycles: The case of the eurozone, *JEP*, 3: 145–166.

The significance of these arguments varies from the perspective of different countries that might one day join the euro. In the UK, the independence of monetary policy plays an important role in the political debate. The UK trades intensively with its former colonies and with the USA; its external trade thus is less integrated with the rest of the EU than most continental countries (see Chapter 1). Moreover, the UK industry has structural differences to the rest of Europe: a smaller agricultural sector, a bigger financial services sector, and oil reserves in the North Sea. These structural differences imply that the British economy may be subject to different business cycles, and thus in need of a different monetary policy from continental Europe. Moreover, the UK has more private home ownership financed by variable rate mortgages, which makes ordinary people directly dependent on the central bank interest rate.[40] These arguments suggest that Britain may in fact be better off outside the 'optimum currency area'.

These arguments are less applicable to other countries. For example, Denmark is economically more integrated with the rest of the EU, and its industry structure more similar to its neighbours. Hence it is hard to argue that Denmark should be outside the optimum currency area. The domestic political debate prior to the referendum in September 2000, when Denmark rejected joining the euro, focused primarily on issues of national sovereignty. As Denmark has a solid track record in macroeconomic policy, and the exchange rate of the Danish crown has been pegged to the euro anyway, it made little substantive difference, apart from Danes paying slightly higher interest rates on their mortgage due to the residual currency risk (and not having to contribute to the bailout of Southern European countries). The Baltic States have even smaller economies that are highly integrated with European trade. However, with only a short period of solid macroeconomic policy, their currencies were still seen as less solid than the Danish crown. Thus Estonia, Latvia and Lithuania were happy to join in 2011, 2014 and 2015 respectively.

On the other hand, is Greece in the optimum currency area? The economic structure of Greece is less manufacturing oriented, with relatively strong tourism and shipping sectors. The stock market capitalization is lower (Chapter 2, Figure 2.2), service sectors are more regulated, and the tax collection from high-income earners less effective than elsewhere in the eurozone. These structural characteristics suggest that perhaps Greece might not be sufficiently aligned. Turning to the Maastricht Criteria, we note that before 2000 Greece was missing the inflation, deficit and debt targets by a wide margin (see respectively Figures 8.4, 8.5 and 8.6); only in 1999 did it manage to get its budget deficit down to 3.1%, according to IMF data. (Preliminary data submitted to the EU in 1999 suggested it was below 3.0%, but rumours suggested they were fake). Thus the decision to heed Greek politicians' pleading and admit Greece to the eurozone was a political decision, not supported by economic fundamentals. A costly mistake, as it turned out. For the next decade, Greece had a big party – GDP per capita grew by 43% from 1998 to 2007 (Figure 8.8) – funded by growing budget and trade deficits (Figures 8.5. and 8.7). But when the party ended, the hangover was painful.

DEBATES AND EXTENSIONS

LEARNING OBJECTIVE

4   Participate in
     debates over the
     political institutions
     of the EU

Like the rules and regulations in a nation state, the EU institutions are constantly evolving.[41] However, institutional change is more complex than in most nation states because of the decentralized and coordinated modes of decision-making in the political system of the EU. No president has the power to determine the overall direction, and the parliament is not empowered to create and pass laws. The member states continue to dominate decision making in Brussels. Imagine the governors of the states of the USA were to convene in Washington twice a year to haggle over all major policies to be implemented during the next half year. Sounds crazy? Well, it is approximately like that in the EU – because the EU is not a nation state but an association of sovereign nation states. We first review the structure, and then address the question of legitimacy.

The structure of political institutions

The formal structure of the EU resembles the structure of nation states, yet the actual lines of power are quite different. The Lisbon Treaty aimed to reduce inefficiencies in the system by reducing the power of national vetoes and creating new leadership positions. Even so, the political structures of the EU remain complex; the main institutions are the Commission, the Parliament, the Council, and the Court of Justice.

The most important body for policymaking in the EU is the European Council (not to be confused with the Council of Europe), which defines the general political directions and priorities of the EU. It consists of the heads of government of the member states, the President of the Commission, and is chaired by the President of the European Council, a position newly created with the Lisbon Treaty. Donald Tusk of Poland was appointed as the second President in 2014 succeeding Belgian Herman van Rumpoy. The EU High Representative for Foreign Affairs and Security Policy participates in the work of the council.

The highest formal decision-making body is the Council of the European Union, which consists of the ministers of the member states. Depending on the issue on the agenda, each country is represented by the minister responsible for that subject (foreign affairs, finance, social affairs, transport, agriculture, etc.) Decisions are taken by qualified majority voting, with votes for each country weighted by its population size, ranging from 29 votes for the UK, Germany, France and Italy, to three votes for Malta. The presidency of the Council of the EU is held for six months by each member state on a rotational basis.

The European Commission is the EU's executive arm, with a role similar to that of a national government in the responsibility for the day-to-day running of the EU. Most legislation is initially discussed in the Commission, where different national positions are deliberated at length with the aim to find mutually agreeable rules (see Closing Case '*Nokia* goes to Brussels'). The Commission is based in Brussels and organized in departments known as 'Directorate General' (DG), each headed by a Commissioner. It is composed of 26 commissioners, each from a different country,[42] and each with a specific area of responsibility. The President of the Commission is nominated by the European Council, and thus by consensus between the governments of the member states. The parliament has to formally confirm the appointment of the Commission, which it usually does. In 2014, Jean-Claude Juncker of Luxembourg followed José Manuel Barroso of Portugal as President of the Commission.

The European Parliament in Strasbourg has been elected every fifth year since 1979 directly by the citizens of member states in a unique exercise in multinational democracy. The parliament has gradually increased its power and responsibilities. It has to approve European law, it monitors the growing EU bureaucracy, and it shares control over the EU budget. The parliament discusses all forthcoming legislation, and it is thus of critical importance to businesses that wish to anticipate changes in the regulatory framework. Most Members of the European Parliament (MEPs) belong to one of the European parties, which are associations of the national parties that are usually better known to voters. MEPs typically vote along party lines, though they are more independent than in most national parliaments, and on occasion national concerns dominate voting behaviour. The parliament has important monitoring and

European Council
The assembly of heads of governments setting overall policy directions for the EU.

President of the European Council
The person chairing the meetings of the European Council.

Council of the European Union
The top decision-making body of the EU, consisting of ministers from the national governments; it decides by qualified majority voting.

European Commission
The executive arm of the EU, similar to a national government.

Directorate General (DG)
A department of the Commission, similar to a ministry of a national government.

President of the Commission
The head of the EU's executive, similar to a national prime minister.

European Parliament
The directly elected representation of European citizens.

Members of the European Parliament (MEPs)
Parliamentarians directly elected by the citizens of the EU.

co-decision rights, yet it does not hold all the powers of a typical national parliament. Notably, it cannot initiate legislation, raise revenues or choose a head of government. In other words, it is shaping the rules, but not selecting the people.

The EU also has its own judicial system, with a Court of Justice based in Luxembourg, and a General Court. The General Court mainly deals with cases taken by individuals and companies directly before the EU's courts, while the Court of Justice primarily deals with cases taken up by the Commission and cases referred to it by the courts of member states. In addition, national courts are required to enforce the treaties that their country has ratified, and thus the laws enacted under them.

European Court of Justice (ECJ)
The court system of the EU.

Democratic legitimacy

European elections tend to receive much less attention in the media than national elections. Yet the election is for one of the most influential political bodies in the world, and the election is probably the second-largest election in the world (after India). Especially for businesses, most of the relevant rules are decided in the European Parliament – when legislation comes down to national parliaments, they are constrained by what has been decided already in Strasbourg and Brussels. Equally crucial, the European Parliament scrutinizes the budget of the EU, and thus the Commission. Hence it does its best to minimize the money wasted. National politicians may not admit it, but in many areas of politics, true power slipped away from national parliaments a long time ago. But they won't tell you – except when they need a scapegoat.

However, not all is well with European democracy. Many voters feel disenfranchised, because they do not see how they can influence decisions made in Brussels. This feeling may be particularly strong in the UK (In Focus 8.4) but it exists in political groupings across the continent. This aversion to EU decision-making processes is partly due to the complexity of the process, not to mention the many translations, and partly because national newspapers rarely discuss the legislative process in Brussels. Moreover, the larger a group trying to reach a common policy, the more compromises have to be made: in the EU, the representatives of almost 500 million citizens have to agree. Many voters also fail to understand why decisions cannot be made closer to them at national or even local level. The principle of 'subsidiarity' feels rather abstract and does not seem to work in practice. The bureaucrats in Brussels seem a far way off, not unlike voices in Scotland or Galicia complaining about bureaucrats in London and Madrid.

Various parties have been arguing for more democracy in Europe, yet for some this implies securing veto rights wielded by (democratically elected) national governments, whereas for others it means more power to the (democratically elected)

IN FOCUS 8.4

Half in, half out: the British

While many are queuing to get into the EU, one nation sometimes wishes it had never entered. In 1998, the *Financial Times* summarized the British relationship with 'Europe' (which in Britain often means 'the rest of Europe'), as follows:

'Britain lives with its history. The post-war relationship with its European neighbours has been one infused with misery and missed opportunities. To come to terms with what is now the European Union is to come to terms with the retreat from past glory. The nation's leaders have shunned the challenge.'

This quotation from 1998 still rings true almost two decades later. Essential to understanding the ambivalent relationship of the British, or more precisely their political leaders, towards Europe, is to understand that most British politicians of the 20th century never appreciated the EU as a political project, but rather focused on the economic benefits. In the 1950s the UK stayed out of the union, as it still prioritized relationships with its (former) colonies in the Commonwealth over relationships with its European neighbours. It first applied for membership in the 1960s, but was then vetoed by French leader Charles de Gaulle. Eventually the UK joined along with Denmark and Ireland in 1973. Psychologically, many people of Britain see themselves as an independent nation with a major role in the world stage, rather than a part of Europe, to which they geographically belong.

Thus the UK has been reluctant to engage in the deepening of the union. When the SEA laid out the path to the single market in 1986, the British went along with it, because the basic principles – widespread liberalization – reflected Anglo-Saxon principles of a free-market economy, strongly promoted at the time by Prime Minister Margaret Thatcher. However, she negotiated rebates and exceptions for Britain, which won her support at home, but few friends elsewhere. When the Maastricht Treaty introduced coordination of environmental and social issues, she negotiated an opt-out from the social chapter. British firms thus could get away with lesser social standards and shorter notice periods in case they wished to lay off staff. Many people in the rest of Europe – not just trade unions – thought this gave British firms a rather unfair competitive advantage. After a change in government, Britain surrendered this opt-out with the Amsterdam treaty. Britain also stayed out of the eurozone, and passport-free travel in the Schengen area.

Arguably, many of the conflicts over the appropriate form of EU regulation are grounded in the differences between civil and common law (see Chapter 2). The continental approach of detailed regulation sits uneasily with the British tradition that gives more weight to interpretation and case law. However, British businesses are often more euro-friendly than politicians from the two main political parties. While they may see European legislation as overly intrusive, the costs of staying out and thus missing market opportunities on the continent are even higher. On the other side of the Channel, some are getting fed up with British obstinacy. Especially for the political left, the single market project reflects Anglo-Saxon values of free enterprise, and thus an Anglo-Saxon ideological take-over of Europe. Most British people certainly don't see it that way. It will take many more years for the British and their partners to develop a common understanding of what Europe is really about.

Sources: (1) P. Stephens, 1998, UK's view of Europe obscured by past glories, *Financial Times*, January 4; (2) D. Gowland & A. Turner, eds, 1998, *Reluctant Europeans: Britain and European Integration 1945–1998: A documentary history*; London: Pearson; (3) D. Watts & C. Pilkington, 2005, *Britain in the European Union Today*, 3rd ed., Manchester: Manchester University Press; (4) S. Wall, 2008, *A stranger in Europe: Britain and the EU from Thatcher to Blair*, Oxford: Oxford University Press; (5) *The Economist*, 2009, Charlemagne: Those exceptional British, March 28.

European Parliament, possibly including the right for the Parliament to elect the Commission. When politicians join this debate it is helpful to ask where they have their own powerbase; national governments are as likely to vote for strengthening the European Parliament as turkeys to vote for Christmas.

IMPLICATIONS FOR PRACTICE

Businesses operate in a context where the rules and regulations issued by the institutions of the EU (Commission, Council and Parliament) are central to what is permitted, and what is not. In other words, the EU is probably more important in shaping the institutional environment for business in Europe than national governments. Businesses thus need to keep their eyes on what is going in Strasbourg and Brussels (Table 8.4).

First, you need to know the rules, and to identify advantages that your business may achieve within this institutional context. The provisions, stipulations and legal requirements attached to the different EU policy areas require careful audit from businesses operating in the union. You need to know what rights you have when operating in another country and how to comply with existing regulation in your industry.

LEARNING OBJECTIVE

5   Draw implications for action

Table 8.4   Implications for practice

- Know the rules that apply to your industry in the EU
- Anticipate future changes in the rules by monitoring decision-making processes in the EU
- Direct your efforts of lobbying towards the institutions of the EU

Second, you need to think forward and anticipate future changes in rules. At times, policy developments can be quite rapid, and only by staying in touch with discussions in the European sphere, will you be able to stay ahead of your competitors in adapting to institutional change. In the same way, you may recognize opportunities and threats early by following the debates on possible further expansion of the union. To be able to anticipate changes in the institutional framework of the EU, you need to monitor the discussion in the EU, especially the EU parliament.

Third, as a concerned citizen or as a business leader, you may direct your efforts of lobbying towards the institutions of the EU.[43] Lobbying is about making your voice heard and known to decision-makers, with the aim of influencing political processes. As a lobbyist you may be able to influence preferences at an early stage, influence the positions taken by national governments, and – by working with the media – influence public perceptions of European issues. Business lobbies have shifted their attention from national capitals to Brussels and Strasbourg, where decision-makers are seeking information and qualified opinions on issues relevant to business. The Commission and various associated institutions are working on a wide range of regulations likely to affect businesses some day in the future. Any piece of legislation needs to clear three hurdles: the Commission, the Council and Parliament. All three bodies are involved in the decision-making, and may thus be relevant for lobbyists. Once new legislation reaches national parliaments it is usually too late to effect major changes, even though the media may only pick up issues at that stage.

lobbying
Making your voice heard and known to decision-makers with the aim of influencing political processes.

CHAPTER SUMMARY

1 Explain the origins and the evolution of the EU

- European integration started with the Treaties of Rome aiming to overcome the historical divisions of Europe.
- The EU has continuously been enlarged, starting with the UK, Denmark and Ireland in 1973, and most recently Croatia in 2013.
- The integration in the EU has continuously been deepened through a series of inter-governmental treaties, often known by the cities where they were signed. Most important are the single European Act (1986), the Maastricht Treaty (1992), and the Lisbon Treaty (2007).

2 Explain how and why the institutional framework created by the EU is pivotal for business

- The single market is based on the four freedoms of movement of goods, capital, people and services. It is implemented though harmonized regulation in some sectors, and mutual recognition of national regulation in other sectors.
- The EU aims to facilitate free movement of people within the union. This aim is supported by the Schengen Agreement for passport-free travel, and the Bologna Process for European higher education.
- The euro has become a common currency in 16 countries that have transferred their monetary policy to the European Central Bank.
- EU competition policy aims to ensure that a competitive environment is maintained in cases of mergers and acquisitions, cartels and collusion, and state aid.

3   Discuss the merits and drawbacks of the euro as a common currency

- The common currency reduces the cost of doing business, but also constrains policy options for national governments.

- The empirical evidence suggests that the eurozone may be larger than an optimum currency area.

4   Participate in debates over the political institutions of the EU

- The formal political structures of the EU resemble a national government, yet governments of

member states wield considerable power through the Council.

- The decision-making processes in the EU are based on democratic principles, yet they often are far removed from the individual citizens in member countries.

5   Draw implications for action

- With major institutional changes being decided at European level, businesses need to be informed about current rules and expected future change, and they may direct their lobbying to Brussels and Strasbourg.

KEY TERMS

Bologna Process	European Convention on	Monetary union
Central and Eastern Europe	Human Rights	Mutual recognition
Comecon	European Council	Optimum currency area
Common market	European Court of Human Rights	Political union
Copenhagen Criteria	European Court of Justice (ECJ)	President of the Commission
Council of Europe	European Parliament	President of the European Council
Council of the European Union	European Stability Mechanism (ESM)	Schengen Agreement
Customs union	European Union (EU)	Schengen Area
Directorate General (DG)	Eurozone	Schengen Visa
Economic transition	Four freedoms of the EU single market	Single European Act (SEA)
Economic union	Free trade area	Single market
Erasmus Programme	Harmonized sector	State aid
EU Presidency	Lobbying	Subsidiarity
Euro	Maastricht Criteria	Subsidy competition
European Central Bank (ECB)	Maastricht Treaty	Treaties of Rome
European Commission	Members of the European	
European Constitution	Parliament (MEPs)	

CRITICAL DISCUSSION QUESTIONS

1   When should the EU issue regulation that is binding for all businesses in all countries, and when should it instead leave regulation to the nation states?

2   Some trade unions fear that the free movement of people depresses wages of ordinary workers because immigrants from other European countries are willing to work for lower wages. Should the free movement of people within the thus be restricted?

3   Review Figures 8.4 to 8.9. Can you offer an explanation as to why the Greek economy fared

particularly badly during and after the financial crisis of 2009?

4   From the World Economic Outlook Database (www.imf.org/external/pubs/ft/weo/2014/02/weodata/index.aspx) download data for the past decade for a European country of your interest. Analyzing these data, how was the economy influenced by the decision join or not to join the eurozone?

5   As a business leader, how can you influence future European legislation?

RECOMMENDED READINGS

D. Dinan, 2014, Europe Recast: A History of European Union, 2nd ed., Palgrave-Macmillan – a detailed historical account of the EU.

J. Fernández-Villaverde, L. Garicano & T. Santos, 2013, Political credit cycles: The case of the eurozone, JEP, 3: 145–166 – a good analysis on why some eurozone economies struggled after 2010 that adds additional insights to the interpretation of Figures 8.4 to 8.8.

J. Pelkmans, 2006, European Integration: Methods and Economic Analysis London: Prentice

Hall – an economics perspective on how the EU works.

G. Suder, 2011, Business in Europe, 2nd ed., Los Angeles: Sage – a textbook covering the institutional context of the EU and business practice in the EU.

H. Wallace, W. Wallace, M. Pollack, 2005. Policy-Making in the European Union, 5th ed., Oxford: Oxford University Press – a collection of articles describing and analyzing political processes in the EU.

CLOSING CASE

The Eco-design Directive: Nokia goes to Brussels

In August 2007, a new EU directive came into force that harmonized regulation of environmental standards with respect to energy-using products. This 'Directive on the Eco-design of Energy-using Products' (EuP) aims to lower negative environmental impact over the entire life cycle of products. It is gradually being applied to an increasing range of products, and has profound implications for manufacturers and importers of, for example, mobile handsets. Yet it did not come as a surprise to industry leaders, such as *Nokia* of Finland. As market leader for mobile phone handsets, *Nokia* emphasized not only technological features but design and image in its product development and marketing. This included taking a lead on social and environmental sustainability issues.

Environmental policy debates were shifting from focus on environmentally friendly production to environmentally friendly products. Traditionally, environmental pressure groups would, for example, focus on the emissions from a specific production plant. However, around the year 2000, this was shifting to a product focus. Thus manufacturers were challenged to consider the environmental impact of their products over the entire life cycle, including the disposal of the product when consumers would eventually discard it. For example, the car industry has been pressured in some countries to assume costs associated with the scrapping of cars. This pressure led firms to change

their designs to reduce the use of materials that were costly to recycle. In the mobile phone sector, such issues were a potential issue because of the use of metals in the electronics that, if disposed of inappropriately, could lead to environmental hazards.

The EU Commission took the initiative for new environmental regulation that would harmonize national regulations. New proposed directives aimed, firstly, to ensure that new environmental standards would not vary across countries in ways that inhibit free trade in the union, and, secondly, to raise the environmental standards. Two initiatives were discussed from September 2000 among the departments (DGs) of the Commission. The DG Enterprise drafted a directive on the impact on the environment of electrical and electronic equipment (EEE), while the DG Transport and Energy was working on a directive on energy efficiency requirements for end-use equipment (EER).

The discussions were of concern to companies like *Nokia*, which were closely following the policy debates both nationally and in Brussels. *Nokia* had established a representative office in Brussels specifically to deal with EU related matters. In the debate over new environmental standards for electronics products, several issues were of concern to *Nokia*. First, would national governments be allowed to enact stricter requirements within their boundaries? As a company selling in many markets, *Nokia* naturally preferred a standardized approach with little variation of laws across countries. Second, should there be a full-scale life cycle assessment? This would not only be costly and

time-consuming, but also require assessing potential impacts that are simply not known, such as pollution arising from discarded mobile phones. Third, should small and medium-sized businesses be given simplified requirements? If this was the case, it might make it difficult to source components from such firms. Fourth, should the EU's own environmental management system be mandatory for all firms? *Nokia* preferred to continue using ISO 14001, which is also recognized outside the EU.

Nokia principally had several avenues by which it could hope to influence policy decision-making processes in Brussels. First, it might approach its national government, which might aim to influence decisions in the Council of Ministers. In this case, the Finnish government acknowledged the responsibility of the Commission, and thus the national politics route was not given priority. Second, Nokia might work through industry associations of which it is a member, and that have established communication channels to the relevant DGs of the Commission and to the Parliament. In this case, Nokia worked with the European Information, Communications, and Consumer Electronics Technology Industry Association (EICTA). A drawback of this approach is that industry associations normally represent what all members can agree on as a common position, i.e. the lowest common denominator. This is not necessarily in the interest of those players in an industry that have already established above-average standards.

Third, companies may form ad hoc coalition with other companies with similar interests, thus sharing each other's lobbying resources. Fourth, a large company like *Nokia* might aim to directly influence the Commission via the relevant DGs. At the time, Erkki Liikanen from Finland was Commissioner for Enterprise and Information Society, and *Nokia* had good relationships with him and his team. *Nokia* worked with industry associations as well as ad hoc coalitions of leading players in the industry to develop such direct channels, including bilateral meetings on issues where industry associations found it difficult to build a consensus.

The legislative process progressed in multiple iterations of discussions within the Commission. In November 2002, the two separate legislative processes were merged, and in August 2003 the new 'Directive on Establishing a Framework for the Setting of Eco-design Requirements for **E**nergy-**u**sing **P**roducts' (EuP) was formally proposed. Following further consultations and negotiations it was formally approved as Directive 2005/32/EC by the Council and the Parliament in April 2005, and came into force in August 2007. *Nokia* found its interests reasonably well accommodated, though the data collection and reporting requirements established by the new directive are quite substantial. However, a harmonized regulation helps those businesses already operating across Europe, while high standards help businesses that have already established competences in managing to a high standard.

The new directive led to industry-specific regulation, so-called Integrated Product Policy (IPP), which establishes the best available practice and the standards thus to be used. The development of IPPs was initiated by a series of pilot studies, and *Nokia* volunteered to lead the pilot study for mobile phones. With a collaborative approach to working with the Commission and a reputation for being an environmentally responsible company, *Nokia* found that its views were heard and respected by policymakers. The pilot study on mobile handsets found that the environmental impact would be less than in other industries, and it thus did not become a priority for the Commission to regulate this industry.

Nokia continues to build its environmental reputation, not only by compliance with the regulatory requirements, such as this directive, but by acting proactively. An element of this environmental strategy is to anticipate new requirements, and thus to lead in their implementation. An ear on the ground in Brussels helps anticipating future requirements that may translate into new EU directives, or that may be promoted by influential NGOs.

CASE DISCUSSION QUESTIONS:

1 How can companies get into the discussions on new legislation at an early stage when the major direction is likely to be decided?

2 What are the merits of using the alternative venues for lobbying: (1) national governments, (2) industry associations, (3) ad hoc coalitions, and (4) direct approach to the Commission?

3 What are the merits of using a cooperative approach to working with the Commission (or a national government)?

Sources: (1) P. Kautto, 2007, Industry-government Interaction in the preparation of a new directive: Nokia, Industry Associations and EuP, *European Environment,* 17: 79–91; (2) P. Kautto, 2009, Nokia as an environmental policy actor: Evolution of collaborative corporate political activity in a multinational company, *JCMS,* 47: 103–125. (3) European Commission, no date, *Eco-Design of Energy-Using Products,* (ec.europa.eu); (4) Nokia, no date, *Environmental Strategy* (www.nokia.com).

NOTES

'For journal abbreviation, please see page xx-xxi.'

1 E. Spolaore, 2013, What is European integration really about? *JEL* 27: 125–144; D. Dinan 2014. *Europe Recast: A History of European Union,* 2nd ed., Basingstoke: Palgrave Macmillan.

2 Original document is available at: www.eurotreaties.com/rometreaty.pdf (accessed February 2014).

3 H. Grabbe, 2002, European Union conditionality and the acquis communautaire, *International Political Science Review*, 23: 249–268.

4 K.E. Meyer, 1995, Direct foreign investment in the early years of economic transition, *EoT*, 3: 301–320; N. Crespo & M. Fontoura, 2007, Integration of CEES into EU market, *JCMS*, 45: 611–632.

5 *The Economist*, 2009, Holding together: A special report on the euro area, supplement (16 pages), June 13.

6 European Commission, no date, Historical overview (ec.europa.eu, accessed December 2014).

7 D. Phinnemore, 2004, *Treaty establishing a constitution for Europe*, Chatham House Briefing Paper, London: Chatham House; A. Moravcsik, 2005, A too perfect union? Why Europe said 'No', *Current History*, 104: 355–359.

8 C. Reh, 2009, The Lisbon Treaty: De-constitutionalizing the European Union? *JCMS*: 47: 635–650.

9 J. Pelkmans, 2006, *European Integration: Methods and Economic Analysis*, 3rd ed., Harlow: Pearsons (Chapters 5 to 10); G. Suder 2011, *Doing Business in Europe*, 2nd ed., Los Angeles: Sage .

10 European Commission, no date, A single market for goods (ec.europa.eu, accessed June 2014).

11 D. Smallbone, A. Cumbers, S. Syrett & R. Leigh, 1999, The single European market and SMEs, *Regional Policy*, 33: 51–62.

12 *The Economist*, 2008, Regulating pesticides: A balance of risk, July 3.

13 J. Knudsen, 2005, Breaking with tradition, in: A. Verdun & O. Groci, eds, *The European Union in the Wake of Eastern Enlargement*, Manchester: Manchester University Press; European Commission, no date, Freedom to provide services / Freedom of establishment (ec.europa.eu, accessed, February 2014).

14 S. Schmidt, 2005, Reform in the shadow of community law: Highly regulated economic sectors, *German Politics*, 14: 157–173.

15 F. Mustilli & J. Peltmans, 2012. Securing EU growth from services, CEPS special report #67, London: CEPS; J. Springford, 2012. How to build European services markets, report, Centre for European Reform;

B. Dettmer, 2015, Trade effects of the European Union's service directive, *WE*, advance online.

16 L. Quaglia, R. Eastwood & P. Holmes, 2009, The financial turmoil and EU policy cooperation in 2008, *JCMS*, 47: 63–87; E. Grossman & P. Leblond, 2011, European Financial Integration: Finally the Great Leap Forward? *JCMS*, 49: 413–435; A. Gehringer, 2013, Growth, productivity and capital accumulation: The effects of financial liberalization in the case of European integration, *International Review of Economics & Finance*, 25: 291–309.

17 U. Elleman-Jensen, 2010, Island melder sig ud af verden, *Berlingske Tidende*, January 6; M. Huden, 2010, Iceland can refuse debt servitude, *Financial Times*, January 6.

18 Citizen of new member countries may benefit from the full freedom of movement only after a transition period of often several years.

19 European Commission, 2005, Directive 2005/36/EC on the recognition of professional qualifications.

20 European Commission, 2014. Erasmus+ Program Guide, ec.europa.eu (accessed December 2014).

21 Auswärtiges Amt (German Foreign Ministry), no date, The Schengen Agreement and the Convention Implementing the Schengen Agreement (www.auswaertiges-amt.de, accessed December 2014).

22 Auswärtiges Amt, no date, *as above*.

23 S. Bishop & M. Walker, 1999, *Economics of E.C. Competition Law*, London: Sweet & Maxwell; M. Furse, 2008, *Competition law of the EC and UK*, 6th ed., Oxford: Oxford University Press; X. Vines, ed., 2009, *Competition Policy in the EU*, Oxford: Oxford University Press.

24 E.J. Morgan & S. McGuire, 2004, Transatlantic divergence: GE-Honeywell and the EU's merger policy, *JEPP* 11: 39–56; Y. Akbar & G. Suder, 2006, The new EU merger regulation, *TIBR*, 48, 667–686.

25 A. Wigger & A. Nölke, 2007, Enhanced roles of private actors in EU business regulation and the erosion of Rhenish capitalism: The case of antitrust enforcement, *JCMS* 45: 487–513; E.J. Morgan, 2009, Controlling cartels – Implications of the EU policy reforms, *EMJ*, 27: 1–12.

26 European Commission, 2014, *Report on Competition Policy 2013*, Brussels: EU (page 4).

27 European Commission, various years, *Report on Competition Policy*, Brussels: EU.

28 *The Guardian*, 2014, Dane investigating EU tax deals says Luxleaks trail will lead to fair play, December 19.

29 D. Currie, 1998, *Will the Euro work?* London: Economist Intelligence Unit; S. Mercado, R. Welford & K. Precott, 2000, *European Business*, 4th ed., London: Pearsons (Chapter 4); D. March 2009. *The Euro: The Politics of the New Global Currency*, Yale University Press; The

Economist, 2009, Holding Together: A Special Report on the Euro Area (supplement, 16 pages), June 13; P. De Grauwe, 2009, *Economics of the Monetary Union*, 8th ed., Oxford: Oxford University Press.

30 G. Zestos, 2006, *European Monetary Integration: The Euro* (p. 64), Cincinnati, Ohio: Cengage South-Western.

31 *The Economist*, 2005. A survey of Italy (16 pages), November 25.

32 S. Ruhkamp, 2009. Der Euro gewinnt weltweit an Gewicht, *Frankfurter Allgemeine Zeitung*, July 9.

33 *The Economist*, 2009, The euro at ten: Demonstrably durable, January 3; H. Sinn, 2014, Austerity, growth and inflation, *WE*, 37: 1–13.

34 T. Barber, 2008, Fiscal rules reform allows budget deficits to rise, *Financial Times*, November 4; B. Benoit, 2009, Germany set to suffer record deficit, *Financial Times*, May 14.

35 L. Papademos, 2001, Opening address: The Greek economy, in: R. Bryant, N. Garganas & G. Tavlas, eds, *Greece's Economic Performance and Prospects*, Bank of Greece and Brookings Institution (p. xxxvii).

36 C. Dustmann, B. Fitzenberger, U. Schönberg & A. Spitz-Oener, 2014, From sick man of Europe to economic superstar, *JEL* 28(1): 167–88.

37 J. Fernández-Villaverde, L. Garicano, & T. Santos, 2013, Political credit cycles: The case of the eurozone, *JEP*, 3: 145–166.

38 R. Mundel, 1961, A theory of optimum currency area, *AER*, 51: 657–65; P. Krugman, 2012, Revenge of the optimum currency area, *NBER Macroeconomics Annual*, 27: 439–448; K. O'Rourke & A. Taylor, 2013, Cross of euros, *JEP*, 27: 167–192.

39 *The Economist*, 2009, California's budget crisis: Meltdown on the ocean, July 11.

40 M. Bainbridge, B. Burkitt & P. Whyman, 1998, *Is Europe ready for EMU?* Bruges Group Occasional Paper #30.

41 S. Hix, 2005, *The Political System of the European Union*, 2nd ed., Basingstoke: Palgrave MacMillan; J. Peterson & M. Shackleton, eds, 2006, *The Institutions of the European Union,* 2nd ed., Oxford University Press; M. Nugent, 2003, *The Government and Politics of the European Union*, 5th ed., Basingstoke: Palgrave Macmillan.

42 Countries whose nationals hold position of President of the European Council or of High Representative for Foreign Affairs do not appoint Commissioners.

43 P. Bouwen, 2002, Corporate lobbying in the EU, *JEPP*, 9, 365–390; D. Coen, 2007, Empirical and theoretical studies in EU lobbying, *JEPP*, 14: 333–345. G. Suder, 2011, *Business in Europe*, 2nd ed., Los Angeles: Sage (Chapter 9); A. Dür & G. Mateo, 2012, Who lobbies the European Union? *JEPP*, 19: 969–987; H. Klüver, 2013, Lobbying as a collective enterprise, *JEPP*, 20: 59–76.

CHAPTER NINE

GLOBAL INTEGRATION AND MULTILATERAL ORGANIZATIONS

LEARNING OBJECTIVES

After studying this chapter, you should be able to

1 Explain the multilateral institutions of the global trade system, and their current challenges

2 Explain the multilateral institutions of the global monetary system, and their current challenges

3 Explain the advantages and disadvantages of regional and bilateral economic integration

4 Participate in policy debates on the institutional framework for global economic integration

5 Draw implications for action

OPENING CASE

WTO mediates between Airbus *and* Boeing

Two of the mightiest companies have been battling for leadership of the global market for large and very large aircraft. Yet this is not only a battle between two firms, but between governments backing their respective champions. Caught in the middle,

the World Trade Organization (WTO) is tasked with creating a level playing field for international competition.

Boeing has been the world's leading aircraft manufacturer since the 1950s, exploiting its capabilities of building military aircraft during World War II. Of its two domestic competitors, *Lockheed Martin* exited the large aircraft market in 1986, and *McDonnell Douglas* was acquired by *Boeing* in 1997. Since that time, the world market for large civil aircraft has been a duopoly of *Boeing* and *Airbus*.

Airbus was created in 1970 as a Franco-German joint venture with government backing and the explicit objective to challenge the monopoly of US manufacturers. The A300 launched in 1974 and the A320 launched in 1988 became *Airbus'* flagship products, and challenged the dominance of the USA. In 2001, *Airbus* for the first time won more new orders than its US rival. In the same year, it became an independent company wholly owned by *EADS*, a European air, space and military conglomerate (but with far smaller military operations than *Boeing*).

The European governmental support displeased *Boeing* and American politicians. Initially, the subsidies were tolerated because of the 'infant industry' nature of the support, and the small market share of *Airbus*. At the same time, European observers felt that *Boeing* gained an unfair advantage from its close association with the US Air Force, by far the world's largest buyer of military aircraft and technology. In 1992, the EU and the USA signed an agreement defining and limiting the support provided to their aircraft manufacturers. In particular, they banned direct production and sales subsidiaries, but allowed certain forms of launch aid in the form of state-guaranteed loans and spillovers from military to civil aviation research and product development.

However, the 1992 agreement was widely considered as unsatisfactory because it legitimized subsidies – and thus transfers from taxpayers to businesses. In 2004, *Boeing* convinced the US government to terminate the 1992 agreement, and to lodge a formal complaint against the EU for subsidies allegedly in violation of WTO regulation. The EU responded in kind and submitted a complaint against the US government support for *Boeing*. Ever since, the WTO has been trying to negotiate peace between the two potent adversaries and their powerful political supporters.

The US complaint focuses on so-called launched aid provided by European governments for the next generation aircraft, the A380. This launch aid is in the form of loans (according to the USA) at interest rates below market rates that only need to be repaid in line with sales of the commercialized aircraft (Table 9.1). Secondary complaints focus on infrastructure investments and research contracts benefiting *Airbus*. The EU maintains that interest rates on launch aid loans are at market rates, and do not distort competition. Moreover, further support mentioned in the US complaint is that given to general business and the travelling public (in the case of the airport extension in Hamburg).

The EU complaint focuses on the close relation between *Boeing* and the US military. *Boeing* participates in major research contracts with the defence

How do *Boeing* and *Airbus* fight their competitive battle for leadership in the global market?

Table 9.1   Claims and counter-claims (simplified)

	Boeing against *Airbus*	*Airbus* against *Boeing*
Complaints	• 'Launch aid' loans by European governments distort competition by lowering the financing risk for *Airbus*. • Interest rates paid by *Airbus* for government guaranteed loans are below market rates. • Government-supported construction of infrastructure, for example the extension of the runway at Hamburg Airport. • Direct capital injections by governments as shareholders. • Research contracts for the European aviation and space industry.	• Indirect subsidization of the civil arm of *Boeing* via R&D contracts from the defence ministry, NASA and other government institutions, with a lack of transparency. • Tax concession and financial support from US states, in particular Washington. • Export promotion via tax advantages for export-oriented companies and loans from the Export-Import Bank. • Launch aid from the government of Japan for the development of major components of the 787.
Responses	• Launch aid is effectively granted at market interest rates, and aims to correct for inefficiencies in long-term capital markets. • Infrastructure investment benefits all businesses and individuals in the area. • Military research links are much smaller than in the US.	• Research contracts are awarded based on competitive bidding that is in principle open to all businesses. • Demand for transparency would endanger national security. • Export promotion schemes have been discontinued following an earlier WTO ruling.

ministry, NASA and other institutions, to develop new technologies for military and space applications. So, new knowledge in one part of *Boeing* directly benefits other areas, namely civil aviation – and the development of the 787 Dreamliner in particular. A major concern is that these relationships lack transparency, which inhibits assessment of the financial benefits received by *Boeing*. Yet the call for more transparency conflicts with the US concern about secrecy in national security matters.

The WTO handled both complaints in separate procedures. In March 2010, the ruling of the WTO regarding the US complaint was notified to the participating parties. The public relations departments of both firms went into overdrive to 'spin' the outcome and to claim victory. Unsurprisingly, the US media reported victory for *Boeing*, while the European media emphasized the large number of aspects where *Airbus*' position was upheld. In 2011, the WTO also ruled that *Boeing* had received subsidies inconsistent with

WTO agreements. Yet these rulings only triggered new rounds of tit-for-tat. In 2015, the WTO established a new panel to investigate EU complaints about significant tax breaks provided by Washington State to *Boeing* for large civil aircraft manufacture.

However, the complexity of supply chains of *Boeing* suppliers in Europe and *Airbus* suppliers in the USA make it very difficult to assess which national economies really benefit from the current regime. In addition, both sides are spending substantial legal costs and top management time while Chinese competitors are plotting their entry into the industry.

Sources: (1) N. Pavcnik, 2002, Trade disputes in the commercial aircraft industry, *WE*, 25: 733–751; (2) E. Heyman, 2007, Boeing v Airbus, *Deutsche Bank Research*, Frankfurt: Deutsche Bank; (3) *The Economist*, 2009, Boeing and Airbus argue about subsidies, August 15; (4) P. Clark, 2010, Airbus claims WTO win over Boeing, *Financial Times*, March 24; (5) *Financial Times*, 2011, WTO rules Boeing had illegal subsidies, January 31; (6) M. Dalton, 2015, EU Files Complaint With WTO About Boeing, *Wall Street Journal*, December 19; (7) www.wto.org.

When companies such as *Boeing* and *Airbus* have a disagreement about the rules of the game, how do they sort out their differences? What if even their two (or more) governments don't agree? There must be some place where countries can discuss their differences, resolve their conflicts and agree on common rules. In setting common rules, multilateral organizations have attained a central role in setting rules and in helping resolve disputes between countries. The world 'multilateral' here indicates that they are based on an agreement between many countries, as opposed to bilateral agreements between two countries. In the area of international trade, the World Trade Organization (WTO) is designed to resolve trade disputes, while the International Monetary Fund (IMF) is the guardian of the global monetary system. At a regional level, integration agreements such as the European Union (Chapter 8) and ASEAN facilitate international business within regions of the world. Other institutions, such as free-trade areas, are based on bilateral agreements between countries or groups of countries.

For businesses, the question is how these supra-national institutions affect the institutional frameworks under which they operate. Specifically, how do changes in the rules of the game via global and regional economic integration, as emphasized by the institution-based view, enable firms to better develop and leverage their capabilities, as highlighted by the resource-based view?

This chapter first introduces multilateral institutions of international trade and monetary systems, and then discusses regional and bilateral economic integration. The debates and extensions section extends the discussion to other areas of international policy coordination: economic development, climate change and financial sector regulation. The 'rules of the game' that nation states have agreed on for their economic interactions are becoming more and more complex, which makes this chapter possibly the most challenging to study – yet also the most important for understanding the driving forces shaping globalization.

> **multilateral organizations**
> Organizations set up by several collaborating countries.

THE MULTILATERAL TRADE SYSTEM

Benefits of global integration by trade

Recall from Chapters 5 and 6 that, theoretically, there are economic gains when firms from different countries freely trade and invest. However, in the 1920s and 1930s, virtually all governments imposed protectionist policies through tariffs and quotas, trying to protect domestic industries. Collectively, these beggar-thy-neighbour policies triggered retaliation that further restricted trade, which worsened the Great Depression and eventually contributed to World War II. In the late 1940s, the world community, mindful of the mercantilist trade wars during the 1930s, initiated several developments aimed at fostering economic and political integration, including the foundation of the United Nations, the creation of the Bretton Woods institutions (IMF and World Bank), and the General Agreement on Tariffs and Trade (GATT) – the predecessor of the World Trade Organization (WTO).

The WTO is now the main multilateral organization establishing rules for international trade and resolving trade-related conflicts between nations worldwide. The WTO serves:

- **to handle disputes constructively.** With increasing international trade, conflicts between nations over the rules applied to trade have also increased. The WTO's dispute resolution mechanism (discussed later in this chapter) has become the preferred mechanisms to settle disputes. Since 1995, over 400 disputes have been brought to the WTO, and in 90% of cases the

> **LEARNING OBJECTIVE**
>
> 1 Explain the multilateral institutions of the global trade system, and their current challenges

> **World Trade Organization (WTO)**
> The organization underpinning the multilateral trading system since 2005.

rulings of the WTO have been complied with by responding countries.[1] Notwithstanding a small number of long-standing conflicts, such as the fight between *Airbus* and *Boeing* (Opening Case), this is a good track record.

- **to make life easier for all participants.** A common set of rules applying to all trading partners makes life easier for businesses, because they don't have to learn about new institutions for each market to which they export. The goal of common rules is promoted by the WTO through its non-discrimination principle. Specifically, a country cannot discriminate among its trading partners. Every time a country lowers a trade barrier, it has to do the same for *all* WTO member countries (except when giving preference to regional partners – discussed later). Such non-discrimination makes life easier for all. The alternative would be continuous bilateral negotiations with numerous countries. Each pair may end up with a different deal, significantly complicating trade and investment. Small countries may individually end up with substantially reduced bargaining power.

- **to raise income, generate jobs and stimulate economic growth.** International trade increases competition and thereby reduces prices for consumers (Chapter 5). The WTO estimates that US household incomes have on average increased by €8000 as result of reduced trade barriers. At the same time, the WTO estimates that EU consumers annually pay €1300 per family *more* because of remaining trade barriers for agricultural products, while Korean protection of their car industry increases prices of cars by 43%.[2] In addition, more and better jobs are created, while consumers have a wider choice of goods to buy. In the EU, exports of goods and services add up to about 15% of GDP, and the share of jobs indirectly dependent on international trade is about three times as high.

Historical roots

The origins of today's World Trade Organization (WTO) are in the General Agreement on Tariffs and Trade (GATT), created in 1948. It was technically an agreement but *not* an organization. Its major contribution was to reduce the level of tariffs by sponsoring 'rounds' of multilateral negotiations. As a result, the average tariff in developed economies dropped from 40% in 1948 to 3% in 2005. In other words, the GATT facilitated some of the highest growth rates in international trade recorded in history. Between 1950 and 1995 (when the GATT was phased out to become the WTO), world GDP grew about five-fold, but world merchandise exports grew by about 100 times!

Despite the GATT's phenomenal success in bringing down tariff barriers, by the mid-1980s it was clear that reforms would be necessary.[3] Such reforms were triggered by three concerns. First, because of the GATT's focus on merchandise trade, neither trade in services nor intellectual property protection was covered. Both of these areas were becoming increasingly important, especially to developed economies. Second, in merchandise trade, there were a lot of loopholes that called for reforms. The most (in)famous loophole was the Multi-fibre Arrangement (MFA), which aimed to protect the textile industry in advanced economies by establishing quotas for the imports of textiles and clothing from potential exporting countries. Thus the MFA was designed to *limit* free trade in textiles, which was a direct violation of the letter and spirit of the GATT. Finally, the GATT's success in reducing tariffs, combined with the global recessions in the 1970s and 1980s, led many governments to invoke non-tariff barriers (NTBs), such as subsidies and local content requirements (see Chapter 5). Unlike tariff barriers that were relatively easy to verify and challenge, NTBs were subtler but

Figure 9.1 Six main areas of the WTO

Umbrella	Agreement establishing the WTO		
Three main areas	Goods (GATT)	Services (GATS)	Intellectual property (TRIPS)
Conflict resolution	Dispute settlement mechanism		
Transparency	Trade policy reviews		

Source: World Trade Organization, 2003, *Understanding the WTO* (p. 22), Geneva: WTO.

pervasive, thus triggering a growing number of trade disputes. The GATT, however, lacked effective dispute resolution mechanisms.

To address the lack of enforcement mechanisms within the GATT, the WTO was created. It turned the GATT from a treaty serviced by an *ad hoc* secretariat into a fully-fledged international organization, headquartered in Geneva, Switzerland. Significantly broader than the GATT, the WTO has six main areas (Figure 9.1):

- An umbrella agreement, simply called the Agreement Establishing the WTO.

- An agreement governing the international trade of goods, still using the old title as the General Agreement on Tariffs and Trade (GATT). Hence the GATT continues to live as part of the new organization.

- An agreement governing the international trade of services, the General Agreement on Trade in Services (GATS). The GATS aims to open up markets in service industries such as insurance, telecommunications, tourism and transportation, which requires member countries to liberalize these traditionally tightly-controlled sectors to let foreign companies compete.

- An agreement governing intellectual property rights, the Trade-Related Aspects of Intellectual Property Rights (TRIPS). This agreement establishes rules regarding intellectual property rights used in international trade, which were a particular concern to MNEs in developed countries wishing to exploit their copyrights, patents, trademarks and geographic names. It was not popular among developing countries that now faced more payments for, for example, urgently needed medicines first developed by Western MNEs.

- Trade dispute settlement mechanisms, which allow for the WTO to adjudicate trade disputes between countries in a more effective and less time-consuming way (discussed next).

- Trade policy reviews, which enable the WTO and other member countries to 'peer review' a country's trade policy.

To the disappointment of developing countries, the WTO did not require developed countries to open up their agricultural sectors. However, overall, the WTO has a far wider scope, incorporating trade in services, intellectual property, dispute settlement and peer review of policy. The membership of the WTO has been continuously growing, with Russia joining in 2012 (In Focus 9.1) and bringing the membership to 160 countries by 2014. The next two sections outline two of its major initiatives: dispute settlement and the Doha Development Agenda.

General Agreement on Trade in Services (GATS) A WTO agreement governing the international trade of services.

Trade-Related Aspects of Intellectual Property Rights (TRIPS) A WTO agreement governing intellectual property rights.

IN FOCUS 9.1

Russia in the WTO

In August 2012, Russia finally joined the WTO after 18 years of negotiations. Since China joined the WTO in 2001, Russia has been the largest economy outside of the WTO and has thus faced higher trade barriers when exporting to virtually all other countries. WTO membership has opened up markets to Russia but it also requires that Russia reduces its tariffs over the next eight years. By 2020 the weighted average of tariffs applied to Russian imports was scheduled to fall to 5.8% from 13.0% in 2011.

Russia's trade structure is quite unusual in that 71% of its exports are fuels and mining products, whereas 75% of its imports are in manufacturing. Commentators varied in their assessments of the likely impact of WTO membership. Optimists predicted that liberalization would lead to intensified competition in manufacturing and service sectors, and better access to latest technology. Therefore, the manufacturing and service sectors would be strengthened. Pessimists pointed to the removal of tariffs that protected the agricultural machinery, truck manufacturing and airline manufacturing industries especially. This could lead to the collapse of these sectors under import competition, and therefore a re-enforcement of the natural resource dependency of the Russia economy.

Russia's WTO membership also has potentially important impact on EU external trade, as Russia is the fourth-largest market outside the EU for EU firms (6.8% of extra-EU exports), and the second-largest source for extra-EU imports (12.2%), behind China (16.6%) but ahead of the USA (11.6%). Eastern members of the EU especially have a high share of their

Figure 9.2   Russia as EU export destination (in % of total exports)

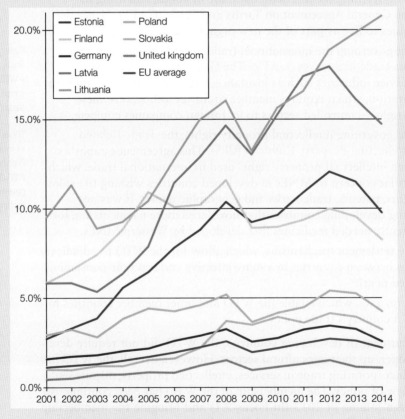

Source: Authors' creation using data from Eurostat.

international trade with Russia. Since the EU had earlier granted Russia most-favoured nation status, the main impact of WTO membership on EU-Russia relationship was expected in service industries, which Russia committed to liberalize and open to international competition.

A major change of actual WTO membership, as opposed to most-favoured nation status, is participation in the WTO's dispute settlement. The first dispute against Russia was filed by Japan in 2013 over a recycling fee that Russia imposes on imported cars, but not on (most) domestically produced cars. Russia called for WTO dispute settlement for the first time in January 2014 over the EU's procedures for calculating dumping margins in anti-dumping investigations.

Did the WTO membership actually benefit EU-Russia trade? Figure 9.2 shows exports to Russia from selected EU countries as a percentage of their total exports. Russia's role as customer for EU products and services has steadily grown, especially for countries in closer geographic proximity. In addition to Russia's strong economic performance, this trend reflects that many trade liberalization measures had been phased in before actual WTO membership in 2012. Contrary to expectations, in the first two years of WTO membership, EU exports to Russia actually dropped from €123 billion to €103 billion (from 2.7% of EU exports to 2.2%) due to adverse economic and political developments. In particular, the EU and Russia imposed trade sanctions on each other due to the dispute over the Russian annexation of the Crimea, and the conflicts in eastern Ukraine. The WTO could not prevent these trade sanctions.

Sources: (1) *The Economist*, 2012, Industry in Russia: Lurching into the fast lane, July 14; (2) O. Shepotylo & S. Tarr, 2012, Impact of WTO accession and the customs union on the bound and applied tariff rates of the Russia Federation, Policy Research Working Paper #6161, World Bank; (3) V. Evseev & R. Wilson, 2012, WTO Accession: Implications for Russia, *Russian Analytical Digest*, no. 199, p.11–16; (3) WTO, 2012–2014, various news items, www.wto.org/emgilsh/news_e/news_e.htm/; (4) WTO, 2015, trade profiles, stat.wto.org/Home/WSDBHome.aspx?/Language=E; (4) Day P., 2014, A tale of two sanctions, BBC podcast, http://www.bbc.co.uk/programmes/b04stlw4.

Trade dispute settlement

One of the core activities of the WTO is its dispute settlement mechanism, which aims to resolve conflicts between governments over trade-related matters.[4] Before the WTO, the old GATT mechanisms experienced (1) long delays, (2) blocking by accused countries and (3) inadequate enforcement. The WTO dispute settlement mechanism addresses these three problems.

dispute settlement mechanism
A procedure of the WTO to resolve conflicts between governments over trade-related matters.

The preferred approach is to facilitate negotiations between the two countries to help them settle the dispute themselves. When a country submits a formal complaint to WTO, the first stage is thus a period of mandatory bilateral consultations. If this consultation fails, the WTO establishes a panel of experts to investigate the case, hear the opinions of the two parties, and eventually issue a report. This report is the basis for the ruling of the WTO. As it can only be rejected by consensus, it generally is the same as the final ruling. The whole process follows a tight timeline for each stage, and lasts about 12 months (or 15 months if a country appeals). This process avoids the long delays of the old GATT system, and it makes it impossible for countries to block rulings against them. WTO decisions are final.

In terms of enforcement, the WTO does *not* have its own enforcement capability. The WTO simply recommends that the losing countries change their laws or practices and, if they do not do so, may authorize the winning countries to use tariff retaliation to compel the offending countries' compliance with the WTO rulings. That is more than the old GATT could do, yet still lacks real enforcement 'teeth'. A country that has lost a dispute case can choose its own options: (1) change its laws or practices to be in compliance or (2) defy the ruling by doing nothing and be willing to suffer trade retaliation by winning countries, known as 'punitive duties'. Trade sanctions are of course a dubious measure, because they involve raising tariffs and imposing additional costs on the winning country's own importers. It can be effective if used strategically to hit the other country in a sensitive area. Yet for small countries in dispute with a big country, it can be mainly symbolic.[5]

Fundamentally, a WTO ruling is a *recommendation* and not an order; no higher level entity can order a sovereign government to do something against its wishes. In other words, the offending country retains full sovereignty in its decision on whether or not to implement a panel recommendation. Most of the WTO's trade dispute rulings are resolved without resorting to trade retaliation. As shown in the 'shrimp-turtle' case (In Focus 9.2), even some of the most powerful countries, such as the USA, have lost cases and have painfully adjusted their own laws and practices to be in compliance with the WTO rulings. However, certain 'big' cases, such as the conflict between *Airbus* and *Boeing* (Opening Case), have been in dispute for decades. The WTO tends to condemn subsidies, but as long as both the EU and US support their aircraft makers, and favour their own firms in military procurement, no end is in sight.

IN FOCUS 9.2

Beef and shrimp: is the WTO over-reaching?

The purpose of the WTO's Appellate Body is to settle trade conflicts between countries, and to eliminate national regulations that create unjustified trade barriers. But when is a regulation justified to protect the health of the citizens, or of the environment, and when does it constitute an unfair trade barrier? Social and environmental activists often disagree with the assessments of the WTO, which has led to deep suspicion of the WTO, and large demonstrations.

To illustrate the issues underlying the conflict, let us consider two long-running disputes. In the USA, it has long been common practice that cattle are treated with growth hormones, which speed up the growth of meat in animals. Since there are no specific labelling requirements regarding hormone treatment, US consumers are often unaware of this, and it is not a big issue in domestic politics. However, many other countries, including the EU, consider hormone treatment of cattle as either harmful to the animals, harmful to human health, or both. Following extensive lobbying by consumer groups, the EU thus issued a directive in 1989 that outlawed hormone treatment, as well as the import of hormone-treated meat.

The USA has been trying to push its hormone-treated beef into global markets ever since, calling laws such as these an unfair trade barrier. Unfortunately, there exists no scientific consensus on whether or not hormone-treated beef is indeed harmful to human health. Underlying this dispute is a different attitude to risk: European nations are often following a precautionary principle in designing their rules, whereas the USA tend to ban only 'proven harmful' substances. The World Organization for Animal Health declined to rule on the matter, whereas the UN Food and Agriculture Organization voted in 1991 against a motion on the matter brought by the USA. However, the WTO Appellate Body ruled in 1998 that the EU import ban of hormone-treated beef was in violation of free trade principles because it was not based on adequate scientific evidence. The EU nevertheless left the ban in place, but it has remained a major conflict in EU-USA relations ever since, including the negotiations over TTIP. In bilateral FTAs with other partners, the USA have been able to open markets for their beef.

In other cases, the USA were at the receiving end of the WTO's predominance of free trade reasoning. For example, the WTO ruled against the US import ban of shrimp from countries that did not adequately protect turtles in their shrimp fishing operations. The USA claimed that shrimp trawlers from India, Malaysia, Pakistan and Thailand often caught shrimp with nets that trapped and killed an estimated 150 000 sea turtles each year. The four countries complained to the WTO, arguing that the US Endangered Species Act was an illegal trade barrier. The WTO panel ruled in their favour and provoked a firestorm of criticism from environmentalists. In its final ruling, the WTO Appellate Body argued that the USA lost the case *not* because it sought to protect the environment, but because it violated the principle of non-discrimination.

It provided countries in the Caribbean technical and financial assistance to equip their fishing boats, but did not give the same assistance to the four complaining countries. After its appeal failed, the USA reached agreements with the four countries to provide similar technical and financial assistance.

The beef hormone case and the shrimp-turtle case are cause célèbre among anti-WTO advocates, who fear that the WTO regime is undermining democracy by allowing judges in Geneva to constrain national authorities' ability to implement policies aimed at protecting health standards and the natural environment.

Sources: (1) W. Kerr & J. Hobbs, 2002, The North American–European Union dispute over beef produced using growth hormones, WE, 25(2): 283–292; (2) D.L. Prost, 2006, The precautionary principle and risk assessment in international food safety, Risk Analysis, 5: 1259–1273; (3) A. Walter & G. Sen, 2009, Analyzing the Global Political Economy, Princeton: Princeton University Press; (4) S. Epstein, 2010, Hormones in U.S. Beef, Huffington Post, March 18; (5) D. Rodrik, 2011, The Globalization Paradox, Oxford: Oxford University Press; (6) J. Polti & J. Chaffin, 2013, US-EU talks, Financial Times, April 17.

The Doha Development Agenda

Since 2001, trade negotiators have been discussing how global trade can become more inclusive and help the world's poor. Consequently, the next round of WTO negotiations carried the official title of Doha Development Agenda (named after the city of Doha, in Qatar). Its ambitions included: (1) to reduce agricultural subsidies in developed countries to facilitate exports from developing countries, (2) to slash tariffs, especially in industries that developing countries might benefit from (such as textiles), (3) to free up trade in services[6] and (4) to strengthen intellectual property protection. The first two items were pushed primarily by developing countries (and several NGOs), the other two by developed economies (led by the USA and the EU). In these trade negotiations the EU is representing all its member countries, such that Europe speaks with one voice – though it is often difficult for the members to agree what that EU voice should say.

The negotiations require bringing divergent interests of the 160 members together. The 'hot potato' is often agriculture. Australia and most developing countries demanded that Japan, the EU and the USA reduce farm subsidies. Yet the politically influential farm lobbies in the USA, the EU and Japan continue to undermine such efforts. On the other hand, many developing countries, led by India, resist tightening protection of intellectual property rights (IPR), notably on pharmaceuticals because they need drugs to fight national emergencies, such as HIV/AIDS and other pandemics. However, as negotiations progress, the power within the WTO has been shifting towards Asia because of both the strong economic growth and the greater trade interdependence in global supply chains.[7]

After several rounds of negotiations, in December 2013 in Bali, Indonesia, 159 members struck a trade facilitation agreement (TFA) – a pledge to cut red tape at customs posts in all countries. Although the TFA was far narrower and less ambitious than the sweeping deal envisioned when the Doha Agenda was first launched, it was viewed as a big win. However, it collapsed when India withdrew its support. The 'hot potato' again turned out to be food subsidies (see In Focus 9.3). The sheer complexity of an agreement on 'everything' among 159 member countries proved to be a challenge too far.

The negotiations are further complicated by new issues added to the agenda: Europe and North America are increasingly paying attention to issues such as labour and environmental standards, and as they are increasing requirements at home, they also want to make sure imported goods live up to the same standards (Chapter 10). Emerging economies, in contrast, often see a lot of this 'CSR agenda' as a new form of protectionism.

Doha Development Agenda
A round of WTO negotiations started in Doha, Qatar, in 2001 focusing on economic development.

IN FOCUS 9.3

Food versus trade?

In December 2013 in Bali, Indonesia, member countries of the WTO struck a trade facilitation agreement (TFA) – a pledge to cut red tape at customs posts around the world. Limited in scope, the deal would simplify customs red tape, rather than tackling the thornier problems on the negotiation agenda, such as agricultural subsidies and intellectual property. Still, it was estimated to add up to $400 billion a year to the global economy.

However, in July 2014, India withdrew its support, thus delaying the implementation of the deal. India, like many developing countries, is concerned about its 'food security' policies, in other words, its dependence on imports and highly-volatile world market prices. India's subsidies for food would soon grow large enough to violate WTO rules, which dictate that no developing country could subsidize more than 10% of the total value of harvests to farmers. Already spending $19 billion (1% of GDP) on such subsidies, India may exceed the 10% limit in the near future. When that happens, India could be subject to a WTO

challenge. The new Narendra Modi administration, elected into power in early 2014, insisted that it would not sacrifice food security on the altar of global trade. Even the WTO's efforts to let India have four extra years (until 2017) of immunity from challenge were not viewed as good enough. In other words, India would not trade food security for trade.

India is hardly the only protectionist country when it comes to agricultural subsidies. According to *The Economist*, 'the rich countries are the worst culprits'. Japanese rice and sugar tariffs are, respectively, 778% and 328%. The EU dishes out 40% of its budget to farmers. But, by giving up the gains from more smooth trade, India is also hurting itself. Its food subsidies lead to huge stockpiles of unwanted products and they fan corruption. In the end, the biggest loser seems to be the WTO.

Sources: (1) *The Economist*, 2013, The Indian problem, November 23; (2) *The Economist*, 2013, Unaccustomed victory, December 14; (3) *The Economist*, 2014, Bailing out from Bali, August 9; (4) *The Economist*, 2014, No more grand bargains, August 9; (5) M. Kumar & T. Miles, 2014, India says WTO deal is not dead, *Reuters*, August 1.

THE MULTILATERAL MONETARY SYSTEM

LEARNING OBJECTIVE

2   Explain the multilateral institutions of the global monetary system, and their current challenges

International Monetary Fund (IMF)
A multilateral organization promoting international monetary cooperation and providing temporary financial assistance to countries with balance of payments problems.

Recall from Chapter 7 that, after World War II, a fixed exchange rate system was created with the US dollar as the anchor currency. Along with this Bretton Woods system the International Monetary Fund (IMF) was created to help countries maintain the fixed exchange rate.[8] Since the 1970s, the IMF no longer acts to secure stable exchange rates, but its mandate shifted to promoting international monetary cooperation and providing temporary financial assistance to member countries to help overcome balance of payments problems. The IMF performs three primary activities on behalf of its 188 member countries: (1) monitoring the global economy, (2) providing technical assistance to developing countries and (3) lending to countries in financial difficulties.

The lending activity of the IMF is focused on helping countries experiencing severe balance of payments problems. The IMF can be viewed as a lender of last resort, to assist member countries should they get into financial difficulty. By definition, the IMF's lending refers to loans, not free grants. IMF loans usually have to be repaid in one to five years. Although there are some extensions for payments, no member country has defaulted. The ideal scenario for the IMF to make a difference is that when a country suffers from a balance of payments crisis (for example, rapid outflow of capital) that may trigger a financial crisis, the IMF can step in and inject funds in the short term.

While an IMF loan provides short-term financial resources, it also comes with strings attached – policy reforms that the recipient country must undertake as condition for receiving the loan. The aim of this IMF conditionality is to fight the sources of macroeconomic imbalances, notably inflation and government deficits – and should ensure that the country is *able* to repay the loan and to finance its capital needs through normal financial markets.[9] Thus the IMF typically imposes conditions that entail belt-tightening, by pushing governments to embark on reforms that they probably would not have undertaken otherwise. The details – where to cut government expenditures or to raise revenues – are normally negotiated with the government of the country. For instance, when the IMF provided a $30 billion loan to Brazil in 2002, the Brazilian government agreed to maintain a budget surplus of 3.75% of GDP or higher to pay for government debt. After a few years of relative calm, the IMF became again the 'global economic fireman' during the global crisis of 2008/09, providing rapid-fire bailouts to several countries, mostly in Europe (see Figure 9.3). While these bailouts required painful adjustments, they helped

IMF conditionality
Conditions that the IMF attaches to loans to bail out countries in financial distress.

Figure 9.3 The largest IMF bailouts since 2000 (in billion euros)

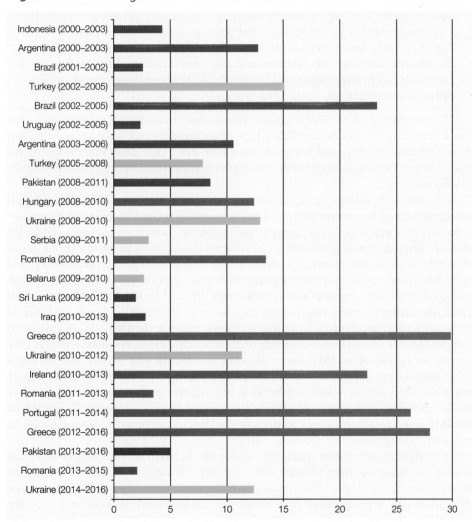

Notes: The 25 largest stand-by arrangements (SBR) and extended arrangements (EFF). Colour codes: red = EU member; green = other European countries; blue = non-European countries.

Source: Authors' creation using data extracted from various pages at www.inf.org (accessed March 2015).

most of these economies to recover by 2011.[10] However, in the following years, the eurozone was under stress, and the IMF provided some of the largest loan facilities in its history to Greece, Portugal and Ireland (also see Chapter 8). Somewhat embarrassingly for Europe, the IMF as an organization traditionally mainly helping developing countries recently had to turn its main attention to relatively advanced economies.

While the IMF comes to the rescue, it is not necessarily popular in the countries that it helps. That is because the conditions attached to bailout loans are often unpopular among those concerned. MIT Professor Simon Johnson, formerly a senior economist with the IMF, observes that as an IMF adviser, 'you're never at the top of anyone's dance card' because, essentially, the 'IMF specializes in telling its clients what they don't want to hear'. The advice that political and financial leaders don't like to hear boils down to this: desperate economic situations are often caused by elites overreaching themselves – and the necessary reforms involve cutting the financial wealth, as well as the political influence of these elites. In Johnson's words:

> 'Eventually, as the oligarchs in Putin's Russia now realize, some within the elite have to lose out before recovery can begin. It's a game of musical chairs: there just aren't enough currency reserves to take care of everyone, and the government cannot afford to take over private-sector debt completely. So the IMF staff looks into the eyes of the minister of finance and decide whether the government is serious yet. The fund will give even a country like Russia a loan eventually, but first it wants to make sure Prime Minister Putin is ready, willing, and able to be tough on some of his friends.'[11]

The complexity of the IMF's actions means that it cannot please everyone. One line of criticism centres on the IMF's lack of accountability.[12] IMF officials are not democratically elected, and some of them may even lack deep knowledge of the host country. Consequently, IMF-induced adjustment programmes can be politically explosive.

A second and perhaps more challenging criticism is that the IMF's 'one-size-fits-all' strategy may be inappropriate.[13] Deficit spending is used by many Western governments as a major policy weapon to pull a country out of an economic crisis. Yet the IMF often demands governments in vulnerable countries, in the midst of a major economic crisis, to balance their budgets by slashing spending (such as cutting petrol subsidies). Some argue that these actions often make the crisis far worse than it needs to be. After the IMF came to rescue economies affected by the 1997 Asian financial crisis, the unemployment rate temporarily went up threefold in Thailand, fourfold in South Korea, and tenfold in Indonesia. Some criticize the IMF for sticking to its policies despite inconclusive evidence of their merits. However, demonstrating the success or failure of an IMF rescue package is difficult: you would have to know what would have happened without the rescue package. Obviously, times are tough when the IMF arrives – but is it because of excessive and unsustainable spending before the crisis, or because the IMF is 'too tough'? Some critics actually argue that the IMF is too soft – allowing countries to run deficits that are not sustainable in the medium to long term.

The IMF has continuously modified its approach, based on experiences and analyses of various crises over the past three decades.[14] Since no two countries – or two crises – are identical, the IMF constantly faces a dilemma when going into action: how to design a programme that brings the country back to economic stability, while limiting social disruptions? The financial crisis of 2008/09 has led to renewed debates around the pros and cons of IMF conditionality and has led to some reform initiatives – notably to take a longer view on balancing government budgets to reduce the pain of austerity.[15]

REGIONAL AND BILATERAL ECONOMIC INTEGRATION

Evolution of regional integrations

Some integration and coordination is taking place worldwide, yet other initiatives of great practical relevance to business occur at a regional level. In Chapter 8, we discussed European integration, yet regional integration is not limited to Europe, it is also a common feature in other parts of the world. In particular, trade liberalization in the form of regional and bilateral free trade areas (FTAs) has proliferated. FTAs exist on all continents:

- The North American Free Trade Agreement (NAFTA) between Canada, Mexico and the USA came into effect in 1994 and enabled trilateral merchandise trade to grow from $289 billion in 1993 to $1.1 trillion in 2014 – a nearly fourfold increase. US trade with Canada tripled, and US trade with Mexico increased by 506% – while US trade with the rest of the world grew 279%. Canada and Mexico are the largest importers of US goods and each absorb more US imports than Britain, France and Germany combined.[16]

- In Asia, the longest-standing and most successful integration is the Association of Southeast Asian Nations (ASEAN), founded in 1967 (In Focus 9.4).

- The South Asian Free Trade Area (SAFTA), founded in 2004, brings together India, Pakistan, Bangladesh, Sri Lanka, the Maldives, Nepal and Bhutan, and commits partner countries to eliminate all tariffs on trade between member countries by 2016.

LEARNING OBJECTIVE

3 Explain the advantages and disadvantages of regional and bilateral economic integration

free trade area (FTA) A group of countries that remove trade barriers among themselves.

North American Free Trade Agreement (NAFTA) A free trade agreement between Canada, Mexico and the USA.

Association of Southeast Asian Nations (ASEAN) The organization underpinning regional economic integration in Southeast Asia.

South Asian Free Trade Area (SAFTA) Free trade area covering India, Pakistan, Bangladesh, Sri Lanka, The Maldives, Nepal and Bhutan.

IN FOCUS 9.4

ASEAN integrates regional economies

The ten member countries of ASEAN represent together a population of 617 million people, more than the 28-member EU. In 1992, ASEAN set up the ASEAN Free Trade Area (AFTA), which accelerated intra-ASEAN trade. In addition to the free trade agreement, ASEAN members have signed a number of further cooperation agreements regarding investment, trade in services, and single aviation market, as well as cultural and sport events. ASEAN has the ambition of moving from an FTA to a common market with the creation of the ASEAN Economic Community. The original implementation date has been postponed from January 1, 2015 to December 31, 2015, and some experts suggest that industries in some countries need even more time to prepare.

The benefits of regional integration are however limited by the fact that intra-ASEAN trade accounts for on average only 24.2% of exports of ASEAN countries, varying from 14.9% for Vietnam and 19.1% for the Philippines to 42.1% for Myanmar and 63.4% for Laos. ASEAN countries' main trading partners – China (11.7%), Japan (11.4%), the EU (9.8%) and the USA (8.3%) – are outside the region. The benefits of AFTA, thus, may be unequally distributed. Moreover, ASEAN is subject to considerable internal political tensions and cultural diversity. Most member countries have experienced authoritarian regimes in the recent past, but have moved towards democracy. In contrast, Myanmar (Burma) is run by an authoritarian military regime that until 2013 was subject to trade boycotts from many countries outside the region. Moreover, economic, cultural and religious diversity is considerably

Figure 9.4   ASEAN summit in Naypyitaw, Myanmar, November 2014

MYANMAR, 2014

17th ASEAN – JAPAN SUMMIT
Nay Pyi Taw, Myanmar, 12 November 2014

higher in ASEAN compared to the EU: per capita GDP in 2012 varied from €48 600 in Singapore and €34 000 in Brunei to €990 in Myanmar and €890 in Cambodia. Hence people in Singapore earn almost 50 times as much as those in Cambodia. Despite this internal economic diversity and persistent differences in political systems, economic integration is progressing.

ASEAN is also acting as a group in negotiating trade agreements with other countries, including agreements and regular summits with the EU. ASEAN is an important trading partner of the EU, accounting for 5.8% of EU imports and 4.7% of EU exports in 2013. Since 2007, ASEAN has signed bilateral FTAs with Korea, Japan, India, Australia

and New Zealand. Politically most significant may be the ASEAN China Free Trade Agreement (ACFTA), which came into effect in 2010, creating the largest FTA among emerging economies. ASEAN is also negotiating with all six regional neighbours about a far-reaching 'regional comprehensive economic partnership' (RCEP).

Sources: (1) ASEAN, 2008, *ASEAN Economic Community Blueprint*, www.aseansec.org (accessed February 2010); (2) *The Economist*, 2010, Banyan: Asia's never-closer union, February 6; (3) ASEAN, 2014, Intra- and extra-ASEAN trade 2013, www.asean.org (accessed March 2015); (4) DG Trade, 2014, European Union trade in goods with ASEAN, trade.ec.europa.eu (accessed March 2015).

- In the Middle East, the Gulf Cooperation Council (GCC) has since 1981 advanced political and economic integration between Saudi Arabia, Kuwait, Bahrain, Oman, Qatar and the United Arab Emirates. The GCC common market and customs union have been fully implemented in 2015.

- Based on a Chinese initiative, the Shanghai Cooperation Organization (SCO) brings together China, Russia and the Central Asian nations of Kazakhstan, Kyrgyzstan, Tajikistan and Uzbekistan. Originally a forum for military cooperation, the SCO also took various initiatives to facilitate economic cooperation, but not aiming for a deep comprehensive integration.

In South America, two regional integration schemes are competing with each other: Andean Community and Mercosur. Members of the Andean Community (launched in 1969) and Mercosur (launched in 1991) are mostly countries on the *western* and *eastern* sides of the Andean mountains respectively. The two integration initiatives reflect not only historical animosities between countries, but differences in economic systems: Mercosur countries tend to have more state intervention and trade protection, whereas the Andean Community is more free market and pro-free trade.[17] Membership in both initiatives has been changing over time, and initiatives for deeper integration are periodically aired but rarely implemented.[18] One obstacle is the lack of trade complementarity, as only about 5% and 20% of members' trade is within the Andean Community and Mercosur respectively. Their largest trading partner, the USA, lies outside the region. Thus Chile, Colombia, Panama and Peru signed bilateral FTAs with the USA to focus on North America rather than their hard to predict neighbours.[19]

In Africa, numerous regional integration initiatives are overlapping. While African countries are interested in reaping the benefits from regional economic integration, there is relatively little trade within Africa (amounting to less than 10% of the continent's total trade). Regional integration played an important role in West Africa, where ECOWAS reduced tariffs and customs barriers, an important measure in a part of the world where customs have a reputation for being slow and corrupt. The French-speaking countries of West Africa went even further, and introduced a common currency, the CFA franc, which is tied to the euro, and contributed to monetary stability in the region.[20]

Challenges to regional integration

Regional integration initiatives among emerging economies face (at least) four major challenges. First, neighbouring countries often face historical conflicts, some even wars, and fundamental ideological differences regarding their economic and political system. This inhibits commitments to opening borders and aligning regulatory regimes.

Second, the benefits of integration may be unequally distributed, such that some local production is replaced by imports, while in other sectors production is expanded on the back of rising exports. Yet workers may not be able to move easily from one sector to the other. For example, in Mexico, *maquiladora* (export assembly) factories blossomed under NAFTA, with jobs peaking at 1.3 million in 2000. Beyond *maquiladoras*, the export boom NAFTA caused reportedly accounted for more than half of the 3.5 million jobs created in Mexico. In the USA, political interest groups stirred up fears of widespread job losses – yet what is the evidence? Studies estimate that about 300 000 US jobs were lost due to NAFTA, which, on the other hand, added about 100 000 jobs. This net loss is small for an economy generating two million new jobs *every* year. Moreover, this count of jobs misses a pervasive but subtle benefit. NAFTA has allowed US firms to *preserve* US jobs, because 82% of the components used in Mexican assembly plants are US-made, whereas factories in Asia use far fewer US parts. Without

Gulf Cooperation Council (GCC)
Political and economic integration involving Saudi Arabia, Kuwait, Bahrain, Oman, Qatar and the United Arab Emirates.

Shanghai Cooperation Organization
Organization facilitating military and economic cooperation among China, Russia and four of the Central Asian nations.

Andean Community
A customs union in South America that was launched in 1969.

Mercosur
A customs union in South America that was launched in 1991.

ECOWAS
Economic integration in West Africa.

CFA franc
Common currency of French-speaking countries in West Africa.

NAFTA, entire industries might be lost rather than just the labour-intensive portions.[21]

Third, countries face structural differences in their economies, which makes them subject to asymmetric external shocks. Such asymmetries can inhibit deeper integration because countries might lose their ability to use economic policy to adjust to such shocks. For example, ideas for regional monetary unions have been discussed in Latin America, Southern Africa and Southeast Asia, but apart from the CFA franc, none have been implemented. The tensions in the eurozone further discourage emerging economies from experimenting with a monetary union.

Fourth, many neighbouring emerging economies share similar same kinds of comparative advantages, and therefore their main trading partner is either the USA or the EU. For example, most African countries have comparative advantages in export raw materials (oil, minerals and precious metals) or agricultural produce (coffee, cacao and fruit). Hence they would benefit most from access to European or North American markets, while the gains from regional trade are comparatively small.

Generalized System of Preferences (GSP)
A system of tariff reductions facilitating less and least developed country's access to EU markets.

To counter this challenge, countries have been negotiating 'North-South' trade agreements. The EU has been running a system of Generalized System of Preferences (GSP) since 1971, which gives many less-developed countries, mostly former colonies of France and the UK, easier access to EU markets. The most extensive benefits are offered to the least developed (poorest) countries, which face much-reduced tariff barriers when exporting to the EU.[22]

Two more ambitious initiatives aim to integrate the USA with regional FTAs. In Latin America, negotiations on the Free Trade Area of the Americas (FTAA) have been ongoing since 1998. Free trade oriented countries around the Pacific Ocean have been discussing a Trans-Pacific Partnership (TPP), but progress is slow.[23]

Bilateral trade and investment agreements

Australia-New Zealand Closer Economic Relations Trade Agreement (ANZCERTA)
A bilateral trade agreement between Australia and New Zealand.

In addition to regional integration, bilateral trade and investment treaties have been proliferating. One of the first was the Australia-New Zealand Closer Economic Relations Trade Agreement (ANZCERTA), launched in 1983, which has over time removed tariffs and NTBs between the two neighbouring countries. Citizens from both countries can also freely work and reside in the other country.

The USA has been leading the more recent trend of bilateral trade agreements. Starting with Israel in 1985, the USA has entered 20 bilateral free trade and investment agreements with countries as diverse as Australia, Singapore, Peru, Oman and Jordan.[24] US policymakers see bilateral agreements as an opportunity to push trade liberalization further than what could be achieved in multilateral forums like the WTO (where everyone has to agree on the same standards), while encouraging partner countries to pursue economic reforms that the USA believes to be beneficial, including, for example, service sector liberalization and the protection of intellectual property.

EU Canada Comprehensive Economic and Trade Agreement (CETA)
A economic integration agreement in negotiation between the EU and Canada.

Likewise, the EU has signed a number of bilateral trade agreements, mainly with neighbouring countries, and negotiations are under way with Canada over a EU Canada Comprehensive Economic and Trade Agreement (CETA) (see Integrated Case 'EU and Canada negotiate CETA') and with the USA over a Transatlantic Trade and Investment Partnership (TTIP).[25]

Transatlantic Trade and Investment Partnership (TTIP)
An economic integration agreement in negotiation between the EU and USA.

China joined the trend in 2005 with bilateral FTA deals with Chile and Pakistan, which were followed by many more. The Sino-Swiss FTA, which came into effect in 2014, was the first FTA between China and a European country. It frees most of Switzerland's industrial exports fully or partly from customs duties, while other tariffs will be phased out over the next 5 to 10 years; in some cases even 15 years (liquid pumps, filling machines, heat exchangers, industrial ovens).[26]

Early FTAs were concerned with the free movement of goods, and hence the removal of tariffs and basic non-tariff barriers, such as customs procedures. Over time, these agreements have become more and more ambitious with respect to the trade barriers they aim to remove. With the rise of service sectors, FTAs also aim to create platforms for service firms to internationalize – and in practice that means opening service sectors to foreign direct investment and creating a 'level playing field' between them and local firms. Thus FTAs are often connected to international investment agreements (IIAs) that aim to protect the interests of foreign direct investors.[27]

This makes these deals both more complex, and potentially controversial, for at least three reasons. First, liberalization of service sectors, like telecommunication or electricity networks, and opening them up to foreign investors, is not supported by all political stakeholders. Second, to facilitate foreign direct investment, the treaties also contain commitments not to change the rules of the game in the future in ways that would undermine the business of the foreign investor. Such commitments are controversial among those who foresee the need to regulate industries more tightly in the future, for example, for ethical, environmental or human health reasons. Third, many treaties include a commitment to settle conflicts between MNEs and host governments using investor-state dispute settlement (ISDS) by independent tribunals that are outside the national and supranational court systems (In Focus 9.5).

international investment agreements (IIAs)
Agreements between states to protect foreign direct investment between countries.

investor-state dispute settlement (ISDS)
Legal processes using tribunals that are outside the national and supranational court systems.

IN FOCUS 9.5

Disputes over ISDS tribunals

What happens if a foreign investor believes they have been treated unfairly in a host country? As a basic principle of international law, in each country the laws of that country apply and they are enforced by national courts. However, businesses operating across national borders have long included stipulations in their contracts that disputes between the contracting partners shall be referred to an international tribunal, such as the *Arbitrage Institute of the Stockholm Chamber of Commerce.*

Many international trade and investment treaties between countries introduce such tribunals also for conflicts between host governments and foreign investors, mostly the *International Centre for Settlement of Investment Disputes (ICSID),* an organization associated with the World Bank and based in Washington, DC. By moving such conflicts to ISDS tribunals, possible home biases of domestic courts are eliminated. Worldwide, 3268 different international treaties include investor protection and commitments to arbitrage procedures. A total of 608 cases have been brought to such tribunals over the past 20 years, with an increasing trend.

However, some of the rules and processes of these ISDS tribunals are considered unsatisfactory by campaigners and some political parties. For example, the tribunals consist of corporate lawyers, not judges appointed by a democratically legitimated authority, which raises concerns regarding their impartiality as well as their legitimacy. Thus in its *2012 World Investment Report* (page 88), UNCTAD noted:

'The shortcomings of the ISDS system have been well documented. Concerns include (i) an expansive use of IIAs [International Investment Agreements] that reaches beyond what was originally intended; (ii) contradictory interpretations of key IIA provisions by ad hoc tribunals, leading to uncertainty about their meaning; (iii) the inadequacy of ICSID's annulment or national judicial review mechanisms to correct substantive mistakes of first-level tribunals; (iv) the emergence of a 'club' of individuals who serve as counsel in some cases and arbitrators in others, often obtaining repeated appointments, thereby raising concerns about potential conflict of interest; (v) the practice of nominating arbitrators who are likely to support

the position of the party appointing him/her; (vi) the high costs and considerable length of arbitration proceedings; and (vii) overall concern about the legitimacy and equity of the system.'

At a more fundamental level, questions were raised over whether private tribunals would undermine national sovereignty and the independence and democratic legitimization of courts of law. One former judge of the German constitutional court argued that the special rights for investors not only violate the principles of the German constitutions, but also represent a systemic break of international law. Specifically, the equality before the law would be undermined if corporations with deep financial pockets can use private tribunals that are not accessible to private individuals or interest groups, or unaffordable for small businesses.

Public debates on ISDS tribunals were informed by high profile cases. Many recent cases are based on the Energy Charter Treaty, and involve foreign investors objecting to changes in national laws changing rates of subsides or taxation for renewable energy plants, notably in Spain and the Czech Republic. In Germany, the government faced a major conflict with the Swedish energy company *Vattenfall*. In the aftermath of the Fukushima nuclear meltdown in Japan, the German government decided to stop all use of nuclear power, and therefore shortened operating licences for existing power stations. The industry cried foul and demanded compensation. The normal process in such a case would be to directly negotiate, or if that fails, to sue the government in the domestic courts – which is what the owners of nuclear power stations, German *E.ON* and *RWE* as well as Swedish *Vattenfall*, did. However, *Vattenfall* enjoyed investor protection under the Energy Charter Treaty and therefore in addition went to the ICSID to sue for €4.7 billion in compensation. Those concerned about the general safety of nuclear power found the compensation frivolous, but even business-friendly politicians found the additional avenue that *Vattenfall* could use to extract compensation from German taxpayers inconsistent with an equal playing field.

In Canada, another case incensed political observers. *Lone Pine*, an energy company incorporated in the USA (but headquartered in Calgary), had made preparatory investments to extract shale gas below the St Laurence River. But the Quebec government, under pressure from environmental groups, issued a moratorium on fracking until the environmental risks had been better analyzed. In 2012, *Lone Pine* used a clause in the NAFTA treaty to sue the Canadian government for the infringement of its rights by a province of Canada. Specifically, *Lone Pine* argued that the moratorium represented an expropriation of its property rights, and it thus should be compensated by the Canadian government. Canadian companies, operating under Canadian law, cannot claim compensation under environmental protection laws and regulation.

The most controversial is the use of such arbitrage tribunals by the tobacco industry. For example, Australia introduced new labelling laws for cigarette packages in 2012. *Philip Morris* sued the Australian government in Australian courts and lost hands-down. But *Philip Morris* moved its brand ownership rights to *Philip Morris Asia* in Hong Kong before the new Australian rules came into effect. *Philip Morris Asia* then sued Australia under a 1993 bilateral trade and investment treaty between Hong Kong and Australia in an international tribunal, which dragged on for several years, at great cost to the government.

Neither of the three cases has been decided at the time of writing, nor are any substantive interim decisions publicly available on the pertinent legal websites.

Sources: **ISDS operations**: (1) UNCTAD, 2012, *World Investment Report 2012*; (2) UNCTAD, 2014, *Recent developments in ISDs*, IIA Issues Note 1/2014; (3) UNCTAD, 2015, *Recent Trends in IIAs and ISDS*, IIA Issues Note 1/2015; (4) R. Hank, 2015, Wozu braucht es Schiedsgerichte, *Frankfurter Allgemeine Zeitung*, February 2. **Legal and political objections**: (1) S. Bross, 2014, *Freihandelsabkommen,* Report #4/2014, Hans-Böckler-Foundation (18 pages); (2) T. Fitz, 2015, *Analyze und Bewertung des EU-Kanada Freihandelsabkommens CETA*, Hans-Böckler-Foundation (51 pages); (3) C. Crouch, 2015, Democracy at a TTIP'ing point, Juncture 21(3), www.ippr.org; (4) G. Monbiot, 2015, The TTIP trade deal will throw equality before the law on the corporate bonfire, *The Guardian*, January 13; (5) S. Liebrich, 2015, Ex-Verfassungsrichter geisslt geplante TTIP-Schiedsgerichte, *Süddeutsche Zeitung*, January 20. **Vattenfall case**: (1) International Institute for Sustainable Development, 2012, *The German Nuclear Phase-Out put to the test in international investment arbitration*, Briefing Note, June; (2) International Institute for Sustainable Development, 2014, *Der aktuelle Stand bei Vattenfall geg. Deutschland II*, December 2014. (3) M. Balser & M. Bauchmüller, 2014, Vattenfall fordert Milliarden Euro Schadenersatz, *Süddeutsche Zeitung*, October 15; (4) *Handelsblatt*, 2015, Hoffnung auf Schadensersatz sorgt für Auftrieb, January 28; (5) Tribunal documents at: italaw.com/cases/1654. **Lone Pine case**: (1) J. Gray, 2012, Quebec's St. Lawrence fracking ban challenged under NAFTA, *Globe and Mail*, November 22; (2) I. Solomon, 2013, No Fracking Way, *Huffington Post*, March 10; (3) Tribunal documents at: www.italaw.com/cases/1606. **Phillip Morris case**: (1) The Telegraph, 2011, Philip Morris sues Australian government over tobacco packaging, November 11; (2) *BBC News*, 2011, Philip Morris sues Australia over cigarette packaging, November 21; (3) P. Martin, 2012, Smoke signals: plans of Big Tobacco plain to see, *Sydney Morning Herald*, August 29; (4) Tribunal documents at: www.italaw.com/cases/851.

Trade creation or trade diversion?

Advocates of regional and bilateral FTAs see them as a convenient substitute for global free trade. Critics argue that they (1) permit countries with large markets to use their bargaining power more effectively, (2) lead to a hub-and-spoke system of international trade that further strengthens the countries at the hubs, (3) create fragmented rules for businesses operating in multiple countries and (4) increase trade diversion. The trade diversion effect happens when trade no longer follows comparative advantages (Chapter 5) but the political lines of FTAs.[28] For example, France and other southern European countries may have competitive advantages in clothing manufacturing *relative to* Germany and other northern European countries. With free trade inside the EU common market but an external EU tariff barrier, France may thus specialize in clothing and thus 'divert' trade, as Germans would buy textiles 'made in France' instead of importing them from China or Bangladesh. However, once the common tariffs are removed, French manufacturers face painful adjustment processes – as happened in 2005 when the MFA agreement expired and the EU thus allowed free import of textiles and clothing.

Many economists see bilateral agreement not only as a poor substitute for multilateral agreements, but also as an obstacle to future multilateral agreements. By design, regional and bilateral integration provides preferential treatments to members and thereby *discriminates* against non-members (which is allowed by WTO rules). It is still a form of protectionism centred on 'us versus them', except 'us' is now an expanded group of countries. For example, simulation studies of the EU-USA agreement TTIP suggest that EU countries and the US would benefit from TTIP, but other countries around the world may suffer considerable negative effects due to loss of exports to the US or the EU (Figure 9.5).[29]

Critics, such as esteemed trade economist Jagdish Bhagwati, argue that rather than walking on two legs (global and regional), 'we have wound up on all fours' – crawling with slow progress.[30] As FTAs proliferate, non-members feel that they are squeezed out and begin plotting their own regional and bilateral deals. Soon, the world may end up with a global 'spaghetti bowl' of different rules.

trade diversion
A change in trade pattern away from comparative advantages due to trade barriers.

DEBATES AND EXTENSIONS

The WTO and the IMF are probably the two most important multilateral organizations for global business. However, global coordination is also taking place in many other areas, and political leaders of the world continuously see need to address the challenges of the global economy, and societies in general. Thus lots of political meetings and multilateral organizations aim to facilitate the way we live together on this globe. The largest and most ambitious multilateral organization is the United Nations (UN), whose mission is to secure world peace. Here we extend the discussion on global integration with three more specific agendas of political negotiations and collaboration: (1) economic development, (2) stopping climate change, and (3) securing stability of the banking system (Table 9.2).

LEARNING OBJECTIVE

4 Participate in policy debates on the institutional framework for global economic integration

The development agenda

A major challenge for the global economy is the inequality between nations, and persistent poverty in many developing countries. This challenge has been recognized since the 1950s, and multilateral banks have been established to help fund development projects. In particular, the World Bank, based in Washington, DC,

World Bank
A multilateral bank designed to help developing countries, especially with project finance.

Figure 9.5 Estimated trade creation and diversion effects of TTIP

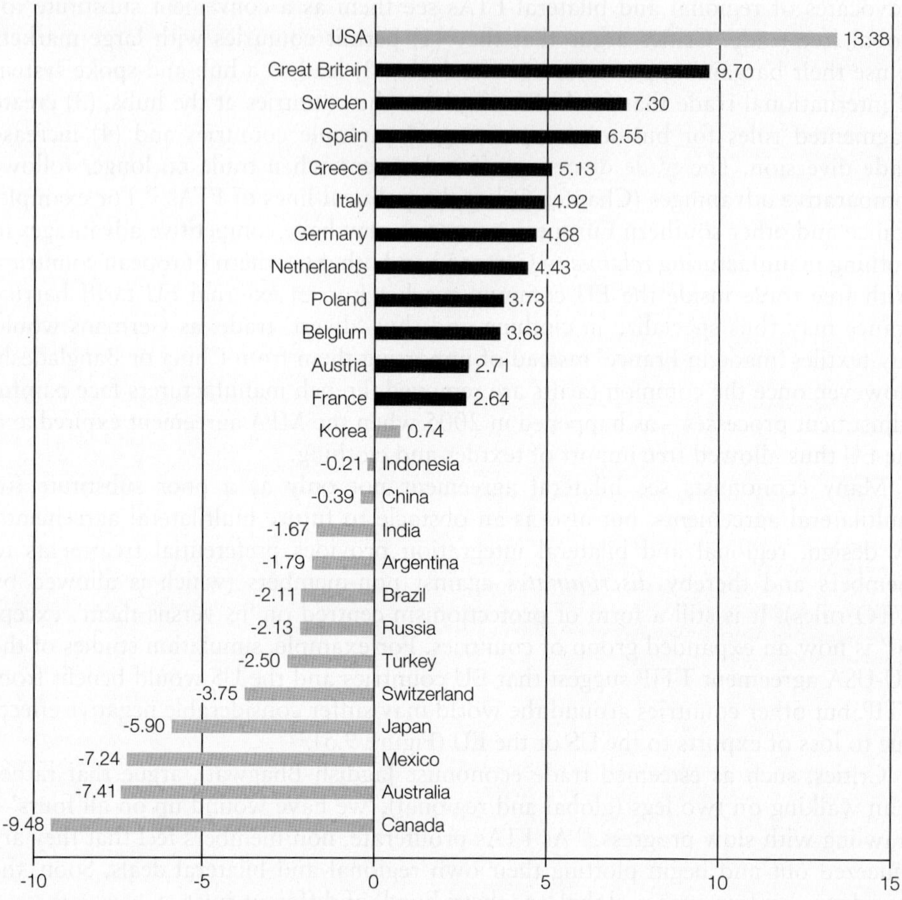

Note: Estimated change in long-term real GDP in per cent. Green = USA; blue = EU member countries; orange = other countries.

Source: G.J. Felbermayr & M. Larch (2013), The transatlantic trade and investment partnership (TTIP): Potentials, problems and perspectives, *CESifo Forum* 2, 49–60.

Table 9.2 Selected multilateral organizations

Policy agenda	Global	Regional
Trade	WTO	EU (common market), NAFTA, ASEAN, Mercosur
Monetary	IMF	EU (eurozone), CFA franc
Peace	United Nations	OSCE
Development finance	World Bank	ADB, AfDB, EBRD, IDB
Climate change	Kyoto Agreement, Copenhagen Accord	—
Financial sector regulation	Basel Committee	—

USA, provides loans for large projects, such as transport infrastructure, agricultural irrigation projects or banking sector reform. The World Bank specialized in projects that, because of their scale or country risk, would not be financed alone by the private sector, mainly in the poorest countries of the world. Specialized capabilities in project finance in developing countries and the support by the governments of the world (the World Bank's owners), enable financing projects that private investment bankers may consider as too risky. Recipients of the loans are normally the respective country's governments, or projects secured by government guarantees.[31]

In addition, the World Bank has a large pool of economic advisors who assess projects, and otherwise advise governments on a wide range of issues, such as how to facilitate economic growth, or run an effective government administration – a critical contribution in countries that only recently attained independence. Moreover, the World Bank and the IMF are running major research projects on economic development, and compile and publicize economic data. Some observers see these research, advisory and information collection functions as even more important than the project finance. As a student, you can benefit from this activity directly: when preparing an assignment or dissertation you may find databases such as the World Development Indicators or the International Financial Statistics valuable and up-to-date sources of information (and more reliable than data found in newspapers).

However, talking of the World Bank, it is important to remember that it is a bank, and not a charity. Banks give loans, not gifts (though the slightly lower interest rate charged may be considered a gift). Hence money received from the World Bank (like IMF loans) needs to be repaid, and projects thus need to generate more in revenues than they cost. In contrast, charities, national governments, or multilateral organizations like UNDP or UNCTAD may provide money or services for free – as a gift. Such official or private development aid is a gift from generous donors wishing to help societies suffering extreme poverty or the consequences of a major disaster, such as droughts, earthquakes, hurricanes or the Indian Ocean tsunami in 2004.

development aid
A gift from generous donors wishing to help developing countries.

The World Bank is complemented by regional development banks, such as the Asian Development Bank (ADB) based in Manila, the African Development Bank (AfDB) headquartered in Abidjan, Côte d'Ivoire, and the Inter-American Development Bank (IDB) based in Washington, DC, USA. In Europe, the European Bank for Reconstruction and Development (EBRD), based in London, serves transition economies. Established in 1991, when the economies of Central and Eastern Europe broke away from central and planning, the EBRD is heavily involved in the restructuring of former state-owned enterprises, and (differently from the World Bank) the EBRD is temporarily taking small equity stakes in selected privatized companies. In 2015, it added Greece to it countries of operation.[32] The BRICS countries announced in 2014 the intention to establish their own 'New Development Bank' as a financing mechanism for development projects in developing countries, which would both complement and compete with the World Bank in financing development projects.[33]

European Bank for Reconstruction and Development (EBRD)
A multilateral bank designed to help transition economies.

For businesses, development projects funded by the World Bank or other development banks provide opportunities to engage in infrastructure development. The backing of the World Bank reduces the risks normally associated with such projects in developing countries. In transition economies, the EBRD may also become a partner for a foreign investor, for example when acquiring an equity stake in a joint venture.

The climate change agenda

A major concern of the 21st century is the environmental impact of human activity.[34] International agreements cover a wide range of issues, from the conservation of rainforests to the protection of whales. A major focus of the environmental discussion has become the warming of the Earth's atmosphere as a result of greenhouse gas (GHG) emissions.

Kyoto Protocol
An agreement committing developed countries to limit their greenhouse gas emissions.

The Kyoto Protocol signed in 1997 was an attempt to achieve something immensely difficult. Under this protocol, developed countries pledged by 2012 to have cut emissions by 6% from 1990 levels. Each country was thus allowed to emit a certain quantity of CO_2. Governments issue emission permits to polluting firms within their borders, and such permits (essentially rights to pollute) can be bought and sold by firms worldwide. Through this emissions trading system, polluting firms can pay someone else (at home or in other participating countries) to cut emissions and claim credit.[35]

While the EU and Japan took Kyoto very seriously, the USA, which had been the world's number one emitter of GHG until recently, refused to ratify it during the Bush presidency. Developing countries, who were not leading polluters at the time, were not asked to commit to limits on emissions. They argued that the developed countries had caused the problem and thus needed to resolve it – and moreover, developing countries ought to be given a chance to develop first. Kyoto had a substantial impact on European businesses, where emission trading schemes stabilized pollution. However, the worldwide effects were limited because Kyoto did not cover the world's top-emitting country, the USA, and placed no limits on India and China, which developed faster than anticipated, making China the biggest source of GHG.

Recently, the scientific evidence about climate change has become stronger, showing for example that the average temperature on Earth has increased by 1 °C since the Industrial Revolution. Over a decade after Kyoto, GHGs in the atmosphere were still increasing. Worse, they were increasing at an accelerating rate. Because GHGs stay in the atmosphere for decades (and often centuries), continuous creation of GHGs is predicted to lead to global warming of as much as 5 °C by the end of this century, with disastrous ramifications. In addition to more volatile weather conditions, it would cause rising sea levels that result in the permanent flooding of many low-lying coastal areas (including whole countries and major ports), famine and possibly wars. Clearly, climate change is a global problem. The solution has to be global.

While world leaders agree, in principle, with the necessity to do something, they strongly disagree what each of them need to do. Since there is no 'free environmental lunch', the debate boils down to who has to give up most to stop global warming. In the past, developed countries have created most GHGs on a per capita and cumulative basis, while 1.6 billion people in the developing world still suffer from poverty and lack access to electricity. The World Bank urged developed countries to take aggressive action to reduce their own emissions, which 'would free some "pollution space" for developing countries, but more importantly, would stimulate innovation and the demand for new technologies so they can be rapidly scaled up'.[36]

A crucial bone of contention is coal-fired power plants. Relative to oil, gas, nuclear, wind, solar and biofuel sources, coal is not only the cheapest and the dirtiest, but also the most widely-used energy source in countries such as China. New sources of energy, such as wind, solar, and biofuel are still more expensive, such that they stand little chance in the absence of subsidies (or taxes on 'old' technologies). Not surprisingly, few politicians in the coal-dependent countries advocate the aggressive displacement of coal in power plants. Even Germany continues to rely on lignite, a particularly polluting type of coal, because of the country's determination to phase out nuclear fuels.

Proposals are numerous but solutions are few, because every new proposal generates new loopholes. Extending the emissions certificate scheme created in Kyoto (and implemented in Europe) would create a major allocation problem. A key sticking point in the debate on tradable emission certificates is the allocation of certificates: should every one of 7 billion people in the world receive the same quantity of certificates or should past pollution be the benchmark? The latter implies that those who polluted most in the past also get the rights to pollute more in the future. Critics argued that this would be a stealth tax that would be a job killer, encouraging firms to shift more production abroad. In fact, empirical estimates suggest that a country unilaterally committing to Kyoto standards may lose 13% of the export revenues.[37] So, if only some countries adapt higher standards, should they impose import duties on goods from countries that have more lax rules on emissions? Not surprisingly, China and other developing countries vehemently oppose such 'climate protectionism'. Thus *The Economist* suggests that climate change 'is a prisoner's dilemma, a free-rider problem, and the tragedy of the commons all rolled into one'.[38]

In 2009, world leaders agreed a new Copenhagen Accord which aimed to limit the level of global warming to no more than 2°C by the century's end. Developed countries committed to reducing their GHG emissions by 80% by 2050, while no targets were set for developing countries. Most European governments – and even more so NGOs – were deeply disappointed by the lack of a binding agreement.[39] In essence, countries agreed to keep talking. Subsequent rounds of talks, such as Durban 2011 and Lima 2014, created a lot of 'hot air' in terms of speeches urging the world community to act, but few hard and enforceable commitments.[40]

Copenhagen Accord
A declaration by developed and developing countries to combat climate change.

For businesses, this state of affairs implies that standards and incentive schemes are likely to continue to vary across countries, and that the expected stimulus for new technologies remains weak and uncertain. Energy-intensive industries, on the other hand, face fewer pressures for urgent (costly) adjustment than might have happened under more stringent commitments.

The financial sector regulation agenda

Banks take in savings and invest them in a variety of assets, from loans to businesses to government bonds. Banks are private businesses. Yet in contrast to most other businesses, the bankruptcy of a bank can have major consequences for large numbers of people – if not the entire economy. Throughout the last 200 years, several major recessions around the world have been triggered by 'bank runs' – people queuing outside the banks trying to take their savings out because they suddenly fear that their money is not longer safe.[41] In consequence, countries have created regulatory frameworks that aim to guarantee the stability of the financial sector. They require banks, for example, to hold minimum capital levels, report activities in great detail, and participate in insurance schemes.

Such regulations have reduced the frequency of major banking crises and scandals – but they have not eliminated them. In 2008, UK mortgage bank *Northern Rock* collapsed, soon to be followed by Icelandic *Landisbanken* and US investment bank *Lehman Brothers*. Others were rescued through emergency take-overs, like *Bear Stearns* in the US and *HBOS* in the UK. However, the consequences of these banking collapses were felt far beyond the countries concerned. More generally, changes in investing and risk-taking behaviour quickly spread around the world, even when there is no major crisis, which adds to the volatility of financial markets.[42] Hence a key concern on the international policy agenda became, do we need international coordination of bank regulation and supervision?

International standards for banks have been created by the Basel Committee for Banking Supervision (Basel Committee, in short), a group of central bankers from the major economies of the world. This committee established minimum regulatory standards, which have been revised in 2004 and 2011, known as Basel II and Basel III. In particular, these rules establish minimum capital requirements for banks – how much equity they need to have relative to the investments they make. The regulatory standards also link the capital requirements to the riskiness

Basel Committee
A group of central bankers establishing standards for banking supervision.

Basel II/Basel III
The name of a set of rules for banking regulation.

of the portfolio of investments of a bank.[43] For example, government bonds are less risky than shares in companies, or loans to small businesses. Moreover, a portfolio of different types of investment is less risky than putting 'all your eggs in a single basket'.

risk-rating agencies
Agencies that assign ratings to assets such as bond that indicate the level of riskiness of the asset.

While banks may use their own methods for assessing risks, in practice, risk-rating agencies such as *Moody's* and *Fitch* play an important role. They assign ratings (such as AAA, AA, A) to different assets, and these ratings then (indirectly) determine how much equity banks need to hold. In other words, the Basel criteria force banks to use ratings of a small number of agencies for their investment decisions. This has two undesirable side-effects.[44] First, changes in ratings trigger similar investment or divestment decision by different investors, such that small changes in ratings permeate quickly through the financial system. Hence the fact that everyone uses the same risk indicators actually *increases* systemic risk (In Focus 9.6).

IN FOCUS 9.6

Why are the rating agencies so powerful?

Banking regulations Basel II and Basel III require banks to use formal models and use external risk indices to assess the risk of their investment portfolio. These models and external risk indices are thus critical for key performance variables of the banks.

General established risk metrics have the advantage of creating objective criteria to assess how risky a bank is – and whether our savings with the bank are safe. However, if everyone is using the same risk models and the same external indicators provided by *Moody's* and *S&P* this has undesirable side-effects. First, before the financial crisis, the agencies did not rate certain complex assets correctly, in particular mortgage-backed deposit certificates in the USA, with fatal consequences for some investors.

Second, small changes in any of the indices can result in all the banks having to make adjustments in their investment portfolio – in other words they have to rebalance the risk profile of their portfolio quickly, to prevent their own rating from being affected. Hence a downgrading of an asset will trigger a lot of sales of that asset in a short time, resulting in a substantive change in the price, and consequently increased volatility of the price of the asset. Consequently, having all banks use the same risk metrics actually *increases* systemic risk – i.e. the chance that many banks experience financial difficulties at the same time.

The third flaw became apparent in 2011, when each blink from a rating agency triggered a flurry of trading activity in government bonds of various countries. Essentially, even the expectation of a change in a rating makes it more expensive for a borrower to get money from the banks or to rollover credits. The leading rating agencies are private, US-based financial institutions that produce the indices for their clients, who pay for the privilege. They (may) know how financial markets work in the USA, but their understanding of financial instruments used elsewhere appears sometimes limited.

These problems are not easy to fix. To reduce systematic risk, regulators would have to allow for (and encourage) a greater diversity of risk metrics. However, as long as *Moody's* and *S&P* are the gold standards of risk indices, those using other indices face unfavourable assessments by financial analysts and investors, and may thus be traded at a discount.

Sources: (1) F. Heid, 2007, The cyclical effects of the Basel II capital requirements, *JBF*, 31, 3885–3900; (2) N. Kuls & C. Tigges, 2007, A. Greenspan: Die Ratingagenturen wissen nicht was sie tun, *Frankfurter Allgemeine Zeitung*, September 22; (3) O. Henkel, 2009, *Die Abwracker: Wie Zocker und Politiker unsere Zukunft verspielen*, München: Heyne; (4) P. Slovnik, 2012, Systematically important banks and capital regulation challenges, *OECD Economics Department Working Papers*, No. 916.

Second, when assessing sovereign bonds – that is bonds issued by national governments – the rating agencies assess for example the possible impact of political events and of government spending plans. Since the verdict of the agencies has direct impact on the country's ability to raise capital on the markets, the agencies have considerable power to influence political decisions. Countries like Italy and Greece have thus been very critical about their supposedly unfair criteria.[45]

The regulatory standards came in for considerable criticism in the aftermath of the financial crisis because banks failed to protect against risks in those countries that were traditionally believed to have the most developed financial markets – the US and UK.[46] In particular, measures of risk failed to capture rare events that occur only once in a generation, so-called black swan events, because they employed data from only the most recent two decades.[47] Moreover, risk models focused each asset in isolation, and insufficiently (or not at all) considered the interdependence of different assets. They thus underestimated the risk in banks' investment portfolio as a whole.[48]

black swan events
Rare events that occur only once in a generation.

Reforms of banking regulation focus on two issues: the basic capital requirements, and the procedures of assessing the risk of banks' investment portfolios.[49] First, higher capital requirements force banks to reduce their lending to high-risk customers; unsurprisingly small and medium-sized enterprises have been complaining that it is getting more difficult for them to obtain bank loans. The policy objectives of providing finance to entrepreneurs and of securing stability of financial markets appear to be in conflict. Second, stress tests aim to assess the vulnerability of banks to different types of economy-wide shocks, yet the stress tests themselves introduce new forms of uncertainty into financial markets. It is not easy to be a banker in the age of new banking regulation.

IMPLICATIONS FOR PRACTICE

This chapter has introduced some of the rules of the game shaping global and regional economic integration. How does this knowledge help managers? Managers need to combine the insights from the institution-based view with those from the resource-based view to come up with strategies and solutions to capitalize on opportunities presented by global and regional economic integration. Three broad implications for action emerge (Table 9.3).

First, managers need to understand the rules of the game at both global and regional levels. Changes in the rules induced by, for example, FTAs change the viability of business models, and may force firms to rethink their strategies. For example, when the MFA was phased out in 2005, numerous managers at textile firms who had become comfortable under the MFA's protection complained about their lack of preparation. In fact, they had 30 years to prepare for this event. When the MFA

LEARNING OBJECTIVE

5   Draw implications for action

Table 9.3   Implications for action

- Managers need to understand the rules of the game at both global and regional levels to assess challenges and opportunities.

- Firms ought to make the most of their home region, as they are often better prepared to compete on regional rather than global levels.

- Managers need to be aware of and possibly engaged in political discussions, as these discussions are likely to shape the business environment of the future.

was signed in 1974, it was agreed that it would be phased out by 2005. The attitude that 'we don't care about (trade) politics' thus can lead to a failure in due diligence. In another example, firms that developed 'green' technologies early may benefit from new government policies aimed to address climate change – even though international treaties do not spell out mandatory policies – yet! The best managers expect their strategies to shift over time in response to changes in the 'big picture', taking advantage of new opportunities brought by global and regional integration.

Second, the proliferation of FTAs suggests that firms ought to make the most of them. The majority of international trade by EU countries is with other EU countries (Chapter 1). Likewise, the majority of the multinational enterprises (MNEs) generate most of their revenues in their home markets or their home region.[50] The largest MNEs may have a presence around the world, but their centre of gravity (measured by revenues) is often still close to home. Neighbouring countries within a region share some cultural, economic and geographic similarities – as well as FTAs. From a resource-based standpoint, most firms are better prepared to compete on regional rather than global levels. Managers, in short, need to think both local and global to design their strategies based on resources that they may be able to access anywhere in the world.[51]

Third, managers need to be aware of and possibly engaged in the political discussions shaping the business environment of the future. In the broadest sense, these debates are about capitalism as a unifying worldwide economic system. In theory (Chapter 5), the economic benefits of international trade are evident. Yet so are numerous conflicts over the distribution of these benefits and over undesirable side-effects. The discussion of multilateral institutions has highlighted the political nature of many of the rules governing international trade and investment. The widespread perception that the burden of the global economic crisis – caused by rich bankers in rich countries – falls strongly on the poor and the unskilled has given new impetus to critics of global integration. Even *The Economist* is concerned:

> 'For Western liberals, even ones who believe in open markets as unreservedly as this paper, that means facing up to some hard facts about the popularity of their creed. Western capitalism's victory over its rotten communist rival does not ensure it an enduring franchise with voters. As Karl Marx pointed out during globalization's last great surge forward in the 19th century, the magic of comparative advantage can be wearing – and cruel. It leaves behind losers in concentrated clumps (a closed tyre factory, for instance), whereas the more numerous winners (everybody driving cheaper cars) are desperate. It makes the wealthy very wealthy: in a global market, you will hit a bigger jackpot than in a local one. And capitalism has always been prone to spectacular booms and busts.'[52]

Businesses acting on this global stage of international trade, investment and finance are at the forefront of many of these debates. They thus face pressures to explain their role and their contributions to society to enhance their legitimacy, as well as the legitimacy of the system that allows them to prosper. MNEs have power and influence that enable them to make contributions to some of the issues discussed in this chapter. How and why companies assume responsibilities that go beyond generating profits for their shareholders, we discuss in the next chapter.

CHAPTER SUMMARY

1 Explain the multilateral institutions of global trade system, and their current challenges

- There are both political and economic benefits for global integration by trade.

- The GATT (1948–1994) significantly reduced tariff rates on merchandise trade.

- The WTO (1995–present) was set up not only to incorporate the GATT but also to cover trade in services, intellectual property, trade dispute settlement and peer review of trade policy.

- The Doha Development Agenda, aimed at promoting more trade and development, has thus far failed to accomplish its goals.

2 Explain the multilateral institutions of the global monetary system, and their current challenges

- The IMF promotes monetary cooperation and provides temporary financial assistance with balance of payments problems.

- IMF loans are usually conditional macro-economic or financial reforms, which is often controversial in the countries concerned.

3 Explain the advantages and disadvantages of regional and bilateral economic integration

- Regional economic integration brings together groups of likeminded countries, and thus is easier to negotiate than global agreements.

- In Latin America, Africa and some parts of Asia, regional trade agreements are often not very effective because countries' main export markets are outside the region.

- Bilateral FTAs often include commitment not only to reduce tariffs but to liberalize service sectors and adjust industry regulations.

4 Participate in policy debates on the institutional framework for global economic integration

- Development banks such as the World Bank provide loans for projects such as infrastructure in developing countries.

- The Kyoto Protocol and the Copenhagen Accord aim to combat climate change but are widely criticized for lacking tangible commitments.

- International banking standards promoted by the Basel Committee are being revised in view of the experiences of the global financial crisis.

5 Draw implications for action

- Managers need to understand the rules of the game at both global and regional.

- Many firms may be better prepared to compete on regional as opposed to global levels.

- Managers need to be aware of and possibly engaged in the political discussions likely to shape the business environment of the future.

KEY TERMS

Andean Community
Association of Southeast Asian Nations (ASEAN)
Australia-New Zealand Closer Economic Relations
    Trade Agreement (ANZCERTA)
Basel II/Basel III
Basel Committee
Black swan events
CFA franc
Comprehensive Economic and Trade Agreement (CETA)
Copenhagen Accord
Development aid
Dispute settlement mechanism
Doha Development Agenda
ECOWAS
EU Canada Comprehensive Economic and Trade
    Agreement (CETA)

European Bank for Reconstruction and
    Development (EBRD)
Free trade area (FTA)
General Agreement on Tariffs and Trade (GATT)
General Agreement on Trade in Services (GATS)
Generalized System of Preferences' (GSP)
Gulf Cooperation Council (GCC)
IMF conditionality
International investment agreements (IIAs)
International Monetary Fund (IMF)
Investor-state dispute settlement (ISDS)
Kyoto Protocol
Mercosur
Multilateral organizations
Non-discrimination principle
North American Free Trade Agreement (NAFTA)

Risk-rating agencies
Trade diversion
Transatlantic Trade and Investment Partnership (TTIP)
Shanghai Cooperation Organization (SCO)
South Asian Free Trade Area (SAFTA)

Trade-Related Aspects of Intellectual Property Rights
  (TRIPS)
World Bank
World Trade Organization (WTO)

CRITICAL DISCUSSION QUESTIONS

1 The WTO negotiations collapsed because many
   countries believed that no deal was better than a bad
   deal. Do you agree or disagree with this approach?
   Why?

2 Critics argue that the WTO promotes trade at the
   expense of the environment (see In Focus 9.3).
   Therefore, trade, or more broadly, globalization,
   needs to slow down. What is your view on the
   relationship between trade and the environment?

3 Who should be in charge of regulating and
   supervising banks that operate internationally? What
   principles should guide such regulation?

4 You are an IMF official going to a country whose
   export earnings are not able to pay for imports. The
   government has requested a loan from the IMF.
   Which areas would you recommend the government
   to cut: (1) education, (2) salaries for officials, (3) food
   subsidies, and/or (4) tax rebates for exporters?

RECOMMENDED READINGS

**B.M. Hoekman & M.M. Kostecki, 2009, *The Political
Economy of the World Trading System*, 3rd
ed., Oxford: Oxford University Press** – a book
explaining how the WTO has evolved and how it
works in practice.

**A. Narlikar, M. Daunton & R. Stern, 2012, *Oxford
Handbook of the World Trade Organization*,
Oxford: Oxford University Press** – a collection of
analytical papers on various aspects of the WTO.

**D. Rodrik, 2011, *The Globalization Paradox*, Oxford:
Oxford University Press** – a highly critical assessment
of globalization and the institutions shaping it.

**J. Stiglitz, 2002, *Globalization and its Discontents*,
New York: Norton** – a Nobel prize-winning
economist formerly associated with the IMF gives
a critical account of the state of globalization with a
special focus on the role of the IMF.

**A. Walter & G. Sen, 2009, *Analyzing the Global
Political Economy*, Princeton: Princeton
University Press** – explains how the global
economy works with focus on political forces and the
role of multilateral institutions.

CLOSING CASE

The future of globalization: Wärtsilä scenarios

Wärtsilä is a Finnish MNE that develops, manufactures
and services very large scale engines for ships and
power stations in particular. It prides itself in delivering
'complete lifecycle power solutions' and aims to 'offer
innovative products, services and solutions, based
on constantly better and environmentally compatible
technologies'. Following a sequence of acquisitions of
manufacturers and service providers around the world

over the past decade, *Wärtsilä* has become a global
leader in this sector of the energy industry, with a
turnover in 2014 of €4.8 billion and 17 700 employees
in 70 countries around the world.

The future of the energy industry is highly uncertain, and contingent on changes in consumer behaviour, politics and technology. How can a company in
such an uncertain environment plan for the future?
Wärtsilä decided to look into the future using a scenarios approach. It brought together experts inside

and outside the company to essentially develop stories describing what the future *might* look like. Their primary goal was to develop insights into the changes that they and their customers may face in the future.

The scenario team developed three scenarios that explore how the tensions between living standards of a growing population and climate change may shape the paths of globalization, and the energy sector in particular. In order to develop a broad perspective, an international and cross-functional team spent about 8000 hours discussing issues such as macroeconomics, geopolitics and the natural environment. Top managers from Wärtsilä thus engaged in discussions with academics, NGOs, business leaders, government representatives and other experts. A key theme throughout the scenarios was power – not only in the sense of energy, but influence: who can influence events and why?

The first scenario was named the 'green earth'. It envisages a consumer-driven cultural change that is based on a general awareness of the scarcity of resources and of the causes of climate change. This process leads to the adoption of energy-conserving technologies and behavioural changes, for example in the use of transportation. In parallel, governments adopt stringent environmental standards for the life-cycle of products and services. In consequence, for example, mass transportation and electrical vehicles become the preferred modes of transport; the demand for oil is reduced, and the demand for natural gas and renewable energy sources increases. The

geopolitical situation remains stable and the world economy grows at a modest pace.

The second scenario, called blue globe, predicts major changes in technology that enable economic growth while curbing emission. World leaders make substantive commitments to reducing greenhouse gas emissions, which spurs innovation in the energy sector. Technologies such as carbon-capture and storage, nuclear power and large-scale wind parks thus support continued economic growth. At the same time, transportation is electrified, which reduces its impact on the environment, and stops the rise of the price of oil. The reduced demand for oil leads to changes in geopolitics, with reduced political tensions.

The third scenario, called grey world, is more pessimistic. It envisages increased scarcity of resources, with energy security becoming the pivotal issue driving international business and politics. Research into new technologies does not lead to viable new solutions, while public opinion prevents the construction of new nuclear power stations. With leading economies dependent on imported energy, the bargaining power of oil- and gas-exporting countries increases. Energy production is largely based on fuels available locally, or traded based on bilateral trade agreements. Political tensions run high, and regional wars over energy and raw materials are a distinct possibility. Lack of intergovernmental agreements thus undermines the potential for economic prosperity.

Wärtsilä shared the scenarios with its business partners to stimulate discussions on future business

opportunities – and threats. Often the discussions triggered by the scenarios were the most interesting outcome. None of these scenarios was expected to come true exactly as described, but the future was likely to be a blend of all three. In this sense, the scenarios challenged conventional modes of thinking, and supported strategic planning and decision-making.

CASE DISCUSSION QUESTIONS

1 From a resource-based perspective, how is technological change likely to influence future paths of globalization?

2 From an institution-based perspective, how are national and international politics likely to influence future paths of globalization?

3 If you were an executive in the energy sector, how would you prepare your business for the future?

Sources: (1) Wärtsilä Corporation, 2008, *Powerscenarios 2023*, mimeo, Helsinki; (2) V. Riihimaki (Vice President of Wärtsilä Power Plants), 2009, *Keynote speech*, 10th Vaasa International Business Conference; (3) Wärtsilä Corporation, 2009, Corporate website www.wartsila.fi (last accessed May 2015).

NOTES

'For journal abbreviations please see page xx–xxi.'

1 WTO, 2014, 10 things the WTO can do, Geneva: WTO (p.12).
2 WTO, 2014, *as above* (p. 7). However, some argue that these estimates may be too optimistic. See J. Stiglitz & A. Charlton, 2005, *Fair Trade for All* (p. 46), New York: Oxford University Press.
3 D. Rodrik, 2011, *The Globalization Paradox*, Oxford: Oxford University Press (Chapter 4).
4 C. Bown & J. Pauwelyn, 2010, *The Law, Economics and Politics of Retaliation in WTO Dispute Settlement*, Cambridge: Cambridge University Press; A. Narlikar, M. Daunton, R. Stern, 2012, *Oxford Handbook of the World Trade Organization,* Oxford: Oxford University Press (Chapters 22 to 25).
5 M.L. Busch & E. Reinhardt, 2002, Developing countries and GATT/WTO dispute settlement, *JWT*, 37: 719–735; C. Bown & R. McCullogh, 2010, Developing countries, dispute settlement, and the Advisory Centre on WTO Law, *Journal of International Trade & Economic Development*, 19(1): 33–63.
6 J. Francois & B. Hoekman, 2010, Services trade and policy, *JEL*, 48: 642–692.
7 R. Baldwin, M. Kawai & G. Wignaraja, eds., 2014, *A World Trade Organization For The 21st Century*, Cheltenham: Elgar.
8 P. Kenen, 1985, Macroeconomic theory and policy, in: P. Kenen & R. Jones, *Handbook of International Economics*, Amsterdam: North Holland; E. Conway, 2014, *The Summit*, London: Little Brown.
9 M. Arabaci & S. Ever, 2014, The IMF and the catalytic Effect, *WE*, 37: 1575–1588.
10 *The Economist*, 2010, East European economies: Fingered by fate, March 20.
11 S. Johnson, 2009, The quiet coup, *The Atlantic*, May.
12 J. Stiglitz, 2002, *Globalization and Its Discontents*, New York: Norton; M. Copelovitch, 2010, Master or Servant? *International Studies Quarterly*, 54: 49–77.
13 S. Radelet & J. Sachs, 1998, The onset of the East Asian financial crisis, *NBER working paper* #6680; P. Krugman, 2008, *The Return of Depression Economics and the Crisis of 2008,* London: Penguin.
14 A.O. Krueger, 1998, Whither the World Bank and the IMF, *JEL*, 36, 1983–2020.
15 Ghosh, M. Chamon, C. Crowe, J. Kim & J. Ostry, 2009, Coping with the crisis: Policy options for emerging market countries, *IMF staff position paper*, Washington: IMF
16 *Business Week*, 2013, The stranger next door, May 6: 8–9
17 *The Economist*, 2006, Trade in South America, August 26.
18 *The Economist*, 2006, Mercosur's summit: Downhill from here, July 29; *The Economist*, 2011, Regional Integration in Latin America, April 9; *The Economist*, 2012, South American integration: Mercosur RIP?, July 14.
19 *Business Week*, 2014, Latin America's great divide, June 9
20 P. Masson, 2008, Currency unions in Africa, *WE*, 31: 533–547.
21 *Business Week*, 2001, NAFTA's scorecard, July 9.
22 DG Trade, 2014, Revised EU trade scheme to help developing countries applies on 1 January 2014, trade.ec.europa.eu (accessed March 2015).
23 *The Economist*, 2012, Partners and Rivals: Another trade agreement gets bogged down, September 22.
24 Office of the US Trade Representative, no date, Free Trade Agreements, www.ustr.gov (accessed March 2015).

25 *BBC News*, 2015, Transatlantic trade deal text leaked to BBC, February 26.

26 See publications linked from website of the Swiss Chinese Chamber of Commerce in China cn.swisscham.org/sha/fta (accessed January 2015).

27 S. Jandhyala & R. Weiner, 2014, Institutions sans frontières, *JIBS*, 45: 649–669.

28 M. Fratanni & C. Oh, 2009, Expanding RTAs, trade flows, and the multinational enterprise, *JIBS*, 40: 1206–1227; S. Urata & M. Okabe, 2014, Trade creation and diversion effects of regional trade agreements, *WE*, 37: 267–289.

29 G. Felbermayr & M. Larch, 2013, The transatlantic trade and investment partnership (TTIP), *CESinfo*, 14(2): 49–60.

30 J. Bhagwati, 2002, *Free Trade Today* (p. 119), Princeton, NJ: Princeton University Press.

31 M. Gavin & D. Rodrik, 1995, The World Bank in a historical perspective, *AER*, 85, P&P 329–334; Krueger, 1998, *as above*.

32 A. MacDonald, 2015, EBRD to launch funding in Greece, promoting enterprise, *Reuters*, March 3.

33 R. Desai & J. Vreeland, 2014, What the new bank of BRICS is all about, *Washington Post*, July 17; B. Eichengreen, 2014, Do the BRICS need their own development bank? *The Guardian*, August 14.

34 K.P. Gallagher, ed., 2008, *Handbook on Trade and the Environment*, Cheltenham: Elgar; D. Helm & C. Hepburn, 2009, *The Economics and Politics of Climate Change*, Oxford: Oxford University Press; J. Howard-Grenville, S. Buckle, B. Hoskins & G. George, 2014, Climate change and management, *AMJ*, 57: 615–623.

35 L. Goulder, 2013, Markets for pollution allowances, *JEP*, 27(1): 87–102; R. Newell, W. Piser & D. Raimi, 2013, Carbon markets 15 years after Kyoto, *JEP*, 27(1): 123–46.

36 World Bank, 2009, *World Development Report 2010*, Washington: World Bank; *The Economist*, 2009, The grass is always greener, April 24.

37 R. Aichele & G. Felbermayr, 2013, Estimating the effects of Kyoto on bilateral trade flows using matching econometrics, *WE*, 26: 303–330.

38 *The Economist*, 2009, A special report on climate change and the carbon economy, December 5.

39 *New York Times*, 2009, Climate deal announced, but falls short of expectations, December 18; *The Guardian*, 2010, various articles: If you want to know who's to blame for Copenhagen, look to the US Senate (December 21), How do I know China wrecked the Copenhagen deal? (December 22), Blame Denmark, not China (December 28).

40 *The Economist*, 2011, A Deal in Durban, December 17.

41 K. Galbraith, 1957, *The Great Crash* (reprinted: 1992, London: Palgrave); P. Krugman, 2008, *as above*.

42 S. Claessens, H. Tong & S. Wei, 2012, From financial crisis to the real economy, *Journal of Financial Intermediation*, 88: 375–387; V. Bruno & H. Shin, 2014, Globalization of corporate risk taking, *JIBS*, 45: 800–820.

43 F. Heid, 2007, The cyclical effects of the Basel II capital requirements, *JBF*, 31, 3885–3900.

44 H.O. Henkel, 2009, *Die Abwracker: Wie Zocker und Politiker unsere Zukunft verspielen*, München: Heyne.

45 S. Foley, 2014, Italy accuses S&P of not getting 'la dolce vita', *Financial Times*, February 4.

46 A. Walter & G. Sen, 2009, *Analyzing the Global Political Economy*, Princeton: Princeton University Press.

47 N. Taleb, 2010, *The Black Swan,* New York: Random House.

48 A.G. Haldane, 2009, Why Banks failed the stress Test, mimeo, Bank of England, February; R.M. Stulz, 2009, 6 ways companies mismanage risk, *HBR*, 87(3): 86–94.

49 *The Economist*, 2010, Reforming banking: Base camp Basel, January 23.

50 A. Rugman, 2005, *The Regional Multinationals*, Cambridge: Cambridge University Press; A. Rugman & A. Verbeke, 2004, A perspective on regional and global strategies of multinational enterprises, *JIBS*, 35: 3–18.

51 C.K. Prahalad & M. Krishnan, 2008, *The New Age of Innovation*, New York: McGraw Hill.

52 *The Economist*, 2009, So much gained, so much to lose, November 7

CHAPTER TEN

SOCIALLY RESPONSIBLE BUSINESS

LEARNING OBJECTIVES

After studying this chapter, you should be able to

1 Articulate a stakeholder view of the firm

2 Articulate CSR challenges faced by firms operating in the global economy

3 Explain how institutions influence firms' corporate social responsibility activities

4 Participate in three leading debates concerning corporate social responsibility

5 Draw implications for action

OPENING CASE

Starbucks: *standards in the spotlight*

Founded in 1971, *Starbucks* took off in 1987 after being purchased by Howard Schultz. Starting with a single store in Seattle, USA, *Starbucks* grew to 21 366 stores in 2014 (of which 10 713 were company-operated and 10 653 were licensed), and of which 6764 were outside the US. It generated worldwide revenues of about €16.4 billion, of which close to

€2.4 billion come from overseas operations. Around the world, *Starbucks* has created coffee houses where people feel comfortable to relax.

Since its 1987 (re)birth, *Starbucks* has tried to position itself as a company that, in the words of Schultz, 'puts people first and profits last'. In the 1990s, *Starbucks* developed an environmental mission statement, created a corporate social responsibility (CSR) department, named a senior vice-president

What is ethical practice for growing coffee?

for CSR, and began working with non-governmental organizations (NGOs). However, even so, NGOs frequently criticize *Starbucks* for failing social obligations.

In 2000, *Global Exchange*, an NGO promoting the idea of 'Fair Trade', launched a campaign against *Starbucks*. The Fair Trade movement advocated a minimum 'fair' price of US$1.26 per pound to ensure a 'living wage' for coffee producers – regardless of the highly volatile market price, which was only 64 cents per pound in 2000. In early 1999, *TransFair USA*, a third-party licensing organization, launched the Fair Trade Certified label. In November 1999, *TransFair* and *Starbucks* met to discuss Fair Trade coffee. While discussions were in progress, *Global Exchange* turned up the heat on *Starbucks* in February 2000 by demonstrating in front of a San Francisco store after a local TV station aired a clip on child labour on Guatemalan coffee farms. A few days later, during the open forum portion of the Starbucks shareholders meeting, *Global Exchange* activists took the microphone and demanded that Starbucks offer Fair Trade coffee. Things got heated and these activists were physically removed from the meeting.

Why did *Global Exchange* target *Starbucks* rather than any other company – there must have been firms with lower standards? From the perspective of an NGO seeking publicity, *Starbucks* presented an ideal target: (1) the firm itself claimed to be highly responsible, but appeared to fall short of other organizations' standards, (2) its popularity among the middle classes and intellectuals meant it was directly relevant to the

NGO's most likely supporters and (3) its geographic spread meant that customers around the world care about it – and might join campaigns against it. Protests might not only damage *Starbucks*' image but would also make it *physically* difficult for customers to enter and leave stores. Financially, buying Fair Trade coffee ($1.26 per pound) would not be prohibitively expensive, since *Starbucks* was already paying a premium price of $1.20 per pound. However, the price wasn't the key issue for *Starbucks*: the main obstacle was that Fair Trade co-ops could not deliver the consistent volume and quality of coffee beans that *Starbucks* required to consistently serve the same quality of drinks throughout its restaurants.

Starbucks could have ignored *Global Exchange*, fought back, or capitulated. However, *Starbucks* chose a middle ground, agreeing to sell Fair Trade coffee in its domestic company-owned stores. Soon, *Starbucks* became the largest US purchaser of Fair Trade coffee, purchasing 20 million pounds, or 6% of its coffee purchases in 2007. *Starbucks* accounted for 10% of all Fair Trade certified coffee worldwide (and 20% of Fair Trade certified coffee imported to the USA). In addition to purchasing Fair Trade coffee, *Starbucks* launched its own Coffee and Farmer Equity (CAFE) guidelines to 'ensure the sustainable supply of high quality coffee, achieve economic accountability, promote social responsibility within the coffee supply chain, and protect the environment', By 2009, Starbucks had a fleet of CAFE practice 'verifiers' (inspectors) and purchased 77% of its coffee from CAFE practice suppliers.

However, staying on side with campaigners for social environmental causes is challenging. Its high visibility has made *Starbucks* a target for a wide range of campaigners. For example, in the USA, activists threatened to boycott *Starbucks* for allowing customers to carry guns on their premises, which triggered opposition attacks from pro-gun lobbyists to 'buycott' (buy more) as long as they can come in with their guns. In Europe, *Starbucks* was framed as an aggressive tax avoider (see Chapter 6). *Reuters* news agency estimated that *Starbucks* paid only €12 million in corporate tax on €4.35 billion sales in the UK over 14 years, because it managed to transfer profits to the Netherlands through a licence fee of 6% of turnover and high interest rates on intra-company loans. In China, *Chinese Central Television* (CCTV) attacked *Starbucks* high prices and profits: many types of coffee cost as much as 50% more in China than in the US or the UK, enabling *Starbucks* to earn a healthy 32% profit margin, compared to 21% in the USA and 2% in Europe.

Since 2001 *Starbucks* has been publishing a Corporate Social Responsibility Annual Report. The report for the financial year 2013 lists ten goals for environmental and social performance indicators, and tracks the development of these indicators over six years, along with a target value for 2015. For example, on ethical sourcing, 95% of coffee was ethically sourced in 2013 through an externally audited system such as CAFE or Fairtrade, up from 77% in 2008. The target for 2015 is 100%. Other goals concern energy consumption, recycling and staff hours given to social purposes.

Schultz expresses his personal commitment:

'As Starbucks continues to grow, we will never stop exploring innovative solutions to effect positive change. We will continue to challenge ourselves, to set aspirational goals, always refusing to accept the status quo. This is who we are. I am proud that we continue to push, to learn, and to take big swings, knowing that sometimes we may miss. But we must continue to ask ourselves, what can Starbucks do to live up to our responsibility to all the people and communities we serve?'

While Schultz clearly believes that doing business ethically is important, getting everyone in the company to pull in the same direction is an on-going challenge. More challenging, perhaps, is that not everyone agrees on what 'ethical business' really means.

Sources: (1) P. Argenti, 2004, Collaborating with activists, *California Management Review*, 47: 91–116; (2) D. Vogel, 2005, The low value of virtue, *Harvard Business Review*, June: 26; (3) *Business Week*, 2007, Saving Starbucks' soul, April 9: 56–61; (4) M. Venkatraman & T. Nelson, 2009, From servicescape to consumptionscape: a photo-elicitation study of Starbucks in the New China, *JIBS*, 1010–1026; (5) *Reuters*, 2012, Special Report – Starbucks's European tax bill disappears down $100 million hole, November 1; (6) *CNN*, 2013, Starbucks to customers: Please don't bring your guns! September 18; (7) *Wall Street Journal*, 2013, Starbucks Is Criticized by Chinese State Media for Higher Prices, October 21. (8) Starbucks, 2014, *FY2013 Global Responsibility Report*, www.starbucks.com.

corporate social responsibility (CSR)
The consideration of, and response to, issues beyond the narrow economic, technical and legal requirements of the firm to accomplish social benefits along with the traditional economic gains which the firm seeks.

Many people believe that firms should contribute to the pivotal social and environmental issues in their communities. Although many regard *Starbucks* as a socially responsible firm, the Opening Case raises crucial questions: Should firms assume responsibility for social issues of the world? How should companies react to pressures to take responsibilities beyond their legal obligations? There are no easy answers to these questions. This chapter helps you to answer these and other questions concerning corporate social responsibility (CSR), defined as

'firms' consideration of, and response to, issues beyond the narrow economic, technical, and legal requirements of the firm to accomplish social benefits along with the traditional economic gains which the firm seeks.'[1]

A critical aspect of CSR is that it is voluntary. Hence in this chapter we will discuss (mainly) activities that firms do *beyond* their legal obligations. CSR activities are pursued not solely in the quest to increase profits, but to address important concerns of the wider society.

The advance of globalization has put several environmental and social issues on the agenda of both policymakers and MNEs (Chapter 9). A key concern is sustainability, which is defined as the ability 'to meet the needs of the present without compromising the ability of future generations to meet their needs'.[2] Once firms cross borders they are operating in multiple societies and thus are confronted with multiple sustainability concerns. In addition to formal and informal norms of each country, they may also face pressures at home with respect to their activities abroad – think of journalists investigating the practices of sub-suppliers in distant locations. Several multilateral organizations have developed statements expressing these multi-dimensional expectations, summarized in Table 10.1. Thus globalization is creating new challenges in terms of both the moral complexity of the issues – what is 'right' to do where? – and the operational complexity of implementing CSR practices throughout a global operation. Firms have responded these evolving expectations by developing triple bottom line strategies that take into account their *economic, social* and *environmental* performance.[3]

This chapter first introduces a stakeholder view of the firm to explain the evolution of CSR before looking at CSR issues arising specifically in the global operations of multinational enterprises (MNEs). Then we discuss how the institution-based view can explain international variations in CSR practices and communications, and apply the resource-based view to explore how companies may benefit from CSR. Debates and extensions follow.

sustainability
The ability to meet the needs of the present without compromising the ability of future generations to meet their needs around the world.

triple bottom line
The economic, social and environmental performance that simultaneously satisfies the demands of all stakeholder groups.

Table 10.1 CSR for MNEs: recommendations from international organizations

MNEs and host governments
- Should not interfere in the internal political affairs of the host country. (OECD, UN)
- Should consult governmental authorities and national employers' and workers' organizations to ensure that their investments conform to the economic and social development policies of the host country. (ICC, ILO, OECD, UN)
- Should reinvest some profits in the host country. (ICC)

MNEs and laws, regulations and politics
- Should respect the right of every country to exercise control over its natural resources. (UN)
- Should refrain from improper or illegal involvement in local politics. (OECD)
- Should not pay bribes or render improper benefits to public servants. (OECD, UN)

MNEs and technology transfer
- Should develop and adapt technologies to the needs of host countries. (ICC, ILO, OECD)
- Should provide reasonable terms and conditions when granting licences for industrial property rights. (ICC, OECD)

MNEs and environmental protection
- Should respect the host country laws and regulations concerning environmental protection. (OECD, UN)
- Should supply to host governments information concerning the environmental impact of MNE activities. (ICC, UN)

MNEs and consumer protection
- Should preserve the safety and health of consumers by disclosing appropriate information, labelling correctly and advertising accurately. (UN)

MNEs and employment practices
- Should cooperate with host governments to create jobs in certain locations. (ICC)
- Should give advance notice of plant closures and mitigate the adverse effects. (ICC, OECD)
- Should respect the rights for employees to engage in collective bargaining. (ILO, OECD)

MNEs and human rights
- Should respect human rights and fundamental freedoms in host countries. (UN)

Sources: (1) ICC: *The International Chamber of Commerce Guidelines for International Investment*, www.iccwbo.org; (2) ILO: *The International Labour Office Tripartite Declarations of Principles Concerning Multinational Enterprises and Social Policy*, www.ilo.org; (3) OECD: *The Organization for Economic Cooperation and Development Guidelines for Multinational Enterprises*, www.oecd.org; (4) UN: *The United Nations Code of Conduct on Transnational Corporations*, www.un.org.

STAKEHOLDERS OF THE FIRM

LEARNING OBJECTIVE

1 Articulate a stake-holder view of the firm

stakeholder
Any group or individual who can affect or is affected by the achievement of the organization's objectives.

At the heart of CSR is the concept of a stakeholder, which is 'any group or individual who can affect or is affected by the achievement of the organization's objectives'.[4] Shown in Figure 10.1, while shareholders are an important group of stakeholders, other stakeholders include managers, non-managerial employees (hereafter 'employees'), suppliers, customers, communities, governments, and social and environmental groups. A major debate on CSR is whether managers' efforts to promote the interests of these stakeholders are at odds with their fiduciary duty to safeguard shareholder interests. As firms' primary function is to serve as economic enterprises, they are unable to resolve all the social problems of the world. Yet on the other hand, firms have the power to contribute to solving some of the issues, especially when they act together. Therefore, the key is how to prioritize.[5]

Primary and secondary stakeholder groups

primary stakeholder groups
The constituents on which the firm relies for its continuous survival and prosperity.

The stakeholder view of the firm propagates that companies should take a broader view on who they are responsible to. Instead of only pursuing an economic bottom line, such as profits and shareholder returns, firms are expected to simultaneously address the demands of all stakeholder groups.[6]

Stakeholders vary in their importance to a firm.[7] Primary stakeholder groups are constituents on which the firm relies for its continuous survival and prosperity.

Figure 10.1 A stakeholder view of the firm

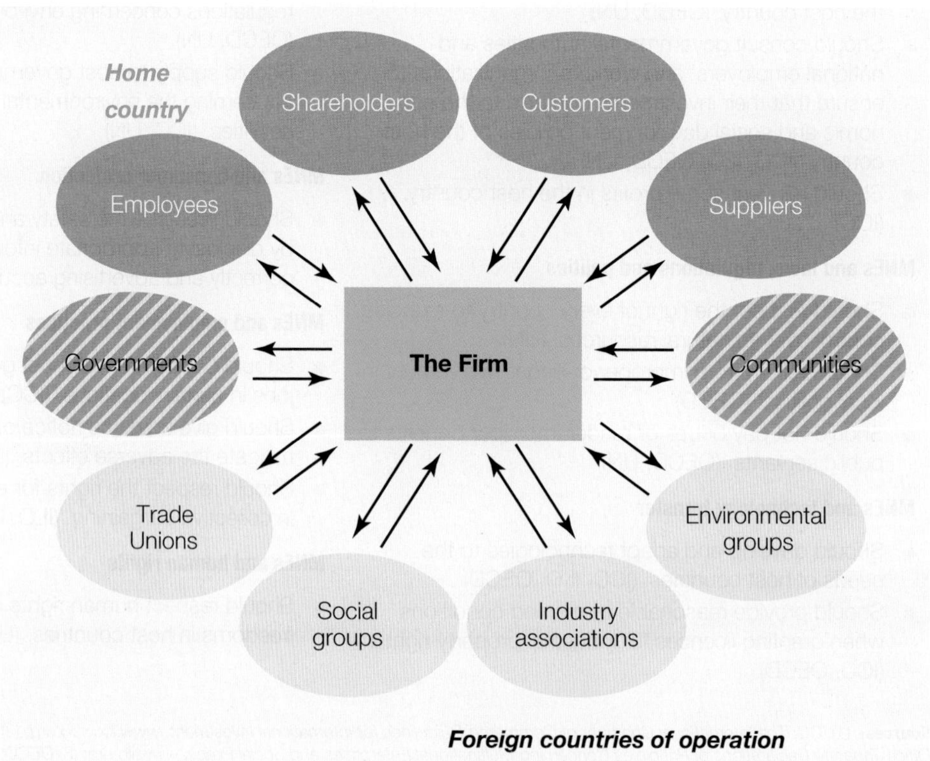

Note: Orange = primary stakeholders; yellow = secondary stakeholders.

Shareholders, managers, employees, suppliers, customers – together with governments and communities whose laws and regulations must be obeyed and to whom taxes and other obligations may be due – are typically considered primary stakeholders.

Secondary stakeholder groups are defined as 'those who influence or affect, or are influenced or affected by, the corporation, but they are not engaged in transactions with the corporation and are not essential for its survival'.[8] Environmental groups (such as *Greenpeace*) often take it upon themselves to promote pollution-reduction technologies. Trade unions and organizations concerned about labour practices (such as the *Fair Labor Association*) frequently challenge firms that allegedly fail to provide decent labour conditions for employees at home and abroad. Organizations such as these are known as non-governmental organizations (NGOs). They increasingly assume the role of monitor – and in some cases enforcer – of social and environmental standards.[9] Although firms do not depend on NGOs and other secondary stakeholders for their survival, such groups may have the potential to cause significant embarrassment and damage to a firm – as illustrated by the confrontation between *Starbucks* and *Global Exchange* (Opening Case).

In international business, the stakeholder map is complicated by the fact that stakeholders are distributed around the world, and therefore not only have widely varying interests, but also hold different values. What appears to be a sensible adaptation to local stakeholders to some may conflict with the views of other stakeholders (In Focus 10.1).

secondary stakeholder groups
Those who influence or affect, or are influenced or affected by, the corporation, but are not engaged in transactions with the corporation and are not essential for its survival.
non-governmental organizations (NGOs)
Organizations, such as environmentalists, human rights activists and consumer groups that are not affiliated with governments.

IN FOCUS 10.1

IKEA *adapts in Saudi Arabia*

In October 2012, Swedish furniture company *IKEA* was lambasted on the *BBC World Service* radio for air brushing women out of their catalogues distributed in Saudi Arabia. Women's rights activists in Sweden were outraged, and so was the *BBC* reporter. The story was first brought by Swedish newspapers, then discussed by British media like the *BBC* and *The Guardian*, and eventually travelled around the world. As the story spread, *IKEA* felt pressured to issue an apology, stating that this marketing brochure was inconsistent with its culture and did not reflect its approach to equality of women in society.

What went wrong? From the perspective of a marketing manager of the *IKEA* store in Saudi Arabia, the decision seems to be straightforward: to distribute a catalogue, it needs to comply with the law of the country. Yet the catalogue pictures from headquarters contain pictures of women. So, a version without women in Western clothes was needed. In fact, close inspection of the photos suggests that *IKEA* provided two sets of photos – with and without people – and

the Saudi subsidiary combined these as it saw fit. Some pictures in the Saudi catalogue had no people at all, while others had juice glasses replacing wine glasses. The picture that circulated through the world media had a man helping two children in the bathroom. Nothing suspicious you might think. Except that it was paired with a version of the same picture from the Swedish catalogue, which had, in addition, a woman standing in the middle. With these two versions side by side, it appeared that the woman had been erased, an act that was interpreted as condoning what many Northern Europeans consider the suppression of women in Saudi society.

One of the basic ideas of international business is the need to adapt products and marketing strategy to local contexts. With pictures of women who are not totally covered being illegal, using the original Swedish pictures obviously is not an option for the Saudi country manager. At the same time, he (let's assume it is a male) wanted to convey the idea of a Northern European lifestyle, so editing the pictures seemed an obvious approach. Most pictures in advertising are heavily photoshopped anyway, why not do a bit more photoshopping? What he overlooked is an ethical challenge of the interconnected world: local practices must also be acceptable to stakeholders back home – even though they may not understand the local context, and why local people (or, in this case, local law) would not accept the original.

A more sensitive designer might have designed a brochure showing no people at all. While this is an easy approach, it becomes difficult to illustrate how consumers use a locally unfamiliar product. Alternatively, people in local clothes could populate the pictures, though that doesn't convey Swedish values of

the *IKEA* brand. So, perhaps drawing abstract depictions of people might solve the problem?

But perhaps showing women is possible after all: the 2014 online version of the catalogue does have some women in the pictures!

Sources: (1) *Metro* (Stockholm), 2012, Här är Ikeas bilder – med och utan kvinnor, October 1; (2) *Svenska Dagbladet*, 2012, Kvinnor raderade i saudisk Ikeakatalog, October 1; (3) *BBC WorldService*, 2012, radio broadcast, October 2; (4) N. Malik, 2012, No women please, we're Saudi Arabian Ikea, *The Guardian*, October 2; (5) *IKEA*, 2015, Saudi Arabia catalogue, onlinecatalogue.ikea.com/SA/ar/IKEA_Catalogue/ (accessed March 2015).

Who are the most important stakeholders? At a recent meeting in Copenhagen, Danish CSR managers were asked 'who is your most important audience?' The almost unanimous answer was: 'employees and future employees'.[10] In other words, *you* as a potential future employee are perhaps the most important target of CSR initiatives. Why? Most of the firms present at the meeting operate in high technology industries, where the attraction and retention of talented young people is key to their success. One way to attract highly motivated young people is to offer a work environment that they appreciate – and that includes shared values that they can identify with. Hence CSR is, at least in Denmark, an important means of recruiting the best graduates from business schools and universities.

Why shareholders matter: two perspectives

instrumental view
A view that treating stakeholders well may indirectly help financial performance.

Two different lines of argument have evolved as to why firms ought to pay attention to their stakeholders. First, the instrumental view suggests that treating stakeholders well may indirectly help the financial performance of the firm.[11] For example, good environmental practice may reduce wastage, well-treated employees are more productive, and a reputation for social responsibility may strengthen a brand and thus attract more customers – all of which can enhance revenues. Hence proponents of this argument suggest that good ethics may be a useful instrument to help make good profits. They thus advocate only CSR initiatives believed to enhance profitability.

normative view
A view that firms ought to be self-motivated to 'do it right' because they have societal obligations.

In contrast, the normative view suggests that firms *ought* to be self-motivated to 'do it right' because they have societal obligations. Authors developing their arguments out of moral philosophy or religious value systems tend to assert a moral duty for firms that goes beyond respecting the law and generating profits.[12] Hence they argue that firms ought to do what is right independent of a direct link to financial performance. Codes of conduct thus ought to express values that organizational members view as central and enduring.[13] Proponents of this view may prefer a narrower definition of CSR that only includes activities that are not aimed at increasing profits: a new recycling facility counts as CSR only to the extent that sales of the recycled products do not cover the additional costs.

shared value creation
An approach to CSR that focuses on activities that are good for both the firm and its stakeholders.

A managerial approach that bridges between the normative and instrumental views is shared value creation.[14] This approach suggests focusing corporate CSR on activities that in the long run are expected to create value for *both* the firm and for the broader community. This can be done in three ways. First, firms can look for unmet social needs in the community, and design new products or business models to serve this community, while earning profits on the products or services they provide.

Do MNEs have moral duties towards local communities?

Second, firms can review their practices to identify ways to create modifications that increase benefits for external stakeholders. For example, changes in the sourcing practices in form of additional training of suppliers may reduce negative effects such as pollution, while reducing the firm's supply chain risk. Third, initiatives can be launched that create value for a local community but indirectly create value for the company, for instance by enhancing the company's reputation among consumers or potential employees. For example, *Nestlé* has over five decades been deeply involved with the local community around its factory in Moga, India. By investing in tangible and intangible infrastructure that helps develop the local community, *Nestlé* also enabled the community to provide resources that *Nestlé* itself needs, such as milk supplies and qualified employees.[15] This activity started long before the term shared value creation was invented, and highlights that sustainable shared value arises from long-term commitments by both firms and communities.

Critics of the shared value approach, however, argue that many activities reported under 'shared value creation' are just good business practice and do not reflect a particular notion of taking responsibility for social or environmental issues.[16] Thus how can we distinguish between CSR and good (profitable) business practice?

Stakeholder conflicts

While some CSR debates pitch shareholders against other stakeholders, different stakeholder groups also disagree with each other (Figure 10.2). Hence the challenge is not only to balance between shareholders and other stakeholders, but between different groups of stakeholders. For example, producing food for millions of people certainly addresses a social concern that CSR should be advocating – who would want to be responsible for widespread famine? However, food production also uses a lot of environmental resources. Cattle in particular eat a lot of grains and soya – which in turn require land that otherwise could be used for human food production. Cattle also emit a large amount of methane, a gas contributing to global warming. With rising incomes, many people in emerging economies are increasing the meat content of their diets, which aggravates the environmental problems of cattle farming. Some advocate vegetarianism as a solution, yet few are really willing to forgo meat.

Figure 10.2 An example of conflicting objectives

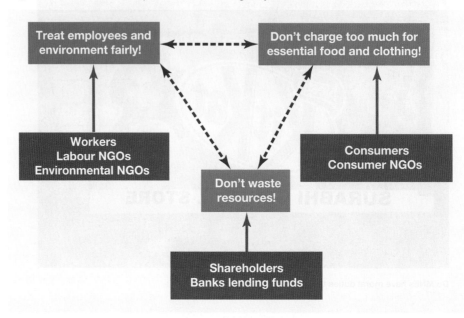

Similar controversies surround fish: for a long time, overfishing of the oceans was seen as a major environmental problem, and fish farming ('aquaculture') was seen as a solution. Yet it gradually emerged that aquaculture too can be a source of environmental damage (In Focus 10.2). Different stakeholders disagree with each other how best to address these issues. Another area of conflict between stakeholders concerns the production of garments. Many consumers chase low prices, either because they are too poor to afford products produced at higher social standards, or because they are not concerned about the conditions under which the products were made. These consumers 'voting with their purse' are at odds with the advocates of higher labour standards. In fact, empirical evidence suggests that consumers around the world may support ethical products when asked in opinion polls, but act quite differently when they make their own purchasing decisions.[17]

IN FOCUS 10.2

Farming salmon

There has been an explosion in the global supply of salmon recently. This rising supply is not due to an increase of wild salmon catch, which has been in steady decline for decades, because of dams, pollution and overfishing. As the wild Atlantic salmon disappear, fish farming (aquaculture) has been on the rise.

Starting in Norway as a cottage industry in the late 1960s, salmon farming spread to Britain, Canada, Iceland and Ireland in the 1970s, the USA in the 1980s, and Chile in the 1990s. Farm-raised salmon live in sea cages. They are fed pellets to speed up their growth (twice as fast as in the wild), pigments to replicate the pink wild salmon flesh, and pesticides to kill the lice that go hand in hand with an industrial feedlot. Atlantic

salmon farming (still dominated by Norwegian firms) has exploded into a $9 billion a year global business that produces approximately two million tons of fish annually. About 60% of the world's salmon production is farmed, including almost all Atlantic salmon. In essence, it is aquaculture companies that have brought you most of the delicious and nutritious Atlantic salmon, which has been transformed from a rare, expensive seasonal delicacy to a common chicken of the sea to be enjoyed year round. In addition, salmon farming takes commercial fishing pressure off wild salmon stocks and provides employment to coastal regions. For example, in Norway, about 6000 people work in the aquaculture industry, mostly related to salmon farming.

But here is the catch: farm-raised salmon have (1) fouled the nearby sea, (2) spread diseases and sea lice, and (3) led to a large number of escaped fish. Each of these problems has become a growing controversy. First, a heavy concentration of fish in a tiny area – up to 800 000 in one floating cage – leads to food and faecal waste that promotes toxic algae blooms, which in turn have led to closure of shell-fishing in nearby waters. Second, sea lice outbreaks at fish farms in Ireland, Norway and Scotland have devastating effects on wild salmon and other fish. The third, and probably most serious problem, is the escaped salmon. Many salmon escape when seals chew through pens, storms demolish cages, or fish are spilled during handling. In Scotland, for example, nearly 300 000 farmed fish escaped in 2002. Research

has found that escaped salmon interbreed with wild salmon. In Norwegian rivers that are salmon spawning grounds, 10% to 35% of the 'wild' fish are found to be escaped salmon.

Wild salmon are an amazing species, genetically programmed to find their spawning grounds in rivers after years of wandering in the sea. Although at present only one egg of every 4000, after maturing to become a fish, is likely to complete such an epic journey, salmon have been magical fish in the legends of Iceland, Ireland, Norway and Scotland. These legends are threatened by the escaped farm-raised salmon and the hybrid they produce with wild salmon, because genetically homogeneous salmon, descended from aquaculture fish, are ill-suited to find these rivers and could also leave the species less able to cope with threats, such as disease and climate change. In short, the biodiversity of the wild salmon stocks, already at dangerously low levels, is threatened by fish farming. Defenders of fish farming, however, argue that *all* farming alters, and sometimes damages, the environment. They argue that, compared to the production of beef or chicken, fish farming uses fewer natural resources and hence is a more environmentally-friendly form of nutrition.

Sources: (1) *Business Week*, 2006, Fished out, September 4; (2) *Economist*, 2003, A new way to feed the world, August 9; (3) *Economist*, 2003, The promise of a blue revolution, August 9; (4) F. Montaigne, 2003, Everybody loves Atlantic salmon: Here's the catch, *National Geographic*, 204 (1): 100–123; (5) *Marine Harvest ASA*, 2014, Salmon farming Industry Handbook 2014, www .marineharvest.com/investor (accessed March 2015).

child labour
Working people under the age of 16.

Other conflicts concern the indirect consequences of transferring rules across countries. For example, NGOs in Europe and North America expect firms not to employ child labour, work by people under the age of 16. Yet are the children really better off without a job?[18] There is an implicit assumption in this argument that children would spend their time in meaningful education and that they have enough food to eat – in developing countries these assumptions may not hold. Children that have work may well be better off than those that do not. For example, a study of the long-term implications of the campaign to abolish child labour in the manufacture of footballs in the Sialkot district of Pakistan found that the campaign benefited MNEs and NGOs, yet many poor women and children were worse off: they used to work as sub-contractors in their own home, but now no longer had access to work.[19] Many of them depended on the income; some even were the main breadwinner of the family. In consequence, poverty increased in the local areas, and children had less to eat – and even less chance to earn access to education. A better solution for the children might have been to combine work and education.

Assessing the merits of different stakeholder claims is further complicated by the fact that some vocal groups inside or outside the firm may pursue opportunistic goals of their own. Even the process of developing a CSR strategy can be captured by organizational politics and interest groups within a firm.[20] Moreover, the interests of stakeholders 'at home' may conflict with the interest of stakeholders abroad: expanding overseas, especially toward emerging economies, may provide employment to people in host countries and develop these economies at the 'base of the pyramid', all of which have noble CSR objectives. However, this is often done at the expense of domestic employees and communities. They fear being laid off and becoming dependent on social welfare programmes. Thus some media, unions and politicians may argue that MNEs' actions shirk their CSR by increasing the social burdens of their home countries.

The conflicting stakeholder objectives and interests come to the fore when the media put their spotlight on a specific issue, such as pollution of a local river, or complaints by disgruntled former employees that may or may not have merit.[21] Rarely do journalistic reports provide a comprehensive and balanced assessment of a firm's overall positive and negative contributions to society. Handling of the media thus is a challenging task for companies that aspire to build a reputation as a responsible company.

CSR IN THE GLOBAL ECONOMY

LEARNING OBJECTIVE

2   Articulate CSR challenges faced by firms operating in the global economy

Acting on the global stage exposes MNEs to more complex ethical issues that increase the importance of creating appropriate CSR policies. One important area is corruption, which we have already discussed in Chapter 3. Recall that for companies originating in OECD countries, legislation in home countries penalizes those who bribe overseas. This is an unusual case of legislation extending beyond national borders. On many other issues, MNEs have to figure out themselves what is 'right', considering formal and informal institutions in *both* home and host countries. We next discuss two areas where these issues are particular pertinent: (1) environmental standards, and (2) labour standards.

Environment: arbitraging or raising standards?

MNEs are running some of the largest industrial operations around the world, and hence they are also amongst the biggest polluters. However, are they to blame for pollution around the world? One side of the debate argues that because of heavier environmental regulation in developed economies, MNEs may have an incentive to arbitrage on differences in environmental costs. Thus they would shift pollution-intensive production to 'pollution havens' in developing countries, where environmental standards may be lower. This argument suggests that MNEs in highly-polluting industries relocate production to locations with less stringent regulations, or they might use the threat of such relocation to pressure politicians not to raise environmental standards.[22] To attract foreign direct investment, developing countries may thus enter a 'race to the bottom' by lowering (or at least not tightening) environmental standards.[23]

The other side argues that MNEs may actually have positive effects on the environment in developing countries, for four reasons (Table 10.2). First, MNEs are likely to adopt higher CSR standards than local firms, because they are more closely monitored by various stakeholders in their home and host countries. Second, they may gain scale advantages from implementing common standards across operations in different countries. It is easier to manage a global operation if everyone follows the same standards and procedures. This implies that standards are likely to be higher than the local requirements at any specific location. Third, firms exposed to higher environmental regulations may become early movers into new technologies, which may translate into long-term competitive advantages when other countries follow in upgrading their standards.[24] Fourth, higher standards reduce risk of catastrophic events such as a fire destroying production facilities, or a high profile media report detecting pollution the firm itself was not aware of. Such events can settle firms with major liabilities and lawsuits.

Some MNEs go even beyond their own operations and work with local governments to raise environmental standards, such as advising on legislation or contributing to training officials. For example, *Dow Chemical* partnered in China with the national authorities to develop an integrated preventive strategy for environmental processes, not only for its own plants, but for local small and medium-sized enterprises.[25] Higher and more consistently enforced standards may actually be in the interest of the MNEs: they create barriers for some (potential) low-cost competitors. Hence many MNEs have several economic reasons to *voluntarily* apply environmental standards higher than those required by host countries.[26]

Recent empirical evidence suggests that the pollution haven effect is important in some industries, such as natural resource extraction, construction, food processing and utilities, while in industries such as automotive and communications, more stringent environmental rules actually attract more investors.[27] Moreover, in regions with strong human capital, FDI is negatively associated with pollution, while less advanced regions with weak human capital tend to attract more polluting FDI projects.[28]

pollution haven
Countries with lower environmental standards.
race to the bottom
Countries competing for foreign direct investment by lowering environmental standards.

Table 10.2 Pressures on standards

Pressures on MNEs to lower standards	Pressures on MNEs to raise standards
• Lowering costs by standards arbitrage, i.e. producing where regulations imposes least costs. • Using the threat of relocation to prevent governments from raising legal requirements ('race to the bottom').	• Closer monitoring by stakeholders at home and abroad. • Scale advantages of common practices and standards throughout the organization. • Opportunities for first mover advantages in new technologies and practices. • Lower risk of catastrophic disruptions.

Compared to local firms in the same industry, MNEs typically deploy higher standards.[29] One study finds that governmental pressures lead to harmonization of environmental outcome standards, industry pressures lead to standardization of processes, while consumer pressures mainly affect firms' communications.[30] Another study finds that US capital markets significantly reward environmental practices, thus refuting the perspective that being green constitutes a liability that depresses market value.[31] However, MNEs are often associated with industrialization (which host countries appreciate), and industrialization increases pollution.[32] Hence MNEs as a group do not appear to substantially add to the environmental burden in developing countries, though there may be exceptions in particularly sensitive industries.

Labour: how to treat those who work for you abroad

Workers around the world complain about their working conditions. While some may have exaggerated expectations on the privileges they ought to enjoy, at the other end there are undoubtedly many who live and work under unimaginably poor conditions (see In Focus 10.3). Often this is an outcome of the poverty of the country. The working poor may live under horrible conditions in the eyes of a Western idealist. Yet they may still be better off with the job than unemployed and begging in the slums.

labour standards
Rules for the employment of labourers including working hours, minimum pay, union representation and child labour.

When they are sourcing from developing countries, MNEs are confronted with low labour standards in terms of working hours, minimum pay, union representation and child labour.[33] The 1980s and 1990s saw an acceleration of extended supply chains to poorer countries, and initially MNEs were not particularly fussed about how their shoes or T-shirts were manufactured, as long as the quality and the price were right. Major publicity campaigns targeting well-known brands such as *Nike* put an end to such a naïve approach to international sourcing.

The economics of labour standards are similar to those of environmental standards (Table 10.2). There are gains from producing where costs are lowest, but there are countervailing pressures for MNEs to raise standards above local norms. However, there are crucial differences. The typical environment polluter is a big plant in the chemicals or paper industry, which requires large capital investments and is stuck at its location once the construction of the plant is completed. This reduces the bargaining power of such firms negotiating with regulators. In contrast, many labour-intensive operations are 'footloose plants' that require little set-up costs (apart from staff training) and can easily relocate when regulations change. Thus the pressures to lower standards (left column in Table 10.2) are relatively strong.

footloose plant
Plants that can easily be relocated.

In their own operations in developing countries, MNEs often provide professional training, higher wages and better working conditions than local competitors.[34] They try to attract some of the best people, and after investing in their training, they are keen to keep them. Even so, MNEs are being criticized: local firms may complain that the best people do not want to work for them because MNEs pay 'too high' wages. Meanwhile, trade unions back home may complain about the 'too low' wages paid in developing countries that put pressures on wages in developed countries.

The real challenges, however, emerge when MNEs buy products or components from local firms. In Europe, many consumers – and NGOs – expect that their shoes and their clothes are made by people being paid and treated fairly. This raises two questions: are MNEs responsible for what happens in legally independent firms, and how can they be sure what actually happens in a sub-supplier's plant?

The first question is often answered differently from a legal and a normative perspective. Legally, firms are responsible for their operations, not those of other firms. Moreover, the relevant laws are normally those of the country where the factory is

IN FOCUS 10.3

Working poor

The miserable working conditions in some parts of the world are periodically highlighted in news reports and in scholarly studies. The following quotations illustrate some of the worst examples. In El Salvador, a government study of maquiladora factories found that

'. . . in the majority of companies, it is an obligation of the personnel to work overtime under the threat of firing or some other kind of reprisal. This situation, in addition to threatening the health of the workers, causes family problems in that [the workers] are unable to properly fulfil obligations to their immediate family. On some occasions, because the work time is extended into the late hours of the night, the workers find themselves obligated to sleep in the factory facilities, which do not have conditions necessary for lodging of personnel.' (Source 2)

The conditions become alive in the recollections of individual workers, such as the following statement by a 26-year-old worker in a maquiladora factory in Mexico:

'We have to work quickly with our hands, and I am responsible for sewing 20 steering wheel covers per shift. After having worked for nine years at the plant, I now suffer from an injury in my right hand. I start out the shift okay, but after about three hours of work, I feel a lot of sharp pains in my fingers. It gets so bad that I can't hold the steering wheel correctly. But still the supervisors keep pressuring me to reach 100 per cent of my production. I can

only reach about 70 per cent of what they asked for. These pains began a year ago and I am not the only one who suffered from them. There are over 200 of us who have hand injuries and some have lost movement in their hands and arms. The company has fired over 150 people in the last year for lack of production. Others have been pressured to quit.' (Source 1)

Another source emphasizes that the working conditions are below what ordinary newspaper readers can even imagine:

'The manner in which these women lived, the squalidness and unhealthy location and nature of their habitations, the impossibility of providing for any of the slightest recreations or moral or intellectual culture or of educating their children can be easily imagined: but we assure the public that it would require an extremely active imagination to conceive this reality.' (Source 3)

Actually, this report is referring to textile factories in New York, and it was published in the New York Daily Tribune in the year 1845. It illustrates that poor treatment of workers is not specific to certain cultures – if anything it is a typical of early stages of industrialization.

Sources: (1) P. Varley, C. Mathiasen & M. Voorhes, 1998, *The Sweatshop Quandry: Corporate Responsibility on the Global Frontier*. Washington, DC: Investor Responsibility Research Center (p. 68); (2) D.A. Arnold & N.E. Bowie, 2003, Sweatshops and Respect for Persons, *BEQ*, 13, 221–242 (p. 230); (3) L.P. Hartman, B. Shaw & R. Stevenson, 2003, Exploring the Ethics and Economics of Global Labor Standards, *BEQ*, 13, 193–220 (p. 195).

located – not those of the country of origin of the MNE. Such a legalistic view was adopted by many firms in the 1970s and 1980s, but it is less common now. MNEs concerned with their brand reputation accept that normative pressures are also relevant in defining the appropriate standards in both their own operations and the operations of their suppliers and sub-suppliers.[35]

Standards and compliance

Faced with pressures from a variety of sources, including legal requirements, industry self-regulation, and NGOs, MNEs have introduced 'codes of conduct' (also known as 'standards of engagement' or 'code of ethics') that they impose on their own employees as well as their suppliers.[36] For example, labour standards may specify minimum

code of conduct
(standards of engagement, code of ethics)
Written policies and standards for corporate conduct and ethics.

standards for working hours, age of workers, health and safety, wages and other aspects of operating a manufacturing plant. Other standards concern health, safety and the environment (HSE), as well as procedures designed to prevent corruption.

health, safety and environment (HSE)
A common term to cover the areas for which companies have mandatory standards.

Companies introduce such codes for three types of reasons: (1) to comply with legal obligations, (2) to reduce the risk of costly accidents, and (3) to demonstrate their social and environmental responsibility. In practice these goals are mutually reinforcing: for example, higher standards regarding the emission of poisonous gases reduce the chances of conflicting with legal requirements, but also reduce the risk of major accidents, and look good to the wider community. In a narrower interpretation of the concept, however, the first two motivations may not count as CSR because they primarily help to reduce financial losses. However, in practice, firms do not distinguish these motivations, and operate with one set of codes of conduct, which they then include in their CSR report.

compliance
Procedures to monitor and enforce standards for employees and suppliers.
compliance training
Mandatory training and tests designed to ensure that every employee knows the relevant codes of conduct.

With codes of conduct comes compliance, sets of monitoring and enforcement procedures designed to assure that everyone meets the standards, while – after appropriate warnings – discontinuing relationships by firing non-compliant employees or suppliers.[37] In MNEs in sensitive sectors such as banking or pharmaceuticals, every employee has to go through compliance training, and sit a test every year(!) for the leadership to be confident that every one of their representatives around the world knows the rules. For example, test questions may ask: 'A client brings you a bottle of wine along with the mortgage loan application, what do you do?' Or, 'A sales agent regularly claims higher travel expenses than would normally be needed for the type of trips he does; what do you do?' Such extensive compliance procedures are both costly and time-consuming, as they require detailed record keeping, reporting and attention from top management. Even so, sometimes employees in overseas subsidiaries conspire to circumvent rules, notably when operating in non-transparent markets and facing stiff sales targets (see Integrative Case *GSK*).

Some NGOs argue that compliance procedures, especially with respect to suppliers in emerging economies, are insufficient. They allege that monitors are insufficiently independent and don't publish all their reports, and that unsatisfactory suppliers are not kicked out rigorously enough.[38] One recent study interviewed workers outside their place of work in southern China, and presents allegations that suppliers not only fail to meet the standards they have committed to, but have developed tactics to systematically mislead monitoring teams.[39] More progress has been achieved by MNEs that shift from a focus on compliance with the standards of engagement to a commitment approach that involves knowledge transfer, diffusion of best practice, and joint problem solving with the operative staff of suppliers.[40] Others use independent third-party monitors to enhance the assurance of their compliance regime.[41]

INSTITUTIONS, STAKEHOLDERS AND CSR

LEARNING OBJECTIVE

3 Explain how institutions influence firms' corporate social responsibility activities

Debates and practices of CSR vary across countries and they change over time. The roots of such differences are often differences in formal and informal institutions.[42] In fact, international debates over CSR sometimes suffer miscommunication due to differences in cultural values. People in liberal market economies (LMEs) and coordinated market economies (CMEs) have different understandings of what firms are, and what their role in the society is. Yet if we don't agree about the purpose of the firm, it is difficult to agree on its obligations.

Liberal market economies

Recall from Chapter 2 that in LMEs like the USA and the UK, firms are unambiguously considered an economic enterprise that exist to serve the shareholders' interest. In line with this view, Milton Friedman, a University of Chicago economist, eloquently suggested: 'The social responsibility of business is to increase its profits.'[43] This line of thought draws upon the idea that pursuit of economic self-interest (within legal constraints) promotes the welfare of society as a whole. Hence firms' first and foremost stakeholders are shareholders, whose interests managers have a legal duty to look after. With this primacy of shareholders and a strong belief in the efficiency of the market mechanism comes strong support for the instrumental view of CSR: 'it is good if it helps profits'. Economists such as Milton Friedman extend the argument to suggest that if firms attempt to attain social goals, such as providing employment and social welfare, managers will lose their focus on profit maximization (and its derivative, shareholder value maximization) and thus cause greater harm than good.[44] Some even argue that workers would be worse off if firms unilaterally raised standards because the firm would lose competitiveness and in consequences workers would lose their jobs.[45]

In the USA, the leading LME, firms have a high degree of discretion over their activities, since regulations are less constraining, and markets are to a large degree self-organized by businesses rather than regulated by the state. At the same time, the financial system requires a high degree of transparency, the education system is largely private, the cultural system values individual freedom but also 'giving back to society' – that is, sharing the wealth with others. These features of the institutional context induce firms to voluntarily assume responsibilities for societal concerns (Table 10.3, Figure 10.3).[46] This explicit CSR includes issues that might be covered by government activities in CMEs, such as support for universities, health care or employee training. It may be strategic in the sense that the CSR activity aims to achieve certain specified benefits for society as well as for the firm itself.[47] Explicit CSR is supported by a culture that simultaneously appreciates people who make a lot of money, and people who voluntarily help others. Thus philanthropy – donations for cultural, environmental, scientific or other benefits of the wider society – has a long tradition in the USA.[48]

explicit CSR
Voluntarily assuming responsibilities of societal concerns.

philanthropy
Donations for purposes that benefit the wider society.

Table 10.3 Explicit and implicit CSR compared

Explicit CSR	Implicit CSR
• Describes corporate activities that assume responsibility for the interests of society.	• Describes corporations' role within the wider formal and informal institutions for society's interests and concerns.
• Consists of voluntary corporate policies, programmes and strategies.	• Consists of values, norms and rules that result in (often codified and mandatory) requirements for corporations.
• Incentives and opportunities are motivated by the perceived expectations of different stakeholders of the corporation.	• Motivated by the societal consensus on the legitimate expectations of the roles and contributions of all major groups in society, including corporations.

Source: D. Matten & J. Moon, 2008, 'Implicit' and 'Explicit' CSR, *AMR*, 33, 404–424. Reproduced with permission.

Figure 10.3 Implicit and explicit CSR, and varieties of capitalism

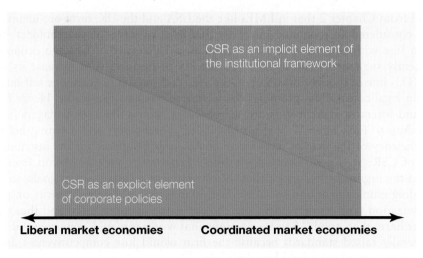

Source: D. Matten & J. Moon, 2008, Implicit and Explicit CSR, *AMR*, 32, 404–424. Reproduced with permission.

Coordinated market economies

In CMEs like those in Western Europe, most firms are also owned by private share-holders. Managers have to act in the interest of the shareholders, yet a wide range of formal and informal constraints impose other obligations on firms. Cooperative arrangements, such as standards set by industry associations and collective bargaining with trade unions, establish standards and processes that firms have to accommodate. Interest groups, political parties and the media often implicitly adopt a normative view when discussing CSR, though they may disagree on what the relevant norms are. Shareholders' rights are thus constrained. At the same time, the state has a far more active role in a CME. Regulations of many aspects of business are more specific and the state is supplying a wide range of services to society, financed by taxes raised from individuals and firms.

This is supported by cultures that consider many aspects of the welfare state as the responsibility of the state, and expect firms and individuals to help the state with its responsibilities by firstly paying taxes (that are higher than in the USA) and by obeying laws and regulations. These cultural differences became evident in a recent survey in which opinion leaders were asked to what extent they agree with the statement 'The social responsibility of business is to increase profits.' The highest percentage of agreement was reported for the United Arab Emirates (over 80% 'strongly agree' or 'somewhat agree'), with Japan, India, South Korea, Singapore and Sweden also scoring over 60%. Anglo-Saxon countries are in the middle of the table, whereas in Brazil, China, Germany, Italy and Spain less than 40% agree with the statement.[49]

implicit CSR
Participating in the wider formal and informal institutions for the society's interests and concerns.

In CMEs, firms see much less reason to engage in explicit CSR by voluntarily doing *more* than what they are expected to do. Rather, they engage in implicit CSR, that is participation in the wider formal and informal institutions for the society's interests and concerns.[50] Hence they take into consideration the interests of other stakeholders by following the formal and informal rules of the society for such interaction with stakeholders. Hence they do good things for society, but not on a voluntary basis as an explicit CSR. Firms pursuing implicit CSR would not be inclined to claim special credit for doing so, and they would not be able to gain any special reputation because all firms in the same context follow the same rules. Thus

European observers shake their head about some CSR initiatives in the US: even the highlighted 'responsible' practices may fall short of legal requirement in many European countries, especially on labour issues such as employee representation within the firm, working time, or redundancy procedures. For example, *Starbucks* (Opening Case) announced in 2004 a CSR initiative to pay health care benefits for all those they employed for more than 20 days per month. In many European countries they would be obliged to do so by law, even for part-time employees.[51]

The differences in institutional pressures are reflected in standards of engagement used by firms around the world; they vary considerably across firms, industries and countries.[52] US codes of conduct tend to focus on secondary stakeholder issues, such as labour standards in the supplier network and welfare of the community. European codes concentrate more on production activities, such as quality management and the environmental footprint. Hong Kong codes tend to focus on corruption prevention but pay less attention to broader CSR issues because corruption is perceived to be a major concern.

Convergence?

In recent years, the institutional context for CSR has changed in two ways: (1) CSR has moved up the corporate agenda around the world and (2) there has been some degree of convergence between CMEs and LMEs. First, why have so many stakeholder groups become more vocal, and been able to influence corporate agendas? On the one hand, this may be a result of increasing wealth. Social and environmental concerns become important to people once their basic needs such as food, clothing and accommodation have been met. In a way, caring for others is like a luxury good that rich people can afford. Less affluent people and societies tend to be less concerned. On the other hand, formal and informal institutions have evolved over time. Since the 1970s, the world has seen an increasing focus on 'shareholder value', and government policies have actively promoted the market as the predominant (or only) coordination mechanism, especially during the Reagan years in the USA and the Thatcher years in the UK. The CSR movement of the 1990s and 2000s can be seen as counter-movement to firms' increased focus on shareholder value.

Second, why are LMEs and CMEs converging? On the one hand, LMEs have introduced more regulation on a number of issues, such as the environment and corporate governance. In fact, the UK may be located at an intermediate point of Figure 10.3, in part as a result of legislation introduced with the European social charter (Chapter 8). On the other hand, firms in CMEs realized that playing by the rules may not be enough when operating across borders. As local rules in host countries vary, and may be below those of the home country, MNEs face social pressures not unlike those in LMEs to explicitly state how they manage, for example, labour issues in supplier firms. Thus US firms have started the trend of introducing explicit corporate codes of conduct, yet this practice has quickly spread to MNEs based in Europe.

DEBATES AND EXTENSIONS

The subject of CSR is full of debates. Probably, most of you as readers have found something in the previous pages that you would like to debate. In corporate boardrooms, CSR has become a hot issue that needs to be balanced with the quest for profit, which is why this chapter is a central part of this book. Here, we discuss three questions: (1) if active CSR is good for the firm itself, notably its financial performance, (2) if CSR is good for the stakeholders that are the object of this policy and (3) hypernorms versus local norms.

LEARNING OBJECTIVE

4 Participate in three leading debates concerning corporate social responsibility

Is CSR good for financial performance?

Is there a link between CSR and economic performance, such as profits and share-holder returns? Many scholars have investigated this question, but the answer is inconclusive. While some studies indeed report a positive relationship,[53] others find a negative relationship,[54] or no relationship.[55] A meta-analysis (a study that aggregates findings of earlier studies) suggests that – on average – social responsibility and, to a lesser extent, environmental responsibility, are on average associated with better financial performance.[56]

There can be a number of explanations for these inconsistent findings. A resource-based explanation suggests that a good reputation may be a value-creating, rare, hard to imitate and organizationally-embedded (VRIO) resource, especially in industries with a poor reputation. A reputation takes a long time to build – consumers are not impressed by fancy announcements, they look for a track record of activity. On the other hand, because of capability constraints and market positioning, some firms are not cut out for a CSR-intensive (differentiation) strategy. For example, companies like *Primark*[57] or *Asda* that compete in very price-sensitive market segments are less likely to benefit from proactive CSR than companies like *Selfridges* or *Marks & Spencer* (Closing Case) that compete on the basis of their brand image.

More detailed studies suggest that consistent CSR policies over long time periods have a positive effect, while short-term or temporary initiatives do not. This is because CSR benefits a firm when it can build a credible reputation as a responsible firm – and that does not happen overnight. Thus 'it takes time for being socially responsible to translate into higher financial returns and . . . it is the consistent application of a strategy of social responsibility that ultimately pays off in financial terms'.[58] Moreover, too much of a good thing may not be that good: some firms may be 'overdoing their goodness' in ways that actually harm their financial performance. In summary, because each firm is different (a basic assumption of the resource-based view), not every firm's economic performance is likely to benefit from CSR.

Is CSR good for society?

Some critics describe CSR activity as mere 'window dressing', and assert that firms only do what is good for themselves. In other words, CSR is seen mainly as a public relations exercise, with few benefits for workers in sub-supplier plants or for the natural environment they claim to be protecting. These critics point to the efforts that companies spend on communicating their activities and on converting CSR into brand value – and thus into market share and profits.[59] We can interpret these debates as a conflict between the instrumental view and the normative view. Recall, that the *instrumental view* asserts that CSR is good *if* it helps corporate performance and is a dominant norm in corporate boardrooms, many business schools, and university departments of economics.[60]

In contrast, many NGOs, journalists and politicians have adopted a *normative view*, asserting that firms also have other obligations to their stakeholders. These critics often do not appreciate initiatives by managers doing CSR with an eye on financial performance to satisfy their obligation to shareholders and their own share option plans. Since this conflict is essentially about values, there is no 'right or wrong' answer to it. However, *if* there is a link between CSR, corporate reputation and consumers buying the products, *and if* the reputation depends on outcomes of CSR rather than on public relations, *then* we would expect that even instrumentally-motivated CSR is creating benefits for the stakeholders that consumers care about. The empirical evidence on this complex causal link is however inconclusive.

Some CSR initiatives indeed do *not* create value for the stakeholders. Good intentions are not sufficient to create positive impact on stakeholders. Creating impactful CSR initiatives requires a good understanding of how initiatives of the firm interact with the local context. This is a particular concern for initiatives aimed at improving incomes or living conditions at the 'bottom of the pyramid'. We earlier mentioned children losing their job as a result of anti-child labour campaigns. As another example, a study of local community development projects organized by oil multinationals in local communities where they operate in Nigeria found that MNEs made many mistakes that governmental aid agencies made decades ago, due to naïve understanding of the social structure of the local society, which led to their contributions having low impact.[61] Even a *Harvard Business Review* paper claims that 'feel-good stories aside, it's been nearly impossible to gauge the efficacy of these ventures'.[62] Thus companies need to work hard to engage with local stakeholders to develop initiatives that help the local community in the long run, for example by strengthening indigenous capabilities.

Other critics suggest that CSR is mainly making up for damage caused by the same MNEs earlier. For example, a German magazine commented on the publicity about Fair Trade chocolate in the UK by pointing out that it really is a response to problems caused by the firms themselves:

> *'Five giants control about 80% of international cocoa trade. Especially during the 1990s, they pressed the prices to such an extent that it was impossible for farmers to invest in better crops, plant protection, and new tools. In the past 12 months, the harvest was the worst in 14 years due to heavy rainfalls, pest and fungal diseases.'*[63]

As a result, cocoa prices have been surging and manufacturers are concerned about the long-term security of their supplies. By investing in cocoa production and paying farmers a higher price, they hope to secure their supplies, and this also helps to attain Fair Trade certification.

A similar link has been suspected behind *Wal-Mart*'s recent drive to increase environmental standards in its value chain. Many NGOs targeted *Wal-Mart* due to the combination of its size (and thus bargaining power) and its relentless focus on 'everyday low prices', which induced suppliers to cut corners whenever they could. In the words of a Chinese expert cited in the *Washington Post*:

> *'They are the rule setters. Before,* Wal-Mart *only cared about price and quality, so that encouraged companies to race to the bottom of environmental standards. They could lose contracts because competition was so fierce on price. [Now, they changed.]* Wal-Mart *says if you're over the compliance level, you're out of business. That will set a powerful signal.'*[64]

Wal-Mart did take action, for example, by suspending 126 suppliers for a year due to unsatisfactory compliance, and permanently halting purchasing from 35 – out of about 10 000 suppliers in China. However, *Wal-Mart* itself faces conflicting institutional pressures; in the words of an executive: 'Our customers care, they just don't want to pay more'.[65]

A recent study by MIT professor Richard Lorke suggests that these examples are indicative of broader evidence. After studying labour practices around the world, he offers four conclusions:[66]

- Codes of conduct alone have negligible effect on labour practices.
- Helping suppliers through knowledge transfer helps.
- Collaborative relationships with suppliers that share productivity gains help even more.

- The origin of unsatisfactory labour standards are often in the manufacturers own business models, especially just-in-time delivery, minimization of inventories, short life cycles and last-minute design changes – combined with stiff penalties on suppliers failing to deliver.

In other words, the pressures created by buyers – companies further down the value chain – combined with asymmetric bargaining power create conditions where suppliers face tough choices between substantial financial loss (losing orders or paying penalties for late delivery) and pushing their own workforce to work at conditions below minimum standards (as set by local law, ILO standards or contractual commitments). Looking at *Apple*'s supply chain from this perspective, it appears obvious that companies like *Foxconn* or *Pegatron* are under enormous pressure: large volumes of a new product are to be delivered by the official launch date, design changes are on-going, and inventories are avoided at (almost) all cost, because the product value depreciates sharply once the next update becomes available.

Local norms versus hypernorms

A central idea of international management is that MNEs need to adapt to local institutions (see Chapters 2 and 3). Hence the relevant rules of the game are those of the host country! Yet this idea seems to be at odds with some of the ideas developed in this chapter, namely that MNEs develop global standards of practice, under pressure of stakeholders that are based (primarily) in their home country. When and how much should they adapt to local norms, and when should headquarters prevail?

One view promoted by Tomas Donaldson of the Wharton School, and widely adopted in business schools, suggests that there are certain hypernorms – norms considered valid anywhere in the world – that MNEs ought to respect wherever they operate.[67] Donaldson identified three such hypernorms (Table 10.4), namely: (1) respect for human dignity, (2) universally agreed basic rights, and (3) good citizenship in the host society.[68] The first two points suggest that there are certain values and rights that all individuals have, and that are independent of local cultures. The norms advocated by international organizations (Table 10.1) fall into this category. In contrast, the third point acknowledges the existence and the need to respect for local institutions.

Conflicts between local norms and hypernorms are common but rarely as evident as during the apartheid era in South Africa, when local laws required racial segregation of the workforce. Following the idea of hypernorms, some MNEs such as *BP* deliberately bypassed or ignored these local laws to challenge, breach and seek to dismantle the apartheid system. Emboldened by the successful removal of the apartheid regime in South Africa in 1994, CSR advocates have unleashed a new campaign, stressing the necessity for MNEs to promote hypernorms (or 'universal values'), in particular, in the human rights area. *Shell*, after its widely criticized (lack of) action in Nigeria, has explicitly endorsed the United Nations Declaration on

hypernorms
Norms considered valid anywhere in the world.

Table 10.4 Managing ethics overseas: three 'middle-of-the-road' approaches

- Respect for human dignity
- Respect for universal basic rights
- Good citizenship in the host society, respecting their institutional context

Sources: (1) T. Donaldson, 1996, Values in tension: Ethics away from home, *Harvard Business Review*, September–October: 4–11; (2) J. Weiss, 2009, *Business Ethics*, 5th ed., Cincinnati, OH: Cengage Learning.

Human Rights and supported the exercise of such rights 'within the legitimate role of business' since 1996.

But when exactly should hypernorms dominate over local norms? Almost every country has local laws and norms that some foreign MNEs may find objectionable. In Malaysia, ethnic Chinese are discriminated against by law. In many Arab countries, women are expected to 'cover up' in public places. In Asian countries, such as China, *independent* trade unions are illegal. At the heart of this debate is whether foreign MNEs should spearhead efforts to remove some of these discriminatory practices or conform to host country laws and norms. This is obviously a non-trivial challenge.

IMPLICATIONS FOR PRACTICE

In view of diverse pressures pertaining to firms, it has become very tricky for MNEs to pursue a defensive strategy of denying their responsibility when confronted with an ethical issue. They may win in court, but unless their customers are in the low income bracket (and hence highly price sensitive) they may lose their customers or other stakeholders. Many leading MNEs nowadays at least pursue an accommodative strategy, in which they demonstrate their responsibility by applying norms and standards advocated by NGOs even when they are not (yet) enshrined in law. For example, after denial strategies in the 1990s, *Nike* and the entire sportswear industry became very sensitive to concerns about labour standards, thus accommodating concerns raised by NGOs before they spill out as major scandals. Instead of treating NGOs as threats, firms like sportswear manufacturer *adidas* (Chapter 1, Opening Case) have their sourcing policies certified by NGOs.

The idea of shared value creation provides a starting point for firms that want to pursue a proactive strategy by 'going beyond the call of duty' without losing the support of financial investors. Table 10.5 indicates four different types of initiatives. First, businesses may focus their innovation activities on areas of social and environmental needs. For example, at the Copenhagen Climate Summit in December 2009, many businesses were demonstrating how their technologies may help addressing the issues politicians were debating, for example by improving the efficiency of energy use (for example more fuel-efficient cars), efficiency improvements in energy generation (for example changes in existing power plants), power generation from renewable sources (for example wind and solar energy), bio-combustibles, nuclear and carbon capture (i.e. putting carbon created by power stations underground).[69] By demonstrating the feasibility of new technologies, firms may even be able to influence the standards set by regulatory authorities.

Second, proactive firms often engage in *voluntary* activities that go beyond what is required by law.[70] For bigger impact, they may not do so alone, but through joint initiatives. For example, overseas subsidiaries of German firms collaborate in the German Chamber of Commerce not only to represent their interests *vis-à-vis* local

LEARNING OBJECTIVE

5   Draw implications
    for action

defensive strategy
A strategy that focuses
on regulatory compliance
with little top management
commitment to CSR causes.
accommodative strategy
A strategy that is
characterized by some
support from top managers,
who may increasingly
view CSR as a worthwhile
endeavour.
proactive strategy
A strategy that endeavours
to do more than is required
in CSR.

Table 10.5 Implications for action

CSR strategies need to be balance corporate and societal interests:

- Businesses may focus their innovation activities on areas of social and environmental needs.
- Businesses may collaborate to voluntarily set and implement standards.
- Businesses may benefit from collaborative relationships with NGOs.
- CSR publicity should match CSR capabilities.

authorities, but in social initiatives such as the creation and support of vacation training programmes (see Integrative Case German Chamber of Commerce).

Third, proactive firms often build alliances with stakeholder groups, for example with NGOs.[71] Because of historical tensions and distrust, these 'sleeping-with-the-enemy' alliances may not be easy to handle. The key lies in identifying manageable projects of mutual interest. For instance, *Unilever* Indonesia commissioned *Oxfam*, a UK-based charity, to comprehensively explore and document its impact on poverty and development. The report provided a basis for both *Unilever* and local stakeholders to improve their practices. It showed, for example, that *Unilever* paid a lot of taxes to the Indonesian government, provided employment and shared best practices in the local economy. It treated its employees better than local firms, paying entry-level employees 123% of the minimum wage, spending €180 million on local supplies, and reinvesting profits of €130 million in the local economy. Even so, it contributed little to people living in poverty, the prime concern of *Oxfam*.[72]

Fourth, managers need to match their CSR publicity with their core business strategy and capabilities. Imitating practices from high profile cases without knowing enough about your own firm may lead to some disappointing outcomes. Rather, firms need to design CSR practices that fit with their core business and their *existing* capabilities,[73] while building new capabilities needed to achieve higher goals in the future. For example, engine maker *MAN Diesel & Turbo* tried to communicate the importance of 'safety at work' to all its employees and customers in China. Its CSR initiative to give every employee a free child car seat not only supported the families of the staff, but also reinforced the central message that this company cares about everyone's safety.[74] In particular, firms only benefit from CSR statements if they can actually live up to their standards, and demonstrate progress towards their stated goals. Failed standards and unachieved goals invite attacks from NGOs.

What determines the success and failure of firms around the world? No doubt CSR has become an important part of the answer. The best-performing firms are able to integrate CSR activities into their core economic functions to address social and environmental concerns.[75] The globally ambiguous and varying CSR standards, norms and expectations make many managers uncomfortable. As a result, they may relegate CSR to the backburner. However, this does not seem to be the right attitude for current and would-be managers who are studying this book – that is, *you*. Managers, as a unique group of stakeholders, have an important and challenging responsibility to safeguard and advance the world economy. From a CSR standpoint, this means building more humane, more inclusive and fairer firms that not only generate wealth and develop economies, but also respond to changing needs of societies around the world.

CHAPTER SUMMARY

1 Articulate a stakeholder view of the firm

- A stakeholder view of the firm urges companies to consider not only shareholders but other interested parties.

- An instrumental view advocates attention to stakeholders if that helps financial performance; in contrast a normative view believes in the moral obligation of companies to treat stakeholders responsibly.

- Stakeholders often disagree with each other, creating complex moral challenges and needs for effective communication.

2 Articulate CSR challenges faced by firms operating in the global economy

- MNEs face opposing economic incentives to produce where environmental regulation is less tight, and to implement standards higher than the legal minimum.

- Labour standards in foreign subsidiaries and supplier networks are subject to scrutiny by NGOs as well as the MNEs themselves.

3 Explain how institutions influence firms' corporate social responsibility activities

- Institutional differences explain why views on CSR differ between countries.

- Due to institutional difference, American firms are more likely to pursue voluntary, 'explicit CSR', while European firms pursue 'implicit CSR'.

4 Participate in three leading debates concerning corporate social responsibility

- The relationship between CSR and financial performance is highly disputed among scholars.

- Not all CSR initiatives create benefits for society.

- MNEs have to strike a sometimes difficult balance between their own global norms, and the norms of the host society.

5 Draw implications for action

- Businesses may focus their innovation activities on areas of social and environmental needs.

- Businesses may collaborate to voluntarily set and implement standards.

- Businesses may benefit from collaborative relationships with NGOs.

- CSR publicity should match CSR capabilities.

KEY TERMS

Accommodative strategy	Health, safety and environment (HSE)	Primary stakeholder groups
Child labour	Hypernorms	Proactive strategy
Code of conduct (standards of engagement, code of ethics)	Implicit CSR	Race to the bottom
	Instrumental view	Secondary stakeholder groups
Compliance	Labour standards	Shared value creation
Compliance training	Non-governmental organizations (NGOs)	Stakeholder
Corporate social responsibility (CSR)		Sustainability
Defensive strategy	Normative view	Triple bottom line
Explicit CSR	Philanthropy	
Footloose plant	Pollution haven	

CRITICAL DISCUSSION QUESTIONS

1 In your opinion, how should MNEs act when legal requirements on labour or environmental issues vary between the different countries in which they operate? Should they remain politically neutral and adopt practices and laws of the host country, or should they stick to the rules that would apply to the same operation back home?

2 Some argue that investing in emerging economies greatly increases the economic development and standard of living of the base of the global economic pyramid. Others contend that moving jobs to low-cost countries not only abandons CSR for domestic employees and communities in developed economies, but also exploits the poor in these countries and destroys the environment. How would you participate in this debate if you were (1) CEO

of an MNE headquartered in a developed economy moving production to a low-cost country, (2) the leader of a labour union in the home country of the MNE that is losing lots of jobs, or (3) the leader of an environmental NGO in the low-cost country in which the MNE invests?

3 You find out that one of your suppliers, contrary to your code of conduct, is employing people aged 14 to 16 years of age. How do you react?

4 You are the PR officer of a major MNE in the chemicals industry. The media in your home country allege that your company is covering up an environmental disaster caused by your subsidiary in India, in which several people died. How do you react?

RECOMMENDED READINGS

A. Crane, D. Palazzo, L. Spence & D. Matten, 2014, Contesting the value of 'creating shared value', CMR, 56: 130–153 – a critical assessment of the 'shared value' idea and its applications in view of the broader debate of business in society and the role of stakeholders.

J.H. Dunning, ed., 2004, *Making Globalization Good: The Moral Challenges of Global Capitalism,* Oxford: Oxford University Press – a collection of essays by scholars as well as political and religious leaders about the moral challenges of global capitalism.

L.A. Hartman, D.G. Arnold & R.E. Wokutch, 2003, *Rising above Sweatshops: Innovative Approaches to Global Labor Challenges,* Westport, CT: Praeger – A study that investigated several initiatives by firms and industry organizations to raise labour standards in firms supplying Western MNEs.

D. Matten & J. Moon, 2009, 'Implicit' and 'Explicit' CSR: A conceptual framework for a comparative understanding of corporate social responsibility, *AMR,* 33, 404–424 – a theoretical articles that explains why the driving forces of CSR differ between Europe and North America.

M. Porter & M. Kramer, 2011, Creating shared value, HBR, 89(1–2): 62–77 – the most influential recent article shaping the thinking of boardrooms on social responsibility.

A.G. Scherer & G. Palazzo, eds, 2008, *Handbook on Research on Global Corporate Citizenship,* Cheltenham: Elgar – a collection of essays outlining and reflecting over the state of the art in research on CSR in a global context.

R. Van Tulder & A. van der Zwart, 2006, **International Business-Society Management, Abington: Routledge** – a textbook that explores the role of companies' CSR practices within the conflicting pressures of markets, state and civil society.

M. Yaziyi & J. Doh, 2009, *NGOs and Corporations: Conflicts and Collaboration,* Cambridge: Cambridge University Press – analyzes the relations between firms and NGOs from both sides, exploring the potential (and limits) for mutually beneficial interaction.

CLOSING CASE

M&S: . . . because there is no 'Plan B'

Founded in 1884, *Marks & Spencer* (M&S) is a leading UK retailer, specializing in clothing and premium food products. As the UK's largest clothing retailer, it holds 12% market share, and also holds 4% of the UK food retail market. In 2014, M&S had 86 000 employees operating 798 stores in the UK and 455 stores in 54 other territories.

As a premium brand, M&S has long been concerned about its social reputation. Yet traditionally M&S was mainly engaged in compliance and philanthropy, that is fulfilling regulatory and industry standards, and donating money to charitable causes. However, in 2007, M&S launched an initiative that was to transform the way everyone at M&S thinks about CSR – not a separate activity but a foundation of its business values. Its ambitious corporate-wide Plan A addressed some of

the biggest social and environmental challenges with 100 concrete commitments that it aspired to achieve by 2012.

As a premium brand serving increasingly environmentally-aware middle class consumers, M&S has a high percentage of employees supporting pro-active approaches to CSR. Therefore, Plan A was backed by a strong business case that recognized the potential for business growth if supported by responsible business practices. Although motivated by considerations for social responsibility, M&S did not call it a 'CSR' plan. The committee in charge was called the 'How We Do Business' (HWDB) Committee, and was headed by the CEO. Where did the term 'Plan A' come from? According to Plan A's website: 'We're calling it Plan A because we believe it's now the only way to do business. There is no Plan B.'

The original Plan A was divided into five areas (with leading examples):

- Climate change: becoming carbon neutral for all its UK and Irish operations.

- Waste reduction: sending no waste to landfills.

- Sustainable raw materials: tripling sales of organic food.

- Fair partnership with suppliers: introducing random checking of suppliers to ensure that M&S's global sourcing principles are being adhered to at all times.

- A healthy lifestyle for customers and employees: introducing more nutritionally-balanced food.

In Plan A's first year (2007), M&S reduced energy-related CO_2 emissions from its stores and offices by 55 000 tons, opened three pilot 'eco-stores', and completed a carbon footprint assessment for its food business. As an example of a specific initiative, plastic shopping bags were traditionally given away free of charge in the UK. M&S argued that, from an environmental standpoint, plastic bags are not 'free' because they are not biodegradable and will be stuck in landfills forever. In a pilot scheme, 50 stores in south-west England and Northern Ireland gave customers a free cloth 'bag for life'. After four weeks, these trial stores started charging 10 pence for each 'bag for life' (which would be replaced free of charge when worn out), and 5 pence for each plastic food carrier bag. The effect was immediate: in pilot stores, the customers' use of food carrier bags dropped by over 70%. Overall, M&S reduced its use of plastic bags by 11% across all its stores in 2007 – a total of 37 million fewer bags given out. Following these successful trials, M&S rolled out its programme to charge for shopping bags in all its UK and Irish stores.

Over the years, Plan A shifted M&S corporate culture in two ways. First, collaboration with other businesses and non-business associations are important, as expressed by CEO Marc Bolland: 'We know we can't deliver Plan A 2020 alone. That's why we're stepping up our efforts to "lead with others" by participating in broader coalitions to deliver sector-wide change.' (page 1)

Second, M&S emphasized the need to develop a culture that supports socially responsible thinking and acting, rather than relying on standards and measurable performance indicators. In the words of Plan A director Mike Barry: 'Risks are getting more complex, for example the interaction between food, water and energy. These interactions defy simple standard setting. We can never have enough standards to cover every social and environmental issues . . . Instead we need our employees and people working in our supply chains to see Plan A not as a matter of compliance, but as a way of working that delivers social, environmental and economic benefit.' (page 2)

Plan 2020, launched in 2014, was organized around four themes: inspiration, intouch, integrity and innovation. Under these four pillars, 100 specific commitments were made. For example,

- Commitment #6 (under inspiration) aims 'to help our customers give clothes a second life by recycling 20 million items of clothing each year by 2020. In 2013/14, customers donated 4 million garments and the initiative raised £4.2 for *Oxfam*, a charity.

- Commitment #14 (under intouch) aims to offer over 10 years work placements to 15 000 people from disadvantaged groups. In 2013/14, 3200 such placements were offered.

- Commitment #55 (under integrity) requires all of *M&S* top clothing factories to install energy efficient lightning, and improve insulation and temperature controls to reduce energy usage by 10% by 2015. In the period 2011 to 2014, 85 of 100 suppliers met this target.

- Commitment #86 (under innovation) aims to improve fuel efficiency of UK and Ireland stores by 35% by 2015. Staying on target, fuel efficiency was reduced by 32% from 2556 litres per store in 2006/07 to 1746 litres in 2013/14.

Starting in its first year, Plan A earned numerous kudos from various CSR groups. *M&S* led the global retail sector in the *Dow Jones* Sustainability Index. It received over 190 awards over eight years of operating Plan A including, for example, as first retailer, triple certification by all *Carbon Trust* standards for respectively carbon, water, and waste management.

CASE DISCUSSION QUESTIONS

1 Why is the Plan A agenda important to *M&S*?

2 What are the disadvantages and risks of giving 'how we do business' such a central role in a firm's identity?

3 What could they do even better?

Sources: Based on (1) *The Economist*, 2008, Just good business, January 19: 3–6; (2) M&S, 2007, Plan A News, plana. marksandspencer.com; (3) M&S, 2008, Plan A: Year 1 Review, January 15, plana.marksandspencer.com; (4) M&S, 2011, How We Do Business Report 2011, plana.marksandspencer.com; (5) M&S, 2014, Introducing Plan A 2020, planareport.marksandspencer.com.

NOTES

'For journal abbreviations please see page xx–xxi.'

1 K. Davis, 1973, The case for and against business assumption of social responsibilities (p. 312), *AMJ*, 16: 312–322.

2 World Commission on Environment and Development, 1987, *Our Common Future* (p. 8), Oxford: Oxford University Press; also see A. Carroll & A. Buchholtz, 2015, *Business & Society*, 9th ed., Stamford, CT: Cengage Learning.

3 A. Scherer & G. Palazzo, 2011, The new political role of business in a globalized world, *JMS*, 48: 899–931.

4 E. Freeman, 1984, *Strategic Management: A Stakeholder Approach* (p. 46), Boston: Pitman.

5 B. Husted & D. Allen 2006, CSR in the MNE, *JIBS*, 37: 838–849; G. Kassinis & N. Vafeas, 2006, Stakeholder pressures and environmental performance, *AMJ*, 49: 145–159; P. David, M. Bloom & A. Hillman, 2007, Investor activism, managerial responsiveness, and corporate social performance, *SMJ*, 28: 91–100; B. Parmar, E. Freeman & J. Harrison, 2010, Stakeholder theory: State of the art, *AMA*, 4: 403–445.

6 T. Donaldson & L. Preston, 1995, The stakeholder theory of the corporation, *AMR*, 20: 65–91.

7 R. Mitchell, B. Agle & D. Wood, 1997, Toward a theory of stakeholder identification and salience, *AMR*, 22: 853–886; T. Kochan & S. Rubinstein, 2000, Toward a stakeholder theory of the firm, *OSc*, 11: 367–386; C. Eesley & M. Lenox, 2006, Firm responses to secondary stakeholder action, *SMJ*, 27: 765–781.

8 M. Clarkson, 1995, A stakeholder framework for analyzing and evaluating corporate social performance (p. 107), *AMR*, 20: 92–117.

9 J. Doh & T. Guay, 2006, CSR, public policy, and NGO activism in Europe and the United States, *JMS*, 43: 47–73; M. Yaziyi & J. Doh, 2009, *NGOs and Corporation*, Cambridge: Cambridge University Press; A. Kourula & S. Laasonen, 2010, Nongovernmental Organizations in Business and Society, Management, and International Business Research, *B&S*, 49: 35–67.

10 Klaus Meyer, participant observation.

11 T. Jones, 1995, Instrumental stakeholder theory, *AMR*, 20: 404–437; M. Orlitzky, F. Schmidt & S. Reyes, 2003, Corporate social responsibility and financial performance, *OSt*, 24: 403–441.

12 A. Scherer & M. Smid, 2000, The downward spiral and the US model business principles, *MIR*, 40: 351–371; D. Arnold, 2003, Philosophical foundations, in: L. Hartman, D. Arnold & R. Wokutch, *Rising above Sweatshops: Innovative Approaches to Global Labor Challenges*, Westport, CT: Praeger; J. Dunning, ed., 2004, *Making Globalization Good*, Oxford: Oxford University Press.

13 C. Robertson & W. Crittenden, 2003, Mapping moral philosophies, SMJ, 24: 385–392; J. van Oosterhout, P. Heugens & M. Kaptein, 2006, The internal morality of contracting, AMR, 31: 521–539.

14 M. Porter & M. Kramer, 2006, Strategy and society, HBR, 84/12: 78–92; M. Porter & M. Kramer, 2011, Creating sharedvalue, HBR, 89/1–2: 62–77.

15 A. Biswas, C. Tortajada, A. Biswas-Tortajada, Y. Joshi & A. Gupta, 2014, Creating Shared Value: Impacts of Nestlé in Moga India, Heidelberg: Springer.

16 A. Crane, D. Palazzo, L. Spence & D. Matten, 2014, Contesting the value of 'creating shared value', CMR, 56: 130–153.

17 T. Devinney, P. Auger & G. Eckhardt, 2010, The Myth of the Ethical Consumer, Cambridge: Cambridge University Press.

18 J. French, 2009, Children's labor market involvement, household work, and welfare, JBE, 92: 63–78.

19 F. Khan, 2004. Hard times recalled: The child labour controversy in Pakistan's soccer ball industry, in: F. Bird, E. Raufflet & J. Smucker, International Business and the Dilemmas of Development, Basingstoke: Palgrave-Macmillan, pp. 132–156.

20 S. Banerjee, 2007, Corporate Social Responsibility, Cheltenham: Elgar; K. Bondy, 2008, The paradox of power in CSR, JBE, 82: 307–323.

21 D. Spar, 1998, The Spotlight and the Bottom Line, FA, 77: 7–12.

22 H. Leonard, 1988, Pollution and the Struggle for a World Product, Cambridge: Cambridge University Press; N. Mabey & R. McNally, 1998, Foreign direct investment and the environment, WWF-UK Report, (www.wwf-uk.org/filelibrary/pdf/fdi.pdf); L. Zarsky, 1999, Havens, halos and spaghetti: Untangling the evidence about FDI and the environment, conference paper, Paris: OECD, January 28–29.

23 D. Spar & D. Yoffie, 1999, Multinational enterprises and the prospect for justice, JIA, 52: 557–581.

24 M.E. Porter & C. van der Linde, 1995, Toward a new conception of the environment-competitiveness relationships, JEP, 9: 97–118.

25 China Business Review, 2007, Dow partners with China's SEPA, May-June: 17.

26 A. Rugman & A. Verbeke, 1998, Corporate strategy and international environmental policy, JIBS, 29: 819–833; P. Christmann & G. Taylor, 2006, Firm self-regulation through international certifiable standards, JIBS, 37: 863–878.

27 D. Marconi, 2012, Environmental regulation and revealed comparative advantage in Europe, RIE, 20: 616–625; S. Poelhekke & F. van der Ploeg, 2015, WE, advance online.

28 J. Lan M. Kakinaka & X. Huang, 2012, Foreign direct investment, human capital and environmental pollution in China, Environmental and Resource Economics, 51: 255–275.

29 A. King & M. Shaver, Are aliens green? SMJ, 22, 1069–1085; R. Hoffmann, C. Lee, B. Ramasamy & M. Yeung, 2005, FDI and pollution, JID, 17: 311–317.

30 P. Christmann, 2004, Multinational companies and the natural environment, AMJ, 47: 747–760.

31 G. Dowell, S. Hart & B. Yeung, 2000, Do corporate global environmental standards create or destroy market value? MS, 46: 1059–1074.

32 J. He, 2006, Pollution haven hypothesis and environmental impacts of foreign direct investment, EE, 60: 228–245.

33 T. Palley, 2002, The child labor problem and the need for international labor standards, JEI, 36: 601–615; D. O'Rourke, 2003, Outsourcing Regulation: Analyzing nongovernmental systems of labor standards and monitoring, PSJ, 31: 1–29.

34 B. Aitken, A. Harrison & R. Lipsey, 1997, Wages and foreign ownership, JIE 43: 103–132. N. Driffield & S. Girma, 2003, Regional foreign direct investment and wage spillovers, OBES, 65: 453–474; F. Heyman, F. Sjöholm & P. Tingvall, 2007, Is there really a foreign ownership wage premium, JIE, 73: 355–376.

35 E. Lee, 1997, Globalization and Labour Standards, ILR, 136: 173–188; J. Surroca, J. Tribo & S. Zahra, 2013, Stakeholder pressure on MNEs and the transfer of socially irresponsible practices to subsidiaries, AMJ, 56: 549–572.

36 L. Preuss, 2010, Codes of conduct in organization context, JBE, 94: 4711–487; G. Garegnani, E. Merlotti & A. Russo, 2015, Scoring firms' codes of ethics, JBE, 126: 541–557; M. Kaptein, 2015, The Effectiveness of Ethics Programs, JBE, advance online.

37 B. Bulgurcu, H. Cavusglu & I. Benbasat, 2010, Information system policy compliance, MIS Quarterly, 34: 523–548; C. Parker & V. Lehmann-Nielsen, eds, 2011, Explaining Compliance: Business Responses to Regulation, Cheltenham: Elgar; N. Egels-Zanden, 2014, Revisitng supplier compliance with MNC codes of conduct, JBE, 119: 59–75; Q. Hu, T. Dinev, P. Hart & D. Cooke, 2014, Managing employee compliance with information security policies, Decision Sciences, 43: 615–660.

38 O'Rourke, 2003, as above.

39 N. Egels-Zandén, 2007, Suppliers' compliance with MNCs' codes of conduct, JBE, 75: 45–62.

40 S. Frenkel & D. Scott, 2002, Compliance, collaboration, and codes of labor practice: The adidas connection', CMR, 45: 29–49; R. Locke, M. Amengual & A. Mangla, 2009, Virtue out of necessity, P&S, 37: 319–351.

41 P. Perego & A. Kolk, 2012, Multinationals' accountability on sustainability, JBE, 110: 173–190.

42 S. Charreine Petit & J. Surply, 2008, Du whistleblowing à l'americaine à l'alerte éthique à la française, M@n@gement, 11: 113–135; A. Temple & P. Walgenbach, 2007, Global standardization of organizational forms and practices? JMS, 44: 1–24.

43 M. Friedman, 1970, The social responsibility of business is to increase its profits, *New York Times Magazine*, September 13.

44 M. Jensen, 2002, Value maximization, stakeholder theory, and the corporate objective function, *BEQ* 12: 235–256.

45 D. Henderson, 2001, *Misguided Virtue*, London: Institute for Economic Affairs; *The Economist*, 2001, Curse of the Ethics Executive, November 17. Note that his argument implicitly assumes (as is common in economics) that markets are efficient. In other words, consumer goods markets competition is based on price (and not, for example, reputation), labour markets with free entry and exit from contracts, full information of workers signing an employment contract, and no imbalanced bargaining power. If these assumptions are substantially violated the argument collapses.

46 D. Matten & J. Moon, 2009, 'Implicit' and 'Explicit' CSR, *AMR*, 33: 404–424; A. Apostolakou & G. Jackson, 2010, corporate social responsibility in Western Europe, *JBE*, 94: 371–394.

47 M. Porter & M. Kremer, 2006, Strategy and society, *HBR*, 84(December), 78–92.

48 S. Brammer & S. Pavlin, 2005, Corporate community contributions in the United Kingdom and the United States, *JBE*, 56: 15–26; S. Brammer, S. Pavelin & L. Porter, 2009, Corporate charitable giving, multinational companies and countries of concern, *JMS*, 46: 575–596.

49 *The Economist*, 2011, Attitudes to business: Milton Friedman goes on tour, January 29.

50 Matten & Moon, 2008, *as above*.

51 Matten & Moon, 2008, *as above*.

52 G. Weaver, 2001, Ethics programs in global businesses, *JBE*, 30: 3–15; A. Kolk & R. van Tulder, 2004, Ethics in international business, *JWB*, 39: 49–60; I. Maignan & D. Ralston, 2002, CSR in Europe and the US, *JIBS*, 33: 497–514.

53 Y. Eiadat, A. Kelly, F. Roche, & H. Eyadat, 2008, Green and competitive? *JWB*, 43: 131–145; P. Godfrey, C. Merrill & J. Hansen, 2009, The relationship between CSR and shareholder value, *SMJ*, 30: 425–445; B. Lev, C. Petrovits & S. Radhakrishnan, 2010, Is doing good for you? *SMJ*, 31: 182–200; M. Sharfman & C. Fernando, 2008, Environmental risk management and the cost of capital, *SMJ*, 29: 569–592; H. Wang & C. Qian, 2011, Corporate philanthropy and corporate financial performance, *AMJ*, 54: 1159–1181; I. Lorenço, M. Branco, J. Curtoi & T. Eugénio, 2012, How does the market value corporate sustainability performance? *JBE*, 108: 417–428.

54 S. Ambec & P. Lanoie, 2008, Does it pay to be green? *AMP*, November: 45–62; D. Vogel, 2005, The low value of virtue, HBR, June: 26.

55 B. Agle, R. Mitchell & J. Sonnenfeld, 1999, What matters to CEOs? *AMJ*, 42: 507–525; A. McWilliams & D. Siegel, 2000, CSR and financial performance, *SMJ*, 21: 603–609.

56 Orlitzky, Schmidt & Reyes, 2003, *as above*.

57 S. Happel, 2015, Warum Primark kein Skandal schadet, *Handelsblatt*, February 11.

58 S. Brammer & A. Millington, 2008, Does it pay to be different? *SMJ*, 29: 1325–1343.

59 Banerjee, 2007, *as above*.

60 M.W. Peng & H. Shin, 2008, How do future business leaders view globalization? *TIBR*, 50: 175–182

61 G. Frynas, 2005, The false developmental promise of corporate social responsibility, *IA*, 81: 581–598.

62 T. London, 2009, Making better investments at the base of the pyramid, *HBR*, 87 (5): 106–113

63 *Der Spiegel*, 2010, Warum Schokogiganten auf politisch korrekten Kakao setzen, January 3, translated by Klaus Meyer.

64 S. Mufson, 2010, In China, Wal-Mart presses suppliers on labor, environmental standards, *Washington Post*, February 28.

65 Mufson, 2010, *as above*. A similar message arises from the study by Devinney et al., 2010, *as above*.

66 R. Locke, 2012, *Beyond Compliance: Promoting Labor Rights in a Global Economy*, New York: Cambridge University Press; *The Economist*, 2012, Working conditions in factories: When the jobs inspector calls, March 31

67 T. Donaldson & T.W. Dunfee, 1994, Toward a unified conception of business ethics, *AMR*, 19: 252–284; G.G. Brenkert, 2009, ISCT, hypernorms and business, *JBE*, 88: 645–658; T. Donaldson, 2009, Compass and dead reckoning, *JBE*, 88: 659–664.

68 T. Donaldson, 1996, Values in tension: Ethics away from home, *HBR*, September–October: 4–11.

69 *El País*, 2009, Gran negocio verde en Copenhague, December 13.

70 P. Bansal & K. Roth, 2000, Why companies go green, *AMJ*, 43: 717–737.

71 D. Spar & L. LaMure, 2003, The power of activism, *CMR*, 45(3): 78–101; S. Vachani, J.P. Doh & H. Teegen, 2009, NGO's influence on MNE's social development strategies in varying contexts, *IBR*, 18: 446–456; M. Seitanidi & M. Crane, 2009, Implementing CSR through Partnerships, *JBE*, 85: 413–429; M. van Huijstee & P. Glasbergen, 2010, NGOs Moving Business, *B&S*, 49: 591–618.

72 Yaziyi & Doh, 2009, *as above*.

73 A. McWilliams & D. Siegel, 2001, Corporate social responsibility, *AMR*, 26: 117–127.

74 Personal communication with Klaus Meyer.

75 B. Husted & J. Salazar, 2006, Taking Friedman seriously, *JMS*, 43: 75–91.

PART FOUR

THE FIRM ON THE GLOBAL STAGE

11   Starting International Business

12   Foreign Entry Strategies

13   Competitive Dynamics

14   Global Strategies and Acquisitions

CHAPTER ELEVEN

STARTING INTERNATIONAL BUSINESS

LEARNING OBJECTIVES

After studying this chapter, you should be able to

1 Explain the different options for firms to start engaging in international business

2 Explain how firms develop resources for international business

3 Explain how institutions influence exporting behaviour

4 Participate in two leading debates on early stage internationalization

5 Draw implications for practice

OPENING CASE

Kaspersky Lab *is scaling the globe*

by Anna Gryaznova and Olga Annushkina

Kaspersky Lab, the fourth-largest antivirus software vendor in the world – with 2008 revenues that exceeded US$0.3 billion – was founded in Moscow in 1997 by four young and ambitious software engineers, including a young couple, Natalya and Eugene Kaspersky. Back in 1994, Natalya, a graduate of Moscow Institute of Electronic Engineering, started working in *KAMI*

Information Technologies Center, where she was manager of the antivirus software development group set up by Eugene. The couple established *Kaspersky Lab* three years later: Eugene was in charge of antivirus software development, while Natalya, the company's chief executive, was responsible for definition and implementation of the business model. At that time, this required strenuous digging for clients – corporate clients, dealers and distributors that would help the company to reach private clientele.

In the mid 1990s, the market for antivirus software was just starting in Russia and worldwide, and at that time in Russia *Kaspersky Lab* was not very lucky in finding many clients willing to pay for something they couldn't touch (software). The start of the company in 1997 was a very big challenge. *Kaspersky Lab* had 19 people as staff, and revenues were insufficient to survive. At that time, attracting external investments in Russia for a software start-up was impossible. Help came from an unexpected source. In 1996, *Kaspersky Lab* had entered OEM agreements by licensing its AV engine to two of its competitors – Finnish *F-Secure* and German *G Data*. In late 1997, Natalya went to Finland and reached agreement with *F-Secure* that they would pay *Kaspersky Lab* advanced royalties on a monthly basis. This arrangement saved *Kaspersky Lab* in its first years.

Natalya started actively searching for potential sales partners for *Kaspersky Lab* in different countries. The first contracts came from Switzerland, Germany, Poland, the Netherlands and the USA. Natalya called her initial approach a 'water strategy': to enter every regional market possible with one focused product, by catching any selling opportunity at any price. The product itself – antivirus software packages for privates and companies – needed only very small adaptations for international markets, mainly the translation of the product description into a local language. With the help of local partners, *Kaspersky Lab* localized its products in 14 languages; and in just three years, it started to sell its software in more than 20 countries.

While growing, the company decided to launch its own local offices to increase its international presence. Its first offices opened in the UK, Poland, Holland and China. Later, Germany, France, the US and Japan were added. The UK office was the most difficult, as it was the first. The company made all the possible mistakes entering the UK, and initially experienced very slow growth. Yet the team learned a lot from that experience, and the UK office eventually became one of the most successful local operations of *Kaspersky Lab*.

One of the key points concerning the local office launches for *Kaspersky Lab* was getting the right people on board. That is why Natalya, when taking on a new local manager, would often agree to open the company office close to the manager's home (for instance in Ingolstadt instead of Berlin, or in Oxfordshire instead of London), just for the sake of keeping them interested. That way the chosen manager has built the office and hired local people there.

Another challenge was to get the resources for development. During the internet boom of the late 1990s, no investor was interested enough to provide *Kaspersky Lab* with the financial resources it needed for the international marketing campaign. After Natalya's worthless trip to Wall Street, the company decided to cut its appetite and get by on its own. This strategy did not allow the company big marketing campaigns, so it needed to be smart. *Kaspersky Lab* decided to focus on its main strength – technological capability. The company took part in all possible

antivirus software tests, contests and rankings – with excellent results. The 'word of mouth' spread first among 'geeks' and later reached the mass market. To maintain its 'technological' selling proposition, the company was among the first to issue daily and then hourly antivirus updates, having the fastest reaction in the world against new viruses.

While technologically advanced private users all over the world were happy to install *Kaspersky Anti-Virus,* the corporate world was much more closed, partially because *Kaspersky Lab* came to the market much later than its competitors. Once a company had *Symantec* or *McAfee* it was not inclined or motivated to search for an alternative solution. So, Natalya decided to focus on the small and medium business segment, leaving the large corporate market for the future.

This strategy proved to be successful. Ten years after its foundation, *Kaspersky Lab* was among the top four companies in the world revenue-wise after

Symantec, *McAfee* and *Trend Micro*. The number of users of *Kaspersky* software increased from 200 million in 2010, to 400 million in 200 countries in 2015. Even the *BBC* noted that '*Kaspersky Lab* is regarded outside Russia as one of the country's few business success stories not related to the energy sector' and the *Fast Company* magazine ranked it among the Top 50 Most Innovative Companies worldwide. *Kaspersky Lab* has repeatedly exposed serious cyber-security problems, and its software engineers are frequently quoted by the media as experts on cyber-security issues. This is an amazing recognition for a company that never had a financial investor.

Source: The case was originally prepared by Anna Gryaznova of Moscow State University and Olga Annushkina of SDA Bocconi School of Management based on field research.
Update sources: (1) *BBC News*, 2011, Russian police free software tycoon Kaspersky's son, April 24; (2) www.kaspersky.com; (3) *The Economist*, 2015, The Kaspersky equation, February 21.

What are the steps that *Kaspersky Lab* had to go through to build an international brand? How can a small entrepreneurial business from Russia realistically reach such diverse and distant markets? How does it learn to do business in the countries it was targeting? How does it organize its operations and supply chain? More generally, what are the challenges that small and medium-size enterprises (SMEs) face when launching into international markets? These are the sorts of questions that we will be discussing in this and the following chapters.

Compared with domestic business, transaction costs are higher in international business. On the one hand, there are numerous differences in formal institutions and informal norms (see Chapters 2 and 3). On the other hand, it is harder to assess if the potential partner is trustworthy. SMEs, here defined as companies with less than 500 employees, have fewer resources than large firms, and thus cannot simply buy up local firms to establish a foothold in a foreign market. In view of high costs, some small firms simply say 'Forget it!' when receiving an unsolicited order from abroad. Conceptually, this is an example of transaction costs being so high that many firms may choose not to pursue international opportunities.

However, as we will show in this chapter, SMEs have many options to extend their business model in a profitable way to new countries. Such foreign entry requires entrepreneurs, who are leaders identifying opportunities and taking decisions to exploit them.[1] In many start-ups like *Kaspersky Lab*, a group of people, known as the entrepreneurial team, shares responsibilities and contributes complementary capabilities and experiences. This chapter focuses on the challenges of entrepreneurial firms at early stages of internationalization and on the basic transactions they may undertake. Then, we discuss how companies progress from their first steps to higher levels of international business, and why some firms, known as 'born globals', are able to jump ahead and internationalize early.

The remainder of Part 4 discusses strategic challenges to more established firms. The next chapter focuses on the establishment of subsidiaries abroad in the form of,

small and medium-sized enterprises (SMEs)
Firms with fewer than 500 employees.

entrepreneur
Leader identifying opportunities and taking decisions to exploit them.

entrepreneurial team
A group of people jointly acting as entrepreneurs.

for example, joint venture, acquisition or greenfield. The division is that Chapter 11 covers non-equity modes, which are especially relevant to firms at early stage of international business. Chapter 12 then reviews equity investments – that is, foreign direct investment (FDI) – which is mainly relevant for medium- and large-sized businesses. Chapter 13 analyzes the strategies of firms that have achieved a position on the global stage, while Chapter 14 discusses the dynamics of collaboration and competition of such firms.

GOING INTERNATIONAL

LEARNING OBJECTIVE

1 Explain the different options for firms to start engaging in international business

exporter
Seller of products or services to another country.

importer
Buyer of goods or services from another country.

direct exports
The sale of products made by firms in their home country to customers in other countries.

Principally, firms can act as sellers or buyers or both. In international trade, the sellers are known as exporters, and the buyers as importers. In this section, we review these basic transactions from the perspective of smaller and entrepreneurial firms that do not have the resources to set up an FDI (which will be covered in the next chapter). First, we look at exporters and importers of goods, then those buying and selling services, before reviewing a range of contractual forms that combine exchanges of goods, services and rights (Table 11.1).

Managing exports and imports

Many firms start international business through direct exports, which is the sale of products to customers in another country. This strategy is attractive for less experienced firms because they can reach foreign customers directly. It can start with an unsolicited enquiry from customers who learned about the products, for example

Table 11.1 Non-equity internationalization strategies (examples)

	Seller (Exporting)	Buyer (Importing)
Good	● Direct exports ● Indirect exports via domestic intermediary ● Indirect export with foreign distributor or agent	● Direct import ● Indirect import ● Subcontracting of manufacturing
Service	● Delivering services to customers abroad ● Attracting foreign customers to your location	● Hiring consultants based abroad ● Subcontracting of services
Combination of goods, services and rights	● Licensor ● Franchisor ● Build turn-key projects ● Build-operate-transfer contracts ● Management contract	● Licensee ● Franchisee ● Subcontracting ● R&D contracts

at a trade fair,[2] and took the initiative for the transaction. To actively and systematically pursue export customers requires a more systematic investment in export marketing.

Delivering an export order however creates practical challenges for an inexperienced firm. One essential question to clarify with your trading partner is who is in charge of moving the goods from your place to theirs. If you are a regular user of *eBay*, you already know that you need to pay attention to whether the seller offers to send the product, or expects you to pick it up. It gets more complicated in international trade; a whole vocabulary has developed for traders to negotiate who is responsible for that (Table 11.2). The most important terms to remember are fob and cif. If your contract states 'fob' the seller has to deliver 'free on board' the ship or train at a specified port. If it states 'cif', the seller in addition has to pay the 'costs of insurance and freight' of the transport to a destination port. There are also other contract options, but these two are the most common. Once the goods are loaded on the ship, the shipping company will issue a bill of lading (B/L), which the seller can use to claim the delivery of the goods. For

fob (free on board)
Contract clause: the seller has to deliver goods free on board of a ship or train.

cif (costs of insurance and freight)
Contract clause: the seller has to pay all transportation costs to a destination port.

bill of lading (B/L)
Document certifying the delivery of the goods to a ship or train.

Table 11.2 The trader's vocabulary

Term	Meaning	Explanation
Trade documents		
AWL	Airway bill	Document issued by an airline to certify receipt of merchandise. Contrary to B/L, it does not entail a legal title to the products.
B/L	Bill of lading	Document issued by a courier or shipping company certifying that the merchandise has been delivered, and paid for. Only the person holding the B/L has the right to claim the products.
LOC	Letter of credit	A document certifying that the importer's bank will pay a specific sum of money to the exporter upon delivery of the merchandise.
Contract terms		
CIF	Cost, insurance & freight	The seller pays all costs of transport, including insurance and freight.
DDP	Delivered duty paid	The seller will deliver the goods to a specified place, and pay the necessary customs duties.
EXW	Ex works	Buyer has to pick up good from the seller's specified factory or warehouse.
FOB	Free on board	The seller delivers the goods on board a boat or train, put does not pay for the transport.

people working in shipping or logistics (see Chapter 17), this vocabulary is their daily bread.

A further concern is how to overcome the lack of trust when a firm receives an export order from an unknown customer abroad. Businesses receive many offers for collaboration via e mail, but how can you distinguish a genuine customer from a fraudster? For example, in Figure 11.1, the US exporter does not trust the Chinese importer, but banks on both sides can facilitate this transaction by a letter of credit (L/C), which is a financial contract that states that the importer's bank (*Bank of China* in this case) will pay a specific sum of money to the exporter upon delivery of the merchandise. It has several steps:

letter of credit (L/C)
A financial contract that states that the importer's bank will pay a specific sum of money to the exporter upon delivery of the merchandise.

- While the unknown Chinese importer's assurance that it will promptly pay for the merchandise may be questioned by the US exporter, a L/C from the highly reputable *Bank of China* will assure the US exporter that the importer has good creditworthiness and has sufficient funds for this transaction. If the US exporter is not sure about whether *Bank of China* is a credible bank, it can consult its own bank, *Bank of America*, which will confirm that an L/C from *Bank of China* is 'as good as gold'.

- With this assurance through the L/C the US exporter can release the merchandise, which goes through a US freight forwarder, then a shipping company, and then a Chinese customs broker. Finally, the goods will reach the Chinese importer.

- Once the US exporter has shipped the goods, it will present to Bank of America the L/C from *Bank of China* and shipping documents such as the B/L. On behalf of the US exporter, *Bank of America* will then collect payment from *Bank of China*, which, in turn, will collect payment from the Chinese importer.

Overall, instead of having unknown exporters and importers deal with each other, transactions are facilitated by banks on both sides that know each other quite well because of numerous such dealings. In other words, the L/C reduces transaction costs.

Figure 11.1 An export/import transaction

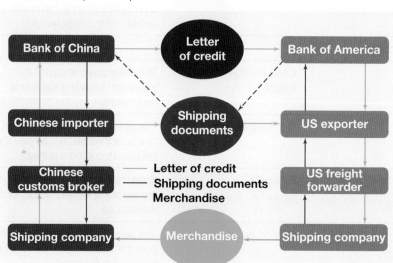

Direct exports represent the most basic mode, capitalizing on economies of scale in production concentrated in the home country and affording better control over distribution.[3] This strategy essentially treats foreign demand as an extension of domestic demand. Sporadic exports may work if the export volume is small; it is not optimal when the firm has a large number of foreign buyers. Marketing considerations suggest that the firm needs to be closer, both physically and psychologically, to its customers. Yet many SMEs do not have the resources to build a local marketing operation. They may thus reach overseas customers through indirect exports – exporting through an intermediary.[4]

Trade intermediaries

Export intermediaries are based in the same country as the exporter, but have the expertise to perform an important 'middleman' function by linking sellers and buyers overseas that otherwise would not have been connected.[5] Such intermediaries include trading companies and export management companies that help SMEs in their internationalization. In some countries, they play an important role in facilitating exports, handling for example about 50% of total exports in Japan and South Korea, and 38% in Thailand. In Europe and the USA they are less prominent, handling typically less than 10% of exports from SMEs.[6] Intermediaries are more common for standardized products and commodities (such as textiles, woods and meats), where competition focuses primarily on price.[7]

Export via intermediaries not only enjoys the economies of scale in domestic production (similar to direct exports), but it is also relatively worry-free because the intermediary handles cross-cultural communication, international payments, and other activities that small firms may find rather burdensome. However, they have some drawbacks because of the introduction of third parties with their own agendas and objectives that are not necessarily the same as the exporter's.[8] The primary reason exporters choose intermediaries is because of information asymmetries concerning risks and uncertainties associated with foreign markets. Intermediaries with international contacts and knowledge essentially make a living by taking advantage of such information asymmetries. They may have a vested interest in making sure that such asymmetries are not reduced.

If exporters are interested in learning more about how their products perform overseas, they may employ their own local agent or distributor. The difference is that sales agents receive a commission on sales, while distributors trade on their own account; in other words, they buy the products and then sell them on in the local market at their own risk and using their own channels.[9] Such local intermediaries normally provide knowledge of the local market and network relationships with local customers, thus facilitating both access to customers and after-sales service. However, this kind of arrangement entails the risk that the distributor effectively controls the local market and shares information only selectively. Distributors may, for example, repackage products under their own brand, and monopolize the communication with customers. For example, *Nilfisk*, a Danish producer of commercial vacuum cleaners, worked successfully for many years with its Spanish distributor *Nilfisk Aspiradoras*. Yet the distributor acted fiercely independently, and *Nilfisk* found it difficult to integrate the operations more tightly. In an industry where after-sales service is essential, local customers had built loyalty with the distributor rather than with the manufacturer. This gave the distributor considerable bargaining power when it came to rearranging the distributor agreements.[10]

Some firms that have negative experiences with intermediaries subsequently move back to direct exports. This is likely to be appropriate in particular for exporters that

indirect exports
A way for SMEs to reach overseas customers by exporting through domestic-based export intermediaries.

export intermediary
A firm that performs an important 'middleman' function by linking sellers and buyers overseas.

sales agent
An intermediary receiving commission for sales.

distributor
An intermediary trading on their own account.

What are the merits of participating in a trade fair?

deal with a small number of customers and with products that require a high degree of direct interaction between the manufacturer and the user. Direct exports may thus be used for instance by manufacturers of technologically complex machines, or producers of customized intermediate products. A particular challenge for such firms may be after-sales service: how do you fix a defective machine at the other end of the world? The internet helps to deliver many aspects of after-sales service, for example performance analysis and error identification. Yet customers may still develop more confidence to a supplier with a local operation, which may necessitate establishment of a sales subsidiary (see Chapter 12).

The opposite side of the coin to exporting is importing. Many textbooks focus on the exporter as the primary decision-maker, but importers are equally important in driving international trade. In many ways, the activities are the same, but from a buyer's perspective. Initially, firms may engage in sporadic imports by ordering from a supplier they met at a trade fair, or via the internet. For small transactions with a trustworthy source, they may simply pay in advance using their credit card. You can also do that as an individual, but remember that you will be liable to pay customs and duties when the products arrive in your country (unless it is an intra-EU transaction and value-added tax has been paid in the country of origin, see Chapter 8). For larger transactions, a letter of credit (Figure 11.1), guarantees importers that their payment is only released when they have received the goods. For regular imports, firms would develop supplier relationships that involve extensive exchange of knowledge and, usually, a firmer contractual arrangement.

Alternatively, importers may employ specialized intermediaries to find suitable suppliers, and to negotiate appropriate terms of delivery. Trading houses such as *Li & Fung* of Hong Kong have taken this role of trade intermediary so far as to coordinate the entire supply chain for their customers. For instance, a European department store may order shirts to a particular specification, and *Li & Fung* would source all the components across Asia, arrange for their assembly at a low-cost location, organize transportation and customs clearance, and deliver the finished shirts to a warehouse in Europe.[11]

Managing international services

Traditionally, international trade meant sending goods across borders. Yet globalization – especially advances in communication and transport technologies – has changed that. Countries like Greece and Cyprus earn more through exports of services than through exports of goods, mainly due to their shipping and tourism industries. The UK, the largest exporter of services among the EU countries, earned €215 billion in 2008 through export of services, compared to exports of goods worth €317 billion.[12] Traditionally, services had to be produced at the site of delivery – serving a meal normally requires a cook and a kitchen at the site where the customer wants to eat. However, regulatory and technological changes facilitate trade in services, taking two different forms: (1) cross-border services, and (2) servicing foreign residents.

First, cross-border services are services that are sent across national borders. A wide range of services falls in this category, and they have been growing fast in recent years. Airlines transport people around the globe; courier companies deliver parcels and letters, while maritime shipping companies coordinate fleets of cargo and container ships on the world's oceans. Some forms of cross-border supply involve people travelling to another country on a temporary basis, for example a university may send a teacher, a hospital sends a specialist doctor, or a rock band gives a concert. Similarly, construction engineers, architects and other consultants may design a bridge or write a report in their main office with occasional visits to see the site. Such transactions count as exports in the balance of payment because they earn money for the national economy. For example, if the government of Vietnam hires a Sweden-based professor to prepare a report on ecological changes of the Mekong Delta, this counts as service export from Sweden. If, however, a Swedish aid organization pays for the report, then it does not count as export, even if the field research is conducted in Vietnam.

Other cross-border supplies of services do not require a physical movement of people: a software application can be sent over the internet, and a call centre can counsel clients by phone. The internet has created entirely new opportunities for such cross-border supply of services based on web applications, such as online learning, or international business process outsourcing (Chapter 4) including data entry, processing of financial transactions or proofreading of documents (such as this book).

Second, servicing foreign residents involves delivery of services to people living in other countries. This form of service export is driving the internationalization of, for example, tourism, education and health care businesses. In tourism, every firm is a potential exporter, even your neighbourhood take-away and your local bed-and-breakfast (B&B). However, it is only really meaningful to talk about international business when businesses systematically target international customers. A hotel may, for instance, offer English language menus, a souvenir shop, and tourist guides trained in cross-cultural communication. The internet offers inexpensive opportunities for small firms, such as B&Bs, to increase their exposure to potential clients around the world, and thus to compete with larger hotel chains.[13] Beyond advertising, they may accept bookings online, backed up by an online credit card payments system. Larger tourism businesses, such as entertainment parks or hotel chains, may systematically target international customers by advertising in magazines abroad or cooperating with travel agents (In Focus 11.1).

cross-border services Supplying services across national borders.

servicing foreign residents Supplying services to customers coming from abroad.

IN FOCUS 11.1

Tourism: exporting experiences

Selling to tourists is like exports in reverse: rather than sending goods to your customers, the customers come to the goods. But what is it that this industry sells: hotel beds, fine dinners and bus rides? People can get these services in a lot of locations, even at home. What are they looking for when on holiday? The distinctive quality – or competitive advantage – lies in the 'experiences' that particular activities offer at the location. Tourists thus vary in their appreciation of tourist activities, each with their own personal experience of interacting with the local context.

This reverse nature of tourism 'exports' creates challenges for those who provide the services. An important aspect is the communication of the values and unique experience associated with the event or location. Thus tourism service providers often collaborate to create and market brand values associated with a city, a region or a country, for example: 'Wonderful Copenhagen', 'Greece, A Masterpiece you can Afford' or 'Malaysia, truly Asia'.

Another challenge is to deliver experiences that the tourists appreciate. Tourists come from different cultures and thus normally lack understanding and appreciation of the local culture, yet many seek to experience local culture as part of their holiday. They would like to participate in the activities of the locals, but do tourists experience the event in the same way? Or does the event itself change its nature because of the presence of tourists? Some tourism operators thus create staged authenticity, with events adapted to suit foreign perspectives of 'native folk dances' or, in Britain, 'medieval banquets'. Tourism service providers thus are acting as mediators of culture, helping foreigners to interpret and appreciate what they are experiencing.

Some tour operators, such as Australian *Intrepid* and Chinese *WildChina,* thus focus on small-group travel with groups of, on average, ten travellers. This allows travellers to get off the beaten track, use local accommodation and transport, and really get to know the culture. Itineraries focused on introducing local knowledge and experience can provide unique, authentic insights into local lives. The small-group adventures style strikes a balance between pre-planned activities and spontaneous adaptation to travellers' interests. Thereby they can manage the creative tension between the demand for authenticity and the barriers to communicating cultural values and traditions.

Sources: (1) C.S. Ooi, 2002, *Cultural Tourism & Tourism Culture*, Copenhagen: CBS Press; (2) T. O'Dell & P. Billing, eds, 2005, *Experiencescapes*, Copenhagen: CBS Press; J.C. Holloway & N. Taylor, 2006, *The Business of Tourism*, 7th ed., Harlow: Pearson; (3) www.intrepidtravel.com; (4) www.wildchina.com.

The internationalization of education is driven by individuals' desire to tap into knowledge and experience available abroad.[14] Educational institutions recruit potential students by marketing in target countries, and by activating their international alumni networks. Language schools have been leading the trend: scores of continental European teenagers come to England every Easter and every summer to brush up on their English – and to have a good time. Others, from boarding schools to senior management executive training, have been developing programmes aimed at international audiences. For example, British universities market their programmes through the government-backed British Council and specialized agencies to potential students around the globe.

In the health care sector, international clients are still a relatively new phenomenon. Traditionally, internationalization was inhibited by high travel costs, information asymmetries, and the national structure of health insurance systems. Yet hospitals in some emerging economies offer treatments at much lower costs than in the USA or in Western Europe, and they attract patients not covered by health insurance.[15] For example, 1000-bed Narayana Hrudayala Hospital in Bangalore, India, has developed a cost-efficient business model that allows surgeons to focus on and build experience in very specific areas by performing vast numbers of operations of a similar type. Their lower costs attract some of the estimated six million US citizens seeking affordable medical care outside of the USA.[16] Similarly, South African hospitals have specialized in beauty treatment: tell your friends you are off on a safari and out of sight, and return mystically rejuvenated three weeks later.[17]

Managing international contracts

Most international business transactions are not one-off transactions, but they are embedded in longer term contractual relationships. A wide range of contracts have been developed that combine exports and imports of goods and services, transfer of rights, define of contributions, and allocate profits and risk of a business operation. This section provides a brief glance at some of them: (1) licensing, (2) franchising, (3) turnkey and build-own-operate projects, (4) subcontracting and (5) management contracts.

Manufacturers may earn revenues on their capabilities, without physically producing the goods, by licensing or franchising. The basic idea of these contracts is to transfer property rights (see Chapter 2) for a royalty fee, but without necessarily becoming involved in the local operation. Licensing refers to an agreement in which a Firm A, (the licensor), gives a Firm B (the licensee) the rights to use A's proprietary technology (such as a patent) or trademark (such as a corporate logo) for a royalty fee paid to A by B. For example, a software developer like *SAP*, *Microsoft* or *Kaspersky Lab* (Opening Case) may license its software to other firms. These other firms are then allowed to use the software under term defined in the contract, yet they may (normally) not share it with other users. Franchising represents a similar idea, but typically covers entire business concepts: not only the product, service and trademark, but also the marketing strategy, operation manuals, and quality control procedures. Many world famous brands such as *McDonalds*, *Starbucks* or *Benetton* are managed as franchise chains. Thus the relationship between giver of the franchise (the franchisor) and the recipient (franchisee) involves extensive training and continuing communication.[18]

A great advantage is that licensors and franchisors can expand abroad with relatively little capital of their own.[19] Entrepreneurs interested in becoming licensees/franchisees have to put their own capital up front. Thus the licensor/franchisor does not have to bear the full costs and risks associated with foreign expansion. For example, *Bang & Olufsen* runs most sales outlets for its designer consumer electronics as

licensing
Firm A's agreement to give Firm B the rights to use A's proprietary technology (such as a patent) or trademark (such as a corporate logo) for a royalty fee paid to A by B.

licensor
The company granting a licence.

licensee
The company receiving a licence.

franchising
Firm A's agreement to give Firm B the rights to use a package of A's proprietary assets for a royalty fee paid to A by B.

franchisor
The company granting a franchise.

franchisee
The company receiving a franchise.

franchise operations. Their UK subsidiary employs only 40 people who provide training and support to franchisees in the UK, Ireland and the Benelux countries.[20]

On the other hand, the licensor/franchisor does not have tight control over production and marketing, and thus how their technology and brand names are used.[21] If a foreign licensee was producing sub-standard products that damage the brand and refuses to improve quality, the licensor would be left with the difficult choices of (1) suing its licensee in an unfamiliar court abroad or (2) discontinuing the relationship, both of which are complicated and costly. For example, *Starbucks* franchised its coffee shop concept to a joint venture with German department store chain *Karstadt*. The venture lost both partners a lot of money before *Starbucks* bought out the partner to take full ownership control in 2004, and tried to make a new start to grow in Germany, where it had only 157 outlets, compared to 764 in the UK.[22]

Becoming a licensee or franchisee of a foreign brand is an opportunity for an entrepreneur to build their business. Foreign licensors and franchisors will provide training and technology transfer – for a fee, of course. Entrepreneurs consequently can learn a great deal about how to operate at world-class standards. Further, they do not have to be permanently under the control of licensors and franchisors. If enough learning has been accomplished and enough capital has been accumulated, it is possible to discontinue the relationship and to reap greater entrepreneurial profits. For example, in Thailand, *Minor Group*, which had held the *Pizza Hut* franchise for 20 years, broke away from the relationship. Its new venture, *The Pizza Company*, is now the market leader in Thailand.[23] Most franchise contracts would however rule out direct competition.

Third, turnkey projects refer to projects in which clients pay contractors to design and construct new facilities. At project completion, contractors will hand clients the proverbial 'key' to facilities ready for operation – hence the term *turnkey*. This form of contracting is particularly common in the construction and civil engineering industries. Companies such as *ALSTOM*, with core competences in designing and implementing large projects such as power stations, motorways or airports, would thus manage the entire design and construction process on site, in part through expatriate experts (see Chapter 3, Opening Case).

For larger projects, the tasks get more complex, more specialized competences have to be combined, and long-term risks have to be shared. The contract thus is often more than a simple construction order, but for example a design-and-build contract, which includes architectural work as well as the physical construction. Infrastructure projects are often designed as build-operate-transfer (BOT) agreements, which include the management of the facility after the construction has been completed. After completion of the project, the consortium would operate the facility and collect user fees over a specified period of time (for instance 20 years) before ownership is transferred to the local party, typically the host government. For example, *Safi Energy*, a consortium among *GDF Suez* (France), *Mitsui* (Japan) and *Nareva Holdings* (Morocco), has been awarded a BOT power generation project in Morocco.[24] Such complex contracts increasingly replace traditional 'build-transfer' type of turnkey projects. Often several firms get together to establish a consortium, which is a project-focused temporary business, owned and managed jointly. Consortia may then jointly bid for contracts and implement the work (In Focus 11.2). Some construction companies have moved into the operation of large infrastructure projects. For example, *Ferrovial* of Spain is operating London *Heathrow* and other British airports.

Fourth, subcontracting combines the export of raw materials with the import of finished goods. Firms use subcontracting to outsource an intermediate stage of their value chain to a location where this particular activity can be done more cheaply. The subcontractor would work to the exact specification of the main manufacturer.[25]

turnkey project
A project in which clients pay contractors to design and construct new facilities and train personnel.

design-and-build (DB) contract
A contract combining the architectural or design work with the actual construction.

build-operate-transfer (BOT)
A contract combining the construction and temporary operation of a project eventually to be transferred to a new owner.

consortium
A project-based temporary business owned and managed jointly by several firms.

subcontracting
A contract that involves outsourcing of an intermediate stage of a value chain.

IN FOCUS 11.2

Building bridges

Construction is big business – in more than one sense! One of the largest bridges the world has ever seen is currently being constructed between the countries of Qatar and Bahrain in the Arabian Gulf. The Qatar-Bahrain Causeway connecting the two countries will be 40 kilometres long coast-to-coast, with 18 kilometres of embankments where the sea is shallow, and 22 kilometres of viaducts and bridges over deep water, including two arch bridges over shipping channels. It is expected to cut the travel time by car from six hours to just 30 minutes. The construction is expected to take five years to build and cost in the range of €3 billion. No single company would be able to handle all the design, construction and commission of such a big project: a wide range of different capabilities needs to be brought together and integrated. Moreover, the construction of such a mega infrastructure project creates complex interfaces between the public sector and the private sector, as many governmental agencies become involved, and many businesses from around the world compete for a share of the work. Businesses thus use a complex net of contracts to codify their contributions, their obligations, and their share in the risk.

At an early stage of this project, Danish consultants *COWI* conducted preliminary engineering and environmental investigations in 2001/2. They carried out surveys and investigated on land and at sea, compared alternative alignments, conducted costs and environmental impact assessments, and presented a preliminary conceptual design of the bridge. Key issues in this work concerned the arrangements of the tolling and border crossing facilities, and the necessary navigational clearances to ensure that shipping lines were not disrupted.

In May 2008, following a worldwide **tender**, the Qatar-Bahrain Causeway Foundation representing the two governments of Qatar and Bahrain awarded a 'design and build' contract to a consortium led by *Vinci Construction* (of France) and involving *Hochtief* (of Germany, later acquired by *ACS* of Spain) and *CCC* (of Greece) and *Qatari Diar–Vinci Construction* (of Qatar), while dredging work and construction of embankments were awarded to *Middle East Dredging Company* (partially owned by *Dredging International* of Belgium).

A separate **project management contract** was awarded to *KBR* (USA) and *Halcrow* (UK), for design management, project management and construction management services. They will be overseeing the contracting consortium on behalf of the two governments. The construction was expected to start in 2009, but has been repeatedly delayed and, rather than 2015, the completion is now expected to be only shortly before the 2022 *FIFA World Cup* in Qatar. Once finished, it will truly be an international bridge!

Sources: (1) *New Civil Engineer* (www.nce.co.uk); (2) *Construction Week* (www.constructionweekonline.com); (3) *Arabian Business* (www.arabianbusiness.com), (4) COWI website (www.cowi.com); (5) Halcrow website (www.halcrow.co.uk, last accessed May 2009).

The advantage is that this allows saving costs on labour-intensive processes, such as sewing in garments manufacture. The disadvantage is the limited control over what is going on inside the subcontractors' plant. For instance, it has become a major concern to NGOs that subcontractors in developing countries are not maintaining international labour standards; companies thus have to create special training and monitoring procedures to ensure high standards (see Chapter 10).[26] Skilful use of subcontracting allows small firms, such as Danish publisher *Skandinavia A/S*, to leverage their resources (In Focus 11.3).

Some firms have taken the idea of subcontracting from labour intensive processes and applied it to outsourcing design and development work. Such R&D contracts allow firms to tap into the best locations for certain innovations at relatively low costs, such as IT work in India and aerospace research in Russia.[27] However, three drawbacks may emerge. First, given the uncertain and multidimensional nature of

tender
A competition for a major contract.

project management contract
A contract specifying what products and services a contractor is to deliver during a project.

R&D contract
A subcontracting of R&D between firms.

IN FOCUS 11.3

Scandinavia A/S: *a small publisher for small people worldwide*

You do not have to be big to run a global business. Copenhagen-based *Scandinavia A/S* publishes illustrated children's books (such as Hans Christian Andersen fairy tales), inspirational books, and gift books all over the world, which are translated in over 80 different languages. Yet it achieved this with a workforce of only eight people. How does it run the business?

Scandinavia focuses on its core competencies of product development, finance, production, quality control, marketing and sales in Copenhagen, while all other functions involving the printing, finding of authors, illustrators and shipping are outsourced to firms specializing in those activities. Essentially, *Scandinavia* is the centre of a global network of subcontractors. This gives the firm the opportunity to find artists appreciated beyond its native Denmark, access the latest printing technology (while keeping fixed costs low), and flexibly shift production from one country or printer to another depending on cost and quality considerations.

The Copenhagen hub serves as a knowledge base, everything else is outsourced. For example, product development is a combination of in-house ideas, ideas from illustrators with new concepts, printers introducing

new technologies, and other parties. *Scandinavia* works with illustrators from diverse countries such as Argentina, Denmark, France, Holland, Indonesia and Spain. The challenge is trying to find a style that will appeal to as many cultures and countries as possible. Meanwhile, production is sourced out to printers in China, Hong Kong, Singapore, Poland, Slovakia, Belarus, Japan and other countries.

This business model allows *Scandinavia* to focus on the high value-added part of the value chain, in particular to ensure that the final product is of a quality that *Scandinavia A/S* would be proud of. *Scandinavia* sells the concept with the design and the combination of the book. The publisher in the respective country does the translation into their language and sends their print files to *Scandinavia,* which then combines the printing of the same title to the various publishers in a combined print run. The publishers in the respective countries are free to change the text, but not the illustrations or the concept. This type of production, known as co-production in the industry, enables small firms to develop a global reach with limited resources and low fixed costs.

Source: Klaus Meyer's interview with Anthony Steen Hoglind, who spent ten years in managerial roles with *Scandinavia A/S*.

R&D, these contracts are often difficult to negotiate and enforce. Although delivery time and costs are relatively easy to negotiate, quality is often difficult to assess. Second, such contracts may nurture competitors. A number of Indian IT firms, nurtured by such work, are now on a global offensive to take on their Western rivals. Finally, firms that rely on outsiders to perform a lot of R&D may in the long run lose some of their core R&D capabilities.

Fifth, firms may know how to run a business, but they do not want to assume the financial risks of large real estate investments. A management contract would allow them to run the business, even though they don't own it. This is common, for example, in the hotel business or for infrastructure operators. Next time you stay at a *Sheraton* or *Hilton* hotel, remember that the bed you are sleeping in is unlikely to be owned by *Sheraton* or *Hilton*. More likely, it is owned by a local business and managed either by the international chain under a management contract, or by a local franchisee.[28] This business model has been pushed furthest by *Intercontinental*, a British hotel chain owning the *Holiday Inn* and *Crown Plaza* brands,[29] and French chain *Accor*, which owns *Ibis, Mercure, Novotel* and other budget hotel brands across Europe.[30]

management contract
A contract over the management of assets or a firm owned by someone else.

RESOURCES AND INTERNATIONALIZATION

Internationalization process models

How do companies move from their first steps abroad to becoming major players on the global stage? How do they build the resources required to succeed in unfamiliar foreign markets? A single export transaction may capitalize on a specific opportunity. Yet to succeed continuously in other countries requires considerable networks and knowledge on how to do business in each host country. For example, to succeed in Europe, Asian businesses need to learn not only all the rules and regulations, but how to engage with unfamiliar organizations, such as media, trade unions and NGOs.[31] Capabilities in managing in such foreign environments are to a large extent based on experiential knowledge, that is, they have to be learned by engaging in the particular activity and context. This focal role of experiential knowledge leads to a path-dependency in firms' growth: a firm may by chance start to export to Japan, then learn more about the country, and then set up a local sales subsidiary. This path-dependency is reflected in internationalization process models: (1) the Uppsala learning model of internationalization, (2) the network internationalization model and (3) stages models of internationalization.

First, the Uppsala model, by Jan Johanson and Jan-Erik Vahlne, was developed at the University of Uppsala in Sweden.[32] The essence of this model is that internationalization is a dynamic process of learning in which firms take decisions over their next step based on what they know at the time. Thus a firm may make an initial commitment of resources to a market, which provides a basis for learning about the particular environment, and thus allows building context specific experiential knowledge and reduces the liability of outsidership. This knowledge then shapes the firm's ability to recognize business opportunities,[33] its perception of risk, and the cost of deepening its involvement (Figure 11.2). Thus internationalization tends to be a process of incremental decisions that one-by-one reduce market uncertainty. For example, Sweden's *IKEA* took 20 years (1943–1963) before entering a neighbouring country, Norway. Then it focused on building Western European operations over the next decades. Only more recently has it accelerated its internationalization.[34]

LEARNING OBJECTIVE

2 Explain how firms develop resources for international business

experiential knowledge
Knowledge learned by engaging in the activity and context.

Uppsala model
A model of internationalization processes focusing on learning processes.

Figure 11.2 Internationalization processes

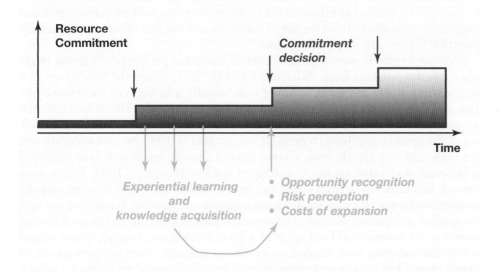

Second, the internationization of a firm is often interdependent with the internationalization of its network. Smaller firms and entrepreneurs especially draw on resources that they do not own, but which they can access through relationships with other businesses (and sometimes government agencies). In particular, networks provide access to assets, talent and technology, as well as knowledge of potential customers, suppliers and competitors. The Uppsala model thus has been extended to incorporate firms' networks.[35] Network relationships play an important role in facilitating access to information and organizational learning, and thus help reduce resource deficiencies. Over time, firms in a network reinforce each other's internationalization processes, thus the expertise in a firm's network grows both with new members joining, and with existing members gaining more experience. For small businesses, these networks often overlap with the personal networks of individual entrepreneurs. For example, a study of small Danish businesses in the Baltic Sea region found that the Estonian-born wife of a CEO was pivotal in building business activity in Estonia, while a Polish-born manager helped another firm to outsource production to Poland.[36]

stages models
Models depicting internationalization as a slow stage-by stage process an SME must go through.

Third, some scholars interpret the internationalization process model as prescribing that firms need to go through distinct stages before they can successfully operate an FDI. These stages models suggest that firms go through this process in a slow, stage-by-stage process.[37] Thus firms would go through a sequence of modes that reflect an increasing degree of commitment, for example, first licensing, then joint ventures, finally wholly-owned subsidiaries. The specific modes vary however across industries and business models.[38] Moreover, there is considerable evidence that distance raises costs of doing business, yet experienced firms are better able to manage the obstacles of distance, and thus face fewer such costs.[39] Hence firms would enter culturally and institutionally close markets first, spend enough time there to accumulate overseas experience, and then gradually move to distant markets, and from more simple modes, such as exports, to more sophisticated strategies, such as FDI.

Accelerating resource acquisition

The internationalization process model provides a good explanation of the patterns of internationalization in the 1950s to the 1980s.[40] However, the Uppsala model has arguably become less powerful in explaining recent expansion paths, as many firms are internationalizing early in their life, and appear to jump over stages of the traditional model. These firms are known as born globals or international new ventures (INV), defined as businesses that, 'from inception, seek to derive significant competitive advantages from the use of resources and the sale of outputs in multiple countries'.[41] How can they achieve that?

born global (international new venture)
Start-up company that from inception, seeks to derive significant competitive advantages from the use of resources and the sale of outputs in multiple countries.

Consider *Logitech*, now a global leader in computer peripherals.[42] It was established by entrepreneurs from Switzerland and the USA, where the firm set up dual headquarters. R&D and manufacturing were initially split between these two countries, and then quickly spread to Ireland and Taiwan through FDI. Its first commercial contract was with a Japanese company. As another example, consider *Genmab*, one of Europe's largest biotech firms. It was created in 1993 by two scientists, one American and one Dutch, with finance from a Danish investor. It was registered in Denmark and listed on the Copenhagen stock exchange in 2000. Yet its main research laboratory was from the outset in the Netherlands, and its main customers are globally operating pharmaceutical companies.[43] Another interesting example is a medical equipment venture, *Technomed*, which was set up in France. From its inception, the founders did not see it as a French company; instead, it was viewed as a global company with English as its official language, very uncharacteristic of French firms. Only nine months after its founding, *Technomed* established a subsidiary through FDI in a key market, the USA.

Table 11.3 Building resources for international business

Traditional processes	Accelerated processes
• Experiential learning and knowledge acquisition • Network building and exploitation	• Recruiting an entrepreneurial team with international experience • Learning by importing and partnering with inward foreign investors • Learning from others operating in the same foreign country • Acquiring resources in the foreign country, possibly entire firms

There is little doubt that international business requires certain resources and capabilities that aspiring entrepreneurs need to build. INVs thus must have found other ways to build their resources and capabilities.[44] Their strategies include (1) building an entrepreneurial team with international competences, (2) cooperating with internationally active firms, (3) learning from others and (4) acquiring resources abroad (Table 11.3).

First, a key differentiator between rapidly and slowly (or not) internationalizing firms is the international experience of the entrepreneurial team, a fact well documented in management research.[45] Personal experience is an important resource, which is particularly important in young firms where the firm itself has not yet built embedded knowledge. Thus entrepreneurs who have previously worked in an international role for a major company are better positioned to engage in international business: they know their industry and potential customers worldwide. Likewise, people who have lived abroad often have networks and local knowledge that help building export relationships.[46] Even studying abroad provides experiences, tacit knowledge and networks that help budding entrepreneurs to go international early. With solid previous experience abroad, doing business internationally is not so intimidating. For example, *Logitech* was established by a team of a Swiss and an Italian, who met when studying at Stanford University in California, and a former manager of *Olivetti* and *IBM*.[47] For them, bridging between Europe and America came naturally.

Second, firms may build competences for international business by working with foreign investors coming into their country. Foreign investors and importers usually work with local suppliers and distributors, and they may help them to upgrade their product quality and supply chain management practices. Such interaction with inward investors provides opportunities for learning, building international networks, and establishing a reputation beyond the home ground. Firms may thus gather their first experience in international business as importers, and then use that experience to develop their own export business.[48] Others find opportunities to develop a domestic supplier relationship with a foreign investor into an international supply contract. For example, one Northern Irish bakery for chilled part-bake bread secured supply contracts with a US firm, *Subway*, in the mid-1990s. So successful was this relationship that the firm became a suppliers to *Subway* franchisees throughout Europe.[49] Similarly, several IT companies in Bangalore, India and car component manufacturers in China have joined the international supply chain of a major multinational, who then helped them to establish operations in third countries.[50] Thus experience in one sort of international activity facilitates acceleration of another international activity.

Third, firms may learn not only from their own experiences but from observing others. Notably, late entrants can learn by observing earlier entrants' successes and failures, and incorporate such knowledge into the design of their operations.[51] More-over, they may imitate the behaviour of others as a means to reduce uncertainty:[52] if others (who presumably did their homework before entering) find it appropriate to use sales agents, then this appears to be an appropriate strategy. Such mimetic behav-iour is a common way for firms to reduce the uncertainty associated with entering unfamiliar countries, and to speed up international growth.[53] However, it can also lead to everyone following the same fad until it eventually collapses: the fact that your rivals are rushing into China does not necessarily mean that now is the time for you to invest in China.

Fourth, ambitious firms may speed up their international growth by acquiring specific resources locally. At a basic level, they may rent offices, buy real estate, source local raw materials, and hire people with specialist technical expertise or local knowledge. More challenging is the acquisition of brand names, distribution networks and legitimacy in the local context. These sorts of resources are rarely available to buy other than by taking over an entire firm. Foreign entrants thus may build relationships with local firms or take over local firms to access to the know-ledge embedded in teams, organizational structures and routines.[54] The acquisition of local firms with sought-after capabilities thus helps overcoming the uncertainty that slows internationalization of firms following the traditional Uppsala model.[55]

INSTITUTIONS AND INTERNATIONALIZATION

The ability of internationally inexperienced firms to engage in international business is to a large extent shaped by (1) the institutional environment of the home country, and (2) the institutional distance between the home country and the host countries.

First, the general institutional environment of the home country shapes firms' incentives, and thus the relative merits of pursuing international growth or domestic business opportunities. For instance, open economies with low trade barriers allow foreign entrants to challenge local firms, and thus indirectly encourage firms to pur-sue their opportunities abroad.[56] On the other hand, high tariffs encourage growth behind these protective barriers, for instance by expanding in related industries or by integrating suppliers. Thus institutional environments have been shown empirically to have a major impact on firms' exports, and the profitability of such exports.[57]

In addition, some countries have designed specific institutions to help SME export-ers to overcome the uncertainty associated with international business. For example, export credit insurances, such as *Euler Hermes*, indemnify exporters against default of trade credits provided to customers abroad, thus reducing the risk of exporting. In the case of certain high-risk countries, governments like Germany assume some of the risk, thus effectively reducing the costs of the insurance.[58] A different type of scheme is operated by the Danish Foreign Ministry: its 'go global' initiative collects information on specific target markets to help smaller businesses in identifying suit-able business partners.[59]

Second, smaller firms will be more sensitive to differences in institutions across countries. Thus they are deterred by institutional distance which is 'the extent of sim-ilarity or dissimilarity between the regulatory, normative and cognitive institutions of two countries'.[60] This includes cultural distance, which is the difference between two cultures in terms of values[61] or subjective affinity. The costs of doing business increase with such distance – both the costs of market transactions and the costs of coordinating with people in the same organization.[62] For example, a recent study has

mimetic behaviour
Imitating the behaviour of others as a means to reduce uncertainty.

3   Explain how institutions influence exporting behaviour

institutional distance
The extent of similarity or dissimilarity between the regulatory, normative and cognitive institutions of two countries.

cultural distance
The difference between two cultures along some dimensions of value or subjective affinity.

shown that trade flows are associated with voting patterns in the Eurovision Song Contest, a proxy for cultural affinity![63]

Internationalization process models suggest that firms normally enter first where the cost of entry and the perceived risks are lowest, which is in culturally similar countries. Based on learning experiences in these countries, they may then venture further afield and enter culturally distant countries in later stages. For example, *Agrana* from Austria first expanded to neighbouring countries in Central and Eastern Europe before making acquisitions further afield (see Integrative Case *Agrana*). *Fan Milk* first developed its business model in Ghana and soon expanded to Nigeria (also an English-speaking country) before entering French-speaking countries in West Africa (see Integrative Case *Fan Milk*). Business between countries that share a language on average is three times greater than between countries without a common language. Similarly, MNEs from emerging economies perform better in other developing countries, presumably because of their closer institutional distance and similar stages of economic development.[64]

However, keep in mind that these distance effects only moderate the basic rationale for doing business.[65] For instance, natural resource-seeking firms have some compelling reasons to enter culturally and institutionally distant countries (such as Papua New Guinea for bauxite, Zambia for copper and Nigeria for oil). For example, a company developing specialized equipment for the oil exploration industry may already in the early stages develop export operations in distant and 'difficult' locations such as Nigeria, Iraq or the Far Eastern parts of Russia.

DEBATES AND EXTENSIONS

Designing and combining entry modes

Foreign entry is often presented first and foremost as a choice between a given set of entry modes. This may be true for firms establishing simple transactions across borders. Yet as businesses mature, they usually develop more complex nets of relationships and contracts.[66] First, they may combine different types of transaction in one business relationship, for instance licensing technologies and exporting components to the same customer. Second, they may serve different segments of a market with different operation modes, for example exporting to a small market while licensing to a mature market where a strong local partner has emerged. Thus the alternative modes introduced in this section are like the building blocks for international business. New forms of contracts are designed to share resources, responsibilities, risk and returns in ways that best suit the partners in the deal.

Moreover, the decision on how to enter a foreign country is interdependent with other activities that a company may already have in the country, and with operations in other locations. An existing distributor may thus become sales agent for a new product line, or an intermediary to negotiate with local suppliers. Therefore, foreign entry decisions are highly interdependent, such that it may be more appropriate to talk about foreign operation modes configuration.[67]

Cyberspace versus conventional entry

The internet provides many avenues to support international business activity, or to create entirely new business models that by their nature transcend national boundaries. Two types of strategy emerge. First, in online-to-offline businesses, the internet can serve to facilitate an offline delivery of a product or service. For example, exporters may increase their sales by using the internet as an advertising board and catalogue, to facilitate communication with suppliers, and to process and track orders.[68] Second, the entire value chain of the business may be created and coordinated online, based on digital products such as data, analytics, software or online games. In particular, the increased connectedness of what is known as the 'internet of things' creates new opportunities to develop new services that help others to optimize their operations, to interpret the mass of data available, or deliver vital information, such as health diagnostics.[69]

From a resource-based perspective, the internet lowers the resource needs of entering international markets because it offers new opportunities for cost-effective cross-national advertising, communication, and coordination. However, firms need to develop new capabilities to utilize these new technologies effectively, and to integrate them with their business models.[70] This includes delivery of goods and services in locations where they do not have a physical presence. For example, *Xiaomi* used the internet as their primary channel to reach customers in China, yet it needed to partner with traditional retailers in India because the distribution infrastructure did not allow efficient delivery of online purchases (see Integrative Case *Xiaomi*).

From an institution-based view, the key question is, whose rules of the game should e-commerce follow? Although pundits argue that the internet is undermining the power of national governments, there is little evidence that the modern nation-state system is retreating. At early stages of new technologies, investors and early commercial users push the boundaries of technology to build their markets – informality rules. As a technology matures, businesses become more concerned about protecting their property rights, while governments feel compelled to intervene to constrain businesses from growing too powerful. Thus, like for earlier waves of technology, we can expect regulation to eventually catch up.[71] National governments, so far, often find it difficult to enforce such rules, as evidenced by the battle of the US authorities with gambling websites based in countries in the Caribbean. However, governments find ways to enforce rules even beyond their territories using inter-governmental negotiations, focusing on the firms operations that are within their territory, and even by implementing screening software that blocs access to unwelcome websites. For example, British online gambling providers face legal obstacles to transactions with US banks (and thus US-based clients).[72] An issue that is particularly contentious between online service providers and national governments is the handling of personal data collected from users. Who has access to what, and what data may be transferred between companies and across national borders under what conditions? For example, *Facebook* negotiated with the EU and the Canadian government about its protection of the privacy of its individual members.[73]

IMPLICATIONS FOR PRACTICE

LEARNING OBJECTIVE

5   Draw implications
      for practice

As an entrepreneur or a small business who finds the home market 'too small for your shoes', how should you go about growing your business on an international stage? This chapter suggests several lessons (Table 11.4). First, a wide range of operation modes is available, even for a small firm (see Table 11.1). The strategic challenge is to analyze both your own resources and capabilities (Chapter 4), and the host context you are targeting (Chapters 2 and 3). On that basis, you can to design an appropriate mode or combination of modes that link capabilities and contexts. Competitive advantage is often gained by finding innovative ways to combine resources to compete in a foreign market.

Second, continuous learning is essential in international business. A lot of this learning has to take place 'in action' rather than in a classroom. Therefore, plan ahead how you will be building your experiences when you design your firm's

Table 11.4 Implications for action

- Design operations to link your capabilities with the local contexts you are targeting.

- Design operations to facilitate learning about IB in general, and the host country in particular.

- Design operations for flexibility to enable later adjustment to changes in both your own capabilities and in the external environment.

- If your medium-term target markets are international, design your business models accordingly from the outset.

international operation. In particular, create interfaces with the local environment, and with customers in particular. A website or a licensing deal may give you quick market access. Yet they provide you with limited customer feedback, and competitors may overtake you by adapting better to the needs of consumers in that country. For example, *Benetton* grew its fashion chain fast by using a franchising model; yet its recent decline is attributed by some to the lack of control over the critical interface with their consumers around the world.

Third, the dynamic view of internationalization implies that initial arrangements need to be built for flexibility. An initial entry mode may not last forever, thus contracts need to be designed to allow for change: switching from one agent to another, taking an equity stake in the agent, or replacing an agent by a sales subsidiary.[74] For example, Danish packing materials manufacturer *Scanbech* appointed sales agents in Germany with explicit buyout options and dual distribution agreements for the time when *Scanbech* would increase its commitment and establish its own sales subsidiary.[75]

Fourth, entrepreneurial teams that think global *from the outset* can design their operations for global markets and supply chains, and avoid creating a domestic organization that later needs to be reorganized.[76] Reorganization is usually a very costly process that may be resisted by some people in the organization. Therefore, entrepreneurial firms without an established domestic orientation (such as *Logitech*, *Genmab* and *Technomed*) may outperform their rivals that wait longer to internationalize. In other words, there may be inherent advantages of being young when venturing abroad, provided the entrepreneurial team can assemble the relevant competences.

CHAPTER SUMMARY

1 Explain the different options for firms to start engaging in international business

- Goods can be exported and imported with and without intermediaries such as agents and distributors.

- Services can be exported by attracting customers to your site, or by sending the outcome of the services across borders.

- A wide variety of contracts is available to combine different transfers of goods, services and rights,

including (1) licensing, (2) franchising, (3) turnkey projects, (4) subcontracting and (5) management contracts.

2 Explain how firms develop resources for international business

- Traditional models of internationalization emphasize the gradual nature of knowledge accumulation and network building processes, which are reflected in stages models.

- Internationalization processes have accelerated as firms find new ways to build the capabilities needed in international business, including (1) building an experienced managerial team, (2) cooperating with experienced firms, (3) mimicking others and (4) acquiring local resources.

3 Explain how institutions influence exporting behaviour

- Institutions of the home environment shape the relative costs and risks associated with international versus domestic growth.

- Cultural and institutional distance increase the costs of doing business, and thus lead many firms to start international business in locations in close proximity of their origins.

4 Participate in two leading debates on early stage internationalization

- A new line of research suggests focusing on the combination of different entry modes.

- The internet creates new challenges for resource exploitation and for interacting with institutions in many countries simultaneously.

5 Draw implications for practice

- Operations abroad should be designed to (1) link with local contexts, (2) facilitate learning, and (3) allow for flexibility.

- Start-up businesses aiming for global markets may benefit from creating global structures from the outset.

KEY TERMS

Born global (international new venture)
Bill of lading (B/L)
Build-operate-transfer (BOT)
CIF (costs, insurance, freight)
Consortium
Cross-border services
Cultural distance
Design-and-build contract
Direct exports
Distributor
Entrepreneurial team
Entrepreneur

Experiential knowledge
Exporting
Export intermediary
FOB (free on board)
Franchisee
Franchising
Franchisor
Importer
Importing
Indirect exports
Institutional distance
Letter of credit (L/C)
Licensee
Licensing

Licensor
Management contract
Mimetic behaviour
R&D contract
Sales agent
Servicing foreign residents
Small and medium-sized enterprises (SMEs)
Stages models
Subcontracting
Tender
Turnkey project
Uppsala model (of internationalization)

CRITICAL DISCUSSION QUESTIONS

1 Some suggest that foreign markets are graveyards for entrepreneurial firms to overextend themselves. Others argue that foreign markets represent the future for SMEs. If you were the owner of a small, reasonably profitable domestic firm, would you consider expanding overseas? Why?

2 Your Kazakh classmate offers you 15% commission if you sell hand-made, fashionable clothing from Kazakhstan to local distributors in your home town. Would you consider this offer?

3 Your company receives an enquiry by email from an unknown customer in Australia. The customer asks for detailed information about your latest high tech products, and envisages a very large order. How do you react?

4 Your former high school buddy invites you to join an entrepreneurial start-up that specializes in cracking the codes of protection software, which protect CDs and DVDs from being copied. He has developed the pioneering technology and lined up financing. The worldwide demand for this technology appears enormous. He offers you the job of CEO and 10% of the equity of the firm. How would you respond to his proposition?

RECOMMENDED READINGS

O. Andersen, 1993, **On the internationalization process of the firm,** *JIBS,* **24: 209–231** – a critical review paper of the internationalization process literature.

M. Forsgren, 2002, **The concept of learning in the Uppsala internationalization model: a critical review,** *IBR,* **11: 257–277** – a review of alternative ways of learning how to do international business.

J. Johanson & J.E. Vahlne, 2009, **The Uppsala internationalization process model revisited: From liability of foreignness to liability of outsidership,** *JIBS,* **40, 1411–1431** – the fathers of the Uppsala model review and extend the literature that builds on their original work published in 1977.

L. Welch, G. Benito & B. Petersen, 2007, *Foreign Operation Methods,* **Cheltenham: Elgar** – a specialized textbook covering a wide range of modes with focus on non-equity modes.

S. Young, J. Hamill, C. Wheeler & J.R. Davies, 1989, *International Market Entry and Development: Strategies and Management,* **Englewood Cliffs, NJ: Prentice Hall** – an older book providing a very concise treatment of alternative modes of foreign entry.

CLOSING CASE

Better generation: the global generation of business

by Amber Guan and Klaus Meyer

Energy efficiency became a hot topic worldwide as governments committed to limit greenhouse gas emissions. One stream of innovations focused on distributed power generation, that is, small-scale generation of electricity with capacities from 1–100 kilowatts, close to the energy user. Individual owners of land or buildings (factories, farmyards, private homes) could install small windmills or solar panels to serve their own needs. However, these new technologies still faced substantial obstacles: high costs of installation, lack of knowledge what technology works where, and inconsistent (or absence) of governmental regulation.

To overcome the technological barriers, Toby Hammond developed a tool called 'Power Predictor', a combined wind and solar power measuring device that collects local data from the site where it is mounted. These data enable an assessment of the specific site's wind and solar generation potential, and thereby allow for forecasting the payback time for renewable energy investments, and to offer recommendations for the most cost-effective form of renewable energy equipment.

With degrees in Environmental Biology and in Sustainable Development, Hammond worked as environmental consultant to private and public sector clients before

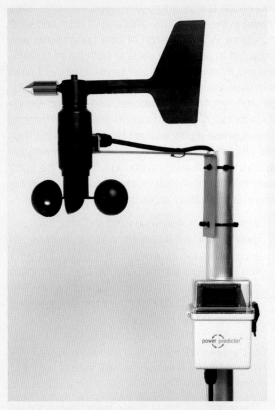

The device is called a 'Power Predictor', it is a combined wind and solar power measuring device that collects local data from the site where it is mounted.

founding *Better Generation* (*BG*) to manufacture and distribute his device. In 2008 he teamed up with Graham Brant, a venture capitalist with 28 years experience in global business, including positions with *Microsoft*, such as CEO of *Microsoft* Hong Kong. After leaving *Microsoft*, he set up a small investment fund, *Beyond Asia Capital*, that invested in hybrid Chinese/Western start-up companies, before focusing full-time on his role as CEO of *BG*. Together, Brant and Hammond could pursue the Power Predictor idea on a global scale.

The essence of *BG*'s business model was to focus on a key bottleneck for micro-generation industry: the difficulties of obtaining detailed data about the viability of individual sites for micro-generation, and of obtaining supplier-neutral advice about the most appropriate solution for the site. Their Power Predictor came in two parts: a measuring device and web-based software. The device collected the data, which are uploaded and analyzed using web-based software and *BG*'s own databases to create reports for individual customers. The most strategic element of this business model was BG's ownership of the data uploaded by the Power Predictor's users. *BG* thus built a global database of renewable energy micro-generation resource data stored in the cloud. This database of solar and wind conditions in a wide range of local geographies was expected to be of great value to both future customers and to developers of new technologies. *BG* used this database to connect turbine manufacturers, distributors, retailers, and installers and thus to reduce the adaptation barriers to micro-generation systems. This business model enabled *BG* to explore distribution channels and to lock-in potential micro-generation system buyers. It also provided a platform for the company to enter the market for micro wind turbines in the future. Graham Brant explains:

'Establishing a worldwide wind and solar resource database is an ambitious plan. It involves an enormous effort to research the worldwide wind and solar micro-generation technologies, complete the list of approved micro-generation system installers and distributors in each country, and distribute Power Predictor worldwide. The way of doing it is to internationalize the business as early as possible. We are learning as we are doing, once the right model is established, we will just copy it to other countries.'

The success of this business model depended on the scale and scope of the operation. The value of the database depends on its volume and reach. Therefore,

international growth and building market share were essential goals for BG. In the words of Graham Brant,

'with our unique product concepts and the value proposition in the market place, we could sell our product at a much higher price than we do now. However, by charging a relatively low price, we are aiming to drive sales volume and grab market share. Therefore, the success of our business is based on building volume. This is the case not just in the UK market, but also for the international market. What we really want to be is the Google of the micro-energy generation industry.'

Better Generation was organized as a group of three companies. *BG Group* based in Hong Kong was the parent company and the operational hub, while *BG UK* was responsible for European marketing and product design. *BG China* was a joint venture with a young technology firm in Chengdu manufacturing wind sensor products and large wind turbine control systems. This structure was designed to support a tax-efficient trading strategy, to operationally integrate the China-based manufacturing unit and to support a cost efficient global sales platform.

The micro-generation industry was boosted by government initiatives around the world in the wake of the Kyoto protocol. However, many incentive schemes and subsidies focused on large-scale energy generation. Micro-generation still faced high initial set-up costs and uncertainty regarding the efficacy of available technologies. Therefore, the perceived market potential was strongly associated with government incentives to help consumers with the high up-front cost. Moreover, local planning permissions for wind turbines created obstacles that varied not only between countries, but also across provinces and towns.

The institutional environment for the renewable energy industry was therefore crucial for prioritizing which potential markets to enter. The market size and the generally supportive policies for micro-generation led *BG* to focus on the USA. For example, the federal government offered tax credits for energy generation from wind turbines, including a special scheme for small wind turbines for home, farm and business use. However, responsibility for the specific regulation of the energy sector and of building policies was mainly up to individual states in the US, which created a very fragmented market. Other countries, such as continental Europe, focused their energy policies on larger scale power generation, and thus offered less immediate market potential for BG. In its initial entry, *BG* used local distributors to reach markets fast, yet carefully designed distributor agreements to be sure to retain the rights to its database.

Other early business opportunities came from unexpected sources. In Haiti, a mobile telecom company was looking for the most efficient way to provide power for each of its mobile phone connection masts across the country. In South Africa, the government offered financial incentives for villages to invest in micro-energy, but wanted a financial feasibility study before disbursing any funds: the Power Predictor report became part of these feasibility studies. In Chile, *BG* also linked up with the government to map the potential for wind energy along the Chilean Pacific coastline.

CASE DISCUSSION QUESTIONS

1 What motivates *Better Generation* to become international very fast?

2 What are the risks of a fast internationalization strategy for *Better Generation*?

3 How can *Better Generation* build the resources required for a fast internationalization strategy?

4 How should *Better Generation* develop its international strategy in terms of countries chosen and entry modes?

Sources: This case was prepared by Amber Guan (MBA Graduate, University of Bath) and Klaus Meyer based on archival data and personal interviews.

NOTES

'For journal abbreviation, please see page xx-xxi.'

1 I. Kirzner, 1973, *Competition and Entrepreneurship*, Chicago: University of Chicago Press; M. Casson, 2010, *Enterpreneurship: Theory, Networks, History*, Cheltenham: Elgar.

2 F. Seringhaus & P. Rossen, 2001, Firm experience and international trade fairs, *JMM*, 17: 877–901; K.E. Meyer & A. Skak, 2002, Networks, serendipity and SME entry into Eastern Europe, *EMJ*, 20: 179–188.

3 L. Leonidou & C. Katsikeas, 1996, The export development process, *JIBS*, 27: 517–551; R. Salomon & J.M. Shaver, 2005, Export and domestic sales, *SMJ*, 26: 855–871; M. Matanda & S. Freeman, 2009, Effects of perceived environmental uncertainty on exporter-importer inter-organizational relationships and export performance improvement, *IBR*, 18: 89–107.

4 G. Balabanis, 2000, Factors affecting export intermediaries' service offerings, *JIBS*, 31: 83–99.

5 M.W. Peng & A.Y. Ilinitch, 1998, Export intermediary firms, *JIBS*, 29: 609–620; H. van Driel, 2003, The role of middlemen in the international coffee trade since 1870, *BH* 45(2): 77–101.

6 M.W. Peng & A. York, 2001, Behind intermediary performance in export trade, *JIBS*, 32: 327–346; P.D. Ellis, 2010, Trade intermediaries and the transfer of marketing knowledge in transition economies, *IBR*, 19, 16–33.

7 M.W. Peng, Y. Zhou & A. York, 2006, Behind make or buy decisions in export strategy, *JWB*, 41: 289–300.

8 D. Skarmeas, C. Katsikeas & B. Schlegelmilch, 2002, Drivers of commitment and its impact on performance in cross-cultural buyer-seller relationships, *JIBS*, 33: 757–783; C. Zhang, S.T. Cavusgil & A. Roath,

2003, Manufacturer governance of foreign distributor relationships, *JIBS*, 34: 550–566; H. Lau, 2008, Export channel structure in a newly industrialized economy, *APJM*, 25: 317–333.

9 C. Solberg & E. Nes, 2002, Exporter trust, commitment and marketing control in integrated and independent export channels, *IBR*, 11: 385–405; F. Wu, R. Sinkovics, S. Cavusgil & A. Roath, 2007, Overcoming export manufacturers' dilemma in international expansion, *JIBS*, 38: 283–302.

10 B. Petersen, D. Welch & L. Welch, 2000, Creating meaningful switching options in international operations, *LRP*, 33: 688–705.

11 J. Margretta, 1998, An interview with Victor Fung, *HBR*, September-October 102–118; V.K. Fung, W.K. Fung & Y. Wind, 2007, *Competing in a Flat World*, Upper Saddle River: Wharton School Publishing.

12 Office for National Statistics (UK), 2009, *Balance of Payment: The Pink Book*, Cardiff: ONS.

13 T. Lituchy & A. Rail, 2000, Bed and breakfast, small inns, and the Internet, *JIMktg*, 8: 86–97.

14 K. Larsen, J. Martin & R. Morris, 2002; Trade in educational services, *WE*, 25, 849–868; OECD, 2004, *Internationalization and Trade in Higher Education; Opportunities and Challenges*, Paris: OECD; M. Czinkota, 2006, Academic freedom for all in higher education, *JWB*, 41, 149–160.

15 P. Ghemawat, 2007, *Redefining Global Strategy*, Cambridge, MA: Harvard Business School Press (Chapter 6).

16 G. Anand, 2009, The Henry Ford of heart surgery, *Wall Street Journal*, November 26.

17 Klaus Meyer's interviews with a hospital director and a B&B host in Johannesburg, South Africa.

18 B. Petersen & L.S. Welch, 2000, International retailing operations: downstream entry and expansion via franchising, *IBR* 9: 479–496; L.S. Welch, G.R.G. Benito & B. Petersen, 2007, *Foreign Operation Methods*, Cheltenham: Elgar (Chapters 3 & 4); J. Barthélemy, 2009, Le choix de la franchise ou de l'intégration verticale, *MI/IM/GI*, 13(4): 65–72.

19 J. Combs & D. Ketchen, 1999, Can capital scarcity help agency theory explain franchising? *AMJ*, 42: 196–207; A. Fosfuri, 2006, The licensing dilemma, *SMJ*, 27: 1141–1158.

20 Klaus Meyer's personal communication with the managing director of Bang & Olufsen UK.

21 A. Arora & A. Fosfuri, 2000, Wholly owned subsidiary versus technology licensing in the worldwide chemical industry, *JIBS*, 31: 555–572; P. Aulakh, S.T. Cavusgil & M. Sarkar, 1998, Compensation in international licensing agreements, *JIBS*, 29: 409–420; P. Aulakh, M. Jiang & S. Li, 2013, Licensee technological potential and exclusive rights in international licensing, *JIBS*, 44: 699–718.

22 W. Streitz, 2004, Karstadt und Starbucks: Das Ende der Frapuccino-Escapaden, *Der Spiegel*, September 29; *Managermagazin*, 2014, Verschlafen in Seattle, March.

23 R. Tesker, 2002, Pepperoni power, *Far Eastern Economic Review*, November 14.

24 United Nations (UN), 2014, *World Investment Report 2014*, Geneva: UN (p. 81).

25 R. Aron & J.V. Singh, 2005, Getting offshoring Right, *HBR*, 83 (December): 135–143; R. Metters & R. Verma, 2007, History of offshoring knowledge services, *JOM*, 26: 141–147.

26 L. Hartman, D. Arnold & R.E. Wokutch, eds, 2003, *Beyond Sweatshops*, New York: Praeger.

27 B. Ambos, 2005, Foreign direct investment in industrial research and development, *RP*, 34: 395–410; A. Lewin, S. Massini & C. Peeters, 2009, Why are companies offshoring innovation? The emerging global race for talent, *JIBS*, 40: 901–925.

28 F. Contractor & S. Kundu, 2003, Modal choice in a world of alliances: analyzing organizational forms in the international hotel sector, *JIBS*, 29, 325–357.

29 *The Economist*, 2009, Hotels: Outsourcing as you sleep, February 21.

30 *The Economist*, 2010, Hotels: Asset-light or asset-right, November 13.

31 K.E. Meyer, 2014, Process perspectives on the growth of emerging economy multinationals, in: A. Cuervo-Cazurra & R. Ramamurti, eds, *Understanding Multinationals from Emerging Markets*, Cambridge: Cambridge University Press.

32 J. Johanson & J. Vahlne, 1977, The internationalization process of the firm, *JIBS*, 4: 20–29; G.R.G. Benito &

L.S. Welch, 1994, Foreign market servicing, *JIMktg* 2: 7–27; J. Johanson & J.E. Vahlne, 2009, The Uppsala internationalization process model revisited, *JIBS*, 40, 1411–1431; Meyer, K.E. (2014): Process perspectives on the growth of emerging economy multinationals, in: A. Cuervo-Cazurra & R. Ramamurti, eds, *Understanding Multinationals from Emerging Markets*, Cambridge: Cambridge University Press, p. 169–194.

33 J. Johanson & J. Vahlne, 2006, Commitment and opportunity development in the internationalization process, *MIR*, 46: 165–178; K.E. Meyer & O. Thaijongrak, 2013, The dynamics of emerging economy MNEs: how the internationalization process model can guide future research, *APJM*, 30: 1125–1153.

34 K. Kling & I. Goteman, 2003, IKEA CEO Anders Dahlvig on international growth, *AME*, 17: 31–45.

35 J. Johanson & L. Mattson, 1988, Internationalization in industrial systems, in. N. Hood & J. Vahlne, eds, *Strategies in Global Competition,* New York: Croom Helm; S. Chetty & D. Blankenburg Holm, 2000, Internationalization of small to medium-sized firms: A network approach, *IBR*, 9: 77–93; N. Coviello, 2006, The network dynamics of international new ventures, *JIBS*, 37: 713–731; K.E. Meyer & M. Gelbuda, 2006, Process perspectives in international business, *MIR*, 46: 143–164; S. Prashantham, 2009, *The Internationalization of Small Firms*, London, Rutledge.

36 K.E. Meyer & A. Skak, 2002, *as above*.

37 A. Hadjikani, 1997, A note on the criticisms against the internationalization process model, *MIR* 37: 1–23; L. Li, D. Li & T. Dalgic, 2004, Internationalization process of small and medium-sized enterprises, *MIR*, 44: 93–116.

38 N. Malhotra & C. Hinings, 2010, An organizational model of understanding internationalization processes, *JIBS*, 41: 330–349.

39 G. Gao, Y. Pan, J. Lu & Z. Tao, 2008, Performance of multinational firms' subsidiaries, *MIR*, 6: 749–768; P.Y. Li & K.E. Meyer, 2009, Contextualizing experience effects in international business, *JWB*, 44: 370–382.

40 Johanson & Vahlne, 2009, *as above*; R. Amdam, 2009, The internationalization process theory and the internationalization of Norwegian firms 1945–1980, *BH* 445–461.

41 B. Oviatt & P. McDougall, 1994, Toward a theory of international new ventures, *JIBS*, 25: 45–64.

42 P. McDougall, S. Shane & B. Oviatt, 1994, Explaining the formation of international new ventures, *JBV*, 9: 469–487.

43 *The Economist*, 2008, Face value: From across the divide, June 14.

44 T. Madsen & P. Servais, 1997, The internationalization of born globals, *IBR* 6: 561–583; G. Knight & S. Cavusgil, 2004, Innovation, organizational capabilities, and the born-global firm, *JIBS*, 35: 124–141; M. Jones &

N. Coviello, 2005, Internationalization: conceptualizing an entrepreneurial process of behaviour in time, *JIBS*, 36: 284–303; S. Sui & M. Baum, 2014, Internationalization strategy, firm resources and the survival of SMEs in the export market, *JIBS*, 45: 821–841.

45 A.B. Reuber & E. Fischer, 1997, The influence of the management team's international experience on the internationalization behaviors of SMEs, *JIBS*, 28: 807–825; S. Chetty, K. Eriksson & J. Lindbergh, 2006, The effect of specificity of experience on a firm's perceived importance of institutional knowledge in an ongoing business, *JIBS*, 37: 699–712; H. Sapienza, E. Autio, G. George & S. Zahra, 2006, A capabilities perspective on the effects of early internationalization on firm survival and growth, *AMR*, 31: 914–933.

46 K. Gillespie, L. Riddle, E. Sayre & D. Sturges, 1999, Diaspora interest in homeland investment, *JIBS*, 30: 623–634; I. Filatotchev, X. Liu, T. Buck & M. Wright, 2009, The export orientation and export performance of high technology SMEs in emerging markets: The effects of knowledge transfers by returnee entrepreneurs, *JIBS*, 40: 1005–1021.

47 V. Jolly, M. Alahuhta & J. Jeannet, 1992, Challenging incumbents, *SC*, 1: 71–82.

48 H. Korhonen, R. Luostarinen & L. Welch, 1996, Internationalization of SMEs: inward-outward patterns and government policy, *MIR*, 36–315–329.

49 J. Bell, R. McNaughton & S. Young, 2001, Born-again global firms (p. 184), *JIM*, 7: 173–189.

50 S. Prashantham, 2015, *Born Globals, Networks, and the Large Multinational Enterprise:Insights from Bangalore and Beyond*, Elsevier; P. Hertenstein et al., 2015, Foreign multinationals, business networks and home country effects, *APJM*, advance online.

51 M. Lieberman & D. Montgomerry, 1998, First mover (dis-)avantages, *SMJ*, 19: 1111–1125.

52 P. Di Maggio & W. Powell, 1983, The iron cage revisited: Institutional isomorphism and collective rationality in organizational fields, *ASQ*, 48: 147–160; J. Lu, 2002, Intra- and inter-organizational imitative behavior, *JIBS*, 33: 19–37.

53 M. Forsgren, 2002, The concept of learning in the Uppsala internationalization process model. *IBR*, 11: 257–277; C. Schwens & R. Kabst, 2009, How early opposed to late internationalizers learn, *IBR*, 18: 509–522.

54 J. Anand & A. Delios, 2002, Absolute and relative resources as determinants of international acquisitions, *SMJ*, 23: 119–134. K.E. Meyer, M. Wright, S. Pruthi, 2009, Managing knowledge in foreign entry strategies: A resource-based analysis, *SMJ*, 31: 557–574; S. Freeman, K. Hutchings, M. Lazaris & S. Zynier, 2010, A model of rapid knowledge development, *IBR*, 19, 70–84.

55 Forsgren, 2002, *as above*.

56 T. Hutzschenreuther & F. Gröne, 2009, Product and geographic scope of multinational enterprises in response to international competition, *JIBS*, 40: 1149–1170.

57 G. Shinkle & A. Kriauciunas, 2010, Institutions, size and age in transition economies: Implications for export growth, *JIBS*, 41: 267–286; G. Gao, J. Murray, M. Kotabe & J. Lu, 2010, A 'strategy tripod' perspective on export behaviors, *JIBS*; 41: 377–396.

58 M. Schilling, 2008, *Die Instrumente der Hermes Exportkreditverischerung*, Bremen: Salzwasser-Verlag.

59 www.goglobal.dk, accessed October 2009.

60 D. Xu & O. Shenkar, 2002, Institutional distance and the multinational enterprise (p. 608), *AMR*, 27: 608–618.

61 B. Kogut & H. Singh, 1988, The effect of national culture on the choice of entry mode, *JIBS*, 19: 411–432.

62 S. Shane & H. Singh, 1998, National cultural distance and cross-border acquisition performance, *JIBS*, 29: 137–158; J. Hennart & J. Larimo, 1998, The impact of culture on the strategy of MNEs, *JIBS*, 29: 515–538; S. Estrin, D. Baghdasaryan & K.E. Meyer, 2009, The impact of institutional and human resource distance on international entry strategies, *JMS*, 46: 1171–1196; N. Prime, C. Obadia & I. Vida, 2009, Psychic distance in exporter-importer relationships, *IBR*, 18: 184–199; D. Dow & S. Ferencikova, 2010, More than national cultural distance, *IBR*, 19, 46–58.

63 G. Felbermayr & F. Toubal, 2010, Cultural proximity and trade, *EER*, 54: 279–293.

64 E. Tsang & P. Yip, 2007, Economic distance and survival of foreign direct investments, *AMJ*, 50: 1156–1168.

65 J. Steen & P. Liesch, 2007, A note on Penrosian growth, resource bundles, and the Uppsala model of internationalization, *MIR*, 47: 193–206.

66 J. Puck, D. Holtbrugge & A. Mohr, 2009, Beyond entry mode choice, *JIBS*, 40: 388–404; D. Tan, 2009, Foreign market entry strategies and post-entry growth, *JIBS*, 40: 1046–1063; G. Benito, B. Petersen & L.S. Welch, 2009, Towards more realistic conceptualizations of foreign operation modes, *JIBS*, 40, 1455–1470.

67 C.G. Asmussen, G. Benito & B. Petersen, 2009, Organizing foreign market activities: From entry mode choice to configuration decisions, *IBR* 18: 145–155.

68 A. Morgan-Thomas & S. Bridgewater, 2004, The Internet and exporting, *IMR*, 21: 393–406; P. Servais, T. Madsen & E. Rasmussen, 2006, Small manufacturing firms' involvement in international e-business activities, *AIM*, 17: 297–317.

69 M. Porter & J. Heppelmann, 2014, How smart, connected products are transforming competition, *HBR*, November.

70 B. Petersen & L.S. Welch, 2003, International business development and the Internet, post-hype, *MIR* 43

(special issue) 7–29; S. Loane, R.B. McNaughton & J. Bell, 2004, The internationalization of Internet-enabled entrepreneurial firms, *CJAS*, 21: 79–96.

71 D. Spar, 2001, *Ruling the Waves: Cycles of Discovery Chaos and Wealth from the Compass to the Internet*, New York: Harcourt.

72 *The Economist,* 2006, Online gambling: Busted flush, October 5; R. Blitz, 2009, Brussels intensifies transatlantic fight over online gambling, *Financial Times*, March 27.

73 D. Gelles, 2009, Canada forces tighter Facebook privacy, *Financial Times*, August 28.

74 B. Petersen, L. Welch & G. Benito, 2010, Managing the internationalization process, *MIR*, 50: 137–154.

75 Petersen, Welch & Welch, 2000, *as above*.

76 E. Autio, H. Sapienza & J. Almeida, 2000, Effects of age at entry, knowledge intensity, and imitability in international growth, *AMJ*, 43: 909–924.

CHAPTER TWELVE

FOREIGN ENTRY STRATEGIES

LEARNING OBJECTIVES

After studying this chapter, you should be able to

1 Explain why MNEs establish subsidiaries abroad (*why* to enter)

2 Identify relevant location-specific advantages that attract foreign investors (*where* to enter)

3 Compare and contrast first- and late-mover advantages (*when* to enter)

4 Compare and contrast alternative modes of entry (*how* to enter)

5 Explain the interdependence of operations and entry strategies

6 Apply the institution-based view to explain constraints on foreign entry strategies

7 Participate in leading debates on foreign entry strategies

8 Draw implications for action

OPENING CASE

Pearl River Piano *enters foreign markets*

A grand piano from a famous maker is the aspiration and passion of pianists around the world. Professionals swear by their favourite brands, like *Bösendorffer* (from Vienna, Austria) or *Steinway* (from New York, USA). Some choose a handmade piano from a traditional family business like *Grotrian-Steinweg* (from Braunschweig, Germany). The manufacture of a piano is a traditional craft that requires highly specialist skills, true to the Latin origins of the word (*manu* = hand). Most people with a passion for music make do with a more mundane brand, such as *Yamaha* (from Yokohama, Japan). *Yamaha* brought together Japanese traditional passion for manufacturing excellence, and a more recent passion for classical music to become the largest piano maker in the world in the 1990s. In 2008, Yamaha acquired the leading European manufacturer *Bösendorffer* for a stronger positioning in the premium segment.

With such a strong field of incumbents, and strong loyalty to traditional brands, it may come as a surprise that a new kid on the block has been rolling up the market: in 2002, *Pearl River* (of Guangzhou, China) overtook *Yamaha* to become the largest piano producer in the world, making about 100 000 pianos every year. How did it achieve that? Given the relatively low prestige associated with Chinese-made goods, few would associate an aspirational product like a piano with 'made in China'. *Pearl River Piano* was founded in 1956 in Guangzhou, next to the Pearl river. *Pearl River*'s centre of gravity has remained in China, where pianos have become more affordable with rising income. The one-child policy induced families to invest heavily in their only child's education. As a result, the Chinese now buy half of the pianos produced in the world.

Pearl River succeeded in becoming the top selling brand in China. This may sound like an attractive market position. Yet rising demand has attracted numerous new entrants, many of which compete at the low end in China. These over 140 competitors have pushed *Pearl River*'s domestic market share from 70% at its peak a decade ago down to about 25% – although it is still the market leader.

Facing price competition at home, *Pearl River* sought new opportunities overseas. In North America, it started exporting in the late 1980s by relying on US-based importers. Making its first ever foreign direct investment (FDI), it set up a US-based sales subsidiary, *Peal River Piano Group America* in California in 1999.

What challenges does a piano maker pace when expanding overseas?

Acknowledging the importance of the US market and the limited international experiences of its management team, *Pearl River* hired an American with long experience in the piano industry, to head the subsidiary. Within two years, the greenfield subsidiary succeeded in getting *Pearl River* pianos into about one-third of the specialized US retail dealers. Within ten years, the *Pearl River* brand became the leader in the low end of the upright piano market in North America.

Efforts to penetrate the high-end market, however, were still frustrated. The *Pearl River* brand suffered from all the usual trappings associated with Chinese brands. 'We are very cognisant that our pricing provides a strong incentive to buy,' Rich noted in a media interview, 'but $6000 is still a lot of money.' In an audacious move to overcome buyers' reservation about purchasing a high-end Chinese product, *Pearl River* made a second strategic FDI in 2000 by acquiring the brand *Ritmüller*. Founded in 1795, *Ritmüller* had manufactured pianos in Göttingen, Germany, for over one hundred years, although the factory had closed during the recession of the late 1920s. The brand continued to be appreciated among connoisseurs of antique pianos, and thus helped *Pearl River* to position itself in the European piano-making tradition and to move up-market. A new office in Munich focused on design, research and development. A newly-designed product line signalled commitment to a classic heritage and standard of excellence. Moreover, *Pearl River* commissioned international master piano designer Lothar

Thomma to integrate German craftsmanship with the latest manufacturing technology. *Pearl River* executives debated with branding experts and media gurus whether the company should invest solely on building the *Pearl River* brand or to inject major resources into reviving the *Ritmüller* brand.

While *Pearl River* is aggressively entering markets around the globe using a combination of exports, greenfield investments and acquisitions, competitors are facing the pressure. Several smaller European piano makers have had to close down; others have been acquired by investors from Japan or Korea. However, European brands remain popular, allowing craftsmanship-driven businesses to occupy the premium segment worldwide. Even German family business *Grotrian-Steinweg*, which builds 500 pianos a year, sell about 80 to 100 pianos in the professional market in China: their agent in Beijing invested €75 000 in English antiques to create an ambience of tradition and luxury for customers who consider spending a small fortune for special sound and prestige of a piano handmade in Germany.

Sources: (1) W. Ding, 2009, The return of the king, *Beijing Review,* May 21; (2) Funding Universe, 2009, Guangzhou Pearl River Piano Group Ltd., www.fundinguniverse.com; (3) Pearl River Piano Group, 2009, www.pearlriverpiano.com; (4) D. Behrendt, 2009, Tradition gibt den Ton an, *Hannoversche Allgemeine Zeitung*, March 4; (5) M.Chmielewski, 2011, Grotiran-Steinweg hakt die Krise ab, *Braunschweiger Zeitung*, November 7; (6) Stadtarchiv Göttingen, no date, *Stationen der Stadtgeschichte*, www.stadtarchiv.goettingen.de.

How do companies such as *Pearl River Piano* enter foreign markets? Why did they start their ambitious international growth in the Hong Kong and later the USA, before entering Europe? Why did *Pearl River Piano* establish a greenfield operation in the USA, but acquire a business in Germany? What are the advantages of building your own brand, and when is a combination with an acquired brand appropriate? These are some of the key questions in this chapter.

Recall from Chapter 6 that multinational enterprises (MNEs) engage in foreign direct investment (FDI) by operating subsidiaries abroad. Chapter 6 has already introduced key theoretical ideas as to why FDI and MNEs exist. This chapter approaches FDI from the perspective of a specific firm considering the establishment of a foreign subsidiary. Preparing such an investment, MNEs need to design an entry strategy that specifies their objectives and how they intend to achieve these objectives.

foreign subsidiary
An operation abroad set up by foreign direct investment.

entry strategy
A plan that specifies the objectives of an entry and how to achieve them.

We here consider foreign entries by mature firms with sufficient resources to establish their own subsidiaries. This complements Chapter 11, which focuses on smaller firms and non-equity modes. We start with a review of the objectives that motivate firms to establish subsidiaries abroad. Foreign entry requires several strategic decisions, including location, timing, entry mode, marketing, human resources and logistics. Most textbooks focus on the entry mode decision: exports, contracts, joint ventures or wholly-owned subsidiaries? However, this choice of entry mode actually

Figure 12.1   The building blocks of an entry strategy

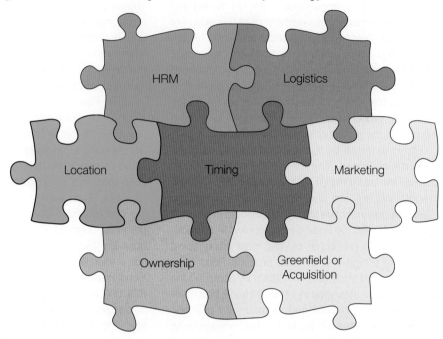

depends on many other aspects of the entry strategy. Our framework integrates these aspects. When designing an entry strategy, MNEs generally have to consider them together, ensuring a good fit between the different elements of the strategy – like the pieces of a jigsaw puzzle (Figure 12.1).

STRATEGIC OBJECTIVES OF ESTABLISHING FOREIGN SUBSIDIARIES

LEARNING OBJECTIVE

1   Explain why MNEs establish subsidiaries abroad (*why* to enter)

If you want to advise a company on how to set up an operation overseas (a popular topic for BA and MSc dissertations), then the first question you should ask the company is 'What *exactly* do you want to achieve?' MNEs establish foreign subsidiaries for a variety of reasons, and each operation contributes to the global MNE in a different way. Hence every entry decision has to be considered in relation to the overall strategy of the MNE, and make best use of both the local context and the global resources of the MNE. There are four common objectives for establishing subsidiaries abroad and thus to engage in FDI:[1]

natural resource-seeking FDI
Investors' quest to pursue natural resources in certain locations.

market-seeking FDI
Investors' quest to go after countries that offer strong demand for their products and services.

- Investors interested in natural resource-seeking aim to access particular resources, such as minerals, oil or renewable resources including timber or agricultural produce that they need in their production processes. Their main questions thus are, where do we find these resources, and how can we best secure access to them?

- Market-seeking investors aim to sell their products or services to new customers. They would identify the relevant market and then seek a central location for sales, marketing and distribution operations. In some industries, the actual production also needs to be located close to the customer or the point of consumption, notably in service industries such as hotels and financial services, and for manufactured goods that face high transportations costs.

Hence market-seeking investors ask, where are our potential future customers, and what do we have to do to reach them better than our competitors do?

● Efficiency-enhancing investors aim to reduce their overall costs of production. They often single out the most efficient locations featuring a combination of low-cost inputs – especially labour force, economies of scale and good transportation linkages. Their main question is, how can we lower the costs of our production and the delivery of products and service to customers? For example, Indian IT company *Tata Consultancy Services* set up operations in Hungary because Hungary offered the best combination of labour costs and proximity to European clients.

efficiency-enhancing FDI
Investors' quest to single out the most efficient locations featuring a combination of scale economies and low-cost factors.

● Capability-enhancing investors aim to access new ideas and technologies that help them to upgrade their own technological and managerial capabilities. Such entries aim to access the knowledge base of the host country, and thus to generate knowledge that may help the entire MNE to advance its organizational learning and growth.[2] Capability builders such as *Tata* and *Geely* (In Focus 12.1) thus ask, where are the latest technologies and ideas that we can connect to our existing technologies and innovation activities? Note that the primary concern of this type of investor is not to build a new subsidiary, but to change the parent organization.

capability-enhancing FDI
Investors' quest for new ideas and technologies that to upgrade their own technological and managerial capabilities.

IN FOCUS 12.1

Tata *and* Geely *acquire capabilities*

When Indian and Chinese MNEs invest overseas their first aim is often to build their own capabilities. Even when they have been highly successful at home, they still face a gap in capabilities, such as technological and managerial competences, marketing to premium customers, engaging with financial advisors and private equity, managing R&D processes and leading creative people.

Consider two examples in the car industry. India's *Tata Group* acquired *Corus Steel*, *Tetley Tea* and *Jaguar Land Rover (JLR)* in the UK. Contrary to typical Western acquisitions, these foreign entries were not (primarily) aiming to sell Indian products in Europe, nor to reduce costs of existing operations, or to access natural resources. In fact, the acquired firms have only been loosely integrated with other member firms of the *Tata Group*. So why did *Tata* make these big and risky investments? In addition to financial motives (risk diversification), *Tata*'s ambition has been to compete in global markets, and therefore it needed to build a range of managerial competences. After the acquisition, the acquired firm was given high operational

autonomy, and additional financial resources for investment. On this basis, *Tata*-owned *JLR* has successfully rebuilt its UK manufacturing operations and its emerging economy market share. At the same time, parent organization *Tata Motors* continued to struggle in its Indian home market.

Similarly, *Geely*, a private Chinese car manufacturer, acquired Swedish premium car maker *Volvo* and the manufacturer of London taxis, *Manganese Bronze*. Like *Tata*, *Geely* was not geared towards European markets (their growth was close to zero at the time). Rather, *Geely* aimed to use the acquired brands and technologies to strengthen its position in the largest and fastest growth market for passenger cars, China. After the acquisition, *Volvo* built a new car assembly plant in China and invested in building its premium brand in China. In 2014 alone, *Volvo* added 30 new dealerships in China to increase its network to 157, and sales surged by 33%. Thus China overtook the USA as *Volvo*'s most important market.

In both cases, the new owners thus helped build bridges to potential customers in emerging economies by investing in new plants, distribution channels and brand marketing. Yet their main objective was even more ambitious: to enhance the parent's capability base with an eye on global market leadership. This strategy requires the transfer and integration of knowledge and capabilities from the acquired firm to the new parent.

This intention is, however, challenging to implement. For example, how can a technological laggard identify the sources of a leader's superior performance? How can knowledge that is embedded in organizational processes, or even the education system, be communicated to recipients in another country? How can capabilities be replicated in a parent organization (the acquirer) with very different organizational structures and culture, say authoritarian leadership in China versus flat hierarchies in Northern Europe? Early indications suggest that both *Tata* and *Geely* found this reverse knowledge transfer quite challenging.

Sources: (1) V. Bajaj, 2012, Tata Motors finds success in Jaguar Land Rover, *New York Times*, August 30; (2) N. Shirouzu, 2013,Geely, Volvo differ over future China look, *Reuters*, September 10; (3) R. Gribben 2015, Jaguar Land Rover: £1.3bn Tata gamble pays off as big cat purrs at last, *The Telegraph*, February 15; (4) A. Sharman, 2015, Volvo drives Geely to record sales, *Financial Times*, February 27; (5) Meyer, K.E., 2015, What is strategic asset seeking FDI? *MBR*, 23(1): 57–66.

These four strategic goals, while analytically distinct, are not mutually exclusive. Thus investors may pursue several objectives when establishing a particular subsidiary. However, it is important to have a fairly clear idea of 'what' you want to achieve, before you consider 'how' to achieve it – in designing foreign entry strategies (as well as your own career, for example). A natural resource-seeker needs to specify the resources sought, and a market-seeker needs to identify the target customers, and so on. Having established the objectives of a foreign entry, we can discuss how firm aim to achieve them.

WHERE TO ENTER?

LEARNING OBJECTIVE

2 Identify relevant location-specific advantages that attract foreign investors (*where* to enter)

location-specific advantages
Advantages that can be exploited by those present at a location.

Like real estate, the motto for international business is 'Location, location, location'. In fact, such a spatial perspective (that is, geography beyond one's home country) is a defining feature of international business.[3] Location decisions involve (at least) two levels: first the country (say, UK), and second the site (say, Abingdon Business Park, near Oxford). The considerations for these between-country and within-country location decisions tend to be similar. Favourable locations in certain countries may give firms operating there access to location-specific advantages, that is, advantages that can be exploited by those present at a location. We may regard the continuous expansion of international business as a continuous search for locational advantages. As we discussed in Chapter 6, locational advantages relate in particular to markets, resource endowments, agglomeration and institutions. Prospective foreign investors access the locational advantages of possible host countries and – critically – match them with their own needs. Thus the weighting of different locational advantages varies for firms with different objectives (Table 12.1).

The quality and costs of local resources are a prime concern of natural resource-seeking and efficiency-enhancing investors. Their key decision parameters are the specific local resources that they require for their operations. For example, oil majors like *Shell* and *BP* seek accessible oil deposits, software developers like *SAP* seek trained software engineers, and manufacturers seek reliable workers and suppliers of intermediate goods. Some of these resources are available only at a limited number of locations, which takes certain industries to far off locations, such as oil exploration in the Middle East, Russia and Venezuela.

The costs and productivity of the local labour force is a prime consideration for efficiency-enhancing investors. Numerous MNEs have entered China with

Table 12.1 Matching strategic goals with locations

Strategic goals	Location-specific advantages	Illustrative locations mentioned in the text
Market-seeking	Strong market demand and customers willing to pay	Marketing and sales of consumer goods anywhere in the world
Natural resource-seeking	Quality and costs of natural resources	Oil exploration in the Middle East, Russia and Venezuela
Efficiency-enhancing	Economies of scale, abundance of low-cost labour force and suppliers, transport and communication infrastructure	Manufacturing in Guandong, China; logistics in Rotterdam, Vienna and Miami
Capability-enhancing	Innovative individuals, firms and universities, industry agglomeration	Chinese acquisitions of technologies and brands in Germany; wind energy in Jutland; IT in Silicon Valley and Bangalore

efficiency-enhancing motives. China now manufactures two-thirds of the world's photocopiers, shoes, toys and microwave ovens; half of its DVD players, digital cameras and textiles; and one-third of its desktop computers.[4] It is important to note that mainland China does not present the absolutely lowest labour costs in the world. However, its attractiveness lies in its ability to enhance foreign entrants' efficiency by lowering total costs. Total costs arise from the combination of costs of labour and the productivity of costs – plus costs of other inputs, and the costs of bring goods to market. Since the key efficiency concern is lowest total costs, it is also not surprising that some nominally 'high-cost' countries (such as the USA) continue to attract significant FDI. For instance, *Grupo Mexico*, the world's third-largest copper producer, has moved some of its energy-thirsty refining operations from 'high-cost' Mexico to 'low-cost' Texas, where electricity costs 4 cents per kilowatt hour as opposed to 8.5 cents in Mexico.[5]

The geography and logistics infrastructure is another consideration high on the list of efficiency-enhancing investors. They prefer locations that combine low labour costs with good local infrastructure and access to major ports, such as electronics assembly in Guangdong Province in southern China, or textile factories in Bing Duong and Dong Nai in southern Vietnam.[6] The location of logistics and coordination activities is even more focused on geography. Rotterdam, for instance, is an ideal stopping point for sea transport entering or leaving continental Europe (see Chapter 5, Opening Case). Vienna is an attractive site for MNEs' regional headquarters for Central and Eastern Europe, as are Singapore and Hong Kong for East Asia. Miami, which advertises itself as the 'Gateway of the Americas', is an ideal location both for North American firms looking south and Latin American companies coming north.

The size and growth potential of a market are the prime attractors for market-seeking investors. They aim to identify patterns of (future) demand for their particular products and services. For consumer goods, they may predict their market demand using demographic data such as per capita incomes and population size. For example, the Japanese appetite and willingness to pay for seafood have motivated seafood exporters around the world – ranging from nearby China and Korea to distant Norway and Peru – to ship their catch to Japan and fetch top dollars (or yen). *Pearl River Pianos* initially focused on the USA because of its sheer market size, and lots of Americans have large private homes to accommodate a piano. However, businesses supplying other businesses focus on the size and growth of their specific local customer industry. Access to markets may require a local sales operation, or even local production, if transportation is costly (for instance due to tariffs), or if the local institutional environment inhibits effective marketing and distribution of imported products.

Existing local capabilities are the main attraction for capability-enhancing investors. Similarly, where do you find the world's most famous piano brands? Where do you find the world's best traditional piano-building skills? These two questions have guided *Pearl River Piano* in their foray into Germany, where they were looking to enhance their design and development capabilities by acquiring a brand and competences in traditional piano-making. Other Chinese investors followed similar motives when they acquired traditional medium-sized German firms because of their technologies and brand reputation in global niche markets. For example in 2005, *SG Group*, a manufacturer of industrial sewing machines, acquired a German company with a global network of operations in the industry, *Dürkopp Adler*. *SG* was at the time losing market share in China to foreign investors. The acquisition in Germany provided it with new technologies and a brand name for the premium segment that enabled *SG* to regain market share in China, in addition to gaining access to new markets abroad (see Integrative Case *SG Group*).[7]

The existing structure of industry is important to all types of investors, as they may join industry clusters (or 'agglomerations'), though for different reasons.[8] Capability-enhancers like to join innovation clusters, such as information technology in Silicon Valley and Bangalore, or wind energy technology in the Jutland peninsula of Denmark. In addition to communities of experts developing new ideas, they may also meet venture capitalists with expertise in their industry. Efficiency-enhancing investors, such as the aforementioned garments and electronics firms in Vietnam and China, are more concerned about the availability of the availability of specialized suppliers and a workforce with industry-specific skills. Market-seeking investors in business-to-business sectors may join industrial clusters where they find their main customers, for example, accountants and consultants would locate in hubs where companies maintain their corporate headquarters.

WHEN TO ENTER?

LEARNING OBJECTIVE

3 Compare and contrast first- and late-mover advantages (*when* to enter)

first-mover advantages
Advantages that first movers obtain and that later movers do not enjoy.
late-mover advantages
Advantages that late movers obtain and that first movers do not enjoy.

Unless a firm is approached by unsolicited foreign customers that may lead to 'passive' entries, conscientious entry timing considerations centre on whether there are compelling reasons to be early or late entrants in certain countries.[9] Market-seekers especially often pursue first-mover advantages, defined as the advantages that first movers obtain and that later movers do not enjoy. Speaking of the power of first-mover advantages, *Xerox*, *FedEx* and *Google* have now become verbs: you will often hear people say 'Google it.' In some parts of Africa, *Colgate* is the generic term for toothpaste, thanks to *Colgate-Palmolive*'s first introduction of the product concept to the continent. *Unilever*, a late mover, is disappointed to find out that its African customers call its competing toothpaste 'the red *Colgate*'! However, first movers may also encounter significant disadvantages, which in turn become late-mover advantages. Table 12.2 shows a number of first- and late-mover advantages.

- First movers may gain advantage through proprietary technology. They also ride down the learning curve in pursuit of scale and scope economies in new countries. In Vietnam, early movers *Toyota* and *Ford* have been learning how to adapt their production and marketing technologies to the local conditions, and were thus prepared to face later entrants, such as *Nissan* in 2010.

- First movers may make pre-emptive investments. A number of Japanese MNEs have 'cherry picked' leading local suppliers and distributors as new

Table 12.2 First-mover advantages and late-mover advantages

First-mover advantages	Late-mover advantages (or first-mover disadvantages)
• Proprietary, technological leadership • Pre-emption of scarce resources • Establishment of entry barriers for late entrants • Relationships and connections with key stakeholders such as customers and governments	• Opportunity to free-ride on first-mover investments • Resolution of technological and market uncertainty • First mover's difficulty to adapt to market changes

members of the expanded *keiretsu* networks in Southeast Asia and blocked access to them by late entrants from the West.[10]

- First movers may erect significant entry barriers for late entrants, such as customer switching costs. Parents, having bought one brand of disposable diapers (such as *Huggies* or *Pampers*) for their first child, often stick with this brand for their other children. Buyers of expensive equipment are likely to stick with the same producers for components, training and other services for a long time. That is why aircraft manufacturers *Airbus* and *Boeing* compete intensely for airline orders: once the airlines build the service infrastructure around one type of aircraft, they will continue using this airline, and need servicing for their existing fleet (also see Integrative Case *Rolls-Royce*).

- First movers may build precious relationships with key stakeholders, such as customers and governments. For example, Danish fashion retailer *Bestseller* entered China in 1995, anticipating the rise of the middle class and thus increasing demand for premium brands. When the economy indeed boomed and young people built affinity to luxury brands, *Bestseller* had built both the infrastructure and prestigious brands like *Vero Moda* and *Jack & Jones* to serve them.[11]

On the other hand, the potential advantages of first movers may be counterbalanced by various disadvantages (see Table 12.2). There are numerous examples of first-mover firms that have lost, such as *EMI* in CT scanners, *de Havilland* in jet airliners, and *Netscape* in internet browsers. They were taken over by more resourceful second movers, respectively *GE*, *Boeing* and *Microsoft (Explorer)*. Specifically, late-mover advantages are manifested in three ways.

- Second movers may be able to free ride on first movers' huge pioneering investments. For example, a first mover in 3G telecommunications technology, such as Hong Kong's *Hutchison Whampoa* that is trying to introduce 3G in nine countries simultaneously, needs to incur huge advertising expenses to educate customers on both what 3G technology is and why its offering is the best. A late mover can free-ride on such customer education by only focusing on why its particular product is the best.

- First movers face greater technological and market uncertainties. After some of these uncertainties are removed, second movers may join the game with massive firepower. Some MNEs such as *IBM* and *Matsushita* are known to have such a tendency.

- As incumbents, first movers may be locked into a given set of fixed assets or reluctant to cannibalize existing product lines in favour of new ones. Second movers may be able to take advantage of first movers' inflexibility by leapfrogging first movers.

Overall, there is some evidence pointing to first-mover advantages, but there is also evidence supporting a second-mover strategy.[12] Although first movers may have an opportunity to win, their pioneering status is not a birthright for success. Empirical research suggests that first movers can maintain their leadership position *if* they continuously commit resources and *if* they actively learn about the local environment. Many first movers, however, did not succeed in creating sustained market leadership.[13] For example, among all three first movers that entered the Chinese automobile industry in the early 1980s, *VW* captured significant advantages, *Chrysler* had very moderate success, and *Peugeot* failed and had to exit. Among later entrants in the late 1990s, while many are struggling, *GM*, *Honda* and *Hyundai* have gained significant market shares. It is obvious that entry timing cannot be viewed in isolation, and entry timing per se is not the sole determinant of success and failure of foreign entries. It is through interaction with other strategic variables that entry timing has an impact on performance.[14]

HOW TO ENTER?

LEARNING OBJECTIVE

4 Compare and contrast alternative modes of entry (*how* to enter)

modes of entry
The format of foreign market entry.

non-equity mode
A mode of entry that does not involve owning equity in a local firm.

equity mode
A mode of entry (JVs that involves taking full or partial) equity ownership in a local firm.

Modes of entry are the format of foreign market entries. The first step is to determine whether to pursue equity or non-equity modes of entry. This crucial decision differentiates MNEs (involving equity modes) from non-MNEs (relying on non-equity modes). Non-equity modes (like exports and contractual agreements) tend to reflect relatively smaller commitments to overseas markets; we have already discussed them in Chapter 11. Also, recall from Chapter 6 that full ownership provides firms with internalization advantages, essentially reducing risks and costs by bringing market transactions in house. For smaller firms, such as *Grotrian-Steinweg Pianos* (Opening Case), non-equity modes are often the cornerstone of their international strategy. For larger firms, such as *Pearl River Piano*, non-equity modes often complement equity modes.

Equity modes (like JVs and wholly-owned subsidiaries) normally require larger, harder-to-reverse commitments. Equity modes establish an organization overseas that the firm owns, at least partially. The distinction between equity and non-equity modes is what defines an MNE: an MNE enters foreign markets via equity modes through foreign direct investment (FDI). A firm that merely exports/imports with no FDI is usually not regarded as an MNE.

Equity modes are particularly preferred when it comes to transferring intangible assets. Many businesses aim to achieve competitive advantages in each of their foreign markets by deploying intangible assets. However, they face asymmetric information regarding the content, value and usage of these assets, which are classic sources of market failures. Thus the more markets are characterized by information asymmetries, the more likely MNEs prefer to handle this transaction internally, and thus to choose an equity mode.[15] Moreover, the transfer of tacit knowledge requires 'learning by doing' and direct face-to-face interaction between people. That is difficult to achieve unless they work in the same company.[16] Thus firms competing especially on the basis of technology, brand names or other intangible assets, are likely to use equity modes rather than contractual collaboration.

Once a firm has decided to use an equity mode, it still has a choice of different entry modes that vary in terms of commitment, risk, return and control.[17] The decision depends essentially on two questions: how do we access complementary local resources? And, how much control will we attain? Figure 12.2 thus depicts the entry modes for foreign investors in a simple 2 x 2 matrix.

Most investors prefer full control over their operations, and thus establish a wholly-owned subsidiary (WOS) in which they are the only owner. The advantage of a WOS is that it provides full control, and thus the ability to integrate the operation

wholly-owned subsidiaries (WOS)
A subsidiary located in a foreign country that is entirely owned by the parent multinational.

Figure 12.2 The choice of FDI entry modes

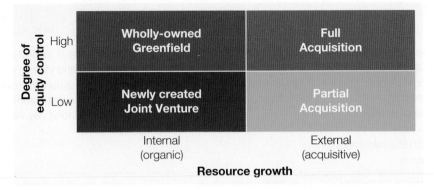

tightly with the parent firm and to determine what the subsidiary should do. In particular, the investor can control the use of knowledge transferred to the affiliate without worrying that a local partner may use it for its own purposes. A WOS can be established in two ways: (1) as a greenfield project, or (2) as a full acquisition.

The resource dimension

Foreign entrants usually need some local resources to complement their own resources, and thus they face a make-or-buy decision: should we develop and deploy our own resources, or should we buy local resources? Moreover, should we buy specific resources one by one, or should we buy an entire local business that has all the relevant resources? Firms seeking to establish a WOS thus have to choose between a greenfield entry and an acquisition entry (Table 12.3).[18]

Greenfield operations – building new factories and offices from scratch (on a proverbial piece of 'greenfield' formerly used for agricultural purposes) – creates three advantages. First, a greenfield operation allows investors to create a new operation from scratch according to their own designs, and thus to match it with their global organization. A greenfield option is thus preferred in particular by MNEs with competitive advantages grounded in the firm's organizational structure and culture. For example, Japanese car manufacturers *Nissan*, *Toyota* and *Honda* have set up their UK plants as greenfield investments because this allows transfer of the work practices that are central for their competitive advantage.[19] In particular, they allow selecting and training suitable people rather than working with a workforce used to a different culture. Second, a greenfield WOS gives an MNE complete equity and management control. This eliminates the headaches associated with JVs and providing better protection of proprietary technology, and allows for centrally coordinated global actions. Third, greenfield investments may be designed to be small initially, and to grow with the market development (especially for sales units), thus limiting the up-front capital commitment.

In terms of drawbacks, a greenfield WOS tends to add new capacity to an industry, which will make a competitive industry more crowded, and thus increases the intensity of competition (Chapter 13). Finally, greenfield operations, relative to acquisitions, suffer from a slow entry speed because it normally takes two or more years to plan and build a new plant and new distribution channels. In terms of risk, greenfield investments reduce the risk of failure due to conflict between the JV partners or with employees in an acquired firm. However, it usually takes quite some time to build a greenfield plant, which means pay-back periods are likely to be long, and investment risks are high.

greenfield operation
Building factories and offices from scratch.

Table 12.3 Equity modes of entry: advantages and disadvantages

Entry modes	Advantages	Disadvantages	Risks
Greenfield (wholly-owned)	• Design operations to fit the parent • Complete equity and operational control • Better protection of know-how • Option to scale operation to needs	• Add new capacity to industry • Slow entry speed (relative to acquisitions)	• No co-owner related risks • No integration failure risk • High investment risk due to large capital commitment and long pay-back periods
(Full) Acquisition	• Complete equity and operational control • Better protection of know-how • Do not add new capacity • Fast entry speed	• Political sensitivity • High up-front capital needs • Post-acquisition integration challenges	• High investment risk due to large up-front capital commitment • Integration process related risks • No co-owner related risks
Joint venture (newly established)	• Sharing costs, risks, and profits • Access to partners' knowledge and assets • Politically acceptable	• Divergent goals and interests of partners • Limited equity and operational control • Difficult to coordinate globally	• Limited investment risk due to lower capital commitment • High risk of coordination failure
Partial acquisition	• Access to operations that the previous owner is reluctant to give up • Previous owners' continued commitment	• Need to restructure and integrate, yet with limited control	• Limited investment risk due to lower capital commitment • High risk of integration problems • High risk of conflicts with co-owners

acquisition
The transfer of the control of operations and management from one firm (target) to another (acquirer), the former becoming a unit of the latter.

The second way to establish a WOS is through the **acquisition** of a local business.[20] An acquisition provides local organizationally-embedded resources, such as human capital and networks with local authorities. Acquisitions are probably the most important mode in terms of the amount of capital involved, representing approximately 70% of worldwide FDI flows. In addition to sharing many benefits of greenfield WOS, acquisitions enjoy two other advantages, namely: (1) adding no new capacity to the industry, and (2) faster entry speed. Foreign entry by full acquisition is particularly feasible when another foreign investor is withdrawing from the market. For example, *Behr*, a German manufacturer of automotive air conditioning and engine cooling systems, acquired its South African operation from a US firm, *Federal Mogul*, who wanted to divest from this sub-segment of the automotive supplier industry. This acquisition allowed *Behr* to strengthen its position as supplier to its key customers *VW*, *Mercedes*, and *BMW*, who had recently upgraded their South African manufacturing plants.[21] Full ownership was desirable for *Behr* because it had to integrate the new operations with its existing operations, and it was feasible because a facility of high technological standard was for sale at that time. As another example, consider *Thai Union Frozen Foods*, who aggressively entered EU markets by acquiring a French company owning brands like *John West* and *Petite Navire* (In Focus 12.2).

IN FOCUS 12.2

Thai Union *acquires market access*

A family business founded in Thailand in 1977 by a Chinese immigrant, *Thai Union Frozen Products Plc* has become one of the world's largest seafood processors, with subsidiaries in France, India, Indonesia, Japan, Norway, the USA and Vietnam. *Thai Union*'s international growth started with exports to Japan and the USA in 1988. In Japan, a JV with a local trading partner soon followed. In the USA, *Thai Union* went step-by-step to build up its market presence. Exports were followed by sales offices. In 1997, *Thai Union* purchased 50% of *Chicken of the Sea*, which was increased to full ownership in 2006; and in 2003, it acquired *Empress International*. In Europe, *Thai Union* made a big splash in 2010 by acquiring *MW Brands*, a French manufacturer and distributor of canned seafood, for €670 million. At the time, this was the second-largest outward FDI in Thai history. In 2014, *Thai Union* added further European brands to its portfolio by acquiring *King Oscar* in Norway and *MerAlliance* in France.

Thai Union's initial strategy focused on exploiting its lower cost base arising from (1) lower-cost skilled labour in Thailand and seafood caught off the Thai coast, and (2) product diversification that enables full exploitation of the raw seafood. The best parts of fish or shrimp become top-end food products; while the residual is used for, for example, pet food.

The purchase of European brands was primarily motivated by market-seeking motives, but also adds fishing and processing capacity. With the acquisition of *MW Brands*, the share of Europe in *Thai Union*'s total sales jumped from 11% to over one-third, thus reducing its dependence on the US market. *MW Brands* became market leader for tuna and other seafood products in France, the UK, Ireland, the Netherlands and Italy, with brands like *John West*, *Petite Navire*, *Conserverie Parmentier* and *Mareblu*. These brands represented a strategic asset that could also be exploited in further European markets. In addition, the acquisition also supported efficiency-seeking motives by adding four processing plants in France, Portugal, Seychelles and Ghana to its existing facilities in Thailand, Indonesia, Vietnam and the USA, and by increasing its fishing fleet from four to nine vessels.

However, the ambitions of CEO Thiraphong Chansiri (the son of the founder) do not end here. In 2015, he pursued a €1.3 billion bid for *Bumble Bee Foods* in the USA in an attempt to move into higher margin premium products.

Sources: (1) K.E. Meyer & O. Thaijongarak, 2013, The dynamics of emerging economy MNEs: How the internationalization process model can guide future research, *APJM*, 30: 1125–1153; (2) M. Peel, 2015, Thai Union plans to real in more Western catches, *Financial Times*, February 2; (3) www.mwbrands.com.

In terms of drawbacks, acquisitions are most likely to attract political resistance from both individuals working in the plant, and from nationalistic sentiments – especially if high-profile companies are involved. In addition, acquisitions have to confront a different and potentially devastating disadvantage – the restructuring and integration of the acquired business (see Chapter 14). The restructuring challenges are particularly acute when acquiring firms that were previously run very inefficiently, such as state-owned enterprises in transition economies. Restructuring challenges are considerably easier when acquiring a business formerly owned by another foreign investor, such as the *Behr* examples above. In terms of risks, acquisitions present high investment risks because of the high capital commitment required up front, and the chance of the integration process going wrong.

The control dimension

joint venture (JV)
A new corporate entity created and jointly owned by two or more parent companies.

A joint venture (JV) is a 'corporate child' that is a new entity jointly owned by two or more parent companies.[22] It has three principal forms: minority JV (the focal firm holds less than 50% equity), 50/50 JV, and majority JV (more than 50% equity). A JV with a local partner has three advantages. First, an MNE shares costs, risks and profits with a local partner, thus limiting the financial risk of the investment. Second, the MNE gains access to knowledge about the host country, and the local firm, in turn, benefits from the MNE's technology, capital and management. Third, JVs may be politically more acceptable.[23]

In terms of disadvantages, first, JVs often involve partners from different backgrounds and goals; conflicts are natural. Second, effective equity and operational control may be difficult to achieve because everything has to be negotiated (and in some cases, fought over). Finally, the nature of the JV does not give an MNE the tight control over a foreign subsidiary that it may need for global coordination (such as simultaneously launching new products around the world). In terms of risks, JVs reduce the investment risks because less capital is committed. However, JVs are highly exposed to internal risks such as conflicts between the parent firms, and they constrain the investors' ability to change its strategy. Hence the risk of not reacting sufficiently flexibly to changing internal or external circumstances is high.

JVs are thus appropriate in special situations, namely when three conditions are met: (1) the new business unit depends on resource contributions from two or more firms, (2) high transaction costs inhibit the markets for these resources or for the expected outputs, and (3) it is not feasible for the entire parent firms to be integrated into one firm, for instance because they are big relative to the envisaged project, or one of them is a state-owned enterprise.[24] In other words, JVs are common where two firms are trying to achieve something that neither could do on its own, and where the outcomes are highly uncertain. An area where JVs are common is entries into emerging economies: MNEs that lack local knowledge and relationships with influential local players in their target markets may best obtain such knowledge and relationships access by collaborating with a local firm (In Focus 12.3). JVs thus provide an avenue to operate in unfamiliar contexts, especially in countries with weak market supporting institutions, such as China or Russia. JVs are also used, for example, when two multinationals want to jointly conduct research and development, or merge a particular business unit (see Chapter 14).

As a consequence of their operational disadvantages, many JVs operate only for a limited lifetime. Some JVs are designed for a specific purpose, and are discontinued once this purpose has been achieved. Other JVs have no explicit termination agreement, but they are subject to conflicts between their parents and shifting interests and bargaining positions. Thus ownership stakes may change, and most JVs are eventually dissolved.[25] Only a few JVs, such as *Fuji-Xerox*, defy the trend and successfully operate for several decades.

IN FOCUS 12.3

Joint venture ZF Kama *in Russia*

by Irina Mihailova

In 2005, *ZF Friedrichshafen (ZF)*, a German automotive industry supplier, and *Kamaz Corporation*, a Russia truck manufacturer, set up a joint venture '*ZF Kama*' to produce transmissions in Russia.

ZF is one of the world's leading suppliers of driveline and chassis technology, with an annual turnover of €12.8 billion, over 72 600 employees and 122 production sites worldwide (of which 31 are in Germany). For *ZF*, the JV in Russia was an important step towards building a strong market position in the Russian market, where *ZF* previously did not have production facilities. The cooperation with *Kamaz* was expected to help this objective by creating an association with a leading local truck manufacturer and its extensive dealer network in Russia. In addition, the technological and managerial capabilities of *Kamaz* were significant criteria for the choice of partner. The Russian JV generated an increase in demand for parts produced in *ZF* plants in Western Europe, and thus contributed to the growth and viability of these established business units.

Kamaz Corporation is one of the largest automobile corporations in Russia with, at the time, 59 000 employees. It operates an integrated production complex that incorporates the whole technological cycle of truck production, from the development, production of components, and assembly of vehicles, to the marketing of vehicles and after-sales services. *Kamaz* produces a wide range of trucks, trailers, buses, tractors, engines, power units and a variety of machine tools, and operates the largest automotive distribution and service network in Russia and neighbouring countries. For *Kamaz*, the primary objective for establishing the JV was to access the advanced technologies of *ZF*, and to ensure the supply of high-quality car components. Hence the primary criterion for the choice of JV partner was the possession of product technology. Moreover, a track record of sincere cooperation initiatives and a willingness to share risks were also important arguments for partnering with *ZF*.

ZF Kama was founded in 2005 to manufacture commercial vehicle transmissions, the first production facility established by *Kamaz* with a foreign partner. The JV is located within the industrial site of *Kamaz* in the city of Naberezhnye Chelny, in Tatarstan. *ZF* holds 51% of the equity of the JV, while *Kamaz* holds the remaining 49%. Both partners actively participate in the management of the JV, and they both have representatives in the management team. *Kamaz*, is responsible for day-to-day operations of the JV, and manages key business relationships with customers,

suppliers and government authorities. *ZF* contributes primarily through product technology and expertise.

In 2014, *ZF Kama* opened a new production plant in Naberezhnye Chelny to manufacture transmission gearboxes and their parts. The main customer of the JV is *Kamaz*, but the JV also supplies truck transmissions to *ZF* plants in Friedrichshafen (Germany), Bouthéon (France), and Eger (Hungary).

After the JV with *ZF*, *Kamaz* has built a range of JVs with other Western partners in the automotive industry, including suppliers *Cummins* and *Federal Mogul* (both from the USA) and *Knorr Bremse* (Germany), agricultural machines with *Case New*

Holland (part of the Italian *Fiat Group*), and construction cranes with *Palfinger* (Austria). The jewel in its portfolio of partnerships is a truck distribution and assembly JV, *Mercedes-Benz Trucks Vostok* with *Daimler* (Germany), which also acquired 11% of the equity of *Kamaz*.

Source: Originally prepared by Irina Mihailova (Aalto University) based on interviews with the companies, and updated by Klaus Meyer. Additional sources: (1) RT, 2009, Daimler announces joint ventures with Kamaz, December 21; (2) ZF Kama, 2012, YouTube Video (www.youtube.com/watch?v=cpj8QM8zPzw); (3) www .zf.com; (4) www.daimler.com; (5) www.palfinger.com; (6) www .kamaz.ru.

partial acquisition
Acquisition of an equity stake in another firm.

Shared control can also be established by an acquisition of an equity stake but not full ownership. Such partial acquisitions occur in particular (1) if a seller is unwilling to sell the business in full, or (2) if the previous owners are still needed to run the operation. For example, privatization agencies in Central and Eastern Europe in the 1990s often sold only a small equity stake, and kept the remainder, or gave it to domestic investors.[26] *France Telecom* acquired a 35% equity stake in *Polish Telecom* in 2000, with local investors and the Polish Treasury holding the remainder. The company needed major improvements in efficiency, as standards of telephone and internet communications were lagging. For example, *Polish Telecom* employed far more people per customer than other European telecom service providers. This restructuring led to tough negotiations with trade unions that resisted layoff and outsourcing of jobs until generous redundancy payments had been agreed.[27]

Partial acquisitions are also common for MNEs buying out entrepreneurial firms: if the entrepreneurs retain an ownership stake, they are probably more motivated to continue to pull their weight for the company. For example, when French luxury goods manufacturer *LVMH* acquired Italian fashion brand *Loro Piana*, the founder retained 20% of the equity and remained involved in the management. The advantage of partial acquisitions is to provide access to a firm that otherwise would be 'not for sale', while limiting the capital commitment. The main disadvantage of partial acquisition is that acquirers may have to implement organizational change without full equity control, and thus without the power to enforce changes in structures or processes. In terms of risks, partial acquisitions face less investment risks because the initial capital investment is limited, and it is often easier to sell again than a stake in a custom-designed JV. However, the risks arising from the integration process and potential conflict with co-owners are likely to be higher than in JVs.

strategic alliance
Collaboration between independent firms using equity modes, non-equity contractual agreements, or both.

JVs and partial acquisitions are special cases of a strategic alliance, that is, collaboration between independent firms in a given economic space and time for the attainment of a set of agreed goals. It can take various organizational forms, including using equity modes, non-equity contractual agreements, or both. However, the term strategic alliance is often used very broadly. Understanding the relationship between two firms normally requires a more detailed specification of contributions, control, and risk-sharing arrangements. Therefore, we prefer to use more specific terms to describe the nature of a relationship between two firms.

HOW TO ORGANIZE YOUR OPERATIONS

LEARNING OBJECTIVE

5   Explain the
    interdependence of
    operations and entry
    strategies

In the classroom we can systematically analyze each aspect of entry strategy in isolation. Yet in the real world they are all interdependent, and decisions over multiple aspects have to be made together. Even operational strategies are important for the design of an entry strategy. Thus at the time of entry it is already necessary to consider how the operation will be run in the future, notably (1) marketing, (2) human resources, and (3) logistics – issues that we will discuss in detail in Chapters 15 to 17.

First, a key issue in marketing is global standardization versus local adaptation of products, processes and brands. Advantages of standardization across the operations of the MNE include economies of scale in the exploitation of capabilities of the global firm, including product development, production and marketing. In contrast, local adaptation strategies aim to accommodate local needs and preferences. They normally require the creation or acquisition of local resources such as mass-market brands. This is common for instance in food and beverage industries. The Polish brewing industry is dominated by three global players: *Heineken*, *SABMiller* and *Carlsberg*. Yet most Polish pub revellers probably don't know this. The leading brands in Poland are *Tyskie*, *Zywiec* and *Okocim*, all of which are local brands owned by one of the big three.[28] These brewing MNEs pursue multi-tier strategies that combine international premium brands with local brands aimed at the mass market – all acquired by taking over local breweries. The importance of local brands, however, implies that first mover advantages and the acquisition of local brands were important, which put constraints on other aspects of entry strategy.

Second, human resources are critical to foreign entry because each subsidiary needs qualified and motivated people, especially to facilitate knowledge sharing within an organization. This involves both the transfer of organizational practices to the new operation and the tapping of headquarters into local knowledge. Foreign investors thus have to send expatriate managers, who lead in recruiting, training, and motivating local staff. Expatriates play a pivotal role in coordinating between headquarters and subsidiaries, as do locally-recruited people who can liaise with other units of the MNE. Firms with a pool of internationally experienced managers are better able to establish a new operation without a local JV partner. On the other hand, firms without locally knowledgeable people are more likely to need contributions from a local JV partner.

Third, logistics is an important aspect of a foreign entry strategy, because lower labour costs are only valuable for a business if the products can be transported to the customer in good time at acceptable cost. Likewise, serving a local market is only feasible if you can get your products to the customer in good condition at acceptable cost. Effective supply chain management practices are thus crucial capabilities for companies aiming to exploit synergies between operations around the globe. For example, modern transportation and communication systems enable MNEs to optimize the integration of their internal operations as well as supplier relations. A foreign entry often triggers changes in these systems. In particular, the choice of location for production sites is interdependent with the choice of logistics systems.

INSTITUTIONS AND FOREIGN ENTRY STRATEGIES

LEARNING OBJECTIVE

6   Apply the institution-
    based view to
    explain constraints
    on foreign entry
    strategies

Foreign entry strategies are often constrained by the institutional environment in the host economy. Institutions may (1) prohibit certain types of operations or transactions, (2) create a need for local knowledge, (3) change the relative (transaction) costs of alternative strategies or (4) motivate tariff-jumping FDI. Table 12.4 illustrates the possible impact of such constraints on entry mode and location decisions.

Table 12.4 Institutional constraints on foreign entry

Types of constraints	Impact of entry mode (examples)	Impact on location (examples)
Certain operations or transactions are not permitted	• Establish JVs where WOSs are not permitted	• Locate where planning permissions are easier to obtain
Need for local knowledge	• Establish JVs to access local knowledge	• Locate in agglomerations of foreign investors that help attaining local knowledge
Higher transaction costs due to costly contract enforcement	• Avoid complex arm's-length contracts with unfamiliar partners	• Locate in areas where local uncertainty is lower
Higher transaction costs due to lack of financial intermediaries	• Avoid full or partial acquisitions of local firms	–
Higher tariffs or other trade barriers	–	• Locate production in the target market

First, some governments discourage or ban wholly-owned subsidiaries (WOSs), thereby leaving JVs with local firms as the only entry choice. For example, the Indian government dictates the maximum ceiling of foreign firms' equity position in the retail sector to be 51%, forcing foreign entrants to set up alliances such as JVs with local firms. The Indian retail market is an attractive target for multinational retailers, as it is still highly fragmented. Yet foreign investors have to accept the ownership constraint. Thus in 2009, American *Wal-Mart* formed a 50/50 JV with *Bharti Retail* with the goal of setting up wholesale cash-and-carry stores throughout India. French *Carrefour* negotiated a similar deal with the *Future Group* of Indian magnate Kishore Biyani, combined with a wholly-owned wholesale operation, as foreign ownership in wholesale trade is not restricted.[29] Legal restrictions such as the building code also affect where hypermarkets are opened. Supposedly, the inability to obtain planning for new stores has been a major reason for the withdrawal of *Wal-Mart* from Germany.[30]

Recently, there has been a general trend towards less restrictive policies, as many governments (such as those in Mexico and South Korea) that historically only approved JVs now allow WOSs. As a result, there has been a noticeable decline of JVs and a corresponding rise of acquisitions in emerging economies.[31] However, despite the general movement toward more liberal policies, many governments still impose considerable requirements, especially when foreign firms acquire domestic assets. For example, only shared ownership is permitted in industries considered strategic, such as automobile assembly in China, and the oil industry in Russia. US regulations only permit up to 25% of the equity of any US airline to be held by foreign carriers, and EU regulations limit non-EU ownership to 49% of EU-based airlines.

Second, the institutional environment in many emerging economies is characterized by idiosyncratic rules and extensive use of networks. Such institutions, often characterized as 'weak institutions' by Western investors, create a need for local knowledge, local network relationships, and other tacit resources held by local firms. For example, even after the legal restrictions have been removed, many foreign entrants use JVs to enter countries like China and Vietnam because they lack the necessary local knowledge and contacts. Hence foreign entrants are likely to see a greater need to cooperate with local partners, for instance by establishing a JV. An alternative route to access local knowledge is to locate near other foreign investors, and to participate in the knowledge exchange within informal 'expatriate networks'.[32]

Third, 'weak institutions' also increase transaction costs, such as such as search costs arising from information asymmetries, and contract enforcement costs associated with inefficient legal systems. This implies that businesses are to a large extent based on relationships rather than arm's-length transactions. Licensing or franchising contracts with a stranger could thus be costly because they are difficult to enforce. Moreover, acquisitions are costly where financial market institutions are underdeveloped, for instance due to the lack of reliable accounting and auditing information and non-existence of intermediaries such as financial advisors and consultants.[33] Foreign investors may thus avoid complex arm's-length relationships, or locate in advanced regions where legal uncertainties have been reduced.

Fourth, institutions inhibiting international trade may in some circumstances actually increase foreign entry with local production facilities. For example, local production allows entrants to overcome tariffs and non-tariffs barriers that inhibit serving a market through an export strategy. For example, *Ford* is operating a production facility in Vietnam at well below its efficient scale; yet it is important to gain access to the Vietnamese market. Another institution that may attract foreign investors is local content requirements that may induce manufacturers to ask their suppliers to set up a local operation.

DEBATES AND EXTENSIONS

This chapter has already covered some crucial debates, such as first- versus late-mover advantages. Here we discuss two *recent* debates: (1) the scale of entry and (2) dynamics of acquisitions.

LEARNING OBJECTIVE

7 Participate in leading debates on foreign entry strategies

Scale of entry: commitment and experience

Small firms facing resource constraints typically enter with a small operation that they gradually expand, as suggested by the internationalization process model (Chapter 11). However, resource-rich companies face a strategic choice regarding the scale of entry between entering with a large up-front investment, or with a small foothold operation. In some highly competitive industries, heavy up-front investment is required to prevent retaliation from incumbents or to realize first-mover advantages, as for branded consumer goods. A number of European financial services firms, such as *HSBC* and *ING Group*, have spent several billion dollars to enter the USA by making a series of acquisitions. The benefits of these large-scale entries demonstrate strategic commitment to certain markets. This both helps assure local customers and suppliers ('We are here for the long haul!') and deters potential entrants. Moreover, in some capital-intensive industries, for instance oil exploration, only large-scale operations are economically viable. The drawbacks of such hard-to-reverse strategic commitment are (1) limited strategic flexibility elsewhere and (2) huge losses if these large-scale 'bets' turn out wrong.

On the other hand, small-scale entry reduces the costs and risks of entry. They focus on organizational learning by getting firms' feet 'wet' – learning by doing – while limiting the downside risk.[34] Such platform investment provides investors with a small foothold from which to observe the local industry and to flexibly react to business opportunities if and when they emerge.[35] For example, to enter the market of Islamic finance in which no interest can be charged (per teaching of the Koran), *Citibank* set up a subsidiary *Citibank Islamic Bank*, *HSBC* established *Amanah*, and *UBS* launched *Noriba*. They were designed to experiment with different interpretations of the Koran on how to make money while not committing religious sins. This capability cannot be acquired outside the Islamic world; it needs to be developed

scale of entry
The amount of resources committed to foreign market entry.

platform investment
An investment that provides a small foothold in a market or location.

locally. Such development of new capabilities internally takes time. The main draw-back of small-scale entries is a lack of strong commitment, which may lead to difficulties in building market share and capturing first-mover advantages.

Acquisition dynamics

Recall from Chapter 11 that internationalizing firms can use a range of different strategies to build resources specific to contexts they want to enter. The acquisition of a local firm can greatly accelerate this process. However, a single acquisition is often insufficient to create the operation that the foreign investor needs to achieve its objectives. Hence acquisitions are often followed by extensive restructuring and additional investments or divestments.[36] This leads to complex strategies involving acquisitions (Table 12.5).

brownfield acquisition
Acquisition where subsequent investment overlays the acquired organization.

In some cases, the subsequent investment completely overlays the acquired organization; we then talk of a brownfield acquisition.[37] In these cases, the foreign investor may be interested only in a particular asset, such as an operating licence, a distribution outlet or a brand name. Yet often this asset is not 'for sale' on its own, and can only be accessed by taking over the entire company. For example, cosmetics company *Beiersdorf* of Germany acquired *Pollonia-Lechia* in Poland, which owned the rights to the *Nivea* brand in Poland, yet had few other assets of interest. *Beiersdorf* added a new, parallel organizational structure to market the *Nivea* brand by Western standards, but operated largely independent of the old structures. This set-up allowed the restructuring to run smoothly. Once the new operation was up and running, the old structure was closed down.[38]

multiple acquisition
A strategy based on acquiring and integrating multiple businesses.

In other cases, foreign investors may want to build an operation that incorporates several local businesses, especially when the local industry is highly fragmented. Thus investors may pursue a strategy of multiple acquisitions, that is, a strategy based on acquiring and integrating several businesses. A single acquisition may be insufficient to build the kind of operation that the foreign investor aspires to, notably economies of scale and a leading market share. The acquisition of smaller firms in a new market may make sense only in the context of a broader strategy that involves further acquisitions. For example, *Carlsberg* in Poland acquired four different breweries – yet they

Table 12.5 Types of acquisitions

Types	Purpose (example)	Risks
Conventional acquisition	• Take over a company that has complementary resources and capabilities	• Not overpaying • Post-acquisition integration
Brownfield acquisition	• Obtain specific asset controlled by another firm, but upgrade it to fit the global operation	• Very high capital investment • Complex post-acquisition upgrading and integration
Multiple acquisitions	• Build a strong market share in a previously highly fragmented market	• Very high capital investment • Integration of multiple local units, as well as integrating them with the global operation
Staged acquisition	• Take over a firm whose sellers are unwilling to let go, or where their continued commitment is important	• Integration process with initially limited control • Uncertainty over long-term ownership structure

still ended up in third place behind two competitors that were even more aggressive: *Heineken* and *SABMiller*.[39]

We have noted before that some acquisitions only involve the acquisition of an equity stake – partial acquisitions. However, this is rarely a stable arrangement. Often the foreign investor soon increases its equity stake, sometimes based on a pre-agreed schedule. In such staged acquisitions the ownership transfer takes place over stages: what looks like a shared ownership arrangement to outsiders is actually a way to implement an acquisition. For example, in the case of *Skoda Auto*, *VW* initially acquired a minority equity stake but attained management control over the company in 1993. Thus *VW* led the restructuring of the company while it was still formally a JV with the Czech state. Only later did *VW* acquire full ownership and then fully integrated *Skoda* in its global operations. The advantages of staged acquisitions are, first, reduced political sensitivity, second, less up-front capital needs, and third, continued commitment of the previous owners. The disadvantages and risks are similar to partial acquisitions (Table 12.3).

staged acquisition
Acquisition where ownership transfer takes place over stages.

IMPLICATIONS FOR PRACTICE

Foreign market entries represent a foundation for overseas actions. Without these crucial first steps, firms will remain domestic players. The challenges associated with internationalization are complex, and the stakes high. Returning to our fundamental question, we ask: what determines the success and failure in foreign market entries? The answer boils down to the two core perspectives: institution- and resource-based views. Consequently, three implications for action emerge (Table 12.6). First, from an institution-based view, managers need to understand the rules of the game, both formal and informal, governing competition in each of your foreign markets. Entry strategies need to 'fit' these institutions, notably by complying with local regulation and informal norms, as well as by building legitimacy with local interest groups.

Second, from a resource-based view, managers need to bring together the capabilities of their MNE with complementary local resources. Few investors would be able to compete in foreign markets solely based on their existing resources: their liability of outsidership works against them. Different entry strategies allow building or acquiring local capabilities in different ways: a gradual entry with a platform investment would emphasize learning along the lines of the internationalization process models (Chapter 11), a JV would facilitate learning from the partner, while an acquisition would provide embedded capabilities of the acquired firm. With competition from both local firms and other foreign investors, managing your resources and capabilities is key to succeeding in foreign countries.

Finally, managers need to match the different elements of an entry strategy with their strategic goals. Decisions on one element influence other aspects. If timing and speed of entry are crucial for an investor – for example when pursuing first-mover advantages – then an acquisition or a JV may offer quick market access. On the other hand, if global integration of marketing, logistics and human resource management

LEARNING OBJECTIVE

8 Draw implications for action

Table 12.6 Implications for action

- Understand the rules of game in the host country – both formal and informal – and fit your strategies to the constraints and opportunities of these institutions.
- Bring together the MNEs' global capabilities and complementary local resources.
- Match the different elements of an entry strategy with the firm's strategic goals.

are important, then the existing structures and practices of an acquired firm may pose major obstacles, and a greenfield entry may be more appropriate. Thus foreign entry decisions have to reflect the complex interdependence of multiple dimensions. Decision makers may develop alternative scenarios and compare their respective merits, for example, an acquisition of a specific firm in the Czech Republic versus a greenfield investment in a specific industrial zone in Poland.

Overall, appropriate foreign market entries, while important, are only a beginning. To succeed overseas, post-entry strategies are equally or more important. These would entail managing competitive dynamics (Chapter 13), developing global strategies (Chapter 14), and creating dynamic and efficient operations (Chapter 15 to 17), all of which will be covered in later chapters.

CHAPTER SUMMARY

1 Explain why MNEs establish subsidiaries abroad (*why* to enter)

- Firms' strategic goals can be grouped into four categories: (1) natural resources, (2) market, (3) efficiency and (4) innovation.

2 Identify relevant location-specific advantages that attract foreign investors (*where* to enter)

- Foreign entrants seek locational advantages that match their strategic objectives.

3 Compare and contrast first- and late-mover advantages (*when* to enter)

- First-movers can attain advantages, such as early brand building, yet there are countervailing benefits for fast followers.

4 Compare and contrast alternative modes of entry (*how* to enter)

- Entry modes vary by the degree of control that entrants attain over the local operation.
- Entry modes provide access to local resources in different ways.

5 Explain the interdependence of operations and entry strategies

- Entry strategies need to take (1) marketing, (2) human resources and (3) logistics operations into account.

6 Apply the institution-based view to explain constraints on foreign entry strategies

- Formal and informal institutions may restrict the options for foreign entry, create needs for local knowledge, and increase transaction costs of certain forms of transaction.

7 Participate in leading debates on foreign entry strategies

- These leading debates are (1) the scale of a foreign entry and (2) acquisition dynamics.

8 Draw implications for action

- From an institution-based view, managers need to fit their strategies to the constraints and opportunities of local institutions.
- From a resource-based view, managers need to bring together the MNEs global capabilities and complementary local resources.
- Managers must match the different elements of an entry strategy with the firm's strategic goals.

KEY TERMS

Acquisition
Brownfield acquisition
Capability-enhancing FDI
Efficiency-enhancing FDI
Entry strategy
Equity mode
First-mover advantages
Foreign subsidiary

Greenfield operation
Joint venture (JV)
Late-mover advantage
Location-specific advantage
Market-seeking FDI
Modes of entry
Multiple acquisition
Natural resource-seeking FDI

Non-equity modes
Partial acquisition
Platform investment
Scale of entry
Staged acquisition
Strategic alliance
Wholly-owned subsidiary (WOS)

CRITICAL DISCUSSION QUESTIONS

1 Since joining the EU, countries like Poland and Hungary have seen an increase of foreign direct investment. Yet some foreign investors move their operations from these countries to locations further East, complaining about rising labour costs. Use institution-based and resource-based views to explain these changes.

2 From institution- and resource-based views, identify the obstacles confronting MNEs from emerging economies interested in expanding overseas. How can such firms overcome them?

3 In what situations should companies consider sharing control over an operation with a local firm that is directly or indirectly owned by the host country's government?

4 In what situations should branded consumer goods manufacturers consider foregoing potential first-mover advantages and delay their entry until after a competitor has entered?

RECOMMENDED READINGS

K.E. Brouthers, 2013, A retrospective on: Institutional, cultural and transaction cost influences on entry mode choice and performance, *JIBS*, **44: 14–22** – an assessment of the state-of-the-art on entry-mode research.

J.H. Dunning & S. Lundan, 2008, *Multinational Enterprises and the Global Economy*, **2nd ed., Cheltenham: Elgar** – the most comprehensive book reviewing scholarly work on how companies are setting up foreign investment.

J.-F. Hennart, 2009, Down with MNE-centric theories! Market entry and expansion as the bundling of MNE and local assets, *JIBS*, **40:**

1432–1454 – a conceptual paper that integrates the perspective of a foreign investor with that of local partner firms.

K.E. Meyer & Y.T.T. Tran, 2006, Market penetration and acquisition strategies for emerging economies, *LRP*, **39: 177–197** – a study that illustrates many of the issues discussed in this chapter, using the case of *Carlsberg*.

A. Verbeke, 2009, *International Business Strategy*, **Cambridge: Cambridge University Press** – a textbook that develops concepts of business strategy out of the economics-based theory of the MNE.

CLOSING CASE

Danone *and* Wahaha: *'failed' joint ventures*

by Sunny Li Sun and Hao Chen

In 1996, France's *Danone SA* established five joint ventures (JVs) with China's *Wahaha Group*. *Danone* owned 51% of each of these JVs and *Wahaha* and its employees owned the remainder. Founded in 1987, *Wahaha* is one of the best-known beverage brands in China. By 2006, the total number of JVs between *Danone* and *Wahaha* had grown from five to 39, with revenues increasing from $100 million in 1996 to $2.25 billion in 2006. These JVs, which cost *Danone*

$170 million, paid *Danone* a total of $307 million in dividends over the past decade. By 2006, they contributed 6% of *Danone*'s total global profits.

In addition to the JVs with *Wahaha*, *Danone* also bought stakes in more than seven Chinese food and dairy firms, spending another $170 million (besides what was spent on *Wahaha*) over the past decade in China. In 2006, *Danone* became the biggest beverage maker by volume in China, ahead of rivals such as *Coca-Cola* and *PepsiCo*. At the same time, *Wahaha* also pursued aggressive growth in China, some of which was beyond the scope of the JVs with *Danone*. By 2006, *Wahaha Group* managed 70 subsidiaries scattered throughout China. All these subsidiaries use the same brand 'Wahaha', but only 39 of them had JV relationships with Danone.

A major dispute erupted concerning Wahaha's other 31 subsidiaries that had no JV relationships with Danone. In 2006, after profits from the 39 JVs jumped 48% to $386 million, Danone wanted to buy Wahaha's other subsidiaries. This would enable Danone to control the Wahaha brand once and for all. This proposal was rejected by Wahaha's founder Zong Qinghou, who served as chairman of the 39 JVs with Danone. Zong viewed this offer as unreasonable, because the book value of the non-JV subsidiaries' assets was $700 million, with total profits of $130 million, while the price/earnings ratio of Danone's $500 million offer was lower than four. Zong also asserted that the buy-out would jeopardize the existence of the Wahaha brand, because Danone would phase it out and promote global brands such as Danone and Evian.

The heart of the dispute stemmed from the master JV agreement between Danone and Wahaha, which granted the subsidiary JVs exclusive rights to produce, distribute and sell food and beverage products under the Wahaha brand. This meant that every product using the Wahaha brand should be approved by the board of the JV. Danone thus claimed that the non-JV subsidiaries set up by Zong were illegally selling products using the Wahaha brand, and were making unlawful use of the JVs' distributors and suppliers. However, Zong claimed that the original JV agreement to grant exclusive rights to use the Wahaha brand was never approved by the Chinese trademark office,

and so was not in force or effect. He further stated that Danone had not made an issue when Wahaha embarked on its expansion and openly used the subsidiary JVs' assets – it seemed that Danone preferred Wahaha to shoulder the risk first. According to Zong, when Wahaha's expansion proved successful, Danone wanted to reap the fruits of his labour. Finally, Zong argued that forcing Wahaha Group to grant the exclusive rights for the Wahaha brand to the JVs with Danone was unfair to Wahaha Group, because Danone was actively investing in other beverage companies around the country and competing with Wahaha. Wahaha suggested that in human marriage terms, these would be extra-marital affairs.

The boardroom dispute spilled into the public domain when Zong publicly criticized Danone in April 2007. In response, Danone issued statements and initiated arbitrations against Wahaha in Stockholm, Sweden. Danone also launched a lawsuit against a company owned by Zong's daughter in the United States, alleging that it was using the Wahaha brand illegally. Outraged, Zong resigned from his board chairman position at all the JVs with Danone. Wahaha's trade union, representing about 10 000 workers of Wahaha Group, sued Danone in late 2007, demanding $1.36 million in damages. This made the dispute worse, and revenues of the JVs only increased 3% in 2007, 17% less than the industry's average growth.

Between 2007 and 2009, both sides spent most of their energy dealing with over 21 lawsuits and arbitrations in several countries. Even the French president and Chinese minister of commerce called for the two parties to stop lawsuits and to settle. Danone spent $83 million in litigation fees in three years but won no victory. Finally, Danone gave up and sold its 51% share in the JVs to Wahaha in September 2009. No financial terms were publicly disclosed. A person familiar with the matter said the settlement amount was 'slightly below' the figure Danone cited in previously published financial accounts as the value of its Wahaha holdings: $555 million.

As observers, we can wonder whether the divorce was caused by opportunism from the start or by 'changed circumstances' as the relationship evolved. Even with the painful divorce, Danone still earned respectable financial returns. A Danone spokesman defended the JV strategy: 'If we now have 30% of our sales in emerging markets and we built this in only ten years, it's thanks to this specific [JV] strategy. We have problems with Wahaha. But we prefer to have problems with Wahaha now to not having had Wahaha at all for the last ten years.' Wahaha's Zong said in the settlement announcement: 'Chinese companies are willing to cooperate and grow with the world's leading peers on the basis of equality and reciprocal benefit.'

CASE DISCUSSION QUESTIONS

1 Was a series of joint ventures the appropriate mode for *Danone* to enter China? What would have been the alternatives?

2 How would you design a joint-venture contract for an entry in China?

3 How would you suggest *Danone* should have managed its relationship with *Wahaha*?

Sources: This case was written by Sunny Li Sun and Hao Chen (both at the University of Texas at Dallas) under the supervision of Professor Mike W. Peng. It was based on (1) *China Daily*, 2007, Chinese drinks giant brands Danone 'despicable' over lawsuit, June 8; (2) finance.sina.com.cn/focus/2007wahaha; (3) M.W. Peng, S.L. Sun, & H. Chen, 2008, Managing divorce: How to disengage from joint ventures and strategic alliances, *Peking University Business Review*, April; (4) *Wall Street Journal*, 2009, Danone pulls out of disputed China venture, October 1.

NOTES

'For journal abbreviation, please see page xx-xxi.'

1 J.H. Dunning & S. Lundan, 2009, *Multinational enterprises and the global economy*, 2nd ed., Cheltenham: Elgar; G. Benito, 2015, Why and how motives (still) matter, *MBR*, 23: 15–24.

2 K.E. Meyer, 2015, What is strategic asset seeking FDI?, *MBR*, 23: in press. Other authors refer to this category as resource augmenting or 'strategic asset seeking', see Dunning and Lundan, 2009, *as above*.

3 J. Dunning, 1998, Location and the multinational enterprise, *JIBS*, 29: 45–66; R. Belderbos, W. van Olffen & J. Zou, 2011, Generic and specific social learning mechanisms in foreign entry location choice, *SMJ* 32(12): 1309–1330; S. Beugelsdijk & R. Mudambi, 2013, MNEs as border-crossing multi-location enterprises, *JIBS*, 44: 413–426; J. Alcácer, C. Denzsö & M. Zhao, 2015. Location choices under strategic interactions, *SMJ*, 36(2): 197–215.

4 Economist Intelligence Unit, 2006, *CEO Briefing* (p. 9), London: EIU.

5 G. Smith, 2003, Mexico: Was NAFTA worth it? (p. 72), *Business Week*, December 22.

6 K.E. Meyer & H. Nguyen, 2005, Foreign investment strategies and sub-national institutions in emerging markets: Evidence from Vietnam, *JMS*, 42: 63–93.

7 S. Sohm, B.M. Linke & A. Klossek, 2009, *Chinese Companies in Germany*, Bielefeld: Bertelsmann Foundation.

8 S. Mariotti & L. Piscitello, 1995, Information costs and locations of FDIs within the host country: Empirical evidence from Italy, *JIBS*, 26: 815–841; M.J. Shaver, & F. Flyer, 2000, Agglomeration economics, firm heterogeneity, and foreign direct investment in the United States, SMJ, 21: 1175–1193; J. Alcacer & W. Chung, 2007, Location strategies and knowledge spillovers, *MSc*, 53: 760–776.

9 M. Lieberman & D. Montgomery, 1988, First-mover advantages, *SMJ*, 9: 41–58; Y. Luo & M.W. Peng, 1998, First mover advantages in investing in transition economies, *TIBR*, 40: 141–163; J. Frynas, K. Mellahi & G. Pigman, 2006, First mover advantages in international business and firm-specific political resources, *SMJ*, 27: 321–345.

10 M.W. Peng, S. Lee & J. Tan, 2001, The *keiretsu* in Asia, *JIM*, 7: 253–276.

11 C. Boutrup, 2011, *Kina Sweet and Sour*, Copenhagen: Gyldendal.

12 L. Fuentelsaz, J. Gomez & Y. Polo, 2002, Followers' entry timing, *SMJ*, 23: 245–264; J. Shamsie, C. Phelps & J. Kuperman, 2004, Being late than never, *SMJ*, 25: 69–84.

13 B. Tan & I. Vertinsky, 1996, Foreign direct investment by Japanese electronics firms in the United States and Canada, *JIBS*, 27: 655–681; T. Isobe, S. Makino & D. Montgomery, 2000, Resource commitment, entry timing, and market performance of foreign direct investments in emerging economies, *AMJ*, 43: 468–484; V. Gaba, Y. Pan & G. Ungson, 2002, Timing of entry in international market, *JIBS*, 33: 39–55.

14 M.W. Peng, 2000, Controlling the foreign agent, *MIR*, 40: 141–165; F. Suarez & G. Lanzolla, 2007, The role of environmental dynamics in building a first mover advantage theory, *AMR*, 32: 377–392.

15 J.F. Hennart, 1982, *The Multinational Enterprise*, Ann Arbor: University of Michigan Press; M. Casson, 1987, *The Firm and the Market*, Cambridge, MA: MIT Press; P. Buckley & M. Casson, 1998, Analyzing foreign market entry strategies, *JIBS*, 29, 539–561.

16 D. Teece, 1977, Technology transfer by multinational firms, *EJ*, 87: 242–261; B. Kogut & U. Zander 1993, Knowledge of the firm and the evolutionary theory of the multinational enterprise, *JIBS*, 24: 625–645.

17 Y. Pan & D. Tse, 2000, The hierarchical model of market entry modes, *JIBS*, 31: 535–554. See also C.W.L. Hill, P. Hwang & W.C. Kim, 1990, An eclectic theory of the choice of international entry mode, *SMJ*, 11: 117–128; K.D. Brouthers, L.E. Brouthers & S. Werner, 2003, Transaction cost-enhanced entry mode choices and firm performance, *SMJ*, 24: 1239–1248; H. Zhao, Y. Luo & T. Suh, 2004, Transaction cost determinants and ownership-based entry mode choice, *JIBS*, 35: 524–544.

18 J.F. Hennart & Y.R. Park, 1993, Greenfield vs. acquisition, *MS*, 39, 1054–1070; J. Anand & A. Delios, 1997, Location specificity and the transfer of downstream assets to foreign subsidiaries, *JIBS*, 28, 579–604; H. Barkema & F. Vermeulen, 1998, International expansion through start-up or acquisition, *AMJ*, 41: 7–26; A.W.K. Harzing, 2002, Acquisitions versus greenfield investments, *SMJ*, 23: 211–227.

19 B. Wilkinson, J. Morris & M. Munday, 1995, The iron first and the velvet globe, *JMS*, 31: 819–830; J. Lowe, J. Morris & B. Wilkinson, 2000, British factory, Japanese factory and Mexican factory, *JMS* 37: 541–560.

20 H. Barkema & F. Vermeulen, 1998, International expansion through start-up or acquisition, *AMJ*, 41: 7–27; K. Brouthers & L. Brouthers, 2000, Acquisition or greenfield start-up? *SMJ*, 21: 89–98; Harzing, 2002, *as above*; K.E. Meyer & S. Estrin, 2007, *Acquisition Strategies in European Emerging Economies*, Basingstoke: Palgrave.

21 S. Gelb & A. Black, 2004, South African case studies, in: S. Estrin & K.E. Meyer, eds, *Investment Strategies in Emerging Markets*, Cheltenham: Elgar, 209–242.

22 K. Harrigan, 1988, Joint ventures and competitive strategy, *SMJ*, 9: 141–158; B. Kogut, 1988, Joint ventures, *SMJ* 9: 319–332.

23 S. Chen & J.F. Hennart, 2002, Japanese investors' choice of joint ventures versus wholly-owned subsidiaries in the U.S., *JIBS*, 33: 1–18; J.F. Hennart & Reddy, 1997, The choice between mergers/acquisitions and joint ventures, *SMJ*, 18: 1–12.

24 P. Buckley & M. Casson, 1998; Models of the multinational enterprise, *JIBS*, 29: 21–44; J.F. Hennart, 2009, Down with MNE-centric theories, *JIBS*, 40: 1032–1054; K.E. Meyer & Y. Wang (2015): Transaction Cost Perspectives on Alliances and Joint Ventures, in: J. Larimo, N.Nummela & T. Mainela, eds, *Elgar Handbook of International Alliances and Network Research*, Cheltenham: Elgar.

25 A. Inkpen & P. Beamish, 1997, Knowledge, bargaining power, and the instability of international joint ventures, *AMR*, 22: 177–200.

26 S. Estrin, 2002, Competition and corporate governance in transition, *JEP*, 16: 101–124; K.E. Meyer, 2002, Management challenges in privatization acquisitions in transition economies, *JWB*, 37, 266–276.

27 P. Kulawczuk, 2007, The purchase of a monopoly: France Telecom acquires TPSA, in: K.E. Meyer & S. Estrin, eds, *Acquisition Strategies in European Emerging Markets*, Basingstoke: Palgrave Macmillan, 133–146.

28 K.E. Meyer & Y. Tran, 2006, Market Penetration and Acquisition Strategies for Emerging Economies, *LRP*, 39: 177–197; M. Bak, 2007, Growth through multiple acquisitions: Carlsberg Breweries in Poland, in: K.E. Meyer & S. Estrin, eds, *Acquisition Strategies in European Emerging Markets*, Basingstoke: Palgrave Macmillan.

29 H. Hauschild, 2010, Carrefour pant Einstieg in Indien, *Handlsblatt*, March 7.

30 A. Verbeke, 2009, *International Business Strategy*, Cambridge: Cambridge University Press. Other commentators attribute *Wal-Mart*'s withdrawal to persistent conflicts with employees and trade unions.

31 M. Desai, C. Foley & J. Hines, 2004, The costs of shared ownership, *JFE*, 73: 323–374; S. Rossi & P. Volpin, 2004, Cross-country determinants of M&As, *JFE*, 74: 277–304; H.K. Steensma, L. Tihanyi, M. Lyles & C. Dhanaraj, 2005, The evolving value of foreign partnerships in transitioning economies, *AMJ*, 48: 213–235; P. Kale & J. Anand, 2006, The decline of emerging economy JVs, *CMR*, 48: 62–76; M.W. Peng, 2006, Making M&As fly in China, *HBR*, March: 26–27.

32 D. Tan & K.E. Meyer, 2011, Country-of-origin and industry agglomeration of foreign investors in an emerging economy, *JIBS*, 42: 502–520.

33 K.E. Meyer, S. Estrin, S. Bhaumik & M.W. Peng, 2009, Institutions, Resources, and Entry strategies in emerging economies, *SMJ*, 31: 61–80.

34 Y. Luo & M.W. Peng, 1999, Learning to compete in a transition economy, *JIBS*, 30: 269–296; M. Lord & A. Ranft, 2000, Organizational learning about new international markets, *JIBS*, 31: 573–589.

35 B. Kogut & N. Kulatilaka, 1994, Options thinking and platform investment, *CMR*, 36(2): 52–71; B. Kogut & S. Chang, 1996, Platform investments and volatile exchange rates, *RES*, 78: 221–232; D. McCarthy & S. Puffer, Strategic investment flexibility for MNE success in Russia, *JWB*, 32: 293–319.

36 L. Capron, P. Dussage & W. Mitchell, 1998, Resource deployment following horizontal acquisitions in Europe and North America, *SMJ*, 19, 631–661; L. Capron, W. Mitchell & A. Swaminathan, 2001, Asset divesture following horizontal acquisitions: A dynamic view, *SMJ*, 22: 817–844.

37 K.E. Meyer & S. Estrin, 2001, Brownfield entry in emerging markets, *JIBS*, 32: 257–267; S. Estrin & K.E. Meyer, 2009, Brownfield acquisitions: A reconceptualization and extension, *MIR*, 51: 483–510.

38 S. Blazejewski, W. Dorow & H. Stüting, 2003, The case of Beiersdorf-Lechia S.A. Pozan, in: S. Blazejewski, W. Dorow, eds, *Change Management in Transformation Economies,* Basingstoke: Palgrave.

39 Meyer & Tran, 2006, *as above*.

CHAPTER THIRTEEN

COMPETITIVE DYNAMICS

LEARNING OBJECTIVES

After studying this chapter, you should be able to

1 Explain how attacks and counterattacks are used in dynamic competition

2 Explain how and why firms sometimes like to collude

3 Outline how competition policy and anti-dumping laws affect international competition

4 Articulate how resources and capabilities influence competitive dynamics

5 Participate in leading debates concerning competition

6 Draw implications for action

OPENING CASE

Gulf Airlines *challenge a global industry*

Three airlines in the Gulf region are challenging European and American airlines in their most profitable business: long-haul connections. The threesome, *Emirates*, *Etihad Airways* and *Qatar Airways* are intensively competing with each other by investing in modern aircraft and upgrading their airport hubs. Together, they have become the most disruptive force in global aviation.

Launched in 1985 in Dubai, United Arab Emirates (UAE), *Emirates* serves 140 destinations in 70 countries with its all wide-body fleet of 212 planes and

373 more on order. It is the largest customer of the ultra-long-range Boeing 777s and Airbus A380s. With these capable jets, any two cities in the world can be linked with one stop via Dubai. In the financial year 2013/2014, *Emirates* carried 44.5 million passengers and 2.25 million tons of cargo. *Emirates* makes the most of its location. Dubai International Airport (DXB) is an ideal stopping point for air traffic between Europe and Asia, and between Africa and Asia. Connecting 220 destinations, DXB handles over 40 million passengers a year, soon to be expanded to 60 million a year. Since Dubai's own population is fewer than four million, the majority of the passengers are connecting (transit) passengers who are not from or going to Dubai.

Emirates 'super-connector' positioning is directly challenging traditional long-haul carriers such as *British Airways* (*BA*), *Air France-KLM* and *Lufthansa*. These established airlines fear that just like no-frills competitors squeeze their short-haul flights, *Emirates* can threaten their profitable long-haul business. In fact, *Emirates* already has more intercontinental seats than *BA* and *Air France* combined. *Emirates* focuses on secondary (but still sizable) cities, such as Manchester, Hamburg and Kolkata. Passengers flying, for example, from Hamburg to Sydney may not care whether they change planes at Frankfurt or Dubai, especially when *Emirates* flies newer and quieter planes, offers cheaper tickets, and provides nicer amenities. One of *Emirates'* open secrets of success is to fly super-sized planes – one A380 can carry 500 passengers – to reduce the cost per passenger. The savings help to undercut fares of the traditional airlines.

However, *Emirates* faces aggressive competition from two regional rivals that realized that geographic advantage is not a Dubai monopoly. Doha, Qatar, is only 200 miles from Dubai. *Qatar Airways,* founded in 1992, operates 154 aircraft plus 180 on order. In December 2014, it received its first next-generation Airbus, the A350-900, which was put into service on the Doha to Frankfurt connection. Replacing its ageing Doha International Airport (handling 15 million passengers in 2010), Qatar opened a new international airport at Hamad in 2014 with a capacity of 29 million and a projected future capacity of 48 million. Signalling its global ambitions, *Qatar Airways* acquired 9.99% stake in *IAG*, *British Airways'* parent, in 2015. Akbar Al Baker, CEO of *Qatar Airways*, argued that '*IAG* represents an excellent opportunity to further develop our Westwards strategy. Having joined the *Oneworld* alliance it makes sense for us to work more closely together in the near term and we look forward to forging a long-term relationship.'

Closer to Dubai, Abu Dhabi (a fellow emirate in the UAE) launched *Etihad Airways* in 2003. It quickly became the fastest-growing airline in the history of commercial aviation. With 107 aircraft, it has another 213 on order. Only a 45-minute drive from DBX, Abu Dhabi International Airport had a capacity of 20 million in 2012, and plans to expand to 40 million. *Etihad Airways* developed its business by partnering with smaller European airlines facing liquidity difficulties, which it developed as feeder airlines for its global network. Thus *Etihad* acquired a one-third stake in *Air Berlin* of Germany, 49% of Italian *Alitalia*, and 49% of *Air Serbia*.

All three airlines from the gulf are heavily investing in marketing and branding in Europe. Football fans tend to know 'the Emirates' (the home of Arsenal Football Club) and 'the Etihad' (formerly City of Manchester Stadium). *Emirates* also sponsors a veritable portfolio of AC Milan, Real Madrid, Paris Saint-Germain, Hamburger SV and Olympiacos. *Qatar Airways* is aiming very high with its deal with Barcelona FC, while *Etihad* is looking further afield, sponsoring Melbourne FC and New York City FC.

European airlines have been fighting back with their own aggressive pricing and new offerings, but also lobby to restrict the Gulf operators in Europe because of the 'unfair' subsidies their new competitors allegedly receive in the form of cheap fuel and low airport fees. *Emirates* responds that it pays slightly more for fuel at home (DXB) than abroad, because of the lack of refining capacity in the Gulf. Moreover, since Dubai provides few social services to expatriates, *Emirates* spends $400 million a year to provide accommodation, health care, and schools for its staff – a huge expense that rivals do not have to cough up. In 2015, US airlines felt the pinch too, and demanded that the US take action, claiming that the three received hidden aid worth $42 billion, mainly in the form of interest-free loans and guarantees.

At home, Dubai, Abu Dhabi and Doha are raising their investment in airport capacity. In fact, Dubai is building an even larger airport, Dubai World Central-Al Maktoum International (DWC), with five parallel runways and a projected passenger capacity of 160 million. Thus the three 'super-connectors' from the Gulf continue to compete intensely with each other, while jointly taking market share from established European airlines. Recently, *Turkish Airlines* joined the competition, investing in new routes connecting through Istanbul, while European, Asian and American airlines upgrade their facilities and partnerships. Will there be enough air traffic for all of them? Some analysts speculate that there may only be two survivors of the 'super-connectors'. Who will be the survivors of this intensive competition?

Sources: (1) *Aviation News*, 2011, Dubai International Airport, December: 34–39; (2) *Bloomberg Businessweek*, 2010, Emirates wins with big planes and low costs, July 5: 18–19; (3) *The Economist*, 2010, Rulers of the new silk road, June 5: 75–77; (4) *The Economist*, 2010, Super-duper-connectors from the Gulf, June 5: 21; (5) A. Parker & S. Kerr, 2013, Emirates: In a sweet spot, *Financial Times*, December; (6) *Handelsblatt*, 2014, Etihad-Einstieg bei Air Berlin erst 2015, November 29; (7) R. Wright, 2015, US airlines seek help on Gulf rivals, *Financial Times*, March 6; (8) J. Gapper, 2015, Stop trying to ground the Gulf airlines, *Financial Times*, March18.

Emirates has been plotting its strategy for building a leading position in its chosen market for a long time. It made strategic investments to build rare capabilities. At the same time, it is engaged in head-to-head competition with its rivals, reacting to their moves in terms of pricing, frequent flyer schemes, or auxiliary services. Once *Emirates* makes a move, how do *Etihad*, *Turkish Airlines* and *Lufthansa* respond? How can they compete so fiercely, yet earn handsome profits for their owners?

When business leaders talk of the big ideas on how they engage with the competition, they often refer to the 'strategy'. What is strategy? Essentially, a strategy consists of broadly defined objectives and a set of actions to achieve those goals.[1] For businesses, objectives often refer to markets in which the company wants to compete and the market position the company wants to achieve.[2] The actions include, for example, acquisition of key capabilities, or entry into key market segments. In your personal life, you may also have a strategy: you may have a career objective of one day leading a major international business, and the actions you take to achieve that objective include studying this course. For business, developing strategy is first and foremost about where, when and how to compete.

This chapter thus first deals with the dynamics of competition, and with the ways firms cooperate to undermine competition by collusion and signalling. Then, we draw on institution- and resource-based views to shed light on competitive dynamics. Debates and extensions focus on strategies to face challenging market situations such as recession or overwhelming foreign entrants in your home market.

strategy
Objectives and a set of actions to achieve those objectives.

DYNAMICS OF COMPETITION

oligopoly
A market structure with only a small number of competing firms.

competitive dynamics
The actions and responses undertaken by competing firms.

competitor analysis
The process of anticipating a rival's actions in order to both revise a firm's plan and prepare to deal with rivals' responses.

attack
An initial set of actions to gain competitive advantage.

counter-attack
A set of actions in response to an attack.

AMC framework
A conceptual framework of awareness, motivation, capability indicating when firms are likely to attack and counterattack each other.

blue ocean strategy
A strategy of attack that avoids direct confrontation with incumbents.

When there are only a few companies competing an industry, we call it an oligopoly. In an oligopoly, firms don't compete by driving down prices; they rather interact in strategic ways to beat their competitor, yet make handsome profits at the same time. These actions and responses undertaken by competing firms are known as competitive dynamics.[3] Since one firm's actions are rarely unnoticed by rivals, the initiating firm would naturally like to predict rivals' responses *before* making its own move. Anticipating rivals' actions, the initiating firm may want to both revise its plan and prepare to deal with rivals' responses in the next round. This process is called competitor analysis, advocated a long time ago by the ancient Chinese strategist Sun Tzu's teaching 'If you know the enemy and know yourself, your victory will not stand in doubt.' The key word is *interaction* – how firms interact with rivals.

While militaries fight over territories, firms compete in markets.[4] Obviously, military principles cannot be directly applied in business because the marketplace, after all, is not a battlefield where the motto is 'kill or be killed'. Fighting to the death would destroy the value firms create, and nothing would be left. In fact, if your competitor has to shut down, the media and the competition authorities will subject your actions to greater scrutiny, which is not necessarily a good position to be in. Thus businesses compete to win, but not necessarily to kill the competitor. Moreover, businesses fight for market share because it helps their profitability, thus their aggressiveness will be tempered by the need to protect profits. Hence business is often simultaneously rivalry and cooperation.[5]

At any time, businesses can intensify their competitive efforts by launching an attack, defined as an initial set of actions to gain competitive advantage, which may take the form of price cuts, advertising campaigns, market entries, new product introductions, or lawsuits. An attack is worthwhile if it is expected to yield a stronger position and/or higher profitability, at least in the longer run. When companies enter a new market, or attack an existing rival in a new way, they tend to think of that rival as it is 'today'. However when attacked, rivals may launch a counter-attack, defined as a set of actions in response to an attack. Firms considering an attack thus need to anticipate possible reactions.

The awareness, motivation, capability (AMC) framework gives some indication of rivals' likely response:[6]

- **Awareness** is a prerequisite for any counterattack. If an attack is so subtle that rivals are not aware of it, then the attacker is likely to succeed. A new competitor is more likely to be noticed when making a high-profile entry, for example, by acquiring another firm, or by launching a major marketing campaign. Moreover, rivals with very similar operations and marketing practices are more aware of each other than of rivals operating in very different ways. Limited interaction and low similarity reduce managers' cognisance of the relationship with a competitor, and thus their awareness of the potential threat.[7] For example, importers may be perceived as less threatening than competitors setting up a local subsidiary.[8]

  One interesting idea is the 'blue ocean strategy' that avoids attacking core markets defended by rivals.[9] A direct attack on rivals' core markets is likely to result in a quick retaliation in the form of a price war, legal action or massive marketing aimed at the entrant's target audience. This can be avoided by creating a new product or customer experience that incumbents do not perceive as a threat, and hence do not trigger any strategic actions. A classic example is *Cirque du Soleil*, a new form of entertainment experience that initially was not seen as a direct competitor by traditional circus and event organizers, but which has steadily gained market share in the broader defined 'entertainment market'. Taking small steps to establish a foothold in an occupied niche, an entrant is less likely to get much attention from the incumbent. However, growing out of a niche is not easy either. For example, *Haier* was inspired by the blue ocean idea in its entry into the USA, yet it got stuck in the niches it targeted (In Focus 13.1).

- **Motivation** is also crucial. Rivals will launch a counterattack if they expect long-term benefits from doing so. These benefits are likely to be large if the incumbent has a lot to lose, for example, when market dominance is crucial for the incumbent's profitability. On the other hand, if the attacked market segment is of marginal value, as compact refrigerators are in the USA, managers may decide *not* to counterattack. Moreover, incumbents operating in a competitive environment and under private ownership have stronger incentives to react than firms in regulated industries that mainly depend on interaction with policymakers.

IN FOCUS 13.1

Haier *pursues niche in the USA*

White goods maker *Haier* dominated its home country, China, with a broad range of products. Yet it chose to enter the US market in a low-profile segment: compact refrigerators for hotels and student residences. Does anyone remember the brand of the refrigerator in the last hotel room you stayed in? Evidently, not only you failed to pay attention to that brand, but incumbents such as *GE* and *Whirlpool* also dismissed this segment as peripheral and low margin. In other words, they were not aware of the competitive threat until *Haier* had built a substantive operation in the USA. *Haier* developed products for related niches, such as wine cooling cabinets, and convinced retail chains like *Wal-Mart* and *Target* to carry its products. With this strategy it achieved a 50% US market share in the niche market of compact refrigerators.

Haier also invested more than $30 million to build a factory in South Carolina. Why would a Chinese multinational, blessed with a low-wage work force at home, operate a plant in high-wage USA? *Haier* officials suggest that shipping refrigerators across the Pacific is costly and can take 40 days, thus offsetting China's wage advantage. Better to build close to the customer and place the 'Made in USA' tag on the product. But perhaps more importantly, it sends a strong signal to

both competitors and distributors: we are here to stay! This commitment to the US market increases retailers' confidence in carrying the brand. To competitors, it said, 'Don't pick a price war or play anti-dumping tricks, we can do the same.'

In China, *Haier* went from strength to strength, earning itself a reputation for fast-paced innovation, creative new business models to serve even remote areas of China, and empowering management practices (in a country known for authoritarian leadership style). Yet in the US, *Haier* remained for a decade a niche player in the low-price segment. Of 80 000 employees worldwide, only 470 worked in the US, of which 250 were in the production plant in South Carolina. Recalls of freezers made in China but sold under the same *Haier* brand as products made in South Carolina further dampened the brand reputation. To escape its small, low-margin business, *Haier* invested in 2012 in a new strategy by establishing an R&D centre in the US to study consumers and develop products locally.

Sources: Based on (1) R. Crawford & L. Paine, 1998, The Haier Group (A), Harvard Business School case 9–398–101; (2) M. Zeng & P. Williamson, 2003, The hidden dragons, *HBR*, 81 (10): 92–104; (3) B. Einhorn, 2012, China's biggest brands try to raise their profile, Bloomberg, July 26; (4) B. Fischer, U. Lago & F. Liu, 2013, *Reinventing Giants*, London: Jossey-Bass; (5) *Bloomberg Businessweek*, Haier recalls 41K chest freezers due to fire risk, April 2.

- **Capability** is the ability to engage in a battle for markets. Even if an attack is identified and a firm is motivated to respond, it requires strong capabilities to carry out counterattacks. First, firms with strong financial resources are able to make critical investments, or to engage in a price war. For example, *Microsoft* has fought back *Apple*'s near double-digit share of the PC-software market (with the Mac selling for US$2700) and a new generation of US$500 'netbook' computers that run on the free Linux operating system. Leveraging its deep pockets (a hard-to-imitate capability), *Microsoft* charged PC makers only US$15 for Windows, which was normally priced at US$70. As a result, Mac sales stopped increasing, and Linux has disappeared from most netbooks. In 2009, approximately 95% of netbooks run Windows, up from 10% in 2008.[10] *Apple*, however, did not sit idle and in turn launched a counterattack on *Microsoft* by launching its iPad in 2010.

Second, technological capabilities are crucial for firms to react to entrants using new technologies. To succeed against innovative competitors, firms have to connect new knowledge with existing knowledge, and to transform it for application in their own context. Firms with strong human capital and innovation-facilitating organizational structures are better positioned to exploit such knowledge spillovers.[11]

Overall, minimizing the awareness, motivation and capabilities of actual or potential competitors increases the chances of a successful attack. Carrying out frontal, simple and predictable attacks will find rivals ready to launch a counterattack. Rivals, however, will also be subtle in their counterattacks, launching attacks where they can catch the attacker unaware. Winning firms excel at making subtle, complex, but unpredictable moves.

LEARNING OBJECTIVE

2   Explain how and why firms sometimes like to collude

collusion
Collective attempts between competing firms to reduce competition.

tacit collusion
Firms indirectly coordinate actions by signalling their intention to reduce output and maintain pricing above competitive levels.

explicit collusion
Firms directly negotiate output, fix pricing and divide markets.

cartel
An entity that engages in output- and price-fixing, involving multiple competitors.

prisoners' dilemma
In game theory, a type of game in which the outcome depends on two parties deciding whether to cooperate or to defect.

game theory
A theory on how agents interact strategically to win.

COMPETITION AND COLLUSION

Competition is at the core of interaction between firms, and thus the main focus of economic analysis. However, the real world of competition is more ambiguous. 'People of the same trade seldom meet together, even for merriment and diversion,' wrote Adam Smith in *The Wealth of Nations* (1776), 'but their conversation often ends in a conspiracy against the public.' In modern jargon, this means that competing firms in an industry may have an incentive to engage in collusion, defined as collective attempts to reduce competition.

To collude or not to collude?

Collusion can be tacit or explicit. Firms engage in tacit collusion when they indirectly coordinate actions by signalling their intention to reduce output and maintain pricing above competitive levels. Explicit collusion occurs when firms directly negotiate output, pricing, or division of markets. Explicit collusion leads to a cartel – an output- and price-fixing entity involving multiple competitors. As we will discuss in the next section, such collusion is usually illegal.

Collusion, like other strategic decisions, can be a rational decision for a firm.[12] Yet powerful incentives also work to prevent collusion. Chief among these incentives is the prisoners' dilemma.[13] The term 'prisoners' dilemma' is used in game theory (a theory on how agents interact strategically to win) to describe a situation where two prisoners are suspected of a major joint crime (such as burglary), but the police do not have strong evidence. The two prisoners are separately interrogated and told that if either one confesses, the confessor will get a one-year sentence while the other will go to jail for ten years. If neither confesses, both will be convicted of a lesser charge (such as trespassing) and go to jail for two years. If both confess, both will go to jail for ten years. At first glance, the solution seems clear enough. The maximum *joint* payoff would be for neither of them to confess. However, both prisoners have strong incentives to confess – otherwise known as defect.

Translated to an airline setting, Figure 13.1 illustrates the payoff structure for both airlines A and B in a given market, let's say, the connection between Paris and Rome. Assuming a total of 200 passengers, cell 1 represents the ideal outcome for both airlines to maintain the price at €500, and each gets 100 passengers and makes €50 000; the 'industry' revenue reaches €100 000. However, both airlines can increase their own revenues by lowering prices and attracting their competitors' customers. In cell 2, if B maintains its price at €500 while A aggressively drops it to €300, B is likely to lose all customers. Assuming perfectly transparent pricing information on the internet, who would want to pay €500 when they can get a ticket for €300? Thus A may make €60 000 on 200 passengers and B gets nothing. In cell 3, the situation is reversed. In both cells 2 and 3, although the industry *decreases* revenue by 40%, the price drop *increases* the revenues of the firm charging the lower price by 20%. Thus both A and B have strong incentives to reduce price. Yet if both do so simultaneously, they end up in cell 4, where each still gets 100 passengers but with a 40% reduction in revenue. A key insight from this application of game theory is that even if A and B have a prior agreement to fix the price at €500, both still have strong incentives to cheat, thus pulling the industry to the competitive outcome in cell 4 where consumers benefit from lower prices, but both firms are worse off due to lower profits.

However, what happens if the situation remains the same over several periods of time? Of course, in a repeated game both players know the trade-offs in the next period, and that affects their behaviour in the first round. If someone plays 'aggressive' in a repeated game, they can expect to be punished in the next round of the game. This expected punishment, however, can prevent aggressiveness in the first place. Hence if the two airlines in the theoretical example compete in a stable market for many years, they actually have some incentives to accommodate each other, and thus to remain in cell 1, knowing that any attempt to get to the more favourable outcome in cell 2 or 3 would invariably lead them into cell 4 in the next period.

repeated game
A game plays over several periods of time.

Figure 13.1 A prisoners' dilemma for airlines

		Airline A	
		'Accomodative' A keeps price at €500	'Aggressive' A drops price to €300
Airline B	'Accomodative' B keeps price at €500	*(Cell 1)* A: €50 000 B: €50 000	*(Cell 2)* A: €60 000 B: 0
	'Aggressive' A drops price to €300	*(Cell 3)* A: 0 B: €60 000	*(Cell 4)* A: €30 000 B: €30 000

tit-for-tat
A strategy of matching the competitors move being either aggressive or accommodative.

Hence companies can play a game of 'tit-for-tat', which means that they would react aggressively once their opponent plays 'aggressive', but act 'accommodative' when the other acts 'accommodative'.[14] If both firms understand the rules of tit-for-tat, they will play 'accommodate' and thus not deviate from a situation that suits them both. In fact, experiments have shown that in real life situations players do best when they play 'tit-for-tat' but occasionally play 'accommodate' when the other plays 'aggressive' because some actions perceived as aggressive are actually based on misunderstandings, which can unintentionally lead to a path permanent aggressive play from both sides.

Market structure and collusion

concentration ratio
The percentage of total industry sales accounted for by the top four, eight or twenty firms.
price leader
A firm that has a dominant market share and sets 'acceptable' prices and margins in the industry.
capacity to punish
Sufficient resources possessed by a price leader to deter and combat defection.

Given the benefits of collusion and incentives to cheat, which industries are conducive to collusion? Five factors emerge (Table 13.1). The first is the number of firms or, more technically, concentration ratio, the percentage of total industry sales accounted for by the top four, eight, or 20 firms. In general, the higher the concentration, the easier it is to organize collusion.

Second, the existence of a price leader – defined as a firm that has a dominant market share and sets 'acceptable' prices and margins in the industry – helps tacit collusion. The price leader needs to possess the capacity to punish defectors. The most frequently used punishment entails undercutting the defector by flooding the market, thus making the defection fruitless. Such punishment is costly because it brings significant financial losses to the price leader in the short run. The price leader needs to have both willingness and capacity to punish and bear the costs. For example, prior to the 1980s, *GM* played the price leader role in the US automobile industry, announcing in advance the percentage of price increases. Ford and Chrysler would follow; otherwise, *GM* would punish them. More recently, with declining market share, *GM* is no longer able to play this role. Thus the industry has become much more turbulent and competitive.

Third, in an industry with homogeneous products in which rivals are forced to compete on price, it is easier to collude than if everyone offers slightly differentiated products. This is because it is easier to observe whether rivals stick to the agreement. Firms in commodity industries may have stronger incentives to collude because their price competition is often cut-throat, and it is easier to monitor members' compliance with the agreement. In other words, the more transparent the market, the easier it is to identify those who 'cheat' on a collusive agreement. This is a paradox.

Table 13.1   Industry characteristics and possibility of collusion *vis-à-vis* competition

Collusion possible	Examples
Few firms (high concentration)	Sugar, cement
Existence of an industry price leader	US automotive industry in the 1980s (GM as price leader), crude oil (Saudi Arabia)
Homogeneous products	Electricity, steel tubes, railway tracks
High entry barriers	Aircraft, aircraft engines
High market commonality (mutual forbearance)	Brewing in Central and Eastern Europe

Normally, market transparency helps consumers. However, it also helps cartels to quickly identify cheaters, and to increase awareness of potential competitors. For example, price comparison websites set up to help consumers to find the cheapest price for their gas or electricity supplier have the side-effect of facilitating (tacit) collusion between the firms.

Fourth, an industry with high entry barriers for new entrants (such as airlines) is more likely to facilitate collusion than an industry with low entry barriers (such as taxis).[15] New entrants are likely to ignore the existing industry 'order' and to introduce less homogeneous products with newer technologies (in other words, 'disruptive technologies') or different forms of service delivery. As 'mavericks', new entrants 'can be thought of as loose cannons in otherwise tranquil industries'. For example, *Virgin Atlantic* upset the cosy competition in transatlantic air travel between the UK and the USA in the 1990s after overcoming high barriers to enter the industry.

Finally, multimarket competition occurs when firms engage the same rivals in multiple markets. Multimarket firms may respect their rivals' spheres of influence in certain markets, and their rivals may reciprocate, leading to tacit collusion.[16] For example, companies competing in several European countries have reasons not to upset each other too much. If two firms have a high degree of overlap between their markets, this also affects the intensity of rivalry. They are more likely to restrain from aggressively going after each other. Such mutual forbearance primarily stems from (1) deterrence and (2) familiarity. Deterrence is important because under a high degree of market commonality, if a firm attacks in one market, its rivals have the ability to engage in cross-market retaliation, leading to a costly all-out war that the businesses do not really want – though consumers might love the lower prices. Familiarity is the extent to which tacit collusion is enhanced by a firm's awareness of the actions, intentions, and capabilities of rivals.[17] Repeated interactions lead to such familiarity, resulting in more mutual respect. For example, *GE* has tremendous respect for traditional rivals like *Siemens*, *Philips* and *Rolls-Royce*. *GE* knows how to compete with them; they will never destroy *GE*. However, firms from emerging economies, such as *Mindray*, *Goldwind* and *Haier* may introduce new products that create a new price-performance paradigm, and thereby disrupt the patterns of competition.[18]

multimarket competition
Firms engage the same rivals in multiple markets.

market commonality
The overlap between two rivals' markets.

cross-market retaliation
The ability of a firm to expand in a competitor's market if the competitor attacks in its original market.

Cooperation and signalling

Some firms choose to compete and attack, and others choose to cooperate. How can a firm signal its intention to cooperate to *reduce* competitive intensity? Short of illegally talking directly to rivals, firms have to resort to signalling through their actions:

- Firms may enter new markets not really to challenge incumbents but to seek mutual forbearance by establishing multimarket contact. Thus MNEs often chase each other, entering one country after another.[19] For example, across Central and Eastern Europe, the big four global brewing MNEs (*Heineken, SABMiller, AB InBev* and *Carlsberg*) dominate the market in every country.[20] However, in each country, there are only two or three of the big four. They say that they aspire to market leadership in each market in which they compete, and exit those markets where they do not foresee becoming at least number two. This strategy also reduces the intensity of competition compared to a hypothetical market where all four go head-to-head. Similarly, airlines that meet on many routes are often less aggressive than airlines that meet on one or a few routes.[21]

- Firms can send an open signal for a truce. As *GM* faced grave financial difficulties in 2005, *Toyota*'s chairman told the media *twice* that *Toyota* would 'help *GM*' by raising *Toyota* prices in the USA. As far as signalling goes, *Toyota*'s signal could not have been more unambiguous, short of talking directly to *GM*, which would be illegal. *Toyota*, of course, was self-interested. Should GM indeed declare bankruptcy, *Toyota* would attract all the 'machine-gun fire' from protectionist backlash (as indeed happened in 2010). Nevertheless, US anti-trust authorities reportedly took note of *Toyota*'s remarks – they interpreted the message as an invitation to *GM* for price fixing.[22]

- Firms can also use certain pricing schemes that discourage competitors from aggressively underbidding them. In particular, it is legal in many countries to offer a price-match guarantee: 'if you see the same product in the local area for a lower price, we pay you the difference'. Such a strong commitment sends two signals: to consumers it says 'we have the lowest price', to competitors it says 'don't try to compete on price'. And so they don't. Hence the firm can gradually raise prices to the levels of the competitors.

- Sometimes firms can send a signal to rivals by enlisting the help of governments. Because direct negotiations with rivals on what consists of 'fair' pricing are often illegal, holding such discussions is legal under the auspices of government investigations. Thus filing an anti-dumping petition or suing a rival does not necessarily indicate a totally hostile intent. Sometimes, it signals to the other side: 'We don't like what you are doing; it's time to talk.' *Cisco*, for instance, filed anti-dumping complaints against its new rival from China, *Huawei*, but dropped them after both firms negotiated a solution.

- Some alliances and joint ventures may also be used to reduce the competition, for example, when two competitors form a joint venture for their operations in the same industry.[23] Such alliances are however subject to competition policy review, and thus only feasible between non-leading firms in a market.

INSTITUTIONS GOVERNING COMPETITION

LEARNING OBJECTIVE

3 Outline how competition policy and anti-dumping laws affect international competition

competition policy
Policy governing the rules of the game in competition in a country.
anti-trust policy
American term for competition policy.

In their aspiration for market share and profitability, it is important for firms to 'play by the rules'. In particular, collusion to enhance profits is usually against the rules. These rules are set by the legislators to protect consumers and smaller businesses. In the EU, the European Commission is responsible for monitoring and enforcing competition rules for businesses operating across countries, with national authorities retaining responsibility for purely domestic matters (Chapter 8). The institution-based view emphasizes that managers need to be well versed in these rules of the game governing competition.

The formal institutions governing competition are known as competition policy (or anti-trust policy in the US). These institutions shape the mix of competition and cooperation within a market economy.[24] Without competition policy, firms are likely to sooner or later collude, for instance by forming cartels, or agreeing not to invade each other's market. This might be good for corporate profits, but it would be bad for consumers: prices rise.[25] Consumer prices vary considerably across countries (Table 13.2). European consumers often pay higher prices than Americans: for example, British consumers pay the highest prices for agriculture and fishery products, cars and professional products, while Dutch consumers pay most for drugs and for petrol. Competition policy is probably a major cause of such differences (though probably not the only one), and the authorities have been getting tougher in enforcing the

Table 13.2 International price comparisons (ratio of domestic retail prices to world market prices)

	Australia	Canada	Germany	Japan	Netherlands	UK	US
Agriculture and fisheries	**1.067**	1.112	1.529	1.584	1.080	*1.648*	1.158
Processed food	**1.086**	1.192	1.447	*2.099*	1.299	1.202	1.090
Textiles	1.111	1.163	1.101	*1.478*	1.140	1.237	**1.051**
Printing and publishing	1.120	1.205	1.024	1.186	*1.342*	1.029	**1.005**
Drugs and medicines	**1.001**	2.680	2.643	1.217	*3.349*	1.845	3.105
Petroleum and coal	2.127	1.320	2.847	3.359	*4.335*	4.067	**1.007**
Motor vehicles	1.224	1.197	1.315	**1.000**	1.648	*1.680*	1.106
Professional goods	1.125	1.082	1.379	1.077	1.369	*1.586*	**1.074**
Weighted means	1.266	1.270	1.539	*1.567*	1.541	1.480	**1.118**

Note: Bold typeface indicates the lowest price in this category; *italics* indicate the highest price in this category.

Source: OECD, 2004, Product market competition and economic performance in the United States (p. 14), Economics Department working paper no. 398, Paris: OECD.

Table 13.3 EU competition policy

Fairness of competition	Creation and protection of competition
• Price fixing cartels • Market dividing agreements • Anti-competitive practices by dominant firms	• Mergers and acquisitions (Chapter 14) • Liberalization of regulated or state-controlled industries (Chapter 8) • Limits on subsidies from states to firms (Chapter 8)

rules. Here we focus on (1) collusion to raise prices, (2) collusion to divide markets, and (3) anti-competitive practices by dominating a market (Table 13.3).

First, classic cartels of the 19th and early 20th century included agreements between major companies to keep prices in a given market at a higher than competitive level. Such collusive price setting has been outlawed in many countries. By the end of the 20th century, trade liberalization had opened many formerly protected markets, which created new motivations for firms to collude across borders.[26] Competition watchdogs in Europe and North America reacted to this trend by increasing their collaboration to investigate international cartels.[27] The largest cartel ever convicted was the global vitamin cartel in operation in the 1990s. It involved four firms that controlled more than 75% of worldwide production: (1) *Hoffman-La Roche* of Switzerland, (2) *BASF* of Germany, (3) *Rhône-Poulenc* of France (now *Aventis*), and (4) *Eisai* of Japan. Its discovery led to numerous convictions and fines by US, EU, Canadian, Australian and South Korean competition authorities. The victims were vitamin consumers around the world, paying on average 30% to 40% more. The total illegal profits were estimated to be $9 to $12 billion, of which 15% accrued in the USA and 26% in the EU. Firms and managers in this conspiracy paid a heavy price: worldwide, firms paid record fines of almost €4 billion.[28]

collusive price setting
Price setting by monopolists or collusion parties at a higher than competitive level.

In the EU, the position of Competition Commissioner has become one of the most powerful positions in Brussels. Recent office holders Mario Monti (Italy), Neelie Kroes (Netherlands), Joaquín Almunia (Spain), and, since 2014, Margarethe Vestager (Denmark) have taken on some of the biggest names in business. In parallel, national authorities continue to investigate collusion of firms with their national boundaries, for example, in Germany the Kartellamt has investigated and penalized firms in a wide range of industries (In Focus 13.2).

When regulators catch companies colluding at the costs of consumers, punishments tend to be severe. In countries such as the USA, the UK and Ireland, not only companies are fined, but individuals involved in the price fixing can receive personal fines and jail sentences. How are cartels that operate in secrecy caught? Both the EU and the USA have 'leniency programmes' that take advantage of the prisoners' dilemma discussed earlier: under certain circumstances, firms that are first to report a cartel (and thus 'defect' from the collusion) get a lesser punishment than others caught in the same cartel. This increases the incentives for members of a cartel to cheat on each other, and hence makes it less likely that cartels are established in the

leniency programme
A programme that gives immunity to members of a cartel that first report the cartel to the authorities.

IN FOCUS 13.2

Caught colluding in Germany

The German competition authorities, known as Kartellamt, have been busy cartel busting, claiming the scalps of some of the biggest names in German and international business. In 2014, they fined 67 businesses and 80 individuals a record €1.01 billion. Some of these cartels have been operating for many years, and the investigations by the Kartellamt stretched over several years, as proof of collusion is often hard to construct. High profile cases concern consumer goods like beer, sugar, coffee and sausages, as well as industrial goods like cement, steel tubes and railway tracks. The office investigates not only market power by sellers, but also by buyers. For example, supermarkets – where the four largest chains control 85% of the market – have been investigated for abusing their buyer power to the detriment of their suppliers, including farmers.

If found guilty, penalties can be stiff. The Kartellamt works on the presumption that stiff penalties have a deterrent effect. For example, the beer cartel involved some of the largest brewers in Germany, both domestic and international players. Since the German beer market is more fragmented than other European markets, brewers in Germany tend to be a bit frustrated that their profit margins are lower than elsewhere in Europe. Yet collusion eventually backfired. According

to investigations, the collusion increased the price of beer by €1 per crate of 24. Fines totalling €340 million were levied against 11 breweries, including market leaders *Carlsberg* and *Radeberger* as well as numerous smaller regional breweries. *Beck's* (owned by *AB-InBev*) benefited from the leniency programme, and got away penalty-free. A similarly large total of fines was levied against the 21 members of the sausage cartel (€338 million).

However, the legal troubles of the cartel are not over with the payment of a fine. Customers who can prove that they have incurred financial losses can sue the cartel members for compensation. For example, in the railway track case, *Deutsche Bahn* (Germany's railway network operator) obtained compensation of about €150 million from *Thyssen-Krupp* and €50 million from *Voest-Alpine*. In the sugar case, sweets, cookie and bread manufacturers were preparing to sue the cartel, and experts estimated that the compensation could be as high as €3 billion – ten times the fine imposed by the Kartellamt!

Sources: (1) *Frankfurter Allgemeine Zeitung*, 2014, Ein Euro zu viel je Kasten Bier, April 2; (2) *Frankfurter Allgemeine Zeitung*, 2014, Das Amt will die Supermärkte bändigen, September 24; (3) *Frankfurter Allgemeine Zeitung*, 2014, July 19; Das Wurstkartell zockte die Verbraucher bei Aldi ab; (4) Bundeskartellamt, 2014, Jahresrückblick, press release, December 23; (5) V. Vottsmeier, C. Kapalschinski & K. Ludowig, 2015, Bitterer Nachgeschmack, *Handelsblatt*, March 20 (p. 1 & 6).

first place.[29] For example, in the lifts and escalators cartel in the Benelux countries, *Kone* of Finland was first to come forward and received immunity for Belgium and Luxembourg, whereas *Otis* of the USA received immunity with respect to the cartel in the Netherlands. Even so, the Commission imposed the largest cartel fines ever – a total of €992 million. The largest share, €480 million, was borne by *ThyssenKrupp* of Germany.[30] In addition to these fines, the companies faced indirect costs from legal and consulting fees, the pressure on management time, and the negative publicity. Hence if you are colluding and fear being caught, it actually pays to be the first to 'blow the whistle'. Moreover, once under investigation, it pays to collaborate early with the regulators!

In contrast, regulators in emerging economies often have neither the capabilities to investigate cartels, nor the legal means to punish wrongdoing. For example, in Mexico, the authorities had to give notice to targets of their investigations before conducting a search – you can guess how much evidence they found. Also, the maximum penalty was limited to about €5 million – compared with 10% of the offender's sales in the EU. Thus, for a long time, collusion in Mexico has been profitable even if it was detected. This abnormality was corrected with new laws in 2010; mobile phone operator *Telcel* was one of the first to be caught, receiving a fine of almost €1 billion for abuse of a dominant market position. This signalled a shift in the policies and enforcement regarding competition, though law enforcement often remains an uphill struggle.[31] Similarly, other emerging economies like Brazil[32] and China[33] have been getting tougher on colluding businesses.

Second, in market division collusion, companies may divide markets between each other. This is a major concern in Europe, because many market leaders have traditionally dominated their home market, and the option of invading each other's home market emerged only when the single European market came into effect in 1993. Moreover, it is difficult for an outsider to objectively assess whether two companies stay out of each other's home market because they lack the capability to compete in that market, or because of (tacit) collusion. Even so, the European Commission has prosecuted a number of cases. For example, *Carlsberg* and *Heineken* fiercely compete in many countries, but they stayed out of each other's home markets, Denmark and the Netherlands respectively, until the Commission intervened. In another case, the Commission fined gas suppliers *E.ON* (Germany) and *Gaz de France* (France) €553 million *each* because they had agreed to divide markets, i.e. not to sell gas in the partner's home market.[34]

market division collusion
A collusion to divide markets amongst competitors.

Third, dominant players in a particular market may use anti-competitive practices to inhibit competition, in particular by using their market power to dominate related markets, or raise barriers to entry for potential competitors. For example, it sounds fairly reasonable that a food manufacturer offering a retailer a free display freezer stipulates that this freezer may be used exclusively for products of this manufacturer and not for competitors' products. However, if this manufacturer is the sole supplier of certain goods, then this tactic allows a dominant firm to keep out potential challengers. Dutch-British food MNE *Unilever* used to provide display freezers to small shops in Ireland at low/no costs, provided that the freezers were used exclusively for *Unilever*-made ice creams. This exclusivity agreement inhibited the entry into the Irish ice cream market by *Mars*, a US confectionary producer. *Mars* complained to the competition authorities, and the European Commission eventually decided in its favour, declaring the exclusivity agreement an anti-competitive practice of a dominant firm. This decision was upheld by the European Court of Justice (ECJ), and *Unilever* eventually had to pay *Mars* compensation.[35]

anti-competitive practices (by a dominant firm)
Business practices by a dominating firm that make it more difficult for competitors to enter or survive.

Anti-competitive practices by dominant players are a major issue in industries where one firm controls a crucial element of the infrastructure, such as telecommunications, software and internet services. For example, the Commission argued that

Deutsche Telekom was using its control of telecom networks in Germany to inhibit potential entrants competing with its telecom operations business. Specifically, the price that *Deutsche Telekom* charged other operators for the use of the network was too high, according to a ruling of the Commission.[36] Another focus of Commission investigation has been various information technology sectors (see Closing Case). In several such cases, the EU has taken a tougher interpretation of what constitutes an anti-competitive practice by a dominant firm than US courts did in comparable cases.[37]

predatory pricing
An attempt to monopolize a market by setting prices below cost and intending to raise prices to cover losses in the long run after eliminating rivals.

A related practice is predatory pricing, defined as (1) setting prices below cost, *and* (2) intending to raise prices to cover losses in the long run after eliminating rivals ('an attempt to monopolize'). In a rare case in the 1990s, British bus company

IN FOCUS 13.3

Is anti-dumping discriminatory?

To most people, 'fair competition' also implies that governments play 'fair' and don't use legal tricks, such as dumping investigations, to prevent foreign entry. However, the actual practice of anti-dumping raises considerable concerns. Anti-dumping cases are usually filed by a domestic firm with the relevant domestic government authorities. In the US, these authorities would then request comprehensive, proprietary data on their cost and pricing, in English, using US generally accepted accounting principles (GAAP), within 45 days. Many foreign defendants fail to provide such data on time because they are not familiar with US GAAP. The investigation can have the four following outcomes:

- If no data are forthcoming from abroad, the data provided by the accusing firm become the evidence, and the accusing firm can easily win.

- If foreign firms do provide data, the accusing firm can still challenge their validity. For example, in the case of Louisiana versus Chinese crayfish growers, the authenticity of the $9 *per week* salary of Chinese workers was a major point of contention.

- Even if the low-cost data are verified, US and EU anti-dumping laws allow the complainant to argue that these data are not 'fair'. In the case of China, the argument goes, its cost data reflect huge distortions due to government intervention, because China is still a 'non-market' economy; the wage may be low, but workers may be

provided with low-cost housing and benefits subsidized by the government. The crayfish case thus boiled down to how much it would cost to raise hypothetical crayfish in a market economy (in this particular case, Spain was mysteriously chosen). Because Spanish costs were about the same as Louisiana costs, the Chinese, despite their vehement objections, were found guilty of dumping in America by selling below *Spanish* costs. Thus 110% to 123% import duties were levied on Chinese crayfish.

- The fourth possible outcome is that the defendant wins the case. But this happens in only 5% of the anti-dumping cases in the USA.

Simply filing an anti-dumping petition (regardless of the outcome), one study finds, may result in a 1% increase of the stock price for US-listed firms. Evidently, Wall Street expects 'Uncle Sam' to be on the side of US businesses. It is thus not surprising that anti-dumping cases have proliferated throughout the world. Joseph Stiglitz, a Nobel laureate in economics and then chief economist of the World Bank, wrote that anti-dumping duties 'are simply naked protectionism' and one country's 'fair trade laws' are often known elsewhere as 'unfair trade laws'.

Sources: (1) S. Marsh, 1998, Creating barriers for foreign competitors, *SMJ*, 19: 25–37; (2) T. Prusa, 2001, On the spread and impact of anti-dumping (p. 598), *CJE*, 34: 591–611; (3) J. Stiglitz, 2002, *Globalization and Its Discontent* (p. 172–173), New York: Norton; (4) J. Lindeque, 2007, A firm perspective of anti-dumping and countervailing duty cases in the United States, *JWT*, 41: 559–579.

Stagecoach was found guilty of predatory pricing when it offered free rides on certain lines where it had a serious competitor, and not on others. However, it is difficult to prove predatory pricing. First, it is not exactly clear what 'cost' is. Second, even when firms are found to be selling below cost, courts would want to see evidence that the initially incurred loss will subsequently be recovered, which is hard to provide. These two legal tests have made it extremely difficult to win a predation case within the EU or in the USA.

However, the argument prevails in international trade. Foreign competitors competing on price often find themselves accused of 'dumping', which is defined as (1) an exporter selling below cost abroad, and (2) planning to raise prices after eliminating local rivals. Many countries have rules that allow investigation of dumping allegations, and the introduction of anti-dumping duties (see Chapter 5) designed to increase the price to the presumed fair price. However, these rules are often used (some would say abused) for protectionist purposes (In Focus 13.3). An OECD study in Australia, Canada, the EU and the US reports that 90% of the practices found to be unfairly dumping in these countries would never have been questioned under their own anti-trust laws if used by a domestic firm in making a domestic sale.[38]

dumping
An exporter selling below cost abroad and planning to raise prices after eliminating local rivals.

In addition to collusion and anti-competitive practices, EU competition policy also covers issues discussed elsewhere in this book: the control of mergers and acquisitions (Chapter 14), state aid and liberalization of regulated industries (Chapter 8). Competition policy is often a subject of bitter disputes between businesses and the regulators, be they national or at the EU level. Businesses complain that the procedures are too bureaucratic, and that they cannot be challenged sufficiently in independent courts.[39] On the other hand, consumers feel that MNEs still have too much market power to dictate prices, especially in utilities such as telecommunications, gas supplies and transport.

RESOURCES INFLUENCING COMPETITION

A number of resource-based imperatives, informed by the VRIO framework outlined in Chapter 4, drive decisions and actions associated with competitive dynamics. The key question is whether the firm has sufficient resources to engage in a competitive battle.

LEARNING OBJECTIVE

4 Articulate how resources and capabilities influence competitive dynamics

Value-creation

Firm resources must create value when engaging rivals in dynamic competition. To stay ahead in the competition, moreover, a firm has to create more value for its customers than its competitors do. Otherwise, customers will defect to the rival – no matter how shrewd a competitive game is played. In addition, firms may need resources to persevere in a competitive battle. For example, the ability to attack in multiple markets – of the sort *Apple* and *Samsung* possessed when launching their smartphones in numerous countries simultaneously – throws rivals off balance, thus adding value. Likewise, the ability to rapidly lower prices depends on the availability of resources.[40] Another example of a strong resource is a dominant position in key markets (such as flights in and out of London Heathrow by *British Airways*). Similarly, Saudi Arabia's vast oil reserves enable it to become the enforcer (price leader) of OPEC cartel agreements. Such a strong sphere of influence poses a credible threat to rivals, who understand that the firm will defend its core markets vigorously.

Rarity

Either by nature or nurture (or both), certain assets are very rare, thus generating significant advantage in competitive dynamics. Dubai Airport, the home base of *Emirates* (Opening Case), has a rare advantage over other airports striving to be hubs for intercontinental long-distance flights: it is conveniently located between Europe and Asia, it faces few constraints to expansion because the surrounding area is essentially desert, and it faces few constraints on night flights. Airports elsewhere, such as London Heathrow or Paris Charles de Gaulle, face more constraint due to their proximity to big cities and local political opposition to expansion and night flights. By using Dubai as a home base, *Emirates* has a rare geographic advantage that *British Airways* or *Air France* cannot imitate, because they cannot easily change their global hubs.

Imitability

Most rivals watch each other and probably have a fairly comprehensive (although not necessarily accurate) picture of how their rivals compete. However, the next hurdle lies in how to imitate successful rivals. It is well known that fast-moving rivals tend to perform better.[41] Even when armed with this knowledge, competitively passive and slow-moving firms will find it difficult to imitate rivals' actions. Many major airlines have sought to imitate successful discount carriers, such as *Southwest* and *Ryanair*, but failed.

Another barrier to imitation is patenting, which is a particularly effective means of preventing the imitation of the products created by rivals. Patents provide rights to technology that may be value-creating. Whoever is first to patent a new technology can prevent others from imitating the technology. Thus firms are expanding their scale and scope of patenting, resulting in a 'patent race'.[42] Yet according to some estimates, only about 5% of patents end up having any economic value.[43] So why do firms spend so much money on the patent race (on average, half a million dollars in R&D for one patent)? The answer is in part defensive and competitive. The proliferation of patents makes it very easy for one firm to unwittingly infringe on rivals' patents. When being challenged, a firm without a defensive portfolio of patents is at a severe disadvantage: it has to pay its rivals for using their patents. On the other hand, a firm with strong patents can challenge rivals for their infringements, thus making it easier to reach some understanding – or mutual forbearance. Patents thus become a valuable weapon in fighting off rivals (In Focus 13.4).

patent race
A competition of R&D units where the one first to patent a new technology gets to dominate a market.

IN FOCUS 13.4

Patent lawsuits: competing in the courts

The number of patent lawsuits has skyrocketed. In the hotly contested smartphone arena, *Apple* sued *Samsung*, *Nokia* and *HTC* for patent violations. In retaliation, *Samsung*, *Nokia* and *HTC* countersued *Apple* for patent violations. *Kodak* also sued *Apple* and *Blackberry*. *Oracle* and *Xerox* sued *Google*. Hardly a week goes by without a new lawsuit in 'patent wars'. Worldwide, *Apple* and *Samsung* fought over 20 cases in nine countries, which not only include the USA and South Korea, but also Australia, Britain, France, Germany, Italy, Japan and the Netherlands. In the USA, *Apple* won a $1 billion ruling in its favour. But its home court advantage did not go very far. *Samsung* appealed and was able to reduce the damages to $290 million. In another US lawsuit, *Apple* won $120 million in damages. However, *Samsung* won favourable rulings in South Korea, Japan and Britain. In South Korea, *Apple* was found to infringe on two *Samsung* patents, while *Samsung* was found to violate one *Apple* patent. The court awarded small damages to *Samsung*. In Japan, *Samsung* was not found to violate *Apple*'s patents, and *Apple* had to reimburse *Samsung*'s legal costs. In Britain, *Samsung* won. *Apple* was required to publish a statement on its own website and in the media that *Samsung* did not violate *Apple*'s intellectual property.

In many rapidly evolving industries, inadvertently tripping over someone else's patents is a real danger. The open secret, according to *The Economist*, is that 'everyone infringes everyone else's patents in some way'. This creates an incentive for firms to engage in an 'arms race' in filing and hoarding patents. In patent wars, patents are both defensive and offensive weapons.

Contrary to popular thinking, many patents are not truly novel and non-obvious. In 2006, *Business-Week* opined that the USA was 'awash in a sea of junk patents'. This over-patenting costs firms a lot of money: on average, one patent costs half a million dollars. However, strategically patenting a portfolio of inventions around some core technologies allows firms to gain an upper hand in patent lawsuits and negotiations. Patent lawsuits are becoming very predictable. Firm A sues Firm B for patent infringement. B digs through its own patent portfolio and discovers that some of its own patents are infringed by A. So B countersues A. To avoid costly and mutually destructive exchange of lawsuits, they eventually reach cross-licensing deals that, after exchanging small sums of money, give each other the rights to the patents.

But here is a catch: to be a party to such exchange, a firm needs to have a sufficiently large hoard of patents. Prior to 2011, *Google* had only 307 mobile-related patents. As a result, *Google* was vulnerable when compared with *Blackberry*'s 3134 mobile-related patents, *Nokia*'s 2655, and *Microsoft*'s 2594. That was a key reason behind *Google*'s $12.5 billion purchase of *Motorola Mobility*, a handset maker that was losing money. *Google* was not really interested in the handset business. Instead, it was buying *Motorola*'s hoard of over 1000 mobile-related patents. *Google* sold the handset business to *Lenovo* shortly thereafter, but kept most of the patents.

Less predictable but no less damaging effects of this obsession with patenting are attacks by patent 'sharks' (or 'trolls'). Trolls are patent-holding individuals or (often small) firms that sue manufacturers for patent infringement in order to receive damage awards for the illegitimate use of trolls' patents. Traditionally, such 'non-operating entities' would license their patents to manufacturers that would pay a licensing fee. But many trolls hope to be infringed and thus keep patents as invisible as possible until the patents are used by unsuspecting manufacturers. Trolls then pounce in surprise attacks, demanding compensation exceeding what they would reasonably expect from real licensing fees up front.

In 1990, individual inventor Jerome Lemelson sued toymaker *Mattel* for infringing a coupling technology used in toy trucks. Although the court determined that *Mattel* inadvertently (not wilfully) infringed Lemelson's patent, the court nevertheless awarded him $24 million – which is a lot of toy trucks! Most experts agreed that if Lemelson and *Mattel* had negotiated up front, Lemelson would not have been able to extract a licensing fee close to this astronomical sum. Such cases have motivated a lot of trolls. Although ethically dubious, such a strategy is not only profitable but also perfectly legal. 'Operating entities' (manufacturers), especially high-tech ones, are well advised to prepare for shark attacks. Beefing up patent law expertise has become a crucial institution-based capability.

Sources: (1) *BusinessWeek*, 2006, The patent epidemic, January 9: 60–62; (2) M. Reitzig, J. Henkel & C. Heath, 2007, On sharks, trolls, and their patent prey, *Research Policy*, 36: 134–154; (3) *The Economist*, 2010, The great patent battle, October 23; (4) *Bloomberg Businessweek*, 2011, Android's dominance is patent pending, August 8; (5) *The Economist*, 2011, Inventive warfare, August 20; (6) *The Economist*, 2012, iPhone, uCopy, iSue, September 1; (7) *Bloomberg Businessweek*, 2012, Apple vs. Samsung: The longer view, September 3; (8) W. Watkins, 2014, *Patent Trolls*, Washington DC: Independent Institute.

Organization

Some firms are better organized for competitive actions, such as stealth attacks and willingness to answer challenges 'tit-for-tat'. The intense 'warrior-like' culture not only requires top management commitment but also employee involvement down to the 'soldiers in the trenches'. It is such a self-styled 'wolf' culture that has propelled *Huawei* from China to become *Eriksson*'s and *Cisco*'s leading challenger. It is difficult for slow-moving firms to suddenly wake up and become more aggressive.[44]

On the other hand, more centrally coordinated firms may be better mutual for-bearers than firms whose units are loosely controlled. For an MNE competing with rivals across many countries, a mutual forbearance strategy requires some units, out of respect for rivals' sphere of influence, to sacrifice their maximum market gains by withholding some efforts. Of course, such coordination helps other units with dominant market positions to maximize performance, thus helping the MNE as a whole. Successfully carrying out such mutual forbearance calls for organizational reward systems and structures (such as those concerning bonuses and promotions) that encourage cooperation between units. Conversely, if a firm has competitive reward systems and structures (for example, bonuses linked to unit performance), unit managers may be unwilling to give up market gains for the greater benefits of other units and the whole firm, thus undermining mutual forbearance.[45]

DEBATES AND EXTENSIONS

LEARNING OBJECTIVE

5 Participate in leading
   debates concerning
   competition

Competition is relatively easy when new markets are opening up, waiting to be conquered. However, markets do not always grow, sometimes they shrink. The global recession that followed the financial crisis in 2008 raised awareness of the fast changing nature of competition. We here discuss (1) survival strategies, (2) long-term strategic thinking and (3) competition against overwhelming rivals.

Survival strategies

survival strategy
A strategy designed to ensure survival by ensuring liquidity and positive cash flow.

During a recession, rather than seeking to outgrow their rivals, firm first and foremost are concerned about their own survival. Competition is much harder in shrinking markets.[46] Survival strategies focus on liquidity and the immediate preservation of resources.[47] For example, during a credit crunch, companies find it more difficult to raise capital by borrowing from the banks or by raising equity. Hence retention of cash flow becomes a priority. Similarly, a slump in demand requires firms to adjust their output to cut costs or to focus on markets that are likely to be resilient (Table 13.4).

What are people and businesses likely to do *more* of during a recession? Reflecting over this question points to business opportunities during the recession. For example, in the 'value for money' segment of consumer goods, retailers such as *Asda* and *Primark* in the UK, and *Aldi* and *Lidl* in Germany reported substantive sales growth during the 2008 recession. Likewise, manufacturers focus on 'value for money' products.[48] This may involve innovations that aim not at modifying products, but at production processes and business models that deliver almost the same benefits to customers at much lower costs.[49] In business-to-business markets, suppliers face customers tightening their budgets. For example, if IT budgets are cut by 25%, while 70% of the budget is spent on maintenance, then only 5% of the budget is available for new acquisitions of hardware or software. Thus opportunities for IT service providers like *SAP* or *Microsoft* are very limited, unless they can help their customers to save costs elsewhere in the organization.

Another industry that tends to be fairly resilient to economic downturns is entertainment. People may spend less on long-distance travel and expensive days

Table 13.4 Resilient strategies

Opportunity	Examples	Challenging decisions
Low-cost retail	Discount supermarkets for food and clothing	Is it worthwhile going downmarket, thus taking the risk of downgrading the brand?
Basic needs goods	Non-branded consumer goods, foods	How can we innovate to deliver essentials at lower costs?
Help customers save costs	IT system providers, energy saving technologies	How can we convince customers that recession is a good time to invest?
Career breaks	Education, especially post-experience programmes, gap-year travel, social work	How can we invest in new programmes when our customers' budgets are tight?
Entertainment	Domestic tourism, home entertainment, take-away food, sports	How can we develop 'budget' services during a recession by preparing to go upmarket when the economy picks up?

out, but they are substituting such activities with stay-at-home entertainment. This creates opportunities for businesses that provide for an enjoyable day at home, or nearby. Survival strategies thus include focus on consumer experiences such as sports (both spectator and participant), video games, children's toys, take-aways and ready-to-eat meals (substituting for days eating out). Similarly, tourism may suffer from a decline of long-distance travel, but benefits from people returning to domestic tourism sites. In the recession of 2008, British hotels reported brisk trading: not only did the British seek nearby tourist spots for their holidays, but the depreciation of the British pound made Britain cheaper for foreign visitors.

Resilient strategies also target people who wish to use their involuntary career break (more commonly known as unemployment) in a useful way. In particular, they may invest in their own future and enrol for education programmes, especially mid-career programmes (such as an MBA), and career-preparing programmes (such as MSc). Thus applications for all sorts of university courses went up in 2009, creating growth opportunities for entrepreneurial higher education institutions.

Long-term strategies and strategic positioning

Survival strategies may achieve just that – survival – but not prosperity in the longer term. Like farmers using the winter to fix their tools for the next spring, businesses have to think ahead – even during a deep crisis – to use the downturn to position themselves for the next upswing. For example, *Renishaw*, a British engineering company specializing in precision measurement systems, continued to invest in R&D during the crisis of 2008, while laying off half of its 2000-strong workforce and cutting salaries by 20%. By 2009, its turnover grew by 17% on the basis of its R&D investment.[50]

Entrepreneurs may view a crisis as an opportunity. They ask, how are we going to benefit from the next economic upswing? How can we take advantage of rivals that drop out – headhunting their best people, invading their markets, or acquiring the bankrupt business? These questions resemble those you may have asked yourself when choosing your course at university: what skills will be in demand in a few years when you graduate? These questions concern the strategic positioning of the firm (or yourself) during the next economic cycle. Answering these questions, however, requires a vision of what the market will be like in the future.

Conventionally, businesses try to look into the future by economic forecasting. This approach employs complex econometric models that incorporate estimated relationships between key variables, and extrapolations of trends. These models generate point estimates of the most likely future state of the world, along with a range ('confidence interval') in which the actual outcome will be with, say, 90% probability. In a stable environment, such forecasts provide reasonably good guidance for decision-makers. However, forecasts may be insufficient in highly volatile environments. Indeed, the precision of point estimates can be misleading. For example, a crisis may induce people to change their shopping habits, which changes key parameters in the econometric model. Therefore, forecasts are usually not very good at predicting when trends change, and they provide few insights into the range of possible developments.

An alternative is scenario planning.[51] Scenario approaches emphasize uncertainty and the range of *possible* outcomes rather than focusing on the *most likely* outcome. Scenario planning brings together a diverse set of experts to speculate about the future, generate ideas, and then to condense these ideas into 'scenarios' capturing key variations. The experts would aim to identify the dimensions that are most crucial for shaping the future of the industry (see Chapter 9 Closing Case for an example). Different combinations allow envisaging possible future states of the world. For example, at the onset of the financial crisis in 2008, consultants *McKinsey* developed possible scenarios for the world economy in 2010 along the dimensions of 'severe *versus* moderate global recession' and 'global credit and capital markets reopen and recover *versus* close down and remain volatile'.[52] Discussing the scenarios with internal and external experts may be as important as the written-up scenarios: this process provides decision-makers with insights into the factors likely to be important in the future. Other scenarios look even further into the future, such as those developed by *Wärtsilä* for the global energy industry.

Scenarios serve several purposes. First, they create a mindset aware of the nature of uncertainty, framing the future in terms of possibilities rather than probabilities. Decision-makers – as well as those who have to implement decisions – thus are mentally and practically prepared for having to change their course of action at short notice. Second, they provide a basis for assessing the robustness of alternative strategies.[53] Businesses would want their strategies to generate profitable operations under most of the likely scenarios. Hence assessing the likely outcomes of proposed strategies under a set of alternative scenarios provides insights in their robustness.

Third, scenarios provide a basis for contingency plans that may be implemented when certain events happen or benchmarks are reached. Contingency plans allow preparation for both offensive as well as defensive actions, and may address questions such as, what acquisitions might be attractive on what terms? What new products might be launched under different scenarios? Which conditions would trigger a market exit, and how can an exit be managed while minimizing losses?

Local firms versus big MNEs

Some firms face competitors that are much bigger than themselves, yet sometimes they win. How is that possible?[54] They can adopt four strategic postures depending on (1) the industry conditions, and (2) the nature of their firm's competitive assets. Shown in Figure 13.2, these factors suggest four strategic actions.[55]

---

economic forecasting
A technique using econometric models to predict the likely future value of key economic variables.

scenario planning
A technique generating multiple scenarios of possible future states of the industry.

contingency plans
Plans devised for specific situations when things could go wrong.

Figure 13.2 How local firms may respond to MNE actions

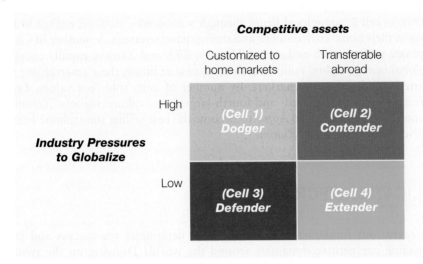

Source: N. Dawar & T. Frost, 1999, Competing with giants: Survival strategies for local companies in emerging markets (p. 122), *HBR*, March–April: 119–129.

In Cell 3, in some industry segments, the pressures to globalize are relatively low, and local firms' strengths lie in a deep understanding of local markets. Therefore, a defender strategy, which leverages local assets in areas in which MNEs are weak, is often called for. For example, in Israel, facing an onslaught from MNE cosmetics firms, a number of local firms turned to focus on products suited to the Middle Eastern climate and managed to defend their turf. *Ahava* has been particularly successful, in part because of its unique components extracted from the Dead Sea that MNEs cannot find elsewhere.[56] In essence, a defender strategy is making the best of local resources to compete in domestic and regional markets where the local firm has unique advantages that allow it to stay ahead of its foreign competitors. Even in highly global industries such as brewing, local firms may find a niche market where they can avoid head-on competition with the global players. For example, *Innis & Gunn*, a Scottish speciality brewer, grew to sell 500 000 cases of bottled ale a year within five years after foundation. Yet it isn't even brewing the beer itself – the brewing is outsourced to one of the large brewers. *Innis & Gunn* solely focuses on building and selling the brand. It found a niche market where it can compete, and even export.[57]

defender strategy
This strategy centres on leveraging local assets in areas in which MNEs are weak.

In cell 4, in some industries with less pressure for globalization, local firms may possess skills and assets that are transferable overseas, thus leading to an extender strategy. This strategy centres on leveraging home-grown competencies abroad. For instance, *Asian Paints* controls 40% of the house paint market in India. *Asian Paints* developed strong capabilities tailored to the unique environment in India, characterized by thousands of small retailers serving numerous poor consumers, who only want small quantities of paint that can be diluted to save money. Such capabilities are not only a winning formula in India, but also in much of the developing world.

extender strategy
This strategy centres on leveraging home-grown competencies abroad.

Cell 1 depicts a most difficult situation for local firms that compete in industries with high pressures for globalization. Thus a dodger strategy is necessary, which involves some form of collaboration. For example, local firms may cooperate through joint ventures (JVs) with MNEs and sell-offs to MNEs. In the Chinese automobile industry, *all* major local automakers have entered JVs with MNEs. The essence of this strategy is that to the extent that local firms are unable to successfully

dodger strategy
This strategy centres on cooperating through joint ventures (JVs) with MNEs and sell-offs to MNEs.

contender strategy
This strategy centres
on a firm engaging in
rapid learning and then
expanding overseas.

compete head on against MNEs, cooperation becomes necessary. In other words, if you can't beat them, join them!

Finally, in cell 2, some local firms, through a contender strategy, engage in rapid learning in their home environment and then expand overseas. A number of Chinese smartphone makers, such as *Lenovo, Huawei, ZTE* and *Xiaomi*, rapidly caught up with global heavyweights. Following their success at home, these smartphone makers started entering foreign markets. By number of units sold (not value), *Lenovo* and *Huawei* are now the third- and fourth-largest smartphone makers. *Xiaomi* has dethroned both *Samsung* and *Apple* to become the best-selling smartphone brand in China (see Integrative Case '*Xiaomi*').

IMPLICATIONS FOR PRACTICE

LEARNING OBJECTIVE

6 Draw implications
   for action

Let us revisit our fundamental question: what determines the success and failure in managing competitive dynamics around the world? Drawing on the two core perspectives (institution- and resource-based views), we suggest that to successfully manage competitive dynamics, managers not only need to become masters of manoeuvres (both confrontation and cooperation) but also experts in government regulations if they aspire to successfully navigate the global landscape.

Consequently, three clear implications for action emerge for managers (Table 13.5). First, managers need to understand their competitors, and how they are likely to react to any competitive move. The reaction depends on the competitor's awareness, motivation and capability, but also on their ability to use the institutional context to their advantage.

Second, managers need to understand how the rules of the game governing competition vary around the world, and how they can use these rules to their advantage. For example, if you are drawn into collusion with a competitor, or you discover someone else in your company is, it is important to understand the nature of leniency programmes: often it pays to get out quickly and report your collaborators to the authorities; otherwise you may face very large fines indeed. Likewise, in antidumping cases or patent protection, firms with capabilities in managing legal processes and interactions with the regulatory authorities are often one step ahead of their competitors.

Third, managers need to strengthen their capabilities to more effectively compete and/or cooperate. In attacks and counterattacks, subtlety, frequency, complexity and unpredictability are often helpful to improve a firm's market position. In cooperation, market similarity and mutual forbearance may be better. As Sun Tzu advised 2500 years ago, you, as a manager, need to 'know yourself' – including your unit, your firm and your industry.

Table 13.5 Implications for action

- Analyze your competitor to be able to predict likely reactions and counterattacks.
- Understand the rules of the game governing domestic and international competition around the world.
- Strengthen resources and capabilities that more effectively compete and/or cooperate.

CHAPTER SUMMARY

1 Explain how attacks and counterattacks are used in dynamic competition

- Attackers need to consider possible counterattacks, which are driven by (1) awareness, (2) motivation, and (3) capability.

2 Explain how and why firms sometimes like to collude

- Collusion may enable firms to collectively earn higher return at the expense of their customers and/or suppliers.

- Industries primed for collusion tend to have (1) a smaller number of rivals, (2) a price leader, (3) homogeneous products, (4) high entry barriers, and (5) high market commonality.

- Without talking directly to competitors, firms can signal to rivals by various means.

3 Outline how competition policy and anti-dumping laws affect international competition

- Competition policies outlaw (1) price-raising cartels, (2) division of markets, and (3) anti-competitive practices by dominant firms.

- Internationally, anti-dumping laws discriminate against foreign firms and protect domestic firms.

4 Articulate how resources and capabilities influence competitive dynamics

- Resources meeting the VRIO criteria are necessary for long-term success in a competitive battle.

5 Participate in leading debates concerning competition

- Survival strategies focus on liquidity and preservation of resources.

- Strategies for the next upswing focus on the strategic positioning in post-recession markets.

- Faced with overwhelming foreign competitors, local firms still have several strategic options.

6 Draw implications for action

- Analyze your competitor to be able to predict likely reactions and counterattacks.

- Understand the rules of the game governing competition around the world.

- Strengthen resources and capabilities that more effectively compete and/or cooperate.

KEY TERMS

AMC framework
Anti-competitive practices
    (by a dominant firm)
Anti-trust policy
Attack
Blue ocean strategy
Capacity to punish
Cartel
Collusion
Collusive price setting
Competition policy
Competitive dynamics
Competitor analysis
Concentration ratio

Contender strategy
Contingency plans
Counterattack
Cross-market retaliation
Defender strategy
Dodger strategy
Dumping
Economic forecasting
Explicit collusion
Extender strategy
Game theory
Leniency programme
Market commonality
Market division collusion

Multimarket competition
Oligopoly
Patent race
Predatory pricing
Price leader
Prisoners' dilemma
Repeated game
Scenario planning
Strategy
Survival strategy
Tacit collusion
Tit-for-tat

CRITICAL DISCUSSION QUESTIONS

1 As CEO, you feel the price war in your industry is undermining profits for all firms. However, you have been warned by corporate lawyers not to openly discuss pricing with rivals, who you know personally (you went to school with them). How would you signal your intentions?

2 As a CEO of a French firm, you are concerned that your firm and your industry in the EU are being devastated by non-EU imports. Trade lawyers suggest filing an anti-dumping case against leading foreign rivals in China and assure you a win. Would you file an anti-dumping case or not? Why?

3 As part of an attack, your firm (firm A) announces that in the next year, it intends to enter country X, where the competitor (firm B) is very strong. Your firm's real intention is to march into country Y, where B is very weak. There is actually *no* plan to enter X. However, in the process of trying to 'fool' B, customers, suppliers, investors and the media are also being intentionally misled. What are the ethical dilemmas here? Do the pros of this action outweigh its cons?

4 You are running a restaurant and wish to serve your country's leading brands of wine and beer to your customers. The distributor of these brands is happy to supply you on the condition that you exclusively sell these brands. How do you react?

RECOMMENDED READINGS

M.J. Chen, 1996, Competitor analysis and inter-firm rivalry, *AMR*, 21: 100–134 – theoretical paper that introduces the awareness, motivation and capability framework on dynamic competition.

G.S. Day & D.J. Reibstein, 1997, Wharton on Dynamic Competitive Strategy, New York: Wiley – a collection of essays by professors associated with Wharton sharing their ideas on practical aspects of how to compete.

A. Dixit & B. Nalebuff, 1991, Thinking Strategically, New York: Norton – a very practical book that extracts ideas from game theory that helps businesses (and individuals) make decisions in competitive situations.

E.J. Morgan, 2009, Controlling cartels – Implications of the EU policy reforms, *EMJ*, 27: 1–12 – a synthesis of the institutional framework regarding collusion and cartels in the EU.

D.F. Spulber, 2007, *Competitive Strategy*, Cambridge: Cambridge University Press – a strategy textbook that focuses on competition in the global economy.

CLOSING CASE

Brussels vs Microsoft and Google

The European Commission is fighting not only old incumbents of utilities networks, but applies the same principles of market dominance and anti-competitive practices to big players in computer, software and internet industries. In particular, *Microsoft* has been the target of several investigations, due to the dominance of its Windows operating system. In one case, triggered in 1998 by *Sun Microsystems*, also a US firm, the Commission ruled that *Microsoft* had to make more information available about its proprietary software code to facilitate other software firms developing software products that link into Windows. This highly controversial case went on for many years, and in 2007 *Microsoft* was fined €899 million due to failure comply with a 2004 ruling on monopolistic business practices. Essentially the Commission considers Windows a basic infrastructure, similar to the cables used by telecom companies, and thus infers that others have to have access to the system.

In a separate case, the Commission investigated whether *Microsoft* was freezing out competing products by bundling its Media Player and its browser

(Explorer) into the Windows operating system. Such bundling enabled *Microsoft* to pull customers away from its competitor *Netscape*, which eventually led to the demise of that browser. In 1995, *Netscape* had 90% of the market, but by 1999 *Microsoft* had become market leader with 70% thanks to the bundling strategy. In 2010, the Commission and *Microsoft* agreed that *Microsoft* offers a 'choice screen' from which users can themselves choose which browser they want to use. By then *Netscape* had disappeared from the market, while Chrome (developed by *Google*) and Firefox (developed by *Mozilla*) were emerging as the main competitors, with 23% and 12% market share respectively. In 2013, the EU slapped an additional €700 million fine on *Microsoft* for lapsing in its commitment to offer consumers a choice of browsers, increasing the cumulative total of fines for anticompetitive behaviour to €2.5 billion.

Google came under scrutiny by the Commission because of its dominant position in internet search, where its European market share was around 90%. Since 2010, the Commission has been investigating whether *Google* is abusing this dominance to provide preferential links to its own businesses (or businesses it was associated with) by manipulating the sequence of search results. To avoid a fine, *Google* agreed to make concessions on how to display competitors' links on its website. The settlement would let three rivals display their logos and web links in a prominent box and content providers would be able to decide what material *Google* can use for its own services. However, competitors would need to pay for the display, based

on an auction. This promoted a furious response from critics who considered that the settlement did not go far enough. Even so, Competition Commissioner Joaquin Almunia intended to end the four-year investigation despite the 'very negative' feedback on *Google*'s concessions.

A separate investigation focused on *Google*'s Android smartphone platform, estimated to be installed on 85% of new smartphones worldwide in 2014, compared to 12% for *Apple*'s iOS and 2.7% for *Microsoft*'s Windows Phone. According to *Google*, Android was actively used by 1 billion users every month in 2014, up from 500 000 in 2013. The investigation was triggered by complaints from competitors including *Microsoft* and *Nokia*. The Commission is considering, first, whether *Google* obstructs or delays the launch of smartphone devices using competing operating systems or rival mobile services and, second, whether *Google* is abusing Android's market dominance to promote its own services. In 2011 to 2014, the Commission sent three rounds of questionnaires to participating companies requesting documents such as e-mail messages, faxes, letters, meeting transcripts, and presentations related to agreements with *Google* as far back as 2007.

Google's troubles did not end there. In addition to competition authorities, *Google* was also in conflict with European and national authorities over issues such as protection of privacy, copyright of newspapers, and tax avoidance. In November 2014, the European Parliament even passed a resolution to call for a breakup of *Google*. Although the parliament does not have the power to break up a company, this non-binding resolution put pressure on the Commission to take a hard line on the search giant.

CASE DISCUSSION QUESTIONS

1 As *Google*, how would you develop your business in Europe?

2 As a software entrepreneur in Europe, how would the dominance of *Microsoft* and *Google* in their respective segment influence your strategy?

3 As a member of the European Parliament, is there any action that you should take?

Sources: (1) P. Windrum, 2004, Leveraging technological externalities: Microsoft's exploitation of standards in the browser war, *RP*, 33: 385–394; (2) E. Morgan, 2009, Controlling cartels – Implications of the EU policy reforms, *EMJ*, 27: 1–12; (3) *The Economist*, 2010, Google and Antitrust: Engine trouble, December 4; (4) *The Economist*, 2012, Google and antitrust: Over to you, and hurry, May 26; (5) *Financial Times*, 2013, Google face Brussels probe over android licensing, June 13; (6) *Globe Investor*, 2014 Google avoids fine with European Union antitrust deal, February 5; (7) *The Guardian*, Google facing European antitrust scrutiny of Android device deals, July 31; (8) *InformationWeek*, 2014, Google Breakup: Wrong Answer To EU Antitrust Concerns, Dec, 1; (9) *Netmarketshare*, 2014, Desktop Top Browser Share Trend, December 30; (10) M. Ahmed, 2015, Google loses its way in Europe, *Financial Times*, February 26.

NOTES

'For journal abbreviation, please see page xx-xxi.'

1 R. Rumelt, 2011, *Good Strategy Bad Strategy*, London: Profile Books.

2 M. Porter, 1998, *Competitive Strategy*, New York: Free Press.

3 K. Coyne & J. Horn, 2009, Predicting your competitors' reaction, *HBR*, April: 90–97; N. Kumar, 2006, Strategies to fight low-cost rivals, *HBR*, December: 104–112.

4 V. Rindova, M. Becerra & I. Contardo, 2004, Enacting competitive wars, *AMR*, 29: 670–686; G. Markman, P. Gianiodis & A. Buchholtz, 2009, Factor-market rivalry, *AMR*, 34: 423–441.

5 A. Brandenburger & B. Nalebuff, 1996, *Co-opetition*, New York: Currency Doubleday.

6 M. Chen, 1996, Competitor analysis and interfirm rivalry, *AMR*, 21: 100–134.

7 M. Chen, K. Su & W. Tsai, 2007, Competitive tension: The awareness-motivation-capability perspective, *AMJ*, 50: 101–118; J. McMullen, D. Shephard & H. Patzelt, 2009, Managerial (In)attention to competitive threats, *JMS*, 46: 157–181.

8 T. Hutzschenreuter & F. Gröne, 2009, Product and geographic scope changes of multinational enterprises in response to international competition, *JIBS*, 40: 1149–1170.

9 W. Kim & R. Mauborgne, 2005, Blue Ocean Strategy, *HBR*, 82: October; W. Kim & R. Mauborgne, 2005, Blue Ocean Strategy; *CMR*, 47: 105–121.

10 *Business Week*, 2009, How Microsoft is fighting back (finally), April 20.

11 M. Blomström & A. Kokko, 2003, The economics of foreign direct investment incentives, NBER Working Paper #9489; J. Spencer, 2008, The impact of multinational enterprise strategy on indigenous enterprises, *AMR*, 33: 341–361.

12 O. Bertrant, F. Lumineau & E. Fedorova, 2014, The supportive factors of firms' collusive behavior, *OSt*, 35: 881–908.

13 G. Tullock, 1985, Adam Smith and the prisoners' dilemma, *QJE*, 100, 1073–1081; J.B. Baker, 1999, New developments in antitrust economics, *JEP*, 13, 181–194.

14 R. Axelrod & W. Hamilton, 1983, The evolution of cooperation, *Science*, 211, 1390–1396; D. Midgey, R. Marks & L. Cooper, 1997, Breeding Competitive Strategies, *MS*, 43: 257–275.

15 A. Mainkar, M. Lubatkin & W. Schulze, 2006, Toward a product-proliferation theory of entry barriers, *AMR*, 31: 1062–1075.

16 F. Smith & R. Wilson, 1995, The predictive validity of the Karnani and Wernerfelt model of multipoint competition, *SMJ*, 16: 143–160; M. Semadeni, 2006, Minding your distance, *SMJ*, 27: 169–187.

17 G. Kilduff, H. Elfenbein, & B. Staw, 2010, The psychology of rivalry, *AMJ*, 53: 943–969; R. Livengood & R. Reger, 2010, That's our turf! *AMR*, 35: 48–66.

18 J. Immelt, V. Govindarajan & C. Trimble, 2009, How GE is disrupting itself, *HBR*, October: 56–65.

19 F. Knickerbocker, 1973, *Oligopolistic Reaction and Multinational Enterprise*, Boston: Harvard Business School Press; J. Anand & B. Kogut, 1997, Technological capabilities of countries, firm rivalry, and foreign direct investment, *JIBS*, 28: 445–465; K. Ito & E. Rose, 2002, Foreign direct investment location strategies in the tire industry, *JIBS*, 33: 593–602.

20 K.E. Meyer & Y. Tran, 2006, Market penetration and acquisition strategies for emerging economies, *LRP*, 39: 177–197.

21 J. Baum & H. Korn, 1996, Competitive dynamics of interfirm rivalry, *AMJ*, 39: 255–291.

22 *USA Today*, 2005, Price remarks by Toyota chief could be illegal, June 10.

23 T. Tong & J. Reuer, 2010, Competitive consequences of interfirm collaboration, *JIBS*, 41: 1056–1073

24 M. Motta, 2004, *Competition Policy: Theory and Practice*, Cambridge: Cambridge University Press; M. Furse, 2008, *Competition Law of the EC and UK*, Oxford: Oxford University Press; D. Bartalevich, 2015, EU competition policy and U.S. antitrust: a comparative analysis, *European Journal of Law and Economics*, advance online.

25 J. Clougherty, 2005, Antitrust holdup source, cross-national institutional variation, and corporate political strategy implications for domestic mergers in a global context, *SMJ*, 26: 769–790.

26 S. Evenett, M. Levenstein & V. Suslow, 2001, International cartel enforcement, *IE*, 24: 1221–1245.

27 C. Damro, 2006, The new trade politics and EU competition policy, *JEPP*, 13: 867–886; S. McGuire & M. Smith, 2008, *The European Union and the United States*, Basingstoke: Palgrave.

28 *The Guardian*, 2001, Vitamin cartel fined for price fixing, November 21; C. Hobbs, 2004, The confession game, *HBR*, September: 20–21.

29 S. Brenner, 2011, Self-disclosure at international cartels, *JIBS*, 41(2): 221–234; C. Hoang, K. Huschelrath, U. Laitenberger & F. Smuda, 2014, Determinants of self-reporting under the European corporate leniency program, *International Review of Law and Economics*, 40(10): 15–23.

30 E.J. Morgan, 2009, Controlling cartels, *EMJ*, 27: 1–12.

31 *The Economist*, 2011, Monopolies in Mexico: Compete – or else, May 7.

32 *The Economist*, 2011, Competition policy in Brazil: Too little, too late, July 9.

33 *Frankfurter Allgemeine Zeitung*, 2014, Chinas Kartellamt geht gegen Audi vor, August 6.

34 *Frankfurter Allgemeine Zeitung*, 2009, Milliarden-Bußgeld für Eon und GdF, July 9.

35 P. Meller, 2003, European court tells Unilever it can't restrict store freezers, *New York Times*, October 24; European Court of Justice, 2006, *Unilever v Commission*, C-552/03 P.

36 European Court of First Instance, 2008, *Deutsche Telekom v Commission*, T-271/03.

37 J. Vickers, 2009, Competition policy and property rights, Department of Economics Discussion paper Series #436, University of Oxford.

38 OECD, 1996, *Trade and Competition: Frictions after the Uruguay Round* (p. 18), Paris: OECD.

39 *The Economist*, 2010, Antitrust in the European Union: Unchained watchdog, February 20.

40 J. Baum & S. Wally, 2003, Strategic decision speed and firm performance, *SMJ*, 24: 1107–1129; V. Terpstra & C. Yu, 1988, Determinants of foreign investment of US advertising agencies, *JIBS*, 19: 33–55.

41 W. Ferrier, K. Smith & C. Grimm, 1999, The role of competitive action in market share erosion and industry dethronement, *AMJ*, 42: 372–388.

42 D. Fudenberg, R. Gilbert, J. Stiglitz & J. Tirole, 1983, Preemption, leapfrogging and competition in patent races, *EER*, 22: 3–31.

43 *The Economist*, 2005, A market for ideas, October 22.

44 C. Pegels, Y. Song & B. Yang, 2000, Management heterogeneity, competitive interaction groups, and firm performance, *SMJ*, 21: 911–923.

45 B. Golden & H. Ma, 2003, Mutual forbearance, *AMR*, 28: 479–493; A. Kalnins, 2004, Divisional multimarket contact within and between multiunit organizations, *AMJ*, 47: 117–128.

46 J. Schumpeter, 1939, *Business Cycles*, vol. II, New York: McGraw Hill; K. Galbraith, 1957, *The Great Crash of 1929*, London: Penguin; P. Krugman, 2008, *The Return of Depression Economics*, London: Penguin.

47 K.E. Meyer, 2009, Thinking strategically during the global downturn, *AIB Insights* 9(2): 2–7.

48 J. Quelch & K. Jocz, 2009, How to market in a recession, *HBR*, April: 52–62.

49 P. Williamson & M. Zeng, 2009, Value-for-money strategies for recessionary times, *HBR*, March: 66–74.

50 P. Yuk, 2010, Investing in new products and markets pays dividends, *Financial Times*, March 12.

51 P.J.H. Shoemaker, 1995, Scenario planning: A tool for strategic thinking, *SMR*, 36: 28–40; H. Courtney, 2001, *20/20 foresight: Crafting strategy in an uncertain world*, Cambridge, MA: Harvard Business School Press.

52 L. Bryan & D. Farrel, 2008, Leading through uncertainty, *MQ*, December, p. 1–13.

53 P. Goodwin & G. Wright, 2001, Enhancing strategy evaluation in scenario-planning, *JMS*, 38, 1–16.

54 Ferrier, et al., 1999, *as above*. K. Smith, W. Ferrier & C. Grimm, 2001, King of the hill, *AME*, 15: 59–70.

55 N. Dawar & T. Frost, 1999, Competing with giants, *HBR*, March–April: 119–129.

56 D. Lavie & A. Fiegenbaum, 2000, Strategic reaction of domestic firms to foreign MNC dominance, *LRP*, 33: 651–672.

57 A. Bolger, 2010, The accidental beer business, *Financial Times*, March 10.

CHAPTER FOURTEEN

GLOBAL STRATEGIES AND ACQUISITIONS

LEARNING OBJECTIVES

After studying this chapter, you should be able to

1 Articulate the strategic advantages and types of strategies of globally operating firms

2 Explain why global firms engage in mergers and acquisitions, and alliances

3 Apply the institution-based view to explain patterns of acquisitions

4 Apply the resource-based view to explain when acquisitions are likely to succeed

5 Participate in leading debates on global strategies and acquisitions

6 Draw implications for action

OPENING CASE

Danisco: *the rise and sale of a global leader*

When *Danisco* announced the completion of the sale of its sugar division to its German competitor *Nordzucker*, many Danes rubbed their eyes. For them, the name '*Danisco*' was synonymous with sugar.

What was *Danisco* doing? The answer is that *Danisco* had been undergoing a steady transformation for over 20 years. Experts in the industry and financial analysts had been following the remarkable transformation of one of Denmark's leading companies. Yet the wider public knew little about what they actually were doing. Why? Because most people know companies with famous consumer brand names. *Danisco*, however, had become a market leader in business-to-business markets – apart from its now-sold sugar division.

After the transformation, *Danisco* was positioned as a specialized supplier of food ingredients based on natural raw materials. Its customers included global food giants such as *Unilever, Kraft, Danone* and *Nestlé*, as well as regional and local players in all major economies. *Danisco* specialized in ingredients that alter the properties of processed foods, such as yoghurts, ice cream, sauces and bread. Its business model included not only the development and manufacture of these ingredients, but the development of applications for the ingredients jointly with customers. For example, *Danisco* has been involved in the creation of *Magnum* ice cream, which is successfully marketed by major brand manufacturers around the world. To emphasize the innovation-driven nature of their business, *Danisco* adopted the slogan 'First you add knowledge'.

When the global financial crisis hit in 2008, *Danisco*'s first priority was to advance ingredients that would help its customers save costs. A major market research project investigated how people change their food-purchasing

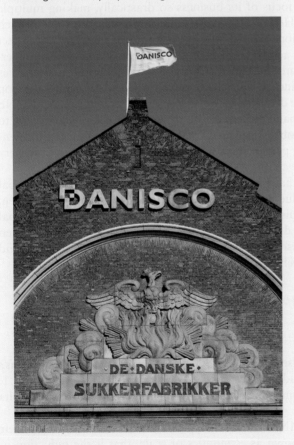

behaviour during the recession. On this basis, *Danisco* determined which kinds of solutions were required in specific food industry sectors and focused its marketing on product properties that help reduce costly ingredients (like fats) or extend shelf life. For example, they advanced a functional stabilizer that enables efficient replacement of egg without any alteration to processing lines, while also being easier and cheaper to store than liquid egg yolk.

How did *Danisco* become a global market leader in this niche? *Danisco* was created in 1989 by a merger of three companies aiming to create a strong Danish company that could compete in the EU common market after its completion in 1992. It was hoped that the merger would keep traditional businesses in Danish hands and enhance their viability. The new company was a diversified conglomerate, operating mainly in Denmark and other parts of Northern and Western Europe. From the outset the company aimed to focus its profile and to strengthen its core businesses. In the first annual report (1989/1990), the corporate strategy was 'to be a first-class supplier to the international food industry on the global market and be a supplier of high quality foods and branded goods on selected European markets'. Over the next years, the foods, food ingredients and packaging businesses were grown, while businesses in the machine-building segment were sold.

In the sugar sector, *Danisco* first consolidated its dominant position in Denmark, and then grew by acquisitions around the Baltic Sea in Sweden, (East) Germany, Poland and Lithuania. The sugar market was shaped by EU regulation that aimed to protect sugar beet farmers, but that also constrained the intensity of competition and limited the scope for aggressive growth. Liberalization of this market had long been anticipated, and it finally came into effect in 2009.

In 1999, *Danisco* announced a new strategy that focused solely on food ingredients, and acquired Finnish ingredients manufacturer *Cultor OY* to cement this strategic shift. At the same time, *Dansico* began to sell its businesses in branded foods and food packaging, including Danish icon brands like *Aalborg Snaps*. Two divisions thus remained: *Danisco Ingredients* developed, manufactured and distributed emulsifiers, stabilizers, flavours and enzymes, while *Danisco Sugar* dominated Northern European sugar markets. During this transformation, the internationalization of sales rapidly increased, with sales outside Denmark rising from 69% in 1995 to 88% in 2004, and over 95% after the sale of the sugar division. In 2009, *Danisco* generated €1.7 billion turnover, of which 38% came from Europe, 40% from the Americas and 17% from Asia-Pacific. *Danisco* employed 6800 people in 17 countries, in part to serve local markets, such as China, and in part to process natural ingredients only found in specific locations, such as Chile. Expansion in Europe, North America and Australia occurred mainly through acquisitions, while business in emerging markets grew to a larger extent by greenfield projects. However, the integration of the acquired companies took time, and only after that process had been completed, the share price began to rise again.

The sale of the sugar division in 2009 thus was the logical consequence of the two-decade long transformation process. The synergies between the sugar and ingredients divisions had diminished, while liberalization of the EU sugar regime led to the expectation of changing competitive dynamics in the sector. However, before completing the sale to *Nordzucker* of Germany, clearance needed to be obtained from competition authorities in those countries where both *Nordzucker* and *Danisco* held substantive market shares.

In spring of 2011, the history of *Danisco* took another turn: US chemicals giant *DuPont* launched a takeover bid! As a focused company, *Danisco* had become an attractive target, and would provide *DuPont* a launch pad into the food ingredients business. Yet shareholders drove a hard bargain and managed to drive the share price up by about 60% before agreeing to sell. *DuPont* moved fast to integrate the Danish company, which is now called *DuPont Nutrition and Health*.

Sources: (1) J. Cortzen, 1997, *Merchants and Mergers: The Story of Danisco*, Copenhagen: Børsens Forlag; (2) K.E. Meyer & I.B. Møller, 1998. Managing Deep Restructuring: Danish Experiences in Eastern Germany, *EMJ*, 16: 411–421; (3) K.E. Meyer, 2006, Globalfocusing, *JMS*, 43(5): 1109–1144; (4) Danisco (various years): Danisco annual reports; (5) DuPont Nutrition Health (2014): Latest News, www.danisco.com (accessed January 2015); (6) J. Kongskov, 2012: *Dansen om Danisco: Med i kulissen ved rekordsalget af et industriklenodie* Copenhagen: Gyldendal Business.

Why did *Danisco* change the focus of its business so drastically, making multiple acquisitions and divestments? How do companies like *Danisco* create value in such dispersed yet integrated operations around the world? And, how does *DuPont* expect to create even more value by acquiring apparently well-run *Danisco*? The diversity of the global economy creates both challenges and opportunities for companies transcending borders and continents. This chapter explores how companies develop **global strategies**. Exploiting the diversity of the world, global strategies spread MNE operations across the world, making the best use of whatever each location has to offer. The implementation of global strategies usually requires acquiring complementary businesses, or establishing partnerships with firms that control complementary resources or stages of the value chain.

We review the advantages that firms may be chasing when they develop global strategies, and try to create value by integrating operations across the world. Then, we explore how firms use acquisitions and alliances to develop the kinds of global operations that allow them to deploy these strategies on the global stage. We then discuss how institution- and resource-based views help explaining the patterns and performance of acquisitions. Debates and extensions follow.

global strategies
Strategies that take advantage of operations spread across the world.

STRATEGIZING GLOBALLY

Competitive advantages of the global firm

Why are multinational enterprises (MNEs) often more competitive than local firms? They can develop competitive advantages in several ways, as outlined in Table 14.1. These potential advantages complement each other, but not every MNE exploits each of these advantages.[1]

First, a basic advantage of MNEs over their typical domestic rivals is simply their size. Advantages of size are known as **economies of scale**, that is the reduction in unit cost that is achieved by increasing the volume of production. In manufacturing,

LEARNING OBJECTIVE

1 Articulate the strategic advantages and types of strategies of globally operating firms

economies of scale
Reduction in unit costs achieved by increasing volume.

Table 14.1 Strategic advantages of global firms

- Global scale advantages reduce costs in production, product development and marketing.
- Global sourcing provides access to a wider range of inputs.
- Global knowledge management enhances innovation.
- Global operation allows better servicing of global customers.
- Risk diversification reduces the corporate risk profile.

economies of scale arise from higher capacity utilization, or from larger production facilities. Thus the fixed costs of setting up a factory or a production line are distributed over a larger number of products. Large volume production thus reduces the costs of each unit.

In addition, scale advantages at other stages of the value chain are of increasing importance. For example, MNEs may share their costs of designing and developing new products across products manufactured and sold at multiple locations. In sectors such as the car industry, these scale advantages of development can be enormous. Selling more cars by serving many countries makes a big difference to the prices that the manufacturers like *VW*, *GM* or *Toyota* have to charge to recoup their R&D investment. Cars produced around the world vary in their design. Yet they often share a common platform of technologies and components, which greatly reduces the development costs of new models. Similarly, scale economies increase volumes of purchasing and sales, and thus bargaining power *vis-à-vis* suppliers and distributors.

Second, global sourcing allows MNEs to access resources in a variety of locations. Hence they can source every input where it is available at the best quality or the lowest price. Small cost differences for raw materials, components or labour can make a big difference to a firm's cost structure – provided they are not eaten up by transport costs. Moreover, global sourcing enables firms to access specific qualities of raw materials available only at a limited number of locations. For example, *Danisco* (see Opening Case) set up a specialized plant to processes specific types of algae that were only available in the sea off the coast of southern Chile.

global sourcing
Buying inputs all over the world.

Sourcing around the world enables MNEs to exploit comparative advantages (Chapter 5). Exporters and importers also exploit comparative advantages. Yet MNEs do so internally, and thus with greater operational flexibility, which enables smooth shifts of production from one site to another when circumstances change.[2] Activities that have low set-up costs can be moved in response to, for example, changes in exchange rates or labour costs.[3]

Third, global companies can tap into innovation clusters and talent around the world by placing their R&D centres in strategic locations. For example, software businesses head for Silicon Valley, California, while biotechnology firms cluster around Cambridge, England or Copenhagen, Denmark. Such dispersed yet interconnected centres of excellence offer four types of benefits:[4]

centres of excellence
Specialized centres for innovation that serve the entire MNE.

1 They can overcome the potential replication and inconsistency of standards that may evolve in case of disconnected R&D activity.

2 The interaction between R&D units at different locations enhances creativity and idea generation, and thus innovation. Bringing together people living in different environments within one organization allows to exchange

knowledge, experiences and competences, which in turn facilitates the generation of new ideas and innovations.

3 Centres of excellence allow exploitation of comparative advantages in, for example, specialized human resources, such as IT skills in India.

4 R&D centres around the world provide interactions with different customers, and hence projections on future market trends.

Fourth, global firms can better serve clients that themselves are operating at multiple locations. Such global clients, also known as global key accounts, may source their inputs internationally.[5] In other words, they negotiate contracts with suppliers who can provide the same product or service at multiple sites. The automotive industry has been at the forefront of developing supply networks on a global scale. Manufacturers like *VW* or *Toyota* work closely with suppliers such as *Bosch, Continental, Senso* or *Delphi* when developing new models, and expect them to deliver modules or components at any of their assembly sites. *Danisco* (Opening Case) was similarly developing relationships with global key accounts, such as food manufacturers *Nestlé, Danone* and *Unilever*. Firms with a global distribution network and production close to key locations of their customers have a distinct advantage in serving such global clients.

Fifth, risk diversification, by operating in multiple countries, reduces the financial risk profile of a company. Like portfolio investment, sales revenues from a variety of sources reduce the overall risk profile, as long as they are less than perfectly positively correlated. It is rare that a recession hits every country at the same time. Thus companies with global sales may be able to shift the focus of their activities to locations that are doing relatively well. In consequence, their global sales are less volatile over time than sales generated in a single market. Similarly, locating production at multiple sites reduces exposure to adverse events affecting any particular site, including not only economic events (such as a recession) but also natural disasters, wars and terrorism or a flu pandemic. With increased frequency of unexpected events disrupting global trade, risk management practices that allow companies to react flexibly to the unexpected can be a vital competitive advantage.

Global business models

How can globally operating firms best realize the potential benefits of globalization? Every firm will have a different answer to this question; such is the nature of the pursuit for strategic advantage. To keep an overview, IESE Professor Pankaj Ghemawat introduced an AAA typology of global strategies: aggregation adaptation, and arbitrage. The prevalence of these strategy types varies across industries, but also between firms within the same industry (Table 14.2).[6]

First, aggregation strategies focus on synergies between operations in different locations by integrating them above the national level. It does not necessarily imply standardization; it may simply involve sharing of resources and integration of processes. For example, R&D laboratories serving a variety of activities may be pooled at a small number of strategic locations. Aggregation strategies are designed both to exploit economies of scale, and to foster innovation and knowledge management. At the same time, activities that are best done differently may be located close to local resources and customers. For example, product development, sourcing and finance are often handled in regional or global business units, while sales, marketing and human resources are typically managed locally.

Aggregation is often at a regional rather than global level, thus reflecting the regional nature of a lot of business. Global brand companies like *Dell* and *Toyota* in fact have region-based supply chains, with separate hubs in Asia, Europe and North

global key account
Customer served at multiple sites around the world, but that negotiates centrally.

risk diversification
Reduction of the risk profile of a company by investing in different countries and industries.

AAA typology
Aggregation, adaptation and arbitrage strategies.

aggregation strategies
Strategies that focus on synergies between operations at different locations.

Table 14.2 AAA typology of global strategies

Strategy type	Primary ideas	Industry examples
Aggregation	Global integration: exploit scale advantages and create knowledge globally	Consumer electronics, machine tools
Adaptation	Local responsiveness: deliver consumers in each location what they need	Food and beverage, media and entertainment
Arbitrage	Global production and sourcing: exploit comparative advantages across countries	Mining, oil and gas, agriculture and forestry

Sources: (1) P. Ghemawat, 2007, Redefining Global Strategy, Boston: Harvard Business School Press; P. Ghemawat, P. 2007, Managing differences, *HBR*, (March): 58–68; (2) S. Estrin & K.E. Meyer, 2014, Local context and global strategy, *GSJ*, 4(1): 1–19.

America.[7] Large organizations can vary their levels of aggregation, say global R&D, regional supply chains and local sales operations to fine-tune operations. Such varied aggregation allows optimizing synergies, yet it also increases complexity and thus cooperation challenges.

Aggregation often follows geography: country, region and global. Yet in some industries other dimensions, such as cultural, administrative and linguistic communalities are more important. For example, consultancy and call centre-based services may pool customers sharing a common language because communicating in the customers' own language is essential for the quality of their services. Alternatively, they may locate in areas like Greater London, where qualified staff fluent in many languages are readily available, a benefit of immigration from a wide range of countries and cultures.

Second, adaptation strategies aim to deliver locally adapted products in each market. They aim to serve consumers on their local terms despite differences in their needs, preferences and purchasing power. The skill of designing adaptation strategy is to deliver locally adapted products while making the most of the global organization. Ghemawat proposes four levers of adaptation (Table 14.3):

adaptation strategies
Strategies that deliver locally adapted products in each market.

1 Companies may focus on those activities and products where only a minimum of adaptation is required. For example, fast-moving consumer goods MNEs may focus on young urban consumers whose consumption patterns vary less across countries than older or rural people. Firms may also focus on stages of the value chain that require less adaptation, or sell the same product but position it in a different segment. A standard product from Western Europe may be positioned as a premium brand in an emerging economy, and thus be sold using different marketing and sales processes.[8] For example, *Heineken* and *Carlsberg* are considered mainstream brands in their home countries, yet in countries such as Vietnam they compete for leadership in the premium segment.[9]

2 MNEs may externalize the costs of adaptation by working with local partners that contribute investment and local knowledge. For example, they may focus on business-to-business segments providing high-value added components that are incorporated in a variety of customized products by downstream partners, such as *Wärtsilä* building engines for ships constructed around the world, and *Hella* making headlights for cars of many different brands. Other MNEs, such as *McDonalds* or *KFC*, have developed franchising models that empower local franchisees to vary products within the scope of the corporate brand and to carry the costs and risks associated with such adaptation.

Table 14.3 Levers of adaptation

Ideas	Examples
• Focus on activities and products that require less adaptation across markets	• Marketing to young urban consumers with cosmopolitan values • Specialize in technologies or components used in a variety of final products
• Externalize the costs of adaptation by working with local partners	• Allow local franchisees and distributors to modify products and service delivery • Enable users to modify the products to fit their needs
• Design the basic product in ways that increase flexibility of the final product to be produced for different markets	• Design products with shared platforms that economize on base technologies • Design modular products that can be variously combined for different purposes
• Organize innovation processes with effectiveness of variation in mind	• Localize innovation to capitalize on local knowledge. • Recombine competences across the multiple locations

Source: P. Ghemawat, 2007, *Redefining global strategy*, Boston: Harvard Business School Press.

3 Adaptability can be achieved through business models designed to share some communalities, but allow for adaptation to specific user groups or locations. For example, car manufacturers have developed their models around platforms and modules that allow production of a wide range of different cars with a small range of components and technologies.

4 Local innovation allows creation of new products by locally knowledgeable people that can combine products or services of the MNE with business ideas of local entrepreneurs, and geared towards local needs. This increases variety of products without stretching central research and development units.

arbitrage strategies
Strategies that exploit differences in prices in different markets.

Third, arbitrage strategies exploit differences in prices in different markets. International variations in prices are the basis for international trade (see Chapter 5) and provide many opportunities to earn money by moving products from one location to another. MNEs may be better positioned to exploit arbitrage, as their subsidiaries can access local markets directly.[10]

Traditionally, arbitrage opportunities were associated with labour, capital and natural resources. Strategies of labour arbitrage exchange the services of a labour force, and thus allow exploiting low-cost labour or specialist human capital. Natural resource arbitrage exploits variation in geology and climate to trade energy resources (such as oil, gas and coal), minerals (such as copper, aluminium, zinc, gold, silver, diamonds) as well as agriculture, forestry and fishery products. Capital arbitrage can be achieved through overseas listing, which provides access to capital at lower costs when foreign capital markets are more internationalized and more liquid. For example, many Chinese companies like *Alibaba* and *Sina.com* list on NASDAQ, while others like *Tsingdao* brewery or *Lenovo* raised capital on the Hong Kong stock market. Similarly, South African firms such as *SABMiller* and Australians like *Rio Tinto* are listed in London.

overseas listing
Raising capital by listing on a stock exchange abroad.

Location-bound human capital also gives rise to arbitrage of knowledge-intensive services. For example, educational institutions – from boarding schools and language classes to universities – sell their services to students, who come to their classrooms from all parts of the world. Similarly, entertainment experiences attract global audiences, such as musicals in London and New York, opera in Milan and Verona, or gambling in Monaco, Las Vegas and Macau. Recently, medical services for patients worldwide are provided by hospitals in Singapore, Thailand, South Africa (beauty treatments!), and Eastern Europe who offer operations at much lower prices than for example in Western Europe.

The AAA strategies are not exclusive, as many MNEs combine aspects of two or even all three strategies. However, trying to realize all three strategies at the same time may well overstretch organizational capabilities. Thus choosing the right strategy is about finding a business model that best fits the specific firm, and its global competitive environment.

GROWTH BY ACQUISITIONS

Global operations provide competitive advantages, yet how do firms build global operations? One possibility would be organic growth with successive opening of new operations across the world. However, few firms choose this path – it simply takes too much time. Companies with global ambitions thus typically grow through mergers and acquisitions (M&As).

An acquisition is a transfer of the control of operations and management from one firm (target) to another (acquirer), the former becoming a unit of the latter. For example, *DuPont* acquired *Danisco* (Opening Case) and integrated it in its own operations; *Danisco* ceased to exist as a firm. A merger is the combination of operations and management of two firms to establish a new legal entity. For instance, the merger in 2005 between *Interbrew* (Belgium) and *Ambev* (Brazil) created *Inbev*, which merged in 2009 with *Anheuser Busch* (USA) to form *AB InBev*. Similarly, cement and construction companies *Holcim*, headquartered in Switzerland, and *Lafarge*, from France, merged in 2014 to create *Lafarge-Holcim*, with operations in 90 countries and headquartered in Switzerland.[11]

However, only 3% of M&As are mergers (Table 14.4). Even many so-called 'mergers of equals' turn out to be one firm taking over another; *Daimler*'s acquisition of *Chrysler* is an example (see Closing Case). Hence in practice, we can use the terms 'M&As' and 'acquisitions' interchangeably.[12] Another important distinction is that in partial acquisitions, the acquirer does not attain full ownership (see Chapter 12).

Most large M&As are cross-border (international) M&As; they account for approximately 30% of all M&As. In the record year of 2007, M&A deals topped €2.9 trillion, of which €1.3 trillion involved European companies. During the recession of 2009, the worldwide value of M&As dropped to €1.5 trillion, and stayed around that level for the next few years.[13] M&As represent the largest proportion of FDI flows, reaching approximately 70% of worldwide FDI. UNCTAD recorded 12 199 major international M&A deals in 2007; by 2013 that number had fallen to 8624.[14] Most of the largest MNEs of the world have grown by acquisitions, as have many MNEs from emerging economies that recently entered the global stage, such as Brazilian *Embraer*, Chinese *Sany* and *Lenovo*, and Indian *Tata* and *Bharti Airtel* (see Integrative Case).

Most managers contemplating the acquisition of another company aim to acquire full equity control, that is 100% of the shares of the company. In this way, they can call the shots, and reorganize the target company to fit their own strategic objectives. However, in some cases, investors only acquire an equity stake. Such partial acquisitions can arise from different motives. First, some investors are mainly interested in financial motives, such as risk diversification, but do not want to pursue organizational synergies. This includes, for example, sovereign wealth funds

LEARNING OBJECTIVE

2 Explain why global firms engage in mergers and acquisitions, and alliances

M&A
Popular shorthand for 'mergers and acquisitions'.
acquisition
The transfer of the control of operations and management from one firm (target) to another (acquirer), the former becoming a unit of the latter.
merger
The combination of operations and management of two firms to establish a new legal entity.

Table 14.4   The variety of cross-border mergers and acquisitions

Type	Sub-type	Examples
Mergers	Merger of equals	*Anhauser-Busch* (USA) and *Inbev* (Belgium) to form *AB InBev*
		Lafarge (France) and *Holcim* (Switzerland) to form *Lafarge-Holcim*
	Statutory merger	*Daimler* (Germany) → *Chrysler* (USA)
Acquisitions	Increase equity stake to majority position or full ownership	*AB InBev* (Belgium) → *Grupo Modelo* (Mexico)
		Unilever (UK) → *Hindustan Lever* (India)
	Full acquisition	*DuPont* (USA) → *Danisco* (Denmark)
		Shanghui Holdings (China) → *Smithfields Foods* (USA)
Partial acquisitions	Minority stake without strategic control	*China Investment Corporation* → 10% of *Heathrow Airport*
		Etihad Airlines → 49% of *Al Italia*
	Majority stake taking strategic control	*LVMH* (France) → 80% of *Loro Piana* (Italy)
		Softbank (Japan) → 51% *Supercell* (Finland)

(see Chapter 6) like *China Investment Corporation* acquiring a minority stake in infrastructure businesses like *Heathrow Airport*. Second, majority acquisition may be inhibited by legal constraints. This is typical for acquisitions in emerging economies, but may also happen in Europe. For example, airlines still need to be majority-owned in the country of operation, thus *Etihad Airways* expanded in Europe by taking minority stakes in *Alitalia* and *Air Berlin* (see Chapter 13, Opening Case). Third, investors may want to secure the commitment of the entrepreneurs who once created a company and thus leave them an equity stake, as did for example *LVMH* acquiring *Loro Piano* or *Softbank* acquiring *Supercell* from the founders.

Motives for acquisition

synergies
Value created by combining two organizations that together are more valuable than the two organizations separately.

What drives acquisitions? Table 14.5 shows three drivers: (1) synergies, (2) hubris and (3) managerial motives.[15] First, synergies between two merging organizations mean that the new organization is more valuable than the two organizations separately. Such synergy value can be created for example by sharing head office functions or distribution channels. For this reason, acquisitions often lead to cost-cutting and lay-offs of middle managers in the acquired firm. Other acquisitions help firms to build the global operations they aspire to, adding for example complementary market positions, production facilities or operational capabilities. The strategic complementarity of the resources of the two (or more) organizations thus forms the basis for synergies, and thus for the creation of value in the M&A.[16]

For example, when *MOL*, the Hungarian-integrated oil refinery and distribution company, took over its Slovakian counterpart *Slovnaft*, it identified a wide range of synergies, including optimization of refinery production, linking of logistics networks, shared R&D, coordinated sales and marketing, and integrated financial management. However, not all these synergies could be realized, for example in the area of logistics,

Table 14.5 Motives for acquisitions

Synergistic motives	• Leverage superior organizational capabilities • Enhance market power • Reduce costs by eliminating duplicate units and exploiting scale economies • Access to complementary resources • Tax avoidance effects, for example by moving the company to a location of lower corporate taxation
Hubris motives	• Managers' overconfidence in their own capabilities
Managerial motives	• Self-interested actions, such as prestige, empire building and bonuses

while synergies in marketing and finance exceeded expectation.[17] The realization of synergies is a challenging managerial task that only some firms have mastered.

A related M&A driver is to establish a strong market position, or to enhance market power.[18] *Mittal Steel*'s acquisition of European market leader *Arcelor* in 2007, propelled the Indian-owned MNE into a global leadership position, with almost 10% of world steel output. *Arcelor*'s high-tech steel plants, particularly in France and Belgium, added new capabilities to *Mittal*'s existing less sophisticated facilities, and enabled it to raise the quality of its products, especially for technologically demanding buyers, such as the car industry. Moreover, the acquisition gave *Mittal* a bridgehead into new Latin American markets.[19]

While synergistic motives, in theory, add value, other motives can reduce shareholder value. Hubris refers to managers' overconfidence in their capabilities.[20] Managers of acquiring firms make two strong statements. The first is, 'We can manage *your* assets better than you [target firm managers] can!' The second statement is even bolder. Given that acquirers of publicly listed firms have to pay an acquisition premium, this is essentially saying: 'We can achieve something no one else can.' Capital markets are (relatively) efficient and the market price of target firms reflects their intrinsic value. Yet an acquirer offering a premium suggests to create more value in the acquired firm than other owners, usually due to expected synergies. Empirical studies, however, show that very often the premium is too high, and acquiring firms have overpaid.[21] Yet the appropriate price for a company is often hard to determine. For example, Andrew Witty, the CEO of *GSK*, argued that many valuations in the 2015 acquisitions wave in the pharma industry were overvaluing target companies (also see Integrative Case *GSK*). Yet some investment bankers challenged *GSK*, arguing that they were missing major growth opportunities.[22] Investment bankers and other advisors who are paid commission as a percentage of the deal value naturally have incentives to encourage high valuations.

While the hubris motive suggest that managers may *unknowingly* overpay for targets, managerial motives posit that for self-interested reasons, some managers may *knowingly* overpay for target firms in their personal quest for more power, prestige and money. This behaviour is caused by agency problems. Managers as 'agents' are supposed to act in shareholders' best interest, yet they can use their inside knowledge to advance their own goals, because shareholders lack effective mechanisms of control. While managerial self-interest is usually hard to prove, it is often suggested by opponents of a deal. For example, when German state railway company *Die Bahn* took over British bus and train operator *Arriva*, several politicians suggested that managers were pursuing their own interests rather than those of the owners, in this case the German state.[23]

hubris
A manager's overconfidence in his or her capabilities.

Managing acquisitions

Even if the potential synergies between two firms make an acquisition look promising, it still requires skilful management of the process both before and after the actual acquisition (Table 14.6). Because of these challenges of post-acquisition integration, acquisitions are often considered a high risk strategy.[24]

An acquisition actually starts well before the contracts are signed. The first step is due diligence, which is the assessment of the target firm's financial status and its resources, and the fit between the target and the acquirer. At a basic level, due diligence aims to discover hidden liabilities of the target firm: are there environmental hazards on any of the firm's real estate? Have they signed contracts that are difficult to terminate? Is their technology well protected by patents? The lack of due diligence can lead to spectacular losses: for example, after *HP* acquired *Autonomy*, a UK internet start-up, for US$11 billion, they quickly wrote-off three-quarters of the value. They later sued *Autonomy*'s founders for having misled them, while the founders countered that *HP* had mismanaged the process. Whatever the merits of the legal arguments, the damage of poor due diligence cannot be undone.[25]

At a higher level, due diligence concerns the feasibility of realizing the aspired synergies. This concerns, first, strategic fit, which is about the effective matching of complementary strategic capabilities that allow for jointly achieving more, or achieving the same at lower costs.[26] In addition, but often not considered as carefully, it is crucial that the two firms have good organizational fit, which concerns the compatibility of cultures, systems and structures.[27] On paper, *Daimler* and *Chrysler* had great strategic fit in terms of complementary product lines and geographic scope, but there was very little organizational fit. These cultural clashes led to an exodus of American managers from *Chrysler* – a common phenomenon in acquired firms – and eventually the failure of the merger (see Closing Case).

After the acquisition the operational managers take over. Their main challenge is to manage the post-acquisition integration, the process that aims to integrate two formerly independent firms. The key challenge is to realize the synergies that motivated the merger in the first place, which involves the often conflicting objectives of creating new capabilities and exploiting existing resources in the larger organization. Getting people from previously competing organizations to work together, and adapt to each other can be quite challenging, especially if they used to see each other as arch-enemies.

due diligence
The assessment of the target firm's financial status, resources and strategic fit.

strategic fit
The effective matching of complementary strategic capabilities.

organizational fit
The similarity in cultures, systems and structures.

post-acquisition integration
The process that aims to integrate two formerly independent firms after an acquisition.

Table 14.6 Managing M&As

	Challenges for all M&As	Particular challenges for cross-border M&As
Pre-acquisition: overpayment for targets	• Managers overestimate their ability to create value • Inadequate pre-acquisition due diligence • Poor strategic fit	• Lack of familiarity with foreign cultures, institutions and business systems • Nationalistic concerns against foreign takeovers (political and media levels)
Post-acquisition: failure in integration	• Poor organizational fit • Failure to address multiple stakeholder groups' concerns	• Clashes of organizational cultures compounded by clashes of national cultures • Nationalistic concerns against foreign takeovers (firm and employee levels)

Post-acquisition integration unusually involves realizing efficiency gains, which often includes laying off some people. For example, after the merger, the company does not need two corporate headquarters, two corporate procurement offices, etc. Sometimes, some redundant business units need to be spun off as acquisitions swallow both the excellent capabilities and mediocre units of target firms.[28] Hence some acquisitions are followed by the disposal of selected business units. In this process, integration managers need to address the genuine concerns of many different stakeholders, who may fear loss of status, power or even their job, and who thus may try to undermine the efforts of the new owners. Insensitive management of these human aspects of M&As often results in low morale and key people leaving the company.[29]

In cross-border M&As, integration difficulties may be worse because clashes of organizational cultures are compounded by clashes of national cultures.[30] The French-Swiss *Lafarge-Holcim* merger almost unravelled because of conflicts of personalities and organizational culture between the boards of the two companies.[31] The French-American *Alcatel-Lucent* merger had to overcome cultural differences throughout both organizations. At a gathering at an *Alcatel-Lucent* European facility, employees threw fruit and vegetables at executives announcing another round of restructuring. The merger failed to produce the expected synergies, there were significant write-downs of *Lucent*'s assets, and eventually the episode cost both CEOs their jobs.[32] Even more difficult to manage are interfaces between Asian and American cultures, as *Nomura* painfully experienced (In Focus 14.1).

IN FOCUS 14.1

Nomura

In September 2008, *Lehman Brothers* went bankrupt. *Lehman*'s assets in Asia and Europe were purchased by *Nomura* for the bargain price of $200 million. Founded in 1925, *Nomura* is the oldest and largest securities brokerage and investment bank in Japan. Although *Nomura* had operated in 30 countries prior to 2008, it had always been known as a significant, but still primarily regional (Asian), player in the big league of the global financial services industry. The tumultuous year of 2008 became the opportunity of a lifetime for *Nomura*. Within a lightning 24 hours, CEO Kenichi Watanabe decided to acquire *Lehman*'s remnants in Asia and Europe. By cherry-picking *Lehman*'s Asia and Europe operations and adding 8000 employees, who tripled *Nomura*'s size outside Japan, Nomura transformed itself into a global heavyweight overnight. The question was: 'Does *Nomura* have what it takes to make this acquisition a success?'

The answer was a decisive 'No!' from *Nomura*'s investors, who drove its shares down by 70% by

2012. Since there was little evidence that *Nomura* had overpaid, the biggest challenge was post-acquisition integration, merging a hard-charging New York investment bank with a hierarchical Japanese firm practising lifetime employment.

Lehman's most valuable assets were its talents. To ensure that *Nomura* retained most of the talent, *Nomura* set aside a compensation pool of $1 billion and guaranteed all ex-*Lehman* employees who chose to stay not only their jobs but also their 2007 pay level (including bonuses) for three years. About 95% of them accepted *Nomura*'s offer. During the financial meltdown in 2008 and 2009 (which was triggered by *Lehman*'s collapse), many employees at other firms lost their jobs. The fact that *Nomura* guaranteed both jobs and pay levels was appreciated by ex-*Lehman* employees, who otherwise would have been devastated.

However, integrating *Lehman* introduced significant stress to *Nomura*'s long-held traditions. One key challenge was pay level. Most senior executives at *Lehman* made, on average, over $1 million in 2007. On average,

Nomura employees only received half the pay of their *Lehman* counterparts. Not surprisingly, guaranteeing ex-*Lehman* employees such an astronomical pay level (viewed from a *Nomura* perspective) created a major problem among *Nomura*'s Japanese employees. In response, *Nomura* in 2009 offered its employees in Japan higher pay and bonuses that would start to approach the level of ex-*Lehman* employees, in exchange for less job security – in other words, they could be fired more easily if they underperformed.

Another challenge was the personnel rotation system. Like many leading Japanese firms, *Nomura* periodically rotated managers to different positions. While these practices produced well-rounded generalist managers, they generated a rigid hierarchy: a manager in a later cohort year, no matter how superb his (always a male) performance was, was unlikely to supervise a manager in an earlier cohort year. *Nomura*'s conservative values and HR practices clashed with the hard-driving norms of an Anglo-American finance culture at *Lehman*: (1) key players were specialists with deep expertise but little knowledge of the organization as a whole, and (2) superstars were typically on a fast track, motivated by huge performance-related bonuses. Moreover, *Nomura* Europe was dominated by Europeans, whereas headquarters in Tokyo had an entirely Japanese top management.

Four years after the acquisition, the performance was disappointing. In 2009, *Nomura* moved its investment banking headquarters to London to demonstrate its commitment to break into the top tier. In Europe, *Nomura* became by 2011 number 13 in underwriting equities and number 15 in advising on mergers. In Asia outside of Japan and in the United States, it was a distant number 24 and number 22, respectively, in underwriting equity offerings. In contrast, *Nomura*'s dominance in Japan was strengthened by the *Lehman* deal. *Nomura*'s market share in advising Japanese acquirers that made deals overseas shot up from 10% in 2007 to 25% in 2011.

Integration continued to be *Nomura*'s headache number one. Outside Japan, *gaijin* (foreigners) were running most of the show. *Nomura* undertook a campaign to expunge the long shadows of the *Lehman* hangover. Both symbolically and comically, mentioning the 'L'-word (such as 'This is how we did it at *Lehman*') during senior executive meetings in London would cost executives £5 every time – they had to toss the money into a box as a penalty. In 2012, Jesse Bhattal, a former Asia Pacific CEO of *Lehman*, who rose to deputy president of the *Nomura* group, resigned amid heavy losses. Bhattal got frustrated about his interactions with the board, and failed to agree how to reposition the operation in view of ongoing losses. His resignation was one of many bye-byes of ex-*Lehman*ites after the pay guarantees ran out in 2010. Following massive cost cutting in the European operations in 2012, a smaller and more integrated *Nomura* Europe finally turned the corner in 2014, six years after the acquisition.

Sources: (1) *Bloomberg*, 2012, Nomura reeling from Lehman hangover, February 28; (2) E. Choi, H. Leung, J. Chan, S. Tse & W. Chu, 2009, How can Nomura be a true global financial company? Case study, University of Hong Kong; (3) *The Economist*, 2009, Numura's integration of Lehman, July 11; (4) A. Huo, E. Liu, R. Gampa and R. Liew, 2009, Nomura's bet on Lehman, case study, University of Hong Kong; (5) S. Baker & T. Hyuga, 2012, Nomura reeling from Lehman as Shibata vows not to retreat, *Bloomberg*, February 28; (6) M. Arnold & D. Schafer, 2014, Nomura's London are rises from Lehman legacy, *Financial Times*, September 14.

Acquisitions vs strategic alliances

strategic alliances
Collaboration between independent firms using equity modes, non-equity contractual agreements, or both.

An alternative to a full takeover of another firm is collaboration with that firm, also known as **strategic alliance**. We have already discussed one form of strategic alliance, namely joint ventures (JVs), as a means to enter new markets (Chapter 12). Here we look at two further forms of strategic alliances: (1) business unit joint ventures (JVs), and (2) joint production, marketing or distribution arrangements.

business unit JV
A JV in which existing business units from two firms are merged.

First, some major MNEs pool their activities in specific industry segments with a competitor or another firm offering complementary resources. For example, *Ericsson* formed a **business unit JV** with *Sony* to develop and market mobile phones, combining *Ericsson*'s technological expertise and *Sony*'s design competences. Similarly, *Nokia* has pooled is network operating systems with *Siemens* in *Nokia Siemens Networks*, and *Siemens* pooled its white goods business with *Bosch* in *Bosch-Siemens-Hausgeräte*, while competing with *Bosch* as an automotive supplier. Why do companies pool business units in such a JV under shared ownership?

Like other JVs (Chapter 12), business unit JVs draw on the competences of two (or more) parent firms. They are an attractive option if three conditions are met:

1 The two entities can together achieve something that neither could achieve on its own, for example market leadership in their industry or next-generation innovations.

2 The merged unit depends on inputs, such as technologies, from both parent firms that may be disrupted by legal separation (in other words, market transaction costs are high).

3 A full takeover is not feasible, perhaps because the competition authorities would object.

Business unit JVs can develop a life of their own and become long-running success stories in their industry: *Bosch-Siemens-Hausgeräte* and *Sony-Ericsson* mobile phones have been key players in their industries for several years. Even longer, *Fuji Xerox*, a Japanese-American JV has been manufacturing printers since 1962. In other cases, JVs are discontinued when the original purpose has been achieved. For example, *HP* and *Ericsson* created a JV at a time when telecommunications and computer industries were merging. They set out to jointly develop new technologies to conquer the emerging telecommunications network market. After several years of a volatile relationship, these objectives were achieved, and *Ericsson* took over the JV.[33]

Second, a strategic alliance may consist of far-reaching operational collaboration without equity investment. Such alliances are common for example in the airline industry, where national flag carriers have formed alliances that allow them to connect to all major travel destinations. Their collaboration includes, for example, code-sharing and shared frequent flyer programmes, which enable both (or more) partners to offer services that draw on resources of the partner. For example, when buying a *Lufthansa* ticket from Germany to Bangkok, you may actually be flying on a *Thai Air* aircraft.

operational collaboration A form of strategic alliance that includes collaboration in operations, marketing or distribution.

Other strategic alliances connect firms at different stages of the value chain, especially in industries where the development of new products requires extensive collaboration between these firms. For example, in the PC and laptop industry, brand manufacturers like *Dell* and *HP* collaborate with original equipment manufacturers like *Foxconn* or *Pegatron*, chip makers like *Intel* or *Qualcomm*, design houses like *frog* or *ideo*, and even basic materials manufacturers like *Bayer MaterialScience* or *Evonik*. The core players in new product development collaboration tend to make long-term commitments to each other, while peripheral suppliers are contracted on shorter-term basis.

INSTITUTIONS GOVERNING ACQUISITIONS

Mergers and acquisitions are subject to formal and informal institutions such as restrictions on foreign ownership (Chapter 12), often simultaneously in several countries. Managers pursue M&As to enhance the profitability of their firms (or to further their personal interest), yet such mergers are not necessarily in the best interest of consumers. Therefore, legislators have created competition policy that merging firms have to respect in every market in which they are operating. For example, when US firms *GE* and *Honeywell* wished to merge in 2001, the European Commission intervened, fearing negative implications for European markets. However, authorities use different processes and criteria to approve or disallow proposed mergers, which implies that multiple approvals may be required. In the

LEARNING OBJECTIVE

3 Apply the institution-based view to explain patterns of acquisitions

GE/Honeywell case, this led to conflicting decisions in Europe and the USA.[34] Eventually, the Commission lost some parts of its case in the courts, and *GE* and *Honeywell* were allowed to merge. Subsequently, the EU has refined its processes and guidelines and hired more economists specializing in competition analysis, which contributes to convergence of regulatory practice in the EU and the USA. Thus merging firms now act within a somewhat clearer and more predictable institutional framework.[35] For businesses contemplating an M&A, the key concerns are: (1) what are regulators looking for in horizontal M&As, (2) what are regulators looking for in vertical M&As and (3) how can merging companies get approvals even when there are initial concerns?

- **Horizontal M&A.** The key criterion for M&As within the same industry is whether the removal of competition will allow the merging companies to attain a dominant market position after the merger, and thus to raise prices or create barriers to potential market entrants but simultaneously lock-in key customers (Table 14.7). Traditionally, the main way to assess this criterion has been the joint market share. Yet in recent years regulators have shifted to also consider potential positive effects of reduced costs and accelerated innovation for consumers. Moreover, the definition of the market focuses on substitutability of the products and services, as many competitors are not exactly in the same market, but sell close substitutes. These assessments based on new methods of economic analysis that had first been introduced in the USA, and are increasingly applied by the EU as well. For example, the European Commission prohibited the merger between Irish airlines *Ryanair* and *Aer Lingus*, which both had their main hub in Dublin, and together accounted for 80% of passengers on many short-haul routes between Dublin and European destinations. *Ryanair* argued that it was operating in a different market segment, 'budget travel', and its customers choose between 'not travelling versus *Ryanair*' rather than '*Ryanair* versus *Aer Lingus*'. The Commission investigated this claim not just by economic analysis but also by a questionnaire survey of passengers using Dublin airport, and ruled that indeed the two companies were direct competitors, and thus the merger was not allowed to go ahead.[36]

  Companies know these rules, and they design their acquisition strategies accordingly. For example, *Heineken* (Netherlands) had long wished to take over *Scottish and Newcastle* (S&N) to enter the attractive UK beer market. Yet in other countries such as France, they both held large market shares,

Table 14.7 What regulators are looking for when assessing mergers & acquisitions

Horizontal M&A	Vertical and conglomerate M&A
Will the merged firm attain a dominant market share?	Will the merged firm have the ability to use its control over multiple stages of the value chain to limit access to suppliers or customers for competitors operating in only one stage?
Will consumers benefit from cost savings or accelerated innovation in the merged firm?	Will the merged entity have economic incentives to behave in such manner?
Will the removal of competition enable the merged firm to raise prices?	Will such behaviour give rise to significant impediment to effective competition?

and the competition authorities would not have approved the merger. Meanwhile, *Carlsberg* was keen to acquire *S&N* because of their co-owned business in Russia and other attractive operations in emerging economies. Yet the British authorities would not have approved a merger of two of the four largest brewers in the UK. Thus *Heineken* and *Carlsberg* launched a surprise joint attack: they acquired *S&N*, and then sliced it up in such a way that no national competition authority would have reasons to object. Thus *Heineken* took over the operations in the UK, Finland, Belgium and Portugal, while *Carlsberg* took over *S&N*'s share in the joint operation in Russia (also see Chapter 2, Closing Case) as well as businesses in France and Greece. The *Kronenbourg* brand is thus now owned by *Carlsberg* in France, but by *Heineken* in the UK. Otherwise, the two arch-rivals continue to compete in many countries, softened by even stronger multi-point competition.

- **Vertical M&A.** Vertical acquisitions tends to give less rise to competition concerns, as efficiency gains between the partners are more likely due to the cost reductions that come with the internalization of markets. Usually, vertical mergers do not lead to a loss of direct competition. However, competition authorities may intervene if the merged entity is able to use its control over multiple stages of a value chain to make it harder for rivals competing in only one of the stages. For example, a vertically integrated company with dominance in the upstream stage may make it more difficult for rivals who compete in the downstream stage, because they would depend on the merged firm's inputs ('input foreclosure'). As a hypothetical example, if a dominant supplier of essential goods, such as milk, was to acquire a retail chain, the competition authorities may object because they fear that the merged firm might use its control over the milk market to the disadvantage of other retailers.

  Likewise, a vertically integrated firm with dominance over the downstream stage may make it difficult for companies competing only in the upstream segment because they would have to sell their output to one of their competitors ('output foreclosure'). As a hypothetical example, an electricity grid operator that also operates power plants may grant competing power

input foreclosure
Practice of a vertically integrated firm to cut off a competitor from key suppliers.

output foreclosure
Practice of a vertically integrated firm to cut off a competitor from key customers.

How did the takeover of *Scottish and Newcastle* affect the competition between *Carlsberg* and *Heineken*?

generators access to its network under less favourable conditions than its own plants. Thus a vertical integration between a network operator and its suppliers would be a concern to competition authorities. When assessing vertical mergers, the European Commission would look for ability, incentives and detrimental effects of such behaviours (Table 14.7). In practice, these issues are important in the assessment of anti-competitive behaviour (Chapter 13), yet there have been few blocked vertical mergers, apart from the *GE/Honeywell* case, which ultimately went ahead.

- **Remedial actions**. If a regulator is concerned that a merger negatively affects competition, it can (1) prohibit the merger, (2) ask for divestment of selected operations or (3) ask for commitment to specific actions that ensure competition.

  First, an outright prohibition is the simplest solution because it is easiest to implement and monitor, yet it does not allow the merging partners to achieve their goals. Second, the regulators may ask the merging firm to sell a business unit to ensure that competition is maintained in a particular market. This solution is however more tricky than might seem at first sight: it is essential that the sold unit is a viable business that will emerge as a substantive competitor in the hands of the new owners. As many businesses depend on knowledge transfer, licences or distribution channels shared with their parent firm, this condition is not easy to meet. If the regulator forces a sale, the merged firm has incentives to create a weak competitor that does not pose a substantial threat. For example, when *AB InBev* acquired full ownership of the brewing activities of Mexican brewery *Grupo Modelo*, the US authorities forced *AB InBev* to sell *Modelo*'s operations in the US because of the concern of market dominance in the USA. *AB InBev* complied by selling the US operations and the rights to the *Modelo* brands in the USA to *Constellation Brands*, a wine and liquor producer with no major operations in beer.[37] Similarly, to meet the conditions of EU approval, when *Kraft* took over *Cadbury* they sold *Cadbury*'s Polish *Wedel* operation to Japanese-Korean *Lotte* (who had no prior activities in European confectionary markets), and when *Lafarge* merged with *Holcim*, they sold €6.5 billion worth of European assets to Irish *CRH* (who was a small player in the global cement industry).[38]

  Third, the regulator may impose behavioural constraints, such as a commitment to give rivals access to critical infrastructure on a non-discriminatory basis, or to licence technologies. Such a commitment was used for example when *Vivendi*, the owner of *Canal+*, merged with *Seagram*, which owned *Universal*, one of Hollywood's prime movie studios. Concerns were raised that preferred access by *Canal+*, a leading pay TV operator, to *Universal*'s movies would make life more difficult for competing pay TV operators. Thus the merging parties committed not to grant *Canal+* 'first window rights' covering more than 50% of *Universal*'s new releases.[39] Such commitments are naturally difficult to assess and to monitor; thus regulators see them as a less preferred option.

A major concern of businesses about the competition policy is that the EU Commission has to deal with very complex matters, yet it has far fewer people working on these issues than comparable authorities in the USA. Thus, rulings are often less evidently supported by sophisticated economic analysis (a nice revenue earner for economics professors in the USA) and may take quite some time, especially if they are challenged in the European Court of Justice. In response to such criticism, the EU Commission has increased the resources it has allocated to its competition policy monitoring work.

RESOURCE-BASED PERSPECTIVES ON ACQUISITIONS

Value creation?

Do acquisitions create value? Obviously managers pursuing acquisitions believe that they would add value, mainly by exploiting synergies. However, the overall performance of M&As is sobering. As many as 70% of acquisitions reportedly fail. On average, acquiring firms' performance does not improve after acquisitions.[40] Target firms, after being acquired and becoming internal units, often perform worse than when they were independent firms. The only identifiable group of winners is shareholders of target firms, who may experience increase in their stock value during the period of the transaction – thanks to the acquisition premium (the difference between the acquisition price and the market value of target firms).

Acquirers of EU firms on average pay an 18% premium, and acquirers of US firms pay even more, from 20 to 30% premium.[41] Shareholders of acquiring firms experience a 4% loss of their stock value during the same period. The combined wealth of shareholders of both acquiring and target firms is marginally positive, less than 2%.[42] Thus, on average, M&As destroyed value.[43] For example, in 2006, *Google* paid $1.6 billion to acquire *YouTube*, a 20-month-old video-sharing site with *zero* profits. *Microsoft* CEO Steven Ballmer commented that 'there's no business model for *YouTube* that would justify $1.6 billion'.[44] One company that is distinctly better known for the quality of its products than for the vision of its M&A strategies is *Daimler* (see Closing Case).

However, some acquisitions do indeed create value, that is the merged organization is worth more than the two independent firms. Empirical evidence suggests that such value creation is primarily associated with realizing operational synergies, including efficiency gains, and less with tax or market power effects.[45] The creation of this value however depends not only on the potential synergies but, as discussed above, on the successful management of both pre- and post-acquisition processes. Firms with capabilities to manage these processes are able to create value in acquisitions, even when others cannot.

Rarity, imitability and organization

Although many firms undertake acquisitions, a much smaller number have mastered the art of post-acquisition integration.[46] The high failure rate of acquisitions in combination with strong track records of some firms, such as *General Electric*, in managing acquisitions, suggests that capabilities to manage acquisition are indeed quite rare. For example, *GE Capital*, a finance firm associated with *General Electric*, developed acquisition competences by conducting one acquisition after another. They integrated the process over four stages: pre-acquisition, foundation building, rapid integration and assimilation, which includes drawing lessons for the next acquisition.[47]

These acquisition process-related capabilities are grounded in tacit knowledge in various units of *GE Capital*, and thus they are hard to imitate. As another example, at *Northrop*, integrating acquired businesses is down to a 'science'. Each must conform to a carefully orchestrated plan listing nearly 400 items, from how to issue press releases to which accounting software to use. Unlike its bigger defence rivals, such as *Boeing* and *Raytheon*, *Northrop* thus far has not stumbled with any acquisitions.

The capabilities to manage M&A processes are complex and specific to each organization. Hence they would be both hard to identify and imitate by outsiders, and they are embedded in the organization. They involve both manuals and 'to-do lists',

LEARNING OBJECTIVE

4 Apply the resource-based view to explain when acquisitions are likely to succeed

acquisition premium
The difference between the acquisition price and the market value of target firms.

but also processes and assessments that draw on tacit knowledge of teams and individuals managing the post-acquisition integration.

DEBATES AND EXTENSIONS

This chapter has introduced a number of debates (such as the merits of acquisitions), and this section discusses two debates of concern to contemporary medium-sized European businesses: (1) hidden champions and (2) globalfocusing.

Hidden champions

International business is often presented as primarily a matter of big MNEs competing for market share, especially in American textbooks. Smaller firms are often seen as fringe players in local or regional markets. With limited human and financial resources, how can a firm of, say, 1000 employees implement a global strategy?

Across Europe, many firms with 1000 to 5000 employees operate on the global stage in specific niche industries. Germany's infamous *Mittelstand* (medium-size) firms have achieved market leadership in such global niche markets. They are often family-owned, operate in business-to-business markets, and are not widely known. Thus they are often nicknamed hidden champions, a term coined by professor-turned-consultant Hermann Simon.[48] They are leaders in their selected niche markets, with competitive advantages grounded in highly specialized technological competences that are exploited worldwide.[49] Some of them have built quite a substantive position in the Chinese market,[50] especially automotive suppliers and machine tool manufacturers like *Wuerth, Junghans* and *Dürr* (see Chapter 15, Closing Case).

hidden champions
Market leaders in niche markets keeping a low public profile.

Family ownership is common among these firms, but does not necessarily imply that the company is managed by a family member. For example, the 300-year-old pharmaceutical company *Merck* is still owned by the descendants of the founder, yet they employ professional managers to lead the business. The 151 family members elect a family board that acts similarly to a supervisory board in a listed company. Yet as the family takes a longer term perspective than typical financial investors, *Merck* can invest with longer time horizons.[51] While *Merck* has occasionally made acquisitions in its history, transferring the family business culture to a previously listed company has been a substantial operational challenge.

Firms resembling the German hidden champions are also found in many other continental European countries with traditions in family businesses and commitment to manufacturing excellence, especially in Italy, Switzerland and the Nordic countries. In fact, the governments of UK and France have initiated projects to learn from the German experience.[52] Medium-sized firms are also common in the USA, yet their financing structure tends to be different: while German firms rely more on bank finance, private equity is more common in the USA.[53]

Focus strategies

divestment
The sale or closure of a business unit or asset.

Globalization has made global strategies more attractive. Yet how can companies formerly diversified in a local or regional market develop a global strategy? The answer is, in part, that acquisitions and divestments, the sale of business units, are often closely related.[54] Many entrepreneurial companies initially experiment with a variety of different businesses ideas before succeeding with a particular product or business model, and henceforth focusing all development on this line of business.

Other focused companies have their roots in diversified conglomerates of the 1950s and 1960s. They mainly focused on their home countries because barriers to trade and investment were substantial. Yet with the reduction of trade barriers, they changed their strategies from competing in several industries in their home country to a global scope within a much more sharply defined industry. Such a globalfocusing strategy, which is the conversion of a domestic conglomerate to a global niche player, has motivated many acquisitions and divestments.[55] This strategic change is driven by external pressures of institutional change, and consequently shifts in the ways in which the firm's resources can add value. The change process itself involves a realignment of the firm's resources, and thus acquisition and sale of business units, as we have seen in the evolution of *Danisco* (Opening Case).

globalfocusing
A strategic shift from diversification to specialization which increases the international profile.

In the pharmaceutical industry, a recent trend has been for companies to divest businesses that lack scale to compete globally, while acquiring businesses that strengthen their core or start-ups with promising new drugs. For example, in an €18 billion deal, British *GSK* swapped its cancer drugs business for Swiss *Novartis*' vaccines unit, while also creating a joint venture to pool both companies' consumer healthcare business. In the USA, *AbbVie* paid €19 billion for bio-tech start-up *Pharmacyclics* because of a single promising new leukaemia drug. *Johnson & Johnson* was also eager to acquire *Pharmacyclics*, but lost in the bidding war. Even so, they proceeded with their focusing strategy by selling *Cordis*, which makes medical devices, for €1.8 billion. Meanwhile, in Germany, *Bayer* acquired the consumer healthcare division of *Merck* for €13 billion.[56] One sure winner of the M&A frenzy is the investment banks advising the companies. Whether shareholders win remains to be seen.

However, restructurings are rarely permanent. Many companies go through repeated periods of radical change. For example, *Nokia* (In Focus 14.2; Figure 14.1) has transformed itself since the 1990s from a Finnish conglomerate into a global mobile phone handset developer, and lately a network service provider.

The relative merits of alternative corporate growth paths, and hence the optimal scope in terms of product diversification and internationalization, are grounded in the transferability of the firm's resources across industries and countries. Some capabilities may be specific to a country, but may be profitably transferred to other industries within this country. For example, the in-depth knowledge of consumers and marketing practices may enable strategies of 'brand extension' to loosely related products. Other resources are more specific to an industry but may be exploited in this industry in other countries. For example, technological expertise for product development can be a foundation for international growth.

A focused strategy, however, also entails greater exposure to market volatility. With dependence on one particular industry, any new regulation, new technologies or new competitors will have a major impact on the company. To some extent this may be compensated for by being less dependent on the business cycles of a particular country. Yet with globally integrated markets specialists will often be more vulnerable, and their share price will probably fluctuate more.

A focused company is more likely to become a takeover target. This would be an upside risk for financial investors and for board members remunerated in stocks or stock options. However, people in the local communities where the company is operating may see this quite negatively, as key jobs may move away from the community. The reason why a focused company is a more attractive acquisition target is that an acquirer – *DuPont* in the case of *Danisco* – is typically looking for a specific business that complements its existing operations, and they would be less interested in a acquiring lots of associated businesses that have no synergies with their core. Thus it was only after the sale of the sugar division to *Nordzucker* that *Danisco* became an attractive acquisition target.[57]

IN FOCUS 14.2

Focusing and refocusing Nokia

Nokia became known as brand for mobile headsets, yet two decades ago the mobile phone business generated a mere 10% of the revenues of what was then an industrial conglomerate in Finland. *Nokia* quite literally 'hit gold' with its mobile handset design and marketing, and thus focused its resources on exploiting this goldmine, selling its other business units along the way. The main restructuring occurred in one major wave in the early 1990s, which created foundations to grow its competences in mobile telephony globally, and to exploit these competences by developing and marketing related communications devices.

The transformation of the company can be traced through its annual reports. In 1990, Nokia presented itself as

> 'a European technology company, . . . 84 per cent of turnover comes from EFTA and EC countries. The group is divided into six divisions... Main products are colour TVs and monitors, microcomputers and terminals, mobile phones, digital telephone exchanges and telecommunication networks, cables and cable machinery as well as tyres and chemicals for forest industry.'

In contrast, in 2009, the *Nokia* website introduced the company thus:

> 'We make a wide range of mobile devices with services and software that enable people to experience music, navigation, video, television, imaging, games, business mobility, and more. Developing and growing our offering of consumer internet services, as well as our enterprise solutions and software, is a key area of focus. We also provide equipment, solutions, and services for communications networks through Nokia Siemens Networks.'

However, the synergies between the mobile phone handset business and the network business gradually diminished. Mobile phones were increasingly about design, fashion and user software, which required different types of capabilities from a technology business like network infrastructure. After a successful run in mobile phones, Nokia lost its leadership to new competitors like *Apple* and *Samsung. Nokia's* turnover dropped from a peak of €51.0 billion in 2007 to €30.2 billion in 2012. A partnership with *Microsoft* in 2011 was supposed to help turn the company around, but could not stop the slide. Initially, *Nokia's* sales in emerging economies held up while sales in Europe were dropping, but in 2012 China sales took a big hit, dropping from €7.1 billion in 2010 to €2.5 billion in 2012.

Under pressure, *Nokia* went through another major transformation in 2013. First, it acquired *Siemens'* stake in *Nokia Siemens Networks* to become the sole owner. Second, *Nokia* sold all of its mobile phone business along with licences for its patents and mapping services for €5.4 billion to *Microsoft*. Third, in 2015, it strengthened its network business by taking over *Alcatel Lucent*, thus challenging the global leaders *Ericsson* of Sweden and *Huawei* of China.

Nokia thus became a much smaller and more focused company, reporting a turnover of just €13.8 billion in 2014. It focused on three lines of business: the network infrastructure business, now called *Nokia Networks*, generated almost 90% of its sales; the location intelligence business, called *HERE*, provided software and services for navigation tools and other applications, and *Nokia Technologies*, focused on technology development and intellectual property rights activities. *Nokia Technologies* quickly returned to the consumer market with a tablet device in 2014, developed jointly with *Foxconn*.

Sources: (1) K.E. Meyer, 2009, Globalfocusing: Corporate Strategies under Pressure, *SC*, 18: 195–207; (2) *The Economist*, 2011, Nokia at the crossroads: Blazing platforms, February 12; (3) *Financial Times*, 2014, Nokia hopes it is on cusp of its greatest transformation yet, October 28; (4) *Financial Times*, 2014, Nokia's broadband gamble pays off, October 23; (5) *Financial Times*, 2014, Nokia partners with Foxconn to take on Apple with tablet device, November 18; (6) Nokia, various years, *Annual Report*.

Figure 14.1 Nokia OY 1990–2014

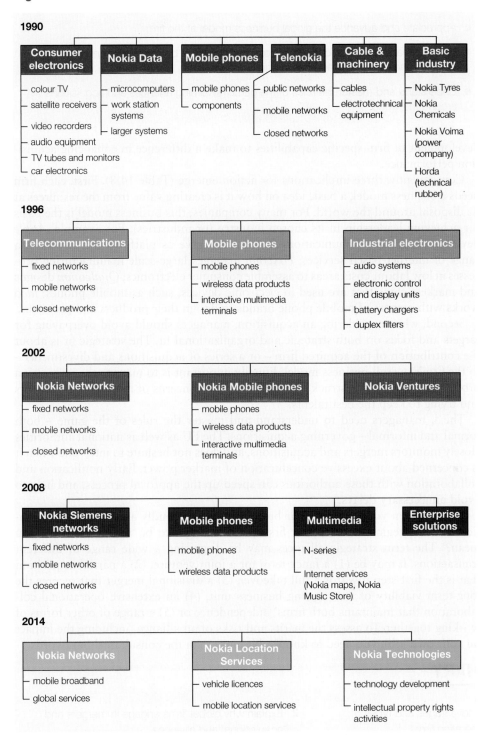

IMPLICATIONS FOR PRACTICE

What determines success and failure in global strategies? Our two core perspectives shed light on this 'big question'. The institution-based view argues that thorough understanding and skilful manipulation of the rules of the game governing acquisitions are often behind the fate of acquisitions. The resource-based view calls for the

LEARNING OBJECTIVE

6 Draw implications for action

Table 14.8 Implications for action

- Appreciate and advance the global business model of the firm.

- When managing acquisitions, do not overpay, focus on both strategic and organizational fit, and thoroughly address integration concerns.

- Understand and master the rules of the game governing alliances and acquisitions around the world.

development of firm-specific capabilities to make a difference in enhancing acquisition performance.

Consequently, three implications for action emerge (Table 14.8). First, each firm needs a business model, a basic idea on how it is creating value from the resources at its disposal around the world. For many companies, this business model is the basis for achieving leadership in its chosen industry (or industries). For example, *Apple* develops personal communication devices that serve as platform for providing a range of internet-based services; *Foxconn* manages large-scale manufacturing processes in low labour costs areas to assemble consumer electronics; *Qualcomm* designs and markets chips that are used in electronic devices, such as mobile phones; *ideo* works with owners of mobile phone brands to design their products and processes.

Second, when considering an acquisition, managers should avoid overpaying for targets and focus on both strategic and organizational fit. The strategic fit is about the contribution of the acquired firm – or a series of acquisitions and divestments – to the firm's overall business model. Equally important is to manage the integration process after the deal is struck, by addressing the concerns of multiple stakeholders and trying to keep the best talents.

Third, managers need to understand and master the rules of the game – both formal and informal – governing acquisitions. The EU as well as national authorities closely monitors mergers and acquisitions, and does not hesitate to intervene when it is concerned about excessive concentration of market power. Early notification and collaboration with these authorities can speed up the approval process, and help to avoid unnecessary delays.

Finally, when your boss or your business partner proudly announces the formation of a 'strategic alliance', your first question ought to be 'what exactly do you mean?' The term strategic alliances may be disguising a wide range of different transactions. It may be (1) a fancy term for a joint venture, (2) a partial acquisition that is the first step towards a full takeover, (3) a divisional merger that secures the long-term viability of a struggling business unit, (4) an extensive operational collaboration that maintains both firms' independence or (5) a range of other forms of working together. To assess the merits and risks of an alliance (including the impact on your own job), you need to know a bit more than the consultants' buzzwords.

CHAPTER SUMMARY

1 Articulate the strategic advantages and types of strategies of globally operating firms

- Advantages include global scale advantages, global sourcing, global knowledge management, servicing of global customers, and risk diversification.

- Global strategies can be characterized by a mix of aggregation, adaptation and arbitrage strategies.

2 Explain why global firms engage in mergers and acquisitions, and alliances

- Acquisitions may be driven by expected synergies, by managerial hubris, or by self-interest of the individuals involved.

- Alliances provide an alternative to a full acquisition, for example by merging business units, or collaborating on operations.

3 Apply the institution-based view to explain patterns of acquisitions

- Horizontal acquisitions may not be permitted if they result in a reduction of competition that is judged to be harmful to consumers.

- Vertical acquisitions may not be permitted if they allow a dominant player to inhibit competition in an upstream or downstream industry.

- Remedial measures include prohibition of the merger, required divestments or behavioural constraints.

4 Apply the resource-based view to explain when acquisitions are likely to succeed

- The impact of resources on acquisitions is illustrated by the VRIO framework.

5 Participate in leading debates on global strategies and acquisitions

- They concern (1) how hidden champions can succeed and (2) how globalfocusing allows conglomerates to become global specialists.

6 Draw implications for action

- Managers need to understand and master the rules of the game governing alliances and acquisitions around the world.

- When managing acquisitions, the savvy manager should focus on both strategic and organizational fit.

KEY TERMS

AAA typology
Acquisition
Acquisition premium
Adaptation strategies
Aggregation strategies
Arbitrage strategies
Business unit JV
Centres of excellence
Divestment
Due diligence

Economies of scale
Global key accounts
Global sourcing
Global strategies
Globalfocusing
Hidden champions
Hubris
Input foreclosure
M&A
Merger

Operational collaboration
Organizational fit
Output foreclosure
Overseas listing
Post-acquisition integration
Risk diversification
Strategic alliances
Strategic fit
Synergies

CRITICAL DISCUSSION QUESTIONS

1 As an employee in a middle management role, you hear that your company has been acquired by a competitor based in a different country. What are your immediate and long-term concerns? What actions might you take?

2 As an investor, would you rather put your money in a domestic firm operating in multiple industries, or in a global company specialized in a single industry? What are the risks associated with either type of strategy?

3 As a CEO, you are trying to acquire a foreign firm. The size of your firm will double, and it will become the largest in your industry. On the one hand, you are

excited about the opportunity to be a leading captain of industry and the associated power, prestige and income (you expect your salary, bonus and stock option to double next year). On the other hand, you have just read this chapter and are troubled by the fact that 70% of M&As reportedly fail. How would you proceed?

4 During the courtship and negotiation stages of a merger, managers often emphasize equal partnerships and do not reveal (or try to hide) their true intentions. What are the ethical dilemmas here?

RECOMMENDED READINGS

P. Ghemawat, 2007, *Redefining Global Strategy*, Boston: Harvard Business School Press – a practitioner-oriented book outlining ideas how companies can develop global strategies.

J. Haleblian, C. Devers, G. McNamara, M. Carpenter & R. Davison, 2009, Taking stock of what we know about mergers and acquisitions, *JM*, 35: 469–502 – a review article summarizing current scholarly thinking on M&As.

P.C. Haspeslagh & D.B. Jemison, 1989, *Managing Acquisitions*, New York: Free Press – a classic book grounded in the resource-based view on how to manage acquisitions.

K.E. Meyer, 2006, Globalfocusing: From domestic conglomerates to global specialists, *JMS*,

43: 1 109–1 144 – a study following acquisitions and divestments of two companies over time, and interpreting the process from an resource-based view by introducing the concept of globalfocusing.

A. Verbeke & H. Merchant, 2012, *Handbook of Research on International Strategic Management*, Cheltenham: Elgar – a collection of essays reviewing the state of the art of theories linking international business and strategic management.

G.S. Yip & G.T.M. Hult, 2012, *Total Global Strategy*, 3rd ed., Upper Saddle River: Prentice Hall – a textbook targeted at MBA students with the ambition to lead global firms.

CLOSING CASE

Daimler *merges and demerges*

The *Daimler AG* builds some of the best cars, mostly sold under its Mercedes-Benz brand. Yet *Daimler* has also been involved in numerous other technology businesses, often with limited success. In two periods of its recent history, *Daimler*'s top management pursued ambitious growth strategies, yet overestimated the potential for synergies between acquired businesses, and their own ability to integrate a complex business organization.

In the 1980s, *Daimler* developed the vision of an integrated technology group, acquiring in a single year, 1985 three German businesses with distinguished histories of their own: defense contractor *MTU*, small aircraft manufacturer *Dornier*, and white goods conglomerate *AEG*. However, *Daimler*'s plan to become a leading provider of military hardware took a hit when the Iron Curtain fell in 1990 and governments around Europe cut their military expenses. Addressing the challenge proactively, *Daimler* decided to focus on civilian aircrafts and acquired the Dutch business jet builder *Fokker*. Yet global competition proved too strong for the already struggling company and 1996 *Fokker* went into insolvency after *Daimler* had lost DM 800 million from the deal. According to one study, *Daimler*'s buying and selling of companies during that

period was estimated to have destroyed the value of the company by DM 36 million. *Dornier* was sold to *Fairchild*, and *AEG* was liquidated (the white goods brand *AEG* is today owned by *Electrolux*).

In the late 1990s the vision of an integrated technology group was replaced by a vision of a global leader in the car industry. Rather than diversifying into related industries, *Daimler* aimed to build a presence in all three major continents. In 1998, *Daimler* paid US$35 billion to acquire *Chrysler*, a 40% premium over market value. *Daimler* CEO Jürgen Schremp and *Chrysler* CEO Bob Eaton announced the largest transatlantic merger a 'marriage made in heaven'. Observers were critical from the outset. Rather than strong synergies, they suspected high levels of hubris and significant managerial self-interests. On paper, *Daimler* and *Chrysler* had great strategic fit in terms of complementary product lines and geographic scope, but there was very little organizational fit. For example, American managers resented the dominance of German managers, while the Germans disliked being paid two-thirds less than their *Chrysler* colleagues. These clashes led to an exodus of American managers from *Chrysler*.

In 2000, *Daimler* also acquired a 34% stake in Japan's *Mitsubishi* and 10.44% in Korean *Hyundai*, expecting these strategic alliances to provide channels

into emergent Asian markets and access small car brands and technologies. In this way, *Daimler* would become the global number one with significant positions in Europe, Asia and North America.

Yet the marital bliss did not last long. The equity stake in *Hyundai* was sold in 2004 with a substantial profit, while the struggling *Mitsubishi* was soon also sold at a loss. In 2007, under new leadership of Dieter Zetsche, *Daimler* sold *Chrysler* to *Cerberus Capital*, a private equity firm, for US$7.4 billion – four-fifths of the value had been lost (either *Daimler* over-paid, or the value was destroyed after the acquisition). In consequence, *Daimler* fell behind its German rivals *BMW* and *Audi,* especially in growing Asian markets.

The new vision was to focus on its core brand, *Mercedes Benz*, and to be the best rather than the biggest car manufacturer. In 2013, *Daimler* sold the rest of its 15% share in *EADS*, the French-German owner of *Airbus*, and thus completely withdrew from military and aircraft businesses. In 2015, *Daimler* even sold its 4% share in Californian e-car innovator *Tesla* – but this time making a healthy profit.

Instead, *Daimler* invested in automotive technology including new internet-based technologies integrated in cars. The brand was modernized and expanded, and a new marketing drive in China aimed to catch up with its German peers *Audi* and *BMW* who had successfully build market share in this growing market.

In 2014, *Daimler* thus established in a new joint venture with Beijing based *BAIC* to manufacture *Mercedes Benz* cars for the Chinese market. By 2015, this strategy eventually paid off. Turnover grew in Europe and China, the share price outperformed the DAX index for several months, and profit numbers almost reached those of *Audi* and *BMW*.

CASE DISCUSSION QUESTIONS

1 What are the merits and risks of converting *Daimler* into an integrated technology group like *Siemens* or *GE*?

2 What are the merits and risks of converting *Daimler* into a multi-brand global car maker, like *Unilever* or *Nestlé* in consumer goods?

3 What are the merits and risks of *Daimler* focusing exclusively on its *Mercedes Benz* brand for passenger cars and trucks?

Sources: (1) G. Steinmetz & G. White, 1998, Chrysler's Executive Pay Draws Fire From Overseas, *Wall Street Journal*, May 26; (2) *The Economist*, 2004, DaimlerChrysler: The wheels come off, April 19; (3) Der Spiegel, 2004, Ende der Partnerschaft, May 12; (4) H. Jakobs, 2010, Totale Überbezahlung für eine totale Pfeife, *Süddeustche Zeitung*, May 17; (5) *Handelsblatt*, 2011, Daimlers teure und erfolglose Einkaufstour, February 11; (6) *Handelsblatt*, 2013, Daimler entledigt sich letzter EADS-Anteile, April 16; (7) *Handelsblatt*, 2014, Daimler vergoldet die Anteile in Tesla, October 21; (8) *Handelsblatt*, 2014, Daimler übertrifft bereits in September das Vorjahr, December 12; (9) T. Mitchell, 2014, Daimler has high hopes for China joint venture with BAIC, *Financial Times*, December 15.

NOTES

'For journal abbreviation, please see page xx–xxi.'

1 S. Ghoshal, 1987, Global strategy, *SMJ*, 8: 425–440; G. Yip, 1989, Global strategy … In a world of nations? *SMR*, 31, 29–41; J. Dunning & S. Lundan, 2008, *Multinational Enterprises and the Global Economy*, 2nd ed, Cheltenham: Elgar; P. Buckley, 2009, Internalization thinking, *IBR*, 18: 224–235.

2 M. Kenney & R. Florida, eds, 2004, *Locating Global Advantage*, Stanford: Stanford University Press; T.J. Sturgeon 2002, Modular production networks, *ICC*, 11, 451–496; P.J. Buckley, 2009; The impact of the global factory on economic development, *JWB*, 44, 131–143.

3 B. Kogut, 1985, Designing global strategies: Profiting from operational flexibility, *SMR* 27: 27–38; B. Kogut & N. Kulatilaka 1994. Option thinking and platform investment, *CMR*, Winter, 52–71.

4 R. Mudambi, 2001, Knowledge management in multinational firms, *JIM*, 8: 1–9; N.J. Foss & T. Pedersen, 2001, Transferring knowledge in MNCs, *JIM*, 8: 49–67; N. Noorderhaven & A.Harzing, 2009, Knowledge-sharing and social interaction within MNEs, *JIBS*, 40: 719–741.

5 S. Lacoste, Vertical coopetition: The key account perspective, *IMM*, 41: 649–658; I. Davies & L. Ryals, 2014, The effectiveness of key account management practices, *IMM*, 43: 1182–1194; W. Murphy & N. Li, 2015, Key account management in China, *JBR*, 1234–1241.

6 P. Ghemawat, 2007a, *Redefining Global Strategy*, Boston: Harvard Business School Press; P. Ghemawat, P. 2007b., Managing differences, *HBR*, (March): 58–68.

7 Ghemawat, 2007a, *as above* (p. 144–156).

8 N. Dawar & A. Chattopadhay 2002. Rethinking marketing programs for emerging markets, *LRP*, 35: 457–474; T. London & S. Hart, 2004, Reinventing strategies for emerging markets, *JIBS*, 35: 350–370; C.K. Prahalad. 2004, *The Fortune at the Bottom of the Pyramid*, Philadelphia: Wharton School Publishing.

9 K.E. Meyer & Y. Tran, 2006, Market penetration and acquisition strategies for emerging economies, *LRP*, 39: 177–197.

10 B. Kogut, 1985, Designing Global Strategies: *SMR*, 26(3): 15–28; S. Rangan, 1998, Do multinationals operate flexibly? *JIBS*, 29: 217–237.

11 A. Som, 2014, Lafarge-Holcim a merger of equals? Blog, knowledge.essec.edu, April 30.

12 J. Haleblian, C. Devers, G. McNamara, M. Carpenter & R. Davison, 2009, Taking stock of what we know about mergers and acquisitions, *JM*, 35: 469–502.

13 *Financial Times Online*, 2010, Mergers and acquisitions data 2000–2009, March 17.

14 UNCTAD, 2014, *World Investment Report 2014* (Web Table 12), www.unctad.org/wir.

15 K. Brouthers, P. van Hastenburg & J. van den Ven, 1998, If most mergers fail why are they so popular? *LRP*, 31: 347–353; A. Seth, K. Song & R. Pettit, 2000, Synergy, managerialism, or hubris? *JIBS*, 31: 387–405.

16 R. Larsson & S. Finkelstein, 1999, Integrating strategic, organizational, and human resource perspectives on mergers and acquisitions, *OSc*, 10: 1–26; D. Loree, C. Chen & S. Guisinger, 2000, International acquisitions, *JWB*, 35: 300–315; D. Schweiger & P. Very, 2001, International M&As special issue, *JWB*, 36: 1–2; J. Anand & A. Delios, 2002, Absolute and relative resources as determinants of international acquisitions, *SMJ*, 23: 119–134; T. Saxton & M. Dollinger, 2004, Target reputation and appropriability, *JM*, 30: 123–147.

17 Z. Antal-Mokos & K. Tóth, 2007, The emergence of the Central European MNE: MOL, in: K.E. Meyer & S. Estrin, eds, *Acquisition Strategies in European Emerging Economies*, Basingstoke: Palgrave, 190–202.

18 S. Bhattacharyya & A. Nain, 2011, Horizontal acquisitions and buying power, *Journal of Financial Economics*, 99: 97–115.

19 P. March, 2009, Steel magnate steered Mittal to success with Arcelor, *Financial Times*, December 30.

20 R. Roll, 1986, The hubris hypothesis of corporate takeovers, *JB*, 59: 197–216; F. Vermeulen, 2010, *Business Exposed*, London: PrenticeHall-FT.

21 P.R. Haunschild, A. Davis-Blake & M. Fichman, 1994, Managerial overcommitment in corporate acquisition processes, *OSc*, 5: 528–540; S. Moeller, F. Schlingemann & R. Stulz, 2004, Firm size and the gains from acquisitions, *JFE*, 73: 201–228.

22 A. Ward, 2015, GSK chief warns of bad medicine in pharma M&A, *Financial Times*, May 12 (page 1 headline).

23 *Handelsblatt*, 2010, Deutsche Bahn tätigt teuersten Zukauf ihrer Geschichte, April 22.

24 H. Bresman, J.M. Birkinshaw & R. Nobel, 1999, Knowledge transfer in international acquisitions, *JIBS*, 30: 439–469; R. Larsson & S. Finkelstein, 1999, Integrating strategic, organizational, and human resource perspectives on M&As, *OSc*, 10: 1–26; J. Reuer, O. Shenkar & R. Ragozzino, 2004, Mitigating risk in international M&As, *JIBS*, 35: 19–32.

25 *BBC News*, 2015, HP sues former Autonomy leaders for $5.1bn, alleging fraud, March 15, http://www.bbc.co.uk/news/business-32131529.

26 J. Kim & S. Finkelstein, 2009, The effects of strategic and market complementarity on acquisition performance, *SMJ*, 30: 617–646.

27 S. Cartwright & C. Cooper, 1993, The role of culture compatibility in successful organizational marriage, AME, 7: 57–70; P. Puranam, H. Singh & M. Zollo, 2006, Organizing for innovation, AMJ, 49: 263–280; M. Brannen & M. Peterson, 2009, Merging without alienating, JIBS, 40: 468–489; R. Chakrabarti, S. Gupta-Mukherjee & N. Jayaraman, 2009, Mars-Venus marriages, JIBS, 40: 216–236.

28 L. Capron, 1998, Resource redeployment following horizontal acquisitions in Europe and North America, SMJ, 19: 631–661; O. Bertrant & L. Capron, 2014, Productivity enhancement at home via cross-border acquisitions, SMJ, advance online.

29 J. Birkinshaw, H. Bresman & L. Håkanson, 2000, Managing the post-acquisition integration process, JMS, 37: 395–425; A. Zaheer, X. Castañer & D. Souder, 2011, Synergy sources, target autonomy, and integration in acquisitions, JM, 39: 604–632; J. Birkinshaw, H. Bresman & R. Nobel, 2011, Knowledge transfer in international acquisitions: A retrospective, JIBS, 41:21–26.

30 P. Morosini, S. Shane & H. Singh, 1998, National cultural distance and cross-border acquisition performance, JIBS, 29: 137–158; J. Child, D. Faulkner & R. Pitkethly, 2001, The Management of International Acquisitions, Oxford: Oxford University Press; R.M. Sarala & E. Vaara, 2010, Cultural differences, convergence, and crossvergence as explanations of knowledge transfer in international acquisitions, JIBS, 2010: 41365–1390.

31 S. Gordon & A. Massoudi, 2015, A merger of ego (FT Big Read: M&A), Financial Times, March 24.

32 Bloomberg Businessweek, 2011, Alcatel-Lucent chops away at years of failure (p. 29), May 2.

33 B. Büchel, 2002, Joint venture development, JWB, 37: 199–207.

34 E. Morgan & S. McGuire, 2004, Transatlantic divergence: GE-Honeywell and the EU's merger policy, JEPP, 11: 39–56; S. Anwar 2005, EU's competition policy and the GE-Honeywell merger fiasco, TIBR 47: 601–626; Y. Akbar & G. Suder, 2006, The new EU merger regulation, TIBR, 48: 667–686.

35 C. Damro, 2006, The new trade politics and EU competition policy, JEPP, 13: 867–886; S. McGuire & M. Smith, 2008, The European Union and the United States, Basingstoke: Palgrave.

36 A. Weitbrecht, 2008, Ryanair and more – EU merger control in 2007, ECLR, 29: 341–348.

37 CNN, 2013, AB InBev and Modelo merger set to move forward, April 19.

38 Gordon & Massoudi, 2015, as above.

39 M. Motta, M. Polo & H. Vasconcelos, 2007, Merger remedies in the European Union: An overview, Antitrust Bulletin, 52: 603–632.

40 D. King, D. Dalton, C. Daily & J. Covin, 2004, Meta-analyses of post-acquisition performance, SMJ, 25: 187–200; K. Uhlenbruck, M. Hitt & M. Semadeni, 2006, Market value effects of acquisitions involving Internet firms, SMJ, 27: 899–913.

41 C. Moschieri & J. Campa, 2009, The European M&A industry (p. 82), AMP, November: 71–87.

42 G. Andrade, M. Mitchell & E. Stafford, 2001, New evidence and perspectives on mergers, JEP, 15: 103–120.

43 J. Doukas & O. Kan, 2006, Does global diversification destroy firm value? JIBS, 37: 352–371.

44 Business Week, 2006, Ballmer: They paid how much for that? October 23.

45 L. Capron & N. Pistre, 2002, When do acquirers earn abnormal returns? SMJ, 23: 781–795; E. Devos, R. Kadapakkam & S. Krishnamurthy, 2009, How Do Mergers Create Value? Review of Financial Studies, 22: 1179–1211.

46 J. Haleblian, J. Kim & N. Rajagopalan, 2006, The influence of acquisition experience and performance on acquisition behavior, AMJ, 49: 357–370.

47 R. Ashkenas, L. Demonaco & S. Francis, 1998, Making the deal real: how GE Capital integrates acquisitions, HBR, (January-February): 5–15.

48 H. Simon, 1996, Hidden Champions, Boston, MA: Harvard Business School Press.

49 B. Venohr, 2006, Wachsen wie Wuerth, Frankfurt, Campus; H. Simon, 2009, Hidden Champions of the 21st Century, New York: Springer; B. Venohr & K.E. Meyer, 2009, Uncommon common sense, BSR, 20(1): 38–43; The Economist, 2011, Economic Focus: Vorsprung durch exports, February 5.

50 The Economist, 2011, Germany's Mittelstand: Beating China, July 30.

51 O. Helvadjian, 2014, More than 300 years of a family, German Chamber Ticker (China), no 3: 52–53.

52 The Economist, 2012, Mid-sized companies France: Why Doesn't France have a Mittelstand? October 20.

53 The Economist, 2012, Mid-sized companies America: The mighty middle, October 20.

54 L. Capron & W. Mitchell, 1998, Bilateral resource redeployment and capabilities improvement following horizontal acquisitions, ICC, 7: 453–484; L. Capron & M. Guillen, 2009, National corporate governance institutions and post-acquisition target reorganization, SMJ, 30: 803–833; L. Capron, W. Mitchell & A. Swaminathan, 2001, Asset divesture following horizontal acquisitions, SMJ, 22: 817–844.

55 Meyer, 2006, Globalfocusing: from domestic conglomerates to global specialists, JMS, 43: 1109–1144. K.E. Meyer, 2009, Globalfocusing: Corporate strategies under pressure, SC, 18:195–207.

56 A. Ward & J. Fontanells-Khan, 2015, J&J and GSK-Novartis deals seen as 'precision' M&As, Financial Times, March 3; A. Ward, 2015, AbbVie victory adds to pharma M&A frenzy, Financial Times, March 6.

57 J. Kongskov, 2012, Dansen om Danisco: Med i kulissed ved rekordsalget af et industriklenodie, Copenhagen: Gyldendal Business.

PART FIVE

OPERATIONS IN THE GLOBAL MNE

15 Organizing and Innovating in the MNE

16 People in the MNE

17 Customers and Suppliers of the MNE

CHAPTER FIFTEEN

ORGANIZING AND INNOVATING IN THE MNE

LEARNING OBJECTIVES

After studying this chapter, you should be able to

1   Articulate the relationship between multinational strategy and structure

2   Outline the challenges associated with learning, innovation and knowledge management

3   Explain how institutions affect strategy and structure

4   Explain how institutions and resources affect strategy and structure

5   Participate in two leading debates on organizing and innovating in the MNE

6   Draw implications for action

OPENING CASE

The global organizational design of the 'Big Four'

by Mehdi Boussebaa

The global accountancy profession is dominated by four players that offer their services virtually all over the world: *PricewaterhouseCoopers* (*PwC*), *Deloitte Touche Tohmatsu*, *Ernst & Young* and *KPMG*. These 'Big Four', like other professional service firms such as management consultancies and law firms, are very important for today's economy because they broker complex business transactions and offer managerial advice to the world's largest companies. They offer a diversified range of intangible, knowledge-based services that go beyond their traditional core offerings – audit and assurance – to include financial advice and management consulting. These services are targeted at Fortune 500 corporations as well as smaller, local clients and government agencies. The

421

Big Four are also important because they are often held to be organizations of the future towards which other types of enterprise are converging. In the past, exemplary organizations were generally drawn from the manufacturing and retailing sectors but in the present era professional service firms such as the Big Four are regarded as *the* source of managerial and organizational inspiration.

Over the last few decades, the Big Four have continued to expand internationally, becoming enormous multinational organizations as a result. For instance, *PwC*, the largest of the Big Four, employs more than 160 000 people in 757 offices across 151 countries. In comparison, *General Motors* operates in 34 countries and *Wal-Mart* in 15. Such an international spread creates significant managerial and organizational challenges for the firms. In particular, the Big Four face the major challenge of serving large multinational clients who expect not only cutting edge and customized professional expertise but also seamless cross-national service. These clients also expect their advisors not only to provide different professional services but also to know about the countries and the industries in which they operate, creating a pressure on the Big Four to be structurally differentiated along three different axes: service line, geographic location and industry/market. This differentiation in turn requires the integration of competencies held by individuals and teams in different parts of the professional service firm, often in different places around the world.

How do the Big Four respond to these managerial and organizational challenges? Research conducted in these firms shows that they have been developing a 'multiplex' organizational form that consists of

a unique mélange of both structural and cultural features. Specifically, the multiplex form has three core elements. First, it is characterized by several axes of deep specialization: professional expertise (produced through service lines), client expertise (developed through industry and market research), and geographical expertise (built through an international network of local offices). For example, *Ernst & Young* offers not only a range of services (for example, assurance, advisory services and tax) but also claims expertise in 14 major industries (for example, energy, financial services, health care and pharmaceuticals). The firm is also organized into several geographical regions through which client service delivery is coordinated. Second, the multiplex form operates a sophisticated client management system, which connects teams of professionals drawn from the different expertise axes, and focuses their efforts on the task of satisfying client needs. Third, the multiplex is supported by a culture of reciprocity that holds the firm together and ensures that the differentiation forces do not overpower the effectiveness of its client management system. This culture of reciprocity is achieved by building relationships across the different specialization axes and reinforcing these through the development of an array of organizational processes, including career, communication, recruitment and socialization practices.

Sources: This case was prepared by Mehdi Boussebaa, University of Bath, based on R. Greenwood, T. Morris, S. Fairclough & M. Boussebaa, 2010, The organizational design of transnational professional service firms. *Organizational Dynamics*, 39, 39: 173–183. See also M. Boussebaa, 2009, Struggling to organize across national borders: The case of global resource management in professional service firms. *Human Relations*, 62: 829–850.

How can multinational enterprises (MNEs) such as *PwC* and *KPMG* organize their operations to be successful both locally and internationally? How can they make sure that people within the organization work together constructively? How can they foster the exchange of knowledge and improve the odds for better innovation? These are some of the key questions we address in this chapter.

MNEs operate in many different local contexts, and their ability to make connections between local contexts is crucial to achieve competitive advantage in global strategies (Chapter 14).[1] However, realizing such competitive advantages requires complex organizations that have to achieve many things simultaneously. Global MNEs are rarely hierarchical monoliths where the boss knows and decides everything, and thousands of people implement the decisions. Such central decision-making would kill creativity and initiative in the organization, and thus undermine many of the firm's capabilities. MNEs are typically knowledge-intensive firms, that is, firms where the creation, dissemination and/or exploitation of knowledge are essential for their competitive advantage. Hence how MNEs organize creative people and diverse subunits in distinct local contexts is at the core of this chapter.

We start by introducing a traditional view on organizing the MNEs based on the conflicting pressures for global integration and local responsiveness, followed by a modern view focused on knowledge management. Next, the institution- and resource-based views shed additional light on these issues. Debates and extensions follow.

ORGANIZATIONAL STRUCTURES IN MNES

The integration-responsiveness framework

The trade-offs between arbitrage and adaptation strategies (Chapter 14) provide the foundation for a popular conceptual framework known as the integration-responsiveness framework. First, global integration helps realizing aggregation benefits, such as economies of scale, global innovation and global sourcing, while local responsiveness accomodates idiosyncratic local consumer demand and institutions.[2] Pressures for local responsiveness arise from different consumer preferences and host country institutions, formal and informal. Consumer preferences vary tremendously around the world. For example, *McDonalds* beef-based hamburgers obviously would find few (or no) costumers in India, a land where cows are sacred. Thus *McDonalds* developed vegetarian product offerings specifically for India. Likewise, throughout Europe, Canadian firm *Bombardier* manufactures an Austrian version of railcars in Austria, a Belgian version in Belgium, and so on. *Bombardier* believes that such local responsiveness is essential for making sales to railway operators in continental Europe, which tend to be state-owned.

Being locally responsive may please local customers and other stakeholders, but these adaptations may increase cost because they reduce the potential for economies of scale. Given the universal interest in lowering cost, some globally operating MNEs downplay (or ignore) the different needs and wants of various local markets and market a 'global' version of their products and services – ranging from the world car to the global iPod. Integration and responsiveness, however, may not be incompatible. Management gurus Chris Bartlett and Sumantra Ghoshal argue that MNEs may be able to pursue both objectives simultaneously.[3] Hence integration-responsiveness is not a scale, but can be depicted as a 2 × 2 matrix with four strategies: (1) home replication, (2) localization, (3) global standards and (4) transnational strategy (Figure 15.1, Table 15.1). Each strategy has a set of pros and cons.[4]

Home replication strategy, often known as 'international' strategy, is based on replication of home country-based competencies, such as production scales, distribution efficiencies and brand positioning. Essentially, the operation abroad is built to resemble the home operation in the belief that this is the best way to transfer competences of the firm. This strategy is relatively easy to implement and may be used by firms venturing abroad for the first time.

A disadvantage is that this strategy suffers from a lack of local responsiveness. This makes sense when the majority of a firm's customers are back home. However, when the firm aspires to broaden its international scope to reach more foreign customers, failing to be mindful of foreign customers' needs and wants may result in their alienation. For instance, *Wal-Mart*, when entering Brazil, set up an exact copy of its stores in the USA, with a large number of American footballs (the oval ones). Obviously, in Brazil, the land of 'real' football, nobody (other than perhaps a few homesick US expatriates) plays American football. Setting up an exact replica only makes sense as a starting point for experimentation and learning on how best to adapt while retaining the core features of the business model.[5]

LEARNING OBJECTIVE

1 Articulate the relationship between multinational strategy and structure

integration-responsiveness framework
A framework of MNE management on how to simultaneously deal with two sets of pressures for global integration and local responsiveness.
local responsiveness
The necessity to be responsive to different customer preferences around the world.

home replication strategy
A strategy that emphasizes international replication of home country-based competencies such as production scales, distribution efficiencies and brand power.

Figure 15.1 Multinational strategies and structures: The integration-responsiveness framework

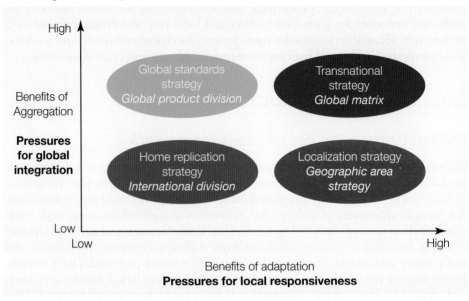

Note: In some other textbooks, 'home replication' may be referred to as 'international' strategy, 'localization' as 'multidomestic' strategy, and 'global standards' as 'global' strategy. Some of these labels are confusing because one can argue that all four strategies here are 'international' or 'global'. The present set of labels is more descriptive and (hopefully) less confusing.

localization (multidomestic) strategy
A strategy that focuses on a number of foreign countries/regions, each of which is regarded as a stand-alone 'local' (domestic) market worthy of significant attention and adaptation.

Localization (multidomestic) strategy is an extension of the home replication strategy. It considers each country or region as a stand-alone 'local' market worthy of significant attention and adaptation. Although sacrificing global efficiencies, this strategy is effective when there are clear differences between national and regional markets and few pressures for global economies of scale. When first venturing overseas, *MTV* started with a home replication strategy (literally, broadcasting American

Table 15.1 Four strategic choices for multinational enterprises

	Advantages	Disadvantages
Home replication	• Leverages home country-based advantages • Relatively easy to implement	• Lack of local responsiveness • May result in foreign customer alienation
Localization	• Maximizes local responsiveness	• High costs due to duplication of efforts in multiple countries • Too much local autonomy
Global standards	• Leverages economies of scale • Emphasizes integrated innovation	• Lack of local responsiveness • Too much centralized control
Transnational	• Cost-efficient while being locally responsive • Engages in global learning and diffusion of innovations	• Organizationally complex • Difficult to implement

programming). It then gradually moved to a localization strategy with eight channels, each in a different language, for Western Europe alone.

In terms of disadvantages, the localization strategy has to shoulder high costs due to duplication of efforts in multiple countries. The costs of producing such a variety of programming at *MTV* are obviously greater than the costs of producing one set of programming. As a result, this strategy is only appropriate in industries where economies of scale are not substantial. Another drawback is potentially too much local autonomy. Each subsidiary regards its country to be unique, and it is difficult to introduce corporate-wide changes. For example, *Unilever* had 17 country subsidiaries in Europe in the 1980s, and it took as long as four *years* to 'persuade' all 17 subsidiaries to introduce a single new detergent across Europe.

As the opposite of the localization strategy, the global standards strategy is sometimes simply referred to as 'global strategy'. Its hallmark is the development and distribution of standardized products worldwide to reap the maximum benefits from economies of scale and shared product development. Global standards do not imply that all core operations are based at home. In a number of countries, the MNE may designate centres of excellence, defined as subsidiaries explicitly recognized as a source of important capabilities that are leveraged by and/or disseminated to other subsidiaries.[6]

Global standards also help serving global clients.[7] MNEs in business-to-business markets, such as the Big Four accountancy firms (Opening Case) serve global key accounts, that is, customers who themselves operate at multiple sites and expect delivery of products or services across various countries. Most original equipment manufacturers (OEMs) – namely, contract manufacturers that produce goods *not* carrying their own brands (such as the makers of *Nike* shoes and *HP* computers) – use this structure. Singapore's *Flextronics*, the world's largest electronics OEM, has dedicated global accounts for *Dell*, *Palm* and *Sony Ericsson*. Hence all negotiations with these clients are channelled through the same person (or office), the global key account manager.

In terms of disadvantages, a global standards strategy sacrifices local responsiveness. It makes sense in industries where pressures for cost reduction are paramount and pressures for local responsiveness are relatively minor. For example, Japanese consumer electronics firms conquered the world in the 1980s with fairly standardized radios, CD-players and other gadgets. However, as noted earlier, in numerous industries, ranging from automobiles to foods, a one-size-fits-all strategy may be inappropriate.

A transnational strategy aims to capture the best of both worlds by endeavouring to be cost-efficient and locally responsive.[8] A hallmark of this strategy is global learning and diffusion of innovations. Traditionally, the diffusion of innovations in MNEs was a one-way flow from the home country to various host countries. Underpinning such a one-way flow was the assumption that the home country is the best location for generating innovations, an assumption that is increasingly challenged, for two reasons. First, given that innovations are inherently risky and uncertain, there is no guarantee that the home country will generate the highest quality innovations.[9] Second, for many large MNEs, their subsidiaries have acquired a variety of innovation capabilities, some of which may have the potential for wider applications elsewhere.[10] *GM* has ownership stakes in *Daewoo*, *Opel*, *Vauxhall*, *Subaru* and *Suzuki* as well as the *Shanghai GM* joint venture with China's *SAIC*. Historically, *GM* employed a localization strategy, and each subsidiary could decide what cars to produce by themselves. Consequently, some of these subsidiaries developed locally formidable but globally underutilized innovation capabilities and patents. It makes sense for *GM* to tap into some of these local capabilities (such as *Opel*'s prowess in what Americans call 'compact' cars) for wider applications. MNEs that engage in a

global standards strategy
A strategy that relies on the development and distribution of standardized products worldwide to reap the maximum benefits from low-cost advantages.

centre of excellence
An MNE subsidiary explicitly recognized as a source of important capabilities, with the intention that these capabilities be leveraged by and/or disseminated to other subsidiaries.

global key accounts
Customers who themselves operate at multiple sites where they expect delivery.

transnational strategy
A strategy that endeavours to be cost-efficient, locally responsive and learning-driven simultaneously around the world.

transnational strategy promote global learning and diffusion of innovations. Hence knowledge flows from the home country to host countries (which is the traditional flow) but also from host countries to the home country and among subsidiaries in multiple host countries.[11]

The IR framework is well established but it is not without problems. First, a transnational strategy is organizationally complex and difficult to implement. The large amount of knowledge sharing and coordination may slow down decision speed. Simultaneously trying to achieve cost efficiencies, local responsiveness and global learning places contradictory demands on MNEs (discussed later in this chapter). Second, the IR framework does not take account of other important dimensions of global strategy, such as the stage in the value chain of the subsidiary.[12]

Four organizational structures

Also shown in Figure 15.1, there are four organizational structures approximately matching the four strategic choices just outlined: (1) international division structure, (2) geographic area structure, (3) global product division structure and (4) global matrix structure.

international division
A structure bundling all international activities in one unit, often associated with a home replication strategy.

An international division is typically set up when firms initially expand abroad, often engaging in a home replication strategy. For example, for many years *Starbucks* bundled all non-USA-based coffee shops into one international division, complementing its four product divisions that primarily focus on the USA (Figure 15.2). Although this structure is intuitively appealing, it often leads to two problems. First, foreign subsidiary managers, whose input may be channelled through the international division, are not given sufficient voice relative to the heads of domestic divisions.[13] Second, by design, the international division serves as a 'silo' whose activities are not coordinated with the rest of the firm that focuses on domestic activities. Consequently, such an organizational structure is mainly used by firms where international sales contribute only a small share of their revenues. As international operations become more important, firms tend to reorganize. For example, in 2011, *Starbucks* created three regional divisions for, respectively, the Americas, Asia Pacific, and Europe, Middle East and Africa.[14]

geographic area structure
An organizational structure that organizes the MNE according to different countries and regions.

A geographic area structure organizes the MNE according to different geographic areas. It is the most appropriate structure for a localization strategy. Figure 15.3 illustrates such a structure for *Arcelor-Mittal*, a Europe-based, Indian-owned steel

Figure 15.2   International division structure at *Starbucks* before 2011

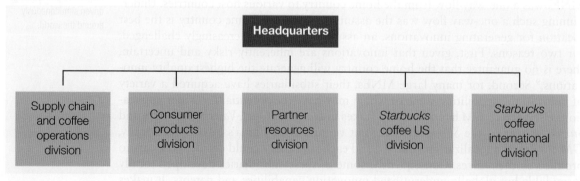

Note: Headquartered in Seattle, USA, *Starbucks* operated coffee houses around the world.

Source: (1) www.cogmap.com; (2) www.starbucks.com.

Figure 15.3 Geographic area structure at *ArcelorMittal* steel

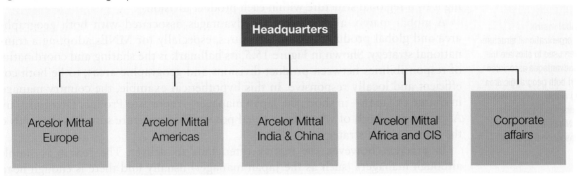

Note: Headquartered in London, UK, *Mittal Steel* was the world's largest steelmaker. After its merger with *Arcelor* in 2007, it moved to a mixed geographic/product structure.

Source: www.mittalsteel.com (accessed March, 2007).

Figure 15.4 Global product division structure at *Airbus*

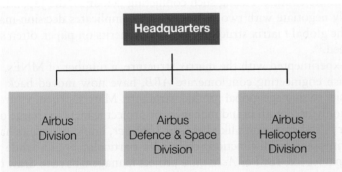

Note: Headquartered in Munich, Germany, and Paris, France, *Airbus* is the largest commercial aircraft maker and the largest defence contractor in Europe.

Source: eads.com.

company. A geographic area can be a country or a region, led by a country or regional manager. Each area is largely stand-alone. In contrast to the limited voice of subsidiary managers in the international division structure, country and regional managers carry a great deal of weight in a geographic area structure. Interestingly and paradoxically, *both* the strengths and weaknesses of this structure lie in its local responsiveness. Although being locally responsive can be a virtue, it also encourages the fragmentation of the MNE into autonomous, hard-to-control 'fiefdoms'.[15] Few global companies still use such a structure, unless they are focused on a single line of business.

A global product division structure, which is the opposite of the geographic area structure, supports the global standards strategy. Figure 15.4 shows such an example from *Airbus*. This structure treats each product division as a stand-alone entity with full worldwide – as opposed to domestic – responsibilities. This structure greatly facilitates attention to pressures for cost efficiencies because it allows for consolidation on a worldwide (or at least regional) basis and reduces inefficient duplication in multiple countries. For example, *Unilever* reduced the number of soap-producing factories in Europe from ten to two after adopting this structure. Most MNEs operating in more

country or regional manager
The business leader of a specific geographic area or region.

global product division
An organizational structure that assigns global responsibilities to each product division.

global matrix
An organizational structure often used to alleviate the disadvantages associated with both geographic area and global product division structures, especially for MNEs adopting a transnational strategy.

than one line of business have adopted a product division structure, some supplementing it by a regional structure within each product division.

A global matrix alleviates the disadvantages associated with both geographic area and global product division structures, especially for MNEs adopting a transnational strategy. Shown in Figure 15.5, its hallmark is the sharing and coordination of responsibilities between product divisions and geographic areas, to be both cost efficient and locally responsive. In this hypothetical example, the country manager in charge of Japan – in short, the Japan manager – reports to Product Division 1 and Asia Division, both of which have equal power. This structure supports the goals of the transnational strategy.

In practice, however, the matrix often fails to deliver. The reason is simple: although managers (such as the Japan manager) usually find there is enough headache dealing with one boss, they do not appreciate having to deal with two bosses, who are often in conflict! For example, Product Division 1 may decide that Japan is too tough a nut to crack and that there are more promising markets elsewhere, thus ordering the Japan manager to *curtail* investment and channel resources elsewhere. However, Asia Division, which is evaluated by how well it does in Asia, may beg to differ. It argues that to be a leading player in Asia, it cannot afford to be a laggard in Japan. Therefore, Asia Division demands that the Japan manager *increase* investment in the country. Facing such conflicting demands, the Japan manager has to constantly negotiate with two bosses, which complicates decision-making. Consequently, the global matrix structure, despite its merits on paper, often slows down decision speed.[16]

Having experimented with the matrix structure, a number of MNEs, such as the Swiss-Swedish engineering conglomerate *ABB*, have now moved back to the simpler and easier to manage global product structure. Matrix structures are nowadays more commonly used with brand managers or project leaders in charge of the 'row': in consumer brand companies like *P&G* or *Unilever*, brand managers have to coordinate activities across all functions to build a particular brand, while in business service companies like *IBM* or *Accenture* project managers have to draw on different units to design and implement a project for a particular client.

Figure 15.5 A hypothetical global matrix structure

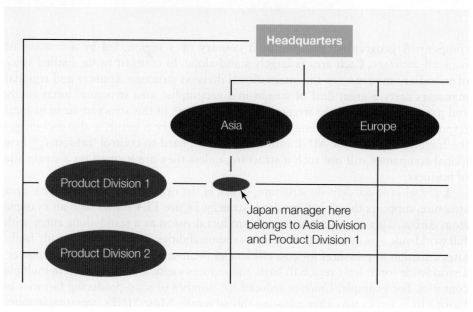

Neither strategies nor structures are static. They evolve typically from the relatively simple international division through either geographic area or global product division structures. Structures also change in response to external pressures.[17] In Europe, many MNEs traditionally pursued a localization strategy supported by the geographic area structure. However, the single market of the European Union has made such a structure obsolete. Consequently, more MNEs have now moved toward a pan-European strategy with a region-wide structure.

MANAGING KNOWLEDGE IN GLOBAL MNES

Knowledge is created at many places in the MNE. Each subsidiary is generating knowledge through the interactions of people within the subsidiary, and through the interaction of the subsidiary with (1) other units of the MNE, and (2) with people and organizations in its local context, but outside the MNE (Figure 15.6). Many MNEs deliberately invest in innovation-seeking activities abroad, aiming to tap into such local knowledge.[18] As a result, MNEs themselves are embedded in multiple local contexts (countries) at home and in multiple host countries.[19] The opportunities of accessing and creating knowledge around the world are vast, yet the challenges of knowledge management in such a complex setting are equally vast.

LEARNING OBJECTIVE

2 Outline the challenges associated with learning, innovation and knowledge management

Transforming knowledge

Many of the capabilities that are the foundation of MNEs' competitiveness are grounded in knowledge. Food ingredients manufacturer *Danisco* (Chapter 14, Opening Case) recognized this in its slogan '*First you add Knowledge*'. Some scholars argue that knowledge management is *the* defining feature of MNEs.[20] Knowledge management can be defined as the structures, processes and systems that actively develop, leverage and transfer knowledge.

knowledge management
The structures, processes and systems that actively develop, leverage and transfer knowledge.

Figure 15.6   Multinational enterprises and local context

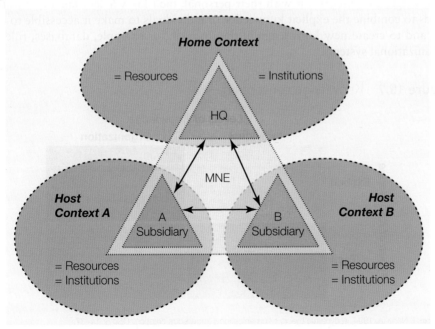

Knowledge is a broad concept that includes not only factual information, but also the know-how and know-why held by individuals and by the firm as a whole. Hence sophisticated information technology (IT), such as software provided by *SAP* (Chapter 4, Opening Case), is an important foundation, but knowledge management concerns also the informal social relationships within the MNE that facilitate the creation and sharing of knowledge. This is because there are two categories of knowledge:

- Explicit knowledge is codifiable (that is, can be written down and transferred with little loss of its richness). Virtually all the knowledge captured, stored and transmitted by IT is explicit.

- Tacit knowledge is non-codifiable and its acquisition and transfer require hands-on practice.[21] For instance, mastering a driving manual (containing a lot of explicit knowledge) without any road practice does not make you a good driver. Tacit knowledge is evidently more important and harder to transfer and learn; it can only be acquired through learning by doing (driving, in this case).

Knowledge is often held by individuals – you know how to study and get a good mark in your exam, employees in companies individually 'know' how to do their specific job. However, there is also knowledge held by the team or organization. For example, a football team knows how to launch an attack, or defend, based on patterns of interaction between the members of a team. This organizational (or team-embedded) knowledge is more than the sum of the knowledge held by individuals; it is held by the organization either in shared repositories of documents and data, or embedded in the practices and routines of the members of the team. Based on the two distinctions explicit/tacit knowledge and individual/organizational knowledge, Japanese scholar Ikujiro Nonaka identified four types of knowledge that organizations have to manage (Figure 15.7).

Knowledge management requires transformation of different forms of knowledge, such that knowledge held by individuals can be shared, and individuals utilize knowledge held in the organization in their own work. Thus tacit knowledge of individuals (cell 3) has to be made explicit (cell 1), for example, by writing manuals or by entering it into databases. At the same time, individuals have to adopt the explicit knowledge, and integrate it with their personal, tacit knowledge. The organization needs to combine the explicit knowledge of individuals to make it accessible to others, and to create new knowledge in the form of, for example, databases, rules or organizational systems.

Figure 15.7   Knowledge conversion

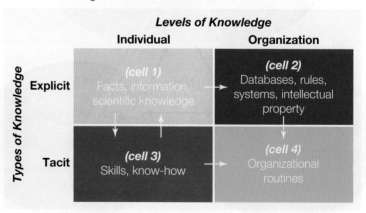

Source: I. Nonaka, 1994, A dynamic theory of organizational knowledge creation, *OSc* 5: 14–37.

However, organizations 'know' more than the content of their databases. Think of a professional football team, such as Manchester United: they may have video recordings and analyses of their main competitors, such as Real Madrid, codified in databases. However, individual players may have played against them before, or they have experiences competing with Spanish teams playing a similar style. They develop organizational routines (such as how to launch a counter-attack, how to score from a free kick or a corner) partly by studying the organizational explicit knowledge, and partly by sharing knowledge from player to player in a process known as socialization (cell 4). As a result, the team shares organizational knowledge that is more than the sum of the knowledge of individuals and that, due to its tacit nature, is hard to describe. Yet everyone knows it is there. Football teams that have played together for a long time have more such team-embedded knowledge than those just recently assembled for a game. That is why teams with few star players sometimes can beat the teams composed of many stars – think of 'minnows' such as Croatia, Denmark or Greece beating major football nations such as Spain or Germany in the European Championships.

Managing knowledge in football teams is easy – compared to MNEs. There are only 11 players (plus their support staff) and they all work at the same location, the football pitch. However, many MNEs comprise thousands of people dispersed all over the world. How can they manage their knowledge? We start by looking at the four types of strategy.

Knowledge management in four types of MNEs

Knowledge flow from the centre to the periphery is the essence of a home replication strategy. Subsidiaries largely adapt and leverage parent company competencies. Thus the parent company develops knowledge about new products and technologies, and then transfers it to subsidiaries in a traditional one-way flow. To be able to do that, the company has to make the tacit knowledge of its people explicit in, for example, manuals that can then be transferred across the organization – and to subsidiaries abroad. The most famous historical example of such a process is Henry Ford's Model T in the 1920s. Before that, cars would be individually built by skilled craftsmen. With the standardization of processes in mass production, *Ford* codified the knowledge and thus made it transferable to new employees who do not need the craftsman training.[22] In the same way, the knowledge could also be transferred to new plants abroad. More recent examples of such a strategy are *McDonalds'* hamburgers, *Starbucks'* coffee houses, or *Subway* sandwiches. Codification makes organizational knowledge explicit and thus allows its transfer abroad.

In MNEs adopting a localization strategy, most knowledge exchange takes place within subsidiaries, with limited knowledge transfer between units. Initially, the subsidiary may be set up with a knowledge transfer from headquarters, but then the subsidiary develops a life of its own, developing knowledge that can best tackle local markets. From the 1950s to the 1980s, *Ford* developed cars in Europe for European customers with limited flows of knowledge from and to headquarters.

In MNEs pursuing a global standards strategy, the interdependence is increased. Knowledge is developed and retained at headquarters and a few centres of excellence at other locations. Consequently, there is an extensive flow of knowledge and people from these centres to other subsidiaries. Knowledge flows within the centre(s) thus involves the full cycle of knowledge creation and codification, while knowledge from the centre may be codified to facilitate the transfer. For example, *Yokogawa Hewlett-Packard*, *HP*'s subsidiary in Japan, won a coveted Japanese Deming Award for quality. The subsidiary was then charged with transferring such knowledge to the rest of the *HP* family, which resulted in a tenfold improvement in *corporate-wide* quality in ten years.[23]

Table 15.2 Knowledge management in four types of multinational enterprise

Strategy	Home replication	Localization	Global standards	Transnational
Interdependence	Moderate	Low	Moderate	High
Role of foreign subsidiaries	Adapting and leveraging parent company competencies	Sensing and exploiting local opportunities	Implementing parent company initiatives	Differentiated contributions by subsidiaries to integrated worldwide operations
Development and diffusion of knowledge	Knowledge developed at the centre and transferred to subsidiaries	Knowledge developed and retained within each subsidiary	Knowledge mostly developed and retained at the centre and key locations	Knowledge developed jointly and shared worldwide
Flow of knowledge	Extensive flow of knowledge and people from headquarters to subsidiaries	Limited flow of knowledge and people to and from the centre	Extensive bilateral flow of knowledge and people between the centre and subsidiaries	Extensive flow of knowledge and people in multiple directions, also across subsidiaries

Sources: (1) C. Bartlett & S. Ghoshal, 1989, Managing across Borders: The Transnational Solution (p. 65), Boston: Harvard Business School Press; (2) T. Kostova & K. Roth, 2003, Social capital in multinational corporations and a micro-macro model of its formation (p. 299), *Academy of Management Review*, 28 (2): 297–317.

reverse knowledge transfer
Knowledge created in a subsidiary being transferred from the subsidiary to a parent organization.

Such reverse knowledge transfer – new knowledge created in a subsidiary being transferred from the subsidiary to a parent organization – is of increasing importance in a global interconnected world (see In Focus 15.1).[24] Yet operationally it is often not easy, for three reasons. First, headquarters usually combine a high degree of power with some degree of 'not invented here' syndrome. Thus there may be inherent resistance, and the ability to block initiatives coming from subsidiaries. Second, if a subsidiary is technologically more advanced, then the headquarters may lack the competences to assess the technology and its potential applications within headquarter operations. The third challenge is particularly relevant for emerging economy firms seeking to tap into technology and managerial knowledge in Europe or North America: that sought knowledge is often embedded in organizational routines and cultures; the effective transfer of best practice would thus require major changes in the organizational culture of the parent organization, which is difficult to achieve given the often steep hierarchies and personal loyalties permeating many emerging economy businesses.[25]

Transnational MNEs are built on extensive and multi-directional flows of knowledge.[26] For example, extending a popular ice cream developed in Argentina based on a locally popular caramelized milk dessert, *Häagen-Dazs* introduced the flavour, Dulce de Leche, to the USA and Europe. Within one year, it became the second most popular *Häagen-Dazs* ice cream (second only to vanilla).[27] Particularly fundamental to transnational MNEs is knowledge flows between dispersed subsidiaries.

Instead of a top-down hierarchy, the MNE thus can be conceptualized as an integrated network of subsidiaries (sometimes called the 'N-form'), each not only developing locally relevant knowledge, but also aspiring to contribute globally beneficial knowledge that enhances corporate-wide competitiveness of the MNE as a whole.

IN FOCUS 15.1

Reverse innovation at McDonalds

Faced with increasing competition from new fast food chains like *Subway*, *Five Guys* and *Chipotle*, *McDonalds* was losing market share in its home market, the USA. Younger people especially were no longer drawn to its hamburger diet and were looking for fresh and ethically sourced foods, yet still with the convenience of fast service.

In response, *McDonalds* has unleashed across the USA the McWrap, a 20-centimetre white-flour tortilla wrapped around 85 grams of chicken, plus lettuce, spring greens, sliced cucumbers, tomatoes and cheese – all for US$3.99. Customers can choose their preferred dressing: ranch, sweet chilli or creamy garlic. Made to order, the McWrap can be prepared in under 60 seconds. When served, it comes with a cardboard wrapper whose top can be zipped open. The whole thing can fit vertically in a cup holder in a car (important in the USA!). The two-year efforts to fix *McDonalds* freshness problem illustrates how a multinational can change its strategy by tapping into its global organization. Dissecting the launch of McWrap, we can see at least three things.

First, the idea did not come from the USA. It came from three operations in Europe. In 2004, *McDonalds* in the Czech Republic started selling the Chicken Roll Up. In 2005, *McDonalds* in Poland introduced a pancake, inspired by popular street food. In 2009, Austria pioneered the nifty cardboard container that can be unzipped. Thanks to a European food studio (which would be called an R&D lab in many other firms), these local innovations were noticed and adapted by *McDonalds*.

Second, the McWrap idea was attractive to headquarters because of its strategic search for fresher and healthier items to outcompete local rivals offering fresher ingredients. Specifically, it was the search for local responsiveness – in this case in *McDonald's* home country, the USA – that identified the wrap to be a good potential fit. Americans are changing their eating habits, eating more chicken, and preferring more fresh food, and the wrap might enable *McDonalds* to respond to such change.

Third, significant experimentation and learning went into the process. Led by Dan Courfreaut, executive chef and vice president of 'culinary innovation', *McDonalds* menu innovation team undertook intense

How did European pancakes inspire *McDonalds* in the USA?

research and numerous experiments that ultimately took two years to complete. The food had to be tasty, low-cost, and fast to serve – without compromising quality. To enhance freshness, two slices of English cucumber were added for the first time to *McDonalds* offerings. While adding a tiny bit of cucumber does not sound like a big deal, it was actually quite a challenge to *McDonalds* supply chain structure, as farmers had to be recruited to farm the particular variety. Initial tests used half a chicken breast. But focus groups thought the wrap was a salad – with too many vegetables. Despite the rising health awareness, customers actually wanted more meat. So, the final version of the wrap had a full breast of chicken. The wrap's name also went through intense testing. In the first trial in Chicago, it was called the Grande Wrap. But customers could not figure out what 'grande' was. Then the name Fresh Garden Wrap was tested in Orlando, and it flopped too. Eventually, McWrap was chosen.

Sources: (1) Mike Peng's interviews, (2) *Bloomberg Businessweek*, 2013, McFresh, July 8: 44–49; (3) *Wall Street Cheat Sheet*, 2013, 8 reasons McDonald's is praying the McWrap is a smash hit, July 10, wallstcheatsheet.com; (4) www.mcdonalds.com.

Communities of practice

community of practice (CoP)
Group of people doing similar or related work and sharing knowledge about their practices of work.

Most knowledge creation takes place in groups of people doing similar or related tasks, known as a community of practice (CoP).[28] When people work, their practices may not follow the rules laid down in manuals exactly, but they evolve with experimentation and innovation on the job. If people doing the same or similar types of work are closely connected by a social network, they can exchange such new knowledge before it gets codified. Knowledge exchange within a CoP thus is more timely and relevant to the participants' practice than the traditional process of codifying knowledge, and then sharing it with relevant parties. A CoP can be a powerful forum to share knowledge within a firm. Thus firms may foster social interaction between people doing similar jobs. One simple way to do that is to offer free coffee in the office: the coffee machine becomes a point where people meet, gossip and exchange practical knowledge about their job.

Organizing CoPs is more complex in MNEs operating across multiple locations, and where people speak different languages and originate from different cultures. Some MNEs take deliberate steps to facilitate the formation of CoPs. For example, *Shell* recognizes the contribution of CoPs to innovation, and systematically supports initiatives by staff to establish them.[29] CoPs can operate through face-to-face interaction, for instance by bringing experts on specialist topics together in workshops and 'away days'. Other CoPs operate as virtual communities of practice, sharing information on the intranet of the MNE. If members of a virtual CoP share common professional qualifications and other tacit knowledge, they can perhaps share tacit knowledge more effectively than corporate databases.[30] For example, *Siemens* introduced a system for knowledge sharing through codification and shared databases (In Focus 15.2). Yet beyond identifying the relevant experts, the more effective means to share knowledge often remains direct interaction within a CoP.

virtual community of practice
Community of practice interacting via the internet.

On a local level, CoPs can easily cross organizational boundaries: think of IT geeks in Silicon Valley hanging out at the same parties exchanging tacit knowledge about the latest trends in the industry. A presence in different local contexts with varying institutions and resources is an important stimulus to innovation. Overseas R&D provides a vehicle to access a foreign country's local talents and expertise.[31] Collaborative research with external partners, such as other firms or university research labs, provides important sources of innovation.[32] However, connecting such a local CoP with the MNE's internal (virtual) CoP is a challenge that few firms have accomplished.[33] Thus multiple embeddedness creates complex managerial

IN FOCUS 15.2

Siemens' *ShareNet: a knowledge management system*

Siemens, headquartered in Munich, is an engineering conglomerate that produces power generation equipment, transportation systems, medical devices and numerous other industrial products. In the early 1990s, *Siemens* was, in the words of its then CEO, 'an introverted, some would say arrogant, company, particularly in Germany, where 50% of our business and more than 50% of the people were still located at that time'. Yet by 2013, 228 000 of *Siemens'* 413 000 employees were working outside of Germany, and 85% of sales were generated internationally. A critical element in the transformation to a global organization was to develop processes to connect and rejuvenate its employees' comprehensive knowledge and expertise that was geographically dispersed in 190 countries. Thus *Siemens* invested heavily in developing new knowledge management (KM) systems that would develop, sustain and exploit its corporate memory.

A major initiative, called 'ShareNet', was launched in 1998 and went through four steps. First, the concept definition envisioned ShareNet not only to handle explicit knowledge but also tacit knowledge. To overcome the drawbacks of traditional, repository-based KM systems, the new system had to integrate interactive components, such as a forum for urgent requests and a platform for sharing rich knowledge. Pilot tests were carried out in Australia, China, Malaysia and Portugal to gain cross-cultural insights from users far from Munich.

The second step was the global rollout for 39 countries. Balancing global integration and local responsiveness, strategic direction for the project came from Munich, with ShareNet managers in each local subsidiary. These people from local subsidiaries were to become the nucleus in their regions. ShareNet managers held local workshops and encouraged participants to post an unsolved problem as an urgent request that would be sent to all users worldwide. Without exception, by the end of the day, the posting would get at least one reply, and inevitably the person who had posted it would be 'stunned'.

The third step was generating momentum. Many people said: 'I don't have time for this.' Others put it more bluntly: 'Why do I have to share?' In the early stages, *Siemens* provided incentives for country managers and rewarded a country's overall participation. For a successful sale resulting from ShareNet collaboration, a bonus was given to both the country that had contributed the knowledge and the country that used it. Individual contributors were rewarded with gifts and prizes, such as mobile phones, books and even trips to visit knowledge exchange partners. Contrary to expectations, the average number of contributed knowledge pieces per contributor in China (16.67) was much higher than in the USA (3.29). Indian employees were also enthusiastic. The ShareNet team suspected that this was in part because rewards were more attractive to Chinese and Indian employees (who were usually paid less) than to US employees. In India, some employees became overzealous, made low-quality contributions, and even neglected their 'day jobs'. The ShareNet team consequently adjusted rewards.

The fourth step was consolidating and sustaining performance. By 2002, ShareNet had 19 000 users in more than 80 countries, supported by 53 ShareNet managers in different countries. After the initial establishment, the ShareNet team was trimmed to fewer than ten members worldwide. User behaviour also changed substantially. There was a noticeable decline in knowledge contributions, although the level of urgent requests was maintained. The rationale was simple: an urgent request could directly help to solve an immediate problem in a tough time, whereas knowledge contributions did not yield an immediate payoff to the contributor. To demonstrate value added, the ShareNet team documented €5 million direct profits that had been generated by the KM system.

Sources: (1) *Economist*, 2007, European business: Home and abroad, February 10; (2) www.siemens.com; (3) T. Stewart & L. O'Brien, 2005, Transforming an industrial giant, *Harvard Business Review*, February: 115–122; (4) S.C. Voelpel, M. Dous & T. Davenport, 2005, Five steps to creating a global knowledge-sharing system: Siemens' ShareNet, *Academy of Management Executive*, 19: 9–23; (5) *Siemens*, 2015, Annual Report 2014.

challenges for MNEs to convert opportunities of knowledge creation into success stories.

More than most, the Big Four accountancy firms have to deal with complex challenges of knowledge management (Opening Case). They have created structures in which individual consultants are embedded in three types of CoP: line of service (assurance, M&A advisory, etc.), geographic (Americas, EMEA [Europe, Middle East and Africa], Far East, etc.) and customer industries (consumer products, pharmaceuticals, health sector, etc.). For every customer contract, a team is assembled that brings together the relevant expertise from different CoPs and different locations around the world.[34]

Knowledge governance

What organizational structures and mechanisms do MNEs use to facilitate the creation, integration, sharing and utilization of knowledge? This question is the essence of knowledge governance.[35] It is easy to show the benefits of knowledge exchange across an organization, yet the individual people in the MNE may not behave in ways that optimize knowledge flows. The challenges to be tackled include knowledge retention, knowledge sharing, knowledge transmission and knowledge utilization (Table 15.3).[36]

A basic problem is the retention of knowledge. Since knowledge, especially tacit knowledge, is often embedded in individuals, the departure of key individuals, such as star designers or R&D personnel, can lead to the loss of knowledge-based capabilities. In the worst case, employees may take their knowledge to competitors.[37]

In knowledge sharing, the key question is whether those who have knowledge are willing to share this knowledge with those in the organization who need it. Specifically, managers of the source subsidiary may view outbound sharing of knowledge as a diversion of scarce time and resources, asking 'How does it help me/us?' Further, some managers may believe that 'knowledge is power', and monopolizing certain knowledge may be viewed as the currency to acquire and retain power within the MNE.[38] Even when certain subsidiaries are willing to share knowledge, inappropriate transmission channels may still undermine the effectiveness knowledge

knowledge governance
The structures and mechanisms MNEs use to facilitate the creation, integration, sharing and utilization of knowledge.

Table 15.3 Selected challenges in knowledge governance

Elements of knowledge governance	Challenges	Common obstacles
Knowledge retention	Can the firm keep the knowledge it has accumulated?	Employee turnover and knowledge leakage
Knowledge sharing	Are people willing to share knowledge with others inside the firm?	'How does it help me?' syndrome and 'knowledge is power' mentality
Knowledge transmission	Is knowledge communicated effectively between people and business units?	Inappropriate channels, language barriers
Knowledge utilization	Do potential recipients appreciate and utilize knowledge available elsewhere in the organization?	'Not invented here' syndrome, lack of absorptive capacity

Source: A. Gupta & V. Govindarajan, 2004, *Global Strategy and Organization* (p. 109), New York: Wiley.

sharing.[39] Virtual CoPs help, but they are less effective than face-to-face interaction. Finally, recipient subsidiaries may present two problems that block successful knowledge inflows. First, the 'not invented here' syndrome causes some managers to resist accepting ideas from other units. Second, recipient subsidiaries may have limited absorptive capacity – the 'ability to recognize the value of new information, assimilate it, and apply it'.[40]

absorptive capacity
The ability to recognize the value of new information, assimilate it and apply it.

As solutions to combat these problems, corporate headquarters can manipulate the formal rules of the game, such as (1) tying bonuses to measurable knowledge outflows and inflows, (2) using high-powered, corporate- or business-unit-based incentives (as opposed to individual- and single-subsidiary-based incentives) and (3) investing in codifying tacit knowledge. *Siemens* used some of these measures when promoting its ShareNet (In Focus 15.2). However, these formal policies fundamentally boil down to the very challenging (if not impossible) task of how to accurately measure inflows and outflows of tacit knowledge. The nature of tacit knowledge simply resists such formal bureaucratic practices. Moreover, high powered incentives may undermine a corporate culture of sharing knowledge, as individuals focus on initiatives that are measured and rewarded, while reducing informal means of sharing that can be more timely and effective. In other words, large bonuses can undermine a cooperative culture.[41]

Consequently, MNEs often rely on a great deal of informal integrating mechanisms, such as (1) facilitating management and R&D personnel networks among various subsidiaries through joint teamwork, training and conferences and (2) promoting strong organizational (that is, MNE-specific) cultures and shared values and norms for cooperation among subsidiaries.[42] The key idea is that instead of using traditional, formal command-and-control structures that are often ineffective, knowledge management is best facilitated by informal social capital, which refers to the informal benefits individuals and organizations derive from their social structures and networks.[43] Because of the existence of social capital, individuals are more likely to go out of their way to help friends and acquaintances. Consequently, managers of the China subsidiary are more likely to help managers of the Chile subsidiary if they know each other and have some social relationship. Otherwise, managers of the China subsidiary may not be as enthusiastic to provide such help if the call for help comes from managers of the Cameroon subsidiary, with whom there is no social relationship. Overall, informal interpersonal relationships among managers of different units may greatly facilitate inter-subsidiary cooperation among units.

social capital
The informal benefits individuals and organizations derive from their social structures and networks.

Subsidiary mandates

If MNEs are no longer monolithic, hierarchical organizations, and if knowledge originates throughout the global network of the MNE, then subsidiaries have more important roles than implementing decisions by headquarters. This leads subsidiaries to attain, potentially, considerable autonomy within the MNE, and the possibility of becoming worldwide leaders in certain specializations. Many MNEs have created centres of excellence with a worldwide (or global) mandate – namely, the charter to be responsible for one MNE function throughout the world. *HP*'s Singapore subsidiary, for instance, has a worldwide mandate to develop, produce and market all *HP* handheld products.

worldwide (or global) mandate
The charter to be responsible for one MNE function throughout the world.

Many MNEs provide subsidiaries the autonomy to design their own *subsidiary-level* strategies and agendas.[44] These activities are known as subsidiary initiatives, defined as the proactive and deliberate pursuit of new opportunities by a subsidiary to expand its scope of responsibility.[45] For example, managers in *Honeywell*'s Canadian subsidiary anticipated that their sub-scale operation may be closed down when North American economic integration gathers pace. Therefore, they approached

subsidiary initiative
The proactive and deliberate pursuit of new opportunities by a subsidiary to expand its scope of responsibility.

their US-based headquarters to propose themselves as a global centre for excellence for certain product lines. In exchange, they agreed to shut down some inefficient lines. Negotiations followed and eventually the Canadian subsidiary was designated as a *Honeywell* centre of excellence for valves and actuators.[46] Other initiatives concern changing the product portfolio in ways not envisaged by the global strategy, as did *Schenck Shanghai Machinery*, a subsidiary of the German *Dürr* group (see Closing Case).

Providing subsidiary managers with the freedom to act entrepreneurially in their own markets is a powerful way to elicit their best ideas and initiatives. Yet subsidiary autonomy also makes it more difficult to realize the benefits of integration, in particular, economies of scale and shared standards and practices. When headquarters want to introduce common practices throughout the organization (such as quality circles), some subsidiaries may be happy to comply, others may pay lip service, and still others may object, citing local differences.[47] In such situations, subsidiary employees often argue that headquarters, especially those staffed by parent country nationals only, take decisions in more or less ignorance about the local context of the subsidiary, and that practices imported from, say, the USA will do more harm than good.

From the perspective of corporate headquarters, it is often hard to distinguish between good-faith subsidiary initiatives and opportunistic 'empire building'. For instance, a lot is at stake when determining which subsidiaries become centres of excellence with worldwide mandates.[48] Subsidiaries that fail to attain this status may see their roles marginalized and, in the worst case, their facilities closed. Subsidiary managers often identify with the subsidiary and the host country, and naturally prefer to strengthen their subsidiary. The challenge thus is to create systems of international competition and performance assessment that constrain self-seeking behaviours while encouraging entrepreneurial initiatives.

INSTITUTIONS AND THE CHOICE OF ORGANIZATIONAL STRUCTURE

MNEs face different sets of institutions that influence the ways in which they can organize their business, including institutions (1) in their home country and (2) in their host countries. We discuss them in turn.

Home country institutions

MNEs are subject to the national institutional frameworks in each context in which they are operating. These institutional differences influence organizational forms in several ways, including the adaptation of the multi-divisional form. Historically, most firms were organized either as holding companies (if they operated in multiple businesses), or by functions along the value chain, separating purchasing, manufacturing and sales units (if they operate in a small number of industries). However, with increasing diversity of products and markets, such an organizational form was no longer appropriate. Starting in the USA in the 1950s, companies started introducing product division structures or geographic division structures discussed earlier.[49] These 'multi-divisional' forms were favoured in particular by outside financial investors who wanted clearer transparency and more efficient stock markets. The new forms were soon adopted by British MNEs that faced a similar institutional context as US firms, especially the financial market.[50] Yet in France and Germany, individual owners, bankers and the state play a larger role in the context of a coordinated market economy (Chapter 2). This institutional context led to considerably slower adaptation of multi-divisional forms in French or German firms.[51] Similarly, institutional differences explain why US and British firms tend to be more focused on a single line of business, whereas German, French and Japanese businesses tend to have a higher degree of product diversification.[52]

The four modern organizational structures also vary across home countries. US companies traditionally were more likely to use home replication strategies and, due to the huge size of their home market, many of them continue to use an international division structure, even if this division is allowed to localize its strategy. European MNES were operating traditionally in very distinct national markets, which encouraged localization strategies and geographic division structures. With the introduction of the EU single market in 1993, these differences diminished, and reduced the case for a geographic structure, leading firms to integrate operations more across countries and moving to product division or matrix structures.

Host country institutions

Host country governments, on the other hand, often attract or encourage MNEs into undertaking activities. For example, basic manufacturing generates low-paying jobs, but does not provide substantial technology spillovers to local businesses, and carries little prestige. Advanced manufacturing, R&D and regional headquarters, on the other hand, generate higher-paying jobs and provide more technology spillovers.[53] Therefore, host country governments often use a combination of 'carrots' (such as tax incentives and free infrastructure upgrades) and 'sticks' (such as threats to block market access) to attract MNE investments in higher value-added activities (see Chapter 6).

Many government incentive schemes specifically focus on attracting MNEs that contribute to the science and technology base of the country by establishing R&D units. Numerous subsidy schemes and tax breaks have been created to attract R&D operations. However, MNEs tend to look more broadly for the institutional framework influencing innovation activity, also known as national innovation systems.[54] Thus MNEs locate their R&D units near quality universities and research laboratories, and where networks between business and academia facilitate knowledge flows.[55]

national innovation systems
The institutions and organizations that influence innovation activity in a country.

There are also numerous elements of informal institutions when dealing with *host* countries. For instance, *Airbus* spends 40% of its procurement budget with US suppliers. While there is no formal requirement for *Airbus* to 'farm out' supply contracts, its sourcing decisions are guided by the informal norm of reciprocity: if one country's suppliers are involved with *Airbus*, airlines based in that country are more likely to buy *Airbus* aircraft. Such informal norms of producing or sourcing locally are particularly important when selling to government entities that are under political pressures to 'keep jobs at home'.

RESOURCE-BASED CONSIDERATIONS

LEARNING OBJECTIVE

4 Explain how institutions and resources affect strategy and structure

The resource-based view – exemplified by the VRIO framework – adds a number of insights.[56] First, when making structural changes, whether the new structure (such as matrix) adds concrete value is crucial. Similarly, when do innovations actually create value? The vast majority of innovations fail to reach the market, and most new products that do reach market end up being financial failures. R&D by definition contains a lot of experimentation: finding out what works and what does not.

Hence some innovations can be expected not to add value. The crucial questions for firms are whether their R&D programme as a whole creates value, and whether the organizational structure helps or hinders value-creating innovations.

A second question is rarity. Certain strategies or structures may be in vogue at one point in time. When rivals all move toward a global integration, this strategy cannot become a source of differentiation. To improve global coordination, many MNEs spend millions of dollars to equip themselves with enterprise resource planning (ERP) packages provided by *SAP* and *Oracle*. However, such packages are available to many, thus providing no firm-specific advantage for the adopting firm. Rarity comes not from adopting textbook structures or buying in systems and software; it comes from making it work by developing the tacit organizational knowledge that connects those systems with the needs of the firm.

Even when capabilities are valuable and rare, they have to pass a third hurdle, namely, imitability. Formal structures are easier to observe and imitate than informal structures. This is one of the reasons the informal, flexible matrix has been fashionable. The informal, flexible matrix 'is less a structural classification than a broad organizational concept or philosophy, manifested in organizational capability and management mentality'.[57] It is obviously a lot harder, if not impossible, to imitate an intangible mentality than to imitate a tangible structure.

The last hurdle is organization – namely, are MNEs organized, both formally and informally, to exploit the values they are creating. A crucial difference exists between an innovator and a *profitable* innovator. The latter not only has plenty of good ideas but also lots of complementary assets (such as appropriate organizational structures and marketing muscles) to add value to innovation (see Chapter 4). *Philips*, for example, is a great innovator, having invented rotary shavers, videocassettes and compact discs (CDs). However, its abilities to profit from these innovations lag behind those of *Sony* and *Matsushita*, which have much stronger complementary assets.

DEBATES AND EXTENSIONS

LEARNING OBJECTIVE

5   Participate in two leading debates on organizing and innovating in the MNE

The question of how to manage complex MNEs has led to numerous debates, some of which have been discussed earlier (such as the debate on the matrix structure). Here, we outline two of the leading debates not previously discussed: (1) top management teams and (2) relocating divisional headquarters.

Top management teams

An important element in the structure of an MNE is the composition of the top management team, and the leadership of subsidiaries. The nationality of the head of foreign subsidiaries is such an example.[58] MNEs essentially can have three choices when appointing a head of a subsidiary:

- a parent country national as the head of a subsidiary (such as a French person for a subsidiary of a French MNE in India)
- a host country national (such as an Indian for the same subsidiary)
- a third country national (such as a Briton for the same subsidiary).

MNEs from different countries follow different norms when making these appointments. Most Japanese MNEs seem to follow an informal rule: heads of foreign subsidiaries, at least initially, need to be Japanese nationals.[59] In comparison, European MNEs are more likely to appoint host and third country nationals to lead subsidiaries. These staffing approaches reflect strategic differences.[60] Home country nationals, especially those long-time employees of the same MNE, are more likely to have developed a thorough understanding of the informal workings of the firm and to be better socialized into its dominant norms and values. Consequently, the Japanese propensity to appoint Japanese nationals is conducive to their preferred global standards strategy, which values globally coordinated and controlled actions.[61] Conversely, the European comfort in appointing host and third country nationals is indicative of European MNEs' traditional preference for a localization strategy.

Beyond the nationality of subsidiary heads, the nationality of top executives at the highest level (such as board chair, CEO, and board members) seems to follow another informal rule: they are (almost always) parent country nationals. However, in the eyes of stakeholders, such as employees and governments around the world, a top echelon consisting of largely one nationality does not bode well for an MNE aspiring to globalize everything it does. Thus many MNEs have started to internationalize their board, first by appointing individuals with expensive international experience, and second by appointing foreigners to the board, or even to a CEO position.[62] Consequently, such major MNEs as *SAP* (Chapter 4, Opening Case) and *Bayer* have appointed foreign-born bosses to top posts, and this strategy is gathering pace worldwide. The most famous foreign-born boss is probably Carlos Ghosn, who became CEO of Japanese carmaker *Nissan* in 1999, and was promoted to CEO in Nissan's French parent company *Renault* in 2005. Born in Brazil to Lebanese immigrants, Ghosn was educated in France and rose through the ranks in French MNEs *Michelin* and *Renault*.

Such foreign-born bosses bring substantial diversity to the organization, which may be a plus, especially for firms that have a high share of foreign owners, and/or of foreign sales.[63] However, such diversity puts an enormous burden on these non-native top executives to clearly articulate the values and exhibit behaviours expected of senior managers of an MNE associated with a particular country.[64] Even in Japan, Carlos Ghosn did not remain alone as a foreign-born CEO. He was joined by Craig Naylor of *Nippon Steel Glass*, Howard Stringer at *Sony*, Michael Woodford of *Olympus*, and Christophe Weber of *Takeda*.[65] Their distinct contribution is often an ability of a (semi-)outsider to implement radical cost-cutting in a company facing severe difficulties (as *Nissan* and *Sony* did at the time respectively that Ghosn and Stringer were appointed), and the more international outlook that companies gain.[66] Yet they may also face stiff resistance: Michael Woodford soon discovered quite a few 'skeletons in the cupboard' at *Olympus*, and fierce resistance from the old guard when he tried to clean up.

Moving (business unit) headquarters overseas

Some MNEs aggregate operations by locating *business unit* headquarters (HQ) away from home, while some are even moving their *corporate* HQ away from their country of origin. The question is: why?

At the business unit level, the answer is straightforward: the 'centre of gravity' of the activities of a business unit may pull its HQ toward a host country.[67] For example, the Danish *East Asiatic Company* moved its operational HQ from Copenhagen to Singapore because most of its markets were in Asia or Latin America. Others move key functions overseas to be closer to their business partners. For example, IBM moved its global procurement office to Shenzhen, China, in 2006.

At the corporate level, there are at least four strategic rationales. First, HQ location is a clear signal to various stakeholders that the firm is a global – rather than domestic or local – player. *News Corporation*'s corporate HQ relocation from Melbourne, Australia to New York in 2004 is indicative of its global status, as opposed to being a remote firm from 'down under'. *Lenovo*'s credibility among its US-based customers after the takeover of *IBM*'s laptop division has been greatly enhanced by the establishment of its worldwide HQ in the USA.

Second, it may facilitate access to capital markets. A corporate HQ in a major financial centre such as New York or London facilitates direct communication with institutional shareholders, financial analysts, and investment banks. The MNE also increases its visibility in a financial market, resulting in a broader shareholder base and greater market capitalization. As a result, three leading (former) South African firms, *Anglo American*, *Old Mutual* and *SABMiller* moved their HQ to London, and later joined the FTSE 100 – the top 100 UK-listed firms by capitalization.

Third, moving corporate HQ to a new country clearly indicates a commitment to that country's market. *HSBC*'s move to London in 1992 signalled its determination to become a more global player, and its commitment to the customers of *Midland Bank*, a major retail bank it had acquired in the UK. However, in an interesting twist of events, *HSBC*'s CEO and the principal office of the CEO relocated back to Hong Kong in February 2010. Technically, *HSBC*'s corporate headquarters are still in London, and it will remain domiciled in the UK for registration and tax purposes. However, the symbolism of the CEO's return to Hong Kong symbolizes that *HSBC* is keen to demonstrate its commitment to growing markets in Asia, which is where *HSBC* started (*HSBC* was set up in Hong Kong in 1865 as the *Hong Kong and Shanghai Banking Corporation*).[68]

Finally, as discussed in Chapter 6, some firms may be able to reduce their tax burden by moving the place of their incorporations (see In Focus 6.4).

IMPLICATIONS FOR PRACTICE

LEARNING OBJECTIVE

6   Draw implications
for action

MNEs are the ultimate large, complex and geographically dispersed business organizations. What determines the success and failure of multinational strategy, structure, and learning? The answer boils down to the institution- and resource-based dimensions. The institution-based view calls for thorough understanding and skilful manipulation of the rules of the game both at home and abroad. The resource-based view focuses on the development and deployment of firm-specific capabilities to enhance the odds for successful MNE management.

Consequently, three implications emerge for managers (Table 15.4). First, they must appreciate external rules influencing the critical trade-off between global integration and local responsiveness. For example, local rules may require localization of product design, or the establishment of allegedly separate entity with partially local ownership. Such institutional constraints need to be accommodated, though they may necessitate full operational localization.

Table 15.4   Implications for action

- Appreciate the external rules of the game affecting the organizational structures of MNEs in home and host countries.
- Understand and be prepared to adapt the internal rules of the game governing MNE management.
- Develop learning and innovation capabilities to leverage multinational presence as an asset – 'act local, think global'.

Second, managers need to understand and be prepared to change the internal rules of the game governing MNE management. Different strategies and structures call for different internal rules of the game. Some facilitate and others constrain MNE actions. Excessive centralization kills local initiative and innovation, and undermines context-sensitive adaptation. Complete decentralization, on the other hand, undermines the MNEs ability to create synergies and exploit economies of scale, while allowing local fiefdoms to persist. The leadership challenge thus is to balance these opposing pressures as the complexities of multiple embeddedness increase.

Finally, managers need to actively develop learning and innovation capabilities to leverage multinational presence. A winning formula is 'act local, think global'. Subsidiaries of MNEs thus need to engage not only in local CoPs to access local knowledge, but with internal CoPs within the MNE to share such knowledge throughout the company.

CHAPTER SUMMARY

1 Articulate the relationship between multinational strategy and structure

- The integration-responsiveness framework provides a tool to analyze multinational strategy and structure.

- There are four strategy/structure pairs: (1) home replication strategy/international division structure, (2) localization strategy/geographic area structure, (3) global standards strategy/global product division structure, and (4) transnational strategy/global matrix structure.

2 Outline the challenges associated with learning, innovation and knowledge management

- The main challenges for knowledge management arise from the tacitness of knowledge.

- The transnational strategy requires more comprehensive knowledge flows across the organization than the other three organizational strategies.

- Communities of practice (CoPs) are an important means to share knowledge in MNEs.

- Governance mechanisms for knowledge face difficult trade-offs between hard incentives and social capital as conduit for knowledge exchange.

3 Explain how institutions affect strategy and structure

- Institutions in the home country, especially ownership and governance structures, affect the strategies and structures adopted by MNEs.

4 Explain how institutions and resources affect strategy and structure

- Institutions in host countries, such as incentive schemes and the national innovation system, affect the types of activities MNEs locate in a country.

5 Participate in two leading debates on organizing and innovating in the MNE

- The debates are (1) foreign nationals in top management teams, and (2) moving business unit or corporate headquarters overseas.

6 Draw implications for action

- Appreciate the external rules of the game affecting the organizational structures of MNEs in home and host countries.

- Understand and be prepared to adapt the internal rules of the game governing MNE management.

- Develop learning and innovation capabilities to leverage multinational presence as an asset – 'act local, think global'.

KEY TERMS

Absorptive capacity
Centre of excellence
Community of Practice (CoP)
Country (regional) manager
Explicit knowledge
Geographic area structure
Global key accounts
Global matrix
Global product division
Global standards strategy

Home replication strategy
Integration-responsiveness
    framework
International division
Knowledge governance
Knowledge management
Localization (multidomestic) strategy
Local responsiveness
National innovation systems

Organizational (team-embedded)
    knowledge
Reverse knowledge transfer
Social capital
Subsidiary initiative
Tacit knowledge
Transnational strategy
Virtual community of practice
Worldwide (global) mandate

CRITICAL DISCUSSION QUESTIONS

1 In this age of globalization, some gurus argue that all industries are becoming global and that all firms need to adopt a global standards strategy. Do you agree? Why or why not?

2 You are the manager of the best-performing subsidiary in an MNE. Because bonuses are tied to subsidiary performance, your bonus is the highest among managers of all subsidiaries. Now headquarters is organizing managers from other subsidiaries to visit and learn from your subsidiary. You worry that if your subsidiary is no longer the star unit when other subsidiaries' performance catches up, your bonus will go down. What are you going to do?

3 You are a corporate R&D manager at *EADS* and are thinking about transferring some R&D work to China, India and Russia, where the work performed by a €70 000 German, French or Spanish engineer reportedly can be done by an engineer in one of these countries for less than €7000. However, engineers at *EADS'* existing plants have staged protests against such moves. French politicians are similarly vocal concerning job losses. What are you going to do?

4 Some companies organize or support social events such as an annual party, sports competitions or art exhibitions that bring together employees from different countries. Are such activities a useful way to support knowledge management or are they just a fringe benefit for spoiled employees?

RECOMMENDED READINGS

C. Bartlett & S. Ghoshal, 1989, *Managing across Borders*, Boston: Harvard Business School Press – classic book outlining the integration responsiveness framework and its implications.

J. Birkinshaw, 2001, *Entrepreneurship in the Global Firm*, London: Sage – a book discussing how managers in global MNEs, especially leaders of subsidiaries, can lead their unit entrepreneurially.

J. Birkinshaw, S. Ghoshal, C. Markides, J. Stopford & G. Yip, eds, 2003, *The Future of the Multinational Company*, London: Wiley – essays in memory of Sumantra Ghoshal,

exploring various aspects of how best to manage a multinational company, and the integration-responsiveness framework in particular.

N.J. Foss & S. Michailova, 2009, *Knowledge Governance: Processes and Perspectives*, Oxford: Oxford University Press – scholarly essays on knowledge processes with focus informal and informal governance mechanisms.

A. Gupta & V. Govindarajan, 2004, Global Strategy and Organization (p. 104), New York: Wiley – discusses how companies can be organized to make best use of global opportunities, especially knowledge management.

CLOSING CASE

Subsidiary initiative at Schenck Shanghai Machinery

German machine tool maker *Dürr* has been operating sales and manufacturing subsidiaries in China since the mid-1990s, providing state-of-the-art machines for the fast-growing car industry in particular. Its flagship division built and installed paint shops, the technologically most complex part of a car assembly line. Initially, its main customers were foreign-Chinese joint ventures, such as *Shanghai Volkswagen*, but local businesses were also increasingly demanding cutting-edge machines like those offered by *Dürr*. In the quest to improve their products, Chinese producers sought machines from a global leader.

However, not all German-engineered machines sold well in China. *Schenck*, a division of *Dürr*, produced in Germany one of the best balancing machines for armatures (small engines), achieving world-leading performance in accuracy and speed by balancing an armature in less than five seconds. Customers in high-cost countries appreciated the highly automated machine that helped to eliminate manual labour. Yet for several years, its Chinese subsidiary, *Schenck Shanghai Machinery* (*SSM*), could not sell a single one of these machines in China. China-based manufacturers considered the machine 'over-engineered', and at a unit price of around €500 000 much too expensive. What to do?

The main purchasing criteria of customers for machines in the lower price segment were brand name, price, quality, after-sales service and delivery period. *Schenck* had a very good brand name and it sold expensive high-quality machines in other segments in China. However, the delivery period for *Schenck* was longer than its competitors, as its machines were tailor-made and had to go through rigorous testing before being delivered to customers. Two Japanese competitors served the 'good enough' market with machines manufactured in China priced at around €100 000. They dominated the segment that *SSM* found difficult to penetrate as its cost base was too high, even after relocating production to China.

The management of *SSM* believed that there was a market in China for balancing machines for armatures if they could be offered at the right price. Yet serving the 'good enough' segment was not in line with *Dürr*'s global strategy, which focused on the premium segment, offering the best of German engineering. The subsidiary leadership faced a difficult choice: should

they give up this market segment or should they take some action? If so, should they take the machine made in Germany and strip it down to the essentials? Or, should they develop a new machine from scratch for the China market?

In 2005, SSM started to develop its own machine 'for China' by forming a development team of five engineers. The team liaised closely with marketing teams familiar with potential local customers, and with sourcing staff who could identify suitable components and suppliers in China. The work of this development team was kept very low profile, without engaging HQ or other units outside China. At the time, the subsidiary leadership believed that it would be difficult to convince HQ and engineers in Germany to develop the machine for China only by developing a machine first, the local leadership team expected to be able to earn the support from German-based engineers.

The new machine was an automatic balancing machine for armatures with grinding and drilling functions. The Shanghai-based development team developed the machine entirely from local components, apart from the measuring unit, which they bought from Germany. Once it was done, they presented a prototype of the new machine to HQ.

The subsidiary leadership was somewhat nervous how HQ would react. The German leadership team did not favour adding lower-quality machines to the product portfolio because of the potential damage to the brand image. The idea of a less sophisticated machine under the Schenck name conflicted with the positioning of Schenck. How would clients in Europe react if they learned that Schenck offered a similar machine in China at a much lower price? Moreover, the Dürr leadership in Germany at that time did not have in-depth understanding of the imperatives of the Chinese markets, nor did German-based R&D teams have great trust in their China-based colleagues.

Thus SSM invested considerable efforts in communicating with colleagues in Germany, and found that managing the relationship with HQ was less difficult than anticipated. Key players in Germany quickly realized that it was probably the right approach for the China market. Essentially, the prototype convinced

HQ that their China-based development team was both technically capable and had deep insight into their local market. On this basis, engineers from Germany and from China worked together to finalize the development.

Once the product was ready for market, SSM quickly secured orders. Customers were surprised to see that Schenck was able to produce a machine suitable for the China market because, in their minds, Schenck had not been in this market for quite a few years. Priced at the same level as the machines by DSK and Kokusai, the machine quickly attracted customers away from these Japanese competitors.

The new machine benefited not only from the Schenk brand name and the reputation of its technology, but from SSM's ability to provide a range of different machines and integrated solutions. Thus by leveraging the Schenck name and the combined capabilities of German and Chinese engineers, SSM successfully built a leadership position in the balancing machines for armatures in China in this particular segment, with a market share of 35 to 40%. The machines were also exported, especially to Southeast Asia, where local government encouraged the development of local car manufacturing industries.

CASE DISCUSSION QUESTIONS

1 From a resource-based perspective, what resources are needed to develop a machine for a distance market, such as China, and where in the MNE are those to be found?

2 What kinds of adaptations are needed to compete in the 'good enough' segment in China?

3 What internal processes do MNEs like Schenck need to develop and manufacture different product specifications for different market segments across a wide range of countries?

Sources: (1) Klaus Meyer's field research in Shanghai; (2) Handelsblatt, 2014, Für Dürr is in China der Lack noch nicht ab, March 24, 2014; (3) K.E. Meyer & J. Zhu, 2014, Dürr AG: A German Premium Manufacturer Goes Mid-Market in China, Shanghai: CEIBS.

NOTES

'For journal abbreviation, please see page xx-xxi.'

1 U. Andersson, M. Forsgren & U. Holm, 2007, Balancing subsidiary influence in the federative MNC, *JIBS*, 38: 802–818; M. Forsgren, U. Holm & U. Andersson, 2007, *Managing the Embedded MNC*, Cheltenham: Elgar; K.E. Meyer, R. Mudambi & R. Narula, 2011, Multinational enterprises and local contexts: the opportunities and challenges of multiple-embeddedness, *JMS*, 48: 235–253.

2 J. Stopford & L. Wells, 1972, *Managing the Multinational Enterprise*, New York: Basic Books; C.K. Prahalad & Y. Doz, 1987, *The Multinational Mission*, New York: Free Press; J. Birkinshaw, S. Ghoshal, C. Markides, J. Stopford & G. Yip eds, 2003, *The Future of the Multinational Company*, London: Wiley.

3 C.A. Bartlett & S. Ghoshal, 1989, *Managing across Borders: The Transnational Solution*, Boston, MA: Harvard Business School Press.

4 A. Harzing, 2000, An empirical analysis and extension of the Bartlett and Ghoshal typology of MNCs, *JIBS*, 31: 101–120; S. Venaik, D.F. Midgley & T.M. Devinney, 2005, Dual paths to performance: the impact of global pressures on MNC subsidiary conduct and performance, *JIBS*, 36: 655–675; K.E. Meyer & Y. Su, 2015, Integration and responsiveness in subsidiaries in emerging economies, *JWB*, 50: 149–158.

5 G. Szulanski & R. Jensen, 2006, Presumptive adaptation and the effectiveness of knowledge transfer, *SMJ*, 27: 937–957.

6 J. Birkinshaw, 2001, Entrepreneurship in the Global Firm, London: Sage; T. Frost, J. Birkinshaw & P. Ensign, 2002, Centers of excellence in MNCs (p. 997), *SMJ*, 23: 997–1018; U. Andersson & M. Forsgren, 2000, In search of centers of excellence, *MIR*, 40: 329–350.

7 J. Birkinshaw & S. Terjesen, 2003, The customer-focused multinational, in Birkinshaw et al., eds, *The Future of the Multinational Company* (p. 115–127).

8 Bartlett & Ghoshal, 1989, *as above*.

9 J. Cantwell, J. Dunning & O. Janne, 2004, Towards a technology-seeking explanation of US direct investment in the United Kingdom, *JIM*, 10: 5–20; H. Berry, 2006, Leaders, laggards, and the pursuit of foreign knowledge, *SMJ*, 27: 151–168; N. Anand, H. Gardner & T. Orris, 2007, Knowledge-based innovation, *AMJ*, 50: 406–428.

10 J. Birkinshaw & N. Hood, 1998, Multinational subsidiary evolution, *AMR*, 23: 773–796; J. Manea & R. Pearce, 2006, MNEs' strategies in Central and Eastern Europe, *MIR*, 46: 235–255; A. Rugman & A. Verbeke, 2001, Subsidiary-specific advantages in MNEs, *SMJ*, 22: 237–250.

11 J. Cantwell & R. Mudambi, 2005, MNE competence-creating subsidiary mandates, *SMJ*, 26: 1109–1128; K. Ruckman, 2005, Technology sourcing through acquisitions, *JIBS*, 36: 89–103.

12 Venaik et al., 2005, *as above*; A. Rugman, A. Verbeke & W. Yuan, Re-conceptualizing Bartlett and Ghoshal's classification of national subsidiary roles in the multinational enterprise, JMS, 48(2): 253–277.

13 B. Lamont, V. Sambamurthy, K. Ellis & P. Simmonds, 2000, The influence of organizational structure on the information received by corporate strategies of MNEs, *MIR*, 40: 231–252; Y. Ling, S. Floyd & D. Baldrige, 2005, Toward a model of issue-selling by subsidiary managers in MNCs, *JIBS*, 36: 637–654.

14 *Starbucks*, 2011, Financial Release, July 11.

15 R. Edwards, A. Ahmad & S. Ross, 2002, Subsidiary autonomy, *JIBS*, 33: 183–191; S. Miller & L. Eden, 2006, Local density and foreign subsidiary performance, *AMJ*, 49: 341–355.

16 L. Burns & D. Wholey, 1993, Adoption and abandonment of matrix management programs, *AMJ*, 36: 106–139; T. Devinney, D. Midgley & S. Venaik, 2000, The optimal performance of the global firm, *OSc*, 11: 674–695.

17 T. Murtha, S. Lenway & R. Bagozzi, 1998, Global mind-sets and cognitive shift in a complex MNC, *SMJ*, 19: 97–114; G. Benito, B. Grøgaard & R. Narula, 2003, Environmental influences on MNE subsidiary roles, *JIBS*, 34: 443–456; R. Whitley, G. Morgan, W. Kelley & D. Sharpe, 2003, The changing Japanese multinational, *JMS*, 40: 643–672.

18 P. Almeida, 1996, Knowledge sourcing by foreign multinationals, *SMJ*, 17: 155–166; W. Kuemmerle, 1999, The drivers of FDI into R&D, *JIBS*, 30: 1–24; K. Asakawa & M. Lehrer, 2003, Managing local knowledge assets globally, *JWB*, 38: 31–42; R. Belderbos, 2003, Entry mode, organizational learning, and R&D in foreign affiliates, *SMJ*, 24: 235–255; M. von Zedtwitz, O. Gassman & R. Boutellier, 2004, Organizing global R&D, *JIM*, 10: 21–49.

19 U. Andersson, M. Forsgren & U. Holm, 2002, The strategic impact of external networks, *SMJ*, 23: 979–996; R. Reagans & B. McEvily, 2003, Network structure and knowledge transfer, *ASQ*, 48: 240–267.

20 B. Kogut & U. Zander, 1993, Knowledge of the firm and the evolutionary theory of the multinational corporation, *JIBS*, 24: 625–645; R. Grant, 1996, Toward a knowledge-based theory of the firm, *SMJ*, 17: 109–122; H. Bresman, J. Birkinshaw & R. Nobel, 1999,

Knowledge transfer in international acquisitions, *JIBS*, 30: 439–462; N. Foss & T. Pedersen, 2005, Organizing knowledge processes in the MNC, *JIBS*, 35: 340–349.

21 X. Martin & R. Salomon, 2003, Knowledge transfer capacity and its implications for the theory of the MNE, *JIBS*, 34: 356–373; U. Schultze & C. Stabell, 2004, Knowing what you don't know? *JMS*, 41: 549–573; T. Felin & W. Hesterly, 2007, The knowledge-based view, *AMR*, 32: 195–218.

22 R. Grant, 2008, *Contemporary Strategy Analysis*, 7th ed., Chichester: Wiley.

23 M. Porter, H. Takeuchi & M. Sakakibara, 2000, *Can Japan Compete?* (p. 80), Cambridge, MA: Perseus.

24 Q. Yang, R. Mudambi,& K. Meyer, 2008, Conventional and reverse knowledge flows in multinational corporations, *JM* 34: 882–902; R. Corredoira & L. Rosenkopf, 2010, Should auld acquaintance be forgot? *SMJ*, 31: 159–181; R. Mudambi, L. Piscitello & L. Rabiosi, 2014, Reverse Knowledge Transfer in MNEs, *LRP*, 47: 49–63.

25 K.E. Meyer, 2015, What is Strategic Asset Seeking FDI? *MBR*, in press.

26 Y. Luo & M.W. Peng, 1999, Learning to compete in a transition economy, *JIBS*, 30: 269–296; T. Frost & C. Zhou, 2005, R&D co-practice and 'reverse' knowledge integration in MNCs, *JIBS*, 36: 676–687; M. Kotabe, D. Dunlap-Hinkler, R. Parente & H. Mishra, 2007, Determinants of cross-national knowledge transfer and its effect on firm innovation, *JIBS*, 38: 259–282; Q.A. Yang, R. Mudambi & K.E. Meyer, 2009, Conventional and reverse knowledge flows in multinational corporations, *JM*, 34: 882–902.

27 Y. Doz, J. Santos & P. Williamson, 2001, *From Global to Metanational*, Boston: Harvard Business School Press.

28 J. Brown & P. Duguid, 1991, Organizational learning and communities of practice, *OSc*, 2: 40–57; E. Wenger & W. Snyder, 2000, Communities of practice, *HBR*, (January/February): 139–145; J. Roberts, 2006, Limits to communities of practice, *JMS*, 43: 623–639.

29 J. McGee, H. Thomas & D. Wilson, *Strategy: Analysis & Practice*, London: Wiley (p. 615).

30 M. Ahuja & K. Carley, 1999, Network structure in virtual organizations, *OSc*, 10: 741–757; A. Ardichvili, M. Mauer, W. Li, T. Wentling & R. Stuedemann, 2006, Cultural influences on knowledge sharing through online communities of practice, *JKM*, 10: 94–107; J. Gammelgaard & T. Ritter, 2008, Virtual communities of practice, *IJKM*, 4: 46–61.

31 M.W. Peng & D. Wang, 2000, Innovation capability and foreign direct investment, *MIR*, 40: 79–83; J. Penner-Hahn & J.M. Shaver, 2005, Does international R&D increase patent output? *SMJ*, 26: 121–140.

32 J. Hagedoorn & G. Duysters, 2002, External sources of innovative capabilities, *JMS*, 39: 167–188; A. Lam, 2003, Organizational learning in multinationals,

JMS, 40: 673–703; M. Mol, P. Pauwels, P. Matthyssens & L. Quintens, 2004, A technological contingency perspective on the depth and scope of international outsourcing, *JIM*, 10: 287–305; R. Narula & G. Duysters, 2004, Globalization and trends in international R&D alliances, *JIM*, 10: 199–218.

33 S. Tallman & A. Chacar, 2010, Knowledge Accumulation and Dissemination in MNEs, JMS48: 278–304.

34 M. Bousssebaa, 2009, Struggling to Organize Across National Borders, *HR*, 62: 829–850; R. Greenwood, T. Morris, S. Fairclough & M. Boussebaa, 2010, The organizational design of transnational professional service firms, *OD*, 39: 173–183.

35 A. Grandori, 2001, Neither hierarchy nor identity: knowledge governance mechanisms and the theory of the firm, *JMS*, 29: 459–483; N. Foss & S. Michailova, eds, *Knowledge Governance: Perspectives, Process and Problems*, Oxford: Oxford University Press; N. Foss, K. Husted & S. Michailova, 2010, Governing knowledge sharing in organizations, *JMS*, 47: 455–482.

36 A. Gupta & V. Govindarajan, 2004, *Global Strategy and Organization* (p. 104), New York: Wiley.

37 K. Asakawa & A. Som, 2008, Internationalizing R&D in China and India, *APJM*, 25: 375–394; Q. Yang & C. Jiang, 2007, Location advantages and subsidiaries' R&D activities, *APJM*, 24: 341–358.

38 S. Michailova & K. Husted, 2003, Knowledge sharing hostility in Russian firms, *CMR*, 45: 59–77; I. Björkman, W. Barner-Rasmussen & L. Li, 2004, Managing knowledge transfer in MNCs, *JIBS*, 35: 443–455; R. Mudambi & P. Navarra, 2004, Is knowledge power? *JIBS*, 35: 385–406.

39 R. Nobel & J. Birkinshaw, 1998, Innovation in MNCs, *SMJ*, 19: 479–496.

40 W. Cohen & D. Levinthal, 1990, Absorptive capacity, *ASQ*, 35: 128–152; J. Jansen, F. v.d. Bosch & H. Volberda, 2005, Managing potential and realized absorptive capacity, *AMJ*, 48: 999–1015; D.B. Minbaeva, T. Pedersen, I. Björkman, C.F. Fey & H.J. Park, 2003, MNC knowledge transfer, subsidiary absorptive capacity, and HRM, *JIBS*, 34: 586–599; S. Schleimer & T. Pedersen, 2014, The effects of MNC parent effort and social structure on subsidiary absorptive capacity, *JIBS*, 45: 303–320.

41 M. Osterloh & B. Frey, 2000, Motivation, knowledge transfer and organizational form, *OSc*, 11: 538–550; M. Robertson & J. Swan, 2003, Control – what control? *JMS*, 40: 831–858.

42 H. Kim, J. Park & J. Prescott, 2003, The global integration of business functions, *JIBS*, 34: 327–344; S. O'Donnell, 2000, Managing foreign subsidiaries, *SMJ*, 21: 525–548; M. Subramaniam & N. Venkatraman, 2001, Determinants of transnational new product development capability, *SMJ*, 22: 359–378.

43 T. Kostova & K. Roth, 2003, Social capital in multinational corporations and a micro-macro model of its formation, AMR, 28: 297–317; A. Inkpen & E. Tsang, 2005, Social capital, networks, and knowledge transfer, AMR, 30: 146–165; P. Gooderham, D.B. Minbaeva & T. Pedersen, 2010, Governance mechanisms for the promotion of social capital for knowledge transfer in multinational corporations, JMS, 48: 123–150; E. Tippmann, P. Scott & V. Mangematin, 2012, Problem solving in MNCs, JIBS, 43: 746–771.

44 J. Taggart, 1998, Strategy shifts in MNC subsidiaries, SMJ, 19: 663–681; W. Newburry, 2001, MNC interdependence and local embeddedness influences on perception of career benefits from global integration, JIBS, 32: 497–507; M. Geppert, K. Williams & D. Matten, 2003, The social construction of contextual rationalities in MNCs, JMS, 40: 617–641; B. Ambos & B. Schlegelmilch, 2007, Innovation and control in the MNC, SMJ, 28: 473–486.

45 J. Birkinshaw, 2000, Entrepreneurship in the Global Firm, London: Sage; T.C. Ambos, U. Andersson & J. Birkinshaw, 2010, What are the consequences of initiative-taking in multinational subsidiaries? JIBS, 41: 1 099–1 118.

46 Birkinshaw, 2000, as above.

47 D. Vora, T. Kostova & K. Roth, 2007, Roles of subsidiary managers in MNCs, MIR, 47: 595–620; T. Ambos, U. Andersson & J. Birkinshaw, 2010, What are the consequences of initiative-taking in multinational subsidiaries? JIBS, 41: 1099–1118; F. Ciabuschi, H. Dellestrand & O. Martin, 2011, Internal embeddedness, headquarters involvement, and innovation importance in MNEs, JMS, 48: 1612–1638.

48 C. Dörrenbacher & J. Gammelgaard, 2010, MNCs, inter-organizational networks, and subsidiary charter removals, JWB, 45: 206–216; J. Balogun, P. Jarzabkowski & E. Vaara, 2011, Selling, resistance, and reconciliation, JIBS, 42: 765–786; H. Dellestrand, 2011, Subsidiary embeddedness as a determinant of divisional headquarters involvement in innovation transfer processes, JIM, 17: 229–242; A. Schotter & P. Beamish, 2011, Performance effects of MNC headquarters-subsidiary conflict and the role of boundary spanners, JIM, 17: 243–259.

49 A. Chandler, 1990, Scale and Scope, Cambridge, MA: Harvard University Press.

50 G. Jones, 1997, Great Britain, in Chandler F. Amatori & T. Hikino, eds, Big Business and the Wealth of Nations, New York: Cambridge University Press.

51 R. Whitley, 1994, Dominant forms of economic organization in market organizations, OSt, 15: 153–182; M. Mayer & R. Whittington, 2004, Economics, politics and nations: Resistance to the multidimensional form in France, Germany and the United Kingdom, 1983–1993, JMS, 41: 1057–1082.

52 B. Kogut, D. Walker & J. Anand, 2002, Agency and institutions: National divergence in diversification behavior, OSc, 13: 162–178; K.E. Meyer, 2007, Globalfocusing: From domestic conglomerate to global specialist, JMS, 43: 1 109–1 144.

53 S. Feinberg & S. Majumdar, 2001, Technology spillovers from foreign direct investment in the Indian pharmaceutical industry, JIBS, 32: 421–437; M. Wright, I. Filatotchev, T. Buck & K. Bishop, 2002, Foreign partners in the former Soviet Union, JWB, 37: 165–179; R. Narula & C. Bellak, 2009, EU enlargement and consequences for FDI assisted industrial development, TNC, 18: 69–89.

54 B. Lundvall, ed., 1992, National Systems of Innovation, London: Pinter; R. Nelson, 1993, ed., National Innovation Systems: A Comparative Analysis, New York: Oxford University Press.

55 J. Niosi, 1997, The globalization of Canada's R&D, MIR, 37: 387–404; R. Narula, 2003, Globalization and Technology, Cambridge: Polity; L. Davis & K.E. Meyer, 2004, Subsidiary research and development, and the local environment, IBR, 13: 359–382.

56 P. Cloninger, 2004, The effect of service intangibility on revenue from foreign markets, JIM, 10: 125–146; A. Delios & P. Beamish, 2001, Survival and profitability, AMJ, 44: 1 028–1 039; E. Danneels, 2002, The dynamics of product innovation and firm competences, SMJ, 23: 1095–1122; S. Tallman, 1991, Strategic management models and resource-based strategies among MNEs in a host country, SMJ, 12: 69–82.

57 Bartlett & Ghoshal, 1989, as above (p. 209).

58 N. Noorderhaven & A. Harzing, 2003, The 'country-of-origin effect' in MNCs, MIR, 43: 47–66.

59 P. Beamish & A. Inkpen, 1998, Japanese firms and the decline of the Japanese expatriate, JWB, 33: 35–50; R. Belderbos & M. Heijltjes, 2005, The determinants of expatriate staffing by Japanese multinationals in Asia, JIBS, 36: 341–354.

60 Y. Paik & J. Sohn, 2004, Expatriate managers and MNCs' ability to control international subsidiaries, JWB, 39: 61–71; R. Peterson, J. Sargent, N. Napier & W. Shim, 1996, Corporate expatriate HRM policies, internationalization, and performance in the world's largest MNCs, MIR, 36: 215–230.

61 J. Johansson & G. Yip, 1994, Exploiting globalization potential, SMJ, 15: 579–601; J. Sohn, 1994, Social knowledge as a control system, JIBS, 25: 295–325.

62 P. Greve, T. Biermann & W. Ruigrok, 2015, Foreign executive appointments, JWB, advance online.

63 L. Oxelheim, A. Gregoric, T. Randoy & S. Thomsen, 2013, On the internationalization of corporate boards: The case of Nordic firms, JIBS, 44(3): 173–194.

64 L. Palich & L. Gomez-Mejia, 1999, A theory of global strategy and firm efficiency, JM, 25: 587–606; O. Richard,

T. Barnett, S. Dwyer & K. Chadwick, 2004, Cultural diversity in management, firm performance, and the moderating role of entrepreneurial orientation, *AMJ*, 47: 227–240.

65 D. Pilling & K. Itagaki, 2015, A Frenchman in Tokyo, *Financial Times*, April 6.

66 J. Soble, 2011, Japan's changing 'gaijin' CEOs, *Financial Times*, July 5.

67 Birkinshaw, et al. 2006, as above. G.R.G. Benito, R. Lunnan & S. Thomassen, 2010, Moving abroad: Foreign located division headquarters in multinational companies, *JMS* 48: 373–394.

68 *Wall Street Journal*, 2009, HSBC re-emphasizes its 'H', September 26.

CHAPTER SIXTEEN

PEOPLE IN THE MNE

LEARNING OBJECTIVES

After studying this chapter, you should be able to

1 Distinguish ethnocentric, polycentric and geocentric management practices

2 Explain how MNEs manage expatriates

3 Explain how MNEs manage employees in subsidiaries abroad

4 Discuss how the institution-based view sheds additional light on HRM

5 Discuss how the resource-based view sheds additional light on HRM

6 Participate in two leading debates concerning people in the MNE

7 Draw implications for action

OPENING CASE

EADS: *managing human resources in a European context*

by Christoph Barmeyer and Ulrike Mayrhofer

The *European Aeronautic Defence and Space Company* (EADS) was created by a merger of the French *Aérospatiale-Matra*, the German *DASA* and the Spanish *CASA*. It aimed to join the strengths of three European engineering traditions and to achieve market leadership and compete with world leaders such as Boeing. However, managing a firm with major units in three different countries requires a unifying organizational culture that integrates and respects the different national cultures.

451

What are the challenges of managing people in an organization influenced by three distinct national cultures?

Individuals from the three companies were selected to work on project teams outside their home country. These expatriates served important roles in facilitating the integration process. At the cultural 'interface', they were to mediate between different systems of meaning and action in order to achieve mutual adaptation. English was adopted as an official language to enable expatriates to effectively communicate within their team. However, expatriates also faced the challenge of integrating into another culture. Even though it was one company, the national culture where they worked was quite different. *EADS* considered this cultural diversity an advantage, because it stimulated creativity and favoured the dynamics of the group. In fact, expatriates had the opportunity to learn about different values, which enabled them to develop new ideas and solutions to the problems they faced.

However, it created personal challenges for the members of the teams, as they were confronted with different ways of communicating and collaborating. Certain concepts of management, such as cooperation or leadership, had different meanings and interpretations in France and in Germany, which often led to misunderstandings. For instance, for French engineers, the notion of cooperation implies that the goal should be achieved through work on an individual basis, whereas for German engineers, the term cooperation means teamwork with the objective to obtain a common goal. Consequently, when working in German teams, the French sometimes felt frustrated by their lack of freedom and the necessity to reach a consensus. In the same way, when working in France, Germans attempted to find a consensus and had the impression that their French partners were individualists and difficult to predict. In the same way, expatriates learned about different conceptions of leadership. For example, German expatriates discovered that their French colleagues employed more paternalistic styles and personal powers, and thus favoured centralized management structures. In contrast, French expatriates were surprised that German authority was mainly oriented towards function and professional competence and that German managers and engineers often graduated from public universities (in contrast with France where most managers and engineers graduate from highly selective and prestigious French 'grandes écoles' like École Polytechnique and École Centrale).

Two metaphors highlight these different culturally embedded characteristics and conceptions of cooperation and leadership. The German organization has been described as a 'well-oiled machine': there is a clear technical structure to the regulation of functions in terms of tasks and responsibilities, and of processes in terms of sequential flow. The organization is understood as a *heterarchical* structure, the functions and goals of which are achieved – detached from personalized authority – according to its own agreed rules. In contrast, the French organization is like a 'pyramid of people': management holds a position of authority at the top of the pyramid, with subordinate participants below. The organization is understood as a *hierarchical* structure, in which interpersonal relations develop and personalized authority figures are needed to regulate power relations. As power is concentrated at the top of the pyramid, the people below have to defend themselves by acting individually.

Human resource managers of *EADS* were aware that it was important to systematically explain such cultural characteristics and differences in order to avoid conflicts that are likely to arise in cross-cultural teams. The company therefore created its own corporate university for executive education, called the *Corporate Business Academy (CBA),* which offered intercultural training seminars and helped to prepare expatriates for their work experience abroad. *EADS* also developed specific processes to build a new

organizational culture based on teamwork. The experiences of the expatriates and the initiatives taken to build a new corporate culture allowed *EADS* to successfully manage its human resources in an organization that even after several changes of shareholders retains its distinct Franco-German identity.

Sources: This case was originally prepared by Christoph Barmeyer (Passau University) and Ulrike Mayrhofer (Université Lyon 3) and updated by Klaus Meyer. Based on: (1) C. Barmeyer & U. Mayrhofer, 2002, Le management interculturel: facteur de réussite des fusions-acquisitions internationales?, *Gérer et Comprendre,* 70: 24–33; (2) C. Barmeyer & U. Mayrhofer (2007), Culture et relations de pouvoir: une analyse longitudinale du groupe EADS, *Gérer et Comprendre,* 88: 4–12; (3) C. Barmeyer & U. Mayrhofer, 2008, The contribution of intercultural management to the successes of international mergers and acquisitions: An analysis of the EADS group, *IBR,* 17: 28–38.

People working in a multinational enterprise (MNE) face some distinct challenges due to their multilocational and multicultural work environment. How can individuals best thrive in such an environment? And, how can MNEs manage their people, for example, to select, train and motivate people to take on postings in other countries? These are some of the crucial questions we address in this chapter from both an individual and the MNE perspective.

In an MNE, the activities to attract select and manage employees are known as **human resource management (HRM).**[1] This term emphasizes that people are key resources of the firm to be actively managed and developed. HRM is thus increasingly recognized as a strategic function that, together with other crucial functions such as finance and marketing, helps accomplish organizational effectiveness and financial performance.[2] In fact, 90% of CEOs name the 'people agenda' as one of their top priorities.[3] An annual survey in China finds that, year after year, executives in both Chinese and foreign-owned firms put 'finding and retaining talent' as their biggest challenge.[4]

Thus HRM plays a particularly crucial role in MNEs, where a great diversity of people work together at multiple locations, and where people frequently have to move between locations. This chapter first outlines three distinct approaches to international HRM. We then explore the management of (1) people sent abroad by the MNE and (2) local employees in subsidiaries abroad. Then, we employ the institution- and resource-based views to shed further light on these issues. Debates and extensions follow.

human resource management (HRM)
Activities that attract, select and manage employees.

LEARNING OBJECTIVE

1 Distinguish ethno-
centric, polycentric
and geocentric man-
agement practices

APPROACHES TO MANAGING PEOPLE

There are three primary approaches to managing people in MNEs.[5] An **ethnocentric approach** emphasizes the norms and practices of the parent company (and the parent country of the MNE). Hence subsidiaries are run largely in the same way as operations in the home country. The MNE will typically have comprehensive procedures and standards developed in the home country, and compliance with them is emphasized throughout its worldwide operations. To facilitate the consistent implementation of

ethnocentric approach
An emphasis on the norms and practices of the parent company (and the parent country of the MNE) by relying on expatriates.

Table 16.1 Multinational management practices

Management practices	Typical top managers at local subsidiaries	Advantages
Ethnocentric	Parent country nationals	Strategies can be implemented most consistently; skills base at home is fully utilized.
Polycentric	Host country nationals	Local adaptation through local knowledge; career opportunity for local staff.
Geocentric	A mix of parent, host and third country nationals	Utilization of the broadest worldwide talent pool; equal career opportunities for everyone.

expatriate (expat)
A non-native employee who works in a foreign country.
parent (home) country national
An employee who comes from the parent country of the MNE and works at its local subsidiary.
host country national
An individual from the host country who works for an MNE.
polycentric approach
An emphasis on the norms and practices of the host country.

management practices, subsidiaries are often led by expatriates, who are non-native employees that work in the foreign country. In ethnocentric MNEs, these expatriates are typically parent country nationals who have been sent out specifically to work in this subsidiary. They not only facilitate control and coordination by headquarters, but they contribute specific skills for the job because they have been trained in the home country (Table 16.1). An ethnocentric approach can be motivated by an (actual or perceived) lack of talent of host country nationals, or by the need for headquarters to effectively communicate with the leader of the subsidiary.

The opposite of an ethnocentric approach, a polycentric approach focuses on the norms and practices of the host country. In short, 'when in Rome, do as the Romans do'. Who will be the best managers if we have an operation in Rome? Naturally, Roman (or Italian) managers. As host country nationals, they face no language and cultural barriers in the local environment, and hence may be better at engaging with local customers, suppliers and government officials. Unlike parent country nationals who often pack up and move after a few years, local employees stay in their positions longer, thus providing more continuity of management. Further, placing host country nationals in top subsidiary positions sends a morale-boosting signal to other local employees who may feel that they, too, can reach the top (at least in that subsidiary). However, in some experienced MNEs, local employees in leadership positions may find it difficult to effectively communicate with headquarters.

geocentric approach
A focus on finding the most suitable managers independent of nationality.
third country national
An employee who comes from neither the parent country nor the host country.

Disregarding nationality, a geocentric approach focuses on finding the most suitable managers, who may be parent, host, or third country nationals, which come from neither the parent country nor the host country. In other words, a geocentric approach treats all employees the same. Geocentric firms develop a pool of managers recruited from a wide range of countries, trained in multiple locations and serving in management roles across the MNE. For a geographically dispersed MNE, a geocentric approach can facilitate the emergence of a corporate-wide culture and identity. For example, the 400 top managers of *Reckitt Benckiser*, a leading household goods manufacturer, represent 55 different nationalities, with no country being recognized as 'home country', and many subsidiaries being run by a third country national.[6] Likewise, *EADS* (Opening Case) is developing a geocentric approach, in part because of its tri-national roots (French, German, Spanish). Even so, the Opening Case illustrates the problems of implementing such an approach. Developing managers from a variety of nationalities into a coherent team is a lot more complex than integrating individuals from two (parent and host) countries.

global talent management
The attraction, selection, development and retention of talented employees in the most strategic roles within an MNE.

The challenge managing human resources in an MNE is thus to support very diverse types of people and careers. At the one end, high-flyers have the capability, potential and ambition to one day take on leadership roles in the company. They like to be known as 'global talent'. Hence a pivotal area of modern HRM is global talent management, defined as the attraction, selection, development and retention of talented employees in the most strategic roles within an MNE.[7] Employees selected to the global talent pool are systematically prepared to assume leadership roles in the MNE, and thus given expatriate assignments both to develop their capabilities and to serve in strategically important roles in the MNEs worldwide operation. At the other end of the spectrum are local employees hired for specific tasks with a unit of the MNE. They would not normally be expected to be promoted beyond the local unit, though some may join the global talent pool if they are exceptionally competent. We first discuss global talents serving in expatriate roles, before turning our attention to locally recruited employees.

global talent pool
Employees that are systematically prepared to assume leadership.

EXPATRIATES

People posted abroad by an MNE are known as expatriates. As home or third country nationals, they play a critical role in managing subsidiaries of MNEs, and in facilitating communication between different units of the MNE. Shown in Figure 16.1, expatriates can play at least five important roles:[8]

LEARNING OBJECTIVE

2 Explain how MNEs manage expatriates

- Expatriates may be *strategists* who lead the design and implementation of the subsidiary's strategies. This CEO-type role requires integration of local knowledge with the strategies and values of the parent, a combination of expertise that global talents are destined for.

- Expatriates may act as *monitors* who ensure the parent's control over the operations of the subsidiary. Especially expatriates in the role of chief financial officer primarily serve to ensure the financial results and accounting standards meet the parent's expectations. This monitoring role aims to secure that subsidiaries fit into the MNE's global 'orbit'.

- Expatriates are also *ambassadors*.[9] Representing headquarters' interests, they build relationships with host country stakeholders, such as local managers, employees, suppliers, customers and government officials. At the same time, expatriates also act as ambassadors representing the interests of the subsidiaries when interacting with headquarters.

Figure 16.1 The roles of expatriates

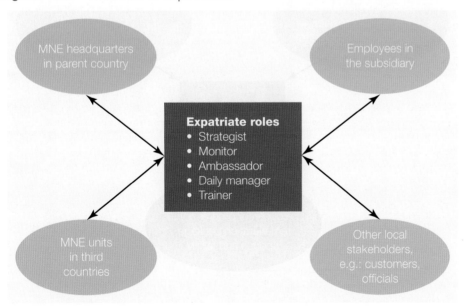

- Expatriates may act as *daily managers* to run the operations and lead the local workforce. One of the reasons they are sent in the first place is often the lack of local management talent that fits the needs of the MNE.

- Finally, expatriates are *trainers* for local staff, including their own replacements, thus transferring knowledge from headquarters to subsidiaries.[10] Hence not all expats are managers; some are specialists, such as engineers seconded for a specific assignment.

Selection of expatriates

An expatriate assignment is demanding, both as a leadership role and as a personal experience. Selecting the right people for expat assignments is thus crucial for their success.[11] Figure 16.2 outlines who influences expatriate selection. In addition to personal preferences, requirements of both headquarters and subsidiaries have to be considered. Headquarters may focus on loyalty to the company and leadership skills in implementing actions mandated from the top (Figure 16.2). Subsidiaries may be more concerned about sensitivity to local culture and in filling specific capability gaps.[12] In some Asian countries, where seniority is highly respected, younger expatriates may be ineffective. Also, it is preferable for expatriates to have some command (or better yet, mastery) of the local language.

In terms of individual dimensions, a wide range of capabilities is required that goes beyond what is needed to succeed in the home environment.[13] One study suggests that in addition to the specific functional skills required for the job, successful expatriates combine three sets of capabilities:[14]

- Intellectual capabilities: knowledge of international business and the capacity to learn about new business contexts.

- Psychological capabilities: openness to different cultures and the capacity to change, along with receptiveness for new ideas and experiences.

Figure 16.2   Factors in expatriate selection

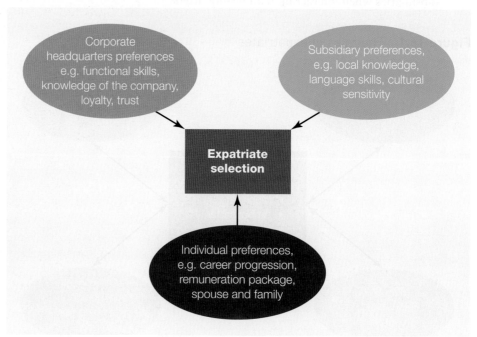

- Social capabilities, including the ability to form connections, to bring people together, and to influence stakeholders that have a different cultural background (for example, colleagues, clients, suppliers and regulatory agencies).

That is quite a demanding capability profile! In addition, personality traits such as an open mindset and emotional stability help expatriates to adjust.[15] Last (but certainly not least), spouse and family preferences have to be considered. The accompanying spouse may have to leave behind a career and a social network. He or she has to find meaningful endeavours abroad (In Focus 16.1). Personal frustrations of family members are a frequent cause of expatriate failure.

In practice, MNEs often face the difficult choice between sending (1) a senior person with extensive industry experience and well-embedded in the company, and (2) an eager, young person who knows the local language and culture, but has limited understanding of the business. First, middle-aged expatriates

IN FOCUS 16.1

Expatriate spouses

You may be excited when you are offered an expatriate assignment, but what will your spouse think about it? Traditionally, it was men who went on expatriate assignments with their wives dutifully tagging along, taking care of home and children while socializing with other expatriate wives. Yet in the age of dual career couples and women as the main breadwinner of the family, this is getting more complicated. To start with, finding a job for the spouse is often challenging because many countries make it difficult to obtain a spouse work permit. Few companies would offer matching expat assignments for a couple; their operations are simply not big enough. One option for spouses is to work freelance in jobs that are location-independent – such as IT consultants, journalists or novelists – but that does not suit everyone. Also, teachers may find their expertise sought after in local schools.

Yet many spouses face the prospect of temporarily suspending their own career to support their partner during a challenging period in his/her life. For Northern Europeans used to women pursuing their own careers, this can be quite challenging, both practically and psychologically. Stories abound about unhappy wives feeling diminished in their self-esteem, playing a reduced role in a foreign culture. How best to pre-empt this challenge?

Lotte Nørgreen, a successful career woman, experienced this challenge when her husband was posted by

Novozymes to an attractive job in Tianjin, near Beijing. The culture shock hit her in many ways, some quite unexpected. One surprise was the local community of Danes she joined: many of the fellow expatriate wives were living a much more traditional wife role than was common in urban Denmark, focusing on children and household, and gossiping with their neighbours.

Experts working with expatriate families offer three pieces of advice for those following their partners to an expatriate assignment. First, in the first couple of weeks, you likely need to focus on supporting your family and making local arrangements, such as supporting children joining an unfamiliar new school. Second, you should actively engage in the local community and learn the local language, do not get stuck in the 'expat bubble' in your fancy villa district. Third, set yourself specific objectives as to what you want to achieve while living abroad: define your own project – say, acquire a new skill or write the book you have always dreamt about!

Sources: (1) M. Shaffer & D. Harrison, 2001, Forgotten partners of international assignments, *Journal of Applied Psychology*, 86: 238–254; (2) R. Brown, 2008, Dominant stressors on expatriate couples during international assignments, *IJHRM* 19: 1018–1034; (3) J. Lauring & J. Selmer, 2009, The supportive spouse, *IBR*, 19: 59–69; (4) L. Mäkelä, M. Känsälä & V. Suutari, 2011, The roles of expatriates' souses among dual career couples, *CCM*, 18: 185–197; (5) C. Bostrup, 2011, *Kina Sweet & Sour: Erfaringer fra danskere, der tør sates på Kina* (Chapter 13), Copenhagen: Gyldendal.

(forty-somethings) often combine best experience, industry competence, ambition and adaptability. Yet they are the most expensive, because the employer often has to provide heavy allowances for children's education. High-quality schools are very expensive. For example, schools teaching a British curriculum in places such as Beijing, Shanghai or Tianjin, cost €25 000 to €35 000 per year.[16] Unfortunately, these expatriates also have the highest percentage of failure rates, in part because of their family responsibilities. An alternative would be to send relatively older managers who no longer have school-age children at home, but unless they have a track record of international assignments, they may find it more difficult to adapt to cultural differences.

Second, MNEs may promote younger managers with high career ambition and interest in the local culture – perhaps even fluency in the local language. Thus expatriates in their late 20s and early 30s are often easier to motivate to take on a challenging assignment in an unfamiliar environment. Moreover, they are less costly to relocate because they may not yet have established a family (and have no school-age children), and have not yet bought a house. The second preference has strong implications for students studying this book now: these overseas opportunities may come sooner than you expect – are *you* ready?

Pre-departure training for expatriates

training
The specific preparation to do a particular job.

Before sending key people on important assignments, MNEs ought to prepare them for the task by providing language and cross-cultural training.[17] However, about one-third of MNEs do not provide cross-cultural training for expatriates – other than wishing them 'good luck' – because many appointments are made on too short notice to allow for in-depth preparation.[18] While the share of companies providing systematic preparation has been increasing over the years, often it is still up to the individual expatriate to ensure that they are well prepared for their assignment.

The extent of training should vary with the length of stay for expatriates. Longer and more rigorous training is imperative for stays of several years, especially for first-time expatriates. Three levels of training can be distinguished.[19] At a basic level, training focuses on providing information on practicalities in so-called area briefings, cultural briefings, and the use of interpreters. Language training may focus on survival phrases (such as 'good morning', 'thank you' and 'please take me to this address'). At an intermediate level, the training would include cultural assimilation training, including, for example, role plays and discussion of cases and critical incidences in groups that include experienced expatriates.

full immersion training
Intensive exposure to a foreign culture and language by living within that culture.

At an advanced level, a full immersion training can intensively expose an expat-to-be to the foreign culture and language. For example, expats may spend a few days at the new location in a situation resembling the future role, but with a mentor at hand to explain and to teach the language. More enlightened firms involve the spouse and children in expatriate training, as they will be sharing the expat experience, and can be an important source of personal support – or stress. Large MNEs usually also provide practical assistance, sometimes through specialist relocation service firms providing a comprehensive package for expatriates, including a suitable place to live, the removal of furniture, identifying suitable schools for the children, and taking care of visa and work permit-related matters.

Expatriates in action

Many of the practical challenges for expatriates are similar to experiences of students going abroad on exchange or to study for a degree course – except that few MNEs provide the sort of pastoral care that many universities offer their students. Arriving at the place of an expat assignment, the initial concerns are usually very practical matters such as finding your way to the office, home and local shops, and 'who does what' and 'who is who' at work (In Focus 16.2). Once these essentials have been taken care of, you can settle down and get on with work – and life.

After a while abroad, essentially every expatriate experiences culture shock, defined as the expatriate's reaction to a new, unpredictable and therefore uncertain environment.[20] Recall from Chapter 3 that societies vary in their culture, which concerns not only visible artefacts, but also values and norms, as well as underlying assumptions. Since such differences are not directly observable, someone entering an unfamiliar society will experience behaviours that are inconsistent with his or her own culture, and needs to figure out what values and norms are guiding the actions of people in that society. Without such knowledge social interactions are ineffective, and individuals are likely to feel frequently confused.

Students like yourself studying abroad also often experience culture shock; some of your classmates may indeed be going through this experience as your are taking your international business course. Essentially, when living in a different culture,

culture shock
An expatriate's reaction to a new, unpredictable and therefore uncertain environment.

IN FOCUS 16.2

Practical tips for getting started in Asia

If you live in a foreign country, you need to take care of a few practicalities right from the start. These tips may help you as you take your first steps. First, in the early days, the support of a local person is invaluable to communicate with other locals what your situation is, and what needs to be done. This includes getting your work permit, opening a bank account and setting your account up with the employer's personnel office. If you are not being offered help, ask for someone to come along with you to make these initial visits – if your account is set up in the wrong way it will come to hound you later. In Taiwan, a basic need is to get a Chinese name: the university computer system reads only Chinese, and without being in that computer I (Klaus Meyer) would not have received my salary. I also urgently needed a name stamp because this is the normal means of identification, for example, when withdrawing money from the bank. Other important issues to do in the first week are to get a mobile phone (or a local SIM card), and learn how to use the local buses and trains (taxis are expensive in the long run).

Second, a major issue for many expatriates is food. Compared to Europe, people in Asia are more likely to eat out at one of the small corner shops than to eat

at home – the food is much cheaper and there really isn't much point in cooking yourself. If you don't read the local language, you may find it useful to memorize where your favourite dish is on the restaurant menu, or the supermarket shelf. However, if you are craving specific dishes from back home you will find that ingredients are hard to find and expensive, and home cooking may often still be the best. In reverse, I have often been bemused by Asian students learning how to cook *after* arriving in England because there it is very expensive (compared to Asia) to go out for meals, and English food doesn't please their tastes.

Third, talk with expats and locals who have been to your country. They will be better able to help you with practicalities and with cross-cultural issues, because they appreciate the differences in cultures. People who have never been abroad often find it difficult to explain their own country to outsiders because they lack understanding of your situation – or have their own prejudices (like 'foreigners don't eat whole fish' just because earlier American visitors apparently have problems facing a whole fish with its head on the table). Friends with whom you can discuss your experiences help a lot to pre-empt, or overcome, your culture shock.

Figure 16.3   Sources of stress for expatriates

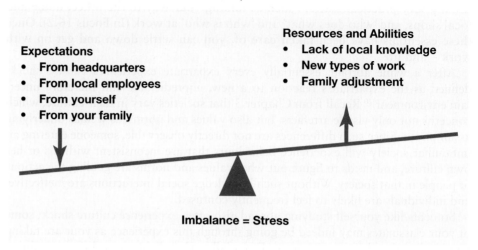

Imbalance = Stress

your selective perception and interpretation systems don't function, you need to spend more effort on interpreting what local people do or say, and you find it more difficult to make yourself understood. Particularly troubling is that unconscious ways of communicating (such as body language) do not work, and hence the expat may not understand why he or she is less effective.[21] For example, when people raised in Northern Europe hear loud shouting, they will intuitively think some major conflict is happening; yet in Cairo, Mumbai or Hong Kong, this may merely signal a routine bargaining over a price. Our cognitive system of interpreting what is happening is grounded in our culture and, when entering another culture, the home culture's perceptive system becomes ineffective. Another source of personal frustration of expatriates is to miss activities that used to be a normal part of daily life, notable 'oral pleasures' of speaking and enjoying entertainment in their own language, and eating familiar foods.[22]

At the same time, when you work as an expat, you are normally under high expectations from both yourself and from your company. This imbalance between the effectiveness of your actions and your expectations causes expatriate stress (Figure 16.3). Even with a lot of financial and psychological support, few expatriates can simultaneously play these challenging multidimensional roles effectively.[23] Thus it is common that expatriates fail to achieve all they set out to achieve, though this phenomenon appears to be more common for US expatriates[24] than for Australian or Nordic expatriates.[25]

Culture shock tends to set in after a few weeks in the new culture. Initially, expatriate managers, like exchange students, are enthusiastic about all the new experiences (Figure 16.4). This initial enthusiasm – or honeymoon period – wears off after a while however. The pressures of work set in, and you may miss your friends back home. For students, unfortunately, this period often coincides with the time when the first assignments are due – to be written and assessed under rules that you are not familiar with. However, this period passes, you become more familiar with the local culture and – hopefully – the language, and you make new friends with both other expats and locals. Thus the mood recovers, and by the time the assignment ends, many would rather stay a bit longer.

When you are experiencing culture shock, the most important thing to know is that most other people also go through it. It is not a disease, but rather a *natural* response to living in an unfamiliar culture. In fact, culture shock is a *positive*

expatriate stress
Stress caused by an imbalance between expectations and abilities affected by culture shock.

Figure 16.4 Culture shock: from honeymoon to normalization

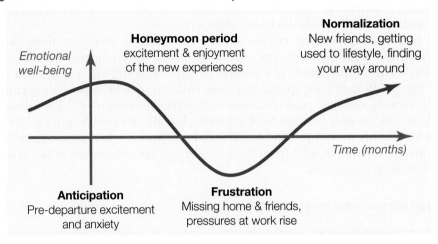

sign of deep involvement with the host culture, rather than remaining isolated in an expatriate ghetto.[26] What can expatriates (or you as a student studying abroad) do to ease the impact of the culture shock? Past experiences suggest that different activities work for different individuals; Table 16.2 offers some suggestions. Some expatriates use extensive physical exercise, while others use meditation and relaxation techniques. Building new social networks with both locals and the expatriate community is particularly important.[27] For example, in many cities around the world, expat communities have organized social jogging events (known as 'hash') that promote fitness and community. A particular powerful idea is 'stability zones', which is where the expatriate would spend most of the time 'totally immersed' in the host culture, but retreat into a 'stability zone' that closely resembles home, such as an international club or a church gathering. For example, Danish expatriates in Hong Kong meet every first Tuesday in the month at a restaurant that serves Biksemad and Pariserbøf for the occasion. Likewise, Spaniards in Shanghai socialize at the *Casa España*, or watch Spanish language movies at the *Instituto Cervantes*. For one evening, they chat in their native tongue and

Table 16.2 Dos and don'ts for expatriates experiencing culture shock

Dos	Don'ts
● Physical exercise	● Blame the host nationals
● Meditation and relaxation techniques	● Blame the company
● 'Stability zones', such as groups in your own cultural community	● Blame your spouse
● Meet others in a similar situation, such as fellow expats and internationally experienced locals	
● Modify expectations on the job	
● Decorate your home-away-from-home with items reflecting your own heritage	

exchange gossip about business, local culture and latest news from back home. Similarly, Chambers of Commerce bring together expatriates in formal and informal setting to facilitate the exchange of experiences.

If you are experiencing culture shock-related stress, there are three things you should *not* do: blame the host nationals, blame the company, or blame your spouse.[28] The culture shock is a natural experience and there is not much that they can do. In fact, your spouse and your children may be experiencing culture shock as well, and they need (and usually deserve) your support.[29] The advice of Table 16.2 is not only relevant for expatriates, but also for people hosting foreigners who recently moved to their country: did you notice a foreign classmate who recently appeared to be a bit frustrated? Maybe you can engage him or her in some of the activities suggested.

Returning expatriates (returnees)

Coming home may seem easier than leaving home, yet it presents challenges of its own. Many returnees (returning expatriates) are surprised by the extent of their readjustment challenges in both (1) professional re-entry and (2) private life (Table 16.3).[30] Unfortunately, many MNEs are not doing a good job managing repatriation – the process of facilitating the return of expatriates.

Professionally, chief among the problems is career anxiety. A key concern is, 'What kind of position will I have when I return?' Some large MNEs have systematic career development plans that include not only commitments by the employee to the company, but commitments by the company specifying what the employee will receive if certain performance objectives are met. In large European MNEs, international experience thus is typically an asset, if not prerequisite, for top management positions, and returnees are likely to find themselves working with colleagues that have gone through similar experiences. In many firms, however, commitments are informal and non-binding. Prior to departure, many expatriates are encouraged by their boss: 'You should take (or volunteer for) this overseas assignment. It's a smart move for your career.' Theoretically, this is known as a psychological contract – an informal understanding of expected delivery of benefits in the future for current services.[31] However, a psychological contract is easy to violate. Bosses may change their mind. Or they may be replaced by new bosses. Violated psychological contracts naturally lead to disappointments.

The international experience of a returning expat is less valued by smaller MNEs that are not using expats extensively, and that may have an ethnocentric view of

returnee
Returning expatriate.

repatriation
The process of facilitating the return of expatriates.

psychological contract
An informal understanding of expected delivery of benefits in the future for current services.

Table 16.3 Challenges of repatriation

Professional re-entry	• Career anxiety – what kind of position will I have when I return (if I do have a position)?
	• Work adjustment – from a big fish in a small pond (at the subsidiary) to a small fish in a big pond (at headquarters).
	• Loss of status and pay – expatriate premiums are gone; chauffeured cars and maids are probably unavailable.
Private Life	• Friends and family have moved on, and cannot relate to the 'exotic' tales of the returnee.
	• Difficult for the spouse and children to adjust to a more mundane life back home.

their firm. Your boss may not appreciate how your rich experience may help the firm. Few (or no one) at headquarters seem interested in learning from expatriates' overseas experience and knowledge. Having been 'big fish in a small pond' in subsidiaries, returnees often feel like 'small fish in a big pond' at headquarters. The initial job back home may be very similar to what you did before you left, and your performance will be similar to your pre-departure job (your boss' perspective) and less than what you did when abroad (your own perspective), which leads to stress. Returning expatriates may also experience a loss of status. Overseas, they are 'big shots', rubbing shoulders with local politicians and visiting dignitaries. They often command expatriate salaries, plus chauffeured cars and maids. However, most of these perks disappear back home. Encouragingly, however, scholarly studies show that international experience tends to accelerate performance improvements, and thus promotions, in the long run.[32]

Moreover, returnees experience a reverse culture shock, a common phenomenon, but less well understood than culture shock. When abroad, images of 'the green, green grass of home' often keep expatriates going. Yet coming home they realize that home is not what it used to be:

reverse culture shock
Culture shock experience by persons returning to their country of origin.

- the country has changed
- the company has changed
- the expatriate him/herself has changed. In particular, the personality and expectations have subtly changed under the experience of living abroad: some things that seemed to be important way back then (like the local sports club where your friends spend all their spare time) just aren't that important when seen from afar.

Even at work returnees may find it hard to adjust to the work culture, because their own perspective, personality and habits have changed. For example, after eight years in China, one returnee to Germany complained:

'It is nice that my team members actually give some feedback on my ideas rather than just wait for me to make all the decisions. But then the discussions are never ending, they always have something to say, it takes so much more time until people actually do something!'[33]

Many also realize that they held idealistic views when abroad that were not true anyway – the streets aren't as clean and the food isn't always as good as you imagined. Re-establishing links with old friends can also be challenging, because you may have quite literally developed away from each other. Some friends have moved, married and had children and their interests have shifted from, say, mountain climbing to playing with the kids. Moreover, many cannot relate to your experiences and may treat your constant temptation of telling stories from distant places as showing off, partly being jealous and partly just being annoyed. Thus a typical experience for a returnee is that: *'I came back with so many stories to share, but my friends and family couldn't understand them. It was as if my years overseas were unshareable.'*[34]

Overall, repatriation, if not managed well, can be traumatic not only for expatriates and their families but also for the firm. Unhappy returning expatriates do not last very long.[35] Approximately one-in-four leaves the firm within one year. Since MNEs make a heavy investment in each expatriate over the duration of a foreign assignment, losing that individual can wipe out any return on investment.[36] The best way to prevent returnees from leaving is a career development plan that comes with a personal mentor (also known as a champion, sponsor or 'godfather').[37] The mentor helps alleviate the 'out of sight, out of mind' feeling by ensuring that the expatriate is not forgotten at headquarters, and by helping to secure a challenging position upon return.

MANAGING PEOPLE ABROAD

Over time, MNEs usually aim to reduce the number of expensive expatriates, calling for expatriates to train local employees.[38] In fact, many subsidiary managers consider the recruitment and retention of a capable and committed workforce their biggest challenge. For example, in the ongoing quest for talent in China, whether employers can provide better training and development opportunities often becomes a key determining factor on whether top talent abroad is retained or not. To stem staff turnover, many MNEs now have formal career development plans and processes for local employees in countries like China.

Attracting a committed workforce

recruitment
The identification, selection and hiring of staff.

How do you find people to work for you? Recruitment concerns the identification of suitable local employees, convincing them to apply for a job, and selecting the most suitable candidates for each job. In many countries, working for an MNE is a very popular career path. Hence the main challenge is to sift through a large number of curriculum vitas (CVs) and to identify the most suitable candidates. Compared to HRM back home, foreign subsidiaries face two additional challenges. First, the candidates need to have not only the functional skills required for the job, but the ability to fit in with a multicultural work environment and to communicate with foreign employees, often in English. This creates difficult trade-offs and challenges in assessing the applicants' abilities. Some MNEs like to hire graduates with degrees in foreign languages and train them in functional skills, rather than hiring people with specialist degrees (say, engineers) whom they would have to train in English. Second, MNE subsidiaries, especially recently established ones, lack knowledge of how the local labour market works. For example, how do you make contact with the best university graduates? How to use job interviews most effectively in a different culture? Due to the need for such local knowledge, the HRM function is often among the most localized units in an MNE subsidiary.

At the top end of the organization, the challenges are quite different. In rapidly developing countries like China, management talent for leadership roles is often quite scarce (In Focus 16.3). People who can lead a major unit within a cross-cultural context are especially almost as scarce as expatriates. The main challenge is thus not to sort through a large numbers of applicants, but to find good people and convince them to apply. For this purpose, firms often employ headhunter (or 'executive search') companies that specialize in finding suitable people for senior positions, working through personal networks to identify those who may seek promotions but didn't get promoted in their own firm. While using headhunters, MNEs naturally don't want their people to be headhunted. Thus the ideal candidate shows a high degree of commitment to the MNE, which is hard to find in rapidly changing business environments.

headhunter company
A company specializing in finding suitable people for senior positions.

Compensation, appraisal and retention

compensation
The determination of salary and benefits.

migrant workers
Workers from rural areas temporarily working in factories in the cities.

As an HRM area, compensation refers to the determination of salary and benefits.[39] At the bottom end of the compensation scale, low-level workers, especially those in developing countries, have relatively little bargaining power. They may be migrant workers who left their village behind to earn better pay in a textile or electronics assembly plant for a few years before returning home. They are willing to accept wage levels substantially lower than those in developed countries, which is why some industries move assembly operations to developing countries in the first place. However, once trained, MNEs would like to keep them for a few years, and thus not only typically pay *higher* wages relative to similar positions in local firms, but support the families and communities (see Integrative Case 'German Chamber of Commerce').

On the other hand, local employees in management and professional positions have increasing bargaining power because local supply of top talent is often limited, especially in emerging economies. Top software engineers and analysts in India and China are scarce, their salaries have been rising by up to 30% per year, while staff turnover even in top outsourcing firms is 15 to 20%.[40] It is not surprising that high-calibre local employees, because of their scarcity, will fetch more pay (In Focus 16.3). MNEs unwilling to pay top local talent top salaries may end up losing such local talent to competitors that are willing to do so. The quest for talent results in a competitive bidding, and eventually individuals qualified for top positions and internationally mobile will earn international rates regardless of nationality.[41]

Pay increases, however, depend on performance. Thus firms conduct some form of performance appraisal, defined as the evaluation of employee performance for

performance appraisal
The evaluation of employee performance for promotion, retention or termination purposes.

IN FOCUS 16.3

Competing for talent in China

This may be hard to believe, but the most populous country in the world has a shortage of managers. Chinese and foreign firms need globally competitive executives in China, yet few executives have the required combination of skills. Thus MNEs of all stripes are going after the same pool of talent, and the pickings are especially slim at the top. Although the average annual pay rise has been 10% or more in recent years, it can be much more for top talent. Top talent is often snatched up, quickly promoted, and then, all too often, headhunted away. Even middle managers quickly quit when offered a slightly higher salary down the road. One study finds that every year, 43% of executives in China voluntarily quit, compared with 5% in Singapore and 11% in Australia. Another study puts the average turnover at 14%. Although estimates vary, China probably now has the world's highest turnover rate for managers.

In a tight job market, money clearly matters. But beyond compensation, training and development are key to staff retention, with inpatriation in the MNE's parent country being one of the most sought-after prizes. At GE China, 60% of the salaried employees are under 35. Young managers take on responsibilities that twenty-something employees elsewhere can only dream about. A position that takes ten years to reach in Japan or five years to reach in the West often takes only three years to get to in China; otherwise, the MNE risks losing such talent. GE finds that its executives are especially vulnerable after three years. This is the crucial point at which they have soaked up enough training and responsibility to make themselves attractive, but they are not yet really loyal to GE. In response, GE tries hard to stimulate, recognize and nurture promising managers, and thereby to reduce its executive turnover to 'only' 7%.

Adding to the heat, Chinese firms have entered the fray. *Alibaba, Tencent, Haier, Huawei, Lenovo* and *Xiaomi* are successfully raiding the managerial ranks of *Microsoft, Google* and other MNEs. This reflects a sea change. Ten years ago, no self-respecting executive would quit a Fortune 500 MNE to join a local outfit. Now such moves are considered very smart, and many MBA graduates aspire to work for local internet start-ups or venture capitalists, rather than for MNEs. Although Chinese firms do not necessarily outbid the MNEs in compensation, Chinese firms offer something that is hard to beat: no glass ceiling, no expats and unlimited promotion opportunities.

Sources: (1) Authors' interviews in China; (2) *Business Week*, 2006, Management grab, August 21: 88–90; (3) *Business Week*, 2005, Stealing managers from the big boys, September 26; (4) V. Hulme, 2006, Short staffed, *China Business Review*, March–April: 18–23; K. Lane & F. Pollner, 2008, How to address China's growing talent shortage, *McKinsey Quarterly*.

promotion, retention or termination purposes. Although initial compensation is negotiated upon entering a firm, follow-up compensation usually depends on performance appraisal. It focuses on decision-making (to determine pay and promotion), development, documentation and subordinate expression. In MNE subsidiaries, performance appraisal is in part provided by expatriates, which creates challenges for all parties involved.

When expatriates evaluate local employees, cultural differences may create problems. Western MNEs emphasize feedback sessions, with the opportunity for subordinates to express themselves. However, high power-distance countries in Asia and Latin America would not foster such an expression, which would potentially undermine the power and status of supervisors. Employees themselves do not place a lot of importance on such an expression.[42] Thus Western expatriates pushing local employees in these cultures to express themselves in performance appraisal meetings may be viewed as indecisive and lacking integrity.

Eventually, it is important for MNEs to retain the best of their local employees, which can be quite challenging in locations where staff frequently jump from one employer to another when better pay packages are offered. Even though Asian cultures traditionally emphasize loyalty and long-term employment, dynamic, competent and ambitious young people frequently depart from this traditional norm. Thus MNEs have to create attractive career prospects, including training, travel and eventually leadership roles to keep their best people on board.[43]

INSTITUTIONS AND HUMAN RESOURCE MANAGEMENT

LEARNING OBJECTIVE

4 Discuss how the institution-based view sheds additional light on HRM

HRM is significantly shaped by formal and informal rules of the game both at home and abroad, especially by employment law and practice. Let us start with *formal* institutions. Every country has rules, laws and regulations governing employment relations, which set formal constraints for HRM. For example, the USA has very strict anti-discrimination laws that some foreign firms find difficult to accommodate. Yet in Japan, firms routinely discriminate against women and minorities. When Japanese MNEs engage in such practices in the USA, they often face legal challenges. Knowing such rules, some of which may be informal, helps MNEs avoid unnecessary conflicts in their overseas operations (Table 16.4).

On the other hand, US firms investing overseas are often amazed at how difficult it is to lay off staff in countries such as France, Germany or India. For example, American tyre manufacturer *Goodyear* had been trying to restructure its two production sites in Amiens, France since 2007. After prolonged negotiations, *Goodyear* decided in January 2013 to close down the plant. But the trade unions continued to fight the management, culminating in two executives being taken hostage. In January 2014, *Goodyear* and the unions eventually agreed redundancy packages rumoured to be about €120 000 per worker. Although less than 10% of workers in France are organized in trade unions, they wield enormous power, much to the dislike of foreign investors, especially those from the USA.[44]

Other formal institutions relate to the education system. Many continental European countries have a vocational training system ('apprenticeships') that is organized jointly by firms, Chambers of Commerce, and schools supported by the state. Access to skilled non-university educated staff *de facto* requires firms to participate in the system. Moreover, with certificates of their craftsmanship, staff would expect to be treated with a certain respect and status, and be entrusted with more complex tasks and responsibilities, than semi-skilled labourers in, for example, the UK.[45] Likewise, they would expect their bosses to have functional

Table 16.4 Some blunders in international HRM

- An American expatriate made a presentation to the prime minister of a small Caribbean country and his cabinet members by starting with 'Honourable Mr Tollis and esteemed members of the cabinet'. The prime minister immediately interrupted him and asked him to start over. This went back and forth several times. Eventually, someone advised the bewildered and then embarrassed expatriate that Mr Tollis was the *former* prime minister, who had been deposed by the current prime minister (the man sitting in front of the expatriate).

- A Spanish company sent a team of expatriates to Saudi Arabia, including a number of young women dressed in the height of current style. Upon arrival, the Saudi immigration official took a look at their miniskirts and immediately sent the entire team back on the next flight back to Spain. The expatriate team belatedly learned that women in Saudi Arabia are not allowed to show their bare legs in public.

- In Malaysia, an American expatriate was introduced to an important potential client he thought was named 'Roger'. He proceeded to call this person 'Rodge'. Unfortunately, this person was a 'rajah', which is an important title of nobility. In this case, the American tendency to liberally use another person's first name – and to proactively shorten it – appeared disrespectful and insensitive. The rajah walked away from the deal.

- A Japanese subsidiary CEO in New York, at a staff meeting consisting entirely of Americans (except him), informed everybody of the firm's grave financial losses and passed the request from headquarters in Japan that everybody redouble efforts. The staff immediately redoubled their efforts – by sending their CVs out to other employers.

- A female South Korean expatriate at a textile plant in Vietnam confronted a worker. She yelled in Korean 'Move!' The Vietnamese worker did not move because he did not understand Korean. The South Korean expatriate then kicked and slapped him. According to the media, in South Korea, it is common for employers to scold or even beat employees if they make a big mistake. But in this case, ten Vietnamese colleagues retaliated by beating up the expatriate, who was wounded, hospitalized and then deported. The workers went on to strike for four days and obtained 10 to 15% pay rises.

Sources: (1) P. Dowling & D. Welch, 2005, *International Human Resource Management*, 4th ed. (p. 59), Cincinnati, OH: Cengage South-Western; (2) R. Linowes, 1993, The Japanese manager's traumatic entry into the United States, *Academy of Management Executive*, 7 (4): 21–38; (3) D. Ricks, 1999, *Blunders in International Business*, 3rd ed. (pp. 95–105), Oxford: Blackwell.

'Workers unite against shareholders': how can MNEs manage the expectation of a multicultural workforce?

knowledge, and be able to do or explain critical tasks when the need arises. In reverse, German or Japanese managers are often frustrated about the low levels of basic skills, such as numeracy, in British workforces.[46] These differences in educational systems thus translate into differences in skill profiles, which make it difficult to transfer management practices between continental Europe, Japan and Anglo-American countries.[47] For example, a German manufacturing company tried to improve its work practices in an acquired subsidiary in the UK. It thus launched a 'back to the workbench' initiative that asked middle and top managers to work on the shop floor for two weeks to better understand the operational challenges. While several German managers took up the challenge, none of their British colleagues did. Not only was the idea of working on the shop floor a violation of their status (or 'class'), but they lacked the skills needed for the shop floor.[48] Managers that have experienced, however brief, working in the lower ranks of a company, for example as apprentices, can communicate more effectively with the people they are supposed to lead. Manual workers will rarely be impressed by the latest management gimmick – but a manager who can explain how best to fix a broken machine has a good chance of earning their respect.

Home country institutions also influence the HR practices employed in subsidiary. Often there is no legal obligation that would force MNEs to transfer practices developed under the specific institutions conditions of their home environment, such as vocational training and employee participation processes. However, the internal consistency of the operations of an MNE is often enhanced by shared HR practices.[49] Hence some German MNEs introduce apprenticeship-style training in overseas affiliates as far away as Japan. However, when *VW* tried to introduce German-style work councils in its plants in Chattanooga, Tennessee, USA, it ran into massive opposition from local politicians. Yet the failure to bring global employee representation to the US affiliate triggered hostile reactions from union representatives of other *VW* plants.[50]

PEOPLE AS RESOURCES

LEARNING OBJECTIVE

5   Discuss how the resource-based view sheds additional light on HRM

Many businesses claim that people are their most important resources. Applying the VRIO framework, managers' first question is *which* people in the organization add *value*?[51] Consider two examples. Low-skill workers add little value, and correspondingly their wages are low. However, the more training employees receive, the more they – potentially – create value. Results pooled from 397 studies found that, on average, training adds value by leading to approximately 20% performance improvement for that individual.[52] Thus training can be seen as a means to enhance the value of human resources.

Next, are particular human resources practices *rare*? Many individuals have highly specialized skills that can add value to organizations at different places around the world. Such individuals, such as entertainers, consultants or management gurus are rare and thus can charge huge fees for their services. Other human resources are embedded in teams of people, such as a football team, that together create rare values.

Further, how *imitable* are human resources? It is relatively easy to imitate specific skills by undergoing a training course; however, it is much more difficult to imitate complex capabilities consisting of multiple, mutually reinforcing abilities, skills and knowledge of a team. Consider the *Portman Ritz-Carlton* hotel in Shanghai. Its expatriate general manager personally interviews *every* new hire. It selects local employees genuinely interested in helping guests. It deeply cares about employee satisfaction, which has led to superb guest satisfaction. Each single practice here may be imitable, and the *Portman Ritz-Carlton* has been meticulously studied by its rivals and around the world. Yet none has been able to successfully imitate its system.

Finally, do human resources help the *organization* accomplish its goals, or do they only benefit the individual employee? If you have very unique skills that you can easily apply in different organizations and in different countries, then you will have a lot of bargaining power, and can negotiate high fees. Think of football stars or banking executives. For a company, such employees can be dangerous: they may be able to attract a lot of the value created, leaving little for everyone else, including shareholders. On the other hand, if skills are specific to an organization and not transferable, or if the effectiveness of an individual depends on the entire team, then the human resources are organizationally embedded and create value for the firm and not just for the individual.

DEBATES AND EXTENSIONS

Changes within global yet continuously evolving MNEs is creating new organizational forms for work, and hence new challenges for both employees and their HR managers. Our debates and extensions discuss two such challenges: (1) multicultural teams and (2) non-traditional forms of expatriation.

LEARNING OBJECTIVE

6   Participate in two leading debates concerning people in the MNE

Multicultural teams

If you work for an MNE in a managerial role, you will soon find yourself working in multicultural team, where members represent a variety of different cultures. In fact, you are likely to experience multicultural teams already in your education, for example, if you participate in an Erasmus exchange programme or when you are assigned to highly diverse teams to work on an assignment (as is normal practice in MBA programmes around the world).

Many firms promote teamwork and diversity because they believe that diverse teams are more innovative, and can engage with a variety of clients and other stakeholders. Yet it is challenging to leverage such team diversity to enhance performance. On the one hand, cultural diversity increases creativity and satisfaction; on the other hand it leads to losses due to conflicts and lower social integration.[53] However, to what extent the potential losses and gains are realized depends on the configuration and leadership of the team.[54]

If you are a member, or even leader, of a multicultural team, the following three ideas should help you.[55] First, success depends on members' awareness of the cultural diversity and the willingness to be open minded about teammates' work styles and values. Spending time together socializing outside work usually helps to build better basic understanding. Especially if your team is not physically located in the same space, occasional face-to-face meetings greatly help to create team spirit, shared working practices, and a common sense of purpose. Second, certain disagreements may be helpful to promote learning in teams, yet too many arguments may lead to conflicts and can torpedo team effectiveness. Hence you need to avoid making conflicts emotional and, as a leader, may need to intervene to round up a discussion. Third, variable structuring of the interactions between team members can help bringing out the best of every member. For example, if a meeting is led by someone other than the boss, members may be more open to expressing their view.

Leading multicultural teams is not easy, and needs practice. The ability to lead a multicultural team is related to cultural intelligence, global identity and openness to

multicultural team
A work team with members representing multiple cultures.

cultural diversity,[56] which are highly tacit competences, best learned through experience rather than reading textbooks. Yet with these abilities you can open yourself international career opportunities.

Non-traditional assignments

Traditionally, expat assignments consisted of a three- to five-year 'tour of duty' abroad, after which a career would advance elsewhere in the MNE. However, such traditional assignments are quite expensive for employers, such that many MNEs have moved to shorter assignments and non-traditional forms of expatriation, such as contract work, commuter assignments and virtual teams.[57] First, firms use contract work when they need experts to implement specific tasks, for example in major construction projects, such as power stations and bridges (see Chapter 3, Opening Case). These expatriates thus stay for shorter periods, and are often sent from one assignment to the next. Second, commuter assignments send people on a weekly or biweekly basis to work in another country, while keeping residency (and family) back home. Common within Europe, such commuter assignments enable firms to manage operations without an expatriate being 'on site' year-round. Both contract work and commuter assignments are more flexible and often less costly (no family relocation). However, individuals on frequent short-term assignment experience problems in maintaining their social and family life, and they have to deal with a lot of complex, regulatory regimes regarding, for example, work visas and income taxes.[58]

Third, globally operating firms often assemble project teams for a specific task or contract, drawing on the best people in the organization wherever in the world they are based. The teams working on these projects often operate as a virtual team, which rely heavily on communication technologies, such as telephone, email and video conferences rather than face-to-face interactions. The idea is to harness talent from anywhere in the world to jointly solve business problems that may relate to internal tasks (such as developing a new IT infrastructure) or external contracts (such as advising a specific global client).[59] Virtual teams are particularly common in global service businesses, such as accounting, engineering and consulting firms (Chapter 15, Opening Case). However, virtual teams often have to overcome substantial communication barriers and obstacles to building personal relationships. For example, video conferences can hardly show body language, and provide little scope for informal chats. Hence virtual teams amplify both the benefits and the costs of teamwork, and thus require extra effort in managing the team dynamics.[60] In fact, many executives believe that face-to-face meetings are often necessary, and recent evidence suggests that site visits enhance the quality of collaboration.[61] Thus global executives spend a lot of time on aeroplanes. Yet as travel is both costly and stressful (see Chapter 8, Opening Case), virtual teams are an increasingly common feature of international business, and managers have to learn how to make them work effectively.[62]

Fourth, MNEs increasingly use inpatriates – relocating employees of a foreign subsidiary to the MNE's headquarters for the purposes of (1) filling skill shortages at headquarters and (2) developing a global mindset for such inpatriates.[63] The term *inpatriate* of course is derived from *expatriate*, and most inpatriates are expected to eventually return to their home country to replace expatriates (see Closing Case). Examples would include IT inpatriates from India to work at *IBM* in the USA, and telecom inpatriates from China to work at *Alcatel* in France. Technically, these inpatriates are expatriates from India and China, who will experience similar problems to expatriates discussed earlier in this chapter. Often such inpatriate assignments primarily serve to develop future leaders for the overseas operation.

---

contract work
A short assignment for a specific project or contract.

commuter assignment
Assignments that involve regular stays abroad but with the main base remaining back home.

virtual team
A team that is geographically dispersed and interact primarily through electronic communication.

inpatriate
Employees of a foreign subsidiary relocated to the MNE's headquarters for the purposes of (1) filling skill shortages at headquarters, and (2) developing a global mindset for such inpatriates.

IMPLICATIONS FOR PRACTICE

What determines the success or failure of HRM around the world? This chapter has outlined the challenges of managing people in an MNE. What qualifications do you need to succeed in an HRM role? We suggest four capabilities (Table 16.5) based on the four Cs developed by Susan Meisinger, president of the *Society for Human Resource Management*.[64] First, HR managers need to be *curious*. They need to be well versed in the numerous formal and informal rules of the game governing HRM in worldwide operations. They must be curious about emerging trends of the world (such as the rise of outsourcing) and create people strategies to respond to these trends.

Second, HR managers must be *competent*. From its roots as an administrative support function, HRM is now acknowledged to be a more strategic function that directly contributes to the bottom line. As a result, HR managers need to develop organizational capabilities that drive business success. This starts with broadening the competencies of HR managers, who may have been trained more narrowly. Now, HR managers not only must contribute to the strategy conversation by enabling the firm to recruit, develop and retain the people who can eventually implement the CEO's strategic vision.

Third, HR managers must be *courageous*. As employee advocates, HR managers sometimes need to be courageous enough to disagree with the CEO and other line managers if necessary. GE's recently retired head of HR, William Conaty, is such an example. 'If you just get closer to the CEO, you're dead,' Conaty shared with a reporter. 'I need to be independent. I need to be credible.'[65] GE's CEO Jeff Immelt called Conaty 'the first friend, the guy that could walk in my office and kick my butt when it needed to be' – as a trusted business partner should be. Fourth, HR managers must be *caring* for people. As guardians of talent, HR managers need to nurture and develop employees, and provide personal support when individuals face career challenges such as conflicts with their bosses.

This chapter also has direct implications for any ambitious young managers in an MNE. You need to have proactive career management to develop a global mind-set.[66] Given that international experience is now a prerequisite for reaching the top at many firms, managers need to prepare by investing in their own technical expertise, cross-cultural adaptability, and language training. Some of these investments (such as language) are long-term in nature, and just-in-time preparation will not cut it. This point thus has strategic implications for students who are studying this book *now*: have you picked up a foreign language? Have you spent one semester or year abroad? Have you made some friends from abroad who are studying in this class together with you now? Imagine a scenario for expatriate selection five to ten years down the road: wouldn't you hate it when your colleague is tipped to go to Latin America as a high-profile expat, but you are passed over because you have

LEARNING OBJECTIVE

7 Draw implications for action

Table 16.5 Implications for action

- Be *curious* – need to know formal and informal rules of the game governing HRM in all regions of operations.
- Be *competent* – develop organizational capabilities that drive business success.
- Be *courageous* – challenge the leaders of your firm to take people and career issues seriously.
- Be *caring* – as guardians of talent, HR managers need to nurture and develop people.

never studied Spanish? The difference may be that your colleague started investing in learning Spanish five to ten years ago, and you didn't. To make yourself 'expat ready', you have to start now. The point, of course, is not just about Latin America. You can pick any country likely to be an attractive place to do business in the future. It is about arming yourself with the knowledge now, making proper investments and preparing yourself to be picked. In the global economy, *your* career is in your hands.

CHAPTER SUMMARY

1 Distinguish ethnocentric, polycentric and geocentric management practices

- International staffing may use ethnocentric, polycentric and geocentric approaches.
- Expatriates play multiple challenging roles and often have high failure rates. They need to be carefully selected, taking into account a variety of factors.

2 Explain how MNEs manage expatriates

- Expatriates play many crucial roles in MNE subsidiaries, and therefore need a variety of both financial and personal abilities.
- Pre-departure language tuition and cross-cultural training is essential but not always provided.
- Expatriates typically experience a period of culture shock caused by their limited understanding of the local context and pressures at work.
- Returnees face problems of reintegration both professionally and privately.

3 Explain how MNEs manage employees in subsidiaries abroad

- Training and development of local employees are now an area of differentiation among many MNEs.

- Retention of local top talent requires competitive pay, ongoing training, clear career prospects and culture-sensitive performance appraisal.

4 Discuss how the institution-based view sheds additional light on HRM

- HRM is significantly shaped by formal and informal rules of the game, both at home and abroad.

5 Discuss how the resource-based view sheds additional light on HRM

- People are resources that can add value both for their organization, and for themselves.

6 Participate in two leading debates concerning people in the MNE

- These are (1) non-traditional forms of expatriation, and (2) managing cross-cultural teams.

7 Draw implications for action

- HR managers need to have the four Cs: being curious, competent, courageous and caring about people.
- All managers in an MNE need to proactively develop an international career mindset.

KEY TERMS

Commuter assignment
Compensation
Contract work
Culture shock
Ethnocentric approach
Expatriate (expat)
Expatriate stress
Full immersion training
Geocentric approach
Global talent management

Global talent pool
Headhunter company
Host country national
Human resource management
   (HRM)
Inpatriate
Migrant workers
Multicultural team
Parent (home) country national
Performance appraisal

Polycentric approach
Psychological contract
Recruitment
Repatriation
Returnee
Reverse culture shock
Third country national
Training
Virtual team

CRITICAL DISCUSSION QUESTIONS

1 You have been offered a reasonably lucrative opportunity for an expatriate assignment for the next three years, and your boss will have a meeting with you next week. What would you discuss with your boss?

2 As HR director for an oil company, you are responsible for selecting 15 expatriates to go to work in Iraq. However, you are personally concerned about their safety there. How do you proceed?

3 You are general manager of an MNE subsidiary in India. For the third time in as many months, one of your best engineers has been poached by one of your competitors. What are you going to do prevent further departures of key people?

4 You have been assigned to an international team to develop a report on environmental pollution in the Mekong river delta in Southeast Asia. Experts joining the team are based in the Stockholm, Paris, Singapore and Sydney offices of your company. How are you going to make this team work effectively?

RECOMMENDED READINGS

N.J. Adler & A. Gundersen, 2008, *International Dimensions of Organizational Behavior*, 5th ed., Cincinnati, OH: South-Western – a very practically oriented textbook focusing on expats, international teams and careers.

N.A. Boyacigiller, R.A. Goodman, M.E. Phillips & J.L. Pearce, eds, 2004, *Crossing Cultures: Insights from Master Teachers*, London: Routledge – a book with practical tips and class room exercises for hands-on learning on cross-cultural management issues.

D. Collings, G. Wood & P. Caligiuri, eds, 2014, *The Routledge Companion to International Human Resource Management*, Abingdon: Routledge – a collection of essays by leading scholars of the state of the art of research in the field.

P.J. Dowling, M. Festing & A.D. Engle, 2013, *International Human Resource Management*, 6th ed., London: Cengage – a textbook focused on international aspects of human resource management.

G.K. Stahl, I. Björkman & S. Morris, eds, 2012, *Handbook of Research in International HRM*, 2nd ed., Cheltenham: Elgar – a collection of essays by leading scholars of the state of the art of research in the field.

CLOSING CASE

Dallas vs Delhi

Prashant Sarkar is director for corporate development for the New Delhi, India, subsidiary of the US-based *Dallas Instruments*. Sarkar has an engineering degree from the Indian Institute of Technology and an MBA from the University of Texas, Dallas. After obtaining his MBA, he worked at a *Dallas Instruments* facility in Richardson, Texas (a suburb of Dallas), and obtained a green card (US permanent residence) while maintaining his Indian passport. When *Dallas Instruments* opened its first Indian subsidiary in New Delhi, Sarkar was tipped to be one of the first managers sent from the USA. The India of the early 21st century is certainly different from the India that Sarkar had left behind more than a decade earlier. Reform is in the air, MNEs are coming in left and right, and an exhilarating self-confidence permeates the country.

As a manager, Sarkar has shined in his native New Delhi. His wife and two children are also happy. After all, curry in New Delhi is a lot more authentic and fresher than that in Indian grocery stores in Dallas. Grandparents, relatives and friends are all happy to see the family back. In Dallas, Prashant's wife, Neeli, a teacher by training, taught on a part-time basis but couldn't secure a full-time teaching position because she didn't have a US degree. Now she is principal of a great school. The two children are enrolled in the elite New Delhi American School, the cost of which is paid for by the company. New Delhi is not perfect, but the Sarkars feel good about coming back.

'Prashant, I have great news for you!' the American CEO of the subsidiary tells Sarkar one day 'Headquarters wants you to move back to Dallas. You'll be in charge of strategy development for global expansion, working directly under the group vice president. Isn't that exciting? They want someone with proven success. You are my best candidate. I don't know what design they have for you after this assignment, but I suspect it'll be highly promising. Don't quote me, but I'd say you may have a shot to eventually replace me or the next American CEO here. While I personally enjoy working here, my family sometimes still complains a bit about the curry smell. Or folks in Dallas may eventually want you to go somewhere else. Frankly, I don't know, but I'm just trying to help you speculate. I know it's a big decision. Talk to Neeli and the kids. But they lived in Dallas before, so they should be fine going back. Of course, I'll put you in touch with the folks in Dallas directly so that you can ask them all kinds of questions. Let me know what you think in a week.'

CASE DISCUSSION QUESTIONS

1 Going from Dallas to New Delhi, Sarkar, with his Indian passport, would be a host country national. With his green card, he could also be considered a US national, and thus an expatriate. Now if he goes from New Delhi to Dallas, would he be an expatriate or an inpatriate? What difference does that make?

2 What questions should Sarkar ask the people at headquarters in Dallas?

3 Will Neeli and the children be happy about this move? Why?

4 Should Sarkar accept or decline this opportunity? Why?

Source: Based on Mike Peng's interviews. All individual and corporate names are fictitious.

NOTES

'For journal abbreviation, please see page xx–xxi.'

1 G. Stahl, I. Björkman & S. Morris, eds, 2012, *Handbook of Research in International HRM*, 2nd ed. Cheltenham: Elgar.

2 H. Scullion & K. Starkey, 2000, In search of the changing role of the corporate human resource function in the international firm, *IJHRM*, 11: 1061–1081; D. Bowen, C. Galang & R. Pillai, 2002, The role of HRM, *HRM*, 41: 103–122.

3 H. Scullion & D. Collings, eds, 2011, *Global Talent Management*, Abington: Routledge (p. 3).

4 J. Fernandez, B. Xu, D. Zhou, M. Puyuelo & J. Li, 2014, *China Business Survey 2014*, Shanghai: China Europe International Business School.

5 H. Perlmutter, 1969, The tortuous evolution of the multinational corporation, *CJWB*, 4: 9–18.

6 B. Becht, 2010, Building a company without borders, *HBR*, (April): 103–106.

7 Scullion & Collings, 2011, *as above* (p. 6–7).

8 N. Boyaçigiller, 1990, The role of expatriates in the management of interdependence, complexity and risk in multinational corporations, *JIBS*, 21: 357–381; A. Harzing, 2001, Of bears, bumble-bees, and spiders, *JWB*, 36: 366–379; R. Marschan, D.E. Welch & L.S. Welch, 1996, Control in less hierarchical multinationals, *IBR*, 5: 137–150; D. Tan & J. Mahoney, 2006, Why a multinational firm chooses expatriates, *JMS*, 43: 457–484.

9 M. Janssens, T. Cappellen & P. Zanoni, 2006, Successful female expatriates as agents, *JWB*, 41: 133–148; D. Vora & T. Kostova, 2007, A model of dual organizational identification in the context of the multinational enterprise, *JOB*, 28: 327–350.

10 Y. Chang, Y. Gong & M. Peng, Expatriate knowledge transfer, subsidiary absorptive capacity, and subsidiary performance, *AMJ*, 55: 927–948.

11 H. Brewster & H. Scullion, 2001, The management of expatriates: Messages from Europe, *JWB*, 36: 346–365.

12 S. Toh & A. DeNisi, 2005, A local perspective to expatriate success, *AME*, 19: 132–146.

13 R. Takeuchi, P. Tesluk, S. Yun & D. Lepak, 2005, An integrative view of international experience, *AMJ*, 48: 85–100; P. Caligiuri, 2006, Developing global leaders, *HRMR*, 16: 219–228; S. Shin, F. Morgeson & M. Campion, 2007, What you do depends on where you are, *JIBS*, 38: 64–83; H. Cheng & C. Lin, 2009, Do as large enterprises do? *IBR*, 18, 60–75.

14 M. Javidan, M. Teagarden & D. Bowen, 2010, Managing yourself: Making it overseas, *HBR*, (April): 109–113.

15 V. Peltokorpi & F. Froese, 2012. The impact of expatriate personality traits on cross-cultural adjustment, *IBR*, 21, 734–746.

16 W. Mansell, 2011, Expat guide to China: schools, *The Telegraph*, April 11.

17 M.E. Mendenhall & G.K. Stahl, 2000, Expatriate training and development, *HRM* 39: 251–265; E. Drost, C. Frayne, K. Lowe & J.M. Geringer, 2002, Benchmarking training and development practices, *HRM*, 41: 67–86.

18 Brookfield Global Relocation Services, 2010, Global Relocation Trends Survey, www.brookfieldgrs.com/insights_ideas/grts/ (accessed April 2010).

19 M.E. Mendenhall, E. Dunbar & G. Oddou, 1987, Expatriate selection, training and career-pathing, *HRM*, 26: 331–345.

20 J. Black, 1990, Locus of control, social support, stress, and adjustment in international assignments, *APJM*, 7: 1–29; N. Adler & A. Gundersen, 2008, *International Dimensions of Organizational Behaviour*, 5th ed., Mason, OH: Thomson-Southwestern.

21 J. Selmer, 1999, Culture shock in China? *IBR*, 8: 515–534.

22 J. Usunier, 1998, Oral Pleasures and expatriate satisfaction, *IBR*, 7: 89–110.

23 R. Takeuchi, D. Lepak, S. Marinova & S. Yun, 2007, Nonlinear influence of stressors on general adjustment, *JIBS*, 38: 928–943; C. Brewster, J. Bonache, J. Cerdin & V. Suutari, 2014, Exploring expatriate failure, *IJHRM*, 25: 1921–1937; B. Firth, G. Chen, B. Kirkman & K. Kim, 2014, Newcomers abroad, *AMJ*, advance online.

24 J. Black, M. Mendenhall & G. Oddou, 1991, Toward a comprehensive model of international adjustment, *AMR*, 16: 291–317; R. Tung, 1982, Selection and training procedures for US, European, and Japanese multinationals, *CMR*, 25: 57–71.

25 P. Dowling & D. Welch, 1988, International human resource management: An Australian perspective *APJM*, 6: 39–65; I. Björkman & M. Gertsen, 1993, Selecting and training Scandinavian expatriates, *SJM*, 9: 145–164.

26 Adler & Gunderson, 2008, *as above*.

27 C. Farh, K. Bartoil, D. Shapiro & J. Shen, 2010. Networking abroad, *AMR*, 35, 434–454; A. Mahjan & Toh, 2014, Facilitating expatriate adjustment, *JWB*, 49: 476–487 .

28 Adler & Gunderson, 2008, *as above*.

29 H. de Cieri, P. Dowling & K. Taylor, 1991, The psychological impact of expatriate relocation on partners, *IJHMR*, 2: 377–414; R. Takeuchi, 2010, A critical review of expatriate adjustment research through a multiple stakeholder view, *JoM*, 36, 1040–1064.

30 M. Lazarova & J. Cerdin, 2007, Revisiting repatriation concerns, *JIBS*, 38: 404–429.

31 A. Haslberger & C. Brewster, 2009, Capital gains: expatriate adjustment and the psychological contract in international careers, *HRM*, 48, 379–387.

32 G. Stahl, E. Miller & R. Tung, 2002, Toward the boundaryless career, *JWB*, 37: 216–237; V. Suutari & C. Brewster, Expatriation, *IJHRM*, 14: 1132–1151; S. Carraher, S. Sullivan & M. Crocitto· 2008, Mentoring across global boundaries, *JIBS*, 39, 1310–1326.

33 Personal communication with Klaus Meyer, 2014.

34 Adler & Gunderson, 2008, as above (p. 287).

35 S. Fineman, 2006, On being positive, *AMR*, 31: 270–291; M. Lazarove & J. Cerdin, 2007, Revisiting repatriation concerns, *JIBS*, 38: 404–429.

36 L. Bassi & D. McMurrer, 2007, Maximizing your return on people, *HBR*, March: 115–123; Y. McNulty, H. de Cieri & K. Hutchings, 2009, Do global firms measure expatriate return on investment? *IJHRM*, 20: 1309–1326; D.Welch, A. Steen & M. Tahvanainen, 2009, All pain, little gain? *IJHRM*, 20: 1327–1343.

37 J. Mezias & T. Scandura, 2005, A needs-driven approach to expatriate adjustment and career development, *JIBS*, 36: 519–538.

38 K. Law, L. Song, C. Wong & D. Chen, 2009, The antecedents and consequences of successful localization, *JIBS*, 40: 1359–1373.

39 K. Lowe, J. Milliman, H. De Cieri & P. Dowling, 2002, International compensation practices, *HRM*, 41: 45–66; E. Chang, 2006, Individual pay for performance and commitment: HR practices in South Korea, *JWB*, 41: 368–381; J. DeVaro, 2006, Strategic promotion

tournaments and worker performance, *SMJ*, 27: 721–740; Y. Yanadori & J. Marler, 2006, Compensation strategy, *SMJ*, 27: 559–570.

40 *The Economist*, 2013, Indias outsourcing business, January 13.

41 T. Gardner, 2005, Interfirm competition for HR, *AMJ*, 48: 237–256; B.S. Reiche, 2009, To quit or not to quit, *IJHRM*, 20: 1362–1380.

42 J. Milliman, S. Nason, C. Zhu & H. De Cieri, 2002, An exploratory assessment of the purposes of performance appraisals in North and Central America and the Pacific Rim, *HRM*, 41: 87–102.

43 A. Vo, 2009, Career development for host country nationals, *IJHRM*, 20: 1402–1420.

44 G. Parussini, 2014, Goodyear tire workers in France take two bosses hostage, *Wall Street Journal*, January 6; D. Jolly, 2014, Goodyear reaches severance deal with French union, *New York Times*, January 22; P. Gumbel, 2014, In France, where unions rule, *Reuters*, January 29.

45 G. Delmestri & P. Walgenbach, 2005, Mastering techniques or brokering knowledge? Middle managers in Germany, Great Britain and Italy, *OSt*, 26: 197–220.

46 J. Lowe, J. Morris & B. Wilkinson, 2000, British Factory, Japanese Factory and Mexican Factory, *JMS*, 37: 541–560.

47 G. Hofstede, 1993, Cultural constraints in management theories, *AME*, 7: 81–94; A. Klarsfield, 2004, Management Development in Europe: Do National Models Persist? *EMJ*, 22: 649–658; C. Carr, 2005, Are German, Japanese and Anglo-Saxon Decision Styles Still Divergent in the Context of Globalization? *JMS*, 42: 1155–1188.

48 F. Moore, 2011, Holistic ethnography, *JIBS*, 42: 654–671.

49 T. Kostova & K. Roth, Adoption of an organizational practice by subsidiaries of multinational corporations, *AMJ*, 45: 215–233; N. Beck, R. Kabst & P. Walgenbach, 2009, The cultural dependence of vocational training, *JIBS*, 40: 1374–1395.

50 The Economist, 2014, *Chattanooga shoo-shoo*, February 22: 57.S. Greenhouse, 2014, Labor regroups in South after VW vote, *New York Times*, February 16; *Handelsblatt*, 2014, VW-Betriebsrat droht US-Politikern, February 19.

51 K. Law, D. Tse & N. Zhou, 2003, Does HR matter in a transition economy? *JIBS*, 34: 255–265; S. Kang, S. Morris & S. Snell, 2007, Relational archetypes, organizational learning, and value creation, *AMR*, 32: 236–256.

52 W. Arthur, W. Bennett, P. Edens & S. Bell, 2003, Effectiveness of training in organizations, *JAP*, 88: 234–245.

53 V. Govindarajan & A. Gupta, 2001, Building an effective global business team, *SMR*, 42(4): 63–71; C. Boone, W. Olffen, A. van Witteloostuijn & B. Brabander, 2004, The genesis of top management team diversity, *AMJ*, 47: 633–656; G. Stahl, M. Maznivsk, A. Voigt & K. Jonson, 2010, Unraveling the effects of cultural diversity in teams, *JIBS*, 41: 609–709.

54 L. Zander & C. Butler, 2010, Leadership modes, *SJM*, 26: 158–267; A. Zimmermann, 2011, Interpersonal relationships in transnational, virtual teams, *IJMR*, 13: 59–78.

55 J. Brett, K. Behfar & M. Kern, 2006, Managing multicultural teams, *HBR*, November: 84–91; M. Zellmer-Bruhn & C. Gibson, 2006, Multinational organization context, *AMJ*, 49: 501–518; R. Dibble & C. Gibson, 2013, Collaboration for the Common Good, *JOB*, 34: 764–790; K. Ferrazzi, 2014, Getting virtual teams right, *HBR*, 92(12): 120–123.

56 A. Lisak & M. Erez, 2015, Leadership emergence in multicultural teams, *JWB*, 50: 3–14.

57 H. Mayerhofer, L. Hartmann, G. Michelitsch-Riedl & I. Kollinger, 2004, Flexpatriate assignments, *IJHRM*, 15: 1371–1390; M. Meyskens, M. von Glinow, W. Werther & L. Clarke, 2009, The paradox of international talent, *IJHRM*, 20: 1439–1450.

58 M. Tahvanainen, D.E. Welch & V. Worm, 2005, Implications of short-term international assignments, *EMJ*, 23: 663–673; T. Starr & G. Currie, 2009, Out of sight but still in the picture: short-term international assignments and the influential role of family, *IJHRM*, 20: 1421–1438.

59 C. Gibson & S. Cohen, eds, 2003, *Virtual teams that Work*, San Francisco: Jossey-Bass.

60 Ferrazzi, 2014, *as above.*

61 P. Hinds & C. Crampton, 2014, Situated coworker familiarity, *OSc* 25: 975–814.

62 D. Welch, V. Worm & M. Fenwick, 2003, Are virtual assignments feasible? *MIR*, 43: 95–114; S. Krumm, K. Terwiel & G. Hertel, 2013, Challenges in norm formation and adherence, *Journal of Personnel Psychology*, 12: 33–44; C. Cramton & P. Hinds, 2014, An embedded model of cultural adaptation in global teams, *OSc*, 25: 1056–1081.

63 M. Harvey, C. Speier & M. Novicevic, 2001, The role of inpatriation in global staffing, *IJHRM*, 10: 459–476; B.S. Reiche, 2006, The inpatriate experience in multinational corporations, *IJHRM*, 19: 1572–1590.

64 S. Meisinger, 2005, The four Cs of the HR profession, *HRM*, 44: 189–194.

65 *Business Week*, 2007, Secrets of an HR superstar (p. 66), April 19: 66–67.

66 T. Cappellen & M. Janssens, 2005, Career paths for global managers, *JWB*, 40: 348–360; M. Dickman & H. Harris, 2005, Developing career capital for global careers, *JWB*, 40: 399–408; O. Levy, S. Beechler, S. Taylor & N. Boyacigiller, 2007, What we talk about when we talk about 'global mindset', *JIBS*, 38: 231–258; D. Thomas, M. Lazarova & K. Inkson, 2005, Global careers, *JWB*, 40: 340–347; T. Khanna, 2014, Contextual intelligence, *HBR*, 92(9).

CHAPTER SEVENTEEN

CUSTOMERS AND SUPPLIERS OF THE MNE

LEARNING OBJECTIVES

After studying this chapter, you should be able to

1 Explain how companies may analyze consumer behaviour abroad

2 Articulate the four Ps in international marketing (place, product, price and promotion)

3 Articulate the three As in supply chain management (agility, adaptability and alignment)

4 Discuss how institutions affect marketing and supply chain management

5 Discuss how resources affect marketing and supply chain management

6 Participate in two leading debates concerning marketing and supply chain management

7 Draw implications for action

OPENING CASE

Zara *rewrites the rules on marketing and supply chain management*

Zara is one of the hottest fashion chains of the 21st century. Founded in 1975, *Zara*'s parent, *Inditex*, has become one of the leading global apparel retailers. Since its initial public offering (IPO) in 2001, *Inditex* tripled its sales and profits and doubled the number of its stores of eight brands, of which *Zara* contributes two-thirds of total sales. As of March 2015, the market cap of *Inditex* reached around €86 billion, greater than *Nike* (market cap: US$82 billion) and *H&M* (market cap: US$57 billion). *Zara* succeeds by breaking and then rewriting rules on marketing and supply chain management.

Rule number one: The place of origin of a fashion house critically shapes its brand image. However, *Zara* does not hail from *Milan* or *Paris* – it is from *Arteixo*, a town of only 25 000 people in Galicia, a remote province of north-western Spain. Yet *Zara* is active in Europe, the Americas, Asia, Australia and Africa. By 2014, *Inditex* was operating 6500 stores in 88 countries, including 2500 *Zara* stores. *Zara* stores occupy some of the priciest locations: Paris's Champs-Elysées, Tokyo's Ginza and New York's Fifth Avenue.

Rule number two: Avoid stock-outs (a store running out of items in demand). But *Zara* believes that occasional shortages contribute to an urge to buy now. With new items arriving at stores *twice* a week, experienced *Zara* shoppers know that if you see something and don't buy it, you can forget about coming back for it, because it will be gone. The small batch of merchandise during a short window of opportunity for purchasing motivates shoppers to visit *Zara* stores more frequently. In London, shoppers visit the average store four times a year but frequent *Zara* 17 times annually. There is a good reason to do so: *Zara* makes about 20 000 items a year, about triple what *Gap* does. As a result, 'At *Gap*, everything is the same,' according to a *Zara* fan, 'and buying from *Zara*, you'll never end up looking like someone else.'

Rule number three: Bombard shoppers with ads. *Gap* and *H&M* spend on average 3 to 4% of their sales on advertising. *Zara* devotes just 0.3% of its sales to ads. The high traffic in the stores alleviates some of the need for advertising in the media, most of which only serves as a reminder to visit the stores.

Rule number four: Outsource. *Gap* and *H&M* do not own any production facilities. However, outsourcing production (mostly to Asia) requires a long lead time, usually several weeks. Again, *Zara* deviates from the norm. By concentrating (major parts of) its production in-house and in Spain, *Zara* has developed a super-responsive supply chain. It designs, produces and

How does Zara manage to deliver affordable fashion?

delivers new garments to its stores worldwide in a mere 15 days, a pace that is unheard of in the industry. The best speed the rivals can achieve is two months. Outsourcing may not necessarily be 'low cost', because errors in prediction can easily lead to unsold inventory, forcing retailers to offer steep discounts. The industry average is to offer 40% discounts across all merchandise. In contrast, *Zara* sells more at full price, and when it discounts, it averages only 15%.

Rule number five: Strive for efficiency through large batches. In contrast, *Zara* intentionally deals with small batches. Because of its flexibility, *Zara* does not worry about 'missing the boat' for a season. When new trends emerge, *Zara* can react quickly. More interestingly, *Zara* runs its supply chain like clockwork, with a fast but predictable rhythm: every store places orders on Tuesday/Wednesday and Friday/Saturday. Trucks and cargo flights run on established schedules – like a bus service. From Spain, shipments reach most European stores in 24 hours, US stores in 48 hours, and Asian stores in 72 hours. Not only do store staff know exactly when shipments will arrive, regular customers do too, thus motivating them to check out the new merchandise more frequently on those days. Mr Isla, *Inditex*'s CEO,

thus emphasizes that the success of *Inditex* is not just about speed, but about understanding customers, responding to them: '*Instead of designing a collection long before the season, and then working out whether clients like it or not, we try to understand what our customers like, and then we design it and produce it.*'

Focused initially on Western Europe, *Zara* has expanded in the 2000s to emerging economies; more than 50% of new shops opened are in places such as China, Russia, Poland and Mexico. *Zara* adapts its business model as appropriate, using fewer but larger outlets. In 2010, *Zara* launched its first online boutique, serving six European countries. By 2014, the online presence has been extended to 27 of its countries of operation. Online sales jumped 42% in 2014, reaching €533 million.

Sources: (1) K. Ferdows, M. Lewis & J.A.D. Machuca, 2004, Rapid-fire fulfilment, *HBR*, November: 104–110; (2) *Business Week*, 2006, Fashion conquistador, September 4; (3) C. Rohwedder, 2009, Zara grows as retail rivals struggle, *Wall Street Journal*, March 26; (4) *The Economist*, 2011, Fashion for the masses: Global stretch, March 12; (5) *The Economist*, 2012, Inditex: Fashion Forward, March 24; (6) T. Buck, 2014, Fashion: A better business model, *Financial Times*, June 18; (7). www.zara.com.

How can firms such as Zara continuously attract customers in different countries? Having attracted customers, how can firms ensure a steady supply of products and services? This chapter deals with these and other important questions associated with marketing and supply chain management. Marketing refers to efforts to create, develop and defend markets that satisfy the needs and wants of individual and business customers. In international markets, a key challenge for marketing is to create appropriate variations of both products and processes across countries.[1] A supply chain is the flow of products, services, finances and information that passes through a set of entities from a source to the customer. Supply chain management refers to activities that plan, organize, lead and control the supply chain.[2] As the Opening Case illustrates, marketing and supply chain management are closely intertwined. Marketing will only succeed if the supply chain gets the right products to the right customers at the right time. Therefore, we discuss them together in this chapter.[3]

We start by briefly outlining the challenges of understanding diverse consumer behaviours around the world. Then, we discuss how MNEs use marketing and supply chain management to deliver products that these diverse customers value. The institution- and resource-based views add further insights on the variations of marketing and supply chain management. Finally, debates and extensions round up this chapter.

marketing
Efforts to create, develop and defend markets that satisfy the needs and wants of individual and business customers.

supply chain
Flow of products, services, finances and information that passes through a set of entities from a source to the customer.

supply chain management
Activities to plan, organize, lead and control the supply chain.

UNDERSTANDING CONSUMERS AROUND THE WORLD

What consumers want varies across countries for lots of reasons discussed throughout this book. Cultural differences (Chapter 3) are probably most important in explaining such differences, but differences in the regulatory environment (Chapter 2) and in resource endowments and incomes matter too. Marketers have a tool box – the

LEARNING OBJECTIVE

1 Explain how companies may analyze consumer behaviour abroad

marketing mix – of techniques to sell to different customers, but before deploying their tool box, they first need to understand their customers' needs. Often, this is more than asking customers what they want, but studying customer behaviours and coming up with new ideas to enhance their lives. For example, when Swedish truck maker *Volvo* started selling coaches in India, many wondered how they could succeed: local buses are so much cheaper, and few travellers would be able and willing to pay substantially extra simply for the luxury of travelling in a *Volvo* bus. However, *Volvo*'s Indian marketers realized that their buses provided coach operators with a number of benefits. Most importantly, they were more reliable – and *Volvo* offered a service guarantee to repair buses breaking down en route. Stronger engines provided advantages in mountainous terrain, and more robust air-conditioned design made bus travel more comfortable. Last, not least, luggage could be stored inside the bus (rather than on the roof, as in traditional Indian buses) which reduced theft and damage by adverse weather conditions – a major concern during monsoon season. Thus by understanding the needs of bus operators (as customers) and travellers (as the customers' customers), *Volvo* was able to create an attractive product offering that led to rapid growth of its market share.[4]

More generally, when companies want to adapt their marketing to consumers in different countries, they need to understand their (potential) consumers, media and distribution channels.[5] This can be quite challenging if the consumers are far removed from the corporate boardrooms where marketing strategies are being designed. Three approaches can be considered: (1) experimental adaptation, (2) survey-based research and (3) anthropological studies. First, an experimental approach would transfer the firm's practices to the new location, and then use a trial-and-error approach to learning about consumers and identifying the optimal solution for each market through incremental changes. This approach reduces the initial costs of entry, but risks making major marketing blunders that others may be laughing about for years to come (Table 17.1).

A particular challenge is the translation of brand and product names. What can you do if your brand has an ambiguous meaning in a foreign language? An experimental approach suggests to try it out, but be flexible and creative in responding

Table 17.1 Linguistic challenges for marketers

- One US toymaker received numerous complaints from American mothers because a talking doll told their children, 'Killing mommy!' Made in Hong Kong, the dolls were shipped around the world. They carried messages in the language of the country of destination. A packing error sent some Spanish-speaking dolls to the USA. The message in Spanish '*Quiero mommy!*' means 'I love mommy!' (This is also a supply chain blunder.)

- Spanish speakers have their fun with products such as a photocopier named Olympia Roto (*roto* means 'broken' in Spanish), and cars named Lada Nova (*no va* means 'no go'), Mazda Laputa (*la puta* means 'prostitute') and Mitsubishi Pajero (*pajera* is a derogatory term for people masturbating).

- French speakers may smile over Gerber baby food, which in French means 'vomiting', over Persil washing powder (*persil* means 'parsley') and over GE's product GPT (Gravel Pack Tool), which in French is pronounced as *J'ai pété* ('I have farted').

- Portuguese people needed some convincing to buy Nescafé, as they would hear *N'es café* ('this is not coffee').

- Literal translations from Chinese to English resulted in Chinese firms marketing the following products: White Elephant brand batteries, Sea Cucumber brand shirts, Pansy men's shirts, and Maxipuke brand poker cards (the two Chinese characters, *pū kè*, mean 'poker', and they should have been translated as Maxi brand poker cards – but its package said 'Maxipuke').

Sources: (1) T. Dalgic & R. Heijblom, 1996, International marketing blunders revisited – some lessons for managers, *Journal of International Marketing*, 4 (1): 81–91; (2) D. Ricks, 2006, *Blunders in International Business*, 4th ed., Oxford: Blackwell; (3) *Handelsblatt*, 2014, Fehlgriff Markenname, April 11.

to consumers. For example, Japanese fashion chain *Uniqlo* was very aware that in German the name would be pronounced 'uni-klo' and be associated with university toilets. They delayed entry in Germany until after they established themselves in other large European markets, and then took the plunge – with their original brand name.[6] Only time will tell if they will succeed in challenging market leaders *H&M* and *Zara* (Opening Case).

Second, consumer research has evolved as a major area of applied research, analyzing very large datasets. Traditionally, the main source of data was surveys of (potential) consumers that have been analyzed and condensed in concise marketing reports by professional marketing consultants.[7] You have probably been asked many times to complete little questionnaires by companies. Such survey data allow, for example, for testing specific hypotheses about likely consumer responses to changes in prices or new product variations. However, indices developed from surveys are often difficult to compare across countries, because cultural differences also affect how respondents interpret the questions that market researchers ask them.[8] Recently, different types of data have become a rich source of information for consumer research, namely the user data that all of us leave behind each time we visit a website on the internet. Such 'big data' are a gold mine of marketing information![9]

Third, an innovative approach is to directly observe potential consumers and to study their behaviours from an anthropological and ethnographic perspective. Embedded market researchers participate in social groups to understand what people do with their products and how they talk about them. For example, embedded researchers at *Nestlé* saw housewives in India adding fresh vegetables and garnish to their instant noodles. *Nestlé* responded by supplementing its own instant noodles with vegetables. Also, after witnessing first-hand India's small kitchens and vulnerability to rodent infestations, they reduced pack sizes.[10] Going one step further, one British entrepreneur built her business by filming the life of ordinary people and arranging such visual insights for decision-makers in corporate boardrooms (In Focus 17.1).

IN FOCUS 17.1

Honest Films

Companies operating on the global stage often aim to sell to consumers in a wide variety of countries. Yet these consumers live under different circumstances, and thus use globally standardized products in different ways, and perceive different benefits from the same product. Such subtle differences of lifestyle and culture are therefore critical for the reception of marketing. However, local managers often experience challenges in communicating subtleties of local culture to senior managers and decision-makers in corporate headquarters, who often spend only a few days in places like Asia. The statistics and graphs generated in traditional marketing reports are insufficient; so marketing agencies turn to anthropology – a science traditionally used to study the cultures of remote tribes.

Have you ever been in a Chinese home? Imagine you are visiting a young middle-class couple in Shanghai, the primary target group for consumer goods marketers. You walk up a narrow staircase, you are welcomed at the door and offered slippers to wear in the home, you are invited to sit down on the couch, and your eyes wander around the small room . . . what do you notice? The furniture is space-saving and functional, combining traditional and modern designs, yet some decorative items are given special space – what is the significance of these objects? On the wall you see pictures from the couple's holidays in Tokyo and Venice – how do these experiences influence their reception of Western consumer goods?

Faced with the challenge of communicating such experiences to Westerners, British entrepreneur Sarah Thomas developed her business idea for Honest Films.

She joined forces with anthropologist film-makers, documentary film-makers and strategic planners to study life where it happens, as it happens. Their films about the lives of ordinary people uncover insights normally overlooked by traditional market research. They thus provide business decision-makers with a first-hand look at the issues, and engage and inspire them in a way no written report can. Such a real-life perspective on how products might be used provides an alternative to statistics-filled consumer research reports, and facilitates innovations from customized advertising messages to new product developments.

Sources: (1) Presentation by the entrepreneur at the University of Bath, February 2009; (2) www.honestfilms.net (accessed January 2015).

THE MARKETING MIX

LEARNING OBJECTIVE

2   Articulate the four Ps in international marketing (place, product, price and promotion)

marketing mix
The four underlying components of marketing: product, price, promotion and place.

product
The offerings that customers purchase.

Consumer research is one side of the coin of international marketing; the other side is the marketing mix deployed by companies to reach that consumer through: (1) product, (2) price, (3) promotion, and (4) place (Figure 17.1).[11] In this section, we explore how companies address these marketing challenges when operating across several national markets.

Product

Product refers to offerings that customers purchase. Although the word *product* originally referred to a physical product, its modern use includes services (such as delivery, maintenance and upgrades). Even for a single category (such as women's clothing or sports cars), product attributes vary tremendously. For firms interested in doing business around the world, a key concern is standardization versus localization.[12] Localization is natural. *McDonalds*, for example, supplements its core burger menu with wine in France, beer in Germany, mutton pot pies in Australia, and Maharaja Mac and McCurry Pan in India. What is interesting is the rise of standardization, which is often attributed to Theodore Levitt's 1983 article, 'The Globalization of Markets'.[13] This article advocated globally standardized products to exploit advantages of scale; a model followed by, for example, *Hollywood* movies and *Coke Classic*. However, numerous 'global products' failed outside their home market, for example, *Ford*'s world car and *MTV*'s global (essentially American) programming. Thus one size does

Figure 17.1   A simple model of consumer marketing

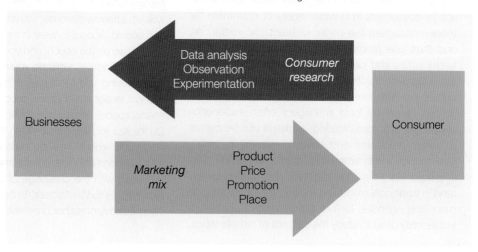

not fit all, but most firms cannot afford to create entirely new products and services for each group of customers. Thus how much to localize remains a challenge, especially when entering markets that are very different from the home market, or that are internally very diverse (such as large emerging economies).[14]

As noted in Chapter 15, localization is appealing (in the eyes of local consumers and governments) but expensive. A sensible solution is to share many product components to reduce the development cost and exploit scale advantages, but vary those aspects of most concern to customers. Consider the two global weekly business magazines, US-based *Bloomberg Businessweek* and UK-based *The Economist*.[15] In addition to its US edition, *Bloomberg Businessweek* publishes two English language editions for Asia and Europe and a Chinese edition for China. Although these four editions share certain content, there is a lot of local edition-only material that is expensive to support and produce. In comparison, each issue of *The Economist* has the following regional sections: (1) the Americas (excluding the USA), (2) Asia (excluding China), (3) Britain, (4) China, (5) Europe (excluding Britain), (6) Middle East and Africa and (7) USA. Although the content for each issue is identical, the order of appearance of the regional sections varies. For US subscribers, their *Economist* starts with the USA section; for Asian subscribers, their magazine starts with the Asia section, and so forth. By doing that, *The Economist* adapts to its customers – both advertisers and readers – with different regional interests without incurring the costs of running multiple editions for different regions, as *Bloomberg Businessweek* does. Therefore, how many editions does one issue of *The Economist* have? We can say one – or six if we count the six different ways of stapling regional sections together and six different sets of advertisements.

One of the major concerns for multinational enterprises (MNEs) is to decide whether to market global brands (such as *Nestlé*) or local brands in their portfolio.[16] The key is market segmentation – identifying segments of consumers who differ from others in purchasing behaviour.[17] There are limitless ways of segmenting the market (males versus females, university versus high school-educated, urban dwellers versus rural residents, French versus Italians). The million dollar question for marketers is: how does one generalize from such a wide variety of market segmentation in different countries to generate products that can cater to a few of these segments *around the world*?

market segmentation
A way to identify consumers who differ from others in purchasing behaviour.

Some brands, such as *Coca-Cola* or *Apple*, indeed appeal to customer groups around the world (Table 17.2). Yet for consumer goods, local brands often have the largest market share, with many consumers being unaware that many such brands are actually owned by a major MNE.[18] For example, in Poland, the leading brand of chocolate is *Wedel*, and the leading brands of beer are *Tyskie*, *Zywiec* and *Okocim*. Yet *Wedel* has been in foreign hands since 1991: it was acquired by *PepsiCo* who sold it to *Cadbury* UK in 1998. When *Cadbury* was acquired by *Kraft* USA in 2010, they sold *Wedel* to the Japanese-Korean *Lotte* group to comply with a requirement by the EU competition authority (see Chapter 14).[19] The three beer brands are owned respectively by MNEs *Heineken*, *SABMiller* and *Carlsberg*.[20] MNEs thus serve diverse consumer preferences with multi-tier branding, a portfolio of different brands targeted at different consumer segments: global brands for the premium segment, national brands for the mid-markets and/or for mass-markets, and further brands for specific niche markets.

multi-tier branding
A portfolio of different brands targeted at different consumer segments.

Overall, Ted Levitt may have been *both* right and wrong. A large percentage of consumers around the world indeed have converging interests and preferences centred on global brands. However, a substantial percentage of them also resist globally standardized brands, products and services. As a rule of thumb, products deeply embedded in culture, such as foods, tend to require more adaptation than, say, electronic gadgets like computers and televisions.

Table 17.2 Top 20 global brands, 2004 to 2014

Rank 2014	Rank 2009	Rank 2004	Brand	Rank 2014	Rank 2009	Rank 2004	Brand
1	20	43	Apple (USA)	11	15	17	**BMW (Germany)**
2	7	n.a.	Google (USA)	12	9	5	Intel (USA)
3	1	1	Coca-Cola (USA)	13	10	6	Disney (USA)
4	2	3	IBM (USA)	14	14	16	Cisco (USA)
5	3	2	Microsoft (USA)	15	43	66	Amazon (USA)
6	4	4	GE (USA)	16	24	28	Oracle (USA)
7	19	21	Samsung (Korea)	17	11	12	Hewlett-Packard (USA)
8	8	9	Toyota (Japan)	18	13	15	Gillette (USA)
9	6	7	McDonalds (USA)	19	16	44	**Louis Vuitton (France)**
10	12	11	**Mercedes-Benz (Germany)**	20	18	18	Honda (Japan)

Note: Nokia dropped from 5th in 2009 to 98th in 2014.

Source: www.interbrand.com (accessed December 2014).

PRICE

price
The expenditures that customers are willing to pay for a product.
price elasticity
How demand changes when prices change.

Price refers to the expenditures that customers are willing to pay for a product. Most consumers are 'price-sensitive'. The jargon is price elasticity – how demand changes when prices change. Basic economic theory of supply and demand suggests that when prices drop consumers will buy more and generate stronger demand, which in turn will motivate firms to expand production to meet this demand. This theory, of course, underpins numerous firms' relentless drive around the world to cut costs and then prices. The question is *how* price-sensitive consumers are. Holding the product (such as shampoo) constant, in general, the lower income of the consumers, the more price sensitive they are. In Europe, retail chains like *Aldi*, *Lidl* and *Asda* cater for these price-sensitive consumers.

This segment is even more important in emerging economies, where many people still live on low incomes. For example, in India, shampoo is often sold in single-use packets, each costing about one to ten (euro) cents, because many consumers there find the cost of a bottle of shampoo prohibitive. How to overcome such price elasticity is thus crucial as India develops its mass retailing.

However, not all consumers are highly price-sensitive. Luxury products that are status symbols of upwardly mobile middle classes attain their status exactly because not everyone can afford these products. Thus luxury goods usually compete on brand appeal and differentiation, not on price. In fact the prices – and the absence of discounts – are important indicators of the prestige of many luxury brands. For example, Danish start-up company *Pandora* is designing and marketing jewellery that has become highly fashionable among women across Europe. Their marketing combines fashion appeal with collector passion: a simple bracelet for €29 can be complemented with 'charms' that can be added and rearranged by the wearer – and they costs up to €399. *Pandora's* model is highly successful, with a profit margin of, reportedly,

How do you sell consumer goods to poor people?

45%. Yet it is a risky business model, as fashion trends are highly volatile; the share price of *Pandora* thus has been highly volatile since its IPO in 2010.[21]

In addition to the price at the point of purchase, another dimension of price is the total cost of ownership. An example is the *Nescafé* Espresso machine. Prices for the machine start at €78 (and even less if you find a special offer), while a box of 16 capsules of coffee costs €4.71. Hence if you drink two cups a day, this adds up to €212 for the coffee per year – much more than the machine.[22] The total costs of ownership for drinking two cups of coffee per day for one year thus adds up to €290, which is more than twice the price of good old-fashioned home-brewed coffee. Although many consumers may not pay explicit attention to the total cost of ownership, it is certainly important to business customers and is often explicitly evaluated prior to purchase decisions. Moreover, after-sales services and spare parts are less price-sensitive and thus have a higher margin.[23] In fact, the lowest price that successful companies charge is zero. For example, business networking sites *LinkedIn* and *Xing* allow you to sign up and use their services for free. Yet the companies are fairly profitable based on the sale of supplementary services, especially to corporate customers. More generally, many firms compete on winning the initial sale with a low price, with the aim of capturing more revenue through after-sales products and services.

total cost of ownership
Total cost needed to own a product, consisting of initial purchase cost and follow-up maintenance/service cost.

Promotion

Promotion refers to all the communications that marketers insert into the marketplace. Promotion includes TV, radio, advertising, social network campaigns, as well as coupons, direct mail, billboards, direct marketing (personal selling) and public relations. Marketers face a strategic choice of whether to standardize or localize promotional efforts. Standardized promotion can not only save a lot of money on advertising agencies, but project a globally consistent message, which may be critical for global luxury brands targeting frequent travellers, such as *Gucci, Hermès* or *YSL*.

However, there is a limit to the effectiveness of standardized promotion. The messages communicated in advertising are often culturally embedded, which implies that they would be received differently in different countries.[24] In the 1990s, *Coca-Cola* ran a worldwide campaign featuring a cute polar bear cartoon character. Research later

promotion
Communications that marketers insert into the marketplace.

showed that viewers in warmer weather countries had a hard time relating to this ice-bound animal with which they had no direct experience. In response, *Coca-Cola* switched to more costly but more effective country-specific advertisements. For instance, the Indian subsidiary launched a campaign that equated *Coke* with *thanda*, the Hindi word for 'cold'. The German subsidiary developed commercials that showed a 'hidden' kind of eroticism that would upset conservative consumers back in the USA.[25] As another example, consider fashion retailer *C&A*'s ill-conceived attempts to save costs through a Europe-wide standardization strategy (In Focus 17.2). These examples suggest that even highly global brands can benefit from localized promotion.

IN FOCUS 17.2

C&A: *failed European standardization*

C&A is a fashion retailer with German and Dutch roots, operating across Europe. After more than a hundred years of profitable growth, *C&A* fell on hard times in the late 1990s. It had failed to move with changing trends of fashion and shopping habits. Traditionally, *C&A* was positioned as affordable fashion for working-class people, yet even these customers were no longer satisfied with *C&A*'s sturdy but old-fashioned image. *C&A* offered low prices, but consumer surveys showed its image to be lagging behind competitors such as *Marks & Spencer* in the UK. Sales dropped to levels last seen in the early 1980s, and in 1998 *C&A* recorded a loss of about €130 million.

The management reacted by focusing on cost savings and synergies. Like in many European businesses, national subsidiaries were traditionally operating quite independently. Thus there should be efficiency gains somewhere, shouldn't there? Centralization to headquarters in Amsterdam and Düsseldorf was seen as the answer: a Europe-wide fashion line communicated with a uniform marketing campaign featuring the same clothes and the same models, designed with the help of external designers. However, the strategy went spectacularly wrong. National differences were overlooked by designers and marketers in Düsseldorf. For example, Italian designers changed the suits to look great on the slim and sporty models featured in the ads. Yet they failed to recognize that the typical male customer of *C&A* in Germany was middle-aged with a tendency to be overweight. After a number of faux pas like this, subsidiary managers revolted against the new centralization.

The Spanish subsidiary was especially aggrieved. Children's clothes in violet colours wouldn't sell in Spain, where that colour is associated with mourning.

Ads showing children as clowns didn't fit with how Spaniards like to see their children. Women's evening dresses designed in Germany were too short for Spanish culture. Men in swimsuits had body hair, another no-go in Spain. Many of these miscommunications might easily have been rectified through effective internal communication, but feeling overruled from above, local staff aggravated small conflicts, and undermined the strategy. In 2000, *C&A* pulled back, returned more autonomy to the national subsidiaries, and focused on its traditional cheap but fashionable market appeal. The return to basic values turned *C&A* back to profitability, though it was too late for some – the UK operation was closed down.

Over the next decade, *C&A* adapted a more measured adaptation strategy for its 18 countries. This balanced localization is illustrated by *C&A*'s internet presence: the front pages of national websites show a common layout, featuring the same fashion model. Yet beyond the front door, variations abound. The German site features online shopping services not available in other countries, while the Dutch site emphasizes the latest lines of fashion by two Dutch fashion designers. The same images are used in many national websites, reflecting extensive standardization of designs. Yet the Russian site features more low-cost sturdy clothing, similar to the traditional ware offered in Western Europe before the 1990s. Meanwhile, in China, *C&A* entered the market with a more upmarket positioning.

Sources: (1) B. Weiguny, 2005, *Die geheimnisvollen Herren von C&A*, Munich: Piper; (2) *Handelsblatt*, 2007, Billigheimer C&A gründet Tiefstpreiskette, November 11; (3) *Handelsblatt*, 2009, C&A widersetzt sich Kaufhaus-Krise, April 22; (4) *Die Welt*, 2011, Ein Streifzug durch 100 Jahre C&A, June 5; (5) websites of C&A in multiple countries.

In addition to the traditional domestic versus international challenge, a new challenge lies in the pursuit of marketing via the internet.[26] Online ads are a feature of a wide range of websites, such as search engines, news sites, blogs and social network platforms, and can be focused at very specific target groups. In the 2010s, teens and twenty-somethings spend a lot of time on *Facebook*, *Instagram* or *Twitter*. They 'do not buy stuff because they see a magazine ad,' according to one expert, 'they buy stuff because other kids tell them to online.'[27] How can marketers reach 'generation Y' and 'generation Z' that have developed substantially different ways of social interaction and of accessing and processing information?[28] Firms such as *Apple* and *Procter & Gamble* (*P&G*) experiment with a variety of formats, including sponsorships and online forums, with some hits, some misses, and lots of uncertainty. A key challenge of using such interactive media is that advertisers lose some control over their brands: this brand image evolves with the contributions of participants in online forums.[29] However, this also entails a risk of unwanted images or stories spreading quickly and widely.

Place

The 'place' in marketing place refers to the location where a product is sold, which can be a physical location or a virtual location on the internet. In international business, a key decision is often when to enter which market – and in what sequence. Four sets of considerations come into play: (1) market potential, (2) costs, (3) strategic motives and (4) distribution channels. First, the potential of a market is usually estimated based on the size and growth of the market for the specific products, taking into consideration trends that may affect potential customers' buying behaviour. This initial analysis makes use of industry-level market statistics, but usually entrants employ additional customer surveys to assess the likely consumer behaviour. Second, expected revenues need to be converted to estimates of *net* revenues, taking into account both cost of the initial entry, and the unit costs that may be higher due to the adaptation of products and marketing programmes.

Third, strategic motives for the choice of market include test markets, which are markets where trials are rolled out before a worldwide (or Europe-wide) introduction of new products. For example, Nordic countries are a popular test market because they resemble other European markets, but product introduction is much less expensive and errors can be rectified much more easily. Moreover, bridge markets may offer avenues to enter broader markets, such as Latin American firms entering the Spanish market in view of eventually conquering Europe-wide markets. Fourth, the question of place is closely related to the question of distribution channel, how to bring the products to the customer. This is nowadays primarily related to the question of how best to use online channels, without undermining traditional distribution partners in the 'bricks and mortar' channels – which brings us to the topic of supply chain management.

place
The location where products and services are provided.

SUPPLY CHAIN MANAGEMENT

To be able to market their product, firms need a distribution channel – the set of business units and intermediaries that facilitate the movement of goods to consumers. Traditionally, firms used to have separate 'purchasing' and 'sales' units that would interact with suppliers and customers respectively, and intermediaries on either side. With changes in transportation, data processing and communication technologies, these two aspects of business operations have converged. The new challenge is thus how to manage the longer channel from suppliers (and contract manufacturers) all the way to consumers (see Figure 17.2). Consequently, a new term, supply chain, has been coined, and now almost replaces the old-fashioned 'distribution channel'. The

LEARNING OBJECTIVE

Articulate the three As in supply chain management (agility, adaptability and alignment)

distribution channel
The set of business units and intermediaries that facilitates the movement of goods to consumers.

Figure 17.2   Supply chain management

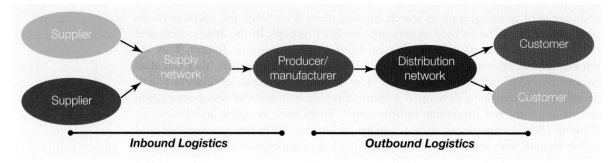

sales and purchasing functions are increasingly interdependent as the entire process is managed 'on time', and the purchase of a component may be triggered by a customer ordering a final product, as in the case of Dell computers. Strategy guru Michael Porter thus distinguishes 'inbound logistics' (purchase) and 'outbound logistics' (sales) to indicate that the two functions complement each other like opposite sides of the same coin.[30] A supply chain thus covers all movements of goods at any stage of the value chain, encompassing both inbound and outbound logistics (see Chapter 4).

Traditionally, business logistics was a low-prestige support function. However, if the supply chain covers the entire value chain, then supply chain management essentially handles the entire process of value creation. Consequently, supply chain management has now taken on new strategic importance and gained tremendous prestige. One indication of the more central role of supply chain management is the rapid growth of support companies, such as transportation service providers *UPS* and *DHL*. On any given day, 2% of the world's GDP can be found in *UPS* trucks and planes. These companies not only transport packages from A to B, but help businesses optimize their entire supply chain.[31] Similarly, the rise of e-commerce giants like *Amazon* in the USA, and *JD.com* and *Yihaodian* in China is closely associated with their ability to manage the logistics from the producers of a product to the doorstep of the consumer (In Focus 17.3). Next, we discuss three ways to strengthen supply chains: (1) agility, (2) adaptability and (3) alignment.

inbound logistics
Purchasing and the coordination of intermediaries on the supply side.
outbound logistics
Sales and the coordination of intermediaries on the customer side.

IN FOCUS 17.3

Online shop #1

Internet shopping has become the new normal in urban China. Rather than heading for a local supermarket, many consumers in Shanghai turn to the web; click and pay – and a few hours later a motorcycle deliveryman drops a box of food, household goods or the latest fashion at the doorstep. Why carry a crate of beer from the supermarket home, and then up to the 23rd floor? Let the deliveryman do it for you! A revolution of retailing is under way!

The latest entry into this market is *Yihaodian* – literally translated '#1 Shop'. Founded in 2008, it has in only five years become the third-largest internet retailer in China – after *Alibaba* and *JD.com*. It was founded by Gang Yu, a Chinese-American returnee who was a professor of logistics and worked for a while with Dell and Accenture. His strategy focused on speed, and creating an entirely new supply practice based on the latest scholarly research.

Yihaodian started with food, beverages and household goods, and already by 2009 had expanded into cosmetics and consumer electronics. Clothing is

Why is the 'last mile' cheaper to manage in China than in Europe?

Yihaodian's latest offering. The growth has been spectacular. In 2009, Yihaodian celebrated receiving 1000 orders an hour – by 2014 that number had increased to 300 000 to 400 000. *Yihaodian* is counting its customer base in tens of millions and employs 10 000 people, mainly in the 'last mile' delivery.

The strategy is supported by the latest technology and supply chain management practices. The company does all its technological development in-house, and controls its information systems, including supplier relationships, warehouse management and delivery stations. Thus 10% of employees are IT engineers. In the central control room, 16 screens allow the management to track online traffic in real time, including by region, by categories of products, etc. For example, one screen displays a word cloud with the keywords most frequently entered in the search engine on *Yihaodian*'s website in the last minute. Such tools enable 'instant' capturing of new consumer trends, and targeting of consumers far more precisely than in traditional retail outlets. This includes customers on the move: with the spread of smartphones and tablets in China, the mobile sector has become an important part of e-commerce in China, accounting for 10% of e-commerce in 2013 and predicted to reach 20% in 2016.

In 2011, *Wal-Mart* acquired 51% of the capital of *Yihaodian*, but the companies operate largely independently, apart from some cooperation in sourcing and supplier management. Both companies believe that they can learn a lot from each other. *Wal-Mart* has long been famous for its capabilities in supply chain management, yet it has been less successful in translating that expertise to e-commerce. *Yihaodian* thus becomes a source of new ideas – and inspiration. At one meeting, *Wal-Mart* shared their ambition to develop in the next two years a system that allows fulfilling every order within two days. *Yihaodian* executives laughed. Their ambition is to fulfil every order in Shanghai in three hours. They are not quite at that target yet, but close. In part, this capability is based on high urban concentration and relatively cheap 'last mile delivery' using deliverymen on electric motorcycles. Yet it is enabled by groundbreaking new technologies that analyze huge amounts of data and coordinate many different players in a supply chain.

Sources: (1) Interviews and participant observation; (2) D. Jolly, 2013, Comment Yihaodian est devenu en cinq ans le troisième supermarché virtuel chinois; blog, *Les Echos*, March 3.

Agility

Agility refers to the ability to quickly react to unexpected shifts in supply and demand. Firms such as *Zara* thrive in large part because of the agility of their supply chain (see Opening Case). *Zara*'s agility permeates throughout its entire operations,

agility
The ability to quickly react to unexpected shifts in supply and demand.

starting with design processes. As soon as designers spot certain trends, they create sketches and go ahead with ordering fabrics without finalizing designs. This speeds things up, because fabric suppliers require a long lead time. Designs are finalized when reliable data from stores come. Production commences as soon as designs are complete. In addition, *Zara*'s factories normally only run one shift, easily allowing for overtime production if demand calls for it. Its distribution centres are also highly efficient, allowing it to handle demand fluctuation without creating bottlenecks.[32]

Agility may become more important in the 21st century because supply chains are more complex and therefore more sensitive to disruptions triggered by a wide range of different causes, including man-made disasters such terrorist attacks, political unrests or strikes, and natural disasters such as flu epidemics, earthquakes, typhoons or volcanic eruptions. Under external shocks, an agile supply chain can rise to the challenge while a static one can pull a firm down.[33] Firms that have (or can quickly find) alternative intermediaries or suppliers can continue to supply their customers, as well as new ones. Consider how mobile phone makers *Nokia* and *Ericsson* reacted differently to a fire induced by a thunderstorm in 2000 at a New Mexico factory of their handset chip supplier, *Philips*. The damage was minor, and *Philips* expected to resume production within a week. However, *Nokia* took no chances, and it quickly carried out design changes so that two other suppliers, one in Japan and another in the USA, could manufacture similar chips for *Nokia*. *Nokia* then quickly placed orders with these two suppliers. In contrast, *Ericsson*'s supply chain had no such agility: it was set up to function exclusively with chips from the damaged *Philips* plant – in other words, *Ericsson* had no plan B. Unfortunately, *Philips* later found out that the damage was greater than first reported, and production would be delayed for months. By that time, *Ericsson* scrambled to contact the other two suppliers, only to find out that *Nokia* had locked up all of their output for the next few months. The upshot? *Ericsson* was driven out of the handset market as an independent player (it remained in the market with a joint venture with *Sony* called *Sony Ericsson*).[34] Similarly, many firms' supply chain agility was tested buy the Icelandic volcano eruption in 2010 (In Focus 17.4).

IN FOCUS 17.4

A volcano focuses minds on supply chain agility

The eruption of the Icelandic volcano Eyjafjallajökull made Europeans aware how dependent they have become on air travel, and highlighted to businesses the value of supply chain agility. Businesses could respond in two ways, either tell customers that it was a *force majeure* (an unpredictable event) for which they have no legal obligations, or they can go beyond their call of duty and help the customer. Airline customers in particular experienced both sorts of reactions: some travellers were left stranded at stopovers with nowhere to go, and airlines providing little information and support. Other airlines couldn't get customers to their destination either, but showed respect and offered at least moral support, accommodation and food for their customers. Guess whose customers came back after the crisis, and who binned their frequent flyer cards? Crises are great opportunities for a company to show that care for customers is not just an advertising slogan.

Budget airlines work with minimum service, and offer nothing more than exactly what was contracted – with no intention of helping in case of minor disruptions. The trick of two single tickets instead of a return reduces their legal obligation to help stranded customers. Those flying frequently find that the real

How can a company handle major supply chain disruptions caused by natural disasters such as a volcano eruption?

costs of budget airlines are just not worth the hassle. But mainstream airlines have also in recent years been 'cutting slack' to save costs. This may not have had direct effects on services, but it reduces their flexibility. Companies that have a bit of slack – and a motivated workforce – are much more able to react to crisis, and 'go the extra mile' to keep customers satisfied. Others, like *British Airways*, have for years told their shareholders how much they care for them, and focused on efficiency (read 'cut costs'). Consequently, their workforce was quite demotivated and even went on strike during those difficult weeks. Disgruntled customers were looking for alternatives. More generally, a highly motivated workforce together with a moderate amount of slack helps companies handling unexpected disruptions.

The volcano crisis suggests that the transport industry has become too dependent on the jet engine. Finding alternative modes of transport should be a major challenge for engineers around the world. The UK has been leading in Europe in the development of budget air travel; many believe this is due to early deregulation and hence greater competition in the airline industry. However, there is another reason: the infrastructure for surface transportation – rail and motorways – is weaker than in continental Europe. Without fast, affordable and reliable railways, the option to travel out of town to the airport, and then to fly, is much less attractive. From a risk management perspective, it helps to have alternatives in case one mode of travel/transport is disrupted – whether you plan a holiday or want to ship products to a customer!

Adaptability

While agility focuses on flexibility that can overcome short-term fluctuation in the supply chain, adaptability refers to the ability to change supply chain configurations in response to long-term changes in the environment and technology. Enhancing adaptability often entails making a series of make-or-buy decisions. This requires firms to continuously monitor major geopolitical, social and technological trends, make sense of them, and reconfigure the supply chain accordingly.[35] The damage for failing to do so may not be visible immediately, but across a number of years, firms failing to do so may be selected out of market.

Consider American telecommunications equipment giant *Lucent*. In the mid-1990s, *Lucent* faced competitive pressures from rivals *Siemens* and *Alcatel* that benefited from low-cost, Asia-based production. *Lucent* responded by adapting its

adaptability
The ability to change supply chain configurations in response to long-term changes in the environment and technology.

supply chain through phasing out production in high-cost developed economies, and setting up plants in China and Taiwan. However, *Lucent* then failed to adapt continuously. It owned its production in Asia, whereas rivals outsourced manufacturing to Asian suppliers that became more capable of taking on more complex work. In other words, *Lucent* used foreign direct investment (FDI) to 'make', whereas rivals adopted outsourcing to 'buy.' Ultimately, *Lucent* was stuck with its own relatively higher cost (although Asia-based) plants and was overwhelmed by rivals. By 2006, *Lucent* lost its independence and was acquired by its arch-rival *Alcatel*.

Alignment

alignment
The alignment of interest of various players.

Alignment refers to the alignment of interests of various players in the supply chain. In a broad sense, each supply chain is a strategic alliance involving a variety of players, each of which is a separate profit-maximizing firm.[36] As a result, conflicts are natural. However, players associated with one supply chain must effectively coordinate to achieve mutually desirable outcomes.[37] Thus supply chains are better at resolving conflicts of interest may be able to outperform other supply chains. For example, for *Boeing*'s 787 Dreamliner, some 40% of the $8 billion development cost is outsourced to suppliers: *Mitsubishi* makes the wings, *Messier-Dowty* provides the landing gear, and so forth.[38] Many suppliers are responsible for end-to-end design of whole subsections. Headed by a vice president for global partnerships, *Boeing* treats its suppliers as partners, has 'partner councils' with regular meetings, and fosters long-term collaboration. Even so, the alignment did not meet expectations. Disruptions in the supply chain were chief reasons for the repeated delay of the launch of the Dreamliner.

Conceptually, there are two key elements to achieve alignment: power and trust.[39] Not all players in a supply chain are equal, and more powerful players such as *Boeing* naturally exercise greater bargaining power.[40] Having a recognized leader exercising power facilitates the legitimacy and efficiency of the whole supply chain. Otherwise, time-consuming negotiation and bargaining between supply chain members of more or less equal standing may reduce the effectiveness of the entire chain.

Trust stems from perceived fairness and justice from all supply chain members.[41] Although supply chains have become ever more complex and extended, modern practices, such as low (or zero) inventory, frequent just-in-time (JIT) deliveries, and more geographic dispersion of production, have made all parties more vulnerable if the *weakest* link breaks down. Therefore, it is in the best interest of all parties to invest in trust-building mechanisms to foster more collaboration.

For instance, *7-Eleven* Japan exercises a great deal of power by dictating that vendors resupply its 9000 stores at three specific times of the day. If a truck is late by more than 30 minutes, the vendor has to pay a penalty equal to the gross margin of the products carried to the store. This may seem harsh, but it is necessary. This is because *7-Eleven* Japan staff reconfigures store shelves three times a day to cater to different consumers at different hours, such as commuters in the morning and schoolchildren in the afternoon. Time literally means money. However, *7-Eleven* Japan softens the blow by trusting its vendors. It does not verify the contents of deliveries. This allows vendors to save time and money, because after delivery, truck drivers do not have to wait for verification and can immediately move on to their next stop. The alignment of interest of such a supply chain is legendary. Hours after the Kobe earthquake in January 1995, when relief trucks moved at two miles an hour (if they moved at all) on the damaged roads, *7-Eleven* Japan's vendors went the extra mile by deploying seven helicopters and 125 motorcycles to deliver 64 000 rice balls to the starving city.

third-party logistics (3PL)
A neutral intermediary in the supply chain that provides logistics and other support services.

Sometimes, introducing a neutral intermediary (middleman) – more specifically, third-party logistics (3PL) providers – may more effectively align the interests in the supply chain. In the case of outsourcing in Asia, buyers (importers) include large

Western retail businesses such as *Gap*, *H&M* and *Toys "R" Us*, while suppliers (exporters) are often smaller Asian manufacturers. Despite best intentions, both sides may still distrust each other. MNE buyers are not sure of the quality and timeliness of delivery. Further, MNE buyers are unable to control labour practices in supplier factories, some of which may be dubious (see Chapter 10). For example, *Apple*'s reputation took a severe hit due to alleged questionable labour practices at its supplier factories. However, suppliers may also be suspicious. Since most contracts for shoes, clothing, toys and electronics are written several months ahead, suppliers are not confident about MNE buyers' ability to correctly forecast demand. Suppliers thus worry that in case of lower than anticipated demand, buyers may reject shipments to reduce excess inventory by citing excuses such as labour practices or quality issues.[42] One solution lies in the involvement of 3PL intermediaries, such as the Hong Kong–based *Li & Fung* (Closing Case) that may add value by aligning the interests of all parties, and by providing related services such as quality control and trade financing.[43]

INSTITUTIONS, MARKETING AND SUPPLY CHAIN MANAGEMENT

Formal and informal institutions in both target and home countries constrain the options for marketing and supply chain management. For example, standards in advertising – formal rules designed by governments to protect consumers – vary considerably across countries. Companies marketing controversial products, such as tobacco or alcoholic beverages, must be particularly adept at interpreting local rules and customs.[44] Other companies also occasionally fall foul of advertising standards. The British Advertising Standards Authority (ASA) issues about a dozen rulings every week, and frequently bans ads – including online ads and statements on companies' own websites. Recent cases include misleading statements on the extent of free services included in a package, the nature of 'unlimited' data access, or the placement of violent ads where children may encounter them.[45] The challenge in international advertising is often to know what sort of proof may have to be provided when making claims about a product, as this varies considerably across country. Moreover, some countries such as Germany do not permit direct performance comparisons with competing products.

LEARNING OBJECTIVE

4 Discuss how institutions affect marketing and supply chain management

standards in advertising
Formal rules designed by governments to protect consumers.

Other constraints on marketing strategies arise from ownership restrictions. For example, until 2003, India did not allow FDI in the retail sector at all, while in China foreign retailers still are only allowed to operate through joint venture stores. Even so, leading foreign retailers like *Carrefour* (from France), *Tesco* (from the UK), and *Wal-Mart* (from the USA) find it hard to turn their retail operations in China profitable. *Tesco* eventually sold the majority stake in its China business to its local partner. *Wal-Mart* struggled with its 'bricks and mortar' operation, as employees used accounting tricks to mislead their US bosses by inflating sales.[46] However, *Wal-Mart* smartly invested in online retail start-up *Yihaodian* (see In Focus 17.3), which is where people in Shanghai do their weekly shopping. This minority stake provides *Wal-Mart* with opportunities to learn how to run the logistics for online marketplaces more efficiently.

Informal rules do not lead to official sanctions, but they can undermine the effectiveness of market strategies. In marketing, most of the blunders happen due to firms' failure to appreciate the deep underlying differences in cultures, religions and norms – all part of the informal institutions.[47] Marketing managers thus need to be particularly sensitive to how informal norms affect consumers' perceptions of their products and promotions, as exemplified in In Focus 17.2 on *C&A*.

Supply chains not only create interdependencies between firms, they themselves can become a channel for the diffusion of practices and norms. If consumers expect their T-shirts to be produced by certain minimum labour standards, then retailers use codes of conduct to translate these standards (along with documentation) on all manufacturers in a supply chain (Chapter 10). Similarly, many European firms adopted the ISO 9000 series of quality management systems. They then imposed the standard on their suppliers and partners throughout the world because every product is only as reliable as any of its components. Over time, these suppliers and partners spread ISO 9000 to other domestic firms. By 2010, more than one million sites around the world had been ISO 9001 certified. Similarly, the environmental standards of ISO 14000 quickly spread through supply chains across the world.[48] In other words, suppliers and partners that export goods and services in a supply chain may be simultaneously *importing* their customers' norms and practices.[49] Thus ISO 9000 and ISO 14000 informally became rules worldwide.

RESOURCES, MARKETING AND SUPPLY CHAIN MANAGEMENT

LEARNING OBJECTIVE

5   Discuss how resources affect marketing and supply chain management

We can evaluate marketing and supply chain management activities based on the VRIO criteria. First, do these activities add *value*?[50] Marketing creates value for a firm if it helps to increase revenues by either increasing sales volumes or raising prices that can be charged to customers. It may also create value for consumers if it helps them to identify products that best suit them. Supply chain management creates value for customers by providing products in a more timely manner, which increases value for customers, for instance, by lowering inventory costs. However, marketers need to constantly reassess which techniques actually add value. While online media are popular, managers often lack tools to quantify the benefit of advertising on websites and in social media. This is especially unsettling in a cross-cultural context. How consumers react to the messages of online advertising depends not only on how they engage with the internet, but also on the correspondence of the message with their own values. Likewise, new practices in supply chain management may add value when transportation linkages run smoothly. Yet dependence on certain suppliers and channels may destroy value at times of disruption, such as earthquakes, volcanic eruptions or political upheavals.

Second, managers need to assess the *rarity* of marketing and supply chain activities. If all rival firms advertise on *Google* and use *DHL* to manage logistics (all of which do add value), these activities, in themselves, are not rare. First movers into new techniques may attain rare advantages. For example, when radio frequency identification (RFID) tags were first introduced, they created extra benefits because they were rare.[51] However, as RFID has become more available, its rarity has diminished.

Third, having identified valuable and rare capabilities, managers need to assess how likely it is for rivals and partners to *imitate*.[52] Potential imitators are not just distant copycat producers, but also partners in a firm's own supply chain. As more Western MNEs outsource production to suppliers, it is always possible that some of the aggressive contract manufacturers may bite the hand that feeds them by imitating and eventually competing with Western MNEs. It is natural for ambitious contract manufacturers to flex their muscle. Such muscle is often directly strengthened by the Western MNEs themselves, which willingly transfer technology and share know-how, which is often known as supplier (or vendor) development.[53] China's *Haier* (household appliances) and *Xiaomi* (mobile phones) have become global leaders in just that way. While it is possible to imitate and acquire world-class manufacturing capabilities, marketing prowess and brand power are more intangible and thus harder to imitate. Hence Western MNEs often protect themselves by (1) being careful about what they outsource, and (2) strengthening customer loyalty to their brands to fend off contract manufacturers.[54]

Finally, managers need to ask: is our firm *organizationally* ready to accrue the benefits of improved marketing and supply chain management? Oddly, in many firms, Marketing and Sales units do not get along well – to avoid confusion, here we write the two terms with a capital letter to refer to these functional units. When revenues are disappointing, the blame game begins: Marketing blames Sales for failing to execute a brilliant plan, and Sales blame Marketing for setting the price too high and burning too much of the budget in high-flying but useless promotion. Marketing staff tend to be better educated, more analytical, and disappointed when certain initiatives fail. In contrast, Sales people are often 'street smart', persuasive, and used to regular rejection. It is not surprising that Marketing and Sales have a hard time working together.[55] Yet work together they must. Some leading firms have disbanded Marketing and Sales as separate functions, and have created an integrated function.

DEBATES AND EXTENSIONS

There are some long-standing debates in this field, such as the standardization versus localization debate discussed earlier. Here we focus on two important debates not previously discussed: (1) business-to-business marketing and (2) country of origin, a liability or an asset?

LEARNING OBJECTIVE

6   Participate in two leading debates concerning marketing and supply chain management

Business-to-business marketing

So far we have assumed that the customer is also the one who makes the decision to purchase a product. This is usually the case in business-to-consumer (B2C) industries, where products are eventually consumed by ordinary people – perhaps after having gone through one or two trade intermediaries, such as your local supermarket. However, this is not the case for firms operating in business-to-business (B2B) industries. In B2B markets, the customer uses the product for goods that may go through several transformations before they reach a consumer. Imagine you are manufacturing natural food ingredients like *Danisco* (Chapter 14), fine chemicals like *Dow Chemical* or *Lanxess*, or plastics like *Evonik* or *Bayer MaterialScience* (In Focus 17.5). How do you market such products?

The first challenge is to understand the value chain that your product feeds into. Figure 17.3 shows a very simplified image of a value chain. The brand manufacturer and the tier 1 supplier are often the ones who decide exactly what materials should be used, down to a list of two or three approved suppliers. Technically, the tier 2 supplier may be the customer who buys (and pays) for the materials. Yet the purchasing decision critically depends on other players. Thus the challenge for a materials provider is how to influence the key decision-makers in the value chain, without being their direct supplier.

Figure 17.3 illustrates three ideas that can influence decision-makers. First, the supplier can get involved with the innovation teams of the brand manufacturer, or with design companies like *frog* or *ideo* that develop new products for many brands of, for example, mobile phones. Such relationship marketing, defined as a focus to establish, maintain and enhance relationships, helps to lock in customers.[56] If a new design is based on a supplier's specification of, say, plastics, then this supplier is likely to earn long-term supply contracts in the future.

business-to-consumer (B2C) marketing
Marketing to final consumers of a product.
business-to-business (B2B) marketing
Marketing to other businesses that will further process the product.

relationship marketing
A focus to establish, maintain and enhance relationships with customers.

IN FOCUS 17.5

B2B marketing: BMS plastics for laptops

Laptops are marketed by companies like *Hewlett-Packard, Dell, Lenovo, Acer* or *Toshiba,* known as OEMs. Consumers associate them with the development and production of the laptop. Yet in fact OEMs are sitting at the top of complex value chains. Like an iceberg, only the tip is visible to the untrained eye, and what is below the surface is much bigger than what is visible.

Somewhere in that iceberg, *Bayer MaterialScience* (*BMS*) is developing and selling polycarbonate, a material used to make the plastic parts of laptops and many other products. They sell polycarbonate resin to moulders of plastic parts, which are then sold to the manufacturer of the computer. Often it is not the OEM that puts its brand name on it, but a contract manufacturer like *Pegatron, Inventec,* or *Foxconn,* known as ODM, specializing in large-volume assembly work. Most of these ODMs are based in Asia, with Taiwan serving as hub for design and coordination, while the actual manufacturing takes place in mainland China.

Most OEMs source from multiple ODMs to diversify their risks and to enhance the flexibility of their global supply chain. ODMs in turn work with multiple suppliers and sub-suppliers for components and materials, such as polycarbonate. They too normally designate lead suppliers – often firms involved in product development processes. Lead suppliers are expected to provide more technical support and supply several manufacturing sites around the world; services for which *BMS* has a competitive advantage due to its global presence. In return, lead suppliers are paid a small price premium, and enjoy a long-term supply relationship.

The direct customers of *BMS* are moulders, to whom they deliver the material. Moulders tend to be very price conscious and pay close attention to product properties such as the flow of the material within moulds, as even tiny irregularities would increase the number of product faults, and hence their costs. However, they operate to very specific instructions of OEMs and ODMs when selecting materials. Hence working with OEMs and ODMs is essential to secure orders from moulders for *BMS*.

In 'open innovation' collaborations, OEMs, ODMs and other suppliers collaborate to jointly develop the next generation devices. Traditionally, OEMs would take the lead, but some design initiatives originate from ODMs or independent design firms. The division of responsibilities between these companies is evolving over time. Many ODMs have developed competences not only in managing manufacturing processes, but in designing components (hence the term 'ODM'). Other OEMs keep the design process in-house, and then specify a product characteristic, say a particular colour scheme, and let the ODM work out how to implement the idea.

The complexity and fast pace of change of the industry value chain makes industrial marketing very challenging for *BMS*. Every client has a different way of operating, and different demands on services. *BMS's* industrial marketing unit thus not only gathers information on the constantly evolving industry structure and on new product ideas, but develops relationships with key designers and decision-makers to participate in their open innovation processes.

Source: Interviews by Klaus Meyer with company and industry experts.

---

ingredient branding
Creating a brand identity for a component of a product.

Second, suppliers can try to build an ingredients brand for their component. The most famous example for this is *Intel*, whose slogan '*Intel* inside' stares at many computer users. Similarly, *DuPont* successfully developed the 'Teflon' brand for its material uses in 'non-stick' cooking utensils. This strategy has been imitated many times. For example, *GE* brands its medical devices as '*GE* Caring First', hoping customers would select hospitals using *GE* equipment. Yet evidence of such strategies actually returning profits is thin, because of the very indirect benefits of such a brand – even if you are a Borussia Dortmund fan (the club sponsored by *Evonik*), do you care what plastics are used in your computer or your car?

The third idea is lobbying of regulatory authorities with the aim of influencing regulatory standards (also see Chapter 8). Such standards may concern the safety of

Figure 17.3 Indirect marketing in B2B markets

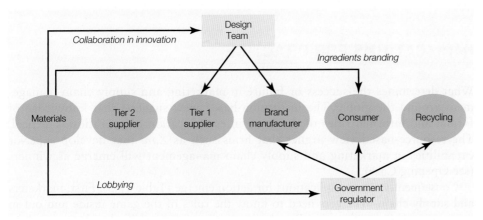

manufacturing plants, the safety of consumers using a device, or the emissions created when a device is disposed of or recycled. Companies that are able to deliver fine chemicals that meet higher standards may benefit from regulation that pushes low price-low quality competitors out of the market.

Country of origin as liability or asset

Being an outsider, especially a foreigner, is often seen as a disadvantage. However, under certain circumstances, being foreign can be a competitive advantage. For example, in the 1880s, British industry lobbied their government to protect them, by requiring importers to attach a 'Made in . . .' label to their products. To their great disappointment, 'Made in Germany' quickly became a mark of quality and reliability, and ensured German manufacturing enduring success in the UK, interrupted by two world wars. Similar positive country-of-origin effects emerged elsewhere in the world. American cigarettes are 'cool' among smokers in Central and Eastern Europe. Anything Korean – ranging from handsets and TV shows to *kimchi* (pickled cabbage) flavoured instant noodles – is considered hip in Southeast Asia. Conceptually, the country-of-origin effect refers to the positive or negative perception of firms and products from a certain country.[57]

Marketers have to decide whether to enhance or downplay such a country-of-origin effect.[58] This can be very tricky. *Disneyland Tokyo* became popular in Japan because it played up its American image. But *Disneyland Paris* received relentless negative press coverage in France because it insisted on its 'wholesome American look'.[59] Thus some consumers may be attracted by the 'Americanness' of *Disney* entertainment, *McDonalds* hamburgers or *KFC* chickens, while others are appalled by it. Since businesses only care about their (potential) consumers, this may not be a major concern to them. Yet broad social resentment against a brand can be harmful to both the brand, and the country of origin.[60]

Others deliberately associate with a different country. *Giordano* downplays its Asian origin by adopting an Italian-sounding brand of clothing line, made by a Hong Kong company that has no connection with Italy. Yet *Giordano* believed that Italy has a positive country-of-origin image from which it can benefit. Likewise, *Häagen-Dazs* managed to make its customers believe that it is Scandinavian, when in fact it hails from the USA, while *New Yorker* hails from Germany, and *Costa Coffee* from the UK. German- and Italian-sounding names are popular in China, even with minimal actual association with Europe. For example, the kitchen knife brand

country-of-origin effect
The positive or negative perception of firms and products from a certain country.

Klaus Meyer claims a historical link to Solingen, Germany,[61] but the brand is not known in Germany (and has absolutely no association with your author!)

IMPLICATIONS FOR PRACTICE

LEARNING OBJECTIVE

7   Draw implications for action

What determines the success or failure in marketing and supply chain management around the globe? The institution-based view suggests that knowledge of formal and informal rules of the game in each location of operation is critical. The resource-based view argues that firms such as *Zara* that develop superior capabilities in marketing and supply chain management will emerge as winners (see Opening Case).

Consequently, three implications for action emerge (Table 17.3). First, marketers and supply chain managers need to know the rules of the game inside and out in order to craft their strategies. Regulations arising from specific legislation, such as advertising standards or employment law, force firms to adapt their strategies. In addition, informal norms exist in all societies, and they vary across countries. Violating informal norms may not trigger a lawsuit, but it can trigger negative media exposure and consumer protests that severely harm a firm's reputation. Your local competitors will be ready to pounce on your errors to mobilize allies against the 'foreign invader undermining our culture'. This holds for essentially all countries – including your own!

Second, in marketing, focus on the four Ps! You know this from marketing class. However, in international marketing, managers need to understand the behaviours of local consumers from a different culture who consequently react differently to marketing communications, and even use the same product in a different way. Thus before you roll out your 4P marketing toolbox, invest some time and resources in consumer research using both qualitative and quantitative methods.

Finally, in supply chain management, enhance your flexibility and responsiveness by focusing on the triple A. Underestimating the importance of a flexible response, many firms deliver only container loads to minimize the number of deliveries and freight costs. When demand for a particular product suddenly rises these firms are slow to react; they have to wait until the container (or truck) is full. Such a practice may delay shipment, and thus cause stock-outs in stores, which disappoints consumers. When the container eventually arrives, the shop may have excess inventory because consumer fashion has moved on. To get rid of such inventory, as much as a third of the merchandise carried by department stores is sold at a discount. Such discounts not only destroy profits, but also undermine brand equity by upsetting consumers who recently bought the discounted items at full price. In contrast, the triple A urges savvy supply chain managers to focus on agility, adaptability and alignment of interests of the entire chain.

Table 17.3 Implications for action

- Know the formal and informal rules of the game on marketing and supply chain management inside and out.
- In marketing, study local consumers behaviours, preferences and norms to avoid blunders.
- In supply chain management, focus on agility, adaptability and alignment (the triple A).

CHAPTER SUMMARY

1 Explain how companies may analyze consumer behaviour abroad.

- Using marketing surveys and non-conventional methods, international marketers need to study consumer behaviours in the markets they wish to enter.

2 Articulate the four Ps in international marketing (place, product, price and promotion).

- In international marketing, the number one concern about products is standardization versus localization.
- Price elasticity varies not only across market segments, but across countries.
- In promotion, marketers need to decide whether to enhance or downplay the country-of-origin effect.
- The place of sale has to do with what sequence and through what channels to enter foreign markets.

3 Articulate the three As in supply chain management (agility, adaptability and alignment)

- The complexity of international *supply chain management* is growing, with increased outsourcing to suppliers, contract manufacturers and 3PL providers.
- Agility deals with the ability to quickly react to unexpected shifts in supply and demand.
- Adaptability refers to the ability to reconfigure supply chain in response to longer term external changes.

- Alignment focuses on the alignment of interests of various players in the supply chain.

4 Discuss how institutions affect marketing and supply chain management

- Formal and informal rules such as advertising standards and employment law significantly impact these two areas.

5 Discuss how resources affect marketing and supply chain management

- Managers need to assess marketing and supply chain management based on the VRIO criteria.

6 Participate in two leading debates concerning marketing and supply chain management

- The debates are (1) B2B marketing and (2) asset versus liability of country of origin.

7 Draw implications for action

- Knowing the formal and informal rules of the game will enable managers to answer challenges in marketing and supply chain management.
- To avoid marketing blunders, managers should study consumer behaviour before deploying their marketing mix.
- Managers can enhance supply chain management by focusing on agility, adaptability and alignment (triple A).

KEY TERMS

Adaptability	Inbound logistics	Price elasticity
Agility	Ingredient branding	Product
Alignment	Market segmentation	Promotion
Business-to-business (B2B) marketing	Marketing	Relationship marketing
	Marketing mix	Standards in advertising
Business-to-consumer (B2C) marketing	Multi-tier branding	Supply chain
	Outbound logistics	Supply chain management
Country-of-origin effect	Place	Third-party logistics (3PL)
Distribution channel	Price	Total cost of ownership

CRITICAL DISCUSSION QUESTIONS

1 Consider a novel product (such as a wearable IT device) and a country you know very little about (say China or Brazil). How are you going to find the information you need to design a marketing strategy?

2 In Hollywood movies, it is common to have product placement (products, such as cars, from sponsored companies appear in movies without telling viewers that these are commercials). As a marketer, you are concerned about the ethical implications of product placement via Hollywood, yet you know the effectiveness of traditional advertising is declining. How do you proceed?

3 You are brand manager for branded chocolate bars. How can you use social networking sites such as *Facebook* to promote your product without putting off users tired of seeing too much advertising on their favourite site?

4 You are a supply chain manager at a UK firm. A volcano breaks out in Iceland, disrupting air travel across Europe. On the one hand, you are considering switching to local suppliers in the UK. On the other hand, you feel bad about abandoning your Asian suppliers, with whom you have built a pleasant personal and business relationship, and who – in the long run – may be able to deliver products much more cheaply. Yet your tightly coordinated production cannot afford to miss one supply shipment. How do you proceed?

RECOMMENDED READINGS

J. Mangan, C. Lalwani & T. Butcher, 2008, *Global Logistics and Supply Chain Management*, **Chichester: Wiley** – a textbook on the international supply chain aspects of this chapter.

P. Marsh, 2012, *The New Industrial Revolution: Consumers, Globalization, and the End of Mass Production*, **New Haven: Yale University Press** – a *Financial Times* journalist analyzes how globalization has changed the way manufacturing and global supply chains are organized.

M. de Mooij, 2011, *Consumer Behaviour and Culture*, **2nd ed., London: Sage** – explores how variations across Europe affect consumer behaviour and its implications for marketing.

D. Ricks, 2006, **Blunders in International Business, 4th ed., Oxford: Blackwell** – humorously tells the story of mistakes made by international business people, mostly in the area of marketing.

J.C. Usunier & J. Lee, 2012, **Marketing across Cultures, 6th ed., London: Prentice Hall** – a marketing textbook focusing on international and cross-cultural issues.

CLOSING CASE

Li & Fung: *from trading company to supply chain manager*

From its roots as a Hong Kong trading company, *Li & Fung* has emerged as the largest sourcing firm in the world. It manages the supply chain of high-volume, time-sensitive consumer goods (especially clothes and toys) produced throughout Asia for some of the major retail brands, such as *Limited Brands* (with brands such as *Victoria's Secret* and *Bath and Body Works*), *Liz Claiborne*, *Talbots*, *Timberland*, *Toys "R" Us* and *Sanrio*, the Japanese merchandiser of *Hello Kitty*.

Although *Li & Fung* has over 300 offices and distribution centres in more than 40 countries, it does not own any factories. As an intermediary, it adds

How did Victor Fung and his company build a mega-business, managing supply chains for retailers such as *Toys "R" Us*?

value by linking smaller suppliers in Asia and larger retailers in the developed world. *Li & Fung* maintains a network of 15 000 suppliers and factories throughout Asia. By bargaining on behalf of the 'small guys', *Li & Fung* enhances their bargaining power vis-à-vis multinational buyers. In exchange, *Li & Fung* enforces a code of conduct that prevents substandard quality and labour abuses. Suppliers found to violate this code are excluded from accessing *Li & Fung*'s buyers. On the other hand, *Li & Fung* keeps multinational buyers honest. If they refuse shipments due to their own problems (such as faulty forecast or demand collapse), *Li & Fung* denies them future access to its supplier network. Of course, *Li & Fung*'s buyers and suppliers pay a fee for its services, but the fee is lower than the transaction costs associated with the haggling, uncertainties and headaches when buyers and suppliers bargain directly.

Life as a trader and now a supply chain manager is not easy. In an effort to disintermediate, both buyers and suppliers relentlessly imitate *Li & Fung*'s capabilities. Intermediaries such as *Li & Fung* thrive by working with small- and medium-sized client firms on both sides. When buyers grow and expand their purchasing volume from Asia, they often set up their own procurement channels in Asia directly. Therefore, *Li & Fung* would be bypassed. On the other hand, when suppliers become more successful overseas, their export

volume justifies their investment to set up their own distribution channels in the West, again bypassing the likes of *Li & Fung*. Thus *Li & Fung* lives in a precarious world, constantly under the threat of being bypassed from both sides of its clients. For *Li & Fung*, the solution is to constantly develop and leverage its intimate knowledge of its markets and business partners to develop added services, such as customs handling, quality control and trade finance. By offering more than trade intermediation, and managing sourcing better than some in-house procurement departments, *Li & Fung* made itself indispensable.

However, *Li & Fung*'s business model has recently come under pressure. In a three-year plan (2014–2016) it outlined the new key strategy of refocusing on global supply chain management for consumer goods. As a first step, it spun-off its brand and licensing business into a separated listed company. The second step was to strengthen its logistics capabilities by acquiring *China Container Line*, a freight forwarding business. This allows *Li & Fung*'s logistics business to offer a more complete logistics solution to its customers. Third, in view of rising labour costs in Asia, *Li & Fung* changed its supplier management by offering them extended services, such as procurement support for raw materials and parts, compliance training, risk management, product testing and trade credit services.

CASE DISCUSSION QUESTIONS

1 From a resource-based perspective, what distinguishes *Li & Fung* from suppliers, buyers and other intermediaries?

2 From an institutional perspective, how can you explain the role of trade intermediaries in international supply chains?

3 Intermediaries such as *Li & Fung* need to be paid. Why do buyers and suppliers still find it valuable

to deal with *Li & Fung* as an intermediary? In other words, why don't they trade directly?

Sources: (1) V. Narayanan & A. Raman, 2004, Aligning incentives in supply chains, *HBR*, November: 94–102; (2) V. Fung, W. Fung & Y. Wind, 2008, *Competing in a Flat World*, Philadelphia: Wharton School Publishing; (3) *Business Week*, 2009, How not to sweat the retail details, May 25: 52–54; (4) A. Chintakananda, A. York, H. O'Neill & M.W. Peng, 2009, Structuring dyadic relationships between export producers and intermediaries, *EJIM*, 3: 302–327; (5) *Financial Times*, 2014, Li & Fung's strategy to make the maths work, June 2; (6) Li & Fung, 2014, Interim Report.

NOTES

'For journal abbreviation, please see page xx-xxi.'

1 J. Quelch & K. Jocz, 2012, *All Business is Local*, New York: Portfolio Press.

2 G.T. Hult, D. Ketchen & S. Slater, 2004, Information processing, knowledge management, and strategic supply chain performance, *AMJ*, 47: 241–253; T. Choi & D. Krause, 2006, The supply base and its complexity, *JOM*, 24: 637–652.

3 D. Ketchen & G.T. Hult, 2007, Bridging organization theory and supply chain management, *JOM*, 25: 573–580.

4 J. Lehy, 2009, How Volvo took a lead in India, *Financial Times*, September 1.

5 C.S. Craig & S.P. Douglas, 2001, Conducting international marketing research in the twenty-first century, *IMR*, 18: 80–90; M. De Mooij, 2005, *Consumer Behaviour and Culture*, London: Sage.

6 *Handelsblatt*, 2014, Mit langweiliger Kleidung gegen H&M, April 11.

7 M. Solomon, G. Bamossy, S. Askegaard & M.K. Hogg, *Consumer Behaviour: A European Perspective*, 3rd ed., Harlow: Prentice Hall.

8 C. Jarvis, S. Mackenzie, P. Podsakoff, D. Mick & W. Bearden, 2003, A critical review of construct indicators and measurement model misspecification in marketing and consumer research, *JCR*, 30, 199–218.

9 H. Chen, R. Chiang & V. Storey, 2012, Business intelligence and analytics, *MIS Quarterly*, 36: 1165–1188; T. Davenport, P. Barth & R. Bean, 2012, How 'big data' is different, SMR, July; H. Varian, Big data, *JEP*, 28(2): 3–28; Buck, C. Horbel, T. Kessler & C. Christian, 2014, Mobile consumer Apps, *Marketing Review St. Gallen*, 31: 26–35.

10 L. Lucas, 2010, Brands get up close and personal, *Financial Times*, October 13.

11 P. Kotler & K. Keller, 2005, *Marketing Management*, 12th ed., Upper Saddle River, NJ: Prentice Hall.

12 S. Jain, ed., 2003, *Handbook of Research in International Marketing*, Cheltenham; Elgar; D. Dow, 2006, Adaptation and performance in foreign markets, *JIBS*, 37: 212–226; C. Katsikeas, S. Samiee & M. Theodosiou, 2006, Strategy fit and performance consequences of international marketing standardization, *SMJ*, 27: 867–890.

13 T. Levitt, 1983, The globalization of markets, *HBR*, May–June: 92–102.

14 M. Harvey & M. Myers, 2000, Marketing in emerging and transition economies, *JWB*, 35: 111–113; D. Rigby & V. Vishwanath, 2006, Localization, *HBR*, April: 82–92.

15 As the page numbers differ for different editions of these magazines, we do not report page numbers in our references, but suggest students searching for an article to type the title of the article in the magazine's website search function.

16 J. Townsend, S. Yeniyurt & M. Talay, 2009, Getting to global, *JIBS*, 40: 539–558.

17 T. Beane & D. Ennis, 1987, Market segmentation, *EJM*, 21: 20–42; F. Hofstede, J. Steenkamp & M. Wedel, 1999, International market segmentation based on consumer-product relations, *JMR*, 36: 1–17; D. Yankelovich & D. Meer, 2006, Rediscovering market segmentation, *HBR*, February: 122–131.

18 A. Schuh, 2000, Global standardization as a success formula for marketing in Central Eastern Europe? *JWB*, 35: 133–148.

19 www.wedel.com/#history (accessed March 2015).

20 K.E. Meyer & Y. Tran, 2006, Market penetration and acquisition strategies for emerging economies, *LRP*, 39: 177–197; A. Schuh, 2007, Brand strategies of Western MNCs as drivers of globalization in Central and Eastern Europe, *EMJ*, 41: 274–192.

21 C. Schlautmann, 2010, Pandora ist ein Glücksfall für Juweliere, *Handelsblatt*, March 13; *Børsen*, 2011, Sådan forklarede Pandora sin chokmelding, August 2; *Børsen*, 2011, Pandora tager hul på ny æra, December 9.

22 Price example from Carrefour (www.carrefour.fr).

23 M. Cohen, N. Agrawal & V. Agrawal, 2006, Winning in the aftermarket, *HBR*, May: 129–138.

24 J. Usunier & J. Lee, 2009, *Marketing across Cultures*, 5th ed., London: Pearson.

25 K. Macharzina, 2001, The end of pure global strategies? (p. 106), *MIR*, 41: 105–108.

26 J. Schibrowsky, J. Peltier & A. Nill, 2007, The state of internet marketing research, *EJM*, 41: 722–733.

27 *Business Week*, 2005, The MySpace generation (p. 92), December 12: 86–96.

28 S. Noble, D. Haylo & J. Phillips, 2009, What drives college-age generation Y consumers? *JBR*, 62: 617–628.

29 J. Kietzmann, K. Hermkens, I. McCarthy & B. Silvestre, 2011, Social media? Get serious! *BH*, 54: 241–251. H. Pereira, M. Salgueiro & I. Mateus, 2014, Say yes to Facebook and get your customers involved! *BH*, 57: 695–702.

30 M. Porter, 1985, *Competitive Advantage*, New York: Free Press.

31 *The Economist*, 2006, The physical internet, June 17: 3–4.

32 The following discussion draws heavily on H. Lee, 2004, The triple-A supply chain, *HBR*, October: 102–112.

33 Y. Sheffi & J. Rice, 2005, A supply chain view of the resilient enterprise, *SMR*, 47: 41–48; B. Avittathur & P. Swamidass, 2007, Matching plant flexibility and supplier flexibility, *JOM*, 25: 717–735.

34 *Economist*, 2006, When the chain breaks, June 17: 18–19.

35 R. Belderbos & L. Sleuwaegen, 2005, Competitive drivers and international plant configuration strategies, *SMJ*, 26: 577–593; F. Rothaermel, M. Hitt & L. Jobe, 2006, Balancing vertical integration and strategic outsourcing, *SMJ*, 27: 1033–1056.

36 J. Murray, M. Kotabe & J. Zhou, 2005, Strategic alliance-based sourcing and market performance, *JIBS*, 36: 187–208.

37 D. Griffith & M. Myers, 2005, The performance implications of strategic fit of relational norm governance strategies in global supply chains, *JIBS*, 36: 254–269; M. McCarter & G. Northcraft, 2007, Happy together? *JOM*, 25: 498–511.

38 C. Niezen & W. Weller, 2006, Procurement as strategy, *HBR*, September: 22–23.

39 R.D. Ireland & J. Webb, 2007, A multi-theoretic perspective on trust and power in strategic supply chains, *JOM*, 25: 482–497.

40 W. Benton & M. Maloni, 2005, The influence of power driven buyer/supplier relationships on supply chain satisfaction, *JOM*, 23: 1–22; T. Crook & J. Combs, 2007, Sources and consequences of bargaining power in supply chains, *JOM*, 25: 546–555.

41 D. Krause, R. Handfield & B. Tyler, 2007, The relationships between supplier development, commitment, social capital accumulation, and performance improvement, *JOM*, 25: 528–545; C. Rodriguez & D. Wilson, 2002, Relationship bonding and trust as a foundation for commitment in US-Mexican strategic alliances, *Journal of International Marketing*, 10: 53–76.

42 N. Morgan, A. Kaleka & R. Gooner, 2007, Focal supplier opportunism in supermarket retailer category management, *JOM*, 25: 512–527.

43 M.W. Peng, 1998, *Behind the Success and Failure of US Export Intermediaries*, Westport, CT: Quorum; V. Narayanan & A. Raman, 2004, Aligning incentives in supply chains, *HBR*, November: 94–102.

44 H. Saffer & F. Chaloupka, 2000, The effect of tobacco advertising bans on tobacco consumption, *JHE*, 19: 1117–1137; H. Saffer & D. Dave, 2002, Alcohol consumption and alcohol advertising bans, *AE*, 34: 1325–1334.

45 *The Guardian*, 2010, various news items on various dates: www.guardian.co.uk/media/asa; *Advertising Standards Authority*, 2015, various news items: www.asa .org.uk/Rulings/Adjudications.aspx.

46 *Bloomberg*, 2014, How Wal-Mart made its crumbling China business look so good for so long, December 12.

47 K. Fam, D. Waller & B. Erdogan, 2004, The influence of religion on attitudes towards the advertising of controversial products, *EJM*, 38: 537–555.

48 International Standards Organization, www.iso.org (accessed December 2014).

49 I. Guler, M. Guillén & J.M. Macpherson, 2001, Global competition, institutions, and the diffusion of organizational practices, *ASQ*, 47: 207–232; O. Boiral, 2003, ISO 9000, *OS*, 14: 720–737.

50 J. Anderson, J. Narus & W. Rossum, 2006, Customer value propositions in business markets, *HBR*, March: 91–99; R. Priem, 2007, A consumer perspective on value creation, *AMR*, 32: 219–235.

51 C. Chao, J. Yang & W. Jen, 2007, Determining technology trends and forecasts of RFID by a historical review and bibliometric analysis from 1991 to 2005, *Technovation,* 27: 268–279; E. Ngai, K. Moon, F. Riggins & C. Yi, 2008, RFID Research, *IJPE*, 112: 510–530.

52 F. Pil & S. Cohen, 2006, Modularity: Implications for imitation, *AMR*, 31: 995–1011.

53 S. Modi & V. Mabert, 2007, Supplier development, *JOM*, 25: 42–64; K. Rogers, L. Purdy, F. Safayeni & P.R. Dimering, 2007, A supplier development program, *JOM*, 25: 556–572.

54 S. Fournier & L. Lee, 2009, Getting brand communities right, *HBR*, April: 105–111.

55 P. Kotler, N. Rackham & S. Krishnaswamy, 2006, Ending the war between sales and marketing, *HBR*, July: 68–78.

56 L. Berry, 1995, Relationship marketing of services, *JAMS*, 23: 236–245; G. Hoetker, 2005, How much do you know versus how well I know you, *SMJ*, 26: 75–96.

57 J. Knight, D. Holdsworth & D. Mather, 2007, Country-of-origin and choice of food imports, *JIBS*, 38: 107–125; P. Verlegh, 2007, Home country bias in product evaluation, *JIBS*, 38: 361–373.

58 L. Brouthers, E. O'Connell & J. Hadjimarcou, 2005, Generic product strategies for emerging market exports into Triad nation markets, *JMS*, 42: 225–245; J. Usunier, 2006, relevance in business research: the case of country-of-origin research in marketing, *EMR*, 3: 60–73; J. Knight, D. Holdsworth & D. Mather, 2007, Country-of-origin and choice of food imports, *JIBS*, 38: 107–125.

59 M. Brannen, 2004, When Mickey loses face, *AMR*, 29: 593–616.

60 J. Johansson, 2005, *In Your Face: How American Marketing Excess is Fuelling Anti-Americanism*, Upper Saddle River: Prentice-Hall.

61 www.klausmeyer.cc (accessed December 2014).

PART SIX

INTEGRATIVE CASES

1 Xiomi Challenges Global Smartphone Leaders

2 Rolls Royce: From Insolvency to World Leadership

3 Agrana: From Local Supplier to Global Player

4 Bharti Airtel Acquires Resources and Companies

5 Enhancing UK Export Competitiveness

6 Canada and the EU Negotiate CETA

7 German Chamber of Commerce Develops Social Responsibility in China

8 Tackling Corrupt Practices: GSK China

9 Fan Milk in West Africa

10 ESET: From Living-room to Global Player in Antivirus Software

11 The LG-Nortel Joint Venture

12 Beko Washes Clothes Across Europe

13 SG Group: Managing European Acquisitions

14 Just another move to China?

XIAOMI CHALLENGES GLOBAL SMARTPHONE LEADERS

Klaus Meyer and Jianhua (Jenny) Zhu
CEIBS

In December 2014, surprised newspaper readers around the world learned that the most valuable start-up company was a Chinese company that most had never heard of: smartphone maker *Xiaomi* (valued at $45 billion) overtook the worldwide operating taxi-booking company *Uber* (valued at $40 billion). Within only four years, *Xiaomi* became number one in China by units sold, ahead of *Samsung*, *Apple* and *Lenovo*. In the second quarter of 2014, *Xiaomi* had overtaken *Samsung* to become volume market leader with a 14 per cent market share. Worldwide, *Xiaomi* rose to sixth place in 2014, behind *Samsung*, *Apple*, *Lenovo*, *LG and Huawei* (Table 1). What explains the phenomenal success of *Xiaomi*?

The Chinese smartphone market has grown to become the largest in the world, overtaking the USA in 2012, with 31.8 million units sold. The industry was driven by rapid evolution of smartphone technologies and the availability of Wi-Fi, cheap components, specialized contract manufacturers and a vast domestic market of budget-conscious consumers. Local Chinese companies compete head-on against *Apple*, *Samsung* and other major global brands, who still sold about 20 per cent of their global sales in China. Six of the top eight vendors are Chinese firms that compete intensely among themselves: computer maker *Lenovo*, telecom equipment giants *Huawei* and *ZTE*, consumer electronics firms *TCL* and *Coolpad* and start-up *Xiaomi*. *Samsung* and *Apple* target the high-end market with handsets for about €500, while domestic competitors target lower market segments with selling prices set between €100 and €150.

Only a few years ago, the hottest brand in town was *HTC*. Once a manufacturer of phones for Western brands, *HTC* started its own branded smartphone in 2007, and became the top Android-based smartphone in the USA in 2010. Driven by a fast innovation culture, *HTC* aimed to launch a new version every month. Yet with an undifferentiated product and a mid-price positioning, *HTC* soon found itself squeezed

Table 1 Estimated world smartphone market share (units sold)

	2011	2013	2014
Samsung	16.8%	32.5%	28.0%
Apple	10.2%	16.6%	16.4%
Lenovo	n/a	4.9%	7.9%
LG	n/a	4.3%	6.0%
Huawei	9.5%	4.4%	5.9%
Xiaomi	nil	2.2%	5.2%
Coolpad	n/a	3.6%	4.2%
ZTE	6.9%	3.2%	3.1%
Sony	n/a	4.1%	3.9%
Nokia	30.1%	3.0%	n/a
Other	26.6%	21.2%	19.4%

Source: Technavio, Gartner, author's estimates.

between *Apple* and *Samsung* at the high end and Chinese players such as *Huawei* and ZTE at the low end. HTC's global market share slipped to 2.2 per cent in the third quarter of 2012. In the next two years, HTC launched new high-end phones, but despite awards and rave reviews, sales remained modest.

ENTREPRENEURSHIP, CHINESE STYLE

One entrepreneur who observed and learned from *HTC* was Lei Jun. A graduate from Wuhan University, he spent his early years as a software engineer, later a CEO, at *Kingsoft*, a software company competing with *Microsoft* in China. His first major success as an entrepreneur was *zhuoyue.com*, an online book retailer, he sold to *Amazon* in 2004, earning him €10 million. After *Kingsoft* was listed on the *Hong Kong Stock Exchange* in 2007, Lei resigned as CEO and started a new career as a venture capitalist, investing in online commerce and social media businesses.

In 2011, Lei Jun founded *Xiaomi*. At this time, the smartphone industry was rapidly maturing, with specialist providers at different stages of the value chain. Upstream were hardware manufacturers (like *Qualcomm* for chips) and software providers, for operating systems (such as Android) and software applications (like WeChat and Weibo). In the mid-stream, companies like *Foxconn* integrated the hardware and software to manufacturers of the physical products, smartphones. Further downstream, brand owners like *Nokia*, *Apple*, *Samsung*, *HTC*, *Huawei* and *Lenovo* marketed the products, and also led product innovation. Smartphones were usually sold via distributors, including telecom operators *China Mobile*, *China Telecom* and *China Unicom*, and retails stores like *Gome*, *Suning*, *JD.com* or *Taobao*.

With a good dozen established smartphone brands, how could *Xiaomi* differentiate itself? First, *Xiaomi* only used the suppliers for *Apple* and *Samsung* to establish a reputation as a top-tier brand. For example, *Xiaomi*'s chip suppliers were *Nvidia* and *Qualcomm*, and its manufacturers were *Foxconn* and *Inventec*. Second, *Xiaomi* developed its own operating system, MIUI, based on *Google*'s Android system, yet using creative designs to make it more user-friendly for Chinese consumers.

Third, Lei Jun developed an innovative business model to reach consumers while reducing costs. *Xiaomi* spent next to nothing on adverting, but sold its phones exclusively through the internet. In this way, it not only saved the margin the retailer would earn, but dramatically reduced the need to keep inventories. Building on his experiences in e-commerce and social media from his earlier entrepreneurial ventures, Lei Jun designed innovative online marketing and distribution channels. Initially, *Xiaomi* targeted technology-savvy IT engineers and college students via an online *Xiaomi* forum. Thus *Xiaomi*'s official website is its main sales channel, complemented by online malls, such as *Taobao*. Lei Jun moreover developed a pre-selling model to reduce expenses for inventory. *Xiaomi*'s cell phones were usually offered with limited supply, and customers had to register online before being able to bid online for a *Xiaomi* smartphone. As a result, 150 000 units were often sold online within minutes. A *Financial Times* correspondent observed:

> offering sleek, high-spec kit at low prices, *Xiaomi* has overtaken more venerable rivals to become the country's most popular smartphone brand. Its models sell for hundreds of dollars less than the latest *Apple* or *Samsung* phones, yet on the streets of Beijing or Shanghai they have become objects of lust.

However, the true source of *Xiaomi*'s success may not be the product, but the community of fans that *Xiaomi* has built. Before launching its products, *Xiaomi* already recruited tech enthusiasts to help testing its MIUI operating system. *Xiaomi* engages directly with its fans both online, for example, through social media communications and early bird offers, and offline, by inviting them to product launches or parties in nightclubs across China. With intensive online communication, *Xiaomi* developed a fashionable image beyond online geeks. As CEIBS professor Jane Wang observed (source 15):

> Everyone around us has the iPhone6 and iPhone6 plus. But Xiaomi stands out as something different. What does this say about its users? It says: I'm experimental, I'm willing to give new ideas a try and I'm really leading the trend.

As the brand matured, it also became popular as a gift young people gave to the grandparents: good value for money, and easy to use. This market however was less emphasized by *Xiaomi*, as it adds less to its aspired brand image.

Xiaomi's innovation strategy focuses on fast prototyping with very short 'launch-test-improve' cycles, a strategy found in many Chinese technology start-ups. Thus products are launched in quick succession, customer feedback is collected via online forums, and engineers quickly incorporate new ideas in the next product ideas, especially in software. While every change is small, cumulatively this process generates quite substantive innovations in the operating software, MIUI, and the apps that come with the *Xiaomi* phone.

This business model enables *Xiaomi* to offer innovative products while undercutting rivals with rock-bottom prices; many *Xiaomi* models are available online for prices around €100, whereas *Samsung*'s Galaxy smartphones retail for €500 and more. Thus in 2014, *Xiaomi* sold 61.1 million smartphones (a 227 per cent increase over 2013) and earned sales revenue of almost €10 billion (135 per cent increase). However, some observers expected *Xiaomi* to drive smartphones to commoditization – a process of competition by which differentiated products that command high prices and high margins lose their comparative advantage. *Xiaomi* focused on building volume and market share, and expected profits to come later once market leadership had been consolidated, thus following a strategy common in boom years in Silicon Valley. However, with thin margins, the business model was also sensitive to disruptions, as *Xiaomi* had little financial buffer to absorb unexpected shocks.

COMPETITION, CHINESE STYLE

As *Xiaomi* became the most popular Android-based smartphone brand, it was recognized as the most 'threatening' competitor for *Samsung* in China. In the third quarter of 2014, *Samsung*'s market share in China fell to 24.4 per cent, down from 32.1 per cent a year before, and for five consecutive quarters

Samsung reported falling earnings, because it was squeezed by *Apple*'s iPhone6 and Chinese local rivals like *Xiaomi*.

Moreover, *Xiaomi* also ate market share of local players like *Huawei* and ZTE. In response, *Huawei* and ZTE launched mobile phones with similar configurations at competitive prices. Thus *Xiaomi* launched Redmi Note at the price of €110, which was in direct competition with *Huawei*'s Honor 3X, priced at €130. The intense competition between Chinese brands raises the question whether or not *Xiaomi* has sustainable competitive advantages. Some commentators suggest that the loyal fan base and the associated online platforms are rare and hard to imitate resources. However, CEIBS Strategy professor Sam Park has his doubts (source 15):

> There is nothing that warrants any type of sustained advantage for *Xiaomi* even in the local market... Given the lack of unique competences, *Xiaomi* is, and will continue to be, easily challenged by other local companies. Most of these, including *Lenovo* and *Huawei,* already launched a similar business model in part of their operations. For local companies, once competition heats up, and the margins become thin, it becomes difficult to survive.

Moreover, the lack of patents has become *Xiaomi*'s Achilles heel. *Huawei* has built a portfolio of 22 169 patents, one of the largest number, not just in China, but worldwide. Likewise, *Lenovo* has accumulated 14 493 patents, including 2300 patents acquired with the takeover of *Motorola Mobility.* In contrast, *Xiaomi* had only seven patents, quite literally a technology dwarf among the giants of the telecom industry.

This lack of patents came to haunt *Xiaomi* as it challenged the leaders. In November 2014, lawyers for *Huawei* and ZTE sent letters to *Xiaomi* about the latter's patent infringements. Yet neither *Huawei* nor ZTE actually sued *Xiaomi* in court. The reason was twofold. *Xiaomi*'s hardware supplier *Qualcomm* owned 80 per cent of the patents for CDMA communications. *Qualcomm* also signed reverse patent authorization whenever it worked for a different mobile phone vendor, which meant that *Qualcomm* was able to integrate all kinds of patents on one smartphone chip. As a result, the *Xiaomi* chip provided by *Qualcomm* was safe. On the other hand, due to the IP protection environment in China, even if *Huawei* or ZTE won the lawsuit, the reimbursement fee for each patent was only €10 000, which would hardly dent *Xiaomi*.

INTERNATIONAL AMBITIONS

Focused on the vast and fast-growing Chinese market, *Xiaomi* sold only 3 per cent of its smartphones outside of China, compared to *Lenovo*'s 16 per cent and *Huawei*'s 41 per cent. Following the example of its Chinese peers, *Xiaomi* decided to first focus on other emerging economies, starting in India and then Brazil and Russia.

Xiaomi's first major international venture was in India, where its €90-a-piece smartphones undercut key competitors including global players *Samsung* and *Apple,* as well as local start-ups *Micromax, Karbonn* and *Spice.* However, *Xiaomi* found India more difficult to penetrate than China. While both are emerging economies, the Chinese experience was only of limited use in India. In particular, the online sales channels were – so far – less effective: first, *Xiaomi* does not enjoy the same attention in online tech circles and hence did not gather the same extent of buzz. In part, this was because many Chinese like *Xiaomi* because it represents the Chinese entrepreneurial spirit, an appreciation that is difficult to replicate abroad. Second, online retailing was still in its infancy in India, mainly because the physical infrastructure to bring online ordered products to consumers is not in place. Thus *Xiaomi* adapted its business models by collaborating with phone operator *Bharti Airtel* and electronics retailer *MobileStore* to develop more traditional distribution channels – but this increases its costs.

A different challenge of internationalization is the possibility of global competitors claiming intellectual property rights (IPR) infringement. IPR disputes are common among smartphone giants; *Apple* and *Samsung* have been fighting court battles in several countries for years. While the nature of IPR is often disputed, claims of IP infringement have become an effective, if costly, weapon of competition. In China, many

IPR that are not specifically registered in China cannot be enforced. Yet once companies operate outside of China, and become big enough to be able to pay large fees, they become the targets of IPR lawyers. Thus *Xiaomi* and other Chinese smartphone makers have armed themselves with *Google* executives and Silicon Valley lawyers seasoned at navigating the perilous waters between war and peace in IPR.

Xiaomi experienced its first foreign IPR conflict in India. In December 2014, *Ericsson* sued *Xiaomi* in an Indian court for IPR infringement, and the Delhi High Court ordered *Xiaomi* to suspend its sales in India. A few days later, the ban was reduced to a specific product with a specific chip made by *MediaTek* of Taiwan. Yet the ban was reintroduced a few months later when that particular phone was found to still be on sale in India through an online retailer that *Xiaomi* claimed was not an authorized retailer. While sorting out this specific legal battle, *Xiaomi* had to prepare itself for bigger battles to be expected when it entered other markets around the world.

Sources: (1) *BBC News*, 2014, China's Xiaomi becomes most valuable tech start-up, December 30; (2) CCID Consulting, 2012, Strategic Analysis on Chinese Smartphone Industry; (3) *South China Morning Post*, 2014, Chinese companies drive commoditisation of smartphone market, August 18; (4) *Wall Street Journal*, 2014, HTC One (M8), March 25; (5) C. Clover, 2015, Self-made in China, a smartphone billionaire, *Financial Times*, January 3; (6) Xiaomi's microblog, 2013, www.weibo.com, November 28, accessed March 2015; (7) E. Dou, 2015, Five things Xiaomi does to cultivate fans, *Wall Street Journal*, April 6; (8) C. Clarke, 2015, Rebel, geek, or both? *CEIBS Link* (Alumni Magazine), no 1, p. 38–44; (9) T. Hout & D. Michael, 2014, A Chinese approach to management, *HBR*, September, 103–107; (10) T. Bradshaw, 2015, Xiaomi Mi Note, *Financial Times*, February 27; (11) *South China Morning Post*, 2014, Chinese companies drive commoditisation of smartphone market, August 18; (12) K. Benner, 2015, Xiaomi's passage to India, Bloomberg view (blog), April 1; (13) S. Mundy & S. Jung-A, 2015, Profits blow sends Samsung back down to earth, *Financial Times*, January 9; (14) *Sohu*, 2014, The price war between Xiaomi and Huawei, roll.sohu.com/20140322/n397023827.shtml, accessed March 2015; (15) J. Coughin, 2015, Mobile Battlefield, *CEIBS Link* (Alumni Magazine), no 1, p. 28–31; (16) S. Yu, 2014, Why Huawei and ZTE cannot sue Xiaomi for patent infringement? tech.sina.com.cn/t/2014–11–26/doc-iavxeafr5; (17) *Bloomberg Businessweek*, 2014, Samsung's China problems come to India, October 27: 44–45; (18) *The Economist*, 2014, Smartening up their act, October 25; (19) J. Crabtree & C. Clover, 2014, India ban threatens Xiaomi's overseas expansion, *Financial Times*, December 11; (20) J. Crabtree, 2015, Indian court to investigate Xiaomi in Ericsson case, *Financial Times*, February 5.

DISCUSSION QUESTIONS

From an institution-based view:

1 How has *Xiaomi* been able to leverage the institutional environment in China to challenge global players such as *Samsung* and *Apple*?

2 What obstacles would it have to overcome to similarly succeed in India or Brazil?

From a resource-based view:

3 What resources has *Xiaomi* been able to create to enable its growth in China? Do you believe it has a sustainable advantage in China?

4 What obstacles to transferring resources to India and Brazil is *Xiaomi* likely to experience, and how to you suggest overcoming them?

ROLLS ROYCE: FROM INSOLVENCY TO WORLD LEADERSHIP

Klaus Meyer
CEIBS

*R*olls-Royce Plc (*RR*) sticks out from the crowd: it is a rare case of a large British company leading in a high-technology manufacturing industry: aircraft engines. Although Britain has been the cradle of the industrial revolution, it has more than other European countries shifted in the latter part of the 20th century to a service-driven economy. The share of manufacturing in British GDP fell to little more than 11 per cent in 2009, making *RR* look like the leftover of a bygone era. In fact, *RR* effectively went bankrupt in 1971, and was taken over by the government. Yet since privatization in 1997, it has gone from strength to strength, rising to second place behind *General Electric* (*GE*) in the market for civil aircraft engines.

How did *RR* achieve its leadership position under such adverse conditions? This case traces the history of the company (see Table 1) in search of the roots of its long-term success (Table 1). Before we start, we need one clarification: in the 21st century, *RR* does not make cars – the famous *Rolls-Royce* motorcar brand is now owned by *BMW* of Germany.

ENTREPRENEURIAL ORIGINS

Rolls-Royce was founded in 1904 by two entrepreneurs, Henry Royce, a perfectionist engineer, and Charles Rolls, a persuasive salesman. From the outset, the company integrated Royce's perfectionist approach and his attention to detail with Rolls' ability to relate customers' wishes, and engineering feasibility shaped the credo of the company. Soon the media called their cars 'the best cars in the world'.

World War I changed the priorities for *RR*. It started constructing aero engines, initially under a licence from *Renault*, but soon based on Royce's own engine designs. *RR* drew on its extensive experience of building engines for motorcars, but needed major innovations, because it takes far more energy to keep an aircraft in the air than it does to keep a car rolling along a road. This success helped both the firm and the nation: *RR* built the engines for half of all WWI aeroplanes of the Allies.

Table 1 Timeline

1906	Foundation of *RR* by Henry Royce and Charles Rolls.
1914	Manufacture of *RR*'s first aircraft engine.
1931	Acquisition of carmaker *Bentley*.
1930s	At *Rover*, Frank Whittle leads early research into turbojet engines.
1941	*GE* obtains a licence to build turbojet engines in an intergovernmental deal, *Pratt & Whitney* follows in 1947.
1943	*RR* takes over Whittle's jet engine project from *Rover*, in exchange for its tank development programme.
1945	*RR* gained a clear lead in gas turbines as the era of the piston engine comes to a close; a team of *RR* engineers takes out patents for a three-shaft turbojet engine.
1958	*RR*'s Avon is the first jet-turbine engine to power commercial passenger services across the Atlantic.
1959	*RR* starts manufacture of nuclear reactors for submarines.
1966	*RR*'s acquisition of *Bristol Siddeley* completes the consolidation of the UK aircraft engine industry.
1968	Contract to develop and deliver RB211 engine for *Lockheed*.
1970	Rescue package led by the Bank of England offers loans of £13 million.
1971	Effective bankruptcy and nationalization by the Conservative government (Heath).
1973	Separation of the automobile company from *RR Plc*.
1974	Labour government (Macmillan) elected; *RR* is placed under control of the National Enterprise Board.
1979	Conservative government (Thatcher) elected.
1985	*RR* returns to profitability.
1987	Privatization of *RR* raises £1.36 billion for the government.
1989	Acquisition of *Northern Engineering Industries* (*NEI*).
1990	Establishment of JV with *BMW* to manufacture engine for regional and corporate jets.
1992	Recession hits sales in both civilian and military segments of aerospace industry, *RR* suffers operating loss of £172 million.
1993	Rationalization programme announced, closing six of twelve manufacturing sites and laying off 2900 people (6 per cent of the workforce).
1995	Acquisition of Allison Engine Company (USA), a military engine supplier.
1998	Limit on foreign ownership raised to 49.5 per cent.
1999	Acquisition of *Vickers* (UK), *Cooper Rolls* (UK) and *National Automotive* (USA), and of *BMW*'s 50.5 per cent shareholding of their joint venture in Germany.
2007	Construction of a new test facility in Dahlewitz, near Berlin, Germany.
2008	A new business unit focuses on engines for the nuclear power industry.

2009	£151.5 million government scheme to support technology-based field, of which £130 million is channelled through *RR*. Plant extension and divisional headquarters for the marine sector located in Singapore.
2011	*RR* creates a 50-50 joint venture with *Daimler* to acquire German diesel engine manufacturer *Tognum AG* (formerly *MTU*), later renamed *Rolls Royce Power Systems*.
2012	New manufacturing plant for Trent 300 engines opened in Singapore.
2014	*RR* acquires *Daimler*'s 50 per cent equity stake in *Rolls Royce Power Systems*.

In the 1920s, the car sector boomed, and *RR* developed a premium brand, known for both the reliability of its engines and the originality of its designs. Its leading position was further strengthened by the acquisition of *Bentley* in 1931. However, technologies for aeroplanes and cars increasingly evolved along different trajectories, such that the synergies between the two lines of business declined.

While *RR* was market leader for aircraft engines at the end of WWI, competition increased during the 1920s, especially from US manufacturers. In popular racing competitions manufacturers could show off their latest technologies (a bit like Formula 1 motorcar racing). The main product at the time, an engine called Merlin, used a piston technology similar to that used in cars, but scaled up to produce the much higher levels of power needed in aviation. The Merlin reached its peak during WWII, when 165 000 Merlin engines helped the Allied war efforts, of which 55 000 were built under licence by *Packard* in the USA. Royce' s philosophy of building ever better engines yielding constant improvements compelled the company forward. This philosophy of perfection established by the founder continued as the core of the company's corporate culture long after Royce's death in 1930.

In the early 1930s, an independent engineer, Frank Whittle, invented a completely new form of engine, the jet engine. In 1941, his first plane powered by a jet engine took to the air, and in 1943, *RR* took over Whittle's entrepreneurial operation, and put jet engines into mass production. By the end of the war, the new jet engine technology had largely replaced piston engines, and *RR* was leading in this technology.

COMPETITION AND INDUSTRY CONSOLIDATION

After WWII, *RR* focused on the fast-growing civilian airline sector. Its Avon engine became the first gas turbine to power passenger services across the Atlantic. However, US competitor *Pratt & Whitney* also invested in advanced gas-turbine technologies, notably with a new technology for turbine fan blades, and was able to leapfrog *RR* in the civilian airline market. Losing its leadership in this market in the 1950s taught *RR* two lessons that, according to later CEO Ralph Robbins, shaped the strategic thinking over the next generation: First, 'engines must be sized for the world market and for a wide range of applications' and second, 'once introduced, they must be developed continually'. With long development cycles for new models, new technologies have often been researched over several years, or even decades, before their introduction to the market.

The 1950s and 1960s saw a rapid consolidation of the UK aero engine industry from seven independent manufacturers to just one. The process was completed when *RR* acquired *Bristol Siddeley* in 1966 for £63.6 million, in part to prevent a link-up between *Bristol Siddeley* and their prime competitor, *Pratt & Whitney*. This acquisition, however, tied up considerable financial resources because *Bristol Siddeley* owned shares in other businesses, and it took *RR* a while to sell them off to recover the costs of the acquisition. However, with that acquisition, RR had secured its position as number one manufacturer of aero engines in the UK – and in Europe. In the late 1950s, *RR* also became involved with nuclear energy, designing and manufacturing the reactors for the British nuclear submarine fleet.

Yet in this industry competition was already taking place on a global scale, as *RR* belatedly realized. The American competitors were flying ahead, in part because of government support. Since the 1920s, *Pratt & Whitney* had benefited from government-funded research and subsidies to aerospace industry. During WWII, the British handed their American Allies jet engine technology, which allowed *General Electric* to enter the aircraft engine industry. Dual licensing requirements by the US military led to this technology being shared with *Pratt & Whitney* from 1947 onwards. Both firms took up these new ideas and advanced their own jet engines. The technology received during WWII became the basis for *GE*'s next generation turbofan engines, which it supplied to the US navy and air force, the biggest customer for military aircraft. In the 1960s, *GE* became the world's biggest aircraft engine manufacturer, though it did not enter the commercial aircraft market until 1971. Meanwhile, *Pratt & Whitney* became the prime supplier of engines to the rapidly growing American commercial airlines.

In the 1960s, *RR* was trying to catch up with its American competitors. A creed of engineering excellence guided the company, and it was reproduced generation after generation through recruitment and internal training. Employees tended to join the company young, and stayed with the company for most of their working life. The top management of *RR* were mostly internally promoted engineers, who took great pride in their history and their engineering skills. The pursuit of engineering excellence became the core of *RR*'s organizational culture, and informed key decisions – excessively so, according to some commentators who felt that too little attention was paid to timing and cost considerations.

AN AMBITION TOO FAR

In the early 1960s, *RR* started developing a new generation of larger scale turbofan engines. For this scale of engine, the two-shaft design of turbojet engines hit its technical limitations, and *RR* started developing engines using a three-shaft configuration, which were expected to develop better aerodynamics, and thus be suitable for larger scale engines. In this development work, *RR* could draw on patents taken out by *RR* engineers in 1945. *RR* competed for major contracts with *Boeing*, but lost out to its American competitors *GE* and *Pratt & Whitney*.

In 1967, *RR* started negotiations with *Lockheed* to supply their new L-1011 aircraft, which were widely expected to provide *RR* with a breakthrough into the American market. *RR* promised to develop a technological superior engine that was cheaper to run and easier to maintain, and met the demands of the next generation of aircraft. Eager to sign the deal, *RR* agreed to deliver the new engine at a price that undercut its American rivals: £200 000 compared to $250 000 (*GE*) and £280 000 (*Pratt & Whitney*). *Lockheed* announced the deal in March 1968 with an initial order of 450 engines, known as RB211 at the time. The news was well received by British financial markets and politicians.

However, the development of the new engine was a mammoth task, and entailed considerable economic risk. Not only was the new engine considerably bigger than any of *RR*'s existing designs, it was in a different shape and thus required major investments in new machinery and new welding techniques. The development of the RB211 became *RR*'s prime objective; about half of its 84 000 strong workforce worked on the task. The British government supported the effort with initially £47 million of 'launch aid' (effectively an R&D subsidy).

At the time, the three-shaft design was still an unproven technology, and it was difficult to raise capital on the market for such a long-term and high-risk project. The challenge increased with changes in *Lockheed*'s design of the aircraft, which triggered the need for further adjustments of the engine. The aircraft became larger and heavier during the development process, which required even stronger engines. At the same time, *RR* encountered technological problems. The envisaged new carbon fibre fan blades failed the so-called 'bird-strike test', which led to a restart of fan blade designs, which increased both the weight and the costs of the engine. Various technical problems caused delays, and raised the prospect of having to pay severe late-delivery penalties.

The stress of the technological development started hitting financial numbers, and in 1970 *RR* reported £10 million in losses. At the same time, the costs of developing the RB211 surged: initial estimates in September 1968 suggested £68 million, yet this number increased to £170.3 million in September 1970 and to 202.7 million in January 1971. The estimated production costs increased from originally £154 000 to £237 000 in 1970, which would translate as a loss of £37 000 for each engine sold.

When the crisis became apparent in September 1970, a rescue package was negotiated that included a further £42 million of launch aid from the British government, and loans from the Bank of England and commercial banks. A turnaround plan was initiated, yet it was already too late. On February 4, 1971 *RR* went into receivership. Eventually, the attempt to develop the RB211 for the *Lockheed* drove *RR* into bankruptcy.

GOVERNMENT TO THE RESCUE

Faced with the possible bankruptcy of one of the most prestigious British manufacturing enterprises, the Conservative government decided to nationalize *RR*. This move was motivated primarily by the importance of *RR* as a defence contractor, which made it a national interest. *RR*'s car business was separated in 1973, and privatized again. Initially, cancellation of the RB211 was considered, which would have implied a massive downsizing of the company. However, the government soon thought better of it, and provided new launch aid for *RR* to continue its development, while renegotiating the terms of the contract with *Lockheed*. The government appointed new board members to join *RR* who were sympathetic to the RB211, but also had a sharp eye for the company's finances. As one insider later described it 'the first thing we had to learn was that the company was not just a playground for engineers to amuse themselves'. After tough negotiations, the government gave the management of *RR* operational freedom to develop the company – and the RB211 programme – while retaining ultimate control over strategic decisions.

PRIVITIZATION

When Margret Thatcher became Prime Minister in 1979, privatization was given a high policy priority. However, it took another eight years until *RR* returned to private ownership. The RB211 went into production eventually, but the aviation industry was hit by a severe recession in the early 1980s. *RR* recorded losses of £58 million in 1979, which accelerated to a loss of £193 million in 1983. In 1983 and 1984 it sold only 126 new engines, far fewer than a 'worst case' prediction of 350 published in 1982. *RR* drastically cut its workforce from 62 000 to 41 000, while the government provided further launch aid of £437 million (of which £118 million was repaid from sales levies) in the 1980s.

At the height of the new crisis, *RR* considered exiting as an independent competitor from the large-scale engine market. It entered a collaborative development with *GE* in 1984. *RR* took a 15 per cent stake in *GE*'s latest high-thrust development project, while *GE* took a 15 per cent stake in the development of a new medium-size engine aimed at the *Boeing* 757. However, in a recovering aircraft market, *RR*'s leadership soon realized that they might not have to give up just yet. Engineers found new ways to increase the thrust of their engines without increasing the fan diameter. By 1986, *RR* was marketing its own high-thrust engine, in direct competition with the joint project with *GE*. Understandably, the Americans were not amused, and the collaboration was soon terminated.

New engine developments during the 1980s were building on the designs and technologies of the 1970s and 1960s – and patents obtained back in the 1930s. The experience of the 1970s taught RR that the complexity of the technologies necessitated that new engine programmes be grounded in the R&D experience of the development team, and in previously demonstrated technologies. Thus *RR* pursued a strategy of continuous development of technologies, well ahead of their market introduction.

Eventually, *RR* started making profits again: in 1986, it recorded pre-tax profits of £120 million. In 1987, after 16 years under government ownership and massive financial injections, RR was privatized. The flotation raised £1.36 billion for the government, a handsome return on its investment (estimated to be £833 million since nationalization). The government, however, retained a golden share in the company (which it still holds in 2015) because of the national defence interests in the company. Foreign ownership was initially limited to 25 per cent, but under pressure of EU competition policy this was raised to 28.5 per cent in 1989 and to 49.5 per cent in 1998.

MORE RESTRUCTURING AND TAKE-OFF

In the first years after privatization, *RR* experienced spectacular growth as its three-decade long investment in the three-shaft jet engine technology of the RB211 finally paid off. Its market share in the civil aircraft market grew from 5 per cent at the time of privatization to 20 per cent in 1990. Under new ownership, the strategy focused on core businesses, while more activities were outsourced. New management practices such as lean manufacturing, total quality management and business process reengineering aimed to cut costs and enhance productivity. Spending on R&D continued to rise in absolute values, staying at 6 per cent to 7 per cent throughout the 1990s.

In 1989, *RR* acquired Newcastle-based *Northern Engineering Industries*, a power station equipment and heavy engineering group. This acquisition launched a diversification strategy that added gas turbines for energy and marine uses. New engines for the maritime sector, especially the navy, utilized technologies developed in aircraft-related research, for example, advances in fan blade technologies.

With continued emphasis on technology development, *RR*'s stock market performance from 1987 to 2001 lagged the development of the stock market. The management was willing to accept lower short-term financial performance, by focusing on building its technologies and market positions. However, another recession in the early 1990s exposed *RR*'s low profitability. *RR* responded by further restructuring its operations, including (from 1993 onwards) the layoff of 2900 people and the closure of six of the company's twelve manufacturing plants in the UK.

The privatized *RR* was a very focused company – limited to the largest segments of the aero engine market, and thus highly dependent on the fluctuations of this market. At the same time, *RR* was much smaller than its two American rivals, and lacked the possibility to utilize its technologies across segments. To diversify its activities and to utilize its technologies in a broader market, *RR* entered a JV with *BMW* of Germany in 1990. The JV was to develop new engines for two specific segments of the aircraft industry: medium-sized 100-seat aircraft and long-range business jets. *BMW* had historically manufactured aero engines, but left the industry in the 1960s.

The JV succeeded in becoming market leader in the business jet market. The regional jet market, on the other hand, declined when a major customer, *Fokker*, ceased business, while new entrants such as *Embraer* opted for a new technology supplied by *GE*. However, *BMW-RR* achieved a turnover well ahead of initial projections of US$727 million in 1999. Eventually, *BMW* decided to refocus its strategy. *RR* bought the JV in 1999 and renamed it *Rolls-Royce Deutschland*.

ORGANIC AND ACQUISITIVE GROWTH

From the late 1990s, *RR* shifted its strategic priorities to engine technologies in the power industry and the marine sector. By now *RR* was a highly profitable business with a proven technology and a strong order pipeline, which made it much easier to raise capital on the stock market.

After regaining a profitable position in the industry, *RR* pursued a path of expansion both organically and by acquiring other businesses. In 1995, *RR* acquired *Allison Engine Company* in Indiana, USA for

£328 million, following a cooperation that dated back to the 1960s. *Allison* strengthened *RR*'s position in the USA, the world's largest aviation market, and provided access to the US military, the largest buyer of aircraft engines. However, the acquisition was subject to a special investigation into its national security implications, and *RR* was required to manage *Allison* as a separate company under a proxy board. Indiana henceforth became the hub of *RR*'s North American operations, employing over 9000 people.

RR expanded its business in areas where its knowledge of building engines to highest standards was believed to be applicable: marine propulsion, power generation (especially nuclear power), and gas pumping. Navies around the globe shifted from piston engines to gas turbines to increase the power generated on limited space, while reducing maintenance costs. *RR* achieved leadership in this technology and supplied more than 50 navies around the globe.

A major step in building the marine business was the acquisition in 1999 of *Vickers*, a British company with a long-standing engineering tradition almost equal to that of *RR*. For £576 million, *RR* obtained capabilities for marine power systems in particular, which enabled *RR* to pursue a leadership position for commercial ship engines. In the early 2000s, the marine sector was the fastest-growing division of *RR*, increasing turnover from £275 million in 1997 to £2.5 billion in 2013 (see Figure 1). The shipbuilding industry has moved increasingly to Asia, with Korean shipyards taking the lead first, and more recently Chinese shipyards emerging as major players. Consequently, *RR* moved the headquarters of its marine division to Singapore, to be closer to the main hubs of the shipbuilding industry in 2009.

The energy division received a major boost in 2008 with the announcement that *RR* would enter the nuclear power industry. This coincided with a policy shift of the British government. Reversing its earlier policy, the Labour government announced that several new nuclear power stations would be built in the UK to cope with the diminishing capacity in traditional coal- and gas-fired power stations. Politicians quickly added that such a major investment should be driven by British engineering. Yet not having built any nuclear power stations for over two decades, such competences needed to be regained and upgraded to the state-of-the art. *RR* strengthened its capabilities for nuclear technologies by acquiring two businesses providing management and engineering services to nuclear plants, *R Brooks Associates* in 2011 and *PKMJ Technical Services* in 2013.

In November 2011, *RR* teamed up with *Daimler AG* to acquire the German engine manufacturer *Tognum AG*, with both partners holding 50 per cent of the equity. *Tognum* was manufacturing reciprocating engines, propulsion, and distributed energy systems under the *MTU* brand, and was a leading supplier of engines for high-speed trains. For example, *MTU* engines were contracted to drive *Hitachi*'s future high-speed trains that would go into service in the UK in 2017. The JV invested in new facilities, notably a new engine plant in Poland. In March 2014, *RR* acquired full equity control by buying out *Daimler AG* and fully integrating it into *RR* as *Rolls Royce Power Systems*.

Figure 1 *Rolls Royce* revenues (million £)

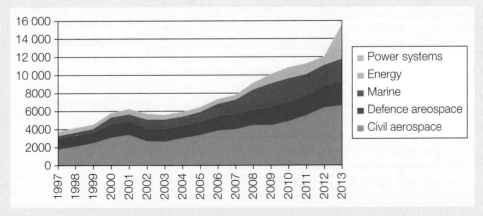

COMPETITIVE DYNAMICS OF THE 21ST CENTURY

The dynamics of competition in *RR*'s core business shifted substantially around the beginning of the new millennium. The technological achievements of modern aero engines are truly amazing, even for engineers. The contemporary Trent engine generates about a million horsepower (hp) at take-off. Each single turbine blade develops more than 900 hp – more than a Formula 1 racing car! Yet power alone is not sufficient to stay ahead in the engine industry.

First, the manufacture and servicing of engines is becoming more integrated. *RR* engineers are monitoring the performance of *RR* engines in real time: data collected from engines are directly transmitted from the aircraft to the *RR* service centre. In case of malfunction, the service centre initiates corrections or sends instructions for work to be done once the aircraft has landed. Thus maintenance (and if necessary repairs) can be completed more quickly, and the aircraft is up in the air again much more quickly. This new form of servicing blurs the boundary between manufacturing and servicing, and opens new business opportunities to *RR* to exploit its competences. Independent maintenance businesses would not be able to draw on *RR*'s extensive engineering competences and its databases. In the 2010s, *RR* earned more money through after-sales services and spare parts than through the manufacture of engines. In the civil aircraft division, as many as 70 per cent of aircraft were sold with a fleet management contract (see Figure 2). This shift to services and long-term contracts made the business less sensitive to the volatilities of the aircraft construction industry.

Second, *RR* needed a global footprint of both manufacturing and service sites to be not too far from its main clients, the airline companies. Notably, *RR* built a new engine plant in Singapore to take advantage of skilled labour and government support available in the city state. Similarly, its service units had to be present in all major hubs where airlines would conduct their maintenance operations.

Third, *RR* benefited from a moderate shift in British industrial policy. The importance of developing capabilities or the engineering sector was recognized by the British government in 2008, when the dangers of focusing on the financial sector as the primary driver of the British economy became apparent. A new strategy provided funding of £151.5 million to manufacturing in technology-driven fields, of which 86 per cent was being channelled through *RR*.

However, *RR* also faced operational challenges. In November 2010, a *Qantas* flight using the latest *Airbus* 380 made an emergency landing in Singapore after parts of one of its engines had blown off and

Figure 2   Percentage of revenues in services

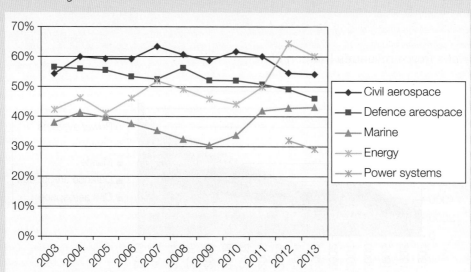

landed in a village in Indonesia. *Qantas* and *Airbus* quickly briefed the press, apologized, and promised an investigation. It quickly transpired that the *RR* Trent 900 engines were at fault, the latest model from *RR*, causing *RR* share prices to drop by 10 per cent. After a few days, *RR* explained publicly where they saw the problem and what they intended to do about it, leading to a partial recovery of the share price. *Qantas* grounded its fleet with *RR* engines for several days, suffering economic damage for which *RR* later agreed to pay A$95 million in compensation.

Once the financial crisis was overcome, airlines, especially those in emerging economies, made new large orders for aircraft, such that *RR*'s sales and profits recovered by 2010. The share price surged to new heights, trading at over 880p in November 2012, which is 60 per cent higher than its peak before the financial crisis in 2007. As a leader in one of the most globalized industries, *RR*'s main challenges remained to manage the cyclical demand for its products, and to stay ahead of competitors worldwide.

Sources: (1) Department for Business, Innovation & Skills, 2010, Manufacturing in the UK: Supplementary Analysis, Economics Paper 10B; (2) M. Donne, 1981, Leader of the Skies: Rolls-Royce, London: Muller; R. Robins, 2005, *Rolls-Royce Centenary Lecture: Striving for perfection,* lecture notes, Derby: Rolls Royce; (3) K. Hayward, 1989, the British Aircraft Industry, Manchester: Manchester University Press; (4) B. O'Sullivan, 2008, Nuclear co-operation – 50 years no, *Rolls-Royce Magazine,* issue 117, p. 30–32; (5) W. Lazonick & A. Principe, 2005, Dynamic capabilities and sustained innovation, *Industrial and Corporate Change,* 14: 501–542; (6) P. Pugh, 2001, *The Magic of a Name: The Rolls-Royce Story Part 2,* Cambridge: Icon Books; (7) D.J. Smith, 2003, Strategic alliances and competitive strategy in the European aerospace industry: The case of BMW Rolls Royce GmbH, *European Business Review* 15, 262–276; (8) Rolls Royce Annual Report 2013, p. 23; (9) S. Reed, D. Brady & B. Einhorn, 2005, Rolls-Royce at your service, *Business Week,* November 14; *The Economist,* 2009, Rolls-Royce: Britain's lonely high-flier, January 10; (10) S. Syed, 2012, Rolls Royce gears up for Singapore production, *BBC News,* February 2; (11) *The Economist,* 2011, Rolls-Royce: Per ardua, February 5.

DISCUSSION QUESTIONS

From the perspective of the institutional view:

1 How did WWI and WWII influence the long-term development of the company?
2 How did US defence policy influence the development of *RR*?
3 How did UK government policy influence the development of *RR*?

From the perspective of resource-based view:

4 Which resources are the sources of competitive advantage for *RR* in 2014?
5 What dynamic capabilities does *RR* have that have helped it at different stages of its development?
6 If there was a new entrant in the market for aircraft engines, where would you expect it to come from?

AGRANA: FROM LOCAL SUPPLIER TO GLOBAL PLAYER

Erin Pleggenkuhle-Miles
University of Nebraska

Headquartered and listed in Vienna, Austria, *Agrana* is one of the leading suppliers to multinational brands around the world. With revenues of €3.0 billion and capitalization of €1.1 billion in 2014, *Agrana* is a world leader in fruit preparations and fruit juice concentrates, and one of Central Europe's leading sugar and starch companies.

Agrana was formed in 1988 as a holding company for three sugar factories and two starch factories in Austria. Since then, it has become a global player with 52 production plants in 26 countries with three strategic pillars: sugar, starch and fruit. *Agrana* supplies most of its fruit preparations and fruit juice concentrates to the dairy, baked products, ice cream and soft-drink industries. In other words, you may not know *Agrana*, but you have probably enjoyed many *Agrana* products. How did *Agrana* grow from a local supplier serving primarily the small Austrian market to a global player?

FROM CENTRAL AND EASTERN EUROPE TO THE WORLD

In many ways, the growth of *Agrana* mirrors the challenges of regional integration in Europe and then with global integration of multinational production. There are two components of European integration. First, EU integration accelerated throughout Western Europe in the 1990s. This means that firms such as *Agrana*, based in a relatively smaller country, Austria (with a population of 8.2 million), needed to grow its economies of scale to fend off the larger rivals from other European countries blessed with larger home country markets and hence larger scale economies. Second, since 1989, Central and Eastern European (CEE) countries, formerly off limits to Western European firms, have opened their markets. For Austrian firms such as *Agrana*, the timing of CEE's arrival as potential investment sites was fortunate. Facing powerful

This case was written by Erin Pleggenkuhle-Miles (then University of Texas at Dallas) under the supervision of Professor Mike Peng, and updated by Alexandra Han and Klaus Meyer.

rivals across Western Europe but being constrained by its smaller home market, *Agrana* has aggressively expanded its foreign direct investment (FDI) throughout CEE. Most CEE countries have become EU members since then. As a result, CEE provides a much larger playground for *Agrana*, allowing it to enhance its scale, scope, and thus competitiveness.

At the same time, multinational food production by giants such as *Nestlé, Unilever, Coca-Cola, PepsiCo* and *Danone* has been growing, reaching almost all parts of the world. Emerging as a strong player not only in Austria and CEE but also in the EU, *Agrana* has 'chased' these corporate customers by investing in and locating supplier operations around the world. This strategy has allowed *Agrana* to better cater to the expanding needs of its corporate buyers.

Until 1918, Vienna had been capital of the Austro-Hungarian Empire, whose territory not only included today's Austria and Hungary but also numerous CEE regions. Although formal ties were cut during the Cold War, informal ties never disappeared. These ties have been reactivated since the end of the Cold War, providing a foundation for Austrian firms to enter CEE. Thus Austrian firms have been pushed by pressures arising from the EU integration and pulled by the attractiveness of CEE. However, among hundreds of Austrian firms that have invested in CEE, not all are successful. How did *Agrana* emerge as a winner from its forays into CEE? The answer boils down to *Agrana's* firm-specific resources and capabilities.

PRODUCT-RELATED DIVERSIFICATION

Agrana has long focused on sugar and starch production in CEE. However, the liberalization of the EU sugar market put pressure on the sugar industry. Traditionally, the EU allocated quotas to sugar farmers and thereby limited competition between both sugar beet farmers and sugar refineries. Anticipated for several years, in 2006, the EU passed reforms reducing subsidies, and abolishing the quota system over a four-year transition period. Sugar refineries acted ahead of the reforms by either diversifying into related sectors, or by consolidating across Europe (also see Chapter 14, Opening Case '*Danisco*').

Agrana focused on diversification in processed fruit and fruit juices, a major customer industry for sugar and starch. This diversification also capitalized on its core competence – the refining and processing of agricultural raw materials, in particular sugar beets, cereals and potatoes (Table 1). First,

Table 1 Agrana divisions

Sugar	*Agrana* Sugar maintains ten sugar factories in five EU countries (Austria, Czech Republic, Slovakia, Hungary and Romania) plus Bosnia-Herzegovina. It is one of the leading sugar companies in Central Europe with number one market positions in Austria and Hungary. The sugar *Agrana* processes is sold to both consumers and manufacturers in the food and beverage industries. Within this sector, *Agrana* maintains customer loyalty by playing off its competitive strengths, which include high product quality, matching product to customer needs, customer service and just-in-time logistics.
Starch	*Agrana* operates four starch factories in three countries (Austria, Hungary and Romania). The products are sold to the food and beverage, paper, textile, construction chemicals, pharmaceutical and cosmetic industries. To maintain long-term client relationships, *Agrana* works in close collaboration with its customers and develops 'made-to-measure solutions' for its products. As a certified manufacturer of organic products, *Agrana* is Europe's leading supplier of organic starch.
Fruit	The fruit division operates 39 production plants across every continent. Like the starch division, the fruit division does not make any consumer products, limiting itself to supplying manufacturers of brand-name food products. Its principal focus is on fruit preparations and the manufacturing of fruit juice concentrates. Fruit preparations are customized products made from a combination of high-grade fruits and sold in liquid or lump form. Manufacturing is done in the immediate vicinity of *Agrana* customers to ensure a fresh product. Fruit juice concentrates are used as the basis for fruit juice drinks and are supplied globally to fruit juice and beverage bottlers and fillers.

entry into the fruit sector ensured additional growth and complemented *Agrana*'s position in the starch sector. Since the starch division was already a supplier to the food and beverage industry, this allowed *Agrana* to benefit from those relationships previously developed when it entered the fruit sector. Second, because the fruit sector is closely related to *Agrana*'s existing core sugar and starch businesses, *Agrana* could employ the expertise and market knowledge it had accumulated over time, thus benefiting its new Fruit Division.

Agrana's CEO, Johann Marihart, believes that growth is an essential requirement for the manufacturing of high-grade products at competitive prices. Economies of scale have become a decisive factor for manufacturers in an increasingly competitive environment. In both the sugar and starch segments, *Agrana* developed from a locally active company to one of Central Europe's major manufacturers in a very short time. Extensive restructuring in the sugar and starch divisions has allowed *Agrana* to continue to operate efficiently and competitively in the European marketplace.

ACQUISITIONS

How did *Agrana* implement its expansion strategy? Acquisitions. Between 1990 and 2001, *Agrana* focused on expansion into CEE sugar and starch markets by expanding from five plants to 13, almost tripling its capacity. As the sugar division reached a ceiling in its growth potential due to EU sugar reforms, *Agrana* began searching for a new opportunity for growth. Diversifying into the fruit industry aligned with *Agrana*'s goal to be a leader in the industrial refinement of agricultural raw materials.

Agrana diversified into the fruit segment in 2003 through the acquisition of five firms. With the acquisition of Denmark's *Vallø Saft* Group (fruit juice concentrates) in April 2003, *Agrana* gained a presence in Denmark and Poland. The acquisition of an interest (33 per cent) in Austria's *Steirerobst* (fruit preparations and fruit juice concentrates) in June 2003 strengthened *Agrana*'s presence in Austria, Hungary and Poland, while also establishing a presence in Romania, Ukraine and Russia. *Agrana* fully acquired *Steirerobst* in February 2006. *Agrana* began acquiring France's *Atys* Group (fruit preparations), initially by making a partial acquisition of 25 per cent of their equity in July 2004, which was increased to 100 per cent in December 2005. With *Atys*, *Agrana* acquired 20 plants across all continents. In 2004, *Agrana* also acquired Belgium's *Dirafrost* (fruit preparations) and two months later (January 2005) Germany's *Wink* Group (fruit juice concentrates). *Agrana* also established a 50-50 joint venture with *Xianyang Andre Juice Co Ltd*, a manufacturer of fruit juice concentrates in China. These acquisitions allowed *Agrana* within only two years to become a global player in the fruit segment. Table 2 provides an overview of *Agrana*'s plant locations around the globe.

The strategy of *Agrana* is laid out in its 2006–2007 annual report: '*Agrana* intends to continue to strengthen its market position and profitability in its core business segments . . . and to achieve a sustainable increase in enterprise value. This will be done by concentrating on growth and efficiency, by means of investments and acquisitions that add value, with the help of systematic cost control and through sustainable enterprise management.' *Agrana*'s growth strategy, consistent improvement in productivity, and value added approach enable continual increases in its enterprise value and dividend distributions to shareholders. The key to *Agrana*'s global competitiveness in the fruit segment is not only its many acquisitions but its ability to integrate those acquired into the group to realize synergistic effects.

By 2006, *Agrana* thus was a related-diversified conglomerate focused on the processing of agricultural products primarily for the processed food industry, with the fruit division becoming the largest unit in terms of sales. With expected changes in dietary habits of consumers around the world, great potential was expected in this sector. *Agrana* also entered production of bio-ethanol, an environmentally friendly fuel that can be produced as by-product of starch production.

Table 2 *Agrana* by division as of 2014

Region	Country	Sugar plants	Starch plants	Fruit plants	Revenues (€ million)	Employees
European Union	Austria, Belgium, Czech Republic, Denmark, France, Germany, Hungary, Poland, Romania, Slovakia	9	5	19	2 492.8	4 711
Other Europe	Bosnia-Herzegovina, Russia, Serbia, Turkey, Ukraine	1	—	5	151.3	992
North America	USA, Mexico	—	—	4	249.0	1 108
South America	Argentina, Brazil	—	—	2	31.5	204
Asia	China, South Korea	—	—	3	59.1	263
Australia & Oceania	Australia, Fiji	—	—	2	38.9	119
Africa	Egypt, Morocoo, South Africa	—	—	4	20.9	1 532
Total		10	5	39	3 043.4	8 929

Source: AGRANA 2013–2014 Annual Report

CONSOLIDATION AND PRICE PRESSURES

Following the period of rapid acquisition-driven growth in 2004 to 2006, came a period of consolidation and organic growth. *Agrana* focused on the expansion and modernization of the plants it had acquired around the world, while integrating operations and introducing the *Agrana* brand name across its business unit. Further expansions happened at a more gradual pace, notably with a joint venture in fruit preparation in Egypt in 2010. The Chinese operations were reorganized in 2011/12, when Agrana first took over its local partner and then build an entirely new plant in Dachang.

However, the market environment was challenging. Globally prices for sugar and starch experienced several years of decline. The effect was particularly strong in Europe as a consequence of the liberalization of the EU sugar market. Also, fruit preparations and fruit juices experienced slow growth and competitive pricing. In 2014, *Agrana*'s sales were down about 15 per cent in many segments due to price pressures and recession in some of the countries it was operating in (Table 3). Therefore, by 2015, *Agrana* was under pressure to reconsider its options to enhance both growth and profitability.

Table 3 *Agrana* revenues by division (in € million)

	Sugar	Starch	Fruit	Total
2005–2006	1 040.0 (49.9%)	314.0 (15.1%)	730.6 (35.0%)	2 084.7
2012–2013	1 121.5 (36.6%)	804.3 (26.2%)	1 140.1 (37.2%)	3 065.9
2013–2014	1 022.8 (33.6%)	848.5 (27.9%)	1 172.1 (38.5%)	3 043.4

Source: *AGRANA* Annual Reports, various years.

Sources: Based on media publications and company documents. The following sources were particularly helpful: (1) *Agrana* investor information provided by managing director, Christian Medved, to Professor Mike Peng at the Strategic Management Society Conference, Vienna, October 2006; (2) *Agrana* Company Profile 2007; (3) Sugar Traders Association, www.sugartraders.co.uk/ (accessed May 4, 2007); (5) N. Merret, 2007, Fruit segment drives Agrana growth, *Food Navigator.com Europe,* January 12; (6) N. Merret, 2006, Agrana looks east for competitive EU sugar markets, Confectionery News.com, November 29; (7) C. Blume, N. Strang, & E. Farnstrand, *Sweet Fifteen: The Competition on the EU Sugar Markets,* Swedish Competition Authority Report, December 2002; (8) Agrana, 2014, Annual Report 2013/14; (9) Baader Bank, 2015, Agrana Beteiligungs-AG, investor presentation.

DISCUSSION QUESTIONS

1 From an institution-based view, what opportunities and challenges have been brought by the integration of EU markets in both Western Europe and CEE?

2 Compare how *Danisco* (Chapter 13, Opening Case) and *Agrana* have responded to reforms of the EU sugar market institutions. What are the similarities and differences? Which strategy is more successful in the long run?

3 From a resource-based view, what is behind *Agrana's* impressive growth?

4 From an international perspective, how do you foresee the future international strategy for *Agrana* in view of competitive international markets?

BHARTI AIRTEL ACQUIRES RESOURCES AND COMPANIES

Ajit Nayak
University of Exeter

In June 2010, *Bharti Airtel* acquired *Zain Africa BV* for $10.7 billion. *Zain Africa* was one of the leading mobile telecom companies in Africa, with operations in 18 countries. Sunil Mittal, the charismatic entrepreneur and founder of *Bharti Airtel* stated:

> This agreement is a landmark for global telecom industry…a pioneering step towards South-South cooperation and strengthening of ties between India and Africa. With this acquisition, *Bharti Airtel* will be transformed into a truly global telecom company with operations across 18 countries fulfilling our vision of building a world-class multinational.

This deal came hot on the heels of *Bharti Airtel*'s acquisition of a 70 per cent stake in Bangladesh's *Warid Telecom International*, a subsidiary of UAE's *Dhabi Group*, in January 2010.

Few people in Europe or the US would have heard of these companies. *Bharti Airtel* is India's largest mobile network operator and, with around 300 million customers, it is the fourth-largest in the world by subscription base. Its customer base grew by around 68 per cent every year from 2001 to 2009, reaching 100 million subscribers. As impressive as that growth is, the subscriber base doubled to 200 million between 2009 and 2012, and surpassed 300 million in 2014. The *Zain Africa* and *Warid* deals demonstrate *Bharti Airtel*'s ambition and capability to raise capital globally during a global recession to finance deals. It also signals, as Sunil Mittal stated, *Bharti Airtel*'s 'intent to further expand our operations to international markets where we can implant our unique business model and offer quality and affordable telecom services'. Is the *Bharti Airtel* case evidence of new confidence of emerging economies MNEs as they attempt to become the new kids on the global stage?

Bharti Airtel's growth story is remarkable. Started in 1995 by Sunil Mittal, it has grown to become a major player on the world telecom stage, and now acts as a beacon for Indian firms looking to expand globally. *Bharti Airtel* is much more global than it looks at first glance. The *Zain* and *Warid* deals mean that *Bharti Airtel* now operates in 18 countries. Prior to 2010 it only operated in India, Sri Lanka and the Seychelles. But a closer look reveals the global scope of this firm in terms of its value chain, leadership and mindset.

First, in stark contrast to India's outsourcing destination for call centre services tag, *Bharti Airtel* counter-intuitively outsourced several parts of its value chain, including IT to *IBM* and network equipment to *Nokia*, *Siemens* (now merged) and *Ericsson*. This move is key to *Airtel*'s strategy of disaggregating the value chain; one that it has pioneered in the telecom industry, which has high-cost passive infrastructure. In 2014, *Bharti* divested its tower business in Africa to *Helios Towers* (a company backed by George Soros, Madeleine Albright and Jacob Rothschild) and to *Eaton Towers* and *IHS Towers*, two leading tower business companies in Africa. It also outsourced some of the network operation of the former *Zain* operation to *Huawei* and *Ericsson*. Imagine that: an Indian company outsourcing its activities to Western multinationals!

However, this innovative way of thinking about the telecom business model is central to Airtel's strategy. According to Akhil Gupta, one of the architects of *Bharti*'s strategy, the company followed three key questions in outsourcing parts of the value chain: 'First, who has the better domain knowledge, is it us or somebody else, and forget about core and non-core; second, who can attract better human capital; and third, who has better economies of scale? If the answer to all three was somebody else, then we definitely outsourced.' Irrespective of established norms and practices, *Bharti Airtel* aimed to simplify and innovate in terms of the business model to grow. By outsourcing to major international players, and developing business models that incentivized all parties to improve and grow the mobile network services, *Airtel* created a new low-cost high-growth business model.

Second, *Airtel*'s 'minutes factory model' focuses on increasing subscribers who spend little, compared to the traditional model that focuses on average spend per subscriber. *Airtel* is not one of the leading telecom companies in the world by revenues, but by focusing on increasing its subscriber base it has focused on understanding the world population that is under-served by other telecom companies. The hallmark of entrepreneurs and firms from emerging economies is that they have to improvise and innovate from a low cost base, inferior technology and underdeveloped home markets. By turning all three negatives into opportunities, *Airtel* aimed to rewrite the rules of the game globally.

Third, *Bharti Airtel* has developed significant global presence on its board of directors since 1997. The British telecom company *BT* had a 44 per cent stake in *Bharti* until 1999. Donald Cameron, *BT*'s former Director (New Ventures), joined the *Bharti* board in 1999. Sunil Mittal also invited PM Sinha, President and CEO of *Pepsi*, N Kumar, Vice-Chairman of the *Sanmar Group*, Wong Hung Khim, Group Chairman & CEO of *DelGro* Group of Companies, Singapore and Pulak Prasad, Managing Director, *Warburg Pincus*. In announcing these appointments, the company emphasized the importance of people with global exposure and global mindsets:

> We welcome the new independent directors, who come into *Bharti* with their vast wealth of professional expertise … These corporate leaders will help us to further focus sharply on shareholder value, guide us in ensuring the best of corporate governance and assist us in making *Bharti* a company that is managed by leading edge, world class values, processes and practices.

Arguably, it is the involvement of the private equity firm *Warburg Pincus* that acted as a catalyst for *Airtel*'s global ambitions. As Sunil Mittal recalled: '*Warburg Pincus* let us think big.' They invested US$292 million to finance *Bharti*'s growth, and worked closely with *Airtel*'s management team to shape the strategy. Equally important was the involvement and investment from *SingTel*, Singapore's largest telecom company, which holds around 30 per cent stake in *Bharti Airtel*. And its CEO (Chua Sock Koong) and nominees are represented on the board of directors of *Bharti Airtel*. Gupta recalls the significance of *SingTel*'s involvement:

> We had great relations with *Vivendi, BT* and *Italia Telecom,* but we realized that when the going got tough in their home turf, their first reaction was to get out of Asia. For all of them, Europe came first. But for *SingTel,* Asia comes first. India is its biggest jewel today.

One would be hard pressed to find other MNEs with such an internationally diverse board, let alone an Indian company.

Sunil Mittal may have been inspired by his namesake LN Mittal and the *Mittal Arcelor* deal, or by the *Tata Corus* deal, both in 2006. But this was different. This was an Indian firm going global by looking at strategically prioritizing other emerging economies. Whereas the *Mittal Arcelor* and the *Tata Corus* deals in the steel industry were motivated by acquiring production capacity, strategic assets and technology, and access to western markets, *Bharti Airtel* aimed to expand its successful low-cost 'minutes factory' business model into other emerging economies. The perceived similarities to the Indian markets enabled *Bharti Airtel* to use and build on its existing capabilities. However, as with the *Mittal Arcelor* deal, which became a highly politicized merger, the role and significance of governments in protecting their largest firms and determining cross-border acquisitions was apparent in *Airtel's* African safari. As Manoj Kohli, the then-CEO of the Africa operation recognized:

> The governments of each of the 15 countries were extremely positive, extremely delighted to welcome *Bharti Airtel* . . . They gave us blessings for our agenda . . . The agenda clearly is about rural coverage, it is about affordability, it is about creating more employment at small towns, villages where we will spread our services and of course important CSR initiatives which *Bharti* has taken in India and now we will spread those initiatives in Africa too.

Similarly, the Bangladeshi government was very keen to attract the $300 million investment into its telecom industry through the *Warid* deal. As Manoj Kohli remarked, 'The Government of Bangladesh, the regulator, telecom minister, all senior government officials have supported and encouraged us to complete this deal expeditiously.' The *Zain* acquisition did pose significant hurdles in terms of getting support from the various African countries. For example, the government of Gabon had objected to the deal and the Tanzanian government would be a 40 per cent partner in the operations.

A consistent mark of Mittal's and *Bharti's* entrepreneurial strategy is the disruption of established wisdom and models. The challenge to innovate and create dynamic capabilities to continually reconfigure and transform existing capabilities is now taken up by the new generation of leaders at *Airtel*. Sunil Mittal's son, Kavin Mittal, as head of strategy and new product development at *Bharti SoftBank*, a joint venture between *Bharti Enterprises* and Japan's *SoftBank Corp*, has launched 'Hike' and 'Hoppr' apps, to find new revenue streams for telecom companies. In 2014, *Airtel Africa* appointed Frenchman Christian de Faria as CEO, ushering in a new wave of global talent at the company. Continuing the South-South strategy, *Airtel* signalled its move towards alliances in procuring devices and equipment and in developing 4G technology with *China Mobile*, the world's largest telecom company. By procuring jointly, both companies aim to benefit from lower costs and to share testing and validation practices with vendors and suppliers. Working together on 4G and further innovations in spectrum technologies will also enable the two companies to create standardized ecosystems for mobile technologies and platforms in the future. In particular, *China Mobile* leads the way in developing TDD-LTE mobile technology for 4G services. As Mittal stated, 'This partnership will provide a major platform for development and deployment of 4G and future mobile technology standards as both countries enter a phase of explosive data led growth.'

Sources: This case was written by Ajit Nayak (University of Exeter) based on personal interviews with the company and (1) *Economic Times (India)*, 2010, Zain, Bharti Airtel to ink Africa deal on Tuesday 29 March; (2) N. Karmali, 2010, Sunil Mittal Seals Zain Deal, *Forbes*, March 30; (3) N. Karmali, 2010, Bharti Airtel Dials Bangladesh, *Forbes*, January 12; (4) *Economic Times (India)*, 2010, Airtel will make a strong mark in Bangladesh, January 12; (5) www.airtel.in; (6) www.bharti.com (both accessed January-April 2015); (7) *Business Standard (India)*, 2014, Airtel sells 3500 towers to Eaton in Africa, September 9; (8) A.S. Mankotia, 2015, Bharti Airtel enters into a partnership with China Mobile to develop 4G technology, buy devices & equipment, *Economic Times (India)*, March 4.

DISCUSSION QUESTIONS

1 From a resource-based view, what are *Bharti Airtel's* main resources? How were these resources built, and how do they shape its ongoing path of growth?

2 From an institution-based view, how are the challenges of entering emerging economies such as Bangladesh and Africa different from entry in West European economies?

3 Compare *Bharti Airtel's* approach to internationalization with that of European MNEs. To what extent is *Bharti Airtel's* model unique to emerging economy MNEs?

4 What are the implications of the rise of emerging economy MNEs such as *Bharti Airtel* for globalization?

ENHANCING UK EXPORT COMPETITIVENESS

Mike W Peng
University of Texas at Dallas

Klaus E Meyer
CEIBS

The UK has over the past decades experienced persistent deficits on its trade balance. While service industries, in particular the financial sector, regularly generated a surplus, the manufacturing sector has recorded persistent deficits. The oil and gas sector used to record surpluses in the 1990s, but with depletion of North Sea oil reserves, even this sector recorded a deficit. The sharp depreciation of the pound at the onset of the financial crisis in 2008 helped the slide, but was insufficient to trigger a turnaround.

In view of this situation, the UK government launched a major consultation on how to strengthen the UK manufacturing sector. Among other experts, the authors of this textbook have been asked to share their views. Below is an abbreviated version of the recommendations delivered in our report early 2013. The full 55-page report is available at www.bis.gov.uk/foresight. Following the framework of this textbook, we have derived our first three recommendations (1–3) from a resource-based view, and our next six recommendations (4–9) – the bulk of our advice – primarily from the institution-based view.

This case is an abbreviated excerpt from a consulting report commissioned by the UK Government Office for Science as part of the two-year (2011–2013) Foresight Project 'The Future of Manufacturing'. The report was published as M.W. Peng & K.E. Meyer, 2013, Winning the future markets for UK manufacturing output, Future of Manufacturing Project Evidence Paper 25, London: Foresight, Government Office for Science. It is in the public domain at www.bis.gov.uk/foresight. The views expressed are those of the authors and do not represent the policy of any government or organization. Reprinted with permission. © Crown copyright.

Figure 1 UK balance of trade in goods and services (in £ billion)

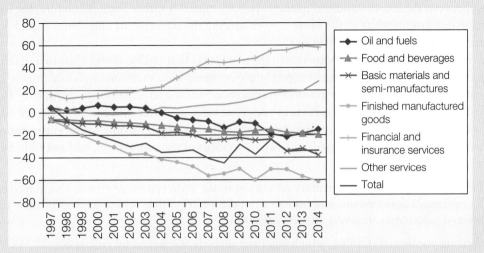

Source: Authors' creation using data from Office of National Statistics (www.ons.gov.uk).

NINE RECOMMENDATIONS FOR GOVERNMENT POLICYMAKERS

1: Support pre-competitive manufacturing capabilities and future technology platforms

The UK government, like all EU governments, is restricted in the ability to provide direct subsidies to firms. In global competition, this may place UK (and EU) firms at a disadvantage relative to their rivals in the US and Asia, which can benefit from more direct government support. However, there are ways for the UK government to be more active. For example, the Technology Strategy Board (2012) announced its funding of at least £50 million a year to support pre-competitive manufacturing capabilities and future technology platforms. Such much-needed investments will speed up the process for successful commercialization, and help firms jump through the hurdles associated with the 'valley of death' (good ideas flame out before emerging technologies become competitively and commercially successful).

2: Push firms to reach for the high end and do not support competition on low cost for the sake of jobs

Bucking the trend that low-cost manufacturing jobs are migrating to low-cost countries is neither advisable nor realistic. The UK government should encourage firms to reach for the high end, which thrives on high productivity. Focusing on low cost may generate short-run benefits, but will in the long run result in severe stagnation of manufacturing productivity. Thus the UK should steer away from attempts to compete on lower cost – for example, through policy measures that lower labour cost and lengthen permissible work time. Such policies may encourage manufacturing in sectors where the UK would be competing with countries that have much lower per capita income (such as Eastern Europe or East Asia). In the medium term, the UK would be squeezed out of this market segment. In other words, attempts to build such low-cost sectors (such as final assembly of low-end electronics or cars) may generate job growth in the short run, but are not sustainable in the long run – unless the UK is willing to accept a fall in average incomes to the level of, say, Poland or Romania.

3: Strengthen human capital to enable advanced manufacturing

While hardly an original recommendation, this point must be emphasized: UK manufacturing will not (re) gain world-class competitiveness in the absence of high-level human capital. UK firms' endeavours to build high-end, high-productivity-based capabilities are essentially efforts to engage in human capital-intensive manufacturing. Effective government support can help to build human resources that enable such advanced manufacturing. This leads to two ideas. First, the UK has leading-edge universities and technology clusters, yet the gap between the top end and the 'average' human capital is rather large. Therefore, the UK ought to foster its elite institutions while at the same time enhancing the diffusion of knowledge and skills from the elite institutions to the second and third tier.

Second, the UK needs to build capabilities in the *workforce* that enable world-class manufacturing. This would entail investing heavily in human capital development. Such investment should in part come from the government. This is because the positive spillovers of skills and capabilities (especially from low to medium levels) from productive individuals to society at large are substantive. Essentially we advocate the raising of skills beyond the elite institutions, because sustaining a high income for an entire nation requires high performance capabilities possessed by a broad segment of the population, and not only by the elites. Specific priorities can be:

- Providing more resources for primary education in the state system to enable children to enter a path of personal development and human capital formation that is independent of their parents' ability and willingness to invest in their education.

- Prioritizing vocational training, which has been severely weakened by past policies. One stream of action may extend initiatives to re-introduce vocational training through apprenticeships, which requires multi-year courses in collaboration between industry and educational institutions.

4: Remove uncertainty by clarifying the UK's commitment to stay within the EU

As rules of the game, institutions serve to reduce uncertainty. Managers hate uncertainty, especially when it comes to long-term commitments such as constructing a new manufacturing plant. Despite the EU's problems, the UK's periodic threats to leave the EU – such as Prime Minister David Cameron's speech in January 2013 (while we were in the middle of doing this research) – heighten uncertainty and undermine UK trade and investment. In view of the large and growing importance of regional integration in supply chains and of the fact that the EU accounts for more than 50 per cent of UK exports, an exit of the UK from full EU integration would be *disastrous* for much of UK manufacturing. Given that emerging economies only collectively purchase less than 8 per cent of UK exports, the loss of exports to the EU will not be compensated by the additional exports to emerging economies.

Uncertainty over the status of the UK's membership in the EU – and hence the specific rules applying to trade between the UK and other EU countries – is in particular likely to depress inward FDI, especially manufacturing investment by non-EU firms in regional platform investment. Historically, the UK has been quite successful in attracting investors looking for a base to serve EU markets – *Toyota*, *Nissan* and *Honda* come to mind. But such investment in particular will be on hold or go elsewhere if the uncertainty about the future status is not removed. Moreover, participation in regional value chains (and hence intra-regional trades in components) enables benefiting from exports of downstream products eventually destined for countries outside the EU. Given the relatively slow growth in the EU, future marginal increases of benefits for the UK to stay within the EU may be less than what they have been in the past. However, we see no reason to put at risk the existing benefits, which are very substantial (i.e. over half of UK exports).

5: Enhance certainty by negotiating more free trade agreements (FTAs)

Firms from FTA member countries typically increase their trade and investment activities due to the tremendous certainty brought by FTAs. The EU currently has FTAs with 28 countries: Albania, Algeria, Andorra, Bosnia and Herzegovina, Chile, Colombia, Croatia, Egypt, Faroe Islands, Iceland, Israel, Jordan, Lebanon, Liechtenstein, Macedonia, Mexico, Montenegro, Morocco, Norway, Palestinian Authority, Peru, San Marino, Serbia, South Africa, South Korea, Switzerland, Tunisia and Turkey. The EU recently concluded negotiations with Singapore, and is also currently negotiating with three individual countries (India, Japan and Russia) and three regional entities (Association of South Eastern Asian Nations [ASEAN], Gulf Cooperation Council [GCC] and Mercosur).

Firms clearly prefer multilateral agreements to bilateral FTAs. Bilateral FTAs tend to create different rules applying to different pairs of export/import countries, which greatly increase the bureaucracy that exporters and importers have to deal with and reduce the scope for scale economies. Therefore, we prefer a multilateral FTA between the EU and ASEAN to a bilateral FTA, for example, between the UK and Singapore. Thus we recommend that the UK advocate more EU efforts to negotiate the following FTAs, a transatlantic FTA with the United States and Canada, an FTA with the Australia-New Zealand Closer Economic Relations Trade Agreement and, in the long run, with China.

6: Create a tax regime that is competitive, stable and fair

Global competition is also about tax competition. While the UK corporate tax rate of 28 per cent appears to be relatively pro-business, the tax regime has recently given a decidedly *mixed* message to UK firms. Legislation designed to encourage R&D spending in the UK was followed by cutbacks in tax deductions for capital expenditure (PwC, 2009: 33). Some of the UK's competitors have aggressively used favourable tax as a means to lure investment and jobs. For example, Ireland only levied 10 per cent corporate income tax on manufacturing income between the 1980s and 2002 and 12.5 per cent since 2002, thus attracting many investors to locate in Ireland. In addition, new EU members Hungary and Bulgaria have aggressively reduced their corporate income rates to 16 per cent and 10 per cent, respectively.

A tax system will, however, only be stable if it is generally accepted by the population (i.e. the electorate in a democracy) to be fair. Some corporate taxation systems *de facto* do not tax firms at the location where the profit is generated, but (by default or through consciously created loopholes) allow firms to shift profits from high tax locations to low tax locations through practices such as transfer pricing and excessively high licensing fees. This is likely to undermine the legitimacy of an international system of tax competition. In other words, if nations compete on taxes, there also need to be commonly agreed rules (i.e. institutions) by which this competition takes place. Perhaps surprising for most UK observers, the UK may actually benefit from more integration in the EU on this matter because it would prevent incidences such as *Google* and *Starbucks* paying virtually no tax in the UK.

7: Attract more inward FDI and promote more outward FDI

Given that foreign multinationals generate approximately half of UK manufacturing exports, it seems imperative that the UK continues to attract inward FDI in order to increase exports. The most important policies to this end are the same that also promote domestic investment in manufacturing: free trade within the region and valuable, rare and hard-to-imitate resources that foreign investors can tap into.

Exports are generated by a combination of 'push' and 'pull' effects. While UK-based firms (including UK-based foreign multinationals) 'push' exports, UK multinationals – via outward FDI abroad – 'pull' UK exports into their host economies, often in the form of high-end products, components and service exports. Given that the UK has the second-largest stock of outward FDI, it seems natural that efforts be strengthened to promote more outward FDI, especially into downstream and service activities. Incorporating the protection of FDI into FTAs (fostering a formal institution) and promoting the views of businesses 'out in the world' as ambassadors and supporters of the British economy (creating an informal institution) are likely to help.

8: Facilitate the mobility of highly qualified individuals into and out of the UK

Mobility of people is an essential precondition for successful international trade, especially in the high end of both manufacturing and services. The UK benefits from being a more multicultural society than most of its EU peers. This attraction enables many knowledge-based, creative industry sectors to thrive, and facilitates the coordination of global operations out of the UK. In this regard, the UK government policy has been confusing to say the least. On the one hand, Deputy Prime Minister Nick Clegg (2013) wrote in *The Economist*: 'We will continue to be one of the most open economies on the planet, welcoming trade and investment and welcoming talented individuals who wish to make a contribution to Britain.' On the other hand, shrinking immigration quotas, more visa application procedures, abstention from Schengen area free-travel arrangements, and increased requirements in citizenship tests all send a very strong, disconcerting message that – in a complete reversal of UK policies over the past century or more – the UK no longer welcomes skilled immigrants or temporary workers. In summary, if the UK is serious about promoting export competitiveness, it will have to be serious about making it less cumbersome for highly qualified individuals to move into and out of the UK.

9: Lead efforts to lift regulatory trade barriers such as the EU arms embargo on China

Removing regulatory trade barriers can obviously facilitate more UK exports and generate more jobs. Commanding a 6 per cent world share, aerospace and defence represent one of the UK's most globally competitive manufacturing industries. China has expressed an interest in importing arms from the UK. But the UK has declined, because of an institution-based trade barrier: the EU arms embargo on China since 1989 due to the Tiananmen Square incident.

From a resource-based perspective, the defence sector – and the aerospace industry in particular – is an area where the UK has cutting-edge capabilities that it can exploit, but needs to continuously renew to remain globally competitive at the high end. From an institution-based view, already in 2004, the EU planned to lift the embargo by 2005. But intense US pressures forced the EU to abandon the plan. In 2009, UK Business Secretary Peter Mandelson stated that the ban should be phased out. China is an officially recognized Strategic Partner of the EU. Not surprisingly, China has called the ban 'absurd, puzzling and political discrimination' against a Strategic Partner.

CONCLUSION*

In global competition, no advantage is forever. As the first industrial nation, the UK enjoyed significant first-mover advantage. In 1900, with 2.2 per cent of the world's population it generated 15 per cent of exports. But it is not realistic to sustain this level of pre-eminent performance in the face of increasingly strong global competition. However, it is important to note that the UK is still punching *above* its weight: with 0.9 per cent of the world's population, it currently generates approximately 3.3 per cent of the world's exports – including 6.6 per cent of service exports and 2.6 per cent of goods exports.

What does the future hold for UK manufacturing exports? Lacking crystal balls, we have to gain a deeper understanding of the past if we endeavour to engage in the perilous exercise of predicting the future. The data that we have analyzed suggest that the UK's relative decline in manufacturing appears to have accelerated in the last decade, not only *vis-à-vis* emerging economies, but also relative to European peers. In the 1980s and 1990s, there was a widespread belief in the UK that service growth would more than compensate for the relative loss of manufacturing capabilities. Today, in part as a consequence of policies launched two or three decades ago, the UK is indeed a global leader in many service sectors with a service trade surplus. The problem, however, is that the corresponding deficit in the trade of goods is so large and growing that it cannot be compensated by the success of service exports. In the future, reviving and strengthening UK manufacturing seems to be a must.

In conclusion, our review suggests that UK manufacturing firms have good opportunities to compete in both old and new segments within 'high-end' industries, if they can create and occupy *deep niches* for themselves. To this end, we recommend focusing policy efforts on developing world-class competitiveness of both individuals and firms (and hence of the nation), and to enhance an open and pro-competition trade and investment environment. From the resource-based and institution-based views, the key to winning the future markets for UK manufacturing exports lies in (1) UK firms' possession of valuable, rare and hard-to-imitate resources and capabilities that can translate into products appreciated by customers, and (2) the UK government's resolve and courage to embrace policy challenges that will ultimately make the nation more competitive and prosperous.

*This is the conclusion to the entire 55-page report, not just the recommendations above.

DISCUSSION QUESTIONS

1 From a resource-based view, how can UK firms and their managers enhance their export competitiveness?

2 From an institution-based view, how can the UK government help British firms to enhance export competitiveness? Drawing from the list of recommendations, what specific actions do you recommend to undertake in the short run, medium run, and long run?

3 Recommendation 9 on military exports triggered considerable debate between the co-authors. How should government policy makers balance economic interests and geo-political considerations?

CANADA AND THE EU NEGOTIATE CETA

Klaus Meyer
CEIBS

In September 2014, after five years of negotiations, Canadian Prime Minister Stephen Harper and European Commission President José Manuel Barroso signed a deal that was expected to transform business relationships between Europe and Canada. The deal is more comprehensive than other free trade treaties, not only in the extent of tariff reductions, but in terms of the depth of regulatory institutions that should allow businesses from either side of the Atlantic to compete on equal footing on the other side. Canada and the EU already trade €75 billion worth of goods and services each year, making EU the second-largest partner for Canada in terms of both exports and import, after the USA. The ambition of the 1500-page-long Canada-EU comprehensive economic and trade agreement (CETA) was to grow bilateral trade by 23 per cent. The ratification was expected to take two years, because it required the support of Canadian provinces and EU member states.

Businesses were pleading for a rapid ratification, eager to capitalize on new market opportunities. Many Canadian businesses saw the CETA as a golden opportunity to reduce their dependence on the USA as export market. The CETA would integrate Canada with one of the largest economies with very favourable trade conditions. At the same time, it would facilitate European investment in Canada, and develop Canada as a platform to serve the US market. Meanwhile, citizens on both sides of the Atlantic would benefit from more choice of imported goods on their supermarket shelves, and lower prices due to intensified competition.

AMBITIONS

The main objectives of the agreement were (1) the removal of tariffs and quotas, (2) the reduction of non-tariff barriers (NTBs), (3) new opportunities for individuals, (4) protection of foreign direct investors, and (5) creating effective investor-state dispute settlement (SSDS) processes (Table 1).

Table 1 Aspired benefits of the CETA

Aspired benefits	Examples
• Remove import tariffs and quotas	• 98 per cent of tariff lines are set to zero per cent from day one • Most quotas are substantially raised or eliminated
• Align regulatory regimes to remove non-tariff barriers	• EU and Canada open public sector procurement to firms from the partner economy • Patent and copyright rules are better aligned • Consultation processes when regulatory changes are being prepared
• Make it easier for individuals to work in the other economy	• Framework for mutual recognition of professional qualifications • Temporary work permits for international businesses persons
• Create a level playing field for foreign direct investors	• Commitments to fair, equal, and non-discriminatory treatment of foreign businesses
• Create effective conflict resolution mechanism	• ISDS process with independent tribunals and generally open hearings

Sources: (1) Government of Canada, no date, 'Technical Summary of Final Negotiated Outcomes', actionplan.gc.ca/ceta, (downloaded March 2015); (2) DG Trade, 2014, Comprehensive Trade and Economic Agreement (CETA), updated December 2014 ec.europa.eu/trade/policy/in-focus/ceta/ (accessed March 2015).

First, the main component of the agreement is the abolishment of tariffs and quotas, with a very limited number of exceptions. Most duties will be eliminated immediately, with a transition of seven years for some products. For industrial goods, on the day that the contract comes into force, the EU will set 99.3 per cent of tariffs lines to zero, while Canada will set 99.6 per cent of tariff lines to zero. The remainder, which mainly concerns the automotive sector, will be set to zero within the next seven years. This elimination of tariffs on industrial goods will save European exporters €470 million, according to EU estimates. At the same time, most quotas are raised or eliminated. For example, the Canadian car manufacturers will be able to export 100 000 vehicles without payment of duty to Europe, which is far higher than then the previous limit of 8000 vehicles.

For agriculture fisheries and forestry products the treaty allows more exemptions. On the first day, Canada will set 92 per cent of its agricultural tariff lines to zero, and eliminate all its seafood tariffs. The EU will set 93.5 per cent of agricultural tariffs lines to zero, eliminating for example, the 8 per cent tariff rate on Canadian maple syrup. A particular concern for Canadians was EU tariffs for fresh and frozen seafood, of which 95.5 per cent will be set to zero on day one. Canadian cattle farmers, among many other businesses, were getting ready for new opportunities, preparing to adjust their breeding practices and marketing strategies to the new consumers. Xavier Poncin, an industry spokesperson commented:

The big beef thing in Europe, of course, is to have no hormones, so it will be a good challenge for some Canadian farmers to change the way they do things. ... It's a big market, so let's go for it.

Second, the treaty commits both sides to remove non-tariff barriers, and thus make certain changes to their existing rules of the game. For example, EU companies will be allowed to bid for public contracts at all levels of government in Canada, and the Canadian government will set up a single electronic procurement website to facilitate this process. Canada also agreed to extend patent protection of pharmaceuticals from 20 years to 22 years to align it closer to the rules in the EU. This would benefit European pharmaceutical companies marketing their drugs in Canada. Alcoholic beverages are another tricky area for Canada, because alcohol can only be sold through special province-licensed shops, with a number of exceptions of shops selling only Canadian wines. With the CETA, in principle no provincial shop may discriminate between Canadian and European wines. Yet thanks to active industry lobbying, there are exemptions. Ontario and British Columbia may operate up to 292 and 60 shops respectively that sell Canadian wines exclusively.

Third, the treaty aims to make it easier for EU and Canadian citizens to work in each other's territory. For this purpose, the treaty establishes processes for the mutual recognition of professional qualifications, which is expected to create more job opportunities. In consequence, skilled professionals in Canada can more easily go to European countries to work; for example, architects in Montreal may move to Paris for work. Moreover, temporary entry of businesspeople will be made easier, thus enabling businesses to send employees abroad, for example to implement services delivery or partake in the management of subsidiaries.

Fourth, the treaty establishes the principle of equal treatment between domestic firms and those owned by foreign investors from the partner economy. Thus, except for very specific exceptions named in the treaty, legislation and government procedures are not allowed to discriminate between Canadian and EU businesses. Canada and the EU also commit that they will not impose new restrictions on foreign shareholdings. These regulations are especially important for service sectors, such as financial services, which contribute an increasing part of international trade. Moreover, future liberalizations are locked in, meaning that once a sector is privatized, such liberalization becomes part of the treaty. This 'ratchet mechanism' ensures that foreign investors in liberalized service sectors are protected from re-nationalization.

Fifth, conflicts between foreign investors and host country governments at national and local levels are referred to investors-state dispute settlement (ISDS) tribunals for arbitrage. These tribunals shall protect foreign investors from discrimination in the form of, for example, restrictions on foreign shareholdings, quotas on employee numbers, or forcing foreign firms out by limiting the number of firms that can operate in a given sector (see Chapter 9, In Focus 9.4).

CITIZENS' CONCERNS

While the goal of free trade receives strong support, there have also been plenty of critical voices. The concerns arise in five areas (Table 2): (1) losers from free trade, (2) change in existing regulatory institutions, (3) foreigners may take locals' jobs, (4) commitments that may restrict government from introducing new rules in the future, and (5) the ISDS process is unsatisfactory in many ways.

First, when there is free trade, those who historically benefited from protection may lose out to more competitive foreign rivals. For example, Canadian cheese producers were concerned that free trade may damage their livelihood, as the colder climate of Canada limits their ability to compete with Dutch or French cheese producers. The treaty opens Canadian cheese markets, but also stipulates a quota limiting EU cheese product imports to 17 000 tons. Nevertheless, cheese manufacturers lobbied the Canadian government for financial compensation. Frédéric Kaplan, the head of economic affairs at the French embassy in Canada, commented:

> There is good Canadian cheese and these guys don't export to Europe. They are crying for compensation, saying the bad Europeans are coming in, and I say to them, 'Ask for compensation to get (some) help to support selling their cheese in the EU.'

Similarly, the Ontario wine industry was concerned about the new competition of French and Spanish wines, but could not secure quotas. On the European side, quotas limit the import of Canadian beef

Table 2   Concerns about the CETA

Issue	Canadian example	European example
Removal of tariffs may cost jobs in previously protected industries	• Cheese and wine producers	• Beef and pork farmers
Alignment of regulatory regimes may lead to changes that citizens don't want	• Health sector costs increase due to longer patents for pharmaceuticals • Municipalities lose ability to support local employment through their procurement processes	• Need for 'scientific proof' may make it difficult to defend certain food quality standards based on ethical or human health considerations
Individuals working in the other economy may take locals' jobs	—	—
The protection of the rights of foreign investors may create obstacles to modernizing the regulatory system when required	• Privatization of services	• Health and environmental standards legislation
The conflict resolution mechanism lacks judicial transparency and democratic legitimacy	• Moratorium on fracking in Quebec	• Phasing out of nuclear power in Germany

and pork as well as automobiles, albeit new quotas are much higher than before. Since most decision-makers believe in the principle of free trade because of its beneficial effects for consumers – greater variety and lower prices – these arguments did not lead to fundamental objections. Yet some interest groups made forceful interventions: Newfoundland province suspended its participation in the ratification process because it felt the conditions attached to the compensation fund for its potentially negatively impacted fishery industry were too stringent.

Second, the required changes in the regulatory regime have negative side effects on some groups. For example, the extension of patent protection for pharmaceuticals by two years would also increase the costs of drugs for the Canadian public health care system because the introduction of generic drugs will be delayed. Canadian Premier Harper promised the provinces (who in Canada are in charge of health care) that the health-care system would be compensated by the national government for any extra expenses.

Also, Canada's commitment to opening all its public sector procurement is controversial because previously it was normal practice for provincial or local authorities to discriminate in favour of local companies, or require a certain number of local people to be employed. Such discrimination has been made illegal in Europe in the context of the common market legislation in the early 1990s. Now, some local authorities are concerned that they no longer can secure that the local community benefits from government contracts. In fact, Europeans may have better access to some provincial or municipal contracts than firms from other Canadian provinces. This fuelled a debate in Canada on 'free trade begins at home', suggesting that first barriers to inter-province trade should be eliminated before such barriers *vis-à-vis* European competitors are removed.

In Europe, environmental groups and consumer health advocates were concerned that the treaty would indirectly open doors for food products previously banned in Europe for ethical or health reasons. In particular, genetically modified foods, hormone treated beef and certain processes for handling meat in slaughterhouses are outlawed in the EU, but common practice in North America. Especially US-based lobby groups have been pushing hard to ease the access for these types of foods; for example, the US Department of Agriculture and the Foreign Agricultural Service complained about 'long delays in reviews of biotech products [that] create barriers to US exports of grain and oil seeds products'. In contrast, many leading European politicians and NGOs believe that these products, known in Europe as genetically modified foods, should never ever be allowed in – or if they are permitted they should be clearly labelled as such. Labelling requirements, however, are not acceptable to US soybean producers either, because it would require extensive tracing of origins to be able to declare processed foods as 'GMO free'.

The treaty states a commitment to protect the environment and health, while also emphasizing the promotion of efficient science-based processes in the context of 'biotechnology products' (that's 'genetically modified foods' to most people). The concern by NGOs is firstly that European bureaucrats may go easy on regulations under pressure from lobbying US multinationals, that the requirement for scientific evidence will enable large US-based multinationals to challenge certain EU regulations in court whenever scientific evidence is not entirely conclusive (which it rarely is). Since US firms operate in Canada under NAFTA and may thus serve Europe through a Canadian affiliate, this issue also affects the EU-Canada CETA.

Third, free movement of people always raises concerns about 'too much' immigration is some parts of the local populations. In fact, the CETA set limits for the entry permits to be issued under this scheme. Hence the free movement of people has not become an issue in the public debates on CETA.

Fourth, what happens if some government in the future wants to change the rules? For example, new evidence is likely to emerge that some substance is damaging to the environment or human health and governments may want to introduce restrictions in its use. Can such restrictions also be imposed on foreign investors, or do they attain rights to do their business unhindered? For example, could the EU introduce rules that restrict or tax fuel extracted from oil sands, which is big business in Alberta, but viewed as environmentally harmful by many outside of Alberta? In the WTO, the critical criterion is whether scientific evidence exists to justify the restriction. Yet environmental or consumer advocacy groups may lobby for restrictions ahead of evidence becoming conclusive. Thus parliaments may introduce new regulation following the precautionary principle; and public opinion regarding such new legislation (and hence parliamentary majorities) is likely to move at different speeds in different countries. If such regulation affects foreign investors, however, this may affect the profitability of their business. Would foreign investors then have to be compensated? Several legal experts thus raised concerns that CETA may restrict future governments' ability to regulate markets.

Similar concerns were raised by trade unions. For example, Canadian public sector union NUPGE raised concerns that once local authorities decide to privatize a service such as water treatment they (or their successors, after an election) will not be able to revert back to public service because the foreign service provider might see that as an infringement of their rights, and hence to take the council to international arbitrage for expropriating its rights. British unions raised similar concerns regarding the British National Health Service. The bigger issue is, when do treaty commitments become a constraint on national sovereignty and the basic principle of democracy that citizens have the right to determine – through established procedures – the principles by which they want to live?

Fifth, the commitment to ISDS tribunals was also challenged on several grounds. On the one hand, fundamental questions were asked about whether ISDS tribunals were consistent with the general principles of law enforcement, including equity before the law and the independence of judges. Thus the practices of ISDS, which had previously not received much attention, were discussed in the wider public. Canadians thus learned about *Lone Pine*'s compensation claim over the fracking moratorium in the St Lawrence River, while Germans got heated up over *Vattenfall*'s compensation for the nuclear phase-out imposed by the German government (Chapter 9, In Focus 9.5).

Moreover, critics suggested that the mandate for ISDS in the treaty were either too broad, or too ambiguous. For example, the draft of CETA stated that:

A Tribunal may take into account . . . whether a Party (government) created a legitimate expectation . . . upon which the investor relied in deciding to make or maintain an investment.

The interpretation of what constituted a 'legitimate expectation', especially in the context of politicians that may be replaced in democratic elections, is unclear. Vague statements are bound to create extensive legal wrangling of which the main winners are the lawyers.

Thus proposals were discussed to replace the private tribunals with an international court system that more closely resembles the public court systems in nation states, with greater transparency, avenues for appeal – and losers bearing the costs of a tribunal (as is common in European legal practice, but not North America). Opponents of this idea suggested that this would unduly delay the creation of CETA.

Business Associations such as the BDI in Germany disagreed with concerned citizens groups and political parties, and lobbied hard for incorporation of ISDS tribunals in CETA. German companies find North American courts, especially US courts, very difficult and costly to navigate, and therefore fear the costs of legal processes when they do business in North America. They expected ISDS tribunals to help them establish a more level playing field.

In Europe, the debate over CETA ratification took place while negotiations with the USA over a similar treaty, known as TTIP, progressed. These negotiations raised similar issues, but of greater complexity due to even larger variations in industry regulation and legal systems between the EU and the USA. EU Trade Commissioner Karel de Gucht described the CETA as 'template' for the ongoing negotiations with the USA over TTIP. If CETA was agreed, it would pave the way for free trade and investment not just between the EU and Canada but also with the USA.

Sources: (1) WTO, 2014, Country Profile Canada, www.wto.org; (2) The Economist, 2013, 'Atlantic Record' and 'Canada doesn't get any sexier than this', October 26; (3) Government of Canada, 2013, Technical Summary of Final Negotiated Outcomes', actionplan.gc.ca/ceta (downloaded March 2015) (p. 5); (4) European Commission Directorate-General for Trade ('DG Trade'), 2014, Comprehensive Trade and Economic Agreement (CETA), updated December 2014 ec.europa.eu/trade/policy/in-focus/ceta/ (accessed March 2015); (5) C. Ley, 2015, The view from Europe on free trade with Canada, Canadian Cattlemen, January 2; (6) DG Trade, 2014, as above; W. Robson & D. Schwanen, 2014, Agreement with Europe a major step forward for Canada, National Post, September 25; (7) B. Fox, 2014, What the leaked EU-Canada trade paper means for TTIP, EU Observer, August 18; (8) T. Fitz, 2015, Analyse und Bewertung des EU-Kanada Freihandelsabkommens CETA, study , Hans-Böckler-Foundation (51 pages); (9) L. Berthiaume, 2013, Here's who wins and loses in the Canada-EU trade deal, National Post, October 18; (10) T. Talaga, 2014, French try to ease Canadian fears over free trade deal, The Star, December 3; (11) S. Bailey, 2015, Newfoundland and Labrador says it won't participate in ongoing trade talks, Globe and Mail, January 19; (12) E. Reguly, 2015, Trade minister firm on buy America, Newfoundland at CETA talks, Globe and Mail, January 21; (13) A. Raj, 2012, Provinces failing to defend themselves in Canada-EU free trade negotiations, says lawyer, Huffington Post, September 7. A. Rexer, 2014, Leaked CETA treat: major blow to buy local, The Tyee, August 14; (14) B. McKenna, 2014, Free trade begins at home, Globe and Mail, August 31; (15) S. Lunn, 2014, Premiers to talk trade at annual summer meeting in Charlottetown, CBC News, August 28; (16) C. Hecking 2014, Freihandelsabkommen hebelt deutsche Gen-Politik aus, Der Spiegel, November 14; (17) N. Kwasniewski, 2015, Mit TTIP kommt Gentechnik in die Supermärkte, Der Spiegel, January 12; (18) F. Harvey, 2014, EU under pressure to allow GM food imports from US and Canada, The Guardian, September 5; (19) C. Crouch, 2015, Democracy at a TTIP'ing point, Juncture 21(3), www.ippr.org; (20) M. Lessard, 2014, Free trade agreement attack democracy and human rights, Huffington Post, August 25; (21) P. Inman & L. Elliott, 2015, TTIP under pressure from protesters as Brussels promises extra safeguards, The Guardian, February 19; (22) J. Gray, 2012, Quebec's St. Lawrence fracking ban challenged under NAFTA, Globe and Mail, November 22; (23) M. Balser & M. Bauchmüller, 2014, Vattenfall fordert Milliarden Euro Schadenersatz, Süddeutsche Zeiting, October 15; (24) D. Sturn, 2015, Wie Gabriel die Angst vor dem Freihandel bekäpft, Die Welt, February 23; (25) P. Pinzler, 2015, Kann er nicht oder will er nicht, Die Zeit, January 24; (26) Legal Tribune, 2015, Investitionsgerichtshof als Ausweg? February 25; (27) Handelsblatt, 2014, Gabriels Freihandels-Dilemma, September 29.

DISCUSSION QUESTIONS

1 How will CEFTA change the institutions governing international trade between Canada and the EU?'

2 How is the CEFTA likely to impact on international trade between EU and Canada?

3 Why are some interest groups opposed to liberalizing trade through CEFTA?

4 If you were a member of the European Parliament, would you vote for or against the treaty?

Disclaimer: *This case has been prepared solely for classroom discussion and is not meant as a basis for business decisions. In preparing this case, the author had to assume sources to be accurate. Therefore representation may be imprecise and the final wording of the treaty is likely to be adjusted as it goes through the legislative process. Research assistance by Ethan Huang and fruitful discussions with Sui Sui (Ryerson University) are gratefully acknowledged.*

GERMAN CHAMBER OF COMMERCE DEVELOPS SOCIAL RESPONSIBILITY IN CHINA

Klaus Meyer
CEIBS

German companies have been operating in the Greater Shanghai area since 1984 when *Volkswagen* (*VW*) established the first major foreign joint venture in the area. *VW* was soon followed by numerous suppliers, and over the next 30 years, German companies became an integral part of the industrial infrastructure of the region. This time represented a period of rapid economic growth and social change in China, and consequently also changing relations between foreign-owned companies and the host society. By the 2010s, young people started to look for more than a salary when choosing their job; social organizations were highlighting poor practices, and national and local governments put pressures on firms to raise their standards for labour, environment and transparency. Relevant legislation had been in place for many years, and gradually law enforcement was tightened.

German companies operating in China were generally enjoying high respect on account of their leading technology, long-term commitments in China, and attractive employment and career prospects. However, even long-term residents in China felt that they were not really part of the society. For example, Rolf Köhler, who for over two decades headed various *Freudenberg* businesses from Shanghai, China, said:

> Even though China has become a very important market, we Germans often feel we're outsiders in this country. Although ties in the economic and political sphere are getting closer, many companies still find it astonishingly difficult to become deeply rooted here. (Source 3, page 56)

In view of the evolving challenges in Chinese society, and the wish to grow deeper roots in the society, the German Chamber of Commerce (GCC) launched an initiative entitled 'China – more than a market'. Its starting point was the belief that German traditions such as the tradition of the 'honest merchant' entail many values and practices that provide a solid foundation to develop what is popularly known as corporate social responsibility (CSR). Large companies such as *VW* or *Bosch* often had well-developed programmes of engagement with their diverse sets of stakeholders. However, many mid-size companies had ad hoc initiatives, but lacked resources for a comprehensive approach to CSR in China. They were looking for new ideas to enhance their social engagement, both as individual companies and as a community of German-owned companies.

In discussing their social responsibilities, German firms in China were concerned in particular with three sets of stakeholders (in addition to customers and suppliers). First on their mind were their local employees, along with the employees' families and the communities in which they lived. The recruitment and retention of skilled employees had become a major challenge for businesses in China, as young people in particular were quick to change jobs when offered a better salary or financial incentives. Thus offering employees more than a job and a salary was seen as essential to enhance the identification of employees with the company, and hence employee loyalty.

Second, an important stakeholder in all social activities was the Chinese government as represented by its various local entities. Principally, social policy was a responsibility of government in China, and business initiatives had to complement rather than compete with the official policy. Otherwise, unwelcome bureaucratic obstacles might arise. Bernd Reitmeier, an entrepreneur operating a business incubator in Kunshan, near Shanghai, describes the situation:

> Good government relations are essential for any foreign company in China, but in our case particularly so, since the Kunshan government sponsors our project by providing land and factory buildings. Besides bringing investment and jobs to the city, our aim is also to support the local government by promoting higher standards, qualifying further workers and becoming a platform for further personal development with regular training offers for surrounding companies. (Source 3, page 32)

The relationship between businesses and social activities in China had shifted at the time of the Sichuan earthquake in 2008. To cope with the consequences of the disaster, the Chinese government invited companies–local and foreign ones – to contribute to its efforts by making donations to various initiatives, either in the form of cash or items in need – from tents to medical equipment. Since that time, companies had become involved in numerous initiatives such as poverty relief, environmental clean up, or education in rural areas.

Third, corporate headquarters are an important stakeholder because ultimately they have to be convinced to allocate resources to social causes. Many mid-sized German companies were very active in their local communities in their home base, especially those originating from smaller towns where they are a major employer. Yet from the perspective of corporate boards in Germany, stakeholders in China were not a primary concern, and they also lacked deep understanding what types of initiatives would be appreciated in China.

Many member firms of the GCC supported social initiatives in China, though not communicating these initiatives very actively. GCC board members believed that this was in part due to reservations among traditional mid-sized German firms about 'boasting' about things that they considered just good practice. In fact, some saw it as an unwelcome 'American' habit to talk too much about the social activities they considered a normal part of doing business.

Members of the GCC board believed that German firms could – and should – do more. First, more and better communication about ongoing activities would help their reputation in China. Second, forums were needed to facilitate the exchange of best practice: ideas developed by one member firm are likely to stimulate initiatives by others, and help better targeting initiatives to stakeholders. Third, the GCC aimed to get companies together to launch joint initiatives, and provided practical support for those exploring new ideas. Fourth, board members wondered if an annual award was appropriate to recognize outstanding social engagement.

To get the ball rolling, the GCC partnered with the *Bertelsmann Stiftung,* a charitable foundation, to launch a high profile initiative. The first step was a study to review companies' ongoing CSR activities, priorities and perspectives. This review of existing activities served as input for a GCC workshop that would discuss how to take the social engagement to a higher level. A common theme arising was that companies preferred initiatives that directly involved their own employees, or donations of their own products. Financial philanthropy was seen as creating only weak links between the mission of their business and the social causes they are supporting.

The study identified a wide variety of activities:

1 Many German executives prioritized engagement in education in China, notably vocational training. This took many different forms, from helping local colleges to develop their curriculum, to offering work placements. For example, *Schenck* (a subsidiary of *Dürr*) and *Krones* support classes at local colleges that train employees in skills needed in the machine tool industry. Such initiatives help firms to develop human capital, especially skilled manual workers, an increasing challenge in the Shanghai area because talented young people often see manual work as unattractive.

2 Staff welfare in a broader sense is also high on the agenda. By engaging and supporting the families of their employees, companies aim to grow deeper roots in the local community. Some organize family days with sport activities for all generations; others invite family members to visit the workplace or open their sport facilities for family members on the weekend. An initiative particularly pertinent to the Chinese context is holiday camps for the children of migrant workers, especially those who live with their grandparents in distant villages and would not normally see their parents outside the New Year holiday season.

3 Wider education-related initiatives include, for example, collaboration with universities in curriculum development, research support or sponsorships. For example, *Bayer* collaborates with Tonji University in Shanghai by sponsoring a Chair for Intellectual Property, an Eco-construction Academy, and an annual Sustainable Development Forum. At the other end of the education spectrum, employees volunteer to teach in primary schools or orphanages. For example, *Freudenberg* rebuilt a local school damaged by the 2008 Sichuan earthquake, and then continued to support it; in a yearly summer camp, *Freudenberg* employees organize activities for the students.

4 Companies support volunteer work by their employees. For example, *SAP* gives its employees a 'social sabbatical' that they can spend on volunteer work in social organizations, and also makes its software available to NGOs. *Bayer* created a staff volunteer association, and grants each employee two days of volunteer leave. Such activities contribute not only to the target communities, but to the personal development and team spirit of the participating employees.

5 Many products offered by German companies contribute to key government policy agendas, notably in areas such as environmental pollution, universal health care and food security. German businesses were continuously innovating technologies to meet rising standards in Europe, and such technology was also sought after in China. In promoting these technologies to China, companies also thus help broader social and environmental objectives.

6 Beyond providing technologies, companies are promoting health, safety and environmental (HSE) standards. In the first instance, they target their employees, suppliers and customers. With a strong record of best practice, then, some companies are reaching out to provide training to social and governmental organizations, to advise regulatory authorities or to contribute to public awareness of HSE.

7 Continuing with a tradition that started with support for relief action after the Sichuan earthquake, many companies donated equipment or volunteer staff in local or national emergencies. For example, medical companies donated medical equipment, and pharmaceuticals companies provided drugs that were in short supply. After the 2013 earthquake in Ya'an, employees in many companies spontaneously collected donations, often topped up with donations by the company itself.

Some large-scale initiatives brought together several organizations to pool resources for a common cause:

• Many German-owned companies participate in, or initiate, social events in their host communities. For example, in several cities, including Tianjin, Guangzhou and Taicang (a district near Shanghai) they organize an annual 'Octoberfest'. Elsewhere, football is the centre of an annual day of family entertainment. In Beijing, teams from twelve local German companies kicked off in 2014, and in the final *Siemens* beat *Volkswagen Finance* after a penalty shootout. In a similar event in Tianjin, *Volkswagen* had the upper hand over *Siemens* in the final.

- A vocational training school was set up in Jinan City, Shandong province, by six German companies (*Festo, ZF, VOSS, Hydrometer, Continental* and *Stihl*) in collaboration with the GCC and the Chinese Ministry of Education. Following the German dual education structure, the centre offers a three-year apprenticeship programme in which young people would work in the participating companies and receive formal training by the centre. The centre moreover offered two-week training courses for college teachers from across China, and became a role model for other initiatives by the Shandong government.

- Similarly, a Sino-German automotive vocational education initiative by five automotive companies – *Audi, BMW, Daimler, Porsche* and *VW* – aimed to advance the vocational training of car mechatronic assistants. Its goal was to create a network of 25 pilot schools that would offer courses matching the German dual educational system, thus providing qualified employees to participating companies and their partners.

- A large group of German companies cooperated with the local Chambers of Commerce in Hunan and Chengdu in a 'fair markets campaign'. Addressing the sensitive area of corruption, the campaign offered training workshops to small and medium enterprises on compliance issues, published a handbook on setting up compliance structures, and designed an educational computer game, all of which aim to help companies to fend of demands for bribes, and to detect suspicious transactions.

- The *Taicang Round Table*, a network of Austrian, German and Swiss companies, launched an initiative that is highly unusual for China: a factory that employs people with disabilities. In China, the inclusion (or even respect for) handicapped people is not yet well developed, and this factory provides them a rare opportunity to participate in a normal work life.

The GCC invited senior executives of key companies in the Shanghai area for a whole-day forum to explore further ways to engage with Chinese society. Participants cleared their busy work schedules for a day, switched off their mobile phones, and joined in for a day of discussions, reflections and creative thinking about the topic of 'more than a market'. The agenda was broad: the GCC wanted to develop channels for sharing best practice, facilitate collaborative initiatives between firms, and develop a broad and self-sustaining agenda to encourage more engagement and impactful initiatives with their host society.

For the evening, the Consul General of Germany in Shanghai had invited all participants for a reception and dinner. Would they be able to share concrete results and commitments with him?

Sources: (1) Participant observations and interviews; (2) *German Chamber Ticker* (China), 2014, various news items, various issues; (3) B. Bartsch, K. Hellkötter & M. Menant, 2015, *More Than a Market*, Gütersloh: Bertelsmann Stiftung. All quotations and named examples are drawn from the published sources; orally communicated examples are presented anonymously.

DISCUSSION QUESTIONS

1 What are the social responsibilities of foreign-owned firms in a host society?

2 Is the creation of vocational training institutions a CSR activity, or 'just' good human resource management practice?

3 How can smaller companies with limited financial resources demonstrate their social and environmental values abroad?

4 What sort of initiatives could mid-sized companies fruitfully take together?

5 The GCC was considering creating an award to recognize outstanding initiatives by German firms in China. How would you design such an award?

TACKLING CORRUPT PRACTICES: GSK CHINA

Klaus Meyer
CEIBS

In the summer of 2013, four senior managers of British pharmaceuticals company *GlaxoSmithKline* (*GSK*) suddenly found themselves in a Chinese jail. What had happened? They stood accused of a massive bribery network, using travel companies as intermediaries to channel 3 billion yuan (€400 million) to bribe doctors and hospital officials. *GSK*'s China CEO, Mark Reilly, was also personally accused of bribing government officials in Beijing and Shanghai. Chinese prosecutors claimed that the cost of the alleged bribes was passed on to Chinese consumers as *GSK* drugs sold in China at much higher prices than in other countries. As an immediate consequence, *GSK*'s sales in China dropped 20 per cent in 2013 – quarterly results in July to September 2013 were even down by 61 per cent.

The internal investigations were complex and had to cut across different divisions of *GSK*'s China operation, and also landed an independent British investigator in jail for unrelated charges. Eventually, *GSK* admitted that some of its executives had broken Chinese laws and apologized for employees apparently acting outside of its internal controls. At the same time, *GSK* denied the sums of money being anything like as high as those circulated in the media. After a one-day trial in September 2014, Mark Reilly and four others were sentenced to suspended prison terms of four years, but allowing for prompt deportation to the UK. In a statement apparently negotiated with the Chinese authorities, *GSK*:

> fully accepts the facts and evidence of the investigation, and the verdict of the Chinese judicial authorities. . . . GSK PLC sincerely apologises to the Chinese patients, doctors and hospitals, and to the Chinese government and the Chinese people.

While this settled legal proceedings in China, *GSK* still faced the prospect of further penalties from the UK's Serious Fraud Office and the US justice department, because overseas bribery is also punishable in home countries too.

PHARMA INDUSTRY IN CHINA

Following economic reforms since the 1980s, the medical industry in China was growing fast. Hospitals became economically independent and had to survive under market conditions. In consequence, those who could pay for service would be served best – in 2000, the WTO ranked China's health system as one of the most unequal in the world – 188 out of 191. Further reforms laid the foundation for both better access and further growth: the share of citizens with health care increased from 43 per cent to 95 per cent. At the same time, the market for pharmaceuticals had grown from €22 to €58 billion in only five years from 2006 to 2011. China thus was the third-largest pharma market in the world (after the USA and Japan), and expected to soon overtake both.

In China's pharmaceutical industry, 80 per cent of drugs were sold through hospitals, of which 90 per cent were public hospitals. In other words, public hospitals accounted for over 72 per cent of the sales of drugs, and were thus the most important sales channel. However, public hospitals are chronically underfunded, and looking for additional revenue streams. About 40 per cent of their revenue comes from their in-house pharmacies (in some regions even 70 per cent); thus hospitals have an interest in doctors prescribing more medicines. The doctors worked under a lot of pressure, they would commonly see over 100 patients a day, which translated to barely five minutes per patient. Individual attention thus was rare. Yet the salaries that doctors received were just 19 per cent higher than a factory worker. According to a survey conducted in all three star public hospitals in Guangzhou in 2014, the basic annual salary for a doctor was only around RMB46 000, yet this was improved by a monthly bonus (around RMB10 000 per month) and an annual bonus (around RMB20 000 to 30 000) that adds up to a total annual salary around RMB180 000 to 200 000. In addition, doctors could earn 'grey income'. It was well known that physicians would receive commissions from pharmaceutical companies. Moreover, surgeons often received payments directly from patients. It was well-established practice for patients to bring 'red envelopes' (cash payments) to ensure prompt attention when they needed surgery. Another source of income was private consulting for drug companies, often in return for a generous fee. Many doctors depended on such outside earning for their income.

Commissions from pharma sales agents were common in this environment for physicians. One sales agent described to a German journalist how it works:

> Experienced agents don't go to the hospital . . .; they catch doctors on the way to work, name the medications they provide and then hold up their fingers. Five fingers stretched up mean for every unit. there will be 5 yuan reward. … Normally, a doctor gets 10% to 20% of the price of a medication.

Some sales agents shared with Chinese media the common practices:

> *Twenty* per cent is the common commission rate, if it is higher than that, it will eat too much of our own profit. If it is lower than that, no doctor will be willing to help us.

As a result of the commission on pharmaceuticals, 'some doctors would only pick the most expensive drug, not the most effective drug. Others will over-prescribe drugs to patients.' In practice, sales agents would give doctors credit cards. Once a drug is prescribed, commissions will be received via credit cards the next day.

Another channel to reach doctors is conferences. Since new medications require training, it is legitimate that pharmaceutical companies invite doctors to conferences – all expenses paid – where they provide training and introduce new drugs. That is common around the world. However, in China, insiders suggest that only the nurses would show up at the presentations, while the doctors enjoy themselves on the golf course. Conference locations are often in holiday locations; in one case that hit the Chinese media, doctors travelled – all expenses paid – to Taiwan or Thailand. In the opinion of David Zweig, Professor at Hong Kong University of Science and Technology, it is challenging to do business with Chinese hospitals:

> It's very hard to do business in the Chinese health care and pharmaceutical sectors without doing pay-offs. Everyone else pays bribes. *Glaxo* just got caught.

His comment was echoed by Professor Gu Xin, from the School of Management, Peking University:

If all the pharmaceutical companies are bad guys, they are not the root of the problem. It is the problem with Chinese pharmaceutical industry.

WHY DO PEOPLE PAY BRIBES?

In cases such as *GSK*, we can never be quite sure who exactly did what – the relevant court cases in China are not conducted in public. Yet we can look at the individuals involved in the case, and analyze the formal and informal institutions they face. This will allow us to get some idea of what happened, and allow us to draw lessons from the incident.

Bribery typically emerges where poorly paid people make decisions about the use of resources valuable to others. Think of customs: lowly customs officers decide when to process shipments at the border, yet any delay costs importers a lot of money. Hence importers have an incentive to pay the customs official 'under the table' to expedite their shipment. In hospitals, the situation is a bit more complicated, but the basic incentive problem is similar. Doctors decide which medicine is prescribed to which patient, yet the bill for the medicine is for the health insurance (typical in Europe), or the national health system (in the UK, for example). Even when patients pay themselves (typical in China), they are often poorly informed and depend on the doctors' recommendation as to what medication is best for them. Hence doctors have a lot of decision power over resources they do not own. Pharmaceutical companies technically sell their products to health insurances or patients, but they know the actual decision-maker is the doctor. Thus their sales agents have strong incentives to provide under the table benefits to doctors. This used to be major concerns in the US and Europe two or three decades ago, before rules were tightened, often under pressure from health insurance companies.

Let us now look at the different people involved. First, the doctors in major hospitals faced informal institutions suggesting that accepting payments from patients or pharma agents was normal practice, as discussed above. They were likely aware that it was illegal, but they also believed that they had few other options to finance their hospital, and their own lifestyle. It appears to be accepted practice, and prosecutions were rare and limited to extreme cases.

The global leadership of the multinational enterprise, here *GSK*, would be concerned about their reputation. Pharmaceutical companies were subject to extensive scrutiny by various stakeholders because their activities touch on many sensitive aspects of peoples' lives, and their health in particular. In dealing with complex ethical decisions, companies like *GSK* have developed codes of conduct that all employees are instructed to follow. Moreover, CEO Andrew Witty took a number of initiatives to enhance the company's social profile, such as opening clinical trials to greater scrutiny and appointing a chief compliance officer reporting directly to the CEO. At the same time, *GSK* has been keen on growing its business in China: the Chinese market was growing fast, yet *GSK* had only three per cent of its global sales from China. The conflicting tensions were summarized by the *Financial Times* as follows:

[Andrew Witty's] public spirited approach has earned him many fans in governments and health organizations around the World. But the China scandal revealed a disconnect between his lofty rhetoric and behaviour in the field. And his good corporate citizenship will count for nothing unless he can show that it also benefits shareholders.

Third, sales agents faced two sets of internal rules. On the one hand, they face *GSK*'s compliance procedures aimed at enforcing their corporate code of conduct. Specifically, only some types of expenses were permitted (bribes not being among them), and they needed to be documented through appropriate receipts. On the other hand, they faced ambitious sales targets – and the knowledge that should they fail to meet the targets, they would not get their bonus and may even lose their job. Faced with an environment where commissions were common, and the prospects of failing their sales targets, such lowly sales agents had strong incentives to find a way to pay a bribe, while also cheating internal controls. Apparently, in GSK not only individual agents but the entire China operation gave in to such temptations. According to the Chinese prosecutors, GSK China organized fictitious conferences, overbilled for training sessions, and in various other ways filing fake expense claims for which the cooperating travel agencies would issue bogus receipts. That enabled the GSK executives to get reimbursed by their company with money they could use for bribes, while the travel agencies earned a fee for themselves. Sales agents fired by GSK didn't think it was their fault, and filed labour disputes against GSK. They complained to the media:

> GSK China should be responsible for non-compliance behaviour, not sales representatives. These bribes were approved by supervisors. In some cases, the management even instructed them to purchase fake receipts for reimbursement.

Fourth, the Chinese authorities were aware of the corruption in the hospital sector, but for a long time did little, because cutting off the 'red envelopes' and commission would force them to pay doctors higher salaries. However, the new party leadership made it their mission to curb corruption and other practices, such as lavish spending by government officials, and they initiated a major crackdown on corruption and other disapproved practices. Hospital doctors were only one of many groups of officials that suddenly faced much closer scrutiny.

Fifth, the law enforcement officers in China faced pressures to take action on corruption. They knew corruption was widespread, but they lacked the resources or incentives to address it comprehensively. So, picking a few high profile cases could demonstrate their commitment and earn them credit with the political leadership. Yet picking on a state-owned pharmaceutical giant might not be a terribly good idea; that enterprise is likely run by party members closely associated with the law enforcement officer's bosses. Hence targeting a foreign company would send a strong message without causing too much embarrassment to the political leadership.

AN INDUSTRY RESPONDS

Indeed, the message from the Chinese authorities was heard. Doctors in hospitals across China reduced or even completely stopped direct interaction with drug companies. A marketing research company surveying doctors discovered an atmosphere of anxiety: doctors were concerned to be drawn into this scandal, or caught in whatever the next law enforcement initiative might be. Informal visits by medical representatives, which were common before the scandal broke, were completely rejected now. The proportion of doctors receiving formal visits also significantly declined from 87 per cent to 74 per cent. While this affected all drug companies, GSK was most affected, as 40 per cent of doctors decreased or even discontinued prescribing their medicines.

Yet GSK did not give up on the China market. GSK's chief executive Andrew Witty publicly stated that he had 'zero tolerance' of the practices GSK was being accused of, and promised to both tighten internal controls, and stay committed to the Chinese market. Although China accounted only for a small portion of GSK's revenue – about €1 billion of nearly €32 billion worldwide, this was of major concern, because the market potential was seen as huge. GSK already had 6000 employees as well as large manufacturing and R&D facilities in China. In cleaning up its China operations, GSK tightened its internal control and reimbursement policies, and targeted 1000 sales agent for dismissal, one-third of its sales force in China. Moreover, GSK announced that it would change the incentive scheme for sales representatives and no longer offer pharmaceutical commissions to doctors.

However, the consequences went beyond GSK. Several multinational pharma companies rotated their top executives out of China as a precautionary measure. Moreover, they increased their focus on compliance, including training for sales agents and education of doctors on what is and what is not acceptable practice. Some distributors and hospitals in tier 3 cities were dropped because the pharma multinationals recognized that it was not possible to ensure compliance in those areas. Everyone was grappling with the fundamental challenge of building market share in this fast growing market when the rules of the game were changing, and still not fully transparent.

A CONCERNED COMMUNITY

For foreign-owned businesses in China the *GSK* investigation represented part of a bigger trend. They appreciated that the new government was tightening law enforcement, and they expected benefits for the Chinese economy in the long run. Yet many foreign investors felt that they were first in line whenever the interpretation of a law was tightened. It was widely believed that Chinese pharma companies paid doctors red envelopes, yet *GSK* was the first to be pursued in spring of 2013. Other foreign investors like *Sanofi*, *Roche*, *Novartis*, *Astra Zeneca* and *Bayer* also received visits from the investigators; in the case of *Novartis* a former employee launched accusations of bribery at hospitals in Beijing. In September 2013, *Chia Tia Tianping Pharmaceutical* (owned by Hong Kong-listed *Sino Biopharmaceutical*) became the first Chinese company to be investigated for corrupt practices, following an investigative report aired on China's national TV station *CCTV*. Was *GSK* the tip of an iceberg? And what would happen to all those that had stayed below the radar screen so far?

Other issues surfaced in the years 2013 and 2014. It was widely known that Chinese companies talk to each other about pricing. Yet when the competition law enforcement was tightened, the first big fines went to German carmaker *Audi* (€30 million), US carmaker *Chrysler* (€4 million) and twelve Japanese car part suppliers (€160 million). In response, all major carmakers including *Audi*, *Mercedes Benz*, *BMW*, *Jaguar*, *Land Rover*, *Honda* and *Toyota* lowered car and components prices on their own initiative. In an even larger case, US chipmaker *Qualcomm* was fined 6.09 billion yuan (€874 million) in February 2015 for abusing its monopoly market position in the market for chips used in mobile phones. As a third example, after a major factory accident near Suzhou, local authorities in the province increased the frequency of factory inspections. This was quite sensible in itself, given the apparently low safety standards in some places. Yet European manufacturers felt that they had to bear a disproportionate share of the burden of additional inspections and not well thought-through new requirements by local authorities.

The point is that the rules themselves often make sense. Yet the perception of foreigners in Shanghai was that law enforcement was unequal, and concerns were raised by both the European and the US chambers of commerce. Specifically, the US chamber noted that the anti-monopoly legislation (AML)

has the potential to stimulate a new round of dynamic growth . . . However, . . . the patterns of AML enforcement give rise to growing concerns about the quality of fairness of enforcement, and they raise legitimate questions about China's commitment to the global antitrust commons.

The president of the EU Chamber of Commerce, Jörg Wuttke, commented during the World Economic Forum meeting in Tianjin:

The problem with the recent cases is that they are so non-transparent that they leave a lot of speculation about the possible intention. . . . We have yet to see if it (recent anti-monopoly cases) has an impact on business investment but certainly the mood sours. *[If high consumer prices were the main concern]*, there are a lot of monopolies that consumers could pinpoint that would give them more bang for their buck *[such as state-monopolized gasoline production]*.

In response to concerns by the foreign investor community, the Chinese authorities emphasized that the law was applied to both domestic and foreign firms, with the aim of protecting consumers. To reinforce the message, Chinese Prime Minister Li Keqiang made formal statement declaring that the investigations were conducted

legally, transparently, and fairly. . . . These measures are absolutely not targeting certain types of enterprises and are not selective in nature. Based on my understanding, foreign companies are only 10 per cent of those impacted by antitrust investigations.

Sources: (1) *The Economist*, 2013, Bitter pill, July 20: 56–57; (2) *BBC News*, 2–14, UK executive accused in GlaxoSmithKline China probe, May 14; (3) *BBC News*, 2014, GlaxoSmithKline fined $490m by China for bribery, September 19; (4) C. Gracie, 2014, GlaxoSmithKline's China scandal: A cautionary tale? *BBC News*, July 1; (5) GSK, 2014, GSK plc Statement of Apology to the People of China, www. gsk-china.com/asp/News/client/newconten/919201492228.htm (accessed December 2014); (6) A. Köckritz & A. Kunze, 2013, Fragen Sie nie den Arzt, *Die Zeit*, August 22; (7) *Xinhua*, 2015, 'GSK bribery case, who benefits from the high profit margin of pharmaceutical industry' (葛兰素史克贿赂案曝光 医药行业暴利谁在买单一举), news.xinhuanet.com/fortune/2014–05/16/c_126510975.htm (accessed January 2015); (8) Li Xiaohong, The Average Salary for a doctor in Beijing is around RMB180, 000 (李晓红, 北京大医院一线医生月收入税前约 18 万), finance. sina.com.cn/china/20140328/071518641331.shtml (accessed January 2015); (9) 'GSK and the bribery in hospitals: 20% commission rate'(GSK 事件牵扯出的药圈潜规则：医院拿药提成 20%回扣是行规, available finance.huanqiu.com/data/2013–07/4148092.html (accessed January 2015); (10) GSK China Bribery Case (葛兰素史克中国行贿事件), baike.baidu.com/link?url=emqgdo2xnn31OKBW9T2mU1mKM_4k_js5--C27tol2QYVuX2AQ6 KZhtIhweCIwjBMqCulZTXNRPWjfdSLoWlSq_ (accessed January 2015); (11) P. Waldmair, 2013, Chinese group accused of bribery, *Financial Times*, September 13; (12) D. Barboza, 2013, Glaxo Used Travel Firms for Bribery, China Says, *New York Times*, July 15; (13) Dai Xiuhui and Dai Leilei, 'GSK Bribery Case and the Pricing Mechanism of Pharmaceuticals' (代秀慧・戴磊磊・'GSK 行贿案与我国药价定区暴露的药品定价机制回顾'), *Legal Weekly*, www.legalweekly.cn/index.php/Index/article/id/6659 (accessed January 2015); (14) A. Ward, 2015, Fixing reputation in China fits a broader 'social' vision, *Financial Times*, May 12; (15) K. Bradsher & C. Buckley, 2014, China Fines GlaxoSmithKline Nearly $500 Million in Bribery Case, *New York Times*, September 19; (16) Xu Manman, 2014, GSK China fired more than 1000 employees who prepared to file labour disputes (徐曼曼, '葛兰素史克中国裁员报道计一〈 多地区已被准起诉', finance.sina.com.cn/chanjing/gsnews/20140606/094619334493.shtml (accessed January 2015); (17) *Caijin, Financial News*, 2014, GSK case no cure for Chinese corruption, May, 14; (18) N. Extier, 2014, Notes on a Scandal, *German Chamber Ticker*, June, p.48–49; (19) Survey conducted by Psyma Business Research China; (20) *Caijing Financial News*, 2014, China to punish Audi, Chrysler for 'monopoly' acts. August 7; (21) Zhu, S.S. 2015, US$975 fine for anti-trust breach, *Shanghai Daily*, February 11 (main story on page 1); (22) Authors' interviews; (23) US Chamber of Commerce, 2014, Competing interests in China's competition law enforcement, (p. ii), policy report, www.uschamber.com (accessed January 2015); (24) European Chamber, 2014, European business in china position paper 2014/15, policy report, www.europeanchamber.com.cn (accessed January 2015); (25) Martina, M. 2014, EU lobby piles in on foreign criticism of China's antitrust enforcement, *Reuters*, September 9.

DISCUSSION QUESTIONS

1 What institutions impact of the sales of pharmaceuticals in China, and why does it seem so difficult to navigate them?

2 As board member of the global *GSK*, how do you prevent similar scandals to happen in the future?

3 As CEO of the Chinese subsidiary of a competing European pharmaceuticals enterprise, how would you lead the company's growth in China?

4 As representative of the British Chamber of Commerce (or as Commercial Attaché of the British Embassy), how would you advise the Chinese authorities? Or would you stay silent?

5 As a middle-aged doctor in a Chinese hospital, how do you cope with the changes around you?

FAN MILK IN WEST AFRICA

Will Mitchell
University of Toronto, Rotman School of Management

Fan Milk is a manufacturer and retailer of refrigerated beverages and frozen dairy products, with leading positions in several West African countries. Its products include FanYogo (one of the world's first frozen yogurts), FanExtra (frozen yogurt with vitamins), Fanice (frozen dessert), FanGold (ice cream), Fantastic (flavoured yoghurt drink), FanChoco and FanVanille (flavoured beverages), FanDango (energy fruit drink) and Tampico (fruit drink). Most products are sold in single-serving pouches and stackable containers.

Fan Milk offers its frozen dairy products, juice and juice drinks in Ghana, Nigeria, Togo, Benin, Burkina Faso and Côte d'Ivoire, countries with a total population of almost 300 million – including 120 million urban consumers. By 2012, *Fan Milk* reached sales of about $150 million across West Africa, up from $108 million in 2008 (Table 1). It distributed through a network of regional agents and 31 000 independent vendors, selling 1.8 million products daily.

The sight and sound of blue-shirted sellers pushing white *Fan Milk* carts and riding bicycles with coolers, while ringing their bells looking for sales, is part of the landscape of most cities in the region. Brand recognition for *Fan Milk* is high: reaching 94 per cent in Nigeria, 97 per cent in Ghana and 100 per cent in Togo in a 2012 survey. Across its markets, consumers view the brand as being affordable, fresh, tasting good, and for everyone.

Fan Milk's business in West Africa dates back to the 1950s. During several visits to West Africa, a Danish entrepreneur, Erik Emborg, saw a potential market for locally produced dairy products. Several West African countries had recently gained independence and the region was thriving. The combination of national pride within the new countries, available infrastructure from the colonial and local heritages, strong agriculture bases, and potential for new industry paved the way for high hopes. Although refrigerated dairy products were not part of consumers' tastes or broader cultural values at the time, Emborg decided it would be worth experimenting with producing and distributing small containers of refrigerated milk directly into local communities, which he hoped would be attractive in the hot climates.

Table 1 *Fan Milk International* A/S (Denmark) financials (in $US million)

	2012	2011	2010	2009	2008
Revenue	$150	$128	$132	$108	$108
Of which: Ghana	$77.3	$55.7	$69.8	$57.7	$43.2
Nigeria	n/a	$47.3	$42.3	$38.8	$39.9
Gross profit	$88	$73	$74	$63	$57
EBIT	$26	$22	$25	$20	$15
Profit after tax	$10	$10	$10	$8	$6
Gross profit %	59%	57%	57%	58%	52%
Return on sales	7%	8%	8%	8%	5%

By country: 2012 results	Revenue share	EBITDA	Employees
Ghana	48%	33%	444
Nigeria	37%	24%	355
Togo Group (Togo, Benin, Burkina Faso)	11%	13%	
Côte d'Ivoire	4%	down	
Liberia	closed 2012		

In 2013, *Fan Milk International,* the Danish parent of the *Fan Milk* businesses in West Africa, was acquired by the French food conglomerate *Danone* (with a 49 per cent stake) and Dubai-based private equity investor *Abraaj Group* (with a 51 per cent stake) for about $300 million. In the coming years, *Danone* plans to acquire a controlling stake in the *Fan Milk* business. The acquisition is part of *Danone's* expansion in Africa. In 2012, for instance, Danone paid $700 million to increase its 29 per cent stake of *Centrale Laitiere* in Morocco (the country's leading dairy business, with about $750 million sales and $50 million net revenue) to a 67 per cent holding.

GHANA

Combining his skills in trading with his connections to people in Denmark and expertise in dairy technology, Erik Emborg created one of the first dairy businesses in Ghana in 1960. Dairies and fresh milk were not widely available in West Africa, so the manufacturing process reconstituted milk from milk powder, sourced from Denmark. In 1962, the Fan logo was introduced and the company became known as *Fan Milk Limited,* offering ice cream, yoghurt and ice-lollies in addition to milk. The company quickly became profitable.

Fan Milk's Ghana business is headquartered in the capital, Accra, whose 2.3 million people are about 9 per cent of the country's population. It also has a distribution centre in Kumasi, about 250 kilometres and a three-and-a-half-hour drive inland from Accra. Kumasi, which also has more than 2 million people, is the only other metropolitan region in Ghana with population of more than 1 million.

Fan Milk distributes its products through a network of bicycle vendors, pushcarts and kiosks throughout the country. *Fan Milk* supplies the carts, bicycles and refrigerated containers for the products, typically selling or renting them to the vendors. Vendors purchase the items and then sell them at a mark-up, with their earnings based on sales. The *Fan Milk* logo is a common sight on ice cream carts and bicycles on beaches and streets selling the products.

Fan Milk Limited was among the first companies to be listed on the Ghana Stock Exchange, in 1990. As of the 2000s, its top two shareholders held more than half of the equity, with the Danish parent *Fan Milk International* holding 37 per cent and the Danish government-backed *Industrialization Fund for Developing Countries (IFU)* holding 25 per cent.

In 2013, the managing director of *Fan Milk Limited* was a Danish expat, supported by local executives in roles such as sales, human resources, IT, internal audit, project management and production. Board members include several highly experienced leaders from Ghana and elsewhere in Africa, as well as the Managing Director of *Fan Milk International* in Denmark. Following the acquisition by *Danone* and *Abraaj* in 2013, two executives from *Abraaj* joined the board.

NIGERIA

In 1961, Erik Emborg created a sister company to the Ghanaian business, *Fan Milk Nigeria Plc*. The Nigerian company began operations in 1963, with a recombination plant in Ibadan (the capital city of Oyo State, 125 kilometres north of Lagos, about 90 minutes by road) and a distribution centre in Lagos, with fewer than 30 employees. Initially, the product range was white milk, chocolate milk, cottage cheese and set yoghurt. As in Ghana, the main outlet was bicycle vendors, who were supplied with cold products from a group of smaller depots.

Fan Milk Nigeria expanded during the 1970s and 1980s. In the 1970s, it introduced yoghurt drinks, ice-lollies, ice cream and recent advances in *Tetra Pak* packaging (developed in Sweden). The new products became popular and generated financial resources to set up more distribution depots. In 1981, *Fan Milk Nigeria* established a second recombination plant in Kano (about 1000 kilometres north-east of Lagos).

When the Nigerian company was established, the foreign owners held 96 per cent of *Fan Milk Nigeria*. In the late 1970s, though, the government introduced the Nigerian Enterprises Promotion Decree, which required major local ownership. In response, *Fan Milk Nigeria* increased its capital and invited Nigerians to invest, which led to 60 per cent Nigerian participation.

During the 1980s and 1990s, import restrictions, economic difficulties, political coup d'états, devaluations and shortages of fuel in Nigeria – and throughout West Africa – weakened *Fan Milk Nigeria*. In 1998, the foreign investors and *IFU* in Denmark agreed to an infusion of capital, which helped *Fan Milk Nigeria* restructure finances, refurbish cold rooms, increase the number of depots, and introduce a new fruit drink, Tampico.

Tampico succeeded rapidly in Nigeria and was introduced to *Fan Milk*'s other markets. The investment in distribution and logistics supported *Fan Milk*'s spread throughout Nigeria. The expansion and rehabilitation programme returned the Nigerian business to profitability by the early 2000s.

With the new investment, and following democratization of Nigerian politics in 1999, control of the company returned to Danish hands. In 2011, *Fan Milk International*, which continues to maintain its headquarters in Aalborg, Denmark, held controlling interest of 62 per cent of the shares of *Fan Milk Nigeria*, while the IFY held 19 per cent.

Fan Milk Nigeria has continued to expand in Nigeria. In 2011, for instance, the company set up a distribution centre in Benin City (300m east of Lagos), by leasing a one-million-litre capacity cold room in the city to serve markets in east Nigeria. The managing director of the Nigerian operation was a Danish expat, supported by a board that included Danish, Nigerian and West African members. The board chair was chancellor of a Nigerian university and president of the Nigeria Stock Exchange. By 2014, *Fan Milk Nigeria* had 21 offices and distribution outlets, including thirteen of the country's 36 states and Federal

Capital Territory of Abuja. It directly employed about 400 people, while providing indirect employment to thousands of others, from bicycle distributors to agents and franchise holders, as well as suppliers and vendors across the spectrum of its business activities.

OTHER WEST AFRICA

Fan Milk International operates subsidiaries in several other countries in West Africa, including Togo, Benin, Burkina Faso and Côte d'Ivoire. Investment in Togo began in 1985, in collaboration with *IFU*. Political and economic development in the francophone countries led to trade agreements, which created opportunities for *Fan Milk* to develop sales and distribution companies in the neighbouring countries. Exports from Ghana started to Benin began in 1992, to Burkina Faso in 1996, and to Côte d'Ivoire in 2002. The company further expanded to Liberia in 2009, but closed this operation in 2012 when the market did not live up to expectations.

BUSINESS MODEL ACROSS MARKETS

Fan Milk's business model follows several principles across its markets. First, it emphasizes urban markets, with lesser coverage in suburban and rural locations. This simplifies its logistics activities, while targeting areas with density of potential demand.

Second, it has begun to expand its market segments, now offering larger packages that cater to families, hotels and restaurants. Nonetheless, over 90 per cent of sales continue to be individual servings in the 'on-the-go' channel. Hence its products continue to be 'impulse buys' sold outdoors in traffic, in front of schools and office buildings.

Third, in most countries, *Fan Milk* relies strongly on intermediaries as agents, who manage the independent distributors. This allows the company to work with people who have strong local knowledge of demand conditions and of potential employees in the distribution network.

The widespread distribution network sometimes creates control issues. During 2012, for instance, *Fan Milk* acknowledged that children below the age of 18 had been selling the company's products on the streets in Liberia, contrary to the nation's goals for child education and in violation of the company's policies. *Fan Milk*'s country manager in Liberia, though, said that the company was not responsible for the violations, because distribution agents employed the children. *Fan Milk* closed the Liberian business shortly after the controversy surfaced.

Moreover, *Fan Milk* has been adapting the agent model to local conditions. In Nigeria, they partially switched to a more tightly controlled agent network after losses at *Fan Milk* Nigeria in the mid 2000s. The difference tends to reflect both the availability of potential intermediary partners and how reliably they can defend contractual relationships in local legal systems.

Fourth, while *Fan Milk*'s markets continue to be West Africa, the company has built a global supply chain to support the end market business. *Fan Milk* continues to import raw materials and packaging materials as well as equipment for its dairy plants and distribution of finished goods. As it has grown, the company has built a global supply chain that includes more than 200 suppliers in Europe, Africa, China and elsewhere.

A central sourcing and logistics group, *Emidan* (based in Denmark), handles the majority of purchases for the *Fan Milk* businesses. *Emidan*'s products include raw materials (for example, milk powder, vegetable oils, stabiliser and flavours), packaging materials (for example, plastic wrappings, cups and containers), and other materials (for example, freezers and coolers, crates, pallets and bicycles). In addition to serving *Fan Milk, Emidan* provides sourcing services for other firms.

ONGOING EXPERIMENTATION

Throughout its history, *Fan Milk* has had a philosophy of 'working out ways that work'. The company has experimented actively within and across countries with products and business models. It has then used what it has learned from the experiments to build robust local businesses.

Through its experiments, *Fan Milk* has developed new distribution techniques to keep up with the changing competitive climate. For example, over time they have added motorbikes and solar-powered kiosks to the network. Recent experiments with mobile kiosks, initiated in Nigeria, are responding to growth in more sophisticated retail infrastructure. In another initiative, *Fan Milk* partnered with the Lagos city government on traffic initiatives, as well as an effort to combine sales of *Fan Milk* products with related collection of refuse.

Product development has also benefited from experiments in the company's markets. Development activities now typically involve cooperation between the local *Fan Milk* companies in West Africa with international suppliers and laboratories, and the technical staff in Denmark.

EVOLVING MARKET ENVIRONMENT

The market environment in *Fan Milk*'s West African markets is constantly evolving (Table 2). On the back of high prices for raw materials such as oil, gas, gold, cacao and coffee, local economies had spurts of strong economic growth. Yet uncertainty regarding both the economic development and the political climate (notably in Nigeria), remains high. Other challenges arise from changing demographics and consumer behaviours:

- **Demographics.** The markets are young, with the main consumer group being between 16 and 34; this young group earns over half the national income.

- **Urbanization.** Much of the population base is shifting to cities. Urbanization is increasing at about 4 per cent per year in the region.

- **Convenience food.** Demand for convenience food is rising along with urbanization and the demographic trend of younger consumers.

- **Retail channels.** Informal retail channels continue to dominate, but there is growing interest in larger indoor retail venues in the largest cities. Growth of indoor retail includes chains such as *Spar* (from the Netherlands) and *Shoprite* (from South Africa), smaller non-chain formats, and many informal corner stores that over time expand their premises and upgrade facilities with cool storage. Despite growth rates, large supermarkets will likely remain a marginal phenomenon for the next decade or so, while the informal 'mom and pop' stores will be more relevant drivers of the retail revolution in West Africa.

- **Media.** Internet and social media channels are increasingly important, with more than half of urban consumers having internet access and owning smart phones. Nonetheless, television and word of mouth remain critically important.

Table 2 West African countries

Country	Official language	Population (million) 2013	Largest city share of population	Top 3 cities share	GDP/capita (PPP) 2012	GDP growth 2012/2002
Fan Milk presence						
Nigeria	English	175	12%	16%	$2 294	156%
Ghana	English	27	9%	19%	$1 765	157%
Côte d'Ivoire	French	22	17%	24%	$1 757	99%
Burkina Faso	French	16	15%	27%	$1 304	136%
Benin	French	10	8%	13%	$1 364	106%
Togo	French	10	26%	58%	$906	108%
Liberia	English	4	28%	47%	$564	110%
No Fan Milk presence						
Niger	French	17	21%	60%	$573	94%
Mali	French	15	12%	15%	$1 047	114%
Senegal	French	14	18%	41%	$1 675	114%
Guinea	French	11	13%	15%	$921	101%
Sierra Leone	English	6	13%	28%	$1 171	146%
Guinea-Bissau	Portuguese	2	20%	41%	$1 028	97%
Gambia	English	2	35%	66%	$1 679	105%
For comparison						
Denmark	Danish	5			$32 333	102%

Sources: (1) www.fanmilk.com; (2) www.fanmilk-gh.net; (3) www.fanmilk-nig.net/ – all accessed September 2014; (4) TV2 Nyhederne, 2009, Production & distribution in Ghana (in Danish), www.youtube.com/watch?v=GQ5rt4MhpMw [accessed March 2015];
(5) Fan Milk, 2012, Lait Vanille (ad, in French): www.youtube.com/watch?v=krcFkkCNmuw [accessed March 2015]; (6) Bloomberg Africa TV, 3/2014, Post-acquisition strategy in Ghana: www.youtube.com/watch?v=dH5F6idcY-U [accessed March 2015]; (7) Fan Milk, 2013–2015, Fan Milk Nigeria YouTube channel: www.youtube.com/user/fanmilkplc [contains further ads, accessed March 2015].

DISCUSSION QUESTIONS

1 How has a Danish entrepreneur been able to build a successful business in Africa?
2 How did Fan Milk as a Ghanaian business manage the challenges of expanding to other African countries?
3 How should Fan Milk respond to ongoing changes in retail channels and consumer demand?
4 How would you recommend Danone manages its newly acquired business Fan Milk?

ESET: FROM LIVING ROOM TO GLOBAL PLAYER IN ANTIVIRUS SOFTWARE

Arnold Schuh
Vienna University of Economics and Business

E*SET, spol. s r.o.** is a global vendor of security software for companies of all sizes and households. Its software solutions deliver instant, comprehensive protection against evolving computer security threats. The company pioneered and continues to lead the industry in proactive threat detection. Founded by six Slovak IT engineers in the Slovakian capital Bratislava in 1992, *ESET* has grown into one of the top five global players in the antivirus software market. How did it accomplish such amazing growth? How did it successfully market around the world mission-critical software that was originally developed in Slovakia?

BEGINNING BEHIND THE IRON CURTAIN

During the Cold War (1945–1989), two young Slovak programming enthusiasts, Peter Pasko and Miroslav Trnka, were asked to help sort out a virus problem at a Slovak nuclear power plant. They were indeed able to discover the virus, one of the world's first. They dubbed it 'Vienna' and wrote a programme for its detection and elimination that formed the basis for their first antivirus product named NOD. NOD stood for 'Nemocnica na Okraji Disku' or 'hospital on the edge of the disk'. Inspired by a popular Slovak TV series with the same title, NOD was the first antivirus software with graphical user interface and an integration of detection, fixing and prevention. The whole production process of NOD – recording, labelling and packaging of diskettes – took place in the living room. They distributed their programme mostly for free in a small network of friends and IT enthusiasts. Selling to state-owned companies was complex and difficult, due to a bureaucratic sourcing process. Exporting was impossible. Thus the two inventors had a brilliant product, yet limited opportunities for commercialization under the given political conditions.

*spol. s r.o. refers to private limited liability company (LLC), according to Slovak law.

In 1989 the communist regime in Czechoslovakia ended in a non-violent revolution, known as the Velvet Revolution. After 42 years under communist rule, the country became a democracy and opened up to the Western world. The new government started the transformation of a (mostly) state-owned and centrally planned economy into a market-based economy with private entrepreneurship as a key element. The transformation process was accompanied by a re-orientation of exports from former Eastern bloc countries toward Western markets. At this time many Czechoslovak products were of mediocre quality, selling at a discount and with some difficulty in the West. The GDP per capita was about 25 per cent of that of neighbouring Austria. The first years after the system change were chaotic. Private businesses were expanding quickly in Czechoslovakia, but legislation and administration lagged behind.

Because the internet was not yet developed, software sales relied on physical distribution. Computer viruses had a limited spread and the security software industry was in its infancy. NOD was still a side business for the founders, whose company was run out of an apartment in Bratislava. Domestic sales grew slowly but continually. In 1990, they started selling NOD in Austria via a local distributor and under the name 'Stopvir'. Although the export business was not very successful in the beginning, in 1991 the first million in local currency (about US$36 000) in revenues was earned.

ESTABLISHMENT OF ESET

In 1992, *ESET, spol. s r.o.* was founded by Rudolf Hruby, Peter Pasko and Miroslav Trnka in Bratislava, in the Slovak part of the then Czechoslovakia, as a privately owned limited liability company (LLC). At this time, the founders did not focus on antivirus software alone. They also saw a business opportunity in developing bookkeeping software. In the early years of the transition process, thanks to the enormous pent-up demand, almost any business was offering attractive growth to entrepreneurs. Although computer usage was still in its infancy, the demand for applications in all types of functional and sectoral areas was growing.

In 1993, their home country, Czechoslovakia, broke up, creating the Czech Republic and the Slovak Republic. Suddenly, *ESET* lost a large part of the former home market, which forced the founders to look for new export markets. In the same year, Trnka began contributing to the column 'Virus Radar' in the leading Slovak periodical *PC Revue*, which helped to build *ESET*'s reputation as an antivirus specialist. In the following years, improved versions of NOD were launched. A turning point was winning the first *Virus Bulletin* award in 1998. *Virus Bulletin* is a British magazine dedicated to providing PC users with regular information about the prevention, detection and removal of computer malware. When this renowned magazine praised *ESET* for its quality, international users became aware of the company and foreign distributors started to ask for sales agreements.

However, the Slovak origin of the company still posed a psychological barrier to prospective foreign buyers and, as a consequence, restrained the growth of sales in foreign markets. Software originating from a relatively unknown, former Eastern bloc country was not perceived as a reliable high-performance product. Management discussed how they could counter this negative country-of-origin effect. In 1999 *ESET LLC* was established in San Diego, California, in the United States, with the help of Anton Zajac. This subsidiary was upgraded to be the international business centre for *ESET*, being responsible for all foreign markets. By selling its software through the US subsidiary, *ESET* got rid of the negative country-of-origin associations, and international revenues began to rise. This dual structure was terminated in 2008 through a merger of the US subsidiary with its parent *ESET, spol. s r.o.* In the meantime, *ESET* had established itself as a leading player in the industry, and was valued above all for its competence and not its country of origin anymore. The choice of the US as a location for the international business centre was also driven by the fact that it was the largest and leading IT market of the world, with a progressive IT industry and demanding customers who would stimulate ESET's innovation efforts.

RAPID INTERNATIONAL EXPANSION AND GROWTH

From the year 2000 on, the company showed remarkable growth. In 2002 the global auditing and consulting company *Deloitte* added *ESET* to its rankings of fastest growing companies, namely 'Deloitte Technology Fast 50 in Central Europe' and 'Fast 500 in EMEA' (Europe, Middle East and Africa). This growth of sales was driven on the one hand by demand, as viruses became a widespread threat through the fast evolution of the Internet, and on the other hand by the improved international presence. In 1990, estimates of new and different computer viruses ranged from 200 to 500 per year. In 2000 the number was 50 000. In 2010 the estimate was 2 million. In 2015, *ESET* records more than 300 000 new pieces of malware *per day*. All statistics show that the number is exponentially growing. A higher penetration of computers, new devices such as smartphones and tablets, widely available mobile broadband technology, cloud computing, and intensified usage have increased the exposure of computer users to malware. The need to protect against these cyber threats has fuelled the sales of *ESET*: sales volume in local currency grew from 2000 to 2014 by a factor of 480! While foreign sales accounted for less than 30 per cent of overall sales in 2003, this share grew to 97 per cent in 2014.

In its first 15 years, the company grew organically. However, in 2008 and 2010 *ESET* acquired two companies in the field of information security services and anti-spam systems. In 2008, *ESET* bought the Czech security company *Setrnet* in order to expand its offering to information security services. Two years later, *ESET* acquired *Comdom Software*, a Slovak software company acclaimed for anti-spam solutions. By acquiring *Comdom*, *ESET* increased its capacity for developing advanced security solutions. In the words of Miroslav Trnka, *ESET*'s then CEO:

> *ESET* is a research and development-oriented company that is going to benefit from this merger by tapping into the potential of this manufacturer of advanced anti-spam solutions. Building on the team of skilled programmers and researchers, we envision introducing new activities, along with injecting new potential into the development of security software.

PEOPLE AND CULTURE AS A BASIS OF SUCCESS

Highly talented and motivated employees are central to *ESET*'s success. Andrew Lee, CEO of *ESET* North America, emphasizes this aspect:

> Great software is the product of great people. *ESET* seeks to recruit people who are not only some of the brightest and best at what they do, but who also fit the positive culture of trust, integrity, innovation, effectiveness and cheerfulness that drives everything that we do as a company. Throughout our organization, each employee is a carefully selected fit for the role, and as such is a key to our success.

This attitude is also expressed in the mission statement: 'Intelligent people develop intelligent products for intelligent customers.' In order to attract and retain this type of employee, *ESET* has to pay salaries according to West European standards. Team building events, skills training, language courses, pension schemes and health insurance contribute to a high level of employee satisfaction and low employee turnover. Owners and management cultivate an informal and personal style in the interaction with their employees and try to know not only their professional skills and strengths, but also their personal life.

Due to the fast growth of the company it became more difficult to find excellent software programmers in Slovakia alone, a country of five million inhabitants. Therefore, *ESET* opened a new R&D centre in Krakow, Poland, in 2008. The purpose was to strengthen its research base and to accelerate innovation in countering the growing volumes and sophistication of cyber threats. Krakow is a major centre of education in Poland and Central Europe, with around 210 000 students and well-known technical universities. It is a place where the IT community is very strong and well organized (with about 320 IT firms). Krakow has even been dubbed as 'Europe's Silicon Valley'.

ESET's portfolio of products serves all types of computer users – home users, small- and medium-sized companies, and large corporate and institutional customers. NOD32 Antivirus is the basic product for homes and businesses. *ESET* Mobile Security protects smartphones. *ESET* Smart Security, the flagship consumer product, provides a comprehensive protection combining antivirus, firewall and anti-spam. Cybersecurity for Macs was developed for *Apple* users. The superior antivirus performance of *ESET* is documented in several tests by industry magazines. The NOD32 Antivirus programme holds the world record for the largest consecutive number of the Virus Bulletin 'VB100%' awards since 1998, and has never missed a single 'in-the-wild' virus (a virus that spreads uncontained among infected computers in the general public) since the launch of the test.

A distribution network of partners and resellers parallel to sales offices in all major markets secure a presence in more than 180 countries worldwide. More than 100 million people use *ESET* security software. Almost 1000 employees generated a turnover of €328 million in 2014, nearly all of it outside of Slovakia. The company grew by close to 139 per cent over five years (2010–2014). According to *IDC*, a global market intelligence firm in the information technology sector, *ESET* held fifth place in the global antivirus market in 2013, with a market share of 4.5 per cent (Table 1). With an annual growth rate of 23 per cent, *ESET* has grown six times faster than the whole market.

The foundations of *ESET*'s strategy have not changed markedly since its inception. Despite its growth from a 'living room' company to a global player, it continues to be driven by an entrepreneurial spirit and built on technological competence. The goal is to develop high-performance, mission-critical security solutions for private and business users to keep out all known and emerging forms of malware. The focus on research and continuous product development is crucial for the superior performance of its NOD product. Top management and employees are living these values, creating a culture that is characterized by responsibility, reliability and innovation. Antivirus business is built on the user's trust and this is mirrored in the culture of *ESET*. What changed over the last 23 years is the scope of operations. A broader range of solutions is offered today to home users, companies of all sizes, and mobile phone users worldwide. In February

Table 1 Worldwide antivirus vendor market shares (by revenue, 2013)

Vendor	Market Share
1. *Symantec*	31.5%
2. *McAfee* (an *Intel* company)	15.6%
3. *Trend Micro*	9.7%
4. *Kaspersky Lab*	7.6%
5. *ESET*	4.5%
6. *Sophos*	3.5%
7. *AVG Technologies*	2.9%
8. *IBM*	2.2%
9. *F-Secure*	2.0%
10. *Panda Security*	1.7%

Source: IDC, Charles J. Kolodgy, Worldwide Endpoint Security 2014–2018 Forecast and 2013 Vendor Shares, August 2014, p. 4.

2015, *ESET* launched an all-new range of next-generation business security products that offer maximum proactive protection with enhanced usability for all sizes of company, highlighting the new strategy focus on business customers.

The international scope of the business is not only reflected in a larger volume and share of foreign sales but also in R&D centres on all continents. *ESET* runs malware research and R&D centres in Europe (Bratislava, Kosice, Krakow and Prague), the Americas (Buenos Aires, Montreal and San Diego) and Asia (Singapore). Spreading its malware research centres over many time zones allows *ESET* to respond effectively to the rise of cyber threats and technological challenges. This is the only way to learn quickly about new cyber threats and to monitor trends. It also gives access to programming talent and knowledge hubs that are located all over the world.

Sources: (1) Company Report of ESET, spol. s.r.o., Amadeus (Bureau van Dijk) database, March 2015, and personal interviews with M. Trnka and B. Ondrasik in February and March 2015; (2) K. Dyba & J. Svejnar, 1992, Stabilization and transition in Czechoslovakia, in O. Blanchard, K. Froot, & J. Sachs eds., *The Transition in Eastern Europe*, Volume 1 (pp. 93–122), Chicago: University of Chicago Press; (3) ESET website, March 2015, www.eset.com/int/about/history/ and www.eset.com/us/; (4) IDC, Charles J. Kolodgy, Worldwide Endpoint Security 2014–2018 Forecast and 2013 Vendor Shares, August 2014, p. 4; (5) M. Trnka on the History of ESET, 2012, Presentation at the 4 Grow East Congress, March 7, Vienna, Austria; (6) IDC, 2014, Worldwide Endpoint Security 2014–2018 Forecast and 2013 Vendor Shares, report, August.

DISCUSSION QUESTIONS

1 How could entrepreneurs in Slovakia create a leading global player in the antivirus software industry?

2 From a resource-based view, what are *ESET*'s sources of competitive advantage?

3 From an institution-based view, country of origin images reflect the view and perceptions of (potential) customers regarding the rules of the game in the country of origin. How does this affect companies in Central and Eastern Europe?

4 What can companies do to address negative country of origin perceptions?

THE LG-NORTEL JOINT VENTURE

Bill Turner, Joe Bentz, Steve Caudill, Christine Pepermintwalla and Ken Williamson
University of Texas at Dallas

Peter MacKinnon, chairman of the recently formed *LG-Nortel* joint venture (JV), is back in his Dallas office after two hard weeks in South Korea (hereafter Korea). Next week, he is off to Europe for a well-deserved vacation with his family. In his office, MacKinnon surrounds himself with family photos, awards and souvenirs from around the world. He is highly dedicated to the *LG-Nortel* JV and currently spends two weeks each month in Korea. When in Dallas, he leaves the headquarters in Korea in the capable hands of *LG-Nortel* JV CEO Jae Ryung Lee.

MacKinnon tackles his work and personal challenges with 100 per cent dedication, as shown in his drive to make the *LG-Nortel* JV a success. He has a passion for life, and is one of those executives who 'works hard and plays hard'. This is evident by the ice hockey stick sitting an arm's length from his desk chair and the fact that he plays in three hockey leagues when visiting Korea. Finding a balance between work and personal life remains a challenge with the current heavy workload and extended travel to Korea each month.

Having travelled around the globe and having been an expatriate in Europe previously, MacKinnon is no stranger to international travel. He describes some interesting cultural aspects of doing business in Korea and highlights 'respect' and 'knowledge for the cultural differences' as important. He is keenly aware of the dynamics of the corporate culture in Korea and its implications on the success of the JV, given the mixed management of Koreans and a few North Americans living in Korea.

This case was written by Bill Turner, Joe Bentz, Steve Caudill, Christine Pepermintwalla and Ken Williamson (University of Texas at Dallas, EMBA 2007) under the supervision of Professor Mike Peng. The purpose of the case is to serve as a basis for classroom discussion rather than to illustrate the effective or ineffective handling of an administrative situation. The authors thank Mr Peter MacKinnon for his time and for sharing his expertise and experiences. The views expressed are those of the authors (in their private capacity as EMBA students) and do not necessarily reflect those of the individuals and organizations mentioned. © Bill Turner. Reprinted with permission.

With MacKinnon's new boss, *Nortel* CEO Mike Zafirovski (Mike Z), driving for management excellence, there is little room for missteps. MacKinnon is currently a very hands-on full-time chairman as demanded by Mike Z. The *LG-Nortel* JV must satisfy the needs of both the corporate parents (*Nortel* and *LG*) as the conduit for their telecom products and also be *Nortel*'s gateway to the Korean telecom market. In addition, MacKinnon must lead and leverage a highly capable and innovative group of Korean engineers to develop new products for the advanced Korean and worldwide telecom markets.

This is MacKinnon's first time chairing a board of directors. Managing this new JV, with a multi-cultural management, is presenting a number of challenges. For the first six months since the JV was established, MacKinnon has been spending 16-hour days tackling a number of 'start-up' problems. He has been driving this mixed cultural team to resolve the recent tactical and operational issues and is working to resolve cross-cultural and management tension. Lately, he has been contemplating how and when to shift to become more strategic and start to be a part-time chairman. His main challenge is how to establish the JV for success in the future and be the strategic part-time chairman that he wants and needs to be.

LG ELECTRONICS BACKGROUND

LG (Korea Stock Exchange: 6657.KS) was established in Korea as a private company in 1958 as *GoldStar*. As a global leader in home appliances, digital media devices and display and information and communications products, *LG* has more than 64 000 employees globally and its 2005 revenues reached over $16.9 billion (unconsolidated). It is comprised of 30 companies with about 130 overseas subsidiaries. As part of the *LG* corporate conglomerate, *LG* Electronics' goal is to enable the intelligent networking of digital products that will make consumers' lives better than ever.

NORTEL BACKGROUND

Nortel (NYSE: NT; Toronto TSX: NT) is a 110-year-old Canadian company doing business in more than 150 countries with 2005 revenues of $10.52 billion. Nortel's portfolio of solutions for telecommunications network providers, government and enterprises includes end-to-end broadband (packet and optical), voice-over IP, multimedia services/applications, wireless networks and wireless broadband networks.

NORTEL'S EXPERIENCE IN NEW MARKETS

Expanding into new global markets, *Nortel* has had its share of successes and failures. Some expansions were accomplished through acquisition of wholly-owned subsidiaries, such as the acquisition of *Matra* in France and others through JVs. MacKinnon discussed one particular learning experience where *Nortel* entered into a 50–50 JV. Unfortunately, voting was deadlocked; the JV became ineffective and had to be shut down.

In 1998, with a presence in North America and Europe, *Nortel* entered into the rapidly expanding South Korean telecom market. This soon turned into a valuable lesson on how *not* to do business in Asia (through an understanding of the local culture but not of the 'business culture'). *Nortel* assumed that to do business in Korea, all you needed was a few local Korean employees in a local office. This was a vital misunderstanding. MacKinnon summed up the challenge by saying, 'You can't just hire a few Koreans and call yourself a Korean company; it's all about relationships.' This first attempt was not successful, and *Nortel* backed out of South Korea.

TELECOM IN SOUTH KOREA: AN INDUSTRY OVERVIEW

South Korea has the 10th-largest economy in the world, and has one of the leading telecommunications infrastructures in the world. This was not true a mere 30 years ago. In the late 1970s, with a population of 40 million, there was barely one phone line to every 160 people. By 2005, there was nearly one phone line to every two people. However, the demand for phone line service is in decline, as more advanced services eliminate the need for basic phone lines. Mobile technology has advanced rapidly, and the subscriber base has grown to nearly 40 million, with an increasing number of these subscribers using their service for wireless digital transfer.

WIRELESS IN SOUTH KOREA: AN ACCELERATING INDUSTRY

South Korea's CDMA Network is the largest EVDO wireless network deployment in the world, and has the most advanced early adopters, with 75 per cent user penetration. As of 2004, Korea already had 11 million subscribers using EVDO. Korea also boasts the most advanced data applications in the world, estimated to be two years ahead of North America. The government originally mandated CDMA wireless technology to be used in South Korea. However, recent mandates to the more widely adopted UMTS technology represent a major technology shift for the country and local equipment providers like *LG*.

THE LG-NORTEL JOINT VENTURE

With the policy shift toward UMTS, *LG* was not prepared and did not have products for UMTS to meet these new government requirements. *LG* now found itself in need of a partner for UMTS products. *Nortel* had had no footprint in the heavily competitive South Korean market since the 1998 retreat, and it needed a way to re-enter South Korea. *LGE* was the leader of the Korean consumer electronics market. It was also a major global force in electronics, information and communications products. Due to *LGE*'s demonstrated innovative technology leadership position in Korea and *Nortel*'s proven UMTS portfolio and worldwide reach, the mutual attraction was inevitable.

On August 17, 2005, *LG* and *Nortel* signed a definitive JV agreement with a contract closure target date of November 1, 2005. Nortel entered into the JV with a $145 million investment. For this investment, *Nortel* would receive ownership of 50 per cent plus one share of the company and control a majority of positions on the board. Gaining 50 per cent plus one share was a 'deal breaker' for *Nortel*, given the past experiences with 50–50 partnerships. MacKinnon was named chairman and Jae Ryung Lee would become CEO. Other key positions were filled accordingly with *Nortel* and *LG* executives (see Figure 2). The JV had over $500 million in sales in the first six months, but not without organizational and cultural issues to deal with.

ISSUES IN THE FIRST SIX MONTHS

Of the 1400 *LG-Nortel* JV employees, 1350 are South Korean and 50 are American and Canadian. While building the JV organization, cultural differences surfaced immediately. A higher than normal attrition rate was seen, in part as the result of placement of younger former *Nortel* employees over older former *LG* employees. This is not acceptable in Korean corporate culture, and thus many Korean employees left.

MacKinnon had also seen the cultural divide when a Korean male employee started holding his hand and confiding in him about some issues the Korean male employee was having. MacKinnon never pulled his hand away, heard the employee's message, and knew immediately that this kind of cultural exchange might happen to Americans and Canadians unaware or less tolerant of these differences in the future.

The burdens of implementing both US GAAP and Korean GAAP have taken their toll and created additional process and stress on the organization. In one instance, contract template issues caused revenue recognition problems, which in turn created a (financially) reported order backlog. The contract template issues were identified, and a plan to correct them was developed. Two contract templates accounted for 60 per cent of the revenue, with another 15 accounting for the other 40 per cent to be corrected. The implementation was now critical to finally recognizing the revenue needed to prove the JV was already a success to both parents, *LG* and *Nortel*.

Pre-JV, *LGE* had been mainly focused on Korea, concentrating on the requirements of the demanding high-growth and innovative local market. Now these highly qualified engineers needed to take a broader worldwide view of product development so products could be funnelled back through *Nortel*'s non-Korean markets.

Nortel cancelled a major project within the JV just as the project was ramping up its development. This decision was made after the most recent planning and forecasting exercises used by *Nortel* had shown that the business case and market outlook would not provide the returns required by *Nortel*. Regardless of sunk costs for development by the JV, the project was cancelled. The shock and awe felt by the Korean members of the JV were hard. They did not agree with this decision and could not understand why this first major project would be killed so early into development. This caused major tension in the relationships between the *LG* and *Nortel* counterparts and with the *Nortel* corporate parent. CEO Lee started asking direct questions, such as 'How could you do this?' and 'Now why are we working together?'

With tensions mounting, small internal conflicts were happening in private. Then one day, in a public meeting, CEO Lee had a very emotional reaction and vented upon MacKinnon many of Lee's frustrations of working with a North American company. Understanding this was not the norm for a Korean executive, MacKinnon listened intently to everything Lee had to say. Once Lee finished, MacKinnon recognized that he must respond and struck back with a ten-minute speech directed at Lee. Afterward, the Korean managers at the meeting asked MacKinnon to go for drinks, but he declined. Seeing that MacKinnon had his hockey equipment with him when leaving, they realized that he had other plans that evening. In fact, MacKinnon had not taken up their offer to go drinking on a number of other occasions, and was always sure to have other plans.

THE FUTURE CHALLENGE OF THE LG-NORTEL JV

MacKinnon is currently a full-time chairman as directed by *Nortel* CEO Mike Z. However, Mike Z is also concerned about the possibility that MacKinnon might be burnt out. MacKinnon himself fully recognizes that eventually he needs to gracefully retreat, become more strategic, and become a part-time chairman. To do this, he ponders how to set up the organization, processes and people to be most effective. In addition, he must ensure success before trade talks between Korea, the United States and Canada conclude, which would lower trade barriers and allow greater competition. The big challenge for MacKinnon is: how can *LG-Nortel* be self-sustaining, and how can he pull away from the day-to-day operations of the JV?

Sources: (1) LGE website: us.lge.com/about/company/c_profile.jsp; (2) Nortel website: www.nortel.com/corporate/index.html; (3) E. Ramstad, 2006, In US-Korea free-trade talks, tense mood highlights the stakes, *Wall Street Journal*, July 11: A6.

DISCUSSION QUESTIONS

1 Did *Nortel* make the right decision by (re)entering South Korea through a JV? What other market entry alternatives did *Nortel* have?

2 Discuss the advantages and disadvantages of having a strategic alliance such as the *LG-Nortel* JV. What are the unique advantages of controlling 50 per cent equity plus one share?

3 What are the skills and attributes that successful JV managers would ideally possess? Does MacKinnon possess these skills and attributes?

4 What can MacKinnon do to reduce cross-cultural conflicts within the JV?

5 What can *Nortel* and *LG* do to improve the odds for the success of this JV?

BEKO WASHES CLOTHES ACROSS EUROPE

Klaus Meyer
CEIBS

If you do your laundry in the UK, chances are that you are using a Turkish washing machine. Many household appliances (commonly known as 'white goods') are produced in Turkey under sub-contracting arrangements for other brands. Yet the best-selling washing machine brand is *Beko*, which is owned and managed by Turkey's largest maker of white goods, *Arçelik*. Europe-wide, *Arçelik* is in 2015 the third-largest manufacturer of home appliances, employing 23 000 people and operating 10 production facilities in Turkey, Romania and Russia – in addition to substantial operations in the Middle East, China and South Africa. In 2014, its turnover reached €4.4 billion.

While *Beko* had success building market share in some countries, *Arçelik* found it challenging to grow sales in other mature markets of Western Europe, and to raise the profitability of its international operations. The *Beko* brand was often perceived as a low-tier brand, and in countries other than the UK brand recognition was low. In Eastern Europe, *Arçelik*'s low-cost strategies matched local demand, but the potential for demand growth was limited. Hence *Arçelik* faced challenging questions as to how to continue its fast growth profitably.

TURKISH ROOTS

Since the 1990s, Turkey has become a hub for the white goods industry. The manufacture of large household appliances was labour-intensive, and their transportation was costly because the machines were quite bulky. Therefore, Turkey provided a good basis for the industry: relatively low labour costs, and geographic proximity to European markets. Following the liberalization of international trade, in particular the customs union with the EU in 1996, trade between the EU and Turkey has become relatively easy (see Chapter 2, Opening Case). Thus foreign and local companies set up production facilities in Turkey.

Arçelik initially grew its washing machine business as an outsourcing partner for major European and American brands. Such partnerships helped *Arçelik* to stay cost competitive while enhancing its own capabilities. At the same time, rising urbanization in Turkey created a catch-up demand from growing middle classes in *Arçelik*'s home market. *Arçelik* developed its proprietary sales channels with its own retail stores branded *Arçelik* or *Beko*, and at the peak held a market share of 60 per cent in Turkey.

Arçelik belonged to one of the largest family-owned business groups in Turkey, the *Koç* Group. Family members held directly and indirectly about 57 per cent of shares of *Arçelik*. The *Koç* Group provided financial support, joint employee training, sharing of management best practices, and synergies in purchasing.

The market liberalization changed the competitive dynamics and created a strong push for *Arçelik* to develop its own technologies. *Arçelik*'s experiences as a manufacturer of other brands helped to develop its own technologies, in particular to improve its product quality, packaging and logistics. From the 1990s onwards, it adopted total quality management practices, and just-in-time and flexible production practices to boost productivity. A major milestone was the establishment of an R&D centre in 1991, which laid the foundation for *Arçelik* to become the leading Turkish company in terms of patent applications, holding 13 per cent of patents issued in Turkey by 2005.

In the 1990s, Arçelik moved into Europe in pursuit of higher income consumers and larger markets. In Eastern countries, such as Russia and Romania, it did not suffer a latecomer advantage as all global brands entered around the same time and there was little brand loyalty. In high income economies in Western Europe, *Arçelik* set up offices in France, Germany and the UK. Its most significant move was the introduction of the *Beko* brand to the UK in 1989. The brand was specifically designed for the export of white goods, including refrigerators, freezers, washing machines, dishwashers and free-standing cooking appliances. The UK and Irish markets were targeted first because they were price-sensitive, not dominated by local brands and, as members of the EU common market, had minimal customs duties.

ACCELERATED GROWTH IN EASTERN EUROPE

In 2001, Turkey experienced a major recession, which triggered *Arçelik* management to think more proactively about growing in foreign markets to spread risk by geographic diversification. *Arçelik* targeted Western Europe, because it felt that it now had developed the required technological and management capabilities.

However, apart from the UK, *Arçelik* lacked locally recognized brands and access to distributors. Thus in 2001, it attempted to acquire *Brandt*, a French company in receivership, but was beaten by *ELCO* of Israel. But, in 2002, *Arçelik* made the big plunge into Europe by acquiring *Blomberg* (Germany), *Elektra Bregenz* (Austria), *Leisure* and *Flavel* (Britain) and *Arctic* (Romania). By choosing an acquisitions route of entry, *Arçelik* could quickly raise its international profile, and acquire brands enjoying strong brand loyalty in their respective home markets. In 2004, *Arçelik* added the rights to the *Grundig* name to its portfolio after acquiring the German TV and radio manufacturer that had gone into liquidation.

The success story continued. *Arçelik*'s Europe-wide market share rose from 7.9 per cent in 2008 to 10.8 per cent in 2013. It thus became the fourth-largest white goods provider in Europe after *Bosch-Siemens-Hausgeräte* (*BSH*) of Germany (17.9 per cent market share), *Indesit* of Italy (13.0 per cent) and *Electrolux* of Sweden (11.0 per cent). In contrast, US manufacturer *Whirlpool* lost market share from 9.4 per cent in 2008 to only 6.7 per cent, while Korean manufacturers *Samsung* (4.9 per cent) and *LG* (3.4 per cent) gained market shares. As a brand, *Beko* became the second bestselling brand by volume with 7.2 per cent in 2013 – up from 4.8 per cent in 2008, with number one positions in the UK and Poland. In Turkey, the *Arçelik* brand was the bestselling brand, and with both *Arçelik* and *Beko* brands together, *Arçelik* held over 50 per cent market share, ahead of domestic competitor *Vestel*. In Romania, *Arçelik*'s *Arctic* brand held the number one position with 35 per cent market share.

BRAND POSITIONING

Beko was the flagship brand for *Arçelik*. In the UK, it was the leading brand for fridges, cookers and free-standing washing machines. Its brand awareness reached 80 per cent. However, while *Beko* was positioned as a mid-market brand in Turkey, it was perceived to be at the lower end of the mid-market in many other countries. Many European consumers associated 'Made in Turkey' with inferior quality. Therefore, *Arçelik* made special efforts to disassociate *Beko* from its Turkish roots and instead to emphasize its international nature and its product quality. First, positioned as a 'world brand', *Beko* is sold in more than 100 countries. For instance, *Beko* sponsors sport events, in particular basketball, including international championships as well as domestic leagues in Russia, Lithuania and Germany. In the UK, *Beko* sponsored a school's football league and launched a 'Mums United' campaign, which provided nutritional advice and decoded soccer jargon for British football mums.

Second, *Beko* took initiatives to link the brand with innovation and quality. Marketing campaigns used the slogan 'smart solutions for everyday life' to emphasize innovation, energy efficiency and ease of use, while highlighting awards received from British consumer magazines. *Arçelik*'s innovation capabilities were supported by nine R&D facilities and over 1000 R&D staff. Coordinated by the R&D centre, *Arçelik* researchers sought to develop technologies that were efficient, environmentally sensitive and enabled consumers to save on energy and water.

Arçelik moreover set out to create an innovative culture. Modern management processes facilitated effective sharing and integration of technological developments across the company. Ideas for new products or improvements were captured from across the company through a yearly idea-gathering process. R&D staff who initiated an innovative project were given funding for six months to develop their concepts. These initiatives generated a string of product innovations. For example, *Beko* developed the world's most energy-efficient washing machine and introduced the first oven with a liquid repellent coating for easy cleaning.

At the same time, the Turkish home base remained critical for *Arçelik*'s cost competitiveness. First, its manufacturing base in Turkey incurred lower logistics costs than Asian competitors that also pursued low cost strategies. Second, *Arçelik*'s unit production costs were lower than those of its West European competitors because its production plants in Turkey had substantially lower unit labour costs than most of Western Europe. Third, *Arçelik* enjoyed larger economies of scale because its production facilities were among the largest white goods plants in the world.

OUTLOOK

Competition in the white goods industry remained intensive as the industry matured and hence consolidated. Over the years, many smaller appliance brands had been taken over by leading players such as *Whirlpool, Electrolux* and *Indesit*. In November 2013, *Fagor*, a Spanish appliance maker, filed for bankruptcy, while, Italian *Indesit* was rumoured to be set for sale by the Merloni family. However, with production sites mainly in relatively high labour cost locations in Italy, competitors were weighing the pros and cons of making a takeover bid.

Arçelik recognized the need to enhance the positioning of *Beko* to keep up with competitors. In markets where it held leading positions, such as Turkey and the UK, *Arçelik* was exploring opportunities to strengthen its leadership, for example by expanding into adjacent product categories, improving retail management, or innovating its global supply chain management. In markets where its market position was weaker, priority questions concerned investments in brand image and product mix through marketing and product innovations, and the continued search for opportunities to acquire or build a premium brand. Last, but not least, *Arçelik* owned the *Grundig* brand, which could potentially by re-launched and re-positioned in the white goods market in Germany, and in the long term also elsewhere.

Sources: (1) F. Bonaglia, A.M. Coplan & A. Goldstein, 2008. Industrial upgrading in the white goods global value chain: The case of Arçelik, *International Journal of of Technological Learning, Innovation and Development*, 1(4): 520–535; (2) T. Gülsoy, O. Ozkanli & R. Lynch, 2012, The role of innovation in the effective international expansion of an emerging-country firm: The case of Arçelik, *Procedia Social and Behavioral Sciences*, 41: 116–129; (3) D. Dombey, 2012, Turkey's Beko claims UK market top spot, *Financial Times,* December 6; (4) Agence France Press, 2013, Spanish company to declare bankruptcy', *Hurriyet Daily News*, November 8; (5) M. Johnson, 'Mondragon feels pain as it cuts off its own arm', *Financial Times*, December 9, 2013; (6) Arcelik, *2013,* Investor Presentation, November www.arcelikas.com/UserFiles/file/20139MIP.pdf ; (7) www.beko.co.uk/Pg/MumsUnitedNews (8) Arcelik A.S., *Annual Report various years.*

DISCUSSION QUESTIONS

1 From an institution-based view, how did the institutional environment of Turkey (also see Chapter 2) influence the growth strategy of *Beko*?

2 From a resource-based view, what capabilities did *Arçelik* have to develop to build market share for *Beko* in different countries of Europe?

3 How would you suggest developing *Arçelik*'s European operations further?

SG GROUP: MANAGING EUROPEAN ACQUISITIONS

Klaus Meyer, Daniel Chng and Jianhua Zhu
CEIBS

One of the first Chinese companies to engage in serial acquisitions in Europe, textile machine manufacturer *ShangGong Group* (*SG Group*) acquired *Pfaff Industrial* and *KSL Keilmann* in 2013, complementing its earlier acquisition of *Dürkopp Adler* (*DA*) in 2005. Through these overseas acquisitions, *SG* became market leader in China and the third largest producer in its industry worldwide. Its household sewing machine brands Butterfly and Flyman were widely known in China, while its German industrial sewing machine brands Dürkopp Adler, Beisler, Pfaff and KSL served high-end customers such as *LV*, *Gucci*, *Hermès*, *Boss* and *Armani* in the clothing, shoes and accessories industry and *Mercedes-Benz*, *BMW*, *Audi* and *GM* in the auto industry.

However, acquiring companies is only one part of international growth. Mr. Zhang Min, *SG Group*'s CEO, was very aware of the challenges of managing the two new acquisitions. He had learned a few lessons from the acquisition of *DA*, yet the strategic and operational challenges were different this time.

THE DÜRKOPP ADLER ACQUISITION

Back in 2005, *SG Group* faced a challenging competitive environment in China. It had been the traditional market leader, yet faced new competition: European producers were offering advanced highly automatic machines, Japanese competitors offered good quality machines for the mid-market at competitive prices, while local entrepreneurial start-ups sold cheap, manually operated machines. Acquiring *DA* provided an opportunity to move into the premium segment: *DA* manufactured high-tech industrial sewing machines under the *DA* and *Beisler* brands for high-end customers, and hence provided an opportunity for *SG* to match its Japanese competitors.

This is an abbreviated version of: Klaus E., Meyer, Daniel H.M. Chng & J. Zhu, 2014, SG Group: A Chinese challenger acquires German premium brands, CEIBS Case Center, 2014. © The authors.

Table 1 Timeline of *SG Group*

October 1965	*Shanghai Industrial Sewing Machine Factory* founded.
September 1993	Listed in Shanghai Stock Exchange, renamed *Shanghai Industrial Sewing Machine Holding Co, Ltd.*
August 1997	Renamed as *ShangGong Holding Co Ltd.*
December 2000	Brands 'Butterfly' and 'Flyman' transferred from *Shanghai Feiren Xiechang Company.*
2005	*ShangGong Shenbei Group Co Ltd.* created holding equity of *ShangGong and Shanghai Shenbei Office Equipment Co Ltd.*
February 2005	Ownership stake of Shanghai government transferred to *Pudong SASAC.*
July 2005	Acquisition of *Dürkopp Adler.*
2006	Establishment of *DA Trading* (Shanghai) and *DA Manufacturing* (Shanghai) as joint ventures between *DA* and *SG* in China.
December 2009	Production site in Hösbach Germany (*Beisler AG*) closed.
March 2010	Strategic partnership between *SG* and private firm *ZOJE.*
July 2010	*DA* sells its materials handling unit to *Knapp AG*, Austria.
January 2011	*DA* (Suzhou) established, equity *ZOJE* 51%, *DA* 25%, *DA Trading* 24%.
March 2013	Acquisition of *Pfaff.*
July 2013	Acquisition of *KSL Keilmann.*

Source: Constructed from *SG* website, *Dürkopp Adler* annual reports and internal documents.

Mr. Zhang saw overseas acquisition as an aggressive, if risky, strategy to address the challenge. He hoped that by acquiring *DA, SG* would not only be able to recover its declining position in China but also open new opportunities in international markets using *DA*'s high-tech products and global sales network.

The roots of *Dürkopp Adler* (DA) were two competing sewing machines companies in Bielefeld, Germany that were acquired by automotive supplier *FAG* and then merged to create *DA*. After the fall of the Iron Curtain in 1990, *DA* pursued new business opportunities in Eastern Europe by acquiring factories in the Czech Republic and in Romania. By 2005, *DA* generated more than 80 per cent of its sales abroad through a global sales and service network with more than 200 partners. It specialized in automated sewing machines for high-end garments and industrial applications.

However, due to weak global demand and a strong euro, both turnover and profits kept declining. *FAG* implemented several restructuring programmes to cut costs and overcapacity. However, these changes proved disruptive and failed to return the company to sustained profitability. Moreover, *FAG* itself was acquired by the *Schaeffler* Group, a leading automotive supplier that had little interest in sewing machines, and thus in 2002 put *DA* up for sale.

Aware of this acquisition opportunity, Mr. Zhang talked to stakeholders of *DA* to understand why *DA* was not profitable. He believed that it was essential to understand the weaknesses of his targets before the acquisition. He noted three key challenges. First, *DA* was not responsive to market changes. The centre of gravity of the textile industry had shifted to south and east Asia; and after the abolishment of textile quotas for products made in China, more than a third of the world's clothing was produced in China by 2003. Hence China became the most important market for sewing machines. However, *DA* had a weak sales network in Asia, serving China until 2002 via a Hong Kong-based distributor. Hence *DA* was not able to capitalize on growing demand in Asia when sales in Europe and USA were declining.

Second, *DA* did not fully exploit opportunities for division of labour among its factories in Europe. Although labour costs in the Czech Republic and Romania were less than half of those in Germany, all four factories produced complete machines, including most parts and accessories. There was little trade in components between the different sites, and hence a lack of scale economies and weak utilization of labour cost differences. Third, *DA* had a large administrative overhead accounting for 30 per cent of sales.

'NOBODY TRUSTED US AT THAT TIME'

Although employees of *DA* had accustomed themselves to the idea that *FAG* would sell *DA*, its sale to a Chinese investor caused a stir among the workforce. This was one of the first acquisitions of a German company by a Chinese state-owned company, and *DA* employees did not know what to expect. Hence *SG* faced a high degree of suspicion from local stakeholders, such as trade unions and the media. Therefore, building trust in the local community was a big concern for Mr. Zhang.

FAG had massively reduced the workforce over two decades, and the number of staff in Bielefeld had been reduced from about 2 500 to 450. Another 167 employees were let go before the acquisition. However, after the takeover, no employee was made redundant and the collective labour agreements continued to apply. The co-determination with two employee representatives on the supervisory board remained unchanged. Above all, no single machine was dismantled. All these actions helped to appease the mood of the workforce.

In November 2005, Mr. Zhang took to the stage at a workers' assembly to announce his strategy:

DA's position as brand management centre and sales management centre will remain unchanged; *DA*'s position as the R&D centre will remain unchanged; *DA*'s position as the production base for high-end products will remain unchanged.

His speech won warm applause from the workers.

Mr. Zhang became the chairman of the supervisory board and worked together with the German CEO to design the overall strategy. The German CEO was responsible for daily operations in production, development and sales, coordinating his activities with his Chinese colleague and CFO, who was in charge of the areas of finance, human resources management and IT.

OPTIMIZING EUROPEAN OPERATIONS

After the acquisition, *SG* aimed to restructure *DA* in two ways; first by optimizing its value chain in Europe, and second by strengthening *DA*'s position in the Chinese market. *DA* had four factories in Europe, two in Germany and one each in the Czech Republic and Romania. Each factory had complete assembly lines and produced sewing machines from scratch. Shortly after the takeover, *DA* strengthened the division of labour among the four sites. The factory in Romania now produced labour-intensive parts, such as hooks and needle bars for subsequent assembly in Europe and China. The plant in the Czech Republic continued to manufacture the main product line. In Germany, the production of *Beisler* in Hösbach (Bavaria) was moved to Bielefeld, and the production facility was closed down in 2009. Bielefeld was thus strengthened as both the main site for high-tech manufacturing and as an R&D centre.

As a result of this clearer division of labour, *DA* was able to significantly lower its production cost, and it achieved a break-even performance at the end of 2005. The evidence of improved economic performance was critical for Mr. Zhang to earn the respect of the German workforce, and the wider community in Bielefeld.

TWO JOINT VENTURES FOR CHINA

The main challenge for *DA* in China was that, despite its reputation for cutting edge technology, *DA* could not sell its machines because of its weak sales and service organization. At the same time, *SG* lacked state-of-the-art manufacturing, managerial and marketing competences to compete in the middle and high-end market segments. To fill these gaps, *DA* and its parent *SG* set up two JVs in China in 2006.

First, *DA Trading* (Shanghai) was to sell *DA* machines to customers in China (later extended to Southeast Asia). *DA* contributed 25 per cent of the equity (later increased to 40 per cent). In 2007, around 3000 sewing machines were sold worldwide in the framework of this JV, which helped turning *SG* profitable.

Second, *DA Manufacturing* (Shanghai) was established in a refurbished part of *SG*'s existing factory, and employed some of its existing workforce. *DA* took 30 per cent equity stake in the JV and contributed especially technical skills and quality management, relocating four managers and engineers from Germany to lead the project. The JV aimed to develop and manufacture sewing machines for the Chinese mid-market. Designs were developed in Germany using CAD technology, and transferred to the China-based development team who would make further adaptations, for instance to incorporate locally available components. Also, a new fast-sewing machine was developed specifically for the Chinese market. The expectation was that a simplified version of the machines made in Germany with the *DA* brand name and German supervision of the manufacturing process would enable the JV to produce reliable yet price-competitive machines, and hence to regain market leadership in China from its Japanese competitors.

However, the JV struggled to achieve German-level precision, durability and reliability. German managers and engineers seconded to China faced both skills gaps and cross-cultural communication barriers that inhibited the transfer of production process knowledge. The quality of manufacturing was not consistent, many machines had substantive defects, and some broke down shortly after the delivery to customers. Consequently, the manufacturing JV failed to turn profitable. Consequently, the production facility in Pudong was closed in 2009.

In reflection, Mr. Zhang noted:

> If I did it all over again, I would not do the same. I overestimated the design capabilities of German staff. I also overestimated the management capabilities of Germans in China. One of our product development strategies after the acquisition of DA was to ask DAs R&D team in Germany to design a lockstitcher against our Japanese competitor and it was produced in Shanghai. It did not work out. Now I understood that it should not be taken for granted that products made in Germany could be made in China. Although Chinese satellites and spaceships have been launched, high-end sewing machines simply could not be made in China. I have learned the lesson. Nowadays, I only introduce mature and suitable products to our Chinese factories step by step and I have to keep the R&D and production of high-end products in Germany for the time being.

CROSS-CULTURAL COMMUNICATION

The Chinese employees held great respect for the quality management skills of their German colleagues. Yet at the same time, they resented German slowness and fussiness. Conversely, German colleagues often interpreted Chinese flexibility and pace of innovation as an inability to implement product designs accurately and consistently. As the innovation manager of DA put it:

> [They] like to improvise and then the quality goes way down . . . as far as our Chinese colleagues are concerned, things are often not fast enough. But our machines call for the highest kind of precision.

However, from a Chinese perspective, such relentless focus on precision was not appreciated because it cost a lot of money and made the products very expensive. Chinese customers at the time did not value durability and reliability as highly as European customers, because they often pursued short-term contracts in highly volatile markets, and hence they were not willing to pay a premium price for more durable products. These differences in the market environment were reflected in the mental models of the engineers: Chinese engineers prioritized speedy adaptation to customers' needs, while German engineers were primarily concerned with reliability and durability of their products.

A related challenge was the management of expectations of customers. *DA* sales managers frequently faced questions such as 'But your machines are now coming from China, aren't they?' Clients in Europe and the USA paid premium prices for machines for safety-sensitive applications, such as the manufacturing of car airbags. Such machines were manufactured in Germany and the Czech Republic; yet customers wanted reassurance of that country of origin, as they would not be willing to pay premium prices for products 'Made in China'.

In the early stages, *SG* and *DA* also experienced cross-cultural misunderstanding in their daily operations, which caused dismay on both sides. For example, Germans got very irritated by the Chinese habit of displaying disinterest if the topics under discussion did not concern them, even falling asleep during meetings. On the other hand, the Chinese found the direct manner with which Germans expressed their opinions, or identified mistakes, to be very snobbish and lacking polite manners, even if they happened to be right.

EVOLVING COMPETITION AND BUSINESS CYCLES

Three years after the takeover, both sides achieved positive financial results. *SG* increased its turnover from RMB1483 million in 2005 to RMB2538 million in 2007, and it returned a small profit for the first time in several years. The acquisition thus helped the turnaround of the parent company. Meanwhile, *DA* was breaking even in 2005. Sales revenues grew from €128.6 million in 2005 to €151.3 million in 2007, while net income increased from €1.4 million to €2.6 million.

However, the financial crisis in 2009 challenged everyone in manufacturing, especially businesses related to the automotive industry. *DA* was no exception. The turnover of its sewing technology unit dropped from €90.7 million to €51.7 million, generating a pre-tax loss of €23.4 million. *SG* responded carrying out a series of restructuring activities. After negotiating with the trade union, 150 *DA* employees were laid off, mostly administrative staff. Moreover, *DA* sold its materials handling unit for €10 million. Mr. Zhang negotiated with *FAG* and the banks to restructure their loans, while *ShangGong* (Europe) wrote off a €10 million loan, which helped to secure bank loans.

DA also established a new JV named *DA (Suzhou)* in Wujiang, with private start-up *ZOJE* taking 51 per cent of the equity, *DA* 25 per cent and its affiliate *DA Trading* (Shanghai) 24 per cent. This JV was to make a fresh push into the large market for standard lockstitcher and simple medium-to-heavy duty stitching machines. The building was provided by *ZOJE*, machines were bought from *DA* Manufacturing, and a fresh production workforce was recruited.

During this difficult time, the Chinese investor stood by *DA*, and made further financial resources available. 'Banks or a German investor would probably cut off the money,' was frequently heard in Bielefeld. Moreover, *DA* maintained its strategy of developing the German location as the global R&D hub for *SG* by investing €5 to €6 million annually in R&D. The main focus was the development of industrial sewing machines for medium and thick materials used for automotive components, such as leather car seats and car interiors.

The fact that *SG* stood by its German affiliate enhanced the respect in which the Chinese investor was held in Bielefeld. The new CEO, Dietrich Eickhoff, commented 'The takeover has developed from a scare scenario to a best-case scenario', while work council leader Klaus-Jürgen Stark said that the takeover '*was the best that could have happened to us*'.

AMBITIOUS NEW ACQUISITIONS

In 2013, *SG* took two more steps in its internationalization by acquiring two German premium brand manufacturers, *Pfaff Industrial* in Kaiserslautern and *KSL Keilmann* in Lorsch, near Frankfurt. *Pfaff* was the second leading premium brand for sewing machines in Europe. *Pfaff Industrial* had top technology for automatic and adhesive sewing machines, and was a long-standing competitor of *DA* in the area of premium products for the automotive industry. *Pfaff Industrial* had also set up a facility to manufacture heavy-duty machines for sewing shoes and leather products in Taicang, near Shanghai. However, *Pfaff*'s annual sales revenues had been declining and were by now only a third of *DA*'s. After years of financial losses, *Pfaff* had accumulated €20 million in debt and was forced into insolvency. For *SG*, the acquisition of *Pfaff* served two strategic goals, to stop *Pfaff*'s competition against *DA* in Europe, and to acquire complementary products and technology.

KSL Keilmann, a family business founded in 1964, was the world's only provider of 3D sewing technology. Operating in a very specific niche *KSL* offered fully automatic sewing machines for customer-tailored solutions. It had sewing technology for specialist applications such as car airbags and carbon fibres used in aeroplane wings and cabin doors. Moreover, its machines allowed for customized pattern stitching used on decorative elements, such as interiors of luxury cars.

After acquiring *Pfaff* and *KSL*, *SG Group* became a global player in the sewing machine industry, with cutting edge technology for many types of industrial sewing machines. Yet it faced new challenges. First, *DA* and *Pfaff* had been competing for 150 years. It was a great challenge to integrate these two previous competitors in terms of R&D, production and sales. The acquisition was motivated in part by the desire to realize operational synergies between *DA* and *Pfaff*. Yet staff at both companies took pride in their brands, and their engineers saw control of their value chain as critical to maintaining their product quality. How could synergies between these erstwhile rivals best be realized? How would specialist manufacturer *KSL* best complement the brand and product portfolio?

Second, *SG* hoped to improve its own R&D capabilities. With its R&D centre in Germany and the market in China, Mr. Zhang also felt there was a need to find new ways to develop good enough products for local markets. As the working hours for machines, climate condition and power pressure were different in Asia from that in Germany, the German R&D team needed a better 'local touch' to design products for the 'good enough' market in China. Yet few R&D team members were willing to relocate to China to study customer needs on site. How could he develop the German brands to better fit the needs of the Chinese market, and how could he use the *ShangGong* brand to fill market niches without undermining the brand value of the German brands?

Sources: Personal interviews by the authors and (1) O. Bonig, 2013. 'Nobody Trusted Us at that Time' (Interview with Zhang Min), in *Unternehmeredition*, August, page 42–43; (2) S. Sohm, B.M. Linke & A. Klossek, 2009. 'Dürkopp Adler and ShangGong Holding: Fit for the Future Together', in: *Chinese Companies in Germany: Chances and Challenges*, Bertelsmann Stiftung; (3) DA annual reports 2009 and 2010; (4) Xin Feng, 2014, High Aspirations, Corner Overtaking, *Shanghai Light Industry*, Issue 3, p.4 (in Chinese); (5) J. Klöckner, 2013, Chinesische Investoren: Freunde in der Krise, *Die Zeit*, March 3.

DISCUSSION QUESTIONS

1 From an institution-based view, what were the key challenges that *SG Group* experienced in integrating its European operations?

2 From a resource-based view, what capabilities did *SG Group* have to develop to (a) compete with Japanese manufacturers in China, and (b) supply the European automotive industry?

3 How should *SG Group* manage its European operations after the two new acquisitions?

JUST ANOTHER MOVE TO CHINA?

Yvonne McNulty

Lisa MacDougall looked at her desk calendar and realized it was the first year anniversary of her employment at John Campbell College. How ironic, she thought, that I might resign today, exactly one year after I started here. As her colleagues dropped by her office throughout the morning to discuss a new research project that she was leading, Lisa felt both elated and sad. She was excited to be embarking on a new chapter in her career, but upset to be leaving behind her first full-time job in nearly a decade. To ease her mind, she took a morning tea break at the campus cafeteria and ordered a latte. Then her mobile phone beeped to alert an incoming message from her husband, Lachlan. As she nervously picked up the phone and read the four-word message – 'it's done, go ahead' – she realized in that instant that there was no going back now: Lachlan had just signed a two-year contract with his employer to move their family to China, and it was happening in six weeks' time.

Taking a deep breath as she walked back to her office, the first task was to write a resignation letter, after which Lisa emailed her boss to request an immediate meeting to tell him she was leaving. Although he took the news in his stride, Lisa knew her boss was upset to be losing her after only a year. The college was building up its research agenda and Lisa, along with a couple of other early-career researchers, had been employed as an integral part of that plan. Lisa knew that her leaving would likely disrupt those plans a little but, she reminded herself, if her boss had ever really understood what made her tick, he perhaps could have seen it coming.

Although it had been roughly six months in the planning to move to China, the decision to go had not been an easy one to make for the MacDougalls. This surprised Lachlan and Lisa, given that they were seasoned expatriates who had moved internationally, as a married couple, at least twice before – first from Sydney to Chicago and then Philadelphia, and six years later a second international move to Singapore, their current home. After 12 straight years 'on the road' and two successful international moves on two continents under their belt, the anticipation of a third move – to China no less – seemed simple enough, and in many ways it was. Good for Lachlan's career? Check – yes. Good for their two young daughters? Check – yes. A wonderful, perhaps life-changing cultural experience for the whole family? Check – definitely, yes. Yet in many ways this move was anything *but* simple; there were so many issues to consider, and so many important decisions to be made that would likely impact their family for years to come, if not for the rest of their lives.

Foremost in Lisa's mind was whether she could work in China. The mere thought of being a stay-at-home 'trailing spouse' again was out of the question. Another concern was going back to the transience of living in rented housing again; needing permission from a landlord to put up a picture or paint the walls would be hard to get used to after having lived in their own home in Singapore for the past four years. Then there was the children's education and the change to a new school. This would be the MacDougalls' first international move with school-aged children, and Lisa had no idea whether international schools in China offered the types of music and sports programmes her children enjoyed. As she mulled over the China decision, Lisa also reflected on what had drawn their family into the expatriate life to begin with. Doing so, she hoped, might help her to understand how their past might now be drawing them to a new adventure in Shanghai.

ALL EXPATRIATE JOURNEYS START SOMEWHERE, AND SOME EVEN IN CHILDHOOD

To many of their friends, Lachlan and Lisa seemed to be made for each other. That they married quite soon after they met, and very soon after that left on their first international assignment to Chicago, came as no surprise to anyone. Lisa was born and raised in Melbourne as the daughter of European migrants and, after an eight-year commission in the Royal Australian Navy living and working on naval establishments all over Australia, she settled in Sydney at the age of 26 to pursue a career in management consulting. She met Lachlan on a rather ordinary Saturday morning at a café in Mosman, when he politely asked if he could borrow the *International Herald Tribune* when she was done reading it. Lachlan wasn't born in Australia; he'd come to Sydney some seven years earlier as a UK backpacker on a three-month holiday that turned into a year-long sojourn, then permanent residency, and finally citizenship. Born and raised mostly in Scotland as the eldest son of a second-generation property developer, Lachlan was an architect by trade with a Bachelor's degree and an MBA from Heriot-Watt University. He'd had an interesting childhood, having moved house (and school) a dozen or more times around Scotland and Ireland as his father bought and sold various properties to expand the family business. Although his father had hoped he would take over the business one day, Lachlan had other ideas.

WHEN EXACTLY DOES A GLOBAL CAREER BEGIN?

Their first move to Chicago was a completely out-of-the-blue opportunity, but one that Lisa and Lachlan accepted immediately and without hesitation. They were newly married, had no family ties in Sydney, and shared a mutual love of travel. Lachlan had changed careers a year earlier into the IT industry, and now worked for a large American technology company with offices around the globe. Although the Chicago job was on local terms – no 'expat package' – the company was willing to pay relocation expenses, and US salaries were much higher than those in Australia. With an expensive mortgage and looking to kick-start a second career, Lachlan knew the opportunity was too good to pass up. Lisa needed no convincing – moving to the US was the fulfilment of a life-long ambition to live and work overseas and she didn't really care where that was. So, they rented out their house and waved goodbye to friends with the promise to 'be back in two years'.

It didn't take long once in Chicago for the MacDougalls to realize that their 'two-year plan' wasn't going to happen. Lachlan was an instant success in his new role, while Lisa relished her newfound status as 'trailing spouse'. Despite Lisa not being permitted to work in the US (they had not known – nor thought to ask – about the availability of work permits for accompanying partners when they accepted the job), she nonetheless found herself loving the freedom to explore a new city without the constraints of a busy, all-consuming and demanding job. They didn't need her salary anyway; Lachlan's career was flourishing, so much so that within 18 months of arriving in Chicago, he was promoted into a regional US role and offered the opportunity to move to Philadelphia. They gladly accepted the move even though, again, it was on local terms with only relocation expenses paid by the company.

By the time they arrived in Philadelphia, Lisa knew that something had changed for her and Lachlan. Their expected return to Sydney in a few months' time was no longer something they talked about. Instead of renting an apartment they bought a house on the 'main line' in leafy, middle class Montgomery County about 30 minutes drive from downtown Philly. They replaced their *IKEA* household goods with more expensive, longer lasting pieces of furniture, bought two cars, and adopted a dog. Rather than seek out an expatriate community, they joined Bryn Mawr Country Club, where they made many American friends and became active in golf and sailing. Because Lachlan's salary was on local terms, they lived and acted like locals, and immersed themselves in the local community with a mindset that they were 'here to stay'. Of course, that would never be the case, given that their H1B visa restricted them to a maximum of six years' residency in the US. But they had another four-and-a-half years until the visa expired, and they intended to stay in Philadelphia until the very last month.

Their move to Asia four years later was, of course, necessary, as their US visa was about to expire with no opportunity to renew. By now the MacDougalls had an 11-month-old daughter, Amelia, who had been born in Philadelphia. Leaving the US was hard for Lisa; their family had put down so many roots over the past six years and made so many American friends, and although they did have the opportunity to apply for a green card which could provide permanent residency, to the surprise of their friends the MacDougalls rejected this option in favour of another international move. They chose Asia because it would be good for both their careers and yet still close enough to Australia to maintain family and professional ties without having to repatriate. Lachlan approached his company about an internal transfer, and secured a new role in Singapore.

Singapore had been everything Lachlan and Lisa had hoped for and they had lived there – again, on a local package – much like they had lived in the US: they bought an apartment, secured permanent residency, sent their daughter to a local pre-school, hired a maid, and joined a local sailing club. Work permits for spouses were easy to get in Singapore, so Lisa had been able to secure part-time employment. Because he had PR status, Lachlan had been able to change employers three years after moving there, and was now a regional expert in his field, being routinely approached by headhunters trying to poach him to accept other job offers. The expatriate community was very well established, so the MacDougalls enjoyed a thriving social life. And it was here, in Singapore, that their second daughter, Emily, was born.

Now, a third move to China was looming, and as Lisa reflected on their expatriate life so far, she knew that this move, more than any before, was a game changer – for her, for Lachlan, and most importantly, for their family. They didn't *have* to leave Singapore; they were permanent residents and they owned their own home, so they could stay as long as they wished and life there was very good. It became abundantly clear that moving to China was a *choice* unlike any other they had had before. Lachlan's employer had asked him to consider a transfer to Shanghai – on a local-plus package no less, with housing and schooling – but if he did not wish to go the company maintained there would be no repercussions, as he was their most senior Asia executive, and they didn't want to lose him. China was, nonetheless, a key strategic market for the company and Lachlan was, by all accounts, perfect for the job. Lisa considered that her husband's career would undoubtedly flourish if they went to China, but she was struck by the fact that, his career aside, there was no other compelling reason to leave Singapore. With this in mind, she knew that if they were to move again, it would need to benefit everyone in the family and not just one person.

BEING A DUAL-CAREER TRAILING SPOUSE IS HARDER THAN YOU THINK

In the months leading up to the China decision, Lisa spent a lot of time reflecting on her trailing spouse journey, trying to piece together what it all meant and what it could mean in a new city like Shanghai. She knew now that without a doubt she was, and probably always would be, the trailing spouse in their family, the person whose job would *not* take them to their next destination, and whose career would require more compromises than Lachlan would need to make in his. After all, he was now a Regional Vice-President for an SME technology firm in Singapore and earning more money than she could ever hope to even as a tenured professor, and that was ok with both of them; his career supported their lifestyle, and she supported their growing family. She was surprised that her trailing spouse status didn't seem to bother her anymore, whereas even a year earlier it had been all she could think about.

Since marrying Lachlan and moving to Chicago, Lisa had not worked full-time for over a decade. The first six years they had spent in the US had been challenging. Chicago had been easy, almost like a long holiday, but that had changed once they moved to Philadelphia and committed to staying in the US for the full duration of their visa. The career she had put 'on hold' back in Sydney, with the intention that she would return to it in a couple of years, was now a thing of the past. With no prospects to legally work in Philly, a husband frequently away on regional business trips, and a waning interest in charity work (which she stereotyped as something 'old ladies' did), Lisa found herself increasingly frustrated and constrained by a trailing spouse life that she had once so willingly embraced. She was bored. Life seemed dull, meaningless and oppressive – and she hadn't yet reached the age of 35! Without a business card and a job title, she felt invisible at the many functions she attended as 'Lachlan's wife'. Instinctively she knew that their decision to move to Philadelphia had resulted in a major loss of her identity, much of which Lisa painfully realized had been tied up in a career that was now impossible for her to continue. She had two choices – commit to a life of resigned acceptance as 'Mrs Nobody' until they repatriated, or do something about it.

Like many trailing spouses often do, Lisa resolved her boredom by turning a negative situation into a life-affirming achievement: she went back to school and obtained a doctorate. On the advice of her doctoral supervisor, she chose a field of research she knew something about – expatriates. As it turned out, Lisa *loved* research and was quite good at it. Being an 'insider' to the expatriate community had many advantages – invitations to speak at international conferences, opportunities to write about her research for industry periodicals, and the chance to start a global mobility website. Slowly, year by year, as her research progressed and her expatriate journey continued, Lisa built a new career for herself and, as she would soon discover, a relatively portable one at that.

It was telling that when the move to Singapore arose she was the one pushing them to go, rather than repatriating to Sydney as Lachlan had thought they would do. As a 'global mobility academic', she perceived there would be few negatives – personally *or* professionally – if they undertook another international assignment, and she had been right: in Singapore she had easy access to a work permit and so was able to do part-time consulting for major corporations as well as adjunct teaching. When she graduated with her PhD, Lisa took a tenure-track position at John Campbell College with the intention that she would spend between three and five years there before considering a move elsewhere. It had been important that she re-enter the full-time workforce, not only professionally but also for her self-esteem and confidence. She felt a deep obligation to financially contribute to the family again, to regain some balance and equality in her marriage, and to be a strong role model as a working mother for her two young daughters. Like many trailing spouses before her, Lisa believed that the longer she remained a 'supportive non-working wife', the harder it would be for her to have a 'voice' in major family decisions where financial considerations would be an over-riding concern.

Now all her thoughts turned to Shanghai. It seemed quite remarkable that in little more than a decade both she and Lachlan had somehow turned their 'expatriate adventure' into thriving global careers – and they weren't done yet. She already had two job offers to consider at local universities in China, having interviewed with institutions when the family went on their familiarization trip a couple of months earlier, but these were predominantly teaching jobs much like the one at John Campbell had turned out to be. Getting a spouse work permit in China would be relatively simple so she found out, but her passion was research and, if she stood any chance of building an academic career, she needed to be in a job that allowed her to publish in good journals. As a foreigner in China with only 'hobby' Mandarin to get her by, how quickly could she establish a new network of contacts to find such a job? And what employment stereotypes and barriers would she face as an 'expat wife'? Although another international move would certainly deepen Lisa's mobility knowledge and experience, moving to China was a career risk – and one that she wasn't sure she needed to take.

COMING FULL CIRCLE TO EMBRACE SHANGHAI

As Lisa drove home from John Campbell College, having resigned from her job earlier that day, she turned on the car radio and listened to a *BBC* World Service programme in which well-known author and publisher, Robin Pascoe, was being interviewed about her newly released book on 'global nomads'. As Pascoe recalled her life as a foreign service spouse, raising two children in four Asian countries during the 1980s and 90s, and spoke of the many times she had reinvented her career as a journalist, author, public speaker, and now publisher, Lisa was struck by how common global careers had become, and by women no less. Although she herself had at times felt somewhat alone in her own journey as a trailing spouse, Lisa nonetheless knew that international mobility was inevitable for many employees as talent management became critical for multinational firms. She and Lachlan were no exception to this phenomenon: they may not have intentionally set out to pursue global careers a decade earlier, but once they had arrived on the international labour market, it made sense that they remain there. They had benefited immensely by doing so, despite the many personal and professional hurdles she had overcome, and even though repatriation to Australia had been an ongoing talking point for years over the dinner table, somehow it just never seemed to factor into any of their plans.

Lisa now clearly saw for the first time that moving to China signalled an important change in their family dynamic: the MacDougalls had acquired the relatively rare skill of 'family mobility' and she instinctively knew that it was a skillset likely to be highly sought after by many global companies. Their 'united nations' global family was, in reality, a valuable commodity. Although she had always had the opportunity to return to a relatively comfortable and stable 'north shore life' in Sydney had she wanted to, Lisa had never really seriously considered it an option; instead, she knew now that she and Lachlan would probably pursue global careers in one form or another for the rest of their lives, as would their children. As Pascoe continued to tell her story on the radio, Lisa began to slowly let go of her fears and to once and for all embrace the Shanghai opportunity. And then she began to wonder . . . retaining their Singapore permanent residency status might not have been necessary after all, given that there were so many other cities they could move to when the Shanghai assignment was complete.

DISCUSSION QUESTIONS

1 In what ways does the MacDougall family represent a rare and valuable resource to a multinational firm?
2 Reflecting on Lisa's dual-career trailing spouse journey, how would you have approached the situation differently?
3 Although not discussed, what impact do you think international mobility has had on the MacDougalls' marriage?

GLOSSARY OF KEY TERMS

AAA typology Aggregation, adaptation and arbitrage strategies.

Absolute advantage The economic advantage one nation enjoys that is absolutely superior to other nations.

Absorptive capacity The ability to recognise the value of new information, assimilate it, and apply it.

Accommodative strategy A strategy that is characterised by some support from top managers, who may increasingly view CSR as a worthwhile endeavour.

Acquisition The transfer of the control of operations and management from one firm (target) to another (acquirer), the former becoming a unit of the latter.

Acquisition premium The difference between the acquisition price and the market value of target firms.

Adaptability The ability to change supply chain configurations in response to long-term changes in the environment and technology.

Adaptation strategy Strategy of delivering locally adapted products in each market.

Administrative practices Bureaucratic rules that make it harder to import foreign goods.

Agglomeration The location advantages that arise from the clustering of economic activities in certain locations.

Aggregation strategy Strategy of realising synergies between operations at different locations.

Agility The ability to quickly react to unexpected shifts in supply and demand.

Alignment The alignment of interest of various players.

Andean Community A customs union in South America that was launched in 1969.

Anti-competitive practices (by a dominant firm) Business practices by a dominating firm that make it more difficult for competitors to enter or survive.

Anti-dumping duty Costs levied on imports that have been 'dumped' (selling below costs to 'unfairly' drive domestic firms out of business).

Anti-trust laws Laws that attempt to curtail anticompetitive collusion by businesses.

Anti-trust policy American term for competition

Appreciation (of a currency) An increase in the value of a currency.

Apprenticeship system Vocational training system for crafts and professions

Appropriability The ability of the firm to appropriate the values for itself.

Arbitrage strategy Strategy of exploiting differences in prices in different markets.

Artefacts of culture Physical objects that represent the visible surface of culture.

Asset specificity An investment that is specific to a business relationship.

Association of South-east Asian Nations (ASEAN) The organisation underpinning regional economic integration in Southeast Asia.

Attack An initial set of actions to gain competitive advantage.

Australia-New Zealand Closer Economic Relations Trade Agreement (ANZCERTA) A bilateral trade agreement between Australia and New Zealand.

AMC framework A conceptual framework of awareness, motivation, capability indicating when firms are likely to attack and counterattack each other.

Balance of payments (BoP) A country's international transaction statement, including merchandise trade, service trade, and capital movement.

Balance of trade The aggregation of importing and exporting that leads to the country-level trade surplus or deficit.

Bandwagon effect The result of investors moving as a herd in the same direction at the same time.

Bargaining power The ability to extract a favourable outcome from negotiations due to one party's strengths.

Base of the pyramid The vast majority of humanity, about four billion people, who make less than €1 500 a year.

Basel Committee A group of central bankers establishing standards for banking supervision.

Basel II/Basel III The name of a set of rules for banking regulation.

Benchmarking An examination of resources to perform a particular activity compared against competitors.

Bid rate The price offered to buy a currency.

Bill of lading (B/L) Document certifying the delivery of the goods to a ship or train

Black swan events Rare events that occur only once in a generation.

Blue ocean strategy A strategy of attack that avoids direct confrontation.

Bologna Process A political process aimed at harmonising European higher education.

Born global (international new venture) Start-up company that from inception, seeks to derive significant competitive advantages from the use of resources and the sale of outputs in multiple countries.

Bretton Woods system A system in which all currencies were pegged at a fixed rate to the US dollar.

581

BRIC Brazil, Russia, India and China.

Brownfield acquisition Acquisition where subsequent investment overlays the acquired organisation.

Build-operate-transfer (BOT) A contract combining the construction and temporary operation of a project eventually to be transferred to a new owner.

Business processing outsourcing (BPO) The outsourcing of business services such as IT, HR or logistics.

Business-to-business (B2B) marketing Marketing to other businesses that will further process the product.

Business-to-consumer (B2C) marketing Marketing to final consumers of a product.

Business unit JV A JV in which existing business units from two firms are merged.

Capability Firm-specific abilities to use resources to achieve organisational objectives.

Capability-enhancing FDI Investors' quest for new ideas and technologies that to upgrade their own technological and managerial capabilities.

Capacity to punish Sufficient resources possessed by a price leader to deter and combat defection.

Capital and financial account (of the BoP) Sales and purchases of financial assets.

Capital flight A phenomenon in which a large number of individuals and companies exchange domestic currencies for a foreign currency.

Captive (in-house) offshoring Setting up subsidiaries abroad – the work done is in-house but the location is foreign.

Cartel An entity that engages in output- and price-fixing, involving multiple competitors.

Case law Rules of law that have been created by precedents of cases in court.

Causal ambiguity The difficulty of identifying the causal determinants of successful firm performance.

Central and Eastern Europe The common name used for the countries east of the former Iron Curtain.

Centres of excellence An MNE subsidiary explicitly recognised as a source of important capabilities, with the intention that these capabilities be leveraged by and/or disseminated to other subsidiaries.

CFA franc Common currency of French-speaking countries in West Africa.

Child labour Working persons under the age of 16.

cif (costs of insurance and freight) Contract clause: the seller has to pay all transportation costs to a destination port.

Civil law A legal tradition that uses comprehensive statutes and codes as a primary means to form legal judgments.

Civilisation The highest cultural grouping of people and the broadest level of cultural identity people have.

Classical trade theories The major theories of international trade that were advanced before the 20th century, which consist of mercantilism, absolute advantage and comparative advantage.

Cluster Countries that share similar cultures together.

Code of conduct Written polities and standards for corporate conduct and ethics.

Cognitive pillar The internalised, taken-for-granted values and beliefs that guide individual and firm behaviour.

Collectivism The idea that the identity of an individual is primarily based on the identity of his or her collective group.

Collusion Collective attempts between competing firms to reduce competition.

Collusive price setting Price setting by monopolists or collusion parties at a higher than competitive level.

Comecon The pre-1990 trading bloc of the socialist countries.

Command economy An economy in which all factors of production are government- or state-owned and controlled, and all supply, demand and pricing are planned by the government.

Common currency Currency shared by a number of countries.

Common law A legal tradition that is shaped by precedents and traditions from previous judicial decisions.

Common market Combining everything that a customs union has, a common market permits free movement of goods and people.

Communities of practice (CoP) Groups of people doing similar or related work and sharing knowledge about their practices of work.

Commuter assignment Assignments that involve regular stays abroad but with the main base remaining back home.

Comparative advantage Relative (not absolute) advantage in one economic activity that one nation enjoys in comparison with other nations.

Compensation The determination of salary and benefits.

Competition policy (anti-trust policy) Policy governing the rules of the game in competition in a country.

Competitive advantage The ability of a firm to outperform its rivals

Competitive dynamics The actions and responses undertaken by competing firms.

Competitor analysis The process of anticipating a rival's actions in order to both revise a firm's plan and prepare to deal with rivals' responses.

Compliance Procedures to monitor and enforce standards for employees and suppliers.

Compliance training Mandatory training and tests designed to ensure that every employee knows the relevant codes of conduct.

Concentration ratio The percentage of total industry sales accounted for by the top 4, 8, or twenty firms.

Consortium A project based temporary business owned and managed jointly by several firms.

Contender strategy This strategy centres on a firm engaging in rapid learning and then expanding overseas.

Contract work A short assignment for a specific project or contract.

Coordinated market economy (CME) A system of coordinating through a variety of other means in addition to market signals.

Copenhagen Accord A declaration by developed and developing countries to combat climate change.

Copenhagen Criteria Criteria the new members have to fulfil to be admitted as members of the EU.

Copyrights Exclusive legal rights of authors and publishers to publish and disseminate their work.

Corporate governance Rules by which shareholders and other interested parties control corporate decisionmakers.

Corporate language The language used for communications between entities of the same MNE in different countries.

Corporate social responsibility (CSR) The consideration of, and response to, issues beyond the narrow economic, technical and legal requirements of the firm to accomplish social benefits along with the traditional economic gains which the firm seeks.

Corruption The abuse of public power for private benefits, usually in the form of bribery.

Cosmopolitans The people embracing cultural diversity and the opportunities of globalisation.

Council of Europe A loose association in which essentially all European countries are members.

Council of the European Union The top decisionmaking body of the EU, consisting of ministers from the national governments; it decides by qualified majority voting.

Counter party risk The risk of a business partner not being able to fulfil a contract.

Counter-attack A set of actions in response to an attack.

Country or regional manager The business leader of a specific geographic area or region.

Country-of-origin effect The positive or negative perception of firms and products from a certain country.

Crawling bands A policy of keeping the exchange rate within a specified range, which may be changing over time.

Cross-border services Supplying services across national borders.

Cross-market retaliation The ability of a firm to expand in a competitor's market if the competitor attacks in its original market.

Cultural distance The difference between two cultures along some identifiable dimensions (such as individualism).

Cultural intelligence An individual's ability to understand and adjust to new cultures.

Culture The collective programming of the mind that distinguishes the members of one group or category of people from another.

Culture shock An expatriate's reaction to a new, unpredictable, and therefore uncertain environment.

Currency board A monetary authority that issues notes and coins convertible into a key foreign currency at a fixed exchange rate.

Currency exchange market A market where individuals, firms, governments and banks buy and sell foreign currencies.

Currency hedging A transaction that protects traders and investors from exposure to the fluctuations of the spot rate.

Currency risk diversification Reducing overall risk exposure by working with a number of different currencies.

Currency swap A currency exchange transaction between two firms in which one currency is converted into another in Time 1, with an agreement to revert it back to the original currency at a specific Time 2 in the future.

Current account (of the BoP) Exports and imports of goods and services.

Customs union One step beyond a free trade area, a customs union imposes common external policies on non-participating countries.

Deadweight loss Net losses that occur in an economy as the result of tariffs.

Defender strategy This strategy centres on leveraging local assets in areas in which MNEs are weak.

Defensive strategy A strategy that focuses on regulatory compliance with little top management commitment to CSR causes.

Democracy A political system in which citizens elect representatives to govern the country on their behalf.

Depreciation (of a currency) A decrease in the value of a currency.

Design and build (DB) contract A contract combining the architectural or design work with the actual construction.

Development aid A gift from generous donors wishing to help developing countries.

Direct exports The sale of products made by firms in their home country to customers in other countries.

Directorate General (DG) A department of the EU commission, similar to a ministry of a national government.

Dispute settlement mechanism A procedure of the WTO to resolve conflicts between governments over trade-related matters.

Dissemination risks The risks associated with unauthorised diffusion of firm-specific know-how.

Distribution channel The set of business units and intermediaries that facilitates the movement of goods to consumers.

Distributor An intermediary trading on their own account.

Divestment The sale or closure of a business unit or asset.

Dodger strategy This strategy centres on cooperating through joint ventures (JVs) with MNEs and sell-offs to MNEs.

Doha Development Agenda A round of WTO negotiations started in Doha, Qatar, in 2001 focusing on economic development.

Domestic outsourcing Outsourcing to a firm in the same country.

Downstream vertical FDI A type of vertical FDI in which a firm engages in a downstream stage of the value chain in two different countries.

Due diligence The assessment of the target firm's financial status, resources and strategic fit.

Dumping An exporter selling below cost abroad and planning to raise prices after eliminating local rivals.

Dynamic capabilities Higher level capabilities that enable an organisation to continuously adapt to new technologies and changes in the external environment.

Economic forecasting A technique using econometric models to predict the likely future value of key economic variables.

Economic system Rules of the game on how a country is governed economically.

Economic transition The process of changing from central plan to a market economy.

Economic union In addition to all features of a common market, members of an economic union coordinate and harmonise economic policies.

Economies of scale Reduction in unit costs achieved by increasing volume.

ECOWAS Economic integration in West Africa.

Efficiency-enhancing FDI Investors' quest to single out the most efficient locations featuring a combination of scale economies and low-cost factors.

Efficiency-enhancing Firms' quest to single out the most efficient locations featuring a combination of scale economies and low-cost factors.

Emerging economies (emerging markets) Economies that only recently established institutional frameworks that facilitate international trade and investment, typically with low- or middle-level income and above average economic growth.

Emerging economy MNEs MNEs that originate from an emerging economy, and are headquartered there.

Entrepreneurial teams A group of people jointly acting as entrepreneurs.

Entrepreneurs Leaders identifying opportunities and taking decisions to exploit them.

Entry strategy A plan that specifies the objectives of an entry and how to achieve them.

Equity mode A mode of entry that involves taking (full or partial) ownership in a local firm.

Erasmus+ Programme An EU programme encouraging student mobility in Europe.

Ethical imperialism The absolute belief that 'there is only one set of Ethics (with a capital E), and we have it'.

Ethical relativism A perspective that suggests that all ethical standards are relative.

Ethics The principles, standards and norms of conduct governing individual and firm behaviour.

Ethnocentric approach An emphasis on the norms and practices of the parent company (and the parent country of the MNE) by relying on PCNs.

Ethnocentric perspective A view of the world through the lens of one's own culture.

EU Canada Comprehensive Economic and Trade Agreement (CETA) A economic integration agreement in negotiation between the EU and Canada.

Euro The currency of the European Monetary Union.

European Bank for Reconstruction and Development (EBRD) A multilateral bank designed to help transition economies.

European Central Bank (ECB) The central bank for the eurozone.

European Commission The executive arm of the EU, similar to a national government.

European Constitution An ambitious project to create a new legal foundation for the EU, which failed.

European Convention on Human Rights A charter defining human rights in Europe.

European Council The assembly of heads of governments setting overall policy directions for the EU.

European Court of Human Rights An international court assessing human rights cases in Europe.

European Court of Justice (ECJ) The court system of the EU.

European Parliament The directly elected representation of European citizens.

European Stability Mechanism (ESM) A fund to support member countries with difficulties raising money on the capital markets.

European Union The political and economic organisation of 27 countries in Europe.

Eurozone The countries that have adopted the euro as their currency.

Exchange rate The price of one currency in another currency.

Exchange rate risk (or currency risk) The risk of financial losses because of unexpected changes in exchange rates.

Expatriate (expat) A non-native employee who works in a foreign country.

Expatriate assignments A temporary job abroad with a multinational company.

Expatriate stress Stress caused by an imbalance between expectations and abilities affected by culture shock.

Experiential knowledge Knowledge learned by engaging in the activity and context.

Explicit collusion Firms directly negotiate output, fix pricing and divide markets.

Explicit CSR Voluntarily assuming responsibilities of societal concerns.

Explicit knowledge Knowledge that is codifiable (that is, can be written down and transferred with little loss of its richness).

Export intermediary A firm that performs an important 'middleman' function by linking sellers and buyers overseas.

Exporter Seller of products or services to another country.

Exporting Selling abroad.

Expropriation Governments' confiscation of private assets.

Extender strategy This strategy centres on leveraging home-grown competencies abroad.

Factor endowment theory (or Heckscher-Ohlin theory) A theory that suggests that nations will develop comparative advantage based on their locally abundant factors.

FDI flow The amount of FDI moving in a given period (usually a year) in a certain direction.

FDI stock The total accumulation of inbound FDI in a country or outbound FDI from a country across a given period of time (usually several years).

Femininity Values traditionally associated with female role, such as compassion, case and quality of life.

First-mover advantage Advantage that first entrants enjoy and do not share with late entrants.

Fixed exchange rate An exchange rate of a currency relative to other currencies.

Floating or (flexible) exchange rate policy The willingness of a government to let the demand and supply conditions determine exchange rates.

Footloose plant Plants that can easily be relocated.

Foreign direct investment (FDI) Investments in, controlling and managing value-added activities in other countries.

Foreign portfolio investment (FPI) Investment in a portfolio of foreign securities such as stocks and bonds.

Foreign subsidiary Operations abroad set up by foreign direct investment.

Formal institutions Institutions represented by laws, regulations and rules.

Forward discount A condition under which the forward rate of one currency relative to another currency is higher than the spot rate.

Forward exchange rate The exchange rate for forward transactions.

Forward premium A condition under which the forward rate of one currency relative to another currency is lower than the spot rate.

Forward transaction A currency exchange transaction in which participants buy and sell currencies now for future delivery, typically in 30, 90, or 180 days, after the date of the transaction.

Four freedoms of the EU single market Freedom of movement of people, goods, services, and capital.

Franchisee The company receiving a franchise.

Franchising Firm A's agreement to give Firm B the rights to use a package of A's proprietary assets for a royalty fee paid to A by B.

Franchisor The company granting a franchise.

Free float A pure market solution to determine exchange rates.

Fob (free on board) Contract clause: the seller has to deliver goods free on board of a ship or train.

Free trade Trade uninhibited by trade barriers.

Free trade area (FTA) A group of countries that remove trade barriers among themselves.

Full immersion training Intensive exposure to a foreign culture and language by living within that culture.

Game theory A theory on how agents interact strategically to win.

General Agreement on Tariffs and Trade (GATT) A multilateral agreement governing the international trade of goods (merchandise).

General Agreement on Trade in Services (GATS) A WTO agreement governing the international trade of services.

Generalised System of Preferences (GSP) A system of tariff reductions facilitating less and least develop country's access to EU markets.

Geocentric approach A focus on finding the most suitable managers, who can be PCNs, HCNs or TCNs.

Geographic area structure An organisational structure that organises the MNE according to different countries and regions.

Global key accounts Customers served at multiple sites around the world, but that negotiate centrally.

Global matrix An organisational structure often used to alleviate the disadvantages associated with both geographic area and global product division structures, especially for MNEs adopting a transnational strategy.

Global product division An organisational structure that assigns global responsibilities to each product division.

Global sourcing Buying inputs all over the world.

Global standards strategy A strategy that relies on the development and distribution of standardised products worldwide to reap the maximum benefits from low-cost advantages.

Global strategies Strategies that take advantage of operations spread across the world.

Global talent management The attraction, selection, development and retention of talented employees in the most strategic roles within an MNE.

Global talent pool Employees that are systematically prepared to assume leadership.

Global virtual teams Teams that are geographically dispersed and interact primarily through electronic communication.

Globalfocusing A strategic shift from diversification to specialisation which increasing the international profile.

Globalisation A process leading to greater interdependence and mutual awareness among economic, political and social units in the world, and among actors in general.

Gold standard A system in which the value of most major currencies was maintained by fixing their prices in terms of gold, which served as the common denominator.

Goodwill The value of a firm's abilities to develop and leverage its reputation.

Greenfield operation Building factories and offices from scratch (on a proverbial piece of 'green field' formerly used for agricultural purposes).

Gross domestic product (GDP) The sum of value added by resident firms, households, and governments operating in an economy.

Gross national income (GNI) GDP plus income from non-resident sources abroad. GNI is the term used by the World Bank and other international organisations to supersede the term GNP.

Gross national product (GNP) Gross domestic product plus income from non-resident sources abroad.

Gulf Cooperation Council (GCC) Political and economic integration involving Saudi Arabia, Kuwait, Bahrain, Oman, Qatar and the United Arab Emirates.

Harmonised sector Sectors of industry for which the EU has created common rules.

Headhunter company A company specialising on finding suitable people for senior positions.

Health, safety and environment (HSE) A common term to cover the areas for which companies have mandatory standards.

Hidden champions Market leaders in niche markets keeping a low public profile.

High-context culture A culture in which communication relies a lot on the underlying unspoken context, which is as important as the words used.

Holy An item or activity that is treated with particular respect by a religion.

Home replication strategy A strategy that emphasises international replication of home country-based competencies such as production scales, distribution efficiencies and brand power.

Horizontal FDI A type of FDI in which a firm duplicates its home country-based activities at the same value chain stage in a host country.

Host country national (HCN) An individual from the host country who works for an MNE.

Hubris A manager's overconfidence in his or her capabilities.

Human resource management (HRM) Activities that attract, select and manage employees.

Human resources Resources embedded in individuals working in an organisation.

Hypernorms Norms considered valid anywhere in the world.

IMF conditionality Conditions that the IMF attaches to loans to bail out countries in financial distress.

Implicit CSR Participating in the wider formal and informal institutions for the society's interests and concerns.

Import quota Restrictions on the quantity of imports.

Import tariff A tax imposed on imports.

Importer Buyer of goods or services from another country.

Importing Buying from abroad.

Inbound logistics Purchasing and the coordination of intermediaries on the supply side.

Indirect exports A way for SMEs to reach overseas customers by exporting through domestic-based export intermediaries.

Individualism The perspective that the identity of an individual is fundamentally his or her own.

Infant industry argument The argument that temporary protection of young industries may help them to attain international competitiveness in the long run.

Inflation The (average) change of prices over time.

Informal institutions Rules that are not formalised but exist in for example norms, values and ethics.

Ingredients branding Creating a brand identity for a component of a product.

In-group Individuals and firms regarded as part of 'us'.

Inpatriate Employee of a foreign subsidiary temporarily relocated to the MNE's headquarters for the purposes of (1) filling skill shortages at headquarters, and (2) developing a global mindset for such inpatriates.

Input foreclosure Practice of a vertically integrated firm to cut off a competitor from key suppliers.

Institutional distance The extent of similarity or dissimilarity between the regulatory, normative and cognitive institutions of two countries.

Institutional framework Formal and informal institutions governing individual and firm behaviour.

Institutional transition Fundamental and comprehensive changes introduced to the formal and informal rules of the game that affect organisations as players.

Institution-based view A theoretical perspective in international business that suggests that firm performance is, at least in part, determined by the institutional frameworks governing firm.

Institutions Formal and informal rules of the game.

Instrumental view A view that treating stakeholders well may indirectly help financial performance.

Intangible assets Assets that are hard to observe and difficult (or sometimes impossible) to quantify.

Integration-responsiveness framework A framework of MNE management on how to simultaneously deal with two sets of pressures for global integration and local responsiveness.

Intellectual property rights Rights associated with the ownership of intellectual property.

Interest rate parity Hypothesis suggesting that the interest rate in two currencies should be the same after accounting for spot and forward in exchange rates.

Internalisation advantages Advantages of organising activities within a multinational firm rather than using a market transaction.

International business (IB) (1) A business (firm) that engages in international (cross-border) economic activities, and/or (2) the action of doing business abroad.

International division A structure that is typically set up when firms initially expand abroad, often engaging in a home replication strategy.

International investment agreements (IIAs) Agreements between states to protect foreign direct investment between countries.

International Monetary Fund (IMF) A multilateral organisation promoting international monetary cooperation and providing temporary financial assistance to countries with balance of payments problems, in order to help secure macroeconomic stability.

Intra-firm trade International trade between two subsidiaries in two countries controlled by the same MNE.

Investor-state dispute settlement (ISDS) Legal processes using tribunals that are outside the national and supranational court systems.

Joint-venture (JV) An operation with shared ownership by several domestic or foreign companies.

Knowledge governance The structures and mechanisms MNEs use to facilitate the creation, integration, sharing, and utilisation of knowledge.

Knowledge management The structures, processes, and systems that actively develop, leverage, and transfer knowledge.

Knowledge spillover Knowledge diffused from one firm to others among closely located firms.

Kyoto Protocol An agreement committing developed countries to limit their greenhouse gas emissions.

Labour standards Rules for the employment of labourers including working hours, minimum pay, union representation, and child labour.

Language A system of shared meanings that enables people to effectively communicate.

Language barriers Communication barriers between people who speak different mother tongues and lack a shared language.

Late-mover advantages Advantages that late movers obtain and that first movers do not enjoy.

Legal certainty Clarity over the relevant rules applying to a particular situation.

Legal system The rules of the game on how a country's laws are enacted and enforced.

Leniency programmes Programmes that give immunity to members of a cartel that first report the cartel to the authorities.

Letter of credit (L/C) A financial contract that states that the importer's bank will pay a specific sum of money to the exporter upon delivery of the merchandise.

Liability of outsidership The *inherent* disadvantage that outsiders experience in a new environment because of their lack of familiarity.

Liberal market economy (LME) A system of coordination primarily through market signals.

Liberalisation The removal of regulatory restrictions on business.

Licensee The company receiving a licence.

Licensing Firm A's agreement to give Firm B the rights to use A's proprietary technology or trademark for a royalty fee paid to A by B.

Licensor The company granting a licence.

Lingua franca The dominance of one language as a global business language.

Lobbying Making your voice heard and known to decision-makers with the aim of influencing political processes.

Local content requirement A requirement that a certain proportion of the value of the goods made in one country originate from that country.

Local responsiveness The necessity to be responsive to different customer preferences around the world.

Localisation (multidomestic) strategy A strategy that focuses on a number of foreign countries/regions, each of which is regarded as a stand-alone 'local' (domestic) market worthy of significant attention and adaptation.

Location advantages Advantages enjoyed by firms operating in certain locations.

Location-bound resources Resources that cannot be transferred abroad.

Location-specific advantages Advantages that can be exploited by those present at a location.

Long-term orientation A perspective that emphasises perseverance and savings for future betterment.

Low-context culture A culture in which communication is usually taken at face value without much reliance on unspoken context.

M&A Popular shorthand for 'mergers and acquisitions'.

Maastricht Criteria Criteria that countries have to fulfil to join the eurozone.

Maastricht Treaty A major treaty deepening integration in Europe.

Managed float The practice of influencing exchange rates through selective government intervention.

Management contract A contract over the management of assets or a firm owned by someone else.

Market commonality The overlap between two rivals' markets.

Market division collusion A collusion to divide markets among competitors.

Market economy An economy that is characterised by the 'invisible hand' of market forces.

Market failure Imperfections of the market mechanism that make some transactions prohibitively costly.

Market seeking FDI Firms' quest to go after countries that offer strong demand for their products and services.

Market segmentation A way to identify consumers who differ from others in purchasing behaviour.

Marketing Efforts to create, develop and defend markets that satisfy the needs and wants of individual and business customers.

Marketing mix The four underlying components of marketing: product, price, promotion and place.

Masculinity Values traditionally associated with male role, such as assertive, decisive and aggressive.

Members of the European Parliament (MEPs) Parliamentarians directly elected by the citizens of the EU.

Mercosur A customs union in South America that was launched in 1991.

Merger The combination of operations and management of two firms to establish a new legal entity.

Migrant workers Workers from rural areas temporarily working in factories in the cities.

Mimetic behaviour Imitating the behaviour of others as a means to reduce uncertainty.

Modern trade theories The major theories of international trade that were advanced in the 20th century, which consist of product life cycle, strategic trade, and national competitive advantage.

Modes of entry The format of foreign market entry.

Monetary union Countries sharing a common currency and monetary policy.

Multicultural team A work team with members representing multiple cultures.

Multilateral organisations Organisations set up by several collaborating countries.

Multimarket competition Firms engage the same rivals in multiple markets.

Multinational enterprise (MNE) A firm that engages in foreign direct investments and operates in multiple countries.

Multiple acquisition A strategy based on acquiring and integrating multiple businesses.

Multi-tier branding A portfolio of different brands targeted at different consumer segments.

Mutual recognition The principle that products recognised as legal in one country may be sold throughout the EU.

National innovation systems The institutions and organisations that influence innovation activity in a country.

Natural resource-seeking FDI Firms' quest to pursue natural resources in certain locations.

Nearshoring Offshoring to a nearby location, i.e. within Europe.

Non-discrimination principle A principle that a country cannot discriminate among its trading partners (a concession given to one country needs to be made available to all other WTO members).

Non-equity mode A mode of entry that does not involve owning equity in a local firm.

Non-governmental organisations (NGOs) Organisations, such as environmentalists, human rights activists and consumer groups that are not affiliated with governments.

Nontariff barrier (NTB) Trade barriers that rely on nontariff means to discourage imports.

Normative pillar The mechanism through which norms influence individual and firm behaviour.

Normative view A view that firms ought to be self-motivated to 'do it right' because they have societal obligations.

North American Free Trade Agreement (NAFTA) A free trade agreement among Canada, Mexico, and the USA.

Not-invented-here syndrome The tendency to distrust new ideas coming from outside of one's own organization or community.

Obsolescing bargain Refers to the deal struck by MNEs and host governments, which change their requirements after the initial FDI entry.

Offer rate The price offered to sell a currency.

Offshore outsourcing Outsourcing to another firm doing the activity abroad.

Offshoring Moving an activity to a location abroad.

OLI paradigm A theoretical framework positing that ownership (O), locational (L), and internalisation (I) advantages combine to induce firms to engage in FDI.

Oligopoly A market form in which a market or industry is dominated by a small number competing firms (oligopolists).

Operation collaboration A form of strategic alliance that includes collaboration in operations, marketing or distribution.

Oportunistic behaviour Seeking self-interest with guile.

Opportunity cost Given the alternatives (opportunities), the cost of pursuing one activity at the expense of another activity.

Optimum currency area A theory establishing criteria for the optimal size of an area sharing a common currency.

Organisational (team embedded) knowledge Knowledge held in an organisation that goes beyond the knowledge of the individual members.

Organisational culture Employees' shared values, traditions, and social norms within an organisation.

Organisational fit The similarity in cultures, systems, and structures.

Original brand manufacturer (OBM) A firm that designs, manufactures, and markets branded products.

Original design manufacturer (ODM) A firm that both designs and manufactures products.

Original equipment manufacturer (OEM) A firm that executes the design blueprints provided by other firms and manufactures such products.

Outbound logistics Sales and the coordination of intermediaries on the customer side.

Out-group Individuals and firms not regarded as part of 'us'.

Outsourcing Turning over an organisational activity to an outside supplier that will perform it on behalf of the firm.

Output foreclosure Practice of a vertically integrated firm to cut off a competitor from key customers.

Overseas listing Raising capital by listing on a stock exchange abroad.

Ownership advantages Resources of the firm that are transferable across borders, and enable the firm to attain competitive advantages abroad.

Parent (home) country national (PCN) An employee who comes from the parent country of the MNE and works at its local subsidiary.

Partial acquisition Acquisition of an equity stake in another firm.

Patent race A competition of R&D units where the first one to patent a new technology gets to dominate a market.

Patents Legal rights awarded by government authorities to inventors of new technological ideas, who are given exclusive (monopoly) rights to derive income from such inventions.

Pegged exchange rate An exchange rate of a currency attached to that of another currency.

Performance appraisal The evaluation of employee performance for promotion, retention or termination purposes.

Philanthropy Donations for purposes that benefit the wider society.

Place The location where products and services are provided.

Platform investment an investment that provides a small foothold in a market or location.

Political risk Risk associated with political changes that may negatively impact on domestic and foreign firms.

Political system A system of the rules of the game on how a country is governed politically.

Political union The integration of political and economic affairs of a region.

Pollution haven Countries with lower environmental standards.

Polycentric approach An emphasis on the norms and practices of the host country.

Post-acquisition integration The process that aims to integrate two formerly independent firms after an acquisition.

Post-Bretton Woods system A system of flexible exchange rate regimes with no official common denominator.

Power distance The extent to which less powerful members within a country expect and accept that power is distributed unequally.

Predatory pricing An attempt to monopolise a market by setting prices below cost and intending to raise prices to cover losses in the long run after eliminating rivals.

President of the Commission The head of the EU's executive, similar to a national prime minister.

President of the European Council The person chairing the meetings of the European Council.

Price The expenditures that customers are willing to pay for a product.

Price elasticity How demand changes when prices change.

Price leader A firm that has a dominant market share and sets 'acceptable' prices and margins in the industry.

Primary resources The tangible and intangible assets as well as human resources that a firm uses to choose and implement its strategies.

Primary stakeholder groups The constituents on which the firm relies for its continuous survival and prosperity.

Prisoners' dilemma In game theory, a type of game in which the outcome depends on two parties deciding whether to cooperate or to defect.

Proactive strategy A strategy that endeavours to do more than is required in CSR.

Product The offerings that customers purchase.

Product life cycle theory A theory that accounts for changes in the patterns of trade over time by focusing on product life cycles.

Project management contract A contract to manage the whole of a project from inception to conclusion.

Promotion Communications that marketers insert into the marketplace.

Property rights The legal rights to use an economic property (resource) and to derive income and benefits from it.

Protectionism The idea that governments should actively protect domestic industries from imports and vigorously promote exports.

Psychological contract An informal understanding of expected delivery of benefits in the future for current services.

Purchasing power parity (PPP) A conversion that determines the equivalent amount of goods and services different currencies can purchase. This conversion is usually used to capture the differences in cost of living in different countries.

Purchasing power parity (PPP) hypothesis Hypothesis suggesting that, in the long run, baskets of goods would cost the same in all currencies ('law of one price').

R&D contract A subcontracting of R&D between firms.

Race to the bottom Countries competing for foreign direct investment by lowering environmental standards.

Recruitment The identification, selection, and hiring of staff.

Regulatory pillar The coercive power of governments.

Relationship marketing A focus to establish, maintain, and enhance relationships with customers.

Relative PPP hypothesis Hypothesis suggesting that changes in exchange rates will be proportional to differences in inflation rates.

Repatriation The process of facilitating the return of expatriates.

Repeated game A game played over several periods of time.

Reshoring Bringing activities back to a firm's home country.

Resource (factor) endowments The extent to which different countries possess various resources (factors), such as labour, land, and technology.

Resource mobility The ability to move resources from one part of a business to another.

Resource-based view A leading perspective in global business that posits that firm performance is fundamentally driven by firm-specific resources.

Returnees Returning expatriates.

Reverse culture shock Culture shock experience by persons returning to their country of origin.

Reverse knowledge transfer Knowledge created in a subsidiary being transferred from the subsidiary to a parent organisation.

Risk diversification Reduction of the risk profile of a company by investing in different countries and industries.

Risk management The identification, assessment and management of risks.

Risk-rating agencies Agencies that assign ratings to assets such as bond that indicate the level of riskiness of the asset.

Sales agent An intermediary receiving commission for sales.

Scale of entry The amount of resources committed to foreign market entry.

Scenario planning A technique generating multiple scenarios of possible future states of the industry.

Schengen Agreement The agreement that laid the basis for passport-free travel.

Schengen Area The area covered by the Schengen Agreement.

Schengen Visa Visa giving non-citizens access to the Schengen Area.

Schuman plan A plan in the 1950s that outlined the path for European Integration.

Secondary stakeholder groups Those who influence or affect, or are influenced or affected by, the corporation, but they are not engaged in transactions with the corporation and are not essential for its survival.

Secular societies Societies where religion does not dominate public life.

Servicing foreign residents Supplying services to customers coming from abroad.

Shanghai Cooperation Organisation Organisation facilitating military and economic cooperation among China, Russia and four of the Central Asian nations.

Shared value creation An approach to CSR that focuses on activities that are good for both the firm and its stakeholders.

Single European Act (SEA) The agreement that established the basis for the single European market.

Single market The EU's term of its common market.

Small- and medium-sized enterprises (SMEs) Firms with fewer than 500 employees.

Social capital The informal benefits individuals and organisations derive from their social structures and networks.

Social complexity The socially complex ways of organising typical of many firms.

South Asian Free Trade Area (SAFTA) Free trade area covering India, Pakistan, Bangladesh, Sri Lanka, The Maldives, Nepal and Bhutan.

Sovereign wealth fund A state-owned investment fund composed of financial assets such as stocks, bonds, real estate, or other financial instruments.

Spot market rate The exchange rate for immediate payment.

Spread The difference between the offered price and the bid price.

Staged acquisition Acquisition where ownership transfer takes places over stages.

Stage models Models depicting internationalisation as a slow stage-by-stage process an SME must go through.

Stakeholder Any group or individual who can affect or is affected by the achievement of the organisation's objectives.

Standards in advertising Formal rules designed by governments to protect consumers.

Standards of engagement (code of conduct, code of ethics) Written policies and standards for corporate conduct and ethics.

State aid Financial support from government to firms through e.g. subsidies or tax rebates.

Strategic alliances Collaborations between independent firms using equity modes, non-equity contractual agreements, or both.

Strategic fit The effective matching of complementary strategic capabilities.

Strategic hedging Organising activities in such a way that currencies of revenues and expenditures match.

Strategic trade policy Government subsidies inspired by strategic trade theory.

Strategic trade theory A theory that suggests that strategic intervention by governments in certain industries can enhance their odds for international success.

Strategy Objectives and set of action to achieve those objectives.

Stereotype A sets of simplistic often inaccurate generalizations about a group that allows others to categorize them.

Subcontracting A contract that involves outsourcing of an intermediate stage of a value chain.

Subsidiarity The EU takes action only if it is more effective than actions taken at lower levels.

Subsidiary initiative The proactive and deliberate pursuit of new opportunities by a subsidiary to expand its scope of responsibility.

Subsidy Government payments to (domestic) firms.

Subsidy competition The competition between governments trying to attract investors by offering subsidies.

Sunk cost Up-front investments that are non-recoverable if the project is abandoned.

Supply chain Flow of products, services, finances, and information that passes through a set of entities from a source to the customer.

Supply chain management Activities to plan, organise, lead, and control the supply chain.

Sustainability The ability to meet the needs of the present without compromising the ability of future generations to meet their needs.

Sustainable competitive advantage The ability to deliver persistently above-average performance.

Survival strategies A strategy designed to ensure survival by ensuring liquidity and positive cash flow.

SWOT analysis An analytical tool for determining a firm's strengths (S), weaknesses (W), opportunities (O), and threats (T).

Synergies Value created by combining two organisation that together are more valuable than the two organisations separately.

Taboo An item or activity considered unclean by a religion.

Tacit collusion Firms indirectly coordinate actions by signalling their intention to reduce output and maintain pricing above competitive levels.

Tacit knowledge Knowledge that is non-codifiable, and whose acquisition and transfer require hands-on practice.

Tangible assets Assets that are observable and easily quantified.

Tariff barrier Trade barriers that rely on tariffs to discourage imports.

Tax avoidance Reducing tax liability by legally moving profits to jurisdictions where tax rates are lower.

Temporary competitive advantage The ability to out-perform rivals for a limited time.

Tender A competition for a major contract.

Theory of absolute advantage A theory suggesting that under free trade, each nation gains by specialising in economic activities in which it has absolute advantage.

Theory of comparative advantage A theory that focuses on the relative (not absolute) advantage in one economic activity that one nation enjoys in comparison with other nations.

Theory of mercantilism A theory that holds the wealth of the world (measured in gold and silver) is fixed and that a nation that exports more and imports less would enjoy the net inflows of gold and silver and thus become richer.

Theory of national competitive advantage of industries (or 'diamond' model) A theory that suggests that the competitive advantage of certain industries in different nations depends on four aspects that form a 'diamond'.

Third country national (TCN) An employee who comes from neither the parent country nor the host country.

Third-party logistics (3PL) A neutral intermediary in the supply chain that provides logistics and other support services.

Tit-for-tat A strategy of matching the competitors move being either aggressive or accommodative.

Total cost of ownership Total cost needed to own a product, consisting of initial purchase cost and follow-up maintenance/service cost.

Totalitarianism (dictatorship) A political system in which one person or party exercises absolute political control over the population.

Trade deficit An economic condition in which a nation imports more than it exports.

Trade diversion A change in trade pattern away from comparative advantages due to trade barriers.

Trade embargo Politically motivated trade sanctions against foreign countries to signal displeasure.

Trade surplus An economic condition in which a nation exports more than it imports.

Trademarks Exclusive legal rights of firms to use specific names, brands, and designs to differentiate their products from others.

Trade-Related Aspects of Intellectual Property Rights (TRIPS) A WTO agreement governing intellectual property rights.

Training The specific preparation to do a particular job.

Transaction costs The costs of organizing economic transactions.

Transatlantic Trade and Investment Partnership (TTIP) An economic integration agreement in negotiation between the EU and USA.

Transnational strategy A strategy that endeavours to be cost efficient, locally responsive and learning driven simultaneously around the world.

Treaties of Rome The first treaties establishing European integration, which eventually led to the EU.

Triad Three regions of developed economies (North America, Western Europe, and Japan).

Triple bottom line The economic, social, and environmental performance that simultaneously satisfied the demands of all stakeholder groups.

Turnkey project A project in which clients pay contractors to design and construct new facilities and train personnel.

Uncertainty avoidance The extent to which members in different cultures accept ambiguous situations and tolerate uncertainty.

Uppsala model A model of internationalisation processes focusing on learning processes.

Upstream vertical FDI A type of vertical FDI in which a firm engages in an upstream stage of the value.

Value chain A chain of activities vertically related in the production of goods and services.

Varieties of capitalisms A scholarly view suggesting that economies have different inherent logics on how markets and other mechanisms coordinate economic activity.

Vertical FDI A type of FDI in which a firm moves upstream or downstream in different value chain stages in a host country.

Virtual team A team that is geographically dispersed and interacts primarily through electronic communication.

Virtual communities of practice Communities of practice interacting via the internet.

Voluntary export restraint (VER) An international agreement in which exporting countries voluntarily agree to restrict their exports.

VRIO framework The resource-based framework that focuses on the value creation (V), rarity (R), imit-ability (I), and organisational (O) aspects of resources.

Waves of globalisation The pattern of globalisation arising from a combination of long-terms trends and pendulum swings.

Western culture An aggregate term for European, North American, Australian and New Zealand cultures.

Wholly owned subsidiaries (WOS) A subsidiary located in a foreign country that is entirely owned by the parent multinational.

World Bank International organisation that provides loans for specific projects in developing countries to support their economic development.

World Trade Organisation (WTO) The organisation underpinning the multilateral trading system.

Worldwide (or global) mandate The charter to be responsible for one MNE function throughout the world.

CREDITS

NAME INDEX

Ahrendts, Angela 99
Albright, Madeleine 526

Barroso, José Manuel 534
Bartlett, Chris 423
Bastiat, Fredric 140
Bhagwati, Jagdish 145, 265
Bhattal, Jesse 402
Biyani, Kishore 354
Björk 70
Brant, Graham 332
Bush, George 37

Christiansen, Ole Kirk 111
Chua Sock Koong 526
Clinton, Hillary 171
Coase, Ronald 32
Colbert, Jean-Baptiste 126

Donaldson, Tomas 298

Eaton, Bob 414
Emborg, Erik 550–1, 552
Erdoğan, Recep Tayyip 30–1, 36
Erhard, Ludwig 40
Eucken, Walter 32, 40–1

Faria, Christian de 527
Fernández de Kirchner, Cristina 180
Friedman, Milton 293

Gang Yu 488
Gauck, Joachim 40
Ghandi, Indira 38
Ghemawat, Pankaj 394
Ghoshal, Sumantra 423
Ghosn, Carlos 441
Gingrich, Newt 37
Gore, Al 37
Guillén, Mauro 13
Gupta, Akhil 526

Hall, Edward 66
Hamel, Gary 97
Hammond, Toby 331–2
Harper, Stephen 534
Heckscher, Eli 129
Hirsch, Seev 131
Hofstede, Geert 60, 63, 67–9, 79
Hollande, François 37
House, Robert 62

Hruby, Rudolf 557
Huntington, Samuel 62

Isla, Pablo 479

Jacobsen, Arne 49
Johanson, Jan 323
Jones, Geoff 14

Kaplan, Frédéric 536
Kaspersky, Eugene 309–11
Kaspersky, Natalya 309–11
Kent, Muhtar 26
Kirchner, Néstor 181
Knudstorp, Jørgen Vig 112–13
Köhler, Rolf 540
Kohli, Manoj 527
Krugman, Paul 143
Kumar, N 526

Layton, Ron 84
Le Pen, Marine 37
Lee, Andrew 558
Lee, Ang 70
Lee, Jae Ryung 561, 563
Lei Jun 507–8
Lemelson, Jerome 379
Lenin 40
Levitt, Theodore 482, 483
Li Keqiang 549
Lipset, Seymour 78
List, Friedrich 140
Lorke, Richard 297
Lyons, Richard 193

MacDougall, Lisa 576–80
MacKinnon, Peter 561–5
Marihart, Johann 522
Marshall, Alfred 162
Meisinger, Susan 471
Mélenchon, Jean-Luc 37
Merkel, Angela 37, 207
Mill, John Stuart 140
Mittal, Kavin 527
Mittal, LN 526
Mittal, Sunil 525, 526
Modi, Narendra 38, 256

Naylor, Craig 441
Nehru, Jawaharlal 38
Nørgreen, Lotte 457
North, Douglass 32

Obama, Barak 37
Ohlin, Bertil 129
O'Rourke, PJ 221

Papademos, Lucas 233
Park, Sam 509
Pasko, Peter 556–7
Piketty, Thomas 13
Porter, Michael 133–4, 488
Prasad, Pulak 526
Putin, Vladimir 54

Reilly, Mark 544
Ricardo, David 128
Robbins, Ralph 511
Robinson, Mary 74
Rodrik, Dani 141
Rolls, Charles 511
Romney, Mitt 37
Ronen, Simcha 62
Rothschild, Jacob 526
Roussef, Dilma 207, 208
Royce, Henry 511

Samuelsen, Paul 141, 143
Sarkar, Prashant 473–4
Sarkozy, Nicolas 37
Schremp, Jürgen 414
Schultz, Howard 278, 280
Schuman, Robert 216
Scott, W. Richard 33
Seldeby, Claes 105
Shakira 70
Shenkar, Oded 62
Simon, Hermann 408
Sinha, PM 526
Smith, Adam 40, 126, 368
Solow, Robert 13
Soros, George 526
Stark, Klaus-Jürgen 574
Stiglitz, Joseph 376
Stolper, Wolfgang 141
Stringer, Howard 441

Tata, Jamseti 78
Teece, David 108
Thatcher, Margaret 515
Thomma, Lothar 339
Trnka, Miroslav 556–7

Vahlne, Jan-Erik 323
Vernon, Raymond 131

NAME INDEX

Wang, Jane 508
Watanabe, Kenichi 401
Weber, Christophe 441
Weber, Max 32
Whittle, Frank 511
Williamson, Oliver 32
Witty, Andrew 399, 546, 547

Wong Hung Khim 526
Woodford, Michael 441
Wuttke, Jörg 548

Yeltsin, Boris 54
Yilmaz, Muharrem 31

Zafirovski, Mike 562, 564
Zetsche, Dieter 415
Zhang Min 570, 571–3, 574, 575
Zong Qinghou 360–1

SUBJECT INDEX

AAA typology 394–7
absolute advantage 126–8, 135
absorptive capacity 437
accommodative strategy 299
accountancy 421–2
acquisition premiums 407
acquisitions 348–50, 356–7, 397–408
adaptability 491–2
adaptation 480–1
adaptation strategies 395–7
administrative practices 139–40
advertising 493
Africa 25–7
agglomeration 162–3, 163–4
aggregation strategies 394–5
agility 489–91
agricultural subsidies 256
aircraft engines 511–16, 518–19
aircraft industry 132
airlines 363–5, 369, 490–1
airway bills 313
AJC (apple juice concentrate) production
    148–9
alignment 492–3
AMC framework 366–8
anthropological studies 481–2
anti-competitive practices 375–6
anti-discrimination laws 466
anti-dumping duties 140, 148–9, 376
anti-trust policy 372–7
antivirus software 309–11, 556–60
ANZCERTA (Australia-New Zealand
    Closer Economic Relations Trade
    Agreement) 262
apartheid 298
apple juice concentrate (AJC) production
    148–9
appraisals 465–6
appreciation of a currency 186–7, 193
apprenticeships 42, 466–8
appropriability 100
arbitrage strategies 396
arbitrage tribunals 263–4
Argentina 180–1, 197
artefacts of culture 60
asset specificity 165–6
attacks 366
Australia-New Zealand Closer Economic
    Relations Trade Agreement
    (ANZCERTA) 262
Austria 520–4
automotive industry 161, 346, 347, 348,
    351–2, 370, 511–19
awareness 366–7

B2B (business-to-business) marketing
    495–7
B2C (business-to-consumer) marketing
    495
balance of payments (BoP) 191–2
balance of trade 123
bandwagon effect 193–4
banking 21, 33, 269–71, 401–2
bargaining power 175
base of the pyramid 17–18
Basel II/Basel III 269–70
beef 254
beer 54–5
benchmarking 101–6, 109
best practices 22–3
bid rate 201
bills of lading (B/L) 313
black swan events 271
blue ocean strategy 366–7
blunders in international HRM 467
blunders in marketing 480
Bologna Process 225–6
BoP (balance of payments) 191–2
born globals 324
BOT (build-operate-transfer) agreements
    320
BPO (business process outsourcing)
    103, 104
brand names 480–1
Brazil 206–8
Bretton Woods system 194–5
brewing 54–5, 353, 371, 374, 383
BRICS countries 17, 267
bridges 321
Britain see United Kingdom
brownfield acquisitions 356
build-operate-transfer (BOT) agreements
    320
business models 412
business process outsourcing (BPO) 103,
    104
business risks 29–32
business unit headquarters 441–2
business unit JVs 402–3
business-to-business (B2B) marketing
    495–7
business-to-consumer (B2C) marketing
    495

CAFE (Coffee and Farmer Equity)
    guidelines 279
Canada 264, 534–9
Canada-EU comprehensive economic and
    trade agreement (CETA) 262, 534–9

candle makers 140
capabilities 90, 93–7, 109, 341–2, 368,
    384
capability-enhancing FDI 341
capacity to punish 370
capital and financial account (of the BoP)
    192
capital flight 194
captive offshoring 105
cartels 368, 371, 373–5
case law 44
causal ambiguity 98
Central and Eastern Europe (CEE) 218,
    220–1, 520–1
centralization of power 38
centres of excellence 393–4, 425
CETA (EU Canada Comprehensive
    Economic and Trade Agreement)
    262, 534–9
CFA franc 261
child labour 288
China 3–4, 23–4, 43, 58–9, 79–81,
    119–22, 143, 148–9, 197, 343, 465,
    488–9, 493, 506–10, 540–3, 544–9,
    570–5, 576–80
chocolate 297
Christmas 72
cif (costs of insurance and freight) 313
civil law 44–5
civilization 62
classic trade theories 126, 134
climate change 267–9
clothes production 286
clusters 61–2, 67–9
CME (coordinated market economies)
    42–3, 294–5
coaches 480
codes of conduct 74–5, 76, 291–2
coffee 278–80
Coffee and Farmer Equity (CAFE)
    guidelines 279
cognitive pillar 33
collectivism 63, 79–80
collusion 368–72
collusive price setting 373–5
command economies 40
commoditization 508
common currency 197
common law 44–5
common markets 215
communities of practice (CoP) 434–6
commuter assignments 470
comparative advantage 128–31, 135,
    145–6

compensation 464–5
competition 363–84
Competition Commissioner 374
competition policy 227–8, 372–7
competitive actions 379–80
competitive advantage 90, 97–8, 100, 133–4, 136
competitive dynamics 366–8
competitor analysis 366, 384
compliance 292
compliance training 292
computer industry 5, 324
concentration ratio 370
consortiums 320
construction 321
consumer electronics 13
consumer protection 141
consumer research 481–2
contender strategy 384
contingency plans 382
contract work 470
convergence 13, 77
cooperation 371–2
coordinated market economies (CME) 42–3, 294–5
CoP (communities of practice) 434–6
Copenhagen Accord 269
Copenhagen Criteria 218
copyrights 48–9
Corn Laws 134, 136
corporate governance 49–50
corporate headquarters 441–2
corporate language 70
corporate social responsibility (CSR) 4, 84, 142, 280–300, 302–4, 540–3
corporate tax 172, 173–4
corruption 75–7, 81, 544–9
cosmopolitans 24
cost of ownership 485
costs of insurance and freight 313
counter party risk 203
counter-attacks 366
country managers 427
country risk analysis 204
country-of-origin effect 497–8
crawling bands 196
crayfish 376
cross-border services 317
cross-cultural training 458
cross-functional capabilities 94
cross-market retaliation 371
CSR (corporate social responsibility) 4, 84, 142, 280–300, 302–4, 540–3
cultural clusters 61–2, 67–9
cultural convergence 77
cultural distance 326–7
cultural generalization 78–9
cultural intelligence 80–1
cultural norms 81
culture 60–9
culture dimensions 63–7, 67–9
culture shock 459–63
currency boards 196, 197

currency exchange market 188–94
currency hedging 200, 203, 204
currency risk 198–202, 206–8
currency risk analysis 204
currency risk diversification 200
currency risk exposure 204
currency risk management strategy 204
currency swaps 201
current account (of the BoP) 192–3
customer interaction 161
customers' needs 480
customs unions 215

dairy products 550–5
DB (design-and-build) contracts 320
deadweight loss 137
defender strategy 383
defensive strategy 299
delivered duty paid 313
democracy 36–9
Denmark 43, 48–9, 163–4, 236
depreciation of a currency 186–7, 193
design-and-build (DB) contracts 320
development agenda 265–7
development aid 267
DG (Directorate General) 237
'diamond' model 133–4
dictatorship 36
direct democracy 38
direct elections 37
direct exports 312–13, 315–16
Directorate General (DG) 237
discrimination 466
dispute settlement 253–4
dissemination risks 167
distribution channels 487–8
distribution effects 141
distributors 315
divestments 408
dodger strategy 383–4
Doha Development Agenda 255
dollar 202
domestic markets 5–6
domestic outsourcing 105
downstream vertical FDI 155
Dubai 171
due diligence 400
dumping 376–7
dynamic capabilities 108

Eco-design Directive 242–4
e-commerce 79–80
economic forecasting 382
economic performance 296
economic pyramid 17
economic systems 40–3
economic transition 218
economic unions 215
economies of scale 392–3
education 319, 466–8
efficiency-enhancing FDI 341
El Salvador 291
elections 36–8

electronics 13
embargoes 142
emerging economies 6–7, 17, 119–22, 176
Energy Charter Treaty 264
energy industry 274–6, 516–17
enterprise resource planning (ERP) packages 88–90, 440
entertainment 380–1
entrepreneurial teams 311, 325
entrepreneurs 311
entry barriers 371
entry strategies 339–40
environmental and social responsibility 142
environmental standards 288–90, 494
equity mode of entry 346
Erasmus+ Programme 225
ERP (enterprise resource planning) packages 88–90, 440
ESM (European Stability Mechanism) 233
ethical imperialism 75
ethical relativism 75
ethics 74–7
ethnocentric approach to managing people 453–4
ethnocentric perspective 22–3
EU Canada Comprehensive Economic and Trade Agreement (CETA) 262, 534–9
EU competition policy 227–8
euro 215, 228–36
European businesses 5–6
European Constitution 222
European Convention on Human Rights 216
European democracy 238
European integration 217
European Stability Mechanism (ESM) 233
eurozone 228, 233–6
ex works 313
exceptionalists 22–3
exchange controls 14
exchange rate risk 198–202
exchange rates 14, 184–204
executive search companies 464
expatriate assignments 7–8
expatriate spouses 457
expatriate stress 460–2
expatriates 454, 455–63, 576–80
experiential knowledge 323
experimental adaptation 480–1
explicit collusion 368
explicit CSR 293
explicit knowledge 167
export credit insurances 326
export intermediaries 315
exporters 312
exporting 119–23, 165–6
expropriation 175
extender strategy 383

factor endowment theory 130
Fair Trade chocolate 297
Fair Trade coffee 279
fashion retail 478–9, 486
FDI (foreign direct investment) 5, 7, 14, 151–78, 180–1
FDI flow 155–7
FDI stock 157, 173–4
femininity 63, 65
financial assets 91
financial crisis 18, 23, 184–6
financial performance 296
financial sector regulation 269–71
first-mover advantages 132, 344–6
first-past-the-post systems 36
fishing 286–7
fixed exchange rates 196
flexible exchange rates 195–6
floating exchange rates 195–6, 197–8
fob (free on board) 313
focus strategies 408–10
food production 285–7
food security 256
footloose plants 290
foreign direct investment (FDI) 5, 7, 14, 151–78, 180–1
foreign entry strategies 353–5
foreign portfolio investment (FPI) 154–5
foreign residents 317
foreign subsidiaries 339–42
formal institutions 33–5, 51–2
forward discount 200–1
forward exchange rate 191
forward premium 200–1
forward transactions 191
four Cs of human resource management 471
four freedoms of the EU single market 222–7
FPI (foreign portfolio investment) 154–5
France 37, 120
franchisees 319, 320
franchising 319
franchisors 319, 320
free float 196
free movement of capital 224
free movement of goods 223
free movement of people 224–7
free movement of services 223–4
free on board 313
free trade 126, 136, 140–2, 146
Free Trade Area of the Americas (FTAA) 262
free trade areas (FTAs) 215, 259–65, 271–2, 530–1
fruit preparations 520–4
full immersion training 458
furniture design 48–9
furniture manufacture 206–8

game theory 368–9
GATS (General Agreement on Trade in Services) 251

GATT (General Agreement on Tariffs and Trade) 249–51
GDP (gross domestic product) 7, 8
General Agreement on Tariffs and Trade (GATT) 249–51
General Agreement on Trade in Services (GATS) 251
Generalized System of Preferences (GSP) 262
geocentric approach to managing people 454
geographic area structures 426–7
Germany 37, 120, 143, 199, 264, 374, 540–3
Ghana 550, 551–2
global business models 394–7
global economic pyramid 17
global economy 18–21
global financial crisis 18, 23
global key accounts 394, 425
global mandates 437
global matrix 428
global product divisions 427–8
global products 482–3
global sourcing 393
global standardization 353
global standards strategy 425
global strategies 392–7
global talent management 454–5
global talent pools 455
globalfocusing 409–10
globalization 12–18, 274–6
GLOBE clusters 62
GNI (gross national income) 8
GNP (gross national product) 8
gold standard 194
goodwill 92
government incentive schemes 439
grand pianos 338–9
Great Britain see United Kingdom
Greece 236
greenfield operations 347
gross domestic product (GDP) 7, 8
gross national income (GNI) 8
gross national product (GNP) 8
GSP (Generalized System of Preferences) 262

harmonized sector 223
headhunter companies 464
headquarters 441–2
health, safety and environment (HSE) 292
health care sector 319
Heckscher–Ohlin theory 130, 133
hedging 200, 203, 204
hidden champions 408
high-context cultures 67
holy 72
home country nationals 454
home replication strategy 423
Hong Kong 79, 197
horizontal FDI 155
horizontal M&As 404–5

hormone treatment 254
hospitality 57–9
host country nationals 454
hotels 322
household appliances 566–9
HRM (human resource management) 451–72
HSE (health, safety and environment) 292
hubris 399
human resource management (HRM) 451–72
human resources 92, 353
Hungary 121, 185–6
Huntington civilizations 62
hypernorms 298–9

I-advantages 158–9, 165–8, 178
IB (international business) 5–11
IIAs (international investment agreements) 263
IMF conditionality 257
imitability 98–100, 378, 407, 440, 468–9, 494–5
implicit CSR 294–5
import quotas 138–9
import tariffs 137–8
importers 312
importing 123, 316
inbound logistics 488
incentive schemes 439
India 37–8, 104, 256, 354, 509–10, 525–7
indirect elections 37
indirect exports 315
individualism 63, 79, 80
industry 4.0 88–90
infant industry argument 140–1
inflation 190
informal institutions 33, 59–60, 80
ingredient branding 496–7
in-groups 79–80
innovation 433–4, 439–40
inpatriates 470
input foreclosure 405
institutional constraints 178
institutional distance 326
institutional framework 32
institutional transition 34
institution-based view 32–5, 80
institutions 32, 33–5, 163, 165 see also formal institutions; informal institutions
instrumental view of stakeholders 284, 296
intangible assets 92
integration-responsiveness framework 423–6
intellectual property rights (IPR) 47–9, 83–4, 255, 509–10
interest rate parity 190–1
internalization advantages 158–9, 165–8, 178

international business (IB) 5–11
international contracts 319–22
international divisions 426
international investment agreements (IIAs) 263
international monetary system 194–8
international new ventures (INV) 324, 325
international strategy 423
international trade 119–46
internationalization 323–9
internet 12, 327–8, 487
internet shopping 488–9
intra-firm trade 166
INV (international new ventures) 324, 325
investment bans 174
investor psychology 193–4
investor-state dispute settlement (ISDS) 263–4
IPR (intellectual property rights) 47–9, 83–4, 255, 509–10
ISDS (investor-state dispute settlement) 263–4
Islamic finance 355
Italy 120

job markets 143–5
joint ventures (JVs) 155, 350–2, 354, 359–61, 372
Jutland 163–4
JVs (joint ventures) 155, 350–2, 354, 359–61, 372

Kartellamt 374
Kenya 83–4
knowledge 167
knowledge economy 109
knowledge governance 436–7
knowledge management 431–6
knowledge spillover 163
Kyoto Protocol 268–9

labour standards 290–2
L-advantages 158–9, 160–5, 178
language 69–71
language barriers 69–70
laptops 496
late-mover advantages 344–6
Latvia 186
L/C (letters of credit) 313–14
legal certainty 45
legal processes 45–6
legal systems 44–6
leniency programmes 374–5
letters of credit (L/C) 313–14
liability of outsidership 11
liberal market economies (LME) 42–3, 293, 295
liberalization 14
Liberia 553
licensees 319, 320
licensing 167, 319

licensors 319, 320
lingua franca 70
LME (liberal market economies) 42–3, 293, 295
lobbying 240, 496–7
local adaptation 353
local content requirements 172
local firms 382–4
local government 199
local knowledge 23–4, 354
local responsiveness 423
localization 483
localization strategy 424–5
locational advantages 158–9, 160–5, 178
location-bound resources 159
location-specific advantages 342
logistics 353, 488
long-term orientation 66
long-term strategies 381–2
low-context cultures 66–7

Maasai 83–4
Maasai Intellectual Property Initiative (MIPI) 84
Maastricht Criteria 229
Maastricht Treaty 222
machine tools 445–6
Malaysia 467
managed float 196
management contracts 322
management teams 440–1
maquiladora factories 291
market commonality 371
market division collusion 375
market economies 40–2
market entries 346–52, 353–5, 355–8
market entry barriers 371
market failure 165
market segmentation 483
market transparency 371
marketing 478–9, 480–1, 495, 498
marketing mix 482–3
markets 160–2
market-seeking investors 340–1
M&As (mergers and acquisitions) 397–408
masculinity 63, 65–6
MBT (Maasai Barefoot Technology) 83
meat 285
Members of the European Parliament (MEPs) 237
MEPs (Members of the European Parliament) 237
mercantilism 126, 135
mergers and acquisitions (M&As) 397–408
Mexico 375
MFA (Multi-fibre Arrangement) 250, 271–2
migrant workers 464–5
migration 14
mimetic behaviour 326

MIPI (Maasai Intellectual Property Initiative) 84
MNE (multinational enterprises) 5, 12, 15, 21, 176
modern trade theories 126, 134
modes of entry 346
monetary unions 215
motivation 367
multicultural teams 469–70
multi-divisional organization 438–9
multidomestic strategy 424–5
Multi-fibre Arrangement (MFA) 250, 271–2
multilateral organizations 249
multilinguists 71
multimarket competition 371
multinational enterprises (MNE) 5, 12, 15, 21, 176
multiple acquisitions 356–7
multi-tier branding 483
mutual recognition 223

NAFTA (North American Free Trade Agreement) 259
national competitive advantage of industries 133–4, 136
national innovation systems 439
national security 141
natural resources 15
natural resource-seeking 340
nearshoring 104
Netherlands 125
networks 324, 354
NGOs (non-governmental organizations) 283
Nigeria 550, 552–3
non-discrimination principle 250
non-equity modes of entry 346
non-governmental organizations (NGOs) 283
non-tariff barriers (NTBs) 137, 138–40, 250–1
normative pillar 33
normative view of stakeholders 284, 296
norms 81, 298–9
North American Free Trade Agreement (NAFTA) 259
not-invented-here syndrome 22
NTBs (non-tarriff barriers) 137, 138–40, 250–1

O-advantages 158–60, 176
OBMs (original brand manufacturers) 107
obsolescing bargain 175
ODMs (original design manufacturers) 107, 496
OEMs (original equipment manufacturers) 107, 425, 496
offer rate 201
offshore outsourcing 105, 167–8
offshoring 103–6, 109
OLI paradigm 158–9

oligopolies 366
operational collaboration 403
opportunistic behaviour 34
opportunity costs 129
optimal currency area 233–6
organization 100
organizational culture 77–8, 92
organizational fit 400
organizational structures 426–9, 438–43
original brand manufacturers (OBMs) 107
original design manufacturers (ODMs) 107, 496
original equipment manufacturers (OEMs) 107, 425, 496
outbound logistics 488
out-groups 79–80
output foreclosure 405–6
outsidership 11
outsourcing 103, 106–8, 167–8
overseas listing 396
ownership, cost of 485
ownership advantages 158–60, 176
ownership restrictions 493

parent country nationals 454
partial acquisitions 352
parties 57–9
patents 48, 378–9, 509
pegged exchange rates 196, 197–8
people management abroad 464–6
performance appraisal 465–6
pharmaceuticals industry 92, 409, 544–9
philanthropy 293
physical assets 91
pianos 338–9
place 487
platform investments 355–6
Poland 104, 184–5, 558–60
political constraint index (POLCON) 51
political risk 39, 50–1, 54–5
political systems 35–9
political unions 215
pollution 288–9
pollution havens 289
polycentric approach to managing people 454
ports 171
post-acquisition integration 400–1
post-Bretton Woods system 195–7
power distance 63
Power Predictor 331–3
PPP (purchasing power parity) 8, 9, 189–90
predatory pricing 376–7
President of the Commission 237
President of the European Council 237
price 484–7
price comparison websites 371
price elasticity 484–5
price leaders 370
price-match guarantees 372
primary resources 90, 91–2

primary stakeholder groups 282–3
prisoners' dilemma 368
proactive strategy 299–300
product 482–3
product life cycle theory 131, 135
product names 480–1
productivity 129–30, 191
project management contracts 321
promotion 485–7
property rights 46–9
proportional representation 36
protectionism 126, 140, 160
psychological contract 462
publishing 322
purchasing power parity (PPP) 8, 9, 189–90

quality management systems 494

race to the bottom 289
radio frequency identification (RFID) tags 494
rarity 97–8, 378, 407, 440, 468, 494
R&D contracts 321–2
recruitment 464
redundancy 466
regional integration 261–2
regional managers 427
regulatory pillar 33
regulatory standards 496–7
relationship marketing 495
relative PPP hypothesis 190
religions 72–4
renewable energy 331–3
renewable resources 15
repatriation 462
repeated games 369
representative democracy 38
reputational resources 92
reshoring 104, 105
resource acquisition 324–6
resource endowments 129–30
resource mobility 136
resource-based view 90, 109
resources 90–7, 162
retail market 354
retention 466
returnees 462–3
reverse culture shock 463
reverse innovation 433–4
reverse knowledge transfer 432
RFID (radio frequency identification) tags 494
risk analysis 204
risk diversification 394
risk management 18, 29–32, 33, 204
risk-rating agencies 270
Ronen and Shenkar clusters 62
Rotterdam 125
Russia 54–5, 252–3, 351–2

SAFTA (South Asian Free Trade Area) 259
sales 495

sales agents 315
salmon 286
sanctions 142
Santiago Principles 178
Saudi Arabia 57–8, 283–4, 467
scale of entry 355
scenario planning 382
Schengen Agreement 226
Schengen area 226–7
Schengen visa 227
Schuman Plan 216
SEA (Single European Act) 221
sea turtles 254–5
seafood 348–9
seals 12
secondary stakeholder groups 283
secular societies 72, 74
servicing foreign residents 317
shared value creation 284–5
shrimp 254–5
signalling 371–2
Singapore 43
Single European Act (SEA) 221
single market 221
Slovakia 186, 556–60
small and medium-size enterprises (SMEs) 311
smartphones 378–9, 506–10
SMEs (small and medium-size enterprises) 311
social capital 437
social complexity 100
social groups 77–8
social responsibility see CSR (corporate social responsibility)
South Africa 174, 298
South Asian Free Trade Area (SAFTA) 259
South Korea 467, 561–5
sovereign wealth funds (SWFs) 176–8
Spain 151–4, 181, 235
sportswear 3–4
spot market rates 191
spread 201
Sri Lanka 142
staged acquisitions 357
stages models 324
stakeholder conflicts 285–8
stakeholders 282–8
standardization 353, 482–3, 486
standards in advertising 493
standards of engagement 291–2
starch 520, 521–3
state aid 228
stereotypes 68–9
strategic alliances 352, 402–3, 412
strategic fit 400
strategic foresight 109
strategic hedging 200, 204
strategic positioning 381–2
strategic trade policy 133
strategic trade theory 131–3, 136
strategies 365

student unions 39
students 225–6
subcontracting 320–1
subcultures 77
subsidiaries 339–42, 346–8, 440–1
subsidiarity 223
subsidiary initiatives 437–8, 445–6
subsidies 138, 247, 255–6
subsidy competition 228
sugar 390–2, 520, 521–3
sunk costs 175
supply chain management 478–9,
    487–93, 498, 500–2
supply chains 23, 479, 494
survival strategies 380–1
sustainability 281
sustainable competitive advantage 100
Sweden 43
SWFs (sovereign wealth funds) 176–8
Switzerland 120
synergies 398–9

taboo 72
tacit collusion 368
tacit knowledge 167
tangible assets 91–2
Tanzania 83–4
tariff-jumping FDI 355
tariffs 14
tarriff barriers 137–8
tax avoidance 172, 173–4, 280
taxes 531
technological advances 13–14
technological resources 92
telecommunications 525–7
temporary competitive advantage 97–8
tenders 321
textile industry 570–5
TFA (trade facilitation agreement) 255–6
third country nationals 454
third-party logistics (3PL) 492–3
tit-for-tat 370

TNI (transnationality index) 21
tobacco industry 50, 264
Togo 550
top management teams 440–1
total cost of ownership 485
totalitarianism 36
tourism 318, 381
toys 72
TPP (Trans-Pacific Partnership) 262
trade barriers 14, 137–8
trade deficit 123, 143
trade diversion 265
trade embargoes 142
trade facilitation agreement (TFA) 255–6
trade surplus 123, 143
trade theories 126, 134
trade unions 466
trademarks 48
Trade-Related Aspects of Intellectual
    Property Rights (TRIPS) 251
training 458
transaction costs 32, 165, 355
Transatlantic Trade and Investment
    Partnership (TTIP) 262, 265
translation 69
transnational strategy 425–6
transnationality index (TNI) 21
Trans-Pacific Partnership (TPP) 262
transportation costs 160
Treaties of Rome 218
triple bottom line 281
TRIPS (Trade-Related Aspects of
    Intellectual Property Rights) 251
trolls 379
TTIP (Transatlantic Trade and
    Investment Partnership) 262, 265
Turkey 29–32, 566–9
turnkey projects 320
turtles 254–5

ultrasound machines 16–17
uncertainty 33–4

uncertainty avoidance 66
unified framework for global business
    9–11
United Kingdom 38, 48–9, 120, 236,
    238–9, 468, 528–33
United States 37, 78, 254–5
unskilled workers 13
Uppsala model 323
upstream vertical FDI 155
US dollar 202

value chains 93–4
value creation 97, 377, 407, 439–40,
    468, 494
varieties of capitalism 42
VERs (voluntary export restraints) 139
vertical FDI 155
vertical M&As 405–6
Vietnam 467
virtual communities of practice 434
virtual teams 470
vitamins 373
volcanic eruption 490–1
voluntary export restraints (VERs) 139
VRIO framework 97–101, 109

waves of globalization 14
Western, educated, industrialized, rich
    and democratic (WEIRD) people 78
Western culture 62
white goods 566–9
wholly-owned subsidiaries (WOS) 346–8,
    354
wind energy 163–4
work councils 468
working conditions 291
World War I 14
worldwide mandates 437
WOS (wholly-owned subsidiaries) 346–8,
    354

ORGANIZATIONS INDEX

ABB 70, 428
Abbey National 152
AbbVie 409
Abertis 156
AB InBev 371, 374, 397, 406
Abraaj Group 551, 552
Abu Dhabi Investment Authority 176
Accenture 104, 105, 107, 428
Accor 322
Acer 5, 496
ACS 153
adidas 3–6, 103, 134, 168, 299
Adobe 173
AEG 414
Aer Lingus 404
Aerolineas Argentinas 181
Aérospatiale-Matra 451
Agrana 327, 520–4
Ahava 383
Air Berlin 364, 398
Air France-KLM 203, 364, 378
Air Serbia 364
Airbus 132–3, 134, 246–8, 345, 415,
    427, 439, 518–19
Alcatel 470, 491, 492
Alcatel Lucent 401, 410
Aldi 380, 484
Alibaba 396, 465
Alipay 80
Alitalia 228, 364, 398
Allied Irish Bank 153
Allison Engine Company 516–17
Alpari 198
ALSTOM 57–9, 320
Amanah 355
Amazon 91, 95, 104, 173, 488, 507
Ambev 397
Amey 153
Andean Community 261
Anglo American 442
Anheuser Busch 397
Antolin 161, 162
Apple 95, 99, 106, 107, 108, 173, 298,
    368, 377, 378–9, 384, 410, 412,
    483, 487, 493, 506–7, 508–9, 559
Applied Materials 173
Arçelik 566–9
Arcelor Mittal 21, 399, 426–7
Arctic 567
Arla 43
Armani 570
Arriva 399
Asda 296, 380, 484

ASEAN (Association of Southeast Asian
    Nations) 259–60
Asian Paints 383
Association of Southeast Asian Nations
    (ASEAN) 259–60
Astra Zeneca 548
Atys Group 522
Audi 415, 543, 548, 570
Automobile Caiova 228
Autonomy 400
Aventis 373

BAA 153
BAE 76
BAIC 415
Bank Burgenland 228
Bank of America 35, 153
Bank Zachodni 153
Barclays 21, 228
Basel Committee 269
BASF 373
Bath 500
Bayer 441, 542, 548
Bayer MaterialScience (BMS) 403, 409,
    495, 496
BBVA 152
Bear Stearns 33, 269
Beck's 374
Behr 348, 350
Beiersdorf 356
Beko 566–9
Benetton 329
Bentley 513
Bertelsmann Stiftung 541
Bestseller 345
Better Generation (BG) 332–3
Beyond Asia Capital 332
BG (Better Generation) 332–3
Bharti Airtel 397, 509, 525–7
Bharti Retail 354
Bharti SoftBank 527
Blackberry 378, 379
Blomberg 567
Bloomberg Businessweek 483
BMS (Bayer MaterialScience) 403, 409,
    495, 496
BMW 92, 95, 121, 348, 415, 511, 516,
    543, 548, 570
BNP Paribas 21
Body Shop 92
Body Works 500
Boeing 132–3, 141, 246–8, 345, 407,
    492, 514, 515

Bombardier 423
Bosch 394, 402, 541, 567
Bosch-Siemens-Hausgeräte 402, 403
Bösendorffer 338
Boss 570
BP 54, 123, 162, 298, 342
Brandt 567
Brasilcel 153
Bristol Siddeley 511
British Airways 364, 377, 378
BT 526
Budimex 153
Bumble Bee Foods 349
Burberry 98, 99, 120

C&A 486, 493
Cadbury 92, 406, 483
Canal+ 406
Cap Gemini 104
Carlsberg 54–5, 353, 356, 371, 374, 375,
    395, 405, 483
Carrefour 167, 354, 493
CASA 451
Case New Holland 352
Cathay Pacific Airways 203
CEMEX 153–4, 160
Centrale Laitiere 551
Cerberus Capital 415
Chia Tia Tianping Pharmaceutical 548
Chicken of the Sea 349
China Construction Bank 21
China Container Line 501
China Investment Corporation (CIC)
    176, 398
China Mobile 507, 527
China Netcom 153
China Telecom 507
China Unicom 507
Chipotle 433
Chrysler 346, 397, 400, 414, 415, 548
CIC (China Investment Corporation)
    176, 398
Cirque du Soleil 366–7
Cisco 372, 380
Citibank 355
Citigroup 104, 176, 228
CML Innovative Technologies 161
CNOOC 171
Coca-Cola 11, 25–7, 77, 483, 485–6, 521
Colgate-Palmolive 344
Comdom Software 558
Conserverie Parmentier 349
Constellation Brands 406

Continental 394, 543
Coolpad 506
Cordis 409
Corus 78, 341, 526
Costa Coffee 497
Council of Europe 216
Council of the European Union 237
Credit Agricole 21
Crown Plaza 322
Cultor OY 391
Cummins 352
Cyprus Airways 228

DA (Dürkopp Adler) 344, 570–5
Daewoo 425
Daimler 92, 352, 397, 400, 407, 414–15, 517, 543
Dallas Instruments 473–4
Damixa 105
Danisco 390–2, 393, 394, 397, 409, 495
Danish Crown 43
Danone 359–61, 391, 394, 521, 551, 552
DASA 451
de Havilland 345
Deere 203
DelGro Group 526
Dell 5, 95, 107, 394, 403, 425, 496
Deloitte Touche Tohmatsu 421
Delphi 394
Delta 83
Deutsche Bahn 374
Deutsche Bank 21, 201, 228
Deutsche Telekom 376
Dhabi Group 525
DHL 103, 488, 494
Diageo 31
Diane von Fürstenberg 83
Die Bahn 399
Dirafrost 522
Disney 497
Dornier 414
Dow Chemical 289, 495
Dubai Ports World 171
DuPont 392, 397, 409, 496
Dürkopp Adler (DA) 344, 570–5
Dürr 408, 438, 445–6, 542

EADS (European Aeronautic Defence and Space Company) 141, 415, 451–3, 454
East Asiatic Company 441
Eastman Kodak 203
EasyJet 95
Eaton Towers 526
eBay 173
EBRD (European Bank for Reconstruction and Development) 267
ECB (European Central Bank) 190, 202, 229
ECJ (European Court of Justice) 238
The Economist 483
ECOWAS 261

ECSC (European Coal and Steel Community) 216
Edeka 159
EEC (European Economic Community) 218
Eisai 373
El Corte Inglés 159
ELCO 567
E.Leclerc 159
Electrolux 414, 567, 568
Elektra 16
Elektra Bregenz 567
Eller & Co 171
Ellinika Nafpigeia 228
Embraer 397, 516
EMI 345
Emidan 553
Emirates 363–5, 378
Empress International 349
Endesa 152, 153, 155
E.ON 264, 375
Ericsson 380, 402, 403, 410, 490, 510, 526
Ernst & Young 421, 422
ESCO 167
ESET 556–60
Etihad Airways 363–5, 398
EU (European Union) 23, 119–22, 213–40, 255
Euler Hermes 326
Euratom (European Atomic Energy Community) 218
European Aeronautic Defence and Space Company (EADS) 141, 415, 451–3, 454
European Atomic Energy Community (Euratom) 218
European Bank for Reconstruction and Development (EBRD) 267
European Central Bank (ECB) 190, 202, 229
European Coal and Steel Community (ECSC) 216
European Commission 237
European Council 237
European Court of Human Rights 216
European Court of Justice (ECJ) 238
European Economic Community (EEC) 218
European Parliament 237
European Union (EU) 23, 119–22, 213–40, 255
Evonik 403, 495
ExxonMobil 203

Facebook 100, 487
FAG 571–2
Fagor 568
Fair Labor Association (FLA) 4
Fairchild 414
Fan Milk 327, 550–5
Federal Mogul 348, 352
FedEx 344

Ferrovial 153, 154, 320
Festo 543
Fiat 30
Fitch 270
Five Guys 433
FLA (Fair Labor Association) 4
Flavel 567
Flextronics 103, 113, 168, 425
Fokker 414, 516
Ford 30, 161, 355, 431, 482
Foxconn 21, 106, 107, 176, 298, 403, 410, 412, 496, 507
France Telecom 352
Freudenberg 542
F-Secure 310
Fuji Xerox 155, 403
Future Group 354

G Data 310
G4S 103
Gap 478, 493
Gaz de France 375
GCC (German Chamber of Commerce) 540–3
GCC (Gulf Cooperation Council) 261
GDF Suez 320
GE (General Electric) 16–17, 132, 228, 345, 367, 371, 403–4, 406, 407, 496, 511, 514, 515
GE Capital 407
GE Healthcare 16–17
Géant 159
Geely 162, 341–2
General Electric (GE) 16–17, 132, 228, 345, 367, 371, 403–4, 406, 407, 496, 511, 514, 515
General Motors (GM) 346, 370, 371–2, 393, 425, 570
Genmab 324, 329
German Chamber of Commerce (GCC) 540–3
Giordano 497
GlaxoSmithKline (GSK) 399, 409, 544–9
Global Broker 198
Global Exchange 279
GM (General Motors) 346, 370, 371–2, 393, 425, 570
Goldwind 371
Gome 507
Goodyear 466
Google 173, 344, 378, 379, 386–7, 407, 465, 494, 507, 510
Government Pension Fund (Norway) 176
Grotrian-Steinweg 338, 339, 346
Grundfos 54
Grundig 567, 569
Grupo Antolin 161, 162
Grupo Mexico 343
Grupo Modelo 406
GSK (GlaxoSmithKline) 399, 409, 544–9
Gucci 98, 99, 120, 485, 570
Gulf Cooperation Council (GCC) 261

Häagen-Dazs 432, 497
Haier 367, 371, 465, 494
Harley-Davidson 97
HBOS 269
Heathrow Airport 177, 398
Heineken 353, 357, 371, 375, 395, 404, 405, 483
Helios Towers 526
Hella 395
Hermès 485, 570
Hewitt Associates 103
Hewlett-Packard (HP) 107, 400, 403, 431, 437, 496
Hitachi 517
H&M 478, 481, 493
Hochtief 153
Hoffman-La Roche 373
Holcim 397, 406
Holiday Inn 322
Hon Hai 21
Honda 346, 347, 548
Honeywell 228, 403–4, 406, 437–8
Hong Kong and Shanghai Banking Corporation 442
HP (Hewlett-Packard) 107, 400, 403, 431, 437, 496
HSBC 21, 201, 355, 442
HTC 107, 378, 506–7
Huawei 107, 171, 372, 380, 384, 410, 465, 506–7, 509, 526
Hutchison Whampoa 345
Hydrometer 543
Hyundai 161, 346, 414–15

Iberdola 152
IBM 88, 97, 103, 104, 105, 107, 109, 203, 325, 345, 428, 441, 470, 526
ICBC 21
ICSID (International Centre for Settlement of Investment Disputes) 181
ideo 412
IFU (Industrialization Fund for Developing Countries) 552
IHS Towers 526
IKEA 160, 283–4, 323
IMF (International Monetary Fund) 18, 195, 256–9
Imperial Tobacco 50
Inbev 397
Indesit 567, 568
Inditex 152, 478
Industrialization Fund for Developing Countries (IFU) 552
Infosys 103, 104, 105, 107, 176
Innis & Gunn 383
Instagram 487
Intel 403, 496
Interbrew 397
International Centre for Settlement of Investment Disputes (ICSID) 181
International Monetary Fund (IMF) 8, 18, 195, 256–9

Intrepid 318
Inventec 496, 507
ISS 103
Italia Telecom 526

Jack & Jones 345
Jaguar Land Rover 78, 83, 169, 341, 548
Japan Tobacco 50
JD.com 488, 507
JLR (Jaguar Land Rover) 78, 83, 169, 341, 548
Jobek do Brasil 206–8
John West 348, 349
Johnson & Johnson 409
JPMorgan 228
Junghans 408

Kamaz Corporation 351–2
Karbonn 509
Kaspersky Lab 309–11, 319
KFC 395, 497
King Oscar 349
Kingsoft 507
Klaus Meyer 498
Knorr Bremse 352
Koç Group 567
Kodak 378
Kone Elevators 71, 375
KPMG 421
Kraft 92, 391, 406, 483
Krones 542
KSL Keilmann 570, 575

Lafarge 397, 406
Lafarge-Holcim 397, 401
Land Rover 78, 83, 169, 341
Landisbanken 269
Lanxess 495
Leclerc 159
Lego 111–13
Lehman Brothers 33, 35, 203, 269, 401–2
Leisure 567
Lenovo 5, 97, 107, 379, 384, 396, 397, 442, 465, 496, 506, 507, 509
LG 506
LG-Nortel 561–5
Li & Fung 103, 316–17, 493, 500–2
Libyan Investment Authority 177
Lidl 380, 484
Limited Brands 500
LinkedIn 100, 485
Liz Claiborne 500
Lockheed 246, 514, 515
Logitech 324, 325, 329
Lone Pine 264, 538
L'Oreal 92, 120
Loro Piana 352, 398
Lotte 406, 483
Louis Vuitton 83
Lucent 491–2
Lufthansa 364, 403
LV 570
LVMH 99, 398

Maasai Barefoot Technology (MBT) 83
Mabey & Johnson 76
McDonalds 77, 173, 190, 395, 423, 431, 433–4, 482, 497
McDonnell Douglas 246
McKinsey 382
Maersk 54
Mahindra 161
MAN Diesel & Turbo 300
Manganese Bronze 341
Mango 152
Manpower 103
Mareblu 349
Marks & Spencer (M&S) 296, 302–4, 486
Mars 375
Matsushita 66, 345, 440
Mattel 379
MBT (Maasai Barefoot Technology) 83
MediaTek 510
MerAlliance 349
Mercedes Benz 95, 348, 415, 548, 570
Mercedes Benz Trucks Vostok 352
Merck 408, 409
Mercosur 261
Merrill Lynch 35
Messier-Dowty 492
Mey Icki 31
Michelin 441
Micromax 509
Microsoft 11, 47–8, 89, 319, 332, 345, 368, 379, 380, 386–8, 410, 465, 507
Midland Bank 442
Mindray 371
Minor Group 320
MIPI (Maasai Intellectual Property Initiative) 84
Mitsubishi 65–6, 414–15, 492
Mitsui 320
Mittal Arcelor 526, 527
Mittal Steel 399
MobileStore 509
MOL 398
Moody's 270
Morgan Stanley 176
Motorola Mobility 379, 509
Mozilla 387
M&S (Marks & Spencer) 296, 302–4, 486
MTU 414
MTV 424, 425, 482
MW Brands 349

Narayana Hrudayala Hospital 319
Nareva Holdings 320
Nescafé 485
Nestlé 95, 285, 391, 394, 481, 521
Netscape 345, 387
New Yorker 497
News Corporation 441–2
Nike 3–4, 103, 168, 299, 425, 478
Nilfisk 315
Nippon Steel Glass 441

Nissan 54, 347, 441
Nokia 107, 108, 121, 242–4, 378, 379, 387, 402, 409, 410, 490, 507, 526
Nokia Siemens Networks 402, 410
Nomura 401–2
Nordzucker 390, 392, 409
Noriba 355
Nortel 561–5
Northern Engineering Industries 516
Northern Rock 269
Northrop Grumman 141, 407
Novartis 92, 409, 548
Novozymes 457
Nvidia 507

OECD 76
Okocim 483
Old Mutual 442
Olivetti 325
Olympus 441
Opel 425
Oracle 89, 102, 378, 440
Orange 107
Ostnor 104, 105
Otis 375
Oxfam 300

Packard 511
Palfinger 352
Palm 425
Pandora 484–5
Parex 186
Pearl River Piano 338–9, 343–4, 346
Pegatron 106, 107, 298, 403, 496
PepsiCo 483, 521, 526
Petite Navire 348, 349
Peugeot 346
Pfaff Industrial 570, 575
P&G (Procter & Gamble) 95, 104, 181, 428, 487
Pharmacyclics 409
Philip Morris 264
Philips 16, 173, 371, 440, 490
The Pizza Company 320
Pizza Hut 320
PKMJ Technical Services 517
P&O 171
Polish Telecom 352
Pollonia-Lechia 356
Porsche 543
Portman Ritz-Carlton hotel 468–9
Pratt & Whitney 511–12, 514
PricewaterhouseCoopers (PwC) 421–2
Primark 296, 380
Procter & Gamble (P&G) 95, 104, 181, 428, 487
Puma 134
PwC (PricewaterhouseCoopers) 421–2

Qantas 518–19
Qatar Airways 364, 365
Qatar Investment Authority 154, 177
Qualcomm 403, 412, 507, 509, 548

R Brooks Associates 517
Radeberger 374
Raytheon 407
RBS (Royal Bank of Scotland) 153, 228
Reckitt Benckiser 454
Reed Isaac 207, 208
Renault 30, 54, 161, 174, 441, 511
Renishaw 381
Repsol 50, 180–1
Rhône-Poulenc 373
Rio Tinto 396
Ritmüller 339
Roche 92, 548
Rockwool 54
Rolls-Royce (RR) 120, 132, 345, 371, 511–19
Royal Bank of Scotland (RBS) 153, 228
RR (Rolls-Royce) 120, 132, 345, 371, 511–19
RWE 264
Ryanair 95, 203, 404

SABMiller 353, 357, 371, 396, 442, 483
Sacyr Vallehermoso 153
Safi Energy 320
SAIC 425
Salesforce.com 89
Samsung 377, 378–9, 384, 410, 506–7, 508–9, 567
Sanmar Group 526
Sanofi 92, 548
Sanrio 500
Santander 152–3, 201
Sany 397
SAP 88–90, 102, 108, 319, 342, 380, 440, 441
Scanbech 329
Scandinavia A/S 322
Schaeffler Group 571
Schenck 445–6, 542
Schenck Shanghai Machinery 438
SCO (Shanghai Cooperation Organization) 261
Scottish and Newcastle (S&N) 404–5
Seagram 406
SEAT 161
Selfridges 296
Senso 394
Serfin 153
Setrnet 558
7-Eleven Japan 492
SG Group 344, 570–5
ShangGong Group 344, 570–5
Shanghai Cooperation Organization (SCO) 261
Shanghai GM 425
Shanghai Machinery (SSM) 445–6
Shanghai Volkswagen 445
ShareNet 435
Sharp 98
Shell 21, 123, 162, 173, 298–9, 342, 434
Siam Cement 203

Siemens 15, 16, 371, 402, 410, 434, 435, 437, 491, 526, 543
Sina.com 396
Singer Sewing Machines 15
SingTel 526
Sino Biopharmaceutical 548
Skoda 357
Slovnaft 398
S&N (Scottish and Newcastle) 404–5
Société Générale 228
Sodexho 103
SoftBank 398, 527
Sony 402, 440, 441
Sony Ericsson 402, 403, 425, 490
Southwest 203
Sovereign Bankcorp 152
S&P 270
Spice 509
SSM (Shanghai Machinery) 445–6
Stagecoach 377
Standard Aero Group 171
Standard Oil 15
Starbucks 84, 167, 278–80, 295, 320, 426, 431
Steiff 104
Steinway 338
Steirerobst 522
Stern GmbH 207, 208
Stihl 543
Subaru 425
Subway 325, 431, 433
Sun Microsystems 386
Suning 507
Supercell 398
Suzuki 425
Swiss National Bank 190, 199
Swissport 153

Taicang Round Table 543
Takeda 441
Talbots 500
Taobao 507, 508
Tata 78, 161, 162, 169, 341–2, 397, 526
TCL 506
TCS 103, 105, 107, 176
Technomed 324, 329
Telcel 375
Telefónica 152, 153
Tencent 465
Tengelmann 159
Tesco 493
Tesla 415
Tetley Tea 78, 169, 341
Texas Instruments 76–7
Thai Air 403
Thai Union Frozen Foods 348–9
3G technology 345
3M 203
Thyssen-Krupp 374, 375
Timberland 500
Tognum 517
Tokyo Electron 173
Toshiba 496

Toyota 102, 161, 200, 347, 371–2, 393, 394, 548
Toys "R" Us 493, 500
TransFair USA 279
Transparency International 76
Triad 17
Tsingdao 396
Turkish Airlines 365
Twitter 487
Tyskie 483

Uber 506
UBS 228, 355
Unilever 95, 173, 300, 344, 375, 391, 394, 425, 427, 428, 521
Uniqlo 481
United Fruit 15
Universal 406
Unocal 171
UPS 488
US Federal Reserve 202

Vallø Saft Group 522
Vattenfall 264, 538
Vauxhall 425
Verizon 107
Vero Moda 345

Versace 98
Vickers 517
Victoria's Secret 500
Videoton 103
Virgin Atlantic 371
Vivendi 406, 526
Voest-Alpine 374
Volkswagen (VW) 121, 155, 161, 346, 348, 357, 393, 394, 468, 540–1, 543
Volvo 341, 480
VOSS 543
VW (Volkswagen) 121, 155, 161, 346, 348, 357, 393, 394, 468, 540–1, 543

Wahaha 359–61
Wal-Mart 21, 95–6, 97, 204, 297, 354, 423, 489, 493
Warburg Pincus 526
Warid Telecom International 525–7
Wärtsilä 274–6, 382, 395
Wedel 406, 483
Whirlpool 367, 567, 568
WildChina 318
Wink Group 522
Wipro 97, 105, 168
World Bank 181, 195, 265–7

World Trade Organization (WTO) 12, 249–56
Wuerth 408

Xerox 344, 378
Xianyang Andre Juice Co Ltd 522
Xiaomi 23–4, 107, 176, 328, 384, 465, 494, 506–10
Xing 100, 485

Yamaha 338
Yihaodian 488–9, 493
Yokogawa Hewlett-Packard 431
YouTube 407
YPF 50, 181
YSL 485

Zain Africa 525–6, 527
Zara 95, 152, 478–9, 481, 489–90, 498
Zelando 95
ZF 351–2, 543
zhuoyue.com 507
ZOJE 574
ZTE 107, 384, 506–7, 509
Zywiec 483